KU-679-321

The 20th Century Book

The 20th Century Book

Its illustration and design

Second Edition

John Lewis

The Herbert Press

To Griselda
whose patience has been infinite during the production of this and many
other books

Copyright © John Noel Claude Lewis 1967, 1984
First edition published in 1967
This new and revised edition first published in Great Britain by
The Herbert Press Limited, 46 Northchurch Road, London N1 4EJ

Designed by John Lewis FSIAD

Printed and bound in Great Britain by W. S. Cowell Ltd, Ipswich, Suffolk

All rights reserved. No part of this publication may be reproduced or used in any
form or by any means — graphic, electronic or mechanical, including photocopying,
recording, taping or information storage and retrieval systems — without permission
of the publishers.

This book is sold subject to the Standard Conditions of Sale of Net Books and may
not be resold in the UK below the net price.

Lewis, John, *1912–*
    The 20th century book. — New and rev. ed
    1. Book design
    I. Title   II. Lewis, John *1912–*
    Twentieth century book
    686   Z116.A3

ISBN 0-906969-41-7

CONTENTS

ACKNOWLEDGEMENTS

A book like this depends on the work of others. My first acknowledgements are to the artists and designers whose work appears here and to the publishers who have given their permission for reproduction and in many cases helped with information. My next are to those who have written about this subject and particularly for the following books:

Dr. G. K. Schauer's *Deutsche Buchkunst 1890–1960,* Mr Albert Kapr's *Buchgestaltung,* Mr Philip Hofer's and Miss Eleanor Garvey's *The Artist and the Book 1860–1960,* Mr David Bland's *A History of Book Illustration,* Mr Percy Muir's *English Children's Books* and the various editions of *The Art of the Book,* published by Studio Ltd.

My thanks are also due to the Trustees of the British Museum for permission to photograph the book illustrated on page 13; to the Victoria and Albert Museum for permission to photograph the books shown on pages 11, 39, 40–1, 82–3, 85, 88–9, 112–13, 114–15, 116–17, 120–1, 122–3, 194–5; to the Bibliothèque Nationale for the photographs on pages 60, 72–3.

My gratitude to all my friends who have helped me either with the loan of books or in other ways including Mr Edward Ardizzone, Mr Tom Balston, Mr R. A. Bevan, Mr Louis Bondy, Mr Max Caflisch, Mr Geoffrey Cumberlege, Mr Robin Don, Mr Charles Ede, Miss Eleanor Garvey, Mr Bob Gill, Mr Felix Gluck, Mr John Hadfield, Mr John Harthan, Mr David Herbert, Mr George Him, Mr Philip Hofer, Mr Blair Hughes-Stanton, M. André Jammes, Mr Jean Koefoed, M. Edy Legrand, Mr James Mosley, Mr John Nash, Mr Walter Neurath, Mr John O'Connor, Mr Francis Odle, Mr David Pearce, Mr James Pfeufer, Mr Hugh Radcliffe-Wilson, Mrs Herta Ryder, Mrs Margaret Rideout, Mr Anthony Rota, Mr Hans Schmoller, Mr Martin Simmons, Mr Geoffrey Smith, Mr Reynolds Stone, Mme J. Veyrin-Forrer.

Also to Messrs John R. Freeman Ltd, Mr John Lunnis, and to Mr Robert Alcock and Miss Shirley Notton of the Butter Market Studio, Ipswich for the care they have taken in photographing several hundred books, and to Mr Ben Clark and all those at the Press in the Butter Market who helped in the production of this book.

And finally to Mr Ruari McLean for helpful advice and for reading the proofs and to Mr John Dreyfus for much valuable criticism and advice at various stages in the production of this book.

PREFACE

This book is not an attempt to catalogue the hundred (or any other arbitrary figure) best books of either this year or of the last sixty or seventy years. The pages and covers from the books shown here are a designer's personal choice. Most of them I like, a few of them I don't, but all of them I feel, were in some way significant. Amongst the books that I like and which are not here are those books whose *raison d'être* relies on superb colour printing and also those whose beauty depends on fine composition and presswork and beautiful paper. In the first case, the futility of trying to re-reproduce by a different process work that has already been done well is fairly obvious, so coffee table books have had to be left out. In the second case, the finely printed private press or even commercially published book with impeccable qualities of precise craftsmanship, is quite beyond the limits of photography and process reproduction. So, the excellent work of such presses as Giovanni Mardersteig's Officina Bodoni is likewise excluded.

In reproduction, the arrangement of type and illustrations on paper, or an individual illustration can be shown. The presswork, unless it is appallingly bad, cannot be seen; and one illustration does not make a book. So this book has become a 'sample tasting', but I hope that by comparison and juxtaposition the tasting may be given some point. The comparative method may produce some pretty odd bedfellows, but widely different attitudes to design were prevailing in different countries at the same time and utterly similar influences were affecting the design of books, that were often separated in time by years or even decades.

There have been a lot of handsome books printed since the beginning of the century. It would not be difficult to fill a book of this size with, say, the best of Scandinavian, or Russian or South American books and none of these appears here. My limitations had to be self-imposed. Amongst my reasons for compiling this book is an attempt to communicate something of my enthusiasm for, and interest in, the design and illustration of books. My livelihood is concerned with the production, editing, designing and publishing of books. My most absorbing and life-long hobby has been the collecting of books – and in particular of illustrated books and of books whose design shows some evidence of 'a directing intelligence'.

As for the book's title, it is fair comment to suggest that the twentieth century began in 1901, but the forces governing the design of the twentieth century book do not fit the calendar so conveniently. The art nouveau movement and the historicism of the first of the English private presses all began before the end of the Victorian era, but they provide the foundations of the design of the modern book.

Auguste Heckscher, in opening a recent A.I.G.A. exhibition of 'Fifty Best Books' in New York said: 'Books used to be made, today they are designed.' After looking at a recent exhibition of 'The Fifty Best Books of the Year' in London, I was forcibly reminded of these words. Though many of the books in this exhibition were well laid out (and, reproduced in miniature in the catalogue, looked well), in fact they were often ill-made, some were ill-printed and often on unsuitable paper, and mostly they were bound in badly blocked, sloppily fitting cases. When a book is *well* made, and is printed on good stock with good presswork, where the binding case fits snugly and is cleanly blocked on nice material, the most unadventurous typographic arrangement will look well. Design is no substitute for craftsmanship. For a book to be a work of art, however, it needs to be both well designed and well made. The feel of a well-made book, its weight in the hand, its texture, even its smell – these qualities that mean so much to anyone who cares for books – the reader of this book will have to take on trust for I cannot show them here.

1893. *Le Voyage d'Urien* by André Gide,
illustrated with lithographs by Maurice Denis,
published by the Librairie de l'Art Indépendant,
Paris. Lithographs printed by Edw. Ancourt, text
printed by Paul Schmidt. Limited to 300 copies.
8″ × 7½″. Lithograph.

1. ART NOUVEAU OR PRIVATE PRESS HISTORICISM?

Since the end of the last century there has been a dichotomy of ideas about the design of books. In the 1890's the two opposing influences were the historicism of the private press movement and the aesthetics of art nouveau. These threads have continued with surprising persistence; though on occasions book designers have moved from camp to camp, sometimes without being aware of their inconsistency. Modern designers are increasingly aware of this dichotomy. It is the modern graphic artist who has made the first real attempt to resolve it – as I hope later pages of this book will show.

One of the first artists in the modern movement to concern himself actively with the relationship of illustration to the design of the book as a whole was Maurice Denis. As a painter he was heavily influenced by Gauguin; but he was more important as a writer on modern art than as a practitioner. His first attempt at illustration was for Paul Verlaine's *Sagesse*. These illustrations, daring in their simplicity of conception, were carried out in 1889, but not published until 1911. André Gide saw them in their unpublished state and asked Denis if he would illustrate his *Le Voyage d'Urien*; the result was a small and little-known book, described by Philip Hofer as a masterpiece of art nouveau. Denis expressed the art nouveau attitude to books when he said, 'A book ought to be a work of decoration and not a neutral vehicle for transmitting a text'; and 'For each emotion, each thought, there exists a plastic equivalent and a corresponding beauty'.

Art nouveau was essentially new art and in no way historical. Its origins, by now only too often explained, were largely oriental, the influences springing from the Japanese prints of Utamaro, Hiroshige, Hokusai and others that were at this time appearing on the bookstalls and in the art shops of Paris, Munich and London.

One of the first Western artists to take a serious interest in this oriental art was James McNeill Whistler, who incorporated in his paintings and in the typography of his books the qualities he found in Japanese prints. He was soon followed by French painters such as Gauguin, Bonnard and Lautrec, and by the poster artists Alphonse Mucha, Jules Chéret and the American Will Bradley. In art nouveau posters, the designs are flat, essentially two-dimensional and without perspective; and the white paper is as important as the flat colours. Although Bradley made full use of art nouveau principles in his posters, in his book work he produced designs that owed more to William Morris's mediaevalism. Alphonse Mucha on the other hand – working, like Bradley, on both posters and book design – used a style that was consistently art nouveau.

Mucha, a Slav from South Moravia, came to Paris when he was twenty-eight to study at the Académie Julian. His work soon developed the characteristics to be seen in his illustrations to *Ilsée, Princesse de Tripoli*. His cover design of lilies is printed in a typical art nouveau 'greenery-yallery' colour scheme; and the lithographed illustrations, which have a feverish, hectic feeling, are mostly in the same greens and yellows. His very solid females, strongly outlined like the leading of a stained glass window, move through a web of febrile tendrils. Mucha, in spite of his origins, was as much France's contribution to art nouveau as Beardsley was England's.

Charles Ricketts, the founder of the Vale Press in Chelsea, was one of the first typographic designers influenced by art nouveau who still based the typography of his books on historic principles.

Before Charles Ricketts founded the Vale Press he practised as a commercial book designer and typographer. He must have been one of the first practising typographers. He designed books for John Lane, and in 1889 laid out several of Thomas Hardy's books, for a London publishing house called Osgood,

1882. *Selections from the Hesperides and Noble Numbers of Robert Herrick.* Illustrated by Edwin A. Abbey. Published by Harper & Brothers, New York. Printed by the Leadenhall Press, London. 11⅝″ × 8⅞″. Case-binding blocked in gold, black, red and green, on a cream-coloured cloth.

McIlvaine, including the first edition of *Tess of the D'Urbervilles.*[1] The most distinctive feature of this book, apart from its art nouveau cover, is the curious asymmetric title-page, with the copy placed high on the page, and a 2-line, drop initial T for 'Tess'. This asymmetry is carried into all the chapter openings. In contrast to the title-page is the equally unconventional contents page, where the copy begins nearly two-thirds of the way down the page. The book gives abundant evidence of an attempt to break away from current commercial convention. It is also clear that Ricketts had taken a look at Whistler's *The Gentle Art of Making Enemies,* but had not reached the assurance or the bravado of the 'Butterfly'.

The effect of art nouveau on the appearance of books and particularly on the covers was very considerable. In 1882 Harper and Brothers, in New York, had published *Selections from the Hesperides and Noble Numbers of Robert Herrick* with drawings by Edwin A. Abbey. The cover design of this book, possibly by Abbey, is one of the earliest examples of this influence, the choice of green and gold on a cream background being typical of many art nouveau colour schemes.

By 1900, art nouveau was already an international style. In Germany, as early as the 1890's, the movement had inspired experiments in the layout of books and in the design of new typefaces. The publication of the journals *Pan* and *Jugend* gave encouragement to such experiments. *Pan,* edited by Julius Meier-Graefe, an art historian, and Otto Julius Bierbaum, an amateur typographer, engaged the services of a number of young designers, who were showing an interest in the typographic arts. These included E. R. Weiss, Peter Behrens and Otto Eckmann. *Pan,* which ran for twenty-one issues, was international in its scope and included articles on Beardsley, Corinth, Toulouse-Lautrec and Van de Velde. *Jugend* was published in Munich and first appeared in 1896; its title (*Youth*) implied a criticism of anything old, and it soon achieved a wide popularity, lending its name to Jugendstil, the German art nouveau movement.

[1] Ricketts, writing in his *A Defence of the Revival of Printing* in 1899, said: 'Some of my earliest experiments in the shaping of books, crude and hesitating as they are, were done for Messrs Osgood, McIlvaine in 1890 and 1891 . . . they were unlike the ordinary books in the matter of title-page, proportion of margin, and in the designs upon their boards.'

1897. *Ilsée Princesse de Tripoli* by Robert de Flers. Illustrated with 132 lithographs by Alphonse Mucha. Lithographed by L'Imprimerie Champenois. Printed and published by L'Édition d'Art. 12⅝" × 10". Cover design printed in blue and yellow on grey-green paper; and illustrated pages.

Painters as book designers

1890. *The Gentle Art of Making Enemies* by J. McNeill Whistler. Published by William Heinemann, London. Printed by the Ballantyne Press, London and Edinburgh. 8″ × 6¼″. Text spread and chapter half-title, showing two variations of Whistler's 'Butterfly' signature.

Whistler v. Ruskin

ART & ART CRITICS

Chelsea, Dec. 1878.

Serious Sarcasm

PARDON me, my dear Whistler, for having taken you *au sérieux* even for a moment.

I ought to have remembered that your penning, like your painting, belongs to the region of " chaff." I will not forget it again ; and meantime remain yours always,

TOM TAYLOR.

LAVENDER SWEEP.
Jan. 9. 1879.

Final

WHY, my dear old Tom, I never *was* serious with you, even when you were among us. Indeed, I killed you quite, as who should say, without seriousness, " A rat ! A rat ! " you know, rather cursorily.

Chaff, Tom, as in your present state you are beginning to perceive, was your fate here, and doubtless will be throughout the eternity before you. With ages at your disposal, this truth will dimly dawn upon you ; and as you look back upon this life, perchance many situations that you took *au sérieux* (art-critic, who knows ? expounder of Velasquez, and what not) will explain themselves sadly—chaff ! Go back !

The World,
Jan. 15, 1879.

THE WHITE HOUSE.
Jan. 10, 1879.

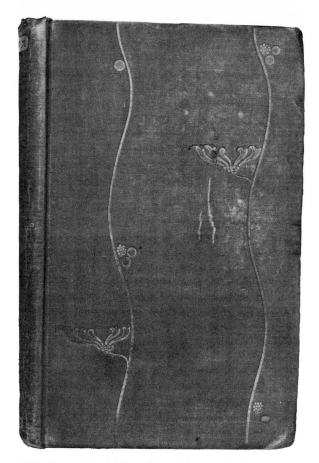

T ESS
OF THE D'URBERVILLES
A PURE WOMAN

FAITHFULLY PRESENTED BY

THOMAS HARDY

IN THREE VOLUMES

VOL. II

'. . . Poor wounded name ! My bosom as a bed
Shall lodge thee.'—W. SHAKSPEARE.

O. M.

ALL RIGHTS
RESERVED

1889. *Tess of the D'Urbervilles* by Thomas Hardy.
Designed by Charles Ricketts; bound in brown
cloth-covered boards, blocked in gold. Published
by J. R. Osgood McIlvaine and Co., London. In
three volumes. Printed by R. & R. Clark,
Edinburgh. $7\frac{1}{2}'' \times 5\frac{1}{2}''$. Case-binding and title-page.

1901. *De Cupidinis et Psyches Amoribus.* A
version by C. I. Holmes. Illustrated with wood
engravings by Charles Ricketts and printed by
Hacon & Ricketts at the Ballantyne Press.
Published by John Lane. $11\frac{1}{2}'' \times 7\frac{3}{4}''$. Text
spread with wood engraving.

celeritate nauigabant. tunc sic iterum momentarius maritus suam
Psychen admonet dies ultima et casus extremus. sexus infestus
et sanguis inimicus iam sumpsit arma et castra commouit et aciem
direxit et classicum personauit. iam mucrone destricto iugulum
tuum nefariae tuae sorores petunt. heu quantis urguemur cladibus,
Psyche dulcissima! tui nostrique miserere religiosaque continentia domum maritum teque et istum paruulum nostrum imminentis ruinae infortunio libera. nec illas scelestas feminas, quas tibi
post interneciuum odium et calcata sanguinis foedera sorores
appellare non licet, uel uideas uel audias, cum in morem Sirenum
scopulo prominentes funestis uocibus saxa personabunt.'
Suscipit Psyche singultu lacrimoso sermonem incertans
'iam dudum, quod sciam, fidei atque parciloquio meo perpendisti documenta, nec eo setius adprobabitur tibi nunc etiam
firmitas animi mei. tu modo Zephyro nostro rursum praecipe,
fungatur obsequio et in uicem denegatae sacrosanctae imaginis
tuae redde saltem conspectum sororum. per istos cinnameos et
undique pendulos crines tuos, per teneras et teretis et mei similes
genas, per pectus nescio quo calore feruidum—sic in hoc saltem
paruulo cognoscam faciem tuam: supplicis anxiae piis precibus
erogatus germani complexus indulge fructum, et tibi deuotae
caraeque Psychae animam gaudio recrea. nec quicquam amplius
in tuo uultu requiro, iam nil officiunt mihi uel ipsae nocturnae
tenebrae: teneo te meum lumen.'
His uerbis et amplexibus mollibus decantatus maritus, lacrimasque eius suis crinibus detergens, facturum spopondit, et
praeuertit statim lumen nascentis diei.
Iugum sororium consponsae factionis, ne parentibus quidem
uisis, recta de nauibus scopulum petunt illum praecipiti cum
uelocitate, nec uenti ferentis oppertae praesentiam licentiosa cum
temeritate prosiliunt in altum. nec immemor Zephyrus regalis
edicti, quamuis inuitus, susceptas eas gremio spirantis aurae solo
reddidit. at illae incunctatae statim conferto uestigio domum penetrant, complexaeque praedam suam, sorores nomine mentientes,
thensaurumque penitus abditae fraudis uultu laeto tegentes, sic
adulant
'Psyche non ita pridem paruula et ipsa iam mater es! quantum
putas boni nobis in ista geris perula! quantis gaudiis totam domum
nostram hilarabis! o nos beatas quas infantis aurei nutrimenta
laetabunt! qui si parentum ut oportet pulchritudini responderit,
prorsus Cupido nascetur.'
Sic adfectione simulata paulatim sororis inuadunt animum,
xii

statimque eas lassitudine uiae sedilibus
refotas et balnearum
uaporosis fontibus
curatas pulcherrime triclinio mirisque illis et beatis edulibus atque tuccetis
oblectat. iubet citharam loqui, psallitur; tibias agere, sonatur; choros canere, cantatur. quae
cuncta nullo praesente dulcissimis modulis animos audientium remulcebant.
nec tamen scelestarum feminarum nequuitia uel illa mellita cantus dulcedine
mollita conquieuit, sed ad destinatam fraudium pedicam sermonem conferentes dissimulanter occipiunt sciscitari, qualis ei
maritus et unde natalium, secta cuia prouenerit. tunc illa simplicitate nimia pristini sermonis oblita nouum commentum instruit, atque maritum suum de prouincia proxima magnis pecuniis negotiantem iam medium cursum aetatis agere, interspersum rara canitie. nec in sermone isto tantillum morata rursum
opiparis muneribus eas onustas uentoso uehiculo reddidit.
Sed dum Zephyri tranquillo spiritu sublimatae domum
redeunt, sic secum altercantur 'quid, soror, dicimus de tam monstruoso fatuae illius mendacio? tunc adulescens modo florenti
lanugine barbam instruens, nunc aetate media candenti canitie lucidus. quis ille quem temporis modici spatium repentina senecta
reformauit? nil aliud repperies, mi soror, quam uel mendacio ista
pessimam feminam confingere uel formam mariti sui nescire.
quorum utrum uerum est, opibus istis quam primum exterminanda est. quod si uiri sui faciem ignorat, deo profecto denupsit
et deum nobis praegnatione ista gerit. certe si diuini puelli—
quod absit—haec mater audierit, statim me laqueo nexili suspendam. ergo interim ad parentes nostros redeamus et exordio
sermonis huius quam concolores fallacias adtexamus.'
xiii   c

13

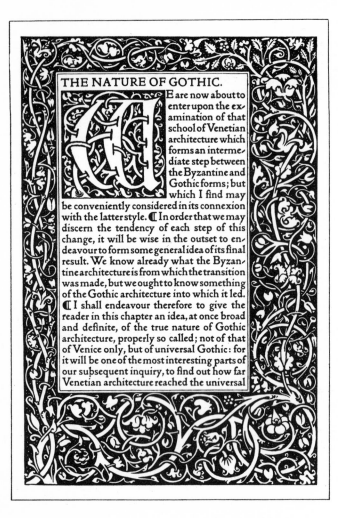

THE NATURE OF GOTHIC.

E are now about to enter upon the examination of that school of Venetian architecture which forms an intermediate step between the Byzantine and Gothic forms; but which I find may be conveniently considered in its connexion with the latter style. ⁋ In order that we may discern the tendency of each step of this change, it will be wise in the outset to endeavour to form some general idea of its final result. We know already what the Byzantine architecture is from which the transition was made, but we ought to know something of the Gothic architecture into which it led. ⁋ I shall endeavour therefore to give the reader in this chapter an idea, at once broad and definite, of the true nature of Gothic architecture, properly so called; not of that of Venice only, but of universal Gothic: for it will be one of the most interesting parts of our subsequent inquiry, to find out how far Venetian architecture reached the universal

A History of NEW YORK

Book VI. Containing the second part of the reign of PETER THE HEADSTRONG, and his gallant achievements on the Delaware.

CHAPTER I. In which is exhibited a warlike portrait of the great PETER— and how General Van Poffenburgh distinguished himself at Fort Casimir

ITHERTO, most venerable and courteous reader, have I shown thee the administration of the valorous Stuyvesant, under the mild moonshine of peace, or rather the grim tranquillity of awful expectation; but now the war-drum rumbles from afar, the brazen trumpet brays its thrilling note, and the rude clash of hostile arms speaks fearful prophecies of coming troubles. The gallant warrior starts from soft repose, from golden visions, and voluptuous ease; where, in the dulcet, "piping time of peace," he sought sweet solace after all his toils. No more in beauty's syren lap reclined, he weaves fair garlands for his lady's brows; no more entwines with flowers his shining sword, nor through the livelong lazy summer's day chants forth his lovesick soul in madrigals. To manhood roused, he spurns the amorous flute; doffs from his brawny back the robe of peace, and clothes his pampered limbs in panoply of steel. O'er his dark brow, where late the myrtle waved, where wanton roses breathed enervate love, he rears the beaming casque and nodding plume; grasps the bright shield and shakes the ponderous lance; or mounts with eager pride his fiery steed, and burns for deeds of glorious chivalry! But soft, worthy reader! I would not have you imagine, that any preux chevalier, thus hideously begirt with iron, existed in the city of New-Amsterdam. This is but a lofty and gigantic mode in which heroic writers always talk of war, thereby to give it a noble and imposing aspect; equipping our warriors with bucklers, helms, and lances, and such like outlandish and obsolete weapons, the like of which perchance they had never seen or heard of; in the same manner that a cunning

Dies Buch kommt wie ein Schiff, befrachtet mit den Koftbarkeiten einer reichen Ferne. Wo es landet, werden Hände voll und Herzen fröhlich. Und manchen lockt's dann hinaus, felber da zu fchürfen und zu pflücken, wo die unermeßlichen Reichtümer warten. So wird dies Buch viele befchenken und einigen ein Führer werden zu dem Goethe, der durchaus mehr war und auch uns mehr fein kann als „der größte deutsche Dichter". Denn nirgends begegnet er uns lebendiger als in feinen Briefen, diefen intimften Dokumenten feines Lebens, feiner Lebenskunft. Zugleich find Goethes Briefe, in denen fich die glänzendfte Epoche des deutschen Geifteslebens und feltfam reizvolle Bilder aus der guten alten Zeit lebendig wiederfpiegeln, auch fachlich von höchftem Intereffe.

Das erfte bis zwölfte Taufend wurde 1906 bei Oscar Brandftetter in Leipzig gedruckt.

Alles um Liebe

Goethes Briefe

aus der erften Hälfte feines Lebens

Herausgegeben von Ernft Hartung

Gefchmückt von Käte Vefper-Waentig

Düffeldorf und Leipzig, verlegt bei Wilhelm Langewiefche-Brandt

The influence of Morris

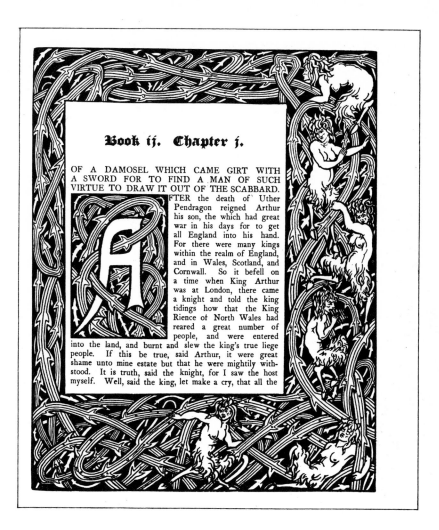

1893–4. *Le Morte d'Arthur* by Sir Thomas Malory. Illustrated by Aubrey Beardsley. Published by J. M. Dent and Co., London. Printed by Turnbull and Spears, Edinburgh. First published in parts and then issued in two volumes. (Second edition issued in a single volume and limited to 1,000 copies for U.K. and 500 for U.S.A.). 10″ × 7⅝″. Chapter opening with border designed by Beardsley.

Opposite left:
1892. *The Nature of Gothic* by John Ruskin. Decorated, printed and published by William Morris at the Kelmscott Press, Hammersmith. Bound in vellum with green silk petersham ties. 8″ × 5½″. First text page with border design by Morris.

Opposite right:
c. 1910. *The Campbell Book* with decorations by Will Bradley. Reproduced from *The Art of the Book* 1914: Studio. Text page, area of illustrations 7¾″ × 5½″.

Opposite:
1906. *Alles um Liebe.* Edited by Ernst Hartung. Designed by Käte Vesper-Waentig. Published by Wilhelm Langewiesche-Brandt, Düsseldorf and Leipzig. 7½″ × 4¾″. Title-page spread.

The German typefounders were soon turning to art nouveau letter forms, and in 1900 Karl Klingspor commissioned Otto Eckmann (an admirer of Beardsley) to design a typeface 'appropriate for the printing of books in the new style'. This Germanic type, called Eckmann-Schmuck, was very like the style of lettering that was appearing on the poster hoardings of Paris and Berlin.

In contrast to art nouveau the historically based work of the English private presses may seem a little humdrum, but the influence they exerted on commercial book production was powerful and lasting. In this revival of fine book printing, the most influential of all the private presses was William Morris's Kelmscott Press in Hammersmith, London. Morris was a mediaevalist and, though his first typeface was based on the fine roman used by Nicholas Jenson in Venice in 1468, all his leanings were towards dark-textured, black-letter books. Morris's pre-occupation with mediaevalism might seem a curious point of departure for modern book design, yet he was really at the beginning of the diverging lines of development in twentieth-century design. Morris contributed much to the decorative arts; for printing, he established the belief in standards of quality in workmanship, and in the use of good materials. Morris aimed at perfection. He stated that he was determined to obtain the very best types, ink and papers as well as the best of illustrations and decorations. His illustrations were always cut on the wood to be printed by the same methods as the type. As far as I know, he never considered using lithography as a method of illustration. Morris's insistence on quality in workmanship, design and materials provided the qualities which were the basis of the revival of fine printing in England and America, in much of the continent of Europe, and particularly in Germany. Morris's interest in early printing was also responsible for producing the last thing he would have wished for — a reactionary revivalism.

1906. *The Dream and the Business* by John Oliver Hobbes. Published by T. Fisher Unwin. Design by Aubrey Beardsley, printed in three colours and mounted on the cover. 6⅝" × 2⅞". This design was also used as a poster for T. Fisher Unwin's 'Pseudonym and Antonym Library'.

In 1893, two years after Morris had started his press, Aubrey Beardsley began work on his drawings for *Le Morte d'Arthur*, for a most enterprising London publisher called J. M. Dent. In spite of the subject, and the Burne-Jones influence, Beardsley's work was the antithesis of everything Morris believed in. The air of decadence in Beardsley's work is an essential part of the aesthetics of art nouveau, itself essentially a cult of the precious. This precious quality can be seen at its best in many fine art nouveau book bindings, but if art nouveau had nothing but this to offer, its influence would not have lasted. Beardsley's sinuous line, his massing of areas of black and white, his choice of subjects, rarefied as hothouse orchids and with a lurking sense of eroticism is the epitome of art nouveau. The most interesting of his qualities as a designer is this use of white space, an ethereal quality which is a component of art nouveau. His cover design for *The Dream and the Business* by John Oliver Hobbes shows this well.

In 1894, Beardsley undertook the art editorship of *The Yellow Book,* to be published by Elkin Mathews and John Lane in England, and by Copeland and Day in Boston. With Henry Harland as editor, and under Lane's supervision, its preliminary announcements had an effect comparable to the notoriety attained by the magazines *Playboy* or *Penthouse* in the 1960's. The first volumes lived up to expectation. The sour yellow covers, with (on the first four books) Beardsley's drawings, the Beardsley title-pages and the wide margins, added up to something quite new and rather shocking. The sheer physical weight, because of the solid board covers and coated stock, the more than adequate printing of Ballantyne's, the writings of Henry James, Max Beerbohm and Baron Corvo *and* Beardsley's exotic drawings, were all factors contributory to the remarkable impact of these quarterly books. These books in some way capture the imagination and are, at least to our eyes, very much of their time.

The Yellow Book ran for thirteen numbers, but Beardsley only stayed with it for the first four. As an indirect result of the Oscar Wilde scandal he was sacked; and with his departure, the fire went out of the series. If Beardsley perhaps found John Lane's rather windy supervision too confining, his next publisher, Leonard Smithers, was quite a different kettle of fish. The new production was to be called *The Savoy* and have Beardsley as art editor and Arthur Symons as literary editor. It had a larger format (quarto) and sold for 2*s* 6*d*, half the price of *The Yellow Book*. The Beardsley covers, for the first two numbers, were printed in black on pink paper-covered boards; abandoning the massed blacks of *The Yellow Book* covers, he used intricate cross hatching to give an engraved effect.

The contributors to the first volume of *The Savoy* included George Bernard Shaw, Havelock Ellis, and Beardsley himself, with the first pages of his novel *Under the Hill*. In Volume 2, Max Beerbohm drew Beardsley and Beardsley drew himself, Sickert showed a drawing of the Rialto and Charles H. Shannon drew a naked girl diving. The standard of illustration in *The Savoy* is much higher than that of *The Yellow Book*; Beardsley had matured in these two years; and his *Under the Hill* drawings are amongst his finest work. *The Savoy* ran for eight volumes; yet, curiously, it is the memory of *The Yellow Book* that lingers on, whilst *The Savoy* is all but forgotten. Yellow always possesses the power to shock, far more than does the dusty cosmetic pink of the first of *The Savoy* covers.

Yellow was always an essential feature of the pulp magazine covers, as for example in the '20's; for the work of Edgar Wallace and Sidney Horler, 'Horler for Excitement!' Gollancz made good use of it in the '30's with the Stanley Morison-designed book jackets. If *The Yellow Book* had been called *The*

The Yellow Book
An Illustrated Quarterly
Volume I April 1894

London: Elkin Mathews & John Lane
Boston: Copeland & Day

Price 5/- Net

The Yellow Book
An Illustrated Quarterly
Volume II July 1894

London: Elkin Mathews & John Lane
Boston: Copeland & Day

Price 5/- Net

The Yellow Book
An Illustrated Quarterly
Volume III October 1894

Price $1.50 Net

London: John Lane
Boston: Copeland & Day

Price 5/- Net

The Yellow Book
An Illustrated Quarterly
Volume IV January 1895

Price $1.50 Net

London: John Lane
Boston: Copeland & Day

Price 5/- Net

1894–5. *The Yellow Book* Volumes 1–4. Edited by Henry Harland. Published by Elkin Mathews and John Lane, London. (Vols 3 and 4 John Lane, Bodley Head). In Boston by Copeland and Day. Printed by the Ballantyne Press, London and Edinburgh. 8″ × 6⅛″. These cover designs for the first four volumes of *The Yellow Book* were by Aubrey Beardsley.

1909. *Histoire de Soliman Ben Daoud et de la Reine du Matin* by Gérard de Nerval. Published by the Eragny Press, Hammersmith. Designed, engraved and printed by Lucien and Esther Pissarro. 8½″ × 5½″. Commissioned by the Society of 'Cent Bibliophiles'. Combined title-page and chapter opening. Gold leaf was used for the printing of the initial letters.

Grey Book, it is doubtful if we would have remembered it. In 1900 Emery Walker, who had been Morris's adviser at Kelmscott (May Morris is reported as saying: 'Without Mr Walker the Kelmscott Press could not have existed — at any rate in the form it took')[2] — went into partnership with T. J. Cobden-Sanderson and started the Doves Press, near the Doves Inn at Hammersmith. The Doves policy was that their books should be free from ornament and owe their design quality to the 'architectural beauty of their pages'. The immaculate productions that resulted from this philosophy are not particularly endearing. The only concessions to decoration were initials drawn for them by Graily Hewitt and Edward Johnston.

Johnston, a pioneer in the teaching of calligraphy in two London art schools, first at the Central School of Arts and Crafts and later at the Royal College of Art, maintained that in the practice of calligraphy the letter cutter and the type designer could learn the fundamentals of their craft. The falling away of this method of teaching is a sad thing. Maybe too many scribes have had their horizons limited to writing Rolls of Honour and the like, yet artists such as Berthold Wolpe, Imre Reiner and Hermann Zapf have successfully carried this craft into the world of type founding and modern graphics. Unhappily there are not many Wolpes, Reiners and Zapfs in each generation.

Of the English private presses at the turn of the century the most interesting was the Eragny. This was run by Lucien Pissarro, a son of the French painter, Camille Pissarro, and a close friend of Ricketts. Lucien married an English girl, Esther Bensusan, and settled in Hammersmith. Together they produced some of the most delightful and, until recently, the least sought after of the private press books. They are beautifully printed and usually decorated with Lucien's coloured woodcuts, which are a curious mixture of his father's down-to-earth impressionism, blended with something derived from Charles Keene's drawings and the whole overlaid with art nouveau decoration. Possibly it is these qualities and particularly the art nouveau influences that have until now detracted from their popularity.

English commercially published books in 1900 showed various influences in their appearance. The most dominant of these was still art nouveau, which showed particularly in decorated covers. John Lane's productions led the field in the elegance of their covers and in their typography. Percy Muir, a partner in another famous book house, wrote: '. . . the actual design and layout (of Lane's Books) were largely the work of two men — Charles Ricketts, who was a genius at that sort of thing . . . and Walter Blaikie, of the firm of T. & A. Constable of Edinburgh, whose unmistakable layout is to be seen in so many of the early productions of the firm'.[3] In illustration the stylistic unrealities of Aubrey Beardsley were mingling with post Pre-Raphaelite illustrators and the robust drawings of William Nicholson, Gordon Browne and Phil May. The airy wide-margined typography of Whistler had had its effect, but so had the eighteenth-century revivalist typography of Pickering and Whittingham and the consciously 'olde worlde' chapbook style of Field and Tuer at the Leadenhall Press. Behind all this confusion lay the heroic work of William Morris at the Kelmscott Press. The commercial publishers of Europe and America had, as yet, paid little heed to Morris's observations about type, presswork and paper. Imitations of Kelmscott proliferated, but, lacking Morris's qualities of design and presswork, were often sorry objects.

[2] *Emery Walker:* C. V. Nordlunde. Copenhagen 1959.

[3] *Minding my own business:* Percy Muir, Chatto and Windus 1956.

2*

THE SAVOY

AN ILLUSTRATED QUARTERLY

No. I

Price **2/6** net

January 1896

AUBREY BEARDSLEY. 1896.

PSYCHE BORNE OFF BY ZEPHYRUS, DRAWN BY EDWARD BURNE-JONES & ENGRAVED BY WILLIAM MORRIS

1898. *A Note by William Morris on his aims in founding the Kelmscott Press.* The last book published by the Kelmscott Press. Frontispiece by Edward Burne-Jones. 8″ × 5¾″.

Opposite:
1896. *The Savoy,* an illustrated quarterly edited by Arthur Symons, with Aubrey Beardsley as art editor. Published by Leonard Smithers. Printed by the Chiswick Press, Charles Whittingham and Co. 10″ × 7⅝″. This publication ran for eight issues. Cover design by Aubrey Beardsley.

The influence of Burne-Jones on Beardsley

The Kelmscott influence was felt in one or two unexpected places, and showed even in Beardsley's work. In his *Le Morte d'Arthur* the decorative borders and initial letters were a direct development of Morris's borders and letters. In all Beardsley's figure drawings, from *Le Morte d'Arthur* to his work for *The Savoy*, there are traces of Edward Burne-Jones's sad elongated, rather sexless creatures. The cross-fertilization of anti-pathetic movements in art is a recurring factor in the design and illustration of twentieth century books. When viewed sixty or seventy years later, their dissimilarities are often submerged by their period flavour.

21

1907. *Riquet à la Houppe* by Perrault with four-colour wood engravings by Lucien Pissarro. Published and printed by the Eragny Press. $5\frac{1}{4}'' \times 4\frac{1}{4}''$. Cover quarter bound in vellum and grey Ingres paper with a printed label. Chapter opening and text spread.

The influence of the English private presses

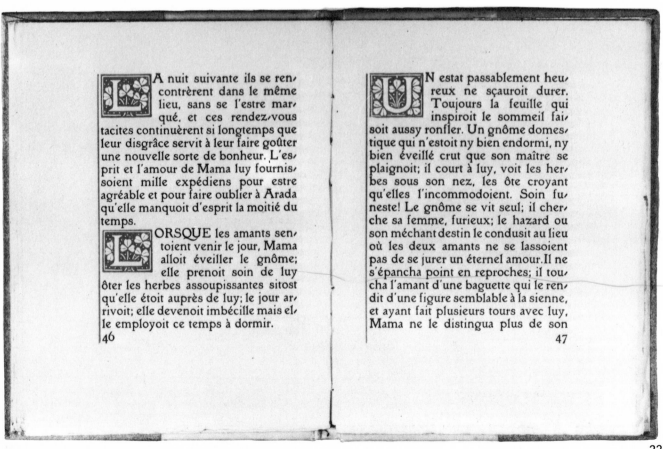

The Autocrat of the
Breakfast-Table by
Oliver Wendell Holmes
author of 'The Poet at
the Breakfast-Table'

London *Walter Scott Limited*
Paternoster Square

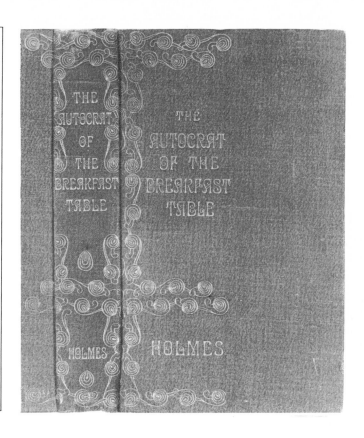

c. 1897. *The Autocrat of the Breakfast Table* by Oliver Wendell Holmes. Published by Walter Scott Ltd, London. Printed by the Walter Scott Press, Newcastle upon Tyne. $6\frac{7}{8}'' \times 4\frac{3}{8}''$. Title-page and red cloth-covered case-binding blocked in gold.

c. 1914. *Routine et Progrès en Agriculture* by R. Dumont. Binding designed by G. Auriol. Published by Maison Larousse. Reproduced from *The Art of the Book* 1914: Studio.

1883–4. *Olde ffrendes wyth newe Faces,* with hand-coloured woodcut illustrations by Joseph Crawhall. Published by Field and Tuer, London and Scribner and Welford, New York. Printed by the Leadenhall Press, London. $11\frac{1}{2}'' \times 8\frac{3}{4}''$. Title-page.

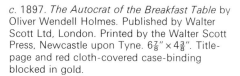

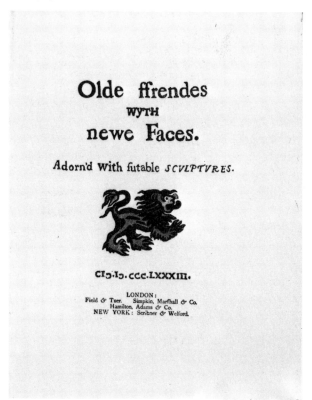

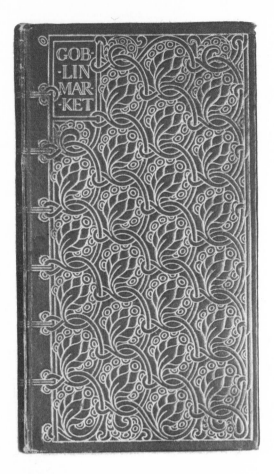

1893. *Goblin Market* by Christina Rossetti,
illustrated by Laurence Housman. Published by
Macmillan and Co. Ltd, London. Printed by
R. & R. Clark Ltd, Edinburgh. $7\frac{1}{8}'' \times 4\frac{1}{8}''$. Green
cloth-covered case-binding, blocked in gold.

To the right:
1896. *Green Arras* by Laurence Housman,
illustrated by the author. Published by John Lane
at the Bodley Head, London. Printed by
R. Folkard and Son, London. $7\frac{1}{2}'' \times 5''$. Green
cloth-covered case-binding, blocked in gold.

The revival of good typography both on the continent and in the U.S.A. was
due largely to the work of the English private presses. The typographic
interests of these press printers were almost exclusively limited to the reviving
of the old style typeface of the fifteenth-century Venetian printers. This
pre-occupation makes them more than a little dull. Good presswork, good
paper, good types and good composition are essential ingredients for the
making of a good book; but they do not necessarily make a visually exciting
one. For example, the charm of the Eragny books is due to other factors than
these, including art nouveau influences and Pissarro's Gallic taste. And however well printed it may be, there is not much charm about a Doves Press page.
The covers of books in the 'nineties were often their most attractive features.
Those for *Goblin Market* and *Green Arras* are both of a smooth sage-green
cloth, with arabesque patterns based on leaves, blocked in gold; on each case
the title on the front is tucked away in the top left-hand corner. These slim
volumes are most elegant little books, both designed and illustrated by
Laurence Housman.

Housman's work appeared in various periodicals and he illustrated a number
of books, including several that he had written himself. His illustrations for
Christina Rossetti's poem are shown in a later chapter of this book. His title
page for his own *Green Arras* is certainly remarkable, not only for the intricate
border, no doubt inspired by William Morris, but also for the extreme economy
of space occupied by the actual copy.

The first illustrated edition of *The Picture of Dorian Gray* was planned to be
published in 1908, the date that actually appears on the title-page; but the
illustrator, Paul Thiriat, fell ill and the book did not appear until 1910. Thiriat's
illustrations are more like magazine drawings than book illustrations. They
have been most skilfully engraved on the wood by E. Dété. This is an attractive
book, with very wide margins, but rather uneven presswork. It has a handsome
case, half bound in white buckram and grey Ingres paper, blocked in gold.
The asymmetric title page, printed in black and red, is evidence of someone's
thought and attention.

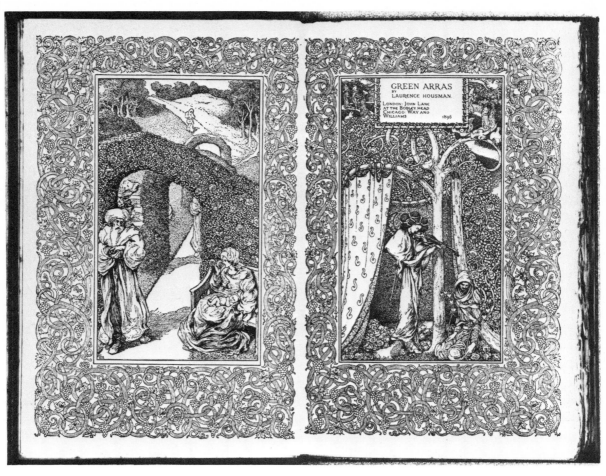

1896. *Green Arras* by Laurence Housman,
illustrated by the author. Published by John Lane
at the Bodley Head, London. Printed by
R. Folkard and Son, London. 7½″ × 5″.
Title-page spread.

1910. *The Picture of Dorian Gray* by Oscar
Wilde. Illustrated by Paul Thiriat (engraved by
E. Dété). Published by Charles Carrington, Paris.
10″ × 7½″. Title-page spread printed in black
and red.

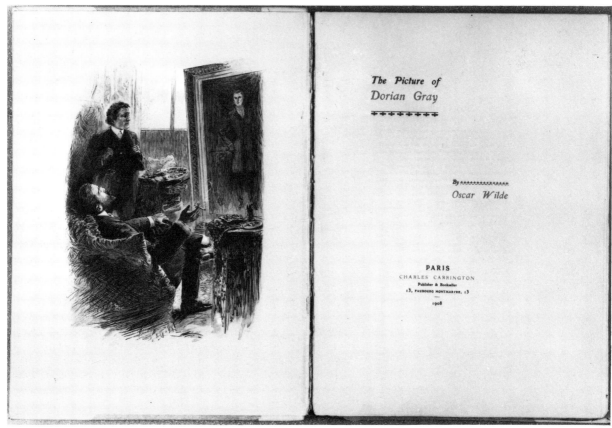

1900. *Vom Lieben Gott und Anderes* by Rainer
Maria Rilke. Illustrated and designed by E. R.
Weiss. Published for Insel-Verlag by Schuster
and Loeffler, Berlin and Leipzig. Printed by

W. Drugulin, Leipzig. Set in Luthersche Fraktur.
8⅜″ × 5⅞″. Title-page. Cased in paper-covered
boards with labels on front and spine printed in
black. End-paper design printed in red.

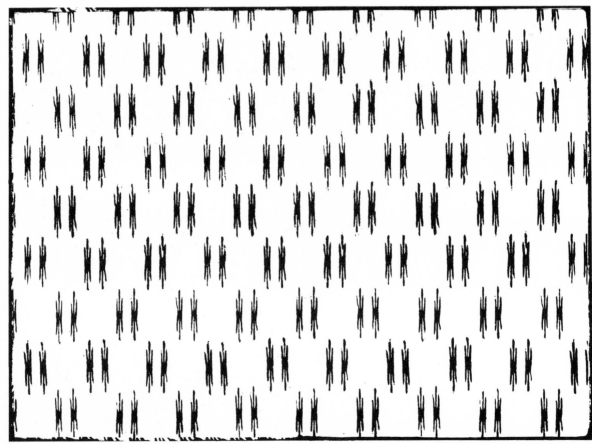

1908. *Ecce Homo* by Friedrich Nietzsche.
Designed by Henry van de Velde. Published by
Insel-Verlag, Leipzig. Printed by Friedrich
Richter. $9\frac{5}{8}'' \times 7\frac{1}{2}''$. Title-page.

Book design in Germany in 1900

Morris had not lived in vain, yet it was not in England but in Germany where
his work had most impact. The revival of good printing in Germany spread
directly from his influence. Amongst the first publishers there to consider
book design as something that mattered were Insel-Verlag of Leipzig, and
J. Fischer and Bruno Cassirer, both of Berlin. Another pioneer of fine book
work in Germany was C. E. Poeschel, the proprietor of the important printing
works Poeschel and Trepte of Leipzig, and for a short while in part control
of Insel-Verlag.

In 1905, Poeschel and Harry Graf Kessler (who later was to have his own
private press) invited Emery Walker to design a series of German classics for
Insel-Verlag. This was the *Grossherzog Wilhelm Ernst* edition. These octavo
books, designed on the proportion of the golden section, with calligraphic
title-pages by Edward Johnston and Eric Gill and attractively cased in limp
calf, had a marked effect upon German book production.

The foremost typographers and book designers in Germany at this time were
Otto Eckmann, Peter Behrens and Rudolf Koch who all designed for the
Klingspor foundry, F. W. Kleukens who designed a series of roman types for
the Stempel foundry, Walter Tiemann who was an instructor at the Royal
Academy of Graphic Arts at Leipzig, and E. R. Weiss who designed for the
Bauer typefoundry. Of these Weiss was the most versatile, and Koch the
most dedicated.

Koch carried Edward Johnston's doctrine to its logical conclusion and most
successfully linked the art of the scribe with the arts of typefounding and
printing. In 1911, Willy Wiegand founded the Bremer Press, and produced
private editions, which followed the style of the Doves Press. The books were
without illustration, but were decorated with fine initial letters drawn by
Anna Simons, a former pupil of Edward Johnston.

27

1902. *Ex Libris* by Bernhard Wenig. Published by Fischer and Franke, Berlin. Privately printed and limited to 500 copies. 9⅝″ × 7″. Bound in grey paper-covered boards, blocked in blue. Title-page.

1898. *Johannes*, a tragedy by Hermann Sudermann. Published by J. G. Cottasche, Stuttgart and Berlin. Printed by Union Deutsche Verlagsanstalt, Stuttgart. 7⅝″ × 4⅞″. Paper cover designed by Otto Eckmann, printed in black and red.

Die zehnte Muse

Dichtungen vom Brettl
∾ und fürs Brettl ∾

Aus vergangenen Jahrhunderten
und aus unsern Tagen gesammelt
von
Maximilian Bern

Sechsundzwanzigstes Tausend.

Recht des Jüngern.
Wer auf des Alten Schultern steht,
Der kann ihm Dank bezeigen;
Doch kann er nicht aus Dankbarkeit
Zu ihm heruntersteigen.
E. F. Ludw. Robert
(1779 1832).

Berlin 1908
Verlag von Otto Elsner

1908. *Die zehnte Muse* edited by Maximilian
Bern. Published by Otto Elsner, Berlin. 8″ × 4½″.
Red cloth-covered case-binding blocked in
white and title-page, set in Eckmann-Schmuck.
Below: 1913 edition cover with paper wrapper
printed in red and green.

Jubiläums-Auflage

86.–100. Tausend!

Maximilian Bern

Die zehnte Muse

Enthält fünfhundert

galante, heitere und ernste

Dichtungen

Romanzen aus realem Leben — Erotische Lyrik
Bunte Lieder — Satiren — Vagabundenlieder
Moderne Fabeln — Sinngedichte — Soziales
Ernste Vorträge   Heitere Vorträge

*Berns Brettlanthologie aus vergangenen Jahr-
hunderten und aus unsern Tagen: „Die zehnte
Muse" ist in ihrer Art klassisch und hat bleiben-
den literarhistorischen Wert.   (Neue Freie Presse.)*

*Dieses Buch kann gar nicht genug gelobt werden.
Die Auswahl ist direkt bewundernswert. (Die Zeit.)*

Preis zwei Mark.

In 1913, Harry Graf Kessler started the Cranach press at Weimar. He had a
special typeface cut by Edward Prince (who had worked for the Kelmscott
Press), under the supervision of Emery Walker: the roman was based on that
used by Jenson in 1470; the italic was designed by Edward Johnston. A
number of English artists worked for Kessler including Eric Gill and Edward
Gordon Craig. Craig produced a set of woodcuts for a truly magnificent edition
of *Hamlet*, based on the designs for his production of the play at the Moscow
Arts Theatre in 1912. He worked on them for seventeen years; so this, one of
the most outstanding of the Cranach books, did not appear until 1929 (in
German) and in 1930 in an English edition.

The classicism of the Cranach *Hamlet* is in marked contrast to Koch's block-
book *Elia*, when, working in a mediaeval tradition, he cut both illustrations and
letters on the wood.

Many years later, Francis Meynell published an edition of *Genesis* from his
Nonesuch Press; its pages had much the same block-book appearance, for
Meynell made use of Koch's Neuland typeface, which combined effectively
with woodcuts by Paul Nash. Maximilian Bern's *Die zehnte Muse*, published
by Otto Elsner in 1908, is set in Eckmann-Schmuck, the typeface Otto Eckmann designed for Klingspor. It was Jugendstil's answer to black letter, and
is comparable to Morris's rejection of the roman typeface. The layout of the
title page for *Die zehnte Muse* is judiciously asymmetric. The paper cover,
from a later edition, is interesting but a poor piece of work in comparison with
the first edition cover.

GOETHES
DRAMATISCHE
DICHTUNGEN
BAND I

LEIPZIG
MDCCCCIX
IM INSELVERLAG

1905–17. *Goethes Dramatische Dichtungen*
Volume I. Grossherzog Wilhelm Ernst Edition.
Pocket edition of the German classics. Layout by
Harry Graf Kessler and Emery Walker, with

titling by Eric Gill. Published by Insel-Verlag.
Printed by Brierkopf and Hartel, Leipzig.
$6\frac{7}{8}'' \times 4''$. Bound in flexible calf and gold
blocked. Case-binding, title-page and text spread.

---

208   FAUST

MEPH. (*zur Hexe*). Und kann ich dir was zu Gefallen tun,
So darfst du mirs nur auf Walpurgis sagen.
DIE HEXE. Hier ist ein Lied! wenn Ihrs zuweilen singt,
So werdet Ihr besondre Wirkung spüren.
MEPHISTOPHELES (*zu Faust*).
Komm nur geschwind und laß dich führen;
Du mußt notwendig transpirieren,
Damit die Kraft durch Inn- und Äußres dringt.
Den edlen Müßiggang lehr ich hernach dich schätzen,
Und bald empfindest du mit innigem Ergetzen,
Wie sich Cupido regt und hin und wider springt.
FAUST. Laß mich nur schnell noch in den Spiegel schauen!
Das Frauenbild war gar zu schön!
MEPH. Nein! Nein! Du sollst das Muster aller Frauen
Nun bald leibhaftig vor dir sehn.
(*Leise.*) Du siehst, mit diesem Trank im Leibe,
Bald Helenen in jedem Weibe.

STRASSE.

Faust. Margarete vorübergehend.

FAUST. Mein schönes Fräulein, darf ich wagen,
Meinen Arm und Geleit Ihr anzutragen?
MARGARETE. Bin weder Fräulein, weder schön,
Kann ungeleitet nach Hause gehn.
(*Sie macht sich los und ab.*)
FAUST. Beim Himmel, dieses Kind ist schön!
So etwas hab ich nie gesehn.
Sie ist so sitt- und tugendreich,
Und etwas schnippisch doch zugleich.
Der Lippe Rot, der Wange Licht,
Die Tage der Welt vergeß ichs nicht!
Wie sie die Augen niederschlägt,
Hat tief sich in mein Herz geprägt;
Wie sie kurz angebunden war,
Das ist nun zum Entzücken gar!

Mephistopheles tritt auf.

FAUST. Hör, du mußt mir die Dirne schaffen!

ERSTER TEIL   209

MEPHISTOPHELES. Nun, welche?
FAUST.   Sie ging just vorbei.
MEPHISTOPHELES. Da die? Sie kam von ihrem Pfaffen,
Der sprach sie aller Sünden frei;
Ich schlich mich hart am Stuhl vorbei,
Es ist ein gar unschuldig Ding,
Das eben für nichts zur Beichte ging;
Über die hab ich keine Gewalt!
FAUST. Ist über vierzehn Jahr doch alt.
MEPHISTOPHELES. Du sprichst ja wie Hans Liederlich,
Der begehrt jede liebe Blum für sich,
Und dünkelt ihm, es wär kein Ehr
Und Gunst, die nicht zu pflücken wär;
Geht aber doch nicht immer an.
FAUST. Mein Herr Magister Lobesan,
Laß Er mich mit dem Gesetz in Frieden!
Und das sag ich Ihm kurz und gut:
Wenn nicht das süße junge Blut
Heut nacht in meinen Armen ruht,
So sind wir um Mitternacht geschieden.
MEPHISTOPHELES.
Bedenkt, was gehn und stehen mag!
Ich brauche wenigstens vierzehn Tag,
Nur die Gelegenheit auszuspüren.
FAUST. Hätt ich nur sieben Stunden Ruh,
Brauchte den Teufel nicht dazu,
So ein Geschöpfchen zu verführen.
MEPHISTOPH. Ihr sprecht schon fast wie ein Franzos;
Doch bitt ich, laßts Euch nicht verdrießen:
Was hilfts, nur grade zu genießen?
Die Freud ist lange nicht so groß,
Als wenn Ihr erst herauf, herum,
Durch allerlei Brimborium,
Das Püppchen geknetet und zugericht't,
Wie's lehret manche welsche Geschicht.
FAUST. Hab Appetit auch ohne das.
MEPHISTOPH. Jetzt ohne Schimpf und ohne Spaß.
Ich sag Euch, mit dem schönen Kind
Gehts ein- für allemal nicht geschwind.
GOETHE VI 14.

VIERTER AKT
FÜNFTE SZENE

England, the messengers presented themselves to the king, giving him Fengons letters; who having read the contents, sayd nothing as then, but stayed convenient time to effect Fengons desire, meane time using the Danes familiarly, doing them that honour to sit at his table (for that kings as then where not so curiously, nor solemnely served as in these our dayes), for in these dayes meane kings, and lords of small revenewe are as difficult and hard to bee seene, as in times past the monarches of Persia used to bee; or as it is reported of the great king of Aethyopia, who will not permit any man to see his face, which ordinarily bee covereth with a vaile. And as the messengers sate at the table with the king, subtile Hamlet was so far from being merry with them, that he would not taste one bit of meate, bread, nor cup of beare whatsoever, as then set upon the table, not without great wondering of the company, abashed to see a yong man and a stranger not to esteeme of the delicate meates and pleasant drinkes served at the banquet, rejecting them as things filthy, evill of tast, and worse prepared. The king, who for that time dissembled what he thought, caused his ghests to be conveyed into their chamber, willing one of his secret servantes to hide himselfe therein, and so to certifie him what speeches past among

DIE TRAGISCHE GESCHICHTE VON

Befürchte nichts für unsere person.
Denn solche göttlichkeit schirmt einen könig:
Verrat, der nur erblickt, was er gewollt,
Steht ab von seinem willen. - Sage, Hamlet,
Was bist du so entrüstet? - Gertrud, laß ihn! -
Sprich, junger mann!
Ham. Wo ist mein vater?
König Tot.
Königin Doch nicht durch ihn.
König Laß ihn nur satt sich fragen. -
Ham. Wie kam er um? Ich lasse mich nicht äffen.
Zur hölle, treu! Zum ärgsten teufel, eide!
Gewissen, frömmigkeit, zum tiefsten schlund!
Ich trotze der verdammnis; so weit kam's:
Ich schlage beide welten in die schanze,
Mag kommen, was da kommt! Nur rache will ich
Vollauf für meinen vater.
König Wer wird euch hindern?
Ham. Mein wille, nicht der ganzen welt gebot.
Und meine mittel will ich so verwalten,
Daß wenig weit soll reichen.
König Höre, Hamlet,
Wenn du von deines teuren vaters tod
Das sichre wissen willst: ist's deiner rache schluß,
Als sieger in dem spiel, so freund als feind,
Unschuldige und schuldge zu vernichten?
Ham. Die schuldgen nur.
König Wollt ihr sie kennen lernen? -
Ham. Den freunden will ich weit die arme öffnen
Und, wie der lebensopfrer pelikan,
Mit meinem blut sie nähren.

140

HAMLET PRINZEN VON DÆNEMARK

Laer. Doch meine hand wird eisen, und nur ein
Gedanke nistet noch in meinem hirn.
König Wie denkt ihr's euch?
Laer. Ihn in der kirch' erwürgen.
König Auf andre art, wenn ihr entschlossen seid.
Laer. Der würger würgte meinen vater hin,
Er würgte meine schwester und wird mich
Erwürgen, doch ich komme ihm zuvor.
König Mit einem wohlgezielten, sichren stoß.
Wollt ihr dies tun, so haltet euch zuhaus.
Kommt Hamlet, soll er wissen ihr seid hier.
Wir laden beide euch zu diesem spiel,
Des ende tödlich sein muß für den prinzen,
Kein wenn und aber ist hier mehr am platz.
Laer. Mit meines hasses gift salb ich die spitze
Des degens.
König Gebt zum apotheker, kauft
Ein richtges gift, ein tödliches: geritzt nur,
Geb er die gottverdammte seele auf.
Doch muß der plan noch einen rückhalt haben.
Ich hab's: wenn ihr vom fechten heiß und durstig
seid -
Ihr müßt deshalb die gänge kräftger machen -
Und er zu trinken fordert, soll ein kelch
Bereitstehn, der, wenn er davon nur nippt,
Entging er etwa eurem giftgen stich,
Noch unsern anschlag sichert.
Laer. Herr, ich zittre,
Dem rüden gleich, der einen eber wittert.

145

VIERTER AKT
SECHSTE SZENE

HARANGUE D'AMLETH
AUX DANOIS
S'il y a quelqu'un d'entre vous, Messieurs de Dannemarch, qui aye encore fraische memoire du tort faict au puissant Roy Horwendille, qu'il ne s'esmeuve en rien, voyant la face confuse et hideusement espouvantable de la presente calamité. S'il y a aucun qui aye la fidelité pour recommandee, et cherisse l'affection qu'on doit a ses parens, et trouve bonne la souvenance des outrages faits a ceur, qui nous ont produits au monde, que celuy ne s'esbabisse, contemplant un tel massacre, et moins s'offense en advisant une si effroyable ruine, et d'hommes, et des plus superbes edifices de tout le pays: car la main qui a execute ceste justice, ne pouvoit en chevir a meilleur marché, et ne luy estoit loisible d'autrement se prevaloir, qu'en ruinant, et l'insensible, et le sensible, pour garder la memoire d'une si equitable vengeance. Je voy bien, Messieurs, bien j'ay cur de cognoistre une telle vostre si affectionnee devotion) que vous estes marris, ayans devant vos yeux Fengon ainsi mutilé, et celuy sans teste, que d'autresfois vous avez recogneu pour chef, mais je vous prie penser que ce corps n'est le corps d'un Roy, ains d'un tyran execrable, et d'un parricide plus detestable.

1929. *Die Tragische Geschichte von Hamlet, Prinzen von Daenemark* by William Shakespeare illustrated with woodcuts by Edward Gordon Craig. Published and printed by the Cranach Press, Weimar. Produced under the direction of J. H. Mason and Max Goertz. 14" × 9½". Text pages.

1921. *Elia*, a block-book with letters and pictures cut on the wood by Rudolf Koch. 11" × 9⅜". Printed by Wilhelm Gerstung, Offenbach-am-Main, in an edition of 200 copies. Double spread.

1902. *The Art of Walter Crane* by P. G. Konody. Published by George Bell and Sons. Printed by the Chiswick Press. $13\frac{1}{2}'' \times 9\frac{1}{2}''$. The title-page design by Walter Crane was also blocked in gold on the cloth cover.

The Arts and Crafts Exhibition Society and art nouveau

Walter Crane was both an illustrator and a book designer. He was also, under William Morris's influence, one of the prime movers in the Arts and Crafts Exhibition Society, a society founded to promote a revival in the decorative arts. Crane stated the aims of this Society with clarity and persuasion in the introductory essay to the catalogue of the 1888 exhibition. The ideas of the various members of the Society were assembled in *Arts and Crafts Essays,* which Morris edited and Rivington, Percival published in 1893. (In this same book was the admirable essay, *Printing,* by Morris and Emery Walker.) Crane was a vociferous opponent of art nouveau, yet his work reveals marked art nouveau characteristics. His earlier illustrations, drawn for the colour printer Edmund Evans, have some charm, but as he became more interested in book *decoration,* as opposed to illustration, so his work became more lifeless. He subordinated everything to the design of the printed page and, though to some extent he avoided the archaism of Morris and Burne-Jones, his work lacked the magnificent quality of inevitability so apparent in all Morris's work. Crane influenced a number of young artists, including Anning Bell, and taught for a number of years at the Royal College of Art. His professional career spanned over half-a-century, during which time he illustrated a great number of books.

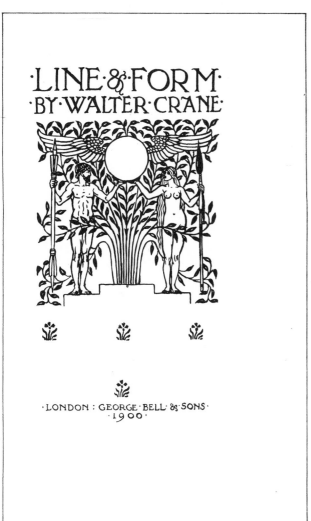

1900. *Line and Form* written and designed by Walter Crane. Published by George Bell and Sons, London. Printed by Charles Whittingham and Co., London. $9\frac{1}{8}'' \times 5\frac{3}{4}''$. The title-page design was also blocked in gold on the cover.

1913. *Le Nouveau Monde* by Villiers de l'Isle-Adam. Illustrated by woodcuts by P. E. Vibert. Published by Georges Crès et Cie, Paris. $9\frac{7}{8}'' \times 6\frac{3}{8}''$. Art Nouveau title-page designed by P. E. Vibert and printed in black, green and orange.

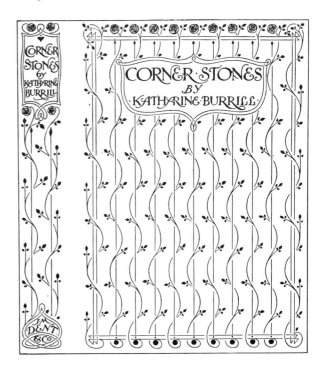

c. 1912. *Corner Stones* by Katharine Burrill. Binding designed by Reginald L. Knowles. Published by J. M. Dent and Sons Ltd, London. Reproduced from *The Art of the Book* 1914: Studio.

1888. *Troy Town* by Q. (Sir Arthur Quiller-Couch). Published and printed by Cassell and Co. Ltd, London. 7¼″ × 5″. Brown cloth cover blocked in gold and black.

The beginning of the illustrated case-binding

Sir Arthur Quiller-Couch's *The Astonishing History of Troy Town* was first published in Cassell's Five Shilling Series in 1888. The cover, by some anonymous artist, is printed in black on a smooth dun-coloured cloth. Only the words 'Troy Town' on the spine are blocked in gold. The letter forms are a firm break away from any traditional roman, and antecede art nouveau with their vaguely oriental characteristics. The history of the late nineteenth- and early twentieth-century illustrated cover is still to be written. The *Troy Town* cover is a relatively modest example of the genus.

In contrast Reznicek's cover for Eduard Fuch's *Die Frau in der Karikatur* is a colourful thing, combining blocking on a suede-finished cloth and a woman's figure printed in colour, cut out and inlaid. The laborious process of mounting four-colour prints on cloth cases, particularly for gift books and children's books, continued well into the 1920's. Though this has been regarded as a bastard process, some pretty covers resulted. The influence of the poster hoarding on such a cover as that for *Die Frau in der Karikatur* is obvious, but it was a golden age for posters and their influence on book covers was considerable.

1906. *Die Frau in der Karikatur* by Eduard
Fuchs. Published by Albert Langen, Munich.
Printed by Hesse and Becker, Leipzig. Bound by
E. R. Enders, Leipzig. 10¾″ × 7⅛″. Case-binding.

1920. *Theodor Hosemann* by Lothar Brieger.
Published by Delphin-Verlag, Munich. With a
catalogue of the works of art by Karl Hobrecker.
9⅜″ × 6¼″. Bound in a rough mustard-coloured
cloth, blocked in black. Sugar-bag blue endpapers. Case-binding, title-page and text spread.

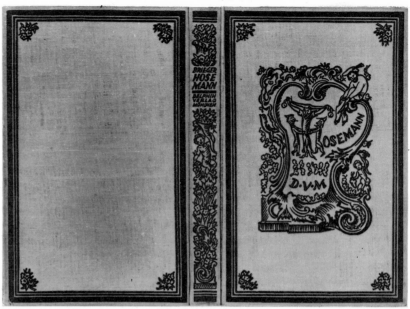

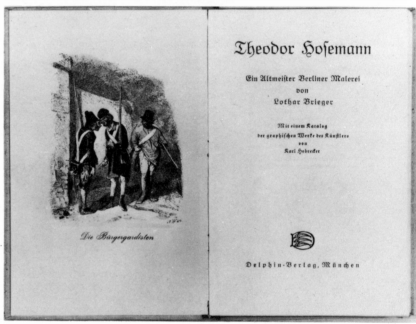

HISTOIRE

DE

L'IMPRIMERIE

EN FRANCE

AU XVᵉ ET AU XVIᵉ SIÈCLE

PAR A. CLAUDIN

LAURÉAT DE L'INSTITUT

TOME PREMIER

PARIS

IMPRIMERIE NATIONALE

MDCCCC

1900. *Histoire de l'Imprimerie en France* by A. Claudin. Published and printed by ·l'Imprimerie Nationale, Paris. 16¾" × 13". Title-page.

Lothar Brieger's monograph on the nineteenth-century German illustrator, Theodor Hosemann, has an interesting cover. The mustard-coloured case is blocked with a design that combines art nouveau, William Morris and rococo motifs. The case-binding is set off with sugar-bag blue end paper. The book, which looks as if it belonged to the end of the nineteenth century, was actually printed and bound in 1920.

The typographic book in France

In French book production more attention was paid to the illustrations than to the typefaces or the *mise-en-page*. But there were exceptions to this amongst publishers and printers; and of these, the Imprimerie Nationale very properly led the field. The French National Printing House at this time was under the enlightened direction of Arthur Christian. In 1900, Christian published Anatole Claudin's monumental *Histoire de l'Imprimerie en France*. This was printing in the grand manner, not seen in France since the times of Barbou and Didot. Typographically traditional, the book was set in large sizes of Garamond and Grandjean typefaces; the folio pages had ample margins and impeccable presswork.

An interest in France in the typographic, illustrated book, rather than the *édition de luxe,* where every other feature was subordinated to the illustration, was largely due to the publisher Édouard Pelletan. Pelletan was almost unique amongst his contemporaries. He demanded a high standard from his printers, was an exacting typographer and made good use of the typefaces of Jannon and Grandjean.

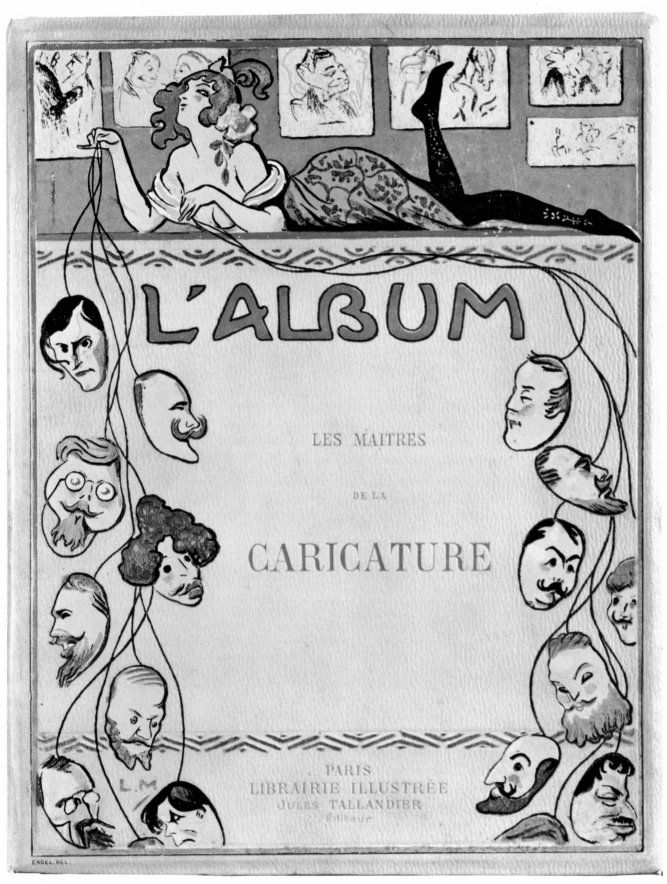

1902. *L'Album: les Maîtres de la Caricature,*
with a preface by Roger-Milès. Published by
Librairie Illustrée, J. Tallandier, Paris. Printed by
l'Imprimerie Générale Lahure, Paris. Bound by
Engel. 12¼" × 9½". Cover design by Lucien
Métivet, printed in full colour, on a cream-
coloured buckram.

CHARLES NODIER

Histoire

du

Chien de Brisquet

PRÉCÉDÉE

D'UNE LETTRE A JEANNE

PAR

M. ANATOLE FRANCE

de l'Académie française

25 Compositions de Steinlen

GRAVÉES PAR DELOCHE, E. FROMENT

ERNEST ET FRÉDÉRIC FLORIAN

KTHMA ES AEI

E   P

PARIS

ÉDOUARD PELLETAN, ÉDITEUR

125, BOULEVARD SAINT-GERMAIN, 125

1900

1900. *Histoire du Chien de Brisquet* by Charles Nodier, with 25 illustrations by Théophile Alexandre Steinlen, engraved by Deloche, E. Froment, Ernest and Frédéric Florian. Published by Édouard Pelletan, Paris. 11⅜" × 9". Title-page printed ih black from a wood engraving and in blue and red, and vignette half-title printed in black and red.

[4] *The New Book Illustration in France* (1924) Léon Pichon, Studio Ltd, London.

When Pelletan established himself as a publisher of 'artistic' books at 125 Blvd. Saint-Germain on 1st February 1896, there was plenty of exciting French book illustration but little good French book design. Léon Pichon, another French publisher of judgment writing nearly thirty years later, stated that at that time the English book, as conceived by William Morris, had a perfect unity; that the German books, derivative though they were (from Morris), matched the character of the race; but that French books were devoid of personality or harmony of style. Above all, Pichon went on, they lacked any 'directing intelligence'.[4] With that last remark, Pichon established the essential factor in book design. The 'directing intelligence' can be publisher, printer, typographer or illustrator, but without such direction, design is absent.

Pelletan, at a time when most French publishers thought only of the illustrations (for this kind of book, Pelletan's 'artistic' book), considered first the book as a whole, then the general typographic arrangement that would help to display the illustrations, and lastly, the illustrations themselves.

He helped to re-establish (at a time of insipidity in French books) a precise classification of the component parts of a book, subordinating everything to the elucidation of the author's text.

Pelletan's typography always took precedence over the illustrations, but this is not to say that he was unaware of the quality of the artists he employed. He used many illustrators, including Steinlen, Daniel Vierge and Willette, but his books, even when illustrated by an artist of the power of Steinlen, were never overpowered by the illustrator's personality. In such a book as Charles Nodier's *Histoire du Chien de Brisquet*, one's first impression on turning the pages is not of the skill of Steinlen's drawings of the woodcutter or his dog, but of the immaculate typography and the superb presswork.

nir chez Jean Paquier. — « As-tu vu nos
« enfants? » lui dit Brisquette.

« Nos enfants? dit Brisquet. Nos enfants?
« mon Dieu! sont-ils sortis? »

« Je les ai envoyés à ta rencontre jusqu'à
« la butte et à l'étang, mais tu as pris par un
« autre chemin. »

Brisquet ne posa pas sa bonne hache. Il

se mit à courir du côté de la butte.

« Si tu menois la Bichonne? »
lui cria Brisquette.

La Bichonne étoit déjà bien
loin.

Elle étoit si loin que Brisquet la perdit bientôt de vue.
Et il avoit beau crier :
« Biscotin, Biscotine! » on
ne lui répondoit pas.

Alors il se prit à pleu-
rer, parce qu'il s'ima-
gina que ses enfants
étoient perdus.

Après avoir couru
longtemps, longtemps,
il lui sembla recon-
noitre la vòix de
la Bichonne. Il
marcha

1900. *Histoire du Chien de Brisquet* by Charles Nodier with 25 illustrations by Théophile Alexandre Steinlen. Published by Édouard Pelletan, Paris. 11⅜" × 9". Text and illustration spread. Cover engraved on the wood by Froment and printed in full colour.

Steinlen's drawings for *Histoire du Chien de Brisquet* were beautifully engraved by Deloche, E. Froment, and Ernest and Frédéric Florian. They marry most happily with the handsome neo-classical typeface. The book is an interesting typographic mixture: the title-page has strong art nouveau influences, particularly in the title lines; the cover belongs to the new age of the French poster. *Histoire du Chien de Brisquet* is a successful example of a book conceived typographically, rather than solely as a vehicle for illustration. It is a beautiful book.

The 1900's might seem to be something of an anti-climax after the splendours of the 'nineties. Yet there was plenty of confidence in the world of books. The development of photographic methods of reproduction led to wide use of illustration, not only inside books but also on their covers. This was the age of the picture cover, sometimes crudely printed, often superbly blocked. In most of these illustrated covers art nouveau motifs can be detected, which were often repeated in the endpapers and title-pages.

But, however lively their covers, the presswork and typography of these books were often deplorable; the papers used were wretched puffed-up antiques, or not very good coated stock (though the bindings were often made up of firm boards and excellent book cloths, well blocked). The wide margins that Whistler had used so successfully in his books helped ro relieve the otherwise rather undistinguished typography. It was only in the private press book and in the work of a few commercial publishers that the typographic virtues one looks for in fine books were to be found.

Histoire du Chien de Brisquet

illustrée par Steinlen

se vend chez Édouard Pelletan aux Éditions d'Art

1900. *Sie*, an album of drawings by Reznicek. Published by Albert Langen, Munich. 14¾" × 11". Bound in calendered unbleached linen, printed in black and Indian red.

[5] See *Victorian Book Design and Colour Printing* by Ruari McLean. Faber and Faber, London 1963.

The illustrated case-binding

The brashness of many of the commercially produced books of the 1900's often has more vitality than the impeccable work of private press productions. This is particularly true of their covers, which were frequently colourful and decorative. They look perhaps a little modest alongside the jewel-like blockings of the '60's and '70's; or against such exotic materials as tortoiseshell or *papier mâché* (which had to be cast in moulds), or cloths such as silk and velvet. Blocking in gold or blind blocking came into use in the 1830's, and the mounting on cloth covers of printed panels of paper some thirty years later.[5] These two techniques provided the hard core of decorative and illustrative bindings well into the twentieth century. The printing of coloured designs on paper-covered boards shown so splendidly by the yellow-backed novels, which were printed in three or four colours from designs cut on wood, fell into disuse. (A development of this method – printing cover designs by offset lithography on cloth – is used rather less often than it might be nowadays.) The cover for *Sie* is by Reznicek and is printed in colour on linen-covered boards. The silhouette treatment of the woman's black dress is worthy of the Beggarstaffs.

The cloth cover for the first American edition (1893) of Robert Louis Stevenson's *Island Nights' Entertainments* is printed in black and a terracotta red. It is an effective and appropriate design by some anonymous designer at Scribner's. The book is illustrated by Gordon Browne and W. Hatherell.

1893. *Island Nights' Entertainments* by Robert
Louis Stevenson. Published by Charles Scribner's
Sons, New York. Printed by Trow Directory,
Printing and Bookbinding Company, New York.
$7\frac{1}{4}'' \times 5''$. Case-binding printed in black and
Indian red on an oatmeal coloured cloth.

1900. *Some Experiences of an Irish R.M.* by
E. Œ. Somerville and Martin Ross. Illustrated by
E. Œ. Somerville. Published by Longmans,
Green and Co., London. $7\frac{1}{4}'' \times 4\frac{3}{4}''$. Case-binding
of dark green cloth blocked in red and black.

1907. *A Tarpaulin Muster* by John Masefield.
Cover designed by 'Mr Symington', reproduced
from *The Inchcape Rock*. Published by E. Grant
Richards. $7\frac{1}{2}'' \times 4\frac{7}{8}''$. Case-binding of unbleached
canvas blocked in navy blue and orange.

1913. *The Pavilion on the Links* by Robert Louis
Stevenson, illustrated by Gordon Browne.
Published by Chatto and Windus, London.
Printed by Ballantyne, Hanson and Co. Ltd,
Edinburgh. $8\frac{1}{8}'' \times 5\frac{1}{4}''$. Case-binding blocked in
six colours on a grey cloth. (*Opposite left.*)

1905. *Ghost Stories of an Antiquary* by
Montague Rhodes James, illustrated by James
McBryde. Published by Edward Arnold, London.
Printed by Billing and Sons Ltd, Guildford.
$8\frac{1}{4}'' \times 5\frac{5}{8}''$. Case-binding of unbleached canvas
blocked in red and black. (*Opposite right.*)

The book covers shown here are very typical of those published at the turn
of the century. The title for *Some Experiences of an Irish R.M.* is blocked in
red and black, on a green cloth from a design by E. Œ. Somerville. The same
treatment is used for the Will Owen design for *A Master of Craft*. Owen, who
was a successful poster artist, illustrated both this book and *At Sunwich Port*,
though the cover design for the latter is by a designer with the initials G.M.W.
The Pavilion on the Links by Robert Louis Stevenson is illustrated with some
very lively drawings by Gordon Browne, who also designed the cover. This
is effectively blocked in white, two yellows, black and dark grey on the mid-
grey cloth. Gold for the letters on the spine brings the total of blocking
operations to six! M. R. James's *Ghost Stories of an Antiquary* makes a
pleasant contrast to these picture covers. It has a square-backed, rough, unbleached canvas cover, blocked in black and red. 'Square-backing' was a
continental rather than an English binding method; the English binders, more
than those of any other country, have remained faithful to rounding-and-
backing.

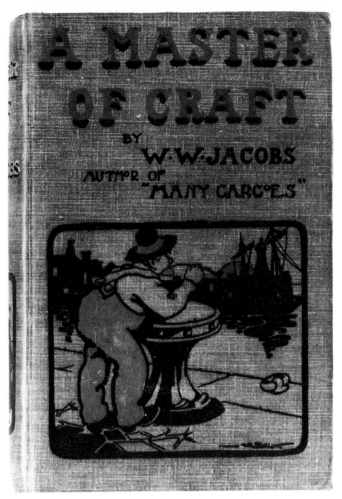

1900. *A Master of Craft* by W. W. Jacobs, illustrated by Will Owen. Published by George Newnes, London. 7¾″ × 5⅛″. Green cloth case-binding blocked in black and orange.

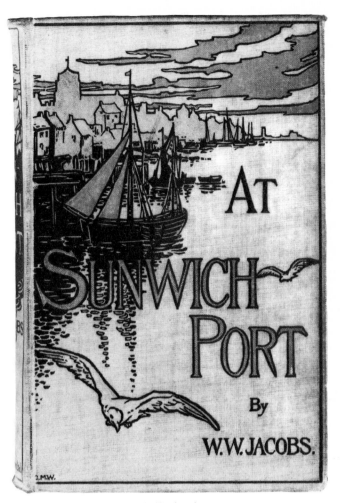

1902. *At Sunwich Port* by W. W. Jacobs, illustrated by Will Owen. Published by George Newnes, London. 7¾″ × 5⅛″. Cloth binding blocked in black, blue and pink.

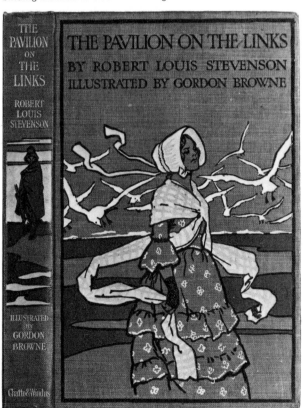

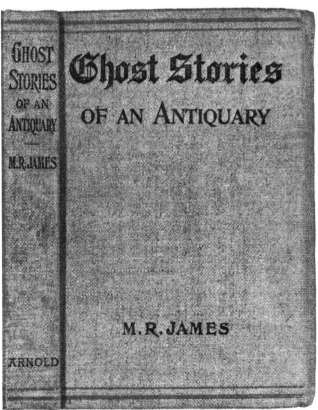

1922. *Printing Types* by Daniel Berkeley Updike.
Published in Great Britain by Oxford University
Press, London; and published and printed by
Harvard University Press, Cambridge, Mass., in
the United States of America. 9¼″ × 6¼″. This
title-page is taken from the second edition, 1937

PRINTING TYPES

THEIR HISTORY, FORMS, AND USE

A STUDY IN SURVIVALS

BY

DANIEL BERKELEY UPDIKE

WITH ILLUSTRATIONS

*"Nunca han tenido, ni tienen las artes otros
enemigos que los ignorantes"*

VOLUME I

SECOND EDITION

GEOFFREY CUMBERLEGE

OXFORD UNIVERSITY PRESS

LONDON

Daniel Berkeley Updike and Bruce Rogers

The effects of Morris's work at Kelmscott were certainly felt in the U.S.A., most strongly in New England, and by no one more so than by Daniel Berkeley Updike. In 1893, Updike started the Merrymount Press. Until that time, from the age of twenty, he had been working for Houghton Mifflin at the Riverside Press. He said: 'None of us were very sensible or businesslike, and if we had been we would have been heard of no more.'[6]

His Merrymount Press achieved an outstanding reputation in both the U.S.A. and Europe for fine typography and presswork and the most painstaking care in every stage of book printing. Updike's career was crowned by the publication in 1922 of his *Printing Types,* of which he wrote 'The book has, by those who know, been called a monumental work, and came, as far as I was concerned, fatally near being so.'[7]

The other great American typographer in the twentieth-century renaissance of book design was Bruce Rogers. Whereas Updike was essentially a scholar-printer, Rogers was an artist who happened to express himself through the design of books. His typographic art, like that of all his contemporaries, was based on the work of the past. His knowledge of period was extensive, yet his books were not slavish copies; he took a period style and made the fullest use of it, producing something quite personal.

[6] Updike: *American Printer and his Merrymount
Press.* Notes on the press by Daniel Berkeley
Updike and essays by Stanley Morison, T. M. Cleland *et alia.* Published by the American Institute of
Graphic Arts, New York, 1947.

[7] *Ib.*

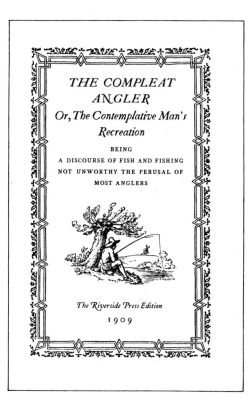

1909. *The Compleat Angler* by Izaac Walton, designed by Bruce Rogers. Published and printed by the Riverside Press, Cambridge, Mass., for Houghton Mifflin Co., Boston. $6\frac{1}{4}'' \times 4\frac{1}{8}''$. Title-page.

Directoire and other period influences

An edition of *The Compleat Angler,* which Bruce Rogers designed in 1909, was printed at the Riverside Press, Cambridge, Mass., and published by Houghton Mifflin Company, from Boston and New York. It is a charming book, square-backed and bound in a brown, crumpled Japanese paper with a simple printed label on the spine. In spite of the very short lines, the setting is remarkably close knit. The title-page has been reproduced many times, but it is so pretty and so typical of its designer that it is worth showing just once again.

By the beginning of the First World War, art nouveau had lost much of its appeal. There was a general return to Directoire (1795–9) and Louis XVI (1774–93) designs. Shepherds, shepherdesses and powdered wigged gallants vied with Pierrots and Columbines as subjects for book decorations. It was a somewhat sentimental period. Popular illustrators in this manner were Emil Preetorius in Germany, Daniel Vierge in France and Hugh Thomson in England. Books continued to look much as they had done for the last twenty years, except for the wider use of coated stock, that was needed for printing halftone illustrations, in monochrome and colour.

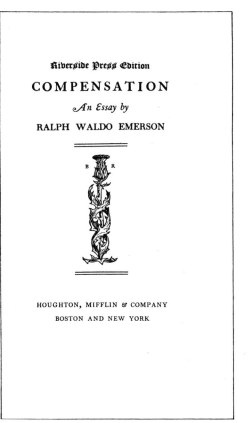

1903 *Compensation,* an essay by Ralph Waldo Emerson. A prospectus designed by Bruce Rogers. Published by Houghton Mifflin and Co., New York. Printed by the Riverside Press. $7\frac{1}{4}'' \times 4\frac{5}{8}''$.

1939. *The Work of Bruce Rogers* published by the Oxford University Press, New York. Half-title for 'Progressive Layouts for On Dry-Cow Fishing' as designed by Bruce Rogers. $9\frac{1}{4}'' \times 5\frac{3}{4}''$.

1913. *Tartarin von Tarascon* by Alphonse Daudet. Translated by A. Gerstmann, with illustrations by Emil Preetorius. Published by Der Gelbe Verlag Mundt and Blumtritt. Printed by M. Müller and Sohn, Munich. 7¾″ × 5¼″. Drawn-on orange coloured paper cover printed in black. Title-page and chapter opening.

Bei den Türken

Die Überfahrt ~ Der Fez in fünf verschiedenen Lagen ~ Am Abend des dritten Tages ~ Erbarmen

Jetzt, mein lieber Leser, möchte ich ein Maler sein, ein großer Maler, damit ich hier bei Beginn des zweiten Teiles unserer Geschichte vor deinen Augen die verschiedenen Lagen skizzieren könnte, die der rote Fez des Herrn Tartarin aus Tarascon an den drei Tagen der Überfahrt von Frankreich nach Algier an Bord des „Zuaven" einnahm. Ich würde ihn zuerst gezeichnet haben bei der Abreise auf der Landungsbrücke. Ach, wie heldenhaft und stolz, wie eine Aureole, schmückt er das schöne tarasconische Haupt.

Dann würde ich ihn zeigen bei der Ausfahrt aus dem Hafen, als der „Zuave" auf den Wellen sich zu wiegen und zu schaukeln begann; man würde ihn zitternd und zagend sehen, als spüre er schon die ersten Vorboten des nahenden Unheils.

Zum dritten würde ich den Fez im Golf du Lion malen. Je breiter hier die Meeresfläche zwischen den Küsten wird,

87

c. 1912. *Briefe der Ninon de l'Enclos* translated by Lothar Schmidt. Illustrated with etchings by Karl Walser. Published by Bruno Cassirer. 7″ × 5″. Title-page and frontispiece.

Series design

The cheap reprints of books dates at least back to the time of the Venetian printer-publisher Aldus, who was producing pocket editions by the first years of the sixteenth century. The great age of mass-produced series of books started with the railway age and railway bookstalls. George Routledge's Railway Library in the 1850's was followed by a number of cheap and (usually) nasty series. The first serious attempt to combine quality with cheapness was made by J. M. Dent, with his Temple Library (1888), followed by his Temple Shakespeare (1894), for which series Walter Crane drew the title-page. The greatest and most lasting success (in the hard-back field) came with Grant Richards' World's Classics in 1901 which the Oxford University Press took over in 1906. Dent's Everyman also began in 1906. Both these series flourish to this day.

The World's Classics were in a small format (6 in. by $3\frac{3}{4}$ in.) with green or maroon cloth-covered binding cases, blocked in gold on the spine with the title and an entwined leaf pattern (by an anonymous designer). The early volumes were well set and well printed by, amongst others, two Edinburgh printing firms, R. & R. Clark and Turnbull and Spears, and the famous East Anglian book house, William Clowes and Sons of Beccles.

The Everyman series was issued in both grey cloth and red leather-covered cases. The format was slightly larger than that of the World's Classics.

For Everyman, J. M. Dent commissioned an English architect called R. L. Knowles to design the covers, endpapers and title-pages. Knowles's designs were made up of swirling, macaroni-like lines, essentially art nouveau in character.

The books were of an ideal size for holding in the hand (or reading in bed) and were extremely legible and well printed by such firms as William Clowes and Sons of Beccles in Suffolk. (The concentration of good printing in East Anglia and Scotland is worth noting.)

1902. *The Opium Eater* by Thomas de Quincey. Published by E. Grant Richards as No. 23 in The World's Classics Series. Spine blocked in gold on a green cloth.

1907. *American Notes and Pictures from Italy* by Charles Dickens. Everyman Library, edited by Ernest Rhys. Published by J. M. Dent and Co. Ltd and in New York by E. P. Dutton. This edition had a gold blocked leather binding and rounded corners. Printed by the Temple Press, Letchworth. $6\frac{3}{4}'' \times 4\frac{1}{8}''$. (*To the right.*)

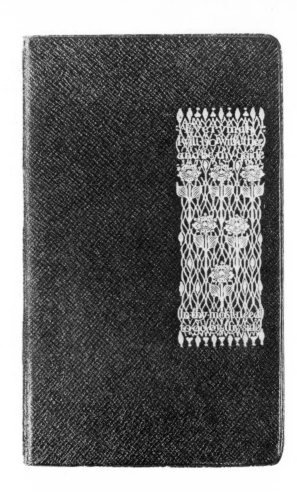

1928. *Memoirs of Mary Wollstonecraft* by William Godwin. Published by Constable and Co., London. Title-page spread. $7'' \times 4\frac{3}{8}''$.

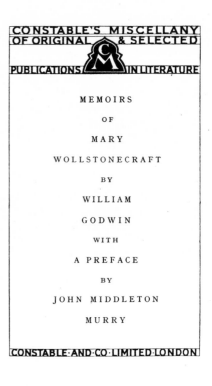

1907. Everyman Library title-page design by
Reginald L. Knowles. Published by J. M. Dent
and Co. Ltd, London.

c. 1905. Everyman Library endpaper design by
Reginald L. Knowles.

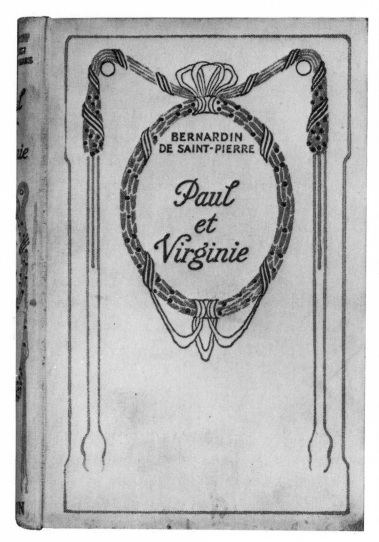

1910. *Paul et Virginie* by Bernardin de Saint-Pierre. Published by Nelson, Paris, London, Edinburgh and New York. Printed in Edinburgh by Nelson. 6⅛" × 4". White cloth case-binding, blocked in green and mauve.

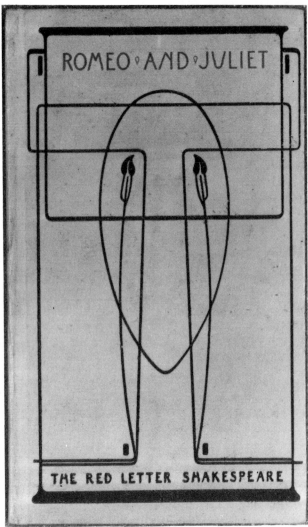

1904. *Romeo and Juliet* by William Shakespeare. The Red Letter Shakespeare. Published by Blackie & Sons Ltd. 6⅛" × 3½". White cloth case-binding blocked in dark green and vermilion, designed by Talwin Morris.

8 *The Art Nouveau Book in Britain:* John Russell Taylor, Methuen, London 1966. If it had not been for Mr Taylor's book, which I saw just as I was completing my proof corrections, I should never have known of Talwin Morris's work and I should also have credited 'The Red Letter Shakespeare' to the Gresham Publishing Company. The volume in my possession had had the original title-pages removed and a replacement leaf had been tipped in with the Gresham Publishing Company's name on it. I can only think it must have come from remainder stock.

In the years before the first war, a number of English publishers entered this cheap reprint field. Most of these series were fairly short lived. The Scottish firm of Nelson brought out one with very pretty white cloth covers, blocked in green and mauve. A white cloth cover was also used by the Gresham Publishing Company for 'The Red Letter Shakespeare', so called because the names of the characters were printed in red.

Blackie and Sons of Glasgow were the publishers of 'The Red Letter Shakespeare'. These little books were designed by Talwin Morris (1865–1911), who came from the south to work for Blackies, as art director. His simple geometric designs were ideal for blocking in gold or colour and were architecturally strong enough to be very effective. His output was enormous. As John Russell Taylor has recently said, Talwin Morris was one of the great purveyors of art nouveau to the fast expanding book buying public.[8]

Various publishers continued to produce reprints in a 'series' format. Amongst these, Constable's 'Miscellany of Original and selected Publications in Literature', was a well-produced series, with smooth light-blue cloth covers blocked in gold and dark blue. One of the most successful and attractive series on either side of the Atlantic is 'The Modern Library'. These little books, published by Random House, the New York publishers, have classically simple covers of smooth grey cloth, with a rectangle of colour on the front and spine, on which the title is blocked in gold. Series designs continued to proliferate, until the overwhelming competition of paperbacks put an effective brake on that kind of publishing.

In England, by the beginning of the 1920's, the beneficial influence of the private press movement was at last having an effect on commercial printing and publishing. One of the last great romantics, Claud Lovat Fraser, nearing the end of his tragically short life, was contributing colour and gaiety both to books and to ephemeral printing for the Curwen Press. The great revival of classic typefaces was under way at Monotype, but in England and America there was little evidence of experimental typography. In Germany the effect of the Jugendstil typographers was not quite exhausted and a new impetus came from the Russian Constructivists and the Swiss Dadaists, resulting in a sudden blaze of typographic innovation.

The typography of George Bernard Shaw's plays

George Bernard Shaw's plays were published in a uniform style. Shaw took a very close interest in every detail of printing and publishing. His *Plays, Pleasant and Unpleasant* was published by Grant Richards, 'that habitual bankrupt', and printed by the Edinburgh firm of R. & R. Clark; but Shaw soon deserted the unstable Grant Richards and himself arranged with Constable to publish his plays on commission. To do this, he had to deal directly with the printer and pay the print bills himself; his connections with W. R. Maxwell at R. & R. Clark is almost unique in the context of author-printer relationships. Shaw had firm ideas about book design and based his page layout and general format on William Morris's *Roots of the Mountains*. He likewise used the same solidly set Long Primer Caslon Old Face. As for a typeface he had little choice; James Shand described the typographic limitations of the times in an article in *Alphabet and Image*, December 1948:

'In 1897 we must remember that there were only two text-types available in most book-houses: Old Style or Modern. More often than not, before mechanical typesetting, there was not even any choice. Publisher and author often had to accept the type of which there happened to be, at any given moment, the greatest amount of "dis".'

It was not until the middle 1920's, when the Limited Collected Edition of his works was proposed, that Shaw was willing to accept machine setting, and then only on the evidence of a specimen page that Maxwell put before him. Maxwell also succeeded in weaning him from his beloved Caslon; the new editions of the Standard Edition were reset in Fournier, in spite of Shaw's saying 'I'll stick to Caslon until I die'!

There have been collected editions of the works of a number of authors, including Macmillan's Pocket Edition of Rudyard Kipling's works. These handsome, slim books were bound in limp maroon calf and blocked in gold.

Three Plays for Puritans: The Devil's Disciple, Cæsar and Cleopatra, & Captain Brassbound's Conversion. By Bernard Shaw.

London: Grant Richards, 48 Leicester Square, W.C.

Androcles and the Lion, Overruled, Pygmalion. By Bernard Shaw.

Constable and Company Ltd. London: 1916.

1901. *Three Plays for Puritans* by Bernard Shaw. Published by E. Grant Richards, London. $6\frac{7}{8}'' \times 4\frac{3}{4}''$. Set in Caslon Old Face. Title-page.

Text spread for *Pygmalion*, set in Caslon Old Face.

1916. *Androcles and the Lion, Overruled and Pygmalion* by Bernard Shaw. Published by Constable and Co. Ltd, London. Printed by R. & R. Clark, Edinburgh. $6\frac{7}{8}'' \times 4\frac{3}{4}''$. Set in Caslon Old Face. Title-page.

---

120   Pygmalion   Act II

when he is neither bullying nor exclaiming to the heavens against some featherweight cross, he coaxes women as a child coaxes its nurse when it wants to get anything out of her.

HIGGINS [*brusquely, recognizing her with unconcealed disappointment, and at once, babylike, making an intolerable grievance of it*] Why, this is the girl I jotted down last night. Shes no use: Ive got all the records I want of the Lisson Grove lingo; and I'm not going to waste another cylinder on it. [*To the girl*] Be off with you: I dont want you.

THE FLOWER GIRL. Dont you be so saucy. You aint heard what I come for yet. [*To Mrs Pearce, who is waiting at the door for further instructions*] Did you tell him I come in a taxi?

MRS PEARCE. Nonsense, girl! what do you think a gentleman like Mr Higgins cares what you came in?

THE FLOWER GIRL. Oh, we are proud! He aint above giving lessons, not him: I heard him say so. Well, I aint come here to ask for any compliment; and if my money's not good enough I can go elsewhere.

HIGGINS. Good enough for what?

THE FLOWER GIRL. Good enough for ye-oo. Now you know, dont you? I'm come to have lessons, I am. And to pay for em too: make no mistake.

HIGGINS [*stupent*] Well!!! [*Recovering his breath with a gasp*] What do you expect me to say to you?

THE FLOWER GIRL. Well, if you was a gentleman, you might ask me to sit down, I think. Dont I tell you I'm bringing you business?

HIGGINS. Pickering: shall we ask this baggage to sit down, or shall we throw her out of the window?

THE FLOWER GIRL [*running away in terror to the piano, where she turns at bay*] Ah-ah-oh-ow-ow-ow-oo! [*Wounded and whimpering*] I wont be called a baggage when Ive offered to pay like any lady.

Motionless, the two men stare at her from the other side of the room, amazed.

Act II   Pygmalion   121

PICKERING [*gently*] What is it you want, my girl?

THE FLOWER GIRL. I want to be a lady in a flower shop stead of selling at the corner of Tottenham Court Road. But they wont take me unless I can talk more genteel. He said he could teach me. Well, here I am ready to pay him—not asking any favor—and he treats me as if I was dirt.

MRS PEARCE. How can you be such a foolish ignorant girl as to think you could afford to pay Mr Higgins?

THE FLOWER GIRL. Why shouldnt I? I know what lessons cost as well as you do; and I'm ready to pay.

HIGGINS. How much?

THE FLOWER GIRL [*coming back to him, triumphant*] Now youre talking! I thought youd come off it when you saw a chance of getting back a bit of what you chucked at me last night. [*Confidentially*] Youd had a drop in, hadnt you?

HIGGINS [*peremptorily*] Sit down.

THE FLOWER GIRL. Oh, if youre going to make a compliment of it—

HIGGINS [*thundering at her*] Sit down.

MRS PEARCE [*severely*] Sit down, girl. Do as youre told. [*She places the stray chair near the hearthrug between Higgins and Pickering, and stands behind it waiting for the girl to sit down*].

THE FLOWER GIRL. Ah-ah-ah-ow-ow-oo! [*She stands, half rebellious, half bewildered*].

PICKERING [*very courteous*] Wont you sit down?

LIZA [*coyly*] Dont mind if I do. [*She sits down. Pickering returns to the hearthrug*].

HIGGINS. Whats your name?

THE FLOWER GIRL. Liza Doolittle.

HIGGINS [*declaiming gravely*]

    Eliza, Elizabeth, Betsy and Bess,
      They went to the woods to get a bird's nes':

PICKERING.   They found a nest with four eggs in it:

HIGGINS.   They took one apiece, and left three in it.

They laugh heartily at their own wit.

The Smoker

The Splendid Wayfaring

1923. *The Book of Lovat* by Haldane McFall.
Projected colour illustration by Lovat Fraser for
The Splendid Wayfaring.

Published by J. M. Dent and Sons Ltd, London.
Printed by the Morland Press. 10¾″ × 8″.

1927. *Das Entfesselte Theater* by Alexander
Tairoff. Published by Gustav Kiepenheuer, Berlin.
Printed by Gebr. Feyl, Berlin. $9\frac{1}{2}'' \times 6\frac{3}{4}''$. Binding
designed by El Lissitsky.

2. THE NEW TYPOGRAPHY IN GERMANY AND FRANCE AND THE ENGLISH AND AMERICAN RENAISSANCE IN PRINTING

The origins of modern book design and the New Typography can be traced back to the work of William Morris, his preoccupation with materials and workmanship and his rejection of the culture of the Italian Renaissance. They also developed from art nouveau with its anti-historical bias. Other influences that contributed to the New Typography were Marinetti and his Futurist Manifesto in 1909, the Dadaists, the Stijlists, the Cubists and the Constructivists. These influences were synthesised at the Bauhaus; and, mainly under the direction of Moholy-Nagy and El Lissitsky, the New Typography grew up with the same philosophical approach as was being applied to building by Walter Gropius.

In 1923, Bauhausverlag was established and, to coincide with the first Bauhaus exhibition, issued its first book. This was *Staatliches Bauhaus in Weimar 1919–1923,* edited by Gropius and Moholy-Nagy. The aim of the school press was to produce a series of books in which problems of art and design could be aired and elucidated.

Moholy-Nagy made the following observations about typography: clarity is of overriding importance, communications should not be constrained by old styles of presentation or preconceived aesthetic ideas, letters and words should not be squeezed into arbitrary shapes, such as a square.

The Bauhaus teachers El Lissitsky, Moholy-Nagy and Joost Schmidt were trying to create a new typographic language, combining freedom of layout and a fresh approach to the materials of printing. This interest in materials sounds a little like the credo of the Arts and Crafts movement, but instead of looking nostalgically to an Utopian idea of the Middle Ages, as the members of the Arts and Crafts movement did, they attempted to come to terms with the twentieth-century machine age.

Half a dozen years after the establishment of Bauhausverlag, Mr Stanley Morison, the most influential and the most rational of English writers on typographical matters, laid down his *First Principles of Typography*. This has, to a large extent, guided the more enlightened English and American printers and publishers since that time. The essence of his closely reasoned, utterly reasonable treatise is that 'typography is the efficient means to an essentially utilitarian and only accidentally aesthetic end'. This was coupled with the statement that the typography of books requires an obedience to convention which is almost absolute – a statement that presupposes a *status quo* for attitudes to design which today seem a little less assured than they did in 1930.

Morison wrote elsewhere, and some thirty years later: 'A designer needs to avoid an uncritical deference to what in some places is publicized as the only correct practice of this age. . . It is just as easy to be superstitious or sentimental about the present as it is about the past. The primary cause of superstition is ignorance of the historical causes of things. . . It is necessary to be aware of the difference between the mere perception of change and an appreciation of the reality underlying it'.[1]

In his *First Principles* Morison limited himself intentionally to composing room practice, to what Charles Peignot recently called *typolecture*, as opposed to *typovision* (or display). He makes no reference to design as such, except for a brief mention of modified margins for pocket books and some firm injunctions against the use of lower case in large sizes for title-pages.

For a postscript to a French edition (1965) of his *First Principles,* Morison makes a plea for tradition, which is, he concludes: 'another word for unanimity about fundamentals which has been brought into being by the trials, errors and corrections of many centuries'. Yet there is little unanimity about the fundamentals of design. However splendid the classical rules of proportion

[1] *The Typographic Book 1450–1935.* Stanley Morison and Kenneth Day, Benn, 1963.

STAATLICHES
BAUHAUS
WEIMAR
1919
1923

WEIMAR-MÜNCHEN

BAUHAUSVERLAG

1923. *Staatliches Bauhaus in Weimar 1919–
1923*. Designed by L. Moholy-Nagy. Published
by Bauhausbücher, Weimar. Title-page.

may be for architecture or book design, there are other rules, other proportions
no less true and no less splendid.

And even the classical proportions may be reassessed.

The Golden Section, used by the Greeks and the artists of the Renaissance,
has provided the basis of the International DIN paper sizes. The use of these
sizes has not had much appeal to book publishers. A more useful related
series of expanding relationships is the Fibonacci series. This Renaissance
series used by Le Corbusier for his Modulor is based on the succeeding
number being obtained by adding together the two preceding numbers i.e.
1, 2, 3, 5, 8. In addition to these there are an almost unlimited variety of ways
in which a square or a rectangle can be subdivided, so that the divisions are
related in a visually satisfying manner. This use of mathematical divisions of
the page area, coupled with a repetition of these proportions throughout a
book provide the essential quality in modern book design, the quality that
Herbert Bayer, former Bauhaus teacher, called 'visual articulation'. That they

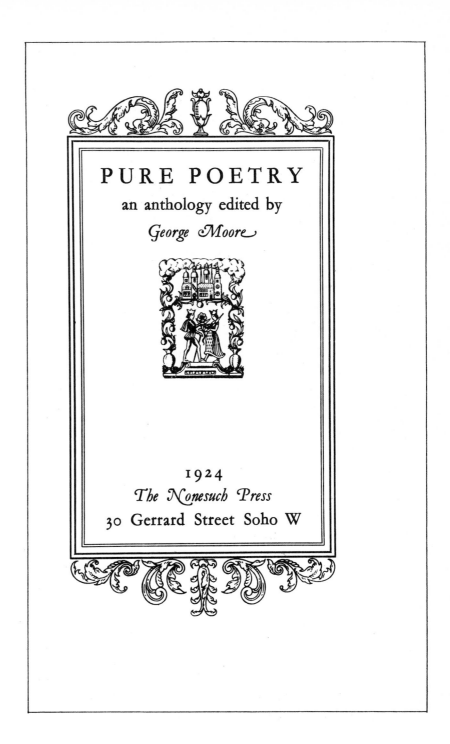

1924. *Pure Poetry* an anthology edited by
George Moore, designed by Francis Meynell.
Published by the Nonesuch Press. Bound in
grey boards, with a gold blocked vellum spine.
$9\frac{1}{4}$" × $5\frac{1}{2}$". Title-page.

apply more to the illustrated book than to the typographic book is obvious.
An infiltration of these features may well improve the look of the latter.

The belief in the importance of 'the historical causes of things' has governed
the attitudes of those involved in the twentieth-century English and New
England renaissance of printing. It has produced standards of book production
that are exceptional, though rarely as excellent as those followed in Germany
or Switzerland by typographers accepting the same historic principles. The
'English Book', as typified by the productions of the Nonesuch Press, or by
the Americans Bruce Rogers and D. B. Updike, is an agreeable thing, with a
feeling of rightness behind it. Sir Francis Meynell founded the Nonesuch
Press to re-issue old titles, because he could not find books he loved in an
acceptable format. (And what better reason, for such a publishing venture,
could one have than that?)

The insularity of England and the nature of English publishers have preserved
English books from the worst excesses of the new movement in typography

1922. *Causeries Typographiques* (No. 6).
Published by M. Audin and Co., 3 Rue Davout,
Lyon. 10¼″ × 6″. Text spread.

1921. *La Poésie* by Jean Epstein. Project for
title-page from *Causeries Typographiques No. 6*
published by M. Audin and Co., Lyon. 10¼″ × 6″.

and deprived them equally of the best features. However at last there are signs of change. It looks as if the New Typography has come to stay, at least for a while. But if it stays in as crystallized a style as sometimes seems possible, it will become even more sterile than the style it seeks to replace. Gropius once said: 'The development of a Bauhaus style would mean a return to academic stagnation and inertia.' Ways of life and methods of communication are changing fast; the design of books must keep pace in type and presentation. It seems to me that much of the sense of Morison's *First Principles* and particularly his statement '. . . any disposition of printing material which, whatever the intention, has the effect of coming between author and reader is wrong . . .', can with advantage be applied to new methods of typography; but with the over-riding proviso that design is a flexible weapon and that even the alphabet itself is liable to be questioned. What seemed a secure tradition in 1930 has changed, perhaps irrevocably, through the influence of the new movement in design.

The French acceptance of *Die Neue Typographie* was typical. They took solid German doctrine and stood it on its head. The spirited examples here are by a lively and erudite printer called Audin who worked at Lyons and periodically issued *Causeries Typographiques*.

In the English and American typographic revivals, borders cast on type bodies played a large part; they ranged from Fournier baroque to Bodoni neoclassical, like Francis Meynell's formal design for both the title and text pages of *Irish Wine*.

By the end of the 1920's, the influence of the Nonesuch Press in England, and of the Riverside and Merrymount Presses in America, was spreading to other commercial printing and publishing houses. *Toulemonde* by Christopher Morley is a sophisticated book, with a pretty title-page, whose title line is set in June, a version of one of Fournier le Jeune's decorative typefaces. This came from Doubleday, Doran, a commercial house which produced many good-looking books.

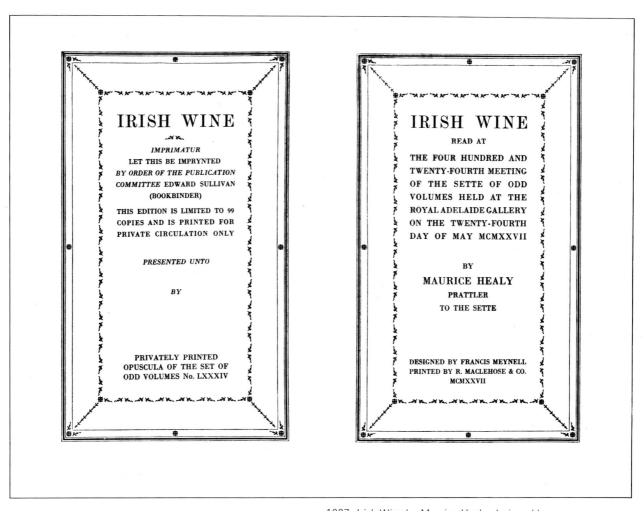

IRISH WINE

IMPRIMATUR
LET THIS BE IMPRYNTED
*BY ORDER OF THE PUBLICATION
COMMITTEE EDWARD SULLIVAN*
(BOOKBINDER)

THIS EDITION IS LIMITED TO 99
COPIES AND IS PRINTED FOR
PRIVATE CIRCULATION ONLY

PRESENTED UNTO

BY

PRIVATELY PRINTED
OPUSCULA OF THE SET OF
ODD VOLUMES No. LXXXIV

IRISH WINE

READ AT

THE FOUR HUNDRED AND
TWENTY-FOURTH MEETING
OF THE SETTE OF ODD
VOLUMES HELD AT THE
ROYAL ADELAIDE GALLERY
ON THE TWENTY-FOURTH
DAY OF MAY MCMXXVII

BY

MAURICE HEALY
PRATTLER
TO THE SETTE

DESIGNED BY FRANCIS MEYNELL
PRINTED BY R. MACLEHOSE & CO.
MCMXXVII

1927. *Irish Wine* by Maurice Healy, designed by Francis Meynell. Printed by MacLehose and Co., Glasgow. Edition limited to 99 copies for private circulation. 8" × 5¼". Title-page spread.

TOULEMONDE

BY
CHRISTOPHER
MORLEY

DOUBLEDAY, DORAN & COMPANY, INC.
GARDEN CITY · 1928 · NEW YORK

The English and American typographic revivals

1928. *Toulemonde* by Christopher Morley. Published by Doubleday, Doran and Co. Inc., New York. 8¾" × 5¾". Title-page.

1931. *Mise en Page* by A. Tolmer. English edition published by Studio Ltd, London. Printed by A. Tolmer, Paris. 10⅜″ × 8¼″. Cover design: quarter-bound paper-covered boards printed in silver, black and yellow. Title-page printed in black and blue.

**The new typography
in France and Germany**

1930. *August Weltumsegler* by Knut Hamsun. Published by Albert Langen, Munich. Project for book design by Ludwig Schierle, Hamburg. Printed by H. Broschek and Co., Hamburg. 7⅝″ × 4¾″. Inset from *Imprimatur II*.

Grundsätzliches zur neuen Typographie

Von Philipp Albinus, Frankfurt am Main

Verlag des Bildungsverbandes der

Deutschen Buchdrucker, GmbH, Berlin

1929

Über die Ausdrucksmittel der neuen Typographie

Was hat das alles mit Typographie zu tun? So wird man unwillkürlich fragen, wenn man die Typographie als ein selbständiges Gebiet des Formschaffens ansieht. Aber das ist sie nie gewesen und kann sie auch niemals sein. Immer war sie gebunden an das Formempfinden ihrer Zeit, und immer wird sie ein Widerschein sein vom Wollen und Vollbringen auf dem Gebiete des formalen Ausdrucks, der Kunst.

Also auch in der Typographie wird man an den grundsätzlichen Änderungen auf dem Gebiet des allgemeinen Formschaffens nicht achtlos vorübergehen können. Das heißt nun keineswegs, daß man etwa die neue Form der Stütze, unten schmal, oben breit, einfach ins Typographische übertragen soll. Nein, auch hier heißt es, aus dem Material heraus im Sinne der neuen Lebensauffassung und des Zeittempos, des gesamten Lebensrhythmus, zu gestalten und zu formen.

Das Bewegungsmoment ist auch für uns ausschlaggebend. Der Empfänger einer Drucksache, die im Stil der geruhsamen Zeit ausgeführt ist, wird unangenehm berührt, wenn er sich plötzlich umstellen muß, sich aus dem Moment der Bewegung, in dem er sich befindet, in das der Ruhe versetzen soll, um die empfangene Drucksache ganz auf sich wirken lassen zu können. Und so ist das charakteristischste Merkmal in der neuen Typographie die Betonung eines Bewegungsrhythmus — die asymmetrische Anordnung der Zeilen und Satzgruppen — gegenüber der Stellung auf Mitte, der Arbeit mit einem Ruhepunkt, der symmetrischen Satzanordnung früherer Zeiten. Es tut dabei nichts zur Sache, daß auch früher gelegentlich einmal eine Verschränkung der Zeilen vorgenommen wurde. Denn es ist doch ein Unterschied, ob man etwas bewußt, als Ergebnis

19

2*

1929. *Grundsätzliches zur neuen Typographie* by Philipp Albinus. Published by Verlag des Bildungsverbandes der Deutschen Buchdrucker, Berlin. Size unknown. Title and text pages. Reproduced from *Books for our time* 1951 by Marshall Lee, published by the Oxford University Press, New York.

Mise en page, written and compiled by a Parisian printer-publisher called A. Tolmer, is an extrovert hotch-potch of type and illustration, published in 1931. It was a book that had a lasting influence on the layout work of the advertising agencies of Paris, London and New York. It is packed with photo-montage and lively illustration. The pictures are much more interesting than the text. M. Tolmer's observations on book design are not particularly illuminating, though his opening remarks on this subject might serve for a fair comment, nearly forty years after they were written: 'The layout of books at the present day, except for a very few *éditions de luxe* produced in the modern spirit, is characterized by a respect for convention which amounts to timidity.'
From Tolmer's *Mise en page* to *Grundsätzliches zur neuen Typographie* by Philipp Albinus is a salutary jump. This book is a good example of 'visual articulation in typography'; that is, a repeating pattern of page design, established in the first place by a grid structure.

A number of German typographers began to lay down rules for the new typography. These designers included Paul Renner, the designer of the sans serif typeface Futura and author of *Die Kunst der Typographie*, and Jan Tschichold, the author of *Die neue Typographie* (1928) and *Typographische Gestaltung* (1935). Tschichold's writings had a very wide influence, and he more than any other writer was able to establish the fundamental principles of the New Typography, the key factors in which were freedom from tradition, geometrical simplicity and the acceptance of the utilitarian purpose of typography. Tschichold's work was much more refined than the earlier Bauhaus work, with which school he was never actually associated.
The project for a cover for Knut Hamsun's *August Weltumsegler* was a prize winner in a competition organized by Die Gesellschaft der Bucherfreunde in Hamburg. It was published in 1931 in the second volume of the German typographic annual, *Imprimatur*. The designer makes the most immaculate use of small, but heavy, grotesque capitals. In a very different vein, and in the same volume, was a lengthy survey of English private presses.

H E N R Y B A R B U S S E

K R A F T

—

VERLAG DIE SCHMIEDE BERLIN

1926. *Kraft* by Henri Barbusse. Binding designed by Georg Salter. Published by Verlag die Schmiede, Berlin. Printed by Jakob Hegner, Hellerau. $7\frac{3}{8}'' \times 4\frac{3}{8}''$. Bound in unbleached linen blocked in blue and red. Binding case and title-page.

1931. *Russland Ja und Nein* by Hans Siemsen. Published by Ernst Rowohlt, Berlin. $8\frac{1}{8}'' \times 5\frac{1}{8}''$. Bound in rough greyish cloth blocked in red, black and grey.

German binding designs

Georg Salter's lively case design for *Kraft*, where blue and red letters are blocked on an oatmeal-coloured cloth, contrasts with the impeccable formality of the book's title-page. (Salter, having made a name for himself as a typographic designer in Germany, has since carved out another career for himself in the United States.) The treatment of the binding case for *Russland Ja und Nein* has banished symmetry from front and spine. The two little American books opposite, one published in 1928 the other in 1934, might belong to a different world. They both come from the hands of distinguished practitioners. *On the Duty of Civil Disobedience* was designed and produced by Carl Purington Rollins from his private press at New Haven. For many years Rollins was the printer to the Yale University Press. The volume of *Emerson-Clough Letters* was designed and printed by William A. Kittredge from the Lakeside Press in Chicago. Kittredge brought distinction to much of the work that passed through the somewhat capacious maw of R. R. Donnelley and Sons. Both Rollins and Kittredge were masters of their craft.

64

1928. *On the Duty of Civil Disobedience* by
Henry David Thoreau, with decorations by
Rockwell Kent. Text set by Carl Purington
Rollins and published by Carl and Margaret
Rollins at the Sign of the Chorobates, New
Haven, Connecticut. 8½″ × 5½″. Edition limited to
300 copies. Title-page and cover.

The American private presses

ON THE DUTY OF
Civil Disobedience
HENRY DAVID THOREAU

New Haven Connecticut
AT THE SIGN OF THE CHOROBATES
Carl & Margaret Rollins

1934. *Emerson-Clough letters* edited by Howard
F. Lowry and Ralph Leslie Rusk. Published by the
Rowfant Club, Cleveland. Printed by William A.
Kittredge at the Lakeside Press, Chicago. Edition
limited to 165 copies. 9¼″ × 6″. Cover of brown
marbled paper with a white label printed in
black. Title-page and cover.

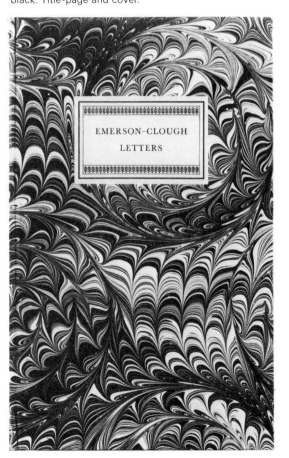

Emerson-Clough
Letters
EDITED BY
HOWARD F. LOWRY
AND
RALPH LESLIE RUSK

Cleveland
THE ROWFANT CLUB
1934

zievů vnějšího světa. činí-li to, musí se tak díti tvůrčím úmyslem analogickým *fotomontáži němého filmu.* to je část úkolů zvukového filmu.

slyšitelná složka zvukového filmu by znamenala sotva obohacení proti filmu němému, rozuměli-li bychom tím zvukové podmalování, zvukovou ilustraci opticky vytvořených montážních částí. co bylo již dosaženo prostředkem — optickým —, je zařazením akustického pochodu jen zeslabeno. kvalitativní vzestup, nová pronikavá výrazová forma vznikne teprve tehdy, až budou zařazovány obě složky ve svém plném rozvinutí, střídavě účinkující. zde začíná skutečná ekonomie i reportážního zvukového filmu.

okamžitý problém zvukového filmu

dříve než můžeme očekávati od zvukového filmu skutečných výkonů, musí býti naše akustická potence chápání značně uvolněna a rozšířena.
›hudebnicie‹ nedospěli dosud ani k produktivnímu využití gramofonové desky, natož rozhlasu a éterových nástrojů.
musí so v těchto oblastech neobyčejně důkladně přeorientovati.
kromě dokumentárního zápisu může zvuková složka filmu obohatiti náš sluch dosud neznámými akustickými účiny.
od akustické složky očekáváme totéž, čeho jsme v němém filmu očekávali po stránce optické a čeho jsme aspoň částečně dosáhli.
přes reprodukční přání obecenstva, zmateného s počátku materiálem, musí býti zvukový film veden k optofonetické synthese. jestliže zvukový film nastoupí cestu k takové synthese, pak to znamená konec konců: abstraktní fonofilm. odtud mohou býti všechny odrůdy filmu opodnány. vedle kategorie ›dokumentárního zvukového filmu‹ a extrémní kategorie ›abstraktního zvukového filmu‹ vzniknou zde organicky ›montážní zvukové filmy‹. nejen montáž optických a akustických částí o sobě, nýbrž obou vzájemně.
znající film měl by nejprve proto předběžně absolvovat období jen zvukových experimentů. to znamená: nejprve isolace od složky optické; prakticky: zvukovou část zvukoobrazového filmového pásma odděliti a jednotlivé kusy z toho zkusmo navzájem kombinovati. (je jasné, že hudební konvence nejsou zde zrovna tak na místě, jako populární žánrové malířství nemůže míti ničeho společného s optickou stránkou filmu.) další etapa, která by však mohla probíhat souběžně s první, musela by přihlížeti k těmto směrnicím:

48 l. moholy-nagy, 1933, fotografika . fotografik . photographic . photographique

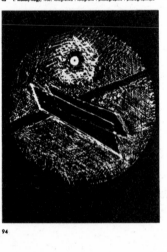

94

46-47 l. moholy-nagy, 1929, fotografie (positiv a negativ) fotografie (positiv und negativ) . photography (positive and negative) . photographie (positive et négative)

1. zhodnocení reálných akustických fenomenů, pokud jsou nám k disposici přírodními šramoty, lidským ústrojím nebo nástrojem.
2. užití zvukových útvarů, opticky zaznamenatelných, ale na reálné existenci nezávislých, které se dají podle plánu předem stanoveného na zvukový filmový proužek nakresliti a pak převésti v reálné tóny. tu tri-ergon systému na příklad světlo-temnými proužky, jejichž abeceda musí býti dříve naučena. poněvadž všechno, co je na zvukový filmový proužek nakresleno, přesazuje projekční aparatura do zvuku nebo šramotu, podaly i mé experimenty s kreslenými profily, sledy písmen, otisky prstů, geometrickými značkami na zvukovém filmovém proužku překvapující zvukové výsledky.) k tomu přistupuje
3. misení obou.
k 1:
a) mluvený film nemusí bezpodmínečně obsahovat souvislou akustickou událost.
akustická složka může působit dvojnásob intensivněji, vystupuje-li nečekaně, jsouc rozdělena v kratší nebo delší časové prostory.
b) jako má optický film možnost, aby různě fixoval objekt snímky shora a zdola, se strany a zpředu, frontálně a ve zkratce, musí něco podobného díti se i se zvukem. různým směrům pohledů musí tedy odpovídati různé směry slyšení (zejména myslíme zde na odstupňované kombinace hudby, řeči a šramotu. k tomu přistupuje akustický close up, snímek časorozptýlný (rozšíření), snímek časosběrný (stažení), skreslování, přeclonění, vůbec prostředky ›zvukové montáže‹: simultánnosti optické musí odpovídati akustická; to znamená: musíme míti odvahu během akustického průběhu dokonce prokládati smyslový proud řeči jinými zvukovými útvary nebo ho pojednou přerušiti a zařaditi jiné akustické dimense, skreslovati, roztahovati, stahovati, a teprve potom pokračovati v původní linii a podobné. urychlením nebo zpomalením normálních zvukových sledů vznikají nejpodivnější překlady, mnoho oktáv nahoru nebo dolů. tyto výsledky jsou opět překombinovatelny. (zde nejsou komice kladeny hranice.)
k 2:
a) správná výše tvůrčího využití bude však u mluveného filmu dosažena teprve tehdy, budeme-li ovládat akustickou abecedu ve formě fotografovatelných projekcí (na příklad u světelných zvukových systémů).
to znamená, že — bez reálných akustických událostí vnějšího světa — budeme plánovitě zaznamenávati na filmovém pásu akustické fenomeny, podle potřeby synchronisovanými s optickými; to znamená: komponista zvukového filmu

95

1936. *L. Moholy-Nagy.* Published by Fr. Kalivoda, Brno. 11¾″ × 8¼″. Text spread.

---

52   An Essay on Typography

mous blobs might be amusing to meet if they were the unaided efforts of some sportive letter designer. But having become common forms they are about as dull as 'Robots' would be if they all had red noses. As machinery & standardised production can only decently turn out the plainest of plain things, we shall have to steel our minds to a very ascetical and mortified future. This will be quite satisfactory to 'highbrows' like ourselves, but it is certain that the masses of the people will not stand it; & designers, who for inscrutable reasons 'must live', will continue to fall over one another in their efforts to design fancy forms which, like a certain kind of figure 9, are all tail and no body (see figure 19, 24).

¶ However, in spite of industrialism, letter designing is still an occupation worthy of the enthusiasm of rational beings, and, though a Q which were all queue & no Q would be 'past a joke', it is difficult to say exactly where a tail should end (see figure 21). The only thing to do is to make ourselves into such thoroughly and completely rational beings that our instinctive or intuitive reactions and responses and sympathies are more or less bound to be rational also. And just as we revolt from smells which are bad for our bodies without reasoning about it, so

Figure 18

shall we revolt against the mentally defective.
¶ A final word may be said about the influence of tools in letter designing. The main stream of lettering to-day is undoubtedly the printed sheet or book. But whatever may be said about the derivation of our letters from the chisel-made or pen-made letters of the past, there is no doubt whatever that neither the chisel nor the pen has now any influ-

1936. *An Essay on Typography* by Eric Gill. Published by Sheed and Ward, London. Printed by Hague and Gill, High Wycombe. 6¾″ × 4¼″. Text spread and (*opposite*) title-page.

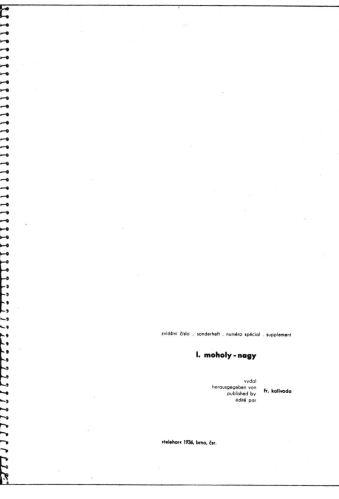

I. moholy-nagy

1936. *L. Moholy-Nagy.* Published by Fr.
Kalivoda, Brno. 11¾″ × 8¼″. Spiral wire binding.
Cover printed in black, and title-page.

AN ESSAY ON TYPOGRAPHY

BY ERIC GILL

Contents:

second edition

LONDON / SHEED & WARD / 1936

A comparison: L. Moholy-Nagy and Eric Gill

László Moholy-Nagy was one of the most influential figures of the modern movement in design. With his influence on typography and photography, his written observations on these subjects, his work as a teacher at the Bauhaus and later at the Chicago Institute of Design, he has played as big a part in shaping the appearance of modern books as any of his typographic contemporaries; yet he was also an architect, a painter and a stage designer.
Moholy, as well as being a brilliant creative thinker, must have acted like a catalyst on the students and designers with whom he came in contact. It is difficult to gauge how much actual book designing he did, but he was certainly largely responsible for the first Bauhaus Press books.

Eric Gill, though older than Moholy-Nagy, played almost as great a part in English twentieth-century typography as the Hungarian did in German typography. Their lines of thought, however, were completely different.
Gill owed much to the teaching of Edward Johnston and was an Arts and Crafts product *par excellence*. Morris's doctrine, 'Every man ought to have joy in his labour', became Gill's credo. For many years he earned a rather precarious livelihood as a letter cutter and sign writer. His belief in tradition was implicit. He wrote: 'Lettering is a precise art and strictly subject to tradition. This is the secret, for letters are things, not pictures of things'. Gill's *An Essay on Typography,* first published in 1931, is an interesting book. It is set in his Joanna typeface, unjustified and freely sprinkled with ampersands and paragraph marks which replace indents. Gill shows here an example of his sans serif, but nothing would have induced him to set a book in a serifless typeface.

Für die neue Typographie sind nicht nur die Schriften und Zeichen des Setz-
kastens Mittel der Gestaltung. Das Bild ist oft besser als das Wort; es bietet oft
mehr und kann manches leichter als Worte vermitteln. Die natürliche Dar-
stellungsweise unserer Zeit ist die Photographie, deren Gebrauch so vielfältig
geworden ist, daß wir ohne sie wohl nicht mehr auskämen. Die Qualität der
Photographie ist für den Wert der ganzen Arbeit mitbestimmend; für sich allein
unterliegt sie Gesetzen, die denen der neuen Gestaltung sinnverwandt sind.

Nicht nur die normale Photographie kann einen Teil neuer Typographie bilden; auch das Photogramm (die kameralose Photographie, deren Technik Moholy-Nagy und Man Ray für uns neu entdeckt und gestaltet haben), das Negativ-
photo, die Doppelaufnahme und weitere Kombinationen, legitimste Möglichkeiten des Lichtbildes (vergleiche das einzigartige Selbstbildnis Lissitzkys), die
Photomontage, die eine Idee verkörpern kann, sollen in den Dienst der typo-
graphischen Mitteilung gestellt werden. Sie können die Aussage verdeutlichen,
anziehend machen und optisch bereichern.

Die Photomontage muß jedoch auf Klarheit des Aufbaus bedacht sein und
unübersichtliche Anhäufungen vermeiden. Die normale Photographie kann als
rechteckige Fläche oder als Silhouette gebraucht werden; beide zusammen geben
neben reinen Größenkontrasten oft erwünschte Kontraste und Abwechslung.
Am Rande abfallende Photoklischees sind hin und wieder sehr wirksam; doch
wird ihr Gebrauch durch die technische Zweckmäßigkeit und ästhetische Er-
wägungen begrenzt. Mehr als eine bis höchstens zwei solcher bis zum Papier-
rande reichenden Photographien sollte man auf der gleichen Seite nicht zeigen.

Photoklischees können auch in einer bunten Farbe gedruckt werden; Über-
schneidungen verschiedenfarbig gedruckter Photos sind gelegentlich sehr wirksam.

Der Gebrauch der Photographie als der wichtigsten Bildform der Gegenwart
schließt den der freien und der Konstruktionszeichnung nicht aus. Beide können
sich ebensogut der Typographie einfügen und an der kontrastierenden Gestaltung teilnehmen. Alle drei können auch nebeneinander erscheinen und neue,
reiche Formen bilden.

Auch die amerikanische Retusche an Maschinendarstellungen und ihre Um-
kehrung als Negativ sind Möglichkeiten, die uns offenstehen und bei passenden
Gelegenheiten benutzt werden können.

Der Bildsatz dagegen, der aus meist eigens gegossenen geometrischen Satz-
elementen Bilder und Darstellungen erzeugt und lange Zeit von gewisser Seite

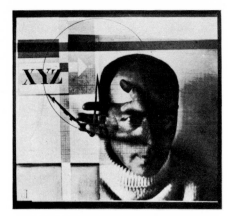

El Lissitzky: *Selbstbildnis* (Photogramm, Doppelbelichtung, Doppelkopie). 1924.

propagiert wurde, kann nur in der Hand zeichnerisch Begabter zu einem brauch-
baren Mittel der Gestaltung werden. So «gesetzte» Schriften sind fast immer
schlechter als selbst die gewöhnlichsten Typen. Jedenfalls ist es ziemlich schwer
und für Ungeübte technisch sehr umständlich, auf diesem Wege Brauchbares
herzustellen. Nicht alles ist so vollendet, wie der Bildsatz von Walter Cyliax-
Krauß, der auf diesem Gebiete das Beste hervorgebracht hat.

Innerhalb einer ganzen Arbeit sind Photo, Zeichnung und Bildsatz nur Teile,
die sich dem Ganzen fügen müssen. Ihre überzeugende Einordnung bestimmt
den Wert ihres Gebrauchs.

1935. *Typographische Gestaltung* designed and
written by Jan Tschichold. Published by Benno
Schwabe and Co., Basel. $8\frac{1}{4}'' \times 5\frac{3}{4}''$. Title-page
and text spread.

1936. *First Principles of Typography* by Stanley
Morison. Published and printed by the University
Press, Cambridge. $6\frac{5}{8}'' \times 4\frac{1}{4}''$. Title-page.

Jan Tschichold:

Typographische Gestaltung

Benno Schwabe & Co . Basel 1935

FIRST PRINCIPLES

OF

TYPOGRAPHY

BY

STANLEY MORISON

CAMBRIDGE
AT THE UNIVERSITY PRESS
1936

is working. While a universal character or typography applicable to all books produced in a given national area is practicable, to impose a universal detailed formula upon all books printed in roman types is not. National tradition expresses itself in the varying separation of the book into prelims, chapters, etc., no less than in the design of the type. But at least there are physical rules of linear composition which are obeyed by all printers who know their job. Let us see what these rules mean.

The normal roman type (in simple form without special sorts, etc.) consists of

ABCDEFGHIJKLMNOPQRSTUVWXYZ&

ABCDEFGHIJKLMNOPQRSTUVWXYZ&

abcdefghijklmnopqrstuvwxyz

ABCDEFGHIJKLMNOPQRSTUVWXYZ&

abcdefghijklmnopqrstuvwxyz

The printer needs to be very careful in choosing his type, realising that the more often he is going to use it, the more closely its design must approximate to the general idea held in the mind of the reader who is

10

accustomed to the normal magazine, newspaper and book. It does no harm to print a Christmas card in black letter, but who nowadays would set a book in that type? I may believe, as I do, that black letter is in design more homogeneous, more picturesque, more lively a type than the grey round roman we use, but I do not now expect people to read a book in it. Aldus' and Caslon's are both relatively feeble types, but they represent the forms accepted by the community; and the printer, as a servant of the community, must use them, or one of their variants. No printer should say, "I am an artist, therefore I am not to be dictated to. I will create my own letter forms", for, in this humble job, such individualism is not helpful to an audience of any size. It is no longer possible, as it was in the infancy of the craft, to persuade society into the acceptance of strongly marked and highly individualistic types—because literate society is so much greater in mass and correspondingly slower in movement. Type design moves at the pace of the most conservative reader. The

11

1936. *First Principles of Typography* by Stanley Morison. Published and printed by the University Press, Cambridge. $6\frac{5}{8}'' \times 4\frac{1}{4}''$. Text spread.

The New Typography and the English and American revivals

Moholy-Nagy, Tschichold and Herbert Bayer on the one side, and Eric Gill, Francis Meynell at the Nonesuch Press and Oliver Simon of the Curwen Press on the other, represent the widely differing continental and English attitudes to book design. The continental New Typography, as we have seen, has close affinities with early twentieth-century movements in art and architecture, such as Cubism and Constructivism. The English style is based somewhat eclectically on the work of the best of the European printers since the time of the fifteenth-century Venetians. It has also been heavily influenced by a renewed interest in calligraphy and by Mr Morison's solid good sense. In comparing the work of the rationalist Morison and the intuitive Tschichold and in particular the title-pages shown on the opposite page, Morison's design is logical with a firm reliance on capital letters; Tschichold's is of an almost Whistlerian waywardness. Tschichold's typography was much less heavy-handed than the early Bauhaus books. In its precision and delicacy it helped to guide the post-war Swiss typographers. Five years after the publication of *Typographische Gestaltung*, Tschichold renounced the doctrine he has helped to establish and returned to an immaculate classicism. This was mainly due, as I have said elsewhere, to a personal reaction against 'militaristic, Nazi-minded New Typography'.[2] Morison stuck to his guns and authorised an unmodified reissue in French of his *First Principles* thirty-five years after its first publication. In a sparkling postscript, he vigorously explained why had had not changed his position.

[2] *Typography: Basic Principles. Influences and Trends since the 19th century:* John Lewis, Studio Vista/Reinhold (2nd Edn 1966).

1919
BAUHAUS
1928

edited by } **HERBERT BAYER
WALTER GROPIUS
ISE GROPIUS**

THE MUSEUM OF MODERN ART · NEW YORK · 1938

1938. *Bauhaus 1919–1928* edited by Herbert
Bayer, Walter Gropius and Ise Gropius.
Typography and cover design by Herbert Bayer.
Published by the Museum of Modern Art, New
York. Printed in the United States of America.
10″ × 7½″. Title-page and cover of light yellow
cloth, blocked in black and red.

Design and typographic doctrine

After the Second World War, while England stuck firmly to her traditions, a
new generation of American designers began to use with fluency and some
freedom the New Typography vernacular, aided and abetted by such Bauhaus
teachers and displaced Europeans as Moholy-Nagy, Herbert Bayer and Georg
Salter. In Europe, the Swiss book designers, such as Max Bill, developed the
new typography into an incredibly precise style. And Jan Tschichold (in
1940) made a complete *volte-face,* back from the New Typography to a rigid
English classicism. In this vein, in the late 1940's, he did a magnificent restyling job for Penguin Books.

1946. *The New Vision and Abstract of an Artist*
by Lázló Moholy-Nagy. Cover and typography
by Paul Rand. Published by Wittenborn and Co.,
New York. Printed by E. L. Hildreth and Co.,
Brattleboro, Vermont. 10″ × 7½″. Title-page.

The documents of modern art: Director ● Robert Motherwell

The New Vision 1928 third revised edition **1946**
and
Abstract of an Artist

László Moholy-Nagy

Wittenborn and Company,   New York, 1946

1945. *Introduction to Typography* written and
designed by Oliver Simon. Published by Faber
and Faber, London. Printed by the Curwen Press,
Plaistow. 8⅜″ × 5¼″. Cover of buff-coloured
cloth printed in blue and red, and title-page.

OLIVER SIMON

INTRODUCTION TO
TYPOGRAPHY

The old artists of the classical school were
never egotists. Egotism has been and
remains responsible for many defects of
modern typography.   *Talbot B. Reed*

LONDON
FABER AND FABER
1945

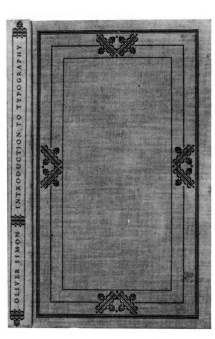

Commentaire du catalogue de l'œuvre
de Sophie Tæuber-Arp
par Hugo Weber

Je connaissais, un peu, l'œuvre de Sophie Tæuber depuis l'exposition bâloise de 1937 qui avait voulu nous présenter les «constructivistes». Je ne la compris pas bien, d'abord, et éprouvai peu d'intérêt. Je me méprenais complètement sur sa signification. C'est peu de semaines avant sa mort que je fis, à Bâle, la connaissance personnelle de Sophie Tæuber. Jean Arp et elle avaient réussi à fuir l'occupation allemande; ils venaient de passer en Suisse. La sincérité de ses enthousiasmes spirituels me fit alors une impression intense; mais je ne pensais guère à son travail, qui était pourtant la source de cette paix rayonnante. Encore moins aurais-je pu imaginer qu'il m'arriverait de me recueillir sur ses ouvrages durant plusieurs semaines dans le calme de son atelier de Meudon. Jean Arp me chargea en effet de dresser le catalogue de son œuvre.

A mon propre étonnement, je me mis un jour à mesurer des tableaux, à les marquer et à rechercher des dates. Mais surtout, je m'engageai dans une vaste contemplation des œuvres de Sophie Tæuber, en constituai le groupement, y distinguai des séries et tentai toutes les possibilités de comparaison qui me semblaient éclairer leurs rapports réciproques. La situation vraiment tragique de notre temps, qui condamne une œuvre aussi riche à s'amasser dans les tiroirs et les recoins d'un atelier, me permit du moins d'en prendre une facile vue d'ensemble. Un classement strictement chronologique présentait des difficultés, car Sophie Tæuber ne signe et date régulièrement ses travaux que dans les deux dernières années de sa vie. C'était un trait de l'esprit Dada de n'attacher aucune importance au temps ni à l'individualité artistique. Quelques points de repère me permirent néanmoins d'établir avec une approximation suffisante mon système de datation; j'eus recours au témoignage de certaines évidences visuelles, dans la mesure où des notes sur photographies, catalogues et publications ou la mémoire de Jean Arp me refusaient d'autres renseignements.

Mon travail ne devint vraiment convaincant que du jour où se dessina un groupement fondé sur les principaux problèmes de forme. Il fallait, pour chacun de ces groupes, déterminer des limites et une appellation, si l'on voulait éviter que le catalogue ne fût qu'un inventaire mécanique et sans vie. Il

serait souhaitable que les artistes puissent eux-mêmes soutenir de leurs conseils une telle entreprise. Avec toute la volonté d'objectivité possible, l'établissement d'un catalogue de ce genre reste une œuvre personnelle. C'est pourquoi je crois utile de commenter ici ma classification et les rapports que j'ai établis entre les diverses séries de cette œuvre.

Il s'avère que Sophie Tæuber reprenait souvent un problème de forme, après l'avoir, parfois durant des années, abandonné pour un autre, qui s'était imposé à elle entre-temps. Pour fixer la chronologie de son évolution dans son ensemble, les dates d'apparition de chacun de ces problèmes sont les plus décisives. Les manifestations ultérieures d'un même problème ont été, dans le catalogue, subordonnées aux premières.

Les premiers travaux de Sophie Tæuber remontent à 1916. Ce sont des compositions planes, ordonnées selon une structure rigoureusement verticale-horizontale. Lorsqu'en 1916 Jean Arp fit la connaissance de Sophie Tæuber à Zurich, elle lui montra ses essais. Elle appliquait des conceptions semblables à toutes espèces de travaux, en broderie et en tissage, sans prétention artistique, mais avec une préoccupation morale très nette, et dont la fermeté, au témoignage de Jean Arp, l'impressionna et l'influença. Par la suite, Sophie Tæuber introduisit, dans le cadre des compositions verticales-horizontales, des figures animées, curvilignes. Souvent c'étaient, réduites à la ténuité de signes, des choses de l'existence extérieure: petits bateaux arborant des drapeaux, oiseaux, vases. Le signe «homme» est rare d'abord.

De tels signes ont eu la vie longue dans l'œuvre de Sophie Tæuber. On peut en retrouver la trace ici ou là dans ses travaux postérieurs.

Dans les gouaches au «pointillisme» libre de 1920 à 1921, dans les compositions en taches de couleur, apparaissent de vagues constellations, rappelant des figures de danse. Mais la plupart se contentent d'un rythme sans gestes, pures formes et couleurs. Ces œuvres font une impression joyeuse et d'une âpre santé. Sophie Tæuber les peignit pourtant durant une période d'incessante tristesse. Du point de vue génétique on les voit se

Compositions verticales-horizontales

Taches quadrangulaires en couleurs

118

119

1948. *Sophie. Taeuber-Arp* edited by Georg Schmidt. Designed by Max Bill. Published by Holbein-Verlag, Basel. Printed by Benteli AG, Bern — Bümplitz, Funke and Saurenmann, Zürich; Georg Rentsch Söhne, Olten-Trimbach. Bound by G. Wolfensberger, Zürich. 11¾″ × 8″. Text spread.

QUI Né LE 24 MAI 1899.
IL BELGE, DE PARIS. AIME
EST LES FUGUES MATELOT À
21 ANS. ATLANTIQUE Nᵉᵗ S
PLUS TARD, VOYAGES EN
AMAZONIE, EN EQUATEUR
AUX INDES ᴱᴺ CHINE. IL EST
ET SE VOUDRAIT AILLEURS,
ESSENTIELLEMᴱᴺᵀ AILLEURS,
AUTRE. IL L'IMAGINE. IL
FAUᵗ BIEN QU'IL L'IMAGINE

1942. *Le Rêve* by Henri Michaux. Designed, printed and published by Pierre Bettencourt. Edition limited to 100 copies. 4¾″ × 3¾″. Text page. The typeface is Peignot, designed by Cassandre.

Swiss and French typography

French interest in typographic developments has been somewhat spasmodic, but a certain number of amateurs of printing have run their own private presses. From amongst these, Pierre Bettencourt and Pierre André Benoit have issued some interesting books. Henri Michaux's *Le Rêve* was published by Bettencourt in 1942, set in two weights of A. M. Cassandre's interesting, little-used typeface Peignot. This curious, half uncial is surprisingly successful, except for the large capital letters. It would have been more logical to have dispensed with these. Francis Picabia's *Parlons d'autre Chose* was published by Benoit in 1953. It is a pleasant book, set in Futura and with decorations by Picabia printed on a heavy grey Ingres paper.

ENSUiTE
ON A UN MONdE de chOSES
À FAiRE, TANT QU'il RESTE de
lA clARTÉ, Si biEN QU'ON A
À pEiNE lE TEMPS dE SE
REGARdER UN pEU.
LAcONTRARiÉTÉpOURNOUS
dANS lA NUiT, c'EST QUANd
il FAUT TRAVAillER, ET il lE
FAUT: il NAÎT dES NAiNS
cONTiNUEllEMENT.

QUANd ON MARchE dANS
lA cAMpAGNE, lUi cONFiE-T-
EllE ENcORE, il ARRiVE QUE
l'ON RENcONTRE SUR SON
chEMiN dES MASSES
cONSidÉRAblES. CE SONT
dES MONTAGNES ET il FAUT

1942. *Le Rêve* text spread.

1953. *Parlons d'autre Chose* by Francis Picabia.
Designed, decorated and printed by Pierre André
Benoit. 7½″ × 5¾″. Edition limited to 75 copies.
Text and illustration spread printed in black on
grey Ingres paper.

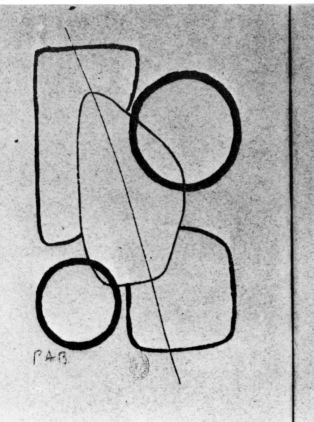

Ne me posez pas de questions
parlons d'autre chose
parlons des lunettes mortes si vous voulez
Botticelli Piero della Francesca
ou Velasquez
ou d'une fille violée
qu'un ramassis d'idiots pensent
qu'ils doivent plaindre

Vous rappelez-vous le vernis de mes tableaux
ils étaient comme des miroirs
où à chaque moment
quelque chose peut surgir
pour se confondre avec les oscillations
de mon cœur fatigué
qui ne sait plus aimer
ni haïr
ni même se transporter
au-dessus des misères intimes

J'ai atteint le comble des souffrances

Francis Picabia

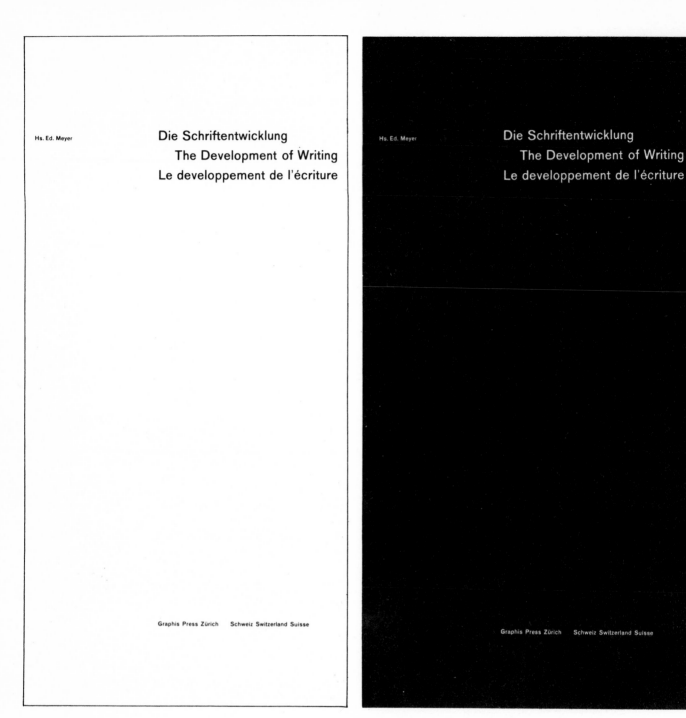

Hs. Ed. Meyer

Die Schriftentwicklung
The Development of Writing
Le developpement de l'écriture

Graphis Press Zürich   Schweiz Switzerland Suisse

Hs. Ed. Meyer

Die Schriftentwicklung
The Development of Writing
Le developpement de l'écriture

Graphis Press Zürich   Schweiz Switzerland Suisse

1958. *Die Schriftentwicklung* by Hs. Ed. Mayer.
Published by the Graphis Press, Zürich. Printed
by Bodmer and Leonardi, Zürich. 11⅝″ × 6⅛″.
Cover and title-page.

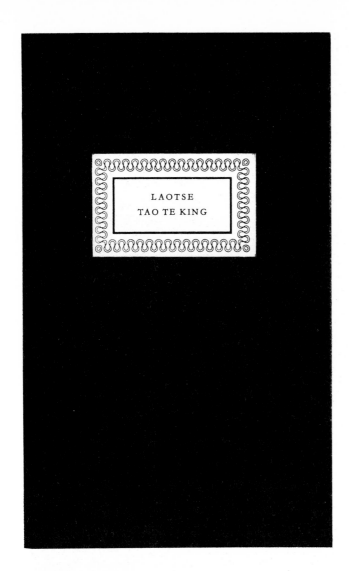

LAOTSE

TAO TE KING

DAS BUCH VOM SINN UND LEBEN

MIT EINEM VORWORT

VON JEAN GEBSER

VERLAG HANS HUBER BERN

UND STUTTGART

1958. *Laotse Tao Te King*, translated from the Chinese by Richard Wilhelm with a foreword by Jean Gebser. Designed by Max Caflisch. Published by Verlag Hans Huber, Bern and Stuttgart. Printed in Switzerland. 8″ × 4⅞″. Cover in black cloth with white paper label printed in black; and title-page.

Swiss book design

Walter Herdeg at Zürich, with his *Graphis* magazine, has done much for the cause of modern design. Hans Meyer's *Die Schriftentwicklung* is an elegant, tall, crisp production, published by the Graphis Press in Zürich. An effective use is made of repeating the title-page design on the cover, but reversing to white on black. Hans Fischli, Director of the School of Arts and Crafts, Zürich, says in his preface to this book: 'The science of calligraphy points to the smallest detail and introduces the laws of order that are the basis of all creative activity, from the architecture of a cathedral to an advertisement in a newspaper'. This discipline is evident in all good printing, and particularly evident in Swiss typography.

Max Caflisch is a German book designer, working in Zürich, and in contrast with so many modern typographers, working in the English style. The main difference between a Caflisch book and those of his English and American opposite numbers is that his books are usually better produced, with better presswork, more precise setting and better-fitting bindings.

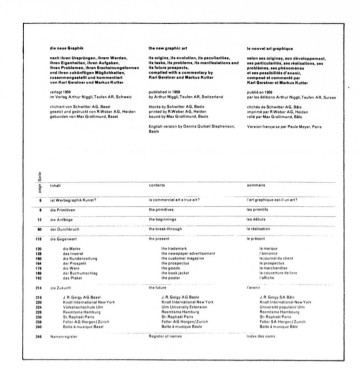

1959. *Die Neue Graphik* by Karl Gerstner and Markus Kutter. Published by Arthur Niggli, Teuffen AR, Switzerland. Printed by R. Weber AG, Heiden. Bound by Max Grollimund, Basel. 9⅛″ × 9″. Cover and contents page.

Gerstner and Kutter's *Die neue Graphik,* published in Switzerland in 1959, is one of the most interesting surveys of graphic design to appear since the last war. It is also a model example of clean layout, based on a grid structure. The book is set in German, English and French, in three unjustified columns, of 8 point Univers, to the page.

1959. *A Newe Booke of Copies 1574* edited by Berthold Wolpe, R.D.I. Designed, published and printed by the Lion and Unicorn Press at the Royal College of Art, London. 9½″ × 8½″. Cover in buff coloured cloth printed in orange and grey and blocked in gold, and title-page.

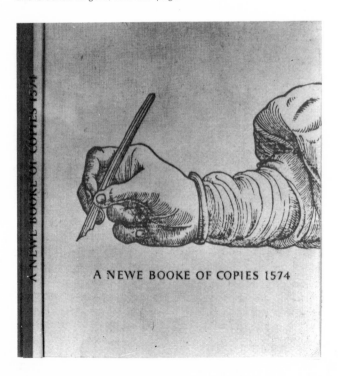

A NEWE
BOOKE OF COPIES
1574

*A facsimile of a unique Elizabethan Writing Book
in the Bodleian Library, Oxford*

*Edited with an Introduction
and Notes by Berthold Wolpe, R.D.I.*

LION AND UNICORN PRESS : LONDON
1959

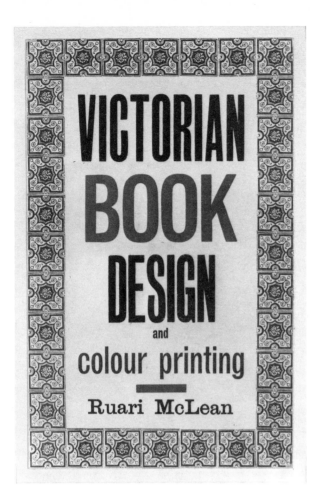

VICTORIAN BOOK DESIGN and colour printing
Ruari McLean

PRINTED EPHEMERA
The changing uses of type and letterforms
in English and American printing

JOHN LEWIS

W. S. COWELL IPSWICH, SUFFOLK

1963. *Victorian Book Design and Colour Printing* by Ruari McLean. Published by Faber and Faber, London. Printed by Shenval Press Ltd, London. $8\frac{1}{2}'' \times 5\frac{1}{4}''$. Jacket design by Ruari McLean printed in black, blue and brown.

1962. *Printed Ephemera* written, compiled and designed by John Lewis. Published and printed by W. S. Cowell Ltd, Ipswich. Distributed by Faber and Faber, London. $12'' \times 9\frac{1}{4}''$. Title-page printed in black and red.

Allusive typography

The reprint of the Elizabethan writing book, *A Newe Booke of Copies*, was carried out at the Royal College of Art by the Lion and Unicorn Press, under the guidance of its editor, Berthold Wolpe. The completely traditional treatment was considered appropriate for a reprint of this nature. The case-binding had a solid orange printing over the back, continuing to the centre of the spine, and in spite of its cutting the title in half, this counterchange treatment made an effective-looking cover, though it called for some precision in the case making.

Ruari McLean's *Victorian Book Design* and my own *Printed Ephemera,* though on different subjects, covered in part the same period of time. The books were published within a year of each other, and we both turned to elongated Victorian sans serif typefaces for jackets, and in the case of *Printed Ephemera* for the title-page as well. There will, I think, always be a place for allusive typography.

The dichotomy of ideas about the design of books continued through the 1960's. *Die Neue Typographie* crystallizes in Germany, and even more so in Switzerland, into a precise rather mechanistic book style.

1963. *Schrift und Bild* compiled by Dietrich Mahlow. Designed by Wolfgang Schmidt. Published by Typos Verlag, Frankfurt-am-Main. Printed by Franz W. Wesel, Baden-Baden. 9⅛″ × 9″. Cover design printed in black on red paper-covered boards; and text spread.

Typos Verlag

Im Zeichen wird die Wahrheit der Dinge und Gedanken durch den Menschen sichtbar, der in dem gleichen Strom mit ihnen schwimmt. Solche Zusammenfassung geistiger Vorgänge muß nicht an lesbare Schrift gebunden sein. Während diese Bindung in Ostasien möglich ist, weil die Schriftzeichen nicht Lautzeichen wie unsere Alphabete sind, sondern ihnen das Abbild zugrunde liegt, formt sich das westliche Zeichen frei von lesbarer Schrift. Damit ist es nicht nur nach der Seite der persönlichen Handschrift des Künstlers offen, sondern auch hinsichtlich seiner Bedeutung. Es geht nicht — oder es muß nicht von Erfahrungen, Empfindungen, Begriffen ausgehen, um dafür Symbole zu schaffen, sondern kann als Zeichenhaftes auch Vorstellungen erzeugen, die noch gar nicht vorhanden waren und die durch uns erst mit Sinn erfüllt werden müssen. Ihre Berechtigung und Schönheit finden diese Zeichen allein in der bildnerischen Sprache, aus der sie entstehen. Darin liegt das Geheimnis der Zeichen, immer wird in ihnen

eine Bewegung sichtbar, die sich auf den Betrachter überträgt und ihn in Gefilde trägt, wo er sich staunend umsieht und sich fragt, warum er dort nicht schon längst zu Hause ist. Jedoch ehe er sich's versieht, wird er in neue Bahnen geworfen, bis er versteht, daß es um die Beschwörung der großen Kraft der Ungewißheit geht.

Grâce à l'homme, la vérité des choses et des pensées, emportées par le même torrent que lui, apparaît, visible, dans le signe. Une telle synthèse de phénomènes d'ordre spirituel n'a pas besoin d'être liée à une écriture lisible. Si, en Asie Orientale, cette liaison est possible, — les signes graphiques n'étant pas des signes phonographiques comme ceux de nos alphabets, mais des signes qui s'appuient sur une représentation —, le signe occidental se forme indépendamment de la lisibilité de l'écriture. C'est ainsi que, non seulement la graphie personelle de l'artiste mais aussi la signification du signe achèvent de modeler ce dernier. Il n'est pas le fruit —, ou plutôt, il n'a pas besoin d'être le fruit d'expériences, de sensations, de concepts pour créer des symboles, sa qualité de signe peut également engendrer des représentations qui n'étaient pas encore présentes et qui ne parviennent à une signification que si nous leur en donnons une. Seul, le langage plastique d'où ils sont issus, confère justification et beauté à ces

signes. C'est là que réside le mystère des signes: ils évoquent toujours un mouvement qui se transmet au spectateur et le transporte dans des sphères où son regard vagabonde, étonné, et où il se demande pourquoi il n'a pas découvert plus tôt cet univers familier. Et cependant, à peine s'est-il retourné, qu'il est déjà projeté sur de nouvelles voies, jusqu'à ce qu'il comprenne qu'il s'agit d'évoquer la grande force d'incertitude.

Willi Baumeister
Spitze Formen

38

Jean Arp
Constellation de six formes noires

39

1963. *The Typographic Book* by Stanley Morison and Kenneth Day. Published by Ernest Benn Ltd, London. Printed by the University Press, Cambridge; and the plates by L. van Leer and Co. Ltd, Amsterdam. 12″ × 9½″. Title-page engraved on the wood by Reynolds Stone, and printed in red. 9⅝″ × 6″ printed area.

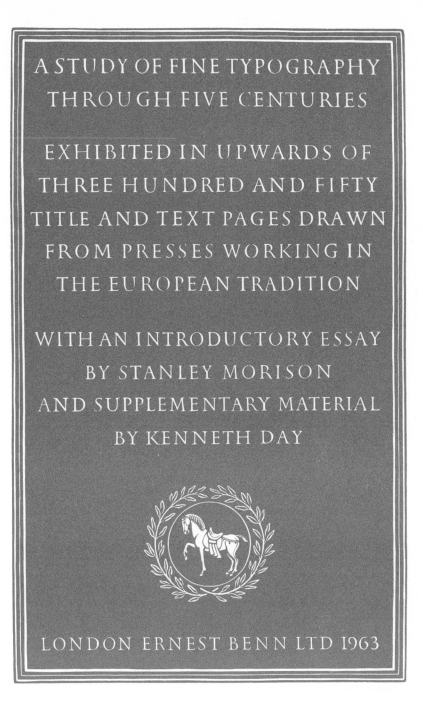

A STUDY OF FINE TYPOGRAPHY
THROUGH FIVE CENTURIES

EXHIBITED IN UPWARDS OF
THREE HUNDRED AND FIFTY
TITLE AND TEXT PAGES DRAWN
FROM PRESSES WORKING IN
THE EUROPEAN TRADITION

WITH AN INTRODUCTORY ESSAY
BY STANLEY MORISON
AND SUPPLEMENTARY MATERIAL
BY KENNETH DAY

LONDON ERNEST BENN LTD 1963

German and English attitudes 1963

The cover of Dietrich Mahlow's *Schrift und Bild* makes an interesting comparison with one of the title-pages of Stanley Morison's *The Typographic Book.* Both books were published in 1963. The *Schrift und Bild* typography is by Wolfgang Schmidt; the engraving for the two title-pages for *The Typographic Book* (this is the second one) is by Reynolds Stone. The text pages show just as great a divergence of thought. *The Typographic Book* has a wide setting, thirteen words to the line of a large size of Monotype Bembo, the most classical of typefaces; and it is printed on a heavy antique paper. *Schrift und Bild* is narrowly set, six words in the line in a small size of Futura (the most machine-drawn of sans serif typefaces) and is printed on a coated paper.

79

1964. *Exercices de Style* by Raymond Queneau. Illustrated by Jacques Carelman with typography by Massin. Published for the Club Français du Livre by Éditions Gallimard. 11″ × 8¾″. Text page and cover.

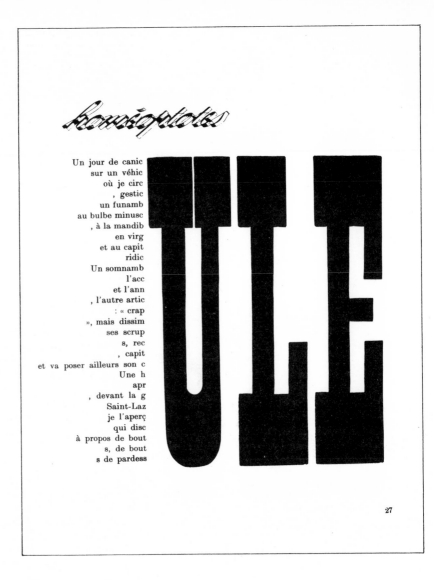

koninghdotas

Un jour de canic
sur un véhic
où je circ
, gestic
un funamb
au bulbe minusc
, à la mandib
en virg
et au capit
ridic
Un somnamb
l'acc
et l'ann
, l'autre artic
: « crap
», mais dissim
ses scrup
s, rec
, capit
et va poser ailleurs son c
Une h
apr
, devant la g
Saint-Laz
je l'aperç
qui disc
à propos de bout
s, de bout
s de pardess

27

EXER
CICES
DE
STYLE

par Raymond Queneau, de l'Académie Goncourt. Edition nouvelle, revue et corrigée.
Avec 33 exercices de style parallèles, dessinés, peints et sculptés par Carelman et
99 exercices de style typographiques de Massin.   Gallimard.

Raymond Queneau's typographic exercises

Raymond Queneau's *Exercices de Style* was published in a limited, illustrated edition by Éditions Gallimard for the Club Français du Livre in 1964. It was a most exciting, witty typographic frolic. Queneau's *Exercices de Style*, in which he tells the same story in many ways and from many points of view, is a perfect exercise for Jacques Carelman's typographic ingenuity. In whatever typographic idiom a designer may work, his ultimate and sole justification is to interpret, and if necessary clarify and point, his author's message. Fortunately, there is still more than one way to do this. The two mainstreams of book design, the German New Typography and the English Historic style, may yet cross-fertilize each other. There is much that each can learn from the other's approach.

3. THE INFLUENCE OF THE FRENCH *ÉDITIONS DE LUXE* ON COMMERCIAL BOOK PRODUCTION IN ENGLAND AND AMERICA

Since the beginning of this century, the most sumptuously illustrated books have come from France. The French have made a speciality of the picture book, particularly the *édition de luxe,* which bears little resemblance to its more restrained English or American counterpart. It is in one way an ancestor of the modern coffee-table book, which, beautifully produced though it may be, with its reproductions of great paintings or photographs of pretty gardens, is only art at second hand. The illustrated *édition de luxe* was, and still is, an excuse for graphically-minded painters and sculptors to express themselves in a new graphic medium. The expensive French limited editions, printed on hand-made paper, were often illustrated by the most illustrious of French contemporary painters. Such typographical virtues as these books may have possessed were of secondary consideration and were usually overwhelmed by the impact of the illustrations and the magnificence of their printing.

Ambroise Vollard, a Parisian art dealer, was one of the first publishers in this field of luxury picture books that were certainly not for children. Vollard issued his first book in 1900: Paul Verlaine's *Parallèlement.* For it Pierre Bonnard lithographed over a hundred illustrations, which were beautiful enough to stand on their own. Nevertheless this is a complete and lovely book. The lithographs, printed in a soft rose-sanguine, are a perfect foil for the superb presswork and for Claude Garamond's italic typeface, and are an integral part of the page. This book sets a standard of quality that Vollard's succeeding artists and printers were rarely able to equal.

Parallèlement was issued, following the French fashion, unsewn in Japanese paper covers, the intention being that the buyer would choose his own binding. But the choice of heavily tooled goat-skin and weighty boards would compress intolerably these ethereal pages; and for myself, I think they are best left free of such expensive constriction.

One of the reasons for the quality of these folios was Vollard's shrewd choice, not only of artists, but also of the craftsmen and printers who interpreted their work by wood engraving, lithography and etching.

Much has been written about these lovely books. Picasso's etchings for Buffon (printed by Lacourière), Georges Rouault's wood engravings and coloured aquatints for *Réincarnations du Père Ubu* and Segonzac's etchings for *Les Georgiques* have been reproduced again and again in reference books and periodicals. (This is the bedevilling effect of this age of endlessly repeated mechanical reproduction.) Because of this and because here we are primarily concerned with the design of books, and the place illustrations can play in this context, there would be little justification for dealing with them at length in these pages. Moreover the quality of the illustrations in these Vollard editions depended greatly on their direct methods of reproduction.

French painters turn freely to etching or lithography as an additional means of expression; and the great contribution made by France to the art of the modern book has been the willingness of her finest painters to move so naturally into the realms of book illustration.

In the years between the wars something of the exuberant quality of these books rubbed off onto the commercial publishers, who were cajoled, or perhaps inspired, by such painters as Fernand Léger in France and Paul Nash in England into publishing rather more colourful books than they otherwise might have done.

The publisher who contributed much to the production of books in this vein was the late George Macy, with his Limited Editions Club and Heritage Press editions in New York. This Book Club still continues with unabated vigour and produces twelve new volumes every year, illustrated, designed and printed by artists, designers and printers from many countries.

Je te veux trop rieuse
Et très impérieuse,
Méchante & mauvaise &
Pire s'il te plaisait,
Mais si luxurieuse!

Ah, ton corps noir & rose
Et clair de lune! Ah, pose
Ton coude sur mon cœur.
Et tout ton corps vainqueur,
Tout ton corps que j'adore!

Ah, ton corps, qu'il repose
Sur mon âme morose
Et l'étouffe s'il peut,
Si ton caprice veut!
Encore, encore, encore!

28

1900. *Parallèlement* by Paul Verlaine, illustrated by Pierre Bonnard with 108 lithographs printed in rose-sanguine and 9 wood engravings printed in black. Lithographs printed by Auguste Clot and the wood engravings by Tony Beltrand. Text printed by l'Imprimerie Nationale, Paris. 11$\frac{7}{8}$″ × 9$\frac{5}{8}$″. Illustration pages.

1928. *Bubu de Montparnasse* by Philippe with etchings by André Dunoyer de Segonzac. Published by Les Trents, Lyon. Illustration.

The press book: France and England

Autographic methods of illustration are in common use in France and, until recently, have been anything but common practice in England or America. Since the time of Whistler, there have been few English artists whose etchings could be compared in their directness and in their quality of drawing with those of André Dunoyer de Segonzac. Sickert was one, and he never illustrated a book. (One could compile an interesting dossier of real illustrators who have never been commissioned to illustrate.)

Stephen Gooden's copper engraving is presented here to show the contrast between the utterly different attitudes prevailing in the two countries. Segonzac's etchings are usually drawn straight to plate, without any preliminary work. His etchings for *Bubu de Montparnasse*, for Vollard, are deliciously free drawings, many of them executed at least in part *au grattoir*,[1] which gives them something of the softness of a lithograph.

His picture of the girl sitting on the edge of a bed is a superb, yet most tentative

[1] With a scraping knife.

84

1933. *The Fables of La Fontaine* translated into English verse by Edward Marsh, with 12 engravings by Stephen Gooden. Published by Heinemann, London. Printed by the Windmill Press. 8⅜" × 5½". The engravings in this edition are reproductions and not printed from the original plates. Illustration: 'The Lion in Love'.

drawing, very lightly inked. No professional engraver or etcher would have been content with these tenuous lines. It is its utterly *unprofessional* quality that gives it its freshness.

In contrast with Segonzac's use of the etching needle, Stephen Gooden's meticulous copperplate engraving might seem somewhat laboured, though the medium is a severely testing one. Such engraving evokes the quiet satisfaction given by any piece of good craftsmanship. Gooden based his style on that of Wenceslaus Hollar, William Marshall and other seventeenth-century engravers. He even re-introduced the engraved title-page. This anachronistic attitude to illustration is one of the odd foibles of the English (and of the Germans); it is an attitude with which the French have little sympathy.

Engraving on copper is a medium well suited to book illustration, but it is little used nowadays, partly because of the difficulty of execution and partly because of the expense of intaglio printing.

1926. *Eclogae et Georgica* by Virgil. Illustrated
by Aristide Maillol. Published by Insel-Verlag
in Leipzig and published and printed by the
Cranach Press, Weimar. 13″ × 10″. Woodcut.

The nude: Maillol and Picasso

Ever since Bonnard's exquisite *Parallèlement*, 'nudes' have been one of the
mainstays of the private press movement, not only in France, but also in
Germany and England. (A national Puritanism seems to have prevented this
happening in the U.S.A.) In 1913 the French sculptor, Aristide Maillol,
completed his illustrations for an edition of Virgil's *Eclogues* for Count Harry
Kessler. This work had been conceived in Greece in 1908, but was delayed
by the war and not published until 1926. It is a handsome book, though the
black line woodcuts, engraved by Eric Gill, give Maillol's nude studies a
somewhat stiff appearance.

MODERN PAINTERS AND SCULPTORS
AS ILLUSTRATORS

1936. *Modern Painters and Sculptors as
Illustrators* edited by Monroe Wheeler. Published
by the Museum of Modern Art, New York.
10″ × 7⅝″. Cover design from an etching by
Picasso from *Les Métamorphoses d'Ovide*,
published by Skira.

[2] *A History of Book Illustration* by David Bland.
Faber and Faber, London 1958.

The cover design for *Modern Painters and Sculptors as Illustrators* is from an
etching by Picasso, illustrating *Les Métamorphoses d'Ovide,* published by
Skira in 1931. This was the finest of Picasso's important illustrated books; he
repeated the same fluid line in a number of other books with classical texts.
David Bland draws attention to the erotic appeal of so many *éditions de luxe*
and quotes a writer in the *Times Literary Supplement* who was of the opinion
that quite half their sales depended on erotic, though rarely pornographic
appeal.[2]

1919. *La Fin du Monde* by Blaise Cendrars,
illustrated by Fernand Léger. Published by
Éditions de la Sirène, Paris. Set in Morland and
printed by Frazier-Soye in Montparnasse and the
stencil colour work by Ateliers de Richard,
Paris. 12½″ × 9⅞″. Title-page.

Fernand Léger: Cubist and Dadaist

La Fin du Monde by Blaise Cendrars, illustrated by Fernand Léger, was
published by Éditions de la Sirène in Paris in 1919. This brown paper-
covered picture book, both Cubist and Dadaist in treatment, makes bold and
decorative use of letterforms.

The typography, in its roughness, is worthy of the Leadenhall Press; the book
is set in 24 point Morland and printed in a rich black with stencil colours. *La
Fin du Monde* was Léger's second book.

Dieu le père est à son bureau américain. Il signe hâtivement d'innombrables papiers. Il est en bras de chemise et a un abat-jour vert sur les yeux. Il se lève, allume un gros cigare, consulte sa montre, marche nerveusement dans son cabinet, va et vient en mâchonnant son cigare. Il se rassied à son bureau, repousse fiévreu-

1919. *La Fin du Monde.* Text spread.

Fernand Léger (1881–1955), mural painter and worker in stained glass, illustrated a number of books. His first was *J'ai tué*, also by Blaise Cendrars, published the year before *La Fin du Monde.* In 1921, Léger cut six woodcuts for André Malraux's *Lunes en Papier*. For the rest of his life he combined the activities of painting, designing and illustration with a catholic freedom. His last book, *Mes Voyages*, was published after his death with an introductory poem by Louis Aragon. Léger, though originally opposed to the Dadaists, incorporated many Dada elements into his *La Fin du Monde.*

ROMANCE A LA VIEILLE DAME
OU NATURE MORTE SENTIMENTALE

à Raoul Dufy.

L'AIR ENTRE PAR LE TROU DE LA SERRURE

Les quatres murs   mur   murent
          si las de t'attester ce qu'ils ont déjà vu
ICI PRÉVAUT LE MOTIF CŒUR

Flore et tenture dont la fanure est la raison
L'ombre des mannequins sentimentaux
                    manteaux à taille
Sur capiton sensible à bergeries

56

1920. *Tour d'Horizon* by Marcel Willard.
Illustrated by Raoul Dufy. Published by Au Sans
Pareil, Paris. 7⅝″ × 5⅝″. Text spread and
illustration.

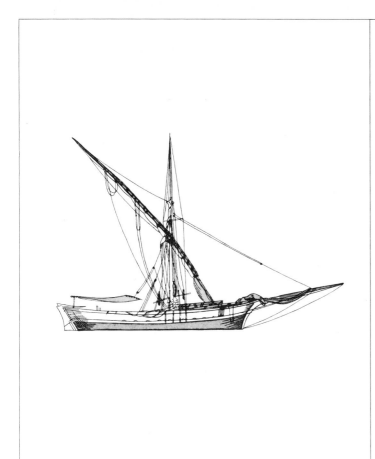

PLATE VII

THE TARTANE

One of the largest vessels in the Mediterranean to-day still preserving the old Lateen sail. Although being slowly superseded, the Tartane were at one time well known, and ships with a similar sail plan are on record as 'Tartan' rigged: A curious point, possibly bearing on this, being the name of 'Dundee,' by which they are still known locally at St. Tropez.

They carry a jib, topsail, and the huge Lateen sail bent to a yard sometimes longer than the vessel herself. This yard or 'antenne' is hoisted by double tyes, as were yards in ships of the sixteenth century, and secured to the mast by a parral. Peak halyards are rove and a vang steadies the yardarm, the lower end being lashed to a short spar at the foot of the mast. Well suited by the light Mediterranean winds, they are engaged in all descriptions of coastal trade.

27

1926. *Sailing Ships and Barges of the Western Mediterranean and the Adriatic* written and illustrated by Edward Wadsworth. Published by Hazelwood Books, Frederick Etchells and Hugh Macdonald. Quarter-bound with a white cloth spine and orange paper-covered boards, blocked in gold. $12\frac{1}{8}'' \times 7\frac{3}{4}''$. Text and illustration spread.

The press book: France and England

Raoul Dufy (1877—1953), influenced by the Fauve painters, is best known for his colourful, short-hand calligraphic paintings of the Côte d'Azur, regattas, casinos and racecourses. Dufy illustrated a number of books, including lithographs for Apollinaire's *Le Poète Assassiné* in 1926 and etchings for *La Belle Enfant* for Vollard in 1930. His designs for Marcel Willard's *Tour d'Horizon* were produced for Au Sans Pareil in Paris and published in an edition of 325 copies in 1920. The illustrations for this typographically eccentric little book were a mixture of etchings and lithographs. Dufy's very free treatment of a sailing ship makes an interesting contrast with Edward Wadsworth's precise etching of a *tartane*. Wadsworth was a member of the Vorticist group and had a deep interest in ships; his book of etchings, *Sailing Ships and Barges of the Western Mediterranean and Adriatic*, is full of precise observation. His linocuts of First World War camouflaged ships are in a very different vein from these engravings.

1932. *Urne Buriall and the Garden of Cyrus* by
Sir Thomas Browne. Illustrated by Paul Nash.
Published by Cassell and Co. Ltd, London.
Printed by the Curwen Press, Plaistow. 12" × 8¾".
Illustration printed by collotype with stencilled
colours.

The French influence in England

The most resolute attempt to combine the best of two worlds, the French
édition de luxe and the English typographic book was made by Desmond
Flower when, in 1932, he produced for Cassells an edition of Sir Thomas
Browne's *Urne Buriall and the Garden of Cyrus* with illustrations by Paul
Nash. This was very well printed by the Curwen Press with typography by
Oliver Simon. The collotype illustrations were hand stencilled. It is a beautiful

1931. *Seven Short Stories* by Walter de la Mare,
with illustrations by John Nash. Published by
Faber and Faber, London. Printed by
R. MacLehose and Co. Ltd, Glasgow. $8\frac{7}{8}'' \times 6\frac{1}{4}''$.
Illustration: 'The Bird of Travel' printed in line
and colour.

piece of work, though the illustrations, considering they come from a most
illustrious painter, seem just a little feeble.

John Nash illustrated in colour for Faber and Faber *Seven Short Stories* by
Walter de la Mare. His somewhat naïve drawings were reproduced by line
and coloured by the stencil process; the result is an attractive and pleasantly
fresh set of illustrations, published the year before his brother's *Urne Buriall*.

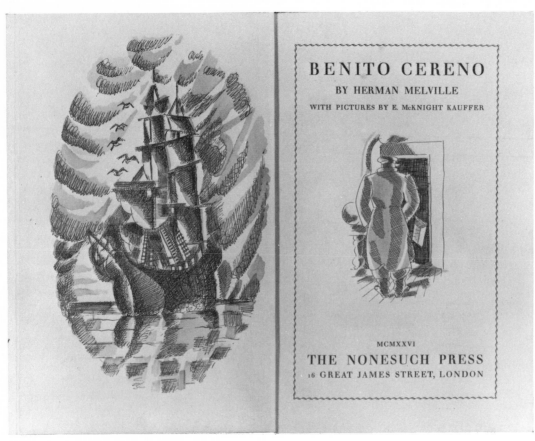

1926. *Benito Cereno* by Herman Melville.
Illustrated by E. McKnight Kauffer. Published by
the Nonesuch Press, London. Printed on a tinted
Van Gelder paper by the Curwen Press, Plaistow.
12″ × 7¾″. Frontispiece and title-page.

ELSIE AND THE CHILD

1

Elsie and her husband Joe were working in the kitchen of Dr.
Raste's abode at the corner of Myddelton Square and Cheval
Street, Clerkenwell, E.C.1. Once they possessed a surname, but
through disuse it had withered away and existed no more—save
in ink on their insurance cards and medical cards. Everybody, high
or humble, called them Elsie and Joe. They thought of themselves

1

1929. *Elsie and the Child* by Arnold Bennett
with stencilled illustrations by E. McKnight
Kauffer. Published by Cassell and Co. Ltd,
London. Printed and stencilled by the Curwen
Press. 10″ × 7½″. Edition limited to 750 copies.
Chapter opening.

1928. *A Sentimental Journey* by Laurence
Sterne, with engravings by J. E. Laboureur.
Published by the Golden Cockerel Press.
9⅛″ × 5½″. Illustration.

Opposite:
1930. *Don Quixote de la Mancha* by Miguel de
Cervantes. Illustrated by E. McKnight Kauffer.
Published by the Nonesuch Press, London.
Printed by the Cambridge University Press.
9″ × 5⅝″. The illustrations are reproduced by
lithography with stencilled colours.

The influence of the French *Livres des Peintres* on English and American
private press books can be seen in productions where processes other than
letterpress have been used. The Nonesuch Press issued a number of illustrated
books. Mostly they were in the conservative English tradition, but there were
exceptions. In 1921, an American graphic artist, E. McKnight Kauffer, who
at that time lived in London, drew a series of stencilled designs for Herman
Melville's *Benito Cereno.* Eight years later, for Cassells, he drew a set of
coloured illustrations for Arnold Bennett's *Elsie and the Child*, which were
stencilled by the Curwen Press, the printers of the book. This attractive and
well-made edition was remaindered, like so many other nice books in the
1930's. Kauffer also used this stencilled technique for his coloured illustrations
for a two-decker Nonesuch edition of *Don Quixote*, where his modern
drawings sit somewhat incongruously alongside the evocative eighteenth-
century typography, and even more uncomfortably within the goatskin
covers. Kauffer's fame rests largely on his achievements as a poster artist, but
his book illustrations are still of interest.

The French painter-illustrators showed little interest in 'costume' illustration,
seeming happiest with either classical or contemporary themes. An exception
to this rule was J. E. Laboureur (1877–1943), who was a prolific illustrator.
Laboureur was a founder member of the Société des Peintres Graveurs
Indépendants and worked with the Cubists, although signs of this are not
very evident in this illustration for the Golden Cockerel edition of Sterne's
Sentimental Journey published in 1928.

1938. *High Street* by J. M. Richards. Illustrated
with lithographs by Eric Ravilious. Published by
Country Life Ltd, London. Printed by the Curwen
Press, Plaistow. 9″ × 5¾″. Lithographed paper-
covered board case-binding. Frontispiece and
title-page.

1938. *High Street*. Illustration for the *Knife Grinder*.

In the 1930's something of the French attitude to book production and the use of autographic methods began to be felt in England by a few artists, of whom Eric Ravilious was one. Ravilious, inspired by Paul Nash, was as happy working in a number of different media as any French artist. He was as much at home on the lithographic stone as he was engraving boxwood or painting murals. In 1938, he collaborated with J. M. Richards, the editor of *The Architectural Review* in producing a book called *High Street*. The illustrations were coloured lithographs of a variety of shop fronts, ranging from a cheese-monger to a clerical outfitter's and throwing in a knife-grinder for good measure. It is a delightful book, beautifully printed (once again by Curwen) and published by Country Life in an ordinary commercial edition.

1931. *Memoirs of an Infantry Officer* by Siegfried
Sassoon. Illustrated by Barnett Freedman.
Published by Faber and Faber, London. Printed
by R. Maclehose and Co. Ltd, Glasgow. 8⅝″ × 5¾″.
Lithographed cloth case-binding and text spread.

that night, so we were rewarded by a mention in the G.H.Q.
communiqué. 'At Mametz we raided hostile trenches. Our party
entered without difficulty and maintained a spirited bombing fight,
and finally withdrew at the end of twenty-five minutes.' This was
their way of telling England. Aunt Evelyn probably read it
automatically in her *Morning Post*, unaware that this minor
event had almost caused her to receive a farewell letter from
me. The next night our Company was in the front line and
I recovered three hatchets and a knobkerrie from No Man's
Land. Curiously enough, I hadn't yet seen a German. I had
seen dim figures on my dark patrols; but no human faces.

The English illustrated book, as produced by the private presses, was nearly always letterpress-printed, often with wood engraved illustrations. Purist bibliophiles held out for a long time against the introduction of lithography. One of the first English artists to change this was Barnett Freedman, an artist who introduced a consummate craftsmanship to the art of book designing and illustrating. He was technically a very skilful lithographer, influenced by the nineteenth-century French trade lithographers rather than by the contemporary School of Paris. To some extent, his lithographic dexterity was a limiting factor, yet within his imposed limitations, he achieved an extraordinary technical consistency in his book illustration. His first important book was Siegfried Sassoon's *Memoirs of an Infantry Officer* published by Faber in 1931; his most successful, Tolstoy's *War and Peace* (1938), for which he lithographed the plates for George Macy's Limited Editions Club of New York. Macy was a great admirer of Barnett Freedman's work, and offered him much greater scope than any English publishers. Freedman drew lithographs for four different titles for the Limited Editions Club. The first of these was *Lavengro* (1935), which Macy wryly described as 'one of the ten finest books we ever issued and one of the ten least popular'. In 1937, Freedman illustrated *War and Peace* for Macy who became enthusiastic about these lithographs. In the *Quarto-Millenary* of the Limited Editions Club, he wrote: 'Some illustrated books are destined for immortality: Botticelli's *Dante,* Delacroix's *Faust,* Blake's *Book of Job,* Flaxman's *Homer.* To that illustrious company I nominate Barnett Freedman's *War and Peace.*' Naturally enough Macy asked Freedman to illustrate one of the twenty-seven volumes of the monumental, Bruce Rogers-designed, edition of Shakespeare. Freedman chose *Henry IV, Part I.* He had some odd bed-fellows amongst the other illustrators, including Graham Sutherland (*Henry VI*), Boardman Robinson (*King Lear*), W. A. Dwiggins (*The Taming of the Shrew*), Edward A. Wilson (*The Tempest*) and Edy Legrand (*Hamlet*). Barnett Freedman's last book for the Limited Editions Club was *Anna Karenina* (1951). Five years later George Macy died, at the early age of fifty-six. By that time, he had published over two hundred and fifty titles, introducing to a wide American public, something of the French attitude to book illustration.

1938. *War and Peace* by Leo Tolstoy. Translated by Louise and Aylmer Maude. Illustrated with lithographs by Barnett Freedman. Designed by John Easton. Printed by R. MacLehose and Co. Ltd, Glasgow. Lithographs printed by the Baynard Press. Bound by Leighton-Straker. Published by the Limited Editions Club, New York. $8\frac{3}{4}'' \times 5\frac{7}{8}''$. Illustrations.

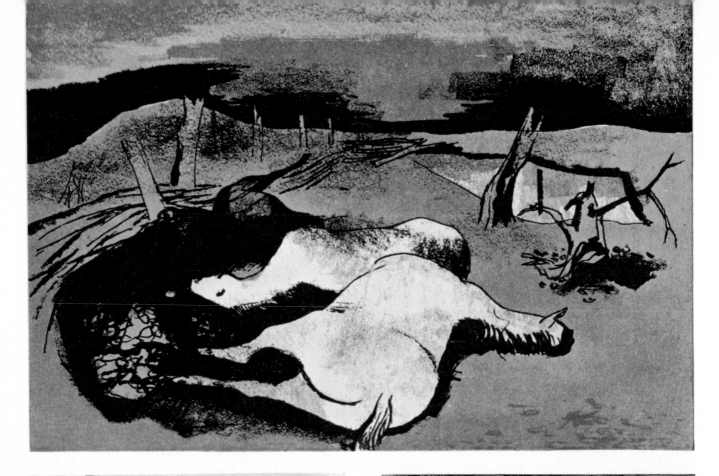

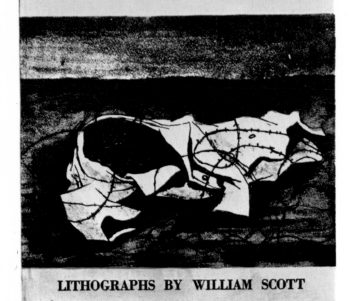

SOLDIERS' VERSE

CHOSEN BY
PATRIC DICKINSON

LITHOGRAPHS BY WILLIAM SCOTT

POEMS OF SLEEP

AND DREAM

Chosen by CAROL STEWART

Lithographs by ROBERT COLQUHOUN

ENGLISH SCOTTISH & WELSH
LANDSCAPE
Verse chosen by
JOHN BETJEMAN and GEOFFREY TAYLOR

Lithographs by JOHN PIPER

Frederick Muller

ENGLISH LANDSCAPE

ENGLISH SCOTTISH & WELSH
LANDSCAPE
Verse chosen by
JOHN BETJEMAN and GEOFFREY TAYLOR

Lithographs by JOHN PIPER

1944. *English, Scottish and Welsh Landscape 1700–c. 1860.* An anthology of poetry chosen by John Betjeman and Geoffrey Taylor, with lithographs by John Piper. Designed and produced by Adprint. Published by Frederick Muller Ltd, London. Printed by the Curwen Press Ltd, Plaistow. Lithograph on the back and front of the cloth case-binding.

Opposite:
1945. *Soldiers' Verse* chosen by Patric Dickinson, With lithographs by William Scott. Produced by Adprint Ltd. Published by Frederick Muller Ltd, London. Printed by W. S. Cowell Ltd, Ipswich. 8¼" × 5½". Cover design and illustration.

1947. *Poems of Sleep and Dream* chosen by Carol Stewart. With lithographs by Robert Colquhoun. Produced by Adprint Ltd. Published by Frederick Muller Ltd, London. Printed by W. S. Cowell Ltd, Ipswich. 8¼" × 5½". Cover design.

In 1938, Walter Neurath, a Viennese publisher, settled in London. Within a few weeks he had established a book production (as opposed to publishing) unit, within the Adprint company. Here he offered a design, production, editorial and ideas service to publishers. As well as producing a number of sociological works, often in collaboration with his namesakes Otto and Marie Neurath, Walter Neurath created a wide-ranging and successful series called 'Britain in Pictures', published by Collins; and towards the end of the 1939–45 war, a series of anthologies 'New Excursions into English Poetry', published by Frederick Muller. These square-backed octavos were illustrated with lithographs by such artists as John Piper, William Scott and Robert Colquhoun. The jacket designs were also printed on the cloth covers. Of these books, *English, Scottish and Welsh Landscape*, with verse chosen by John Betjeman and Geoffrey Taylor and lithographs by John Piper, was probably the most successful. For these illustrations Piper used a limited range of sombre colours, with very effective results.

John Piper, who has done much distinguished work as a stage designer and in stained glass, has also illustrated or decorated a number of books. Amongst his best book illustrations were a fine set of prints for *Brighton Aquatints* in 1939.

In 1945, William Scott, a Scottish-born Ulsterman who had already achieved fame and recognition as a painter, lithographed the illustrations to *Soldiers Verse*, an anthology chosen by Patric Dickinson for this series. Two years later a young Scottish painter called Robert Colquhoun drew the lithographs for another anthology in the same series, called *Poems of Sleep and Dream*. This re-introduction in England of painters as illustrators was belated but welcome.

101

1936. *Green Mansions* by W. H. Hudson, with
illustrations by Miguel Covarrubias. Published
by the Heritage Press in New York and the
Nonesuch Press in London. Printed by the
Haddon Craftsmen and the Duenewald Printing
Corporation in New York. 9⅜″ × 6⅜″. End-papers
and line illustration.

Book Club productions in America

In 1936 the Heritage Press published an interesting edition of W. H. Hudson's
Green Mansions. This romance of the Brazilian rain forests is a fairly stiff
proposition for an illustrator. In Miguel Covarrubias – a Mexican, Hudson
has found a sympathetic interpreter. His line illustrations are just such drawings as an Amerindian might have made and the colour illustrations and endpapers, though rather more sophisticated than the line drawings, still have a
primitive feeling. The reproduction, by four-colour offset, hardly does justice
to these decorative pictures. The cover repeats the jacket design and is
lithographed from an oil painting by Covarrubias. Like the endpapers it depicts
a jungle scene. These illustrations also give some indication of Covarrubias's
work as a mural painter. He has illustrated a number of books, including
Mexico South and *Island of Bali,* both published by Knopf and both written
by the artist.

I found my Indian friends home again

1936. *Green Mansions*. Full page coloured illustration.

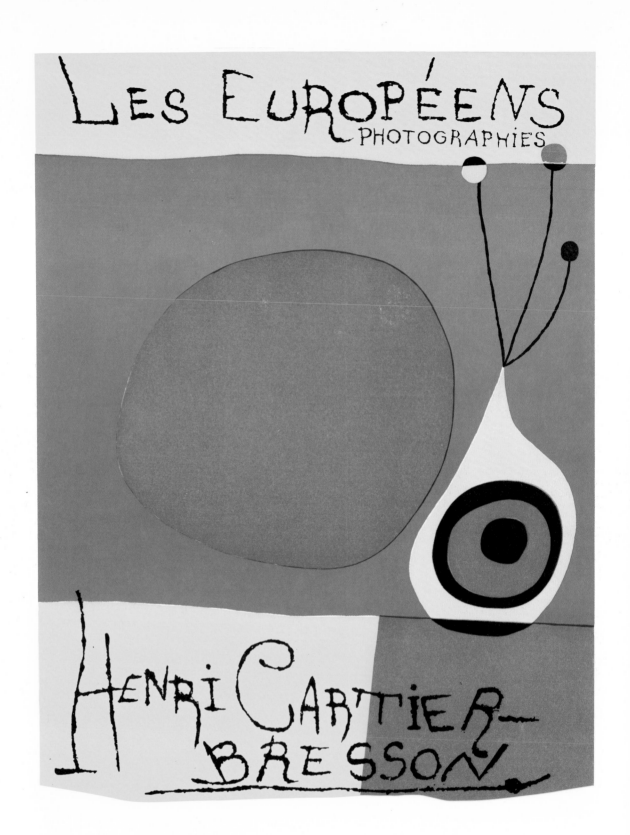

1955. *Les Européens*, photographs by Henri Cartier-Bresson. Published by Éditions Verve, Paris. Printed by Draeger Frères. $14\frac{1}{2}'' \times 11\frac{3}{4}''$. Cover design by Joan Miró, printed in four colours.

I have *faute de mieux* had to leave bookjackets out of this survey. Where jacket designs are printed on the cloth- (or paper-) covered boards, or on drawn-on covers as in paperbacks, I think they do come within my self-imposed limitations. Cartier-Bresson's book of photographs has such a cover. This brilliantly colourful design is by Joan Miró. It is an interesting if unlikely choice for the cover of a book of photographs.

1936. *Transition*. A periodical volume (no. 25). Edited by Eugène Joks. Published in New York. 8" × 6". Cover by Joan Miró, printed in black and blue.

Painters as book designers and illustrators

Miró, a Spanish-born artist who has worked much in Paris, has brought an exceptional quality of colour to the books he has illustrated – a brilliance such as only Matisse had achieved before him. Miró has been both a Cubist and a Surrealist. His work is so individual that it would be difficult for any artist to follow him without being guilty of plagiarism. The cover for the periodical volume *Transition* was done in 1936, and in both these covers Miró's calligraphy adds an almost oriental quality to the designs.

Modern novels are rarely issued with illustrations. In 1950 Heinemann published an illustrated edition of *The Forsyte Saga,* which had been constantly in print since *The Man of Property*, the first of the trilogy, was published in 1920. Anthony Gross, an English artist who has lived and worked for a large part of his life in France, was commissioned to illustrate it. This was an unexpected but inspired choice, for here was a painter, who, like so many French artists, had worked in many media. The book was produced by two printers: the line illustrations, with the text, by one; the coloured plates, printed by offset, by another. The plates were reproduced from colour separations drawn by the artist on sheets of grained plastic, by which method subtle washes of colour could be printed without any screen or chalking. If only the text had been printed as satisfactorily as the coloured illustrations, this would have been a memorable piece of book production. As it is, it will stand as an example of what can be done when a graphically-minded painter turns his hand to illustration.

Soames in Park Lane

1950. *The Forsyte Saga* by John Galsworthy with illustrations by Anthony Gross. Designed by John Lewis. Published by William Heinemann Ltd, London. The colour plates printed by W. S. Cowell Ltd, Ipswich and the text by the Windmill Press, Kingswood. $9\frac{1}{4}'' \times 6\frac{1}{2}''$. Illustration: 'Soames in Park Lane'.

1956. *De Klokken van Chagall* by Bernard
Majorick. Published and printed by Steendrukkerij
de Jong and Co., Hilversum. 9⅝″ × 9¾″.
Lithographed by Chagall.

³ Chagall: *Signature* No. 2 new series 1946.

Romanticism takes different forms in different countries. It is a rare manifestation in France. In the case of Russian artists it nearly always has a
religious significance. Marc Chagall, a Russian-born artist, came to Paris
first in 1920 and was there associated with the Cubists. Michael Ayrton,
writing some years ago about this artist, said, 'The intangible legend and
religion of the Russian-Jew combined with the essentially tangible logic of
French painting explains the strange chemistry of Chagall's art'.³
Chagall's three great works of illustration, Gogol's *Les Ames Mortes,* La
Fontaine's *Fables*, and the *Bible* were all commissioned by Vollard. They were
still unpublished when Vollard died, but the Parisian publisher Tériade came
to the rescue and published the three books between 1948 and 1956. The
illustration shown here is from a lithograph drawn by Chagall at Vence for
Bernard Majorick's essay *De Klokken van Chagall* in 1956. Majorick wrote
this essay because he was intrigued by the frequent recurrence of clocks in
Chagall's work.

107

1978 *Heureux qui comme Iris* written and
illustrated by Karine Huet and Yvon Le Corre.
Published by Gallimard, Paris. 12¼″ × 9⅝″. Cover
and spread.

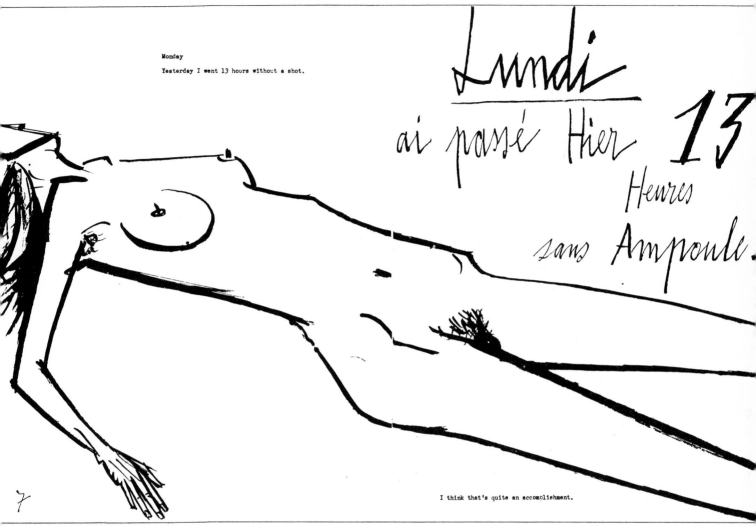

Monday

Yesterday I went 13 hours without a shot.

I think that's quite an accomplishment.

1964–5. *Toxique* by Françoise Sagan, with illustrations by Bernard Buffet. Published by René Julliard in France, E. P. Dutton and Co., in New York and Souvenir Press in London. 12″ × 9¼″. Illustration: 'Yesterday I went 13 hours without a shot.'

[4] 'Iris restaurée par Charles Harker de Abberton, est un smack de moyenne dimension, construit avec peu de tirant d'eau dans le but de draguer les bancs d'huitres devant Bradwell . . . Iris n'est probablement jamais sortie de la Blackwater pendant les trois quarts de sa vie de travail. Si on les utilise comme yachts, les smacks de ce genre, tirant peu d'eau, ne sont pas des bateaux marin, à cause de leur franc-bord bas et de leur grand poids. Par grosse mer, il peuvent être très exposés, voire dangereux' John Lewis *Small Craft Conversion* 1972. Thus Yvon Le Corre was able to make me eat my words!

Something of the French attitude to illustration has rubbed off on the American and English books that I have described in this chapter, but only a little. The last word remains with France.

In 1964 René Julliard published 'a candid diary' of Françoise Sagan's nine days in a special clinic undergoing detoxification from morphine. Mlle Sagan showed this diary to an old friend, the painter Bernard Buffet. The result was *Toxique,* a brilliant series of pages, as effective in their calligraphy as in their spiky, urgent drawings of a tortured, naked girl. The cover, in its simplicity, is a masterpiece. It is a book that only France could have produced.

In the 1970s Yvon Le Corre, a French art teacher, bought the *Iris,* an old Colchester fishing boat which had been beautifully restored by Charles Harker.[4] As Le Corre was setting off for Brittany from the Blackwater river in Essex, Charles Harker said: 'Don't ask too much of her.'

Within a couple of years, Yvon Le Corre had sailed to the Mediterranean and across the Atlantic to Brazil, up to Grenada and Martinique and back to Brittany. *Heureux qui comme* Iris . . . *notes et dessins d'un voyage* is a description of those voyages, largely written by Karine Huet and designed and illustrated by Yvon Le Corre. It is a very French book with vivid illustrations and hand-written text wonderfully intermingled.

1921. *Ali Baba und die Vierzig Räuber.*
Lithographic illustration.

1921. *Ali Baba und die vierzig Räuber* (First edition 1903). Illustrated by Max Slevogt. Published by Bruno Cassirer, Berlin. Printed by W. Drugulin, Leipzig. 12¼" × 9¾". Text pages and line illustrations and title-page.

4. THE EFFECT OF GERMAN IMPRESSIONISM AND EXPRESSIONISM ON BOOK ILLUSTRATION

If this were a history of modern book production and illustration, an entire volume would be needed to do justice to German illustration, even from the time of Adolf Menzel and his great series of pen drawings for *Geschichte Friedrichs des Grossen*. Here, I can only attempt to show the work of a few artists who, since the turn of the century, have affected the general trend of European or American illustration.

From 1892 contemporary art in Munich had been represented by the Secession, which had established by the first decade of this century a form of German Impressionism. Max Slevogt and Lovis Corinth were its leaders. Both artists illustrated books, but Slevogt (1868–1932), who was both a painter and a lithographer, was the more prolific. Slevogt's lithography and pen drawings are full of lively action. In 1903 Bruno Cassirer published his *Ali Baba und die vierzig Räuber,* which was a mixture of line and half-tone drawings, all delightfully free. *Ali Baba* was reprinted a number of times; the illustrations on this page are reproduced from the 1921 edition. In 1908 Slevogt illustrated *Sinbad der Seefahrer* for the same publisher, Bruno Cassirer, and his cousin Paul, who was an art dealer, were amongst the first German publishers to make use of painter-illustrators. When Hitler came to power, Bruno Cassirer left Germany and settled in Oxford.

In the world of books, it is sad to think how many talented painter-illustrators have been neglected by publishers. One of the greatest illustrators who ever lived was the Norwegian Edvard Munch, who never illustrated a book. Munch made countless prints in every graphic process, from woodcuts, zincographs and etchings to lithographs. His woodcut *The Cry* would rank as one of the world's great book illustrations, if it had ever appeared in a book!

1911. *Tubutsch* by Albert Ehrenstein. Illustrated by Oskar Kokoschka. Published by Jahoda and Siegel, Vienna and Leipzig. 12¼″ × 9¾″. Title-page and illustration.

eines Cabkutschers oder eines Karfiolflowaken hülle, die Be=
kanntschaft einer Kanalräumerin zu machen trachte und ihre
eheliche Treue einer Probe unterziehe ...

Nein, das werde ich nicht tun, ich fühle nicht mehr die Kraft
dazu in mir. Der zweifelnde Blick des Hausmeisters hat
meine ganze Energie hinweggenommen! Und als ich im
Schein des zusammensinkenden Wachsstengels aus der Visit=
karte, die auf der Tür meines Kabinetts mit separiertem Ein=
gang prangt, ersah, daß ich der Herr Karl Tubutsch war, da
sagte ich leise, niedergeschmettert, nichts als : "Scho wieder!" ...

Oft in der Nacht fahre ich auf. Was ist? Nichts, nichts!
Will denn niemand bei mir einbrechen? Alles ist voraus=
berechnet. O, ich möchte nicht der sein, der bei mir einbricht.
Abgesehen davon, daß — meinen Stiefelknecht Philipp und
vielleicht noch ein Straßenverzeichnis ausgenommen — bei
mir nichts zu holen ist, ich gestehe offen und ehrlich: ich
kenne den Betreffenden zwar nicht im geringsten, aber ich
habe es auf den Tod des armen Teufels abgesehen. Das
Federmesser liegt gezückt, mordbereit auf dem Nachtkastel.
Philipp, der Stiefelknecht, wacht wurfgerecht darunter ...
will denn niemand bei mir einbrechen ... ich sehne mich nach
einem Mörder.
Wenn ich wenigstens Zahnschmerzen hätte. Ich könnte
dann dreimal "Abracadabra" sagen, auch das heilige Wort
"Zip=zip" dürfte die gleiche magische Wirkung haben ...
und wenn es mit den Schmerzen selbst dann nicht besser
würde, möchte ich keineswegs zum Zahnarzt gehen, nein,
die Schmerzen hegen und pflegen, sie nie erlöschen lassen,

21

1911. *Tubutsch* by Albert Ehrenstein. Illustrated
by Oskar Kokoschka. Published by Jahoda and
Siegel, Vienna and Leipzig. 8″ × 5¾″. Doublespread.

[1] *The Artist and the Book 1860–1960* [by Philip
Hofer and Eleanor M. Garvey], Museum of Fine
Arts, Boston, 1961.

German expressionism

Oskar Kokoschka, born in 1896, an Expressionist painter of 'visionary and
symbolic humanism', had quite a considerable graphic output. In 1911 he drew
in pen the illustrations for Albert Ehrenstein's *Tubutsch*, which was published
in the same year by Jahoda and Siegel in Vienna, in a pleasant format with
handsome wide margins, and in a second edition by Insel-Verlag in 1919.
The *Tubutsch* drawings are typical of Kokoschka's work and indeed of the
whole German Expressionist movement.
Over the last few years there has been a revival of interest, particularly in the
U.S.A., in German Expressionism. Kokoschka has had a considerable influence
as painter, graphic artist and writer, on modern American art. He illustrated
some of his own books, including *Die Träumenden Knaben* which he wrote
and illustrated when he was only twenty-two. 'This book and Slevogt's *Sinbad*
(Berlin 1908) are the first important modern *livres de peintres* from east of the
Rhine.'[1]

1924. *Umbra Vitae* by Georg Heym. Illustrated
with 46 woodcuts by Ernst Ludwig Kirchner.
Published by Kurt Wolff. Munich. 9″ × 8⅛″. Cover
printed in black, yellow and green.

14

15

1924. *Umbra Vitae* by Georg Heym. Illustrated
with 46 woodcuts by Ernst Ludwig Kirchner.
Published by Kurt Wolff. Munich. 9″ × 6⅛″.
Text spread with woodcuts.

Die Brücke Die Brücke, a group of artists founded in 1905, was influenced by Munch
and Gauguin, and by African and Pacific art. These artists would also seem to
have been natural book illustrators, both by the nature of German Expressionist
art, with its concern for the plight of humanity, and technically by their
excellence as wood engravers and print makers. Apparently an unhappy
group — sexually repressed and at variance with the world — they first showed
their distaste for the philistine German middle classes in an illustrated book,
Odi Profanum Vulgus, which has since disappeared.[2]

The animating force in Die Brücke was Ernst Ludwig Kirchner, strongly
supported by Emil Nolde and Karl Schmidt-Rottluff.

Kirchner, the most prolific graphic artist in the group, left over 1,600 prints.
His rather rugged woodcut technique was based on the mediaeval tradition
still practised in Southern Germany. Mediaeval German art, the woodcuts of
the fifteenth and sixteenth centuries, the tensions and obsessions in the work
of Dürer, Altdorfer and particularly Grünewald, all played a part in the
development of Die Brücke artists.

Kirchner's first woodcuts were Jugendstil in manner but soon the influence
of Edvard Munch changed their direction, so that they became powerfully
erotic, in the manner of so many of the Expressionists.

In 1924, eleven years after Die Brücke had been dissolved, Kirchner illustrated
Georg Heym's *Umbra Vitae* with woodcuts that were rough-hewn and brutal
in execution; the book is also interesting typographically, set throughout in a
heavy condensed sans serif, similar to Grotesque No. 9.

As far as I know, neither Nolde nor Schmidt-Rottluff illustrated any books.

[2] See *Expressionism* by Bernard S. Myers. Thames
and Hudson, 1963.

Unser Held, der keinerlei Gepäck hatte, stieg heimlich aus, ohne jemand ein Wort zu sagen, lief flink durch Marseille, immer von der Angst gepackt, das Kamel könne ihm folgen. Und er machte nicht eher Halt, ehe er nicht in einem Coupé dritter Klasse saß und der Zug gemächlich gegen Tarascon schuckerte...

Aber diese Sicherheit war trügerisch gewesen. Zwei Meilen hinter Marseille streckte alles die Köpfe aus den Wagen. Alles schrie und gestikulierte vergnügt. Tartarin seinerseits sah ebenfalls hinaus — und was sah er da? — Er sah das

Kamel, das unvermeidliche Kamel, welches in voller Karriere auf den Schienen hinter dem Bummelzuge herlief und leicht mit ihm Schritt hielt. Entsetzt schloß Tartarin die Augen und drückte sich in die Ecke des Coupés.

Er hatte gehofft, nach dieser verunglückten Expedition wenigstens inkognito nach Tarascon heimkehren zu können, aber die Anwesenheit dieses gottverdammten Vierfüßlers, der zudringlich war wie eine verliebte alte Jungfer, machte eine unmöglich. Ein schöner Triumphzug das, weiß Gott! Kein Geld, kein Ruhm! Kein Löwe! Absolut nichts... nur ein Kamel!

160

1921. *Die Abenteuer des Herrn Tartarin aus Tarascon* by Alphonse Daudet. Illustrated by Georg Grosz. Published by Erich Reiss, Berlin. 9" × 6¼". Illustration spread.

1913. *Tartarin von Tarascon* by Alphonse Daudet. Illustrated by Emil Preetorius. Published by Mundt and Blumtritt, Dachau. 7¾" × 5". Illustration.

Georg Grosz and the 'New Objectivity'

In the Germany of the Weimar Republic grim attitudes were prevailing. Georg Grosz (born 1893), in company with the painter Max Beckmann, became an exponent of the 'New Objectivity'. Grosz, a left-wing Dadaist, was highly, perhaps hysterically critical of post-war Berlin. Many portfolios of his work were issued and in 1923 *Ecce Homo* was published. This extremely scarifying collection of drawings of bordels was confiscated by the police within a few months of publication. Grosz was brought to trial for publishing indecencies. In comparison with *Ecce Homo*, Grosz's illustrations to *Tartarin*, printed on a cheap wood pulp paper, were very mild but effective and witty; they made Preetorius's illustrations to the same book look rather dull.

1921. *Die Abenteuer des Herrn Tartarin aus
Tarascon* by Alphonse Daudet. Illustrated by
Georg Grosz. Published by Erich Reiss, Berlin.
9″ × 6¼″. Illustration.

c. 1928. *Sammelalbum, alte und neue Zeichnungen* by Heinrich Kley. Published by Albert Langen, Munich. 13⅜″ × 10½″. Cover printed in black on yellow cloth. Illustration: 'der Benzinhengit'.

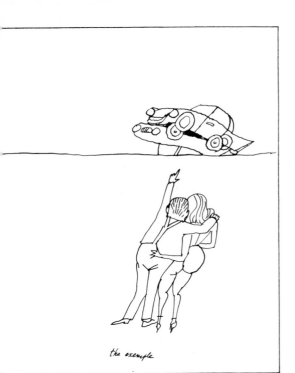

1964. *The Underground Sketchbook of Tomi Ungerer*. Illustration: 'The example'.

Opposite:
1964. *The Underground Sketchbook of Tomi Ungerer*. Published by the Viking Press and the Bodley Head. Printed by William Clowes & Sons Ltd, Beccles. 7" × 8⅜". Illustration without title.

German pre-occupation with sex and violence

The drawings of Heinrich Kley appeared for a number of years in the periodical *Simplicissimus*. An album of his work was published by Albert Langen in Munich in the 1920's, though most of the drawings had appeared many years before. Kley's preoccupation with the sex-war, violence and the imbuing of mechanical contrivances with animal lusts is repeated in the work of Tomi Ungerer. *The Underground Sketchbook of Tomi Ungerer* (1964) certainly makes an interesting comparison with Heinrich Kley's *Sammelalbum* (*c.* 1925), though Ungerer, who is German born and New York domiciled, owes as much to Grosz as to Kley, particularly in his wobbly, sensitive line.

Minimar

c. 1928. *Sammelalbum* by Heinrich Kley. Illustration: 'Minimax'.

Schlag deinen Nächsten tot! Das ist nach der Natur Rechtens, und das gilt allenthalben auf Gottes weitem Erdboden."

„Aber Kinderchen, eure guten Freunde werdet ihr doch nicht verzehren wollen? Ihr denkt 'nen Jesuiten an den Spieß zu stecken, und 's ist euer Schutzpatron, 'n erzabgesagter Feind von euern Feinden, den ihr rösten wollt. Was mich anlangt, ich bin in eurem Lande geboren, und der junge Mann da, is mein Herr, und nichts weniger als 'n Jesuit; hat vielmehr 'nen Jesuiten kaponiert und seine Jacke angezogen, und eben darum habt ihr euch geirrt."

„Damit ihr nun seht, daß ich kein Windbeutel bin, so nehmt den Rock, zeigt ihn an dem ersten Grenzorte von Los Padres und fragt, ob mein Herr nicht 'nen jesuitischen Offizier kalt gemacht. 's ist ja nur 'n Katzensprung bis dahin, und findet ihr, daß ich euch belogen habe, so könnt ihr uns ja noch immer fressen."

„Hat ganz recht!" schrien die Langohren, und sie trugen zwei von den Ältesten des Landes auf, einen Wips nach dem Jesuiterlande zu machen und sich nach der Wahrheit zu erkundigen. Als Leute von Kopf richteten sie ihren Auftrag glücklich aus und brachten gar fröhliche Mär mit.

Die Langohren banden ihre Gefangenen los, erwiesen ihnen ungemein viel Höflichkeiten, setzten ihnen Mädchen und Erfrischungen vor und begleiteten sie bis an die äußersten Grenzen unter dem lauten Jubelgeschrei: „'s ist kein Jesuit nicht! 's ist kein Jesuit nicht!"

44

Siebzehntes Kapitel

Kandide kommt mit seinem Bedienten nach Eldorado.
Was sie da sahen

Wie sie über die Grenzen der Langohren waren, sagte Kakambo zu Kandide: „Sie sehen wohl, diese Hälfte der Erdkugel ist so wenig 'nen Pfifferling wert wie jene. Das Gescheiteste wäre, wir gingen wieder nach Europa, und das je eher, je besser."

Kandide: „Wieder nach Europa? Und wo denn hin? Nach Westfalen? Da schlagen Bulgaren und Abaren tot, was lebenden Odem hat; nach Portugal? Da werde ich verbrannt; und bleiben wir hier, so sind wir keinen Augenblick sicher, gespießt und aufgezehrt zu werden."

Kakambo: „I wissen Sie was! so wollen wir nach Karolina gehen. Dort finden wir Engländer, die ziehen durch die ganze Welt. Helfen tun uns die gewiß; 's sind gar gute Geschöpfe, und Gott wird uns auch beistehen."

Nach Karolina zu kommen, war so leicht eben nicht. Nach welcher Seite ihre Richtung nehmen mußten, wußten sie wohl so ungefähr; allein von allen Seiten her türmten sich ihnen schreckliche Hindernisse entgegen; Gebirge, Flüsse, Abgründe, Straßenräuber und Wilde. Endlich gelangten sie an das Ufer eines kleinen Flusses, das mit Kokosbäumen besetzt war. Da fanden sie wieder Nahrung ihres Lebens und ihrer Hoffnung.

45

1920. *Kandide oder die beste Welt* by Voltaire. Illustrated by Paul Klee. Published by Kurt Wolff, Munich. 9¾" × 7¼". Printed by Spamersche Buchdruckerei, Leipzig. Text spread and illustrations.

A comparison of *Candides*

Paul Klee (1879–1940), a Swiss of German-French parentage, was one of the key figures in modern European art, both as a member of *Der Blaue Reiter* group of painters in Munich and as a teacher at the Bauhaus. Klee's excursions into book illustration were slight. In 1920 he drew the lithographs for a limited edition of Curt Corrinth's *Potzdammer Platz, oder Die Nächte des Neuen Messias*; and in the same year Kurt Wolff published an edition of Voltaire's *Candide* with twenty-six illustrations by Klee. (This was re-issued by Pantheon Books in New York many years later.) These scratchy, slight little pen drawings were actually done in the years between 1906 and 1912. They make an odd marriage with the Fraktur typeface, and an even odder contrast with the English and American illustrated editions of *Candide*. Voltaire's *Candide* is certainly a much illustrated book. In 1922 Routledge in London and E. P. Dutton in New York published an edition, illustrated by Alan Odle, an English artist with a very quirky sense of humour and a Beardsleyesque, art nouveau line. This is an interesting, baroque production. In 1928 Rockwell Kent did the drawings for a Random House edition of the same book, Kent's line drawings being most carefully drawn to match the tone of the Garamond type.

This is an effective and well-balanced piece of book production; the actual illustrations are completely subordinate to the design as a whole; as with all the best of Rockwell Kent's work, the book, rather than the individual illustrations, is the important factor. The opposite could be said of Klee's *Kandide,* for in neither edition did his drawings receive adequate production.

1920. *Kandide oder die beste Welt* by Voltaire.
Illustrated by Paul Klee. Published by Kurt
Wolff, Munich. 9¾″ × 7¼″. Printed by Spamersche
Buchdruckerei, Leipzig. Illustration.

c. 1922. *Candide or the Optimist* by F. A. M. de
Voltaire (*sic*), translated by Henry Morley LL.D.
Illustrated by Alan Odle. Published by George
Routledge and Sons Ltd, London and E. P.
Dutton and Co., New York. Printed by Headley
Brothers, Ashford. 9¾″ × 7¼″. Illustration 'The
Toilet of the Pope's Daughter'.

1930. *Candide* by Jean François Marie Arouet de
Voltaire, translated by Charles Edmund Merrill, Jr.
Illustrated by Rockwell Kent. Published by
Random House, New York. These illustrations
appeared two years earlier in the limited edition
from the same publisher. 10¾″ × 7¼″. Tailpiece.

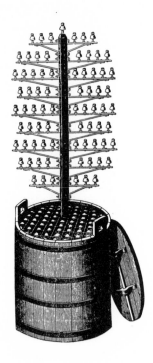

MAX ERNST

LES MALHEURS DES IMMORTELS

révélés par

PAUL ELUARD et MAX ERNST

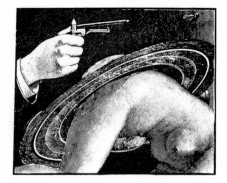

MON PETIT MONT BLANC

La petite personne noire a froid. A peine si trois lumières bougent encore, à peine si les planètes, malgré leur voilure complète, avancent en flottant: depuis trois heures il n'y a plus de vent, depuis trois heures la gravitation a cessé d'exister. Dans les tourbières, les herbes noires sont menacées par le prestidigitateur et restent en terre avec les chauves et la douceur de leur chair que le jour commence à broder de nuages amers.

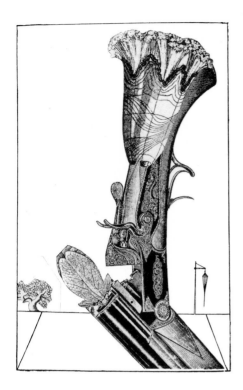

LES AGREMENTS ET L'UTILITE

Personne ne connaît l'origine dramatique des dents. Un jour,
l'équateur a dissipé la peur des chaleurs.

Loin de piller nos récoltes, elle change en miel l'éducation
dure et physique.

Le tapage de ses cloches natales effarouche ses douleurs
et fait sauter son premier enfant de sa bouche construite en
amphithéâtre. Que deviendrait-elle, sans l'horizon des ballons
et des bêtes étourdies? Un ciel sans nom, manié avec la main,
l'a fait connaître et elle nous montre le vieux loup qui, après
l'avoir toute sa vie aimée et combattue, veut vivre avec elle
en bonne intelligence.

Quand elle mourra, je n'aurai que six ans.

37

1922. *Les Malheurs des Immortels* by Paul
Éluard and Max Ernst. Illustrated with collages
by Max Ernst. Published by Librairie Six, Paris.
9½" × 7". Printed on a smooth cream Japanese
paper and set throughout in a sans serif typeface.
Frontispiece, title-page and text spreads.

Surrealism and the book

Max Ernst, born in Cologne in 1891, was a founder member of the Cologne
Dada Group. He established himself in the early 1920's as a Surrealist painter
and showed himself as a master of Surrealist collage, the art of paste-and-
scissors. Surrealism is not solely a perquisite of Max Ernst or of René Magritte,
nor is it confined to them and the more vulgar manifestations of Salvador Dali.
It occurs in the work of the Dadaists, and has had its English exposition in the
books of Lewis Carroll and Edward Lear. Max Ernst, however, has produced
books of exceptional interest. Paul Nash wrote nearly thirty years ago 'It is
not for his alarming ability to horrify that Ernst wins our respect, it is for the
intense poetical imagination working throughout all these conceptions'.[3]
With astonishing technical skill, Ernst has converted Victorian engravings
into illustrations of often startling beauty. *Les Malheurs des Immortels,* which
he produced in collaboration with Paul Éluard in 1922, adds a new dimension
to the illustrated book, and shows how a 'directing intelligence' can cut and
assemble pieces of type and out-dated engravings and make a coherent
lively whole out of the disparate parts. *Les Malheurs des Immortels* was
followed by *Histoire Naturelle* in 1926 and *La Femme 100 Têtes* in 1929,
published by Éditions de Carrefour. Five years later came *Une Semaine de
Bonté, ou les Sept Éléments Capitaux*, with over 150 Surrealist collages,
from Éditions Jeanne Bucher, which was followed, in 1936, by *Rêve d'une
Petite Fille qui voulut entrer au Carmel,* also published by Éditions de
Carrefour.
A renewed interest in Dada and the lasting power of Max Ernst's work is
bearing fruit in Germany. Günther Kieser, a practising graphic designer, was
responsible for producing in 1962 the lively and amusing *Kriminal Sonette* by
Ludwig Rubiner. Jens Rehn's *Das Neue Bestiarium,* published in 1963, has
forty most haunting collage-cum-litho drawings by Marleen Pacha.

[3] Surrealism and the illustrated book. *Signature*
(1st series No. 5, March, 1937).

1962. *Kriminal Sonette* by Ludwig Rubiner,
Friedrich Eisenlohr and Livingston Hahn.
Designed and illustrated by Günther Kieser.
Published by Scherz Verlag, Stuttgart and printed
by Paul Robert Wilk. $7\frac{3}{4}'' \times 6\frac{7}{8}''$. Case-binding
printed in black and purple on white cloth; text
and illustration spread.

Gold

FRED wird in einem braunen Tabakballen
Vom Hafen auf die Zollstation getragen.
Dort schläft er, bis die Schiffsuhr zwölf geschlagen.
Erwacht und schleicht sich in die Lagerhallen.

Am Gold-Depot, wo trunkne Wächter lallen,
Läßt er den kleinen Mörtelfresser nagen,
Bis wie beim Kartenhaus die Mauern fallen.
Dann lädt er Gold in einen Grünkohlwagen.

Als Bauer fährt er sächselnd durch den Zoll.
Doch dort verraten ihn zwei blanke Barren.
Berittne jagen den Gemüsekarren.

Fred sinnt verwirrt, wie er sich retten soll.
Da sitzt DER FREUND in hoher Eberesche
Und schießt ihm pfeiferauchend eine Bresche.

14

1963. *Das Neue Bestiarium* by Jens Rehn.
Illustrated with 40 offset-lithographs by Marleen
Pacha. Published and printed by the Eremiten-
Presse, Stierstadt Schloss, Sanssouris. $10\frac{7}{8}'' \times 6\frac{1}{2}''$.
Drawn-on and wrapped brown paper cover,
printed in black and designed by Günter Bruno
Fuchs. Collage by Marleen Pacha.

c. 1800. Vignetted bookplate engraved on the wood by Thomas Bewick.

1931. *The New Keepsake* illustrated by Rex Whistler and published by T. J. Cobden-Sanderson, London. Vignette.

5. ENGLISH AND AMERICAN TRADITIONS IN ILLUSTRATION

It was not until the early days of the nineteenth century that a distinctive English style of illustration came into being. The literate public developed more quickly in this country than elsewhere because of Britain's pre-eminence in the industrial revolution. Demands for more and more books brought an impossible pressure on intaglio printers of illustrations. It became imperative to find a method of printing *adequate* illustrations at the same time as the text. This brought Thomas Bewick on to the scene; if it had not been Bewick, it would have been someone else. There were at that time plenty of wood engravers capable of cutting crude illustrations for chap-books and broadsides, but they were hardly of a high enough calibre to replace the artist-engravers working on steel and copper plates. Thomas Bewick was actually trained as an engraver on steel and copper. With inspired ingenuity he applied

1838. *The Adventures of Oliver Twist* by Charles Dickens, illustrated by George Cruikshank. Published by Chapman and Hall, London. Illustration: 'Mr Bumble and Mrs Corney taking tea'.

1939. *My Uncle Silas* by H. E. Bates, illustrated by Edward Ardizzone. Published by Jonathan Cape, London. Illustration: 'Finger wet, finger dry'.

1871. *Good Words*. A facsimile wood engraving from a drawing by Arthur Hughes. Illustration: 'The Letter'.

1900. *Sartor Resartus* by Thomas Carlyle. Illustrated by Edmund J. Sullivan. Published by George Bell and Sons, London. Illustration.

exactly the same technique to the end-grain of boxwood, and with consummate skill he produced engravings that could be printed at the same time as the type. As an artist-engraver, working to the limitations of letterpress printing, he gave an incomparable example to hosts of engravers.

The technique of using vignetted engravings as head and tail pieces, as Bewick did, also became a lasting and agreeable fashion in English book design. A hundred years after Bewick's death, Rex Whistler, a master of the *pastiche*, made use of the same technique; but as Bewick had substituted boxwood for the copper plate, Whistler substituted the pen line and zinco for burin and boxwood. Like Bewick, Whistler also formalized his landscapes in a quiet, romantic vein.

George Cruikshank, one of the greatest of English illustrators, also made use of the vignette, first with wood engravings (by another hand), and later with etchings made by himself for a number of books. These included *Sketches by Boz* (1834) and *Oliver Twist* (1837).

As the nineteenth century progressed, the copper or steel plate was finally dropped in favour of the reproduction wood engraving, to avoid the expense of a separate printing process. The influence of Cruikshank lay dormant until an artist signing himself 'Diz' appeared on the scene in the late 1920's. This was Edward Ardizzone, a very English artist of Italian decent, who was to find in the compass of a small vignetted line drawing (and the process line block) a perfect means of expression.

The fantastic dexterity of the nineteenth-century professional wood engraver was no satisfactory substitute for the work of the artist's own hand, though a formidable school of illustration making use of this reproductive process came into being in the 1860's. The artists were either members of, or were heavily influenced by, the Pre-Raphaelite movement. This tradition, established by such artists as Arthur Hughes, was carried into the twentieth century by Edmund J. Sullivan, a very skilful pen draughtsman, whose *tour de force* was an edition of Carlyle's *Sartor Resartus*. In turn Sullivan's influence spread through several generations of illustrators who were trained at Goldsmiths' College School of Art where he taught for many years.

127

1866. *Mrs Caudle's Curtain Lectures* by Douglas
Jerrold, illustrated by Charles Keene. Published
by Bradbury, Evans and Co., London. Illustration:
'The black beetles came into the kitchen'.

1892. *Peter Ibbetson* edited and illustrated by
George du Maurier. Published by James Osgood,
McIlvaine and Co., London. Illustration:
'Bastard! Parricide!'

1891. *Cranford* by Mrs Gaskell illustrated by
Hugh Thomson. Published by Macmillan and Co.,
London. Illustration: 'If you please, my love, will
you call me Matilda'.

1893. *The Adventures of Sherlock Holmes* by
A. Conan Doyle. Published by George Newnes
Ltd, London. Printed by the Gresham Press,
London and Chilsworth. Vignetted half-tone
illustration by Sidney Paget.

1883. *Olde ffrendes wyth newe Faces* illustrated
with hand-coloured woodcuts by Joseph
Crawhall. Published in London by Field and Tuer,
in New York by Scribner and Welford. Woodcut.

1922. *Poems from the works of Charles Cotton*
illustrated by Claud Lovat Fraser. Published by
the Poetry Bookshop, London. Printed by the
Curwen Press, Plaistow. Headpiece.

There are other movements that have played a part in building up this English tradition in illustration. A recurring romanticism keeps cropping up. In the 1880's Field and Tuer at the Leadenhall Press produced a number of chap-books, illustrated by Joseph Crawhall in the crude manner of the seventeenth and eighteenth centuries. Lovat Fraser picked up and made use of the same idiom in the years just before and after the First World War. Charles Keene's unmannered drawings were also an important influence in the late nineteenth century; interpreted by professional engravers and so much admired by Camille Pissarro, they had a lasting influence on certain English and American pen draughtsmen. George du Maurier, though by no means as fine a draughtsman as Keene, also played a part in establishing a style of illustration that endured for many years after his death. When du Maurier's drawings were freed from the hand of the trade wood engraver, as they were in *Peter Ibbetson,* their impact increased enormously. With the introduction of photomechanical reproduction and the line (or half-tone) block, artists such as Hugh Thomson and F. L. Griggs and the American Frederick Remington all made use of their emancipation from the trade engraver.

Though the invention of photo-engraving happened in 1860, the first English book illustrator to use the medium was Hugh Thomson, whose drawings for *Days with Sir Roger de Coverley* (which owed much to the American artist, E. A. Abbey) were reproduced from line blocks. These illustrations first appeared in 1886 in Macmillan's *English Illustrated Magazine* and were reprinted in book form in the same year. Thomson was a prolific illustrator; his books included *Cranford* and *The Vicar of Wakefield* for Macmillan's 'Cranford' series and various volumes in the 'Highways and Byways' series for the same publisher.

With the introduction in Philadelphia in 1896 of the Levy half-tone screen, the illustrator was finally freed from the limitations of line-block or interpretation wood engraving. Sidney Paget made good use of the half-tone process, for his vignetted illustrations for *The Adventures of Sherlock Holmes* — drawings that were originally published in the *Strand Magazine* and later reprinted in book form.

1902. *Ranch Life and the Hunting Trail* by
Theodore Roosevelt. Illustrated by Frederic
Remington. Published by the Century Co., New
York. Printed by the De Vinne Press. $10\frac{1}{2}'' \times 7''$.
Illustration and text spread.

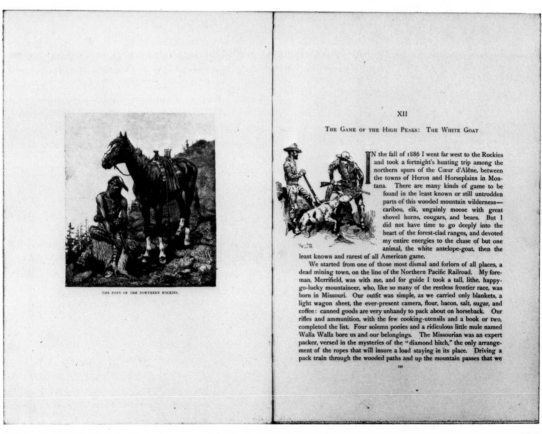

"Hark!" said Tom. "Listen—don't talk."

They waited a time that seemed an age, and then the same muffled boom troubled the solemn hush.

"Let's go and see."

They sprang to their feet and hurried to the shore toward the town. They parted the bushes on the bank and peered out over the water. The little steam ferryboat was about a mile below the village, drifting with the current. Her broad deck seemed crowded with people. There were a great many skiffs rowing about or floating with the stream in the neighborhood of the ferryboat, but the boys could not determine what the men in them were doing. Presently a great jet of white smoke burst from the ferryboat's side, and as it expanded and rose in a lazy cloud, that same dull throb of sound was borne to the listeners again.

"I know now!" exclaimed Tom; "somebody's drownded!"

"That's it!" said Huck; "they done that last summer, when Bill Turner got drownded; they shoot a cannon over the water, and that makes him come up to the top. Yes, and they take loaves of bread and put quicksilver in 'em and set

'em afloat, and wherever there's anybody that's drownded, they'll float right there and stop."

"Yes, I've heard about that, "said Joe. "I wonder what makes the bread do that."

"Oh, it ain't the bread, so much," said Tom; "I reckon it's mostly what they say over it before they start it out."

"But they don't say anything over it," said Huck. "I've seen 'em and they don't."

"Well, that's funny," said Tom. "But maybe they say it to themselves. Of course they do. Anybody might know that."

The other boys agreed that there was reason in what Tom said, because an ignorant lump of bread, uninstructed by an incantation, could not be expected to act very intelligently when sent upon an errand of such gravity.

"By jings, I wish I was over there, now," said Joe.

"I do too," said Huck. "I'd give heaps to know who it is."

The boys still listened and watched. Presently a revealing thought flashed through Tom's mind, and he exclaimed:

"Boys, I know who's drownded—it's us!"

They felt like heroes in an instant. Here was a gorgeous triumph; they were missed; they were mourned; hearts were breaking on their account; tears were being shed; accusing memories of unkindnesses to these poor lost lads were rising up, and unavailing regrets and remorse were being indulged: and best of all, the departed were the talk of the whole town, and the envy of all the boys, as far as this dazzling notoriety was concerned. This was fine. It was worth while to be a pirate, after all.

As twilight drew on, the ferryboat went back to her accustomed business and the skiffs disappeared. The pirates returned to camp. They were jubilant with vanity over their new grandeur and the illustrious trouble they were making. They caught fish, cooked supper and ate it, and then fell to guessing at what the village was thinking and saying about them; and the pictures they drew of the public distress on their account were gratifying to look upon—from their point of view. But when the shadows of night closed them in, they gradually ceased to talk, and sat gazing into the fire, with their minds evidently wandering elsewhere. The excitement was gone, now, and Tom and Joe could not keep back

thoughts of certain persons at home who were not enjoying this fine frolic as much as they were. Misgivings came; they grew troubled and unhappy; a sigh or two escaped, unawares. By and by Joe timidly ventured upon a roundabout "feeler" as to how the others might look upon a return to civilization—not right now, but—

Tom withered him with derision! Huck, being uncommitted as yet, joined in with Tom, and the waverer quickly "explained," and was glad to get out of the scrape with as little taint of chicken-hearted homesickness clinging to his garments as he could. Mutiny was effectually laid to rest for the moment.

As the night deepened, Huck began to nod, and presently to snore. Joe followed next. Tom lay upon his elbow motionless, for some time, watching the two intently. At last he got up cautiously, on his knees, and went searching among the grass and the flickering reflections flung by the camp-fire. He picked up and inspected several large semicylinders of the thin white bark of a sycamore, and finally chose two which seemed to suit him. Then he knelt by the fire and painfully wrote something up-

⋞ 62 ⋟   ⋞ 63 ⋟

Frederic Remington and the English and American impressionist illustrators

1930. *The Adventures of Tom Sawyer* by Mark Twain. Illustrated by Donald McKay. Published by Random House, New York. Printed by the Pynson Printers under the supervision of Elmer Adler. 10⅜" × 7¼". Illustration and text spread.

Joseph Pennell, writing in *Pen Drawing and Pen Draughtsmen* in 1889 about the American artist Frederic Remington, together with the work of two other American illustrators, Arthur B. Frost and E. W. Kemble, said 'Nor has their work any of the slovenliness which characterizes so much English work of the same sort... All will fall under the English critics' ban because they are not pretty or beautiful; but they are more than this, they are real, and genuine realism was the one quality lacking in the brilliant Englishman of thirty years ago'.

Remington was a brilliant portrayer of the Far West. Though much of his work was done in wash, his pen drawings for Theodore Roosevelt's *Ranch Life and Hunting Trail,* published in 1888, were in an impressionist pen technique. He was a prolific painter and illustrated 142 books, including eight of his own. Remington (b. 1861 d. 1909) after a short period as an art student at Yale University (there was only one other art student there at the time), left his home in Up-State New York and made for the Far West. After working as cowboy, cook and ranch hand, he set about recording for posterity the life of the prairies and ranges, before the encroachment of the railways destroyed it. Remington, who possessed a photographic memory, rarely sketched from life, and some of these *Ranch Life* drawings almost look as if they were copied from photographs, so unformalized are the folds and creases in the cowboys' shirts or pants; their realism is certainly genuine enough. Another American artist, Donald McKay, forty years later carried this technique a step further in his illustrations for Mark Twain's *The Adventures of Tom Sawyer* (1930). Here a rather free line has the addition of a scattered green wash; and as this attractive book is printed on a tinted Van Gelder paper, the drawings blend in with the text most beautifully.

131

J. SHERIDAN LE FANU

IN A GLASS DARKLY

With Numerous Illustrations
by
EDWARD ARDIZZONE

LONDON
PETER DAVIES
1929

1929. *In a Glass Darkly* by J. Sheridan Le Fanu, illustrated by Edward Ardizzone. Published by Peter Davies, London. Printed by the Cambridge University Press. 8½″ × 5¼″. Frontispiece and title-page; text and illustration spread.

and about in the house. She hummed tunes to herself, for a time; and then stopped and listened; and then resumed her work again. At last, she was destined to be more terrified than even was the housekeeper.

There was a back kitchen in this house, and from this she heard, as if coming from below its foundations, a sound like heavy strokes, that seemed to shake the earth beneath her feet. Sometimes a dozen in sequence, at regular intervals; sometimes fewer. She walked out softly into the passage, and was surprised to see a dusky glow issuing from this room, as if from a charcoal fire.

The room seemed thick with smoke.

Looking in, ... she very dimly beheld a

monstrous figure, over a furnace, beating with a mighty hammer the rings and rivets of a chain.

The strokes, swift and heavy as they looked, sounded hollow and distant. The man stopped, and pointed to something on the floor, that, through the smoky haze, looked, she thought, like a dead body. She remarked no more; but the servants in the room close by, startled from their sleep by a hideous scream, found her in a swoon on the flags, close to the door, where she had just witnessed this ghastly vision.

Started by the girl's incoherent asseverations that she had seen the Judge's corpse on the floor, two servants having first searched the lower part of the house, went rather frightened upstairs to

inquire whether their master was well. They found him, not in his bed, but in his room. He had a table with candles burning at his bedside, and was getting on his clothes again; and he swore and cursed at them roundly in his old style, telling them that he had business, and that he would discharge on the spot any scoundrel who should dare to disturb him again.

So the invalid was left to his quietude.

In the morning it was rumoured here and there in the street that the Judge was dead. A servant was sent from the house three doors away, by Counsellor Traverse, to inquire at Judge Harbottle's hall door.

The servant who opened it was pale and reserved, and would only say that the Judge was ill. He had had a dangerous accident; Doctor Hedstone had been with him at seven o'clock in the morning.

There were averted looks, short answers, pale and frowning faces, and all the usual signs that there was a secret that sat heavily upon their minds, and the time for disclosing which had not yet come. That time would arrive when the coroner had arrived, and the mortal scandal that had befallen the house could be no longer hidden. For that morning Mr Justice Harbottle had been found hanging by the neck from the banister at the top of the great staircase, and quite dead.

There was not the smallest sign of any struggle or resistance. There had not been heard a cry or any other noise in the slightest degree indicative of violence. There was medical evidence to show that, in his atrabilious state, it was quite on the cards that he might have made away with himself. The jury found accordingly that it was a case of suicide. But to those who were acquainted with the strange story which Judge Harbottle

1939. *My Uncle Silas* by H. E. Bates illustrated
by Edward Ardizzone. Published by Jonathan
Cape, London. Printed by the Camelot Press Ltd.
$9\frac{7}{8}'' \times 7\frac{1}{4}''$. Illustration: 'A Funny Thing'.

Edward Ardizzone, one of the most talented of English illustrators, carried the
tradition of Cruikshank and Leech into the mid-twentieth century. With the
simplest of pen technique, a development of his method of watercolour drawings, he painted a thousand scenes; and all this without much resource to
period properties. When Ardizzone was illustrating Trollope's 'Barchester'
novels or *The Local* (a book about pubs), he established the period and the
place by the attitudes of the figures and by the subtlest characterization.
These drawings were something new in twentieth-century illustration, particularly at a time (in the '30's) when there was much mannered stuff about,
and it took the publishers some little time to realize that here was a *real* book
illustrator.

battell, which you your selfe did appoint: for after that I felt the first Arrow of cruell Cupid within my breast, I bent my bow very strong, and now feare (because it is bended so hard) lest my string should breake: but that thou mayst the better please me, undresse thy haire

and come and embrace mee lovingly: whereupon she made no long delay, but set aside all the meat and wine, and then she unapparelled her selfe, and unattyred her haire, presenting her amiable body unto me in manner of faire Venus, when shee goeth under the waves of the sea. Now (quoth shee) is come the houre of justing, now is come the time of warre, wherefore shew thy selfe like unto a man, for I will not retyre, I will not fly the field, see then thou bee valiant, see thou be couragious, since there is no time appointed when our

56

1947. *The Golden Asse of Lucius Apuleius* translated by William Adlington. Illustrated by Brian Robb and designed by Robert Harling. Published by John Westhouse and printed by W. S. Cowell Ltd, Ipswich. $7\frac{1}{4}'' \times 5\frac{1}{2}''$. Illustrations.

[1] *Signature* II. N.S. 1950.

Ardizzone's first book commission was a handsome edition of Sheridan Le Fanu's *In a Glass Darkly*, published in 1929 by Peter Davis (a publisher who produced a number of well-designed illustrated books). Amongst the most successful of Ardizzone's illustrated books (apart from his children's books) are Anthony Trollope's *The Warden* and *Barchester Towers,* for the Oxford University Press series, and *My Uncle Silas* by H. E. Bates, published in 1939. The last, a book of bucolic and rather bawdy stories, is full of the most lively drawings, each of which shows something of the painter's eye.

Brian Robb was a painter who, for a short period in his career, turned to illustration as a complementary activity. His style as an illustrator varied considerably. During the 1939–45 war, he served as Camouflage Officer to Montgomery's 8th Army, and was with that redoubtable outfit from El Alamein to the end of the Italian campaign. A little book of cartoons that he drew at that time, called *My Middle East Campaigns,* shows one side of his work; they are rather grotesque drawings that reveal a real understanding and a clever and personal observation. Amongst the books he illustrated are a somewhat archaic *Adventures of Baron Münchausen* (1947) and a delightful *Tristram Shandy* (1949). The *Golden Asse* drawings, done in 1947 at the instigation of Robert Harling for John Westhouse, a now defunct publisher, are splendid, rich drawings, discreetly erotic. Edward Ardizzone, as one illustrator writing about another, said of them: '(they) have a truly classical quality, one might say sculptural quality, which has been successfully achieved by a loose, scribbly pen line with much attention to modelling'.[1]

1942. *A Connecticut Yankee in King Arthur's Court* by Mark Twain. Illustrated by Warren Chappell. Published by Heritage Press, New York. Illustration.

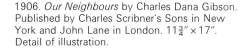

1906. *Our Neighbours* by Charles Dana Gibson. Published by Charles Scribner's Sons in New York and John Lane in London. 11¾″ × 17″. Detail of illustration.

Charles Dana Gibson's books, lavish landscape folios of drawings of America's upper crust, were published in the first decade of the century. His intricate pen painting received kinder treatment from his blockmakers than it would today, for there were at the turn of the century still plenty of trained engravers, who by hand work gave precision to the zinc blocks. Gibson's fame today rests almost solely on his 'Gibson Girls', a type of American beauty he may well be said to have created.

Warren Chappell, an illustrator of some skill, was also a distinguished book designer, who studied type design at Offenbach under Rudolph Koch. In 1939 he designed the typeface Trajanus. Amongst the most successful books he illustrated are *A Connecticut Yankee at King Arthur's Court* (1942) for Heritage, and in 1939 a lively *Don Quixote* for Knopf. Chappell, like Donald McKay, is in the true tradition of American book illustrators — a tradition founded by E. A. Abbey, Howard Pyle, Charles Dana Gibson and, in particular application to Chappell's work, Pennell's trilogy — A. B. Frost, Frederick Remington and E. W. Kemble. Since the time of these father figures, a number of expatriated European artists have brought their disparate talents to enrich and sometimes muddy the stream. Coming from an older tradition, they have sometimes brought vulgarity rather than refinement to the native stock.
But there are other illustrators in the fine native tradition, such as James Daugherty and the painter Thomas Hart Benton. Daugherty's calligraphic draughtsmanship can be seen in *Courageous Companions* (see page 143) and Carl Sandburg's *Abe Lincoln Grows Up*.

1944. *Life on the Mississippi* by Mark Twain, illustrated by Thomas Hart Benton. Published by the Limited Editions Club, New York. Designed by Will Ransom and printed by William E. Rudge's Sons, New York. 9½" × 6⅛". Illustration of a sunken river steamer.

Thomas Hart Benton (b. 1889), a real 'mossback isolationist in art',[2] spent an unprofitable time studying in Paris, before returning to the U.S.A. to find his subject in the life of farming communities in the Middle West. Benton's painting technique was most curious; he made a painted clay model of his subject and then painted from that — a method reminiscent of the English painter Gainsborough, who used to make up little landscape models from pebbles, twigs and bits of parsley.

In 1942 Benton illustrated most vividly *Huckleberry Finn* for the Limited Editions Club, in a version designed by C. P. Rollins, which can more than stand comparison with the original edition illustrated by E. W. Kemble. Two years later he completed a further set of illustrations of Mark Twain's *Life on the Mississippi*, also for the Limited Editions Club.

Lynton Lamb was an impressionist illustrator with a real understanding of fine bookwork. For many years he acted as a consultant to the Oxford University Press, and at the same time practised as a painter and taught lithography at the Slade School of Art. For Oxford, he designed everything from prayer books to wrappers. His wrappers are most effective: economical in their means, often relying on only two workings, consisting of a flat background colour with whites reversed out and a black printing. For the same publisher he illustrated several books, including one of Anthony Trollope's political novels, for a series which Lamb himself designed. (The books in this series were illustrated by different artists, including Edward Ardizzone and Leonard Huskinson.) Lamb drew direct with the pen, with no preliminary working-up. I wrote some years ago about these drawings: 'These are illustrations of "things seen" by a man who observes keenly; and because he is, above all, so intensely interested in personality and character, and also has an abiding interest in the play of light on things and people and in those trappings and furnishings that give an authentic background of time and place, Lamb seems able to evoke naturally and thus successfully the true atmosphere of the author's *mise en scène*'.[3] Lamb was certainly not just a period illustrator; his own book *County Town* is full of the keenest open air observation. Joseph Pennell would have approved.

[2] See *300 years of American Painting*. Alexander Eliot. Time Inc. New York, 1957.

[3] Alphabet and Image 5. *The drawings and book decorations of Lynton Lamb*.

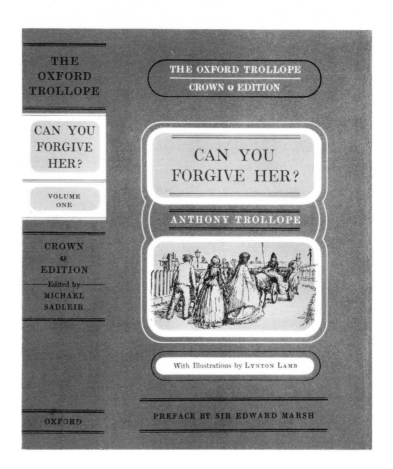

1948. *Can you Forgive Her?* by Anthony Trollope. Designed and illustrated by Lynton Lamb. Published and printed by the Oxford University Press. 8″ × 5″. Series jacket design, lithograph illustration and text spread with line illustration

MR. VAVASOR AND HIS DAUGHTER

seen John Vavasor at the only moment of the day at which he is ever much in earnest. All other things are light and easy to him,—to be taken easily and to be dismissed easily. Even the eating of the dinner calls forth from him no special sign of energy. Sometimes a frown will gather on his brow as he tastes the first half glass from his bottle of claret; but as a rule that which he has prepared for himself with so much elaborate care, is consumed with only pleasant enjoyment. Now and again it will happen that the cook is treacherous even to him, and then he can hit hard; but in hitting he is quiet, and strikes with a smile on his face.

Such had been Mr. Vavasor's pursuits and pleasures in life up to the time at which my story commences. But I must not allow the reader to suppose that he was a man without good qualities. Had he when young possessed the gift of industry I think that he might have shone in his profession, and have been well spoken of and esteemed in the world. As it was he was a discontented man, but nevertheless he was popular, and to some extent esteemed. He was liberal as far as his means would permit; he was a man of his word; and he understood well that code of by-laws which was presumed to constitute the character of a gentleman in his circle. He knew how to carry himself well among men, and understood thoroughly what might be said, and what might not; what might be done among those with whom he lived, and what should be left undone. By nature, too, he was kindly disposed, loving many persons a little if he loved few or none passionately. Moreover, at the age of fifty, he was a handsome man, with a fine forehead, round which the hair and beard was only beginning to show itself to be grey. He stood well, with a large person, only now beginning to become corpulent. His eyes were bright and grey, and his mouth and chin were sharply cut, and told of gentle birth. Most men who knew John Vavasor well, declared it to be a pity that he should spend his time in signing accounts in Chancery Lane.

I have said that Alice Vavasor's big relatives cared but little for her in her early years; but I have also said that they were

4

MR. VAVASOR AND HIS DAUGHTER

careful to undertake the charge of her education, and I must explain away this little discrepancy. The biggest of these big people had hardly heard of her; but there was a certain Lady

Macleod, not very big herself, but, as it were, hanging on to the skirts of those who were so, who cared very much for Alice. She was the widow of a Sir Archibald Macleod, K.C.B., who had been a soldier, she herself having also been a Macleod by birth; and for very many years past—from a time previous to the birth of Alice Vavasor—she had lived at Cheltenham, making short sojourns in London during the spring, when the contents of her limited purse would admit of her doing so.

5

1898. *London Types* by W. E. Henley. Illustrated
by William Nicholson. Published by William
Heinemann, London. 13″ × 11″. Cover design.
Coloured linocut illustration: 'Hammersmith'.

c. 1900. *The Man with the Hoe,* illustrated by Howard Pyle. Published by Doubleday, Page and Co., New York. Reproduced from *Modern Pen Drawings, European and American:* Studio 1901.

1898. *London Types* by W. E. Henley. Illustrated by William Nicholson. Published by William Heinemann, London. 13″ × 11″. Cover design.

The Romantic Movement in illustration

In English book illustration, romanticism made its appearance in the 1880's with the chap-book productions of Field and Tuer, at the Leadenhall Press, where Joseph Crawhall's amusing parodies of eighteenth-century broadsheets were happily wedded to battered old typefaces. William Nicholson, a very talented painter, carried the same thought a stage further with his books, *London Types, An Almanach of Twelve Sports* and *An Alphabet*, all published in the same year, 1898. The illustrations were boldly cut in linoleum and hand-coloured. The books had an immediate success. A contemporary reviewer writing in the *St James's Gazette* said: 'You must turn to your best specimens of Japanese colour-printing to get anything better than these boldly constructed blacks and reds. And what the Eastern world will gain by its delicacy of outline or of tint, it will lose by comparison with the truth of modelling in face and figure which is characteristic of this modern work'. Something of the simplicity of these cuts is to be seen in the posters of the Beggarstaffs, the pseudonym of William Nicholson and James Pryde.

In the same year, 1898, the Beggarstaffs carried their poster technique into the illustrations for Edwin Pugh's book *Tony Drum.*

The American Howard Pyle had a lasting influence on American illustrators, and particularly on the romantic illustrators such as N. C. Wyeth and Edward A. Wilson. In his own lifetime and in his own country he was regarded as a Colossus. Gleeson White, writing in 1897 in the special winter number of *The Studio,* said: 'It is a matter of surprise and regret that Howard Pyle's illustrated books are not as well known as they deserve to be in England . . . anyone with artistic sympathy is completely converted to be a staunch admirer of Pyle's work by a sight of *The Wonder Clock,* a portly quarto published by Harper Brothers in 1894'. He is writing of the Dürer-influenced Pyle, and compares him favourably with Walter Crane. Though the bulk of Pyle's work was done for children, he illustrated a number of other books, including Oliver Wendell Holmes's *One Horse Shay,* and, for Doubleday, Page & Co., *The Man with the Hoe* – which shows a marked Pre-Raphaelite influence.

XIV

I

Maud has a garden of roses
And lilies fair on a lawn ;
There she walks in her state
And tends upon bed and bower,
And thither I climb'd at dawn
And stood by her garden-gate ;
A lion ramps at the top,
He is claspt by a passion-flower.

II

Maud's own little oak-room
(Which Maud, like a precious stone
Set in the heart of the carven gloom,
Lights with herself, when alone

42

1922. *Maud* by Alfred Lord Tennyson. Illustrated by Edmund J. Sullivan. Published by Macmillan and Co. Ltd, London. Printed by R. & R. Clark Ltd, Edinburgh. 9″ × 6″. Text and illustration spread: case-binding design blocked in silver on white cloth.

Mention has already been made of Edmund J. Sullivan. He illustrated a number of books in a romantic vein, including Carlyle's *History of the French Revolution*.

In 1922, Macmillan published an edition of Tennyson's monodrama *Maud*, with line illustrations by Sullivan which had been made some years earlier. It is a charming piece of book making, with a pretty case. The illustrations, some tinted, are as effective as those in *Sartor Resartus*, but freer and more dramatic. The precise intricacy of the *Sartor Resartus* drawings matched Carlyle's turgid prose; but this edition of *Maud* is high Victorian romanticism, half a century out of context.

Sullivan, like Augustus John, another lyrical artist, lived out of his time (possibly an English failing). But he was an artist of considerable erudition,

1915. *The Happy Hypocrite* by Max Beerbohm.
Illustrated by George Sheringham. Published by
John Lane, the Bodley Head, London. Printed by
Spottiswoode Ballantyne and Co. Ltd, London.
10⅛" × 7½". Illustration: 'King Bogey' and chapter
opening initial letter.

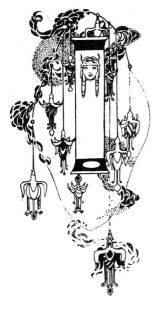

and as well as teaching wrote at length about pen drawing and illustration.
In his book *Line*, he has some salutary things to say about the importance of
the balance of illustration to type, and also of techniques, processes and paper.
After Nicholson's robust cuts and Sullivan's strong chiaroscuro pen work, the
romanticism of George A. Sheringham may seem a little watery. In 1915, he
illustrated Max Beerbohm's *The Happy Hypocrite* which was published by
John Lane. This book, which has a pretty, flowery cover, is a curious mixture
of coloured lithographs and decorative two-colour initials and line drawings.
Sheringham's softly tinted lithographs have an atmosphere of chintz and
pot-pourri. They marked the end of the golden days of pre-1914 England. They
also illustrated the gentler side of Max's evocative but usually astringent prose.

1924. *Iron Men and Wooden Ships*, illustrated
with coloured woodcuts by Edward A. Wilson.
Published by Doubleday, Page and Co., New
York. 12″ × 8¾″. Coloured woodcut: 'Blackbeard'

The mantle of American romanticism has been most ably worn by Howard
Pyle's pupils, N. C. Wyeth and Edward A. Wilson and by James Daugherty.
Wyeth specialized in children's books, Wilson in stories of the sea. Wilson's
illustrations for R. H. Dana's *Two Years before the Mast,* for the Lakeside
Press, were reproduced from the artist's watercolours; for *Iron Men and
Wooden Ships*, which Doubleday, Doran & Co. published in 1924, he used
coloured woodcuts. The cut of Blackbeard here is a rather stiff illustration,
but makes an interesting comparison with Claud Lovat Fraser's book, *Pirates,*
published by Jonathan Cape in 1921, the year that very talented artist died.
The full page illustrations to the *Pirates* were printed in black on sheets of
richly coloured paper.

Lovat Fraser had an instinctive feeling for decorating book pages. He usually
worked with a reed-pen, and often stencilled strong flat colours on to this
rich framework. His colour sense can be appreciated from Haldane McFall's

CAPTAIN JOHN RACKHAM, AND HIS CREW

JOHN RACKHAM was Quarter-Master to *Vane's* Company, till *Vane* was turned out for not fighting the French Man-of-War, and *Rackham* put in Captain in his place, which happened about the 24th day of *November*, 1718. His first cruise was among the *Caribbe* Islands, where he took and plundered several vessels. Afterwards, to the windward of *Jamaica*, he fell in with a *Madeira* Man, which he detained till he had made his market out of her, and then restored her to her Master, suffering *Hosea Tisdel*, a tavern-keeper at *Jamaica*, whom he had taken among his Prizes, to go aboard her, she being bound for that Island.

Afterwards he sailed towards the Island

19

CAPTAIN JOHN RACKHAM

1921 *Pirates* with a foreword and illustrations by C. Lovat Fraser. Published by Jonathan Cape, London. 8¼″ × 6¼″. Text and illustration spread.

Book of Lovat, published by J. M. Dent in 1923. Fulsome though this may be as critical biography, it is a handsome piece of bookmaking greatly enriched with Lovat's colour designs.

James Daugherty's romantic drawing of Spanish galleons is from *Courageous Companions*, published by McKay. These are well designed illustrations.

1929. *Courageous Companions* by Charles J. Finger, illustrated by James Daugherty. Published by McKay, New York. Illustration: size 5½″ × 6¼″.

1916. *Belgium* by Hugh Stokes, illustrated by
Frank Brangwyn. Published by Kegan Paul,
Trench, Trübner and Co. Ltd, London. Printed by
Spottiswoode Ballantyne and Co. Ltd, Colchester.
12″ × 9″. Illustration.

Frank Brangwyn (b. 1867 d. 1956), once reckoned as a giant amongst artists,
is today hardly remembered. His mural paintings, at one time covering acres
of wall space, now lurk in provincial galleries, his railway posters, heroic in
conception, re-appear almost apologetically in anthologies of commercial art.
His working career spanned over half a century and included working for
William Morris on tapestry designs. Brangwyn was already illustrating books
in the 1890's. In 1893 he worked on Robert Leighton's *The Wreck of the
Golden Fleece* for Blackie; in the next year, *The Cruise of the Midge* by Michael
Scott; and in 1896, S. R. Crockett's *Our Coast* for Chatto and Windus. Most
of his book illustration was of sea, ships and ports; his media ranged from oil
painting to pen drawing and wood engraving. His dark, sombre, often melo-
dramatic drawings will surely one day be appreciated again.
There has been an American tradition of sea painting based on first hand
observation that dates at least from the time of Winslow Homer, who used to

1930. *Moby Dick or the Whale* by Herman
Melville. Illustrated by Rockwell Kent. Published
by Random House in New York and
by Cassell and Co. Ltd, London. Printed by
R. R. Donnelley and Sons. 7" × 5¾". Full page
illustration.

work from an open ended shack down on the beach at Prout's Neck on the
coast of Maine.[4] Rockwell Kent has had plenty of first hand observation of the
sea. This illustrator, much of whose work has a kind of factory-production-line
look about it, was a consummate book designer. His books have a unity; the
rather mechanical looking illustrations, line drawings done in the manner of a
steel engraving with evenly ruled lines to suggest receding tones in the sky,
match the even lines of type. Kent's most interesting illustrations were drawn
for his own travel books, but he has illustrated a number of other books,
including an effective edition of Chaucer's *Canterbury Tales* in 1934 for the
Garden City Publishing Co., New York. The full page illustrations for this
book were of single figures, in Kent's simple engraved technique, printed in
black and brown. Rockwell Kent is most widely known for his illustrations to
Moby Dick, which was published first as a three-volume edition by the
Lakeside Press, and in 1930 in a smaller format in one volume.

[4] See *300 years of American Painting*. Alexander
Eliot. Time Inc. New York, 1957.

CHAPTER XXXVI   THE QUARTER-DECK

[Enter Ahab: Then, all]

IT was not a great while after the affair of the pipe, that one morning shortly after breakfast, Ahab, as was his wont, ascended the cabin-gangway to the deck. There most sea-captains usually walk at that hour, as country gentlemen, after the same meal, take a few turns in the garden.

Soon his steady, ivory stride was heard, as to and fro he paced his old rounds, upon planks so familiar to his tread, that they were all over dented, like geological stones, with the peculiar mark of his walk. Did you fixedly gaze, too, upon that ribbed and dented brow; there also, you would see still stranger foot-prints —the foot-prints of his one unsleeping, ever-pacing thought.

← 230 →

But on the occasion in question, those dents looked deeper, even as his nervous step that morning left a deeper mark. And, so full of his thought was Ahab, that at every uniform turn that he made, now at the main-mast and now at the binnacle, you could almost see that thought turn in him as he turned, and pace in him as he paced; so completely possessing him, indeed, that it all but seemed the inward mould of every outer movement.

"D'ye mark him, Flask?" whispered Stubb; "the chick that's in him pecks the shell. T'will soon be out."

The hours wore on;—Ahab now shut up within his cabin; anon, pacing the deck, with the same intense bigotry of purpose in his aspect.

It drew near the close of day. Suddenly he came to a halt by the bulwarks, and inserting his bone leg into the auger-hole there, and with one hand grasping a shroud, he ordered Starbuck to send everybody aft.

"Sir!" said the mate, astonished at an order seldom or never given on ship-board except in some extraordinary case.

"Send everybody aft," repeated Ahab. "Mast-heads, there! come down!"

When the entire ship's company were assembled, and with curious and not wholly unapprehensive faces, were eyeing him, for he looked not unlike the weather horizon when a storm is coming up, Ahab, after rapidly glancing over the bulwarks, and then darting his eyes among the crew, started from his stand-point; and as though not a soul were nigh him resumed his heavy turns upon the deck. With bent head and half-slouched hat he continued to pace, unmindful of the wondering whispering among the men; till Stubb cautiously whispered to Flask, that

← 231 →

1930. *Moby Dick or the Whale* by Herman Melville. Illustrated by Rockwell Kent. Published by Random House in New York and by Cassell and Co. Ltd, London. Printed by R. R. Donnelley and Sons. 7″ × 5⅜″. Chapter opening with illustration and tailpiece.

This second version, a chunky little book (860 pages), was beautifully printed by R. R. Donnelley under the supervision of William A. Kittredge, at the Lakeside Press, Chicago. The drawings may be hard and mannered but it is still a stupendous piece of illustration. All the details of a working sailing craft were familiar stuff to Kent, and beyond this, there is a mystic streak that runs through his work, enabling him, if not to match Melville's magnificent prose, at least to give some pictorial substance to this allegory. Maybe no sperm whale ever reached to the stars as the one illustrated over the page does. Melville makes one feel it could and Kent has recaptured the mood.

Rockwell Kent's travel books began with *Wilderness*, a journal written on Fox Island, Alaska during the winter of 1918–19; his next book was *Voyaging* (1924), a description of a journey in a sailing boat southwards from the Straits of Magellan. These were succeeded half-a-dozen years later by *N by E* and in 1936 by *Salamina*. *N by E* was a most successful example of book design; within its limits, perhaps the most complete, well-balanced piece of book production ever to come out of the U.S.A. From its coarse sailcloth cover, clearly and boldly blocked with a forceful design of a compass rose, and its well-fitting case, to the excellent presswork and perfect balance of illustrations with type, *N by E* is an utterly professional piece of work. These Arctic or Antarctic climes suited Kent's way of drawing, or maybe he drew as he did because of those, cold, clear, bare land and seascapes.

IT IS but an hour or two before midnight and I am sitting on a hill above the little settlement of Godthaab. The sun has nearly set and the red beauty of its light is on the land.

I look over the rolling grassy hills of the foreground, at the stark mountains towering at my back; I look over the calm fiord toward far off peaks clear cut against the glowing sky. It is a breathless evening, breathless! And so profoundly beautiful that it is hard to bear alone. And from the settlement comes laughter and the dance music of the accordion.

So I descend to the village and go to the carpenter-shop where the dance is being held. Crowds of young Greenlanders are there; the place is packed. The girls dressed in their finest stand all in a row. They wear bright colored worsted caps, broad bead-work

* 189 *

1930. *N by E* by Rockwell Kent, designed and illustrated by the author. Published by Putnam, New York (after a Limited Edition from Random House) and by Cassell and Co. Ltd, London.

Printed by the Lakeside Press, Chicago. 8¼″ × 5⅝″. Case-binding, frontispiece, title-page and illustration page.

1893. *Goblin Market* by Christina Rossetti.
Illustrated by Laurence Housman. Published by
Macmillan and Co. Ltd, London. Printed by
R. & R. Clark, Edinburgh. $7\frac{1}{8}'' \times 4\frac{1}{8}''$.
Illustration spread and text page.

GOBLIN MARKET

MORNING and evening
Maids heard the goblins cry
"Come buy our orchard fruits,
Come buy, come buy :

Apples

Art nouveau and decorative book illustration

Art nouveau had a marked influence not only on English book design but also on English book illustration. In 1893–4, Laurence Housman, poet and artist, illustrated two books for Macmillan: *The End of Elfintown* by Jane Barlow and *Goblin Market* by Christina Rossetti. *Goblin Market*, mentioned on page 24, is an interesting, strange piece of book production. Housman's sister engraved, most skilfully, her brother's delicate, swirling lines, and R. & R. Clark printed them impeccably. There is a haunted feeling about them, in which the slack curves of art nouveau play some considerable part.

Other English illustrators working in an art nouveau manner included R. Anning Bell, T. Sturge Moore and Aubrey Beardsley. The latter, a brilliant artist (he was only twenty-five when he died), crammed a fantastic amount of work into the six years of his working life, from the time he left his job as an insurance clerk to his death in 1898.

During the short time he was working with the Guardian Life and Fire Assurance Company, Beardsley used to visit Jones and Evans's book shop just off Cheapside. Here he met Frederick Evans, who was most impressed both with the young man and with his drawings. Evans introduced him to the young publisher, J. M. Dent, and, the result was a contract for Beardsley to illustrate Malory's *Le Morte d'Arthur*. This was a tremendous task of illustration, for there were over three hundred and fifty separate drawings, one on almost every spread. Critics have usually dismissed Beardsley's *Le Morte d'Arthur* as immature, or even as hack work; yet if he had never illustrated another book, this edition of *Le Morte d'Arthur* could stand as a monument of decorative book illustration. Heavily influenced by the Kelmscott books of William Morris and to a lesser extent by Burne-Jones's illustrations, Beardsley already stands as a decorative master in his own right. The borders to his full page illustrations are as virile as Morris's, yet with a strong feeling of art nouveau. His figure

How a devil in Woman's likeness would have tempted Sir Bors

1894. *Le Morte d'Arthur* by Sir Thomas Malory.
Illustrated by Aubrey Beardsley. Published by
J. M. Dent and printed by Turnbull and Spears,
Edinburgh. 10″ × 7¾″. The illustrations are
reproduced from the second edition published
in 1909. Illustration spread; and chapter
opening decoration.

Chap. ir.

drawings, with their massed black and white spaces, are Japanese inspired,
yet possess some of the qualities of a Bonnard or a Lautrec poster. And
through all his work, there is that peculiar *fin de siècle* brooding quality; not
that the creatures of his imagination, unsexed or hermaphrodite, did not have
plenty to brood about.

In *Le Morte d'Arthur* Beardsley learnt his job, but the result is no bungling
student's work. Some of these designs (he never called his drawings
illustrations) stand as models of economy, none is impoverished.

A work that started almost in homage to Morris ended, as Sir Kenneth Clark
has said, as a macabre parody of the Kelmscott style.[5]

[5] From a lecture first given at the Aldeburgh
Festival in 1965.

1894. *Salomé* by Oscar Wilde, illustrated by Aubrey Beardsley. Published by Melmoth and Co., London. $8\frac{1}{2}$" × $6\frac{5}{8}$". The illustrations and sketch for the cover design are reproduced from the 1904 edition. This cover design was later used for *Under the Hill*, published by John Lane in 1904.

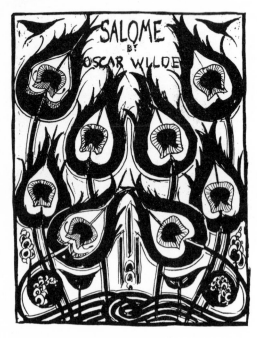

[6] *The Life of James McNeill Whistler* by Elizabeth and Joseph Pennell.

The American artist and critic, Joseph Pennell, on first seeing Beardsley's work, wrote a glowing tribute in the first number of *The Studio*. The result of this was a commission from John Lane to illustrate Oscar Wilde's play *Salomé*. This, perhaps the most feeble of Wilde's plays, had enjoyed a *succès de scandale*, for Sarah Bernhardt was to have appeared in it before the play was banned. Beardsley's drawings, amongst the best he ever did, are a complete send-up; a witty, erotic commentary to Wilde's text.

Salomé resulted in Beardsley's appointment to the art editorship of *The Yellow Book* (see page 15) and after that, to *The Savoy*. The first number of this periodic volume included his drawings for his own rococo novel, *Under the Hill*; in the second number of *The Savoy*, appeared the first of his drawings for *The Rape of the Lock*, the forerunner of a most beautiful set of decorative pen drawings. If with *Le Morte d'Arthur* he had learnt his job, with the drawings for *The Rape of the Lock* he had reached a brilliant maturity, and all this within three years. The Pennells described how James McNeill Whistler, who had been no Beardsley fan, on seeing these drawings, turned to him and said, 'Aubrey, I have made a very great mistake — you are a very great artist'. And the boy burst out crying.[6]

Beardsley by this time was famous, though regarded by many as the very essence of decadence. As a consumptive, his desperate hold on life intensified his every action. His influences were mainly literary, and he was completely self-taught. Beardsley was the prince of decorators and I suppose a failure as an illustrator *per se*; his decorations overwhelmed, but how magnificently, his authors' texts.

In spite of Beardsley, or perhaps because of him, the art nouveau influence on English book illustration lasted for only a short time. One illustrator who was strongly affected by the movement was Robert Anning Bell, whose *The Tempest* (1901) is heavily decorated with art nouveau motifs and borders. By the First World War the movement had petered out.

1896. *The Savoy*. No. 2 an illustrated quarterly,
edited by Arthur Symons. Published by Leonard
Smithers, London. 10″ × 7⅝″. Illustration by
Aubrey Beardsley for *The Rape of the Lock*.

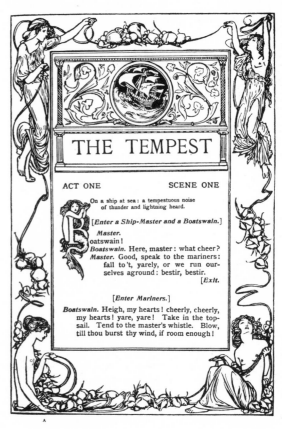

1901. *The Tempest* by William Shakespeare,
decorated by Robert Anning Bell. Published by
Freemantle and Co., London. Printed by
T. and A. Constable, Edinburgh. 9½″ × 6¾″.

1923. *A Box of Paints* by Geoffrey Scott,
illustrated by Albert Rutherston. Published by the
Bookman's Journal, London. Printed by the
Curwen Press, Plaistow. 9½″ × 6¾″. Illustration.

7 *Modern Book Illustration in Great Britain and
America.* Edited by C. Geoffrey Holme and published by The Studio, London and New York, 1931.

Albert Rutherston (brother of Sir William Rothenstein, one time principal of
the Royal College of Art) was also an avowed decorator. His little, coloured
line drawings, often of nubile young women, made charming decorations for
A Box of Paints, a book of poems by Geoffrey Scott published in 1923, and
for the Sitwells' *Poor Young People,* which the Fleuron published in 1925.
This quarto was beautifully manufactured by the Curwen Press and contained sixteen coloured drawings by Rutherston.

Decoration, rather than illustration, has had only a precarious hold on English
books and their publishers. Rex Whistler, however, made good use of mock-
eighteenth-century architectural borders in many of his book jackets and in his
splendid Cresset Press edition of *Gulliver's Travels* (1930).

This book is a most remarkable achievement. Here are pastiche eighteenth-
century engravings, actually drawn by pen and reproduced and printed by
flat-bed photo-gravure. The reproductions are printed in just the sepia colour
an engraving would have and plate-sunk, to boot! The hand colouring at least
is hand-coloured. Yet, though there is plenty for graphic purists to denounce,
the result is one of the most handsome illustrated books ever to be printed
in this country. And the illustrations are ravishing. The frontispiece to Volume 1
depicts a delightful scene outside a dockside, clapboard, bow-windowed pub,
set in a rococo border of dolphins, spars and guns, supported by a mermaid
and her merman. As this has been reproduced at least once before,[7] I have
chosen a plate from Volume II illustrating *A Voyage to Laputa.* In all these
illustrations, Whistler limited his colour (soft blues, pinks and yellows) to the
scene within his architectural borders. These were left in monochrome. All
Whistler's illustrations had a decorative quality, even the little vignetted head
and tail pieces. One of the last books he illustrated was James Agate's
Kingdoms for Horses, which Victor Gollancz published in 1936, and on the
title-page of which is printed: 'With decorations by Rex Whistler'. No mention
here of illustration.

The Lord Munodi
takes him in his chariot
to see the town of LAGADO

1930. *Gulliver's Travels* by Jonathan Swift D.D. illustrated by Rex Whistler. Published by the Cresset Press and printed by the Oxford University Press. Edition limited to 195 copies on hand-made paper. Illustration: 'The Lord Munodi takes him in his chariot to see the town of Lagado' (From Volume II *A Voyage to Laputa*).

1934. *A.B.C. of the Theatre* by Humbert Wolfe,
illustrated by Edward Burra. Published by the
Cresset Press. Printed by Robert MacLehose and
Co. Ltd, Glasgow. 9¾″ × 7⅜″. Cover and
illustration spread.

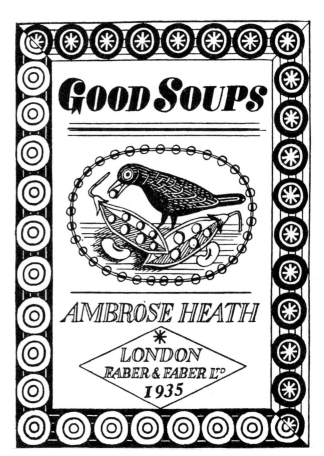

1934. *Good Savouries* by Ambrose Heath
illustrated by Edward Bawden. Published by
Faber and Faber, London. Printed by
R. MacLehose and Co. Ltd, Glasgow. $7\frac{3}{8}'' \times 4\frac{3}{4}''$.
Title-page.

1935. *Good Soups* by Ambrose Heath illustrated
by Edward Bawden. Published by Faber and
Faber, London. Printed by R. MacLehose and Co.
Ltd, Glasgow. $7\frac{3}{8}'' \times 4\frac{3}{4}''$.
Title-page.

1935. *Good Soups* by Ambrose Heath
illustrated by Edward Bawden. Cover design
from lino cuts printed in two colours.

That decoration and humour can go hand-in-hand can be seen in the work of both Burra and Bawden in England, and such artists as Ludwig Bemelmans and Artzybasheff in the U.S.A. As far as I know *A.B.C. of the Theatre* is Edward Burra's only excursion into book illustration; the rest of his working life has been devoted to painting, often religious painting, and always with a great intensity of feeling. His illustrations to Humbert Wolfe's witty lampoons are in a very different vein. There are slight shades of Georg Grosz in some of the drawings but the book as a whole is a success. It had decorated initials designed by Kathryn Hamill and was published by the Cresset Press in 1934. Edward Bawden has illustrated many books, ranging from *Good Food, Good Soups* and *Good Savouries* for Faber in the 1930's to an interesting *Gulliver's Travels* for the Folio Society, a fine edition of *The History of Herodotus* for the Limited Editions Club, and a beautiful set of lithographs of Portugal for *English as she is Spoke* for the Lion and Unicorn Press. He is not only a witty, satirical draughtsman but also a superb decorative craftsman, particularly in his handling of lino cuts. His title-pages for the Ambrose Heath cookery books, drawn fifty years ago, still stand as perfect examples of decorative economy, both in their simplicity of line and in the unfaltering use of the line block.

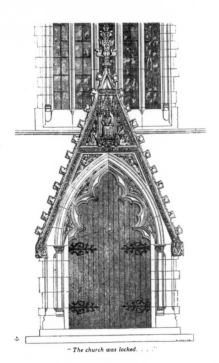

Lines suggested by an advertisement in "The Guardian"
(The Broad Church newspaper)

THE church was locked, so I went to the incumbent—
the incumbent enjoying a supine incumbency—
a tennis court, a summerhouse, deckchairs by the
      walnut tree
and only the hum of the bees in the rockery.
" May I have the keys of the church, your incumbency ? "
" Yes, my dear sir, as a moderate churchman, I
am willing to exchange : light Sunday duty :
nice district : pop 149 : eight hundred per annum :
no extremes : A and M : bicyclist essential
same income expected."
" I think I'm the man that you want, your incumbency.
Here's my address when I'm not on my bicycle,
poking about for recumbent stone effigies—
14, Mount Ephraim, Cheltenham, Glos :
Rector St. George-in-the-Rolling Pins, Cripplegate :
non resident pop in the City of London :
eight fifty per annum (but verger an asset) :
willing to exchange (no extremes) for incumbency,
similar income, but closer to residence."

17

" The church was locked. . . ."

1937. *Continual Dew* by John Betjeman.
Published by John Murray, London. Printed by
William Clowes and Sons Ltd, London. 8″ × 5⅞″.
Illustration spread.

1938. *Pillar to Post* written and illustrated by
Osbert Lancaster. Published by John Murray,
London. Printed by Butler and Tanner Ltd,
Frome. 9¼″ × 6⅝″. Illustration: 'Gothic Revival'.

1939. *Homes Sweet Homes* written and illustrated by Osbert Lancaster. Published by John Murray, London. Printed by Butler and Tanner Ltd, Frome. 9¼" × 6⅝". Illustration: 'Art Nouveau'.

1933. *My Life and Hard Times* by James Thurber. Published by Penguin Books, Middlesex. Printed by Hunt, Barnard and Co. Ltd, London. 7" × 4⅜". Illustration: 'One night while doing the dishes . . .'

Humour and genre

The master of *genre* illustration is Osbert Lancaster, the wittiest of all architectural draughtsmen. His *Pillar to Post* appeared in 1938 and *Homes Sweet Homes* in 1939, both published by John Murray. These books are a joy, leading one through a couple of thousand years of domestic architecture and manners, and enriching the English language with such styles as 'Stockbroker Tudor' and 'By-pass Variegated'. Osbert Lancaster's observation, apart from his wit, is acute, his sense of period almost faultless and his commentary profound.

John Betjeman's *Ghastly Good Taste* (1933) does very much in words what Lancaster does in pictures. The illustration 'the Church was locked . . .' comes from his 'little book of bourgeois verse', called *Continual Dew*. It is, quite apart from the quality of the verse, and its subject matter (which varies from architecture to church livings), a splendid Dada-Surrealist joke. It has a book-jacket by E. McKnight Kauffer, showing a dripping tap, a black-and-gold case-binding, which makes it look like a Victorian prayer book, and pages illustrated with the oddest selection of old engravings and modern drawings. If John Betjeman and Osbert Lancaster typify both English humour and English tradition, James Thurber's drawing (which needs no comment from me) can speak volumes for America and most fittingly bring this chapter — about English and American traditions in illustration — to a close.

1902. *Le Procurateur de Judée* by Anatole France illustrated by Eugène Grasset and engraved on the wood by Ernest Florian. 7½" × 5½". Black line woodcut.

COMMENT SAINT FRANÇOIS, POUR UNE MAUVAISE PENSÉE QU'IL EUT CONTRE FRÈRE BERNARD, COMMANDA AUDIT FRÈRE BERNARD QUE TROIS FOIS LUI MARCHAT AVEC LES PIEDS SUR LA GORGE ET SUR LA BOUCHE

 E très dévot serviteur du Crucifix, monsieur saint François, par l'âpreté de la pénitence et continuel pleurer, était devenu presque aveugle, et à peine voyait la lumière. Une fois entre autres il se partit du couvent où il était, et alla à un couvent où était frère Bernard, pour parler avec lui des choses divines : et venant au couvent, trouva qu'il était dans la forêt en oraison, tout élevé

§

c. 1907. *Les Petites Fleurs* by St Francis of Assisi illustrated by pen drawings on wood by Maurice Denis, engraved by Jacques Beltrand. Published by Rouart et Watelin, Paris.

6. THE WOOD ENGRAVING REVIVAL IN FRANCE AND ENGLAND

The belief in the importance of printing both type and illustration in the same operation was one of the factors in the wood engraving revival. This revival began in France, mainly through the work of trade engravers such as Beltrand, Froment, Bellenger and Florian. Maurice Denis was one of many French artist-illustrators who owed much to his engravers. For *Les Petites Fleurs* by St Francis of Assisi for Rouart et Watelin, he drew his designs on the woodblock and they were engraved by Jacques Beltrand. Paul Gauguin was one of the first artists actually to cut his own woodblocks – for his manuscript book *Noa Noa*. When he was in Paris in 1893, between his voyages to Tahiti, he showed his manuscript to the poet Charles Morice, and with Morice's help the text was published in *La Revue Blanche* in 1901 and, later in the same year, in a single volume.

Gauguin returned to Tahiti and began to enlarge and enrich his original manuscript with watercolour drawings, woodcuts and even a few photographs. From this manuscript, now in the Louvre, various facsimiles have been reproduced and printed. The woodcuts, of particular interest, are a very clear forerunner of the white line engraving that was such a feature of the twentieth-century revival of the craft. The French and English trade engravers were trained to produce black line engravings, by cutting away the wood up to the edge of the drawn black line. This is of course incomparably more difficult than white line engraving, and a denial of the proper use of a burin.

In the year 1902, the publisher Édouard Pelletan wrote in a foreword to *Le Procurateur de Judée*: 'Le livre est avant tout un texte. Le texte se manifeste par la typographie. Donc, le livre, est avant tout, une manifestation typographique . . .' These would hardly have been Vollard's sentiments, even though he brought his first book to the Imprimerie Nationale, who had been responsible for printing *Le Procurateur de Judée*; they were much nearer to the ideas of Ricketts or Morris, Updike or Rogers. French illustrated books, when Pelletan started publishing in 1896, were lacking what another French publisher, Léon Pichon, called 'any directing intelligence'. The woodcut or wood engraving had, by 1900, become an essential part of the typographic conception of a properly illustrated book. Morris's engraved decorations, Ricketts's cuts, Pissaro's coloured woodcuts were all partly responsible for

158

c. 1900. *Noa Noa, Voyage de Tahiti* by Paul
Gauguin and C. Morice. Facsimile of Paul
Gauguin's manuscript, published in Dresden in
1926. Printed by Marée-Gesellschaft Druck.
13" × 10". White line woodcut.

the belief that only the raised surface of box or pearwood could match the
varied surfaces of fine typefaces. Félix Bracquemond in his *Étude sur la
Gravure sur Bois,* published in 1897, stressed the need for unity in a page,
which would only be attained by the woodcut, made up of clear whites and
rich blacks: no half-tones, no cluttering up the pages with ornament.
Bracquemond concluded, 'the fundamental constituent is the white of the
paper'.
The artists who first followed these precepts most faithfully were Raoul Dufy
and André Derain.

1909. *L'Enchanteur Pourrissant* by Guillaume Apollinaire illustrated with 31 woodcuts by André Derain. Published by Henry Kahnweiler, Paris. Printed by Paul Birault. $10\frac{1}{2}'' \times 8''$. Woodcut.

[1] On 3 May 1966 in a sale at Sotheby's of 'Modern French and German Illustrated Books', a copy of this edition of *Le Bestiaire* was sold for £1,800.

In 1909 Derain illustrated with woodcuts *L'Enchanteur Pourrissant,* by Apollinaire, which was published by the art dealer Henry Kahnweiler. This was Kahnweiler's first publication; later he was to rival Vollard in the splendour of his books and the quality of the artists he employed. *L'Enchanteur Pourrissant* was also Derain's first attempt at illustration. These bold, simple designs were cut with a knife along the grain of a soft wood plank.

In 1911, Dufy engraved a vivid *Le Bestiaire*, also for Apollinaire. The original edition of 122 copies sold badly[1] but two fascimile editions were produced

160

LA CARPE.

Dans vos viviers, dans vos étangs,
Carpes, que vous vivez longtemps !
Est-ce que la mort vous oublie,
Poissons de la mélancolie.

1911. *Le Bestiaire ou Cortège d'Orphée* by
Guillaume Apollinaire. With 39 woodcut
illustrations by Raoul Dufy. Published by
Deplanche, Paris and limited to 122 copies.
Printed by Gauthier-Villars. 13″ × 10¼″.
Woodcut: 'La Carpe'.

later, the first (in a smaller format) by Éditions de la Sirène, Paris, in 1919; the
second by Éditions du Cap, Monte Carlo in 1956. The rich black prints of
animals were the forerunners of a great number of French, English and
American books illustrated in the same manner. Derain and Dufy could not
be contained for long by the black and white block, even though theirs was
pioneer work in the revival of wood engraving. Explosive, rich colour was to
be their means of expression.

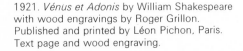

longs cheveux flottants, sans laisser de trace...
L'amour est un esprit tout de feu qui ne tend
point vers la terre, mais vers le ciel.

« Vois ce lit de primevères où je repose : ces
frêles fleurs me soutiennent comme des arbres
robustes ; deux faibles colombes me conduisent
dans les airs, de l'aurore à la nuit, au gré de
mon désir : l'amour peut-il être si léger, doux
enfant, et te paraître un si pesant fardeau ? »

1921. *Vénus et Adonis* by William Shakespeare
with wood engravings by Roger Grillon.
Published and printed by Léon Pichon, Paris.
Text page and wood engraving.

OF MANS First Disobedience, and the Fruit
Of that Forbidden Tree, whose mortal tast
Brought Death into the World, and all our woe,
With loss of Eden, till one greater Man
Restore us, and regain the blissful Seat,
Sing Heav'nly Muse, that on the secret top
Of Oreb, or of Sinai, didst inspire
That Shepherd, who first taught the chosen Seed,
In the Beginning how the Heav'ns and Earth
Rose out of Chaos: or if Sion Hill
Delight thee more, and Siloa's Brook that flow'd
Fast by the Oracle of God; I thence
Invoke thy aid to my adventrous Song,
That with no middle flight intends to soar
Above th' Aonian Mount, while it pursues
Things unattempted yet in Prose or Rhime.
And chiefly Thou O Spirit, that dost prefer

I

1927. *Paradise Lost* by John Milton with
woodcut illustrations by D. Galanis and initial
letters by Anna Simons. Published by the
Cresset Press. Printed at the Shakespeare Head
Press, Oxford. 14" × 10". Designed by Bernard
Newdigate. Opening page with wood engraving.

c. 1920. *Thaïs* by Anatole France. Woodcut
illustration by Emile Charles Carlègle. Reproduced
from *Carlègle* by M. Valotaire, published by
Henry Babou, Paris. $5\frac{7}{8}$" × $4\frac{5}{8}$" size of illustration.

It is a curious fact, but it would seem that few if any of the English wood engravers were familiar with either Derain's *L'Enchanteur Pourrissant* or Dufy's *Le Bestiaire*. John Nash, a founder member (in 1920) of the English Society of Wood Engravers, in discussing this said, 'As far as I know none of us were aware that either Dufy or Derain had ever cut a block or illustrated a book. If one looked back at all, it was to Ricketts and Lucien Pissarro'.

In France many artists, of varying abilities, were soon willing and happy to cut and gouge the end grain of boxwood, or the side grain of pear or cherry. Émile Charles Carlègle, a Swiss who had lived in Paris since 1900, engraved an effective *Daphnis et Chloë* for Léon Pichon in 1913, which owing to the war was not published until 1919. Carlègle specialized in sinuous nudes, white bodies against dark backgrounds; the woodcut was the perfect medium for such modest eroticism.

Publishers who followed Pelletan's lead were Helleu et Sargent (with whom he was associated), Henry Babou and Léon Pichon. Their success was short lived, even on the paperback level with books such as the 'Livre de Demain' series, published by Arthème Fayard for two francs fifty centimes, illustrated by such artists as Hermann Paul, Roger Grillon, Guy Arnoux and Paul-Émile Colin. I can remember these yellow paper-covered books, thirty years ago, amongst the 'remainder' stocks of the Charing Cross Road booksellers. Pelletan's ideals, and his ideas of the 'typographic book', so un-French in their unexuberant attitude, survived his death by barely two decades.

162

COLETTE
(COLETTE WILLY)

MITSOU

16 BOIS ORIGINAUX DE HERMANN PAUL

LE LIVRE DE DEMAIN

ARTHÈME FAYARD & Cⁱᵉ ÉDITEURS PARIS

PRIX : DEUX FRANCS CINQUANTE CENTIMES.

CLAUDE FARRÈRE

LA BATAILLE

27 BOIS ORIGINAUX DE A. ROUBILLE

LE LIVRE DE DEMAIN

ARTHÈME FAYARD & Cⁱᵉ ÉDITEURS PARIS

PRIX : DEUX FRANCS CINQUANTE CENTIMES.

c. 1925. *Mitsou* by Colette illustrated with wood engravings by Hermann Paul. Published by Arthème Fayard and Co., Paris. Printed by l'Imprimerie Bellenand. 9¼″ × 7⅜″. Cover design and woodcut.

Covers for the paper-back series 'Le Livre de Demain'.

c. 1925. *La Bataille* by Claude Farrère illustrated with wood engravings by A. Roubille. Published by Arthème Fayard and Co., Paris. Printed by l'Imprimerie Bellenand. 9¼″ × 7⅜″. Cover design.

c. 1925. *Mitsou* by Colette; wood engraving by Hermann Paul.

1927. *The Chester Play of the Deluge* edited by
J. Isaacs with woodcut illustrations by David
Jones. Published and printed by the Golden
Cockerel Press. 12″ × 9½″. Wood engraving.

The book to encompass the work of artists such as Matisse or Rouault needs
almost to burst the bounds of book-making. There is no place here for the
subordination of such artists to the limitations of text or the wood block.
The revival of interest in wood engraving in England can be traced at least
as far back as the occasional periodical, *The Dial*, which was published by
Ricketts and Shannon between 1889 and 1897, and in which they showed not
only their own cuts, but also the work of Lucien Pissarro and T. Sturge Moore.
Another pioneer, working in Florence in the years before the First World War
was Gordon Craig who cut with the knife, along the grain of soft fruit wood,
the illustrations for *Hamlet* and *The Merchant of Venice*.

1924. *Genesis* with wood engraved illustrations by Paul Nash. Published by the Nonesuch Press – the first book from this press. Printed by the Curwen Press in an edition of 375 copies. $10\frac{1}{2}'' \times 7\frac{1}{2}''$. Wood engraving.

1927. *Poisonous Plants* by W. Dallimore, edited by Dr A. W. Hill, FRS. With wood engravings by John Nash. Published by Frederick Etchells and Hugh Macdonald, London. Printed by the Curwen Press, Plaistow. $12'' \times 7\frac{1}{2}''$. Wood engraving: 'The Horned Poppy'.

1924. *Directions to Servants* by Jonathan Swift D. D., with wood engravings by John Nash. Published and printed by the Golden Cockerel Press. $10'' \times 7\frac{1}{2}''$. Wood engraving: 'Directions to the coachman'.

In 1905, Noel Rooke who like his fellow-student, Eric Gill, had started engraving by this time, was appointed teacher of book illustration at the Central School of Arts and Crafts in London. It was not until 1912, after some opposition, that Rooke was permitted to teach the craft to his students, amongst them Robert Gibbings, who was later to play a great part in the movement, both by his own engraving and by his ownership of the Golden Cockerel Press.

In 1920, the Society of Wood Engravers was formed, amongst whose original members were Lucien Pissarro, Gordon Craig, Gill, Robert Gibbings and John Nash. (The last named, though inspired by his brother Paul to take up the craft, was self taught.)

But the commercial publishers in England were slow to make use of this perfect medium for book illustration, and it was left to the private presses to be the first to exploit this sudden burst of talent. In 1924 Paul Nash did a fine set of engravings for the Nonesuch edition of *Genesis*, which was set in Rudolf Koch's Neuland typeface, producing very much the effect of a block book.

In 1924 John Nash engraved some rather droll cuts for the Golden Cockerel Press edition of Swift's *Directions to Servants*, and two years later the same artist engraved twenty very fine illustrations for *Poisonous Plants*, which was printed by the Curwen Press. The attitude of both John and Paul Nash was similar to that of Derain and Dufy; they were of the modern movement, more interested in design than in representation. However, John Nash's obsession with flowers and plants gives an added authority to the engravings in *Poisonous Plants*; the 'Horned Poppy' is a vivid engraving, evoking in its background the windswept shingle banks of the North Sea. In 1927 David Jones, the Welsh painter, illustrated *The Chester Play of the Deluge* for the Golden Cockerel Press with appropriate and beautifully designed engravings.

I cannot feel enthusiastic about Eric Gill's cuts for the Golden Cockerel's edition of *The Canterbury Tales,* which is spoilt by the insensitive post art nouveau vegetable forms that droop about the pages.

Gill's engravings for *Canticum Canticorum* for Count Harry Kessler's Cranach Press in Germany are, on the other hand, quite delightful. Gill had a healthy liking for the female body and was a very skilful engraver. Blair Hughes-Stanton, another artist interested in the human form, was working at the Gregynog Press in Montgomeryshire between 1931—4. Here he illustrated six books with wood engravings of a delicacy and fineness of line that was quite new to the craft — a delicacy that also made very considerable demands on his pressmen. I suppose that Hughes-Stanton and Gill were the best craftsmen in this English wood engraving revival, though Gill never attempted the intricacies that Hughes-Stanton took in his stride. The fineness of the latter's white line engravings has to be seen in the original, where they are printed on a smooth, cream-coloured Japanese vellum, with impeccable presswork, most sparely inked. No photographic process, however perfect, will reproduce these originals with complete fidelity.

1931. *Canticum Canticorum.* With wood engravings and initials by Eric Gill. Published by Insel-Verlag and printed by the Cranach Press, under the direction of Count Harry Kessler. Set in a version of Jenson's roman specially cut for the Cranach Press by E. P. Prince. 10¼" × 5⅛". Wood engraving.

1929. *The Canterbury Tales* by Geoffrey Chaucer, illustrated with wood engravings by Eric Gill. Set in Caslon Old Face. Published and printed by the Golden Cockerel Press in 4 volumes. 12" × 7½". Text page with illustration.

ARCADES

1933. *Four Poems* by John Milton illustrated
with wood engravings by Blair Hughes-Stanton.
Published and printed by the Gregynog Press.
10″ × 6½″. Wood engraving: 'Arcades'.

1932. *The Adventures of the Black Girl in her Search for God* by George Bernard Shaw, illustrated with wood engravings by John Farleigh. Published by Constable and Co. Ltd. Printed by R. & R. Clark, Edinburgh. 8″ × 5¼″. Cover design.

Title-page.

[2] *Graven Image*: John Farleigh, Macmillan, 1940.

During these years, only slight use had been made by English commercial publishers of the wood engraving process. In 1932, however, Constables had a tremendous success with Bernard Shaw's *The Adventures of the Black Girl in her Search for God*, with wood engravings by John Farleigh. These engravings, influenced to some extent by both Gill and Blair Hughes-Stanton and certainly inspired by his author, are Farleigh's best work. They were printed most faithfully from electros by R. & R. Clark.

Farleigh has described at length[2] the wonders of working with Shaw, who provided rough sketches for many of the illustrations. His description of Shaw's meticulous supervision of his work makes fascinating reading and makes one wish there were a few more authors who could and would take as much interest in the illustrations and production of their books.

Farleigh may not have been a *great* illustrator, but he was a very good craftsman and Shaw provided 'the directing intelligence'. Shaw, too, was a consummate craftsman, who surprisingly permitted his illustrator to order him about in turn, to the tune of asking him to write more copy to fill out a page here and there. This collaboration, like Tenniel's with Lewis Carroll, added a unique quality to this beautiful little book. The endearing little black girl was a figment of Farleigh's imagination, for he never used a coloured model.

The Black Girl is a model example of book planning. It all began with George Bernard Shaw writing to John Farleigh in 1932 in these words:

'Pavlov sitting on a crocodile': John Farleigh's engraving.

'Pavlov sitting on a crocodile': sketch by Shaw.

Whitehall Court
8th May 1932

Dear Sir,

As I am old and out of date I have not the privilege of knowing you or your work. But Mr William Maxwell, of Clark's of Edinburgh, tells me that you can design, draw and engrave pictures as part of a printed book, which, you will understand, is something more than making a picture and sticking it into a book as an 'illustration'. The idea is that you and I and Maxwell should co-operate in turning out a good-looking volume consisting of the story contained in the enclosed proof sheets (please hold them as very private and confidential) and, say, a dozen pictures. Are you sufficiently young and unknown to read the story and make one trial drawing for me for five guineas? That is, if the job interests you.

faithfully,

G. Bernard Shaw

1932. *Twelfth Night* by William Shakespeare illustrated with wood engravings by Eric Ravilious. Published and printed by the Golden Cockerel Press. Engravings printed in sepia and grey. 13" × 9¼" page size. Wood engraving reproduced same size.

1938. *The Writings of Gilbert White of Selborne* edited by H. J. Massingham, illustrated with woodcuts by Eric Ravilious. Published by the Nonesuch Press. 10" × 6¼". Tailpiece same size.

Opposite:
1938. *Cirque de l'Étoile Filante* written and illustrated with etchings and wood engravings by Georges Rouault. Published by Ambroise Vollard, Paris. Etchings printed by Roger Lacourière, text and wood engravings by Henri Jourde. 17¼" × 13¼". Wood engraving by Georges Aubert.

[3] The only comparable illustrated *Selborne* is the edition which John Nash illustrated for the Lutterworth Press in 1951, which was later issued with colour added to the plates by the artist, by the Limited Editions Club of New York in 1972.

Whilst the English artists of the wood-engraving revival were engaged in the crafts of wood cutting and wood engraving, there was a return in France to the use of the professional engraver. One of these, Georges Aubert, was responsible for the engravings in one of the greatest private press books. This was Georges Rouault's *Cirque de l'Étoile Filante*, published by Vollard in 1938. Rouault started work on the designs for this book in 1930. There were a number of coloured etchings and no less than eighty-two large, rich, dark textured wood engravings.

The sheer page size of the Vollard books (17¼ in. by 13¼ in. for the *Cirque*) makes most of the English private press books look a little insignificant. The work of the English artist, Eric Ravilious, is certainly *not* insignificant. His first attempt at illustration by wood engraving was in 1932 for an edition of Shakespeare's *Twelfth Night.* His most successful, the edition of Gilbert White's *Natural History of Selborne* in 1938. Ravilious had a very firmly-developed sense of design, an attribute he shared with his friend Edward Bawden, and which is evident in all his engravings.[3]

Douglas Percy Bliss, the author of the definitive work on the history of wood engraving, illustrated *Border Ballads* for Oxford University Press in 1925 with appropriate Scottish fervour. These ballads, which Bliss had selected, offered admirable scope for his engravings and the book as a whole was also a pleasant piece of design for which the engravings make effective headpieces. Robert Gibbings took over the management of the Golden Cockerel Press in 1924 and ran it for some years. A great, jolly, bearded giant of a man, he was a talented engraver, the strength of whose work is in the clearly defined contrasts of black and white. His method of working was somewhat unusual. He would draw a pen or scraper-board approximation of a woodcut and have this photographed on to the wood block. This preliminary work often showed marked weaknesses of drawing which largely disappeared as soon as he started engraving; it was as if his burin possessed qualities of draughtsmanship that his pen knew nothing about.

171

LITTLE MUSGRAVE AND LADY BARNARD

O wow for day!
And, dear, gin it were day!
Gin it were day, and I were away—
For I ha' na lang time to stay.

I

As it fell on one holy-day,
    As many be in the year,
When young men and maids together did go
    Their matins and mass to hear,

II

Little Musgrave came to the church-door—
    The priest was at private mass—
But he had more mind of the fair women
    Than he had of Our Lady's grace.

III

The one of them was clad in green,
    Another was clad in pall,
And then came in my Lord Barnard's wife,
    The fairest amongst them all.

(30)

JOHNIE ARMSTRONG

I

S U M speiks of lords, sum speiks of lairds,
    And sick lyke men of hie degrie;
Of a gentleman I sing a sang,
    Sum tyme called Laird of Gilnockie.

II

The King he wrytes a luving letter,
    With his ain hand sae tenderly,
And he hath sent it to Johnie Armstrang,
    To cum and speik with him speedily.

III

The Eliots and Armstrangs did convene;
    They were a gallant cumpanie—
' We'll ride and meit our lawful King,
    And bring him safe to Gilnockie.'

IV

' Make kinnen and capon ready, then,
    And venison in great plentie;
We'll wellcum here our royal King;
    I hope he'll dine at Gilnockie! '—

(47)

1925. *Border Ballads* selected, and with wood
engravings, by Douglas Percy Bliss. Published
by the Oxford University Press. Printed by the
Westminster Press. 9¾″ × 6″. Illustrated pages.

1966. *Two Stories: Come and dine and Tadnol:*
T. F. Powys, edited by Peter Riley. Published by
R. A. Brimmell, Hastings. With wood engravings
by Reynolds Stone. 8" × 5½". Wood engraving,
same size.

1952. *The Four Gospels* with wood engraving
illustrations by Reynolds Stone. Published by
Penguin Books Ltd, Middlesex. Headpiece,
same size.

Opposite left:
1934. *Beasts and Saints* by Helen Waddell
illustrated with woodcuts by Robert Gibbings.
Published by Constable and Co. Ltd, London.
Printed by Charles Whittingham and Griggs Ltd,
London. 8" × 6". Woodcut.

Opposite right:
1932. *Iorana a Tahitian Journal* by Robert
Gibbings, with wood engravings by the author.
Published by Houghton Mifflin, Boston and
New York. 9" × 6¼". Wood engraving:
'Pandanus Grove'.

In 1929 Houghton Mifflin sent Gibbings off to Tahiti to collaborate on a book
about that island with James Norman Hall. Gibbings spent four months there
collecting material, by which time Hall had become so involved in the saga
of *The Mutiny on the Bounty* that he had to back out. As a result of this
Gibbings wrote the text of *Iorana*, his first serious attempt at authorship. This
was the forerunner by many years of his autobiographical illustrated writings,
such as *Blue Angels and Whales* (Penguin Books 1938) and the series of
'river' books for Dent, beginning with *Sweet Thames run softly* (1940). His
last work was appropriately called *Till I end my Song* (1957).

Reynolds Stone was trained as a printer at the Cambridge University Press (as
a university graduate apprentice). Whilst still at Cambridge he spent a couple
of weeks at Eric Gill's home learning the rudiments of wood engraving. Since
1934, when he forsook printing, Stone has devoted his time to wood engraving and to cutting letters. His engraved letters are always exquisite pieces of
craftsmanship and on these his reputation stands; but his engraving covers
wider fields than letter cutting. He has engraved many attractive head and tail
pieces, very much on a Bewick scale, including the cuts for the Penguin
edition of the *Four Gospels*.

Joan Hassall is the daughter of John Hassall, famous illustrator and poster
artist. She is a skilled engraver, with a feeling for period illustration. In 1937
she illustrated *Portrait of a Village* by F. Brett Young for Heinemann. In 1940,
Harrap published a new edition of *Cranford* with engravings by Miss Hassall,
including an interesting engraved title-page with a portrait of Mrs Gaskell,
and in 1947 she followed this up with *Our Village* by Mary Russell Mitford,
also for Harrap.

1940. *Cranford* by Mrs Gaskell illustrated with
wood engravings by Joan Hassall. Published by
Harrap. Wood engraving, same size.

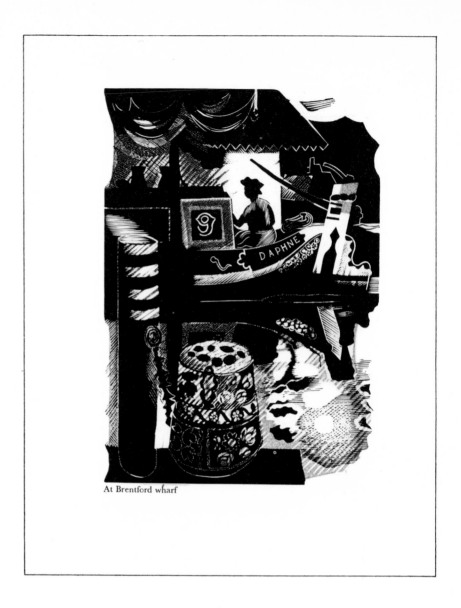

At Brentford wharf

1950. *Canals, Barges and People* by John O'Connor with coloured wood engravings by the author. Published by Art and Technics Ltd, London. Printed by the Shenval Press. $8\frac{1}{4}'' \times 6\frac{3}{8}''$. Coloured wood engraving.

The 1939–45 war broke the continuity of the English wood engraving revival. The steam seemed to go out of the movement. Certainly during the time I was teaching at the Royal College of Art (1950–63) there was only one notable engraving student (David Gentleman). In the years before the war, the R.C.A. had been a forcing house for them, when, in turn, the two Nashes and Eric Ravilious were teaching there. John O'Connor was a pupil of Ravilious at that time. One of the few notable books of engravings since the war is his *Canals, Barges and People* written by the artist and designed by Robert Harling at Art and Technics.

David Gentleman's first essay at wood engraving was in 1953. These engravings were for a slim volume published by the Lion and Unicorn Press, called *A Tale of Two Swannes*. His most ambitious book has been *The Swiss Family Robinson* which was published by the Limited Editions Club, New York, in 1963. These engravings had the addition of a second colour, which had been hand drawn. In 1964 he illustrated *The Shepherd's Calendar* for the

MAY

MAY

Come queen of months in company
Wi all thy merry minstrelsy
The restless cuckoo absent long
And twittering swallows chimney song
And hedge row crickets notes that run
From every bank that fronts the sun
And swathy bees about the grass
That stops wi every bloom they pass
And every minute every hour
Keep teazing weeds that wear a flower
And toil and childhoods humming joys
For there is music in the noise

46

The village childern mad for sport
In school times leisure ever short
That crick and catch the bouncing ball
And run along the church yard wall
Capt wi rude figured slabs whose claims
In times bad memory hath no names
Oft racing round the nookey church
Or calling ecchos in the porch
And jilting oer the weather cock
Viewing wi jealous eyes the clock
Oft leaping grave stones leaning hights
Uncheckt wi mellancholy sights
The green grass swelld in many a heap
Where kin and friends and parents sleep
Unthinking in their jovial cry
That time shall come when they shall lye
As lowly and as still as they
While other boys above them play
Heedless as they do now to know
The unconcious dust that lies below
The shepherd goes wi happy stride
Wi morns long shadow by his side
Down the dryd lanes neath blooming may
That once was over shoes in clay
While martins twitter neath his eves
Which he at early morning leaves
The driving boy beside his team
Will oer the may month beauty dream
And cock his hat and turn his eye
On flower and tree and deepning skye

47

1964. *The Shepherd's Calendar* by John Clare with wood engravings by David Gentleman. Published and printed by the Oxford University Press. 8″ × 5″. Text spread.

1964. *Peter Schlemihls Wundersame Geschichte* by A. von Chamisso with wood engravings by Imre Reiner. Published by Ars Librorum, Frankfurt-am-Main. 8⅛″ × 4⅞″ page size, printed on one side of the paper only. Pages folded and uncut. Tailpiece: 3⅝″ high.

Oxford University Press. This is an attractive book, with a set of most effective engravings, designed as headpieces to each month of the calendar, that give it a very agreeable scale. The engraving in no way overpowers the text.

This wood-engraving revival that started in France and flowered in England never made much headway in the United States. One or two expatriate German artists, such as Fritz Eichenberg and Hans Mueller, have engraved a number of illustrated books for the Limited Editions Club, but the medium has not been in much favour. Today it manifests itself in a livelier manner in Germany, Holland and Scandinavia, where the most potent influence has been Imre Reiner, a Hungarian trained in Germany and influenced to some extent by the German Expressionists. He is a completely cosmopolitan artist, utterly eclectic in his admiration for artists as diverse as Dürer and Bewick. Reiner has illustrated a number of books, making a most highly skilled use of multiple tool engraving. These include Goethe's *Novelle*, Voltaire's *La Princesse de Babilone* and Hugo von Hofmannsthal's *Andreas*.

1886. *Little Lord Fauntleroy* by Frances Hodgson
Burnett illustrated by Reginald B. Birch.
Published by Frederick Warne and Co., London.
Printed by Richard Clay and Sons, Bungay.
$8\frac{3}{8}'' \times 5\frac{3}{4}''$. Illustration: 'Are you the Earl?' said
Cedric, 'I'm your grandson. I'm Lord Fauntleroy'.

7. THE ILLUSTRATION AND DESIGN OF CHILDREN'S BOOKS

Whatever the future may be for illustration generally, there will always be a
place for it in children's books. Children's taste tends to be rather conservative;
books that were old favourites when their parents were children often attract
them. Whether fairy stories will have much of a hold in the space age may be
doubted, but for younger children animal stories look a pretty safe bet. For
older boys and girls, adventure stories may well be surpassed by stories of
real adventure. Pirates and highwaymen may pale into insignificance when
held up to comparison with moon dwellers and the activities of the modern
criminal. And yet, I wonder. There seems to be an indefinite life ahead for the
much loved little books of Beatrix Potter, and *Treasure Island* still 'holds
children from play and old men from the chimney corner'.

If one looks back to the 1880's and '90's, English and American infants (or
their mamas and nannies) were still happily turning over the pages of the
picture books by Caldecott and Kate Greenaway, prettily printed in colour
from wood blocks, most skilfully engraved by Edmund Evans. However, their
tastes were changing; and in the late 1880's there was a spate of new successful children's books, many of them still in print today. I doubt if the American
author Frances Hodgson Burnett has many readers for her *Little Lord
Fauntleroy* (1886), though her charming *The Secret Garden* is still read
widely.

In the 1890's boys still read R. M. Ballantyne's *The Young Fur Traders,* first
published in 1856 as *Snowflakes and Sunbeams* (a singularly unpromising
title that was quickly changed after the first edition).[1] The most successful
writer of English school stories was an energetic young typefounder, by name
Talbot Baines Reed, whose *The Willoughby Captains* and *The Fifth Form at St
Dominic's* both appeared in 1887, and *The Cock House at Felsgarth* in 1891.

[1] *English Children's Books*. Percy Muir, Batsford,
1954.

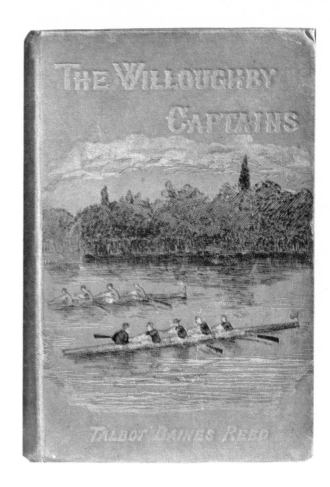

1886. *Little Lord Fauntleroy* by Frances Hodgson
Burnett illustrated by Reginald B. Birch.
Published by Frederick Warne and Co., London.
Printed by Richard Clay and Sons, Bungay.
8⅜" × 5¾". Case-binding, blocked in black, gold
and brown on a grey cloth.

1887. *The Willoughby Captains* by Talbot Baines
Reed illustrated by Alfred Pearse. Published by
Hodder and Stoughton, London. Printed by
Hazell, Watson and Viney Ltd, London. 7¼" × 4¾".
Case-binding blocked in gold, black and colours
on a grey cloth.

1894. *The Young Fur Traders* by Robert Michael
Ballantyne. Published by T. Nelson and Sons,
London. 7⅞" × 4⅞". Chromo-lithographed
frontispiece and title-page by an anonymous
artist.

1903. *With the British Legion* by G. A. Henty illustrated by Wal Paget. Published by Blackie and Sons, London, Glasgow and Dublin. $7\frac{3}{8}'' \times 5\frac{1}{4}''$. Half-tone illustration.

Ballantyne's staying power with his young readers, like Fenimore Cooper's and Marryat's a quarter of a century earlier, owed much to the authentic backgrounds of his books, and particularly of the Canadian arctic, for he had worked as a clerk in the Hudson Bay Company. Ballantyne also took a great deal of trouble over the illustrations for his books, preparing rough pen-and-wash drawings, with copious instructions for the engraver-illustrators.

Whatever one may think of *Little Lord Fauntleroy* as a story, it is certainly an attractive-looking book, with a prettily blocked cover and effective illustrations by the American Munich-trained illustrator, Reginald B. Birch. Joseph Pennell, writing in 1889, thought it was the best thing Birch had ever done.

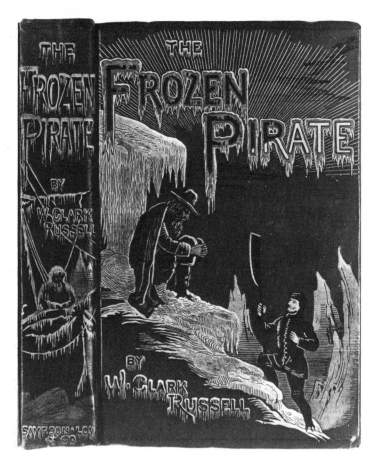

1888. *The Frozen Pirate* by W. Clark Russell illustrated by P. Macnab. Published by Sampson Low, Marston, Searle and Rivington, London. Printed by Gilbert and Rivington Ltd. 7¾″ × 5⅜″. Case-binding blocked in gold and white on a dark green cloth. Scraper-board illustration.

[2] *English Children's Books.* Percy Muir, Batsford, 1954.

[3] Gordon Browne was the son of Hablot K. Browne, the illustrator of so many of the novels of Charles Dickens.

[4] *Talbot Baines Reed*, Stanley Morison. Cambridge University Press, 1960 (privately printed). Also see P. M. Handover's article on Reed in *The Book Collector,* Spring 1963, with a list of his works.

School and adventure stories

Most school stories are too subject to changing manners and times to outlive their period. The early successes in this field were *Tom Brown's Schooldays* (1887), and *Eric or Little by Little* (1858). *Tom Brown's Schooldays* was illustrated by Arthur Hughes and Sydney Prior Hall, and re-issued in 1896 with new illustrations by Edmund J. Sullivan. *Eric or Little by Little* by F. W. Farrar, first illustrated by the Dalziels, passed through thirty-six editions during Farrar's lifetime and, as Percy Muir said, 'achieved an immortality only of derision'.[2]

Most of Talbot Baines Reed's books appeared as serials in the *Boy's Own Paper,* which was published by the Religious Tract Society. His family had close connections with this pious body; but Reed's stories are anything but pious and his boys, drawn by Gordon Browne,[3] H. M. Paget and Alfred Pearse, are, unlike Dean Farrar's, very real boys. 'Between 1906 and 1952 no fewer than ten of his school stories were reprinted, including his first, *The Adventures of a Three Guinea Watch* (1880), and his last, *Tom, Dick and Harry* (1892).'[4]

G. A Henty followed Ballantyne as a writer of adventure stories. His books poured out in an apparently endless succession. He wrote something over ninety books for boys. These were illustrated by several artists, including Gordon Browne, H. M. Paget and Wal Paget – who illustrated, with wash drawings printed by half-tone, Henty's *With the British Legion* (1903). Nearly all these books had colourfully blocked or printed illustrations on their covers. *The Frozen Pirate* by W. Clark Russell is a good example of this kind of case-binding, and the illustrations for it by P. Macnab are an early example of the use of process half-tone, the plates showing considerable evidence of handwork. Until the '90's most children's books were illustrated by line, or line and wash reproduced by wood engraving. The intricately hatched wood blocks blended well with type, giving the books a most agreeable homogeneous quality. Chromo-lithography was widely used for books for young children, often with crude and garish colours, though the delicate title-page for *The Young Fur Traders* is an exception.

1896. *Uncle Remus and his Friends* by Joel
Chandler Harris illustrated by A. B. Frost.
Published by James R. Osgood McIlvaine and
Co., London. Printed by Ballantyne, Hanson and
Co., London. $7\frac{1}{2}'' \times 5''$. Illustration.

1907. *The Tale of Tom Kitten* by Beatrix Potter.
Published by Frederick Warne and Co. Ltd,
London. $5\frac{1}{2}'' \times 4''$. Case-binding.

1904. *The Tale of Benjamin Bunny* by Beatrix
Potter. Published by Frederick Warne and Co.
Ltd, London. $5\frac{1}{2}'' \times 4''$. Illustration spread.

THAT wood was full of
rabbit holes; and in the
neatest sandiest hole of all,
lived Benjamin's aunt and his
cousins — Flopsy, Mopsy,
Cotton-tail and Peter.

Old Mrs. Rabbit was a
widow; she earned her living
by knitting rabbit-wool mittens
and muffetees (I once bought
a pair at a bazaar). She also
sold herbs, and rosemary tea,
and rabbit-tobacco (which is
what *we* call lavender).

15

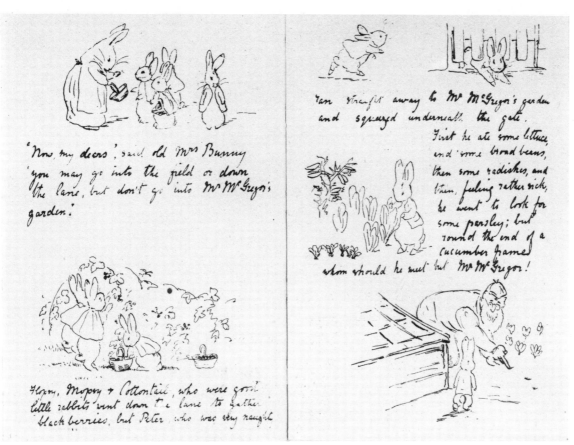

'Now, my dears', said old Mrs Bunny 'you may go into the field or down the lane, but don't go into Mr McGregor's garden.'

Ran straight away to Mr McGregor's garden and squeezed underneath the gate.

First he ate some lettuce, and some broad beans, then some radishes, and then, feeling rather sick, he went to look for some parsley; but round the end of a cucumber frame whom should he meet but Mr McGregor!

Flopsy, Mopsy + Cottontail, who were good little rabbits went down the lane to gather blackberries, but Peter who was very naughty

1893. Facsimile of a letter to Noel Moore telling the original story of Peter Rabbit for the first time. Reproduced from *The Tale of Beatrix Potter* by Margaret Lane, published by Frederick Warne and Co., London and New York, 1946. Original size of letter $7\frac{3}{4}'' \times 5\frac{1}{4}''$.

Beatrix Potter (b. 1866 d. 1943) was a natural illustrator. In her letters to her young friends, she expressed herself as freely by her drawings as in her words. That she should find such a perfect medium for her picture-stories in the three or four-colour half-tone medium is not surprising, for she was quite untutored in any of the autographic processes.

Beatrix Potter was also one of the first illustrators to make a really good use of this half-tone colour process. She was a 'natural', as a book designer as well as a book illustrator; with no training or printing experience she planned every detail of production and layout. Her first two books, *The Tale of Peter Rabbit* (1901) and *The Tailor of Gloucester* (1902), were printed at her own expense and privately published. General publication, in a revised form and with colour, followed, somewhat cautiously, from Frederick Warne who had previously rejected *Peter Rabbit. The Tale of Benjamin Bunny* came out in 1904 and *The Tale of Tom Kitten* in 1907.

The books were originally published at one shilling in paper-covered boards, and one-and-sixpence in a cloth binding. Both versions had a coloured illustration pasted down on the front cover.

Margaret Lane, in her excellent and most moving biography, extols Beatrix Potter's 'great sense of animal beauty, the imaginative truthfulness of her approach and her deeply felt beauty of the countryside'.[5]

Beatrix Potter's books are scaled carefully to a child's needs; they are little and they feel good. She had quite clear ideas of what a small child's book should be like. The books had to be about 5 in. by 4 in. with a coloured picture on every spread, and her text was always limited to no more than one or two simple sentences on each page. Beatrix Potter's rabbits, mice and hedgehogs, even if they are dressed up, are real animals; the illustrations have an intimate, close-up reality, a reality and a viewpoint familiar to any child's eye. Their appeal is just as great today as it was sixty odd years ago. Their anthropomorphism has had many followers and a few antecedents, such as various chapbook editions of Charles Perrault's *Puss-in-Boots*, or Joel Chandler Harris's *Uncle Remus*, published nearly half a century earlier than Beatrix Potter's books. A. B. Frost who illustrated *Uncle Remus* achieved as happy and indissoluble a union with his author as Tenniel had with Lewis Carroll. His animals, like Beatrix Potter's, were quite free from vulgarity.

[5] *The Tale of Beatrix Potter*. Margaret Lane, F. Warne.

1895. *The Blue Fairy Book* edited by Andrew Lang and illustrated by H. J. Ford and G. P. Jacomb Hood. Published by Longmans, Green and Co., London. Printed by Spottiswoode and Co., London. 7″ × 4¾″. Case-binding.

1895. *The Blue Fairy Book*, illustration by H. J. Ford.

1901. *Lion and Unicorn* by John Hassall. Reproduced from *Modern Pen Drawings: European and American*. 8″ × 11⅜″. Published by the Studio, London and New York.

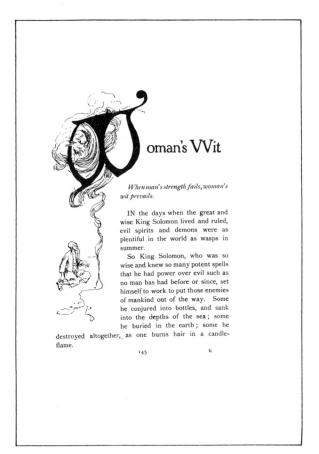

1896. *Twilight Land* written and illustrated by Howard Pyle. Published by J. Osgood McIlvaine and Co., London. Printed by Ballantyne, Hanson and Co., London. 8½″ × 5⅞″. Case-binding, chapter opening and illustration.

Fairy stories

Andrew Lang's series of 'coloured' fairy books was the combined result of his great scholarship and much hard work on the part of his wife. Lang, who came from the border country and had been brought up in an atmosphere of legend and history, was not well served by his illustrators (H. J. Ford who illustrated many of his fairy stories was a feeble draughtsman). The books, however, were pleasantly produced and made a gay showing in their multiplicity of coloured covers. The 'Unicorn' drawing is by John Hassall, an English poster artist with a robust sense of humour – (his poster for the holiday resort of Skegness, of a bouncing fisherman, earned him wide fame). He also illustrated a number of children's books, many of pre-Tudor England. His work was influenced by Boutet de Monvel and other contemporary French illustrators. The 'Unicorn' drawing was done before 1900, but he was still at work in the 1930's. When I was a very young student, I visited him in his studio, which was just like a junk shop, there was so much bric-à-brac lying about. I can remember he showed me how to draw an ear!

Howard Pyle, an American artist who achieved a tremendous reputation in his lifetime, drew in a variety of styles, ranging from the stiff lines of a Dürer engraving to the sketchy impressionism of Daniel Vierge. His first successful book was *The Merry Adventures of Robin Hood*, which came out in 1883. *Twilight Land*, both written and illustrated by Howard Pyle, was first published in England in 1896, by Osgood McIlvaine, a publishing house with a record for producing interesting illustrated books. It is filled with amusing line illustrations, pleasantly set on the page with a lot of white space around them. The typography of the book, presumably by Pyle himself, is less successful; each chapter is headed with somewhat grotesque, very large initial letters and the title-page is decorated with rubrics.

Both *The Blue Fairy Book,* with 390 pages and *Twilight Land,* with 370 pages, really gave young readers something to get their teeth into. And with their heavily blocked, smooth blue cloth covers and gilded heads, they were books to treasure.

1900. *The Bunkum Book* by Aubrey Hopwood
illustrated by Maud Trelawny. Published by
Frederick Warne and Co., London and New York.
Printed by Morrison and Gibb Ltd, Edinburgh.
9" × 11⅞". Illustration.

Undated. *Hauff's Fairy Tales* translated and
adapted by Cicely McDonnell. Illustrated by
Fritz Bergen. Published by Dean and Sons Ltd,
London. 7⅛" × 5⅜". Case-binding.

'The parrot is a Polly Bird,
The Owl a Melancholly Bird,
But I'm the Cockiolly Bird,
And that's a Rara Avis!'

By the 1890's process engraving was in wide use, and the new generation of
illustrators was only too eager to see its drawings appear unaltered by the
hand of the trade engraver. (Amongst the illustrators of children's books,
Howard Pyle was one of the first to make use of the four-colour half-tone.)
However, the chromo-lithographers, particularly in Germany, France and the
United States, were still very active, and continued to be so well into the
twentieth century. *Hauff's Fairy Tales*, translated from the German by Cicely
McDonnell, had a technically ingenious illustrated cover, lithographed and
blocked in heavy relief; and Fritz Bergen's coloured drawings for it were also
chromo-lithographed. *The Bunkum Book* by Aubrey Hopwood, the author
of *The Sleepy King*, with chromo-lithographed illustrations after drawings by
Maud Trelawny, is a strange, poetic creation, almost worthy of Lewis Carroll.
The 'Cockiolly Bird' was a favourite in many British and American nurseries in
the first decade of this century.

Florence and Bertha Upton's series of 'Golliwogg' books (there were ten of
them) was also published in the United States and England at the beginning
of the century. They are the most endearing inventions, very prettily lithographed. The text is hand drawn in an interesting art nouveau letter, so
precisely done it could be mistaken for type.

Gordon Browne was a most versatile illustrator. As well as drawing the
pictures for G. A. Henty's adventure stories and Mrs Ewing's books, he also
illustrated several books for very young children, including an edition of
Rip van Winkle in 1887. Twenty years later, he completed a set of watercolour
drawings for *The Merry Tales of the Wise Men of Gotham.* This little book was
chromo-lithographed sympathetically by Van Leer in Amsterdam, a printing
firm of distinction which is still engaged in the printing of illustrated books.

1903. *The Golliwogg's Bicycle Club* by Bertha
Upton with illustrations by Florence K. Upton.
Published by Longmans, Green and Co.,
London, New York and Bombay. Printed by the
Niagara Lithographic Co., Buffalo, New York.
$8\frac{3}{8}'' \times 11\frac{1}{8}''$. Illustration.

1907. *The Merry Tales of the Wise Men of
Gotham* by F. J. Harvey Darton illustrated by
Gordon Browne. Published by Wells Gardner,
Darton and Co. Ltd, London. Printed by L. van
Leer and Co., Netherlands. $7\frac{1}{4}'' \times 6\frac{1}{2}''$. Cover and
illustration.

"They all splashed into the water."

1905. *Rip van Winkle* by Washington Irving illustrated by Arthur Rackham. Published by William Heinemann, London, and Doubleday, Page & Co., New York. Printed by Richard Clay and Sons Ltd. 9⅞" × 7". Case-binding, illustration and title-page.

BY·WASHINGTON
IRVING
ILLUSTRATED·BY
ARTHUR·RACKHAM

LONDON: WILLIAM·HEINEMANN
NEW·YORK: DOUBLEDAY·PAGE·& Cº

As the twentieth century advanced, and with it the popular acceptance of the three- and four-colour half-tone process, the 'gift' book (virtually the 'Coffee Table' book for children) arrived on the scene, or at least on the nursery table. Arthur Rackham was the most successful English artist in this field; the muted tones and delicate tints of his water-colour drawings combined well with his strong feeling for the grotesque. The 'gift' books were really something for a child to receive. They were heavy and thick, with beautifully blocked covers, they often had a coloured illustration mounted on the front cover, and gilded heads, ornamental headbands and coloured end papers. Inside there would be colour plates, tipped-on to cartridge mounts and protected with tissue. These books were precious objects, to be looked at with awe and handled with care. Among those illustrated by Rackham were *Rip van Winkle* (1905), followed by *Peter Pan in Kensington Gardens* and *Alice in Wonderland*. W. Heath Robinson and his two brothers, and Edmund Dulac also made good use of 'process' and illustrated a number of 'gift' books. Heath Robinson's *The Water Babies* (1915) is full of pretty colour plates and whimsical line drawings, which owe just a little to Beardsley, and which were, at least to me when I was very young, much more acceptable than those in the Linley Sambourne edition. Violent prejudices can develop in one's tender years; I must admit that my affection for Heath Robinson's work may largely be governed by having had his *The Water Babies* and his own *Bill the Minder* (1912) in my nursery. He had a strange, innocent and very personal sense of humour which appeared in all his drawings; also, like Beardsley, he was expert at disposing of massed areas of white or black in his illustrations, as in the drawing here of Mr Grimes and Tom setting off at 3.0 a.m. on a summer's morning for Harthover Place. *Bill the Minder* is full of the strangest fancies, and just as in *The Water Babies*, there is the odd contrast of grotesque black-and-white drawings and very pretty watercolours. That the artist's name should have become a part of the English language has nothing to do with these illustrations. The term 'Heath Robinson' derives from a series of drawings he published in the 1920's in the weekly magazines — drawings of incredibly involved mechanical contrivances designed to solve the simplest problems.

THE WATER BABIES

that that made up for his poaching Sir John's pheasants; whereby you may perceive that Mr. Grimes had not been to a properly-inspected Government National School.

Now, I daresay, you never got up at three o'clock on a midsummer morning. Some people get up then because they want to catch salmon, and some because they want to climb Alps, and a great many more because they must, like Tom. But, I assure you, that three o'clock on a midsummer morning is the pleasantest time of all the twenty-four hours, and all the three hundred and sixty-five days; and why everyone does not get up then, I never could tell, save that they are all determined to spoil their nerves and their complexions by doing all night what they might just as well do all day. But Tom, instead of going out to dinner at half-past eight at night, and to a ball at ten, and finishing off somewhere between twelve and four, went to bed at seven, when his master went to the public-house, and slept like a dead pig, for which reason he was as pert as a game-cock (who always gets up early to wake the maids), and just ready to get up when the fine gentlemen and ladies were just ready to go to bed.

AND SOME BECAUSE THEY WANT TO CLIMB ALPS.

6

ON THEY WENT.

1915. *The Water Babies* by Charles Kingsley illustrated by W. Heath Robinson. Published by Constable and Co. Ltd, London. Printed by Bradbury Agnew and Co. Ltd, London. $8\frac{1}{4}'' \times 6\frac{3}{8}''$. Text and illustration spread.

1912. *Bill the Minder* written and illustrated by W. Heath Robinson. Published by Constable and Co. Ltd, London. $9\frac{5}{8}'' \times 7\frac{1}{8}''$. Printed by T. & A. Constable Ltd, Edinburgh. Illustration.

1935. *Fairy Tales and Legends* by Hans Andersen illustrated by Rex Whistler. Published by Cobden-Sanderson Ltd, London. Printed by the Shenval Press and bound by the Leighton-Straker Bookbinding Company Ltd. Page size 8″ × 5⅜″. Illustrations and case-binding.

The Marsh King's daughter.

From the 1890's the old favourites, *The Arabian Nights* and the stories of the brothers Grimm and Hans Andersen, were meeting increasing competition in the nurseries.

Jacob and Wilhelm Grimm's fairy tales were first published in England in 1823; the first Hans Andersen English translation appeared in 1846. Both books have been through dozens of editions, with a variety of illustrators. The best of the Grimm editions was probably the first English illustrated edition, with George Cruikshank's vivid etchings, and the best Hans Andersen an edition charmingly decorated by Rex Whistler and first published in 1935.

Whistler's Hans Andersen (which is still in print) is a pretty book, bound in a green cloth cover,[6] lettered in gold, with an arabesque pattern, blocked in pale yellow, the same pattern being used for the endpapers. For the illustrations, Whistler used scraper-board with great refinement.

[6] In some editions, the colour of the cloth and blocking varied.

Gerda and Kay: *The Snow Queen.*

1935. *Fairy Tales and Legends* by Hans
Andersen illustrated by Rex Whistler. Published
by Cobden-Sanderson Ltd, London. Printed by
the Shenval Press and bound by the Leighton-
Straker Bookbinding Company Ltd. Page size
8″ × 5⅜″. Illustration: *The Garden of Paradise*.

Wild·Animals·I·Have·KnowN

·and·200·Drawings·

by

Ernest Thompson Seton

NATURALIST·TO·THE·GOVERN-
MENT·OF·MANITOBA·AUTHOR
BIRDS·OF·MANITOBA·♦♦♦
MAMMALS·OF·MANITOBA·♦♦
ART·ANATOMY·OF·ANIMALS
TRAIL·OF·THE·SANDHILL·STAG
BIOGRAPHY·OF·A·GRIZZLY·
LIVES·OF·THE·HUNTED·♦♦♦

Being the Personal Histories of
    Lobo
    Silverspot
    Raggylug
    Bingo
    The Springfield Fox
    The Pacing Mustang
    Wully
    and Redruff

PUBLISHED·BY·HODDER·&·STOUGHTON· LONDON·1920

1898. *Wild Animals I have Known* written and illustrated by Ernest Thompson Seton. Designed by Grace Thompson Seton. Published by Hodder and Stoughton, London. Printed by the Scribner Press, New York. 7⅞″ × 5½″. Title-page reproduced from the 1920 edition.

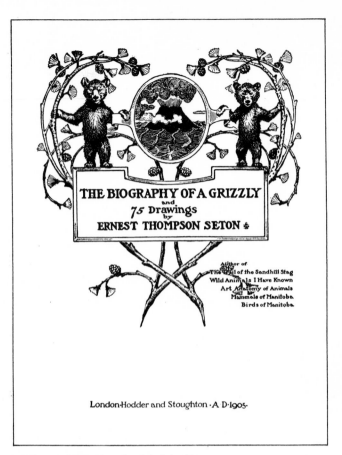

THE BIOGRAPHY OF A GRIZZLY
and
75 Drawings
by
ERNEST THOMPSON SETON ♣

Author of
The Trail of the Sandhill Stag
Wild Animals I Have Known
Art Anatomy of Animals
Mammals of Manitoba
Birds of Manitoba

London·Hodder and Stoughton ·A·D·1905·

1900. *The Biography of a Grizzly* by Ernest Thompson Seton. Published by Hodder and Stoughton, London. Printed in the United States by the De Vinne Press, New York. 7½″ × 5¾″. Title-page reproduced from the 1905 edition.

1899. *The Trail of the Sandhill Stag* by Ernest Thompson Seton. Published by David Nutt Ltd, London. Printed by the De Vinne Press, New York. 7½″ × 5¾″. Half-tone illustration.

Animal stories

In 1898, just over two years before any of Beatrix Potter's books appeared, the first of a series of wild-life books by the American naturalist, Ernest Thompson Seton, was published. The attitude of this author and artist was very different to that of Beatrix Potter or A. B. Frost. He was certainly no anthropomorphist. Seton illustrated his stories of wild animals with most lively, realistic pen drawings and also with wash drawings. The animals jump and run and scutter through the pages of his books, which are themselves interesting pieces of design. They were conceived and laid out by his wife, Mrs Grace Gallantin Thompson Seton, with spacious, open cream-coloured pages, and wide margins, dotted with illustrations. Mrs Seton also drew out the most elaborate asymmetric title pages.

Wild Animals I have Known (1898), *The Trail of the Sandhill Stag* (1899), *The Biography of a Grizzly* (1900) and *Animal Heroes* (1905) were perhaps the most successful of Seton's works. *Wild Animals I have Known* and *Animal Heroes* were bound in a mossy green cloth and blocked in a darker green or in gold. Ernest Thompson Seton, who incidentally signed his drawings 'Ernest Seton-Thompson', was Naturalist to the Government of Manitoba. His books have endeared him to succeeding generations of American and English children. Though the main credit for their success must go to Seton's realistic approach to wild life and his easily read prose, his wife's part as designer of these most attractive-looking books was by no means negligible. Mrs Seton not only designed the books, but was also responsible for the general make-up and the literary revision. The feeling of space and air that runs through these books reflects something of Seton's writing about the 'Old-timers of the Big Plain of Manitoba', to whom *The Trail of the Sandhill Stag* was dedicated. This book was most beautifully printed by the De Vinne Press in New York.

190

Badlands Billy

big and strong; the weaker must move out, and with them Yellow Wolf and the Dusky Cub.

Wolves have no language in the sense that man has; their vocabulary is probably limited to a dozen howls, barks, and grunts expressing the simplest emotions; but they have several other modes of conveying ideas, and one very special method of spreading information—the Wolf-telephone. Scattered over their range are a number of recognized "centrals." Sometimes these are stones, sometimes the angle of cross-trails, sometimes a Buffalo-skull—indeed, any conspicuous object near a main trail is used. A Wolf calling here, as a Dog does at a telegraph post, or a Muskrat at a certain mud-pie point, leaves his body-scent and learns what other visitors have been there recently to do the same. He learns also whence they came and where they went, as well as something about their condition, whether hunted, hungry, gorged, or sick. By this system of registration a Wolf knows where his friends, as well as his foes, are to be found. And Duskymane, following after the Yellow Wolf, was taught the places and uses of the many

124

Badlands Billy

signal-stations without any conscious attempt at teaching on the part of his foster-mother. Example backed by his native instincts was indeed the chief teacher, but on one occasion at least there was something very like the effort of a human parent to guard her child in danger.

The Dark Cub had learned the rudiments of Wolf life: that the way to fight Dogs is to run, and to fight as you run, never grapple, but snap, snap, snap, and make for the rough country where Horses cannot bring their riders.

He learned not to bother about the Coyotes that follow for the pickings when you hunt; you cannot catch them and they do you no harm.

He knew he must not waste time dashing after Birds that alight on the ground; and that he must keep away from the little black and white Animal with the bushy tail. It is not very good to eat, and it is very, very bad to smell.

Poison! Oh, he never forgot that smell from the day when the den was cleared of all his foster-brothers.

125

1898. *Wild Animals I have Known* written and illustrated by Ernest Thompson Seton. Published by Hodder and Stoughton, London. Printed by the Scribner Press, New York. $7\frac{1}{2}" \times 5\frac{1}{2}"$. Dedication page and text spread.

Copyright, 1898, by
Ernest Seton Thompson
for the United States of America

Printed by The Scribner Press, New York. U. S. A.

This Book
Is Dedicated

To Jim

1931. *The Wind in the Willows* by Kenneth Grahame. Illustrated by Ernest H. Shepard. Published by Methuen and Co. Ltd, London. $8\frac{1}{2}'' \times 5\frac{1}{2}''$.
Illustration: 'Toad stared fixedly in the direction of the disappearing motor car'.

1926. *Winnie-the-Pooh* by A. A. Milne. Illustrated by Ernest H. Shepard. Published by Methuen and Co. Ltd, London. Printed by Jarrold and Sons Ltd, Norwich. $7\frac{3}{8}'' \times 4\frac{3}{4}''$. Illustration spread.

The Wind in the Willows by Kenneth Grahame, often described as 'the best-loved children's book of the twentieth century', was first published in 1908, with a rather improbable frontispiece by Graham Robertson.

Illustrated editions followed, the first by Paul Branson in 1913, the next by Nancy Barnhart in 1922 and a third by Wyndham Payne in 1927. It was not until 1930 that an illustrated edition appeared, with drawings by an artist whose work pleased the author. This was Ernest H. Shepard, who was really in sympathy with this whimsical story of Rat, Mole, Badger and Toad, and their doings on the upper reaches of the Thames. Kenneth Grahame died before Shepard had finished his drawings, but not before he had seen enough of the sketches to recognize his little animals as he felt they should be drawn, without any sense of caricature. Shepard's pen drawings for *The Wind in the Willows* are completely successful, except possibly for Mole, who is obviously a difficult subject; Toad is a masterly piece of characterization. Shepard is a most talented draughtsman, whose work has always been full of charm.

Shepard had previously illustrated Kenneth Graham's *The Golden Age* in 1928 and *Dream Days*, by the same author in 1930, both published by John Lane. *The Wind in the Willows* with his drawings, now in paperback form, has passed its 105th edition. The coloured illustrations that were added to a recent hard-backed edition are less successful.

A return to the not-so-real animal book was A. A. Milne's *Winnie-the-Pooh*, which was one of the great, popular successes of the 1920's. This and the succeeding books about Pooh and Christopher Robin were appropriately illustrated in delicate lines by Ernest H. Shepard. The immense success they had, called forth not only wonder but also psychological investigation from a later and less assured generation – an attitude foreshadowed by Dorothy Parker when she wrote in a review of one of these books: 'Here tonstant weader fwowed up'! In spite of the jibes, these were pretty books, nicely cased and blocked and charmingly illustrated.

1894. *Le Bon Roy Henry* by A. Hermant Job.
Published and printed by Alfred Mame and
Son, Tours. $8\frac{3}{4}'' \times 10\frac{1}{2}''$. Illustration spread.

A new look for children's books from France

One of the French contributions to the design and illustration of twentieth-century children's books has been to free the illustrator from the limitations of line blocks and four-colour process. The English publishers' almost total reliance on letterpress printing, at least up to the beginning of the Second World War, was one limiting factor, their lack of courage in this field an even more inhibiting one. The French since the early years of the nineteenth century have been much freer in their use of lithography, gravure, the intaglio processes, and later *pochoir* (the use of stencils) and even the *Jean Berté* process, where the illustrations were printed from rubber blocks with water-colour inks.

In France, by the end of the nineteenth century, lithography had almost completely usurped letterpress printing for the illustration of children's books. Boutet de Monvel's albums, *Nos Enfants, Jeanne d'Arc* and *Chansons de France*, were all illustrated in line and colour and printed by the lithographic press.

A. Hermant Job, the illustrator of *L'Épopée du Costume Militaire*, used the same methods of line and colour for his *Le Bon Roy Henry* (1894). Job, like so many French illustrators, was a very fluent, if literal, draughtsman. Some of his drawings in this book (particularly the one of the assassin François Ravaillac being torn apart by four horses, or the one of a distraught mother being served up with her own baby in a soup tureen, with a large pot of mustard to help it down), are pretty tough fare for the young. The same tradition in draughtsmanship can be seen in the work of Edy Legrand, particularly in his line and *pochoir* drawings for *Bolivar* and *La Fayette*.

In 1919, in rather a different vein, Edy Legrand wrote and illustrated *Macao et Cosmage,* for Éditions de la Nouvelle Revue Française. This was a large square book, printed in black line and stencilled colours, with a hand-written text. It is a gay, boldly drawn, colourful book, whose rather mannered drawings are very much of their time. *Macao et Cosmage* (page 197) was

193

Le 23 mai, comme elle se trouvait à Crespy, elle apprit que la ville de Compiègne était serrée de près par les Anglais et les Bourguignons. Elle s'y porta avec quatre cents combattants et entra dans la ville le 24, à la pointe du jour. Puis, prenant avec elle une partie de la garnison, elle attaqua les Bourguignons. Mais les Anglais vinrent l'assaillir. Les Français reculèrent. « Ne pensez qu'à férir sur eux, criait Jeanne, il ne tient qu'à vous qu'ils soient déconfits! » Mais Jeanne fut entraînée par la retraite des siens. Ramenés sous les remparts de Compiègne, les Français trouvèrent le pont levé et la herse baissée. Cependant, Jeanne, acculée aux fossés, se défendait toujours. Une troupe s'était jetée sur

1896. *Jeanne d'Arc* by M. Boutet de Monvel.
Published by E. Plon, Nourrit et Cie, Paris.
Gravure printed by Ducourtioux and Hulliard,
text by E. Plon. 9″ × 12⅝″. Illustration spread.

something quite new in cheap book production and made a lively contrast to insipid watercolours, printed in three- or four-colour half-tone or the repellent chromo-lithography still in use at that time. Nothing like this had appeared in England or the U.S.A.

One of the first French publishers to produce books of this kind for children was a Parisian printer called A. Tolmer, the author of *Mise en Page*.

In 1921, Tolmer published *Voyages et glorieuses découvertes des Grands Navigateurs et Explorateurs Français* (overleaf). It was vividly illustrated by Legrand and superbly printed by Tolmer with stencilled colours, the variety of these colours and their freshness and subtlety being quite beyond the photographic processes. One of the sadder developments in printing, is the loss of such simple methods; *pochoir* may yet be revived, but almost certainly only for costly and limited editions. In 1929 Tolmer published Edy Legrand's

elle. « Rendez-vous ! » lui criait-on. « J'ai juré et baillé ma foi à un autre qu'à vous, répondait la brave fille, et je lui tiendrai mon serment! » Mais en vain elle résistait. Tirée par ses longs habits, elle fut renversée de son cheval et prise. Du haut des remparts de la ville, le sire de Flavy, gouverneur de Compiègne, assistait à sa capture. Il ne fit rien pour lui porter secours.

Bolivar and *La Fayette*, two attractive books in a landscape format. The drawings were in line, with transparent stencil colours, and the arbitrary placing of the colours and the sensitive line drawings combined to produce a pleasantly fresh effect. Legrand has a natural feeling for placing illustrations on a page. He has illustrated many books for children, including *Line en Nouvelle Calédonie* (1934) for Calmann-Lévy. A year later, in 1935, for the same publisher, he illustrated and designed Madeleine Ley's *La Nuit de la St Sylvaine,* in which the sensitive line of the earlier books had become a little stereotyped. However Edy Legrand over a long career has contributed much to French book illustration, and particularly to the illustration of children's books: *Grands Navigateurs* and *Macao* are far more inventive in their sweeping use of colour than almost anything that has appeared since.

1921. *Voyages et Glorieuses Découvertes des Grands Navigateurs et Explorateurs Français* by Edy Legrand. Published by A. Tolmer, Paris. $14\frac{3}{4}'' \times 10\frac{3}{4}''$. Illustration.

..ILS PURENT TERMINER LA MAISON OÙ ILS VOULAIENT VIVRE..

1919. *Macao et Cosmage* written and illustrated
by Edy Legrand. Published by Nouvelle Revue
Française. Printed by Bellenand, Fontenay-aux-
Roses. Hand coloured by Saude. $13\frac{3}{8}'' \times 12\frac{1}{8}''$.
Illustration.

destiné à être promptement réprimé. La France,
qui n'avait jusqu'alors témoigné qu'une sym-
pathie très vive pour les insurgés, prit nettement
fait et cause pour les Américains.
Elle leur envoya sans tarder subsides
et munitions. Ce n'était pas encore
suffisant pour obtenir un résultat
définitif. La Fayette revint alors en
France pour solliciter de nouveaux
secours. Il fut fêté, acclamé, devint
un héros populaire. Il
représentait une idée
chère à la Nation.

« Antoine l'Enragé » enlève à
l'assaut une forteresse réputée
imprenable.　Le roi le reçut
et l'écouta avec la
plus grande bienveillance, mais l'état
des finances et de l'armée française
empêchait le souverain de prendre
une décision. Habile diplomate,

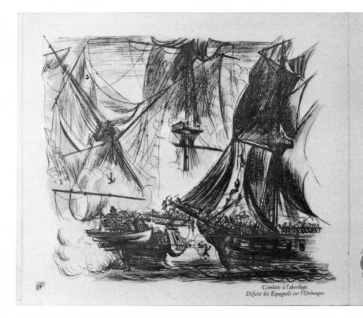

Combats à l'abordage.
Défaite des Espagnols sur l'Orénoque.

au soleil. Beaucoup s'enfuirent. Il faut la flamme de Bolivar pour entraîner les plus
fidèles. Ces hommes à moitié nus, sortant de la forêt tropicale, se trouvent en
quelques jours au milieu d'un désert de glace. L'ascension prend vite l'aspect d'une
vision de cauchemar. Les précipices engloutissent des bataillons entiers.
La faim, la maladie déciment les soldats du Libérateur. Ils réussissent
cependant à traverser la montagne. Bolivar tombe à
l'improviste sur les Espagnols qu'il écrase à Boyaca.
　La magnifique victoire de Carabobo le rendait maître
de la Colombie. Il va au Pérou. Admirablement secondé
par le général Sucre, il est vainqueur à Ayacucho (1824).
Il fait prisonnier le vice-roi, est nommé Président de
la République.
　Bolivar remonte à cheval....
　La Bolivie, l'Équateur sont affranchis....

La traversée des Andes.

Opposite:
1929. *Bolivar* written and illustrated by Edy
Legrand. Published and printed by Tolmer,
Paris. 8¼″ × 9⅝″. Cover and spread.

Opposite:
1929. *La Fayette* written and illustrated by Edy
Legrand. Published and printed by A. Tolmer,
Paris. 8¼″ × 9⅝″. Cover and spread.

1934. *Scaf le Phoque* by Lida with lithographed
illustrations by Rojankovsky. Published by
Flammarion, Paris, in the series Albums du Père
Castor. 8¼″ × 9″. Cover.

In the 1930's a Russian, called Feodor Rojankovsky, working in Paris, lithographed some colourful books for Flammarion. This series, called 'Albums du Père Castor', is still in print.

They were in a landscape format, similar to Legrand's *Bolivar* and *La Fayette*, and were the forerunners of the English Puffin Picture Books. Rojankovsky (he signed his work Rojan) was a skilful lithographer. His earlier books, such as *Panache* (1934), were full of gay, lighthearted drawings of squirrels and pine martens. His *Scaf* (1936) was a rather more ambitious book, with exciting scenes of arctic seas and the Northern Lights, in which the animals are still observed without sentimentality. His later work, drawn for American publishers, has become somewhat vulgar.

1934. *Panache l'Écureuil* by Lida with
lithographed illustrations by Rojankovsky.
Published by Flammarion, in the series Albums
du Père Castor. 8¼″ × 9″. Text and illustration
spread.

Du matin au soir, ils
sautent et dansent sur les
branches. Ils se lancent des
pommes de pin, jouent à
cache-cache, se poursui-
vent comme des enfants.
Et leurs petits yeux vifs
luisent comme des perles
noires. Un beau jour, au
milieu de leurs jeux, Rouquette dit à Quick :

— Et maintenant
assez joué, mon petit mu-
seau. Il est grand temps
que nous nous occupions
de préparer un nid pour
nos enfants. Quelque
chose me dit qu'ils ne vont
pas tarder à naître. Notre
vieux gîte ne vaut plus

4

rien. Je veux que nos petits aient le plus beau nid du monde. Mais il
ne nous tombera pas du ciel! Cherchons. Je vais parcourir toute la forêt,
et que la fouine m'étrangle si je ne trouve pas ce qu'il nous faut! Viens
avec moi. Allons, viens vite!

Quick n'en avait aucune envie. Il aurait préféré continuer à jouer
avec Rouquette, mais elle avait l'air si décidé et si sérieux qu'il n'osa
pas protester. Les deux écureuils prirent leur élan. Sautant de branche en
branche, ils explorèrent la moitié de la forêt sans trouver d'arbre assez
commode pour y installer leur nid.
Celui-ci n'était pas assez haut; les
rameaux de celui-là étaient trop
clairsemés. Ils allaient, enfin, se dé-
cider pour cet autre, quand le vent
leur apporta la détestable odeur
de la fouine. Ils n'eurent pas besoin de renifler deux fois pour se
rendre compte que le terrier de leur
pire ennemie se trouvait juste au-
dessous d'eux. Hop! Hop! Hop!
En trois bonds, les voilà loin.

5

The country of the elephants faded from sight.
The balloon glided noiselessly along in the sky
and Babar and Celeste admired the view.
What a wonderful journey!
The air was warm, a light wind blew.
And there was the sea, the great blue sea.

1935. *Babar's Travels* written and illustrated by Jean de Brunhoff. Published by Methuen and Co. Ltd, London. Printed by W. S. Cowell Ltd, Ipswich. $14\frac{1}{8}'' \times 10\frac{1}{8}''$. Illustration.

1937. *The Seven Simeons* written and illustrated by Boris Artzybasheff. Published by the Viking Press, New York and Cassell and Co. Ltd, London. $11\frac{1}{4}'' \times 8\frac{3}{4}''$. Illustration.

Author-illustrators

In 1934, the first of another successful series of children's books appeared in Paris. This was Jean de Brunhoff's *The Story of Babar* which was later published in England by Methuen. The large paged books ($14\frac{1}{4}$ in. by $10\frac{1}{4}$ in.) are colourful and gay, with rather naïve drawings, and a text written in a clear, childish hand. The series continued with *Babar's Travels* and *Babar the King*; and after Jean de Brunhoff's death, his son, Laurent de Brunhoff, took it further, with some success.

There have also been a number of English authors of children's books, who have illustrated their own works, including Rudyard Kipling (who drew the pen drawings for his *Just So Stories*), Hugh Lofting (who illustrated the odd doings of Dr Dolittle), and Arthur Ransome (who illustrated his books about children and their exciting adventures in small boats). The fact that these authors could hardly draw seems to have carried little weight with their readers, who willingly accept their stiff, awkward drawings as being 'real', because the author must have been there! The success even of an author-illustrator like Edward Ardizzone, who really can draw, must depend at least in part on this quality of authenticity.

Boris Artzybasheff's style has changed considerably over recent years. Thirty odd years ago, he illustrated Padraic Colum's *Orpheus, Myths of the World* with scraperboard drawings. His later work has, much to its advantage, been reduced to an open, often evenly weighted line. For Heritage he has provided yet another version of Balzac's *Droll Stories*, with amusing, rather ribald line drawings. Artzybasheff's own book, *The Seven Simeons*, published by Viking in 1937, is illustrated in line and colour. This is a beautiful piece of decoration.

1908. *Just So Stories for Little Children* written and illustrated by Rudyard Kipling. Published by Macmillan and Co. Ltd, London. Printed by R. & R. Clark, Edinburgh. $6\frac{3}{4}'' \times 4\frac{1}{4}''$. Illustration.

SCOTLAND YARD

1940. *The Big Six* written and illustrated by Arthur Ransome. Published by Jonathan Cape Ltd, London. Printed by the Alden Press, Oxford. $7\frac{7}{8}'' \times 5\frac{1}{4}''$. Illustration.

1929. *Doctor Dolittle in the Moon* written and illustrated by Hugh Lofting. Published by Jonathan Cape Ltd, London. Printed by Butler and Tanner Ltd, Frome. $7\frac{3}{4}'' \times 5\frac{1}{4}''$. Frontispiece and title-page.

"Rigged himself up like a tree"

DOCTOR DOLITTLE IN THE MOON

Told and illustrated by HUGH LOFTING

Published by JONATHAN CAPE LTD LONDON.

H.L.

This was the beginning of many happy days. Lucy loved the life at sea, especially as she had Tim there to tell her about everything. She made great friends with the second mate, and used to tidy his cabin and darn his socks.

This pleased him very much, as he was a bachelor and very

untidy. Often she and Tim would go to the galley, where the cook would tell them wonderful stories of his life at sea.

1938. *Tim and Lucy go to Sea* written and illustrated by Edward Ardizzone. Published by the Oxford University Press, London. Printed by W. S. Cowell Ltd, Ipswich. 10″ × 7⅛″. Illustrated pages.

Edward Ardizzone has been one of the most successful children's author-artists of this century. His first book in this vein was *Little Tim and the Brave Sea Captain*, published in 1936. A wildly improbable story, it is just the kind of dream a very little boy might have when, as a critic on the *New York Herald Tribune* said, 'he has his first sharp attack of sea fever'. This was followed by *Lucy Brown and Mr Grimes*, the story of a friendless old man, who was befriended by a very Victorian little girl. Both books are utterly charming and the successor that brings Tim and Lucy together, *Tim and Lucy go to Sea*, is even better. All have an open, hand-written text, and the artist has no compunction about using 'bubbles' when anyone is talking – as in the illustration here of a ship's cook sitting in his galley talking to the two enthralled children. Ardizzone has a genius for this kind of book, and it is no wonder that they have been equally popular on both sides of the Atlantic. The earlier books had a fine large format, were printed on only one side of the paper and were in colour throughout. The later ones and reprints of the earlier ones have a smaller page size and less colour.

Kathleen Hale's *Orlando* books, describing the adventures of a marmalade cat, have been much loved by children. The first appeared in 1939. The earlier illustrations were lithographed, the later ones were drawn on Plastocowell –

Every morning the Yellow Creature was placed in the front of the ship, where he looked lovely against the sparkling blue sea. Captain Slaughterboard would sit upon a barrel of rum, and watch the Yellow Creature for hours on end.

His pirates had to watch the Yellow Creature too, but they got rather tired of it sometimes.... ......

1945. *Captain Slaughterboard Drops Anchor*
written and illustrated by Mervyn Peake.
Published by Eyre and Spottiswoode, London.
$9\frac{1}{4}'' \times 7''$. Cover and text and illustration spread.

a technique similar to lithography in which the artist draws on a grained plastic sheet. The plastic sheet is then used in the same manner as a photographic positive, the image being printed down on to a deep-etched zinc plate, from which very big runs can be printed with no deterioration of the artist's original work.

Innumerable books for children appear every year, but few stand out from the general run of mediocrity. The ones that do, have, over recent years, mostly come from the United States of America and are the work of professional graphic designers who are taking time off in a less exacting field. There are, however, one or two books, apart from these, that are worth notice.

Early in the last war Mervyn Peake illustrated and wrote *Captain Slaughterboard Drops Anchor*. Unfortunately the edition was destroyed by enemy action. In 1945 Eyre and Spottiswoode reissued it, with flat coloured tints added by the artist to the plates. It was an impoverished edition, printed on wretchedly thin paper, but the drawings are fascinating, horrifying, yet within the scope of a child's imagination. These grotesque figures are the most extraordinary and poetic creations; and the book, I would have thought, is worthy of revival.

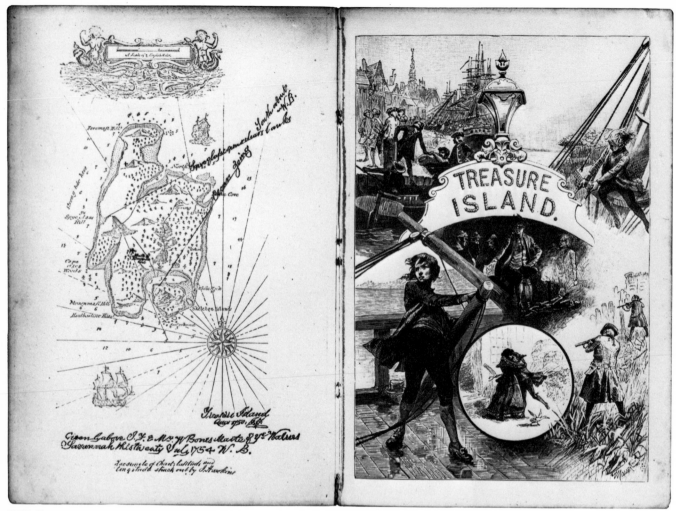

1885. *Treasure Island* by Robert Louis Stevenson illustrated by G. Roux and F. T. Merrill. Published and printed by Cassell and Co. Ltd, London. 7⅛″ × 4¾″. Title-page spread. Reproduced from the 1894 edition.

1911. N. C. Wyeth: 'All day he hung round the cove'.

On re-hashing the classics

By 'classics', I mean books that have a continuing appeal to each new generation. Some are so dependent on their original drawings that there is little point in fresh illustrations; efforts to reillustrate *Alice in Wonderland*, for example, have proved singularly unsuccessful. However, there are books that benefit by new interpretations and fresh illustrations. Such a one is *Robinson Crusoe*. There have been innumerable illustrated versions, ranging from the charming Cruikshank wood-engravings of 1832 to Roger Duvoisin's agreeable pen drawings of 1946. *Tom Sawyer* and *Huckleberry Finn* are also renewed with fresh illustrations for each generation. But of all children's books Robert Louis Stevenson's *Treasure Island* would seem most successfully to lend itself to being illustrated over and over again. Its quality of appealing to adults as much as to children of each new generation — its extreme readability — cannot fail to stir any illustrator with a gleam of romance in his soul into once again re-enacting on paper the scenes on the *Hispaniola* and the quays of Bristol Docks, or Long John Silver wiping his blood-stained knife on a few blades of grass, or the horrific Blind Pew tapping his way into the Admiral Benbow Inn.

I have no idea how many illustrated editions of *Treasure Island* there have been since it was originally published in 1883, for it has been translated into many languages. Cassells were both printer and publisher of the first edition, which had no illustrations except the map. It was an agreeable little book, 7½ in. by 4¾ in., bound in a smooth dark blue cloth, the spine being blocked in gold.

Typographically it was not exceptional, but for a rather nicely displayed opening to the first chapter. The first illustrated edition, which appeared in

1911. *Treasure Island* by Robert Louis Stevenson illustrated by N. C. Wyeth. Published by Charles Scribner's Sons, New York. 9" × 6¾". Title-page printed in colour from trichromatic blocks.

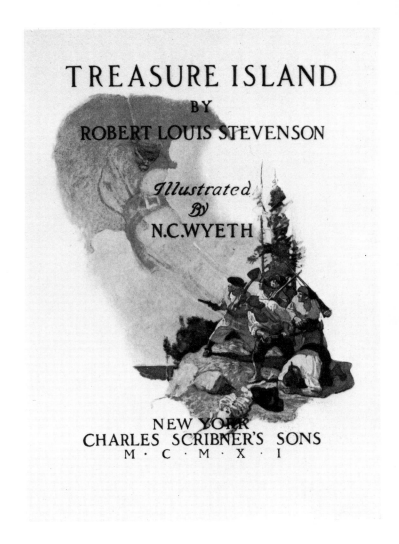

1929. *Treasure Island* by Robert Louis Stevenson illustrated by Rowland Hilder. Published and printed by the Oxford University Press, London. 9⅛" × 6½". Illustration: 'All day he hung round the cove or upon the cliffs with a brass telescope'.

the United States in 1884, published in Boston by Roberts Brothers, had four rather uninspired illustrations by F. T. Merrill. In 1885 the first French edition appeared, with a frontispiece and twenty-two full-page woodcut illustrations by Georges Roux.

In the same year the first English illustrated edition appeared, haphazardly combining the pictures from the French and American editions; the Merrill drawings were printed from zincos and Roux's twenty-two designs from woodcuts were engraved by Ladmiral, Bellenger, F. Moller and various other trade engravers.

It was not until 1899 that a new attempt was made to illustrate this story. In that year Wal Paget drew a fine set of illustrations for a new edition. Wal Paget, one of Henty's illustrators, was the brother of Sidney Paget, the first illustrator of the Sherlock Holmes stories.

Paget's illustrations for *Treasure Island* were reproduced by wood engraving, which gives to his, as it had to the French edition, a pleasant period charm. Paget's edition, however, was in a larger format than the 1885 edition, and was in Cassells' new uniform black binding which they used for all Stevenson's works. His illustrations set the scene pleasantly. To some extent they lack characterization, but this has been a common failing with all the *Treasure Island* illustrators, with one remarkable exception.

It might be reasonable comment to say that a romance like this needs in its illustrations little more than romantic or factual scene setting, and most of the editions shown here admirably answer this need. Between the publication of the Wal Paget edition and its going out of print in 1912 there was only one other illustrated *Treasure Island* of importance. This was published by

1927. *Treasure Island* by Robert Louis Stevenson illustrated by Edmund Dulac. Published by Ernest Benn Ltd, London. Printed by the Whitefriars Press Ltd, London. $9\frac{3}{8}'' \times 7\frac{1}{4}''$. Illustration: 'Black Dog disappears'.

1911. N. C. Wyeth: 'One last tremendous cut'.

1911. N. C. Wyeth: 'Tapping up and down the road in a frenzy' (*Below opposite*)

1899: Wal Paget: 'Now boy', he said, 'take me in to the captain'.

1949. *Treasure Island* by Robert Louis Stevenson illustrated by Mervyn Peake. Published by Eyre and Spottiswoode, London. Printed by the Chiswick Press, London. $8\frac{3}{8}'' \times 5\frac{1}{4}''$. Illustration: 'Now boy', he said 'take me in to the captain'.

THE BLACK SPOT.   35

And he gave it, as he spoke, a wrench, that made me cry out.

"'Now, boy,' he said, 'take me in to the captain'" (*p.* 34).

"Sir," said I, "it is for yourself I mean. The captain is not what he used to be. He sits with a drawn cutlass. Another gentleman——"

1899. *Treasure Island* by Robert Louis Stevenson
illustrated by Wal Paget. Published and printed
by Cassell and Co. Ltd, London. $7\frac{1}{2}'' \times 5''$.
Illustration: 'He lay as we had left him . . .

1947. *Treasure Island* by Robert Louis Stevenson
illustrated by John Minton. Published by Paul
Elek Ltd, London. Printed in the Netherlands.
$9'' \times 5\frac{3}{4}''$. Illustration: 'He lay as we had left him'.

Scribner's in New York in 1911, with N. C. Wyeth's vigorous illustrations; his interesting title-page shows a group of frightened mutineers cowering below the ghost of Captain Flint. The illustrations, packed with action, are reproduced by four-colour half-tone and, of course, printed on coated stock, which is the penalty that illustrators who wished to work in colour had to pay. Books so illustrated immediately become books with plates; book design purists naturally enough object, but not so the generations of American schoolboys who must have delighted in such illustrations as the one of Billy Bones taking a tremendous swipe at the fleeing Black Dog, or that of 'Israel Hands and his companion locked together in deadly wrestle . . .' Wyeth's characters are sturdy specimens of humanity, filling their clothes well; the artist was obviously devoted to action rather than characterization, though his sense of atmosphere was acute. His portrait of Billy Bones standing on a misty Cornish cliff top and that of Pew 'tapping up and down the road in a frenzy' are both effective, even though the Admiral Benbow Inn looks a bit like a Cape Cod farmhouse.

In the late 1920's two interesting editions appeared within two years of each other. These were Ernest Benn's quarto, illustrated by Edmund Dulac, and Oxford University Press's large octavo, illustrated by Rowland Hilder. Both are handsome books, well printed and bound, the Dulac by Whitefriars Press, the Hilder by John Johnson at Oxford. Both made a full use of the four-colour process and both had a very slight scattering of pen-drawings in the text. There the similarity ends. Dulac, famous for his gentle, pretty watercolour illustrations to such books as the *Arabian Nights,* would seem a very odd choice for Stevenson's blood and thunder. Hilder, on the other hand, although a very young man at the time, had already achieved fame for his vigorous romantic draughtsmanship, particularly of ships and the sea.

Yet each book is in its own way successful. Dulac's curious, detached, air-view drawings of the Admiral Benbow and the *Hispaniola* add another dimension to Stevenson's story.

1963. *Treasure Island* by Robert Louis Stevenson illustrated by Peter Roberson. Published by the Folio Society, London. Printed by W. and J. Mackay and Co. Ltd, Chatham. 8¾″ × 5½″. Illustration: 'Our little walk along the quays'.

He made himself the most interesting companion

1929. Rowland Hilder: 'He made himself the most interesting companion'.

1899. Wal Paget: 'Our little walk along the quays'.

Dulac's drawings may not be to the taste of every child, but there are some children who would enter his slightly magical world with eagerness. Hilder's strength comes over, both in the dramatic chiaroscuro and in his knowledge of sailing ships and how they worked. His *Hispaniola*, sailing full-and-bye across the end papers is a real topsail schooner, made of wood, rigged with Italian hemp and with heavy much-patched flaxen sails. This is in the Wyeth tradition and is splendid, vigorous stuff.

Another edition in the same vein was published by George Macy for his Limited Editions Club in New York in 1941, illustrated by Edward A. Wilson with watercolours and a lithographed chalk drawing of Long John Silver for the frontispiece. This particular illustration is a little slick and mannered, and the parrot looks like a crow; Wilson's earlier work was more appealing. Moreover, this *Treasure Island* was not intended for children, but for the subscribers of the Limited Editions Club.

In England, twenty years and another war later than the Dulac and Hilder editions, two more *Treasure Islands* appeared. In 1947 Paul Elek published a series of books which he called the Camden Classics. With the assistance of Denys Sutton, a remarkable short list of illustrated books was issued, including a *Wuthering Heights* with drawings by Anthony Gross, a *Jane Eyre* with lithographs by William Scott, a *Tom Sawyer* with drawings by Keith Vaughan and a *Treasure Island* illustrated by John Minton. This, as it proved from the publisher's point of view, ill-fated series was perhaps too good for its public. The typography, by Peter Ray, with asymmetric title-pages and heavy extended Grotesques for chapter headings was, for dear old England, ahead of its time; sadly enough, a mistake more costly in this conservative country than being behind the times. Looking at this *Treasure Island* now, it does not seem so advanced, with its pleasant if informal typography; but even so it makes a couple of recent editions of the book look a bit fusty. As for Minton's drawings, they are richly black with Minton's own kind of romanticism, for

Robert Louis Stevenson

Treasure Island

Introduction by H. M. Burton

drawings by John Minton

CAMDEN CLASSICS . PAUL ELEK . LONDON

1947. John Minton: Title-page and frontispiece: The Bristol quays.

1885. G. Roux. Illustration: 'I said goodbye to mother'.

he was at the peak of a brief flowering in the 1940's of romantic art in England.

John Minton's drawings match a certain sombreness in the story; they are atmospheric illustration, richly decorative, sultry and tropical, and once again there is little attempt at characterization. The latter charge certainly cannot be levelled at Mervyn's Peake's drawings done some two years later for Eyre and Spottiswoode. Here is a new *Treasure Island* and not a very comfortable one. To appreciate these illustrations it is best to rid one's mind of all previous ideas of how the book ought to be illustrated (though one or two of the scenes in Wal Paget's edition bear comparison). The pirates are dreadful evil old men, capable of terrible deeds. The quizzical expression on Silver's face does not hide the fearful potential of the man. As for Blind Pew, God help any poor boy if that old monster grabbed his arm in a lonely lane on a dark night. Mervyn Peake is the one illustrator amongst those I have mentioned here whose particular abilities have enabled him to dig below the surface of this adventure story, to find the characters that are lurking there. His curious foggy technique of drawing in dots also adds to the mystery of the scene.

Though at least two pleasant enough illustrated editions of this book have appeared since 1948, neither of them has added anything to widen one's appreciation. The Folio Society edition of 1963, illustrated by Peter Roberson, is an attractive piece of book production, and Roberson's drawings of the Bristol docks and of Long John Silver's back view are effective. Otherwise the illustrations are too thinly scattered. The same criticism applies to the equally well produced Nonesuch edition of the same year, illustrated by Robert Micklewright.

I picked *Treasure Island* as a random example for this brief comparative study. There are many other titles that would have done almost as well. As long as such stories are read by children, each succeeding generation will demand new editions and new illustrators to interpret the stories afresh for them.

1927. Edmund Dulac: 'The Apple Barrel'.

1885. G. Roux: 'I got bodily into the apple barrel'.

1963. Peter Roberson: 'The Apple Barrel'.

1929. Rowland Hilder: endpapers.

1949. Mervyn Peake: 'Cleansing his blood-stained knife the while upon a wisp of grass'.

1899. Wal Paget: 'Cleansing his blood-stained knife the while upon a wisp of grass'.

1963. Peter Roberson: Frontispiece.

Hunter brought the boat round under the stern-port, and Joyce and I set to work loading her

1929. Rowland Hilder: 'Hunter brought the boat round under the stern-port'.

1911. N. C. Wyeth: 'About half way down the slope to the stockade, they were collected in a group'.

1963. Peter Roberson: Captain Silver. Blocked in dark blue on blue cloth. Case-binding.

1927. Edmund Dulac: 'Striking the Jolly Roger'.

CHAPTER XVI

Narrative continued by the Doctor: How the Ship was Abandoned

IT was about half-past one—three bells in the sea phrase—that the two boats went ashore from the *Hispaniola*. The captain, the squire, and I were talking matters over in the cabin. Had there been a breath of wind we should have fallen on the six mutineers who were left aboard with us, slipped our cable, and away to sea. But the wind was wanting ; and, to complete our helplessness, down came Hunter with the news that Jim Hawkins had slipped into a boat and was gone ashore with the rest.

It never occurred to us to doubt Jim Hawkins ; but we were alarmed for his safety. With the men in the temper they were in, it seemed an even chance if we should see the lad again. We ran on deck. The pitch was bubbling in the seams ; the nasty stench of the place turned me sick ; if ever man smelt fever and dysentery, it was in that abominable anchorage. The six scoundrels were sitting grumbling under a sail in the forecastle ; ashore we could see the gigs made fast, and a man sitting in each, hard by

123

1927. Edmund Dulac: Chapter opening with pen drawing of the stockade.

1949. Mervyn Peake: Captain Silver.

1911. N. C. Wyeth: 'For all the world, I was led like a dancing bear'.

1941. *Treasure Island* by Robert Louis Stevenson illustrated with water colours and a frontispiece lithographed by Edward A. Wilson. Published by the Limited Editions Club, New York. Printed by the American Book-Stratford Press, New York. $10\frac{1}{2}'' \times 7''$. Illustration: Captain Silver.

PART · 6

CAPTAIN · SILVER

1929. Rowland Hilder: Captain Silver.

wich zurück, kam wieder näher, um sich schließlich, zu meiner größten Überraschung und Bestürzung, auf die Knie zu werfen und die gefalteten Hände flehend zu heben.

Sogleich blieb er wieder stehn.

«Wer bist du?» fragte ich.

«Ben Gunns», erwiderte er, und seine Stimme klang heiser und ungelenk wie ein rostiges Schloß. «Ich bin der arme Ben Gunn, ja, der bin ich, und drei Jahre lang habe ich mit keinem Christenmenschen gesprochen.»

Jetzt konnte ich erkennen, daß er im Weißer war wie ich selber und seine Züge recht angenehm. Seinen Körper allerdings, soweit er entblößt war, hatte die Sonne dunkelbraun gebrannt, sogar seine Lippen waren schwarz, und seine hellen Augen blitzten seltsam widerspruchsvoll aus dem dunklen Gesicht. Von allen Bettlern, die ich gesehen oder mir je vorgestellt hatte, war dieser hier jedenfalls der König der Zerlumptheit. Seine einzige Hülle waren ein paar Fetzen aus altem Segeltuch, und dieses erstaunliche Flickwerk wurde durch ein System der verschiedenartigsten und unzusammengehörigsten Hilfsmittel zusammengehalten wie Messingknöpfe, Taureste und Schlingen von teerbeschmierten Garnaschen. Um den Leib trug er einen alten Ledergürtel mit Messingschnalle, das einzige ganze Stück an seiner Ausstaffierung.

«Drei Jahre!» rief ich. «Hast du den Schiffbruch erlitten?»

«Nein, Maat», sagte er. «Ausgesetzt!»

Davon hatte ich schon gehört, und ich wußte, daß es unter den Freibeutern als eine entsetzliche Strafe galt, wenn man den Missetäter mit etwas Pulver und Blei an Land setzte und auf irgendeiner fernen, verzweifelten Insel zurückließ.

«Vor drei Jahren ausgesetzt», fuhr er fort, «und seither von Ziegen gelebt, von Beeren, von Muscheln. Wo auch ein Mensch ist, sage ich, muß er sich zu helfen wissen. Aber, Maat, mein Herz verlangt dringend nach christlichen Speisen. Hast du nicht zufällig ein Stück Käse bei dir? Nicht? Na ja, so manche lange Nacht habe ich von Käse geträumt – zumeist von gebratenem – und dann bin ich aufgewacht, und da war ich!»

«Wenn ich je wieder an Bord zurück kann», sagte ich, «sollst du pfundweise Käse kriegen!»

Währenddessen hatte er den Stoff meiner Jacke betastet, meine Hände gestreichelt, meine Schuhe gemustert, und zwischen seinen Reden zeigte er immer wieder ein kindliches Vergnügen darüber, daß er sich einem Mitmenschen gegenüber sah. Doch bei meinen letzten Worten schaute er auf; etwas Verschlagenes trat in seinen Blick.

«Wenn du je wieder an Bord zurück kannst, sagst du?» wiederholte er. «Was heißt das? Wer sollte dich daran hindern?»

«Du nicht, das weiß ich», erwiderte ich.

«Und da hast du, wahrhaftig, recht!» rief er. «Na, du – wie heißt du eigentlich, Maat?»

«Jim.»

«Jim, Jim», wiederholte er sichtlich erfreut. «Na, Jim, ich hab ein Leben geführt, so wüst, daß du dich schämen würdest, davon zu hören. Würdest du, zum Beispiel, glauben, wenn du mich anschaust, daß ich eine fromme Mutter gehabt hab?»

«Warum nicht?» erwiderte ich.

«Ja ja, sagte er, «und die hab ich gehabt – und wie fromm ist sie gewesen! Und ich war ein braver, frommer Junge und konnte meinen Katechismus so schnell herunterschnurren, daß man kein Wort vom andern unterschieden hat. Und das ist aus mir geworden, Jim! Mit Pennywerfen auf Grabsteinen hat's angefangen, jawohl, das war das erste, aber dabei ist's nicht geblieben. Und das hat meine Mutter mir auch gesagt, und alles hat sie prophezeit, jawohl, das hat sie, die fromme Frau. Aber die Vorsehung war's, die hat mich hierher geführt. Hier, auf dieser einsamen Insel, hab ich mir das alles zurechtgelegt, und jetzt bin ich wieder zurück bei der Frömmigkeit. Mich wirst du nicht dabei erwischen, daß ich auch nur einen Tropfen Rum trinke. Einen Fingerhut natürlich schon, auf dein Wohl, sobald ich Gelegenheit hab. Ich hab's mir zugeschworen, ich will ein braver Mensch sein, und meinen Weg dazu seh ich auch. Und, Jim, er sah sich um und senkte die Stimme zu einem Flüstern, «ich bin nämlich reich! Jetzt war ich überzeugt davon, daß der arme Teufel in seiner Einsamkeit übergeschnappt war, und diesen Eindruck mußte ich wohl auch auf meinem Gesicht merken gelassen haben, denn er wiederholte seine Erklärung mit größtem Eifer.

«Reich! Reich! sag ich dir! Und noch was will ich dir sagen. Ich werde einen Mann aus dir machen, Jim. Ah, Jim, du wirst die Sterne dafür segnen, daß du der erste bist, der mich gefunden hat.»

Und nun senkte sich plötzlich ein dunkler Schatten über seine Züge, sein Griff um meine Hand verstärkte sich, und er hob drohend den Zeigefinger vor meine Augen.

«Sag mir die Wahrheit, Jim – das ist doch nicht Flints Schiff?» fragte er.

Da hatte ich einen glücklichen Einfall. Es kam mir in den Sinn, daß ich einen Verbündeten gefunden hatte, und so erwiderte ich sogleich:

«Es ist nicht Flints Schiff, und Flint ist tot; aber da du mich doch fragst, will ich dir die Wahrheit sagen – es sind ein paar von Flints Leuten auf dem Schiff, und das ist das Unglück für uns andern.»

«Nicht auch ein Mann – mit einem – Bein?» keuchte er.

«Silver?» fragte ich.

«Ja ja, Silver», rief er. «So hat er geheißen.»

«Er ist der Koch; und der Rädelsführer dazu.»

Noch immer hielt er mich beim Gelenk fest, und jetzt preßte er es mit schmerzhaftem Druck.

«Wenn es der lange John ist, der dich geschickt hat», sagte er, «dann bin ich ein toter Mann, das weiß ich. Aber was wird aus dir? Was glaubst du?»

Da faßte ich einen raschen Entschluß, und statt einer Antwort erzählte ich ihm die ganze Geschichte unserer Reise und machte ihm auch klar, in welcher Patsche wir uns befanden. Mit größtem Interesse hörte er mir zu, und als ich fertig war, streichelte er mir den Kopf.

«Du bist ein guter Junge, Jim, sagte er, «und jetzt seid ihr alle in ein Gedränge gekommen, was? Na, ihr braucht nur Ben Gunn zu vertrauen – Ben Gunn wird's schon schaffen, er ist der rechte Mann dazu. Glaubst du, daß dein Squire sich freigebig zeigen wird, wenn ich ihm helfe? Wenn er doch in der Patsche sitzt, wie du sagst?»

Ich versicherte ihm, daß der Squire der großzügigste Mann auf Erden sei.

«Ja ja, aber verstehst du», erwiderte Ben Gunn. «Ich meine damit nicht, daß er mir ein Tor zu hüten geben soll und mich als Lakai anziehen und so was; das ist's nicht, woran mir gelegen wäre, Jim. Ich meine, glaubst du, er würde, mir, sagen wir mal, tausend Pfund von dem Geld zu geben, das jetzt so zu sagen wie geborgen ist?»

«Alle sollten zu ihren Anteil kriegen», erwiderte ich.

«Ich bin überzeugt, daß er's täte», sagte ich.

«Und die Rückfahrt in die Heimat dazu?» fügte er mit schlauem Zwinkern hinzu.

42

hören konnten; und was das Klima anlangte, war der Doktor bereit, seine Perücke darauf zu verwetten, daß wir, auf dem Moorland gelagert und ohne Medikamente, keine Woche überstehn würden, ohne daß die Hälfte auf dem Rücken lag.

«Und so», setzte er hinzu, «wenn wir nicht vorher alle erschossen worden sind, werden sie froh sein, mit dem Schoner das Weite zu suchen. Es ist immerhin ein Schiff, und vermutlich können sie damit auch wieder Freibeuterei betreiben.»

«Das erste Schiff, das ich je verloren habe», sagte Kapitän Smollett.

Wie ihr euch wohl vorstellen könnt, war ich todmüde; und als ich endlich, nach langem Hin- und Herwälzen, einschlafen konnte, schlief ich wie ein Stück Holz.

Die übrigen waren schon lange wach, hatten bereits gefrühstückt und den Holzvorrat ungefähr um die Hälfte vergrößert, als ich durch Geräusch und lautes Reden geweckt wurde.

«Parlamentärsflagge», hörte ich einen sagen; und gleich darauf einen Schrei der Überraschung: «Silver selber!»

Daraufhin sprang ich auf, rieb mir die Augen und lief zu einer Schießscharte an der Wand.

SILVERS BOTSCHAFT

Da standen tatsächlich zwei Männer vor der Palisade, und einer von ihnen winkte mit einem weißen Tuch; der andere, kein geringerer als Silver höchstselbst, stand friedlich daneben.

Es war noch sehr früh am Morgen, und zwar war es der kälteste Morgen, an den ich mich erinnern konnte, seit ich England verlassen hatte; die Kälte durchschauerte mich bis ins Mark. Der Himmel über uns war hell und wolkenlos, und die Wipfel der Bäume schimmerten rosig in der Sonne. Doch wo Silver mit seinem Spießgesellen stand, lag alles noch im Schatten, und sie wateten knietief in dem weißlichen Bodennebel, der in der Nacht aus dem Moor aufgestiegen war. Kälte und Nebel wußten, zusammengenommen, nichts Gutes vom Klima der Insel zu berichten. Es war offenbar ein feuchter, fieberbrütender, ungesunder Erdenfleck.

«Bleibt im Haus, ihr Männer», ordnete der Kapitän an. «Zehn zu eins, daß dahinter etwas steckt.»

Dann rief er den Freibeuter an.

«Wer da! Stehnbleiben, sonst schießen wir.»

«Parlamentärsflagge!» schrie Silver.

Der Kapitän war auf der Veranda vor der Türe, hielt sich aber vorsichtig in Deckung für den Fall, daß ein Schuß aus dem Hinterhalt geplant war. Er wandte sich um und sagte zu uns:

«Der Doktor mit seiner Wache auf den Posten! Dr. Livesey, Sie gehen an die Nordseite, wenn ich bitten darf, Jim an die Ostseite, Gray nach Westen. Die andere Wache soll sämtliche Musketen laden. Vorwärts, Leute, und gebt gut acht!»

Dann wandte er sich wieder den Meuterern zu.

«Und was wollt ihr mit eurer Parlamentärsflagge?» rief er.

Diesmal war es der andere Mann, der antwortete.

«Käpt'n Silver will an Bord kommen, Sir, und die Sache ins reine bringen.»

«Käpt'n Silver? Kenne ich nicht. Wer ist das?» rief der Kapitän. Und wir hörten wie er zu sich selber halblaut sagte «Gleich Käpt'n? Der ist aber schnell avanciert!»

Jetzt antwortete der lange John selber.

«Ich, Sir. Die armen Burschen haben mich zum Käpt'n gewählt, nachdem Ihr desertiert wart, Sir –», auf das Wort «desertiert» legte er besonderen Nachdruck. «Wir sind bereit, uns zu fügen, wenn wir zu einer Einigung kommen können, und damit

52

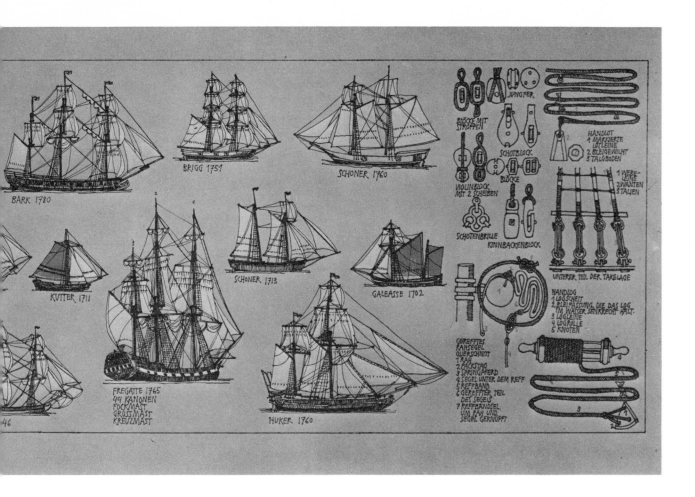

1964. *Die Schatzinsel* by Robert Louis Stevenson, illustrated and designed by Eleonore Schmid. Published by Rene Simmen, Zürich. Printed and reproduced by Käser Press and Graphischen Anstalt Freytag AG, Zürich. $10\frac{3}{4}'' \times 9\frac{3}{16}''$. Drawn-on cover of unbleached cardboard printed in black and orange. Cover printed in black and red. Plate printed on buff laid paper in black, white and orange. Text pages.

'Fünfzehn Mann auf des Totenmanns Kiste,
Jo-ho-ho und die Pulle Voll Rum
Teufel und Trunk bracht' die andern zur Ruhe
Jo-ho-ho und die Pulle voll Rum.'

In 1964, completely new ground was broken by a Swiss edition of Stevenson's book. This was *Die Schatzinsel*, published by Rene Simmen and illustrated and designed by Eleonore Schmid. This is a large square book, with drawn-on covers. The text is set in three columns and the illustrations are limited to vignetted line drawings of all the objects and the fauna that the reader might have encountered if he had shipped aboard the *Hispaniola*. Pistols, cutlasses, a compass and a sextant, turtles and fish, water kegs and meat casks, a sea-lion and a starfish are dotted through the pages. There are also a number of fold-out plates printed in black, white and orange on a buff laid paper. Among these are detailed plans of the *Hispaniola*, the sail plans of contemporary ships, and diagrams of a sailing vessel showing her running, reaching and sailing full and bye. There are also charts of Treasure Island and of the Caribbean, and the various flags used by such pirates of the Spanish Main as Bonnet, Rackham and Tew. There is only one figure drawing in the whole book and that is to show the costume of a seaman in 1750. This is an intriguing approach to illustration. It implies that Stevenson's imagery is quite sufficient and that the purpose of the illustration is to give substance and detail to the props that are the background to the story. The illustrations are completely factual, if freely drawn, renderings from contemporary source material. This almost scientific approach to illustration has, of course, been done before, by such artists as Gordon Macfie with his ship drawings for the Swedish publishers Tre Tryckare or William Fenton with his renderings of locomotives for Hugh Evelyn. The scope is considerable.

215

The graphic designer's book

A new approach to the illustration of books, both in the United States and in England, has been brought about since the 1939–45 war by a number of graphic designers. Exasperated or plain bored by advertising graphics, they have turned their not inconsiderable talents to book production. Their books almost invariably have been for children, and as often as not they have written them themselves. As graphic designers, they have ranged from typographers to advertising art directors. Some, such as Ben Shahn and André François, have limited their graphic work to illustration or lettering. Shahn worked for many years as a litho-artist and François for advertising. And some (highly successful commercial designers on both sides of the Atlantic) have gone right back to base, to the hand press. Applying Morris's doctrine of the value of hand work, they have derived great benefit from the actual printing process, using it as a medium for experiment. Lively effects of overprinting are discovered in this way which are quite beyond the imagination of any artist whose techniques are limited to the drawing board and pots of paint.

Joseph Low, widely known as a designer of advertising work, record sleeves and book jackets, works in this manner and prints on a Colt's Armory Press

1953. *Mother Goose Riddle Rhymes* by Joseph and Ruth Low. Published by Harcourt Brace and Co., New York. Printed in the U.S.A. 8⅜" × 7". Cover design, title-page and text spread.

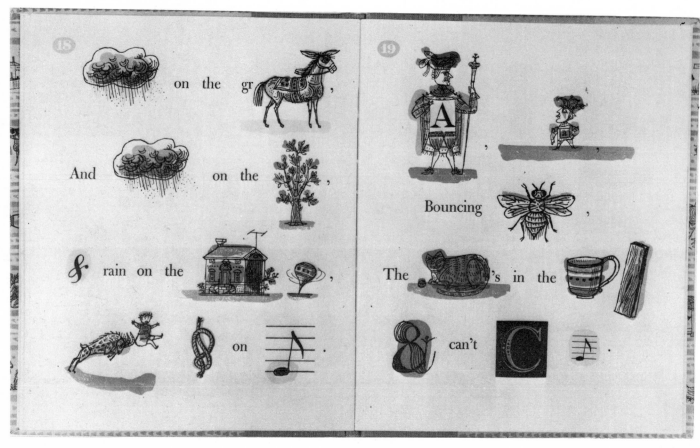

1942. *The Little Red Engine gets a Name* by
Diana Ross. Illustrated by Lewitt-Him. Published
by Faber and Faber Ltd, London. Printed by the
Baynard Press, London. 7¼" × 9¾". Illustration.

at his Eden Hill Press at Newton, Connecticut. He uses the press as a creative
tool, experimenting with type and wood or linocuts. His *Mother Goose Riddle
Rhymes*, a colourful book printed throughout in five colours, was published
in 1953 by Harcourt, Brace and Co. New York. It was preceded by his
Rainbow Dictionary, issued in 1947 by World Publishing with over 1,000
drawings in colour.

George Him was a formidable, successful and endearing figure in the English
graphic scene, with a wealth of graphic experience, who for some years
worked in graphic partnership with Jan Lewitt. They came from Poland to
settle in England in 1937, when their partnership was four years old, and the
work of Lewitt-Him cheered us through the days of the war. In 1942 they
turned from advertising to the production of a children's book, *The Little Red
Engine Gets a Name*, which was published in London by Faber and Faber.
The combination of such diverse personalities was most successful; *The
Little Red Engine* was a delicious book, naïve yet highly sophisticated. The
infusion of such continental talent provided a much needed shot-in-the-arm
to the design of English children's books. George Him, working on his own,
has illustrated some attractive children's books about 'Alexander the Giant',
written by Frank Herrmann. He has also illustrated *Two Plays for Puritans* and
Zuleika Dobson, both for the Limited Editions Club.

O Orang-utan

Sie maß die Beine des Reihers . . .

1960. *Stück für Stück* written and illustrated by Leo Lionni. German translation by James Krüss. Typography by Wolfgang Tiessen. Published by Friedrich Middelhauve Verlag, Cologne and Opladen. 11″ × 9¼″. Illustration spread.

Opposite:
1963. *Eulenglück* written and illustrated by Celestino Piatti. Published by Artemis Verlags-Aktiengesellschaft, Zürich. Printed in Switzerland by Sigg-Set, Sigg Söhne. 8¼″ × 11⅝″. Illustration.

1965. *Celestino Piatti's A.B.C.* Published by Artemis Verlag, Zürich and Ernest Benn Ltd, London. Printed in Switzerland. 8″ × 11½″. Illustration.

1956. *Les Larmes de Crocodile* written and illustrated by André François. Published by Robert Delpire, Paris. Printed by l'Imprimerie Savernoise. 3⁵⁄₁₆″ × 10″. Illustration spread.

The graphic designers whose work appears here have certainly brought fresh life to children's books over the last few years. The common factor running through all their books is the author-artist's reluctance to use more words than are absolutely needful; no doubt a natural enough reaction for graphic designers whose entire work is made up of finding new methods of visual communication. Though many of these graphic designers have been American, one of the most attractive books of recent years has come from an Italian-Swiss, Celestino Piatti, the author of *The Happy Owls.* Piatti has a brilliant decorative colour sense. He is one of the few living graphic designers whose work has the essential quality of communication, yet is intrinsically decorative as well. Another is the Amsterdam-born American, Leo Lionni, who is a painter, a graphic designer and an advertising man. The designs for *Stück für Stück* are cut from tissue-paper; the total effect is one of a dreamy softness, with moments of incisive colour, as in the sharp mustard yellow beak of the heron on this page. André François's *Les Larmes de Crocodile* completes the trilogy of animal books on this spread. François, one of the great advertising artists of this century, here turns his talents to a little book (3¼ in. by 10½ in.) suitable for a child's Christmas stocking.

faut bien sûr trouver la bonne taille

Pas trop long, pas trop court, sinon le crocodile va

llotter dans la LONGUE CAISSE A CROCODILE;

OUNCE

DiCE

TRiCE

BY ALASTAIR REID
DRAWINGS BY BEN SHAHN

1958. *Ounce, Dice, Trice* by Alastair Reid
illustrated by Ben Shahn. Published by Atlantic
Little, Brown and Co., Boston and Toronto.
Printed in the U.S.A. 10″ × 7⅜″. Jacket design.

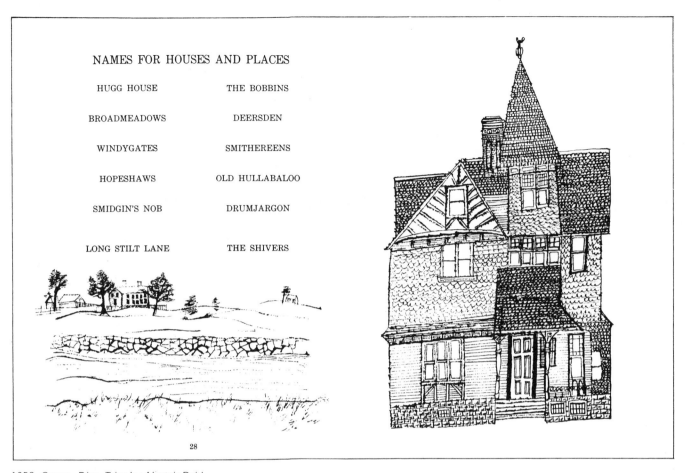

NAMES FOR HOUSES AND PLACES

HUGG HOUSE	THE BOBBINS
BROADMEADOWS	DEERSDEN
WINDYGATES	SMITHEREENS
HOPESHAWS	OLD HULLABALOO
SMIDGIN'S NOB	DRUMJARGON
LONG STILT LANE	THE SHIVERS

28

1958. *Ounce, Dice, Trice* by Alastair Reid,
illustrated by Ben Shahn. Text spread.

Ben Shahn's stature as an artist and as a compassionate commentator on the human scene needs no boost from me. His children's books however have received scant notice, at least in this country, though the same qualities of humour, satire, gentleness and elegance are evident in all his illustrations for *Ounce Dice Trice* by Alastair Reid, published in Boston in 1958. He has interpreted Alastair Reid's 'treasure trove of sounds and images' in a delicious manner. The drawings of houses are particularly effective; he breathes life into bricks and mortar, clapboard and shingle. In *A Partridge in a Pear Tree*, published in 1951 by the Museum of Modern Art in New York, there is additional evidence of his completeness as a graphic artist, for accompanying the archaic drawings is the most beautifully lettered text. For nearly a quarter of a century, from 1913 to 1930, Shahn supported himself mainly by his work as a trade lithographer; and this vigorous discipline, instead of dulling his qualities as an artist, has given his work an unparalleled assurance, for here is an artist who is master of his craft. Ben Shahn's *Love and Joy about Letters* is one of the most handsome books of the last few decades. It is a book for all ages with page after page of his incomparable calligraphy.

WHO iS GOD?*WELL iT iS AN iNViSiBLE
PERSON AND HE LiVES UP iN HEAVEN*
i GUESS UP iN OUTER SPACE*HE
MADE THE EARTH AND THE HEAVEN &
THE STARS AND THE SUN AND THE
PEOPLE*HE MADE LiGHT HE MADE DAY
HE MADE NiGHT*HE HAS SUCH POWER-
FUL EYES HE DOESN'T HAVE MiLLiONS
AND THOUSANDS AND BiLLiONS AND HE
CAN STiLL SEE US WHEN WE'RE BAD*
HE STARTED ALL THE PLANTS GROWiNG*TO
ME i THiNK OF HiM WHO MAKES FLOWERS
& GREEN GRASS & THE BLUE SKY &
THE YELLOW SUN*GOD iS EVERYWHERE
& i DON'T KNOW HOW HE COULD DO iT

35

1963. *Love and Joy about Letters* by Ben Shahn
(English edition 1964). Published by Cory,
Adams and Mackay. Printed by Camera
Publishers, C. J. Bucher Ltd, Lucerne. 10″ × 13⅜″.
Text and illustration spread.

1951. *A Partridge in a Pear Tree* by Ben Shahn.
Published by Doubleday and Co. Inc., New York.
Printed by the Crafton Graphic Co., for the
Museum of Modern Art. 7¼″ × 8½″. Text spread.

ON THE SECOND DAY OF CHRIST-
MAS MY TRUE LOVE GAVE TO ME
TWO TURTLE DOVES AND A PARTRIDGE
                              iN
                              A
                           PEAR
                           TREE

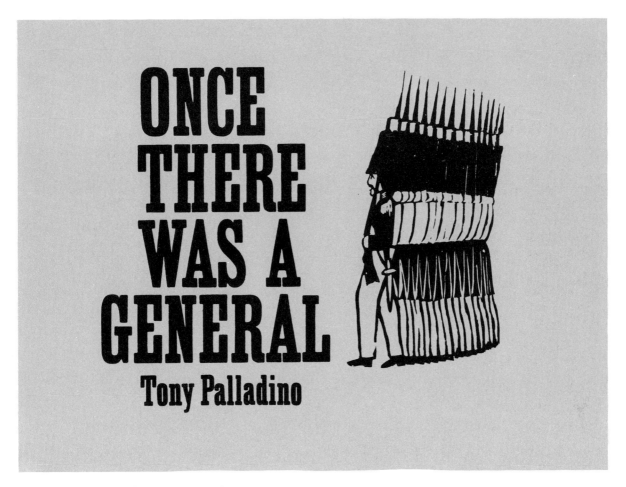

1958. *Once there was a General* written and
illustrated by Tony Palladino. Published by
Franklin Watts. New York. Printed in the U.S.A.
$4\frac{1}{2}'' \times 5\frac{3}{4}''$. Text spread and cover.

The graphic designer's book

Tony Palladino's little book of woodcuts tells a moral tale about a general
whose rise to glory came to nothing but a field of daisies because he had no
wars! Tony Palladino is an Eastside New Yorker who practises as a designer
and illustrator. *The General* began as a single woodcut but slowly developed
into a complete and eminently satisfying story.

Then the general had many more cannons,

many more horses,

a lion. Then, I could trade my zoo for

a tall tower.
(I might keep
one rocking
horse.) Then,
in time, I
could trade
my tall tower
for

1961. *A Balloon for a Blunderbuss* by Bob Gill
and Alastair Reid. Published by Harper and
Brothers, New York. Printed in the U.S.A.
10½″ × 8″. Text spread.

A Balloon for a Blunderbuss is another book by Alastair Reid, this time in
co-operation with Bob Gill, an American graphic designer of great talent who
works mostly in London.
Blind Mice and other Numbers is both written and illustrated with extreme
economy by another talented American designer, Ivan Chermayeff. It is so
sophisticated, that I imagine it may have more appeal to designers than to
their children.

1961. *Blind Mice and other Numbers* designed
and illustrated by Ivan Chermayeff. Published by
Colorcraft, New York. Printed in the U.S.A.
10¾″ × 8⅛″. Text spread.

Up
until
the
eleventh
hour
on the
Twelfth
Night
a
baker's
dozen
days
before
Christmas.

40ty.   end.

Borka was soon
very friendly with
the Captain, Fred
and of course with
Fowler. She coiled
pieces of rope with
her beak, picked up
crumbs from the
floor and helped in
any way she
could. In return
she was
given plenty
of good
food.

1963. *Borka, The Adventures of a Goose with no Feathers* written and illustrated by John Burningham. Published by Jonathan Cape. Printed by L. van Leer and Co., Amsterdam. 10½″ × 8⅜″. Text spread.

John Burningham's *Borka*, the first of a series of children's books by this English artist, had an immediate success. Burningham's books are delightful conceptions brilliantly carried out.

Ann and Paul Rand's *Sparkle and Spin* is another book about words. Paul Rand, who is a leading American artist-designer, here illustrates his wife's words with humour and beauty. The spread here from *Sparkle and Spin* brings this survey of designer-illustrators to a fitting close.

1957. *Sparkle and Spin* by Ann and Paul Rand. Published by Harcourt Brace and Co., New York. Printed in the U.S.A. 10″ × 8¼″. Text spread.

Words are "Yes I will"
and "No I won't,"
but they are polite too
like please and thank you.

1960 *The Fatal Lozenge* written and illustrated by Edward Gorey. Published by Astor, Honor Inc., New York and Ernest Benn, Tonbridge. 6" × 5" page size.
Illustration: 'The Proctor buys the pupil ices
And hopes the boy will not resist
When he attempts to practices vices
Few people even know exist'.

The Proctor *buys a pupil ices,*

And hopes the boy will not resist

When he attempts to practise vices

Few people even know exist.

1964 *The Sinking Spell* written and illustrated by Edward Gorey. Published by Ivan Obolensky Inc., New York and Ernest Benn, Tonbridge. 6" × 5" page size.
Illustration: 'It's gone beneath the cellar floor:
We shall not see it any more'.

1973 *The Juniper Tree and Other Tales from Grimm* translated by Lore Segal and Randall Jarrell. Pictures by Maurice Sendak. Designed by Altha Tehon and Maurice Sendak. Translations copyright © 1973 by Lore Segal. Pictures copyright © 1973 by Maurice Sendak. Reprinted by permission of Farrar, Straus and Giroux, Inc. New York, and the Bodley Head, London. 6¾″ × 5¼″ page size. Illustrations: 'The Twelve Huntsmen' and 'The Three Feathers'.

Since the first edition of this book appeared old reputations have been confirmed and new reputations have been made in the field of children's books. As far as line illustrations go, I think the most significant artists have been Edward Gorey and Maurice Sendak, the most witty Quentin Blake and the most disturbing Ralph Steadman.

Edward Gorey was born in Chicago and graduated at Harvard. He has illustrated and published a number of little books that have as much appeal for adults as they have for children. Many of these have been gathered together and published in the U.S.A. by Putnam under the titles of *Amphigorey* and *Amphigorey Too*. The titles of such fantasies as *The Fatal Lozenge, The Curious Sofa, The Sinking Spell* or *The Pious Infant* (all published in the U.K. by Ernest Benn also) give some indication of this artist's taste for Victorian and *fin de siècle* subjects. Gorey has also illustrated books for other writers. A happy collaboration was with Polly Redford for *The Christmas Bower*, an enchanting book. Gorey's is certainly an original talent. His illustrations have an extra dimension. They give one the feeling that his characters are waiting for something awful to happen.

Maurice Sendak was born in Brooklyn of Polish descent. He has written and illustrated several books for children. His *Where the Wild Things Are* won the Caldecott Medal for Children's Books in 1964. It was published by Harper and Row in America and by the Bodley Head in Great Britain, later appearing as a Puffin Book and going through many editions. Sendak's 'Wild Things' are the most benign-looking monsters, at least to adult eyes. Maurice Sendak started thinking about illustrating Grimm's *Fairy Tales* before this book was completed, but it was not until 1972 that he began work on the actual illustrations. He forsook colour for pen drawing and with an intricate hatchwork of fine lines built up these tonal illustrations. A feature of his drawings is the stockiness of his figures and their large heads. (The head-to-body ratio is about 4.5:1.) The convention works and these are a haunting set of illustrations. The book was called *The Juniper Tree* and was impeccably designed by Altha Tehon and Sendak himself and published in two volumes in a slipcase.

1982 *Roald Dahl's Revolting Rhymes* illustrated by Quentin Blake. Published by Jonathan Cape, London. 10¾″ × 8½″ page size. Illustrations: 'Cinderella' and 'Snow White and the Seven Dwarfs'.

Quentin Blake's deceptively free style conceals a very real talent. The drawings for Roald Dahl's *Revolting Rhymes* look as if they have been knocked off in a few moments. In fact they are the result of much thought. Quentin Blake is a Master of Arts and is the Head of the Department of Illustration at the Royal College of Art. He has also illustrated five other books by Roald Dahl – *The Enormous Crocodile, The Twits, George's Marvellous Medicine, The BFG* and *The Witches.*

Ralph Steadman's fame could rest on his work as a satirical cartoonist in *Private Eye, Punch* and *The Daily Telegraph.* His first successful venture into book illustration was for *The Young Visiters* by Daisy Ashford. In 1967 he illustrated an *Alice in Wonderland* for Dennis Dobson. These drawings are perhaps the most successful attempt to illustrate this book since Sir John Tenniel illustrated the original edition, with the possible exception of Mervyn Peake's. *Cherrywood Cannon,* a doom-laden tale by Steadman's Yugoslavian friend Dimitri Sidjanski, is revealed in all its apocalyptic horror by his brilliant drawings.

Unfortunately there is no space here to show the drawings of a number of contemporary artists who have done noteworthy work for children over the

228

1978 *Cherrywood Cannon* written and
illustrated by Ralph Steadman, based on a story
told to him by Dimitri Sidjanski. Published by
Paddington Press Ltd., New York and London.
12" × 9". Illustration: 'Stuffed the cannon full of
shot'.

last dozen years: illustrators such as Nicola Bayley, who illustrated *The Tiger Voyage* by Richard Adams with richly coloured studies of Victorian interiors, or Jill Barklem, a true successor to Beatrix Potter, with her detailed and wonderfully observed studies of the mice of *Brambly Hedge,* or Elisa Trimby whose book *Mr Plum's Paradise* has the kind of precise detail that children love, or Nancy Ekholm Burkert whose illustrations to an edition of *Snow White and the Seven Dwarfs* owe nothing to Disney. In her pictures Miss Burkert has created a magical version of the late Middle Ages that any child would want to return to again and again.

Monochrome reproduction could do little justice to Errol le Cain's richly coloured illustrations to Perrault's *Cinderella* or to Tomie de Paola's coloured pictures. A delightful book by de Paola is *The Clown of God* which he based on Anatole France's legend of the little juggler and the miracle with which he is involved. Trained as a painter, once a member of a religious order and now living in New Hampshire, Tomie de Paola has drawn on Renaissance sources for his illustrations to this touching little tale. This book reinforces my belief that no matter how beautiful the illustrations may be, unless there is a good story they have little appeal for children.

G

stands for Gnu, whose weapons of Defence
Are long, sharp, curling Horns, and Common-sense.
To these he adds a Name so short and strong,

That even Hardy Boers pronounce it wrong.

20

1899. *A Moral Alphabet* by H. Belloc with illustrations by B.T.B. Published by Edward Arnold, London. $8\frac{1}{4}" \times 6\frac{1}{2}"$. Cover and illustration.

1930. *New Cautionary Tales* by H. Belloc, with illustrations by Nicolas Bentley. Published by Duckworth, London and printed by the Camelot Press Southampton. $8\frac{3}{8}" \times 6\frac{5}{8}"$. Doublespread.

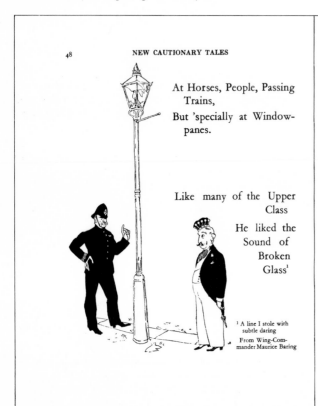

48   NEW CAUTIONARY TALES

At Horses, People, Passing
Trains,
But 'specially at Window-
panes.

Like many of the Upper
Class

He liked the
Sound of
Broken
Glass[1]

[1] A line I stole with subtle daring
From Wing-Commander Maurice Baring

FOR CHILDREN   49

It bucked him up and made him gay:
It was his favourite form of Play.
But the Amusement cost him dear,
My children, as you now shall hear.

JOHN VAVASSOUR DE QUENTIN had
An uncle, who adored the lad:

And often chuckled; "Wait until
You see what's left you in my will!"

D

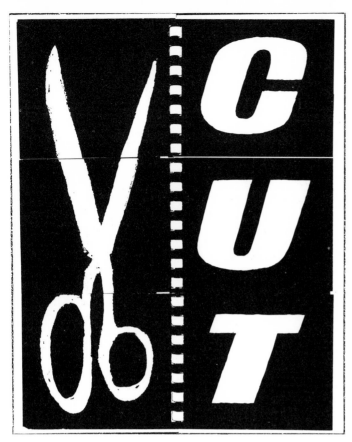

1962. *A to Z* by Bob Gill. Published by Little, Brown and Co., Boston and Toronto. Printed in the U.S.A. $12\frac{1}{4}'' \times 5''$. Text and picture spreads. The book is cut horizontally into three sections.

The sugared pill

Children, understandably enough, have always regarded disguised attempts at instruction with a very proper horror. For a book to be successful in this way calls for considerable ingenuity on the part of the author. Alphabet books, which precede reading books, have provided an outlet for many illustrators, from Bewick to Walter Crane or B.T.B. to Celestino Piatti; Hilaire Belloc's *A Moral Alphabet* (1899) with illustrations by B.T.B. (Lord Basil Blackwood) is an acidulated plum rather than a sugared pill. The mood is set with:

> 'A stands for Archibald who told no lies,
> And got this lovely volume as a prize.'

and concludes with the searching moral:

> 'Idolatry, as you are well aware
> Is highly reprehensible. But there,
> We needn't bother, – when we get to Z
> Our interest in the alphabet is dead.'

The drawings are in open line and mark a kind of half-way stage between Edward Lear and Nicolas Bentley, who illustrated Hilaire Belloc's *New Cautionary Tales.*

The American graphic designer Bob Gill's *A to Z* (1962) uses the old parlour-game 'Heads, Bodies and Legs' technique for his alphabet book. The pages are cut horizontally into three and the intelligent infant is meant to sort out matching colours and words to make up the complete double spread of illustration and word. The book is Plastoic bound so lies flat when open.

231

1930. *1066 and all that* by W. C. Sellar and
R. J. Yeatman, illustrated by John Reynolds.
Published by Methuen and Co. Ltd, London.
Printed by the Mayflower Press, Plymouth.
$7\frac{1}{2}'' \times 4\frac{7}{8}''$. Illustration

In 1930 Walter Carruthers Sellar and Robert Julian Yeatman launched, with
the help of their publishers Methuen & Company, *1066 and all that, A
Memorable History of England*, on to an unsuspecting world. Sellar was a
Charterhouse master, Yeatman a successful advertising copy writer. They
co-opted John Reynolds, son of Frank Reynolds, art editor of *Punch*, to
illustrate their lampoon. The result of their collaboration was quite deadly!
English history after this witty send-up would never be quite the same again.
1066 and all that is more of a poisoned than a sugared pill.

Apart from *1066 and all that*, there have been many attempts to make history
more palatable for the young. The classic example of successfully sugaring a
pill was the late Hendrik Willem van Loon, a Dutch-American historian. Van
Loon had emigrated to the U.S.A. when still a young man. Ever afterwards
he lived in a nostalgic dream of past golden ages, and had an expatriate's
longing for the little fishing port of Veere on the island Walcheren where he
had once lived. Van Loon was a brilliant raconteur and once he had applied
this gift to his writing, he achieved an enormous public. His books bubbled
with endless anecdotes and often, I suspect, much inaccurate information.
Writing was not enough to contain this ebullient giant of a Dutchman, so he
decorated his books with very vital little drawings in colour and black and
white. He was anything but a skilled draftsman and his range of colours was
limited to primaries and a particularly virulent green. These colours came out
of a minute paint box, about two inches long, which he clipped to his thumb.[7]
His books have whetted the appetites of countless children and led them into
wanting to study more solid fare. The illustrations are an essential part of these
racy accounts of history and somehow, by the very fact that they come from
the author's hand, carry more authority than would the work of a separate,
even if more talented illustrator.

Enid LaMonte Meadowcroft's *Benjamin Franklin* shows a rather less frivolous
approach to the teaching of history. The illustrator of this handsome book is
Donald McKay, who a decade earlier had provided the drawings for the
Random House edition of *The Adventures of Tom Sawyer* (see page 131).
McKay's lively drawings are both pleasant and informative.

[7] Van Loon carried this little colour box everywhere. I remember in 1943 lunching with him at
the St Regis Hotel in New York. Something
occurred to him, he pulled his little box out of
his pocket, produced a minute brush, dipped it
into his glass of Chablis and painted a little scene
on the back of the menu.

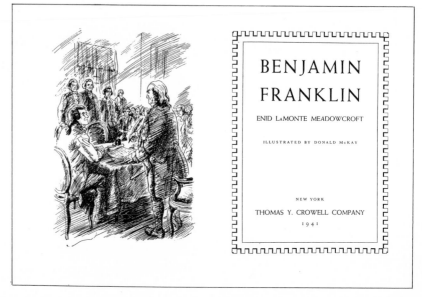

1941. *Benjamin Franklin* by Enid LaMonte
Meadowcroft illustrated by Donald McKay.
Published by Thomas Y. Crowell Co., New York.
$8\frac{3}{4}'' \times 6\frac{1}{2}''$. Frontispiece and title-page.

VAN LOON'S
LIVES

Being a true and faithful account
of a number of highly interesting meetings
with certain historical personages, from
Confucius and Plato to Voltaire
and Thomas Jefferson, about whom
we had always felt a great deal of
curiosity and who came to us
as our dinner guests in a bygone year.
Written and illustrated by

Hendrik Willem van Loon

1942
SIMON AND SCHUSTER
NEW YORK

1942. *Van Loon's Lives* by Hendrik Willem van
Loon with illustrations by the author. Published
by Simon and Schuster, New York. Printed in
the U.S.A. 8$\frac{3}{8}$" × 5$\frac{3}{4}$". Title-page spread and two
illustrations.

The Hospice of St. Bernard amidst the endless snows of winter.

They were playing Mozart's KLEINE NACHTMUSIK.

1947. *The Arabs* by R. B. Sergeant, illustrated by
Edward Bawden. A Puffin Picture Book,
published by Penguin Books Ltd, Middlesex.
Printed by the Curwen Press Ltd, Plaistow.
7" × 8⅝". Illustration spreads.

'Puffin Picture Books' have been one of the most successful attempts at
producing cheap, popular educational books. The first of this lengthy series
of landscape shaped picture books came out in 1940, with the painfully
appropriate title of *War on Land*. Puffin Picture Books were published by
Penguin Books Limited, edited by Noel Carrington, and originally were printed
by W. S. Cowell Limited. These war time productions were an economical
printing of thirty-two pages, printed by offset in full colour on one side of the
sheet and black on the verso. The illustrations of the first Puffins were all
drawn direct to plate by such illustrators as James Holland, James Gardner
and S. R. Badmin. Later volumes included Richard Chopping's *Butterflies in
Britain* (Chopping is the artist who drew most of Ian Fleming's book jackets
for the James Bond stories); R. B. Talbot Kelly's *Paper Birds* and Paxton
Chadwick's *Wild Flowers*.

The format of the Puffin Picture Books was based on the kind of mass
produced illustrated children's books that were being produced in the Soviet
Union. They are also, of course, comparable to such French books as the
Flammarion Père Castor books and to the two Legrand publications, *Bolivar*

234

1964. *The Charge of the Light Brigade* by
Alfred Lord Tennyson, illustrated by Alice and
Martin Provensen. Published by the Golden
Press Inc, New York and Paul Hamlyn Ltd,
London. Printed in the United States of America.
$7\frac{1}{2}'' \times 9\frac{3}{4}''$. Illustration spreads.

and *La Fayette*. After the war, Puffins were given stiff covers. One of the most
attractive post-war volumes was *The Arabs*, with Edward Bawden's illustrations. The subject clearly appealed to the artist as Bawden had spent some
time as an official war artist during the 1939–45 war in the Middle East. It
is a splendidly decorative book.

Alice and Martin Provensen are amongst the most fertile and successful of
contemporary illustrators. In 1964 the Golden Press in New York and Paul
Hamlyn in London published their illustrated edition of Alfred Lord Tennyson's
The Charge of the Light Brigade. This book, in a Puffin format, is one of the
prettiest and wittiest pieces of illustration to appear for a very long time. The
drawings are comparable to an early illumination or to a Mogul painting.
The Provensens' have caught (as their blurb-writer so rightly says) 'the
rigidity, heroism and nobility of the most dramatic and useless battle of the
Crimean War'. Beautiful though the book is, it is strangely moving as well.
Their last illustration succinctly sums up the whole sorry business with a
quote from General Bosquet: 'C'est magnifique, mais ce n'est pas la guerre.'

1941. *The Battle of Britain* by David Garnett and James Gardner. A Puffin Picture Book edited by Noel Carrington. Published by Penguin Books Limited, Harmondsworth, England and New York, U.S.A. Printed by W. S. Cowell Ltd, Ipswich. 7" × 8¾". Cover design.

1941. *Guerra Terrestre* by James Holland. A Puffin Picture Book edited by Noel Carrington. Published by Penguin Books Limited, Harmondsworth, England and New York, U.S.A. Printed by W. S. Cowell Ltd, Ipswich. 7" × 8¾". Cover design.

1946. *Trees in Britain* by S. R. Badmin. A Puffin Picture Book edited by Noel Carrington. Published by Penguin Books Limited, Harmondsworth, England and New York, U.S.A. Printed by W. S. Cowell Ltd, Ipswich. 7″ × 8¾″. Cover design.

1947. *Paper Birds* by R. B. Talbot Kelly. A Puffin Picture Book edited by Noel Carrington. Published by Penguin Books Limited, Harmondsworth, England and New York, U.S.A. Printed by W. S. Cowell Ltd, Ipswich. 7⅛″ × 8¾″. Cover design.

The Russian Churches

Russia had remained a Pagan country until the middle of the tenth century when its ruler, Prince Vladimir, determined to provide a more satisfactory religion for his people, investigated the religious practices of neighbouring countries, and made a study of the Hebrew, Greek, Roman and Mohammedan religions.

He despatched emissaries to consider each of these on the spot. The group that was sent to Constantinople, observing the ritual of the Greek Church reported so favourably, saying "they did not know whether they were on earth or in heaven," that Vladimir decided for the Greek Church and decreed that it be officially adopted throughout Russia. This decision accounts for the curiously Eastern appearance of the Russian Churches, such as S. Basil at Moscow, where the bulbous shapes terminating its octagonal features indicate Tartar origin and contact with the East.

30

S. Basil at Moscow.

1944. *Balbus* written and devised by Oliver Hill and Hans Tisdall. Published by Pleiades Books Ltd, London. Printed by McLagen and Cumming Ltd, London and Edinburgh. 10" × 8".

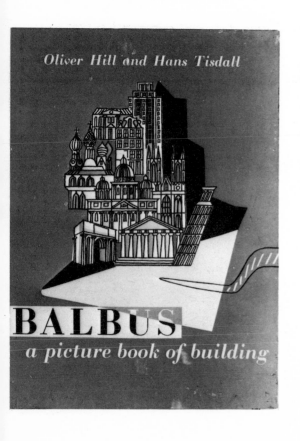

The world around us provides ample material for pictorial educational books. Only too often, the illustration and design of such books is very pedestrian. In 1940, Hans Tisdall, a German artist who had settled in England, collaborated with the architect Oliver Hill to produce a 'picture book of building', which they called *Balbus.* This was printed by the Edinburgh lithographers McLagan and Cumming. The illustrations are reproduced by chromo-lithography, with much use of mechanical stipple tints. This curious, old-fashioned technique is here used most effectively and the illustrations are brilliantly colourful.

Tisdall's was pioneer work. A book like *Geschichte der Schiffahrt,* published in Switzerland in 1962 by Éditions Rencontre and Erik Nitsche International, is now almost a commonplace. A visually articulated presentation and wide use of 'source' material for illustration are the basic ingredients for the modern popular educational books. The use of offset or gravure in place of letterpress has produced much more flexibility in the placing of half-tone or colour illustrations.

However effective 'source' material may be, original drawings are still needed. Nowadays there is a rather more scientific approach to the drafting of such subjects as architecture, furniture, ships, vehicles and locomotives. The English publisher Hugh Evelyn's 'coffee table' books of crisply drawn vintage motor cars are a manifestation of this attitude.

Zeilend door de Eeuwen (the Dutch edition of *Sailing Ships*) is an exquisite little book, originally published by Tre Tryckare, in Göteborg, Sweden. The drawings by Gordon Macfie are almost in the nature of a naval architect's elevation and sail plan. They are printed on a mottled khaki-coloured Ingres paper. The effect of an off-white printing for the sails, against the coloured, textured paper is both subtle and effective.

238

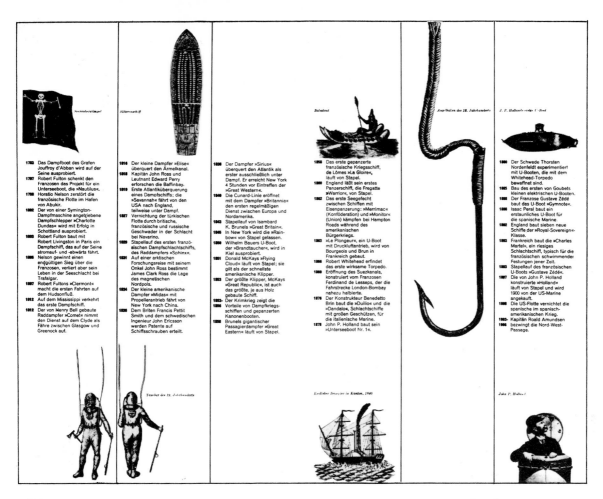

1962. *Geschichte der Schiffahrt* by Courtlandt Canby, translated by Elinor Lipper. Published by Erik Nitsche International. Printed by Heliogravure Centrale S.A., Lausanne. $10\frac{3}{8}'' \times 6\frac{1}{2}''$. Cover and spread.

1964. *Zeilend door de Eeuwen* by Sam Svensson illustrated by Gordon Macfie. Published by P. N. Kampen & Zoon, Amsterdam. $7\frac{1}{2}'' \times 7\frac{1}{2}''$. Illustration printed in black, white and yellow ochre on a tinted Ingres paper.

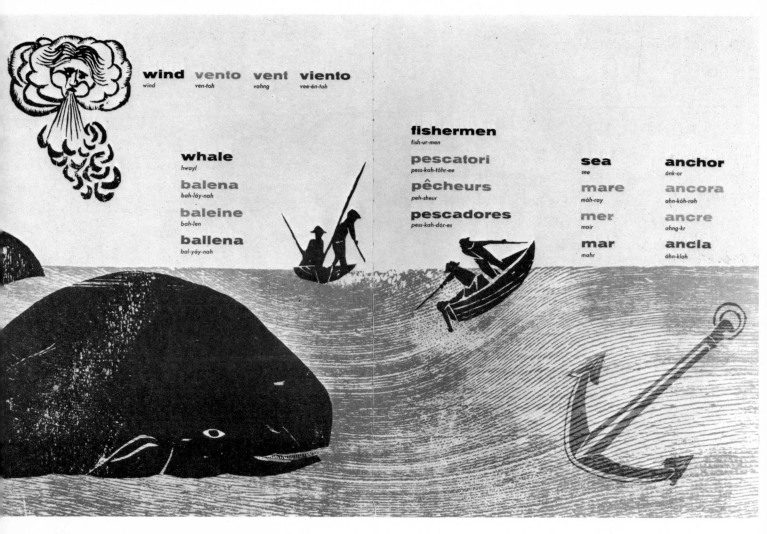

wind vento vent viento
wind *ven-toh* *vahng* *vee-én-toh*

whale
hwayl

balena
bah-láy-nah

baleine
bah-len

ballena
bal-yáy-nah

fishermen
fish-ur-men

pescatori
pess-kah-tóhr-ee

pêcheurs
peh-sheur

pescadores
pess-kah-dór-es

sea
see

mare
máh-ray

mer
mair

mar
mahr

anchor
ánk-or

ancora
ahn-kóh-rah

ancre
ahng-kr

ancla
áhn-klah

1955. *See and Say* written and illustrated by Antonio Frasconi. Published by Harcourt Brace and World Inc, New York. Printed in the U.S.A. $10\frac{3}{8}'' \times 8\frac{1}{4}''$. Spread.

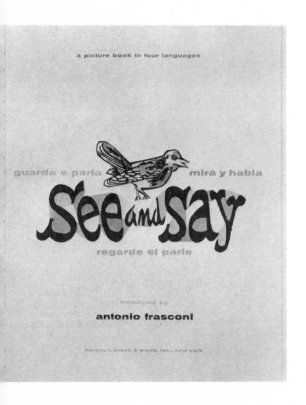

The publishers of school books have been slow to make use of good illustration and design, and by good, I mean illustration and design that do not merely decorate, but help to elucidate and point a text. A fine example of this is Antonio Frasconi's *See and Say*, which was published in 1955.

Frasconi wrote in this book, 'I was brought up in a family where more than one language was spoken . . . the idea that there are many nationalities speaking many languages is to me one of the most important for a child to understand.'

The book is illustrated with coloured woodcuts, the text is in four languages, each printed in a different colour, black for English, blue for Italian, red for French and green for Spanish. The result is one of the most appealing and colourful 'readers'.

Antonio Frasconi was born in Uruguay of Italian parentage and now lives in Connecticut.

1968 *Bauhaus*. Royal Academy of Arts
Exhibition Catalogue prepared by Wulf
Herzogengrath and designed by Herbert Bayer
and Peter Wehr. $8\frac{5}{8}'' \times 8\frac{3}{4}''$. Cover design by
Herbert Bayer.

It is not altogether inappropriate to end this educational section with the cover
of a catalogue commemorating one of the most influential educational estab-
lishments of this century. Fifty years after the Bauhaus was founded, Herbert
Bayer, one of the most distinguished students to come out of the school, was
one of the instigators of the Bauhaus Exhibition, which was sponsored by the
Federal Republic of Germany. The catalogue for the Royal Academy showing
of the exhibition in London was designed by Herbert Bayer and Peter Wehr.
The handsome cover is Bayer's own work. The catalogue itself makes no
pretence at elegance. It is, on the other hand, a highly informative document.

1936. *A Passage to India* by E. M. Forster. Published by Penguin Books Ltd, Harmondsworth. Printed by Wyman and Sons Ltd, London. $7\frac{1}{8}'' \times 4\frac{1}{4}''$. Original cover and series design by Edward Young.

1939. *The Story of Mankind* by Hendrik Willem van Loon. Published by Pocket Books Inc. Printed in the U.S.A. $6\frac{3}{8}'' \times 4\frac{1}{16}''$. Cover design.

8. THE PAPERBACK EXPLOSION AND THE DESIGN OF THE MODERN BOOK

During the first half of the twentieth century, the first significant paperback publishers were Penguin Books in Great Britain and Pocket Books in America. Sir Allen Lane founded Penguin books in 1935, and Robert de Graaf, in association with three directors of the publishers Simon and Schuster, started Pocket Books in 1939. The Penguin story has been fully documented, and much has been written about 'the American paperback explosion'.[1] Our concern here is only with the design of these books and the effect their design has had on the appearance of hard-cover books. Paperbacks began as cheap reprints of hard-cover books. (I am here not taking into account the pulp market, with its cheesecake and blood and thunder covers.) The kind of soft cover books we are considering began in Leipzig in 1841 when Baron von Tauchnitz started on his huge series of reprints (over 5,000 titles) of American and English authors. They were squarish ($6\frac{1}{2}$ in. by $4\frac{5}{8}$ in.) books with white paper covers, printed in black. The titles, set in a mixture of typefaces, were enclosed in a fine rule border with floral corner pieces. They were well printed on quite tolerable, if uncut, pages. Their format and cover remained virtually unchanged for ninety years when a modest restyling took place. It was then given a second new look when the firm was merged with its rival, the Albatross Library in 1936, which had been founded in 1932 in Hamburg by J. Holroyd-Reece, Kurt Enoch and Max Christian Wegner.

The Albatross Library produced the first really good-looking paperbacks. Their covers were designed by Giovanni Mardersteig, the owner of the Officina Bodoni in Verona and one of the greatest of private press printers. The Albatross covers were very simple designs with seven different background colours to differentiate crime, love, travel, biography, psychology, novels and essays, plays and poetry, humour and short stories.

Mardersteig also used the same colour system for his re-design of the Tauchnitz covers when Albatross absorbed the Leipzig firm. The Tauchnitz and Albatross paper-covered books, originally intended for British travellers to while away interminable hours in *wagons lits* and then to throw away, became rather less ephemeral, for they were pleasant books to handle and ideal for reading in bed (whether a *couchette* or a four-poster).

Penguin's first designer was Edward Young. He followed the Albatross format, a convenient one for the pocket. The Penguin cover was a supremely successful design. It was horizontally divided into three panels, a panel of orange at the top and bottom and a white panel between, with the title set in two weights of Gill Sans. Edward Young also drew the penguin trade mark. By that time, in the early 1940's, when he had joined the Navy, Penguins had become a feature of English life and had briefly opened up a new bookselling outlet, through Woolworth 6d. Stores, who at the beginning were their staunchest supporters. By the mid-thirties various English and American publishers had made tentative forays into the paperback market. Most of them retired hurt. In 1929, Charles Boni had started his Paper Books. These attractive books, designed by Rockwell Kent and published at half a dollar, were offered on a subscription basis of twelve titles a year. Perhaps as a result of this, they failed. Alfred Knopf started his Borzoi Books in the 1930's. They were issued in both hard and soft covers and had an almost identical cover design and format for their paperbacks as the Albatross Library.

[1] *The Paperback*. A paper read to the Double Crown Club by Dr Desmond Flower, published by Arborfield Products Ltd, London, 1959, 'Penguin Panorama', by P. G. Burbidge and L. A. Gray in *Printing Review* No. 72. Autumn 1956.

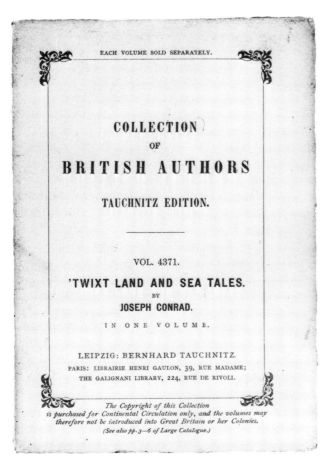

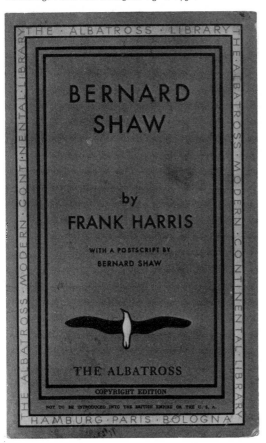

1912. *'Twixt Land and Sea Tales* by Joseph
Conrad. Published and printed by Bernhard
Tauchnitz, Leipzig and Paris. 6⅜″ × 4½″. Cover.

1932. *Bernard Shaw* by Frank Harris. Published
by the Albatross Modern Continental Library,
Hamburg, Paris and Bologna. 7⅛″ × 4 5/16″.

1936. *The Little Wife and other Stories.*
Published by Bernard Tauchnitz, Leipzig, Hamburg
and Paris. 7⅛″ × 4⅜″. Cover design.

c. 1937. *Andalusia* by W. Somerset Maugham. A
Borzoi Book published by Alfred A. Knopf, New
York. Printed in the U.S.A. 7½″ × 4¼″. Cover.

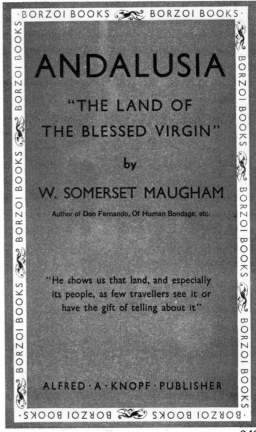

1958. *Tappan's Burro* by Zane Grey. Published by Penguin Books Ltd, Harmondsworth. Printed by Hunt, Barnard and Co. Ltd, Aylesbury. $7\frac{1}{8}'' \times 4\frac{5}{16}''$. Cover design by Dennis Bailey.

1964. *Tiermenschen* by Henry de Montherlant. Published by Deutscher Taschenbuch Verlag, Munich. $7\frac{1}{8}'' \times 4\frac{1}{4}''$. Cover design by Celestino Piatti.

1963. *Billard um halb zehn* by Heinrich Böll. Published by Knaur, Munich and Zürich. Printed by the Süddeutsche Verlagsanstalt und Druckerei GmbH, Ludwigsburg. $7\frac{1}{16}'' \times 4\frac{1}{2}''$. Cover design by Hermann Rastorfer.

1966. *Modern Physics for the Engineer.* Edited by Louis N. Ridenour. Published by McGraw Hill Paperbacks, New York. Printed in the U.S.A. $8'' \times 5\frac{1}{2}''$. Cover designed by Rudolph de Harak.

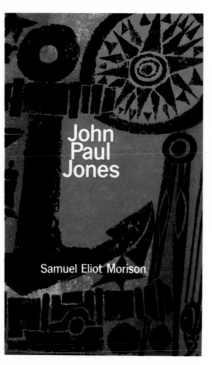

1966. *John Paul Jones* by Samuel Eliot Morison. Published by Time Inc. $8'' \times 5\frac{1}{2}''$. Cover design.

1960. *Münchhausen* by Erich Kästner. Published by Fischer Bücherei Frankfurt-am-Main and Hamburg. Printed in Germany. $7\frac{1}{8}'' \times 4\frac{1}{4}''$. Cover design.

244

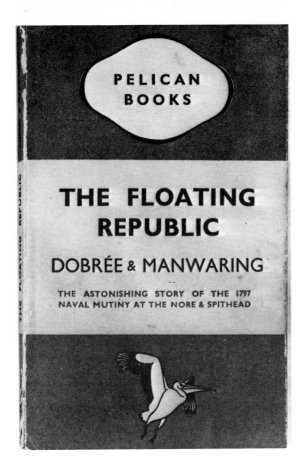

PELICAN BOOKS

THE FLOATING REPUBLIC

DOBRÉE & MANWARING

THE ASTONISHING STORY OF THE 1797
NAVAL MUTINY AT THE NORE & SPITHEAD

1937. *The Floating Republic* by Dobrée and
Manwaring. A Pelican Book published by
Penguin Books Ltd, Harmondsworth. Printed by
Purnell and Sons Ltd. $7\frac{1}{8}'' \times 4\frac{1}{2}''$. Cover design.

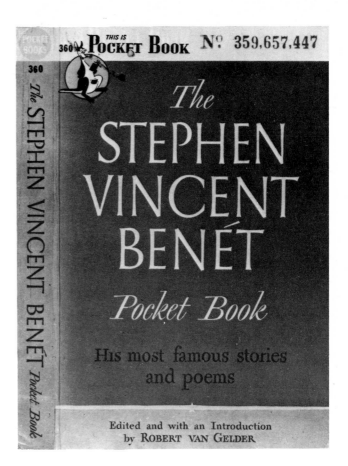

THIS IS
360 **POCKET Book** Nọ 359,657,447

360

The
STEPHEN
VINCENT
BENÉT
Pocket Book

His most famous stories
and poems

Edited and with an Introduction
by ROBERT VAN GELDER

c. 1946. *The Stephen Vincent Benét Pocket Book*
edited by Robert van Gelder. Published by
Pocket Books Inc., New York. Printed in the
U.S.A. $6\frac{3}{8}'' \times 4\frac{1}{16}''$. Cover design.

In England, the firm of Hutchinson had entered the paperback market a year or so later and sold a lot of books. They were followed by Heinemann's pleasant looking Evergreen Books, selling at one shilling, which were an attempt at publishing authors such as Aldous Huxley, John Steinbeck and David Garnett in paperback form. In spite of being printed on fugitive wood pulp paper, they had a slogan 'Evergreen books are books to keep' printed on the jacket flaps.

The jackets on these paperbacks added dignity and kept the covers clean. (Paperback of course is a misnomer, for all these books had drawn-on board covers of at least 2-sheet thickness.)

It was not until 1939 that a venture comparable to Penguins got under way in America. This was Pocket Books. Like Penguins they had sought and found new bookselling outlets through the five-and-ten-cent stores, the news stands, and most important of all, that universal meeting place, the drug store. The format was a little smaller than Penguins, the books were rather more bulky, with glossy laminated covers. Considering the huge runs, they were quite well made and well printed. Within a couple of years a rival firm had sprung up, whose books had an almost identical appearance. These were Avon Books, started by Joseph Myers, who were promptly and unsuccessfully sued by Pocket Books for plagiarism.

After the 1939–45 war, paperback firms sprang up all over the place and many hardback publishers moved into the field once more. Original publications began to supersede reprints and a new move was made into informative, educational publishing. Once again Sir Allen Lane had blazed the trail, with his Pelican series, begun in 1937 with such titles as Shaw's *Intelligent Woman's Guide* and *The Floating Republic* by Dobrée and Manwaring. By this time they had almost grown into a complete home library. The Pelicans were followed by other series, including in 1946 the Penguin Classics. In this series nearly a million copies have been sold of just one title, E. V. Rieu's translation of the *Odyssey*.

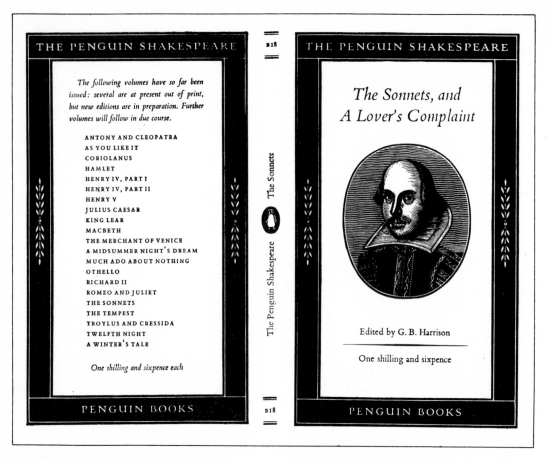

THE PENGUIN SHAKESPEARE

B18

The following volumes have so far been issued: several are at present out of print, but new editions are in preparation. Further volumes will follow in due course.

ANTONY AND CLEOPATRA
AS YOU LIKE IT
CORIOLANUS
HAMLET
HENRY IV, PART I
HENRY IV, PART II
HENRY V
JULIUS CAESAR
KING LEAR
MACBETH
THE MERCHANT OF VENICE
A MIDSUMMER NIGHT'S DREAM
MUCH ADO ABOUT NOTHING
OTHELLO
RICHARD II
ROMEO AND JULIET
THE SONNETS
THE TEMPEST
TROYLUS AND CRESSIDA
TWELFTH NIGHT
A WINTER'S TALE

One shilling and sixpence each

PENGUIN BOOKS

The Sonnets   The Penguin Shakespeare

THE PENGUIN SHAKESPEARE

*The Sonnets, and
A Lover's Complaint*

Edited by G. B. Harrison

One shilling and sixpence

PENGUIN BOOKS

B18

1949. *The Sonnets, and A Lover's Complaint* by William Shakespeare. Designed by Jan Tschichold. A volume from the Penguin Shakespeare published by Penguin Books Ltd, Harmondsworth. Printed by Wyman and Sons, London. 7⅛" × 4⅜". Cover design, printed in black on white board with a wood engraving by Reynolds Stone and text spread.

28   SHAKESPEARE'S

7

*Lo in the Orient when the gracious light,
Lifts up his burning head, each under eye
Doth homage to his new appearing sight,
Serving with looks his sacred majesty,
And having climb'd the steep up heavenly hill,
Resembling strong youth in his middle age,
Yet mortal looks adore his beauty still,
Attending on his golden pilgrimage:
But when from high-most pitch with weary car,
Like feeble age he reeleth from the day,
The eyes ('fore duteous) now converted are
From his low tract and look another way:
    So thou, thyself out-going in thy noon,
    Unlook'd on diest unless thou get a son.*

8

*Music to hear, why hear'st thou music sadly?
Sweets with sweets war not, joy delights in joy:
Why lov'st thou that which thou receiv'st not gladly,
Or else receiv'st with pleasure thine annoy?
If the true concord of well tuned sounds,
By unions married do offend thine ear,
They do but sweetly chide thee, who confounds
In singleness the parts that thou should'st bear:
Mark how one string sweet husband to another,
Strikes each in each by mutual ordering;
Resembling sire, and child, and happy mother,
Who all in one, one pleasing note do sing:
    Whose speechless song being many, seeming one,
    Sings this to thee thou single wilt prove none.*

SONNETS   29

9

*Is it for fear to wet a widow's eye,
That thou consum'st thyself in single life?
Ah; if thou issueless shalt hap to die,
The world will wail thee like a makeless wife,
The world will be thy widow and still weep,
That thou no form of thee hast left behind,
When every private widow well may keep,
By children's eyes, her husband's shape in mind:
Look what an unthrift in the world doth spend
Shifts but his place, for still the world enjoys it:
But beauty's waste hath in the world an end,
And kept unus'd the user so destroys it:
    No love toward others in that bosom sits
    That on himself such murd'rous shame commits.*

10

*For shame deny that thou bear'st love to any
Who for thyself art so unprovident:
Grant if thou wilt, thou art belov'd of many,
But that thou none lov'st is most evident:
For thou art so possess'd with murd'rous hate,
That 'gainst thyself thou stick'st not to conspire,
Seeking that beauteous roof to ruinate
Which to repair should be thy chief desire:
O change thy thought, that I may change my mind,
Shall hate be fairer lodg'd than gentle love?
Be as thy presence is gracious and kind,
Or to thyself at least kind-hearted prove,
    Make thee another self for love of me,
    That beauty still may live in thine or thee.*

The Siege
of Leningrad
Leon Goure
Foreword by Merle Fainsod

McGraw-Hill Paperbacks

Stanford University Press

$2.95

Rudolph deHarak

1965. *The Siege of Leningrad* by Leon Goure.
Published by McGraw-Hill Paperbacks and the
Stanford University Press. Printed in the U.S.A.
8″ × 5⅜″. Cover designed by Rudolph de Harak.

[2] 'On Mass-producing the Classics' by Jan
Tschichold. Translated by Ruari McLean. *Signature No. 3* (New Series) March 1947.
[3] See pages 15 and 250.

Paperbacks for serious reading

Sir Allen intended that the design and typography of his new series should match the quality of the texts, and in 1947 he invited the famous Swiss typographer, Jan Tschichold, to come to England to overhaul the typography of all Penguin productions. Tschichold had already designed a handsome, inexpensive series of books, the Birkhäuser Classics, which were proportioned 5:8 (7 9/16 in. by 4¾ in.). He gave his ideal proportions for trimmed page sizes 3:5 and 5:8.[2]

The Penguin Shakespeares, which he redesigned, were immaculate books, set in Monotype Bembo and (like the Heinemann Evergreen Books) in paper jackets. The series had an effective cover design with a portrait of the bard engraved by Reynolds Stone, set within a wide black border.

Tschichold, with typical thoroughness, applied himself to instilling some Germanic precision into the wayward methods of English printing. And he achieved it. His typography (by then based on Renaissance classicism) was distinguished by its neatness; his title-pages showed impeccable spacing, his colophons on the verso of titles were set in minute (6 point) letter-spaced small capitals. There were few hard-cover books of the late 1940's that typographically could match the looks of these Penguin books.

The design of paperbacks is mainly a matter of packaging. In hard cover books, much money and care is spent on the jackets, but the matter does not end there. The binding case has to be designed and care taken with the layout of text pages, illustrations, cover and end papers. For most paperback publishers, providing they have what they consider to be a good selling cover, the devil can take care of the rest. This, of course, was not the policy of Albatross, Borzoi or Penguin, who remained faithful to their series designs. But even Penguin wavered in the late fifties and started using coloured illustrations on some of their covers. A new format was designed for these books by Abram Games and one or two exciting covers appeared, including Dennis Bailey's vivid drawing for Zane Grey's *Tappan's Burro*. Back in 1938, the Penguin Illustrated Classics under the editorship of Robert Gibbings had made use of wood engraved illustrations on their covers.

Dr Desmond Flower, in the paper that he read to the Double Crown Club in April 1959, said: 'The realization in the early fifties that there did exist a wide market for books concerning themselves with matters above the navel encouraged a number of hard-cover publishers to start soft-cover lines on better paper and at higher prices.' This educational market has come to stay. With large international markets there is also more money available, so that texts can be more easily commissioned, and more can be spent on layout and presentation. An art director is now an obvious necessity, for design becomes an integral part of the concept of the book. Graphic techniques for charts and maps, photography and illustration all play a part, taking a step on from the Tschichold conception of immaculate typography. American publishers such as Prentice-Hall, with their Foundations of Modern Political Science series, McGraw-Hill with their Paperbacks, Harper with their Torchbooks, Time Inc. with their Time and Life Reading Programme, and the various University presses are all producing books that are not only essential student reading but are also exciting to look at.

The narrow format Washington Square Press paperbacks from Pocket Books Inc. show much care in the design of their covers. Two of their titles, which were exhibited in the American Institute of Graphic Arts 1966 Exhibition, show an interesting return to art nouveau letter forms. Both Zane Grey's *The Trail Driver* designed and illustrated by Jerry McDaniel, and Doris M. Stone's *Projects: Botany* designed by Richard Adelson use typefaces that are very like Otto Eckmann's Eckmann-Schmuck.[3]

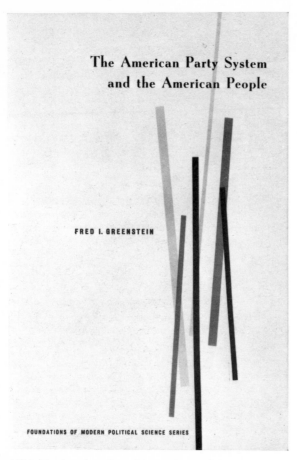

1964. *The American Party System*. Cover design.

1962. *Geometry* by H. G. Forder. A Harper Torch book. Published in their Science Library by Harper and Brothers, New York. 8″ × 5¼″. Cover design.

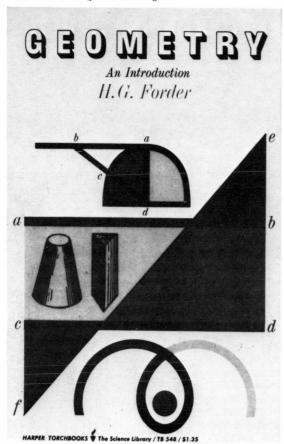

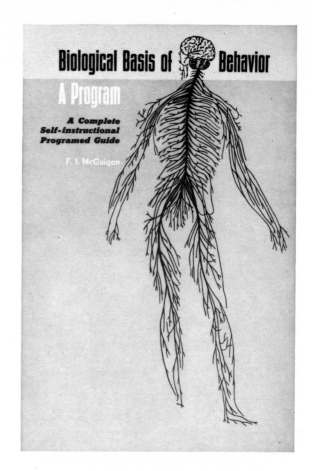

1963. *A Biological Basis of Behavior*. Cover design.

1962. *American Poetry and Poetics* edited by Daniel G. Hoffman. An Anchor Book. Published by Doubleday and Co. Inc, New York. 7⅛″ × 4¼″. Cover design by Ben Shahn.

Citizen Politics: The Behavior of the Electorate

CHAPTER THREE

In the United States, as elsewhere, all citizens
are not equally active in politics. Some Americans have
little political potency. They fail to act on their beliefs even to
the degree of voting. Others, as we saw in Table 3
of Chapter 2, not only vote but also employ a variety of the more
demanding avenues of expression available to the citizen,
such as membership in pressure groups and letter-writing
to public officials. Still others are far more politically active
and potent than virtually anyone caught up in the broad net

18

of the normal public-opinion survey. These are the thousands of individuals in actual leadership positions—for example, elected and appointed
officials at various levels of government, directors of interest groups and
other associations, key figures in the communications industry, and elder
statesmen such as Bernard Baruch and former Presidents Eisenhower,
Truman, and Hoover.

It follows from the uneven distribution of activity that the views of
some citizens have more political impact than the views of others. We
therefore cannot be content with studying the behavior of the undif-
ferentiated "general" public in our assessment of the citizen base of the
political system. We must go on, as we do in the present chapter, to consider the behavior of the *effective* public. After our analysis of groups in
the electorate and their effectiveness, we shall look at the dynamics of
electoral choice.

Groups in the Electorate and Their Behavior

WHO PARTICIPATES IN POLITICS?

Figure 2 provides us with an indication of who the politically active members of the electorate are. Even in the simple act of voting, the range of
participation from group to group is striking. Looking at the extreme cases,
in 1960 nine out of ten of the college-educated voters interviewed by the
University of Michigan Survey Research Center reported that they had
voted. On the other hand, only slightly more than half of the Negro
population seems to have exercised the franchise.

Of course, it is immediately evident that the "groups" shown in
Fig. 2 are not discrete entities. Voters are not *either* college-educated *or*

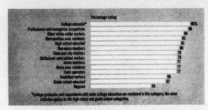

FIGURE 2 *Electoral Turnout of Key American Categoric Groups,
1960 Presidential Election.* Source: National survey conducted in
1960 by Survey Research Center, University of Michigan. Philip Con-
verse of the Survey Research Center has kindly made these findings
available.

19

Citizen Politics: The Behavior of the Electorate

1964. *The American Party System* by Fred I. Greenstein.
In the Foundations of Modern Political Science Series,
editor Robert Dahl, published by Prentice-Hall Inc, N.J.
Designed by Walter Behnke. 9″ × 6″. Text spread.

1963. *A Biological Basis of Behavior* by F. J. McGuigan.
Published by Prentice-Hall Inc, N.J. 9″ × 5⅞″.
Illustration and text spread.

---

28   Receptors

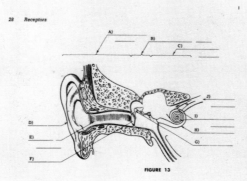

FIGURE 13

A. *External Ear*
B. *Middle Ear*
C. *Inner Ear*
D. *Pinna*
E. *Auditory Canal*
F. *Eardrum*
G. *Ossicles*
H. *Cochlea*
I. *Hair Cells*
J. *Auditory Nerve*

227. In Figure 13, write in the parts of the ear, in
the blanks provided.

228. Without looking at the preceding discussion,
draw a diagram of the parts of the external, the middle, and the inner ear, concluding with the auditory
nerve that runs to the brain. State each step that occurs,
from the point at which a vibrating object sends off
a sound wave, to the point where a nerve impulse is
transmitted to the brain. Be sure to label each part
of the ear. Then check your diagram and steps for
accuracy against the preceding discussion. (Standard
size notebook paper may be used for all drawings that
appear in this book.)

RECEPTORS

Section III: The Eye

auditory

brain

229. We have just seen how the type of energy that
we call an _____ stimulus leaves a
vibrating stimulus object, impinges on the ear, and sets
off a nerve impulse that runs to the _____ .

230. In like manner, we shall now trace the process
by which the type of environmental energy, that we
call a visual stimulus, leaves a stimulus object and
sets off a nerve impulse that runs from the receptor,
eye   called the _____, to the brain.

231. Some stimulus objects emit what we call RADIANT
(rā'dı ont) ENERGY. A light bulb is an example of a
stimulus   _____ object that emits radiant energy.

232. Consider the various stimulus objects, in a
person's environment, that emit RADIANT ENERGY. A
stimulus object, such as a light bulb, itself produces
energy   the radiant _____ that it emits.

233. Other stimulus objects, however, do not produce
radiant   radiant energy, but rather they reflect _____
energy coming from other sources.

234. For example, a light bulb in a room produces
radiant energy that strikes the wall. That radiant
energy is then reflected from the wall and is trans-
receptor   mitted to the organism's visual _____
that we call the eye.

29

249

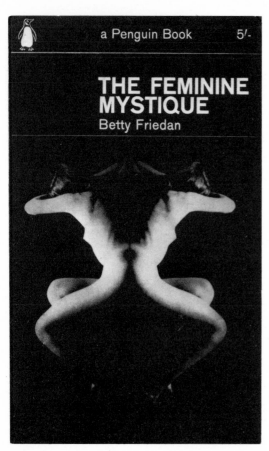

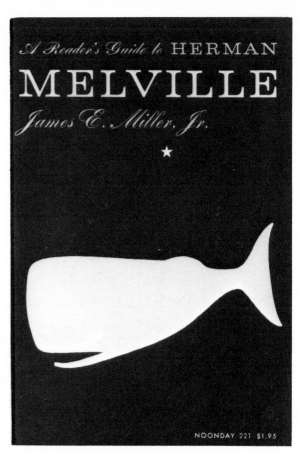

1965. *The Feminine Mystique* by Betty Friedan.
Published by Penguin Books Ltd, Harmondsworth.
Cover designed by Alan Aldridge. 7⅛" × 4¾".

1962. *A Reader's Guide to Herman Melville* by James E.
Miller, Jnr. Published by the Noonday Press, New York.
8" × 5⅝". Cover designed by Robin Fox.

1965. *The Trail Driver* by
Zane Grey. Published by the
Washington Square Press,
Pocket Books Inc, New York.
7" × 4". Cover design by
Jerry McDaniel.

1965. *Projects: Botany* by
Doris M. Stone. Published by
the Washington Square
Press, Pocket Books Inc,
New York. 7" × 4". Cover
designed by Richard Adelson.

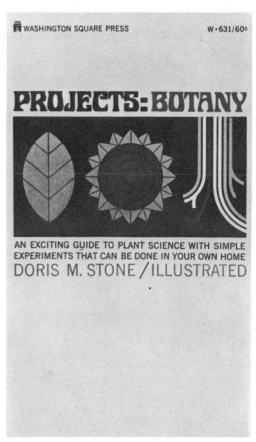

Die russische Revolution 1917

Von der Abdankung des Zaren bis zum
Staatsstreich der Bolschewiki
Herausgegeben von Manfred Hellmann

dtv dokumente

DOCUMENTS SELECTED AND EDITED WITH
NOTES AND INTRODUCTION BY R. W. POSTGATE

Revolution

FROM 1789 TO 1906

HARPER TORCHBOOKS ▼ The Academy Library / TB 1063 / $1.95

1964. *Die russische Revolution 1917* edited by Manfred
Hellmann. Published by dtv, Munich. $7\frac{1}{8}'' \times 4\frac{1}{4}''$.
Cover designed by Celestino Piatti.

1965. *Berlin Alexanderplatz* by Alfred Döblin.
Published by dtv, Munich. $7\frac{1}{8}'' \times 4\frac{1}{4}''$.
Cover design by Celestino Piatti, and title-page.

1962. *Revolution from 1789 to 1906* edited by R. W.
Postgate. A Harper Torchbook. Published by Harper and
Brothers, New York. $8'' \times 5\frac{1}{4}''$. Cover design.

Alfred Döblin:
Berlin Alexanderplatz
Die Geschichte vom Franz Biberkopf

Nachwort von Walter Muschg

Deutscher
Taschenbuch
Verlag

**Alfred Döblin:
Berlin Alexanderplatz
Roman**

And so the Army of the Potomac got a new commander—General Ambrose Burnside (left)—and the army which had not been lucky in its leaders now had the worst. It was Burnside's notion that he could run quickly down the Rappahannock River, jump across before Lee knew he was there, and charge towards Richmond. Not surprisingly, when Burnside got on the river in December, Lee was opposite him and busily entrenching on Marye's Heights behind the town of Fredericksburg. There was no bridge over the river, but Burnside expected to build one— while Lee presumably just sat quietly.

91

1961. *The Civil War as They Knew It* by Abraham Lincoln and Mathew Brady. A Bantam Gallery Edition volume. Published by Bantam Books Inc. Printed in the U.S.A. $6\frac{7}{8}'' \times 4\frac{1}{4}''$. Cover design and text spread.

1964. *L'Église et la République* by Anatole France. No. 5 in the Libertés series published by J. J. Pauvert, Paris. Printed in the Netherlands. $7'' \times 3\frac{1}{2}''$. Cover.

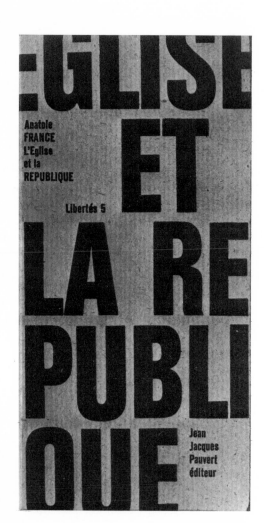

Illustration in paperbacks

In Germany, the gayest looking of all paperbacks are from Deutscher Taschenbuch Verlag, who are known by their initials d t v. These are designed by Celestino Piatti, who uses a simple formula of a white laminated board, with the title set in Aksidenz Grotesk and printed in black, with a boldly drawn illustration vignetted in colour. The insides are immaculately laid out, with title-pages that look as if they belonged to the same world as the covers. Drömersche Verlagsanstalt from Munich publish the Knaur paperbacks with some colourful covers, designed by Hermann Rastorfer.

Paperback publishers were slow off the mark with fully illustrated books. The wide use of offset and gravure has done away with the need to use expensive coated stock for half-tone illustrations. Bantam Gallery Editions with such titles as *The Civil War as they Knew it*, with Mathew Brady's famous contemporary photographs, are a praiseworthy example of intelligent presentation and layout.

The designer of this book makes a lively use of negative prints both for his title-page spread and for section titles, which consist solely of the date of the year, set in an extended Victorian typeface. Dutton Vista Picturebacks edited by David Herbert is the first trans-Atlantic series of comprehensive pictorial surveys to appear in paperback form. These are fully illustrated, well designed books. *New Cinema in Europe* by Roger Manvell, shown here, is one of this series

In spite of indications both in the United States and in Europe of a considerable increase in well made, well laid-out paperbacks, the bulk of the books are still for the *roman policier* and the blood and sex markets. Once again we revert to packaging and find some very lively, good looking covers,

Jour de Fête France 1949. Director Jacques Tati

Pierrot le Fou France 1965. Director Jean-Luc Godard
Anna Karina

1966. *New Cinema in Europe* by Roger Manvell.
Published by Studio Vista Ltd, London and
E. P. Dutton and Co. Inc, New York. A
Dutton Vista Pictureback. Printed by Richard
Clay, Bungay. $7\frac{1}{4}'' \times 4\frac{7}{8}''$. Cover design by
Gillian Greenwood.

1964. *Napoléon le Petit* by Victor Hugo. No. 4
in the Libertés Series published by J. J. Pauvert,
Paris. Printed in the Netherlands. $7'' \times 3\frac{1}{2}''$.
Cover design.

standing out like flowers amongst all the corn. The use of display letters with no illustrations is still a rarity. The French series 'Libertés', published by Jean Jacques Pauvert, has a tall, narrow format, with cover design printed from large black sans serif capitals on brown paper. The texts are carefully set and well printed in Holland. These are thoroughly readable books and though printed on cheap paper, have an elegance about them, which comes from the care and thought that have gone into their production.

Since this book was first published, the great change in the appearance of railway and airport bookstalls has been the flood of Science Fiction titles. Another has been the presence of large-format illustrated paperbacks, increasingly popular especially in the United States. Brian Aldiss, one of the great SF authors, writing in *The Saturday Book* in 1964 drew attention to the cover artists of the old SF magazines such as *Galaxy* and *Fantasy*. He also described the swing towards paperbacks. He concludes prophetically: 'Nowadays the old covers and their mighty white cities, impossible architecture, man-devouring forests and other delectable props are steam engines among the diesel traffic of paperbacks. Their days are numbered. But science fiction, which today reaches a wider and more critical audience than it ever did, goes on; and in another twenty years... someone else may be nostalgically recalling the glories and idiocies of paperback SF covers.'

The two covers shown on page 255 are of a recent selection of Aldiss stories called *New Arrivals, Old Encounters,* and *Foundation,* the first volume of Isaac Asimov's classic trilogy. The artists are Tim Wright and Chris Foss, who more than live up to the traditions of the old SF magazine covers.

Scholem-Alejchem:
Menachem Mendel,
der Spekulant

Knaur

The IPCRESS File/LEN DEIGHTON

Secret File No.1   3/6   Panther

'It's authenticity will make M.I.5 wonder where
he gets his material from'   DAILY SKETCH

1965. *Menachem Mendel, der Spekulant* by Scholem-
Alejchem. Published by Knaur at Munich and Zürich.
Cover design by Cristoph Albrecht. $7\frac{1}{16}'' \times 4\frac{1}{2}''$.

1961. *Borstal Boy* by Brendan Behan. A Corgi Book
published by Transworld Publishers, London.
$7\frac{1}{8}'' \times 4\frac{5}{16}''$. Cover design.

1964. *The Ipcress File* by Len Deighton. A Panther Book,
published by Hamilton and Co. (Stafford) Ltd. $7'' \times 4\frac{1}{4}''$.
Cover design by Raymond Hawkey.

1965. *Le Fils* by Georges Simenon. Published by
Presses de la Cité, Paris. Printed by Bussière at
St Amand. $6\frac{1}{2}'' \times 4\frac{1}{2}''$. Series cover design.

FG1464 A CORGI BOOK 5/-

BORSTAL BOY
BRENDAN BEHAN

THE BAWDY SWAGGERING OUTRAGEOUS BESTSELLER

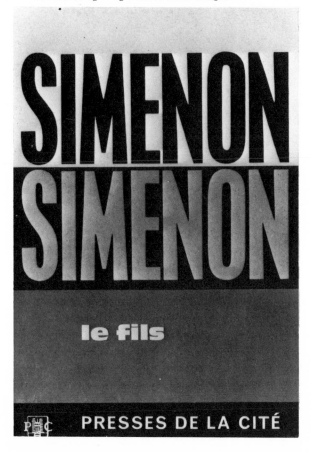

SIMENON
SIMENON

le fils

PRESSES DE LA CITÉ

1980 *Zorba the Greek* by Nikos Kazantzakis. A Touchstone Book published by Simon and Schuster. 8″ × 5¼″. Cover by Seymour Chwaste

1983 *New Arrivals, Old Encounters* by Brian Aldiss. Published by Triad Granada, London. 7″ × 4⅜″. Cover design by Tim White.

1973 *The Case of the Midwife Toad* by Arthur Koestler published by Vintage Books, Random House, New York. 7¼″ × 4⅜″. Cover by Trubshur.

1982 *Foundation* by Isaac Asimov. Published by Granada, London. 7″ × 4⅜″. Cover illustration by Chris Foss.

3
Student Days

It was (I think) in our second session that EB and I, and Sam Heiman, a most cheerful and charming Design student, each had a bed-sitting room in the lodging-house of Miss Helen Groom at 58 Redcliffe Road, South Kensington. We often paid visits to each other's rooms and had great fun with dear Sam who was a Theosophist, a Jew, a Vegetarian, a Pacifist, a Liberal Catholic and much else of the same harmless character. We had breakfast together in the basement. Or rather we were supposed to breakfast together. But Sam preferred to consume mysterious compounds and beverages in the sanctity of his own room. Bawden was always down before me and would be sitting stiffly at table, reading as he ate. He did not look up as I entered. His social temperature was near freezing-point in the morning. When I bustled in announcing that it was a good morning or otherwise, he would go on chewing slowly, his eyes on a book, and would only murmur: 'Is it?' I hated this. I was always ready for conversation in the morning. So I took notice of what EB was reading. I remember that he went steadily through *Anna Karenina*, Fergusson on *Architecture* and Jackson's *History of Wood-Engraving*. He read to learn, unlike Ravilious who read for fun and whose favourite book was *Huckleberry Finn*. Once or twice I found EB deep in a trade periodical on ironmongery and hardware – his father was in that line at Braintree – which he would recommend to me, smiling faintly, 'as good sensible stuff' and 'literature'.

Bawden had a habit of wearing his hat indoors and his hats were dignified, mitre-like ornaments. He used to sit back on his chair at very dangerous angles. Sometimes he tipped the chair too far back until there was a crash. He would get up from the floor, resume his seat, still mitred and expressionless, and join again in the conversation. His hands, like those of William Morris, were always itching to do something (Morris as a school-boy made nets at Marlborough). We had to watch Bawden and catch him before he damaged the landlady's property. He might, bit by bit, during a conversation, with

– 24 –

1931 HOMAGE TO DICKY DOYLE specially drawn to show the use of colour applied by stencilling for the Curwen Press. Reproduced in Curwen Press Miscellany, 1931

– 25 –

1979 *Edward Bawden* by Douglas Percy Bliss, published by the Pendomer Press in England and Canada. 11¼″ × 8″. Illustration spread and jacket printed in black and brown and reproduced from a wallpaper design and typographic borders, both by Edward Bawden. Designed by John and Griselda Lewis.

Art books

Art books still proliferate – more of them appearing in large-format paperback – though it looks as if the day of the coffee-table book is over, which is no bad thing. In no way a coffee-table book was Iain Bain's *The Watercolours and Drawings of Thomas Bewick* which the Gordon Fraser Gallery published in two volumes in 1981. This is an exquisite production, beautifully printed by the Westerham Press. The often minute watercolours (drawn the same size as the final wood engraving) sit on the page like little jewels.

Quite a number of monographs on contemporary artists have appeared, often from presses where the publishing aims have not been solely concerned with profit. The Lion and Unicorn Press at the Royal College of Art produced a handsome book on Stanley Spencer's drawings in 1964. In 1978 a new imprint appeared, the Pendomer Press, a trans-Atlantic venture operating from Godalming in England and Toronto in Canada. The moving spirit behind this was Simon Heneage. His first publication was *John Nash: the painter as illustrator* by John Lewis. This was followed by *Edward Bawden,* a study of the artist by Douglas Percy Bliss. This book was a revelation of Bawden's staying power as an illustrator and designer for books. His work over fifty years has a remarkable consistency.

As an example of the detailed planning of a series, the following account may be of some interest. Studio Paperbacks was a series of introductory handbooks on art and design that was launched in 1963. These books were aimed at the student market and intended to cover the basic principles of different subjects. They had to be relatively inexpensive, to be very fully illustrated, usually with colour, and to be designed in a manner acceptable to students and professional designers. To meet all these requirements meant long runs and economic machining. This was achieved by printing an American and an English edition at the same time, by offset on large machines, giving ninety-six pages printed on two sheets (twenty-four pages to view). These sheets were cut in

1965. *Signs in Action* by James Sutton. A
Studio Vista/Reinhold Art Paperback. Published
in London by Studio Vista Ltd and in New York
by Reinhold Publishing Corporation. Printed in
the Netherlands by Koch and Knuttel, Gouda.
7¾" × 6½". Cover photograph by Herbert
Spencer and text and illustration spread.

1966. *Trademarks* by Peter Wildbur. A Studio
Vista/Reinhold Art Paperback. Published in
London by Studio Vista Ltd and in New York by
Reinhold Publishing Corporation. Printed in the
Netherlands by Koch and Knuttel, Gouda.
7¾" × 6½". Cover design by Peter Wildbur.

Marble Arch, London
Photo Herbert Spencer

German street sign
Photo David Lock and Terry Smith

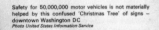

Safety for 50,000,000 motor vehicles is not materially
helped by this confused 'Christmas Tree' of signs –
downtown Washington DC
Photo United States Information Service

These monstrous Christmas Trees are confusing,
difficult to read and hideous. An ill co-ordinated
mass of verbiage.
Is every sign on p. 16 necessary? If the author-
ities tidied up the mess, the driver could see,
clearly, one sign. Even two or three co-ordinated
signs supporting rather than fighting each other
– or repeating the message – can be effective,
but completely different signs saying the same
thing can never be.

How it can be done.

Painted wood sign, Cortina, Italy ▶
Photo Publifoto Milan

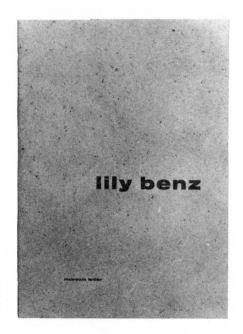

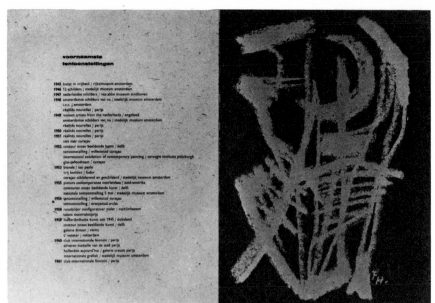

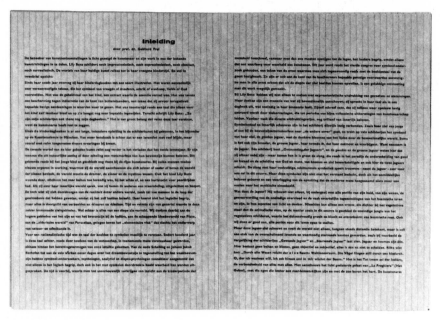

1950–60. Catalogue Covers from the Stedelijk Museum, Amsterdam. Printed on various papers and produced under the direction of Dr Willem Sandberg. Average size 10¼" × 7½".

The Stedelijk Museum catalogues

three, making three sections of sixteen pages. On one side only of one of the sheets, colour would be printed, though in collating for binding this could be scattered fairly widely through the book. The format, a squarish one (7¾ in. by 6½ in.), was perhaps not ideal for a jacket pocket, but most students do not wear jackets nowadays, and this size is far better for displaying illustrations, than, for instance, the upright Albatross-Penguin format. For most of the titles the type was set in a narrow measure, in one or two columns, which gave considerable scope for marginal illustrations, by the simple expedient of dropping one of the columns of type. The covers were printed in full colour, with some conformity of design. The formula proved a success.

New trends in book design have rarely come from the ordinary publishing houses. Such trends appear from other sources such as art galleries or in commercially promoted books, where expense would appear to be of little concern. These books, at their best, can be models of clarity in arrangement and design. They may range from prestige publications to service handbooks and even to catalogues. Where copy has to be made explicit, even appetising,

The Art of the Engineer

The Art of the Engineer

Welsh Arts Council Touring Exhibitions

The Art of the Engineer

Two hundred years in the development
of drawings for the design of transport
on land, sea and air.

1978 *The Art of the Engineer* by Ken Baynes and
Francis Pugh. Produced by Design Systems.
Portfolio cover.

the clever hands of a hundred clever graphic designers have given it order
and clarity.

Exhibition catalogues were first given a new meaning by Dr Willem Sandberg,
the former Director of the Stedelijk Museum in Amsterdam. A brilliantly
exciting series of catalogues was produced under his care. That some of them
are typographically eccentric, with many more words to the line than makes
for comfortable reading, is almost by the way. Here was fresh thinking on the
presentation of type and pictures, and the use of unusual and often inexpensive papers. The Stedelijk Museum catalogues were packed with ideas that
the publishers of picture books might well have followed.

Another and different approach to catalogue design can be seen in the Welsh
Arts Council publication of *The Art of the Engineer*, written by Ken Baynes
and Francis Pugh and produced by Design Systems. This took the form of a
portfolio of twelve folded sheets tracing the development, through two hundred years, of drawings for the design of transport on land, sea or air. The
most effective portfolio cover is taken from a hand-coloured lithograph which
Scott Russell, I. K. Brunel's contractor, had drawn of a section of the *Great
Eastern* after the great ship had been fitted out in 1859.

A particularly notable catalogue was produced in 1972 for the Armand
Hammer Collection, which was exhibited at the Los Angeles County Museum
of Art, the Royal Academy of Arts in London and the National Gallery of
Ireland in Dublin. The catalogue was designed in Los Angeles by James L.
Wood and printed by the Anderson Lithograph Company in Los Angeles, with
a prodigal use of colour, particularly for the reproduction of drawings, some
of which had the merest hint of colour in them. No commercial publisher would
have contemplated such an extravagance, yet if colour reproduction, which
is so costly, in spite of (or maybe because of) great advances in electronic
scanning techniques, could be used for reproducing monochromatic drawings
or even the printed pages of books, it would lift the illustrations right off the
page, in a way that no monochrome reproduction could do.[4]

4 I have noticed, when using 35mm slides, that
colour slides will bring the black and white pages
of books etc. to life in a way that monochromatic
film cannot do. The same lesson applies in the
printing of illustrated books.

1982 *David Gentleman's Britain* written and illustrated by David Gentleman RDI, published by Weidenfeld and Nicolson, London. Cover and illustration page.

1983 *Drain Pig and the Glow Boys in 'Critical Mess'* by Dan Pearce, published by Junction Books, London. $5\frac{3}{4}'' \times 8\frac{1}{4}''$. Cover design.

In conclusion

Some twenty years ago in a leading article in *The Times Literary Supplement* the anonymous writer said: 'For new types of books a new kind of author is emerging, a man who is able to handle words with skill and economy but whose books, in fact, evolve out of a balanced knowledge of both words and techniques of visual communication'.[5] This new kind of author-designer (like the 'directing intelligence' that Léon Pichon talked about) may play a bigger and bigger part in the book of the future, not as one who provides a 'prettifying' element, but as one who can act as an elucidating factor in the graphic presentation of a text, as well as assisting in the economics of production. David Gentleman is such an author. He is a painter, an engraver and a designer who can also handle words. His lavishly illustrated book *David Gentleman's Britain,* published by Weidenfeld and Nicolson in 1982, is an example of this kind of book that combines all the author-artist's skills. Such an approach of course does not apply to books to be read in the train or even in bed. For this, the Renaissance book, as for example those printed by Aldus in Venice in the early years of the sixteenth century and sometimes set in space-saving italic types, is a very satisfactory and utilitarian solution to the arrangement of type on a small page, but it provides no possible guide for the disposition of half-tone illustrations or other pictorial matter in the modern book. The Russian, Hungarian and German typographers of the 1920s made the first real contribution to solving this problem. A quarter of a century later typographers such as Willem Sandberg in Holland, Paul Rand in the United States and Max Bill in Switzerland applied further new thinking to the design of books and catalogues. Little has come from the modern book publisher that can compare in typographic skill with these productions.

As to the future of book design, in spite of radio, television and electronic aids for storing information, it would seem that there may still be a place for books. The question is, what kind of books? One answer would seem to lie in the paperback bookstalls, where the only sign of the designer's hand is in the covers, where, with the rare exceptions of SF titles, colour photographs of naked girls and heavy-handed typography are the main components. In the years since this book first came out there has been a marked decline in the design of such covers. The insides vary from the impeccable typography of Penguins or of the American and English University Presses to the abysmal standards of the pulp printer. As for covers, at the bookstall level I was hard pressed to find even four tolerable new paperback cover designs to include in this edition.

Apart from informative and educational books, the ever expanding market is for children's books. As children are conditioned by television, any stories that appear on the small screen tend to become immediate best sellers in book form. The comic strip either on the TV screen or in the Comics is a form of drawing a child can understand. The success of the adventures of Tintin or of Asterix the Gaul is an indication of where children's tastes lie. The reason for the enormous success of these books is not just in the drawings. Georges Remi (who drew under the pseudonym of Hergé) put much research into his drawings for Tintin, as does Albert Uderzo for Asterix. Both these series of books are compulsive reading (and viewing). There is a lesson here for any publisher or illustrator of children's books. All the design in the world will not compensate for the lack of a good story line and this does not only apply to children's books. Dan Pearce's *Drain Pig and the Glow Boys in 'Critical Mess'* published in 1983 is a strip cartoon book for adults, a brilliant piece of anti-nuclear propaganda that rivets one's attention from the very first page. The reader becomes utterly absorbed in the subterranean adventures of the uncomely little pig. This is the first book by this young cartoonist.

5 *The Times Literary Supplement* 26 April 1963.

S0-CFM-394

Critical Values for Student's *t* Distribution

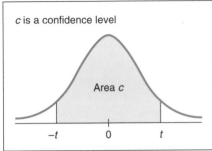

c is a confidence level

Area *c*

−*t*   0   *t*

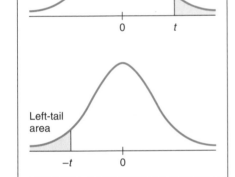

One-tail area

Right-tail area

0   *t*

Left-tail area

−*t*   0

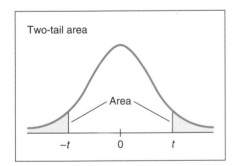

Two-tail area

Area

−*t*   0   *t*

one-tail area	0.250	0.125	0.100	0.075	0.050	0.025	0.010	0.005	0.0005
two-tail area	0.500	0.250	0.200	0.150	0.100	0.050	0.020	0.010	0.0010
d.f. \ c	0.500	0.750	0.800	0.850	0.900	0.950	0.980	0.990	0.999
1	1.000	2.414	3.078	4.165	6.314	12.706	31.821	63.657	636.619
2	0.816	1.604	1.886	2.282	2.920	4.303	6.965	9.925	31.599
3	0.765	1.423	1.638	1.924	2.353	3.182	4.541	5.841	12.924
4	0.741	1.344	1.533	1.778	2.132	2.776	3.747	4.604	8.610
5	0.727	1.301	1.476	1.699	2.015	2.571	3.365	4.032	6.869
6	0.718	1.273	1.440	1.650	1.943	2.447	3.143	3.707	5.959
7	0.711	1.254	1.415	1.617	1.895	2.365	2.998	3.499	5.408
8	0.706	1.240	1.397	1.592	1.860	2.306	2.896	3.355	5.041
9	0.703	1.230	1.383	1.574	1.833	2.262	2.821	3.250	4.781
10	0.700	1.221	1.372	1.559	1.812	2.228	2.764	3.169	4.587
11	0.697	1.214	1.363	1.548	1.796	2.201	2.718	3.106	4.437
12	0.695	1.209	1.356	1.538	1.782	2.179	2.681	3.055	4.318
13	0.694	1.204	1.350	1.530	1.771	2.160	2.650	3.012	4.221
14	0.692	1.200	1.345	1.523	1.761	2.145	2.624	2.977	4.140
15	0.691	1.197	1.341	1.517	1.753	2.131	2.602	2.947	4.073
16	0.690	1.194	1.337	1.512	1.746	2.120	2.583	2.921	4.015
17	0.689	1.191	1.333	1.508	1.740	2.110	2.567	2.898	3.965
18	0.688	1.189	1.330	1.504	1.734	2.101	2.552	2.878	3.922
19	0.688	1.187	1.328	1.500	1.729	2.093	2.539	2.861	3.883
20	0.687	1.185	1.325	1.497	1.725	2.086	2.528	2.845	3.850
21	0.686	1.183	1.323	1.494	1.721	2.080	2.518	2.831	3.819
22	0.686	1.182	1.321	1.492	1.717	2.074	2.508	2.819	3.792
23	0.685	1.180	1.319	1.489	1.714	2.069	2.500	2.807	3.768
24	0.685	1.179	1.318	1.487	1.711	2.064	2.492	2.797	3.745
25	0.684	1.198	1.316	1.485	1.708	2.060	2.485	2.787	3.725
26	0.684	1.177	1.315	1.483	1.706	2.056	2.479	2.779	3.707
27	0.684	1.176	1.314	1.482	1.703	2.052	2.473	2.771	3.690
28	0.683	1.175	1.313	1.480	1.701	2.048	2.467	2.763	3.674
29	0.683	1.174	1.311	1.479	1.699	2.045	2.462	2.756	3.659
30	0.683	1.173	1.310	1.477	1.697	2.042	2.457	2.750	3.646
35	0.682	1.170	1.306	1.472	1.690	2.030	2.438	2.724	3.591
40	0.681	1.167	1.303	1.468	1.684	2.021	2.423	2.704	3.551
45	0.680	1.165	1.301	1.465	1.679	2.014	2.412	2.690	3.520
50	0.679	1.164	1.299	1.462	1.676	2.009	2.403	2.678	3.496
60	0.679	1.162	1.296	1.458	1.671	2.000	2.390	2.660	3.460
70	0.678	1.160	1.294	1.456	1.667	1.994	2.381	2.648	3.435
80	0.678	1.159	1.292	1.453	1.664	1.990	2.374	2.639	3.416
100	0.677	1.157	1.290	1.451	1.660	1.984	2.364	2.626	3.390
500	0.675	1.152	1.283	1.442	1.648	1.965	2.334	2.586	3.310
1000	0.675	1.151	1.282	1.441	1.646	1.962	2.330	2.581	3.300
∞	0.674	1.150	1.282	1.440	1.645	1.960	2.326	2.576	3.291

For degrees of freedom *d.f.* not in the table, use the closest *d.f.* that is *smaller*.

Understandable Statistics
Concepts and Methods

EIGHTH EDITION

Understandable Statistics
Concepts and Methods

Advanced/For Advanced High School Students

Charles Henry Brase
Regis University

Corrinne Pellillo Brase
Arapahoe Community College

HOUGHTON MIFFLIN COMPANY
Boston   New York

This book is dedicated to the memory of
a great teacher, mathematician, and friend

Burton W. Jones

Professor Emeritus, University of Colorado

Publisher: Jack Shira
Sponsoring Editor: Lauren Schultz
Developmental Editor: David George
Editorial Associate: Kasey McGarrigle
Senior Project Editor: Nancy Blodget
Editorial Assistant: Sean McGann
Senior Composition Buyer: Sarah Ambrose
Art and Design Manager: Gary Crespo
Manufacturing Coordinator: Karen Banks
Senior Marketing Manager: Ben Rivera
Marketing Assistant: Lisa Lawler

Cover photographer: Fraser Hall/Robert Harding World Imagery/Getty Images
Viewpoint artist: Lauren Arnest

A complete list of photo credits appears in the back of the book, immediately following the appendices.

TI-83Plus and TI-84Plus are registered trademarks of Texas Instruments, Inc.
SPSS is a registered trademark of SPSS, Inc.
Minitab is a registered trademark of Minitab, Inc.
Microsoft Excel screen shots reprinted by permission from Microsoft Corporation.
Excel, Microsoft, and Windows are either registered trademarks or trademarks of Microsoft Corporation in the United States and/or other countries.

Copyright © 2006 by Houghton Mifflin Company. All rights reserved.

No part of this work may be reproduced or transmitted in any form or by any means, electronic or mechanical, including photocopying and recording, or by any information storage or retrieval system without the prior written permission of Houghton Mifflin Company unless such copying is expressly permitted by federal copyright law. Address inquiries to College Permissions, Houghton Mifflin Company, 222 Berkeley Street, Boston, MA 02116-3764.

Printed in the U.S.A.

Library of Congress Control Number: 2004112994

ISBN
Student Text: 0-618-49658-0
Instructor's Annotated Edition: 0-618-50152-5
Advanced Placement High School Edition: 0-618-50153-3

3 4 5 6 7 8 9—DOW—10 09 08 07 06

▐▌ Contents

viii   Contents

10 Correlation and Regression   580

11 Chi-Square and F Distributions   668

12 Nonparametric Statistics   760

Appendix I: *Additional Topics*   A1

Appendix II: *Tables*   A9

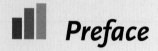
Preface

Welcome to the exciting world of statistics! We have written this text to make statistics accessible to everyone, including those with a limited mathematics background. Statistics affects all aspects of our lives. Whether we are testing new medical devices or determining what will entertain us, applications of statistics are so numerous that, in a sense, we are limited only by our own imagination in discovering new uses for statistics.

Overview

The eighth edition of *Understandable Statistics: Concepts and Methods* continues to emphasize concepts of statistics. Statistical methods are carefully presented with a focus on understanding both the *suitability of the method* and the *meaning of the result*. Statistical methods and measurements are developed in the context of applications.

We have retained and expanded features that made the first seven editions of the text very readable. New definition boxes highlight important terms. New procedure displays summarize steps for analyzing data. Examples, exercises, and problems touch on applications appropriate to a broad range of interests.

Major Content Changes in the Eighth Edition

With each new edition, the authors reevaluate the scope, appropriateness, and effectiveness of the text's presentation and reflect on extensive user feedback. Revisions have been made throughout the text to clarify explanations of important concepts and to update problems.

Introduction of Hypothesis Testing Using *P*-Values

Chapter 9, Hypothesis Testing, has been reorganized. In keeping with the use of computer technology and standard practice in research, hypothesis testing is now introduced using *P*-values. The critical region method is still supported, but not given primary emphasis.

Use of Student's *t* Distribution in Confidence Intervals and Testing of Means

If the normal distribution is used in confidence intervals and testing of means, then the *population standard deviation must be known*. If the population standard deviation is not known, then under conditions described in the text, the Student's *t* distribution is used. This is the most commonly used procedure in statistical research. It is also used in statistical software packages such as Microsoft Excel, Minitab, SPSS, and TI-84Plus/TI-83Plus calculators.

Confidence Intervals and Hypothesis Tests of Difference of Means

If the normal distribution is used, then both population standard deviations must be known. When this is not the case, the Student's t distribution incorporates an approximation for t, with a commonly used conservative choice for the degrees of freedom. Satterthwaite's approximation for the degrees of freedom as used in computer software is also discussed. The pooled standard deviation is presented for appropriate applications ($\sigma_1 \approx \sigma_2$).

Reorganization of Chapter 10, Correlation and Regression

The sample correlation coefficient is presented in Section 10.1, while the equation of the least-squares line is presented in Section 10.2. Inferences regarding predicted values $\hat{y}$, correlation coefficient ρ, and slope β of the least-squares line are now included within a single section, Section 10.3. This organization makes it more convenient to use the option of introducing descriptive components of correlation and regression early.

Runs Test: A New Section in Chapter 12, Nonparametric Statistics

The runs tests for randomness is now included in Chapter 12.

Features in the Eighth Edition

Chapter and Section Lead-ins

- *Preview Questions* at the beginning of each chapter are keyed to the sections.
- *Focus Problems* at the beginning of each chapter demonstrate types of questions students can answer once they master the concepts and skills presented in the chapter.
- *Focus Points* at the beginning of each section describe the primary learning objectives of the section.

Carefully Developed Pedagogy

- *Examples* show students how to select and use appropriate procedures.
- *Guided Exercises* within the sections give students an opportunity to work with a new concept. Completely worked-out solutions appear beside each exercise to give immediate reinforcement.
- *Definition boxes* highlight important definitions throughout the text.
- *Procedure displays* summarize key strategies for carrying out statistical procedures and methods.
- *Labels* for each example or guided exercise highlight the technique, concept, or process illustrated by the example or guided exercise. In addition, labels for section and chapter problems describe the field of application and show the wide variety of subjects in which statistics is used.
- *Section and chapter problems* require the student to use all the new concepts mastered in the section or chapter. Problem sets include a variety of real-world applications with data or settings from identifiable sources. Key steps and solutions to odd-numbered problems appear at the end of the book.

- *Expand Your Knowledge problems* present enrichment topics such as negative binomial distribution; conditional probability utilizing binomial, Poisson, and normal distributions; estimation of standard deviation from a range of data values; and more.

- *Problems incorporating real-world data available on a CD-ROM or text web site* alert students to data available electronically.

- *Cumulative review problem sets* occur after every third chapter and include key topics from previous chapters. Answers to *all* cumulative review problems are given at the end of the book.

- *Data Highlights and Linking Concepts* provide group projects and writing projects.

- *Viewpoints* are brief essays presenting diverse situations in which statistics is used.

- *Design and photos* are appealing and enhance readability.

Technology within the Text

- *Tech Notes* within sections provide brief point-of-use instructions for the TI-84Plus and TI-83Plus calculators, Microsoft Excel, and Minitab.

- *Using Technology* sections have been revised to show the use of SPSS as well as the TI-84Plus and TI-83Plus calculators, Microsoft Excel, and Minitab.

Supplements for Students

- *Text-Specific Web Site* features a number of student resources, including data sets, tutorials, quizzes, glossary, and web links. Go to **http://math.college.hmco.com/ students** and follow the statistics links to the Brase/Brase, *Understandable Statistics, 8e* site.

- *Technology Guide* contains information and examples for the TI-84Plus and TI-83Plus graphing calculators, Minitab software, Microsoft Excel, and SPSS software.

- *Student Solutions Manual* provides solutions to the odd-numbered section and chapter exercises and to all the Cumulative Review exercises in the student textbook.

Supplements for Instructors

- *Instructor's Annotated Edition.* Answers appear in the margins next to *all* of the exercises in the text, while those answers involving larger graphs or tables appear in a special section at the end of the IAE. In addition, teaching comments and general pedagogical suggestions are located in the margins of this text.

- *Instructor's Resource Guide with Complete Solutions* provides the complete solutions to all exercises in the text, sample tests for each chapter, Teaching Hints, and Transparency Masters for the tables and frequently used formulas found in the eighth edition.

- *Text-Specific Web Site.* In addition to the resources found on the student web site, instructors can access digital lessons for use in classroom presentations and classroom management features by going to **http://math.college.hmco.com/instructors** and following the statistics links to the Brase/Brase, *Understandable Statistics, 8e* site.

Alternate Routes Through the Text

Understandable Statistics: Concepts and Methods, Eighth Edition, is designed to be flexible. It offers the professor a choice of teaching possibilities. In most one-semester courses, it is not practical to cover all the material in depth. However, depending on the emphasis of the course, the professor may choose to cover various topics. For help in topic selection, refer to the Table of Prerequisite Material on page 1.

- *Introducing linear regression early.* For courses requiring an early presentation of linear regression, the descriptive components of linear regression (Sections 10.1 and 10.2) can be presented any time after Chapter 3. However, inference topics involving predictions, the correlation coefficient ρ, and the slope of the least-squares line β require an introduction to confidence intervals (Sections 8.1 and 8.2) and hypothesis testing (Sections 9.1 and 9.2).
- *Probability.* For courses requiring minimal probability, Section 4.1 (What Is Probability?) and the first part of Section 4.2 (Some Probability Rules—Compound Events) will be sufficient.

Acknowledgments

It is our pleasure to acknowledge the prepublication reviewers of this text. All of their insights and comments have been very valuable to us. Reviewers of this text include:

Paul Ache, Kutztown University
Delores Anderson, Truett-McConnell College
Robert J. Astalos, Feather River College
Lynda L. Ballou, Kansas State University
Larry Bernett, Benedictine University
Kristy E. Bland, Valdosta State University
John Bray, Broward Community College
Bill Burgin, Gaston College
Toni Carroll, Siena Heights University
Pinyuen Chen, Syracuse University
Jennifer M. Dollar, Grand Rapids Community College
Larry E. Dunham, Wor-Wic Community College
Andrew Ellett, Indiana University
Mary Fine, Moberly Area Community College
Rene Garcia, Miami-Dade Community College
Larry Green, Lake Tahoe Community College
Jane Keller, Metropolitan Community College
Raja Khoury, Collin County Community College
Charles G. Laws, Cleveland State Community College
Michael R. Lloyd, Henderson State University
Beth Long, Pellissippi State Technical and Community College

Lewis Lum, University of Portland
Darcy P. Mays, Virginia Commonwealth University
Charles C. Okeke, College of Southern Nevada, Las Vegas
Peg Pankowski, Community College of Allegheny County
Michael L. Russo, Suffolk County Community College
Janel Schultz, Saint Mary's University of Minnesota
Winson Taam, Oakland University
Jennifer L. Taggart, Rockford College
William Truman, University of North Carolina at Pembroke
Jim Wienckowski, State University of New York at Buffalo
Stephen M. Wilkerson, Susquehanna University
Hongkai Zhang, East Central University
Shunpu Zhang, University of Alaska, Fairbanks

We would especially like to thank Helen Medley for her careful accuracy review of this text, and Lauren Arnest for her creative illustrations that accompany the Viewpoint essays. We are especially appreciative of the excellent work by the editorial and production professionals at Houghton Mifflin. In particular, we thank Lauren Schultz, Kasey McGarrigle, Sean McGann, David George, and Nancy Blodget. Without their creative insight and attention to detail, a project of this quality and magnitude would not be possible. Finally, we acknowledge the cooperation of Minitab, Inc., SPSS, Texas Instruments, and Microsoft Excel.

Charles Henry Brase
Corrinne Pellillo Brase

Table of Prerequisite Material

Chapter	Prerequisite Sections
1 Getting Started	None
2 Organizing Data	1.1, 1.2
3 Averages and Variation	1.1, 1.2, 2.2
4 Elementary Probability Theory	1.1, 1.2, 2.2, 3.1, 3.2
5 The Binomial Probability Distribution and Related Topics	1.1, 1.2, 2.2, 3.1, 3.2, 4.1, 4.2 4.3 useful but not essential
6 Normal Distributions (omit 6.4) (include 6.4)	 1.1, 1.2, 2.2, 3.1, 3.2, 4.1, 4.2, 5.1 also 5.2, 5.3
7 Introduction to Sampling Distributions (omit 7.3) (include 7.3)	 1.1, 1.2, 2.2, 3.1, 3.2, 4.1, 4.2, 5.1, 6.1, 6.2, 6.3 also 6.4
8 Estimation (omit 8.3 and parts of 8.4 and 8.5) (include 8.3 and parts of 8.4 and 8.5)	 1.1, 1.2, 2.2, 3.1, 3.2, 4.1, 4.2, 5.1, 6.1, 6.2, 6.3, 7.1, 7.2 also 5.2, 5.3, 6.4
9 Hypothesis Testing (omit 9.3 and part of 9.5) (include 9.3 and all of 9.5)	 1.1, 1.2, 2.2, 3.1, 3.2, 4.1, 4.2, 5.1, 6.1, 6.2, 6.3, 7.1, 7.2 also 5.2, 5.3, 6.4
10 Correlation and Regression (10.1 and 10.2) (10.3 and 10.4)	 1.1, 1.2, 3.1, 3.2 also 4.1, 4.2, 5.1, 6.1, 6.2, 6.3, 7.1, 7.2, 8.1, 8.2, 9.1, 9.2
11 Chi-Square and F Distributions (omit 11.3) (include 11.3)	 1.1, 1.2, 2.2, 3.1, 3.2, 4.1, 4.2, 5.1, 6.1, 6.2, 6.3, 7.1, 7.2, 9.1 also 8.1
12 Nonparametric Statistics	1.1, 1.2, 2.2, 3.1, 3.2, 4.1, 4.2, 5.1, 6.1, 6.2, 6.3, 7.1, 7.2, 9.1, 9.3

1

Getting Started

To guess is cheap,
To guess wrongly is expensive.

Tell me, I'll forget.
Show me, I may remember.
But involve me and I'll understand.

—Old Chinese Proverbs

**Dragon Gate,
Chinatown,
San Francisco**

Dragon Gate is one of the many landmarks in San Francisco that exemplifies the city's ethnic diversity.

For on-line student resources, visit **math.college.hmco.com/students** and follow the Statistics links to the Brase/Brase, *Understandable Statistics,* 8th edition web site.

Most of the important decisions in life involve incomplete information. Such decisions often involve so many complicated factors that a complete analysis is not practical or even possible. We are often forced into the position of making a guess based on limited information. However, as the first proverb implies, a blind guess is not the best solution. Statistical methods, such as those you will learn in this book, can help you make the best "educated guess."

The authors of this book want you to understand and enjoy statistics. The reading material will *tell you* about the subject. The examples will *show you* how it works. To understand, however, the second proverb says you must *get involved.* Guided exercises, calculator and computer applications, section and chapter problems, and writing exercises are all designed to get you involved in the subject. As you grow in your understanding of statistics, we believe you will enjoy learning a subject that has a world full of interesting applications.

PREVIEW QUESTIONS

◊ Why is statistics important?   (SECTION 1.1)

◊ What is the nature of data?   (SECTION 1.1)

◊ How can you draw a random sample?   (SECTION 1.2)

◊ What are other sampling techniques?   (SECTION 1.2)

◊ How can you design ways to collect data?   (SECTION 1.3)

Where Have All the Fireflies Gone?

A feature article in the *Wall Street Journal* discusses the alarming disappearance of fireflies. In the article, Professor Sara Lewis (of Tufts University) and other scholars express concern about the decline in the worldwide population of fireflies. So far the evidence is anecdotal: stories from around the world about the alarming decline of fireflies. Japan has a tradition that nighttime fireflies are a beautiful reminder of the souls of friends and family who have passed away. For reasons such as this, and possibly for the simple joy of watching fireflies, Japan has a number of special sanctuaries to protect the declining population of fireflies.

There are a number of possible explanations for the world decline in the firefly population. Artificial nighttime lighting might be interfering with the Morse code-like mating ritual of the fireflies. Woodlands, wetlands, and open fields have given way to cities and subdivisions. Chemicals and pesticides may be killing the fireflies.

Fireflies are commercially valuable because they contain two rare chemicals used in research on cancer, multiple sclerosis, cystic fibrosis, and heart disease. The chemicals are also used on spacecraft in electronic detectors designed to look for earth-life forms in outer space. Near St. Louis there is a bounty on fireflies: A chemical company pays 1 cent for each firefly. One family was so successful in collecting fireflies that they were able to send three children to college from the proceeds!

Adapted from Ohio State University Firefly Files logo

3

What does any of this have to do with statistics?

The truth, at this time, is that no one really knows (a) how much the world firefly population has declined or (b) how to explain the decline. The population of all fireflies is simply too large to study in its entirety. In any study of fireflies, we must rely on incomplete information from samples. Furthermore, from these samples we must draw realistic conclusions that have statistical integrity.

You may be sure that a number of very fine scholars in universities across the world are beginning to examine the possible world decline in fireflies. You also may be sure that these scholars will use statistical methods when they collect, analyze, and investigate their data about fireflies.

Ohio State University Department of Entomology does research on anthropods and maintains extensive information about fireflies. For more information about fireflies, visit the Brase/Brase statistics site at **http://math.college.hmco.com/students** and find the link to the Ohio State University Department of Entomology. Then search for *firefly* in the index of the Ohio State site.

Suppose you are conducting a study to compare firefly populations exposed to normal daylight/darkness conditions with firefly populations exposed to continuous light (24 hours a day). You set up two firefly colonies in a laboratory environment. The two colonies are identical except that one colony is exposed to normal daylight/darkness conditions and the other is exposed to continuous light. Each colony is populated with the same number of mature fireflies. After 72 hours, you count the number of living fireflies in each colony.

After completing this chapter, you will be able to answer the following questions.

(a) Is this an experiment or an observation study? Explain.

(b) Is there a control group? Is there a treatment group?

(c) What is the variable in this study?

(d) What is the level of measurement (nominal, interval, ordinal, or ratio) of the variable?

(See Problem 11 of the Chapter 1 Review Problems.)

1.1
What Is Statistics?

FOCUS POINTS

✓ Identify variables in a statistical study.
✓ Distinguish between quantitative and qualitative variables.
✓ Identify populations and samples.
✓ Determine the level of measurement.
✓ Compare descriptive and inferential statistics.

Introduction

Decision making is an important aspect of our lives. We make decisions based on the information we have, our attitudes, and our values. Statistical methods help examine information. Moreover, statistics can be used for making decisions when we are faced with uncertainties. For instance, if we wish to estimate the proportion of people who will have a severe reaction to a flu shot without giving the shot to everyone who wants it, statistics provides appropriate methods. Statistical methods enable us to look at information from a small collection of people or items and make inferences about a larger collection of people or items.

Procedures for analyzing data, together with rules of inference, are central topics in the study of statistics.

Statistics

> **Statistics** is the study of how to collect, organize, analyze, and interpret numerical information from data.

The statistical procedures you will learn in this book should supplement your built-in system of inference—that is, the results from statistical procedures and good sense should dovetail. Of course, statistical methods themselves have no power to work miracles. These methods can help us make some decisions, but not all conceivable decisions. Remember, a properly applied statistical procedure is no more accurate than the data, or facts, on which it is based. Finally, statistical results should be interpreted by one who understands not only the methods, but also the subject matter to which they have been applied.

The general prerequisite for statistical decision making is the gathering of data. First, we need to identify the individuals or objects to be included in the study and the characteristics or features of the individuals that are of interest.

Individuals
Variable

> **Individuals** are the people or objects included in the study.
> A **variable** is the characteristic of the individual to be measured or observed.

For instance, if we want to do a study about the people who have climbed Mt. Everest, then the individuals in the study are all people who have actually made it to the summit. One variable might be the height of such individuals. Other variables might be age, weight, gender, nationality, income, and so on. Regardless of the variables we use, we would not include measurements or observations from people who have not climbed the mountain.

The variables in a study may be *quantitative* or *qualitative* in nature.

Quantitative variable
Qualitative variable

> A **quantitative variable** has a value or numerical measurement for which operations such as addition or averaging make sense. A **qualitative variable** describes an individual by placing the individual into a category or group such as male or female.

For the Mt. Everest climbers, variables such as height, weight, age, or income are *quantitative* variables. *Qualitative variables* involve nonnumerical observations such as gender or nationality. Sometimes qualitative variables are referred to as *categorical.*

Another important issue regarding data is their source. Do the data comprise information from *all* individuals of interest, or from just *some* of the individuals?

Population data
Sample data

> In **population data,** the variable is from *every* individual of interest.
> In **sample data,** the variable is from *only some* of the individuals of interest.

For instance, if we have data from *all* the individuals who have climbed Mt. Everest, then we have population data. On the other hand, if our data come from just some of the climbers, we have sample data.

It is interesting to note that a population is defined in terms of our *desire for knowledge*. The population can be thought of as measurements or observations for the entire group of objects or individuals about which information is desired. In this sense, a population can be an existing set of data, or it can be a set of data that is clear in our understanding but is not yet complete. The ages of all U.S. presidents at the time of inauguration—from George Washington to George W. Bush—can be thought of as an existing set of data. However, the set of ages of all presidents at the time of inauguration from George Washington into the future is not complete. Nevertheless, we have a clear understanding of how this population is to be constructed. In a way, we can think of such an incomplete population as being open-ended.

EXAMPLE 1

Using basic terminology

The Hawaii Department of Tropical Agriculture is conducting a study of ready-to-harvest pineapples in an experimental field.

(a) The pineapples are the *objects* (individuals) of the study. If the researchers are interested in the individual weights of pineapples in the field, then the *variable* consists of weights. At this point, it is important to specify units of measurement and degree of accuracy of measurement. The weights could be to the nearest ounce or gram. Weight is a *quantitative* variable because it is a numerical measure. If weights of *all* the ready-to-harvest pineapples in the field are included in the data, then we have a *population*.

(b) Suppose the researchers also want data on taste. A panel of tasters rates the pineapples according to the categories poor, acceptable, and good. Only some of the pineapples are included in the taste test. In this case, the *variable* is taste. This is a *qualitative* or *categorical* variable. Because only some of the pineapples in the field are included in the study, we have a *sample*.   ◊

Throughout this text, you will encounter *guided exercises* embedded in the reading material. These exercises are included to give you an opportunity to work immediately with new ideas. The questions guide you through appropriate analysis. Cover the answers on the right side (an index card will fit this purpose). After you have thought about or written down *your own response*, check the answers. If there are several parts to an exercise, check each part before you continue. You should be able to answer most of these exercise questions, but don't skip them—they are important.

GUIDED EXERCISE 1

Using basic terminology

Television station QUE wants to know the proportion of TV owners in Virginia who watch the station's new program at least once a week. The station asked a group of 1000 TV owners in Virginia if they watch the program at least once a week.

(a) Identify the individuals of the study and the variable.

⟹ The individuals are the 1000 TV owners surveyed. The variable is the response does, or does not, watch the new program at least once a week.

(b) Do the data comprise a sample? If so, what is the underlying population?

⟹ The data comprise a sample of the population of responses from all TV owners in Virginia.

(c) Is the variable qualitative or quantitative?

⟹ Qualitative—the categories are the two possible responses, does or does not watch the program.

(d) Identify a quantitative variable that might be of interest.

⟹ Age or income might be of interest.

Levels of Measurement: Nominal, Ordinal, Interval, Ratio

We have categorized data as either qualitative or quantitative. Another way to classify data is according to one of the following four *levels of measurement:*

Nominal	Ordinal	Interval	Ratio

Nominal level

Since the *nominal level* is the lowest level, let's examine it first. A dictionary meaning of the word *nominal* is "in name only." This is an easy way to remember the meaning of the nominal level of measurement. Data at this level of measurement consist of "names only," or qualities, with no implied criteria by which the data can be identified as greater than or less than other data items.

The **nominal level of measurement** applies to data that consist of names, labels, or categories.

EXAMPLE 2

Nominal level

The following are examples of data at the nominal level of measurement.

(a) Aspen, Vail, and Breckenridge are names of three ski resorts from the population of names of all ski resorts in Colorado.

(b) Taos, Acoma, Zuni, and Cochiti are names of four Native American pueblos from the population of names of all Native American pueblos in Arizona and New Mexico. ◇

It is clear that the nominal data in Example 2 are not intended for numerical calculation. The specific names or qualities do not contain any implied ordering or numerical significance.

The next level of measurement is the *ordinal level*. Data at the ordinal level may be arranged in some order, but actual differences between data values either cannot be determined or are meaningless.

Ordinal level

> The **ordinal level of measurement** applies to data that may be arranged in order. However, differences between data values either cannot be determined or are meaningless.

EXAMPLE 3

Ordinal level

The following are examples of data at the ordinal level of measurement.

(a) In a fishing tackle catalogue, 17 fishing reels are advertised. Of these reels, 6 were rated as good quality, 4 were rated as better quality, and 7 were rated as best quality.

(b) In a high school graduating class of 319 students, Jim ranked 25th, June ranked 19th, Walter ranked 10th, and Julia ranked 4th.   ◊

In Example 3, we should not try to determine specific quantitative differences between "good," "better," and "best." The difference between June's and Jim's rank is 6, and this is the same difference that exists between Walter's and Julia's rank. However, this difference doesn't really mean anything significant. For instance, if you looked at grade point average, Walter and Julia may have had a big gap between them, whereas June and Jim may have been closer together. In any ranking system, it is only the relative standing that matters. Differences between ranks can be meaningless.

In general, the ordinal level of measurement provides information about relative comparisons, but exact differences are not computed.

The *interval level of measurement* is like the ordinal level, but it has the additional property that meaningful differences between data values can be computed. However, interval-level data may not have an intrinsic zero or starting point. Consequently, *differences* are meaningful, but *ratios* of data values are not.

Interval level

> The **interval level of measurement** applies to data that can be arranged in order. In addition, differences between data values are meaningful.

EXAMPLE 4

Interval level

The following are examples of data at the interval level of measurement.

(a) Years in which Democrats won presidential elections.

(b) Body temperatures (in degrees Celsius) of trout in the Yellowstone River.   ◊

Temperature readings in degrees Celsius (or Fahrenheit) are examples of data at the interval level of measurement. Such values are certainly ordered, and we can compute meaningful differences. However, for Celsius-scale temperatures, there is not an inherent starting point. The value 0°C may seem to be a starting point, but the value of 0°C does not indicate the state of "no heat." Furthermore, it is not correct to say 20°C is twice as hot as 10°C. Calendar times are also interval measurements, since the date 0 A.D. does not signify "no time." However, a time lapse is at a higher level of measurement and is, in fact, an example of our top level of measurement, the *ratio level*.

Ratio level

The *ratio level of measurement* is the highest level. The ratio level is similar to the interval level, but it includes an inherent zero as a starting point for all measurements. Consequently, at this level, both differences *and* ratios are meaningful.

> The **ratio level of measurement** applies to data that can be arranged in order. In addition, both differences between data values and ratios of data values are meaningful. Data at the ratio level have a true zero.

EXAMPLE 5

Ratio level

The following are examples of data at the ratio level of measurement.

(a) The core temperatures of stars in the Milky Way when measured in degrees Kelvin. Notice that in the Kelvin scale of measurement 0°K means "no heat." This is a special temperature scale used primarily by scientists.

(b) Length of trout swimming in the Yellowstone River. A trout 18 inches long is three times as long as a 6-inch trout. Observe that we can divide 6 into 18 to determine the *ratio* of the trout lengths.   ◊

In summary, there are four levels of measurement. The nominal is considered the lowest, and in ascending order we have the ordinal, interval, and ratio levels. In general, calculations based on a particular level of measurement may not be appropriate for a lower level.

Level of Measurement	Suitable Calculation
Nominal	We can put the data into categories.
Ordinal	We can order the data from smallest to largest or "worst" to "best." Each data value can be *compared* with another data value.
Interval	We can order the data and also take the differences between data values. At this level, it makes sense to compare the differences between data values. For instance, we can say that one data value is 5 more than or 12 less than another data value.
Ratio	We can order the data, take differences, and also find the ratio between data values. For instance, it makes sense to say that one data value is twice as large as another.

> **PROCEDURE**
>
> **How to determine the level of measurement**
>
> To determine the level of measurement of data, state the *highest level* (nominal, ordinal, interval, or ratio) that can be justified for the entire collection of data.

GUIDED EXERCISE 2

Levels of measurement

The following describe different data associated with a state senator. For each data entry, indicate the corresponding *level of measurement*.

(a) The senator's name is Sam Wilson.   ⟹   Nominal level

(b) The senator is 58 years old.   ⟹   Ratio level

(c) The years in which the senator was elected to the Senate are 1980, 1986, 1992, and 1998.   ⟹   Interval level

(d) The senator's total taxable income last year was $878,314.19.   ⟹   Ratio level

(e) The senator sponsored a bill to protect water rights. Out of 1100 voters in his district, 400 said they strongly favored the bill, 300 said they favored the bill, 200 said they were neutral, 150 said they did not favor the bill, and 50 said they strongly did not favor the bill.   ⟹   The opinions about the bill are at the ordinal level.

(f) The senator is married now.   ⟹   Nominal level

(g) A leading news magazine claims the senator is ranked seventh for his voting record on bills regarding public education.   ⟹   Ordinal level

Looking Ahead

The purpose of collecting and analyzing data is to obtain information. Statistical methods provide us tools to obtain information from data. These methods break into two branches.

Descriptive statistics

Inferential statistics

Descriptive statistics involves methods of organizing, picturing, and summarizing information from samples or populations.
Inferential statistics involves methods of using information from a sample to draw conclusions regarding the population.

We will look at methods of descriptive statistics in the next two chapters and in Chapter 10. These methods may be applied to data from samples or populations.

Sometimes we do not have access to an entire population. At other times, the difficulties or expense of working with the entire population are prohibitive. In such cases, we will use inferential statistics together with probability. These are the topics of Chapters 4 through 12.

VIEWPOINT

The First Measured Century

The 20th century saw measurements of aspects of American life that had never been systematically studied before. Social conditions involving crime, sex, food, fun, religion, and work have been numerically investigated. The measurements and survey responses taken over the entire century reveal unsuspected statistical trends. *The First Measured Century* is a book by Caplow, Hicks, and Wattenberg. It is also a PBS documentary available on video. For more information, visit the Brase/Brase statistics site at **http://math.college.hmco.com/students** and find the link to the PBS *First Measured Century* documentary.

SECTION 1.1   PROBLEMS

1. *Marketing: Fast Food* USA Today reported that 44.9% of those surveyed (1261 adults) ate in fast-food restaurants from one to three times each week.
   (a) Identify the variable.
   (b) Is the variable quantitative or qualitative?
   (c) What is the implied population?

2. *Advertising: Auto Mileage* What is the average miles per gallon (mpg) for all new cars? Using *Consumer Reports*, a random sample of 35 new cars gave an average of 21.1 mpg.
   (a) Identify the variable.
   (b) Is the variable quantitative or qualitative?
   (c) What is the implied population?

3. *Academic: Student/Faculty Ratio* The students at Eastmore College are concerned about the ratio of number of students to number of faculty at their school. Using *Barron's Profiles of American Colleges*, they took a random sample of 45 colleges in the nation and obtained the student/faculty ratios at these institutions. From this information, they concluded that their student/faculty ratio is higher than those of most colleges in the nation.
   (a) Identify the variable.
   (b) Is the variable quantitative or qualitative?
   (c) What is the implied population?

4. *Archaeology: Ireland* The archaeological site of Tara is more than 4000 years old. Tradition states that Tara was the seat of the high kings of Ireland. Because of its archaeological importance, Tara has received extensive study. For example, when certain types of iron-bearing (ferromagnetic) materials are repeatedly heated in a fire and cooled, a type of permanent magnetism occurs. Because of this, archaeological hearths and other ferromagnetic artifacts are often detected as permanent magnets. Using an instrument called a fluxgate gradiometer, archaeology students are able to locate buried ferromagnetic artifacts (Reference: *Tara: An Archaeological Survey* by Conor Newman, Royal Irish Academy, Dublin). Suppose an archaeologist wants to estimate the density of ferromagnetic artifacts in the Tara region. For this purpose, a random sample of 55 plots, each of size 100 square meters, is used. The number of ferromagnetic artifacts for each plot is determined.
   (a) Identify the variable.
   (b) Is the variable quantitative or qualitative?
   (c) What is the implied population?

5. *Ecology: Wetlands* The Clean Water Act was passed by Congress more than 30 years ago. Since then, government agencies have carefully monitored water quality and its effect on wetlands (Reference: *Environmental Protection Agency Wetland Report* EPA 832-R-93-005). Of particular concern is the concentration of nitrogen in water draining from fertilized lands. Too much nitrogen can kill fish and wildlife. Suppose a student intern working for the Environmental Protection Agency has been studying the nitrogen concentration in a lake receiving drainage from a local golf course. Twenty-eight samples of water were taken at random from the lake. The nitrogen concentration (milligrams of nitrogen per liter of water) was determined for each sample.
   (a) Identify the variable.
   (b) Is the variable quantitative or qualitative?
   (c) What is the implied population?

6. *Education: Teacher Evaluation* If you were going to apply *statistical methods* to analyze teacher evaluations, which question form, A or B, would be better?
   Form A: In your own words, tell how this teacher compares with other teachers you have had.
   Form B: Use the following scale to rank your teacher as compared with other teachers you have had.

1	2	3	4	5
worst	below average	average	above average	best

7. *Student Life: Levels of Measurement* Categorize these measurements associated with student life according to level: nominal, ordinal, interval, or ratio.
   (a) Length of time to complete an exam
   (b) Time of first class
   (c) Major field of study
   (d) Course evaluation scale: poor, acceptable, good
   (e) Score on last exam (based on 100 possible points)
   (f) Age of student

8. *Business: Levels of Measurement* Categorize these measurements associated with a robotics company according to level: nominal, ordinal, interval, or ratio.
   (a) Salesperson's performance: below average, average, above average
   (b) Price of company's stock
   (c) Names of new products
   (d) Room temperature (°F) in CEO's private office

(e) Gross income for each of the past 5 years

(f) Color of packaging

9. *Fishing: Levels of Measurement* Categorize these measurements associated with fishing according to level: nominal, ordinal, interval, or ratio.

(a) Species of fish caught: perch, bass, pike, trout

(b) Cost of rod and reel

(c) Time of return home

(d) Guidebook rating of fishing area: poor, fair, good

(e) Number of fish caught

(f) Temperature of water

1.2
Random Samples

Simple Random Samples

FOCUS POINTS

✓ Explain the importance of random samples.

✓ Construct a simple random sample using random numbers.

✓ Simulate a random process.

✓ Describe stratified sampling, cluster sampling, systematic sampling, and convenience sampling.

Eat lamb—20,000 coyotes can't be wrong!

This slogan is sometimes found on bumper stickers in the western United States. The slogan indicates the trouble that ranchers have experienced in protecting their flocks from predators. Based on their experience with this sample of the coyote population, the ranchers concluded that *all* coyotes are dangerous to their flocks and should be eliminated! The ranchers used a special poison bait to get rid of the coyotes. Not only was this poison distributed on ranch land, but with government cooperation it also was distributed widely on public lands.

The ranchers found that the results of the widespread poisoning were not very beneficial. The sheep-eating coyotes continued to thrive while the general population of coyotes and other predators declined. What was the problem? The sheep-eating coyotes the ranchers had observed were not a representative sample of all coyotes. Modern methods of predator control target the sheep-eating coyotes. To a certain extent the new methods have come about through a closer examination of the sampling techniques used.

In this section, we will examine several widely used sampling techniques. One of the most important sampling techniques is a *simple random sample*.

Simple random sample

A **simple random sample** of *n* measurements from a population is a subset of the population selected in a manner such that

(a) every sample of size *n* from the population has an equal chance of being selected and

(b) every member of the population has an equal chance of being included in the sample.

Notice that two criteria are necessary for a simple random sample of a specified size. Not only must every member of the population have an equal chance of being included, but every sample of the specified size must have an equal chance of being selected as well.

GUIDED EXERCISE 3

Simple random sample

Is open space around metropolitan areas important? Players of the Colorado Lottery might think so because some of the proceeds of the game go to fund open space and outdoor recreational space. To play the game, you pay one dollar and choose any six different numbers from the group of numbers 1 through 42. If your group of six numbers matches the winning group of six numbers selected by simple random sampling, then you are a winner of a grand prize of at least 1.5 million dollars.

(a) Is the number 25 as likely to be selected in the winning group of six numbers as the number 5?

→ Yes. Because the winning numbers constitute a simple random sample, each number from 1 through 42 has an equal chance of being selected.

(b) Could all the winning numbers be even?

→ Yes, since six even numbers is one of the possible groups of six numbers.

(c) Your friend always plays the numbers

1   2   3   4   5   6

Could she ever win?

→ Yes. In a simple random sample, the listed group of six numbers is *as likely as any* of the 5,245,786 groups of six numbers to be selected as the winner. (See Section 4.3 to learn how to compute the number of possible groups of six numbers selected from 42 numbers.)

How do we get random samples? Suppose you need to know if the emission system of the latest shipment of Toyotas satisfies pollution-control standards. You want to pick a random sample of 30 cars from this shipment of 500 cars and test them. One way to pick a random sample is to number the cars 1 through 500. Write these numbers on cards, mix up the cards, and then draw 30 numbers. The sample will consist of the cars with the chosen numbers. If you mix the cards sufficiently, this procedure produces a random sample.

Random-number table

An easier way to select the numbers is to use a *random-number table*. You can make one yourself by writing the digits 0 through 9 on separate cards and mixing up these cards in a hat. Then draw a card, record the digit, return the card, and mix up the cards again. Draw another card, record the digit, and so on. Table 1 in Appendix II is a ready-made random-number table (adapted from Rand Corporation, *A Million Random Digits with 100,000 Normal Deviates*). Let's see how to pick our random sample of 30 Toyotas by using this random-number table.

EXAMPLE 6
Random-number table

Use a random-number table to pick a random sample of 30 cars from a population of 500 cars.

SOLUTION: Again, we assign each car a different number between 1 and 500, inclusive. Then we use the random-number table to choose the sample. Table 1 in Appendix II has 50 rows and 10 blocks of five digits each; it can be thought of as a solid mass of digits that has been broken up into rows and blocks for user convenience.

You read the digits by beginning anywhere in the table. We dropped a pin on the table, and the head of the pin landed in row 15, block 5. We'll begin there and list all the digits in that row. If we need more digits, we'll move on to row 16, and so on. The digits we begin with are

99281   59640   15221   96079   09961   05371

Since the highest number assigned to a car is 500, and this number has three digits, we regroup our digits into blocks of 3:

992   815   964   015   221   960   790   996   105   371

To construct our random sample, we use the first 30 car numbers we encounter in the random-number table when we start at row 15, block 5. We skip the first three groups—992, 815, and 964—because these numbers are all too large. The next group of three digits is 015, which corresponds to 15. Car number 15 is the first car included in our sample, and the next is car number 221. We skip the next three groups and then include car numbers 105 and 371. To get the rest of the cars in the sample, we continue to the next line and use the random-number table in this fashion. If we encounter a number we've used before, we'll skip it.   ◊

◊ **COMMENT** When we use the term *(simple) random sample,* we have very specific criteria in mind for selecting the sample. One proper method for selecting a simple random sample is to use a computer-based or calculator-based random-number generator or to use a table of random numbers as we have done in the example. The term *random* should not be confused with *haphazard!*   ◊

Simulation

Another important use of random-number tables is in *simulation*. We use the word *simulation* to refer to the process of providing arithmetic imitations of "real" phenomena. Simulation methods have been productive in studying a diverse array of subjects such as nuclear reactors, cloud formation, cardiology (and medical science in general), highway design, production control, shipbuilding, airplane design, war games, economics, and electronics. A complete list would probably include something from every aspect of modern life. In Example 7 and Guided Exercise 4 we'll perform brief simulations.

> A **simulation** is a numerical facsimile or representation of a real-world phenomenon.

EXAMPLE 7
Simulation

A well-known theory in stock market analysis is the "random walk" theory (see *A Random Walk Down Wall Street,* 6th Edition, Burton Malkiel, W. W. Norton & Co.). The term *random walk,* as applied to stock prices, means that short-term changes in stock prices cannot be predicted but rather are random. In particular, according to the random walk theory, the next move in the price of a stock (up or down) is completely unpredictable on the basis of what price changes happened before.

Let's use a very simplified model to *simulate* the stock price changes of a hypothetical company, Fun Boards (maker of skateboards, surfboards, snowboards, and

Trading floor, New York Stock Exchange

in-line skates). Suppose the initial price of Fun Boards stock is $50 per share. Use the random-number table to simulate daily price changes for the next 15 trading days in the following way. Notice that we are interested in price *changes*. Days during which the stock does not change price will be ignored.

SOLUTION: The daily stock price change will be dictated by a number from the random-number table. When you encounter an even digit (0, 2, 4, 6, 8), increase the stock price by $1. When you encounter an odd digit (1, 3, 5, 7, 9), decrease the stock price by $1. Do this for a sequence of 15 trading days during which the price changed.

Beginning with line 6, block 2 in Table 1 of Appendix II, we see the 15 random digits

51709   94456   48396

Since the first random digit is odd, we will decrease the price by $1 on the first day. In fact, the next two digits are also odd, so we will decrease the price again by $1 on day 2 and then again on day 3. The next digit is even, so we will increase the price by $1 on day 4. Table 1-1 shows the simulated price changes for the 15-trading-day period.

TABLE 1-1   Simulated Price Moves of Fun Boards Stock

Price	50	49	48	47	48	47	46	47	48	47	48	49	50	49	48	49
Day	Initial	1	2	3	4	5	6	7	8	9	10	11	12	13	14	15
Digit		5	1	7	0	9	9	4	4	5	6	4	8	3	9	6

◇

◇ **COMMENT** Recall that the random samples we have been constructing so far are called *simple random samples*. Throughout this text we will use the term *random sample* to mean simple random sample. All the statistical methods in this text assume that a simple random sampling has been used to collect the data. ◇

GUIDED EXERCISE 4

Simulation

Use a random-number table to simulate the outcomes of tossing a balanced (that is, fair) penny 10 times.

(a) How many outcomes are possible when you toss a coin once?

⟹ Two; heads or tails

(b) There are several ways to assign numbers to the two outcomes. Because we assume a fair coin, assign an even digit to the outcome heads and an

⟹ 7 1 5 4 9 4 4 8 4 3

odd digit to the outcome tails. Then, starting at block 3 of row 2 of Table 1 in Appendix II, list the first 10 single digits.

(c) What are the outcomes associated with the 10 digits?

$\Longrightarrow$ T T T H T H H H H T

(d) If you start in a different block and row of Table 1 in Appendix II, will you get the same sequence of outcomes?

$\Longrightarrow$ It is possible, but not very likely. (In Section 4.3 you will learn how to determine that there are 1024 possible sequences of outcomes for 10 tosses of a coin.)

Sampling with replacement

TECH NOTE Most statistical software packages, spreadsheet programs, and statistical calculators generate random numbers. In general, these devices sample with replacement. *Sampling with replacement* means that although a number is selected for the sample, it is *not removed* from the population. Therefore, the same number may be selected for the sample more than once. If you need to sample without replacement, generate more items than you need for the sample. Then sort the sample and remove duplicate values. Specific procedures for generating random samples on the TI-84Plus/TI-83Plus calculator, Excel, Minitab, and ComputerStat are shown in Using Technology at the end of this chapter. More details are given in the separate Technology Guides for each of these technologies.

Other Sampling Techniques

Although we will assume throughout this text that (simple) random samples are used, other methods of sampling are also widely used. Appropriate statistical techniques exist for these sampling methods, but they are beyond the scope of this text.

Stratified sampling

One of these sampling methods is called *stratified sampling*. Groups or classes inside a population that share a common characteristic are called *strata* (plural of *stratum*). For example, in the population of all undergraduate college students, some strata might be freshmen, sophomores, juniors, or seniors. Other strata might be men or women or in-state students or out-of-state students, and so on. In the method of stratified sampling, the population is divided into at least two distinct strata. Then a (simple) random sample of a certain size is drawn from each stratum, and the information obtained is carefully adjusted or weighted in all resulting calculations.

The groups or strata are often sampled in proportion to their actual percentages of occurrence in the overall population. However, other (more sophisticated) ways to determine the optimal sample size in each stratum may give the best results. In general, statistical analysis and tests based on data obtained from stratified samples are somewhat different from techniques discussed in an introductory course in statistics. Such methods for stratified sampling will not be discussed in this text.

> **Stratified sampling** is a sampling technique in which the entire population is divided into distinct subgroups or strata, based on a specific characteristic such as age, income, education level, and so on. All members of a stratum share the specific characteristic. Random samples are drawn from each stratum.

Systematic sampling

Another popular method of sampling is called *systematic sampling*. In this method, it is assumed that the elements of the population are arranged in some natural sequential order. Then we select a (random) starting point and select every kth element for our sample. For example, people lining up to buy rock concert tickets are "in order." To generate a systematic sample of these people (and ask questions regarding topics such as age, smoking habits, income level, etc.), we could include every 5th person in line. The "starting" person could be selected at random from the first five.

The advantage of a systematic sample is that it is easy to get. However, there are dangers in using systematic sampling. When the population is repetitive or cyclic in nature, systematic sampling should not be used. For example, consider a fabric mill that produces dress material. Suppose the loom that produces the material makes a mistake every 17th yard, but we check only every 16th yard with an automated electronic scanner. In this case, a random starting point may or may not result in detection of fabric flaws before a large amount of fabric is produced.

> **Systematic sampling** is a sampling technique in which members of the population are sequentially numbered. Then, from a starting point, every kth member of the population is included in the sample.

Cluster sampling

Cluster sampling is a method used extensively by government agencies and certain private research organizations. In cluster sampling we begin by dividing the demographic area into sections. Then we randomly select sections or clusters. Every member of the cluster is included in the sample. For example, in conducting a survey of school children in a large city, we could first randomly select five schools and then include all the children from each selected school.

> **Cluster sampling** is a sampling technique in which the entire population is divided into pre-existing segments or clusters. The clusters are often geographic. Then clusters are randomly selected, and every member of each selected cluster is included in the sample.

Convenience sampling

Convenience sampling simply uses results or data that are conveniently and readily obtained. In some cases, this may be all that is available, and in many cases, it is better than no information at all. However, convenience sampling does run the risk of being severely biased. For instance, consider a newsperson who wishes to get the "opinions of the people" about a proposed seat tax to be imposed on tickets to all sporting events. The revenues from the seat tax will then be used to support the local symphony. The newsperson stands in front of a classical music store at noon and surveys the first five people coming out of the store who will cooperate. This method of choosing a sample will produce some opinions, and perhaps some human interest stories, but it certainly has bias. It is hoped that the city council will not use these opinions as the sole basis for a decision about the proposed tax. It is good advice to be very cautious indeed when the data come from the method of convenience sampling.

> **Convenience sampling** is a sampling technique in which data are used from population members that are readily available.

Our discussion of sampling methods is intended to be brief and general. This is not the place for an extensive treatment of the theory and practice of sampling. However, the interested reader is referred to the book *A Sampler on Sampling*, by Bill Williams, John Wiley and Sons, Inc.

VIEWPOINT   *Extraterrestrial Life?*

Do you believe intelligent life exists on other planets? Using methods of random sampling, a Fox News opinion poll found that about 54% of all U.S. men do believe in intelligent life on other planets, whereas only 47% of women believe there is such life. How could you conduct a random survey of students on your campus regarding belief in extraterrestrial life?

SECTION 1.2   PROBLEMS

1. *Sampling: Random*
   (a) In your own words, explain the meanings of the terms *random numbers* and *random samples*.
   (b) Why are random samples so important in statistics?

2. *Sampling: Random* Use a random-number table to get a list of eight random numbers from 1 to 976. Explain your work.

3. *Sampling: Random* Use a random-number table to get a list of six random numbers from 1 to 8615. Explain your work.

4. *Sampling: Random* Use a random-number table to get a list of five random numbers from 43 to 719. Explain your work.

5. *Psychology: Random Selection* How do colds affect analytical thinking performance? Results of a study conducted by McGraw and Schleser were reported in *Psychology Today.* The study showed that under certain conditions, persons with colds do better than their healthy colleagues. The study considered 62 subjects: 40 healthy men and women and 22 suffering from colds or flu. A key component in this study was the formation of two groups of equal size from the 62 participants, with each group containing both healthy and sick participants.
   (a) Describe how you could take the 40 healthy subjects and randomly divide them into two groups of equal size using the random-number table.
   (b) Repeat part (a) for the 22 sick subjects.
   (c) How would you combine the groups of healthy and sick subjects found in parts (a) and (b) to form two groups of equal size so that each group contained both healthy and sick subjects?

6. *Simulation: Coin Toss* Use a random-number table to simulate the outcomes of tossing a quarter 25 times. Assume that the quarter is balanced (i.e., fair).

7. *Computer Simulation: Roll of a Die* A die is a cube with dots on each face. The faces have 1, 2, 3, 4, 5, or 6 dots. The table below is a computer simulation (from the software package Minitab) of the results of rolling a fair die 20 times.

```
DATA DISPLAY
ROW   C1    C2    C3    C4    C5    C6    C7    C8    C9    C10
 1     5     2     2     2     5     3     2     3     1     4
 2     3     2     4     5     4     5     3     5     3     4
```

   (a) Assume that each number in the table corresponds to the number of dots on the face of the die. Is it appropriate that the same number appear more than once? Why? What is the outcome of the 4th roll?
   (b) If we simulate more "rolls of the die," do you expect to get the same sequence of outcomes? Why or why not?

8. *Simulation: Birthday Problem* Suppose there are 30 people at a party. Do you think any two share the same birthday? Let's use the random-number table to simulate the birthdays of the 30 people at the party. Ignoring leap year, let's assume that the year has 365 days. Number the days, with 1 representing January 1, 2 representing January 2, and so forth, with 365 representing December 31. Draw a random sample of 30 days (with replacement). These days represent the birthdays of the people at the party. Were any two of the birthdays the same? Compare your results with those obtained by other students in the class. Would you expect the results to be the same or different?

9. *Sampling: Students in Class* Suppose you are given the number 1, and each of the other students in your statistics class calls out consecutive numbers until each person in class has his or her own number. Explain how you could get a random sample of four students from your statistics class.
   (a) Explain why the first four students walking into the classroom would not necessarily form a random sample.
   (b) Explain why four students coming in late would not necessarily form a random sample.

(c) Explain why four students sitting in the back row would not necessarily form a random sample.

(d) Explain why the four tallest students may not necessarily form a random sample.

10. *Sampling: Quality Control* Products are inspected during production, and equipment is adjusted to correct defects. It is usually not possible to examine every product, so a random sample is examined. For each of the following, give a detailed explanation of how you could get the requested random sample. Be sure to include the random numbers you use to get the random sample.

(a) How would you draw a random sample of 6 of the next 500 stereo headsets coming off an assembly line?

(b) How would you obtain a random sample of 10 men's dress shirts coming off an assembly line from 8 A.M. to 12 noon?

(c) Serial numbers are placed on radios as they come off an assembly line. How could you get a random sample of nine radios with serial numbers from 21942 to 98756?

(d) A truck has just delivered 800 cartons of eggs to a supermarket. How would you get a random sample of 12 cartons to check for broken eggs?

11. *Sampling: General* For each of the following, give a detailed explanation of how you would get the requested random sample. Be sure to include the random numbers you use to get the random sample.

(a) You are a veterinarian. How would you get a random sample of 15 sheep to check for ticks on a farm that has 250 sheep?

(b) You are a medical records technician. Patients from 2000 to the present were given file numbers starting at 1024 and ending with 8342. How would you get a random sample of 10 of these patients?

(c) You are a security agent for an airline. How could you get a random sample of five pieces of luggage that are moving on a conveyor belt in the next 25 minutes?

(d) You are conducting a survey for your sociology class project. How could you get a random sample of 12 adults walking past the information booth at a shopping center between 6 and 7 P.M.?

12. *Education: Test Construction* Professor Gill uses true–false questions. She wishes to place 20 such questions on the next test. To decide whether to place a true statement or a false statement in each of the 20 questions, she uses a random-number table. She selects 20 digits from the table. An even digit tells her to use a true statement. An odd digit tells her to use a false statement. Use a random-number table to pick a sequence of 20 digits, and describe the corresponding sequence of 20 true–false questions. What would the test key for your sequence look like?

13. *Education: Test Construction* Professor Gill is designing a multiple-choice test. There are to be 10 questions. Each question is to have five choices for answers. The choices are to be designated by the letters *a*, *b*, *c*, *d*, and *e*. Professor Gill wishes to use a random-number table to determine which letter choice should correspond to the correct answer for a question. Using the number correspondence 1 for *a*, 2 for *b*, 3 for *c*, 4 for *d*, and 5 for *e*, use a random-number table to determine the letter choice for the correct answer for each of the 10 questions.

14. *Sampling Methods: Health Care* Modern Managed Hospitals (MMH) is a national for-profit chain of hospitals. Management wants to survey patients discharged this past year to obtain patient satisfaction profiles. They wish to use a sample of such patients. Several sampling techniques are described below. Categorize each technique

as *simple random sample, stratified sample, systematic sample, cluster sample*, or *convenience sample*.

(a) Obtain a list of patients discharged from all MMH facilities. Divide the patients according to length of hospital stay (2 days or less, 3–7 days, 8–14 days, more than 14 days). Draw simple random samples from each group.

(b) Obtain lists of patients discharged from all MMH facilities. Number these patients, and then use a random-number table to obtain the sample.

(c) Randomly select some MMH facilities from each of five geographic regions, and then include all the patients on the discharge lists of the selected hospitals.

(d) At the beginning of the year, instruct each MMH facility to survey every 500th patient discharged.

(e) Instruct each MMH facility to survey 10 discharged patients this week and send in the results.

15. *Sampling Methods: Benefits Package* An important part of employee compensation is a benefits package that might include health insurance, life insurance, child care, vacation days, retirement plan, parental leave, bonuses, etc. Suppose you want to conduct a survey of benefit packages available in private businesses in Hawaii. You want a sample size of 100. Some sampling techniques are described below. Categorize each technique as *simple random sample, stratified sample, systematic sample, cluster sample*, or *convenience sample*.

(a) Assign each business in the Island Business Directory a number, and then use a random-number table to select the businesses to be included in the sample.

(b) Use the postal ZIP Codes to divide the state into regions. Pick a random sample of 10 ZIP Code areas and then include all the businesses in each selected ZIP Code area.

(c) Send a team of five research assistants to Bishop Street in downtown Honolulu. Let each assistant select a block or building and interview an employee from each business found. Each researcher can have the rest of the day off after getting responses from 20 different businesses.

(d) Use the Island Business Directory. Number all the businesses. Select a starting place at random, and then use every 50th business listed until you have 100 businesses.

(e) Group the businesses according to type: medical, shipping, retail, manufacturing, financial, construction, restaurant, hotel, tourism, other. Then select a random sample of 10 businesses from each business type.

1.3
Introduction to Experimental Design

FOCUS POINTS

✓ Discuss what it means to take a census.

✓ Describe simulations, observational studies, and experiments.

✓ Identify control groups, placebo effects, and randomized two-treatment design.

✓ Discuss potential pitfalls that might make your data unreliable.

Planning a Statistical Study

Planning a statistical study and gathering data are essential components for obtaining reliable information. Depending on the nature of the statistical study, a great deal of expertise and resources may be required during the planning stage. In this section, we look at some of the basics for planning a statistical study.

> **PROCEDURE**
>
> **Basic guidelines for planning a statistical study**
>
> 1. First, identify the individuals or objects of interest.
> 2. Specify the variables as well as protocols for taking measurements or making observations.
> 3. Determine if you will use an entire population or a representative sample. If using a sample, decide on a viable sampling method.
> 4. In your data collection plan, address issues of ethics, subject confidentiality, and privacy. If you are collecting data at a business, store, college, or other institution, be sure to be courteous and to obtain permission as necessary.
> 5. Collect the data.
> 6. Use appropriate descriptive statistics methods (Chapters 2, 3, 10) and make decisions using appropriate inferential statistics methods (Chapters 8–12).
> 7. Finally, note any concerns you might have about your data collection methods and list any recommendations for future studies.

One issue to consider is whether to use the entire population in a study or a representative sample. If we use data from the entire population, we have a *census*.

Census

> In a **census,** measurements or observations from the *entire* population are used.

When the population is small and easily accessible, a census is very useful because it gives complete information about the population. However, obtaining a census can be both expensive and difficult. Every 10 years, the U.S. Department of Commerce Census Bureau is required to conduct a census of the United States. However, contacting some members of the population—such as the homeless—is almost impossible. Sometimes members of the population will not respond. In such cases, statistical estimates for the missing responses are often supplied.

If we use data from only part of the population of interest, we have a *sample*.

Sample

> In a **sample,** measurements or observations from a *representative part* of the population should be used.

In the previous section, we examined several sampling strategies: simple random sampling, stratified sampling, cluster sampling, systematic sampling, and convenience sampling. In this text, we will study methods of inferential statistics based on simple random samples.

Simulation

As discussed in Section 1.2, *simulation* is a numerical facsimile of real-world phenomena. Sometimes simulation is called a "dry lab" approach, in the sense that it is a mathematical imitation of a real situation. Advantages of simulation are that arithmetic and statistical simulations can fit real-world problems extremely well. The researcher can explore procedures in simulation that might be very dangerous in real life. In the real world you might not want to introduce a high level of a drug into a diabetic person's bloodstream. However, you might want to simulate the injection statistically and study the results. You will harm no one, and the information gained may be of real medical value. Similarly, you might test the effect of wind shear on an airplane wing in a simulated environment rather than with an actual airplane in flight.

Experiments and Observation

When gathering data for a statistical study, we want to distinguish between observational studies and experiments.

> In an **observational study,** observations and measurements of individuals are conducted in a way that doesn't change the response or the variable being measured.
>
> In an **experiment,** a *treatment* is deliberately imposed on the individuals in order to observe a possible change in the response or variable being measured.

EXAMPLE 8

Experiment

In 1778, Captain James Cook landed in what we now call the Hawaiian Islands. He gave the islanders a present of several goats, and over the years these animals multiplied into wild herds totaling several thousand. They eat almost anything, including the famous silver sword plant, which was once unique to Hawaii. At one time, the silver sword grew abundantly on the island of Maui (in Haleakala, a national park on that island, the silver sword can still be found), but each year there seemed to be fewer and fewer plants. Biologists suspected that the goats were partially responsible for the decline in the plants and conducted a statistical study that verified their theory.

(a) To test the theory, park biologists set up stations in remote areas of Haleakala. At each station two plots of land similar in soil conditions, climate, and plant count were selected. One plot was fenced to keep out the goats, while the other was not. At regular intervals a plant count was made in each plot. This study involves an *experiment* because a *treatment* (the fence) was imposed on one plot.

(b) The experiment involved two plots at each station. The plot that was not fenced represents the *control* plot. This is the plot where a treatment was specifically not imposed, but it was similar to the fenced plot in every other way.   ◇

Silver sword plant, Haleakala National Park

Placebo

Statistical experiments are commonly used to determine the effect of a treatment. However, the design of the experiment needs to *control* for other possible causes of the effect. For instance, in medical experiments the *placebo* effect is the improvement or change that is the result of patients just believing in the treatment, whether or not the treatment itself is effective.

> The **placebo effect** occurs when a subject receives no treatment, but (incorrectly) believes he or she is in fact receiving treatment and responds favorably.

To account for the placebo effect, patients are divided into two groups. One group receives the prescribed treatment. The other group, called the *control group,* receives a dummy or placebo treatment that is disguised to look like the real treatment. Finally, after the treatment cycle, the medical condition of the patients in the *treatment group* is compared to that of the patients in the control group.

It is difficult to account for all variables that might influence a patient's response to a treatment. Sometimes patients assigned to a treatment group and a control group are carefully matched by age, gender, level of medical condition, smoker, etc. However, a more common way to assign patients to the treatment and control groups is by using a random process. This is the essence of a *randomized two-treatment experiment.*

Randomized two-treatment experiment

EXAMPLE 9

Randomized two-treatment experiment

Can chest pain be relieved by drilling holes in the heart? For more than a decade, surgeons have been using a laser procedure to drill holes in the heart. Many patients report a lasting and dramatic decrease in angina (chest pain) symptoms. Is the relief due to the procedure, or is it a placebo effect? A recent research project at Lenox Hill Hospital in New York City provided some information about this issue by using a randomized two-treatment experiment. The laser treatment was applied through a less invasive (catheter laser) process. A group of 298 volunteers with severe, untreatable chest pain were randomly assigned to get the laser or not. The patients were sedated but awake. They could hear the doctors discuss the laser process. Each patient thought he or she was receiving the treatment.

The experimental design can be pictured as

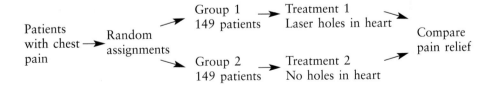

The laser patients did well. But shockingly, the placebo group showed more improvement in pain relief. The medical impacts of this study are still being investigated. ◊

Double-blind experiment

Many experiments are also *double-blind*. This means that neither the individuals in the study nor the observers know which subjects are receiving the treatment. Double-blind experiments help control for subtle biases that a doctor might pass on to a patient.

We have explored only a few features of experimental design. When the effects of several treatments are all being examined at the same time, more complicated designs, including *blocking,* are required. Section 11.6, Introduction to Two-Way ANOVA, gives further examples for such situations.

The study cited in Example 9 has many features of good experimental design.

There is a **control group.** This group received a dummy treatment, enabling the researchers to control for the placebo effect. In general, a control group is used to account for the influence of other known or unknown variables that might be an underlying cause of a change in response in the experimental group. Such variables are called **lurking** or **confounding variables.**

Randomization is used to assign individuals to the two treatment groups. This helps prevent bias in selecting members for each group.

Replication of the experiment on many patients reduces the possibility that the differences in pain relief for the two groups occurred by chance alone.

GUIDED EXERCISE 5

Collecting data

Which technique (sampling, experiment, simulation, or census) for gathering data do you think might be the most appropriate for the following studies?

(a) Study of the effect of stopping the cooling process of a nuclear reactor.

⟹ Probably simulation, since you may not want to risk a nuclear meltdown.

(b) Study of the amount of time college students taking a full course load spend watching television.

⟹ Sampling and using an observational study would work well. Notice that obtaining the information from a student will probably not change the amount of time a student spends watching television.

(c) Study of the effect of a calcium supplement given to young girls on bone mass.

⟹ Experimentation. A study by Tom Lloyd reported in the *Journal of the American Medical Association* utilized 94 young girls. Half were randomly selected and given a placebo. The other half were given calcium supplements to bring their daily calcium intake up to about 1400 milligrams per day. The group

GUIDED EXERCISE 5 continued

getting the experimental treatment of calcium
gained 1.3% more bone mass in a year than the girls
getting the placebo.

(d) Study of the credit hours load of *each* student
enrolled at your college at the end of the
drop/add period this semester.   ⟹   Census. The registrar can obtain records for *every* student.

Surveys

Once you decide whether you are going to use sampling, census, observation, or experiments, a common means to gather data about people is to ask them questions. This process is the essence of *surveying*. Sometimes the possible responses are simply yes or no. Other times the respondents choose a number on a scale that represents their feelings from, say, strongly disagree to strongly agree. Such a scale is called a *Likert scale*. In the case of an open-ended, discussion-type response, the researcher must determine a way to convert the response to a category or number.

A number of issues can arise when using a survey. Are the questions asked in a neutral way, or is conscious or unconscious bias built into the wording? In the case of an interviewer, is he or she giving the respondents subtle feedback that might influence the responses? How can you be sure the respondents are answering truthfully? Is your sample representative of the population? For instance, when conducting election polls, some studies use only registered voters because these are the only people eligible to vote. Other polls use only "likely" voters. They first inquire if the respondent is planning to vote.

Potential pitfalls

Nonresponse

Other problems arise if the selected respondent cannot be contacted or refuses to respond. This is known as *nonresponse*. If the nonresponse is sufficiently high, the study may be biased and some sort of adjustment may need to be made.

Voluntary response

Voluntary response samples often overrepresent people with strong opinions. A Colorado newspaper with statewide distribution asked the question, "Should grazing fees for use of public lands be increased?" Of the people who called in, about 85% said, "No!" However, the results were misleading as an indicator of the opinions held by the population of *all* people in Colorado. The sample who responded were self-selected people. The sample consisted mainly of ranchers who felt strongly enough to call the newspaper. These people did not want their grazing fees on public land increased.

Data from voluntary responses can be useful and interesting. However, the information given is anecdotal in nature. It would be questionable to generalize the results to the entire population of interest. Surveys must be designed and administered carefully for the results to generalize.

Hidden bias

Whenever you gather data, whether by sampling a population, by results of experiment, or by simulation, you should view the data with a critical eye. The way the data are gathered may produce a *hidden bias*. This means that in reality you are not actually measuring what you hoped to measure. For instance, if a uniformed police officer conducts a survey regarding opinions about and use of illegal drugs, the responses might be different than if a casually dressed person asks the same questions. Asking students if parking lots are large enough and safe before asking if they would approve an increase in parking fees might bias responses. Care must be taken to deal with all units or subjects in the same way so that no (conscious or unconscious) preferential treatment or selection can occur.

Other variables

Sometimes our goal is to understand the cause-and-effect relationships between two variables (as might occur in regression and correlation of two variables, presented in Chapter 10). However, the effect of one variable on another can be hidden by other variables for which no data have been obtained. These variables are called *lurking* or *confounding* variables. For instance, a study of ticket price and attendance at a sporting event might show that higher ticket prices and higher attendance are related, since events with higher ticket prices seem to have greater attendance. One might be led to conclude that if you want to increase attendance at an event, you should raise the price of the tickets. What is missing from this analysis is the lurking variable of *event popularity*. A Super Bowl football game is so special that people are willing to pay higher prices just to be there. A preseason football game, however, does not have the drawing power and may need lower ticket prices to ensure a reasonable crowd at the game. Other variables—such as the location of the game, weather, and records of the teams involved—also might influence attendance.

The problem of other variables that influence one or both of the original variables often can be overcome if the researcher not only is familiar with statistics but also is well versed in the field of investigation.

Generalizing results

Some researchers want to generalize their findings to a situation of wider scope than that of the actual data setting. The true scope of a new discovery must be determined by repeated studies in various real-world settings. Statistical experiments showing that a drug had a certain effect on a collection of laboratory rats do not guarantee that the drug will have a similar effect on a herd of wild horses in Montana.

GUIDED EXERCISE 6

Cautions about data

Comment on the usefulness of the data collected as described.

(a) A uniformed police officer interviews a group of 20 college freshmen. She asks each one his or her name and then if he or she has used an illegal drug in the last month.

⟹ Respondents may not answer truthfully. Some may refuse to participate.

(b) Jessica saw some data that show that cities with more low-income housing have more homeless people. Does building low-income housing cause homelessness?

⟹ There may be some other confounding or lurking variables such as the size of the city. Larger cities may have more low-income housing and more homeless.

GUIDED EXERCISE 6 continued

(c) A survey about food in the student cafeteria was conducted by having forms available for customers to pick up at the cash register. A drop box for completed forms was available outside the cafeteria.

⟹ The voluntary response will likely produce more negative comments.

(d) Extensive studies on coronary problems were conducted using men over age 50 as the subjects.

⟹ Conclusions for men over age 50 may or may not generalize to other age and gender groups. These results may be useful for women or younger people, but studies specifically involving these groups may need to be performed.

VIEWPOINT   *Is the Placebo Effect a Myth?*

Henry Beecher, former Chief of Anesthesiology at Massachusetts General Hospital, published a paper in the *Journal of the American Medical Association* (1955) in which he claimed that the placebo effect is so powerful that about 35% of patients would improve simply if they believed a dummy treatment (placebo) was real. However, two Danish medical researchers refute this widely accepted claim in the *New England Journal of Medicine*. They say the placebo effect is nothing more than a "regression effect," referring to a well-known statistical observation that patients who feel especially bad one day will almost always feel better the next day no matter what is done for them. However, other respected statisticians question the findings of the Danish researchers. Regardless of the new controversy surrounding the placebo effect, medical researchers agree that placebos are still needed in clinical research. Double-blind research using placebos prevents the researchers from inadvertently biasing results.

SECTION 1.3   PROBLEMS

1. *Ecology: Gathering Data* Which technique (observational study or experiment) for gathering data do you think was used in the following studies?
   (a) The Colorado Division of Wildlife netted and released 774 fish at Quincy Reservoir. There were 219 perch, 315 blue gill, 83 pike, and 157 rainbow trout.
   (b) The Colorado Division of Wildlife caught 41 bighorn sheep on Mt. Evans and gave each one an injection to prevent heartworm. A year later, 38 of these sheep did not have heartworm, while the other three did.
   (c) The Colorado Division of Wildlife imposed special fishing regulations on the Deckers section of the South Platte River. All trout under 15 inches had to be released. A study of trout before and after the regulation went into effect showed that the average length of a trout increased by 4.2 inches after the new regulation.
   (d) An ecology class used binoculars to watch 23 turtles at Lowell Ponds. It was found that 18 were box turtles, and five were snapping turtles.

2. *General: Gathering Data* Which technique (sampling, experiment, simulation, or census) for gathering data do you think was used in the following studies?
   (a) One way to find information on the Super Bowl football game is to look at the NFL web site. Visit the Brase/Brase statistics site at **http://math.college.hmco.com/students** and find the link to the NFL site. Explore the Super Bowl results. There the winning scores for all the Super Bowl games played to date are given. Using the data for all the games, find the average score for the winning teams.
   (b) A sample of 82 healthy female and male subjects was recruited to participate in a study on pain (*Physical Therapy*, Vol. 70, No. 1). The subjects were divided into two groups. The experimental group received laser stimulation, and the control group received sham stimulation. Tests of pain tolerance were then conducted on each group.
   (c) Computer imaging of runners shows the effect of stride length on running efficiency.
   (d) Do the Chinese like chocolate? Gallup Chinese is conducting surveys in China to answer the question for the U.S. Chocolate Manufacturers Association. Gallup Chinese is surveying a portion of the Chinese population to determine whether there is a market for chocolate in China (*Wall Street Journal*).

3. *General: Gathering Data* Which technique (sampling, experiment, simulation, or census) for gathering data do you think was used in the following studies?
   (a) An analysis of a sample of 31,000 patients from New York hospitals suggests that the poor and the elderly sue for malpractice at one-fifth the rate of wealthier patients (*Journal of the American Medical Association*).
   (b) The effects of wind shear on airplanes during both landing and takeoff are studied by using complex computer programs that mimic actual flight.
   (c) A study of all league football scores attained through touchdowns and field goals was conducted by the National Football League to determine whether field goals account for more scoring events than touchdowns (*USA Today*).
   (d) An Australian study included 588 men and women who already had some precancerous skin lesions. Half got a skin cream containing a sunscreen with a sun protection factor of 17; half got an inactive cream. After 7 months, those using the sunscreen with the sun protection had fewer new precancerous skin lesions (*New England Journal of Medicine*).

4. *Surveys: Manipulation* The *New York Times* did a special report on polling that was carried in papers across the nation. The article points out how readily the results of a survey can be manipulated. Some features that can influence the results of a poll include the following: the number of possible responses, the phrasing of the question, the sampling techniques used (voluntary response or sample designed to be representative), the fact that words may mean different things to different people, the questions that precede the question of interest, and finally, the fact that respondents can offer opinions on issues that they know nothing about.
   (a) Consider the expression "over the last few years." Do you think that this expression means the same time span to everyone? What would be a more precise phrase?
   (b) Consider this question: "Do you think fines for running stop signs should be doubled?" Do you think the response would be different if the question "Have you ever run a stop sign?" preceded the question about fines?
   (c) Consider this question: "Do you watch too much television?" What do you think the responses would be if the only responses possible were yes or no? What do you think the responses would be if the possible responses were rarely, sometimes, or frequently?

5. *General: Randomized Two-Treatment Experiment* How would you use a randomized two-treatment experiment in each of the following settings? Is a placebo being used or not? Be specific and give details.

   (a) A veterinarian wants to test a strain of antibiotic on calves to determine their resistance to common infection. In a pasture are 22 newborn calves. There is enough vaccine for 10 calves. However, blood tests to determine resistance to infection can be done on all calves.

   (b) The Denver Police Department wants to improve its image with teenagers. A uniformed officer is sent to a school one day a week for 10 weeks. Each day the officer visits with students, eats lunch with students, attends pep rallies, and so on. There are 18 schools, but the police department can visit only half of these schools this semester. A survey regarding how teenagers view police is sent to all 18 schools at the end of the semester.

   (c) A skin patch contains a new drug to help people quit smoking. A group of 75 cigarette smokers have volunteered as subjects to test the new skin patch. For one month 40 of the volunteers receive skin patches with the new drug. The other volunteers receive skin patches with no drugs. At the end of two months, each subject is surveyed regarding his or her current smoking habits.

6. *General: Randomized Two-Treatment Experiment* How would you use a randomized two-treatment experiment in each of the following settings? Is this a double-blind experiment or not? Be specific and give details.

   (a) A new high-temperature bonding process is used to manufacture automobile tires. A group of 43 people volunteered to test the new tires on their cars. Out of this group, 25 cars are given the new high-temperature bond tires. The other cars are given new tires without the high-temperature bond. Only the serial numbers on the tires tell which type is being used, and this information is held confidential. After 35,000 miles, all tires are thoroughly examined by the manufacturer.

   (b) The FBI wants to test the Miami Airport security system. The FBI has inserted weapons into 10 out of 250 carry-on bags that agents take through security checks. The agent carrying the bag knows whether or not the bag contains a weapon. Those bags that get through the security check and those that do not are observed by a remote security camera.

   (c) A medical school is investigating new eye drops as a treatment for glaucoma. Out of 63 volunteers, 35 will get the new eye drops. The others will get the currently used (not new) eye drops. The new eye drops come in a grey plastic bottle and the old drops come in a red plastic bottle. Neither the patient nor the doctor knows which color contains which eye drops. After six months, eye pressure on each patient is measured and a sealed report revealing medication is opened.

SUMMARY

In this chapter, you've seen that statistics is the study of how to collect, organize, analyze, and interpret numerical information from populations or samples. First, you looked at classifying data as quantitative or qualitative. Next, you examined levels of measurement. The technique of drawing a simple random sample was discussed along with other sampling methods. Finally, you looked at methods of collecting data and some of the issues involved in experimental design and surveys.

IMPORTANT WORDS & SYMBOLS

Section 1.1 *
Statistics
Individual
Variable
Quantitative variable
Qualitative variable
Population data
Sample data
Levels of measurement
    Nominal
    Ordinal
    Interval
    Ratio
Descriptive statistics
Inferential statistics

Section 1.2
Simple random sample
Random-number table
Simulation
Sampling with replacement
Stratified sample

Systematic sample
Cluster sample
Convenience sample

Section 1.3
Census
Observational study
Experiment
Placebo
Randomized two-treatment experiment
Double-blind experiment
Control group
Treatment group
Confounding variable
Lurking variable
Randomization
Replication
Survey
Nonresponse
Voluntary response
Hidden bias

*Indicates section of first appearance.

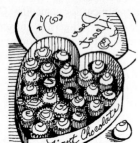

VIEWPOINT   *Is Chocolate Good for Your Heart?*

A study of 7,841 Harvard alumni showed that the death rate was 30% lower in those who ate candy compared with those who abstained. It turns out that candy, especially chocolate, contains antioxidants that help slow the aging process. Also, chocolate, like aspirin, reduces the activity of blood platelets that contribute to plaque and blood clotting. Furthermore, chocolate seems to raise high-density lipoprotein (HDL), the good cholesterol. However, these results are all preliminary. The investigation is far from complete. A wealth of information on this topic was published in the August 2000 issue of the *Journal of Nutrition*. Statistical studies and reliable experimental design are indispensable in this type of research.

CHAPTER REVIEW PROBLEMS

1. *General: Samples and Variables* Find a newspaper or web site article that uses statistics. Are the data from the entire population or just from a sample? What are the variables?

2. *Radio Talk Show: Sample Bias* A radio talk show asked listeners to respond either yes or no to the question, Is the candidate who spends the most on a campaign the most likely to win? Fifteen people called in and nine said yes. What is the implied population? What is the variable? Can you detect any bias in the selection of the sample?

3. *Essay: Levels of Measurement* In your own words, give a complete and careful description of the four levels of measurement. Which level is the highest? Which is the lowest? What are the different suitable uses for each level of measurement?

4. *Personal Data: Levels of Measurement* Write a brief description of yourself in which you list your name, age, year of birth, height, color of your hair and eyes, address, phone number, place of birth, letter grade on test, intended college major (if decided), distance you live from college, and so forth. In one column, list each item in the description of yourself. In a second column to the right of the first, list the level of measurement corresponding to each item in the description.

5. *Colorado Lotto: Simulation* Lotto is the name of the Colorado lottery. The Lotto boards consist of 42 numbers (from 1 to 42). To play, you select six distinct numbers. Every week a drawing machine randomly selects six numbered Ping-Pong balls. If one of your boards contains all six winning numbers, in any order, you've hit the jackpot! You can pick your numbers any way you wish. However, suppose you want to use a random-number table to pick your six numbers. Describe how you would do so, and list your selected numbers. (To play, you must pay $1 to have your selections entered into a computer for a specified week's drawing.)

6. *General: Type of Sampling* Categorize the type of sampling (simple random, stratified, systematic, cluster, or convenience) used in each of the following situations.
   (a) To conduct a preelection opinion poll on a proposed amendment to the state constitution, a random sample of 10 telephone prefixes (first three digits of the phone number) was selected, and all households from the phone prefixes selected were called.
   (b) To conduct a study on depression among the elderly, a sample of 30 patients in one nursing home was used.
   (c) To maintain quality control in a brewery, every 20th bottle of beer coming off the production line was opened and tested.
   (d) Subscribers to the magazine *Sound Alive* were assigned numbers. Then a sample of 30 subscribers was selected by using a random-number table. The subscribers in the sample were invited to rate new compact disc players for a "What the Subscribers Think" column.
   (e) To judge the appeal of a proposed television sitcom, a random sample of 10 people from each of three different age categories was selected and those chosen were asked to rate a pilot show.

7. *General: Gathering Data* Which technique (observational study or experiment) for gathering data do you think was used in the following studies? Explain your answer.
   (a) The U.S. Census Bureau tracks population age. In 1900, the percentage of the population that was nineteen years old or younger was 44.4%. In 1930, the percentage was 38.8%; in 1970, the percentage was 37.9%; and in 2000, the percentage in the age group was down to 28.5% (*The First Measured Century*, T. Caplow, L. Hicks, B. J. Wattenberg).

(b) After receiving the same lessons, a class of 100 students was randomly divided into two groups of 50 each. One group was given a multiple-choice exam covering the material in the lessons. The other group was given an essay exam. The average test scores for the two groups were then compared.

8. *General: Randomized Two-Treatment Experiment* How would you use a randomized two-treatment experiment in each of the following settings? Is a placebo being used or not? Be specific and give details.

(a) A charitable nonprofit organization wants to test two methods of fund raising. From a list of 1,000 past donors, half will be sent literature about the successful activities of the charity and asked to make another donation. The other 500 donors will be contacted by phone and asked to make another donation. The percentage of people from each group who make a new donation will be compared.

(b) A tooth-whitening gel is to be tested for effectiveness. A group of 85 adults have volunteered to participate in the study. Of these, 43 are to be given a gel that contains the tooth-whitening chemicals. The remaining 42 are to be given a similar-looking package of gel that does not contain the tooth-whitening chemicals. A standard method will be used to evaluate the whiteness of teeth for all participants. Then the results for the two groups will be compared. How could this experiment be designed to be double-blind?

9. *Student Life: Data Collection Project* Make a statistical profile of your own statistics class. Items of interest might be

(a) Height, age, gender, pulse, number of siblings, marital status

(b) Number of college credit hours completed (as of beginning of term); grade point average

(c) Major; number of credit hours enrolled in this term

(d) Number of scheduled hours working per week

(e) Distance from residence to first class; time it takes to travel from residence to first class

(f) Year, make, and color of car usually driven

What directions would you give to people answering these questions? For instance, how accurate should the measurements be? Should age be recorded as of last birthday?

10. *Census: Web Site Census and You,* a publication of the Census Bureau, indicates that "Wherever your Web journey ends up, it should start at the Census Bureau's site." Visit the Brase/Brase statistics site at **http://math.college.hmco.com/students** and find a link to the Census Bureau's site, as well as to Fedstats, another extensive site offering links to federal data. The Census Bureau site touts itself as the source of "official statistics." But it is willing to share the spotlight. The web site now has links to other "official" sources: other federal agencies, foreign statistical agencies, and state data centers. If you have access to the Internet, try the Census Bureau's site.

11. *Focus Problem: Fireflies* Suppose you are conducting a study to compare firefly populations exposed to normal daylight/darkness conditions with firefly populations exposed to continuous light (24 hours a day). You set up two firefly colonies in a laboratory environment. The two colonies are identical except that one colony is exposed to normal daylight/darkness conditions and the other is exposed to continuous light.

Each colony is populated with the same number of mature fireflies. After 72 hours, you count the number of living fireflies in each colony.

(a) Is this an experiment or an observation study? Explain.

(b) Is there a control group? Is there a treatment group?

(c) What is the variable in this study?

(d) What is the level of measurement (nominal, interval, ordinal, or ratio) of the variable?

DATA HIGHLIGHTS: GROUP PROJECTS

1. Use a random-number table or random-number generator to simulate tossing a fair coin 10 times. Generate 20 such simulations of 10 coin tosses. Compare the simulations. Are there any strings of 10 heads? of 4 heads? Does it seem that in most of the simulations half the outcomes are heads? half are tails? In Chapter 5, we will study the probability of getting from 0 to 10 heads in such a simulation.

2. Use a random-number table or random-number generator to get a random sample of 30 distinct values from the set of integers from 1 to 100. Instructions for doing this using the TI-84Plus/TI-83Plus, Excel, Minitab, or SPSS are given in Using Technology at the end of this chapter. Generate five such samples. How many of the samples include the number 1? the number 100? Comment about the differences among the samples. How well do the samples seem to represent the numbers between 1 and 100?

LINKING CONCEPTS: WRITING PROJECTS

Discuss each of the following topics in class or review the topics on your own. Then write a brief but complete essay in which you summarize the main points. Please include formulas and graphs as appropriate.

1. What does it mean to say that we are going to use a sample to draw an inference about a population? Why is a random sample so important for this process? If we wanted a random sample of students in the cafeteria, why couldn't we just take the students who order Diet Pepsi with their lunch? Comment on the statement, "A random sample is like a miniature population, whereas samples that are not random are likely to be biased." Why would the students who order Diet Pepsi with lunch not be a random sample of students in the cafeteria?

2. In your own words, explain the differences among the following sampling techniques: simple random sample, stratified sample, systematic sample, cluster sample, and convenience sample. Describe situations in which each type might be useful.

Using Technology

TI-84PLUS/TI-83PLUS • EXCEL • MINITAB • SPSS

General spreadsheet programs such as Microsoft's Excel, specific statistical software packages such as Minitab or SPSS, and graphing calculators such as the TI-84Plus and TI-83Plus all offer computing support for statistical methods. Applications in this section may be completed using software or calculators with statistical functions. Select keystroke or menu choices are shown for the TI-84Plus and TI-83Plus calculators, Minitab, Excel, and SPSS in the Technology Hints portion of this section. More details can be found in the software-specific Technology Guide that accompanies this text.

APPLICATIONS

Most software packages sample *with replacement*. That is, the same number may be used more than once in the sample. If your applications require sampling without replacement, draw more items than you need. Then use sort commands in the software to put the data in order, and delete repeated data.

1. Simulate the results of tossing a fair die 18 times. Repeat the simulation. Are the results the same? Do you expect them to be the same? Why or why not? Do there appear to be equal numbers of outcomes 1 through 6 in each simulation? In Chapter 4, we will see the law of large numbers, which tells us that we would expect equal numbers of outcomes only when the simulation is very large.

2. A college has 5,000 students, and the registrar wishes to use a random sample of 50 students to examine credit hour enrollment for this semester. Write a brief description of how a random sample can be drawn. Draw a random sample of 50 students. Are you sampling with or without replacement?

Technology Hints: Random Numbers

TI-84Plus/TI-83Plus

To select a random set of integers between two specified values, press the **MATH** key and highlight **PRB** with **5:randInt** (low value, high value, sample size). Press Enter and fill in the low value, high value, and sample size. To store the sample in list L1, press the **STO➡** key and then L1. The screen display shows two random samples of size five drawn from the integers between 1 and 100.

```
randInt(1,100,5)
{63 89 13 46 47}
randInt(1,100,5)
{29 82 99 50 41}
```

Excel

To select a random number between two specified values, type the command **=Randbetween(low value, high value)** in the formula bar. Alternatively, access a dialogue box for the command by clicking on the **paste function** f_x key on the menu bar. Then choose **All** in the left drop-down menu and **RANDBETWEEN** in the right menu. Fill in the dialogue box.

A5	▼	=	=RANDBETWEEN(1,100)		
	A	B	C	D	E
1	99				
2	58				
3	69				
4	86				
5	13				

Minitab

To generate random integers between specified values, use the menu selection **Calc ➤ Random Data ➤ Integer.** Fill in the dialogue box to get five random numbers between 1 and 100.

	Worksheet 2 ***
	C1
↓	
1	8
2	35
3	33
4	9
5	15

SPSS

SPSS is a research statistical package for the social sciences. Data are entered in the data editor, which has a spreadsheet format. In the data editor window, you have a choice of data view (default) or variable view. In the variable view, you name variables, declare type (numeric for measurements, string for category), determine format, and declare measurement type. The choices for measurement type are scale (for ratio or interval data), ordinal, or nominal. Once you have entered data, you can use the menu bar at the top of the screen to select activities, graphs, or analysis appropriate to the data.

SPSS supports several random sample activities. In particular, you can select a random sample from an existing data set or from a variety of probability distributions.

Selecting a random integer between two specified values involves several steps. First, in the data editor, enter the sample numbers in the first column. For instance, to generate five random numbers, list the values 1 through 5 in the first column. Notice that the label for the first column is now var00001. SPSS does not have a direct function for selecting a random sample of integers. However, there is a function for sampling values from the uniform distribution of all real numbers between two specified values. We will use that function and then truncate the values to obtain a random sample of integers between two specified values.

Use the menu options **Transform ➤ Compute.** In the dialog box, type in var00002 as the target variable.

Then, in the function box, select the function **RV.UNIFORM(min, max).** Use 1 as the minimum and 101 as the maximum. The maximum is 101 because numbers between 100 and 101 truncate to 100.

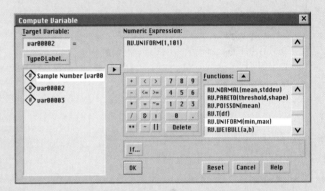

The random numbers from the uniform distribution now appear in the second column under var00002. You can visually truncate the values to obtain random integers. However, if you want SPSS to truncate the values for you, you can again use the menu choices **Transform ➤ Compute.** In the dialogue box, enter var00003 for the target variable. From the functions box, select **TRUNC(numexpr).** Use var00002 in place of numexpr. The random integers between 1 and 100 appear in the third column under var00003.

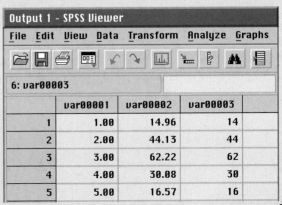

	var00001	var00002	var00003
1	1.00	14.96	14
2	2.00	44.13	44
3	3.00	62.22	62
4	4.00	30.08	30
5	5.00	16.57	16

2

Organizing Data

In dwelling upon the vital importance of sound observation, it must never be lost sight of what observation is for. It is not for the sake of piling up miscellaneous information or curious facts, but for the sake of saving life and increasing health and comfort.

—Florence Nightingale, *Notes on Nursing*

**Florence Nightingale
(1820–1910)**

Florence Nightingale has been described as a "passionate statistician" and a "relevant statistician." She viewed statistics as a science that allowed one to transcend his or her narrow individual experience and aspire to the broader service of humanity. She was one of the first nurses to use graphic representation of statistics, illustrating with charts and diagrams how improved sanitation decreased the rate of mortality. Her statistical reports about the appalling sanitary conditions at Scutari (the main British hospital during the Crimean War) were taken very seriously by the English Secretary at War, Sidney Herbert. When sanitary reforms recommended by Nightingale were instituted in military hospitals, the mortality rate dropped from an incredible 42.7% to only 2.2%.

PREVIEW QUESTIONS

◇ How can you select graphs appropriate for given data sets?   (SECTION 2.1)

◇ What are histograms and ogives? When are they used?   (SECTION 2.2)

◇ What are common distribution shapes?   (SECTION 2.2)

◇ How can you quickly order data and, at the same time, reveal the distribution shape?   (SECTION 2.3)

For on-line student resources, visit **math.college.hmco.com/students** and follow the Statistics links to the Brase/Brase, *Understandable Statistics*, 8th edition web site.

Say It with Pictures

Edward R. Tufte, in his book *The Visual Display of Quantitative Information*, has a number of guidelines for producing good graphics. According to the criteria, a graphical display should

- show the data;

- induce the viewer to think about the substance of the graphic rather than about the methodology, the design, the technology, or other production devices;

- avoid distorting what the data have to say.

As an example of a graph that violates some of the criteria, Tufte includes a graphic that appeared in a well-known newspaper. Figure 2-1(a) shows a facsimile of the problem graphic, whereas part (b) of the figure shows a better rendition of the data display.

After completing this chapter, you will be able to answer the following questions.

(a) Look at the graph in Figure 2-1(a). Is it essentially a bar graph? Explain. What are some of the flaws of Figure 2-1(a) as a bar graph?

FIGURE 2-1

Fuel Economy Standards for Autos

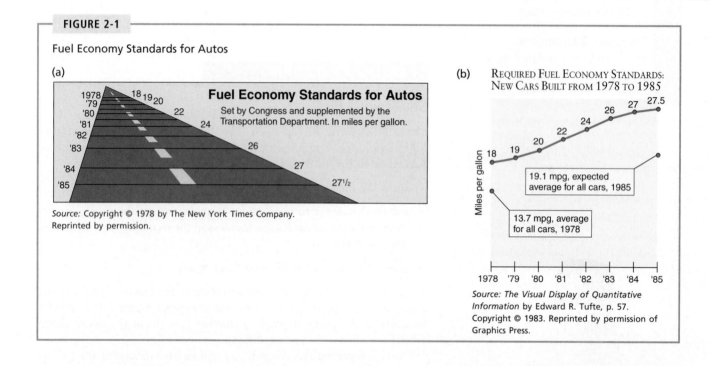

(a)

1978
'79
'80   18 19 20
'81   22
'82   24
'83   26
'84
'85   27
                          27½

Fuel Economy Standards for Autos
Set by Congress and supplemented by the
Transportation Department. In miles per gallon.

Source: Copyright © 1978 by The New York Times Company.
Reprinted by permission.

(b)   REQUIRED FUEL ECONOMY STANDARDS:
        NEW CARS BUILT FROM 1978 TO 1985

Miles per gallon

18   19   20   22   24   26   27   27.5

19.1 mpg, expected
average for all cars, 1985

13.7 mpg, average
for all cars, 1978

1978 '79 '80 '81 '82 '83 '84 '85

*Source: The Visual Display of Quantitative
Information* by Edward R. Tufte, p. 57.
Copyright © 1983. Reprinted by permission of
Graphics Press.

(b) Examine Figure 2-1(b), which shows the same information. Is it essentially a
time-series graph? Explain. In what ways does the second graph seem to display the information in a clearer manner?

(c) Recent changes in fuel economy standards can be found at the Bureau of Transportation Statistics web site. To find the web site, visit the Brase/Brase statistics
site at **http://math.college.hmco.com/students** and use the link. This site indicates
that the fuel economy standard for cars manufactured in 1986, 1987, and 1988
was 26.0 miles per gallon (mpg); for 1989, it was 26.5 mpg, and for model
years 1990 through 1999, it was 27.5 mpg. Make a time-series graph displaying fuel economy standards for new cars by year from 1978 through 1999. What
do you notice about the trend of standards for fuel economy? Were 1999-model
cars required to be more fuel efficient than 1985-model cars?

(d) The Bureau of Transportation Statistics web site also gives the fuel economy
standards for light trucks. By model year, the mpg standards are:

Model year	1982	1983	1984	1985	1986	1987–89
mpg	17.5	19.0	20.0	19.5	20.0	20.5

Model year	1990	1991	1992	1993	1994	1995	1996–99
mpg	20.0	20.2	20.2	20.4	20.5	20.6	20.7

Make a time-series graph displaying these data. Comment about the fuel economy trend for light trucks. How does this trend compare to the trend shown in part (c) for cars?

(See Problem 1 of the Chapter 2 Review Problems.)

2.1
Bar Graphs, Circle Graphs, and Time-Series Graphs

FOCUS POINTS

✓ Determine types of graphs appropriate for specific data.

✓ Construct bar graphs, Pareto charts, circle graphs, and time-series graphs.

✓ Interpret information displayed in graphs.

Open almost any magazine, newspaper, or large web site, and you will find graphs. In fact, because graphs display information so effectively, most word processors and spreadsheet programs include extensive chart- and graph-making tools. In this section, we identify several common types of graphs, show how to construct them, and show how to interpret information presented in graphical form.

Let's start with *bar graphs*. These are graphs that can be used to display quantitative or qualitative data.

Bar graphs

Features of a bar graph

1. Bars can be vertical or horizontal.

2. Bars are of uniform width and uniformly spaced.

3. The lengths of the bars represent values of the variable being displayed, the frequency of occurrence, or the percentage of occurrence. The same measurement scale is used for the length of each bar.

4. The graph is well annotated with title, labels for each bar, and vertical scale or actual value for the length of each bar.

EXAMPLE 1

Bar graph

What's a square foot worth? In retail, annual sales per square foot is an important industry measurement. A recent article in *The Wall Street Journal* gave average annual sales per square foot for nationwide department stores: $147 for Dillard's Inc., $279 for Kohl's Corp., $220 for Marshall Field, $192 for May Department Stores, $357 for Nordstrom, Inc., and $320 for Sears. To make a bar graph of this information, we let the lengths of the bars in Figure 2-2 on the next page represent the sales (in dollars) per square foot. Each store has its own bar.

Usually, it is not necessary to display both the vertical scale and the individual height of each bar. However, the height label gives the reader exact information while the scale display gives the viewer a sense of the range of data values. In addition, the graph is titled and the bars are labeled by store.

From the graph, it is readily apparent that Nordstrom and Sears have the highest sales per square foot. *The Wall Street Journal* reports that Nordstrom's upscale merchandise and Sears' appliance sales push their sales figures up. Among the other four stores that carry similar merchandise, we see that Kohl's has the highest average sales per square foot. ◇

Changing scales

Pareto charts

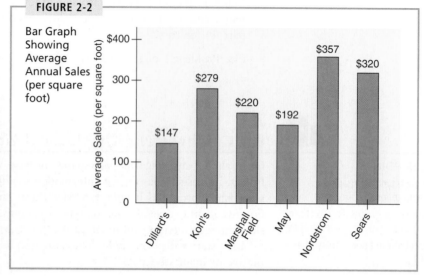

FIGURE 2-2

Bar Graph Showing Average Annual Sales (per square foot)

There are several variations of bar graphs. Figure 2-3 on the next page shows life expectancy for men and women born in specific years. Notice that the bars for men and women are clustered over the year of birth, and a legend identifies which bars are for men and which are for women.

An important feature illustrated in Figure 2-3(b) is that of a *changing scale*. Notice that the scale between 0 and 65 is compressed. The changing scale amplifies the apparent difference between life spans for men and women, as well as the increase in life spans from those born in 1970 to the projected span of those born in 2010.

Changing Scale

Whenever you use a change in scale in a graphic, warn the viewer by using a squiggle ⌐⌐ on the changed axis. Sometimes, if a single bar is unusually long, the bar length is compressed with a squiggle in the bar itself.

Quality control is an important aspect of today's production and service industries. Dr. W. Edwards Deming was one of the developers of total quality management (TQM). In his book *Out of Crisis* he outlines many strategies for monitoring and improving service and production industries. In particular, Dr. Deming recommends the use of some statistical methods to organize and analyze data from industries so that sources of problems can be identified and then corrected. *Pareto* (pronounced "Pah-rāy-tō) *charts* are among the many techniques used in quality-control programs.

A **Pareto chart** is a bar graph in which the bar height represents frequency of an event. In addition, the bars are arranged from left to right according to decreasing height.

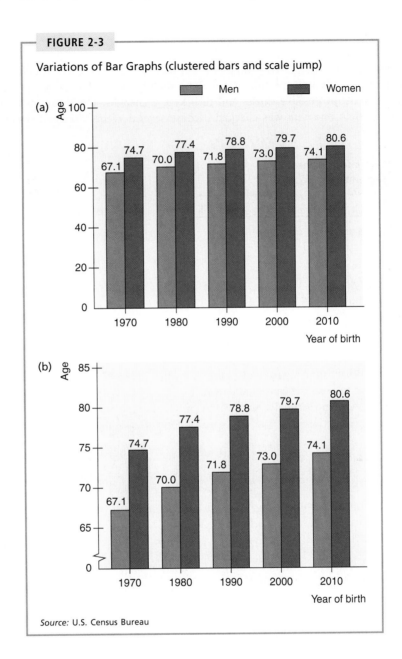

FIGURE 2-3

Variations of Bar Graphs (clustered bars and scale jump)

Source: U.S. Census Bureau

GUIDED EXERCISE 1

Pareto charts

This exercise is adapted from *The Deming Management Method* by Mary Walton. Suppose you want to arrive at college 15 minutes before your first class so that you can feel relaxed when

Continued

GUIDED EXERCISE 1 continued

you walk into class. An early arrival time also allows room for unexpected delays. However, you always find yourself arriving "just in time" or slightly late. What causes you to be late? Charlotte made a list of possible causes and then kept a checklist for 2 months (Table 2-1). On some days more than one item was checked because several events occurred that caused her to be late.

TABLE 2-1   Causes for Lateness
                  (September–October)

Cause	Frequency
Snoozing after alarm goes off	15
Car trouble	5
Too long over breakfast	13
Last-minute studying	20
Finding something to wear	8
Talking too long with roommate	9
Other	3

(a) Make a Pareto chart showing the causes for lateness. Be sure to label the causes, and draw the bars using the same vertical scale.

  FIGURE 2-4 Pareto Chart: Conditions That Might Cause Lateness

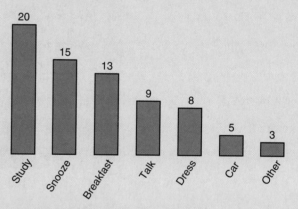

(b) Looking at the Pareto chart, what recommendations do you have for Charlotte?

  According to the chart, rearranging study time, or getting up earlier to allow for studying, would cure her most frequent cause for lateness. Repairing the car might be important, but for getting to campus early, it would not be as effective as adjusting study time.

Circle graphs or pie charts

Another popular pictorial representation of data is the *circle graph,* or *pie chart.* It is relatively safe from misinterpretation and is especially useful for showing the division of a total quantity into its component parts. The total quantity, or 100%, is represented by the entire circle. Each wedge of the circle represents a component part of the total. These proportional segments are usually labeled with corresponding percentages of the total. Guided Exercise 2 shows how to make a circle graph.

> In a **circle graph** or **pie chart,** wedges of a circle visually display proportional parts of the total population that share a common characteristic.

GUIDED EXERCISE 2

Circle graph

How long do we spend talking on the telephone after hours (at home after 5 P.M.)? The results from a recent survey of 500 people (as reported in *USA Today*) are shown in Table 2-2. We'll make a circle graph to display these data.

TABLE 2-2   Time Spent on Home Telephone After 5 P.M.

Time	Number	Fractional Part	Percentage	Number of Degrees
Less than ½ hour	296	296/500	59.2	59.2% $\times$ 360° $\approx$ 213°
½ hour to 1 hour	83	83/500	16.6	16.6% $\times$ 360° $\approx$ 60°
More than 1 hour	121	_____	_____	_____
Total	_____		_____	_____

(a) Fill in the missing parts in Table 2-2 for "More than 1 hour." Remember that the central angle of a circle is 360°. Round to the nearest degree.

⇨ For "More than 1 hour," Fractional Part = 121/500; Percentage = 24.2%; Number of Degrees = 24.2% $\times$ 360° $\approx$ 87°. The symbol $\approx$ means approximately equal.

(b) Fill in the totals. What is the total number of responses? Do the percentages total 100% (within rounding error)? Do the numbers of degrees total 360° (within rounding error)?

⇨ The total number of responses is 500. The percentages total 100%. You must have such a total in order to create a circle graph. The numbers of degrees total 360°.

(c) Draw a circle graph. Divide the circle into pieces with the designated numbers of degrees. Label each piece, and show the percentage corresponding to each piece. The numbers of degrees are usually omitted from pie charts shown in newspapers, magazines, journals, and reports.

⇨ **FIGURE 2-5** Hours on Home Telephone After 5 P.M.

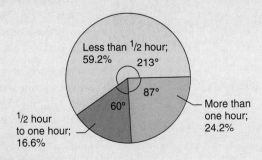

Suppose you begin an exercise program that involves walking or jogging for 30 minutes. You exercise several times a week but monitor yourself by logging the distance you cover in 30 minutes each Saturday. How do you display these data in a meaningful way? Making a bar chart showing the frequency of distances you cover might be interesting, but it does not really show how the distance you cover in 30 minutes has changed over time. A graph showing the distance covered on each date will let you track your performance over time.

Time-series graph

We will use a *time-series graph*. A time-series graph is a graph showing data measurements in chronological order. To make a time-series graph, we put time on the horizontal scale and the variable being measured on the vertical scale. In a basic time-series graph, we connect the data points by lines.

> In a **time-series graph**, data are plotted in order of occurrence at regular intervals over a period of time.

EXAMPLE 2

Time-series graph

Suppose you have been in the walking/jogging exercise program for 20 weeks, and for each week you have recorded the distance you covered in 30 minutes. Your data log is shown in Table 2-3.

TABLE 2-3   Distance (in Miles) Walked/Jogged in 30 Minutes

Week	1	2	3	4	5	6	7	8	9	10
Distance	1.5	1.4	1.7	1.6	1.9	2.0	1.8	2.0	1.9	2.0
Week	11	12	13	14	15	16	17	18	19	20
Distance	2.1	2.1	2.3	2.3	2.2	2.4	2.5	2.6	2.4	2.7

(a) Make a time-series graph.

SOLUTION: The data are appropriate for a time-series graph because they represent the same measurement (distance covered in a 30-minute period) taken at different times. The measurements are also recorded at equal time intervals (every week). To make our time-series graph, we list the weeks in order on the horizontal scale. Above each week, plot the distance covered that week on the vertical scale. Then connect the dots. Figure 2-6 shows the time-series graph. Be sure the scales are labeled.

(b) From looking at Figure 2-6, can you detect any patterns?

SOLUTION: There seems to be an upward trend in distance covered. The distances covered in the last few weeks are about a mile farther than those for the first few weeks. However, we cannot conclude that this trend will continue. Perhaps you have reached your goal for this training activity and now wish to maintain a distance of about 2.5 miles in 30 minutes.   ◇

Time series

Data sets composed of similar measurements taken at regular intervals over time are called *time series*. Time series are often used in economics, finance, sociology, medicine, and any situation where we want to study or monitor a similar measure over a period of time. A time-series graph can reveal some of the main features of time series.

> **Time-series data** consist of measurements of the same variable for the same subject taken at regular intervals over a period of time.

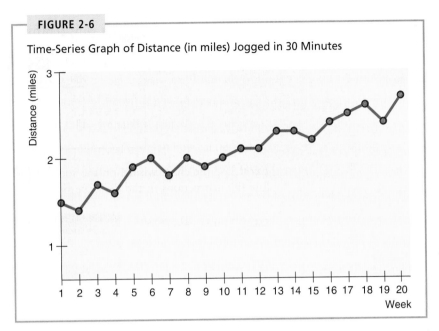

FIGURE 2-6

Time-Series Graph of Distance (in miles) Jogged in 30 Minutes

We've seen several styles of graphs. Which kinds are suitable for a specific data collection?

PROCEDURE

How to decide which type of graph to use

Bar graphs are useful for quantitative or qualitative data. With qualitative data, the frequency or percentage of occurrence can be displayed. With quantitative data, the measurement itself can be displayed, as was done in the bar graph showing life expectancy. Watch that the measurement scale is consistent or that a jump scale squiggle is used.

Pareto charts identify the frequency of events or categories in decreasing order of frequency of occurrence.

Circle graphs display how a *total* is dispersed into several categories. The circle graph is very appropriate for qualitative data, or any data where percentage of occurrence makes sense. Circle graphs are most effective when the number of segments is ten or fewer.

Time-series graphs display how data change over time. It is best if the units of time are consistent in a given graph. For instance, measurements taken every day should not be mixed on the same graph with data taken every week.

For any graph: Provide a title, label the axes, and identify units of measure. As Edward Tufte suggests in his book *The Visual Display of Quantitative Information*, don't let artwork or skewed perspective cloud the clarity of the information displayed.

TECH NOTES *Bar graphs, circle graphs, time-series graphs*

TI-84Plus/TI-83Plus Only time-series. Place consecutive values 1 through the number of time segments in list L1 and data in L2. Press **Stat Plot** and highlight an *xy* line plot.

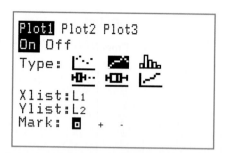

Excel Use the chart wizard on the toolbar . Select the desired option and follow the instructions in the dialogue boxes.

Excel Chart Wizard Menu

Minitab Use the menu selection **Graph.** Select the desired option and follow the instructions in the dialogue boxes.

Minitab Graph Menu

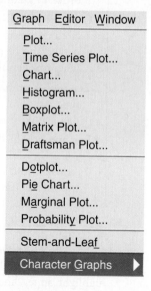

VIEWPOINT   *Do Ethical Standards Vary by the Situation?*

The Lutheran Brotherhood did a national survey and found that nearly 60% of all U.S. adults claim that ethics vary by the situation; 33% claim that there is only one ethical standard; and 7% were not sure. How could you draw a circle graph to make a visual impression of Americans' views on ethical standards?

SECTION 2.1   PROBLEMS

1. *Education: Does College Pay Off?* It is costly in both time and money to go to college. Does it pay off? According to the Bureau of Census, the answer is yes. The average annual income (in thousands of dollars) of a *household* headed by a person with the stated education level is as follows: 16.1 if 9th grade is the highest level achieved, 34.3 for high school graduates, 48.6 for those holding associate degrees, 62.1 for those with bachelor's degrees, 71.0 for those with master's degrees, and 84.1 for those with doctoral degrees. Make a bar graph showing household income for each education level.

2. *Accidents: Child Deaths* How safe is the world for kids? Unfortunately, some children between the ages of 1 and 14 die of injuries every year. United Nations data show that by nation, the annual numbers of deaths from injuries per 100,000 children are as follows: Australia, 9.5; Canada, 9.7; Denmark, 8.1; France, 9.1; Germany, 8.3; Hungary, 10.8; Ireland, 8.3; Italy, 6.1; Japan, 8.4; Korea, 25.6; Mexico, 19.8; New Zealand, 13.7; Netherlands, 6.6; Poland, 13.4; Portugal, 17.8; Spain, 8.1; Sweden, 5.2; Switzerland, 9.6; U.K., 6.1; United States, 14.1. Display these data in a Pareto chart.

3. *Commercial Fishing: Gulf of Alaska* It's not an easy life, but it's a good life! Suppose you decide to take the summer off and sign on as a deck hand for a commercial fishing boat in Alaska that specializes in deep-water fishing for groundfish. What kind of fish can you expect to catch? One way to answer this question is to examine government reports on groundfish caught in the Gulf of Alaska. The following list indicates the types of fish caught annually in thousands of metric tons (Source: *Report on the Status of U.S. Living Marine Resources,* National Oceanic and Atmospheric Administration): flatfish, 36.3; Pacific cod, 68.6; sablefish, 16.0; Walleye pollock, 71.2; rockfish, 18.9. Make a Pareto chart showing the annual harvest for commercial fishing in the Gulf of Alaska.

4. *Archaeology: Ireland* Commercial dredging operations in ancient rivers occasionally uncover archaeological artifacts of great importance. One such artifact is Bronze Age spearheads recovered from ancient rivers in Ireland. A recent study gave the following information regarding discoveries of ancient bronze spearheads in Irish rivers.

River	Bann	Blackwater	Erne	Shannon	Barrow
No. of spearheads	19	8	15	33	14

(Based on information from *Crossing the Rubicon, Bronze Age Studies 5*, Lorraine Bourke, Department of Archaeology, National University of Ireland, Galway.)
(a) Make a Pareto chart for these data.
(b) Make a circle graph for these data.

5. *Lifestyle: Hide the Mess!* A survey of 1000 adults (reported in *USA Today*) uncovered some interesting housekeeping secrets. When unexpected company comes, where do we hide the mess? The survey showed that 68% of the respondents toss their mess in the closet, 23% shove things under the bed, 6% put things in the bathtub, and 3% put the mess in the freezer. Make a circle graph to display this information.

6. *Lifestyle: Fast Food* What meal are we most likely to eat in a fast-food restaurant? A survey of 1261 adults (reported in *USA Today*) revealed that 48.9% of the respondents are most likely to eat lunch at a fast-food restaurant; 7.7%, breakfast; 31.6%, dinner; 10%, a snack; and 1.8% answered "don't know." Display this information in a circle graph.

7. *Education: College Professors' Time* How do college professors spend their time? *The National Education Association Almanac of Higher Education* gives the following average distribution of professional time allocation: teaching, 51%; research, 16%; professional growth, 5%; community service, 11%; service to the college, 11%; and consulting outside the college, 6%. Make a pie chart showing the allocation of professional time for college professors.

8. *Education: College Professors' Age* How old are college professors? The NEA reference in Problem 7 gave the following age distribution in years: under 35 years, 8%; 35–44 years, 29%; 45–54 years, 37%; 55–59 years, 13%; 60–64 years, 9%; and 65 years and over, 4%. Make a pie chart showing the age distribution of college professors.

9. *FBI Report: Hawaii* In the Aloha state, you are very unlikely to be murdered! However, it is considerably more likely that your house might be burgled, your car might be stolen, or you might be punched in the nose. That said, Hawaii is still a great place for a vacation or, if you are very lucky, to live. The following numbers represent the crime rates per 100,000 population in Hawaii: murder, 2.6; rape, 33.4; robbery, 93.3; house burglary, 911.6; motor vehicle theft, 550.7; assault, 125.3 (Source: *Crime in the United States*, U.S. Department of Justice, Federal Bureau of Investigation).
(a) Display this information in a Pareto chart, showing the crime rate for each category.
(b) Could the information as reported be displayed as a circle graph? Explain. *Hint:* Other forms of crime, such as arson, are not included in the information. In addition, some crimes might occur together.

10. *Driving: Bad Habits* Driving would be more pleasant if we didn't have to put up with bad habits of other drivers. *USA Today* reported the results of a Valvoline Oil Company survey of 500 drivers in which the drivers marked their complaints about other drivers. The top complaints turned out to be tailgating, marked by 22% of the respondents; not using turn signals, marked by 19%; 16% marked being cut off; 11% complained about other drivers driving too slowly; and 8% complained about other drivers being inconsiderate. Make a Pareto chart showing percentage of drivers listing each stated complaint. Could this information as reported be put in a circle graph? Why or why not?

11. *Ecology: Lakes* Pyramid Lake, Nevada, is described as the pride of the Paiute Indian Nation. It is a beautiful desert lake famous for very large trout. The elevation of the lake surface (feet above sea level) varies according to the annual flow of the Truckee River from Lake Tahoe. The U.S. Geological Survey provided the following data:

Year	Elevation	Year	Elevation	Year	Elevation
1986	3817	1992	3798	1998	3811
1987	3815	1993	3797	1999	3816
1988	3810	1994	3795	2000	3817
1989	3812	1995	3797		
1990	3808	1996	3802		
1991	3803	1997	3807		

Make a time-series graph displaying the data. For more information, visit the Brase/Brase statistics site at **http://math.college.hmco.com/students** and find the link to the Pyramid Lake Fisheries.

12. *Vital Statistics: Height* How does average height for boys change as the boy gets older? According to *Physician's Handbook,* the average heights at different ages are as follows:

Age (years)	0.5	1	2	3	4	5	6	7
Height (inches)	26	29	33	36	39	42	45	47

Age (years)	8	9	10	11	12	13	14
Height (inches)	50	52	54	56	58	60	62

Make a time-series graph for average height for ages 0.5 through 14 years.

13. *Financial: Two Common Stocks* Thirsty or hungry? Many people think of having a Coke or going to McDonald's when thirst or hunger strikes. However, other people consider the value of the company stock. Which company, Coca-Cola or McDonald's, would be a better investment? To determine the answer, some investors look at historical performance. You can find this kind of information on the web by visiting the Brase/Brase statistics site at **http://math.college.hmco.com/ students** and finding the link to CNN Money. Figure 2-7 on the next page shows the daily close (indicated by the horizontal tick) of each company for a 6-month period. The top of the vertical line represents the highest price of the day, whereas the bottom represents the lowest price of the day. Look at the two parts of the figure, and comment about the general price trend over the 6-month period shown. Note that during that period, the Dow Jones Industrial Average increased by about 10%. Comment on the volatility and performance difference of the stocks. Which increased by the largest percentage during the period shown?

FIGURE 2-7

Time-Series Graphs for Coca-Cola and McDonald's

(a) Stock Price History for
    Coca-Cola

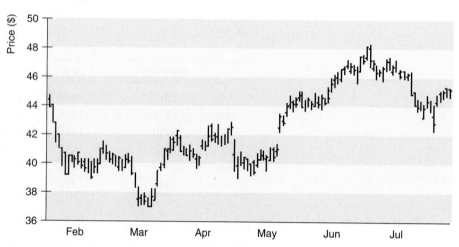

(b) Stock Price History for
    McDonald's

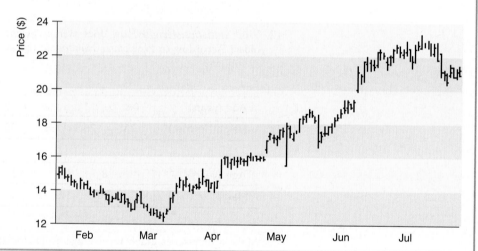

Source: http://money.cnn.com

2.2
Frequency Distributions, Histograms, and Related Topics

FOCUS POINTS

✓ Organize raw data using a
  frequency table.

✓ Construct histograms,
  relative-frequency histograms,
  frequency polygons, and ogives.

✓ Recognize basic distribution
  shapes: uniform, symmetric,
  bimodal, skewed.

✓ Interpret graphs in the context of
  the data setting.

In this section we will study several types of graphs associated with the spread or distribution of a data set. The graphs presented are histograms, relative frequency histograms, frequency polygons, and ogives. Each of the graphs is appropriate for quantitative data. We begin with a study of histograms.

Histograms and Frequency Tables

Suppose you have a large data set and you want to make a visual display of the distribution or spread of the data. A *histogram* provides such a visual display. Histograms are simply bar graphs with special characteristics. In particular, the height of the bars in a histogram show the number of data values that occur in specified intervals of data values. Histograms have other special properties as well.

Histograms

Histograms are bar graphs in which

(a) the bars have the same width and always touch.

(b) the width of a bar represents a quantitative value *x*, such as age, rather than a category.

(c) the height of each bar indicates frequency.

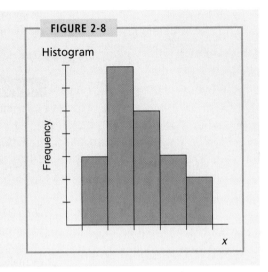

FIGURE 2-8

Histogram

Frequency table

However, before we can make a histogram, we need to organize the data into a *frequency table*. For a frequency table, we first establish distinct data intervals that span all the data. Such intervals are called *classes*. Then we count the number of data values that occur in each of the distinct classes.

A **frequency table** shows the *distribution* of data into classes or intervals. The classes or intervals are constructed so that each data value falls into exactly one class.

The next two examples show how to make a frequency table and corresponding histogram. Pay particular attention to the terminology and methods shown.

EXAMPLE 3

Frequency table

A task force to encourage car pooling did a study of one-way commuting distances of workers in the downtown Dallas area. A random sample of 60 of these workers was taken. The commuting distances of the workers in the sample are given in Table 2-4. Make a frequency table for these data.

(a) First decide how many classes (and corresponding bars in the histogram) you want. Five to 15 classes are usually used. If you use fewer than five classes, you risk losing too much information. If you use more than 15 classes, the data may not be sufficiently summarized, and the corresponding histogram may be too detailed. Let

TABLE 2-4   One-Way Commuting Distances (in Miles) for 60 Workers in Downtown Dallas

13	47	10	3	16	20	17	40	4	2
7	25	8	21	19	15	3	17	14	6
12	45	1	8	4	16	11	18	23	12
6	2	14	13	7	15	46	12	9	18
34	13	41	28	36	17	24	27	29	9
14	26	10	24	37	31	8	16	12	16

the spread of the data and the purpose of the histogram be your guide when selecting the number of classes. In the case of the commuting data, let's use *six* classes.

Class width

(b) Next, find the *class width* for the six classes.

> **PROCEDURE**
>
> **To find the class width**
>
> 1. Compute $\dfrac{\text{Largest data value} - \text{Smallest data value}}{\text{Desired number of classes}}$
>
> 2. Increase the value computed to the next highest whole number.

Note: To ensure that all the classes taken together cover the data, we need to increase the result of step 1 to the *next whole number,* even if step 1 produced a whole number. For instance, if the calculation in step 1 produces the value 4, we make the class width 5.

To find the class width for the commuting data, we observe that the largest distance commuted is 47 miles and the smallest is 1 mile. Using six classes, the class width is 8, since

$$\text{Class width} = \frac{47 - 1}{6} \approx 7.7 \quad \text{(increase to 8)}$$

Class limits

(c) Now we determine the data range for each class.

> The **lower class limit** is the lowest data value that can fit in a class. The **upper class limit** is the highest data value that can fit in a class. The **class width** is the difference between the *lower* class limit of one class and the *lower* class limit of the next class.

The smallest commuting distance in our sample is 1 mile. We use this *smallest* data value as the lower class limit of the *first* class. Since the class width is 8, we add 8 to 1 to find that the lower class limit for the *second* class is 9. Following this pattern, we establish *all* the lower class limits. Then we fill in the upper class limits so that the classes span the entire range of data. Table 2-5 shows the upper and lower class limits for the commuting distance data.

TABLE 2-5   Frequency Table of One-Way Commuting Distances for 60 Downtown Dallas Workers (data in miles)

Class Limits Lower–Upper	Class Boundaries Lower–Upper	Tally	Frequency	Class Midpoint
1–8	0.5–8.5	ℍℍ ℍℍ IIII	14	4.5
9–16	8.5–16.5	ℍℍ ℍℍ ℍℍ ℍℍ I	21	12.5
17–24	16.5–24.5	ℍℍ ℍℍ I	11	20.5
25–32	24.5–32.5	ℍℍ I	6	28.5
33–40	32.5–40.5	IIII	4	36.5
41–48	40.5–48.5	IIII	4	44.5

Class frequency

(d) Now we are ready to tally the commuting distance data into the six classes and find the frequency for each class.

> **PROCEDURE**
>
> **How to tally data**
>
> Tallying data is a method of counting data that fall into a particular class or category.
>
> To tally data into classes of a frequency table, examine each data value. Determine which class contains the data value and make a tally mark or vertical stroke (|) beside that class. For ease of counting, each fifth tally mark of a class is placed diagonally across the prior four marks (|||||).
>
> The *class frequency* for a class is the number of tally marks corresponding to that class.

Table 2-5 shows the tally and frequency of each class.

Class midpoints

(e) The center of each class is called the *midpoint* (or *class mark*). The midpoint is often used as a representative value of the entire class. The midpoint is found by adding the lower and upper class limits of one class and dividing by 2.

$$\text{Midpoint} = \frac{\text{Lower class limit} + \text{Upper class limit}}{2}$$

Table 2-5 shows the class midpoints.   ◇

Constructing a Histogram

Now we are almost ready to make a histogram showing the commuting distances. In a histogram, the bars touch. There is a space between the upper limit of one class and the lower limit of the next class. The halfway points of these intervals are called *class boundaries*. These are shown in Table 2-5.

Class boundaries

> **PROCEDURE**
>
> **How to find class boundaries (integer data)**
>
> To find **upper class boundaries**, add 0.5 unit to the upper class limits.
> To find **lower class boundaries**, subtract 0.5 unit from the lower class limits.

EXAMPLE 4

Histogram

Make a histogram with six bars for the data in Table 2-4 showing one-way commuting distances.

SOLUTION: First we make a frequency table that includes class boundaries (see Table 2-5 on the previous page). Then we draw bars corresponding to each class. The width of each bar is the distance between respective class boundaries. The height of each bar is the corresponding class frequency.

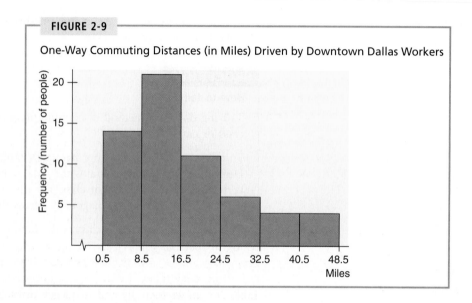

FIGURE 2-9

One-Way Commuting Distances (in Miles) Driven by Downtown Dallas Workers

Figure 2-9 shows the histogram.   ◇

As you can see from Examples 3 and 4, there are a number of steps involved in making a frequency table and a corresponding histogram. The following procedures summarize the steps.

> **PROCEDURE**
>
> **How to make a frequency table**
>
> 1. Determine the number of classes and the corresponding class width.
> 2. Create the distinct classes. We use the convention that the *lower class limit* of the first class is the smallest data value. Add the class width to this number to get the *lower class limit* of the next class.
> 3. Tally the data into classes. Each data value should fall into exactly one class. Total the tallies to obtain each *class frequency*.
> 4. Compute the *midpoint* (class mark) for each class.
> 5. Determine the *class boundaries*.

> **PROCEDURE**
>
> **How to make a histogram**
>
> 1. Make a frequency table with the designated number of classes.
> 2. Place class boundaries on the horizontal axis and frequencies on the vertical axis.
> 3. For each class of the frequency table, draw a bar with width extending between the corresponding class boundaries. The height of the bar is the corresponding class frequency.

◇ **COMMENT** The use of class boundaries in histograms assures us that the bars of the histogram touch and that no data fall on the boundaries. Both of these features are important. But a histogram displaying class boundaries may look awkward. For instance, the mileage range of 8.5 to 16.5 miles shown in Figure 2-9 isn't as natural a choice as a mileage range of 8 to 16 miles. For this reason, many magazines and newspapers do not use class boundaries as labels on a histogram. Instead, some use lower class limits as labels, with the convention that *a data value falling on the class limit is included in the next higher class (class to the right of the limit)*. Another convention is to label midpoints instead of class boundaries. Determine the convention being used before creating frequency tables and histograms on a computer.   ◇

Relative-Frequency Tables and Histograms

Other useful tools for organizing data are *relative-frequency tables* and *relative-frequency histograms*. Once we have made a frequency table, it is easy to construct a relative-frequency table. The relative frequency for a particular class is found by dividing the class frequency by the total of all frequencies (sample size).

$$\textbf{Relative frequency} = \frac{f}{n} = \frac{\text{Class frequency}}{\text{Total of all frequencies}}$$

Table 2-6 on the following page shows the relative frequencies for the commuter data of Table 2-4. Since we already have the frequency table (Table 2-5), the relative-frequency table is obtained easily. The sample size is $n = 60$. Notice that the sample size is the total of all the frequencies. Therefore, the relative frequency for the first class (the class from 1 to 8) is

$$\text{Relative frequency} = \frac{f}{n} = \frac{14}{60} \approx 0.23$$

The symbol $\approx$ means "approximately equal to." We use the symbol because we rounded the relative frequency. Relative frequencies for the other classes are computed in a similar way.

The total of the relative frequencies should be 1. However, rounded results may make the total slightly higher or lower than 1.

PROCEDURE

How to make a relative-frequency table

First make a frequency table. Then, for each class, compute the *relative frequency f/n*, where *f* is the class frequency and *n* is the total sample size.

Using Table 2-6 and Figure 2-9, we can quickly make a relative-frequency histogram (Figure 2-10 on the following page). The horizontal scale will be the same, but the vertical scale will be marked with *relative frequencies f/n* instead of the actual frequencies *f*. The basic shape of the two graphs otherwise will be the same.

TABLE 2-6   Relative Frequencies of One-Way Commuting Distances

Class	Frequency f	Relative Frequency f/n
1–8	14	$14/60 \approx 0.23$
9–16	21	$21/60 \approx 0.35$
17–24	11	$11/60 \approx 0.18$
25–32	6	$6/60 \approx 0.10$
33–40	4	$4/60 \approx 0.07$
41–48	4	$4/60 \approx 0.07$

FIGURE 2-10

Relative-Frequency Histogram for Dallas Commuters:
One-Way Commuting Distances

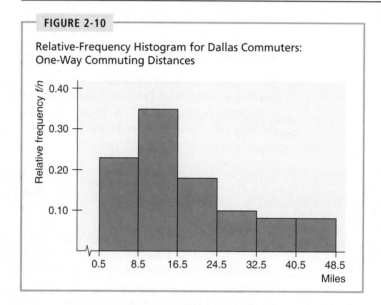

GUIDED EXERCISE 3

Histogram and relative-frequency histogram

One irate customer called Dollar Day Mail Order Company 40 times during the last two weeks to see why his order had not arrived. Each time he called, he recorded the length of time he was put "on hold" before being allowed to talk to a customer representative.

TABLE 2-7 Length of Time on Hold, in Minutes

1	5	5	6	7	4	8	7	6	5
5	6	7	6	6	5	8	9	9	10
7	8	11	2	4	6	5	12	13	6
3	7	8	8	9	9	10	9	8	9

(a) What are the largest and smallest values in Table 2-7? If we want five classes, what should the class width be?

The largest value is 13; the smallest value is 1. The class width is

$$\frac{13 - 1}{5} = 2.4 \approx 3$$

Note that we *increase* the value to 3.

Continued

GUIDED EXERCISE 3 continued

(b) Complete the following frequency table.

TABLE 2-8 Time on Hold

Class Limits			
Lower–Upper	Tally	Frequency	Midpoint
1 – 3	_____	_____	_____
4 – _____	_____	_____	_____
_____ – 9	_____	_____	_____
_____ – _____	_____	_____	_____
_____ – _____	_____	_____	_____

  TABLE 2-9 Completion of Table 2-8

Class Limits			
Lower–Upper	Tally	Frequency	Midpoint
1–3	III	3	2
4–6	ℍℍ ℍℍ ℍℍ	15	5
7–9	ℍℍ ℍℍ ℍℍ II	17	8
10–12	IIII	4	11
13–15	I	1	14

(c) Recall that the class boundary is halfway between the upper limit of one class and the lower limit of the next. Use this fact to find the class boundaries in Table 2-10 and to complete the partial histogram in Figure 2-11.

TABLE 2-10 Class Boundaries

Class Limits	Class Boundaries
1–3	0.5–3.5
4–6	3.5–6.5
7–9	6.5–_____
10–12	_____–_____
13–15	_____–_____

TABLE 2-11 Completion of Table 2-10

Class Limits	Class Boundaries
1–3	0.5–3.5
4–6	3.5–6.5
7–9	6.5–9.5
10–12	9.5–12.5
13–15	12.5–15.5

FIGURE 2-11

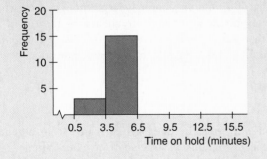

FIGURE 2-12 Completion of Figure 2-11

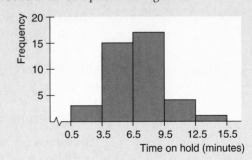

Continued

GUIDED EXERCISE 3 continued

(d) Compute the relative class frequency *f/n* for each class in Table 2-12 and complete the partial relative frequency histogram in Figure 2-13.

TABLE 2-12 Relative Class Frequency

Class	f/n
1–3	3/40 = 0.075
4–6	15/40 = 0.375
7–9	_____
10–12	_____
13–15	_____

TABLE 2-13 Completion of Table 2-12

Class	f/n
1–3	0.075
4–6	0.375
7–9	0.425
10–12	0.100
13–15	0.025

FIGURE 2-13

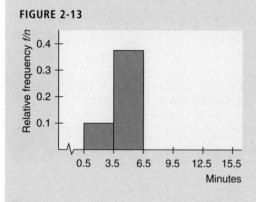

FIGURE 2-14 Completion of Figure 2-13

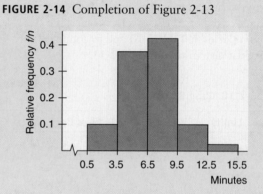

We will see relative-frequency distributions again when we study probability in Chapter 4. There we will see that if a random sample is large enough, then we can estimate the probability of an event by the relative frequency of the event. The relative-frequency distribution then can be interpreted as a *probability distribution*. Such distributions will form the basis of our work in inferential statistics.

Distribution Shapes

Histograms are valuable and useful tools. If the raw data came from a random sample of population values, the histogram constructed from your sample values should have a distribution shape that is reasonably similar to that of the population.

Several terms are commonly used to describe histograms and their associated population distributions.

FIGURE 2-15

Types of Histograms

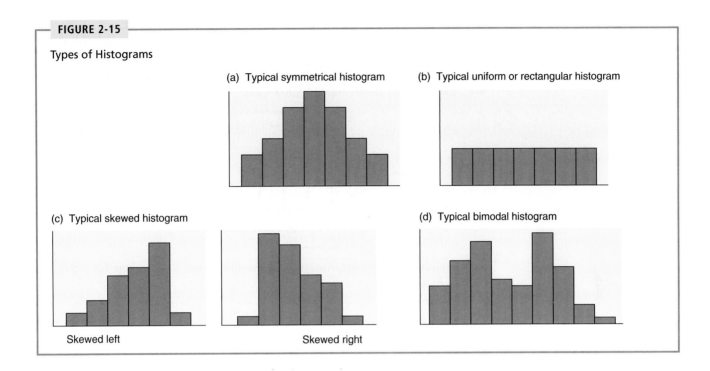

(a) Typical symmetrical histogram

(b) Typical uniform or rectangular histogram

(c) Typical skewed histogram

Skewed left

Skewed right

(d) Typical bimodal histogram

(a) *Symmetrical:* This term refers to a histogram in which both sides are (more or less) the same when the graph is folded vertically down the middle. Figure 2-15(a) shows a typical histogram with a symmetrical shape.

(b) *Uniform or rectangular:* These terms refer to a histogram in which every class has equal frequency. From one point of view, a uniform distribution is symmetrical with the added property that the bars are of the same height. Figure 2-15(b) illustrates a typical histogram with a uniform shape.

(c) *Skewed left or skewed right:* These terms refer to a histogram in which one tail is stretched out longer than the other. The direction of skewness is on the side of the *longer* tail. So if the longer tail is on the left, we say the histogram is skewed to the left. Figure 2-15(c) shows a typical histogram skewed to the left and another skewed to the right.

(d) *Bimodal:* This term refers to a histogram in which the two classes with the largest frequencies are separated by at least one class. The top two frequencies of these classes may have slightly different values. This type of situation sometimes indicates we are sampling from two different populations. Figure 2-15(d) illustrates a typical histogram with a bimodal shape.

TECH NOTE   The TI-84Plus/TI-83Plus calculators, Excel, and Minitab all create histograms. However, each technology automatically selects the number of classes to use. In Using Technology at the end of this chapter, you will see instructions for specifying the number of classes yourself and for generating histograms such as we create "by hand."

The displays show the default histograms for the commuting data of Table 2-4. For each technology, enter the data and then follow the designated menu/key choices.

TI-84Plus/TI-83Plus Press **Stat Plot ➤ On;Histogram Type ➤ Zoom ➤ 9:Zoom-Stat.** Use **Trace** to see the number in a class.

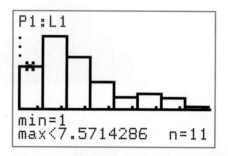

Excel Select **Tools ➤ Data Analysis ➤ Histogram.** Select data range for input and check Chart. In Excel, classes are called bins.

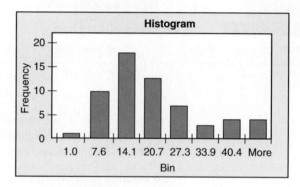

Minitab Select **Graph ➤ Histogram.**

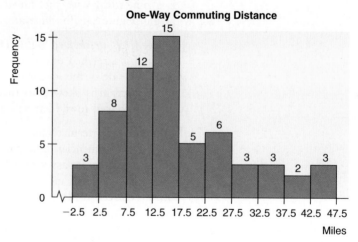

Related Graphs: Frequency Polygons and Ogives

A histogram gives the impression that frequencies jump suddenly from one class to the next. If you want to emphasize the *continuous* rise or fall of the frequencies, you can use a *frequency polygon* or *line graph*.

Frequency polygons

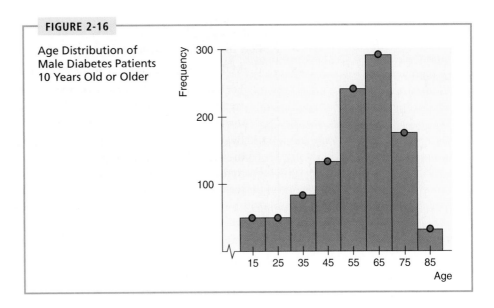

FIGURE 2-16

Age Distribution of
Male Diabetes Patients
10 Years Old or Older

EXAMPLE 5

Frequency polygon

Figure 2-16 shows a histogram of the age distribution of male diabetes patients 10 years and older. Figure 2-17 shows the corresponding frequency polygon.

(a) Notice that the heavy dots in Figure 2-17 occur at points with coordinates (class midpoint, class frequency). These dots are connected.

(b) Consecutive class midpoints differ by the class width. From the histogram, we see that the class width is 10 years. Subtracting 10 from the first class midpoint gives the starting point at 5. Likewise, adding 10 to the last class midpoint gives the ending point at 95.   ◊

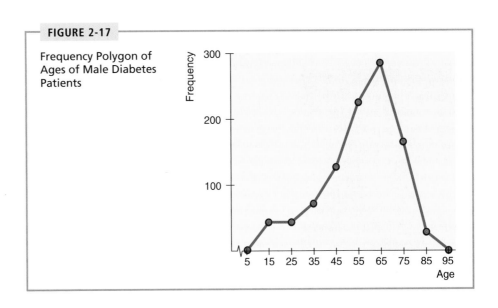

FIGURE 2-17

Frequency Polygon of
Ages of Male Diabetes
Patients

> **PROCEDURE**
>
> **How to make a frequency polygon**
>
> 1. Make a frequency table that shows class midpoints and class frequencies.
> 2. For each class, make a dot over the class midpoint at the height of the class frequency. The coordinates of these dots are (class midpoint, class frequency). Connect these dots with line segments.
> 3. By convention, frequency polygons begin and end with a frequency of zero. On the left end, draw a line segment that meets the horizontal axis *one class width* to the left of the first midpoint. On the right end, draw a line segment meeting the horizontal axis *one class width* to the right of the last midpoint.

Sometimes we want to study *cumulative totals* instead of frequencies or relative frequencies. Cumulative totals can be used to determine how many scores are *above* or *below* a set level.

Cumulative-frequency table

Once we have made a frequency table, it is not hard to make a cumulative-frequency table.

> The **cumulative frequency** for a class is the sum of the frequencies for *that class and all previous classes.*

For example, let's consider the climatologic data published by the U.S. government that gives the daily high temperatures (°F) during the ski season in Aspen, Colorado. In Table 2-14 we see that the cumulative frequency of the second class is 66. This is the sum of the frequencies 23 and 43 from the first and second classes. Likewise, the cumulative frequency for class three is the sum of the frequencies from the first three classes.

Ogives

An *ogive* (pronounced "oh-jive") is a graph that displays cumulative frequencies. It is especially useful for quickly determining the number of data values above or below a specified level.

TABLE 2-14   High Temperatures During the Aspen Ski Season (°F)

| Class Boundaries | | Frequency | Cumulative Frequency |
Lower	Upper		
10.5	20.5	23	23
20.5	30.5	43	66 (sum 23 + 43)
30.5	40.5	51	117 (sum 66 + 51)
40.5	50.5	27	144 (sum 117 + 27)
50.5	60.5	7	151 (sum 144 + 7)

> **PROCEDURE**
>
> **How to make an ogive**
>
> 1. Make a frequency table showing class boundaries and cumulative frequencies.
> 2. For each class, make a dot over the *upper class boundary* at the height of the cumulative class frequency. The coordinates of the dots are (upper class boundary, cumulative class frequency). Connect these dots with line segments.
> 3. By convention, an ogive begins on the horizontal axis at the lower class boundary of the first class.

Table 2-14 shows the cumulative frequencies for high temperatures during the Aspen ski season. The ogive based on this frequency table is shown in Figure 2-18 of Guided Exercise 4. Notice how the points shown in the ogive reflect the information in Table 2-14.

GUIDED EXERCISE 4

Ogive

Ogives are helpful when we want to know how many of our scores are *above* or *below* some level. For instance, the Aspen–Ashcroft area is a world famous center for cross-country skiing on wilderness trails. If the daily high temperature is above 40°F, the surface snow tends to melt. Then at night it freezes again. This can result in a snow crust that makes cross-country skiing faster and more challenging. It also can increase avalanche danger. Let's use the ogive in Figure 2-18 to estimate the percentage of a typical ski season during which the daily high temperatures go above 40°F.

(a) Use Figure 2-18 and find 40.5°F on the horizontal scale. What is the cumulative frequency of number of days with high temperatures less than or equal to 40°F?

⟹ The upper class boundary for temperatures below or at 40°F falls at 40.5°F (Figure 2-19). The cumulative frequency corresponding to 40.5 is 117 (see Figure 2-18).

FIGURE 2-18 Ogive for Daily High Temperatures (°F) During Aspen Ski Season

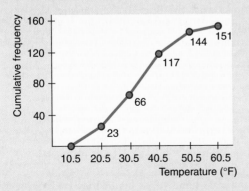

FIGURE 2-19 Segment of Figure 2-18

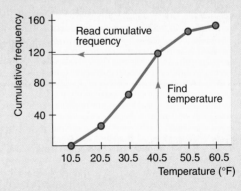

Continued

GUIDED EXERCISE 4 continued

(b) What does the cumulative frequency of 117 at the 40.5°F mark tell us?

➡ The cumulative frequency of 117 tells us that there are 117 days in the season during which the high temperature is 40°F or lower.

(c) How many days are represented in the data set?

➡ The highest cumulative frequency is 151 (see dot over 60.5).

(d) Use the information in parts (b) and (c) to determine how many days the daily high temperature equals or exceeds 40°F. What percentage of the season has temperatures exceeding 40°F?

➡ Because 151 days are represented in the sample and 117 have daily high temperatures at or below 40°F, there are 151 − 117 = 34 days during which the daily high exceeds 40°F. This means that about 23% of the days have temperatures above 40°F.

◇ **COMMENT** Frequency polygons and ogives show different aspects of the data distribution. Among the technical differences, recall that

(a) for a frequency polygon, the points are graphed above the class midpoints, whereas the vertical coordinates represent the class frequencies.

(b) for an ogive, the points are graphed above the upper class boundaries, whereas the vertical coordinates represent the cumulative frequencies. ◇

VIEWPOINT   *Mush, You Huskies!*

In 1925, the village of Nome, Alaska, had a terrible diphtheria epidemic. Serum was available in Anchorage but had to be brought to Nome by dogsled over the 1161-mile Iditarod Trail. Since 1973, the Iditarod Dog Sled Race from Anchorage to Nome has been an annual sporting event with a current purse of more than $600,000. Winning times range from more than 20 days to a little over 9 days.

To collect data on winning times, visit the Brase/Brase statistics site at **http://math.college.hmco.com/students** and find the link to the Iditarod. Make a frequency distribution for these times.

SECTION 2.2   PROBLEMS

For Problems 1–6, use the specified number of classes to do the following:
(a) Find the class width.
(b) Make a frequency table showing class limits, class boundaries, midpoints, frequencies, relative frequencies, and cumulative frequencies.
(c) Draw a histogram.

(d) Draw a frequency polygon.

(e) Draw a relative-frequency histogram.

(f) Draw an ogive.

1. *Sports: Dog Sled Racing* How long does it take to finish the 1161-mile Iditarod Dog Sled Race from Anchorage to Nome, Alaska (*see* Viewpoint)? Finish times (to the nearest hour) for 57 dogsled teams are shown below.

261	271	236	244	279	296	284	299	288	288	247	256
338	360	341	333	261	266	287	296	313	311	307	307
299	303	277	283	304	305	288	290	288	289	297	299
332	330	309	328	307	328	285	291	295	298	306	315
310	318	318	320	333	321	323	324	327			

Use five classes.

2. *Medical: Glucose Testing* The following data represent glucose blood levels (mg/100 ml) after a 12-hour fast for a random sample of 70 women (Reference: *American Journal of Clinical Nutrition,* Vol. 19, pp. 345–351). *Note:* These data are also available with other software on the statSpace CD-ROM.

45	66	83	71	76	64	59	59
76	82	80	81	85	77	82	90
87	72	79	69	83	71	87	69
81	76	96	83	67	94	101	94
89	94	73	99	93	85	83	80
78	80	85	83	84	74	81	70
65	89	70	80	84	77	65	46
80	70	75	45	101	71	109	73
73	80	72	81	63	74		

Use six classes.

3. *Medical: Tumor Recurrence* Certain kinds of tumors tend to recur. The following data represent the lengths of time, in months, for a tumor to recur after chemotherapy (Reference: D. P. Byar, *Journal of Urology,* Vol. 10, pp. 556–561). *Note:* These data are also available with other software on the statSpace CD-ROM.

19	18	17	1	21	22	54	46	25	49
50	1	59	39	43	39	5	9	38	18
14	45	54	59	46	50	29	12	19	36
38	40	43	41	10	50	41	25	19	39
27	20								

Use five classes.

4. *Archaeology: New Mexico* The Wind Mountain excavation site in New Mexico is an important archaeological location of the ancient Native American Anasazi culture. The following data represent depths (in cm) below surface grade at which significant artifacts were discovered at this site (Reference: Woosley, A. I. and

McIntyre, A. J. *Mimbres Mogollon Archaeology,* University of New Mexico Press). *Note:* These data are also available with other software on the statSpace CD-ROM.

85	45	75	60	90	90	115	30	55	58
78	120	80	65	65	140	65	50	30	125
75	137	80	120	15	45	70	65	50	45
95	70	70	28	40	125	105	75	80	70
90	68	73	75	55	70	95	65	200	75
15	90	46	33	100	65	60	55	85	50
10	68	99	145	45	75	45	95	85	65
65	52	82							

Use seven classes.

5. *Environment: Gasoline Consumption* The following data represent highway fuel consumption in miles per gallon (mpg) for a random sample of 55 models of passenger cars (Source: Environmental Protection Agency). *Note:* These data are also available with other software on the statSpace CD-ROM.

30	27	22	25	24	25	24	15
35	35	33	52	49	10	27	18
20	23	24	25	30	24	24	24
18	20	25	27	24	32	29	27
24	27	26	25	24	28	33	30
13	13	21	28	37	35	32	33
29	31	28	28	25	29	31	

Use five classes.

6. *Advertising: Readability* "Readability Levels of Magazine Ads," by F. K. Shuptrine and D. D. McVicker, is an article in the *Journal of Advertising Research.* (For more information, visit the Brase/Brase statistics site at **http://math.college.hmco.com/students** and find the link to DASL, the Carnegie Mellon University Data and Story Library. Look in Data Subjects under Consumer and then Magazine Ads Readability file.) The following is a list of the number of three-syllable (or longer) words in advertising copy of randomly selected magazine advertisements:

34	21	37	31	10	24	39	10	17	18	32
17	3	10	6	5	6	6	13	22	25	3
5	2	9	3	0	4	29	26	5	5	24
15	3	8	16	9	10	3	12	10	10	10
11	12	13	1	9	43	13	14	32	24	15

Use eight classes.

7. *U.S. Senators: Age* Overlaid frequency polygons can be useful for visually comparing two distributions. Let's use frequency polygons to compare the age distributions of U.S. senators in different congresses. *The Macmillan Visual Almanac* gives the following age distributions for the senators in the 95th Congress and in the 103rd Congress:

Age (years)	95th		Age (years)	103rd
30–39	6		30–39	1
40–49	26		40–49	16
50–59	35		50–59	49
60–69	21		60–69	22
70–79	10		70–79	11
≥80	2		≥80	1

(a) Find the class midpoints for the ages, using 84.5 for the class midpoint of the last class.

(b) Make a frequency polygon showing the ages of the senators of the 95th Congress. On the same diagram, superimpose the frequency polygon showing the ages of the senators of the 103rd Congress.

(c) Comment on the age differences of the senators in the two congresses.

8. *U.S. Representatives: Age* How do the ages of U.S. representatives in the House vary from congress to congress? *The Macmillan Visual Almanac* gave the following age distributions for the U.S. representatives in the 95th and 103rd Congresses:

Age (years)	95th		Age (years)	103rd
30–39	81		30–39	47
40–49	121		40–49	153
50–59	147		50–59	131
60–69	71		60–69	89
70–79	15		70–79	12
≥80	0		≥80	3

(a) Find the class midpoints for the ages, using 84.5 for the class midpoint of the last class.

(b) Make a frequency polygon showing the ages of the representatives of the 95th Congress. On the same diagram, superimpose the frequency polygon showing the ages of the representatives of the 103rd Congress.

(c) Comment on the age differences of the representatives in the two congresses.

9. *Business: Profits and Sales* *Fortune* published statistics on its Fortune 500 companies. Forty-eight of the companies were categorized as food companies (using labels such as RJR Nabisco, Pillsbury, General Mills, Quaker Oats, Tyson Foods, Hershey Foods). For 39 of these companies, profits were given as a percentage of sales (with a negative number indicating a loss). The data follow:

2	8	3	2	7	4	5	1	6	5	7	6	5
6	11	6	2	0	8	3	1	4	2	3	0	2
4	2	−1	2	2	10	−3	6	4	1	0	0	1

Also listed in the Fortune 500 companies were 45 electronics companies (including companies such as General Electric, Hewlett-Packard, Texas Instruments). For

44 of these companies, profit as a percentage of sales was also given. The data follow:

7	7	5	6	−6	4	8	6	1	2	9	5	10	16	12
3	5	1	8	1	7	2	5	5	6	5	2	2	11	−3
2	3	5	6	4	−2	2	1	12	5	3	11	6	12	

(a) Make a frequency table and histogram for the food companies, and then make another frequency table and histogram for the electronics companies. Use five classes for each.

(b) By looking at the two histograms, can we determine which category (food or electronics) has the greatest profits as a percentage of sales? Discuss some of the problems involved in comparing these two distributions.

10. *Football: Weights of Professional Players* How do football teams stack up weight-wise? Let's look at two teams in the National Football League. *Lindy's Pro Football* gave the preseason player statistics for all the NFL teams. For the 70 players with the Miami Dolphins, the weights (in pounds) came in as follows:

242	220	224	200	220	222	222	185	223	192
225	196	208	193	202	232	200	225	226	220
198	185	193	190	190	210	192	240	238	227
235	228	237	264	228	235	221	275	275	289
280	275	280	275	295	290	282	295	290	282
295	277	248	182	175	184	234	190	180	238
240	260	270	275	255	280	265	273	280	249

For the 72 players with the San Diego Chargers, the weights were as follows:

213	196	185	119	208	205	203	222	220	214
198	195	180	192	170	200	185	202	198	184
207	223	212	188	206	240	255	242	242	236
246	230	230	230	275	278	280	310	260	280
293	310	295	275	270	275	230	265	305	248
248	165	210	195	188	277	184	300	259	291
237	245	267	271	209	170	285	279	233	195
200	205								

(a) Make frequency tables and histograms for each of the two teams using six classes.

(b) From the histograms, can you tell if either team seems to have the heavier distribution of players' weights? Discuss some of the problems involved in comparing these distributions.

11. *Horse Racing: Winning Times* The Kentucky Derby has been run annually since 1900 at Churchill Downs, Louisville, Kentucky. The distance is 1¼ miles. Since 1900, all the winning times have been over 2 minutes, except for the record time of 1 minute and 59.2 seconds run by Secretariat in 1973 and the 2001 time of 1 minute and 59.97 seconds run by Monarchos. (For more information, visit the Brase/Brase statistics site at **http://math.college.hmco.com/students** and find the link to the Kentucky Derby.) The ogive in Figure 2-20 shows the *seconds over 2 minutes*

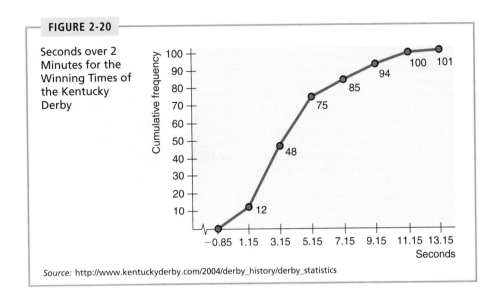

FIGURE 2-20

Seconds over 2 Minutes for the Winning Times of the Kentucky Derby

Source: http://www.kentuckyderby.com/2004/derby_history/derby_statistics

for the winning times. A winning time of 2 minutes and 8.4 seconds has a data entry of 8.4 seconds. Secretariat's record time of 1 minute and 59.2 seconds is a data entry of -0.8 second, since the time is *below* 2 minutes.

(a) Use Figure 2-20 to estimate the number of winning times less than 7.15 seconds (over 2 minutes). There are 101 data values represented. What percentage of the winning times are under 2 minutes and 7.15 seconds?

(b) Use Figure 2-20 to estimate the number of winning times *between* 5.15 and 11.15 seconds (over 2 minutes). What percentage of the winning times are between 2 minutes and 5.15 seconds and 2 minutes and 11.15 seconds?

12. *Insurance: Hospital Costs* The Health Insurance Association of America *Source Book of Health Insurance Data* gave information about the average cost per day per patient in hospitals by state, including the District of Columbia. Figure 2-21 shows a histogram of these data.

(a) Use the information given in the histogram to construct an ogive.

(b) How many states (including the District of Columbia) have average costs per day of less than $690.50?

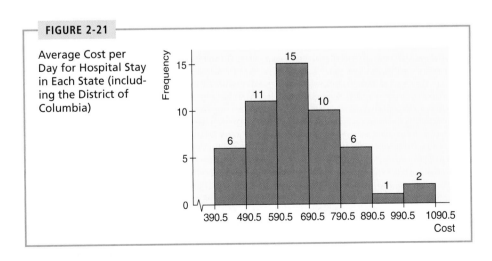

FIGURE 2-21

Average Cost per Day for Hospital Stay in Each State (including the District of Columbia)

FIGURE 2-22

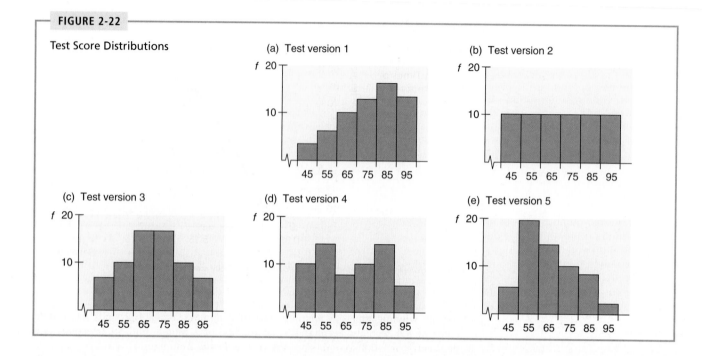

Test Score Distributions

(a) Test version 1

(b) Test version 2

(c) Test version 3

(d) Test version 4

(e) Test version 5

13. *Education: Testing* Professor Silva teaches anatomy and physiology. He has developed five different versions of a test on the same material. On giving each version to a different sample of 60 students, he discovered that the test score distributions looked like those shown in Figure 2-22.
    (a) Categorize the distribution shapes as uniform, symmetric, bimodal, skewed left, or skewed right.
    (b) Comment on some advantages or problems with each test version. As a student, which version might you prefer? Which version would you like the least?

14. *Consumer: Warranty Cards* Many products come with owner registration or warranty cards. Usually, the consumer is asked a few questions about his or her family and household income. Random samples of warranty or registration cards for the indicated product revealed the household income distributions shown in Figure 2-23 on the next page.
    (a) Categorize the distribution shapes as uniform, symmetric, bimodal, skewed left, or skewed right.
    (b) If you were in charge of advertising, how would you use income-distribution information of present customers to target ads for the indicated product?
    (c) How valid do you think income information is on warranty cards?

15. *Agriculture: Wheat Harvest* The following data represent tonnes of wheat harvested each year (1894–1925) from Plot 19 at the Rothamsted Agricultural Experiment Stations, England.

2.71	1.62	2.60	1.64	2.20	2.02	1.67	1.99	2.34	1.26	1.31
1.80	2.82	2.15	2.07	1.62	1.47	2.19	0.59	1.48	0.77	2.04
1.32	0.89	1.35	0.95	0.94	1.39	1.19	1.18	0.46	0.70	

(a) Multiply each data value by 100 to "clear" the decimals.
(b) Use the standard procedures of this section to make a frequency table and histogram with your whole-number data. Use six classes.

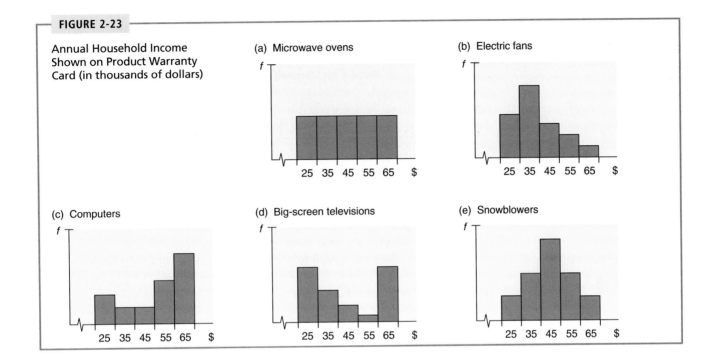

FIGURE 2-23

Annual Household Income Shown on Product Warranty Card (in thousands of dollars)

(a) Microwave ovens

(b) Electric fans

(c) Computers

(d) Big-screen televisions

(e) Snowblowers

(c) Divide class limits, class boundaries, and class midpoints by 100 to get back to your original data values.

16. *Baseball: Batting Averages* The following data represent baseball batting averages for a random sample of National League players near the end of the baseball season. The data are from the baseball statistics section of *The Denver Post.*

0.194	0.258	0.190	0.291	0.158	0.295	0.261	0.250	0.181
0.125	0.107	0.260	0.309	0.309	0.276	0.287	0.317	0.252
0.215	0.250	0.246	0.260	0.265	0.182	0.113	0.200

(a) Multiply each data value by 1000 to "clear" the decimals.
(b) Use the standard procedures of this section to make a frequency table and histogram with your whole-number data. Use five classes.
(c) Divide class limits, class boundaries, and class midpoints by 1000 to get back to your original data.

17. *Expand Your Knowledge: Dotplot* Another display technique that is somewhat similar to a histogram is a *dotplot*. In a dotplot, the data values are displayed along the horizontal axis. A dot is then plotted over each data value in the data set.

PROCEDURE

How to make a dotplot

Display the data along a horizontal axis. Then plot each data value with a dot or point above the corresponding value on the horizontal axis. For repeated data values, stack the dots.

The next display shows a dotplot generated by Minitab (➤**Graph** ➤**Dotplot**) for the number of licensed drivers per 1000 residents by state, including the District of Columbia (Source: U.S. Department of Transportation).

Dotplot for Licensed Drivers per 1000 Residents

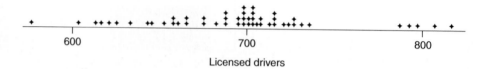

Licensed drivers

(a) From the dotplot, how many states have 600 or fewer licensed drivers per 1000 residents?

(b) About what percentage of the states (out of 51) seem to have close to 800 licensed drivers per 1000 residents?

(c) Consider the intervals 550 to 650, 650 to 750, and 750 to 850 licensed drivers per 1000 residents. In which interval do most of the states fall?

 18. *Dotplot: Dog Sled Racing* Make a dotplot for the data in Problem 1 regarding the finish time (number of hours) for the Iditarod Dog Sled Race. Compare the dotplot to the histogram of Problem 1.

 19. *Dotplot: Tumor Recurrence* Make a dotplot for the data in Problem 3 regarding the recurrence of tumors after chemotherapy. Compare the dotplot to the histogram of Problem 3.

2.3
Stem-and-Leaf Displays

FOCUS POINTS

✓ Construct a stem-and-leaf display from raw data.

✓ Use a stem-and-leaf display to visualize data distribution.

✓ Compare a stem-and-leaf display to a histogram.

Exploratory Data Analysis

Together with histograms and other graphics techniques, the stem-and-leaf display is one of many useful ways of studying data in a field called *exploratory data analysis* (often abbreviated as *EDA*). John W. Tukey wrote one of the definitive books on the subject, *Exploratory Data Analysis* (Addison-Wesley). Another very useful reference for EDA techniques is the book *Applications, Basics, and Computing of Exploratory Data Analysis,* by Paul F. Velleman and David C. Hoaglin (Duxbury Press). Exploratory data analysis techniques are particularly useful for detecting patterns and extreme data values. They are designed to help us explore a data set, to ask questions we had not thought of before, or to pursue leads in many directions.

EDA techniques are similar to those of an explorer. An explorer has a general idea of destination but is always alert to the unexpected. An explorer needs to assess situations quickly and often simplify and clarify them. An explorer makes pictures—that is, maps showing the relationships of landscape features. The aspects of rapid implementation, visual displays such as graphs and charts, data simplification, and robustness (that is, analysis that is not influenced much by extreme data values) are key ingredients of EDA techniques. In addition, these techniques are good for exploration because they require very few prior assumptions about the data.

EDA methods are especially useful when our data have been gathered for general interest and observation of subjects. For example, we may have data regarding the age of applicants to graduate programs. We don't have a specific question in mind. We want to see what the data reveal. Are the ages fairly uniform or spread out? Are there exceptionally young or old applicants? If there are, we might look at other characteristics of these applicants, such as field of study. EDA methods help us quickly absorb some aspects of the data and then may lead us to ask specific questions to which we might apply methods of traditional statistics.

In contrast, when we design an experiment to produce data to answer a specific question, we focus on particular aspects of the data that are useful to us. If we want to determine the average highway gas mileage of a specific sports car, we use that model car in well-designed tests. We don't need to worry about unexpected road conditions, poorly trained drivers, different fuel grades, sudden stops and starts, etc. Our experiment is designed to control outside factors. Consequently, we do not need to "explore" our data as much. We can often make valid assumptions about the data. Methods of traditional statistics will be very useful to analyze such data and answer our specific questions.

Stem-and-Leaf Display

In this text, we will introduce two EDA techniques: stem-and-leaf displays and, in Section 3.4, box-and-whisker plots. Let's first look at a stem-and-leaf display.

> A **stem-and-leaf display** is a method of exploratory data analysis that is used to rank-order and arrange data into groups.

We know that frequency distributions and histograms provide a useful organization and summary of data. However, in a histogram, we lose most of the specific data values. A stem-and-leaf display is a device that organizes and groups data but allows us to recover the original data if desired. In the next example, we will make a stem-and-leaf display.

EXAMPLE 6

Stem-and-leaf display

Many airline passengers seem weighted down with their carry-on luggage. Just how much weight are they carrying? The carry-on luggage weights in pounds for a random sample of 40 passengers returning from a vacation to Hawaii were recorded (see Table 2-15).

To make a stem-and-leaf display, we break the digits of each data value into *two* parts. The left group of digits is called a *stem*, and the remaining group of digits on the right is called a *leaf*. We are free to choose the number of digits to be included in the stem.

The weights in our example consist of two-digit numbers. For a two-digit number, the stem selection is obviously the left digit. In our case, the tens digits will form the stems, and the units digits will form the leaves. For example, for the weight

TABLE 2-15   Weights of Carry-On Luggage in Pounds

30	27	12	42	35	47	38	36	27	35
22	17	29	3	21	0	38	32	41	33
26	45	18	43	18	32	31	32	19	21
33	31	28	29	51	12	32	18	21	26

FIGURE 2-24

Stem-and-Leaf Displays of Airline Carry-On Luggage Weights

(a) Leaves Not Ordered

3	2 represents 32 lb
Stem	Leaves
0	3 0
1	2 7 8 8 9 2 8
2	7 7 2 9 1 6 1 8 9 1 6
3	0 5 8 6 5 8 2 3 2 1 2 3 1 2
4	2 7 1 5 3
5	1

(b) Final Display with Leaves Ordered

3	2 represents 32 lb
Stem	Leaves
0	0 3
1	2 2 7 8 8 8 9
2	1 1 1 2 6 6 7 7 8 9 9
3	0 1 1 2 2 2 2 3 3 5 5 6 8 8
4	1 2 3 5 7
5	1

12, the stem is 1, and the leaf is 2. For the weight 18, the stem is again 1, but the leaf is 8. In the stem-and-leaf display, we list each possible stem once on the left and all its leaves in the same row on the right, as in Figure 2-24(a). Finally, we order the leaves as shown in Figure 2-24(b).

Figure 2-24 shows a stem-and-leaf display for the weights of carry-on luggage. From the stem-and-leaf display in Figure 2-24, we see that two bags weighed 27 lb, one weighed 3 lb, one weighed 51 lb, and so on. We see that most of the weights were in the 30-lb range, only two were less than 10 lb, and six were over 40 lb. Note that the length of the line containing the leaves gives the visual impression that a sideways histogram would present.

As a final step, we need to indicate the scale. This is usually done by indicating the value represented by the stem and one leaf.   ◇

There are no firm rules for selecting the group of digits for the stem. But whichever group you select, you must list all the possible stems from smallest to largest in the data collection.

PROCEDURE

How to make a stem-and-leaf display

1. Divide the digits of each data value into two parts. The leftmost part is called the *stem* while the rightmost part is called the *leaf*.

2. Align all the stems in a vertical column from smallest to largest. Draw a vertical line to the right of all the stems.

3. Place all the leaves with the same stem on the same row as the stem, and arrange the leaves in increasing order.

4. Use a label to indicate the magnitude of the numbers in the display. We include the decimal position in the label rather than with the stems or leaves.

In the example that follows, we show a stem-and-leaf display for data with three digits.

EXAMPLE 7

Selecting the stem

What does it take to win at sports? If you're talking about basketball, one sports writer gave the answer. He listed the winning scores of the conference championship games over the last 35 years. The scores for those games follow below.

132	118	124	109	104	101	125	83	99
131	98	125	97	106	112	92	120	103
111	117	135	143	112	112	116	106	117
119	110	105	128	112	126	105	102	

To make a stem-and-leaf display, we'll use the first *two* digits as the stems (see Figure 2-25). Notice that the distribution of scores is fairly symmetrical.

FIGURE 2-25

Winning Scores of
Conference Basketball
Championship Games

```
08 | 3   represents 083 or 83 points
08 | 3
09 | 2 7 8 9
10 | 1 2 3 4 5 5 6 6 9
11 | 0 1 2 2 2 2 6 7 7 8 9
12 | 0 4 5 5 6 8
13 | 1 2 5
14 | 3
```

GUIDED EXERCISE 5

Stem-and-leaf display

Tel-a-Message is experimenting with computer-delivered telephone advertisements. Of primary concern is how much of the 4-minute advertisement is heard. A study was done to see how long the advertisement ran before the listeners hung up. A random sample of 30 calls gave the information in Table 2-16.

TABLE 2-16   Time Spent Listening to Advertisement (in minutes)

1.3	0.7	2.1	0.5	0.2	0.9	1.1	3.2	4.0	3.8
1.4	3.1	2.5	0.6	0.5	2.1	4.0	4.0	0.3	1.2
1.0	1.5	0.4	4.0	2.3	2.7	4.0	0.7	0.5	4.0

Continued

GUIDED EXERCISE 5 continued

(a) We'll make a stem-and-leaf display using the first digit as the stem and the second as a leaf. What is the leaf unit?

  The trailing digit is in the tenths position, so

$$1 \text{ leaf unit} = 0.1 \text{ min}$$

(b) List all the stem values.

Stem: 0
      1
      2
      3
      4

(c) Complete the stem-and-leaf display, including the unit designation. Order the leaves.

FIGURE 2-26 Time Before Hang-Up

```
1 | 3  represents 1.3 min
0 | 2  3  4  5  5  5  6  7  7  9
1 | 0  1  2  3  4  5
2 | 1  1  3  5  7
3 | 1  2  8
4 | 0  0  0  0  0  0
```

(d) Looking at the stem-and-leaf display, what could you say about the time intervals before people hung up?

Most people hung up before the end of the advertisement. Of those people, more hung up within the first minute than within any other 1-minute interval. Six people listened to the entire advertisement.

◇ **COMMENT** Stem-and-leaf displays organize the data, let the data analyst spot extreme values, and are easy to create. In fact, they can be used to organize data so that frequency tables are easier to make. However, at this time, histograms are used more often in formal data presentations, whereas stem-and-leaf displays are used by data analysts to gain initial insights about the data. ◇

  TECH NOTE   *Stem-and-Leaf Display*

TI-84Plus/TI-83Plus Does not support stem-and-leaf displays. You can sort the data by using keys **Stat ➤ Edit ➤ 2:SortA.**

Excel Does not support stem-and-leaf displays. You can sort the data by using menu choices **Data ➤ Sort.**

Minitab Use the menu selections **Graph ➤ Stem-and-Leaf** and fill in the dialogue box.

Minitab Release 12 Stem-and-Leaf Display (for Data in
Table 2-16)

```
Stem-and-Leaf   of   C1        N=30
LeafUnit=0.10

  10                    0    2345556779
  (6)                   1    012345
  14                    2    11357
   9                    3    128
   6                    4    000000
```

The values shown in the left column represent depth. Numbers above the value in
parentheses show the cumulative number of values from the top to the stem of the
middle value. Numbers below the value in parentheses show the cumulative number of values from the bottom to the stem of the middle value. The number in
parentheses shows how many values are on the same line as the middle value.

VIEWP●INT

What Does It Take to Win?

Scores for NFL Super Bowl games can be found at the NFL web site. Visit
the Brase/Brase statistics site at **http://math.college.hmco.com/students** and find
the link to the NFL. Once at the NFL web site, follow links to the Super
Bowl. Of special interest in football statistics is the spread, or difference,
between scores of the winning and losing teams. If the spread is too large,
the game can appear to be lopsided, and TV viewers become less interested
in the game (and accompanying commercial ads). Make a stem-and-leaf
display of the spread for the NFL Super Bowl games and analyze the results.

SECTION 2.3   PROBLEMS

1. *Cowboys: Longevity* How long did *real* cowboys live? One answer may be found
   in the book *The Last Cowboys* by Connie Brooks (University of New Mexico Press).
   This delightful book presents a thoughtful sociological study of cowboys in West
   Texas and Southeastern New Mexico around the year 1890. A sample of 32
   cowboys gave the following years of longevity:

58	52	68	86	72	66	97	89	84	91	91
92	66	68	87	86	73	61	70	75	72	73
85	84	90	57	77	76	84	93	58	47	

   (a) Make a stem-and-leaf display for these data.
   (b) Consider the following quote from Baron von Richthofen in his *Cattle Raising
       on the Plains of North America:* "Cowboys are to be found among the sons of

the best families. The truth is probably that most were not a drunken, gambling lot, quick to draw and fire their pistols." Does the data distribution of longevity lend credence to this quote?

2. *Ecology: Habitat* Wetlands offer a diversity of benefits. They provide habitat for wildlife, spawning grounds for U.S. commercial fish, and renewable timber resources. In the last 200 years the United States has lost more than half its wetlands. *Environmental Almanac* gives the percentage of wetlands lost in each state in the last 200 years. For the lower 48 states, the percentage loss of wetlands per state is as follows:

46	37	36	42	81	20	73	59	35	50
87	52	24	27	38	56	39	74	56	31
27	91	46	9	54	52	30	33	28	35
35	23	90	72	85	42	59	50	49	
48	38	60	46	87	50	89	49	67	

Make a stem-and-leaf display of these data. Be sure to indicate the scale. How are the percentages distributed? Is the distribution skewed? Are there any gaps?

3. *Health Care: Hospitals* The American Medical Association Center for Health Policy Research included data, by state, on the number of community hospitals and the average patient stay (in days) in its publication *State Health Care Data: Utilization, Spending, and Characteristics*. The data (by state) are shown in the table. Make a stem-and-leaf display of the data for the average length of stay in days. Comment about the general shape of the distribution.

State	No. of Hospitals	Average Length of Stay	State	No. of Hospitals	Average Length of Stay	State	No. of Hospitals	Average Length of Stay
Alabama	119	7.0	Kentucky	107	6.9	N. Dakota	47	11.1
Alaska	16	5.7	Louisiana	136	6.7	Ohio	193	6.6
Arizona	61	5.5	Maine	38	7.2	Oklahoma	113	6.7
Arkansas	88	7.0	Maryland	51	6.8	Oregon	66	5.3
California	440	6.0	Massachusetts	101	7.0	Pennsylvania	236	7.5
Colorado	71	6.8	Michigan	175	7.3	Rhode Island	12	6.9
Connecticut	35	7.4	Minnesota	148	8.7	S. Carolina	68	7.1
Delaware	8	6.8	Mississippi	102	7.2	S. Dakota	52	10.3
Dist. of Columbia	11	7.5	Missouri	133	7.4	Tennessee	122	6.8
Florida	227	7.0	Montana	53	10.0	Texas	421	6.2
Georgia	162	7.2	Nebraska	90	9.6	Utah	42	5.2
Hawaii	19	9.4	Nevada	21	6.4	Vermont	15	7.6
Idaho	41	7.1	New Hampshire	27	7.0	Virginia	98	7.0
Illinois	209	7.3	New Jersey	96	7.6	Washington	92	5.6
Indiana	113	6.6	New Mexico	37	5.5	W. Virginia	59	7.1
Iowa	123	8.4	New York	231	9.9	Wisconsin	129	7.3
Kansas	133	7.8	N. Carolina	117	7.3	Wyoming	27	8.5

4. *Health Care: Hospitals* Using the number of hospitals per state listed in the table in Problem 3, make a stem-and-leaf display for the number of community hospitals per state. Which states have an unusually high number of hospitals?

5. *Expand Your Knowledge: Split Stem* The Boston Marathon is the oldest and best known U.S. marathon. It covers a route from Hopkinton, Massachusetts, to downtown Boston. The distance is approximately 26 miles. Visit the Brase/Brase statistics site at **http://math.college.hmco.com/students** and find the link to Boston Marathon. Search the marathon site to find a wealth of information about the history of the race. In particular, the site gives the winning times for the Boston Marathon. They are all over 2 hours. The following data are the minutes over 2 hours for the winning male runners:

1961–1980

23	23	18	19	16	17	15	22	13	10
18	15	16	13	9	20	14	10	9	12

1981–2000

9	8	9	10	14	7	11	8	9	8
11	8	9	7	9	9	10	7	9	9

(a) Make a stem-and-leaf display for the minutes over 2 hours of the winning times for the years 1961 to 1980. Use two lines per stem.

> **PROCEDURE**
>
> **How to split a stem**
>
> When a stem has many leaves, it is useful to split the stem into two lines or more. For two lines per stem, place leaves 0 to 4 on the first line and leaves 5 to 9 on the next line.

(b) Make a stem-and-leaf display for the minutes over 2 hours of the winning times for the years 1981 to 2000. Use two lines per stem.

(c) Compare the two distributions. How many times under 15 minutes are in each distribution?

6. *Split Stem: Golf* The U.S. Open Golf Tournament was played at Congressional Country Club, Bethesda, Maryland, with prizes ranging from $465,000 for first place to $5000. Par for the course is 70. The tournament consists of four rounds played on different days. The scores for each round of the 32 players who placed in the money (more than $17,000) were given on a web site. For more information, visit the Brase/Brase statistics site at **http://math.college.hmco.com/students** and find the link to golf. The scores for the first round were as follows:

71	65	67	73	74	73	71	71	74	73	71
70	75	71	72	71	75	75	71	71	74	75
66	75	75	75	71	72	72	73	71	67	

The scores for the fourth round for these players were as follows:

69	69	73	74	72	72	70	71	71	70	72
73	73	72	71	71	71	69	70	71	72	73
74	72	71	68	69	70	69	71	73	74	

(a) Make a stem-and-leaf display for the first-round scores. Use two lines per stem. (See Problem 5.)

(b) Make a stem-and-leaf display for the fourth-round scores. Use two lines per stem.

(c) Compare the two distributions. How do the highest scores compare? How do the lowest scores compare?

7. *Astronomy: Motions of Stars* Proper motions are the angular motions of stars across the sky due to effects other than the motion of the earth. These motions primarily reflect the stars' own velocities in space. *Centennial proper motion* indicates that the units are arc seconds per century (per information in an article by K. M. Cudworth, *Astronomical Journal*, Vol. 81, pp. 975–982). The following data represent centennial proper motion for a sample of stars from the global star cluster M92, some of the oldest stars in our galaxy.

1.260	0.251	0.788	0.038	0.050	0.057	0.008
0.219	0.667	0.014	0.759	1.438	0.623	0.173
1.169	1.660	1.808	1.057	1.024	0.216	0.430
0.351	1.616	1.169	0.888	1.260	0.042	0.369

Make a stem-and-leaf display describing the centennial proper motion for these stars using the first two digits as the stem and the last two digits as the leaf.* Do there appear to be any gaps in centennial proper motion for these stars? Would such a discovery be of interest to an astronomer?

8. *Astronomy: Cosmic Radio Signals* Is there an association between the location of cosmic radio sources and particular galaxies? A partial answer might be found in *Astrophysics Journal*, Vol. 148, pp. 321–365. Galaxies and radio sources were randomly studied in the celestial equator between longitudes 10h and 16h and latitudes $-16°$ and 16°. The radio brightnesses (units 10^{-26} watts per square meter per hertz) of the closest radio sources are

9.0	9.5	67.0	11.5	44.0	13.6	9.0	12.5	10.5	11.0
16.5	11.5	9.8	44.0	16.5	16.5	13.5	20.0	9.5	
44.0	28.0	20.0	9.4	11.5	12.5	44.0	13.7	9.5	

After gathering appropriate data, the first activity in many research projects is to perform an initial organization of the data. Make a stem-and-leaf display using one digit as the stem and two digits as the leaf.* *Hint:* 9.0 would be coded as 09.0, so the first digit is considered to be 0. Be sure to label the unit measure. Are there any unusually high or low data values recorded?

Are cigarettes bad for people? Cigarette smoking involves tar, carbon monoxide, and nicotine. The first two are definitely not good for a person's health, and the last ingredient can cause addiction. Problems 9, 10, and 11 refer to Table 2-17, which was taken from the web site maintained by the *Journal of Statistics Education*. For more information, visit the

---

*Technically, if there is more than one digit remaining in the leaf portion, only the leftmost of the leaf digits is considered to be a leaf, and the other digits are truncated. The appropriate scale is listed in the label. For instance, if numbers such as 12,472 are in the data set, and the first two digits comprise the stem, the leaf is the next digit, or 4. Then a label indicates that 12 | 4 represents 12,400. Computer packages such as Minitab follow the convention of truncating numbers so that only one digit is in the leaf portion. In Problems 7 and 8 you are asked to use two digits for each leaf. Place the two digits together and then leave a larger space before listing the next leaf "group" of two digits. In this way you can retrieve actual data values from the display rather than truncated values.

TABLE 2-17   Milligrams of Tar, Nicotine, and Carbon Monoxide (CO) Content for One Cigarette

Brand	Tar	Nicotine	CO	Brand	Tar	Nicotine	CO
Alpine	14.1	0.86	13.6	MultiFilter	11.4	0.78	10.2
Benson & Hedges	16.0	1.06	16.6	Newport Lights	9.0	0.74	9.5
Bull Durham	29.8	2.03	23.5	Now	1.0	0.13	1.5
Camel Lights	8.0	0.67	10.2	Old Gold	17.0	1.26	18.5
Carlton	4.1	0.40	5.4	Pall Mall Lights	12.8	1.08	12.6
Chesterfield	15.0	1.04	15.0	Raleigh	15.8	0.96	17.5
Golden Lights	8.8	0.76	9.0	Salem Ultra	4.5	0.42	4.9
Kent	12.4	0.95	12.3	Tareyton	14.5	1.01	15.9
Kool	16.6	1.12	16.3	True	7.3	0.61	8.5
L&M	14.9	1.02	15.4	Viceroy Rich Light	8.6	0.69	10.6
Lark Lights	13.7	1.01	13.0	Virginia Slim	15.2	1.02	13.9
Marlboro	15.1	0.90	14.4	Winston Lights	12.0	0.82	14.9
Merit	7.8	0.57	10.0				

Source: Journal of Statistics Education web site at http://www.amstat.org/publications/jse. Reprinted with permission.

Brase/Brase statistics site at **http://math.college.hmco.com/students** and find the link to the *Journal of Statistics Education.* Follow the links to the cigarette data.

9. *Health: Cigarette Smoke* Use the data in Table 2-17 to make a stem-and-leaf display for milligrams of tar per cigarette smoked.

10. *Health: Cigarette Smoke* Use the data in Table 2-17 to make a stem-and-leaf display for milligrams of carbon monoxide per cigarette smoked.

11. *Health: Cigarette Smoke* Use the data in Table 2-17 to make a stem-and-leaf display for milligrams of nicotine per cigarette smoked. In this case, truncate the measurements at the tenth position and use two lines per stem (see Problem 5, part a).

 12. *Expand Your Knowledge: Back-to-Back Stem Plot* In archaeology, the depth (below surface grade) at which artifacts are found is very important. Greater depths sometimes indicate older artifacts, perhaps from a different archaeological period. Figure 2-27 is

FIGURE 2-27

Depth (in cm) of Artifact Location

5 | 2 | 0   = 25 cm at Site I and 20 cm at Site II

Site I		Site II
5	2	0 5 5
5 0	3	0 0 0 0 5 5
5 5 5 5	4	0 0 0 5
5 0	5	0 0 5 5
5 5 5 5 5 0	6	0 0 0 5 5 5
5 5 5 5 5 5 0 0	7	
5 5 0 0 0	8	
5 5 0 0	9	
5 5	10	
0	11	0 0 5 5 5
	12	0 0 0 5

FIGURE 2-28

Back-to-Back Stem Plot
Showing Annual Salaries
(in thousands of dollars)
for Full Professors in
California and in New
York

9 | 4 | 5   represents $49,000 for California and $45,000 for New York

California		New York
9	4	5 6 8
9 6 3 0	5	0 1 1 5 6
9 3 0 0 0	6	0 1 1 3 4 5 6 9 9 9
7 7 7 6 6 5 5 5 5 0	7	2 2 4 5 5 6
9 7 5 5 3	8	2 5 6
5 4 4 3	9	3 5 7
4 2	10	0 3
3 2	11	
6 2	12	0 0

---

a *back-to-back stem plot* showing the depths of artifact locations at two different archaeological sites. These sites are from similar geographic locations. Notice that the stems are in the center of the diagram. The leaves for Site I artifact depths are shown to the left of the stem, while the leaves for Site II are to the right of the stem (see *Mimbres Mogollon Archaeology* by A. I. Woosley and A. J. McIntyre, University of New Mexico Press).

(a) What are the least and greatest depths of artifact finds at Site I? at Site II?

(b) Describe the data distribution of depths of artifact finds at Site I and at Site II.

(c) At Site II, there is a gap in the depths at which artifacts were found. Does the Site II data distribution suggest that there might have been a period of no occupation?

13. *Back-to-Back Stem Plot: Salaries* Figure 2-28 is a *back-to-back stem plot* showing the average annual salaries (in thousands of dollars) of full professors in California universities compared to salaries of full professors in New York universities (Source: *The Chronicle of Higher Education.* For more information, visit the Brase/Brase statistics site at **http://math.college.hmco.com/students** and find the link to the *Chronicle of Higher Education.*)

(a) What are the low and high average salaries for professors in California? in New York?

(b) Which state has a greater number of average salaries in the $60,000 range? in the $70,000 range?

(c) In general, which state, California or New York, would you say has higher average salaries for professors in colleges and universities?

SUMMARY

Organizing and presenting data are the main purposes of that branch of statistics called descriptive statistics. In this chapter, we have studied bar graphs, Pareto charts, circle graphs, time-series graphs, histograms, relative-frequency histograms, frequency polygons, ogives, and stem-and-leaf displays. From the viewpoint of future applications, histograms are the most important because the area under a bar can represent the likelihood of data values falling into that class. Histograms and stem-and-leaf displays both reveal distribution properties such as uniformity, symmetry, or skewness.

IMPORTANT WORDS & SYMBOLS

Section 2.1
Bar graph
Pareto chart
Pie chart or circle graph
Time-series graph
Time series

Section 2.2
Frequency
Frequency distribution
Class width
Class, lower limit, upper limit
Class frequency
Class midpoint
Class mark
Frequency table
Class boundaries
Histogram

Relative-frequency table
Relative-frequency histogram
Symmetric distribution
Uniform distribution
Skewed left
Skewed right
Bimodal distribution
Frequency polygon
Cumulative frequency
Ogive
Dotplot

Section 2.3
EDA
Stem
Leaf
Stem-and-leaf display
Back-to-back stem plot

VIEWPOINT   *"This land is your land, This land is my land"**
                                    —Woody Guthrie

But who actually owns the forest? On many maps, forest land (including national forests) is colored green. Such maps give the impression that vast areas of the western United States are public land. This is not the case! *USA Today* gave the following information about ownership of U.S. timber lands: state/local, 17%; federal, 10%; forest industry, 14%; and private nonindustry, 59%. Organize these data for better visual presentation using a Pareto chart and a circle graph.

*Words and music by Woody Guthrie TRO © Copyright 1956 (Renewed) 1958 (Renewed) Ludlow Music, Inc., New York, New York. Used by permission.

CHAPTER REVIEW PROBLEMS

1. *Focus Problem: Fuel Economy* Solve the focus problem at the beginning of this chapter.

2. *Criminal Justice: Prisoners* The time plot in Figure 2-29 on the next page gives the number of state and federal prisoners per 100,000 population (Source: *Statistical Abstract of the United States,* 120th Edition).
   (a) Estimate the number of prisoners per 100,000 people for 1980 and for 1997.
   (b) During the time period shown there was increased prosecution of drug offenses, longer sentences for common crimes, and reduced access to parole. What does

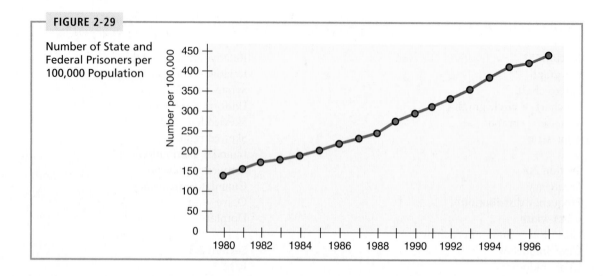

FIGURE 2-29

Number of State and
Federal Prisoners per
100,000 Population

the time-series graph say about the prison population change per 100,000 people?

(c) In 1997, the U.S. population was approximately 266,574,000 people. At the rate of 444 prisoners per 100,000 population, about how many prisoners were in the system? The projected U.S. population for the year 2020 is 323,724,000. If the rate of prisoners per 100,000 stays the same as in 1997, about how many prisoners do we expect to have in the system in 2020? To obtain the most recent information, visit the Brase/Brase statistics site at **http://math.college.hmco.com/ students** and find the link to the Census Bureau.

3. *IRS: Tax Returns* Almost everyone files (or will sometime file) a federal income tax return. A research poll for Turbo Tax (a computer software package to aid in tax-return preparation) asked what aspect of filing a return people thought to be the most difficult. The results showed that 43% of the people said understanding the IRS jargon, 28% said knowing deductions, 10% said getting the right form, 8% said calculating the numbers, and 10% didn't know. Make a circle graph to display this information. *Note:* Percentages will not total 100% because of rounding.

4. *Law Enforcement: DUI* Driving under the influence of alcohol (DUI) is a serious offense. The following data give the ages of a random sample of 50 drivers arrested while driving under the influence of alcohol. This distribution is based on the age distribution of DUI arrests given in the *Statistical Abstract of the United States* (112th Edition).

46	16	41	26	22	33	30	22	36	34
63	21	26	18	27	24	31	38	26	55
31	47	27	43	35	22	64	40	58	20
49	37	53	25	29	32	23	49	39	40
24	56	30	51	21	45	27	34	47	35

(a) Make a stem-and-leaf display of the age distribution.
(b) Make a frequency table using seven classes.

(c) Make a histogram showing class boundaries.

(d) Make an ogive. From the ogive, estimate the percentage of drivers arrested while DUI who are aged 29 or under.

 5. *Agriculture: Apple Trees* The following data represent trunk circumferences (in mm) for a random sample of 60 four-year-old apple trees at East Malling Agriculture Research Station in England (Reference: S. C. Pearce, University of Kent at Canterbury). *Note:* These data are also available with other software on the statSpace CD-ROM.

108	99	106	102	115	120	120	117	122	142
106	111	119	109	125	108	116	105	117	123
103	114	101	99	112	120	108	91	115	109
114	105	99	122	106	113	114	75	96	124
91	102	108	110	83	90	69	117	84	142
122	113	105	112	117	122	129	100	138	117

(a) Make a frequency table with seven classes showing class limits, class boundaries, midpoints, frequencies, relative frequencies, and cumulative frequencies.

(b) Draw a histogram.

(c) Draw a frequency polygon.

(d) Draw a relative-frequency histogram.

(e) Draw an ogive.

6. *Law: Corporation Lawsuits* Many people say the civil justice system is overburdened. Many cases center on suits involving businesses. The following data are based on a *Wall Street Journal* report. Researchers conducted a study of lawsuits involving 1908 businesses ranked in the Fortune 1000 over a 20-year period. They found the following distribution of civil justice caseloads brought before the federal courts involving the businesses:

Case Type	Number of Filings (in thousands)
Contracts	107
General torts (personal injury)	191
Asbestos liability	49
Other product liability	38
All other	21

Note: Contracts cases involve disputes over contracts between businesses.

(a) Make a Pareto chart of the caseloads. Which type of cases occur most frequently?

(b) Make a circle chart showing the percentage of cases of each type.

7. *Archaeology: Tree-Ring Data The Sand Canyon Archaeological Project,* edited by W. D. Lipe and published by Crow Canyon Archaeological Center, contains the stem-and-leaf diagram in Figure 2-30 on the next page. The study uses tree rings to accurately determine the year in which a tree was cut. The figure gives the tree-ring-cutting dates for samples of timbers found in the architectural units at Sand Canyon Pueblo. The text referring to the figure says, "The three-digit numbers in

FIGURE 2-30

Tree-Ring-Cutting
Dates from Archi-
tectural Units at Sand
Canyon Pueblo: *The
Sand Canyon Archaeo-
logical Project*

119	5 6
120	0 0 1 2 3 3 3 3 3 3 3 3 3 3 3 3 3 3 3 3 3 3 3 3 3 3 3 3
120	
121	2
121	5 5
122	0 0 1 1 1 1 2 2 3 4 4 4 4 4 4 4
122	5 8 9
123	0 1 2 3 3 4
123	5 5 5 5 5 5 5 5 5 5 5 5 5 5 6 8 8 9
124	1 2 2 2 2 2 2 2 2 2 2 2 2 2 2 2 2 2 2 2 3 4 4
124	5 6 8 9 9 9 9 9 9 9 9 9
125	0 0 0 0 0 0 0 0 0 0 0 0 0 0 1 1 1 1 1 1 1 2 2 2
125	
126	0 0 0 1 2 2 2 2 2 2 2 2 2 2 2 2 2 4 4 4 4 4 4 4
126	5 5 5 6 6 7
127	0 1 1 1 1 4 4

the left column represent centuries and decades A.D. The numbers to the right represent individual years, with each number derived from an individual sample. Thus, **124 2 2 2** represents three samples dated to A.D. 1242." Use Figure 2-30 and the verbal description to answer the following questions.

(a) Which decade contained the most samples?

(b) How many samples had a tree-ring-cutting date between (and including) 1200 A.D. and 1239 A.D.?

(c) What are the dates of the longest interval during which no tree-cutting samples occurred? What might this indicate about new construction or renovation of the pueblo structures during this period?

8. *Education: Grades* The following relative-frequency histogram is based on information from the *Statistical Abstract of the United States* (112th Edition). In Figure 2-31, the horizontal axis shows high-school grade point average for a person who has received a bachelor's degree. We use a 4-point scale for grading, so A = 4, B+ = 3.5, B = 3, C+ = 2.5, C = 2, D+ = 1.5, and D = 1. The vertical axis gives the relative frequencies for the high-school grade point averages of students who graduated from college.

(a) Comment on the shape of the distribution. Is it skewed? Is it symmetrical? Is it uniform?

(b) The class boundaries are halfway between the class midpoints. Find the class boundaries. *Hint:* Use the fact that the classes are all the same width to find the lower boundary of the first class and the upper boundary of the last class.

(c) Convert the relative frequencies into percentages. Then find the percentage of college graduates who had high-school grade point averages of less than 3.25 (low B). What percentage had high-school grade point averages of less than 3.75 (high B)?

9. *Health Care: Age of Patients* The following data are based on information from the *Statistical Abstract of the United States* (112th Edition). In Figure 2-32, the horizontal axis represents the ages of hospital patients (over 4 years of age on). The vertical axis gives the relative frequencies.

(a) Which age group is the most frequent?

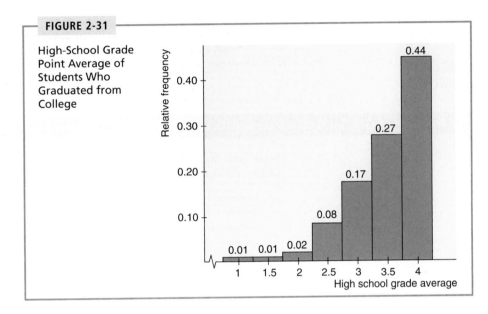

FIGURE 2-31

High-School Grade Point Average of Students Who Graduated from College

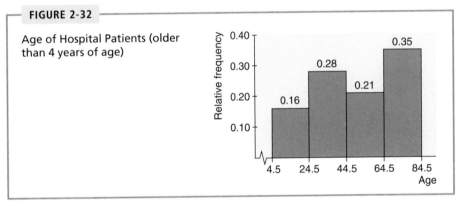

FIGURE 2-32

Age of Hospital Patients (older than 4 years of age)

(b) Convert the relative frequencies into percentages. Then find the percentage of patients older than age 44.

(c) What percentage of patients is 44 years old or younger?

10. *World's Wealthiest People: Age Forbes Richest People* gives the profile of the world's wealthiest men and women. For more information, visit the Brase/Brase statistics site at **http://math.college.hmco.com/students** and find the link to Forbes. Do you have to be old to be worth at least $2 billion? You can answer this question yourself by studying the following data—ages of men and women worth at least $2 billion:

40	66	43	82	52	58	77	52	50	48	47
68	66	73	76	53	67	88	40	79	73	66
65	70	72	77	48	75	82	54	76	41	93
65	60	57	74	70	83	67	68	77	66	34
66	59	48	56	71	40	53	63	52	57	83
52	60	56	71	64	61	53	53	73	70	

(a) Make a stem-and-leaf display.

(b) Make a histogram using seven classes. Describe the shape of the distribution (that is, indicate if it is symmetrical, skewed, or bimodal).

(c) Make an ogive. Estimate the percentage of these very rich people aged 51 or under.

DATA HIGHLIGHTS: GROUP PROJECTS

Break into small groups and discuss the following topics. Organize a brief outline in which you summarize the main points of your group discussion.

1. Examine Figure 2-33, "Everyone Agrees: Slobs Make Worst Roommates." This is a double bar graph because two percentages are given for each response category: responses from men and responses from women. Comment about how the artistic rendition has slightly changed the format of a bar graph. Do the bars seem to have lengths that accurately reflect the relative percentages of the responses? In your own opinion, does the artistic rendition enhance or confuse the information? Explain. Which characteristic of "worst roommates" does the graphic seem to illustrate? Can this graph be considered a Pareto chart for men? For women? Why or why not? From the information given in the figure, do you think the survey just listed the four given annoying characteristics? Do you think a respondent could choose more than one characteristic? Explain your answer in terms of the percentages given and in terms of the explanation given in the graphic. Could this information also be displayed in one circle graph for men and another for women? Explain.

2. Examine Figure 2-34, "Global Teen Worries." How many countries were contained in the sample? The graph contains bars and a circle. Which bar is the longest? Which bar represents the greatest percentage? Is this a bar graph or not? If not, what changes would need to be made to put the information into a bar graph? Could the graph be made into a Pareto chart? Could it be made into a circle graph? Explain.

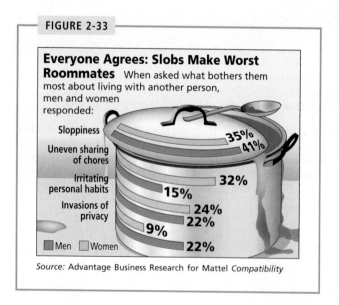

FIGURE 2-33

Everyone Agrees: Slobs Make Worst Roommates When asked what bothers them most about living with another person, men and women responded:

Sloppiness — 35% / 41%
Uneven sharing of chores — 32% / 15%
Irritating personal habits — 24% / 22%
Invasions of privacy — 9% / 22%

■ Men □ Women

Source: Advantage Business Research for Mattel *Compatibility*

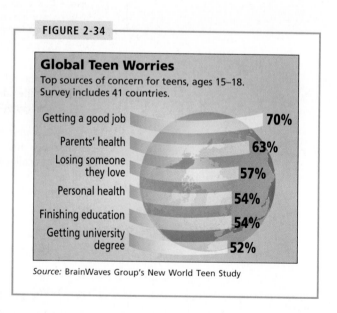

FIGURE 2-34

Global Teen Worries
Top sources of concern for teens, ages 15–18. Survey includes 41 countries.

Getting a good job — 70%
Parents' health — 63%
Losing someone they love — 57%
Personal health — 54%
Finishing education — 54%
Getting university degree — 52%

Source: BrainWaves Group's New World Teen Study

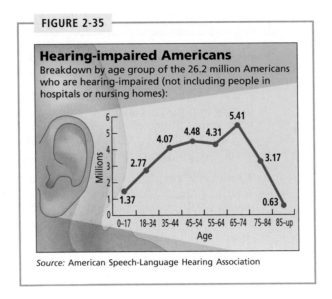

Source: American Speech-Language Hearing Association

3. Examine Figure 2-35, "Hearing-impaired Americans." Is this figure best categorized as a time-series graph, an ogive, or a frequency polygon? What is the midpoint for each class? What would be a reasonable midpoint for the last class? Look at the age classes. For which classes are the class widths equal? Redraw the polygon so that the horizontal scale more accurately represents all the listed intervals. Compare your graph with the given figure. Discuss some reasons you think the designers of the original graphic made the first two classes longer.

4. Examine Figure 2-36, "Markets Diary" (*The Wall Street Journal*). Explain why this could be considered a time-series graph. If you were a trader on the floor of the exchange, a broker in Miami, or just an individual who bought and sold stocks, how could this graph be useful to you? How could the table insert, which is a breakdown of the five most recent trading days, be useful? Explain.

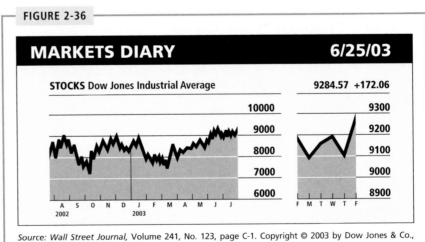

Source: Wall Street Journal, Volume 241, No. 123, page C-1. Copyright © 2003 by Dow Jones & Co., Inc. Reproduced with permission of Dow Jones & Co., Inc. in the format Textbook via Copyright Clearance Center.

LINKING CONCEPTS: WRITING PROJECTS

Discuss each of the following topics in class or review the topics on your own. Then write a brief but complete essay in which you summarize the main points. Please include formulas and graphs as appropriate.

1. In your own words, explain the differences among bar graphs, circle graphs, time-series graphs, Pareto charts, ogives, histograms, relative-frequency histograms, and stem-and-leaf displays. If you have nominal data, which graphic displays might be useful? What if you have ordinal, interval, or ratio data?

2. What do we mean when we say a histogram is skewed to the left? to the right? What is a bimodal histogram? Discuss the following statement: "A bimodal histogram usually results if we draw a sample from two populations at once." Suppose you took a sample of weights of college football players and with this sample you included weights of cheerleaders. Do you think a histogram made from the combined weights would be bimodal? Explain.

3. Discuss the statement that stem-and-leaf displays are quick and easy to construct. How can we use a stem-and-leaf display to make the construction of a frequency table easier? How does a stem-and-leaf display help you spot extreme values quickly?

4. Go to the library and pick up a current issue of *The Wall Street Journal, Newsweek, Time, USA Today,* or other news media. Examine each newspaper or magazine for graphs of the type discussed in this chapter. List the variables used, method of data collection, and general type of conclusion drawn from the graphs. Another source for information is the Internet. Explore several web sites, and categorize the graphs you find as you did for the print media. For interesting web sites, visit the Brase/Brase statistics site at **http://math.college.hmco.com/students** and find links to the Social Statistics Briefing Room, to law enforcement, and to golf.

Using Technology

TI-84PLUS/TI-83PLUS • MINITAB • EXCEL • SPSS

APPLICATIONS

The following tables show the first-round winning scores of the NCAA men's and women's basketball teams.

TABLE 2-18 Men's Winning First-Round NCAA Tournament Scores

95	70	79	99	83	72	79	101
69	82	86	70	79	69	69	70
95	70	77	61	69	68	69	72
89	66	84	77	50	83	63	58

TABLE 2-19 Women's Winning First-Round NCAA Tournament Scores

80	68	51	80	83	75	77	100
96	68	89	80	67	84	76	70
98	81	79	89	98	83	72	100
101	83	66	76	77	84	71	77

1. Use the software or method of your choice to construct separate histograms for the men's and women's winning scores. Try 5, 7, and 10 classes for each. Which number of classes seems to be the best choice? Why?

2. Use the same class boundaries for histograms of men's and of women's scores. How do the scores for the two groups compare? What general shape do the histograms follow?

3. Use the software or method of your choice to make stem-and-leaf displays for each set of scores. If your software does not make stem-and-leaf displays, sort the data first and then make a back-to-back display by hand. Do there seem to be any extreme values in either set? How do the data sets compare?

Technology Hints: Creating Histograms

The default histograms produced by the TI-84Plus/ TI-83Plus calculators, Minitab, and Excel all determine the number of classes to use automatically. To control the number of classes the technology uses, follow the key steps as indicated. The display screens are generated for data found in Table 2-4—Commuting Distances of Dallas Workers—using five classes.

TI-84Plus/TI-83Plus

Determine the class width for the number of classes you want and the lower class boundary for the first class. Enter the data in list L1.

Press **STATPLOT** and highlight On and the histogram plot.

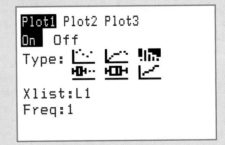

Press **WINDOW** and set Xmin = lowest class boundary, Xscl = class width. Use appropriate values for the other settings.

```
WINDOW
 Xmin=.5
 Xmax=51
 Xscl=10
 Ymin=-5
 Ymax=30
 Yscl=1
 Xres=1
```

Press **GRAPH. TRACE** gives boundaries and frequency.

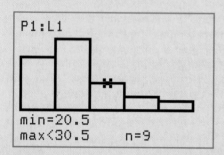

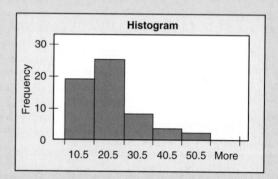

Excel

Determine the upper class boundaries for the five classes. Enter the data. In a separate column, enter the upper class boundaries. Use the menu selection **Tools ➤ Data Analysis ➤ Histogram.**

Put the data range in the Input Range. Put the upper class boundaries range in the Bin Range.

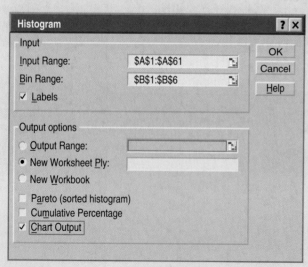

To make bars touch, right click on a bar and select **Format Data Series ➤ Options tab.** Set **gap width** to 0.

Minitab

Determine the class boundaries. Enter the data. Use the menu selection **Graph ➤ Histogram.**

In the Dialogue Box, press **Options.** Then select cutpoints and enter the class boundaries as cutpoint positions.

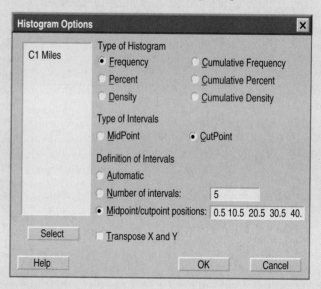

Select **Frame** to adjust scales. Otherwise, press **OK.**

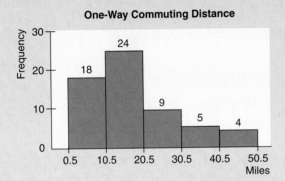

One-Way Commuting Distance

SPSS

The SPSS screenshot at the right shows the default histogram created by the menu choices **Analyze ➤ Descriptive Statistics ➤ Frequencies.** In the dialogue box, move the variable containing the data into the variables window. Click **Charts** and select **Histograms.** Click the Continue button and then the OK button. In

SPSS version 12, there are procedures to control the boundaries (cutpoints) of the histogram.

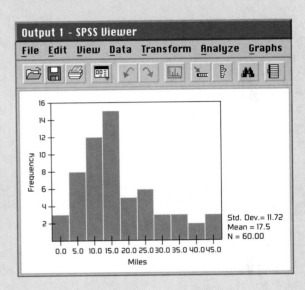

3

Averages and Variation

While the individual man is an insolvable puzzle,
in the aggregate he becomes
a mathematical certainty. You can,
for example, never foretell what any one man
will do, but you can say
with precision what an average number will be up to.

— Arthur Conan Doyle, *The Sign of Four*

Sherlock Holmes

Sherlock Holmes spoke these words to his colleague Dr. Watson as the two were unraveling a mystery. The detective was implying that if a single member is drawn at random from a population, we cannot predict *exactly* what that member will look like. However, there are some "average" features of the entire population that an individual is likely to possess. The degree of certainty with which we would expect to observe such average features in any individual depends on our knowledge of the variation among individuals in the population. Sherlock Holmes has led us to two of the most important statistical concepts: average and variation.

PREVIEW QUESTIONS

◇ What are commonly used measures of central tendency? What do they tell you? (SECTION 3.1)

◇ How do variance and standard deviation measure data spread? Why is this important? (SECTION 3.2)

◇ When data have already been grouped in a frequency table or histogram, how can you estimate the mean and standard deviation? (SECTION 3.3)

◇ How do you make a box-and-whisker plot, and what does it tell about the spread of the data? (SECTION 3.4)

For on-line student resources, visit **math.college.hmco.com/students** and follow the Statistics links to the Brase/Brase, *Understandable Statistics,* 8th edition web site.

96

The Educational Advantage

Is it really worth all the effort to get a college degree? From a philosophical point of view, the love of learning is sufficient reason to get a college degree. However, the U.S. Census Bureau also makes another relevant point. Annually, college graduates (bachelor's) earn on average $17,583 more than high school graduates. This means college graduates earn about 77% more than high school graduates, and according to "Education Pays" on the next page, the gap in earnings is increasing. Furthermore, as the College Board indicates, for most Americans college remains relatively affordable.

After completing this chapter, you will be able to answer the following questions.

(a) Does a college degree *guarantee* someone a 77% increase in earnings over a high school degree? Remember, we are using only *averages* from census data.

(b) Using census data (not shown in "Education Pays"), it is estimated that the standard deviation of college-graduate earnings is about $8,500. Compute a 75% Chebyshev confidence interval centered on the mean ($40,478) for bachelor's degree earnings.

(c) How much does college tuition cost? That depends, of course, on where you go to college. Construct a weighted average. Using the data from "College Affordable for Most," estimate midpoints for the cost intervals. Say 51% are about $3,500; 21% are about $6,000; 6% are about $10,000; 8% are about $14,000; 7% are about $18,000; and 7% are about $25,000. Compute the weighted average of college tuition charged at all colleges. (See Problem 9 in the Chapter Review Problems.)

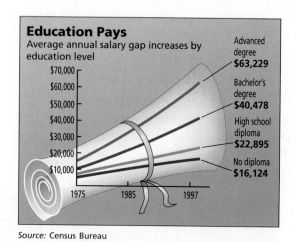

Source: Census Bureau

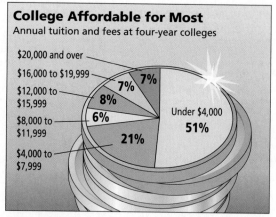

Source: The College Board

3.1   Measures of Central Tendency: Mode, Median, and Mean

FOCUS POINTS

✓ Compute mean, median, and mode from raw data.

✓ Interpret what mean, median, and mode tell you.

✓ Explain how mean, median, and mode can be affected by extreme data values.

✓ What is a trimmed mean? How do you compute it?

✓ Compute a weighted average.

The average price of an ounce of gold is $295. The Zippy car averages 39 miles per gallon on the highway. A survey showed the average shoe size for women is size 8.

In each of the preceding statements, *one* number is used to describe the entire sample or population. Such a number is called an *average*. There are many ways to compute averages, but we will study only three of the major ones.

The easiest average to compute is the *mode*.

The **mode** of a data set is the value that occurs most frequently.

EXAMPLE 1

Mode

Count the letters in each word of this sentence and give the mode. The numbers of letters in the words of the sentence are

5   3   7   2   4   4   2   4   8   3   4   3   4

Scanning the data, we see that 4 is the mode because more words have 4 letters than any other number. For larger data sets, it is useful to order—or sort—the data before scanning them for the mode.   ◊

Median

Not every data set has a mode. For example, if Professor Fair gives equal numbers of As, Bs, Cs, Ds, and Fs, then there is no modal grade. In addition, the mode is not very stable. Changing just one number in a data set can change the mode dramatically. However, the mode is a useful average when we want to know the most frequently occurring data value, such as the most frequently requested shoe size.

Another average that is useful is the *median,* or central value, of an ordered distribution. When you are given the median, you know there are an equal number of data values in the ordered distribution that are above it and below it.

PROCEDURE

How to find the median

The **median** is the central value of an ordered distribution. To find it,

1. Order the data from smallest to largest.

2. For an *odd* number of data values in the distribution,

$$\text{Median} = \text{Middle data value}$$

3. For an *even* number of data values in the distribution,

$$\text{Median} = \frac{\text{Sum of middle two values}}{2}$$

EXAMPLE 2

Median

What do barbecue-flavored potato chips cost? According to *Consumer Reports,* Volume 66, No. 5, the prices per ounce in cents of the rated chips are

19   19   27   28   18   35

(a) To find the median, we first order the data, and then note that there are an even number of entries. So the median is constructed using the two middle values

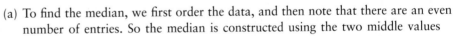

18   19   19   27   28   35

middle values

$$\text{Median} = \frac{19 + 27}{2} = 23 \text{ cents}$$

(b) According to *Consumer Reports,* the brand with the lowest overall taste rating costs 35 cents per ounce. Eliminate that brand, and find the median price per ounce for the remaining barbecue-flavored chips. Again order the data. Note that there are an odd number of entries, so the median is simply the middle value.

18   19   19   27   28

middle value

$$\text{Median} = \text{Middle value} = 19 \text{ cents}$$

(c) One ounce of potato chips is considered a small serving. Is it reasonable to budget about $10.45 to serve the barbecue-flavored chips to 55 people?

Yes, since the median price of the chips is 19 cents per small serving. This budget for chips assumes that there is plenty of other food!   ◇

The median uses the *position* rather than the specific value of each data entry. If the extreme values of a data set change, the median usually does not change. This is why the median is often used as the average for house prices. If one mansion costing several million dollars sells in a community of much lower-priced homes, the median selling price for houses in the community would be affected very little, if at all.

GUIDED EXERCISE 1

Median and mode

Belleview College must make a report to the budget committee about the average credit hour load a full-time student carries. (A 12-credit-hour load is the minimum requirement for full-time status. For the same tuition, students may take up to 20 credit hours.) A random sample of 40 students yielded the following information (in credit hours):

17	12	14	17	13	16	18	20	13	12
12	17	16	15	14	12	12	13	17	14
15	12	15	16	12	18	20	19	12	15
18	14	16	17	15	19	12	13	12	15

(a) Organize the data from smallest to largest number of credit hours.

⇨

12 12 12 12 12 12 12 12 12 12
13 13 13 13 14 14 14 14 15 ⑮
⑮ 15 15 15 16 16 16 16 17 17
17 17 17 18 18 18 19 19 20 20

(b) Since there are an _____ (odd, even) number of values, we add the two middle values and divide by 2 to get the median. What is the median credit hour load?

⇨ There are an even number of entries. The two middle values are circled in part (a).

$$\text{Median} = \frac{15 + 15}{2} = 15$$

(c) What is the mode of this distribution? Is it different from the median? If the budget committee is going to fund the school according to the average student credit hour load (more money for higher loads), which of these two averages do you think the college will use?

⇨ The mode is 12. It is different from the median. Since the median is higher, the school will probably use it and indicate that the average being used is the median.

Note: For small ordered data sets, we can easily scan the set to find the *location* of the median. However, for large ordered data sets of size *n*, it is convenient to have a formula to find the middle of the data set.

For an ordered data set of size n,

Position of the middle value $= \dfrac{n + 1}{2}$

Mean

For instance, if $n = 99$, then the middle value is the $(99 + 1)/2$ or 50th data value in the ordered data. If $n = 100$, then $(100 + 1)/2 = 50.5$ tells us that the two middle values are in the 50th and 51st positions.

An average that uses the exact value of each entry is the *mean* (sometimes called the *arithmetic mean*). To compute the mean, we add the values of all the entries and then divide by the number of entries.

$$\text{Mean} = \frac{\text{Sum of all the entries}}{\text{Number of entries}}$$

The mean is the average usually used to compute a test average.

EXAMPLE 3

Mean

To graduate, Linda needs at least a B in biology. She did not do very well on her first three tests; however, she did well on the last four. Here are her scores:

58   67   60   84   93   98   100

Compute the mean and determine if Linda's grade will be a B (80 to 89 average) or a C (70 to 79 average).

SOLUTION:

$$\text{Mean} = \frac{\text{Sum of scores}}{\text{Number of scores}} = \frac{58 + 67 + 60 + 84 + 93 + 98 + 100}{7}$$

$$= \frac{560}{7} = 80$$

Since the average is 80, Linda will get the needed B.   ◇

◇ **COMMENT** When we compute the mean, we sum the given data. There is a convenient notation to indicate the sum. Let x represent any value in the data set. Then the notation

Σx (read "the sum of all given x values")

means that we are to sum all the data values. In other words, we are to sum all the entries in the distribution. The *summation symbol* Σ means *sum the following* and is capital sigma, the S of the Greek alphabet.   ◇

Formulas for the mean

The symbol for the mean of a *sample* distribution of x values is denoted by $\bar{x}$ (read "x bar"). If your data comprise the entire *population*, we use the symbol μ (lowercase Greek letter mu, pronounced "mew") to represent the mean. The procedure to compute the mean is the same regardless of whether we have population or sample data. If we let n represent the number of entries in a *sample* data set and N represent the number of entries in a *population* data set, the formulas are

$$\text{Sample mean} = \bar{x} = \frac{\Sigma x}{n} \qquad\qquad \text{Population mean} = \mu = \frac{\Sigma x}{N} \qquad (1)$$

● **CALCULATOR NOTE**   It is very easy to compute the mean on *any* calculator: Simply add the data values and divide the total by the number of data. However, on calculators with a statistics mode, you place the calculator in that mode, *enter* the data, and then press the key for the mean. The key is usually designated $\bar{x}$. Because the formula for the population mean is the same as that for the sample mean, the same key gives the value for μ.

We have seen three averages: the mode, the median, and the mean. For later work, the mean is the most important. A disadvantage of the mean, however, is that it can be affected by exceptional values.

Resistant measure

A *resistant measure* is one that is not influenced by extremely high or low data values. The mean is not a resistant measure of center because we can make the mean as large as we want by increasing the size of only one data value. The median, on the other hand, is more resistant. However, a disadvantage of the median is that it is not sensitive to the specific size of a data value.

Trimmed mean

A measure of center that is more resistant than the mean but still sensitive to specific data values is the *trimmed mean*. A trimmed mean is the mean of the data values left after "trimming" a specified percentage of the smallest and largest data values from the data set. Usually a 5% trimmed mean is used. This implies that we trim the lowest 5% of the data as well as the highest 5% of the data. A similar procedure is used for a 10% trimmed mean.

PROCEDURE

How to compute a 5% trimmed mean

1. Order the data from smallest to largest.
2. Delete the bottom 5% of the data and the top 5% of the data. *Note:* If the calculation of 5% of the number of data values does not produce a whole number, *round* to the nearest integer.
3. Compute the mean of the remaining 90% of the data.

GUIDED EXERCISE 2

Mean and trimmed mean

Barron's Profiles of American Colleges, 19th Edition, lists average class size for introductory lecture courses at each of the profiled institutions. A sample of 20 colleges and universities in California showed class size for introductory lecture courses to be

(14)	20	20	20	20	23	25	30	30	30
35	35	35	40	40	42	50	50	80	(80)

(a) Compute the mean for the entire sample.

⇨   Add all the values and divide by 20:

$$\bar{x} = \frac{\Sigma x}{n} = \frac{719}{20} \approx 36.0$$

Continued

GUIDED EXERCISE 2 continued

(b) Compute a 5% trimmed mean for the sample.

⟹ The data are already ordered. Since 5% of 20 is 1, we eliminate one data value from the bottom of the list and one from the top. These values are circled in the data set. Then take the mean of the remaining 18 entries.

$$5\% \text{ trimmed mean} = \frac{\Sigma x}{n} = \frac{625}{18} \approx 34.7$$

(c) Find the median for the original data set.

⟹ Note that the data are already ordered.

$$\text{Median} = \frac{30 + 35}{2} = 32.5$$

(d) Find the median of the 5% trimmed data set. Does the median change because of trimming the data?

⟹ The median is still 32.5. Notice that trimming the same number of entries from both ends leaves the middle position of the data set unchanged.

(e) Is the trimmed mean or the original mean closer to the median?

⟹ The trimmed mean is closer to the median.

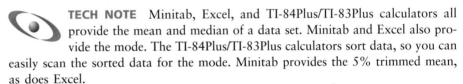

TECH NOTE Minitab, Excel, and TI-84Plus/TI-83Plus calculators all provide the mean and median of a data set. Minitab and Excel also provide the mode. The TI-84Plus/TI-83Plus calculators sort data, so you can easily scan the sorted data for the mode. Minitab provides the 5% trimmed mean, as does Excel.

All this technology is a wonderful aid for analyzing data. However, *a measurement has no meaning if you do not know what it represents or how a change in data values might affect the measurement*. The defining formulas and procedures for computing the measures tell you a great deal about the measures. Even if you use a calculator to evaluate all the statistical measures, pay attention to the information the formulas and procedures give you about the components or features of the measurement.

◇ **COMMENT** In Chapter 1, we examined four levels of data: nominal, ordinal, interval, and ratio. The mode (if it exists) can be used with all four levels, including nominal. For instance, the modal color of all passenger cars sold last year might be blue. The median may be used with data at the ordinal level or above. If we ranked the passenger cars in order of customer satisfaction level, we could identify the median satisfaction level. For the mean, our data need to be at the interval or ratio level (although there are exceptions in which the mean of ordinal-level data is computed). We can certainly find the mean model year of used passenger cars sold or the mean price of new passenger cars. ◇

Weighted Average

Sometimes we wish to average numbers, but we want to assign more importance or weight to some of the numbers. For instance, suppose your professor tells you that your grade will be based on a midterm and a final exam, each of which has

Weighted average

100 possible points. However, the final exam will be worth 60% of the grade and the midterm only 40%. How could you determine your average score to reflect these different weights? The average you need is the *weighted average*.

$$\text{Weighted average} = \frac{\Sigma xw}{\Sigma w}$$

where x is a data value and w is the weight assigned to that data value. The sum is taken over all data values.

EXAMPLE 4

Weighted average

Suppose your midterm test score is 83 and your final exam score is 95. Using the weights of 40% for the midterm and 60% for the final exam, compute the weighted average of your scores. If the minimum average for an A is 90, will you earn an A?

SOLUTION: By the formula, we multiply each score by its weight and add the results together. Then we divide by the sum of all the weights. Converting the percentages to decimal notation, we get

$$\text{Weighted average} = \frac{83(0.40) + 95(0.60)}{0.40 + 0.60}$$

$$= \frac{33.2 + 57}{1} = 90.2$$

Your average is high enough to earn an A.

GUIDED EXERCISE 3

Weighted average

In an investment portfolio, stocks are rated on a scale of 1 to 10 for dividend earning, security, and capital growth potential. On the scale, 1 equals very poor and 10 equals excellent. In one investment strategy favoring security, the dividend rating is given a weight of 2, the security a weight of 5, and the capital growth potential a weight of 3.

(a) Stock A has the ratings shown in Table 3-1. Complete the table and find the weighted average rating of the stock.

TABLE 3-1   Stock A Rating

	Rating x	Weight w	xw
Dividend	7	2	____
Security	8	5	____
Growth	4	3	____
		$\Sigma w =$ ____	$\Sigma xw =$ ____

$\Sigma w = 10$
The last column has entries 14, 40, and 12, and the sum $\Sigma xw = 66$.

$$\text{Weighted average} = \frac{\Sigma xw}{\Sigma w}$$

$$= \frac{66}{10}$$

$$= 6.6$$

Continued

GUIDED EXERCISE 3 continued

(b) Suppose the weight given for dividend increases to 4 while the weight for growth decreases to 1. Would the new weighted average be lower, higher, or the same? Why?

 Higher, since the new weights give more weight to dividend, which has a higher rating and less weight to growth, which has a lower rating. The different ratings will increase the weighted average. The new average is 7.2.

 TECH NOTE The TI-84Plus/TI-83Plus calculators directly support weighted averages. Both Excel and Minitab can be programmed to provide the averages.

TI-84Plus/TI-83Plus Enter the data into one list, such as L1, and the corresponding weights into another list, such as L2. Then press **Stat ➤ Calc ➤ 1: 1-Var Stats.** Enter the list containing the data, followed by a comma and the list containing the weights.

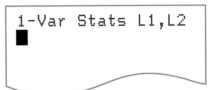

VIEW**P**OINT   *What's Wrong with Pitching Today?*

One way to answer this question is to look at *averages*. Batting averages and average hits per game are shown for selected years from 1901 to 2000 (Source: *The Wall Street Journal*).

Year	1901	1920	1930	1941	1951	1961	1968	1976	1986	2000
B.A.	0.277	0.284	0.288	0.267	0.263	0.256	0.231	0.256	0.262	0.276
Hits	19.2	19.2	20.0	18.4	17.9	17.3	15.2	17.3	17.8	19.1

A quick scan of the averages shows that batting averages and average hits per game are virtually the same as almost 100 years ago. It seems there is *nothing* wrong with today's pitching! So what's changed? For one thing, the rules have changed! The strike zone is considerably smaller than it once was, and the pitching mound is lower. Both give the hitter an advantage over the pitcher. Even so, pitchers don't give up hits with any greater frequency than they did a century ago (look at the averages). However, modern hits go much farther, which is something a pitcher can't control.

1. *Agriculture: Growing Season* The average length of the growing season is often measured in average number of frost-free days. The front range of Colorado (Fort Collins, Boulder, Denver, Colorado Springs, Pueblo) was studied by J. F. Benci and T. B. McKee, from the Department of Atmospheric Science at Colorado State University. Based on data from their Climatology Report No. 77-3, different locations in the Colorado front range had the following average numbers of frost-free days per year:

156	161	152	162	144	153
148	157	168	157	161	157

Compute the mean, median, and mode. Write a brief description of the meaning of these numbers from the point of view of a gardener.

2. *Baseball: Home Runs* Babe Ruth was the American League Home Run Champion 12 times (during the period from 1918 to 1931). The number of home runs he hit to earn the 12 titles were

11	29	54	59	41	46
47	60	54	46	49	46

Find the mean, median, and mode of the number of home runs.

3. *Environmental Studies: Death Valley* How hot does it get in Death Valley? The following data are taken from a study conducted by the National Park System, of which Death Valley is a unit. The ground temperatures (°F) were taken from May to November in the vicinity of Furnace Creek.

146	152	168	174	180	178	179
180	178	178	168	165	152	144

Compute the mean, median, and mode for these ground temperatures.

4. *Ecology: Wolf Packs* How large is a wolf pack? The following information is from a random sample of winter wolf packs in regions of Alaska, Minnesota, Michigan, Wisconsin, Canada, and Finland. (Source: *The Wolf,* by L. D. Mech, University of Minnesota Press.) Winter pack size:

13	10	7	5	7	7	2	4	3
2	3	15	4	4	2	8	7	8

Compute the mean, median, and mode for the size of winter wolf packs.

5. *Medical: Injuries* The Grand Canyon and the Colorado River are beautiful, rugged, and sometimes dangerous. Thomas Myers is a physician at the park clinic in Grand Canyon Village. Dr. Myers has recorded (for a 5-year period) the number of visitor injuries at different landing points for commercial boat trips down the Colorado River in both the Upper and Lower Grand Canyon (Source: *Fateful Journey* by Myers, Becker, Stevens).

Upper Canyon: Number of Injuries per Landing Point Between North Canyon and Phantom Ranch

2	3	1	1	3	4	6	9	3	1	3

Lower Canyon: Number of Injuries per Landing Point Between Bright Angel and Lava Falls

8	1	1	0	6	7	2	14	3	0	1	13	2	1

(a) Compute the mean, median, and mode for injuries per landing point in the Upper Canyon.

(b) Compute the mean, median, and mode for injuries per landing point in the Lower Canyon.

(c) Compare the results of parts (a) and (b).

(d) The Lower Canyon stretch had some extreme data values. Compute a 5% trimmed mean for this region, and compare this result to the mean for the Upper Canyon computed in part (a).

6. *Football: Age of Professional Players* How old are professional football players? The 11th Edition of *The Pro Football Encyclopedia* gave the following information. Random sample of pro football player ages in years:

24	23	25	23	30	29	28	26	33	29
24	37	25	23	22	27	28	25	31	29
25	22	31	29	22	28	27	26	23	21
25	21	25	24	22	26	25	32	26	29

(a) Compute the mean, median, and mode of the ages.

(b) Compare the averages. Does one seem to represent the age of the pro football players most accurately? Explain.

7. *FBI Report: Arson* The annual numbers of arson crimes for a random sample of 12 California suburban areas of about the same size follow:

23	17	35	30	26	39	45	39	13	42	285	394

(Reference: *Crime in the United States*, U.S. Department of Justice, Federal Bureau of Investigation.)

(a) Compute the mean number of arson crimes for all 12 suburban areas.

(b) Compute the median number of arson crimes for all 12 areas and compare your answer with the mean computed in part (a). Which average best describes the level of arson for the majority of the areas?

(c) The highest two entries (285 and 394) were from areas that experienced civil disorder (e.g. riots). Omit these extreme values and calculate the mean and median for the remaining 10 areas.

(d) Compare your answers from part (c) with those from parts (a) and (b). Comment on the effect of extreme values on the mean and median.

8. *Car Theft: Honolulu* A reporter for *Honolulu Star-Bulletin* was doing a news article about car theft in Honolulu. For a given 10-day period, the police reported the following numbers of car thefts:

9	6	10	8	10	8	4	8	3	8

Then, for the next 3 days, for an unexplained reason, the numbers of car thefts jumped to 36, 51, and 30.

(a) Compute the mean, median, and mode for the first 10-day period.

(b) Compute the mean, median, and mode for the entire 13-day period.

(c) Comment on the effect of extreme values on the mean, median, and mode in this problem.

9. *Astronomy: Meteoroids* The College Astronomy Club has been counting meteoroids each night for the past week. Between the hours of 10:00 P.M. and 1:00 A.M., the meteoroid count for each night was

15	12	15	10	17	18	15

Then, for the next two nights there was a meteoroid shower, and the club counted 57 and 62 meteoroids.
(a) Compute the mean, median, and mode for the meteoroid counts on the first seven nights.
(b) Compute the mean, median, and mode for all nine nights.
(c) Comment on the effect of extreme values on the mean, median, and mode in this problem.

10. *Psychology: Performance/Reward Theory* In a course entitled "Experimental Psychology" at Regis University, students train white rats to do various tasks based on a performance/reward theory (for rats).
(a) One event is the hurdles. Times in seconds for seven rats to run the hurdles were

    5.2   3.3   3.3   2.9   2.8   2.3   1.8

Compute the mean, median, and mode.
(b) Another event is the ladder climb. Times in seconds for eight rats to do the ladder climb were

    41.9   7.7   7.9   6.9   6.6   6.6   5.5   5.1

Compute the mean, median, and mode for the ladder climb. The first time (41.9 seconds) was for a rat who got distracted in the middle of the performance. Omit the time for this rat, and recalculate the mean, median, and mode. Comment on the effect on the mean, median, and mode when we leave out the extreme value 41.9.

11. *Leisure: Maui Vacation* How expensive is Maui? If you want a vacation rental condominium (up to four people), visit the Brase/Brase statistics site at **http://math.college.hmco.com/students,** find the link to Maui, and then search for accommodations. *The Maui News* gave the following costs in dollars per day for a random sample of condominiums located throughout the island of Maui.

    89   50   68   60   375   55   500   71   40   350
    60   50   250   45   45   125   235   65   60   130

(a) Compute the mean, median, and mode for the data.
(b) Compute a 5% trimmed mean for the data, and compare it with the mean computed in part (a). Does the trimmed mean more accurately reflect the general level of the daily rental costs?
(c) If you were a travel agent, and a client asked about the daily cost of renting a condominium on Maui, what average would you use? Explain. Is there any other information about the costs that you think might be useful, such as the spread of the costs?

12. *Financial: Credit Cards* Consider the following types of data that were obtained from a random sample of 49 credit card accounts. Identify all the averages (mean, median, or mode) that can be used to summarize the data.
(a) Outstanding balance on each account.
(b) Name of credit card (e.g., MasterCard, Visa, American Express, etc.).
(c) Dollar amount due on next payment.

13. *Student Life: Schedules* Consider the following types of data about courses obtained from a random sample of 35 student schedules. Identify all the averages (mean, median, or mode) that can be used to summarize the data.
(a) Name of department in which each course is offered.

(b) Number of credit hours each student is taking.
(c) Starting time of earliest class on each schedule.

14. *Averages: A Word of Caution* Thriving on Chaos, by Tom Peters, has some excellent cautions about utilizing measurements and averages. In discussing ways to provide superior service, he says, "The use of averages is downright dangerous." He illustrates with examples. Suppose a manufacturing company claims, "on average, we ship parts within 37 hours of order entry." But a careful look at the data shows that for the "worst-off 10 percent of customers," the shipping time was within 89 hours of order entry. Peters' advice is to "focus attention on the worst-off 1, 5, 10, or 25 percent of customers" instead of on the average. Comment on this advice.

15. *General: Mean and Median* Consider a data set of 15 distinct measurements with mean *A* and median *B*.
    (a) If the highest number were increased, what would be the effect on the median and mean? Explain.
    (b) If the highest number were decreased to a value that is still larger than *B*, what would be the effect on the median and mean?
    (c) If the highest number were decreased to a value smaller than *B*, what would be the effect on the median and mean?

16. *General: Mean, Median, Mode* Create a data set with five numbers in which
    (a) the mean, median, and mode are all equal.
    (b) the mean is greater than the median.
    (c) the mean is less than the median.
    (d) the mode is higher than the median or mean.
    (e) all the numbers are distinct and the mean and median are both zero.

17. *Grades: Weighted Average* In your biology class, your final grade is based on several things: a lab score, scores on two major tests, and your score on the final exam. There are 100 points available for each score. However, the lab score is worth 25% of your total grade, each major test is worth 22.5%, and the final exam is worth 30%. Compute the weighted average for the following scores: 92 on the lab, 81 on the first major test, 93 on the second major test, and 85 on the final exam.

18. *Grades: Weighted Average* Suppose the weights for the activities in your biology class changed so that the lab score was still worth 25%, but each of the two major tests also were worth 25%, and the final was worth only 25%. Compute the weighted average for the same set of scores as those in Problem 17: Use 92 on the lab, 81 on the first major test, 93 on the second major test, and 85 on the final exam. Is the weighted average different from that in Problem 17? Since the weights are all the same, did you really need to use a weighted average, or could you simply have taken the mean of the four scores?

19. *Merit Pay Scale: Weighted Average* At General Hospital, nurses are given performance evaluations to determine eligibility for merit pay raises. The supervisor rates the nurses on a scale of 1 to 10 (10 being the highest rating) for several activities: promptness, record keeping, appearance, and bedside manner with patients. Then an average is determined by giving a weight of 2 for promptness, 3 for record keeping, 1 for appearance, and 4 for bedside manner with patients. What is the average rating for a nurse with ratings of 9 for promptness, 7 for record keeping, 6 for appearance, and 10 for bedside manner?

20. *Athletic Awards: Weighted Average* The alumni club of Jefferson College gives a $10,000 award to the most outstanding athlete each year. Since competitive sports include football, basketball, baseball, swimming, and tennis, the rating scale is a way of comparing athletes who participate in any of the sports. Each candidate is

rated on a scale of 1 to 10 (with 10 being the best) for individual performance, win-loss record of team, grade point average, and sportsmanship. The ratings are then averaged using a weight of 5 for individual performance, 2 for win-loss record of team, 1 for grade point average, and 3 for sportsmanship.

(a) One athlete had the following ratings: 9 for individual performance, 7 for team record, 6 for grade point average, and 8 for sportsmanship. Compute the weighted average of the ratings.

(b) Another athlete had ratings of 8 for individual performance, 9 for team record, 5 for grade point average, and 9 for sportsmanship. Compute the weighted average of these ratings. Which athlete had the higher average rating?

21. *Investing: Bonds* Municipal bonds are a good deal for everyone. For the investor they represent tax-free returns. For the local community, they are a loan to help build libraries, theaters, recreation centers, schools, and so on. When you invest in bonds, both the yield (%) and duration (in years) are important. Consider the following information regarding yield and duration of municipal bonds (Reference: Morningstar Research Group, Chicago).

Type of Bond	High Yield	Long Term	Intermediate Term	Short Term
Yield (%)	5.2	3.9	3.6	2.7
Duration (yr)	6.9	8.9	5.2	2.6

Suppose you have an investment in municipal bonds consisting of 15% high yield, 20% long term, 40% intermediate term, and 25% short term.

(a) Compute the weighted average that represents the yield (%) of your entire investment portfolio.

(b) Compute the weighted average that represents the duration (in years) of your entire investment portfolio.

Suppose you have an investment in municipal bonds consisting of $2500 in high yield, $4200 in long term, $7850 in intermediate term, and $11,600 in short term.

(c) Compute the weighted average that represents the yield (%) of your entire investment portfolio.

(d) Compute the weighted average that represents the duration (in years) of your entire investment portfolio.

22. *EPA: Wetlands* Where does all the water go? According to the Environmental Protection Agency (EPA), in a typical wetland environment, 38% of the water is outflow; 47% is seepage; 7% evaporates; and 8% remains as water volume in the ecosystem (Reference: United States Environmental Protection Agency Case Studies Report 832-R-93-005). Chloride compounds as residuals from residential areas are a problem for wetlands. Suppose that in a particular wetland environment the following concentrations (mg/l) of chloride compounds were found: outflow, 64.1; seepage, 75.8; remaining due to evaporation, 23.9; in the water volume, 68.2.

(a) Compute the weighted average of chlorine compound concentration (mg/l) for this ecological system.

(b) Suppose the EPA has established an average chlorine compound concentration target of no more than 58 mg/l. Comment on whether this wetlands system meets the target standard for chlorine compound concentration.

23. *Lifestyle: Gather Your Own Data* For the next week, record the length of time you spend on each telephone or cell phone call you make or receive. Round the times to the nearest minute. Compute the mean, median, and mode. What accounts for some of your shorter phone calls (leaving messages, responding to marketing calls, etc.)?

3.2
Measures of Variation

FOCUS POINTS

✓ Find the range, variance, and standard deviation.

✓ Compute the coefficient of variation from raw data. Why is the coefficient of variation important?

✓ Apply Chebyshev's theorem to raw data. What does a Chebyshev interval tell us?

An average is an attempt to summarize a set of data in just one number. As some of our examples have shown, an average taken by itself may not always be very meaningful. We need a statistical cross-reference that measures the spread of the data.

The range is one such measure of variation.

> The **range** is the difference between the largest and smallest values of a data distribution.

EXAMPLE 5

Range

A large bakery regularly orders cartons of Maine blueberries. The average weight of the cartons is supposed to be 22 ounces. Random samples of cartons from two suppliers were weighed. The weights in ounces of the cartons were

| **Supplier I:** | 17 | 22 | 22 | 22 | 27 |
| **Supplier II:** | 17 | 19 | 20 | 27 | 27 |

(a) Compute the range of carton weights from each supplier.

$$\text{Range} = \text{Largest value} - \text{Smallest value}$$
$$\text{Supplier I range} = 27 - 17 = 10 \text{ ounces}$$
$$\text{Supplier II range} = 27 - 17 = 10 \text{ ounces}$$

(b) Compute the mean weight of cartons from each supplier. In both cases the mean is 22 ounces.

(c) Look at the two samples again. The samples have the same range and mean. How do they differ? The bakery uses one carton of blueberries in each blueberry muffin recipe. It is important that the cartons be of consistent weight so that the muffins turn out right.

Supplier I provides more cartons that have weights closer to the mean. Or put another way, the weights of cartons from Supplier I are more clustered around the mean. The bakery might find Supplier I more satisfactory.   ◊

Blueberry patch

As we see in Example 5, although the range tells the difference between the largest and smallest values in a distribution, it does not tell us how much other values vary from one another or from the mean.

Variance and Standard Deviation

Variance and standard deviation

We need a measure of the distribution or spread of data around an expected value (either $\bar{x}$ or μ). The *variance* and *standard deviation* provide such measures. Formulas and rationale for these measures are described in the next Procedure box. Then examples and guided exercises show how to compute and interpret these measures.

As we will see later, the formulas for variance and standard deviation differ slightly depending on whether we are using a sample or the entire population.

PROCEDURE

How to compute the sample variance and sample standard deviation

Quantity	Description
x	The variable x represents a **data value** or outcome.
Mean $\bar{x} = \dfrac{\Sigma x}{n}$	This is the **average of the data values,** or what you "expect" to happen the next time you conduct the statistical experiment. Note that n is the sample size.
$x - \bar{x}$	This is the **difference** between what happened and what you expected to happen. This represents a "deviation" away from what you "expect" and is a measure of risk.
$\Sigma(x - \bar{x})^2$	The expression $\Sigma(x - \bar{x})^2$ is called the **sum of squares.** The $(x - \bar{x})$ quantity is squared to make it nonnegative. The sum is over all the data. If you don't square $(x - \bar{x})$, then the sum $\Sigma(x - \bar{x}) = 0$ because the negative values cancel the positive values. This occurs even if some $(x - \bar{x})$ values are large, indicating a large deviation or risk.
Sum of squares $\Sigma(x - \bar{x})^2$ or $\Sigma x^2 - \dfrac{(\Sigma x)^2}{n}$	This is an **algebraic simplification of the sum of squares** that is easier to compute. (*See* "Brain Teaser," Problem 18 of this section.) The **defining formula** for the sum of squares is the upper one. The **computation formula** for the sum of squares is the lower one. Both formulas give the same result.
Sample variance $s^2 = \dfrac{\Sigma(x - \bar{x})^2}{n - 1}$ or $s^2 = \dfrac{\Sigma x^2 - (\Sigma x)^2/n}{n - 1}$	The **sample variance** is s^2. The variance can be thought of as a kind of average of the $(x - \bar{x})^2$ values. However, for technical reasons, we divide the sum by the quantity $n - 1$ rather than n. This gives us the best mathematical estimate for the sample variance. The **defining formula** for the variance is the upper one. The **computation formula** for the variance is the lower one. Both formulas give the same result.
Sample standard deviation $s = \sqrt{\dfrac{\Sigma(x - \bar{x})^2}{n - 1}}$ or $s = \sqrt{\dfrac{\Sigma x^2 - (\Sigma x)^2/n}{n - 1}}$	This is **sample standard deviation, s.** Why do we take the square root? Well, if the original x units were, say, days or dollars, then the s^2 units would be days squared or dollars squared (wow, what's that?). We take the square root to return to the original units of the data measurements. The standard deviation can be thought of as a measure of variability or risk. Larger values of s imply greater variability in the data. The **defining formula** for the standard deviation is the upper one. The **computation formula** for the standard deviation is the lower one. Both formulas give the same result.

◇ **COMMENT** Why is *s* called a *sample standard* deviation? First, it is computed from sample data. Then why do we use the word *standard* in the name? We know *s* is a measure of deviation or risk. You should be aware that there are other statistical measures of risk that we have not yet mentioned. However, *s* is the one that everyone uses, so it is called the "standard" (like standard time). ◇

In statistics, the sample standard deviation and sample variance are used to describe the spread of data about the mean $\bar{x}$. The next example shows how to find these quantities by using the defining formulas. Guided Exercise 4 shows how to use the computation formulas.

As you will discover, for "hand" calculations, the computation formulas for s^2 and *s* are much easier to use. However, the defining formulas for s^2 and *s* emphasize the fact that the variance and standard deviation are based on the differences between each data value and the mean.

Defining formulas (sample data)

$$\text{Sample variance} = s^2 = \frac{\Sigma(x - \bar{x})^2}{n - 1} \tag{1}$$

$$\text{Sample standard deviation} = s = \sqrt{\frac{\Sigma(x - \bar{x})^2}{n - 1}} \tag{2}$$

where *x* is a member of the data set, $\bar{x}$ is the mean, and *n* is the number of data values. The sum is taken over all data values.

Computation formulas (sample data)

$$\text{Sample variance} = s^2 = \frac{\Sigma x^2 - (\Sigma x)^2/n}{n - 1} \tag{3}$$

$$\text{Sample standard deviation} = s = \sqrt{\frac{\Sigma x^2 - (\Sigma x)^2/n}{n - 1}} \tag{4}$$

where *x* is a member of the data set, $\bar{x}$ is the mean, and *n* is the number of data values. The sum is taken over all data values.

EXAMPLE 6

Sample standard deviation (defining formula)

Big Blossom Greenhouse was commissioned to develop an extra large rose for the Rose Bowl Parade. A random sample of blossoms from Hybrid A bushes yielded the following diameters (in inches) for mature peak blooms.

2   3   3   8   10   10

Find the sample variance and standard deviation.

SOLUTION: Several steps are involved in computing the variance and standard deviation. A table will be helpful (see Table 3-2 on the next page). Since $n = 6$, we take the sum of the entries in the first column of Table 3-2 and divide by 6 to find the mean $\bar{x}$.

$$\bar{x} = \frac{\Sigma x}{n} = \frac{36}{6} = 6.0 \text{ inches}$$

TABLE 3-2   Diameter of Rose Blossoms (in inches)

Column I x	Column II $x - \bar{x}$	Column III $(x - \bar{x})^2$
2	$2 - 6 = -4$	$(-4)^2 = 16$
3	$3 - 6 = -3$	$(-3)^2 = 9$
3	$3 - 6 = -3$	$(-3)^2 = 9$
8	$8 - 6 = 2$	$(2)^2 = 4$
10	$10 - 6 = 4$	$(4)^2 = 16$
10	$10 - 6 = 4$	$(4)^2 = 16$
$\Sigma x = 36$		$\Sigma(x - \bar{x})^2 = 70$

Using this value for $\bar{x}$, we obtain Column II. Square each value in the second column to obtain Column III, and then add the values in Column III. To get the sample variance, divide the sum of Column III by $n - 1$. Since $n = 6$, $n - 1 = 5$.

$$s^2 = \frac{\Sigma(x - \bar{x})^2}{n - 1} = \frac{70}{5} = 14$$

Now obtain the sample standard deviation by taking the square root of the variance.

$$s = \sqrt{s^2} = \sqrt{14} \approx 3.74$$

(Use a calculator to compute the square root. Because of rounding, we use the approximately equal symbol, $\approx$.)   ◊

GUIDED EXERCISE 4

Sample standard deviation (computation formula)

Big Blossom Greenhouse gathered another random sample of mature peak blooms from Hybrid B. The six blossoms had these widths (in inches):

5   5   5   6   7   8

(a) Again, we will construct a table so we can find the mean, variance, and standard deviation more easily. In this case, what is the value of n? Find the sum of Column I in Table 3-3, and compute the mean.

 $n = 6$. The sum of Column I is $\Sigma x = 36$, so the mean is

$$\bar{x} = \frac{36}{6} = 6 \text{ in.}$$

Continued

GUIDED EXERCISE 4 continued

TABLE 3-3   Complete Columns I and II

I x	II x^2
5	_____
5	_____
5	_____
6	_____
7	_____
8	_____
$\Sigma x =$ _____	$\Sigma x^2 =$ _____

TABLE 3-4   Completion of Table 3-3

I x	II x^2
5	25
5	25
5	25
6	36
7	49
8	64
$\Sigma x = 36$	$\Sigma x^2 = 224$

(b) What is the value of n? of $n - 1$? Use the computation formula to find the sample variance s^2. *Note:* Be sure to distinguish between Σx^2 and $(\Sigma x)^2$. For Σx^2 you square the x values first, and then sum them. For $(\Sigma x)^2$, you sum the x values first and then square the result.

$\Longrightarrow$ $n = 6; \ n - 1 = 5.$

$$s^2 = \frac{\Sigma x^2 - (\Sigma x)^2/n}{n - 1}$$

$$= \frac{224 - (36)^2/6}{5} = \frac{8}{5} = 1.6$$

(c) Use a calculator to find the square root of the variance. Is this the standard deviation?

$\Longrightarrow$ $s = \sqrt{s^2} = \sqrt{1.6} \approx 1.26$

Yes.

Let's summarize and compare the results of Guided Exercise 4 and Example 6. The greenhouse found the following blossom diameters for Hybrid A and Hybrid B:

Hybrid A: mean, 6.0 in.; standard deviation, 3.74 in.

Hybrid B: mean, 6.0 in.; standard deviation, 1.26 in.

In both cases, the means are the same: 6 in. But the first hybrid has a larger standard deviation. This means that the blossoms of Hybrid A are less consistent than those of Hybrid B. If you want a rosebush that occasionally has 10-in. blooms and 2-in. blooms, use the first hybrid. But if you want a bush that consistently produces roses close to 6 in. across, use Hybrid B.

● **ROUNDING NOTE**   Rounding errors cannot be completely eliminated, even if a computer or calculator does all the computations. However, software and calculator routines are designed to minimize the error. If the mean is rounded, the value of the standard deviation will change slightly depending on how much the mean is rounded. If you do your calculations "by hand" or reenter intermediate values into a calculator, try to carry one or two more digits than occur in the original data. If your resulting answers vary slightly from those in this text, do not be overly concerned. The text answers are computer- or calculator-generated.

Population mean variance and standard deviation

In most applications of statistics, we work with a random sample of data rather than the entire population of *all* possible data values. However, if we have data for the entire population, we can compute the *population mean* μ (lowercase Greek letter mu, pronounced "mew"), *population variance* σ^2, and *population standard deviation* σ (lowercase Greek letter sigma) using the following formulas:

$$\text{Population mean} = \mu = \frac{\Sigma x}{N}$$

$$\text{Population variance} = \sigma^2 = \frac{\Sigma(x - \mu)^2}{N}$$

$$\text{Population standard deviation} = \sigma = \sqrt{\frac{\Sigma(x - \mu)^2}{N}}$$

where N is the number of data values in the population, and x represents the individual data values of the population.

We note that the formula for μ is the same as the formula for $\bar{x}$ (the sample mean) and the formulas for σ^2 and σ are the same as for s^2 and s (sample variance and sample standard deviation), except that the population size N is used instead of $n - 1$. Also, μ is used instead of $\bar{x}$ in the formulas for σ^2 and σ.

In the formulas for s and σ we use $n - 1$ to compute s, and N to compute σ. Why? The reason is that N (capital letter) represents the *population size*, while n (lowercase letter) represents the sample size. Since a random sample usually will not contain extreme data values (large or small), we divide by $n - 1$ in the formula for s to make s a little larger than it would have been had we divided by n. Courses in advanced theoretical statistics show that this procedure will give us the best possible estimate for the standard deviation σ. In fact, s is called the *unbiased estimate* for σ. If we have the population of all data values, then extreme data values are, of course, present, so we divide by N instead of $N - 1$.

◇ **COMMENT** The computation formula for the population standard deviation is

$$\sigma = \sqrt{\frac{\Sigma x^2 - (\Sigma x)^2/N}{N}} \quad ◇$$

We've seen that the standard deviation (sample or population) is a measure of data spread. We will use the standard deviation extensively in later chapters.

TECH NOTE Most scientific or business calculators have a statistics mode, and provide the mean and sample standard deviation directly. The TI-84Plus/TI-83Plus calculators, Excel, and Minitab provide the median and several other measures as well.

Many technologies display only the sample standard deviation s. You can quickly compute σ if you know s by using the formula

$$\sigma = s\sqrt{\frac{n - 1}{n}}$$

The mean given in displays can be interpreted as the sample mean $\bar{x}$ or the population mean μ as appropriate.

The following three displays show output for the hybrid rose data of Guided Exercise 4.

TI-84Plus/TI-83Plus Display
Press **STAT ➤ CALC ➤ 1:1-Var Stats.** S_x is the sample standard deviation. σ_x is the population standard deviation.

```
1-Var Stats
 x̄=6
 Σx=36
 Σx²=224
 Sx=1.264911064
 σx=1.154700538
↓n=6
■
```

Excel Display
Menu choices: **Tools ➤ Data Analysis ➤ Descriptive Statistics.** Check the summary statistics box. The standard deviation is the sample standard deviation.

Column 1	
Mean	6
Standard Error	0.516398
Median	5.5
Mode	5
Standard Deviation	1.264911
Sample Variance	1.6
Kurtosis	−0.78125
Skewness	0.889391
Range	3
Minimum	5
Maximum	8
Sum	36
Count	6

Minitab Display
Menu choices: **Stat ➤ Basic Statistics ➤ Display Descriptive Statistics.** StDev is the sample standard deviation. TrMean is a 5% trimmed mean.

N	Mean	Median	TrMean	StDev	SE Mean
6	6.000	5.500	6.000	1.265	0.516

Minimum	Maximum	Q1	Q3
5.000	8.000	5.000	7.250

Now let's look at two immediate applications of the standard deviation. The first is the coefficient of variation, and the second is Chebyshev's theorem.

Coefficient of Variation

A disadvantage of the standard deviation as a comparative measure of variation is that it depends on the units of measurement. This means that it is difficult to use the standard deviation to compare measurements from different populations. For this reason, statisticians have defined the *coefficient of variation,* which expresses the standard deviation as a percentage of the sample or population mean.

Coefficient of variation

> If $\bar{x}$ and s represent the sample mean and sample standard deviation, respectively, then the sample **coefficient of variation** CV is defined to be
>
> $$CV = \frac{s}{\bar{x}} \cdot 100$$
>
> If μ and σ represent the population mean and standard deviation, respectively, then the population coefficient of variation CV is defined to be
>
> $$CV = \frac{\sigma}{\mu} \cdot 100$$

Notice that the numerator and denominator in the definition of CV have the same units, so CV itself has no units of measurement. This gives us the advantage of being able to directly compare the variability of two different populations using the coefficient of variation.

In the next example and guided exercise, we will compute the CV of a population and of a sample and then compare the results.

EXAMPLE 7

Coefficient of variation

The Trading Post on Grand Mesa is a small, family-run store in a remote part of Colorado. The Grand Mesa region contains many good fishing lakes, so the Trading Post sells spinners (a type of fishing lure). The store has a very limited selection of spinners, however. In fact, the Trading Post has only eight different types of spinners for sale. The prices (in dollars) are

2.10	1.95	2.60	2.00	1.85	2.25	2.15	2.25

Since the Trading Post has only eight different kinds of spinners for sale, we consider the eight data values to be the *population.*

(a) Use a calculator with appropriate statistics keys to verify that for the Trading Post data, $\mu \approx \$2.14$ and $\sigma \approx \$0.22$.

SOLUTION: Since the computation formulas for $\bar{x}$ and μ are identical, most calculators provide the value of $\bar{x}$ only. Use the output of this key for μ. The computation formulas for the sample standard deviation s and the population standard deviation σ are slightly different. Be sure that you use the key for σ (sometimes designated as σ_n or σ_x).

(b) Compute the CV of prices for the Trading Post and comment on the meaning of the result.

SOLUTION:

$$CV = \frac{\sigma}{\mu} \times 100 = \frac{0.22}{2.14} \times 100 = 10.28\%$$

The coefficient of variation can be thought of as a measure of the spread of the data relative to the average of the data. Since the Trading Post is very small, it carries a small selection of spinners that are all priced similarly. The CV tells us that the standard deviation of the spinner prices is only 10.28% of the mean.   ◊

GUIDED EXERCISE 5

Coefficient of variation

Cabela's in Sidney, Nebraska, is a very large outfitter that carries a broad selection of fishing tackle. It markets its products nationwide through a catalog service. A random sample of 10 spinners from Cabela's extensive spring catalog gave the following prices (in dollars):

| 1.69 | 1.49 | 3.09 | 1.79 | 1.39 |
| 2.89 | 1.49 | 1.39 | 1.49 | 1.99 |

(a) Use a calculator with sample mean and sample standard deviation keys to compute $\bar{x}$ and s.

⟹ $\bar{x} = \$1.87$ and $s \approx \$0.62$.

(b) Compute the CV for the spinner prices at Cabela's.

⟹ $CV = \dfrac{s}{\bar{x}} \times 100 = \dfrac{0.62}{1.87} \times 100 = 33.16\%$.

(c) Compare the mean, standard deviation, and CV for the spinner prices at the Grand Mesa Trading Post (Example 7) and Cabela's. Comment on the differences.

⟹ The CV's for Cabela's and the Trading Post are pure numbers (no units), so a direct comparison is possible. The CV for Cabela's is more than three times the CV for the Trading Post. Why? First, because of the remote location, the Trading Post tends to have somewhat higher prices (larger μ). Second, the Trading Post is very small, so it has a rather limited selection of spinners with a smaller variation in price. For Cabela's, however, the average price $\bar{x}$ is lower and the variety larger (larger s). It makes sense that the CV for Cabela's is larger than the CV for the Trading Post.

Chebyshev's Theorem

From our earlier discussion about standard deviation, we recall that the spread or dispersion of a set of data about the mean will be small if the standard deviation is small, and it will be large if the standard deviation is large. If we are dealing with a symmetrical bell-shaped distribution, then we can make very definite statements about the proportion of the data that must lie within a certain number of standard deviations on either side of the mean. This will be discussed in detail in Chapter 6 when we talk about normal distributions.

However, the concept of data spread about the mean can be expressed quite generally for *all data distributions* (skewed, symmetric, or other shape) by using the remarkable theorem of Chebyshev, shown on the following page.

Chebyshev's theorem

For *any* set of data (either population or sample) and for any constant k greater than 1, the proportion of the data that must lie within k standard deviations on either side of the mean is *at least*

$$1 - \frac{1}{k^2}$$

Results of Chebyshev's theorem

For *any* set of data:

- at *least* 75% of the data fall in the interval from $\mu - 2\sigma$ to $\mu + 2\sigma$.
- at *least* 88.9% of the data fall in the interval from $\mu - 3\sigma$ to $\mu + 3\sigma$.
- at *least* 93.8% of the data fall in the interval from $\mu - 4\sigma$ to $\mu + 4\sigma$.

The results of Chebyshev's theorem can be derived by using the theorem and a little arithmetic. For instance, if we create an interval $k = 2$ standard deviations on either side of the mean, Chebyshev's theorem tells us that

$$1 - \frac{1}{2^2} = 1 - \frac{1}{4} = \frac{3}{4} \text{ or } 75\%$$

is the minimum percentage of data in the $\mu - 2\sigma$ to $\mu + 2\sigma$ interval.

Notice that Chebyshev's theorem refers to the *minimum* percentage of data that must fall within the specified number of standard deviations of the mean. If the distribution is mound-shaped, an even *greater* percentage of data will fall into the specified intervals (see the Empirical Rule in Section 6.1).

EXAMPLE 8

Chebyshev's theorem

Students Who Care is a student volunteer program in which college students donate work time to various community projects such as planting trees. Professor Gill is the faculty sponsor for this student volunteer program. For several years, Dr. Gill has kept a careful record of x = total number of work hours volunteered by a student in the program each semester. For a random sample of students in the program, the mean number of hours was $\bar{x}$ = 29.1 hours each semester, with a standard deviation of s = 1.7 hours each semester. Find an interval A to B for the number of hours volunteered into which at least 75% of the students in this program would fit.

SOLUTION: According to results of Chebyshev's theorem, at least 75% of the data must fall within 2 standard deviations of the mean. Because the mean $\bar{x}$ = 29.1 and the standard deviation s = 1.7, the interval is

$$\bar{x} - 2s \text{ to } \bar{x} + 2s$$
$$29.1 - 2(1.7) \text{ to } 29.1 + 2(1.7)$$
$$25.7 \text{ to } 32.5$$

At least 75% of the students would fit into the group that volunteered from 25.7 to 32.5 hours each semester.

GUIDED
EXERCISE **6**

Chebyshev interval

The *East Coast Independent News* periodically runs ads in its own classified section offering a month's free subscription to those who respond. In this way, management can get a sense about the number of subscribers who read the classified section each day. Over a period of 2 years, careful records have been kept. The mean number of responses per ad is $\bar{x} = 525$ with standard deviation $s = 30$.

Determine a Chebyshev interval about the mean in which at least 88.9% of the data fall.   ⟹   By Chebyshev's theorem, at least 88.9% of the data fall into the interval

$$\bar{x} - 3s \text{ to } \bar{x} + 3s$$

Because $\bar{x} = 525$ and $s = 30$, the interval is

$$525 - 3(30) \text{ to } 525 + 3(30)$$

or from 435 to 615 responses per ad.

VIEWPOINT   ### *Socially Responsible Investing*

Make a difference *and* make money! Socially responsible mutual funds tend to screen out corporations that sell tobacco, weapons, and alcohol, as well as companies that are environmentally unfriendly. In addition, these funds screen out companies that use child labor in sweatshops. There are 68 socially responsible funds tracked by the Social Investment Forum. For more information, visit the Brase/Brase statistics site at **http://math.college.hmco.com/students** and find the link to social investing.

How do these funds rate compared to other funds? One way to answer this question is to study the annual percent returns of the funds using both the *mean* and *standard deviation*. (See Problems 15 and 16 of this section.)

SECTION 3.2   PROBLEMS

1. *General Concepts: Variance, Standard Deviation* Given the sample data

   | x: | 23 | 17 | 15 | 30 | 25 |

   (a) Find the range.
   (b) Verify that $\Sigma x = 110$ and $\Sigma x^2 = 2568$.
   (c) Use the results of part (b) and appropriate computation formulas to compute the sample variance s^2 and sample standard deviation s.
   (d) Use the defining formulas to compute the sample variance s^2 and sample standard deviation s.

(e) Suppose the given data comprise the entire population of all x values. Compute the population variance σ^2 and population standard deviation σ.

2. *General Concepts: Variance, Standard Deviation* Given the sample data

$$x:\quad 45\quad 23\quad 52\quad 33\quad 29$$

(a) Find the range.
(b) Verify that $\Sigma x = 182$ and $\Sigma x^2 = 7188$.
(c) Use the results of part (b) and appropriate computation formulas to compute the sample variance s^2 and sample standard deviation s.
(d) Use the defining formulas to compute the sample variance s^2 and sample standard deviation s.
(e) Suppose the given data comprise the entire population of all x values. Compute the population variance σ^2 and population standard deviation σ.

3. *Space Shuttle: Epoxy* Kevlar epoxy is a material used on the NASA Space Shuttle. Strands of this epoxy were tested at the 90% breaking strength. The following data represent time to failure (in hours) for a random sample of 50 epoxy strands (Reference: R. E. Barlow, University of California, Berkeley). *Note:* These data are also available with other software on the statSpace CD-ROM. Let x be a random variable representing time to failure (in hours) at 90% breaking strength.

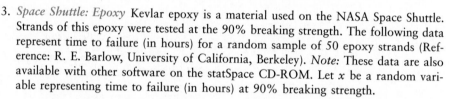

0.54	1.80	1.52	2.05	1.03	1.18	0.80	1.33	1.29	1.11
3.34	1.54	0.08	0.12	0.60	0.72	0.92	1.05	1.43	3.03
1.81	2.17	0.63	0.56	0.03	0.09	0.18	0.34	1.51	1.45
1.52	0.19	1.55	0.02	0.07	0.65	0.40	0.24	1.51	1.45
1.60	1.80	4.69	0.08	7.89	1.58	1.64	0.03	0.23	0.72

(a) Find the range.
(b) Use a calculator to verify that $\Sigma x = 62.11$ and $\Sigma x^2 \approx 164.23$.
(c) Use the results of part (b) to compute the sample mean, variance, and standard deviation for the time to failure.
(d) Use the results of part (c) to compute the coefficient of variation. What does this number say about time to failure? Why does a small CV indicate more consistent data, whereas a larger CV indicates less consistent data? Explain.

4. *Investing: Stocks and Bonds* Do bonds reduce the overall risk of an investment portfolio? Let x be a random variable representing annual percent return for Vanguard Total Stock Index (all stocks). Let y be a random variable representing annual return for Vanguard Balanced Index (60% stock and 40% bond). For the past several years, we have the following data (Reference: Morningstar Research Group, Chicago).

| $x:$ | 11 | 0 | 36 | 21 | 31 | 23 | 24 | -11 | -11 | -21 |
| $y:$ | 10 | -2 | 29 | 14 | 22 | 18 | 14 | -2 | -3 | -10 |

(a) Compute $\Sigma x,\ \Sigma x^2,\ \Sigma y,\ \Sigma y^2$.
(b) Use the results of part (a) to compute the sample mean, variance, and standard deviation for x and for y.
(c) Compute a 75% Chebyshev interval around the mean for x values and also for y values. Use the intervals to compare the two funds.
(d) Compute the coefficient of variation for each fund. Use the coefficients of variation to compare the two funds. If s represents risks and $\bar{x}$ represents expected return, then $s/\bar{x}$ can be thought of as a measure of risk per unit of expected return. In this case, why is a smaller CV better? Explain.

5. *Wildlife: Mallard Ducks and Canada Geese* For mallard ducks and Canada geese, what percent of nests are successful (at least one offspring survives)? Studies in Montana, Illinois, Wyoming, Utah, and California gave the following percentages of successful nests (Reference: *The Wildlife Society Press*, Washington, D.C.).

   x: **Percentage success for mallard duck nests**

56	85	52	13	39

   y: **Percentage success for Canada goose nests**

24	53	60	69	18

   (a) Use a calculator to verify that $\Sigma x = 245$; $\Sigma x^2 = 14,755$; $\Sigma y = 224$; $\Sigma y^2 = 12,070$.
   (b) Use the results of part (a) to compute the sample mean, variance, and standard deviation for x, the percent of successful mallard nests.
   (c) Use the results of part (a) to compute the sample mean, variance, and standard deviation for y, the percent of successful Canada goose nests.
   (d) Use the results of parts (b) and (c) to compute the coefficient of variation for successful mallard nests and Canada goose nests. Write a brief explanation of the meaning of these numbers. What do these results say about the nesting success rates for mallards compared to Canada geese? Would you say one group of data was more or less consistent than the other? Explain.

6. *Archaeology: Ireland* The Hill of Tara in Ireland is a place of great archaeological importance. This region has been occupied by people for more than 4,000 years. In fact, Tara is regarded as the seat of the great High Kings of ancient Ireland. Geomagnetic surveys detect subsurface anomalies in the earth's magnetic field. These surveys have led to many significant archaeological discoveries. After collecting data, the next step is to begin a statistical study. The following data measure magnetic susceptibility (centimeter-gram-second $\times$ 10^{-6}) on two of the main grids of the Hill of Tara (Reference: *Tara: An Archaeological Survey* by Conor Newman, Royal Irish Academy, Dublin).

   Grid E: x variable

13.20	5.60	19.80	15.05	21.40	17.25	27.45
16.95	23.90	32.40	40.75	5.10	17.75	28.35

   Grid H: y variable

11.85	15.25	21.30	17.30	27.50	10.35	14.90
48.70	25.40	25.95	57.60	34.35	38.80	41.00
31.25						

   (a) Compute Σx, Σx^2, Σy, and Σy^2.
   (b) Use the results of part (a) to compute the sample mean, variance, and standard deviation for x and for y.
   (c) Compute a 75% Chebyshev interval around the mean for x values and also for y values. Use the intervals to compare the magnetic susceptibility on the two grids. Higher numbers indicate higher magnetic susceptibility. However, extreme values, high or low, could mean an anomaly and possible archaeological treasure.
   (d) Compute the sample coefficient of variation for each grid. Use the CV's to compare the two grids. If s represents variability in the signal (magnetic susceptibility) and $\bar{x}$ represents the expected level of the signal, then $s/\bar{x}$ can be thought of as a measure of the variability per unit of expected signal. Remember, a

considerable variability in the signal (above or below average) might indicate buried artifacts. Why, in this case, would a large *CV* be better, or at least more exciting? Explain.

7. *Astronomy: Sun Spot Cycles* The National Aeronautics and Space Administration (NASA) has studied data on sun spot cycles collected for the years 1745 to the present. During this time, the mean length of a cycle (maximum to maximum) was 11.01 years, with a standard deviation 2.17 years.
   (a) Use Chebyshev's theorem to find an interval centered about the mean for the cycle length in which you would expect at least 75% of the cycles to fall.
   (b) Use Chebyshev's theorem to find an interval centered about the mean for the cycle length in which you would expect at least 93.8% of the cycles to fall.

8. *Meteorology: Tornados* The U.S. Weather Bureau has provided the following information about the total annual number of reported tornados in the United States for the years 1956 to 1975:

504	856	564	604	616	697	657	464	704	906
585	926	660	608	653	888	741	1102	947	918

   (a) Use a calculator with mean and standard deviation keys to verify that the mean number of tornados per year is 730, with a sample standard deviation of 172 tornados.
   (b) Use Chebyshev's theorem to find an interval centered about the mean for the annual number of tornados in which you would expect at least 75% of the years to fall.
   (c) Use Chebyshev's theorem to find an interval centered about the mean in which you would expect at least 88.9% of the years to fall.

9. *History: Billy the Kid* In 1881, Billy the Kid killed two deputies and escaped from a jail cell in the Lincoln County Courthouse, New Mexico Territory. Famous frontier personalities such as Kit Carson, Jesse Chisum, and Sheriff Pat Garrett (who eventually shot Billy the Kid) also were involved in the notorious Lincoln County Cattle Baron Wars. Before the 1985 renovation of the now famous courthouse, the Museum of New Mexico commissioned anthropologist/historian Yvonne Oakes to do a thorough analysis of the area. The distribution of artifacts (of the 1880s period) for seven excavation sites was

851	596	444	956	576	219	326

(Source: *Museum of New Mexico: Laboratory of Anthropology Notes No. 357.*)

   (a) Compute the range and mean.
   (b) Compute the sample variance and standard deviation.
   (c) Compute the coefficient of variation. Write a brief explanation of the meaning of this number in the context of this problem.
   (d) Use Chebyshev's theorem to find an interval centered about the mean in which at least 75% of the artifact counts for all such excavation sites would fall.

History: Lincoln Country Courthouse Excavation artifacts at the Lincoln County Courthouse (see Problem 9) were examined and labeled according to their functional typology. Table 3-5 gives the mean and coefficient of variation for percentage of artifacts found in excavation sites at the Lincoln County Courthouse. This table will be used in Problems 10 through 14.

TABLE 3-5   Artifacts Found at Lincoln County Courthouse*

Artifact Typology	Mean Percentage	Standard Deviation	CV
Foodstuffs (food storage, processing)	12.5	4.5	36.0
Indulgences (liquor, smoking items)	4.0	1.2	30.0
Domestic routine (tableware, furniture, lamps)	9.3	2.6	28.0
Construction (hardware, tools)	54.1	6.2	11.5
Personal effects (clothing, jewelry)	3.1	1.2	38.7
Entertainment (toys, games, musical instruments)	1.6	0.4	25.0
Arms (ammunition, guns)	0.4	0.1	25.0
Stable	0.2	0.1	50.0
Unknown	27.2	8.2	30.2

*The means were averaged over numerous excavation sites, and they need not total to 100%.

10. Suppose you were looking for antique liquor bottles, spittoons, and so forth (i.e., indulgence typology). With museum permission, you start a new excavation site at the Lincoln County Courthouse. Let P represent the percentage of total artifacts that are of the indulgence typology. Can we estimate a range of values for P before we start the excavation? Use the information of Table 3-5 with Chebyshev's theorem to find an interval centered about the mean in which you expect at least 75% of the Ps (percentage of indulgence artifacts at different sites) to fall.

11. Repeat Problem 10 assuming that you were interested in domestic routine typology.

12. Repeat Problem 10 assuming that you were interested in arms typology.

13. Examine Table 3-5. Would you agree with the statement that construction artifacts were one of the more likely and relatively dependable artifacts to be found? Use the coefficient of variation to explain your answer. (*Hint:* Which typology has the smallest CV and largest mean?)

14. Examine Table 3-5. Arms and stable artifacts have the same standard deviation, but one CV was twice the other. How can this be explained using the mean percentage of artifacts for each?

15. *Investing: Socially Responsible Mutual Funds* Pax World Balanced is a highly respected, socially responsible mutual fund of stocks and bonds (see Viewpoint). Vanguard Balanced Index is another highly regarded fund that represents the entire U.S. stock and bond market (an index fund). The mean and standard deviation of annualized percent returns are shown below. The annualized mean and standard deviation are based on the years 1993 through 2002 (Source: Morningstar).

    Pax World Balanced: $\bar{x} = 9.58\%$; $s = 14.05\%$

    Vanguard Balanced Index: $\bar{x} = 9.02\%$; $s = 12.50\%$

    (a) Compute the coefficient of variation for each fund. If $\bar{x}$ represents return and s represents risk, then explain why the coefficient of variation can be taken to represent risk per unit of return. From this point of view, which fund appears to be better? Explain.

(b) Compute a 75% Chebyshev interval around the mean for each fund. Use the intervals to compare the two funds. As usual, past performance does not guarantee future performance.

16. *Expand Your Knowledge: Moving Averages* You do not need a lot of money to invest in a mutual fund. However, if you decide to put some money into an investment, you are usually advised to leave it in for (at least) several years. Why? Because good years tend to cancel out the bad years, giving you a better overall return with less risk. To see what we mean, let's use a 3-year *moving average* on the Calvert Social Balanced Fund (a socially responsible fund).

Year	1990	1991	1992	1993	1994	1995	1996	1997	1998	1999	2000
% Return	1.78	17.79	7.46	5.95	−4.74	25.85	9.03	18.92	17.49	6.80	−2.38

Source: Morningstar

(a) Use a calculator with mean and standard deviation keys to verify that the mean annual return for all 11 years is approximately 9.45%, with standard deviation 9.57%.

(b) To compute a 3-year moving average for 1992, we take the data values for 1992 and the prior two years and average them. To compute a 3-year moving average for 1993, we take the data values for 1993 and the prior two years and average them. Verify that the following 3-year moving averages are correct.

Year	1992	1993	1994	1995	1996	1997	1998	1999	2000
3-year moving average	9.01	10.40	2.89	9.02	10.05	17.93	15.15	14.40	7.30

(c) Use a calculator with mean and standard deviation keys to verify that for the 3-year moving average, the mean is 10.68% with sample standard deviation 4.53%.

(d) Compare the results of parts (a) and (c). Suppose we take the point of view that risk is measured by standard deviation. Is the risk (standard deviation) of the 3-year moving average considerably smaller? This is an example of a general phenomenon that will be studied in more detail in Chapter 7.

17. *Medical: Physician Visits* In some reports, the mean and coefficient of variation are given. For instance, in *Statistical Abstract of the United States,* 116th Edition, one report gives the average number of physician visits by males per year. The average reported is 2.2, and the reported coefficient of variation is 1.5%. Use this information to determine the standard deviation of the number of visits to physicians made by males.

18. *Brain Teaser: Sum of Squares* If you like mathematical puzzles or love algebra, try this! Otherwise, just trust that the computational formula for the sum of squares is correct. We have a sample of x values. The sample size is n. Fill in the details for the following steps.

$$\Sigma(x - \bar{x})^2 = \Sigma x^2 - 2\bar{x}\Sigma x + n\bar{x}^2$$
$$= \Sigma x^2 - 2n\bar{x}^2 + n\bar{x}^2$$
$$= \Sigma x^2 - \frac{(\Sigma x)^2}{n}$$

19. *Lifestyle: Gathering Data* For the next 2 weeks, record how long it takes you to go from your residence (or job) to your first class. Record the values to the nearest minute. Compute the range, mean, sample standard deviation, and coefficient of variation. Use Chebyshev's theorem to compute an interval in which at least 88.9% of the travel times fall. Were there any unusual data values in your data set? How would you explain them?

3.3
Mean and Standard Deviation of Grouped Data

FOCUS POINTS

✓ Estimate the mean from grouped data.

✓ Estimate the sample variance and standard deviation from grouped data.

If you have a great many data values, it can be quite tedious to compute the mean and standard deviation. Even if you have a calculator, you must punch in the data. In many cases, a close approximation to the mean and standard deviation is all that is needed, and it is not difficult to approximate these two values from a frequency distribution.

The basic plan is as follows:

1. Make a frequency table corresponding to the histogram.

2. Compute the midpoint for each class and call it x.

3. Count the number of entries in each class and denote the number by f.

4. Add the numbers of entries from each class together to find the total number of entries n in the sample distribution.

Treat each entry of a class as though it falls on the midpoint (x) of that class. Then the midpoint times the number of entries in a class (xf) represents the sum of the observations in the class. The formulas for the *mean of grouped data* and *standard deviation of grouped data* are as follows:

Approximating $\overline{x}$ and s from grouped data

Sample mean for a frequency distribution

$$\overline{x} = \frac{\Sigma xf}{n} \tag{5}$$

Sample standard deviation for a frequency distribution (defining formula)

$$s = \sqrt{\frac{\Sigma(x - \overline{x})^2 f}{n - 1}} \tag{6}$$

Computation formula for the sample standard deviation

$$s = \sqrt{\frac{\Sigma x^2 f - (\Sigma xf)^2/n}{n - 1}} \tag{7}$$

where

x is the midpoint of a class,
f is the number of entries in that class,
n is the total number of entries in the distribution, and $n = \Sigma f$.
The summation Σ is over all classes in the distribution.

EXAMPLE 9

Grouped data (defining formula)

FIGURE 3-1

Time in Minutes Before Checkout Begins

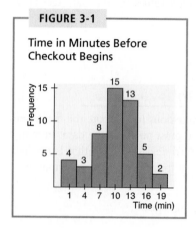

The manager of Pantry Queen Supermarket wants to hire one more checkout clerk. To justify his request to the regional manager, the manager chose a random sample of 50 customers and timed how long each stood in line before a clerk could begin checking the customer out. The written request contained the histogram in Figure 3-1. Approximate the mean and standard deviation of the distribution.

SOLUTION: First, make a table with all the columns necessary to compute the mean and standard deviation (see Table 3-6). (Columns V, VI, and VII are filled in after the mean is computed.) Use the first four columns to find the mean. The value of n is found by summing Column II.

$$n = \Sigma f = 50$$

The mean is

$$\bar{x} = \frac{\Sigma x f}{n} = \frac{509}{50} \text{ from the sum of Column IV}$$

$$\approx 10.2 \text{ min}$$

Once you have the value of the mean, you can complete Columns V, VI, and VII. (They have already been completed for our convenience.)

$$s = \sqrt{\frac{\Sigma(x - \bar{x})^2 f}{n - 1}}$$

$$= \sqrt{\frac{\text{Sum of Column VII}}{(\text{Sum of Column II}) - 1}}$$

$$= \sqrt{\frac{961.40}{50 - 1}} \approx \sqrt{19.62} \approx 4.43$$

Checkout lines

TABLE 3-6   Time in Minutes Before Checkout Begins

I	II	III	IV	V	VI	VII
	Frequency	Midpoint				
Class	f	x	xf	$x - \bar{x}$	$(x - \bar{x})^2$	$(x - \bar{x})^2 f$
0–2	4	1	4	−9.2	84.64	338.56
3–5	3	4	12	−6.2	38.44	115.32
6–8	8	7	56	−3.2	10.24	81.92
9–11	15	10	150	−0.2	0.04	0.60
12–14	13	13	169	2.8	7.84	101.92
15–17	5	16	80	5.8	33.64	168.20
18–20	2	19	38	8.8	77.44	154.88
	$\Sigma f = 50$		$\Sigma x f = 509$			$\Sigma(x - \bar{x})^2 f = 961.40$

Finding $\bar{x}$ and s with repeated data

In the case where our data are not grouped but there are several repeated data values, we can use the techniques of grouped data to find the mean and standard deviation fairly quickly. In such cases, we do not need to find a midpoint of a class interval, since each class consists of a single data value.

GUIDED EXERCISE 7

Mean and standard deviation for repeated data (computation formula)

A random sample of 60 college football players gave the following information (Table 3-7) about recovery time from shoulder injuries, where

x = number of weeks for recovery; f = number of injured players

TABLE 3-7 Recovery Times from Shoulder Injuries

x	1	2	3	4	5	6	7	8
f	5	8	12	19	7	4	3	2

Use the computation formula for grouped data to find the mean and standard deviation of the recovery times.

(a) Looking at the formula for $\bar{x}$ and s,

we see $\bar{x} = \dfrac{\Sigma xf}{n}$

and $s = \sqrt{\dfrac{\Sigma x^2 f - (\Sigma xf)^2/n}{n-1}}$

where $n = \Sigma f$.

Notice that we sum the values f, xf, and $x^2 f$. Make a computation table with x, f, xf, and $x^2 f$ as headers and fill in the values and required totals.

➡ **TABLE 3-8 Recovery Times** (column headers for computation formula for s)

x	f	xf	$x^2 f$
1	5	5	5
2	8	16	32
3	12	36	108
4	19	76	304
5	7	35	175
6	4	24	144
7	3	21	147
8	2	16	128
	$\Sigma f = 60$	$\Sigma xf = 229$	$\Sigma x^2 f = 1043$

(b) Use the formulas to find s and $\bar{x}$.

➡ $n = \Sigma f = 60$

$\bar{x} = \dfrac{\Sigma xf}{n} = \dfrac{229}{60} \approx 3.82$ weeks

$s = \sqrt{\dfrac{\Sigma x^2 f - (\Sigma xf)^2/n}{n-1}}$

$= \sqrt{\dfrac{1043 - 229^2/60}{59}} \approx \sqrt{\dfrac{168.98}{59}} \approx 1.69$

Continued

GUIDED EXERCISE 7 continued

(c) To find the mean and standard deviation of these data, do you think it would be easier to enter all 60 data values directly into your calculator and have the calculator do the work, or use the shortcut method for grouped data?

 When you gain skill in using the grouped-data formula, you will find that it is very efficient. Some calculators, including the TI-84Plus/TI-83Plus, allow you to enter data values and their frequencies as in Table 3-7 instead of entering all 60 data values. Then the calculator will quickly give you values for $\bar{x}$ and s.

 TECH NOTE   The TI-84Plus/TI-83Plus calculators directly support descriptive statistics for grouped data. Both Excel and Minitab can be programmed to accommodate grouped data. (See Using Technology for this chapter.)

TI-84Plus/TI-83Plus   Enter the data into one list, such as L1, and the corresponding frequencies into another list, such as L2. Then press **Stat ➤ Calc ➤ 1: 1-Var Stats.** Enter the list containing the data x, followed by a comma and the list containing the frequencies.

VIEWPOINT   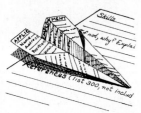 **Are Students Ready for Work?**

Of all high school seniors, 62% say they have "very good" mathematical skills. Only 8% of all employers agree with this claim (*USA Today*). Employers appear to be telling us they need people with *more training* in mathematics, statistics, and general quantitative reasoning skills.

SECTION 3.3   PROBLEMS

1. *Crime: Shoplifting* What is the age distribution of adult shoplifters (21 years of age or older) in supermarkets? The following is based on information taken from the National Retail Federation. A random sample of 895 incidents of shoplifting gave the following age distribution:

Age range (years)	21–30	31–40	41 and over
Number of shoplifters	260	348	287

Estimate the mean age, sample variance, and sample standard deviation for the shoplifters. For the class 41 and over, use 45.5 as the class midpoint.

2. *Anthropology: Navajo Reservation* What was the age distribution of prehistoric Native Americans? Extensive anthropologic studies in the southwestern United States gave the following information about a prehistoric extended family group of 80 members on what is now the Navajo Reservation in northwestern New Mexico. (Source: Based on information taken from *Prehistory in the Navajo Reservation District,* by F. W. Eddy, Museum of New Mexico Press.)

Age range (years)	1–10*	11–20	21–30	31 and over
Number of individuals	34	18	17	11

*Includes infants.

Estimate the mean age expressed in years for this community, the sample variance, and the sample standard deviation. For the class 31 and over, use 35.5 as the class midpoint.

3. *Business Administration: Profits/Assets* What are the big corporations doing with their wealth? One way to answer this question is to examine profits as percentage of assets. A random sample of 50 *Fortune 500* companies gave the following information. (Source: Based on information from *Fortune 500,* Vol. 135, No. 8.)

Profit as percentage of assets	8.6–12.5	12.6–16.5	16.6–20.5	20.6–24.5	24.6–28.5
Number of companies	15	20	5	7	3

Estimate the sample mean, sample variance, and sample standard deviation for profit as percentage of assets.

4. *Agriculture: Water Table* The Bureau of Land Management (BLM) did a study of the water table near Custer, Wyoming, in the month of June. Based on data from the BLM, a random sample of 20 water wells showed that the distances from the ground to the water level (in feet) were

Distance from ground to water level (ft), x	12–14	15–17	18–20	21–23	24–26
Number of wells, f	1	3	8	2	6

Using the midpoints of the depth intervals, estimate the mean depth, the standard deviation, and the coefficient of variation.

5. *Sales: Catalog Shoppers* Based on data from *USA Today,* the ages of a random sample of 300 adults who shop by catalog are

Age	18–24	25–34	35–44	45–54	55–64	65–80
Number	78	75	48	33	33	33

Estimate the mean age of the adults who shop by catalog. Estimate the standard deviation of the age of the shoppers and the coefficient of variation.

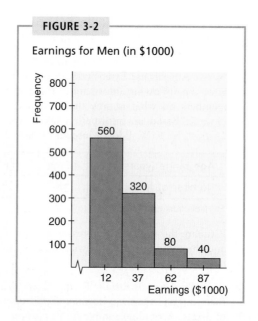

FIGURE 3-2

Earnings for Men (in $1000)

6. *Income: Men versus Women* Based on data from the *Statistical Abstract of the United States*, 116th Edition, a histogram of annual earnings (in thousands of dollars) for a random sample of 1000 men at least 15 years old is shown in Figure 3-2. The histogram in Figure 3-3 shows the earnings (in thousands of dollars) for a random sample of 1000 women who are at least 15 years old.
   (a) Estimate the mean earnings, standard deviation, and coefficient of variation for men.
   (b) Estimate the mean earnings, standard deviation, and coefficient of variation for women.

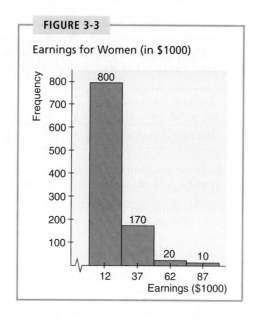

FIGURE 3-3

Earnings for Women (in $1000)

7. *Medical: Hours of Sleep per Day* Alexander Borbely is a professor at the University of Zurich Medical School, where he is director of the sleep laboratory. The his-

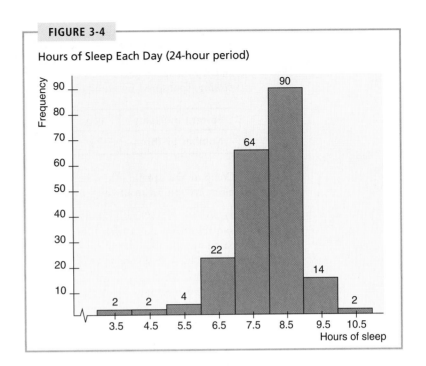

FIGURE 3-4

Hours of Sleep Each Day (24-hour period)

togram in Figure 3-4 is based on information in his book *Secrets of Sleep*. The histogram displays hours of sleep per day for a random sample of 200 subjects. Estimate the mean hours of sleep, standard deviation of hours of sleep, and coefficient of variation.

8. *Ecology: Winter Wolf Packs* How big are winter wolf packs in Minnesota? The following table is based on information taken from *The Wolf*, by L. D. Mech, published by the University of Minnesota Press.

Pack size	1	2	3	4	5	6	7	8	9
Number of packs	15	15	7	9	13	13	9	8	9

Find the sample mean size of the wolf packs, the sample variance, and the sample standard deviation.

9. *Ecology: Life Span of Deer* How long do deer live? In Mesa Verde National Park, deer are not hunted, so the life span of deer in a national park might give a reasonable estimate for the natural life span of deer. The data below are from *The Mule Deer of Mesa Verde National Park*, by G. W. Mieran and J. L. Schmidt, published by the Mesa Verde Museum Association.

Age in years	1	2	3	4	5	6	7	8	9	10
Number of deer	3	7	6	5	4	2	0	1	2	1

(a) Use the methods of grouped data to compute the mean and sample standard deviation of the ages.
(b) Enter the 31 ages individually in a calculator and compute the mean and sample standard deviation of the ages. Are your results the same as in part (a)? Explain why the grouped-data method should give the same results.

10. *Fishing: Bait* What is the mortality rate (percent of fish that die) for trout caught and released using bait with a barbed hook? The following table is based on information taken from regions in British Columbia, Colorado, Michigan, Wisconsin, and Wyoming. (Source: *Proceedings of National Symposium on Catch and Release Fishing,* sponsored by Humboldt State University.)

Percent mortality	35.4	23.0	29.4	38.3	61.5
Number of fish	79	565	136	103	400

Compute the sample mean, sample variance, and sample standard deviation for the mortality rate of trout caught and released (bait on a barbed hook).

11. *Fishing: Lures* What is the mortality rate (percent of fish that die) for trout caught and released using artificial lures with barbed treble hooks? The following table is based on information taken from regions in British Columbia, Colorado, Michigan, Wisconsin, and Wyoming (see source in Problem 10).

Percent mortality	2.8	6.3	1.8	4.8	3.0
Number of fish	145	270	224	271	67

Compute the sample mean, sample variance, and sample standard deviation for the mortality rate of trout caught and released (artificial lure with barbed treble hook).

12. *Fishing: Flies* What is the mortality rate (percent of fish that die) for trout caught and released using artificial flies on barbed hooks? The following table is based on information taken from regions in British Columbia, Colorado, Michigan, Wisconsin, and Wyoming (see source in Problem 10).

Percent mortality	1.3	8.7	11.3	5.9	3.3
Number of fish	75	190	80	51	181

Compute the sample mean, sample variance, and sample standard deviation for the mortality rate of trout caught and released (artificial flies with barbed hook).

3.4
Percentiles and Box-and-Whisker Plots

FOCUS POINTS

✓ Interpret the meaning of percentile scores.
✓ Compute the median, quartiles, and five-number summary from raw data.
✓ Make a box-and-whisker plot. Interpret the results.
✓ Describe how a box-and-whisker plot indicates spread of data around the median.

We've seen measures of central tendency and spread for a set of data. The arithmetic mean $\bar{x}$ and the standard deviation s will be very useful in later work. However, because they each utilize every data value, they can be heavily influenced by one or two extreme data values. In cases where our data distributions are heavily skewed or even bimodal, we often get a better summary of the distribution by utilizing relative position of data rather than exact values.

Recall that the median is an average computed by using relative position of the data. If we are told that 81 is the median score on a biology test, we know that after the data have been ordered, 50% of the data fall at or below the median value of 81. The median is an example of a *percentile*; in fact, it is the 50th percentile. The general definition of the Pth percentile follows.

For whole numbers P (where $1 \leq P \leq 99$), the Pth **percentile** of a distribution is a value such that $P\%$ of the data fall at or below it and $(100 - P)\%$ of the data fall at or above it.

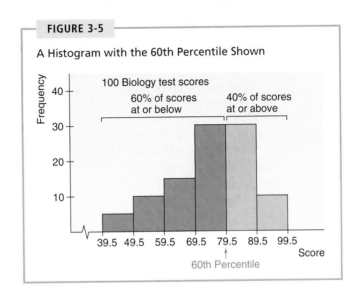

FIGURE 3-5

A Histogram with the 60th Percentile Shown

In Figure 3-5, we see the 60th percentile marked on a histogram. We see that 60% of the data lie below the mark and 40% lie above it.

GUIDED EXERCISE 8

Percentiles

You took the English achievement test to obtain college credit in freshman English by examination.

(a) If your score was at the 89th percentile, what percentage of scores are at or below yours?

The percentile means that 89% of the scores were at or below yours.

(b) If the scores ranged from 1 to 100 and your raw score is 95, does this necessarily mean that your score is at the 95th percentile?

No, the percentile gives an indication of relative position of the scores. The determination of your percentile has to do with the number of scores at or below yours. If everyone did very well and only 80% of the scores fell at or below yours, you would be at the 80th percentile even though you got 95 out of 100 points on the exam.

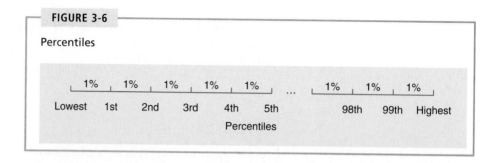

FIGURE 3-6

Percentiles

There are 99 percentiles, and in an ideal situation, the 99 percentiles divide the data set into 100 equal parts. (See Figure 3-6.)

However, if the number of data elements is not exactly divisible by 100, the percentiles will not divide the data into equal parts.

There are several widely used conventions for finding percentiles. They lead to slightly different values for different situations, but these values are close together. For all conventions, the data are first *ranked* or ordered from smallest to largest. A natural way to find the Pth percentile is to then find a value such that P% of the data fall at or below it. This will not always be possible, so we take the nearest value satisfying the criterion. It is at this point that there are a variety of processes to determine the exact value of the percentile.

We will not be very concerned about exact procedures for evaluating percentiles in general. However, *quartiles* are special percentiles used so frequently that we want to adopt a specific procedure for their computation.

Quartiles

Quartiles are those percentiles that divide the data into fourths. The *first quartile* Q_1 is the 25th percentile, the *second quartile* Q_2 is the median, and the *third quartile* Q_3 is the 75th percentile. (See Figure 3-7.)

Again, several conventions are used for computing quartiles, but the following one utilizes the median and is widely adopted.

PROCEDURE

How to compute quartiles

1. Order the data from smallest to largest,

2. Find the median. This is the 2nd quartile.

3. The first quartile Q_1 is then the median of the lower half of the data; that is, it is the median of the data falling *below* the Q_2 position (and not including Q_2).

4. The third quartile Q_3 is the median of the upper half of the data; that is, it is the median of the data falling *above* the Q_2 position (and not including Q_2).

In short, all we do to find the quartiles is to find three medians.

Interquartile range

The median, or second quartile, is a popular measure of the center utilizing relative position. A useful measure of data spread utilizing relative position is the

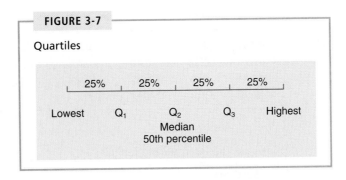

FIGURE 3-7

Quartiles

interquartile range (IQR). It is simply the difference between the third and first quartiles.

$$\text{Interquartile range} = Q_3 - Q_1$$

The interquartile range tells us the spread of the middle half of the data. Now let's look at an example to see how to compute all these quantities.

EXAMPLE 10

Quartiles

In a hurry? On the run? Hungry as well? How about an ice cream bar as a snack? Ice cream bars are popular among all age groups. *Consumer Reports* did a study of ice cream bars. Twenty-seven bars with taste ratings of at least "fair" were listed, and cost per bar was included in the report. Just how much will an ice cream bar cost? The data, expressed in dollars, appear in Table 3-9. As you can see, the cost varies quite a bit, partly because the bars are not of uniform size.

(a) Find the quartiles.

SOLUTION: We first order the data from smallest to largest. Table 3-10 on the next page shows the data in order. Next, we find the median. Since the number of data values is 27, there are an odd number of data, and the median is simply the center or 14th value. The value is shown boxed in Table 3-10.

Median = Q_2 = 0.50

There are 13 values below the median position, and Q_1 is the median of these values. It is the middle or 7th value and is shaded in Table 3-10.

First quartile = Q_1 = 0.33

There are also 13 values above the median position. The median of these is the 7th value from the right end. This value is also shaded in Table 3-10.

Third quartile = Q_3 = 1.00

TABLE 3-9   Cost of Ice Cream Bars (in dollars)

0.99	1.07	1.00	0.50	0.37	1.03	1.07	1.07
0.97	0.63	0.33	0.50	0.97	1.08	0.47	0.84
1.23	0.25	0.50	0.40	0.33	0.35	0.17	0.38
0.20	0.18	0.16					

TABLE 3-10   Ordered Cost of Ice Cream Bars (in dollars)

0.16	0.17	0.18	0.20	0.25	0.33	0.33	0.35
0.37	0.38	0.40	0.47	0.50	0.50	0.50	0.63
0.84	0.97	0.97	0.99	1.00	1.03	1.07	1.07
1.07	1.08	1.23					

(b) Find the interquartile range.

SOLUTION:

$$IQR = Q_3 - Q_1$$
$$= 1.00 - 0.33$$
$$= 0.67$$

This means that the middle half of the data has a cost spread of 67¢.   ◆

GUIDED EXERCISE 9

Quartiles

Many people consider the number of calories in an ice cream bar as important as, if not more important than, the cost. The *Consumer Reports* article also included the calorie count of the rated ice cream bars (Table 3-11). There were 22 vanilla-flavored bars rated. Again, the bars varied in size, and some of the smaller bars had fewer calories. The calorie counts for the vanilla bars follow.

TABLE 3-11   Calories in Vanilla-Flavored Ice Cream Bars

342	377	319	353	295
234	294	286	377	182
310	439	111	201	182
197	209	147	190	151
131	151			

(a) Our first step is to order the data. Do so.

⟹ **TABLE 3-12   Ordered Data**

111	131	147	151	151	182
182	190	197	201	209	234
286	294	295	310	319	342
353	377	377	439		

(b) There are 22 data values. Find the median.

⟹ Average the 11th and 12th data values boxed together in Table 3-12.

$$\text{Median} = \frac{209 + 234}{2}$$
$$= 221.5$$

Continued

GUIDED EXERCISE 9 continued

(c) How many values are below the median position? Find Q_1.

⟹ Since the median lies halfway between the 11th and 12th values, there are 11 values below the median position. Q_1 is the median of these values.

$$Q_1 = 182$$

(d) There are the same number of data above as below the median. Use this fact to find Q_3.

⟹ Q_3 is the median of the upper half of the data. There are 11 values in the upper portion.

$$Q_3 = 319$$

(e) Find the interquartile range and comment on its meaning.

⟹ $IQR = Q_3 - Q_1$
$$= 319 - 182$$
$$= 137$$

The middle portion of the data has a spread of 137 calories.

Box-and-Whisker Plots

Five-number summary

The quartiles together with the low and high data values give us a very useful *five-number summary* of the data and their spread.

> **Five-number summary**
>
> Lowest value, Q_1, median, Q_3, highest value

Box-and-whisker plot

We will use these five numbers to create a graphic sketch of the data called a *box-and-whisker plot*. Box-and-whisker plots provide another useful technique from exploratory data analysis (EDA) for describing data.

PROCEDURE

How to make a box-and-whisker plot

1. Draw a vertical scale to include the lowest and highest data values.
2. To the right of the scale draw a box from Q_1 to Q_3.
3. Include a solid line through the box at the median level.
4. Draw solid lines, called *whiskers*, from Q_1 to the lowest value and from Q_3 to the highest value.

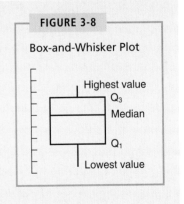

FIGURE 3-8

Box-and-Whisker Plot

The next example demonstrates the process of making a box-and-whisker plot.

EXAMPLE 11

Box-and-whisker plot

Using the data from Guided Exercise 9, make a box-and-whisker plot showing the calories in vanilla-flavored ice cream bars. Use the plot to make observations about the distribution of calories.

(a) In Guided Exercise 9, we ordered the data (see Table 3-12) and found the values of the median, Q_1, and Q_3. From this previous work we have the five-number summary:

low value = 111; Q_1 = 182; median = 221.5; Q_3 = 319; high value = 439

(b) We select an appropriate vertical scale and make the plot (Figure 3-9).

(c) A quick glance at the box-and-whisker plot reveals the following:

(i) The box tells us where the middle half of the data lies, so we see that half of the ice cream bars have between 182 and 319 calories, with an interquartile range of 137 calories.

(ii) The median is slightly closer to the lower part of the box. This means that the lower calorie counts are more concentrated. The calorie counts above the median are more spread out, indicating that the distribution is slightly skewed toward the higher values.

(iii) The upper whisker is longer than the lower, which again emphasizes skewness toward the higher values.

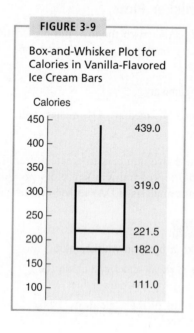

FIGURE 3-9

Box-and-Whisker Plot for Calories in Vanilla-Flavored Ice Cream Bars

◇ **COMMENT** In exploratory data analysis, *hinges* rather than quartiles are used to create the box. Hinges are computed in a manner similar to the way we compute quartiles. However, in the case of an odd number of data values, include the median itself in both the lower and upper halves of the data (see *Applications, Basics, and Computing of Exploratory Data Analysis,* by Paul Velleman and David Hoaglin, Duxbury Press). This has the effect of shrinking the box and moving the ends of the box slightly toward the median. For an even number of data, the quartiles as we computed them equal the hinges. ◇

GUIDED
EXERCISE **10**

Box-and-whisker plot

The Renata College Development Office sent salary surveys to alumni who graduated two and five years ago. The voluntary responses received are summarized in the box-and-whisker plots shown in Figure 3-10.

(a) From Figure 3-10, estimate the median and extreme values of salaries of alumni graduating two years ago. In what range are the middle half of the salaries?

⇨ The median seems to be about $44,000. The extremes are about $33,000 and $54,000. The middle half of the salaries fall between $40,000 and $47,000.

FIGURE 3-10 Box-and-Whisker Plots for Alumni Salaries (in thousands of dollars)

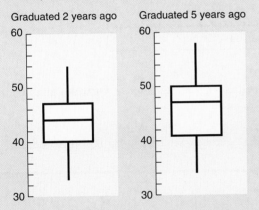

(b) From Figure 3-10, estimate the median and the extreme values of salaries of alumni graduating five years ago. What is the location of the middle half of the salaries?

⇨ The median seems to be $47,000. The extremes are $34,000 and $58,000. The middle half of the data is enclosed by the box with low side at $41,000 and high side at $50,000.

(c) Compare the two box plots and make comments about the salaries of alumni graduating two and five years ago.

⇨ The salaries of the alumni graduating five years ago have a larger spread but begin slightly higher and extend to levels about $4,000 above those graduating two years ago. The middle half of the data is also more spread out with higher boundaries and a higher median.

We have developed the skeletal box-and-whisker plot. Other variations may include *fences*, which are marks placed on either side of the box to represent various portions of the data. Values that lie outside the fences are called *outliers* (see Problem 14 of this section). These values seem to stand by themselves, away from most of the data. They might be exceptional values and deserve closer study. Or they may be the result of data entry error. For a more complete discussion of outliers and variations of box plots, see *Applications, Basics, and Computing of Exploratory Data Analysis,* by Velleman and Hoaglin.

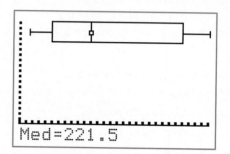

TECH NOTE *Box-and-Whisker Plot* Both Minitab and the TI-84Plus/ TI-83Plus calculators support box-and-whisker plots. On the TI-84Plus/ TI-83Plus, the quartiles Q_1 and Q_3 are calculated as we calculate them in this text. In Minitab and Excel, they are calculated using a slightly different process.

TI-84Plus/TI-83Plus

Press **STATPLOT** ➤ **On.** Highlight box plot. Use **Trace** and the arrow keys to display the values of the five-number summary. The display shows the plot for calories in ice cream bars.

Med=221.5

Excel

Does not produce plot. **Paste Function** ⎣f_x⎦ ➤ **Statistics** ➤ **Quartiles** gives the five-number summary.

Minitab

Press **Graph** ➤ **Boxplot.** In the dialogue box set Display to IQRange Box.

VIEWPOINT

Is Shorter Higher?

Can you estimate a person's *height* from the *pitch* of his or her voice? Is a soprano shorter than an alto? Is a bass taller than a tenor? A statistical study of singers in the New York Choral Society provided information. For more information, visit the Brase/Brase statistics site at **http://math.college.hmco.com/ students** and find the link to DASL, the Carnegie Mellon University Data and Story Library. From the Data Subjects, select music and then singers. Methods of this chapter can be used with new methods we will learn in Chapters 8 and 9 to examine such questions from a statistical point of view.

SECTION 3.4   PROBLEMS

1. *Education: Aptitude Test* Angela took a general aptitude test and scored in the 82nd percentile for aptitude in accounting. What percentage of the scores were at or below her score? What percentage were above?

2. *Education: College Admission* One standard for admission to Redfield College is that the student must rank in the upper quartile of his or her graduating high school class. What is the minimal percentile rank of a successful applicant?

3. *Education: Competency Exam* The town of Butler, Nebraska, decided to give a teacher-competency exam and defined the passing scores to be those in the 70th percentile or higher. The raw test scores ranged from 0 to 100. Was a raw score of 82 necessarily a passing score? Explain.

4. *Education: Test Scores* Clayton and Timothy took different sections of Introduction to Economics. Each section had a different final exam. Timothy scored 83 out of 100 and had a percentile rank in his class of 72. Clayton scored 85 out of 100 but his percentile rank in his class was 70. Who performed better with respect to the rest of the students in the class: Clayton or Timothy? Explain your answer.

5. *Consumer: Pizza Cost* Want a takeout dinner or a dinner that is easy to prepare? Pizza comes to mind for many people. *Consumer Reports* (Vol. 62, No. 1) rated a variety of pizzas from supermarkets. For a 5-ounce serving of supermarket cheese pizza, the costs (in dollars) are

| 0.90 | 0.85 | 0.80 | 1.00 | 0.69 | 0.75 | 0.81 | 0.90 |
| 1.92 | 1.64 | 1.54 | 0.72 | 1.15 | 0.52 | 0.72 | 1.50 |

Compute the five-number summary and interquartile range. Then make a box-and-whisker plot.

6. *Consumer: Pizza Calories* How many calories are in a serving of cheese pizza? The article in *Consumer Reports* referred to in Problem 5 also gave the calories in a 5-ounce serving of supermarket cheese pizza. The calories are

| 332 | 364 | 393 | 347 | 350 | 353 | 357 | 296 |
| 358 | 322 | 337 | 323 | 333 | 299 | 316 | 275 |

Compute the five-number summary and interquartile range. Then make a box-and-whisker plot.

7. *Health Care: Nurses* At Center Hospital there is some concern about the high turnover of nurses. A survey was done to determine how long (in months) nurses had been in their current positions. The responses (in months) of 20 nurses were

| 23 | 2 | 5 | 14 | 25 | 36 | 27 | 42 | 12 | 8 |
| 7 | 23 | 29 | 26 | 28 | 11 | 20 | 31 | 8 | 36 |

Make a box-and-whisker plot of the data. Find the interquartile range.

8. *Health Care: Staff* Another survey was done at Center Hospital to determine how long (in months) clerical staff had been in their current positions. The responses (in months) of 20 clerical staff members were

| 25 | 22 | 7 | 24 | 26 | 31 | 18 | 14 | 17 | 20 |
| 31 | 42 | 6 | 25 | 22 | 3 | 29 | 32 | 15 | 72 |

(a) Make a box-and-whisker plot. Find the interquartile range.
(b) Compare this plot with the one in Problem 7. Discuss the location of the medians, the location of the middle half of the data banks, and the distance from Q_1 and Q_3 to the extreme values.

9. *Consumer: Auto Insurance* Is there a difference in auto insurance cost if you reside in a suburban area or an urban area? *Consumer Reports* (Vol. 62, No. 1) gave suburban and urban costs of auto insurance for several states. In Illinois, the least expensive costs (in dollars) for similar policies were as shown in the following table.

Suburban   **Urban**

1170	1216	1211	1282	1292		2356	2584	2674	2840	2910
808	874	972	986	992		1768	1968	1968	2083	2107

For each group, compute the five-number summary and interquartile range. Then make a box-and-whisker plot for each group and comment on the differences between urban and suburban auto insurance rates.

10. *Sociology: High-school Dropouts* What percentage of the general U.S. population are high-school dropouts? The *Statistical Abstract of the United States*, 120th Edition, gives the percentage of high-school dropouts by state. For convenience, the data are sorted in increasing order.

5	6	7	7	7	7	8	8	8	8
8	9	9	9	9	9	9	9	10	10
10	10	10	10	10	10	11	11	11	11
11	11	11	11	12	12	12	12	13	13
13	13	13	13	14	14	14	14	14	15

(a) Make a box-and-whisker plot and find the interquartile range.
(b) Wyoming has a dropout rate of about 7%. Into what quartile does this rate fall?

11. *Sociology: College Graduates* What percentage of the general U.S. population have bachelor's degrees? The *Statistical Abstract of the United States*, 120th Edition, gives the percentage of bachelor's degrees by state. For convenience, the data are sorted in increasing order.

17	18	18	18	19	20	20	20	21	21
21	21	22	22	22	22	22	22	23	23
24	24	24	24	24	24	24	24	25	26
26	26	26	26	26	27	27	27	27	27
28	28	29	31	31	32	32	34	35	38

(a) Make a box-and-whisker plot and find the interquartile range.
(b) Illinois has a bachelor's degree percentage rate of about 26%. Into what quartile does this rate fall?

12. *Financial: Interpret Graphs* Box-and-whisker plots for the weekly percentage changes in the closing prices of Coca-Cola stock, McDonald's stock, and Disney stock (*Historical Quotes, Dow Jones News Retrieval Service*) are shown in Figure 3-11. Compare the plots. Answer each of the following questions, and explain each answer.
(a) For all the stocks, does the percentage change distribution appear to be skewed right? Explain.
(b) Which stock has a percentage change distribution that is most spread?
(c) Which stock was most volatile during the period shown?
(d) Which stock had a median percentage change that was negative? Which stock had more weekly declines than weekly increases?
(e) If you were a conservative investor interested in purchasing one of these stocks but you wanted the one that had percentage declines that were smallest, which would you select? How do the sizes of the percentage increases in this stock compare with those of the other two?

FIGURE 3-11

Weekly Percentage Change in Closing Price

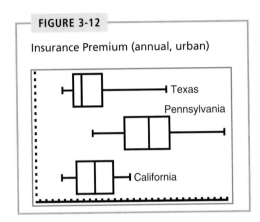

FIGURE 3-12

Insurance Premium (annual, urban)

(f) If you were an investor willing to take risks and you wanted a stock with high growth, which of these stocks would you select? Which one had the highest percentage increases? How do the percentage decreases of this stock compare with those of the other two?

13. *Auto Insurance: Interpret Graphs* Consumer Reports rated automobile insurance companies and gave annual premiums for top-rated companies in several states. Figure 3-12 shows box plots for annual premiums for urban customers (married couple with one 17-year-old son) in three states. The box plots in Figure 3-12 were all drawn on the same scale on a TI-84Plus/TI-83Plus calculator.
    (a) Which state has the lowest premium? the highest?
    (b) Which state has the highest median premium?
    (c) Which state has the smallest range of premiums? the smallest interquartile range?
    (d) Figure 3-13 on the next page gives the five-number summaries generated on the TI-84Plus/TI-83Plus calculators for the box plots of Figure 3-12. Match the five-number summaries to the appropriate box plots.

 14. *Expand Your Knowledge: Outliers* Some data sets include values so high or so low that they seem to stand apart from the rest of the data. These data are called *outliers*. Outliers may be from data collection errors, data entry errors, or simply valid but unusual data values. Regardless of the reason, it is important to identify outliers in the data set and examine the outliers carefully to determine if they are in error. One way to detect outliers is to use a box-and-whisker plot. Data values that fall beyond the limits,

Lower Limit: $Q_1 - 1.5 \times (IQR)$

Upper Limit: $Q_3 + 1.5 \times (IQR)$

where *IQR* is the interquartile range, are suspected outliers. In the computer software package Minitab, values beyond these limits are plotted with asterisks (*).

FIGURE 3-13

Five-Number Summaries for Insurance Premiums

(a)
```
1-Var Stats
↑n=10
 minX=2382
 Q1=2758
 Med=2991
 Q3=3652
 maxX=5715
```

(b)
```
1-Var Stats
↑n=10
 minX=3314
 Q1=4326
 Med=5116.5
 Q3=5801
 maxX=7527
```

(c)
```
1-Var Stats
↑n=10
 minX=2323
 Q1=2801
 Med=3377.5
 Q3=3966
 maxX=4482
```

Students from a statistics class were asked to record their heights in inches. The heights (as recorded) were

65	72	68	64	60	55	73	71	52	63	61	74
69	67	74	50	4	75	67	62	66	80	64	65

(a) Make a box-and-whisker plot of the data.
(b) Find the value of the interquartile range (*IQR*).
(c) Multiply the *IQR* by 1.5 and find the lower and upper limits.
(d) Are there any data values below the lower limit? above the upper limit? List any suspected outliers. What might be some explanations for the outliers?

15. *Salary Increases: Interpret Graphs* The following Minitab display shows box-and-whisker plots for the percentage increases in annual salaries for the university and college faculty in Tennessee (by rank). (Source: *Academe: Bulletin of the American Association of University Professors*, Volume 85, Number 2.)

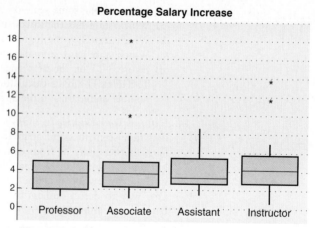

Percentage Salary Increase

(The symbol * represents an outlier.)

Minitab menu selections: ➤ **Graph** ➤ **Boxplot.**

Note: Minitab uses a procedure to find Q_1 and Q_3 that is slightly different from the method shown in this text. As a result, Minitab values for Q_1 and Q_3 will differ slightly from text or TI-84Plus/TI-83Plus values.

(a) Which faculty rank had the smallest median percentage salary increase? Which faculty rank had the single highest percentage salary increase?

(b) Which faculty rank had the largest spread between the first and third quartiles?

(c) Which faculty rank had the smallest spread for the lower 50% of the percentage salary increases?

(d) Which faculty rank had the most symmetric percentage salary increases? If the outliers for the associate professors were omitted, would that distribution appear to be symmetric?

(e) Look at the following descriptive statistics from Minitab.

```
Minitab Display: Descriptive Statistics
VARIABLE     N        MEAN     MEDIAN   TRMEAN   STDEV    SE MEAN
Professo     20       3.685    3.700    3.611    1.766    0.395
Associat     24       4.362    3.750    3.927    3.592    0.733
Assistan     23       4.330    3.500    4.262    2.007    0.419
Instruct     21       4.781    4.100    4.568    3.132    0.684
VARIABLE     MINIMUM  MAXIMUM  Q1       Q3
Professo     1.200    7.500    2.100    4.975
Associat     0.600    17.700   2.350    5.075
Assistan     1.500    8.600    2.900    5.500
Instruct     0.200    13.400   2.850    5.800
```

For the ranks of associate professor and instructor, compute the upper limit for outliers (see Problem 14). Do these ranks show outliers?

SUMMARY

To characterize numerical data, we use both measures of center and of variation. An average is an attempt to summarize the data into just one number. We studied several important averages: the mode, the median, the mean, and weighted averages. We also looked at trimmed means, which are more resistant to the effects of extreme values. However, an average alone can be misleading; we really need another statistical cross-reference. The measure of data spread, or variation, satisfies the purpose. The variations that we looked at most carefully were the range, the variance, the standard deviation, and the interquartile range. Chebyshev's theorem enables us to estimate the data spread. The coefficient of variation lets us compare relative spread from different data sets. A box-and-whisker plot gives a good visual impression of the range of the data and the location of the middle half of the data.

In later work the average we will use most is the mean; the measure of variation we will use most is the standard deviation. Because the mean and standard deviation are so important, we learned how to estimate these values from data already organized in a frequency distribution.

IMPORTANT WORDS & SYMBOLS

Section 3.1
Average
Mode
Median
Mean
Sample mean, $\overline{x}$
Population mean, μ
Summation symbol, Σ
Resistant measure
Trimmed mean
Weighted average

Section 3.2
Range
Sum of squares, $\Sigma(x - \overline{x})^2$
Sample standard deviation, s
Sample variance, s^2

Population standard deviation, σ
Population size, N
Coefficient of variation, CV
Chebyshev's theorem

Section 3.3
Mean of grouped data
Standard deviation of grouped data

Section 3.4
Percentile
Quartile
Interquartile range, IQR
Five-number summary
Box-and-whisker plot
Whisker
Outlier

VIEWPOINT

The Fujita Scale

How do you measure a tornado? Professor Fujita and Allen Pearson (Director of the National Severe Storm Forecast Center) developed a measure based on wind speed and type of damage done by a tornado. The result is an excellent example of both descriptive and inferential statistical methods. For more information, visit the Brase/Brase statistics site at **http://math.college.hmco.com/students** and find the link to the tornado project. Then look up Fujita scale. If we group the data a little, the scale becomes

FS	WS	%
F0 & F1	40–112	67
F2 & F3	113–206	29
F4 & F5	207–318	4

where *FS* represents Fujita scale; *WS*, wind speed in miles per hour; and %, percentage of all tornados. Out of 100 tornados, what would you estimate for the mean and standard deviation of wind speed?

CHAPTER REVIEW PROBLEMS

1. *Consumer: Power Surge Protector* June purchased a new home computer and has been having trouble with voltage spikes on the power line. Such voltage jumps can be caused by the operation of appliances, such as clothes dryers and electric irons,

or just by a power surge on the outside power line. Her friend Jim is an electronics technician and has obtained the following data about voltages when certain electric appliances are turned on and off. Remember, the normal line voltage is 110 volts. All measurements are taken from the line and measured in volts.

| 73 | 140 | 78 | 142 | 80 | 140 | 90 | 133 |

(a) Compute the sample mean, sample standard deviation, coefficient of variation, and range.

Jim advised June to buy a device called a *power surge protector* that protects the computer from strong voltage spikes. Using the power surge protector, Jim again measured voltages to the computer when the same appliances were turned on and off. The results in volts were

| 100 | 120 | 108 | 114 | 105 | 117 | 103 | 114 |

(b) Compute the sample mean, sample standard deviation, coefficient of variation, and range of the voltages using the power surge protector.
(c) Compare your answers for parts (a) and (b). Were the means about the same? Were the voltage distributions different with and without the power surge protector? How did the standard deviation, coefficient of variation, and range reflect this when the mean did not? Explain your answer.

2. *Consumer: Radon Gas* "Radon: The Problem No One Wants to Face" is the title of an article appearing in *Consumer Reports*. Radon is a gas emitted from the ground that can collect in houses and buildings. At certain levels it can cause lung cancer. Radon concentrations are measured in picocuries per liter (pCi/L). A radon level of 4 pCi/L is considered "acceptable." Radon levels in a house vary from week to week. In one house, a sample of 8 weeks had the following readings for radon level (in pCi/L):

| 1.9 | 2.8 | 5.7 | 4.2 | 1.9 | 8.6 | 3.9 | 7.2 |

(a) Find the mean, median, and mode.
(b) Find the sample standard deviation, coefficient of variation, and the range.

3. *Political Science: Georgia Democrats* How Democratic is Georgia? County-by-county results are shown for a recent election. For your convenience, the data have been sorted in increasing order. (Source: *County and City Data Book,* 12th edition, U.S. Census Bureau.)

Percentage of Democratic Vote by Counties in Georgia

31 33 34 34 35 35 35 36 38 38 38 39 40 40 40 40
41 41 41 41 41 41 41 42 42 43 44 44 44 45 45 46
46 46 46 47 48 49 49 49 49 50 51 52 52 53 53 53
53 53 55 56 56 57 57 59 62 66 66 68

(a) Make a box-and-whisker plot of the data. Find the interquartile range.
(b) Make a frequency table using five classes. Then estimate the mean and sample standard deviation using the frequency table. Compute a 75% Chebyshev interval centered about the mean.
(c) If you have a statistical calculator or computer, use it to find the actual sample mean and sample standard deviation. Otherwise, use the values $\Sigma x = 2769$ and $\Sigma x^2 = 132,179$ to compute the sample mean and sample standard deviation.

4. *Grades: Weighted Average* Professor Cramer determines a final grade based on attendance, two papers, three major tests, and a final exam. Each of these activities has a total of 100 possible points. However, the activities carry different weights. Attendance is worth 5%, each paper is worth 8%, each test is worth 15%, and the final is worth 34%.
   (a) What is the average for a student with 92 on attendance, 73 on the first paper, 81 on the second paper, 85 on test 1, 87 on test 2, 83 on test 3, and 90 on the final exam?
   (b) Compute the average for a student with the above scores on the papers, tests, and final exam, but with a score of only 20 on attendance.

5. *General: Average Weight* An elevator is loaded with 16 people and is at its load limit of 2500 lb. What is the mean weight of these people?

6. *Ecology: Blue Spruce Trees* The circumferences (distance around) of 94 blue spruce trees selected at random in Roosevelt National Forest were measured. The results to the nearest inch were grouped in Table 3-13. Using the midpoints of the tree circumference classes, find the mean and standard deviation.

TABLE 3-13   Circumference of Blue Spruce Trees

Circumference (in.)	Number of Trees
10–24	6
25–39	20
40–54	52
55–69	16

7. *Fishing: Line Strength* A certain brand of nylon monofilament fishing line is known to deteriorate in very cold temperatures. A spool of 10-pound test monofilament line was left out overnight at Fairbanks, Alaska, when temperatures dropped to −35°F. A random sample of six pieces of line gave the following breaking strengths (in pounds):

   10.1   6.2   9.8   5.3   9.9   5.7

   (a) Compute the sample mean, sample standard deviation, coefficient of variation, and range.

   A second spool of this line that had not been subjected to extreme cold temperatures gave the following breaking strengths (in pounds) for a random sample of six pieces of line:

   10.2   9.7   9.8   10.3   9.6   10.1

   (b) Compute the sample mean, sample standard deviation, coefficient of variation, and range for these values.
   (c) Compare your answers for parts (a) and (b) and comment on the observed differences. Which line had the more consistent performance? How was this reflected in the sample standard deviations and in the coefficients of variation? In the ranges?

8. *Agriculture: Harvest Weight of Maize* The following data represent weights in kilograms of maize harvest from a random sample of 72 experimental plots on St. Vincent, an island in the Caribbean (Reference: B. G. F. Springer, *Proceedings, Caribbean Food Corps. Soc.*, Vol. 10, pp. 147–152). *Note:* These data are also available with other software on the statSpace CD-ROM. For convenience, the data are presented in increasing order.

7.8	9.1	9.5	10.0	10.2	10.5	11.1	11.5	11.7	11.8
12.2	12.2	12.5	13.1	13.5	13.7	13.7	14.0	14.4	14.5
14.6	15.2	15.5	16.0	16.0	16.1	16.5	17.2	17.8	18.2
19.0	19.1	19.3	19.8	20.0	20.2	20.3	20.5	20.9	21.1
21.4	21.8	22.0	22.0	22.4	22.5	22.5	22.8	22.8	23.1
23.1	23.2	23.7	23.8	23.8	23.8	23.8	24.0	24.1	24.1
24.5	24.5	24.9	25.1	25.2	25.5	26.1	26.4	26.5	26.7
27.1	29.5								

(a) Compute the five-number summary.

(b) Compute the interquartile range.

(c) Make a box-and-whisker plot.

(d) Discuss the distribution. Does the lower half of the distribution show more data spread than the upper half?

9. *Focus Problem: The Educational Advantage* Solve the focus problem at the beginning of this chapter.

10. *Fishing: Atlantic Salmon* What is the mortality rate (percent of fish that die) for Atlantic salmon caught and released using artificial flies with barbed hooks? The following information is based on studies done in Maine (Source: *Proceedings of National Symposium on Catch and Release Fishing*, sponsored by Humboldt State University).

Percent mortality	4.6	12.0	2.6	4.1	3.9
Number of fish	304	52	39	319	77

Compute the sample mean, sample variance, and sample standard deviation for the mortality rate of salmon caught and released (artificial flies with barbed hooks).

11. *Performance Rating: Weighted Average* A performance evaluation for new sales representatives at Office Automation Incorporated involves several ratings done on a scale of 1 to 10, with 10 the highest rating. The activities rated include new contacts, successful contacts, total contacts, dollar volume of sales, and reports. Then an overall rating is determined by using a weighted average. The weights are 2 for new contacts, 3 for successful contacts, 3 for total contacts, 5 for dollar value of sales, and 3 for reports. What would the overall rating be for a sales representative with ratings of 5 for new contacts, 8 for successful contacts, 7 for total contacts, 9 for dollar volume of sales, and 7 for reports?

12. *Agriculture: Bell Peppers* The pathogen *Phytophthora capsici* causes bell pepper plants to wilt and die. A research project was designed to study the effect of soil water content and the spread of the disease in fields of bell peppers (Source: *Journal of Agricultural, Biological, and Environmental Statistics*, Vol. 2, No. 2). It is thought that too much water helps spread the disease. The fields were divided into rows and quadrants. The soil water content (percent of water by volume of soil) was determined for each plot. An important first step in such a research project is to give a statistical description of the data.

Soil Water Content for Bell Pepper Study

15	14	14	14	13	12	11	11	11	11	10	11	13	16	10
9	15	12	9	10	7	14	13	14	8	9	8	11	13	13
15	12	9	10	9	9	16	16	12	10	11	11	12	15	6
10	10	10	11	9										

(a) Make a box-and-whisker plot of the data. Find the interquartile range.

(b) Make a frequency table using four classes. Then estimate the mean and sample standard deviation using the frequency table. Compute a 75% Chebyshev interval centered about the mean.

(c) If you have a statistical calculator or computer, use it to find the actual sample mean and sample standard deviation.

13. *General: Create Examples*

  (a) Is it possible that the range and standard deviation can be equal? If your answer is yes, give an example of a data set for which they are equal.

  (b) Is it possible that the mean, median, and mode can all be equal? Is it possible that they can all be different? If your answer is yes to either question, give an example to illustrate your answer.

DATA HIGHLIGHTS: GROUP PROJECTS

Old Faithful Geyser, Yellowstone National Park

Break into small groups and discuss the following topics. Organize a brief outline in which you summarize the main points of your group discussion.

1. *The Story of Old Faithful* is a short book written by George Marler and published by the Yellowstone Association. Chapter 7 of this interesting book talks about the effect of the 1959 earthquake on eruption intervals for Old Faithful Geyser. Dr. John Rinehart (a senior research scientist with the National Oceanic and Atmospheric Administration) has done extensive studies of the eruption intervals before and after the 1959 earthquake. Examine Figure 3-14. Notice the general shape. Is the graph more or less symmetrical? Does it have a single mode frequency? The mean interval between eruptions has remained steady at about 65 minutes for the past 100 years. Therefore, the 1959 earthquake did not significantly change the mean, but it did change the distribution of eruption intervals. Examine Figure 3-15. Would you say there are really two frequency modes, one shorter and the other longer? Explain. The overall mean is about the same for both graphs, but one graph has a much larger standard deviation (for eruption intervals) than the other. Do no calculations, just look at both graphs, and then explain which graph has the smaller and which has the larger standard deviation. Which distribution will have the larger coefficient of variation? In everyday terms, what would this mean if you were actually at Yellowstone waiting to see the next eruption of Old Faithful? Explain your answer.

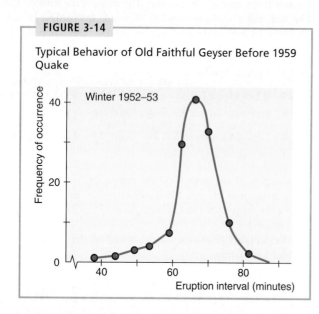

FIGURE 3-14

Typical Behavior of Old Faithful Geyser Before 1959 Quake

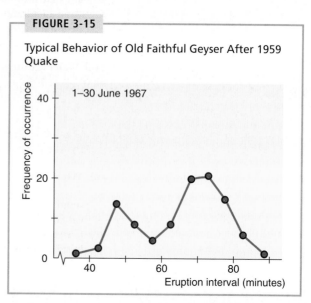

FIGURE 3-15

Typical Behavior of Old Faithful Geyser After 1959 Quake

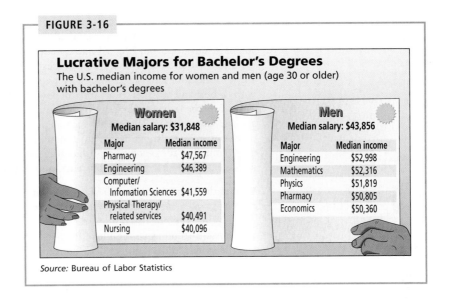

FIGURE 3-16

Lucrative Majors for Bachelor's Degrees
The U.S. median income for women and men (age 30 or older)
with bachelor's degrees

Women
Median salary: $31,848

Major	Median income
Pharmacy	$47,567
Engineering	$46,389
Computer/ Infomation Sciences	$41,559
Physical Therapy/ related services	$40,491
Nursing	$40,096

Men
Median salary: $43,856

Major	Median income
Engineering	$52,998
Mathematics	$52,316
Physics	$51,819
Pharmacy	$50,805
Economics	$50,360

Source: Bureau of Labor Statistics

2. Most academic advisors tell students to major in a field the student really loves. After all, it is true that money cannot buy happiness! Nevertheless, it is interesting to at least look at some of the higher-paying fields of study. After all, a field like mathematics can be a lot of fun, once you get into it. We see that women's salaries tend to be less than men's salaries. However, women's salaries are rapidly catching up, and this benefits the entire work force in different ways. Figure 3-16 shows the median incomes for college graduates with different majors. The employees in the sample are all at least 30 years old. Does it seem reasonable to assume that many of the employees are in jobs beyond the entry level? Explain. Compare the median incomes shown for all women aged 30 or older holding bachelor's degrees with the median incomes for men of similar age holding bachelor's degrees. Look at the particular majors listed. What percentage of men holding bachelor's degrees in mathematics make $52,316 or more? What percentage of women holding computer/information science degrees make $41,559 or more? How do median incomes for men and women holding engineering degrees compare? What about pharmacy degrees?

LINKING CONCEPTS: WRITING PROJECTS

Discuss each of the following topics in class or review the topics on your own. Then write a brief but complete essay in which you summarize the main points. Please include formulas and graphs as appropriate.

1. An average is an attempt to summarize a collection of data into just *one* number. Discuss how the mean, median, and mode all represent averages in this context. Also discuss the differences among these averages. Why is the mean a balance point? Why is the median a midway point? Why is the mode the most common data point? List three areas of daily life where you think either the mean, median, or mode would be the best choice to describe an "average."

2. Why do we need to study the variation of a collection of data? Why isn't the average by itself adequate? We have studied three ways to measure variation. The range, standard deviation, and to a large extent, a box-and-whisker plot all indicate the variation within a data collection. Discuss similarities and differences among these ways to measure data variation. Why would it seem reasonable to pair the median with a box-and-whisker plot and to pair the mean with the standard deviation? What are the advantages and disadvantages of each method of describing data spread? Comment on statements such as the following: (a) The range is easy to compute, but it doesn't give much information; (b) although the standard deviation is more complicated to compute, it has some significant applications; (c) the box-and-whisker plot is fairly easy to construct, and it gives a lot of information at a glance.

3. Why is the coefficient of variation important? What do we mean when we say the coefficient of variation has no units? What advantage can there be in having no units? Why is *relative size* important?

   Consider robin eggs; the mean weight of a collection of robin eggs is 0.72 ounce and the standard deviation is 0.12 ounce. Now consider elephants; the mean weight of elephants in the zoo is 6.42 tons, with a standard deviation 1.07 tons. The units of measurement are different and there is a great deal of difference between the size of an elephant and that of a robin's egg. Yet the coefficient of variation is about the same for both. Comment on this from the viewpoint of the size of the standard deviation relative to the mean.

4. What is Chebyshev's theorem? Suppose you have a friend who knows very little about statistics. Write a paragraph or two in which you describe Chebyshev's theorem for your friend. Keep the discussion as simple as possible, but be sure to get the main ideas across to your friend. Suppose he or she asks, "What is this stuff good for?" and suppose you respond (a little sarcastically) that Chebyshev's theorem applies to everything from butterflies to the orbits of the planets! Would you be correct? Explain.

5. Have each student count the amount of loose change (not paper money) brought to class today. Use a calculator with mean and standard deviation buttons to compute the mean and standard deviation for the class. (Perhaps the professor can enter the data into the calculator while the students tell him or her the numbers.)
   (a) Compute the endpoints of the interval $\bar{x} - 2s$ to $\bar{x} + 2s$. Have each student raise a hand if the amount of loose change that was counted falls into this interval. Explain why you expect about 75% or more of the class to raise their hands.
   (b) Compute the endpoints of the interval $\bar{x} - \sqrt{2}s$ to $\bar{x} + \sqrt{2}s$. Repeat part (a) for this interval. Explain why you expect about 50% or more of the class to raise their hands.
   (c) Suppose we take the point of view that our statistics class is a sample of the entire student body. What percentage of the entire student body do you expect will have from $\bar{x} - 3s$ to $\bar{x} + 3s$ cents in loose change? Is your answer a lower estimate for the actual percentage? Explain.
   (d) Write a paragraph or two in which you discuss how in part (c) we have used inferential statistics to estimate the population (i.e., student body) distribution of loose change using a sample (i.e., our statistics class) from that population.

Using Technology

Raw Data

APPLICATION 1

Using the software or calculator available to you, do the following.

1. Trade winds are one of the beautiful features of island life in Hawaii. The following data represent total air movement in miles each day over a weather station in Hawaii as determined by a continuous anemometer recorder. The period of observation is January 1 to February 15, 1971.

26	14	18	14	113	50	13	22
27	57	28	50	72	52	105	138
16	33	18	16	32	26	11	16
17	14	57	100	35	20	21	34
18	13	18	28	21	13	25	19
11	19	22	19	15	20		

Source: United States Department of Commerce, National Oceanic and Atmospheric Administration, Environmental Data Service. *Climatological Data, Annual Summary, Hawaii,* Vol. 67, No. 13. Asheville: National Climatic Center, 1971, pp. 11, 24.

(a) Use the computer to find the sample mean, median, and (if it exists) mode. Also, find the range, sample variance, and sample standard deviation.

(b) Use the five-number summary provided by the computer to make a box-and-whisker plot of total air movement over the weather station.

(c) Four data values are exceptionally high: 113, 105, 138, and 100. The strong winds of January 5 (113 reading) brought in a cold front that dropped snow on Haleakala National Park (at the 8000 ft elevation). The residents were so excited that they drove up to see the snow and caused such a massive traffic jam that the Park

Service had to close the road. The winds of January 15 and 16 (readings 105 and 138) brought in a storm that created more damaging funnel clouds than any other storm to that date in the recorded history of Hawaii. The strong winds of January 28 (reading 100) accompanied a storm with funnel clouds that did much damage. Eliminate these values (i.e., 100, 105, 113, 138) from the data bank and redo parts (a) and (b). Compare your results with those previously obtained. Which average is most affected? What happens to the standard deviation? How do the two box-and-whisker plots compare?

(d) What is "normal" weather in a region? This is a relevant question, since climate is an important factor in agriculture, commerce, transportation, and tourism. The National Climate Data Center keeps temperature, moisture, wind, and other climate records. It establishes "climatic normals." A "climatic normal" is an arithmetic average of a meteorological element over 30 years. For more information, visit the Brase/Brase statistics site at **http://math.college.hmco.com/students** and find the links to NOAA (National Oceanic and Atmospheric Administration) and *USA Today*. Once at the NOAA site, use the index to find "climatic normals." At the *USA Today* site, select weather.

Technology Hints: Raw Data

TI-84Plus/TI-83Plus, Excel, Minitab

The Tech Note of Section 3.2 gives brief instructions for finding summary statistics for raw data using the TI-84Plus/TI-83Plus calculators, Excel, and Minitab. The Tech Note of Section 3.4 gives brief instructions for constructing box plots on the TI-84Plus/TI-83Plus calculators and in Minitab.

SPSS

Many commands in SPSS provide an option to display various summary statistics. A direct way to display summary statistics is to use the menu choices **Analyze** ➤ **Descriptive Statistics** ➤ **Descriptives.** In the dialogue box, move the variable containing your data into the variables box. Click **Options...** and then check the summary statistics you wish to display. Click Continue and then OK. Notice that the median is not available. A more complete list of summary statistics is available with the menu choices **Analyze** ➤ **Descriptive Statistics** ➤ **Frequencies.** Click the **Statistics** button and check the summary statistics you wish to display.

For box-and-whisker plots, use the menu options **Graphs** ➤ **Interactive** ➤ **Boxplot.** In the dialogue box, place the variable containing your data in the box along the vertical axis. After selecting options you want, click OK.

Grouped Data

APPLICATION 2

Using your software or calculator, do the following.

1. The summit of Longs Peak in Colorado (elevation 14,256 ft) is very beautiful, and in winter very austere. In the following data, x = hourly peak gusts in miles per hour of winter wind on the summit of Longs Peak and f = frequency of occurrence for a sample period of 1518 observation hours.
   (a) Using the class limits, compute each class midpoint. (*Hint:* Compute the first class midpoint. To get the others, just keep adding 10 to the previous class midpoint.)
   (b) Find the approximate sample mean, sample variance, and sample standard deviation of hourly peak gusts on the summit of Longs Peak.

Hourly Peak Gust, mph	Total Hours of Occurrence
0–9	141
10–19	217
20–29	376
30–39	290
40–49	195
50–59	143
60–69	61
70–79	37
80–89	21
90–99	11
100–109	12
110–119	3
120–129	5
130–139	3
140–149	3

(In addition to the values shown in the table, there were three incidences where the wind gusts exceeded 150 mph.)

Source: D. E. Glidden, *Winter Wind Studies in Rocky Mountain National Park.* Estes Park, Colo.: Rocky Mountain Nature Association, 1982, p. 23.

Technology Hints: Grouped Data

TI-84Plus/TI-83Plus

Enter midpoints in list L1 and frequencies in list L2. Then select 1-Var Stats for L1, L2. The final screen will give you the mean and standard deviation for the grouped data.

Excel, Minitab, and SPSS

Neither Excel nor Minitab nor SPSS gives results for grouped data directly. Those familiar with column operations and formula procedures can generate programs to find the mean and standard deviation for grouped data.

```
Grouped-Data Program for Minitab
MTB > # enter midpoints in C1
MTB > # enter frequencies in C2
MTB > SUM C2 put in K1
MTB > Let C3 = C1*C2
MTB > SUM C3 put in K2
MTB > NAME K3 = 'MEAN'
MTB > LET K3 = K2/K1
MTB > LET C4 = (C1 - K3)**2*C2
MTB > SUM C4 put in K4
MTB > LET K5 = SQRT(K4/(K1 - 1))
MTB > NAME K5 = 'STDEV'
MTB > PRINT K3, K5
```

In West Texas, water is extremely important. The following data represent pH levels in ground water for a random sample of 102 West Texas wells. A pH less than 7 is acidic and a pH above 7 is alkaline. Scanning the data, you can see that water in this region tends to be hard (alkaline). Too high a pH means the water is unusable or needs expensive treatment to make it useable (Reference: C. E. Nichols and V. E. Kane, Union Carbide Technical Report K/UR-1). These data are also available with other software on the statSpace CD-ROM. For convenience, the data are presented in increasing order.

x: pH of Ground Water in 102 West Texas Wells

7.0	7.0	7.0	7.0	7.0	7.0	7.0	7.0	7.1	7.1	7.1	7.1
7.1	7.1	7.1	7.1	7.1	7.1	7.2	7.2	7.2	7.2	7.2	7.2
7.2	7.2	7.2	7.2	7.3	7.3	7.3	7.3	7.3	7.3	7.3	7.3
7.3	7.3	7.3	7.4	7.4	7.4	7.4	7.4	7.4	7.4	7.4	7.4
7.5	7.5	7.5	7.5	7.5	7.5	7.5	7.5	7.6	7.6	7.6	7.6
7.6	7.6	7.6	7.6	7.6	7.7	7.7	7.7	7.7	7.7	7.7	7.8
7.8	7.8	7.8	7.8	7.9	7.9	7.9	7.9	7.9	8.0	8.1	8.1
8.1	8.1	8.1	8.1	8.1	8.2	8.2	8.2	8.2	8.2	8.2	8.2
8.4	8.5	8.6	8.7	8.8	8.8						

1. Write a brief description in which you outline how you would obtain a random sample of 102 West Texas water wells. Explain how random numbers would be used in the selection process.

2. Is the given data nominal, ordinal, interval, or ratio? Explain.

3. Make a stem-and-leaf display. Use five lines per stem so that leaf values 0 and 1 are on one line, 2 and 3 are on the next line, 4 and 5 are on the next, 6 and 7 are on the next, and 8 and 9 are on the last line of the stem.

4. Make a frequency table, histogram, relative-frequency histogram, and frequency polygon using five classes. Recall that for decimal data, we "clear the decimal" to determine classes for whole number data and then reinsert the decimal to obtain the classes for the frequency table of the original data.

5. Make an ogive using five classes.

6. Compute the range, mean, median, and mode for the given data.

7. Verify that $\Sigma x = 772.9$ and $\Sigma x^2 = 5876.6$.

8. Compute the sample variance, sample standard deviation, and coefficient of variation for the given data. Is the sample standard deviation small relative to the mean pH?

9. Compute a 75% Chebyshev interval centered on the mean.

10. Make a box-and-whisker plot. Find the interquartile range.

Summary

Wow! In Problems 1–10 you constructed a lot of information regarding the pH of West Texas ground water based on sample data. Let's continue the investigation.

11. Look at the histogram. Is the pH distribution for these wells symmetric or skewed? Are lower or higher values more common?

12. Look at the ogive. What percent of the wells have pH less than 8.15? Suppose a certain crop can tolerate irrigation water with a pH between 7.35 and 8.55. What percent of the wells could be used for such a crop?

13. Look at the stem-and-leaf plot. Are there any unusually high or low pH levels in this sample of wells? How many wells are neutral (pH of 7)?

14. Use the box-and-whisker plot to describe how the data are spread around the median. Are the pH values above the median more spread out than those below? Is this observation consistent with the skew of the histogram?

15. Suppose you are working for the regional water commissioner. You have been asked to submit a brief report about the pH level in ground water in the West Texas region. Write such a report and include appropriate graphs.

4

Elementary Probability Theory

We see that the theory of probabilities is at bottom only common sense reduced to calculation; it makes us appreciate with exactitude what reasonable minds feel by a sort of instinct, often without being able to account for it.

—Pierre-Simon Laplace

This is how the great mathematician Laplace described the theory of mathematical probability. The discovery of the mathematical theory of probability was shared by two Frenchmen: Blaise Pascal and Pierre Fermat. These seventeenth-century scholars were attracted to the subject by the inquiries of the Chevalier de Méré, a gentleman gambler.

Although the first applications of probability were to games of chance and gambling, today the subject seems to pervade almost every aspect of modern life. Everything from the orbits of spacecraft to the social behavior of woodchucks is described in terms of probabilities.

**Pierre-Simon Laplace
(1749–1827)**

This renowned French astronomer and mathematician wrote *The Analytical Theory of Probability.*

PREVIEW QUESTIONS

◇ Why would anyone study probability? *Hint:* Most big issues in life involve uncertainty.   (SECTION 4.1)

◇ What are the basic definitions and rules of probability? (SECTION 4.2)

◇ What are counting techniques, trees, permutations, and combinations?   (SECTION 4.3)

For on-line student resources, visit **math.college.hmco.com/students** and follow the Statistics links to the Brase/Brase, *Understandable Statistics*, 8th edition web site.

How Often Do Lie Detectors Lie?

James Burke is an educator who is known for his interesting science-related radio and television shows aired by the British Broadcasting Corporation. His book *Chances: Risk and Odds in Everyday Life* (Virginia Books, London) contains a great wealth of fascinating information about probabilities. The following quote is from Professor Burke's book:

> *If I take a polygraph test and lie, what is the risk I will be detected?* According to some studies there's about a 72 percent chance you will be caught by the machine.

> *What is the risk that if I take a polygraph test it will incorrectly say that I lied?* At least 1 in 15 will be thus falsely accused.

Both of these statements contain conditional probabilities, which we will study in Section 4.2. Information from that section will enable us to answer the following:

Suppose a person answers 10% of a long battery of questions with lies. Assume that the remaining 90% of the questions are answered truthfully.

1. Estimate the percentage of answers the polygraph will *wrongly* indicate as lies.

2. Estimate the percentage of answers the polygraph will *correctly* indicate as lies.

If the polygraph indicated that 30% of the questions were answered as lies, what would you estimate for the *actual* percentage of questions the person answered as lies? (See Problems 15 and 16 in Section 4.2.)

4.1
What Is Probability?

FOCUS POINTS

✓ Assign probabilities to events.
✓ Explain how the law of large numbers relates to relative frequencies.
✓ Apply basic rules of probability in everyday life.
✓ Explain the relationship between statistics and probability.

Basic concepts

We encounter statements in terms of probability all the time. An excited sports announcer claims that Sheila has a 90% chance of breaking the world record in the upcoming 100-yard dash. Henry figures that if he guesses on a true–false question, the probability of getting it right is 1/2. The Right to Health Lobby claims the probability is 0.40 of getting an erroneous report from a medical laboratory in one low-cost health center. It is consequently lobbying for a federal agency to license and monitor all medical laboratories.

When we use probability in a statement, we're using a *number between 0 and 1* to indicate the likelihood of an event. We'll use the notation $P(A)$ (read, "P of A") to denote the *probability of event A*. The closer to 1 the probability assignment is, the more likely the event is to occur. If the event A is certain to occur, then $P(A)$ is 1.

Probability is a numerical measure between 0 and 1 that describes the likelihood that an event will occur. Probabilities closer to 1 indicate that the event is more likely to occur. Probabilities closer to 0 indicate that the event is less likely to occur.

$P(A)$, read "P of A," denotes the **probability of event A.**
If $P(A) = 1$, the event A is certain to occur.
If $P(A) = 0$, the event A is certain not to occur.

It is important to know what probability statements mean and how to compute or assign probabilities to events, because probability is the language of inferential statistics. For instance, suppose a college counselor claims that 70% of first-year students receive counseling to help plan their schedules. Because of the high percentage of students needing help, he is requesting that an additional counselor be hired. You want to test the counselor's claim. In doing so, you pick a random sample of 30 first-year students and find that only 3 of them got help from a counselor. Can you challenge the counselor's claim on the basis of this random sample in which only 10% of the students got counselor help with their schedules? To answer this question, we need to find the *probability* of picking a random sample of first-year students in which only 10% got counselor help under the assumption that the counselor's claim is correct. This is the kind of question we will consider in hypothesis testing (Chapter 9).

In the meantime, we need to learn how to find probabilities or assign them to events. There are three major methods. One is *intuition*. The sports announcer probably used Sheila's performances in past track events and his own confidence in her running ability as a basis for his prediction that she has a 90% chance of breaking the world record. In other words, the announcer feels that the probability is 0.90 that Sheila will break the world record.

> **Probability assignment based on intuition** is a numerical estimate of the likelihood of an event using past experience, judgment, or opinion.

Relative frequency

The Right to Health Lobby used another method to arrive at its probability statement. It took the *relative frequency* with which erroneous laboratory reports occurred. From a random sample of $n = 100$, it found $f = 40$ erroneous laboratory reports. From this it computed the relative frequency of erroneous laboratory reports via Formula (1).

> **Probability formula for relative frequency**
>
> $$\text{Probability of an event} = \text{Relative frequency} = \frac{f}{n} \qquad (1)$$
>
> where f is the frequency of an event and n is the sample size.

In the case of the laboratory reports, we have

$$\text{Relative frequency} = \frac{f}{n} = \frac{40}{100} = 0.40$$

The relative frequency of erroneous laboratory reports was used as the *probability* of erroneous reports.

The technique of using the relative frequency of an event as the probability of that event is a common way of assigning probabilities and will be used a great deal in later chapters. The underlying assumption we make is that if events occurred a certain percentage of times in the past, they will occur about the same percentage of times in the future. In fact, this can be strengthened to a very general statement called the *law of large numbers*.

Law of large numbers

> **Law of large numbers**
>
> In the long run, as the sample size increases and increases, the relative frequencies of outcomes get closer and closer to the theoretical (or actual) probability value.

The law of large numbers is the reason such businesses as health insurance, automobile insurance, and gambling casinos can exist and make a profit. In Central City, Colorado, there are many casinos with many slot machines. The winnings of a gambler on a single play or even a few plays are uncertain (small sample size). This is one of the reasons gambling is exciting. However, on tens of thousands of plays, the theoretical or actual probability of winning favors the casino. That's why the casino and its owners regard gambling as a business. The house is guaranteed a profit in the long run.

Henry used the third method of assigning probabilities when he determined the probability of correctly guessing the answer to a true–false question. Essentially, he used the probability formula for *equally likely outcomes*.

Equally likely outcomes

Probability formula when outcomes are equally likely

$$\text{Probability of an event} = \frac{\text{Number of outcomes favorable to event}}{\text{Total number of outcomes}} \qquad (2)$$

In Henry's case, there are two possible outcomes. A test answer will be either correct or incorrect. Since he is guessing, we assume that the outcomes are equally likely, and only one is "favorable" to being correct. So, by Formula (2),

$$P(\text{correct answer}) = \frac{\text{Number of favorable outcomes}}{\text{Total number of outcomes}}$$

$$= \frac{1}{2}$$

We've seen three ways to assign probabilities: intuition, relative frequency, and—when outcomes are equally likely—a formula. Which do we use? Most of the time it depends on the information that is at hand or that can be feasibly obtained. Our choice of methods also depends on the particular problem. In Guided Exercise 1, you will see three different situations, and you will decide which way to assign the probabilities. *Remember, probabilities are numbers between 0 and 1, so don't assign probabilities outside this range.*

GUIDED EXERCISE 1

Determine a probability

Assign a probability to the indicated event on the basis of the information provided. Indicate the technique you use: intuition, relative frequency, or the formula for equally likely outcomes.

(a) The director of the Readlot College Health Center wishes to open an eye clinic. To justify the expense of such a clinic, she reports the probability that a student selected at random from the college roster needs corrective lenses. The director took a random sample of 500 students to compute this probability and found that 375 of them needed corrective lenses. What is the probability that a Readlot College student selected at random needs corrective lenses?

⟹ In this case we are given a sample size of 500, and we are told that 375 of these students need glasses. It is appropriate to use a relative frequency for the desired probability:

$$P(\text{student needs glasses}) = \frac{f}{n}$$

$$= \frac{375}{500}$$

$$= 0.75$$

Continued

(b) The Friends of the Library host a fund-raising barbecue. George is on the cleanup committee. There are four members on this committee, and they draw lots to see who will clean the grills. Assuming that each member is equally likely to be drawn, what is the probability that George will be assigned the grill-cleaning job?

⇒ There are four people on the committee, and each is equally likely to be drawn. It is appropriate to use the formula for equally likely events. George can be drawn in only one way, so there is only one outcome favorable to the event.

$$P(\text{George}) = \frac{\text{No. of favorable outcomes}}{\text{Total no. of outcomes}}$$

$$= \frac{1}{4}$$

$$= 0.25$$

(c) Joanna photographs whales for Sea Life Adventure Films. On her next expedition, she is to film blue whales feeding. Her boss asks her what she thinks the probability of success will be for this particular assignment. She gives an answer based on her knowledge of the habits of blue whales and the region she is to visit. She is almost certain she will be successful. What specific number do you suppose she gave for the probability of success, and how do you suppose she arrived at it?

⇒ Since Joanna is almost certain of success, she should make the probability close to 1. We would say $P(\text{success})$ is above 0.90 but less than 1. It is likely the probability assignment was based on intuition.

No matter how we compute probabilities, it is useful to know what outcomes are possible in a given setting. For instance, if you are going to decide the probability that Hardscrabble will win the Kentucky Derby, you need to know which other horses will be running.

Statistical experiment

To determine the possible outcomes for a given setting, we need to define a *statistical experiment*.

> A **statistical experiment** or **statistical observation** can be thought of as any random activity that results in a definite outcome.
>
> An **event** is a collection of one or more outcomes of a statistical experiment or observation.
>
> A **simple event** is an outcome of a statistical experiment that consists of one and only one of the outcomes of the experiment.
>
> The set of all simple events constitutes the **sample space** of an experiment.

Sample space

Usually the outcome of a statistical experiment or statistical observation is in the form of a description, count, or measurement. For example, tossing a coin can be thought of as an experiment. There are only two possible outcomes: heads or tails. These are the simple events of this experiment. The sample space for tossing a coin consists of the two simple events, heads or tails.

It is especially convenient to know the sample space in the case where all outcomes are equally likely, because then we can compute probabilities of various events by using Formula (2).

$$P(\text{event } A) = \frac{\text{Number of outcomes favorable to } A}{\text{Total number of outcomes}} \qquad (2)$$

To use this formula, we need to know the sample space so that we can determine which outcomes are favorable to the event in question as well as the total number of outcomes.

EXAMPLE 1
Using a sample space

Human eye color is controlled by a single pair of genes (one from the father and one from the mother) called a *genotype*. Brown eye color, B, is dominant over blue eye color, ℓ. Therefore, in the genotype Bℓ, consisting of one brown gene B and one blue gene ℓ, the brown gene dominates. A person with a Bℓ genotype has brown eyes.

If both parents have brown eyes and have genotype Bℓ, what is the probability that their child will have blue eyes? What is the probability the child will have brown eyes?

SOLUTION: To answer these questions, we need to look at the sample space of all possible eye-color genotypes for the child. They are given in Table 4-1.

According to genetics theory, the four possible genotypes for the child are equally likely. Therefore, we can use Formula (2) to compute probabilities. Blue eyes can occur only with the $\ell\ell$ genotype, so there is only one outcome favorable to blue eyes. By Formula (2),

TABLE 4-1   Eye Color Genotypes for Child

Father	Mother	
	B	ℓ
B	BB	Bℓ
ℓ	ℓB	$\ell\ell$

$$P(\text{blue eyes}) = \frac{\text{Number of favorable outcomes}}{\text{Total number of outcomes}} = \frac{1}{4}$$

Brown eyes occur with the three remaining genotypes: BB, Bℓ, and ℓB. By Formula (2),

$$P(\text{brown eyes}) = \frac{\text{Number of favorable outcomes}}{\text{Total number of outcomes}} = \frac{3}{4} \qquad \Diamond$$

GUIDED EXERCISE 2

Using a sample space

Professor Gutierrez is making up a final exam for a course in literature of the Southwest. He wants the last three questions to be of the true–false type. To guarantee that the answers do not follow his favorite pattern, he lists all possible true–false combinations for three questions on slips of paper and then picks one at random from a hat.

Continued

GUIDED EXERCISE 2 continued

(a) Finish listing the outcomes in the given sample space.

| TTT | FTT | TFT | _____ |
| TTF | FTF | TFF | _____ |

⟹ The missing outcomes are FFT and FFF.

(b) What is the probability that all three items will be false? Use the formula

$$P(\text{all F}) = \frac{\text{No. of favorable outcomes}}{\text{Total no. of outcomes}}$$

⟹ There is only one outcome, FFF, favorable to all false, so

$$P(\text{all F}) = \frac{1}{8}$$

(c) What is the probability that exactly two items will be true?

⟹ There are three outcomes that have exactly two true items: TTF, TFT, and FTT. Thus,

$$P(\text{two T}) = \frac{\text{No. of favorable outcomes}}{\text{Total no. of outcomes}} = \frac{3}{8}$$

There is another important point about probability assignments of simple events.

The **sum** of the probabilities of all simple events in a sample space must equal 1.

We can use this fact to determine the probability that an event will not occur. For instance, if you think the probability is 0.65 that you will win a tennis match, you assume the probability is 0.35 that your opponent will win.

Complement of an event

The *complement* of an event A is the event that A *does not occur*. We use the notation A^c to designate the complement of event A. Figure 4-1 shows the event A and its complement A^c.

Notice that the two distinct events A and A^c make up the entire sample space. Therefore, the sum of their probabilities is 1.

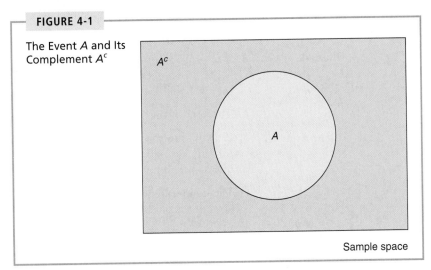

FIGURE 4-1

The Event A and Its Complement A^c

The **complement of event** A is the event that A *does not occur*. A^c designates the complement of event A. Furthermore,

1. $P(A) + P(A^c) = 1$

2. $P(\text{event } A \text{ does } not \text{ occur}) = P(A^c) = 1 - P(A)$ (3)

EXAMPLE 2

Complement of an event

The probability that a college student without a flu shot will get the flu is 0.45. What is the probability that a college student will *not* get the flu if the student has not had the flu shot?

SOLUTION: In this case, we have

$P(\text{will get flu}) = 0.45$

$P(\text{will } not \text{ get flu}) = 1 - P(\text{will get flu}) = 1 - 0.45 = 0.55$ ◇

GUIDED EXERCISE 3

Complement of an event

A veterinarian tells you that if you breed two cream-colored guinea pigs, the probability that an offspring will be pure white is 0.25. What is the probability that an offspring will not be pure white?

(a) $P(\text{pure white}) + P(not \text{ pure white}) = $ _____   ⟹   1

(b) $P(not \text{ pure white}) = $ _____   ⟹ $1 - 0.25$, or 0.75

Summary: Some important facts about probability

1. A **statistical experiment** or **statistical observation** is any random activity that results in a definite outcome. A **simple event** consists of one and only one outcome of the experiment. The **sample space** is the set of all simple events. An **event** A is any subset of the sample space.

2. The probability of an event A is denoted by $P(A)$.

3. The probability of an event is a number between 0 and 1. The closer to 1 the probability is, the more likely the event will occur. The closer to 0 the probability is, the less likely the event will occur.

4. The sum of the probabilities of all simple events in the sample space is 1.

5. Probabilities can be assigned by using intuition, relative frequencies, or the formula for equally likely outcomes. Additional ways to assign probabilities will be introduced in later chapters.

6. The **complement** of an event A is denoted A^c. So, A^c is the event that A does not occur.

7. $P(A) + P(A^c) = 1$

Probability Related to Statistics

We conclude this section with a few comments on the nature of statistics versus probability. Although statistics and probability are closely related fields of mathematics, they are nevertheless separate fields. It can be said that probability is the medium through which statistical work is done. In fact, if it were not for probability theory, inferential statistics would not be possible.

Put very briefly, probability is the field of study that makes statements about what will occur when samples are drawn from a *known population*. Statistics is the field of study that describes how samples are to be obtained and how inferences are to be made about *unknown populations*.

A simple but effective illustration of the difference between these two subjects can be made by considering how we treat the following examples:

Example of a probability application

Condition: We *know* the exact makeup of the *entire* population.
Example: Given 3 green marbles, 5 red marbles, and 4 white marbles in a bag, draw 6 marbles at random from the bag. What is the probability none of the marbles is red?

Example of a statistical application

Condition: We have only *samples* from an otherwise *unknown* population.
Example: Draw a random sample of 6 marbles from the (unknown) population of all marbles in a bag and observe the colors. Based on the sample results, make a conjecture about the colors and numbers of marbles in the entire population of all marbles in the bag.

In another sense, probability and statistics are like flip sides of the same coin. On the probability side, you know the overall description of the population. The central problem is to compute the likelihood that a specific outcome will happen. On the statistics side, you know only the results of a sample drawn from the population. The central problem is to describe the sample (descriptive statistic) and to draw conclusions about the population based on the sample results (inferential statistics).

In statistical work, the inferences we draw about an unknown population are not claimed to be absolutely correct. Since the population remains unknown (in a theoretical sense), we must accept a "best guess" for our conclusions and act using the most probable answer rather than absolute certainty.

Probability is the topic of this chapter. However, we will not study probability just for its own sake. Probability is a wonderful field of mathematics, but we will study mainly the ideas from probability that are needed for a proper understanding of statistics.

Salmon moving upstream

Even though we have only a brief introduction to probability, we will be able to answer questions raised in situations such as the following:

- Commercial salmon fishing is very important in Alaska. Since the salmon are sold by weight, it is useful to know the average weight of a freshly caught salmon. How large a sample of freshly caught salmon is needed if we want to be 95% sure that the mean weight of the sample is within plus or minus 1 ounce of the mean weight of all catchable salmon in Alaskan waters? For the answer to this type of question, see Example 6 in Section 8.4, in which we discuss probability as applied to sample size.

- Retail sales account for about two-thirds of all the money flow in the U.S. economy. For their first job after graduation, many college graduates are either in sales or in charge of a sales team. Whether you are a salesperson or in charge of a sales team, *sales quotas* are important. Suppose you are a bond broker and your job is to sell a particular bond issue by phone. History shows that the probability is about 20% that any one phone call will result in a bond sale. Your sales supervisor claims that you should make at least nine sales each day. How many phone calls should you make if you want to be 99% sure of getting your nine sales? For the answer to this type of question, see Section 5.3, in which we discuss probabilities and quota problems.

- Many practical situations call on us to choose between two competing statements. *Consumer Reports* did a study on the maintenance records of two competing brands of cellular phones. Each brand claims to have the lowest maintenance costs. Is one brand actually better than the other? If there is an apparent difference, is the difference statistically significant at, say, a 1% level (of risk)? For answers to these kinds of questions, see Section 9.5, in which we discuss tests for differences.

All the listed examples require some use of probability. This is why we encourage you to study this chapter carefully. Your time in doing so will be well invested.

VIEWPOINT

What Makes a Good Teacher?

A survey of 735 students at nine colleges in the United States was taken to determine instructor behaviors that help students succeed. Data from this survey can be found by visiting the Brase/Brase statistics site at **http://math.college. hmco.com/students** and finding the link to DASL, the Carnegie Mellon University Data and Story Library. Once at the DASL site, select Data Subjects, then Psychology, and then Instructor Behavior. You can estimate the probability of how a student would respond (very positive, neutral, very negative) to different instructor behaviors. For example, more than 90% of the students responded "very positive" to the instructor's use of real-world examples in the classroom.

SECTION 4.1   PROBLEMS

1. *General: Concepts* In your own words, carefully answer the question: What is probability? List three methods of assigning probabilities.

2. *General: Provide Examples* List examples of how probability might be applied in business, medicine, social science, and natural science. Identify some ways that probability will be useful in the study of statistics.

3. *General: Valid Probabilities* Which of the following numbers cannot be the probability of some event?

   (a) 0.71   (b) 4.1   (c) $\frac{1}{8}$ (d) -0.5

   (e) 0.5   (f) 0   (g) 1   (h) 150%

4. *General: Valid Probabilities*
   (a) Explain why -0.41 cannot be the probability of some event.
   (b) Explain why 1.21 cannot be the probability of some event.
   (c) Explain why 120% cannot be the probability of some event.
   (d) Can the number 0.56 be the probability of an event? Explain.

5. *Probability Estimate: Wiggle Your Ears* Can you wiggle your ears? Use the students in your statistics class (or a group of friends) to estimate the percentage of people who can wiggle their ears. How can your result be thought of as an estimate for the probability that a person chosen at random can wiggle his or her ears? *Comment:* National statistics indicate that about 13% of Americans can wiggle their ears (Source: Bernice Kanner, *Are You Normal?*, St. Martin's Press, New York).

6. *Probability Estimate: Raise One Eyebrow* Can you raise one eyebrow at a time? Use the students in your statistics class (or a group of friends) to estimate the percentage of people who can raise one eyebrow at a time. How can your result be thought of as an estimate for the probability that a person chosen at random can raise one eyebrow at a time? *Comment:* National statistics indicate that about 30% of Americans can raise one eyebrow at a time (see source in Problem 5).

7. *Myers–Briggs: Personality Types* Isabel Briggs Myers was a pioneer in the study of personality types. The personality types are broadly defined according to four main preferences. Do married couples choose similar or different personality types in their mates? The following data give an indication (Source: I. B. Myers and M. H. McCaulley, *A Guide to the Development and Use of the Myers–Briggs Type Indicators*).

Similarities and Differences in a Random Sample of 375 Married Couples

Number of Similar Preferences	Number of Married Couples
All four	34
Three	131
Two	124
One	71
None	15

Suppose that a married couple is selected at random.

(a) Use the data to estimate the probability that they will have 0, 1, 2, 3, or 4 personality preferences in common.

(b) Do the probabilities add up to 1? Why should they? What is the sample space in this problem?

8. *Sociology: Dating Couples* Do couples get engaged or not? If they are engaged, how long did they date before becoming engaged? A poll of 1000 couples conducted by Bruskin and Goldring Research for Korbel Champagne Cellars gave the following information (*USA Today*):

Length of Dating Time Before Engagement

Time	Number of Couples
Never engaged	200
Less than 1 year	240
1 to 2 years	210
More than 2 years	350

(a) Use the data to estimate the probability of each event for a dating couple chosen at random: The couple is not engaged, dated less than 1 year before getting engaged, dated 1 to 2 years before getting engaged, or dated more than 2 years before getting engaged.

(b) Do the probabilities of part (a) add up to 1? Why should they? What is the sample space in this problem?

9. *Psychology: Creativity* When do creative people get their *best* ideas? *USA Today* did a survey of 966 inventors (who hold U.S. patents) and obtained the following information:

Time of Day When Best Ideas Occur

Time	Number of Inventors
6 A.M.–12 noon	290
12 noon–6 P.M.	135
6 P.M.–12 midnight	319
12 midnight–6 A.M.	222

(a) Assuming that the time interval includes the left limit and all the times up to but not including the right limit, estimate the probability that an inventor has a best idea during each time interval: from 6 A.M. to 12 noon, from 12 noon to 6 P.M., from 6 P.M. to 12 midnight, from 12 midnight to 6 A.M.

(b) Do the probabilities of part (a) add up to 1? Why should they? What is the sample space in this problem?

10. *General: Roll a Die*

(a) If you roll a single die and count the number of dots on top, what is the sample space of all possible outcomes? Are the outcomes equally likely?

(b) Assign probabilities to the outcomes of the sample space of part (a). Do the probabilities add up to 1? Should they add up to 1? Explain.

(c) What is the probability of getting a number less than 5 on a single throw?

(d) What is the probability of getting 5 or 6 on a single throw?

11. *Health Care: Flu* "Oh, leave me alone!" How do people want to be treated when they have the flu? A Sterling Health poll of 1000 people gave the following information (*USA Today*).

Want to Be . . .	Number of People
Left alone	770
Waited on hand and foot	160
Treated differently	70

(a) Consider the events: want to be left alone, want to be waited on hand and foot, want to be treated differently. Do these events form a sample space for the way people who have the flu wish to be treated? Use relative frequencies to assign probabilities to these events. Do the probabilities add up to 1? Why should they?

(b) Find the probability of the event "do *not* want to be left alone." Find the probability of the event "do *not* want to be waited on hand and foot."

12. *Agriculture: Cotton* A botanist has developed a new hybrid cotton plant that can withstand insects better than other cotton plants. However, there is some concern about the germination of seeds from the new plant. To estimate the probability that a seed from the new plant will germinate, a random sample of 3000 seeds was planted in warm, moist soil. Of these seeds, 2430 germinated.

(a) Use relative frequencies to estimate the probability that a seed will germinate. What is your estimate?

(b) Use relative frequencies to estimate the probability that a seed will *not* germinate. What is your estimate?

(c) Either a seed germinates, or it does not. What is the sample space in this problem? Do the probabilities assigned to the sample space add up to 1? Should they add up to 1? Explain.

(d) Are the outcomes in the sample space of part (c) equally likely?

13. *Expand Your Knowledge: Odds in Favor* Sometimes probability statements are expressed in terms of *odds*.

The *odds in favor* of an event A is the ratio $\dfrac{P(A)}{P(not\ A)} = \dfrac{P(A)}{P(A^c)}$.

For instance, if $P(A) = 0.60$, then $P(A^c) = 0.40$ and the odds in favor of A are

$\dfrac{0.60}{0.40} = \dfrac{6}{4} = \dfrac{3}{2}$, written as 3 to 2 or 3:2.

(a) Show that if we are given the *odds in favor* of event A as $n{:}m$, the probability of event A is given by $P(A) = \dfrac{n}{n+m}$. *Hint:* Solve the equation $\dfrac{n}{m} = \dfrac{P(A)}{1 - P(A)}$ for $P(A)$.

(b) A telemarketing supervisor tells a new worker that the odds of making a sale on a single call are 2 to 15. What is the probability of a successful call?

(c) A sports announcer says that the odds a basketball player will make a free throw shot are 3 to 5. What is the probability the player will make the shot?

14. *Expand Your Knowledge: Betting Odds Against* Betting odds are usually stated *against* the event happening (against winning).

The odds *against* event W is the ratio $\dfrac{P(not\ W)}{P(W)} = \dfrac{P(W^c)}{P(W)}$.

In horse racing, the betting odds are based on the probability that the horse does *not* win.

(a) Show that if we are given the odds *against* an event W as *a:b*, the probability of *not* W is $P(W^c) = \dfrac{a}{a+b}$. *Hint:* Solve the equation $\dfrac{a}{b} = \dfrac{P(W^c)}{1 - P(W^c)}$ for $P(W^c)$.

(b) In a recent Kentucky Derby, the betting odds for the favorite horse, Point Given, were 9 to 5. Use these odds to compute the probability that Point Given would lose the race. What is the probability that Point Given would win the race?

(c) In the same race, the betting odds for the horse Monarchos were 6 to 1. Use these odds to estimate the probability that Monarchos would lose the race. What is the probability that Monarchos would win the race?

(d) Invisible Ink was a long shot, with betting odds of 30 to 1. Use these odds to estimate the probability that Invisible Ink would lose the race. What is the probability the horse would win the race? For further information on the Kentucky Derby, visit the Brase/Brase statistics site at **http://math.college.hmco.com/students** and find the link to the Kentucky Derby.

15. *Business: Customers* John runs a computer software store. Yesterday he counted 127 people who walked by his store, 58 of whom came into the store. Of the 58, only 25 bought something in the store.

(a) Estimate the probability that a person who walks by the store will enter the store.

(b) Estimate the probability that a person who walks into the store will buy something.

(c) Estimate the probability that a person who walks by the store will come in *and* buy something.

(d) Estimate the probability that a person who comes into the store will buy nothing.

4.2
Some Probability Rules—Compound Events

Conditional Probability and Multiplication Rules

FOCUS POINTS

✔ Compute probabilities of general compound events.

✔ Compute probabilities involving independent events or mutually exclusive events.

✔ Use survey results to compute conditional probabilities.

You roll two dice. What is the probability that you will get a 5 on each die? You draw two cards from a well-shuffled, standard deck without replacing the first card before drawing the second. What is the probability that they will both be aces?

It seems that these two problems are nearly alike. They are alike in the sense that in each case you are to find the probability of two events occurring *together*. In the first problem, you are to find

P(5 on 1st die *and* 5 on 2nd die)

In the second, you want

P(ace on 1st card *and* ace on 2nd card)

The two problems differ in one important aspect, however. In the dice problem, the outcome of a 5 on the first die does not have any effect on the probability of getting a 5 on the second die. Because of this, the events are *independent*.

Independent events

> Two events are **independent** if the occurrence or nonoccurrence of one does *not* change the probability that the other will occur.

In the card problem, the probability of an ace on the first card is 4/52, since there are 52 cards in the deck and 4 of them are aces. If you get an ace on the first card, then the probability of an ace on the second is changed to 3/51, because one ace has already been drawn and only 51 cards remain in the deck. Therefore, the two events in the card-draw problem are *not* independent. They are, in fact, *dependent,* since the outcome of the first draw changes the probability of getting an ace on the second draw.

Probability of A and B

Why does the *independence* or *dependence* of two events matter? The type of events determines the way we compute the probability of the two events happening together. If two events A and B are *independent,* then we use Formula (4) to compute the probability of the event A and B:

Multiplication rule for independent events

$$P(A \text{ and } B) = P(A) \cdot P(B) \tag{4}$$

Conditional probability

If the events are *dependent,* then we must take into account the changes in the probability of one event caused by the occurrence of the other event. The notation $P(A, given B)$ denotes the probability that event A will occur, *given* that event B has occurred. This is called a *conditional probability.* We read $P(A, given B)$ as "probability of A given B." If A and B are dependent events, then $P(A) \neq P(A, given B)$ because the occurrence of event B has changed the probability that event A will occur. A standard notation for $P(A, given B)$ is $P(A \mid B)$. However, we will use the more expanded notation $P(A, given B)$ to remind you that we assume that event B has already occurred. In Appendix I, where Bayes's theorem is discussed, we will revert to the more standard notation $P(A \mid B)$. We use either Formula (5) or Formula (6) to compute the probability of A and B when the events A and B are dependent.

General multiplication rule for any events

$$P(A \text{ and } B) = P(A) \cdot P(B, given \text{ that } A \text{ has occurred}) \tag{5}$$
$$P(A \text{ and } B) = P(B) \cdot P(A, given \text{ that } B \text{ has occurred}) \tag{6}$$

We will use either Formula (5) or Formula (6) according to the information available.

Formulas (4), (5), and (6) constitute the *multiplication rules* of probability. They help us compute the probability of events happening together when the sample space is too large for convenient reference or when it is not completely known.

Note: For conditional probability, observe that the multiplication rule

$$P(A \text{ and } B) = P(B) \cdot P(A, given B)$$

can be solved for $P(A, given B)$, leading to

Conditional probability (when $P(B) \neq 0$)

$$P(A, given B) = \frac{P(A \text{ and } B)}{P(B)}$$

Conditional probability is often designated $P(A \mid B)$.

We will see some applications of this formula in later chapters.

Let's use the multiplication rules to complete the dice and card problems. We'll compare the results with those obtained by using the sample space directly.

EXAMPLE 3
Multiplication rule

Suppose you are going to throw two fair dice. What is the probability of getting a 5 on each die?

SOLUTION USING THE MULTIPLICATION RULE: The two events are independent, so we should use Formula (4). $P(5$ on 1st die *and* 5 on 2nd die$) = P(5$ on 1st$) \cdot P(5$ on 2nd$)$. To finish the problem, we need only compute the probability of getting a 5 when we throw one die.

There are six faces on a die, and on a fair die each is equally likely to come up when you throw the die. Only one face has five dots, so by Formula (2) for equally likely outcomes,

$$P(5 \text{ on die}) = \frac{1}{6}$$

Now we can complete the calculation.

$$P(5 \text{ on 1st die } and \text{ 5 on 2nd die}) = P(5 \text{ on 1st}) \cdot P(5 \text{ on 2nd})$$
$$= \frac{1}{6} \cdot \frac{1}{6} = \frac{1}{36}$$

SOLUTION USING SAMPLE SPACE: The first task is to write down the sample space. Each die has six equally likely outcomes, and each outcome of the second die can be paired with each of the first. The sample space is shown in Figure 4-2. The total number of outcomes is 36, and only one is favorable to a 5 on the first die *and* a 5 on the second. The 36 outcomes are equally likely, so by Formula (2) for equally likely outcomes,

$$P(5 \text{ on 1st } and \text{ on 2nd}) = \frac{1}{36}$$

The two methods yield the same result. The multiplication rule was easier to use because we did not need to look at all 36 outcomes in the sample space for tossing two dice.   ◊

FIGURE 4-2

Sample Space for Two Dice

EXAMPLE 4

Dependent events

Compute the probability of drawing two aces from a well-shuffled deck of 52 cards if the first card is not replaced before the second card is drawn.

MULTIPLICATION RULE METHOD: These events are *dependent*. The probability of an ace on the first draw is 4/52, but on the second draw the probability of an ace is only 3/51 if an ace was drawn for the first card. An ace on the first draw changes the probability for an ace on the second draw. By the multiplication rule for dependent events,

$$P(\text{ace on 1st } and \text{ ace on 2nd}) = P(\text{ace on 1st}) \cdot P(\text{ace on 2nd}, given \text{ ace on 1st})$$

$$= \frac{4}{52} \cdot \frac{3}{51} = \frac{12}{2652} \approx 0.0045$$

SAMPLE SPACE METHOD: We won't actually look at the sample space because each of the 51 possible outcomes for the second card must be paired with each of the 52 possible outcomes for the first card. This gives us a total of 2652 outcomes in the sample space! We'll just think about the sample space and try to list all the outcomes favorable to the event of aces on both cards. The 12 favorable outcomes are shown in Figure 4-3. By the formula for equally likely outcomes,

$$P(\text{ace on 1st card } and \text{ ace on 2nd card}) = \frac{12}{2652} \approx 0.0045$$

Again, the two methods agree.   ◊

FIGURE 4-3

Outcomes Favorable to
Drawing Two Aces

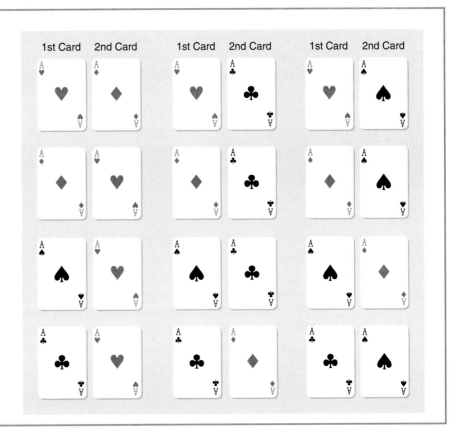

The multiplication rules apply whenever we wish to determine the probability of two events happening *together*. To indicate together, we use *and* between the events. But before you use a multiplication rule to compute the probability of *A* and *B*, you must determine if *A* and *B* are independent or dependent events.

> **PROCEDURE**
>
> **How to use the multiplication rules**
>
> 1. First determine whether *A* and *B* are independent events.
>   If $P(A) = P(A, \text{given } B)$, then the events are independent.
>
> 2. If *A* and *B* are independent events,
>
> $$P(A \text{ and } B) = P(A) \cdot P(B) \tag{4}$$
>
> 3. If *A* and *B* are any events,
>
> $$P(A \text{ and } B) = P(A) \cdot P(B, \text{given } A) \tag{5}$$
> $$\text{or} \quad P(A \text{ and } B) = P(B) \cdot P(A, \text{given } B) \tag{6}$$

Let's practice using the multiplication rule.

GUIDED EXERCISE 4

Multiplication rule

Andrew is 55, and the probability that he will be alive in 10 years is 0.72. Ellen is 35, and the probability that she will be alive in 10 years is 0.92. Assuming that the life span of one will have no effect on the life span of the other, what is the probability they will both be alive in 10 years?

(a) Are these events dependent or independent?

⇒ Since the life span of one does not affect the life span of the other, the events are independent.

(b) Use the appropriate multiplication rule to find *P*(Andrew alive in 10 years *and* Ellen alive in 10 years).

⇒ We use the rule for independent events:

$P(A \text{ and } B) = P(A) \cdot P(B)$

P(Andrew alive *and* Ellen alive)

$= P(\text{Andrew alive}) \cdot P(\text{Ellen alive})$

$= (0.72)(0.92) \approx 0.66$

GUIDED EXERCISE 5

Dependent events

A quality-control procedure for testing Ready-Flash disposable cameras consists of drawing two cameras at random from each lot of 100 without replacing the first camera before drawing the

Continued

GUIDED EXERCISE 5 continued

second. If both are defective, the entire lot is rejected. Find the probability that both cameras are defective if the lot contains 10 defective cameras. Since we are drawing the cameras at random, assume that each camera in the lot has an equal chance of being drawn.

(a) What is the probability of getting a defective camera on the first draw?

⟹ The sample space consists of all 100 cameras. Since each is equally likely to be drawn and there are 10 defective ones,

$$P(\text{defective camera}) = \frac{10}{100} = \frac{1}{10}$$

(b) The first camera drawn is not replaced, so there are only 99 cameras for the second draw. What is the probability of getting a defective camera on the second draw if the first camera was defective?

⟹ If the first camera is defective, then there are only 9 defective cameras left among the 99 remaining cameras in the lot.

$P(\text{defective camera on 2nd draw, }given$

$\text{defective camera on 1st}) = \frac{9}{99} = \frac{1}{11}$

(c) Are the probabilities computed in parts (a) and (b) different? Does drawing a defective camera on the first draw change the probability of getting a defective camera on the second draw? Are the events dependent?

⟹ The answer to all these questions is yes.

(d) Use the formula for dependent events,

$P(A \text{ and } B) = P(A) \cdot P(B, given A \text{ has occurred})$

to compute P(1st camera defective *and* 2nd camera defective).

⟹ $P(\text{1st defective }and\text{ 2nd defective}) = \frac{1}{10} \cdot \frac{1}{11}$

$$= \frac{1}{110}$$

$$\approx 0.009$$

More than two independent events

The multiplication rule for independent events extends to more than two independent events. If you toss a fair coin, then roll a fair die, and finally draw a card from a standard deck of bridge cards, the three events are independent. To compute the probability of the outcome heads on the coin *and* 5 on the die *and* an ace for the card, we use the extended multiplication rule for independent events together with the facts

$$P(\text{head}) = \frac{1}{2}, P(5) = \frac{1}{6}, P(\text{ace}) = \frac{4}{52} = \frac{1}{13}$$

Then

$$P(\text{head }and\text{ 5 }and\text{ ace}) = \frac{1}{2} \cdot \frac{1}{6} \cdot \frac{1}{13}$$

$$= \frac{1}{156}$$

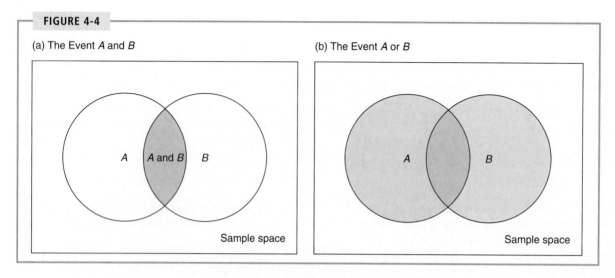

FIGURE 4-4

(a) The Event *A* and *B*

(b) The Event *A* or *B*

Addition Rules

One of the multiplication rules can be used any time we are trying to find the probability of two events happening *together*. Pictorially, we are looking for the probability of the shaded region in Figure 4-4(a).

Probability of A or B

Another way to combine events is to consider the possibility of one event *or* another occurring. For instance, if a sports car saleswoman gets an extra bonus if she sells a convertible or a car with leather upholstery, she is interested in the probability that you will buy a car that is a convertible *or* has leather upholstery. Of course, if you bought a convertible with leather upholstery, that would be fine, too. Pictorially, the shaded portion of Figure 4-4(b) represents the outcomes satisfying the *or* condition. Notice that the condition *A or B* is satisfied by any one of the following conditions:

1. Any outcome in *A* occurs.

2. Any outcome in *B* occurs.

3. Any outcome in both *A* and *B* occurs.

It is important to distinguish between the *or* combinations and the *and* combinations because we apply different rules to compute their probabilities.

GUIDED EXERCISE 6

Combining events

Indicate how each of the following pairs of events are combined. Use either the *and* combination or the *or* combination.

(a) Satisfying the humanities requirement by taking a course in the history of Japan or by taking a course in classical literature

 Use the *or* combination.

Continued

GUIDED EXERCISE 6 continued

(b) Buying new tires and aligning the tires   ⇨   Use the *and* combination.

(c) Getting an A not only in psychology but also in   ⇨   Use the *and* combination.
    biology

(d) Having at least one of these pets: cat, dog, bird,   ⇨   Use the *or* combination.
    rabbit

Once you decide that you are to find the probability of an *or* combination rather than an *and* combination, what formula do you use? Again, it depends on the situation. If you want to compute the probability of drawing either a jack or a king on a single draw from a well-shuffled deck of cards, the formula is simple:

$$P(\text{jack } or \text{ king}) = P(\text{jack}) + P(\text{king}) = \frac{4}{52} + \frac{4}{52} = \frac{8}{52} = \frac{2}{13}$$

since there are 4 jacks and 4 kings in a deck of 52 cards.

If you want to compute the probability of drawing a king or a diamond on a single draw, the formula is a bit more complicated. We have to take the overlap of the two events into account so that we do not count the outcomes twice. We can see the overlap of the two events in Figure 4-5.

$$P(\text{king}) = \frac{4}{52} \quad P(\text{diamond}) = \frac{13}{52} \quad P(\text{king } and \text{ diamond}) = \frac{1}{52}$$

FIGURE 4-5

Drawing a King or a
Diamond from a
Standard Deck

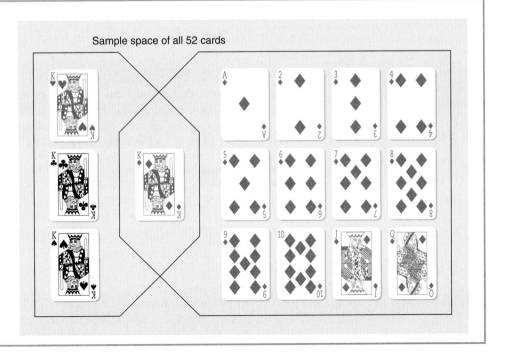

Sample space of all 52 cards

If we simply add $P(\text{king})$ and $P(\text{diamond})$, we're including $P(\text{king } and \text{ diamond})$ twice in the sum. To compensate for this double summing, we simply subtract $P(\text{king } and \text{ diamond})$ from the sum. Therefore,

$$P(\text{king } or \text{ diamond}) = P(\text{king}) + P(\text{diamond}) - P(\text{king } and \text{ diamond})$$

$$= \frac{4}{52} + \frac{13}{52} - \frac{1}{52}$$

$$= \frac{16}{52} = \frac{4}{13}$$

Mutually exclusive events

We say the events A and B are *mutually exclusive* or *disjoint* if they cannot occur together. This means that A and B have no outcomes in common or, put another way, that $P(A \text{ } and \text{ } B) = 0$.

> Two events are **mutually exclusive** or **disjoint** if they cannot occur together. In particular, events A and B are mutually exclusive if $P(A \text{ } and \text{ } B) = 0$.

Formula (7) is the *addition rule for mutually exclusive events* A and B.

> **Addition rule for *mutually exclusive* events *A* and *B***
>
> $$P(A \text{ } or \text{ } B) = P(A) + P(B) \tag{7}$$

If the events are not mutually exclusive, we must use the more general Formula (8), which is the *general addition rule for any events* A and B.

> **General addition rule for any events *A* and *B***
>
> $$P(A \text{ } or \text{ } B) = P(A) + P(B) - P(A \text{ } and \text{ } B) \tag{8}$$

You may ask: Which formula should we use? The answer is: Use Formula (7) only if you know that A and B are mutually exclusive (i.e., cannot occur together); if you do not know whether A and B are mutually exclusive, then use Formula (8). Formula (8) is valid either way. Notice that when A and B are mutually exclusive, then $P(A \text{ } and \text{ } B) = 0$, so Formula (8) reduces to Formula (7).

> **PROCEDURE**
>
> **How to use the addition rules**
>
> 1. First determine whether A and B are mutually exclusive events. If $P(A \text{ } and \text{ } B) = 0$, then the events are mutually exclusive.
>
> 2. If A and B are mutually exclusive events,
>
> $$P(A \text{ } or \text{ } B) = P(A) + P(B) \tag{7}$$
>
> 3. If A and B are any events,
>
> $$P(A \text{ } or \text{ } B) = P(A) + P(B) - P(A \text{ } and \text{ } B) \tag{8}$$

GUIDED EXERCISE 7

Mutually exclusive events

The Cost Less Clothing Store carries seconds in slacks. If you buy a pair of slacks in your regular waist size without trying them on, the probability that the waist will be too tight is 0.30 and the probability that it will be too loose is 0.10.

(a) Are the events too tight or too loose mutually exclusive?

⟹ The waist cannot be both too tight and too loose at the same time, so the events are mutually exclusive.

(b) If you choose a pair of slacks at random in your regular waist size, what is the probability that the waist will be too tight or too loose?

⟹ Since the events are mutually exclusive,

P(too tight *or* too loose)

$= P$(too tight) $+ P$(too loose)

$= 0.30 + 0.10$

$= 0.40$

GUIDED EXERCISE 8

General addition rule

Professor Jackson is in charge of a program to prepare people for a high school equivalency exam. Records show that 80% of the students need work in math, 70% need work in English, and 55% need work in both areas.

(a) Are the events needs math and needs English mutually exclusive?

⟹ These events are not mutually exclusive, since some students need both. In fact,

P(needs math *and* needs English) $= 0.55$

(b) Use the appropriate formula to compute the probability that a student selected at random needs math *or* needs English.

⟹ Since the events are not mutually exclusive, we use Formula (8):

P(needs math *or* needs English)

$= P$(needs math) $+ P$(needs English)

$\quad - P$(needs math *and* English)

$= 0.80 + 0.70 - 0.55$

$= 0.95$

More than two mutually exclusive events

The addition rule for mutually exclusive events can be extended so that it applies to the situation in which we have more than two events that are each mutually exclusive to all the other events.

EXAMPLE 5

Mutually exclusive events

Laura is playing Monopoly. On her next move she needs to throw a sum bigger than 8 on the two dice in order to land on her own property and pass Go. What is the probability that Laura will roll a sum bigger than 8?

SOLUTION: When two dice are thrown, the largest sum that can come up is 12. Consequently, the only sums larger than 8 are 9, 10, 11, and 12. These outcomes are mutually exclusive, since only one of these sums can possibly occur on one throw of the dice. The probability of throwing more than 8 is the same as

$$P(9 \text{ or } 10 \text{ or } 11 \text{ or } 12)$$

Since the events are mutually exclusive,

$$P(9 \text{ or } 10 \text{ or } 11 \text{ or } 12) = P(9) + P(10) + P(11) + P(12)$$
$$= \frac{4}{36} + \frac{3}{36} + \frac{2}{36} + \frac{1}{36}$$
$$= \frac{10}{36} = \frac{5}{18}$$

To get the specific values of $P(9)$, $P(10)$, $P(11)$, and $P(12)$, we used the sample space for throwing two dice (see Figure 4-2 on page 176). There are 36 equally likely outcomes—for example, those favorable to 9 are 6, 3; 3, 6; 5, 4; and 4, 5. So $P(9) = 4/36$. The other values can be computed in a similar way.   ◊

Further Examples

Most of us have been asked to participate in a survey. Schools, retail stores, news media, and government offices all conduct surveys. There are many types of surveys, and it is not our intention to give a general discussion of this topic. Let us study a very popular method called the *simple tally survey*. Such a survey consists of questions for which the responses can be recorded in the rows and columns of a table called a *contingency table*. These questions are appropriate to the information you want and are designed to cover the *entire* population of interest. In addition, the questions should be designed so that we can partition the sample space of responses into distinct (that is, mutually exclusive) sectors.

If the survey includes responses from a reasonably large random sample, then the results should be representative of your population. In this case, we can estimate simple probabilities, conditional probabilities, and the probabilities of some combinations of events directly from the results of the survey.

EXAMPLE 6

Survey

At Hopewell Electronics, all 140 employees were asked about their political affiliations. The employees were grouped by type of work, as executives or production workers. The results with row and column totals are shown in Table 4-2.

TABLE 4-2   Employee Type and Political Affiliation

Employee Type	Political Affiliation			Row Total
	Democrat (D)	Republican (R)	Independent (I)	
Executive (*E*)	5	34	9	48
Production worker (*PW*)	63	21	8	92
Column Total	68	55	17	140 Grand Total

Suppose an employee is selected at random from the 140 Hopewell employees. Let us use the following notation to represent different events of choosing: E = executive; PW = production worker; D = Democrat; R = Republican; I = Independent.

(a) Compute $P(D)$ and $P(E)$.

SOLUTION: To find these probabilities, we look at the *entire* sample space.

$$P(D) = \frac{\text{Number of Democrats}}{\text{Number of employees}} = \frac{68}{140} \approx 0.486$$

$$P(E) = \frac{\text{Number of executives}}{\text{Number of employees}} = \frac{48}{140} \approx 0.343$$

(b) Compute $P(D, \textit{given } E)$.

SOLUTION: For the conditional probability, we *restrict* our attention to the portion of the sample space satisfying the condition of being an executive.

$$P(D, \textit{given } E) = \frac{\text{Number of executives who are Democrats}}{\text{Number of executives}} = \frac{5}{48} \approx 0.104$$

(c) Are the events D and E independent?

SOLUTION: One way to determine if the events D and E are independent is to see if $P(D) = P(D, \textit{given } E)$ [or equivalently, if $P(E) = P(E, \textit{given } D)$]. Since $P(D) \approx 0.486$ and $P(D, \textit{given } E) \approx 0.104$, we see that $P(D) \neq P(D, \textit{given } E)$. This means that the events D and E are *not* independent. The probability of event D "depends on" whether or not event E has occurred.

(d) Compute $P(D \textit{ and } E)$.

SOLUTION: This probability is not conditional, so we must look at the entire sample space.

$$P(D \textit{ and } E) = \frac{\text{Number of executives who are Democrats}}{\text{Total number of employees}} = \frac{5}{140} \approx 0.036$$

Let's recompute this probability using the rules of probability for dependent events.

$$P(D \textit{ and } E) = P(E) \cdot P(D, \textit{given } E) = \frac{48}{140} \cdot \frac{5}{48} = \frac{5}{140} \approx 0.036$$

The results using the rules are consistent with those using the sample space.

(e) Compute $P(D \textit{ or } E)$.

SOLUTION: From part (d) we know that the events Democrat or executive are not mutually exclusive, because $P(D \textit{ and } E) \neq 0$. Therefore,

$$P(D \textit{ or } E) = P(D) + P(E) - P(D \textit{ and } E)$$
$$= \frac{68}{140} + \frac{48}{140} - \frac{5}{140} = \frac{111}{140} \approx 0.793$$

186   Chapter 4   Elementary Probability Theory

GUIDED EXERCISE 9

Survey

Using Table 4-2 on page 184, let's consider other probabilities regarding the types of employees at Hopewell and their political affiliations. This time let's consider the production worker and the affiliation of Independent. Suppose an employee is selected at random from the group of 140.

(a) Compute $P(I)$ and $P(PW)$.

$$P(I) = \frac{\text{No. of independents}}{\text{Total no. of employees}}$$

$$= \frac{17}{140} \approx 0.121$$

$$P(PW) = \frac{\text{No. of production workers}}{\text{Total no. of employees}}$$

$$= \frac{92}{140} \approx 0.657$$

(b) Compute $P(I, \text{given } PW)$. This is a conditional probability. Be sure to restrict your attention to production workers, since that is the condition given.

$$P(I, \text{given } PW) = \frac{\text{No. of independent production workers}}{\text{No. of production workers}}$$

$$= \frac{8}{92} \approx 0.087$$

(c) Compute $P(I \text{ and } PW)$. In this case, look at the entire sample space and the number of employees who are both Independent and in production.

$$P(I \text{ and } PW) = \frac{\text{No. of independent production workers}}{\text{Total no. employees}}$$

$$= \frac{8}{140} \approx 0.057$$

(d) Use the multiplication rule for dependent events to calculate $P(I \text{ and } PW)$. Is the result the same as that of part (c)?

By the multiplication rule,

$$P(I \text{ and } PW) = P(PW) \cdot P(I, \text{given } PW)$$

$$= \frac{92}{140} \cdot \frac{8}{92} = \frac{8}{140} \approx 0.057$$

The results are the same.

(e) Compute $P(I \text{ or } PW)$. Are the events mutually exclusive?

Since the events are not mutually exclusive,

$$P(I \text{ or } PW) = P(I) + P(PW) - P(I \text{ and } PW)$$

$$= \frac{17}{140} + \frac{92}{140} - \frac{8}{140}$$

$$= \frac{101}{140} \approx 0.721$$

Basic probability rules

As you apply probability to various settings, keep the following rules in mind.

Summary of basic probability rules

A statistical experiment or statistical observation is any random activity that results in a recordable outcome. The sample space is the set of all simple events that are the outcomes of the statistical experiment and cannot be broken into other "simpler" events. A general event is any subset of the sample space. The notation $P(A)$ designates the probability of the event A.

1. $P(\text{entire sample space}) = 1$

2. For any event A: $0 \le P(A) \le 1$

3. A^c designates the **complement** of A: $P(A^c) = 1 - P(A)$

4. Events A and B are **independent events** if $P(A) = P(A, \text{given } B)$.

5. Multiplication Rules

   General: $P(A \text{ and } B) = P(A) \cdot P(B, \text{given } A)$

   Independent events: $P(A \text{ and } B) = P(A) \cdot P(B)$

6. Conditional Probability: $P(A, \text{given } B) = \dfrac{P(A \text{ and } B)}{P(B)}$

7. Events A and B are **mutually exclusive** if $P(A \text{ and } B) = 0$.

8. Addition Rules

   General: $P(A \text{ or } B) = P(A) + P(B) - P(A \text{ and } B)$

   Mutually exclusive events: $P(A \text{ or } B) = P(A) + P(B)$

In this section, we have studied some important rules that are valid in all probability spaces. The rules and definitions of probability not only are interesting, but they also have extensive *applications* in our everyday lives. If you are inclined to continue your study of probability a little further, we recommend *Bayes's theorem* in Appendix I. The Reverend Thomas Bayes (1702–1761) was an English mathematician who discovered an important relation for conditional probabilities.

VIEWPOINT   *The Psychology of Odors*

The Smell and Taste Treatment Research Foundation of Chicago collected data on the time required to complete a maze while subjects were smelling different scents. Data for this survey can be found by visiting the Brase/Brase statistics site at **http://math.college.hmco.com/students** and finding the link to DASL, the Carnegie Mellon University Data and Story Library. Once at the DASL site, select Data Subjects, then Psychology, and then Scents. You can estimate conditional probabilities regarding response times for smokers, nonsmokers, and types of scents.

In Problems 1–12, use the appropriate addition or multiplication rules. When possible, verify results by considering the sample space.

1. *General: Candy Colors* M&M plain candies come in various colors. According to the M&M/Mars Department of Consumer Affairs (link to the Mars company web site from the Brase/Brase statistics site at **http://math.college.hmco.com/students**), the distribution of colors for plain M&M candies is

Color	Purple	Yellow	Red	Orange	Green	Blue	Brown
Percentage	20%	20%	20%	10%	10%	10%	10%

Suppose you have a large bag of plain M&M candies and you take one candy at random. Find
(a) P(green *or* blue candy). Are these outcomes mutually exclusive? Why?
(b) P(yellow candy *or* red candy). Are these outcomes mutually exclusive? Why?
(c) P(*not* purple candy).

2. *General: Candy Colors* According to the Department of Consumer Affairs of M&M/Mars, the color distribution of almond M&M candies is

Color	Purple	Yellow	Red	Green	Blue	Brown
Percentage	20%	20%	20%	20%	10%	10%

Suppose you have a large bag of almond M&M candies and you take one candy at random. Compute the probabilities in parts (a) through (c) of Problem 1 for almond M&M candies. Compare the results with those for plain M&M candies. Do you expect any differences? Why or why not?

3. *General: Candy Colors* Dulce de Leche~Caramel M&M candies have another color distribution, utilizing only six colors. The color distribution for these candies is uniform. There are only six colors: brown, red, yellow, orange, green, and blue. Each color comprises about 16.6% of the mix. Compute the probabilities in parts (a) through (c) of Problem 1 for these candies. Compare the results with those for plain M&M candies. Do you expect any differences? Why or why not?

4. *Environmental: Land Formations* Arches National Park is located in southern Utah. The park is famous for its beautiful desert landscape and its many natural sandstone arches. Park Ranger Edward McCarrick started an inventory (not yet complete) of natural arches within the park that have an opening of at least 3 feet. The following table is based on information taken from the book *Canyon Country Arches and Bridges*, by F. A. Barnes. The height of the arch opening is rounded to the nearest foot.

Height of arch, feet	3–9	10–29	30–49	50–74	75 and higher
Number of arches in park	111	96	30	33	18

For an arch chosen at random in Arches National Park, use the preceding information to estimate the probability that the height of the arch opening is

(a) 3 to 9 feet tall   (d) 10 to 74 feet tall
(b) 30 feet or taller   (e) 75 feet or taller
(c) 3 to 49 feet tall

5. *General: Roll Two Dice* You roll two fair dice, a green one and a red one.
   (a) Are the outcomes on the dice independent?
   (b) Find P(5 on green die *and* 3 on red die).
   (c) Find P(3 on green die *and* 5 on red die).
   (d) Find P((5 on green die *and* 3 on red die) *or* (3 on green die *and* 5 on red die)).

6. *General: Roll Two Dice* You roll two fair dice, a green one and a red one.
   (a) Are the outcomes on the dice independent?
   (b) Find P(1 on green die *and* 2 on red die).
   (c) Find P(2 on green die *and* 1 on red die).
   (d) Find P((1 on green die *and* 2 on red die) *or* (2 on green die *and* 1 on red die)).

7. *General: Roll Two Dice* You roll two fair dice, a green one and a red one.
   (a) What is the probability of getting a sum of 6?
   (b) What is the probability of getting a sum of 4?
   (c) What is the probability of getting a sum of 6 *or* 4? Are these outcomes mutually exclusive?

8. *General: Roll Two Dice* You roll two fair dice, a green one and a red one.
   (a) What is the probability of getting a sum of 7?
   (b) What is the probability of getting a sum of 11?
   (c) What is the probability of getting a sum of 7 *or* 11? Are these outcomes mutually exclusive?

9. *General: Deck of Cards* You draw two cards from a standard deck of 52 cards without replacing the first one before drawing the second.
   (a) Are the outcomes on the two cards independent? Why?
   (b) Find P(ace on 1st card *and* king on 2nd).
   (c) Find P(king on 1st card *and* ace on 2nd).
   (d) Find the probability of drawing an ace *and* a king in either order.

10. *General: Deck of Cards* You draw two cards from a standard deck of 52 cards without replacing the first one before drawing the second.
    (a) Are the outcomes on the two cards independent? Why?
    (b) Find P(3 on 1st card *and* 10 on 2nd).
    (c) Find P(10 on 1st card *and* 3 on 2nd).
    (d) Find the probability of drawing a 10 *and* a 3 in either order.

11. *General: Deck of Cards* You draw two cards from a standard deck of 52 cards, but before you draw the second card, you put the first one back and reshuffle the deck.
    (a) Are the outcomes on the two cards independent? Why?
    (b) Find P(ace on 1st card *and* king on 2nd).
    (c) Find P(king on 1st card *and* ace on 2nd).
    (d) Find the probability of drawing an ace *and* a king in either order.

12. *General: Deck of Cards* You draw two cards from a standard deck of 52 cards, but before you draw the second card, you put the first one back and reshuffle the deck.
    (a) Are the outcomes on the two cards independent? Why?
    (b) Find P(3 on 1st card *and* 10 on 2nd).
    (c) Find P(10 on 1st card *and* 3 on 2nd).
    (d) Find the probability of drawing a 10 *and* a 3 in either order.

13. *Marketing: Toys USA Today* gave the information shown in the table about ages of children receiving toys. The percentages represent all toys sold.

What is the probability that a toy is purchased for someone
(a) 6 years old or older?
(b) 12 years old or younger?
(c) between 6 and 12 years old?
(d) between 3 and 9 years old?

A child between 10 and 12 years old looks at this probability distribution

Age (years)	Percentage of Toys
2 and under	15%
3–5	22%
6–9	27%
10–12	14%
13 and over	22%

and asks, "Why are people more likely to buy toys for kids older than I am (13 and over) than for kids in my age group (10–12)?" How would you respond?

14. *Health Care: Flu* Based on data from the *Statistical Abstract of the United States*, 112th Edition, only about 14% of senior citizens (65 years old or older) get the flu each year. However, about 24% of the people under 65 years old get the flu each year. In the general population, there are 12.5% senior citizens (65 years old or older).
   (a) What is the probability that a person selected at random from the general population is a senior citizen who will get the flu this year?
   (b) What is the probability that a person selected at random from the general population is a person under age 65 who will get the flu this year?
   (c) Answer parts (a) and (b) for a community that has 95% senior citizens.
   (d) Answer parts (a) and (b) for a community that has 50% senior citizens.

15. *Focus Problem: Lie Detector Test* In this problem, you are asked to solve part of the Focus Problem at the beginning of this chapter. In his book *Chances: Risk and Odds in Everyday Life,* James Burke says that there is a 72% chance a polygraph test (lie detector test) will catch a person who is in fact lying. Furthermore, there is approximately a 7% chance that the polygraph will falsely accuse someone of lying.
   (a) Suppose that a person answers 90% of a long battery of questions truthfully. What percentage of the story will the polygraph *wrongly* indicate is a lie?
   (b) Suppose that a person answers 10% of a long battery of questions with lies. What percentage of the story will the polygraph *correctly* indicate is a lie?
   (c) Repeat parts (a) and (b) if 50% of the questions are answered truthfully and 50% are answered with lies.
   (d) Repeat parts (a) and (b) if 15% of the questions are answered truthfully and the rest are answered with lies.

16. *Focus Problem: Expand Your Knowledge* This problem continues the Focus Problem. The solution involves applying several basic probability rules and a little algebra to solve an equation.
   (a) If the polygraph of Problem 15 indicated that 30% of the questions were answered with lies, what would you estimate for the actual percentage of lies in the story? *Hint:* Let B = event detector indicates a lie. We are given $P(B) = 0.30$. Let A = event person is lying, so *not A* = event person is not lying. Then

   $$P(B) = P(A \text{ and } B) + P(not \text{ } A \text{ and } B)$$

   $$P(B) = P(A)P(B, \text{ given } A) + P(not \text{ } A)P(B, \text{ given not } A)$$

   Replacing $P(not \text{ } A)$ by $1 - P(A)$ gives

   $$P(B) = P(A)P(B, \text{ given } A) + [1 - P(A)]P(B, \text{ given not } A)$$

   Substitute known values for $P(B)$, $P(B, \text{ given } A)$, and $P(B, \text{ given not } A)$ into the last equation and solve for $P(A)$.
   (b) If the polygraph indicated that 70% of the questions were answered with lies, what would you estimate for the actual percentage of lies in the story?

17. *Life Style: Glasses or Contacts* In the book *Chances: Risk and Odds in Every-day Life*, James Burke says that 56% of the general population wears eyeglasses, while only 3.6% wears contacts. He also says that of those who do wear glasses, 55.4% are women and 44.6% are men. Of those who wear contacts, 63.1% are women and 36.9% are men. Assume that no one wears both glasses and contacts. For the next person you encounter at random, what is the probability that this person is
    (a) a woman wearing glasses?
    (b) a man wearing glasses?
    (c) a woman wearing contacts?
    (d) a man wearing contacts?
    (e) none of the above?

18. *Environment: Alternative Fuels* Gasoline-powered automobiles are a major source of pollution. Alternative fuels such as ethanol or methanol lower some of the hydro-carbon emissions. However, building cars that run on alternative fuels will cost more. A survey in *USA Today* reported how much a person selected at random would be willing to pay for the option of using alternative fuels. As reported, 27.5% of the respondents would not be willing to pay anything, 9.6% would be willing to pay less than $200, 13.5% would be willing to pay from $200 to $599, 2.1% would be willing to pay from $600 to $999, 26.2% would be willing to pay $1000 or more, and 21.1% don't know. Based on this survey, if we picked an adult at random, find the probability that this person would be willing to pay $600 or more for the option of using alternative fuels. What is the probability the person would be willing to pay no more than $199?

19. *Survey: Sales Approach* In a sales effectiveness seminar, a group of sales representatives tried two approaches to selling a customer a new automobile: the aggressive approach and the passive approach. From 1160 customers, the following record was kept:

	Sale	No Sale	Row Total
Aggressive	270	310	580
Passive	416	164	580
Column Total	686	474	1160

Suppose that a customer is selected at random from the 1160 participating customers. Let us use the following notation for events: A = aggressive approach, Pa = passive approach, S = sale, N = no sale. So $P(A)$ is the probability that an aggressive approach was used, and so on.
    (a) Compute $P(S)$, $P(S, given\ A)$, and $P(S, given\ Pa)$.
    (b) Are the events S = sale and Pa = passive approach independent? Explain.
    (c) Compute $P(A\ and\ S)$ and $P(Pa\ and\ S)$.
    (d) Compute $P(N)$ and $P(N, given\ A)$.
    (e) Are the events N = no sale and A = aggressive approach independent? Explain.
    (f) Compute $P(A\ or\ S)$.

20. *Survey: Medical Tests* Diagnostic tests of medical conditions have several results. The test result can be positive or negative, whether or not a patient has the condition. A positive test (+) indicates the patient has the condition. A negative test (−) indicates the patient does not have the condition. Remember, a positive test does not prove the patient has the condition. Additional medical work may be required. Consider a random sample of 200 patients, some of whom have a medical condition and some of whom do not. Results of a new diagnostic test for the condition are shown.

	Condition Present	Condition Absent	Row Total
Test Result +	110	20	130
Test Result −	20	50	70
Column Total	130	70	200

Assume the sample is representative of the entire population. For a person selected at random, compute the following probabilities:

(a) $P(+, \text{given condition present})$; this is known as the *sensitivity* of a test.
(b) $P(-, \text{given condition present})$; this is known as the false-negative rate.
(c) $P(-, \text{given condition absent})$; this is known as the *specificity* of a test.
(d) $P(+, \text{given condition absent})$; this is known as the false-positive rate.
(e) $P(\text{condition present and} +)$; this is the predictive value of the test.
(f) $P(\text{condition present and} -)$.

21. *Survey: Lung/Heart* In an article entitled "Diagnostic accuracy of fever as a measure of postoperative pulmonary complications" (*Heart Lung* 10, No. 1:61), J. Roberts and colleagues discuss using a fever of 38°C or higher as a diagnostic indicator of postoperative atelectasis (collapse of the lung) as evidenced by x-ray observation. For fever ≥ 38°C as the diagnostic test, the results for postoperative patients are

	Condition Present	Condition Absent	Row Total
Test Result +	72	37	109
Test Result −	82	79	161
Column Total	154	116	270

For the meaning of + and −, see Problem 20. Complete parts (a) through (f) from Problem 20.

22. *Survey: Customer Loyalty* Are customers more loyal in the East or in the West? The following table is based on information from *Trends in the United States,* published by the Food Marketing Institute, Washington, D.C. The columns represent length of customer loyalty (in years) at a primary supermarket. The rows represent regions of the United States.

	Less Than 1 Year	1–2 Years	3–4 Years	5–9 Years	10–14 Years	15 or More Years	Row Total
East	32	54	59	112	77	118	452
Midwest	31	68	68	120	63	173	523
South	53	92	93	158	106	158	660
West	41	56	67	78	45	86	373
Column Total	157	270	287	468	291	535	2008

What is the probability that a customer chosen at random

(a) has been loyal 10 to 14 years?
(b) has been loyal 10 to 14 years, given that he or she is from the East?
(c) has been loyal *at least* 10 years?
(d) has been loyal *at least* 10 years, given that he or she is from the West?
(e) is from the West, given that he or she has been loyal less than 1 year?
(f) is from the South, given that he or she has been loyal less than 1 year?

(g) has been loyal *1 or more years,* given that he or she is from the East?
(h) has been loyal *1 or more years,* given that he or she is from the West?
(i) Are the events from the East and loyal 15 or more years independent? Explain.

23. *Survey: Trips to Supermarket* How many times do shoppers go to the supermarket each week? The age group of customers with frequent visits can influence store inventory and marketing methods. The following table is based on information from *Trends in the United States* (see reference in Problem 22). The columns represent number of visits to the primary supermarket in an average week. The rows represent age distribution of customers in years.

Age (years)	One Visit	Two Visits	Three Visits	Four Visits	Five Visits	Six or More Visits	Row Total
18–24	65	58	12	5	4	4	148
25–39	386	230	69	22	17	15	739
40–49	210	161	36	13	9	5	434
50–64	186	102	35	14	7	5	349
65 and over	115	69	18	12	7	3	224
Column Total	962	620	170	66	44	32	1894

What is the probability that a customer chosen at random
(a) has been to the supermarket *at least* 2 times this past week?
(b) has been to the supermarket *at least* 2 times this past week, given that he or she is 25 to 39 years old?
(c) has been to the supermarket *more than* 3 times this past week?
(d) has been to the supermarket *more than* 3 times this past week, given that he or she is *65 or older?*
(e) is *40 or older?*
(f) is *40 or older,* given that he or she has visited the supermarket 4 times this past week?
(g) Are the events age 25–39 years and visits *more than* once a week independent? Explain.

24. *Education: College of Nursing* At Litchfield College of Nursing, 85% of incoming freshmen nursing students are female and 15% are male. Recent records indicate that 70% of the entering female students will graduate with a BSN degree, while 90% of the male students will obtain a BSN degree. If an incoming freshman nursing student is selected at random, find
(a) *P*(student will graduate, *given* student is female).
(b) *P*(student will graduate *and* student is female).
(c) *P*(student will graduate, *given* student is male).
(d) *P*(student will graduate *and* student is male).
(e) *P*(student will graduate). Note that those who will graduate are either males who will graduate or females who will graduate.
(f) The events described by the phrases "will graduate *and* is female" and "will graduate, *given* female" seem to be describing the same students. Why are the probabilities *P*(will graduate *and* is female) and *P*(will graduate, *given* female) different?

25. *Franchise Stores: Profits* Wing Foot is a shoe franchise commonly found in shopping centers across the United States. Wing Foot knows that its stores will not show a profit unless they gross over $940,000 per year. Let *A* be the event that a new Wing Foot store grosses over $940,000 its first year. Let *B* be the event

that a store grosses over $940,000 its second year. Wing Foot has an adminis-trative policy of closing a new store if it does not show a profit in *either* of the first 2 years. The accounting office at Wing Foot provided the following infor-mation: 65% of *all* Wing Foot stores show a profit the first year; 71% of *all* Wing Foot stores show a profit the second year (this includes stores that did not show a profit the first year); however, 87% of Wing Foot stores that showed a profit the first year also showed a profit the second year. Compute the following:

(a) $P(A)$

(b) $P(B)$

(c) $P(B,\ given\ A)$

(d) $P(A\ and\ B)$

(e) $P(A\ or\ B)$

(f) What is the probability that a new Wing Foot store will not be closed after 2 years? What is the probability that a new Wing Foot store will be closed after 2 years?

26. *Therapy: Alcohol Recovery* The Eastmore Program is a special program to help alcoholics. In the Eastmore Program, an alcoholic lives at home but undergoes a two-phase treatment plan. Phase I is an intensive group-therapy program lasting 10 weeks. Phase II is a long-term counseling program lasting 1 year. Eastmore Programs are located in most major cities, and past data gave the following infor-mation, based on percentages of success and failure collected over a long period of time: The probability that a client will have a relapse in phase I is 0.27; the probability that a client will have a relapse in phase II is 0.23. However, if a client did not have a relapse in phase I, then the probability that this client will not have a relapse in phase II is 0.95. If a client did have a relapse in phase I, then the probability that this client will have a relapse in phase II is 0.70. Let A be the event that a client has a relapse in phase I and B be the event that a client has a relapse in phase II. Let C be the event that a client has no relapse in phase I and D be the event that a client has no relapse in phase II. Compute the following:

(a) $P(A)$, $P(B)$, $P(C)$, and $P(D)$

(b) $P(B,\ given\ A)$ and $P(D,\ given\ C)$

(c) $P(A\ and\ B)$ and $P(C\ and\ D)$

(d) $P(A\ or\ B)$

(e) What is the probability that a client will go through both phase I and phase II without a relapse?

(f) What is the probability that a client will have a relapse in both phase I and phase II?

(g) What is the probability that a client will have a relapse in either phase I or phase II?

27. *Medical: Tuberculosis* The state medical school has discovered a new test for tuber-culosis. (If the test indicates a person has tuberculosis, the test is positive.) Experi-mentation has shown that the probability of a positive test is 0.82, given that a person has tuberculosis. The probability is 0.09 that the test registers positive, given that the person does not have tuberculosis. Assume that in the general population the probability that a person has tuberculosis is 0.04. What is the probability that a person chosen at random will

(a) have tuberculosis and a positive test?

(b) not have tuberculosis?

(c) not have tuberculosis and have a positive test?

4.3
Trees and Counting Techniques

FOCUS POINTS

✓ Organize outcomes in a sample space using tree diagrams.
✓ Compute number of ordered arrangements of outcomes using permutations.
✓ Compute number of (nonordered) groupings of outcomes using combinations.
✓ Explain how counting techniques relate to probability in everyday life.

Tree diagrams

When outcomes are equally likely, we compute the probability of an event by using the formula

$$P(A) = \frac{\text{Number of outcomes favorable to the event } A}{\text{Number of outcomes in the sample space}}$$

The probability formula requires that we be able to determine the number of outcomes in the sample space. In the problems we have done in previous sections, this task has not been difficult because the number of outcomes was small or the sample space consisted of fairly straightforward events. The tools we present in this section will help you count the number of possible outcomes in larger sample spaces or those formed by more complicated events.

A *tree diagram* helps us display the outcomes of an experiment consisting of a series of activities. The total number of outcomes corresponds to the total number of final branches in the tree. Perhaps the best way to learn to make a tree diagram is to see one. In the next example we will see a tree diagram and analyze its parts.

EXAMPLE 7

Tree diagram

Jacqueline is in the nursing program and is required to take a course in psychology and one in anatomy and physiology (A and P) next semester. She also wants to take Spanish II. If there are four sections of psychology, two of A and P, and three of Spanish, how many different class schedules can Jacqueline choose from? (Assume that the times of the sections do not conflict with each other.) Figure 4-6 on the next page shows a tree diagram for Jacqueline's possible schedules.

SOLUTION: Let's study the tree diagram and see how it shows Jacqueline's schedule choices. There are four branches from Start. These branches indicate the four possible choices for psychology sections. No matter which section of psychology Jacqueline chooses, she can choose from the two available A and P sections. Therefore, we have two branches leading from *each* psychology branch. Finally, after the psychology and A and P sections are selected, there are three choices for Spanish II. That is why there are three branches from *each* A and P section.

The tree ends with a total of 24 branches. This number of end branches tells us the number of possible schedules. The outcomes themselves can be listed from the tree by following each series of branches from Start to End. For instance, the top branch from Start generates the schedules shown in Table 4-3 on the next page.

Following the second branch from Start, we see all the possible schedules utilizing Section 2 of psychology (see Table 4-4). The other 12 schedules can be listed in a similar manner. ◇

We draw a tree diagram in stages, indicating the possible outcomes for the first event, the second event, and so forth. Guided Exercise 10 will lead you through the process.

FIGURE 4-6

Tree Diagram for Selecting Class Schedules

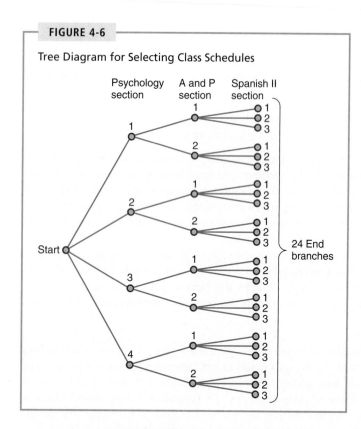

TABLE 4-3 Schedules Utilizing Section 1 of Psychology

Psychology Section	A and P Section	Spanish II Section
1	1	1
1	1	2
1	1	3
1	2	1
1	2	2
1	2	3

TABLE 4-4 Schedules Utilizing Section 2 of Psychology

Psychology Section	A and P Section	Spanish II Section
2	1	1
2	1	2
2	1	3
2	2	1
2	2	2
2	2	3

GUIDED EXERCISE 10

Tree diagram

Louis plays three tennis matches. Use a tree diagram to list the possible win and loss sequences Louis can experience for the set of three matches.

(a) On the first match Louis can win or lose. From Start, indicate these two branches.

FIGURE 4-7 W = Win, L = Lose

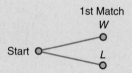

(b) Regardless of whether Louis wins or loses the first match, he plays the second and can again win or lose. Attach branches representing these two outcomes to *each* of the first match results.

FIGURE 4-8

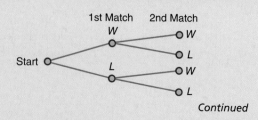

Continued

GUIDED EXERCISE 10 continued

(c) Louis may win or lose the third match. Attach branches representing these two outcomes to *each* of the second match results.

 **FIGURE 4-9**

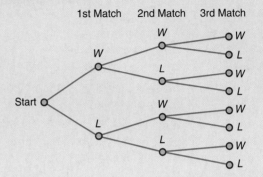

(d) How many possible win–lose sequences are there for the three matches?

⇨ Since there are eight branches at the end, there are eight sequences.

(e) Complete this list of win–lose sequences.

⇨ The last four sequences all involve a loss on Match 1.

1st	2nd	3rd
W	W	W
W	W	L
W	L	W
W	L	L
___	___	___
___	___	___
___	___	___
___	___	___

1st	2nd	3rd
L	W	W
L	W	L
L	L	W
L	L	L

Tree diagrams help us display the outcomes of an experiment involving several stages. If we label each branch of the tree with an appropriate probability, we can use the tree diagram to help us compute the probability of an outcome displayed on the tree. One of the easiest ways to illustrate this feature of tree diagrams is to use an experiment of drawing balls out of an urn. We do this in the next example.

EXAMPLE 8

Probability

Suppose there are five balls in an urn. They are identical except in color. Three of the balls are red and two are blue. You are instructed to draw out one ball, note its color, and set it aside. Then you are to draw out another ball and note its color. What are the outcomes of the experiment? What is the probability of each outcome?

SOLUTION: The tree diagram in Figure 4-10 on the next page will help us answer these questions. Notice that since you did not replace the first ball before drawing the second one, the two stages of the experiment are dependent. The probability associated with the color of the second ball depends on the color of the first ball.

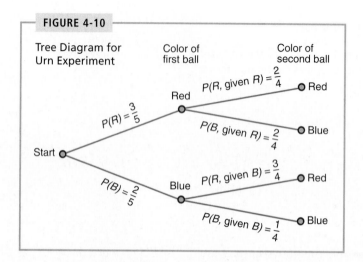

FIGURE 4-10

Tree Diagram for Urn Experiment

For instance, on the top branches, the color of the first ball drawn is red, so we compute the probabilities of the colors on the second ball accordingly. The tree diagram helps us organize the probabilities.

From the diagram, we see that there are four possible outcomes to the experiment. They are

RR = red on 1st *and* red on 2nd

RB = red on 1st *and* blue on 2nd

BR = blue on 1st *and* red on 2nd

BB = blue on 1st *and* blue on 2nd

To compute the probability of each outcome, we will use the multiplication rule for dependent events. As we follow the branches for each outcome, we will find the necessary probabilities.

$$P(R \text{ on 1st } and \text{ R on 2nd}) = P(R) \cdot P(R, \text{ given } R)$$
$$= \frac{3}{5} \cdot \frac{2}{4} = \frac{3}{10}$$

$$P(R \text{ on 1st } and \text{ B on 2nd}) = P(R) \cdot P(B, \text{ given } R)$$
$$= \frac{3}{5} \cdot \frac{2}{4} = \frac{3}{10}$$

$$P(B \text{ on 1st } and \text{ R on 2nd}) = P(B) \cdot P(R, \text{ given } B)$$
$$= \frac{2}{5} \cdot \frac{3}{4} = \frac{3}{10}$$

$$P(B \text{ on 1st } and \text{ B on 2nd}) = P(B) \cdot P(B, \text{ given } B)$$
$$= \frac{2}{5} \cdot \frac{1}{4} = \frac{1}{10}$$

Notice that the probabilities of the outcomes in the sample space add to 1, as they should.   ◊

GUIDED
EXERCISE **11**

Probability

Repeat the urn experiment with the five balls, three of which are red and two of which are blue. This time replace the first ball before drawing the second.

(a) Draw a tree diagram for the outcomes of this experiment. Show the probabilities of each stage on the appropriate branch. (*Hint:* Are the stages dependent or independent?)

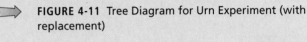

FIGURE 4-11 Tree Diagram for Urn Experiment (with replacement)

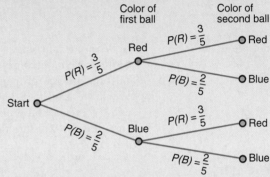

(b) List the four possible outcomes of the experiment (i.e., list the sample space).

Red on 1st *and* red on 2nd
Red on 1st *and* blue on 2nd
Blue on 1st *and* red on 2nd
Blue on 1st *and* blue on 2nd

(c) Use the multiplication rule for independent events and the probabilities shown on your tree to compute the probability of each outcome.

$P(\text{1st } R \text{ and 2nd } R) = P(R) \cdot P(R)$
$$= \frac{3}{5} \cdot \frac{3}{5} = \frac{9}{25}$$

$P(\text{1st } R \text{ and 2nd } B) = P(R) \cdot P(B)$
$$= \frac{3}{5} \cdot \frac{2}{5} = \frac{6}{25}$$

$P(\text{1st } B \text{ and 2nd } R) = P(B) \cdot P(R)$
$$= \frac{2}{5} \cdot \frac{3}{5} = \frac{6}{25}$$

$P(\text{1st } B \text{ and 2nd } B) = P(B) \cdot P(B)$
$$= \frac{2}{5} \cdot \frac{2}{5} = \frac{4}{25}$$

(d) Do the probabilities of the outcomes in the sample space add up to 1?

Yes, as they should.

Continued

GUIDED EXERCISE 11 continued

(e) Compare the tree diagram of this exercise with that of the previous example, in which the first ball was not replaced before the second was drawn. Are the outcomes the same? Are the probabilities of the corresponding outcomes the same?

 The outcomes are the same: *RR, RB, BR,* and *BB.* However, because one experiment did not permit replacement of the first ball before the second was drawn and the other experiment required replacement, the corresponding probabilities of the second stages of the experiment are different. The corresponding probabilities of the final outcomes are also different.

Multiplication rule of counting

When an outcome is composed of a series of events, tree diagrams tell us how many possible outcomes there are. They also help us list the individual outcomes and organize the probabilities associated with each stage of the outcomes. However, if we are interested only in the number of different outcomes created by a series of events, the multiplication rule will give us the total number of outcomes more directly. We state the multiplication rule for an outcome composed of a series of two events.

Multiplication rule of counting

If there are n possible outcomes for event E_1 and m possible outcomes for event E_2, then there are a total of $n \times m$ or nm possible outcomes for the series of events E_1 followed by E_2.

The rule extends to outcomes created by a series of three, four, or more events. We simply multiply the number of outcomes possible for each step in the series of events to get the total number of outcomes for the series.

EXAMPLE 9

Multiplication rule

The Night Hawk is the new car model produced by Limited Motors, Inc. It comes with a choice of two body styles, three interior package options, and four different colors, as well as the choice of automatic or standard transmission. Select-an-Auto Car Dealership wants to carry one of each of the different types of Night Hawks. How many cars are required?

SOLUTION: There are four items to select. We take the product of the number of choices for each item.

$$\left(\begin{matrix}\text{No. of body}\\\text{styles}\end{matrix}\right)\left(\begin{matrix}\text{No. of}\\\text{interiors}\end{matrix}\right)\left(\begin{matrix}\text{No. of}\\\text{colors}\end{matrix}\right)\left(\begin{matrix}\text{No. of transmission}\\\text{types}\end{matrix}\right)$$

$$(2)(3)(4)(2) = 48$$

Select-an-Auto must stock 48 cars to have one of each possible type.   ◊

Sometimes when we consider n items, we need to know the number of different *ordered arrangements* of the n items that are possible. The multiplication rules

> ### GUIDED EXERCISE **12**
>
> ## *Multiplication rule of counting*
>
> The Old Sage Inn offers a special dinner menu each night. There are two appetizers to choose from, three main courses, and four desserts. A customer can select one item from each category. How many different meals can be ordered from the special dinner menu?
>
> (a) Each special dinner consists of three items. List the items and the number of choices per item.
>
> ▷ Appetizer—2; main course—3; dessert—4
>
> (b) To find the number of different dinners composed of the three items, multiply the number of choices per item together.
>
> ▷ $(2)(3)(4) = 24$
>
> There are 24 different dinners that can be ordered from the special dinner menu.

can help us find the number of possible ordered arrangements. Let's consider the classic example of determining the number of different ways in which eight people can be seated at a dinner table. For the first chair at the head of the table, there are eight choices. For the second chair, there are seven choices, since one person is already seated. For the third chair, there are six choices, since two people are already seated. By the time we get to the last chair, there is only one person left for that seat. We can view each arrangement as an outcome of a series of eight events. Event 1 is *fill the first chair,* event 2 is *fill the second chair,* and so forth. The multiplication rule will tell us the number of different outcomes.

Choices for	1st	2nd	3rd	4th	5th	6th	7th	8th	Chair position
	↓	↓	↓	↓	↓	↓	↓	↓	
	(8)	(7)	(6)	(5)	(4)	(3)	(2)	(1)	$= 40{,}320$

In all, there are 40,320 different seating arrangements for eight people. It is no wonder that it takes a little time to seat guests at a dinner table!

The multiplication pattern shown above is not unusual. In fact, it is an example of the multiplication indicated by the factorial notation 8!.

Factorial notation

! is read "factorial"

8! is read "8 factorial"

$8! = 8 \cdot 7 \cdot 6 \cdot 5 \cdot 4 \cdot 3 \cdot 2 \cdot 1$

In general, $n!$ indicates the product of n with each of the positive counting numbers less than n. *By special definition* $0! = 1$.

> **Factorial notation**
>
> For a counting number n,
>
> $$n! = n(n-1)(n-2) \cdots 1$$
>
> $$0! = 1$$
>
> $$1! = 1$$

GUIDED EXERCISE 13

Factorial

(a) Evaluate 3!.

⟹ $3! = 3 \cdot 2 \cdot 1 = 6$

(b) How many different ways can three objects be arranged in order? How many choices do you have for the first position? for the second position? for the third position?

⟹   We have three choices for the first position, two for the second position, and one for the third position. By the multiplication rule, we have

$(3)(2)(1) = 3! = 6$ arrangements

(c) Verify step (b) with a three-stage tree diagram.

⟹   **FIGURE 4-12** Three Choices

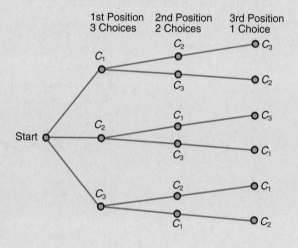

Permutations

We have considered the number of ordered arrangements of n objects taken as an entire group. Specifically, we considered a dinner party for eight and found the number of ordered seating arrangements for all eight people. However, suppose you have an open house and have only five chairs. How many ways can five of the eight people seat themselves in the chairs? The formula we use to compute this number is called the *permutation formula*. As we see in the next example, the *permutations rule* is really another version of the multiplication rule.

Counting rule for permutations

The number of ways to *arrange in order* n distinct objects, taking them r at a time, is

$$P_{n,r} = \frac{n!}{(n-r)!}$$

(9)

where n and r are whole numbers and $n \geq r$. Another commonly used notation for permutations is nPr.

EXAMPLE 10

Permutations rule

Let's compute the number of ordered seating arrangements we have for eight people in five chairs.

SOLUTION: In this case, we are considering a total of $n = 8$ different people, and we wish to arrange $r = 5$ of these people. Substituting into Formula (9), we have

$$P_{n,r} = \frac{n!}{(n-r)!}$$

$$P_{8,5} = \frac{8!}{(8-5)!} = \frac{8!}{3!} = \frac{40,320}{6} = 6720$$

Using the multiplication rule, we get the same results

Chair	1		2		3		4		5	
Choices for	8	×	7	×	6	×	5	×	4	= 6720

The permutations rule has the advantage of using factorials. Most scientific calculators have a factorial key ! as well as a permutations key nPr (see the Tech Note).   ◇

   TECH NOTE   Most scientific calculators have a factorial key, often designated x! or n!. Many of these same calculators have the permutation function built in, often labeled nPr. They also have the combination function that is discussed after the next exercise. The combination function is often labeled nCr.

TI-84Plus/TI-83Plus The factorial, permutation, and combination functions are all under **MATH**, then **PRB**.

Excel Use the **paste function** (f_x), then **all. Fact** gives factorials, **Permut** gives permutations, **Combin** gives combinations.

GUIDED EXERCISE 14

Permutation

The board of directors of Belford Community Hospital has 12 members. Three officers—president, vice president, and treasurer—must be elected from the members. How many different possible slates of officers are there? We will view a slate of officers as a list of three people with one person for president listed first, one person for vice president listed second, and one person for treasurer listed third. For instance, if Mr. Acosta, Ms. Hill, and Mr. Smith wish to be on a slate together, there are several different slates possible, depending on which one will run for president, which for vice president, and which for treasurer. Not only are we asking for the number of different groups of three names for a slate, we are also concerned about order, since it makes a difference which name is listed in which position.

(a) What is the size of the group from which the   ⇒ $n = 12$
slates of officers will be selected? This is the
value of n.

Continued

GUIDED EXERCISE 14 continued

(b) How many people will be selected for each slate of officers? This is the value of *r*.

➡ $r = 3$

(c) Each slate of officers is composed of three candidates. Different slates occur as we arrange the three candidates in the positions of president, vice president, and treasurer. For this reason, we need to consider the number of *permutations* of 12 items arranged in groups of 3. Compute $P_{n,r}$.

➡ $$P_{n,r} = \frac{n!}{(n-r)!}$$

$$P_{12,3} = \frac{12!}{(12-3)!} = \frac{12!}{9!} = \frac{479,001,600}{362,880}$$

$$= 1320$$

There are 1320 different possible slates of officers. An alternative is to use your calculator to compute $P_{12,3}$ directly.

Combinations

In each of our previous counting formulas, we have taken the *order* of the objects or people into account. But what if order is not important? For instance, suppose we need to choose 3 members from the 12-member board of directors of Belford Community Hospital to go to a convention. We are interested in *different groupings* of 12 people so that each group contains 3 people. The order is of no concern, since all 3 will go to the convention. In other words, we need to consider the number of different *combinations* of 12 people taken 3 at a time. Our next formula will help us compute this number of different combinations.

> **Counting rule for combinations**
>
> The number of *combinations* of *n* objects taken *r* at a time is
>
> $$C_{n,r} = \frac{n!}{r!(n-r)!} \tag{10}$$
>
> where *n* and *r* are whole numbers and $n \geq r$. Other commonly used notations for combinations include nCr and $\binom{n}{r}$.

Notice the difference between the concepts of permutations and combinations. When we consider permutations, we are considering groupings *and order*. When we consider combinations, we are considering only the number of different groupings. For combinations, order within the groupings is not considered. As a result, the number of combinations of *n* objects taken *r* at a time is generally smaller than the number of permutations of the same *n* objects taken *r* at a time. In fact, the combinations formula is simply the permutations formula with the number of permutations of each distinct group divided out. In the formula for combinations, notice the factor of *r*! in the denominator.

Now let's look at an example in which we use the *combinations rule* to compute the number of *combinations* of 12 people taken 3 at a time.

EXAMPLE 11

Combinations

Three members from the group of 12 on the board of directors at Belford Community Hospital will be selected to go to a convention with all expenses paid. How many different groups of 3 are there?

SOLUTION: In this case, we are interested in *combinations* rather than permutations of 12 people taken 3 at a time. Using Formula (10), we get

$$C_{n,r} = \frac{n!}{r!(n-r)!} \quad \text{or}$$

$$C_{12,3} = \frac{12!}{3!(12-3)!} = \frac{12!}{3!9!} = \frac{479,001,600}{(6)(362,880)} = 220$$

There are 220 different possible groups of 3 to go to the convention.

Another way to get the solution is to use your calculator to evaluate $C_{12,3}$ directly. Since order is not considered, this number is much smaller than the number of different slates of 3 officers we computed in Guided Exercise 14.   ◊

We have different formulas for permutations and combinations of n objects taken r at a time. How do you decide which one to use? Always ask yourself if order in the groups of r objects is relevant. If it is, use $P_{n,r}$. If order is not relevant, use $C_{n,r}$.

We have introduced you to three counting formulas: the multiplication rule, the permutations rule, and the combinations rule. Other rules apply when the objects are not distinct. Many counting problems are easy to state and fairly difficult to solve. Some have you combine several counting rules. However, the problems for this section are all straightforward. Some ask you to use your counting abilities to compute probabilities.

GUIDED EXERCISE 15

Combinations

In your political science class, you are given a list of 10 books. You are to select 4 to read during the semester. How many different *combinations* of 4 books are available from the list of 10?

(a) Is the order in which you read the books relevant to the task of selecting the books?

⇨ No.

(b) Do we use the number of permutations or combinations of 10 books taken 4 at a time?

⇨ Since the order in which the books are selected is not relevant, we compute the number of *combinations* of 10 books taken 4 at a time.

(c) How many books are available from which to select? How many must you read? What is the value of n? of r?

⇨ There are 10 books from which you must select 4 to read. $n = 10$ and $r = 4$.

Continued

GUIDED EXERCISE 15 continued

(d) Compute $C_{10,4}$ to determine the number of different groups of 4 books from the list of 10.

$$C_{n,r} = \frac{n!}{r!(n-r)!}$$

$$C_{10,4} = \frac{10!}{4!(10-4)!} = \frac{10!}{4!6!} = \frac{3,628,800}{(24)(720)} = 210$$

There are 210 different groups of 4 books to select from the list of 10. An alternate method of solution is to use the nCr key on your calculator.

VIEWP☉INT

Powerball

Powerball is a multistate lottery game that consists of drawing five distinct whole numbers from the numbers 1 through 53. Then one more number from the numbers 1 through 42 is selected as the Powerball number (this number could be one of the original five). Powerball numbers are drawn every Wednesday and Saturday. If you match all six numbers, you win the jackpot, which is worth at least 10 million dollars. Use methods of this section to show that there are 120,526,770 possible Powerball plays. For more information about the game of Powerball and the probability of winning different prizes, visit the Brase/Brase statistics site at **http://math.college.hmco.com/students** and find the link to the Multi-State Lottery Association. Then select Powerball.

SECTION 4.3 PROBLEMS

1. *Tree Diagram*
   (a) Draw a tree diagram to display all the possible head–tail sequences that can occur when you flip a coin three times.
   (b) How many sequences contain exactly two heads?
   (c) *Probability extension:* Assuming the sequences are all equally likely, what is the probability that you will get exactly two heads when you toss a coin three times?

2. *Tree Diagram*
   (a) Draw a tree diagram to display all the possible outcomes that can occur when you flip a coin and then toss a die.
   (b) How many outcomes contain a head and a number greater than four?
   (c) *Probability extension:* Assuming the outcomes displayed in the tree diagram are all equally likely, what is the probability that you will get a head *and* a number greater than four when you flip a coin and toss a die?

3. *Tree Diagram* There are six balls in an urn. They are identical except for color. Two are red, three are blue, and one is yellow. You are to draw a ball from the urn, note its color, and set it aside. Then you are to draw another ball from the urn and note its color.
   (a) Make a tree diagram to show all possible outcomes of the experiment. Label the probability associated with each stage of the experiment on the appropriate branch.

(b) *Probability extension:* Compute the probability for each outcome of the experiment.

4. *Tree Diagram* Repeat the experiment described in Problem 3. However, replace the first ball before you draw the second one.
   (a) Make a tree diagram to show all possible outcomes of the experiment. Label the probability associated with each stage of the experiment on the appropriate branch.
   (b) *Probability extension:* Compute the probability for each outcome of the experiment.

5. *Tree Diagram* Consider three true–false questions. There are two possible outcomes for each question: true or false.
   (a) Draw a tree diagram showing all possible sequences of responses for the three questions. Does your tree diagram look similar to the one in Problem 1? Why would you expect this result?
   (b) *Probability extension:* Only one sequence will contain all three correct answers. Assuming you are guessing and all of the sequences are equally likely to occur when you guess, what is the probability of getting all three questions correct?

6. *Tree Diagram*
   (a) Make a tree diagram to show all the possible sequences of answers for three multiple-choice questions, each with four possible responses.
   (b) *Probability extension:* Assuming that you are guessing the answers so that all outcomes listed in the tree are equally likely, what is the probability that you will guess the one sequence that contains all three correct answers?

7. *Multiplication Rule* Four wires (red, green, blue, and yellow) need to be attached to a circuit board. A robotic device will attach the wires. The wires can be attached in any order, and the production manager wishes to determine which order would be fastest for the robot to use. Use the multiplication rule of counting to determine the number of possible sequences of assembly that must be tested. (*Hint:* There are four choices for the first wire, three for the second, two for the third, and only one for the fourth.)

8. *Multiplication Rule* A sales representative must visit four cities: Omaha, Dallas, Wichita, and Oklahoma City. There are direct air connections between each of the cities. Use the multiplication rule of counting to determine the number of different choices the sales representative has for the order in which to visit the cities. How is this problem similar to Problem 7?

9. *Multiplication Rule* You have two decks of cards (52 cards per deck), and you draw one card from each deck.
   (a) Use the multiplication rule of counting to determine the number of pairs of cards possible.
   (b) There are four kings in each deck. How many pairs of kings are possible?
   (c) *Probability extension:* Assuming all pairs are equally likely to be drawn, what is the probability of drawing two kings?

10. *Multiplication Rule* You toss a pair of dice.
    (a) Use the multiplication rule of counting to determine the number of possible pairs of outcomes. (Recall that there are six possible outcomes for each die.)
    (b) There are three even numbers on each die. How many outcomes are possible with even numbers appearing on each die?
    (c) *Probability extension:* What is the probability that both dice will show an even number?

11. *Multiplication Rule* Barbara is a research biologist for Green Carpet Lawns. She is studying the effects of fertilizer type, temperature at time of application, and water treatment after application. She has four fertilizer types, three temperature zones, and three water treatments to test. Use the multiplication rule of counting to determine the number of different lawn plots she needs in order to test each fertilizer type, temperature range, and water treatment configuration.

12. *Multiplication Rule: Menu Choices* The Deli Special lunch offers a choice of three different sandwiches, four kinds of salads, and five different desserts. Use the multiplication rule of counting to determine the number of different lunches that can be ordered using the Deli Special lunch option, if each lunch consists of one sandwich, one salad, and one dessert.

13. Compute $P_{5,2}$.

14. Compute $P_{8,3}$.

15. Compute $P_{7,7}$.

16. Compute $P_{9,9}$.

17. Compute $C_{5,2}$.

18. Compute $C_{8,3}$.

19. Compute $C_{7,7}$.

20. Compute $C_{8,8}$.

21. *Permutation: Hiring* There are three nursing positions to be filled at Lilly Hospital. Position 1 is the day nursing supervisor; position 2 is the night nursing supervisor; and position 3 is the nursing coordinator position. There are 15 candidates qualified for all three of the positions. Use the permutations rule to determine the number of different ways the positions can be filled by these applicants.

22. *Permutation: Lottery* In the Cash Now lottery game there are 10 finalists who submitted entry tickets on time. From these 10 tickets, three grand prize winners will be drawn. The first prize is one million dollars, the second prize is one hundred thousand dollars, and the third prize is ten thousand dollars. Use the permutations rule to determine the total number of different ways the winners can be drawn. (Assume that the tickets are not replaced after they are drawn.)

23. *Permutation: Objective Exam* Matching questions are sometimes used on objective tests.
    (a) If eight words are to be matched with eight definitions (numbered 1 through 8), use the permutations rule to determine the number of possible word-to-definition matches. (Assume each word corresponds to exactly one definition.)
    (b) If there are eight words but only five definitions, use the permutations rule to determine the number of possible word-to-definition matches.

24. *Counting: Shelving* To emphasize the importance of correct shelving of books, a librarian tells a group of students the number of possible orders in which just six books may be placed on a shelf. What is that number?

25. *Counting: Sports* The University of Montana ski team has five entrants in a men's downhill ski event. The coach would like the first, second, and third places to go to the team members. In how many ways can the five team entrants achieve first, second, and third places?

26. *Counting: Sales* During the Computer Daze special promotion, a customer purchasing a computer and printer is given a choice of three free software packages. There are 10 different software packages from which to select. How many different groups of software packages can be selected?

27. *Counting: Hiring* There are 15 qualified applicants for 5 trainee positions in a fast-food management program. How many different groups of trainees can be selected? (*Hint:* Is order important? If not, use the formula for combinations.)

28. *Counting: Grading* One professor grades homework by randomly choosing 5 out of 12 homework problems to grade.
    (a) How many different groups of 5 problems can be chosen from the 12 problems?
    (b) *Probability extension:* Jerry did only 5 problems of one assignment. What is the probability that the problems he did comprised the group that was selected to be graded?
    (c) Silvia did 7 problems. How many different groups of 5 did she complete? What is the probability that one of the groups of 5 she completed comprised the group selected to be graded?

29. *Counting: Hiring* The qualified applicant pool for six management trainee positions consists of seven women and five men.
    (a) How many different groups of applicants can be selected for the positions?
    (b) How many different groups of trainees would consist entirely of women?
    (c) *Probability extension:* If the applicants are equally qualified and the trainee positions are selected by drawing the names at random so that all groups of six are equally likely, what is the probability that the trainee class will consist entirely of women?

30. *Counting: Lottery* In the Colorado State Lotto game, there are 42 numbers. Players choose any 6. Then the state selects 6 of the numbers at random. The winning tickets (for the grand prize) are those on which the player's 6 numbers match the state's 6 numbers.
    (a) From 42 numbers, how many groups of 6 are possible?
    (b) *Probability extension:* If you buy one lottery ticket, what is the probability of winning the grand prize?
    (c) *Probability extension:* If you buy 10 lottery tickets, what is the probability of winning the grand prize?

SUMMARY

In this chapter we first examined the question: What is probability? We found that probabilities can be assigned to events by intuition, by the method of relative frequency, or by the method of equally likely outcomes. Next, we studied some probability rules. The most important rules are the multiplication rules for independent and dependent events and the addition rules for mutually exclusive and general events. We also looked at some counting techniques useful in computing probabilities. These techniques included tree diagrams, the multiplication rule for counting, combinations, and permutations.

IMPORTANT WORDS & SYMBOLS

Section 4.1
Probability of an event A, $P(A)$
Relative frequency
Law of large numbers
Equally likely outcomes
Statistical experiment
Simple event

Sample space
Complement of event A

Section 4.2
Independent events
Dependent events
A, *given* B

Conditional probability
Multiplication rules of probability (for independent and dependent events)
A and B
Mutually exclusive events
Addition rules (for mutually exclusive and general events)
A or B

Section 4.3
Tree diagram
Multiplication rule of counting
Permutations rule
Combinations rule

VIEWPOINT   *Deathday and Birthday*

Can people really postpone death? If so, how much can the timing of death be influenced by psychological, social, or other influential factors? One special event is a birthday. Do famous people try to postpone their deaths until an important birthday? Both Thomas Jefferson and John Adams died on July 4, 1826, when the United States was celebrating its 50th birthday. Is this only a strange coincidence, or is there an unexpected connection between birthdays and deathdays? The probability associated with a death rate decline of famous people just before important birthdays has been studied by Professor D. P. Phillips, of the State University of New York, and is presented in the book *Statistics, A Guide to the Unknown*, edited by J. M. Tanur.

CHAPTER REVIEW PROBLEMS

1. *Salary Raise: Women* Does it pay to ask for a raise? A national survey of heads of households showed the percentage of those who asked for a raise and the percentage who got one (*USA Today*). According to the survey, of the women interviewed, 24% had asked for a raise, and of those women who had asked for a raise, 45% received the raise. If a woman is selected at random from the survey population of women, find the following probabilities: *P*(woman asked for a raise); *P*(woman received raise, *given* she asked for one); *P*(woman asked for raise *and* received raise).

2. *Salary Raise: Men* According to the same survey quoted in Problem 1, of the men interviewed, 20% had asked for a raise and 59% of the men who had asked for a raise *received* the raise. If a man is selected at random from the survey population of men, find the following probabilities: *P*(man asked for a raise); *P*(man received raise, *given* he asked for one); *P*(man asked for raise *and* received raise).

3. *General: Deck of Cards* Two cards are drawn at random from a standard deck. (A standard deck has 52 cards: 13 hearts, 13 diamonds, 13 clubs, and 13 spades.)
   (a) Are the outcomes of drawing the two cards independent? Why?
   (b) If the first card is replaced before the second is drawn, what is the probability that both cards will be hearts?
   (c) If the first card is not replaced before the second is drawn, what is the probability that both cards will be hearts?

4. *General: Die and Coin* Suppose you throw a fair die and flip a fair coin. Let's represent the outcomes of 3 on the die and heads on the coin by 3H.
   (a) One outcome is 3H. What are the other outcomes? What is the sample space?
   (b) Are all outcomes in the sample space equally likely? Explain.
   (c) What is the probability of getting heads and a number less than 3?

5. *General: Thumbtack*
   (a) Describe how you could use a relative frequency to estimate the probability that a thumbtack will land with its flat side down.
   (b) What is the sample space of outcomes for the thumbtack?
   (c) How would you make a probability assignment to this sample space if, when you drop 500 tacks, 340 land flat side down?

6. *Survey: Reaction to Poison Ivy* Allergic reactions to poison ivy can be miserable. Plant oils cause the reaction. Researchers at Allergy Institute did a study to see the effects of washing the oil off within 5 minutes of exposure. A random sample of 1000 people with known allergies to poison ivy participated in the study. Oil from the poison ivy plant was rubbed on a patch of skin. For 500 of the subjects, it was washed off *within* 5 minutes. For the other 500 subjects, the oil was washed off *after* 5 minutes. The results are summarized in Table 4-5.

TABLE 4-5   Time in Which Oil Was Washed Off

Reaction	Within 5 Minutes	After 5 Minutes	Row Total
None	420	50	470
Mild	60	330	390
Strong	20	120	140
Column Total	500	500	1000

Let's use the following notation for the various events: W = washing oil off within 5 minutes, A = washing oil off after 5 minutes, N = no reaction, M = mild reaction, S = strong reaction. Find the following probabilities for a person selected at random from this sample of 1000 subjects.
   (a) $P(N)$, $P(M)$, $P(S)$
   (b) $P(N$, given $W)$, $P(S$, given $W)$
   (c) $P(N$, given $A)$, $P(S$, given $A)$
   (d) $P(N$ and $W)$, $P(M$ and $W)$
   (e) $P(N$ or $M)$. Are the events N = no reaction and M = mild reaction mutually exclusive? Explain.
   (f) Are the events N = no reaction and W = washing oil off within 5 minutes independent? Explain.

7. *General: Two Dice* In a game of craps you roll two fair dice. Whether you win or lose depends on the sum of the numbers occurring on the tops of the dice. Let x be the random variable that is the sum of the numbers on the tops of the dice.
   (a) What values can x take on?
   (b) What is the probability distribution of these x values (that is, what is the probability that $x = 2$, 3, etc.)?

8. *Academic: Passing French* Class records at Rockwood College indicate that a student selected at random has probability 0.77 of passing French 101. For the student who passes French 101, the probability is 0.90 that he or she will pass French 102. What is the probability that a student selected at random will pass both French 101 and French 102?

9. *Combination: City Council* There is money to send two of eight city council members to a conference in Honolulu. All want to go, so they decide to choose the members to go to the conference by a random process. How many different combinations of two council members can be selected from the eight who want to go to the conference?

10. Compute (a) $P_{7,2}$ (b) $C_{7,2}$ (c) $P_{3,3}$ (d) $C_{4,4}$

11. *Inspection: Food Processing* Freeze Dry Food, Inc., packages all its foods in clear plastic that is sealed. The quality control for the packaging process checks for three items: (1) that the weight shown is correct, (2) that the label is correct, and (3) that the package is properly sealed. These three processes can be done in any order. A computer-operated device directs the packages to the three inspection stations according to backlog in that area. If there is a larger backlog in one area, products are sent to one of the other two areas first. In how many different ways can a package be cycled through the three inspection stations?

12. *Scheduling: College Courses* A student must satisfy the literature, social science, and philosophy requirements this semester. There are four literature courses to select from, three social science courses, and two philosophy courses. Make a tree diagram showing all the possible sequences of literature, social science, and philosophy courses.

13. *General: Multiplication Rule* There are five multiple-choice questions on an exam, each with four possible answers. Use the multiplication rule of counting to determine the number of possible answer sequences for the five questions. Only one of the sets can contain all five correct answers. If you are guessing, so that you are as likely to choose one sequence of answers as another, what is the probability of getting all five answers correct?

14. *General: Multiplication Rule* A coin is tossed six times. Use the multiplication rule of counting to determine the number of possible head–tail sequences that can occur.

15. *General: Combination Lock* To open a combination lock, you turn the dial to the right and stop at a number; then you turn it to the left and stop at a second number. Finally, you turn it back to the right and stop at a third number. If you used the correct sequence of numbers, the lock opens. If the dial of the lock contains 10 numbers, 0 through 9, use the multiplication rule to determine the number of different combinations possible for the lock. (*Note:* The same number can be reused.)

16. *General: Combination Lock* You have a combination lock. Again, to open it you turn the knob to the right and stop at a first number; then you turn it to the left and stop at a second number. Finally, you turn it to the right and stop at a third number. Suppose you remember that the three numbers for your lock are 2, 9, and 5, but you don't remember the order in which the numbers occur. How many permutations of these three numbers are possible?

DATA HIGHLIGHTS: GROUP PROJECTS

Break into small groups and discuss the following topics. Organize a brief outline in which you summarize the main points of your group discussion.

1. Look at Figure 4-13, "Who's Cracking the Books?"

   (a) Does the figure show the probability distribution of grade records for male students? for female students? Describe all the grade-record probability distributions shown in Figure 4-13. Find the probability that a male student selected at random has a grade record showing mostly A's.

   (b) Is the probability distribution shown for all students making mostly A's? Explain your answer. *Hint:* Do the percentages shown for mostly A's add up to 1? Can Figure 4-13 be used to determine the probability that a student selected at random has mostly A's? Can it be used to determine the probability that a female student selected at random has mostly A's? What is the probability?

FIGURE 4-13

Who's Cracking the Books?

Undergraduate Grade Record by Student Characteristic

Student characteristic		C's and D's or lower	B's and C's	Mostly B's	A's and B's	Mostly A's
Gender:	Men	38.8 %	16.6 %	22.6 %	9.6 %	12.4 %
	Women	29.4	16.2	26.2	12.0	16.2
Class level:	Graduating senior	15.8 %	21.9 %	34.5 %	14.7 %	13.0 %
	All other class levels	35.4	15.8	23.6	10.5	14.7
Age:	18 or younger	42.6 %	14.7 %	23.4 %	9.4 %	10.0 %
	19 to 23	38.1	19.0	25.1	9.4	8.3
	24 to 29	33.3	16.9	24.7	10.3	14.9
	30 to 39	23.1	13.2	25.9	14.8	23.0
	40 and older	20.1	10.1	22.0	14.8	33.0

Source: U.S. Department of Education

(c) Can we use the information shown in the figure to determine the probability that a graduating senior has grades consisting of mostly B's or higher? What is the probability?

(d) Does Figure 4-13 give sufficient information to determine the probability that a student selected at random is in the age range 19 to 23 *and* has grades that are mostly B's? What is the probability that a student selected at random has grades that are mostly B's, *given* he or she is in the age range 19 to 23?

(e) Suppose that 65% of the students at State University are between 19 and 23 years of age. What is the probability that a student selected at random is in this age range *and* has grades that are mostly B's?

2. Consider the information given in Figure 4-14, "Vulnerable Knees." What is the probability that an orthopedic case selected at random involves knee problems? Of

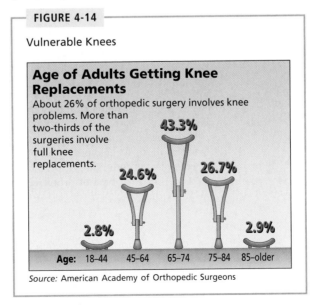

FIGURE 4-14

Vulnerable Knees

Age of Adults Getting Knee Replacements

About 26% of orthopedic surgery involves knee problems. More than two-thirds of the surgeries involve full knee replacements.

43.3%

24.6%

26.7%

2.8%

2.9%

Age: 18–44   45–64   65–74   75–84   85–older

Source: American Academy of Orthopedic Surgeons

those cases, estimate the probability that the case requires full knee replacement. Compute the probability that an orthopedic case selected at random involves a knee problem *and* requires a full knee replacement. Next, look at the probability distribution for ages of patients requiring full knee replacements. Medicare insurance coverage begins when a person reaches age 65. What is the probability that the age of a person receiving a knee replacement is 65 or older?

LINKING CONCEPTS: WRITING PROJECTS

Discuss each of the following topics in class or review the topics on your own. Then write a brief but complete essay in which you summarize the main points. Please include formulas as appropriate.

1. Discuss the following concepts and give examples from everyday life where you encounter each concept. *Hint:* For instance, consider the "experiment" of arriving for class. Some possible outcomes are not arriving (that is, missing class), arriving on time, and arriving late.

   (a) Sample space.

   (b) Probability assignment to a sample space. In your discussion, be sure to include answers to the following questions.

      (i) Is there more than one valid way to assign probabilities to a sample space? Explain and give an example.

      (ii) How can probabilities be estimated by relative frequencies? How can probabilities be computed if events are equally likely?

2. Discuss the concepts of mutually exclusive events and independent events. List several examples of each type of event from everyday life.

   (a) If A and B are mutually exclusive events, does it follow that A and B *cannot* be independent events? Give an example to demonstrate your answer. *Hint:* Discuss an election where only one person can win the election. Let A be the event that party A's candidate wins, and let B be the event that party B's candidate wins. Does the outcome of one event determine the outcome of the other event? Are A and B mutually exclusive events?

   (b) Discuss conditions under which $P(A \text{ and } B) = P(A) \cdot P(B)$ is true. Under what conditions is this not true?

   (c) Discuss conditions under which $P(A \text{ or } B) = P(A) + P(B)$ is true. Under what conditions is this not true?

3. Although we learn a good deal about probability in this course, the main emphasis is on statistics. Write a few paragraphs in which you talk about the distinction between probability and statistics. In what types of problems would probability be the main tool? In what types of problems would statistics be the main tool? Give some examples of both types of problems. What kind of outcome or conclusions do we expect from each type of problem?

Using Technology

TI-84PLUS/TI-83PLUS • MINITAB • EXCEL • SPSS

Demonstration of the Law of Large Numbers

Computers can be used to simulate experiments. With packages such as Excel, Minitab, and SPSS, programs using random-number generators can be designed (see the *Technology Guide*) to simulate activities such as tossing a die.

The following printouts show the results of the simulations for tossing a die 6, 500, 50,000, 500,000, and 1,000,000 times. Notice how the relative frequencies of the outcomes approach the theoretical probabilities of 1/6 or 0.16667 for each outcome. Do you expect the same results every time the simulation is done? Why or why not?

Results of tossing one die 6 times

Outcome	Number of Occurrences	Relative Frequency
⚀	0	.00000
⚁	1	.16667
⚂	2	.33333
⚃	0	.00000
⚄	1	.16667
⚅	2	.33333

Results of tossing one die 500 times

Outcome	Number of Occurrences	Relative Frequency
⚀	87	.17400
⚁	83	.16600
⚂	91	.18200
⚃	69	.13800
⚄	87	.17400
⚅	83	.16600

Results of tossing one die 50,000 times

Outcome	Number of Occurrences	Relative Frequency
⚀	8528	.17056
⚁	8354	.16708
⚂	8246	.16492
⚃	8414	.16828
⚄	8178	.16356
⚅	8280	.16560

Results of tossing one die 500,000 times

Outcome	Number of Occurrences	Relative Frequency
⚀	83644	.16729
⚁	83368	.16674
⚂	83398	.16680
⚃	83095	.16619
⚄	83268	.16654
⚅	83227	.16645

Results of tossing one die 1,000,000 times

Outcome	Number of Occurrences	Relative Frequency
⚀	166643	.16664
⚁	166168	.16617
⚂	167391	.16739
⚃	165790	.16579
⚄	167243	.16724
⚅	166765	.16677

5

The Binomial Probability Distribution and Related Topics

Education is the key to unlock the golden door of freedom.

—George Washington Carver

George Washington Carver (1859–1943)

Carver was a winner of the Spingarn Medal for distinguished service in agricultural chemistry and the prestigious Roosevelt Medal for contributions to science. Carver was also a Fellow in the Royal Society of Arts in London, an honor given to very few Americans.

George Washington Carver won international fame for agricultural research. After graduating from Iowa State College, he was appointed a faculty member in the Iowa State Botany Department. Carver took charge of the greenhouse and started a fungus collection that later included more than 20,000 species. This collection brought him professional acclaim in the field of botany.

At the invitation of his friend Booker T. Washington, Carver joined the faculty of the Tuskegee Institute, where he spent the rest of his long and distinguished career. Carver's creative genius accounted for more than 300 inventions from peanuts, 118 inventions from sweet potatoes, and 75 inventions from pecans.

Gathering and analyzing data were important components of Carver's work. Methods you will learn in this course are widely used in research in every field, including agriculture.

PREVIEW QUESTIONS

◇ What is a random variable? How do you compute μ and σ for a discrete random variable? How do you compute μ and σ for linear combinations of independent random variables? (SECTION 5.1)

◇ Many of life's experiences consist of some successes together with some failures. Suppose you make *n* attempts to succeed at a certain project. How can you use the binomial probability distribution to compute the probability of *r* successes? (SECTION 5.2)

◇ How do you compute μ and σ for the binomial distribution? (SECTION 5.3)

◇ How is the binomial distribution related to other probability distributions, such as the geometric and Poisson? (SECTION 5.4)

For on-line student resources, visit **math.college.hmco.com/students** and follow the Statistics links to the Brase/Brase, *Understandable Statistics*, 8th edition web site.

Personality Preference Types: Introvert or Extrovert?

Isabel Briggs Myers was a pioneer in the study of personality types. Her work has been used successfully in counseling, educational, and industrial settings. In the book *A Guide to the Development and Use of the Myers-Briggs Type Indicators*, by Myers and McCaully, it was reported that based on a very large sample (2282 professors), approximately 45% of all university professors are extroverted.

After completing this chapter, you will be able to answer the following questions. Suppose you have classes with six different professors.

(a) What is the probability that all six are extroverts?

(b) What is the probability that none of your professors is an extrovert?

(c) What is the probability that at least two of your professors are extroverts?

(d) In a group of six professors selected at random, what is the *expected number* of extroverts? What is the *standard deviation* of the distribution?

(e) Suppose you were assigned to write an article for the student newspaper and you were given a quota (by the editor) of interviewing at least three extroverted professors. How many professors selected at random would you need to interview to be at least 90% sure of filling the quota?

(See Problem 22 of Section 5.3.)

◇ **COMMENT** Both extroverted and introverted professors can be excellent teachers. ◇

5.1 Introduction to Random Variables and Probability Distributions

FOCUS POINTS

✓ Distinguish between discrete and continuous random variables.

✓ Graph discrete probability distributions.

✓ Compute μ and σ for a discrete probability distribution.

✓ Compute μ and σ for a linear function of a random variable x.

✓ Compute μ and σ for a linear combination of two independent random variables.

Random Variables

For our purposes, we say that a *statistical experiment* or *observation* is any process by which measurements are obtained. Examples are

1. Counting the number of eggs in a robin's nest

2. Measuring daily rainfall in inches

3. Counting the number of defective light bulbs in a case of bulbs

4. Measuring the weight in kilograms of a polar bear cub

Let x represent a quantitative variable that is measured or observed in an experiment. We are interested in the numerical values that x can take on. So x = number of eggs in a robin's nest and x = weight in kilograms of a polar bear cub would be examples of such quantitative variables. Furthermore, we say that the quantitative variable x is a *random variable* because the value that x takes on in a given experiment is a chance or random outcome. We will study two types of random variables: *discrete random variables* and *continuous random variables*.

Discrete random variable

> When the observations of a quantitative random variable can take on only a finite number of values or a countable number of values, we say that the variable is a **discrete random variable**.

We know what a *finite* number of values is, but what is a *countable* number of values? As an example, let the random variable x be the number of wells an oil prospector drills until the first productive well is found. Then x could be any of the values 1, 2, 3. . . . In theory, we have an infinite number of possibilities for the values of x. The set of values of x corresponds to the set of counting numbers. Therefore, this type of infinity is called *countable*, and we say x has a countable number of values. This is an intuitive approach to the concept of a countable set. The reader interested in a more rigorous discussion is referred to the advanced text *Introduction to Mathematical Statistics* by Hogg and Craig (Macmillan Publishing).

In most of the cases we will consider, a *discrete random variable* will be the result of a count (the terms *countable* and *discrete*, however, have different mathematical meanings). For instance, the number of students in a certain section of a statistics course this term is a discrete random variable. The value must be a counting number such as 25, or 57, or 135, and so forth. The values 25.34 or $25\frac{1}{2}$ are not possible. The cost of tuition to the nearest dollar or nearest cent is another example of a discrete random variable. In this case, we are counting dollars or cents.

Continuous random variable

> When the observations of a quantitative random variable can take on any of the countless number of values in a line interval, we say that the variable is a **continuous random variable**.

For our purposes, we will see most *continuous random variables* occurring as the result of a measurement. For example, the air pressure in an automobile tire represents a continuous random variable. The air pressure could in theory take on any value from 0 lb/in^2 (psi) to the bursting pressure of the tire. Values such as 20.126 psi, 20.12678 psi, and so forth are possible. Another example is the height of students in your statistics class. The height could in theory take on any value from a low of, say, 3 feet to a high of, say, 7.25 feet.

The distinction between discrete and continuous random variables is important because of the different mathematical techniques associated with the two kinds of random variables. Although we will not discuss these techniques at great length in this book, the distinction is very important in the study of advanced mathematical statistics.

In general, measurements of quantities such as length, weight, volume, temperature, or time yield continuous random variables. If the temperature changes from 12°C to 13°C, for example, it must take on all the temperature values between 12 and 13. Temperatures cannot just jump from one reading to the next. Discrete random variables often come from counts, such as the number of passing scores on an exam or the number of weeds in a garden.

GUIDED EXERCISE 1

Discrete or continuous random variables

Which of the following random variables are discrete and which are continuous?

(a) *Measure* the time it takes a student selected at random to register for the fall term.

⇨ Time can take on any value, so this is a continuous random variable.

(b) *Count* the number of bad checks drawn on Upright Bank on a day selected at random.

⇨ The number of bad checks can be only a whole number such as 0, 1, 2, 3, etc. This is a discrete variable.

Continued

GUIDED EXERCISE 1 continued

(c) *Measure* the amount of gasoline needed to drive your car 200 miles.

➩ We are measuring volume, which can assume any value, so this is a continuous random variable.

(d) Pick a random sample of 50 registered voters in a district and find the number who voted in the last county election.

➩ This is a count, so the variable is discrete.

Probability Distribution of a Discrete Random Variable

A random variable has a probability distribution whether it is discrete or continuous.

Probability distribution

> A **probability distribution** is an assignment of probabilities to the specific values of a random variable or to a range of values of the random variable.

> **Features of the probability distribution of a discrete random variable**
>
> 1. The probability distribution has a probability assigned to *each* value of the random variable.
>
> 2. The sum of all the assigned probabilities must be 1.

EXAMPLE 1

Discrete probability distribution

Dr. Mendoza developed a test to measure boredom tolerance. He administered it to a group of 20,000 adults between the ages of 25 and 35. The possible scores were 0, 1, 2, 3, 4, 5, and 6, with 6 indicating the highest tolerance for boredom. The test results for this group are shown in Table 5-1.

(a) If a subject is chosen at random from this group, the probability that he or she will have a score of 3 is 6000/20,000, or 0.30. In a similar way, we can use the relative frequency to compute the probabilities for the other scores (Table 5-2). These probability assignments make up the probability distribution. Notice

TABLE 5-1	Boredom Tolerance Test Scores for 20,000 Subjects
Score	Number of Subjects
0	1400
1	2600
2	3600
3	6000
4	4400
5	1600
6	400

TABLE 5-2	Probability Distribution of Scores on Boredom Tolerance Test
Score x	Probability $P(x)$
0	0.07
1	0.13
2	0.18
3	0.30
4	0.22
5	0.08
6	0.02
	$\Sigma P(x) = 1$

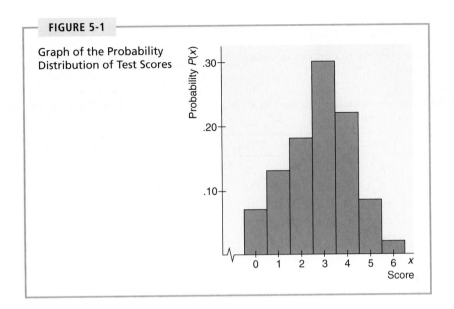

FIGURE 5-1

Graph of the Probability
Distribution of Test Scores

that the scores are mutually exclusive: No one subject has two scores. The sum
of the probabilities of all the scores is 1.

(b) The graph of this distribution is simply a relative-frequency histogram (see
Figure 5-1) in which the height of the bar over a score represents the probability
of that score. Since each bar is one unit wide, the area of the bar over a score
equals the height and thus represents the probability of that score. Since the sum
of the probabilities is 1, the area under the graph is also 1.

(c) The Topnotch Clothing Company needs to hire someone with a score on the
boredom tolerance test of 5 or 6 to operate the fabric press machine. Since the
scores 5 and 6 are mutually exclusive, the probability that someone in the group
who took the boredom tolerance test made either a 5 or a 6 is the sum

$$P(5 \; or \; 6) = P(5) + P(6)$$
$$= 0.08 + 0.02 = 0.10$$

Notice that to find $P(5 \; or \; 6)$, we could have simply added the *areas* of the bars
over 5 and over 6. One out of 10 of the group who took the boredom tolerance test would qualify for the position at Topnotch Clothing.   ◊

GUIDED
EXERCISE **2**

Discrete probability distribution

One of the elementary tools of cryptanalysis (the science of code breaking) is to use relative
frequencies of occurrence of different letters in the alphabet to break standard English alphabet
codes. Large samples of plain text such as newspaper stories generally yield about the same
relative frequencies for letters. A sample 1000 letters long yielded the information in Table 5-3.

Continued

GUIDED EXERCISE 2 continued

(a) Use the relative frequencies to compute the omitted probabilities in Table 5-3.

⟹ Table 5-4 shows the completion of Table 5-3.

TABLE 5-3   Frequencies of Letters in a 1000-Letter Sample

Letter	Freq.	Prob.	Letter	Freq.	Prob.
A	73	——	N	78	0.078
B	9	0.009	O	74	——
C	30	0.030	P	27	0.027
D	44	0.044	Q	3	0.003
E	130	——	R	77	0.077
F	28	0.028	S	63	0.063
G	16	0.016	T	93	0.093
H	35	0.035	U	27	——
I	74	——	V	13	0.013
J	2	0.002	W	16	0.016
K	3	0.003	X	5	0.005
L	35	0.035	Y	19	0.019
M	25	0.025	Z	1	0.001

Source: Elementary Cryptanalysis: A Mathematical Approach, by Abraham Sinkov. Copyright © 1968 by Yale University. Reprinted by permission of Random House, Inc.

TABLE 5-4   Entries for Table 5-3

Letter	Relative Frequency	Probability
A	$\frac{73}{1,000}$	0.073
E	$\frac{130}{1,000}$	0.130
I	$\frac{74}{1,000}$	0.074
O	$\frac{74}{1,000}$	0.074
U	$\frac{27}{1,000}$	0.027

(b) Do the probabilities of all the individual letters add up to 1?

⟹ Yes.

(c) If a letter is selected at random from a newspaper story, what is the probability that the letter will be a vowel?

⟹ If a letter is selected at random,

$$P(a,\ e,\ i,\ o,\ or\ u) = P(a) + P(e) + P(i) + P(o) + P(u)$$
$$= 0.073 + 0.130 + 0.074 + 0.074 + 0.027$$
$$= 0.378$$

Mean and standard deviation of a discrete probability distribution

A probability distribution can be thought of as a relative-frequency distribution based on a very large n. As such, it has a mean and standard deviation. If we are referring to the probability distribution of a *population*, then we use the Greek letters μ for the mean and σ for the standard deviation. When we see the Greek letters used, we know the information given is from the *entire population* rather than just a sample. If we have a sample probability distribution, we use $\bar{x}$ (x bar) and s, respectively, for the mean and standard deviation.

> The **mean** and the **standard deviation of a discrete population probability distribution** are found by using these formulas:
>
> $\mu = \Sigma x P(x)$; μ is called the **expected value** of x
>
> $\sigma = \sqrt{\Sigma (x - \mu)^2 P(x)}$ is called the standard deviation of x
>
> where x is the value of a random variable,
> $P(x)$ is the probability of that variable, and
>   the sum Σ is taken for all the values of the random variable.
>
> *Note:* μ is the *population mean* and σ is the underlying *population standard deviation* because the sum Σ is taken over *all* values of the random variable (i.e., the entire sample space).

Expected value

The mean of a probability distribution is often called the *expected value* of the distribution. This terminology reflects the idea that the mean represents a "central point" or "cluster point" for the entire distribution. Of course, the mean or expected value is an average value, and as such, it *need not be a point of the sample space.*

The standard deviation is often represented as a measure of *risk*. A larger standard deviation implies a greater likelihood that the random variable x is different from the expected value μ.

EXAMPLE 2

Expected value, standard deviation

Are we influenced to buy a product by an ad we saw on TV? National Infomercial Marketing Association determined the number of times *buyers* of a product watched a TV infomercial *before* purchasing the product. The results are shown here:

Number of Times Buyers Saw Infomercial	1	2	3	4	5*
Percentage of Buyers	27%	31%	18%	9%	15%

*This category was 5 or more, but will be treated as 5 in this example.

We can treat the information shown as an estimate of the probability distribution because the events are mutually exclusive and the sum of the percentages is 100%. Compute the mean and standard deviation of the distribution.

SOLUTION: We put the data in the first two columns of a computation table and then fill in the other entries (see Table 5-5).

TABLE 5-5   Number of Times Buyers View Infomercial Before Making Purchase

x (number of viewings)	$P(x)$	$xP(x)$	$x - \mu$	$(x - \mu)^2$	$(x - \mu)^2 P(x)$
1	0.27	0.27	-1.54	2.372	0.640
2	0.31	0.62	-0.54	0.292	0.091
3	0.18	0.54	0.46	0.212	0.038
4	0.09	0.36	1.46	2.132	0.192
5	0.15	0.75	2.46	6.052	0.908
		$\mu = \Sigma xP(x) = 2.54$			$\Sigma (x - \mu)^2 P(x) = 1.869$

The average number of times a buyer views the infomercial before purchase is

$$\mu = \Sigma x P(x) = 2.54 \text{ (sum of column 3)}$$

To find the standard deviation, we take the square root of the sum of column 6:

$$\sigma = \sqrt{\Sigma (x - \mu)^2 P(x)} \approx \sqrt{1.869} \approx 1.37$$ ◇

● **CALCULATOR NOTE** Some calculators, including the TI-84Plus/TI-83Plus models, accept fractional frequencies. If yours does, you can get μ and σ directly by using techniques for grouped data and the calculator's STAT mode.

GUIDED EXERCISE 3

Expected value

At a carnival, you pay $2.00 to play a coin-flipping game with three fair coins. On each coin one side has the number 0 and the other side has the number 1. You flip the three coins at one time and you win $1.00 for every 1 that appears on top. Are your expected earnings equal to the cost to play? We'll answer this question in several steps.

(a) In this game, the random variable of interest counts the number of 1s that show. What is the sample space for the values of this random variable?

⟹ The sample space is {0, 1, 2, 3}, since any of these numbers of 1s can appear.

(b) There are eight equally likely outcomes for throwing three coins. They are 000, 001, 010, 011, 100, 101, _____, and _____.

⟹ 110 and 111.

(c) Complete Table 5-6.

TABLE 5-6

Number of 1s, x	Frequency	P(x)	xP(x)
0	1	0.125	0
1	3	0.375	____
2	3	____	____
3	____	____	____

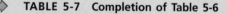

TABLE 5-7 Completion of Table 5-6

Number of 1s, x	Frequency	P(x)	xP(x)
0	1	0.125	0
1	3	0.375	0.375
2	3	0.375	0.750
3	1	0.125	0.375

(d) The expected value is the sum

$$\mu = \Sigma x P(x)$$

Sum the appropriate column of Table 5-6 to find this value. Are your expected earnings less than, equal to, or more than the cost of the game?

⟹ The expected value can be found by summing the last column of Table 5-7. The expected value is $1.50. It cost $2.00 to play the game; the expected value is less than the cost. The carnival is making money. In the long run, the carnival can expect to make an average of about 50 cents per player.

We have seen probability distributions of discrete variables and the formulas to compute the mean and standard deviation of a discrete population probability distribution. Probability distributions of continuous random variables are similar except that the probability assignments are made to intervals of values rather than to specific values of the random variable. We will see an important example of a discrete probability distribution, the binomial distribution, in the next section, and one of a continuous probability distribution in Chapter 6 when we study the normal distribution.

We conclude this section with some useful information about combining random variables.

Linear Functions of a Random Variable

Let a and b be any constants, and let x be a random variable. Then the new random variable $L = a + bx$ is called a *linear function of x*. Using some more advanced mathematics, the following can be proved.

> Let x be a random variable with mean μ and standard deviation σ. Then the **linear function $L = a + bx$** has mean, variance, and standard deviation as follows:
>
> $$\mu_L = a + b\mu$$
> $$\sigma_L^2 = b^2\sigma^2$$
> $$\sigma_L = \sqrt{b^2\sigma^2} = |b|\sigma$$

Linear Combinations of Independent Random Variables

Independent random variables

Suppose we have two random variables x_1 and x_2. These variables are *independent* if any event involving x_1 by itself is *independent* of any event involving x_2 by itself. Sometimes, we want to combine independent random variables and examine the mean and standard deviation of the resulting combination.

Let x_1 and x_2 be independent random variables. Let a and b be any constants. Then the new random variable $W = ax_1 + bx_2$ is called a *linear combination of x_1 and x_2*. Using some more advanced mathematics, the following can be proved.

> Let x_1 and x_2 be independent random variables with respective means μ_1 and μ_2, and variances σ_1^2 and σ_2^2. For the **linear combination $W = ax_1 + bx_2$**, the mean, variance, and standard deviation are as follows:
>
> $$\mu_W = a\mu_1 + b\mu_2$$
> $$\sigma_W^2 = a^2\sigma_1^2 + b^2\sigma_2^2$$
> $$\sigma_W = \sqrt{a^2\sigma_1^2 + b^2\sigma_2^2}$$

Note: The formula for the mean of a linear combination of random variables is valid regardless of whether the variables are independent or not. However, *the formulas for the variance and standard deviation are valid* only if x_1 and x_2 are *independent* random variables. In later work (Chapter 7 on), we will use independent random samples to ensure that the resulting variables (usually means, proportions, etc.) are statistically independent.

EXAMPLE 3

Linear combinations of independent random variables

Let x_1 and x_2 be independent random variables with respective means $\mu_1 = 75$, $\mu_2 = 50$, and standard deviations $\sigma_1 = 16$, $\sigma_2 = 9$.

(a) Let $L = 3 + 2x_1$. Compute the mean, variance, and standard deviation of L.

SOLUTION: L is a linear function of the random variable x_1. Using the formulas with $a = 3$ and $b = 2$, we have

$$\mu_L = 3 + 2\mu_1 = 3 + 2(75) = 153$$
$$\sigma_L^2 = 2^2\sigma_1^2 = 4(16)^2 = 1024$$
$$\sigma_L = |2|\sigma_1 = 2(16) = 32$$

Notice that the variance and standard deviation of the linear function are influenced only by the coefficient of x_1 in the linear function.

(b) Let $W = x_1 + x_2$. Find the mean, variance, and standard deviation of W.

SOLUTION: W is a linear combination of the independent random variables x_1 and x_2. Using the formulas with both a and b equal to 1, we have

$$\mu_W = \mu_1 + \mu_2 = 75 + 50 = 125$$
$$\sigma_W^2 = \sigma_1^2 + \sigma_2^2 = 16^2 + 9^2 = 337$$
$$\sigma_W = \sqrt{\sigma_1^2 + \sigma_2^2} = \sqrt{337} \approx 18.36$$

(c) Let $W = x_1 - x_2$. Find the mean, variance, and standard deviation of W.

SOLUTION: W is a linear combination of the independent random variables x_1 and x_2. Using the formulas with $a = 1$ and $b = -1$, we have

$$\mu_W = \mu_1 - \mu_2 = 75 - 50 = 25$$
$$\sigma_W^2 = 1^2\sigma_1^2 + (-1)^2\sigma_2^2 = 16^2 + 9^2 = 337$$
$$\sigma_W = \sqrt{\sigma_1^2 + \sigma_2^2} = \sqrt{337} \approx 18.36$$

(d) Let $W = 3x_1 - 2x_2$. Find the mean, variance, and standard deviation of W.

SOLUTION: W is a linear combination of the independent random variables x_1 and x_2. Using the formulas with $a = 3$ and $b = -2$, we have

$$\mu_W = 3\mu_1 - 2\mu_2 = 3(75) - 2(50) = 125$$
$$\sigma_W^2 = 3^2\sigma_1^2 + (-2)^2\sigma_2^2 = 9(16^2) + 4(9^2) = 2628$$
$$\sigma_W = \sqrt{2628} \approx 51.26$$

◇ COMMENT: Problem 20 of Section 10.1 shows how to find the mean, variance, and standard deviation of a linear combination of two *linearly dependent* random variables. ◇

SECTION 5.1   PROBLEMS

1. *Random Variables: Classification* Which of the following are continuous variables, and which are discrete?
   (a) Number of traffic fatalities per year in the state of Florida
   (b) Distance a golf ball travels after being hit with a driver
   (c) Time required to drive from home to college on any given day
   (d) Number of ships in Pearl Harbor on any given day
   (e) Your weight before breakfast each morning

VIEWPOINT

The Rosetta Project

Around 196 B.C., Egyptian priests inscribed a decree on a granite slab affirming the rule of 13-year-old Ptolemy V. The proclamation was in Egyptian hieroglyphics with another translation in a form of ancient Greek. By 1799, the meaning of Egyptian hieroglyphics had been lost for many centuries. However, Napoleon's troops discovered the granite slab (Rosetta Stone). Linguists used the Rosetta Stone and their knowledge of ancient Greek to unlock the meaning of the Egyptian hieroglyphics.

Linguistic experts say that because of industrialization and globalization, by the year 2100 as many as 90% of the world's languages may be extinct. To help preserve some of these languages for future generations, 1000 translations of the first three chapters of Genesis have been inscribed in tiny text onto 3-inch nickel disks and encased in hardened glass balls that are expected to last at least 1000 years. Why Genesis? Because it is the most translated text in the world. The Rosetta Project is sending the disks to libraries and universities all over the world. It is very difficult to send information into the future. However, if in the year 2500 linguists are using the "Rosetta Disks" to unlock the meaning of a lost language, you may be sure they will use statistical methods of cryptanalysis (see Guided Exercise 2). To find out more about the Rosetta Project, visit the Brase/Brase statistics site at **http://math.college.hmco.com/students** and find the link to the Rosetta Project site.

2. *Random Variables: Classification* Which of the following are continuous variables, and which are discrete?
   (a) Speed of an airplane
   (b) Age of a college professor chosen at random
   (c) Number of books in the college bookstore
   (d) Weight of a football player chosen at random
   (e) Number of lightning strikes in Rocky Mountain National Park on a given day

3. *Probability Distribution* Consider each distribution. Determine if it is a valid probability distribution or not, and explain your answer.

(a)

x	0	1	2
P(x)	0.25	0.60	0.15

(b)

x	0	1	2
P(x)	0.25	0.60	0.20

4. *Marketing: Age* What is the age distribution of promotion-sensitive shoppers? A *supermarket super shopper* is defined as a shopper for whom at least 70% of the items purchased were on sale or purchased with a coupon. The following table is based on information taken from *Trends in the United States* (Food Marketing Institute, Washington, D.C.).

Age range, years	18–28	29–39	40–50	51–61	62 and over
Midpoint x	23	34	45	56	67
Percent of super shoppers	7%	44%	24%	14%	11%

For the 62 and over group, use the midpoint 67 years.

(a) Using the age midpoints x and the percentage of super shoppers, do we have a valid probability distribution? Explain.

(b) Use a histogram to graph the probability distribution of part (a).

(c) Compute the expected age μ of a super shopper.

(d) Compute the standard deviation σ for ages of super shoppers.

5. *Marketing: Income* What is the income distribution of super shoppers (see Problem 4). In the following table, income units are in thousands of dollars, and each interval goes up to but does not include the given high value. The midpoints are given to the nearest thousand dollars.

Income range	5–15	15–25	25–35	35–45	45–55	55 or more
Midpoint x	10	20	30	40	50	60
Percent of super shoppers	21%	14%	22%	15%	20%	8%

(a) Using the income midpoints x and the percent of super shoppers, do we have a valid probability distribution? Explain.

(b) Use a histogram to graph the probability distribution of part (a).

(c) Compute the expected income μ of a super shopper.

(d) Compute the standard deviation σ for the income of super shoppers.

6. *Sociology: Family Size* The following data are based on information taken from the *Statistical Abstract of the United States* (112th Edition). In this table, x = size of family. The percentage data are the percentages of U.S. families of this size.

x	2	3	4	5	6	7 or more
%	42%	23%	21%	10%	3%	1%

(a) Convert the percentage data to probabilities and make a histogram of the probability distribution for family size.

(b) What is the probability that a family selected at random will have only two members?

(c) What is the probability that a family selected at random will have more than three members?

(d) Compute μ, the expected family size (round families of size 7 or more to size 7).

(e) Compute σ, the standard deviation (round families of size 7 or more to size 7).

7. *Working Conditions: Nursing* The head nurse on the third floor of a community hospital is interested in the number of nighttime room calls requiring a nurse. For a random sample of 208 nights (9:00 P.M. to 6:00 A.M.), the following information was obtained, where x = number of room calls requiring a nurse and f = frequency with which this many calls occurred (i.e., number of nights).

x	36	37	38	39	40	41	42	43	44	45
f	6	10	11	20	26	32	34	28	25	16

(a) If a night is chosen at random from these 208 nights, use relative frequencies to find $P(x)$ when x = 36, 37, 38, 39, 40, 41, 42, 43, 44, and 45.

(b) Use a histogram to graph the probability distribution of part (a).

(c) Assuming that these 208 nights represent the population of all nights at the community hospital, what do you estimate the probability is that, on a randomly selected night, there will be from 39 to 43 (including 39 and 43) room calls requiring a nurse?

(d) What do you estimate the probability is that there will be from 36 to 40 (including 36 and 40) room calls requiring a nurse?

(e) Find the expected number of room calls requiring a nurse.

(f) Find the standard deviation of the x distribution.

8. *History: Florence Nightingale* What was the age distribution of nurses in Great Britain at the time of Florence Nightingale? Thanks to Florence Nightingale and the British census of 1851, we have the following information (based on data from the classic text *Notes on Nursing*, by Florence Nightingale). *Note:* In 1851 there were 25,466 nurses in Great Britain. Furthermore, Nightingale made a strict distinction between nurses and domestic servants.

Age range (yr)	20–29	30–39	40–49	50–59	60–69	70–79	80+
Midpoint x	24.5	34.5	44.5	54.5	64.5	74.5	84.5
Percent of nurses	5.7%	9.7%	19.5%	29.2%	25.0%	9.1%	1.8%

(a) Using the age midpoints x and the percent of nurses, do we have a valid probability distribution? Explain.

(b) Use a histogram to graph the probability distribution of part (a).

(c) Find the probability that a British nurse selected at random in 1851 would be 60 years of age or older.

(d) Compute the expected age μ of a British nurse contemporary to Florence Nightingale.

(e) Compute the standard deviation σ for ages of nurses shown in the distribution.

9. *Fishing: Trout* The following data are based on information taken from *Daily Creel Summary*, published by the Paiute Indian Nation, Pyramid Lake, Nevada. Movie stars and U.S. presidents have fished Pyramid Lake. It is one of the best places in the lower 48 states to catch trophy cutthroat trout. In this table, x = number of fish caught in a 6-hour period. The percentage data are the percentages of fishermen who caught x fish in a 6-hour period while fishing from shore.

x	0	1	2	3	4 or more
%	44%	36%	15%	4%	1%

(a) Convert the percentages to probabilities and make a histogram of the probability distribution.

(b) Find the probability that a fisherman selected at random fishing from shore catches one or more fish in a 6-hour period.

(c) Find the probability that a fisherman selected at random fishing from shore catches two or more fish in a 6-hour period.

(d) Compute μ, the expected value of the number of fish caught per fisherman in a 6-hour period (round 4 or more to 4).

(e) Compute σ, the standard deviation of the number of fish caught per fisherman in a 6-hour period (round 4 or more to 4).

10. *Criminal Justice: Parole* USA Today reported that approximately 25% of all state prison inmates released on parole become repeat offenders while on parole. Suppose the parole board is examining five prisoners up for parole. Let x = number of prisoners out of five on parole who become repeat offenders. The methods of Section 5.2 can be used to compute the probability assignments for the x distribution.

x	0	1	2	3	4	5
P(x)	0.237	0.396	0.264	0.088	0.015	0.001

(a) Find the probability that one or more of the five parolees will be repeat offenders. How does this number relate to the probability that none of the parolees will be repeat offenders?

(b) Find the probability that two or more of the five parolees will be repeat offenders.

(c) Find the probability that four or more of the five parolees will be repeat offenders.

(d) Compute μ, the expected number of repeat offenders out of five.

(e) Compute σ, the standard deviation of the number of repeat offenders out of five.

11. *Fund Raiser: Hiking Club* The college hiking club is having a fund raiser to buy new equipment for fall and winter outings. The club is selling Chinese fortune cookies at a price of $1 per cookie. Each cookie contains a piece of paper with a different number written on it. A random drawing will determine which number is the winner of a dinner for two at a local Chinese restaurant. The dinner is valued at $35. Since the fortune cookies were donated to the club, we can ignore the cost of the cookies. The club sold 719 cookies before the drawing.

(a) Lisa bought 15 cookies. What is the probability she will win the dinner for two? What is the probability she will not win?

(b) Lisa's expected earnings can be found by multiplying the value of the dinner by the probability that she will win. What are Lisa's expected earnings? How much did she effectively contribute to the hiking club?

12. *Spring Break: Caribbean Cruise* The college student senate is sponsoring a spring break Caribbean cruise raffle. The proceeds are to be donated to the Samaritan Center for the Homeless. A local travel agency donated the cruise, valued at $2000. The students sold 2852 raffle tickets at $5 per ticket.

(a) Kevin bought six tickets. What is the probability that Kevin will win the spring break cruise to the Caribbean? What is the probability that Kevin will not win the cruise?

(b) Expected earnings can be found by multiplying the value of the cruise by the probability that Kevin will win. What are Kevin's expected earnings? Is this more or less than the amount Kevin paid for the six tickets? How much did Kevin effectively contribute to the Samaritan Center for the Homeless?

13. *Expected Value: Life Insurance* Jim is a 60-year-old Anglo male in reasonably good health. He wants to take out a $50,000 term (that is, straight death benefit) life insurance policy until he is 65. The policy will expire on his 65th birthday. The probability of death in a given year is provided by the Vital Statistics Section of the *Statistical Abstract of the United States* (116th Edition).

x = age	60	61	62	63	64
P(death at this age)	0.01191	0.01292	0.01396	0.01503	0.01613

Jim is applying to Big Rock Insurance Company for his term insurance policy.

(a) What is the probability that Jim will die in his 60th year? Using this probability and the $50,000 death benefit, what is the expected loss to Big Rock Insurance?

(b) Repeat part (a) for years 61, 62, 63, and 64. What would be the total expected loss to Big Rock Insurance over the years 60 through 64?

(c) If Big Rock Insurance wants to make a profit of $700 above the expected total loss paid out for Jim's death, how much should it charge for the policy?

(d) If Big Rock Insurance Company charges $5000 for the policy, how much profit does the company expect to make?

14. *Expected Value: Life Insurance* Sara is a 60-year-old Anglo female in reasonably good health. She wants to take out a $50,000 term (that is, straight death benefit) life insurance policy until she is 65. The policy will expire on her 65th birthday. The probability of death in a given year is provided by the Vital Statistics Section of the *Statistical Abstract of the United States* (116th Edition).

x = age	60	61	62	63	64
P(death at this age)	0.00756	0.00825	0.00896	0.00965	0.01035

Sara is applying to Big Rock Insurance Company for her term insurance policy.
(a) What is the probability that Sara will die in her 60th year? Using this probability and the $50,000 death benefit, what is the expected loss to Big Rock Insurance?
(b) Repeat part (a) for years 61, 62, 63, and 64. What would be the total expected loss to Big Rock Insurance over the years 60 through 64?
(c) If Big Rock Insurance wants to make a profit of $700 above the expected total loss paid out for Sara's death, how much should it charge for the policy?
(d) If Big Rock Insurance Company charges $5000 for the policy, how much profit does the company expect to make?

15. *Combination of Random Variables: Golf* Norb and Gary are entered in a local golf tournament. Both have played the local course many times. Their scores are random variables with the following means and standard deviations.

Norb, x_1: $\mu_1 = 115$; $\sigma_1 = 12$ Gary, x_2: $\mu_2 = 100$; $\sigma_2 = 8$

In the tournament, Norb and Gary are not playing together, and we will assume their scores vary independently of each other.
(a) The difference between their scores is $W = x_1 - x_2$. Compute the mean, variance, and standard deviation for the random variable W.
(b) The average of their scores is $W = 0.5x_1 + 0.5x_2$. Compute the mean, variance, and standard deviation for the random variable W.
(c) The tournament rules have a special handicap system for each player. For Norb, the handicap formula is $L = 0.8x_1 - 2$. Compute the mean, variance, and standard deviation for the random variable L.
(d) For Gary, the handicap formula is $L = 0.95x_2 - 5$. Compute the mean, variance, and standard deviation for the random variable L.

16. *Combination of Random Variables: Repair Service* A computer repair shop has two work centers. The first center examines the computer to see what is wrong, and the second center repairs the computer. Let x_1 and x_2 be random variables representing the lengths of time in minutes to examine a computer (x_1) and to repair a computer (x_2). Assume x_1 and x_2 are independent random variables. Long-term history has shown the following times:

Examine computer, x_1: $\mu_1 = 28.1$ minutes; $\sigma_1 = 8.2$ minutes

Repair computer, x_2: $\mu_2 = 90.5$ minutes; $\sigma_2 = 15.2$ minutes

(a) Let $W = x_1 + x_2$ be a random variable representing the total time to examine and repair the computer. Compute the mean, variance, and standard deviation of W.
(b) Suppose it costs $1.50 per minute to examine the computer and $2.75 per minute to repair the computer. Then $W = 1.50x_1 + 2.75x_2$ is a random variable representing the service charges (without parts). Compute the mean, variance, and standard deviation of W.
(c) There is a flat rate of $1.50 per minute to examine the computer, and if no repairs are ordered, there is also an additional $50 service charge. Let $L = 1.5x_1 + 50$. Compute the mean, variance, and standard deviation of L.

17. *Combination of Random Variables: Insurance Risk* Insurance companies know the *risk* of insurance is greatly reduced if the company insures not just one person, but many people. How does this work? Let x be a random variable representing the expectation of life in years for a 25-year-old male (i.e., number of years until death). Then the mean and standard deviation of x are $\mu = 50.2$ years and $\sigma = 11.5$ years (Vital Statistics Section of the *Statistical Abstract of the United States*, 116th Edition).

Suppose Big Rock Insurance Company has sold life insurance policies to Joel and David. Both are 25 years old, unrelated, live in different states, and have about the same health record. Let x_1 and x_2 be random variables representing Joel's and David's life expectancies. It is reasonable to assume x_1 and x_2 are independent.

$$\text{Joel, } x_1\text{: } \mu_1 = 50.2 \qquad \sigma_1 = 11.5$$
$$\text{David, } x_2\text{: } \mu_2 = 50.2 \qquad \sigma_2 = 11.5$$

If life expectancy can be predicted with more accuracy, Big Rock will have less risk in its insurance business. Risk in this case is measured by σ (larger σ means more risk).

(a) The average life expectancy for Joel and David is $W = 0.5x_1 + 0.5x_2$. Compute the mean, variance, and standard deviation of W.

(b) Compare the mean life expectancy for a single policy (x_1) with that for two policies (W).

(c) Compare the standard deviation of the life expectancy for a single policy (x_1) with that for two policies (W).

(d) The mean life expectancy is the same for a single policy (x_1) as for two policies (W), but the standard deviation is smaller for two policies. What happens to the mean life expectancy and the standard deviation when we include more policies issued to people whose life expectancies have the same mean and standard deviation (i.e., 25-year-old males)? For instance, for three policies, $W = (\mu + \mu + \mu)/3 = \mu$ and $\sigma_W^2 = (1/3)^2\sigma^2 + (1/3)^2\sigma^2 + (1/3)^2\sigma^2 = (1/3)^2(3\sigma^2) = (1/3)\sigma^2$ and $\sigma_W = \dfrac{1}{\sqrt{3}}\sigma$. Likewise, for n such policies, $W = \mu$ and $\sigma_W^2 = (1/n)\sigma^2$ and

$\sigma_W = \dfrac{1}{\sqrt{n}}\sigma$. Looking at the general result, is it appropriate to say that when we

increase the number of policies to n, the risk decreases by a factor of $\dfrac{1}{\sqrt{n}}$?

5.2
Binomial Probabilities

Binomial Experiment

FOCUS POINTS

✓ List the defining features of a binomial experiment.

✓ Compute binomial probabilities using the formula $P(r) = C_{n,r}\, p^r q^{n-r}$.

✓ Use the binomial table to find $P(r)$.

✓ Use the binomial probability distribution to solve real-world applications.

On a TV quiz show each contestant has a try at the wheel of fortune. The wheel of fortune is a roulette wheel with 36 slots, one of which is gold. If the ball lands in the gold slot, the contestant wins $50,000. No other slot pays. What is the probability that the quiz show will have to pay the fortune to three contestants out of 100?

In this problem, the contestant and the quiz show sponsors are concerned about only two outcomes from the wheel of fortune: The ball lands on the gold, or the ball does not land on the gold. This problem is typical of an entire class of problems that are characterized by the feature that there are exactly two possible outcomes (for each trial) of interest. These problems are called *binomial experiments*, or *Bernoulli experiments*, after the Swiss mathematician Jacob Bernoulli, who studied them extensively in the late 1600s.

Features of a binomial
experiment

Features of a binomial experiment

1. There are a *fixed number of trials*. We denote this number by the letter *n*.

2. The *n* trials are *independent* and repeated under identical conditions.

3. Each trial has only *two outcomes:* success, denoted by *S*, and failure, denoted by *F*.

4. For each individual trial, the *probability of success is the same*. We denote the probability of success by *p* and that of failure by *q*. Since each trial results in either success or failure, $p + q = 1$ and $q = 1 - p$.

5. The central problem of a binomial experiment is to find the *probability of r successes out of n trials*.

EXAMPLE 4

Binomial experiment

Let's see how the wheel of fortune problem meets the criteria of a binomial experiment. We'll take the criteria one at a time.

SOLUTION:

1. Each of the 100 contestants has a trial at the wheel, so there are $n = 100$ trials in this problem.

2. Assuming that the wheel is fair, the *trials are independent,* since the result of one spin of the wheel has no effect on the results of other spins.

3. We are interested in only two outcomes on each spin of the wheel: The ball either lands on the gold, or it does not. Let's call landing on the gold *success* (*S*) and not landing on the gold *failure* (*F*). In general, the assignment of the terms *success* and *failure* to outcomes does not imply good or bad results. These terms are assigned simply for the user's convenience.

4. On each trial the probability *p* of success (landing on the gold) is 1/36, since there are 36 slots and only one of them is gold. Consequently, the probability of failure is

$$q = 1 - p = 1 - \frac{1}{36} = \frac{35}{36}$$

on each trial.

5. We want to know the probability of 3 successes out of 100 trials, so $r = 3$ in this example. It turns out that the probability the quiz show will have to pay the fortune to 3 contestants out of 100 is about 0.23. Later in this section we'll see how this probability was computed.   ◊

Anytime we make selections from a population *without replacement, we do not have independent trials.* However, replacement is often not practical. If the number of trials is quite small with respect to the population, we *almost* have independent trials, and we can say the situation is *closely approximated* by a binomial experiment. For instance, suppose we select 20 tuition bills at random from a collection of 10,000 bills issued at one college and observe if each bill is in error or not. If 600 of the 10,000 bills are in error, then the probability that the first one selected is in error is 600/10,000, or 0.0600. If the first is in error, then the probability that the second is in error is 599/9999, or 0.0599. Even if the first 19 bills selected are in error, the probability that the 20th is also in error is 581/9981, or 0.0582. All these probabilities round to 0.06, and we can say that the independence condition is approximately satisfied.

GUIDED EXERCISE 4

Binomial experiment

Let's analyze the following binomial experiment to determine p, q, n, and r:

According to the *Textbook of Medical Physiology,* 5th Edition, by Arthur Guyton, 9% of the population has blood type B. Suppose we choose 18 people at random from the population and test the blood type of each. What is the probability that three of these people have blood type B? (*Note:* Independence is approximated because 18 people is an extremely small sample with respect to the entire population.)

(a) In this experiment, we are observing whether or not a person has type B blood. We will say we have a success if the person has type B blood. What is failure?

⟹ Failure occurs if a person does not have type B blood.

(b) The probability of success is 0.09, since 9% of the population has type B blood. What is the probability of failure, q?

⟹ The probability of failure is
$$q = 1 - p$$
$$= 1 - 0.09 = 0.91$$

(c) In this experiment, there are $n =$ _____ trials.

⟹ In this experiment, $n = 18$.

(d) We wish to compute the probability of 3 successes out of 18 trials. In this case, $r =$ _____.

⟹ In this case, $r = 3$.

Next, we will see how to compute the probability of r successes out of n trials when we have a binomial experiment.

Computing Probabilities for a Binomial Experiment Using the Binomial Distribution Formula

The central problem of a binomial experiment is to find the probability of r successes out of n trials. Now we'll see how to find these probabilities.

A model with three trials

Suppose you are taking a timed final exam. You have three multiple-choice questions left to do. Each question has four suggested answers, and only one of the answers is correct. You have only 5 seconds left to do these three questions, so you decide to mark answers on the answer sheet without even reading the questions. Assuming that your answers are randomly selected, what is the probability that you get zero, one, two, or all three questions correct?

This is a binomial experiment. Each question can be thought of as a trial, so there are $n = 3$ trials. The possible outcomes on each trial are success S,

TABLE 5-8   Outcomes for a Binomial Experiment with $n = 3$ Trials

Outcome	Probability of Outcome					r (number of successes)
SSS	$P(SSS) = P(S)P(S)P(S)$	$= p^3$	$= (0.25)^3$		≈ 0.016	3
SSF	$P(SSF) = P(S)P(S)P(F)$	$= p^2q$	$= (0.25)^2(0.75)$		≈ 0.047	2
SFS	$P(SFS) = P(S)P(F)P(S)$	$= p^2q$	$= (0.25)^2(0.75)$		≈ 0.047	2
FSS	$P(FSS) = P(F)P(S)P(S)$	$= p^2q$	$= (0.25)^2(0.75)$		≈ 0.047	2
SFF	$P(SFF) = P(S)P(F)P(F)$	$= pq^2$	$= (0.25)(0.75)^2$		≈ 0.141	1
FSF	$P(FSF) = P(F)P(S)P(F)$	$= pq^2$	$= (0.25)(0.75)^2$		≈ 0.141	1
FFS	$P(FFS) = P(F)P(F)P(S)$	$= pq^2$	$= (0.25)(0.75)^2$		≈ 0.141	1
FFF	$P(FFF) = P(F)P(F)P(F)$	$= q^3$	$= (0.75)^3$		≈ 0.422	0

indicating a correct response, or failure F, meaning a wrong answer. The trials are independent—the outcome of any one trial does not affect the outcome of the others.

What is the probability of success on any question? Since you are guessing and there are four answers from which to select, the probability of a correct answer is 0.25. The probability q of a wrong answer is then 0.75. In short, we have a binomial experiment with $n = 3$, $p = 0.25$, and $q = 0.75$.

Now what are the possible outcomes in terms of success or failure for these three trials? Let's use the notation SSF to mean success on the first question, success on the second, and failure on the third. There are eight possible combinations of S's and F's. They are

$$SSS \qquad SSF \qquad SFS \qquad FSS \qquad SFF \qquad FSF \qquad FFS \qquad FFF$$

To compute the probability of each outcome, we can use the multiplication law because the trials are independent. For instance, the probability of success on the first two questions and failure on the last is

$$P(SSF) = P(S) \cdot P(S) \cdot P(F) = p \cdot p \cdot q = p^2q = (0.25)^2(0.75) \approx 0.047$$

In a similar fashion, we can compute the probability of each of the eight outcomes. These are shown in Table 5-8, along with the number of successes r associated with each outcome.

Now we can compute the probability of r successes out of three trials for $r = 0, 1, 2,$ or 3. Let's compute $P(1)$. The notation $P(1)$ stands for the probability of one success. For three trials, there are three different outcomes that show exactly one success. They are the outcomes SFF, FSF, and FFS. Since the outcomes are mutually exclusive, we can add the probabilities. So

$$\begin{aligned} P(1) = P(SFF \text{ or } FSF \text{ or } FFS) &= P(SFF) + P(FSF) + P(FFS) \\ &= pq^2 + pq^2 + pq^2 \\ &= 3pq^2 \\ &= 3(0.25)(0.75)^2 \\ &= 0.422 \end{aligned}$$

In the same way, we can find $P(0)$, $P(2)$, and $P(3)$. These values are shown in Table 5-9 on the next page.

TABLE 5-9 $P(r)$ for $n = 3$ Trials, $p = 0.25$

r (number of successes)	$P(r)$ (probability of r successes in 3 trials)		$P(r)$ for $p = 0.25$
0	$P(0) = P(FFF)$	$= q^3$	0.422
1	$P(1) = P(SFF) + P(FSF) + P(FFS)$	$= 3pq^2$	0.422
2	$P(2) = P(SSF) + P(SFS) + P(FSS)$	$= 3p^2q$	0.141
3	$P(3) = P(SSS)$	$= p^3$	0.016

We have done quite a bit of work to determine your chances of $r = 0, 1, 2,$ or 3 successes on three multiple-choice questions if you are just guessing. Now we see that there is only a small chance (about 0.016) that you will get them all correct.

Table 5-9 can be used as a model for computing the probability of r successes out of only *three* trials. How can we compute the probability of 7 successes out of 10 trials? We can develop a table for $n = 10$, but this would be a tremendous task because there are 1024 possible combinations of successes and failures on 10 trials. Fortunately, mathematicians have given us a direct formula to compute the probability of r successes for any number of trials.

General formula for binomial probability distribution

Formula for the binomial probability distribution

$$P(r) = \frac{n!}{r!(n - r)!} p^r q^{n - r} = C_{n,r} p^r q^{n - r}$$

where n = number of trials

p = probability of success on each trial

$q = 1 - p$ = probability of failure on each trial

r = random variable representing the number of successes out of n trials ($0 \leq r \leq n$)

! = factorial notation. Recall from Section 4.3 that the factorial symbol $n!$ designates the product of all the integers between 1 and n. For instance, $4! = 4 \cdot 3 \cdot 2 \cdot 1 = 24$. Special cases are $1! = 1$ and $0! = 0$.

Table for $C_{n,r}$

$C_{n,r} = \dfrac{n!}{r!(n - r)!}$ is the binomial coefficient. Table 2 of Appendix II gives values of $C_{n,r}$ for select n and r. Many calculators have a key designated nCr that gives the value of $C_{n,r}$ directly.

Note: The binomial coefficient $C_{n,r}$ represents the number of combinations of n distinct objects (n = number of trials in this case) taken r at a time (r = number of successes). For more information about $C_{n,r}$, see Section 4.3.

Let's look more carefully at the formula for $P(r)$. There are two main parts. The expression $p^r q^{n - r}$ is the probability of getting one outcome with r successes and $n - r$ failures. The binomial coefficient $C_{n,r}$ counts the number of outcomes that have r successes and $n - r$ failures. For instance, in the case of $n = 3$ trials, we saw in Table 5-8 that the probability of getting an outcome with one success and two failures was pq^2. This is the value of $p^r q^{n - r}$ when $r = 1$ and $n = 3$. We also observed that there were three outcomes with one success and two failures, so $C_{3,1}$ is 3.

Now let's take a look at an application of the binomial distribution formula in Example 5.

EXAMPLE 5

Compute P(r) using the
binomial distribution formula

Privacy is a concern for many users of the Internet. One survey showed that 59% of Internet users are somewhat concerned about the confidentiality of their e-mail. Based on this information, what is the probability that for a random sample of 10 Internet users, 6 are concerned about the privacy of their e-mail?

SOLUTION:

(a) This is a binomial experiment with 10 trials. If we assign success to an Internet user being concerned about the privacy of e-mail, the probability of success is 59%. We are interested in the probability of 6 successes. We have

$$n = 10 \qquad p = 0.59 \qquad q = 0.41 \qquad r = 6$$

By the formula,

$$P(6) = C_{10,6}(0.59)^6(0.41)^{10 - 6}$$
$$= 210(0.59)^6(0.41)^4 \qquad \text{Use Table 2 of Appendix II or a}$$
$$\text{calculator.}$$

$$\approx 210(0.0422)(0.0283) \qquad \text{Use a calculator.}$$
$$\approx 0.25$$

There is a 25% chance that *exactly* 6 of the 10 Internet users are concerned about the privacy of e-mail.

(b) Many calculators have a built-in combinations function. On the TI-84Plus and TI-83Plus calculators, you can find the combinations function under the math menu. It is designated nCr. Figure 5-2 displays the process for computing $P(6)$ directly on these calculators.

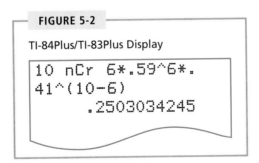

FIGURE 5-2

TI-84Plus/TI-83Plus Display

```
10 nCr 6*.59^6*.
41^(10-6)
       .2503034245
```

Using a Binomial Distribution Table

In many cases we will be interested in the probability of a range of successes. In such cases, we need to use the addition rule for mutually exclusive events. For instance, for $n = 6$ and $p = 0.50$,

$$P(4 \text{ or fewer successes}) = P(r \leq 4)$$
$$= P(r = 4 \text{ or } 3 \text{ or } 2 \text{ or } 1 \text{ or } 0)$$
$$= P(4) + P(3) + P(2) + P(1) + P(0)$$

TABLE 5-10   Excerpt from Table 3 of Appendix II for $n = 6$

n	r	.01	.05	.10 ...	.30 ...	.50 ...	.70 ...	.85	.90	.95
⋮										
6	0	.941	.735	.531 ...	.118 ...	.016 ...	.001 ...	.000	.000	.000
	1	.057	.232	.354 ...	.303 ...	.094 ...	.010 ...	.000	.000	.000
	2	.001	.031	.098 ...	.324 ...	.234 ...	.060 ...	.006	.001	.000
	3	.000	.002	.015 ...	.185 ...	.312 ...	.185 ...	.042	.015	.002
	4	.000	.000	.001 ...	.060 ...	.234 ...	.324	.176	.098	.031
	5	.000	.000	.000 ...	.010 ...	.094 ...	.303 ...	.399	.354	.232
	6	.000	.000	.000 ...	.001 ...	.016 ...	.118 ...	.377	.531	.735

It would be a bit of a chore to use the binomial distribution formula to compute all the required probabilities. Table 3 of Appendix II gives values of $P(r)$ for selected p values and values of n through 20. To use the table, find the appropriate section for n, and then use the entries in the columns headed by the p values and the rows headed by the r values.

Table 5-10 is an excerpt from Table 3 of Appendix II showing the section for $n = 6$. Notice that all possible r values between 0 and 6 are given as row headers. The value $p = 0.50$ is one of the column headers. For $n = 6$ and $p = 0.50$, you can find the value of $P(4)$ by looking at the entry in the row headed by 4 and the column headed by 0.50. Notice that $P(4) = 0.234$.

Likewise, you can find other values of $P(r)$ from the table. In fact, for $n = 6$ and $p = 0.50$,

$$P(r \leq 4) = P(4) + P(3) + P(2) + P(1) + P(0)$$
$$= 0.234 + 0.312 + 0.234 + 0.094 + 0.016 = 0.890$$

Alternatively, to compute $P(r \leq 4)$ for $n = 6$, you can use the fact that the total of all $P(r)$ values for r between 0 and 6 is 1. Then

$$P(r \leq 4) = 1 - P(5) - P(6)$$
$$= 1 - 0.094 - 0.016 = 0.890$$

Note: In Table 3 of Appendix II, probability entries of 0.000 do not mean the probability is exactly zero. Rather, to three digits after the decimal, the probability rounds to 0.000.

EXAMPLE 6

Using the binomial distribution table to find P(r)

A biologist is studying a new hybrid tomato. It is known that the seeds of this hybrid tomato have probability 0.70 of germinating. The biologist plants six seeds.

(a) What is the probability that *exactly* four seeds will germinate?

SOLUTION: This is a binomial experiment with $n = 6$ trials. Each seed planted represents an independent trial. We'll say germination is success, so the probability for success on each trial is 0.70.

$$n = 6 \qquad p = 0.70 \qquad q = 0.30 \qquad r = 4$$

We wish to find $P(4)$, the probability of exactly four successes.

In Table 3, Appendix II, find the section with $n = 6$ (excerpt is given in Table 5-10). Then find the entry in the column headed by $p = 0.70$ and the row headed by $r = 4$. This entry is 0.324.

$$P(4) = 0.324$$

(b) What is the probability that *at least* four seeds will germinate?

SOLUTION: In this case, we are interested in the probability of four or more seeds germinating. This means we are to compute $P(r \geq 4)$. Since the events are mutually exclusive, we can use the addition rule

$$P(r \geq 4) = P(r = 4 \quad or \quad r = 5 \quad or \quad r = 6) = P(4) + P(5) + P(6)$$

We already know the value of $P(4)$. We need to find $P(5)$ and $P(6)$.

Use the same part of the table but find the entries in the row headed by the r value 5 and then the r value 6. Be sure to use the column headed by the value of p, 0.70.

$$P(5) = 0.303 \quad and \quad P(6) = 0.118$$

Now we have all the parts necessary to compute $P(r \geq 4)$.

$$P(r \geq 4) = P(4) + P(5) + P(6)$$
$$= 0.324 + 0.303 + 0.118$$
$$= 0.745 \qquad\qquad\qquad \diamond$$

In Guided Exercise 5 you'll practice using the formula for $P(r)$ in one part, and then you'll use Table 3 (Appendix II) for $P(r)$ values in the second part.

GUIDED EXERCISE 5

Find P(r)

A rarely performed and somewhat risky eye operation is known to be successful in restoring the eyesight of 30% of the patients who undergo the operation. A team of surgeons has developed a new technique for this operation that has been successful for four of six operations. Does it seem likely that the new technique is much better than the old? We'll use the binomial probability distribution to answer this question. We'll compute the probability of at least four successes in six trials for the old technique.

(a) Each operation is a binomial trial. In this case,
$n = $_____, $p = $_____, $q = $_____, $r = $_____.

➡ $n = 6, p = 0.30, q = 1 - 0.30 = 0.70, r = 4$

(b) Use your values of n, p, and q, as well as Table 2 of Appendix II (or your calculator) to compute $P(4)$ from the formula:

$$P(r) = C_{n,r} p^r q^{n-r}$$

➡ $P(4) = C_{6,4}(0.30)^4(0.70)^2$
$= 15(0.0081)(0.490)$
≈ 0.060

Continued

GUIDED EXERCISE 5 continued

(c) Compute the probability of *at least* four successes out of the six trials.

$$P(r \geq 4) = P(r = 4 \text{ or } r = 5 \text{ or } r = 6)$$
$$= P(4) + P(5) + P(6)$$

Use Table 3 of Appendix II to find values of $P(4)$, $P(5)$, and $P(6)$. Then use these values to compute $P(r \geq 4)$.

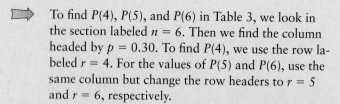 To find $P(4)$, $P(5)$, and $P(6)$ in Table 3, we look in the section labeled $n = 6$. Then we find the column headed by $p = 0.30$. To find $P(4)$, we use the row labeled $r = 4$. For the values of $P(5)$ and $P(6)$, use the same column but change the row headers to $r = 5$ and $r = 6$, respectively.

$$P(r \geq 4) = P(4) + P(5) + P(6)$$
$$= 0.060 + 0.010 + 0.001 = 0.071$$

(d) Under the older operation technique, the probability that at least four patients out of six regain their eyesight is _____. Does it seem that the new technique is better than the old? Would you encourage the surgeon team to do more work on the new technique?

It seems the new technique is better than the old, since, by pure chance, the probability of four or more successes out of six trials is only 0.071 for the old technique. This means one of the following two things may be happening:

(i) The new method is no better than the old method, and our surgeons have encountered a rare event (probability 0.071), or

(ii) The new method is in fact better. We think it is worth encouraging the surgeons to do more work on the new technique.

Common expressions and corresponding inequalities

Many times we are asked to compute the probability of a range of successes. For instance, in a binomial experiment with n trials, we may be asked to compute the probability of four or more successes. Table 5-11 shows how common English expressions such as "four or more successes" translate to inequalities involving r.

TABLE 5-11   Common English Expressions and Corresponding Inequalities (consider a binomial experiment with n trials and r successes)

Expression	Inequality
Four or more successes At least four successes No fewer than four successes Not less than four successes	$r \geq 4$ That is, $r = 4, 5, 6, \ldots, n$
Four or fewer successes At most four successes No more than four successes The number of successes does not exceed four	$r \leq 4$ That is, $r = 0, 1, 2, 3,$ or 4
More than four successes The number of successes exceeds four	$r > 4$ That is, $r = 5, 6, 7, \ldots, n$
Fewer than four successes The number of successes is not as large as four	$r < 4$ That is, $r = 0, 1, 2, 3$

Using Technology to Compute Binomial Probabilities

Some calculators and computer software packages support the binomial distribution. In general, these technologies will provide both the probability $P(r)$ for an exact number of successes r and the cumulative probability $P(r \leq k)$, where k is a specified value less than or equal to the number of trials n. Note that most of the technologies use the letter x instead of r for the random variable denoting the number of successes out of n trials.

TECH NOTE The software packages Minitab and Excel as well as the TI-84Plus and TI-83Plus calculators include built-in binomial probability distribution options. These options give the probability $P(r)$ of a specific number of successes r, as well as the cumulative total probability for r or fewer successes.

TI-84Plus/TI-83Plus Press **DISTR** key, scroll to **binompdf(n, p, r)**. Enter the number of trials n, the probability of success on a single trial p, and the number of successes r. This gives $P(r)$. For the cumulative probability that there are r or fewer successes, use **binomcdf(n, p, r)**.

| $P(r) = 4$ | ```
binompdf(6,.3,4)
           .059535
binomcdf(6,.3,4)
``` |
| $P(r \leq 4)$ | ```
           .989065
``` |

Excel Menu Choice: **Paste Function** $\boxed{f_x}$ ➤ **Statistical** ➤ **Binomdist.** In the dialogue box, fill in the values r, n, and p. For $P(r)$, use false; and for P(at least r successes), use true.

Minitab First, enter the r values 0, 1, 2, . . . , n in a column. Then use menu choice: **Calc** ➤ **Probability Distribution** ➤ **Binomial.** In the dialogue box, select Probability for $P(r)$ or Cumulative for P(at least r successes). Enter the number of trials n, the probability of success p, and the column containing the r values. A sample printout is shown in Problem 17 at the end of this section.

VIEWPOINT

Lies! Lies!! Lies!!! The Psychology of Deceit

This is the title of an intriguing book by C. V. Ford, professor of psychiatry. The book recounts the true story of Floyd "Buzz" Fay, who was falsely convicted of murder on the basis of a failed polygraph examination. During his $2\frac{1}{2}$ years of wrongful imprisonment, Buzz became a polygraph expert. He taught inmates, who freely confessed guilt, how to pass a polygraph examination. (For more information on this topic, see Problem 7.)

SECTION 5.2   PROBLEMS

In each of the following problems, the binomial distribution will be used. Answers may vary slightly depending on whether the binomial distribution formula, the binomial distribution table, or distribution results from a calculator or computer are used. Please answer the following questions and then complete the problem.

What makes up a trial? What is a success? What is a failure?

What are the values of n, p, and q?

1. *Binomial Probabilities: Coin Flip* A fair quarter is flipped three times. For each of the following probabilities, use the formula for the binomial distribution and a calculator to compute the requested probability. Next, look up the probability in Table 3 of Appendix II and compare the table result with the computed result.
   (a) Find the probability of getting exactly three heads.
   (b) Find the probability of getting exactly two heads.
   (c) Find the probability of getting two or more heads.
   (d) Find the probability of getting exactly three tails.

2. *Binomial Probabilities: Multiple-Choice Quiz* Richard has just been given a 10-question multiple-choice quiz in his history class. Each question has five answers, of which only one is correct. Since Richard has not attended class recently, he doesn't know any of the answers. Assuming that Richard guesses on all 10 questions, find the indicated probabilities.
   (a) What is the probability that he will answer all questions correctly?
   (b) What is the probability that he will answer all questions incorrectly?
   (c) What is the probability that he will answer at least one of the questions correctly? Compute this probability two ways. First, use the rule for mutually exclusive events and the probabilities shown in Table 3 of Appendix II. Then use the fact that $P(r \geq 1) = 1 - P(r = 0)$. Compare the two results. Should they be equal? Are they equal? If not, how do you account for the difference?
   (d) What is the probability that Richard will answer at least half the questions correctly?

3. *Sociology: Marriage* The percentage of American men who say they would marry the same woman if they had it to do all over again is 80%. The percentage of American women who say they would marry the same man again is 50% (Source: *Harper's Index*).
   (a) What is the probability that in a group of 10 married men, at least 7 will claim that they would marry the same woman again? What is the probability that less than half will say this?
   (b) What is the probability that in a group of 10 married women, at least 7 will claim they would marry the same man again? What is the probability that less than half will say this?

4. *Sociology: Ethics* The one-time fling! Have you ever purchased an article of clothing (dress, sports jacket, etc.), worn the item *once* to a party, and then returned the purchase? This is called a *one-time fling*. About 10% of all adults deliberately do a one-time fling and feel no guilt about it! (Source: *Are You Normal?*, by Bernice Kanner, St. Martin's Press.) In a group of seven adult friends, what is the probability that
   (a) no one has done a one-time fling?
   (b) at least one person has done a one-time fling?
   (c) no more than two people have done a one-time fling?

5. *Sociology: Mother-in-Law* The ★#@&#★ mother-in-law! Sociologists say that 90% of married women claim that their husband's mother is the biggest bone of contention in their marriages (sex and money are lower-rated areas of contention). (See

the source in Problem 4.) Suppose that six married women are having coffee together one morning. What is the probability that
(a) all of them dislike their mother-in-law?
(b) none of them dislike their mother-in-law?
(c) at least four of them dislike their mother-in-law?
(d) no more than three of them dislike their mother-in-law?

6. *Sociology: Dress Habits* A research team at Cornell University conducted a study showing that approximately 10% of all businessmen who wear ties wear them so tight that they actually reduce blood flow to the brain, diminishing cerebral functions (Source: *Chances: Risk and Odds in Everyday Life,* by James Burke). At a board meeting of 20 businessmen, all of whom wear ties, what is the probability that
(a) at least one tie is too tight?
(b) more than two ties are too tight?
(c) no tie is too tight?
(d) at least 18 ties are *not* too tight?

7. *Psychology: Deceit* Aldrich Ames is a convicted traitor who leaked American secrets to a foreign power. Yet Ames took routine lie detector tests and each time passed them. How can this be done? Recognizing control questions, employing unusual breathing patterns, biting one's tongue at the right time, pressing one's toes hard to the floor, and counting backwards by 7 are countermeasures that are difficult to detect but can change the results of a polygraph examination (Source: *Lies! Lies!! Lies!!! The Psychology of Deceit*, by C. V. Ford, professor of psychiatry, University of Alabama). In fact, it is reported in Professor Ford's book that after only 20 minutes of instruction by "Buzz" Fay (a prison inmate), 85% of those trained were able to pass the polygraph examination even when guilty of a crime. Suppose that a random sample of nine students (in a psychology laboratory) are told a "secret" and then given instructions on how to pass the polygraph examination without revealing their knowledge of the secret. What is the probability that
(a) all the students are able to pass the polygraph examination?
(b) more than half the students are able to pass the polygraph examination?
(c) no more than four of the students are able to pass the polygraph examination?
(d) all the students fail the polygraph examination?

8. *Survey: Cellular Phones* According to an article appearing in the *New York Times Almanac,* about 70% of all U.S. households have a cellular phone. Suppose you are conducting a survey of customer satisfaction regarding cellular phones. If you called 11 households selected at random, what is the probability that
(a) every household has a cellular phone?
(b) more than four households have a cellular phone?
(c) fewer than five households do not have a cellular phone?
(d) more than seven households do not have a cellular phone?

9. *Restaurants: Income* After examination of daily receipts over the past year, it was found that the Green Parrot Italian Restaurant has been grossing over $2200 a day for about 85% of its business days. Using this as a reasonably accurate measure, find the probability that the Green Parrot will gross over $2200
(a) at least 5 days in the next 7 business days.
(b) at least 5 days in the next 10 business days.
(c) fewer than 3 days in the next 5 business days.
(d) fewer than 7 days in the next 10 business days.
(e) fewer than 3 days in the next 7 business days. If this actually happened, might it shake your confidence in the statement $p = 0.85$? Might you suspect that p is less than 0.85? Explain.

10. *Hardware Store: Income* Trevor is interested in purchasing the local hardware/sporting goods store in the small town of Dove Creek, Montana. After examining accounting records for the past several years, he found that the store has been grossing over $850 per day about 60% of the business days it is open. Estimate the probability that the store will gross over $850
   (a) at least 3 out of 5 business days.
   (b) at least 6 out of 10 business days.
   (c) fewer than 5 out of 10 business days.
   (d) fewer than 6 out of the next 20 business days. If this actually happened, might it shake your confidence in the statement $p = 0.60$? Might it make you suspect that p is less than 0.60? Explain.
   (e) more than 17 out of the next 20 business days. If this actually happened, might you suspect that p is greater than 0.60? Explain.

11. *Fishing: Northern Pike* Manitoba northern pike are hardy, tough fish! Using artificial lures with barbed treble hooks, it was found that the hooking mortality rate was only about 5%. This means that only 5% of pike that were caught and released died. (Source: *Proceedings of National Symposium on Catch and Release Fishing,* sponsored by Humboldt State University.) Suppose that a group of anglers caught and released 16 northern pike in Manitoba. What is the probability that
   (a) none of the fish died?
   (b) less than 3 of the fish died?
   (c) all the fish lived?
   (d) more than 14 fish lived?

12. *Marketing: Ice Cream* Supreme Chocolate claims its ice cream tastes so good you can distinguish it from all other brands of chocolate ice cream! Five different brands of chocolate ice cream (one of them Supreme Chocolate) are set before six students who are to pick the one that tastes the best. Assume there is really no difference in the way any of these ice creams taste. However, each student picks one ice cream anyway, not knowing which brand it is because all ice creams are presented in identical dishes without brand labels. What is the probability of (a), (b), and (c) below?
   (a) none of the students choose Supreme Chocolate?
   (b) at least three students choose Supreme Chocolate?
   (c) all six students choose Supreme Chocolate?
   (d) If all six students choose Supreme Chocolate, might this indicate that the given assumption of no difference in taste may be false? Explain.

13. *Psychology: Myers-Briggs* Approximately 75% of all marketing personnel are extroverts, whereas about 60% of all computer programmers are introverts (Source: *A Guide to the Development and Use of the Myers-Briggs Type Indicator,* by Myers and McCaulley).
   (a) At a meeting of 15 marketing personnel, what is the probability that 10 or more are extroverts? What is the probability that 5 or more are extroverts? What is the probability that all are extroverts?
   (b) In a group of 5 computer programmers, what is the probability that none are introverts? What is the probability that 3 or more are introverts? What is the probability that all are introverts?

14. *Sociology: Dating* In *Chances: Risks and Odds in Everyday Life,* James Burke claims that about 70% of all single men would welcome a woman taking the initiative in asking for a date. A random sample of 20 single men were asked if they would welcome a woman taking the initiative in asking for a date. What is the probability that
   (a) at least 18 of the men will say yes?
   (b) fewer than 3 of the men will say yes?
   (c) none of the men will say yes?
   (d) at least 5 of the men will say no?

15. *Health Care: Diabetes* People with diabetes may develop other health complications associated with the disease. The following information is based on a feature in *USA Today* entitled "A Look at Statistics That Shape Our Lives." About 40% of all people with diabetes will also develop hypertension (blood pressure problems), and about 30% of people with diabetes will develop an eye disease. Suppose that you are the director of a health care center that has 10 people with diabetes and no other related health problems. Part of your job is to monitor these patients for symptoms of new illnesses related to diabetes so that corrective measures can be started. What is the probability that
    (a) none of the diabetes patients will ever develop related hypertension?
    (b) fewer than 5 of the diabetes patients will ever develop related hypertension?
    (c) no more than 2 of the diabetes patients will ever develop a related eye disease?
    (d) at least 6 of the diabetes patients will never develop a related eye disease?

16. *Business Ethics: Privacy* Are your finances, buying habits, medical records, and phone calls really private? A real concern for many adults is that computers and the Internet are reducing privacy. A survey conducted by Peter D. Hart Research Associates for the Shell Poll was reported in *USA Today*. According to the survey, 37% of adults are concerned that employers are monitoring phone calls. Use the binomial distribution formula to calculate the probability that
    (a) out of 5 adults, none is concerned that employers are monitoring phone calls.
    (b) out of 5 adults, all are concerned that employers are monitoring phone calls.
    (c) out of 5 adults, exactly 3 are concerned that employers are monitoring phone calls.

17. *Business Ethics: Privacy* According to the same poll quoted in Problem 16, 53% of adults are concerned that Social Security numbers are used for general identification. For a group of 8 adults selected at random, we used Minitab to generate the binomial probability distribution and the cumulative binomial probability distribution (menu selections ➤ **Calc** ➤ **Probability Distributions** ➤ **Binomial**).

Number	r	P(r)	P(<=r)
	0	0.002381	0.00238
	1	0.021481	0.02386
	2	0.084781	0.10864
	3	0.191208	0.29985
	4	0.269521	0.56937
	5	0.243143	0.81251
	6	0.137091	0.94960
	7	0.044169	0.99377
	8	0.006226	1.00000

Find the probability that out of 8 adults selected at random,
    (a) at most 5 are concerned about Social Security numbers being used for identification. Do the problem by adding the probabilities $P(r = 0)$ through $P(r = 5)$. Is this the same as the cumulative probability $P(r \leq 5)$?
    (b) more than 5 are concerned about Social Security numbers being used for identification. First, do the problem by adding the probabilities $P(r = 6)$ through $P(r = 8)$. Then do the problem by subtracting the cumulative probability $P(r \leq 5)$ from 1. Do you get the same results?

18. *Ecology: Wolves* The following is based on information taken from *The Wolf in the Southwest: The Making of an Endangered Species,* edited by David Brown (University of Arizona Press). Before 1918, approximately 55% of the wolves in

the New Mexico and Arizona region were male, and 45% were female. However, cattle ranchers in this area have made a determined effort to exterminate wolves. From 1918 to the present, approximately 70% of wolves in the region are male, and 30% are female. Biologists suspect that male wolves are more likely than females to return to an area where the population has been greatly reduced.

(a) Before 1918, in a random sample of 12 wolves spotted in the region, what is the probability that 6 or more were male? What is the probability that 6 or more were female? What is the probability that fewer than 4 were female?

(b) Answer part (a) for the period from 1918 to the present.

19. *Archaeology: Stone Tools* The following is based on information from *Bandelier Archaeological Excavation Project: Summer 1989 Excavations at Burnt Mesa Pueblo,* edited by Kohler (Washington State University). At an archaeological site in Bandelier National Monument, approximately 15% of the chipped stone tools are made from Jemez obsidian, and 55% are made from basalt.

(a) If 11 chipped stone tools are discovered, what is the probability that at least 3 will be made from Jemez obsidian?

(b) If 5 chipped stone tools are discovered, what is the probability that at least 2 will be made from basalt?

(c) If 10 chipped stone tools are discovered, what is the probability that at least 4 are neither Jemez obsidian nor basalt?

20. *Health Care: Office Visits* What is the age distribution of patients who make office visits to a doctor or nurse? The following table is based on information taken from the Medical Practice Characteristics section of the *Statistical Abstract of the United States* (116th Edition).

Age group, years	Under 15	15–24	25–44	45–64	65 and older
Percent of office visitors	20%	10%	25%	20%	25%

Suppose you are a district manager of a health management organization (HMO) that is monitoring the office of a local doctor or nurse in general family practice. This morning the office you are monitoring has eight office visits on the schedule. What is the probability that

(a) at least half the patients are under 15 years old? First, explain how this can be modeled as a binomial distribution with 8 trials, where success is visitor age is under 15 years old and the probability of success is 20%.

(b) from 2 to 5 patients are 65 years old or older (include 2 and 5)?

(c) from 2 to 5 patients are 45 years old or older (include 2 and 5)? (*Hint:* Success is 45 or older. Use the table to compute the probability of success on a single trial.)

(d) all the patients are under 25 years of age?

(e) all the patients are 15 years old or older?

21. *Binomial Distribution Table: Symmetry* Study the binomial distribution table (Table 3, Appendix II). Notice that the probability of success on a single trial p ranges from 0.01 to 0.95. Some binomial distribution tables stop at 0.50 because of the symmetry in the table. Let's look for that symmetry. Consider the section of the table with $n = 5$. Look at the numbers in the columns headed by $p = 0.30$ and $p = 0.70$. Do you detect any similarities? Consider the following probabilities for a binomial experiment with five trials.

(a) Compare $P(3$ successes$)$ where $p = 0.30$ with $P(2$ successes$)$ where $p = 0.70$.

(b) Compare $P(3$ or more successes$)$ where $p = 0.30$ with $P(2$ or fewer successes$)$ with $p = 0.70$.

(c) Find the value of $P(4$ successes$)$ with $p = 0.30$. For what value of r is $P(r$ successes$)$ the same using $p = 0.70$?

(d) What column is symmetrical with the one headed by $p = 0.20$?

22. *Binomial Distribution: Control Charts* This problem will be referred to in the study of control charts (Section 6.1). In the binomial probability distribution, let the number of trials be $n = 3$, and let the probability of success be $p = 0.0228$. Use a calculator to compute

(a) the probability of two successes.

(b) the probability of three successes.

(c) the probability of two or three successes.

23. *Expand Your Knowledge: Conditional Probability* In the western United States there are many dry land wheat farms that depend on winter snow and spring rain to produce good crops. About 65% of the years there is enough moisture to produce a good wheat crop, depending on the region (Reference: *Agricultural Statistics*, United States Department of Agriculture).

(a) Let r be a random variable that represents the number of good wheat crops in $n = 8$ years. Suppose the Zimmer farm has reason to believe that at least 4 out of 8 years will be good. However, they need at least 6 good years out of 8 years to survive financially. Compute the probability that the Zimmers will get at least 6 good years out of 8, given what they believe is true; that is, compute $P(6 \leq r, given\ 4 \leq r)$. See part (d) for a hint.

(b) Let r be a random variable that represents the number of good wheat crops in $n = 10$ years. Suppose the Montoya farm has reason to believe that at least 6 out of 10 years will be good. However, they need at least 8 good years out of 10 years to survive financially. Compute the probability that the Montoyas will get at least 8 good years out of 10, given what they believe is true; that is, compute $P(8 \leq r, given\ 6 \leq r)$.

(c) List at least three other areas besides agriculture where you think conditional binomial probabilities can be applied.

(d) *Hint for solution:* Review item 6, conditional probability, in the summary of basic probability rules at the end of Section 4.2. Note that

$$P(A, given\ B) = \frac{P(A\ and\ B)}{P(B)}$$

and show that in part (a)

$$P(6 \leq r, given\ 4 \leq r) = \frac{P((6 \leq r)\ and\ (4 \leq r))}{P(4 \leq r)} = \frac{P(6 \leq r)}{P(4 \leq r)}$$

24. *Conditional Probability: Blood Supply* Only about 70% of all donated human blood can be used in hospitals. The remaining 30% cannot be used because of various infections in the blood. Suppose a blood bank has 10 newly donated pints of blood. Let r be a binomial random variable that represents the number of "good" pints that can be used.

(a) Based on questionnaires completed by the donors, it is believed that at least 6 of the 10 pints are usable. What is the probability that at least 8 of the pints are usable given this belief is true? Compute $P(8 \leq r, given\ 6 \leq r)$.

(b) Assuming the belief that at least 6 of the pints are usable is true, what is the probability that all 10 pints can be used? Compute $P(r = 10, given\ 6 \leq r)$.

Hint: See Problem 23.

5.3
Additional Properties of the Binomial Distribution

FOCUS POINTS

✓ Make histograms for binomial distributions.

✓ Compute μ and σ for a binomial distribution.

✓ Compute the minimum number of trials n needed to achieve a given probability of success $P(r)$.

Graphing a Binomial Distribution

Any probability distribution may be represented in graphic form. How should we graph the binomial distribution? Remember, the binomial distribution tells us the probability of r successes out of n trials. Therefore, we'll place values of r along the horizontal axis and values of $P(r)$ on the vertical axis. The binomial distribution is a *discrete* probability distribution because r can assume only whole-number values such as 0, 1, 2, 3, ... Therefore, a histogram is an appropriate graph of a binomial distribution.

PROCEDURE

How to graph a binomial distribution

1. Place r values on the horizontal axis.
2. Place $P(r)$ values on the vertical axis.
3. Construct a bar over each r value extending from $r - 0.5$ to $r + 0.5$. The height of the corresponding bar is $P(r)$.

Let's look at an example to see exactly how we'll make these histograms.

EXAMPLE 7

Graph of a binomial distribution

A waiter at the Green Spot Restaurant has learned from long experience that the probability that a lone diner will leave a tip is only 0.7. During one lunch hour he serves six people who are dining by themselves. Make a graph of the binomial probability distribution that shows the probabilities that 0, 1, 2, 3, 4, 5, or all 6 lone diners leave tips.

SOLUTION: This is a binomial experiment with $n = 6$ trials. Success is achieved when the lone diner leaves a tip, so the probability of success is 0.7 and that of failure is 0.3:

$$n = 6 \qquad p = 0.7 \qquad q = 0.3$$

We want to make a histogram showing the probability of r successes when $r = 0, 1, 2, 3, 4, 5,$ or 6. It is easier to make the histogram if we first make a table of r values and the corresponding $P(r)$ values (Table 5-12). We'll use Table 3 of Appendix II to find the $P(r)$ values for $n = 6$ and $p = 0.70$.

To construct the histogram, we'll put r values on the horizontal axis and $P(r)$ values on the vertical axis. Our bars will be one unit wide and will be centered over the appropriate r value. The height of the bar over a particular r value tells the probability of that r (see Figure 5-3).

The probability of a particular value of r is given not only by the height of the bar over that r value but also by the *area* of the bar. Each bar is only one unit wide, so the area (area = height times width) equals its height. Since the area of each bar represents the probability of the r value under it, the sum of the areas of the bars must be 1. In this example, the sum turns out to be 1.001. It is not exactly equal to 1 because of rounding error.   ◆

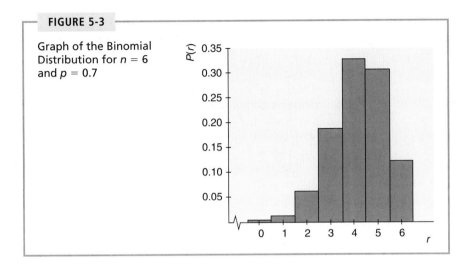

FIGURE 5-3

Graph of the Binomial Distribution for $n = 6$ and $p = 0.7$

TABLE 5-12   Binomial Distribution for $n = 6$ and $p = 0.70$

r	P(r)
0	0.001
1	0.010
2	0.060
3	0.185
4	0.324
5	0.303
6	0.118

Guided Exercise 6 illustrates another binomial distribution with $n = 6$ trials. The graph will be different from that of Figure 5-3 because the probability of success p is different.

GUIDED EXERCISE 6

Graph of a binomial distribution

Jim enjoys playing basketball. He figures that he makes about 50% of the field goals he attempts during a game. Make a histogram showing the probability that Jim will make 0, 1, 2, 3, 4, 5, or 6 shots out of six attempted field goals.

(a) This is a binomial experiment with $n = $ _____ trials. In this situation, we'll say success occurs when Jim makes an attempted field goal. What is the value of p?

⟹ In this example, $n = 6$ and $p = 0.5$.

(b) Use Table 3 of Appendix II to complete Table 5-13 of $P(r)$ values for $n = 6$ and $p = 0.5$.

TABLE 5-13

r	P(r)
0	0.016
1	0.094
2	0.234
3	_____
4	_____
5	_____
6	_____

⟹ **TABLE 5-14   Completion of Table 5-13**

r	P(r)
.	.
.	.
.	.
3	0.312
4	0.234
5	0.094
6	0.016

Continued

GUIDED EXERCISE 6 continued

(c) Use the values of $P(r)$ given in Table 5-14 to complete the histogram in Figure 5-4.

FIGURE 5-4 Beginning of Graph of Binomial Distribution for $n = 6$ and $p = 0.5$

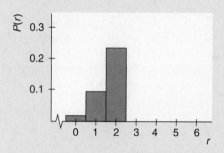

FIGURE 5-5 Completion of Figure 5-4

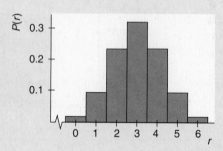

(d) The area of the bar over $r = 2$ is 0.234. What is the area of the bar over $r = 4$? How does the probability that Jim makes exactly two field goals out of six compare with the probability that he makes exactly four field goals out of six?

The area of the bar over $r = 4$ is also 0.234. Jim is as likely to make two out of six field goals attempted as he is to make four out of six.

In Example 7 and Guided Exercise 6, we see the graphs of two binomial distributions associated with $n = 6$ trials. The two graphs are different because the probability of success p is different in the two cases. In Example 7, $p = 0.7$ and the graph is skewed to the left—that is, the left tail is longer. In Guided Exercise 6, p is equal to 0.5 and the graph is symmetrical—that is, if we fold it in half, the two halves coincide exactly. Whenever *p equals 0.5, the graph of the binomial distribution will be symmetrical no matter how many trials we have.* In Chapter 6, we will see that if the number of trials n is quite large, the binomial distribution is almost symmetrical even when p is not close to 0.5.

Mean and Standard Deviation of a Binomial Distribution

Mean and standard deviation of binomial probability distributions

Two other features that help describe the graph of any distribution are the balance point of the distribution and the spread of the distribution about that balance point. The *balance point* is the mean μ of the distribution, and the *measure of spread* that is most commonly used is the standard deviation σ. The mean μ is the *expected value* of the number of successes.

For the binomial distribution, we can use two special formulas to compute the mean μ and the standard deviation σ. These are easier to use than the general formulas in Section 5.1 for μ and σ of any discrete probability distribution.

> **PROCEDURE**
>
> **How to compute μ and σ for a binomial distribution**
>
> $\mu = np$ is the **expected number of successes** for the random variable r
>
> $\sigma = \sqrt{npq}$ is the **standard deviation** for the random variable r
>
> where
>
> > r is a random variable representing the number of successes in a binomial distribution,
> > n is the number of trials,
> > p is the probability of success on a single trial, and
> > $q = 1 - p$ is the probability of failure on a single trial.

EXAMPLE 8

Compute μ and σ

Let's compute the mean and standard deviation for the distribution of Example 7 that describes that probabilities of lone diners leaving tips at the Green Spot Restaurant.

SOLUTION: In that example,

$$n = 6 \qquad p = 0.7 \qquad q = 0.3$$

For the binomial distribution,

$$\mu = np = 6(0.7) = 4.2$$

The balance point of the distribution is at $\mu = 4.2$. The standard deviation is given by

$$\sigma = \sqrt{npq} = \sqrt{6(0.7)(0.3)} = \sqrt{1.26} \approx 1.12 \qquad \Diamond$$

The mean μ is not only the balance point of the distribution; it is also the *expected value* of r. Specifically, in Example 7, the waiter can expect 4.2 lone diners out of 6 to leave a tip. (The waiter would probably round the expected value to 4 tippers out of 6.)

GUIDED EXERCISE 7

Expected value and standard deviation

When Jim (of Guided Exercise 6) shoots field goals in basketball games, the probability that he makes a shot is only 0.5.

(a) The mean of the binomial distribution is the expected value of r successes out of n trials. Out of six throws, what is the expected number of goals Jim will make?

> The expected value is the mean μ:
>
> $$\mu = np = 6(0.5) = 3$$
>
> Jim can expect to make three goals out of six tries.

(b) For six trials, what is the standard deviation of the binomial distribution of the number of successful field goals Jim makes?

> $$\sigma = \sqrt{npq} = \sqrt{6(0.5)(0.5)} = \sqrt{1.5} \approx 1.22$$

Quota Problems: Minimum Number of Trials for a Given Probability

In applications, you do not want to confuse the expected value of r with certain probabilities associated with r. Guided Exercise 8 illustrates this point.

GUIDED EXERCISE 8

Find the minimum value of n for given P(r)

A satellite is powered by three solar cells. The probability that any one of these cells will fail is 0.15, and the cells operate or fail independently.

Part I: In this part, we want to find the least number of cells the satellite should have so that the *expected value* of the number of working cells is no smaller than three. In this situation, n represents the number of cells, r is the number of successful or working cells, p is the probability that a cell will work, q is the probability that a cell will fail, and μ is the expected value that should be no smaller than three.

(a) What is the value of q? of p?

⟹ $q = 0.15$ as given in the problem. p must be 0.85, since $p = 1 - q$.

(b) The expected value μ for the number of working cells is given by $\mu = np$. The expected value of the number of working cells should be no smaller than three, so

$$3 \leq \mu = np$$

From part (a), we know the value of p. Solve the inequality $3 \leq np$ for n.

⟹ $3 \leq np$
$3 \leq n(0.85)$
$\dfrac{3}{0.85} \leq n$ Divide both sides by 0.85.
$3.53 \leq n$

(c) Since n is between 3 and 4, should you round it to 3 or to 4 to make sure that μ is at least 3?

⟹ n should be at least 3.53. Since we can't have a fraction of a cell, we had best make $n = 4$. For $n = 4$, $\mu = 4(0.85) = 3.4$. This value satisfies the condition that μ be at least 3.

Part II: In this part, we want to find the smallest number of cells the satellite should have to be 97% sure that there will be adequate power—that is, that at least three cells work.

(a) The letter r has been used to denote the number of successes. In this case, r represents the number of working cells. We are trying to find the number n of cells necessary to ensure that (choose the correct statement)

(i) $P(r \geq 3) = 0.97$ or

(ii) $P(r \leq 3) = 0.97$

⟹ $P(r \geq 3) = 0.97$

Continued

GUIDED EXERCISE 8 continued

(b) We need to find a value for n so that

$P(r \geq 3) = 0.97$

Try $n = 4$. Then $r \geq 3$ means $r = 3$ or 4 so

$P(r \geq 3) = P(3) + P(4)$

Use Table 3 (Appendix II) with $n = 4$ and $p = 0.85$ to find values of $P(3)$ and $P(4)$. Then compute $P(r \geq 3)$ for $n = 4$. Will $n = 4$ guarantee that $P(r \geq 3)$ is at least 0.97?

⟹ $P(3) = 0.368$

$P(4) = 0.522$

$P(r \geq 3) = 0.368 + 0.522 = 0.890$

Thus $n = 4$ is *not* sufficient to be 97% sure that at least three cells will work. For $n = 4$, the probability that at least three will work is only 0.890.

(c) Now try $n = 5$ cells. For $n = 5$,

$P(r \geq 3) = P(3) + P(4) + P(5)$

since r can be 3, 4, or 5. Are $n = 5$ cells adequate? [Be sure to find new values of $P(3)$ and $P(4)$, since we now have $n = 5$.]

⟹ $P(r \geq 3) = P(3) + P(4) + P(5)$

$= 0.138 + 0.392 + 0.444$

$= 0.974$

Thus $n = 5$ cells are required if we want to be 97% sure that there will be at least three working cells.

In Part I and Part II, we got different values for n. Why? In Part I, we had $n = 4$ and $\mu = 3.4$. This means that if we put up lots of satellites with four cells, we can expect that an *average* of 3.4 cells will be working per satellite. But for $n = 4$ cells there is a probability of only 0.89 that at least three cells will work in any one satellite. In Part II, we are trying to find the number of cells necessary so that the probability is 0.97 that at least three will work in any *one* satellite. If we use $n = 5$ cells, then we can satisfy this requirement.

Quota problems

Quotas occur in many aspects of everyday life. The manager of a sales team gives every member of the team a weekly sales quota. In some districts, police have a monthly quota for the number of traffic tickets issued. Nonprofit organizations have recruitment quotas for donations or new volunteers. The basic ideas used to compute quotas also can be used in medical science (how frequently checkups should occur), quality control (how many production flaws should be expected), or risk management (how many bad loans a bank should expect in a certain investment group). In fact, Part II of Guided Exercise 8 is a *quota problem*. To have adequate power, a satellite must have a quota of three working solar cells. Such problems come from many different sources, but they all have one thing in common: They are solved using the binomial probability distribution.

To solve quota problems, it is often helpful to use equivalent formulas for expressing binomial probabilities. You will see the use of equivalent probabilities in Example 9.

> **PROCEDURE**
>
> **How to express binomial probabilities using equivalent formulas**
>
> $P(\text{at least one success}) = P(r \geq 1) = 1 - P(0)$
>
> $P(\text{at least two successes}) = P(r \geq 2) = 1 - P(0) - P(1)$
>
> $P(\text{at least three successes}) = P(r \geq 3) = 1 - P(0) - P(1) - P(2)$
>
> $P(\text{at least } m \text{ successes}) = P(r \geq m) = 1 - P(0) - P(1) - \ldots - P(m - 1)$
>
> where $1 \leq m \leq$ number of trials
>
> For a discussion of the mathematics behind these formulas, see Problem 24 at the end of this section.

Example 9 is a quota problem. Junk bonds are sometimes controversial. In some cases, junk bonds have been the salvation of a basically good company that has had a run of bad luck. From another point of view, junk bonds are not much more than a gambler's effort to make money by shady ethics.

The book *Liar's Poker*, by Michael Lewis, is an exciting and sometimes humorous description of his career as a Wall Street bond broker. Most bond brokers, including Mr. Lewis, are ethical people. However, the book does contain an interesting discussion of Michael Milken and shady ethics. In the book, Mr. Lewis says, "If it was a good deal, the brokers kept it for themselves; if it was a bad deal, they'd try to sell it to their customers." In Example 9 we use some binomial probabilities for a brief explanation of what Mr. Lewis's book is talking about.

EXAMPLE 9

Quota

Junk bonds can be profitable as well as risky. Why are investors willing to consider junk bonds? Suppose you can buy junk bonds at a tremendous discount. You try to choose "good" companies with a "good" product. The company should have done well but for some reason did not. Suppose you consider only companies with a 35% estimated risk of default, and your financial investment goal requires four bonds to be "good" bonds in the sense that they will not default before a certain date. Remember, junk bonds that do not default are usually very profitable because they carry a very high rate of return. The other bonds in your investment group can default (or not) without harming your investment plan. Suppose you want to be 95% certain of meeting your goal (quota) of at least four good bonds. How many junk bond issues should you buy to meet this goal?

SOLUTION: Since the probability of default is 35%, the probability of a "good" bond is 65%. Let success S represent a good bond. Let n be the number of bonds purchased, and let r be the number of good bonds in this group. We want

$$P(r \geq 4) \geq 0.95$$

This is equivalent to

$$1 - P(0) - P(1) - P(2) - P(3) \geq 0.95$$

Since the probability of success is $p = P(S) = 0.65$, we need to look in the binomial table under $p = 0.65$ and different values of n to find the *smallest value* of n that will satisfy the preceding relation. Table 3 of Appendix II shows that if $n = 10$ when $p = 0.65$, then

$$1 - P(0) - P(1) - P(2) - P(3) = 1 - 0 - 0 - 0.004 - 0.021 = 0.975$$

The probability 0.975 satisfies the condition of being greater than or equal to 0.95. We see that 10 is the smallest value of n for which the condition

$$P(r \geq 4) \geq 0.95$$

is satisfied. Under the given conditions (a good discount on price, no more than 35% chance of default, and a fundamentally good company), you can be 95% sure of meeting your investment goal with $n = 10$ (carefully selected) junk bond issues.

In this example, we see that by carefully selecting junk bonds, there is a high probability of getting some good bonds that will produce a real profit. What do you do with the other bonds that aren't so good? Perhaps the quote from *Liar's Poker* will suggest what is sometimes attempted.   ◊

VIEWPOINT   *Kodiak Island, Alaska*

Kodiak Island is famous for its giant brown bears. The sea surrounding the island is also famous for its king crab. The state of Alaska, Department of Fish and Game, has collected a huge amount of data regarding ocean latitude, ocean longitude, and size of king crab. Of special interest to commercial fishing skippers is the size of crab. Those too small must be returned to the sea. To find locations and sizes of king crab catches near Kodiak Island, visit the Brase/Brase statistics site at **http://math.college.hmco.com/students** and find the link to the StatLib site hosted by the Department of Statistics at Carnegie Mellon University. Once at StatLib, go to crab data. From this information, it is possible to use methods of this chapter and Chapter 8 to estimate the proportion of legal crab in a sea skipper's catch.

SECTION 5.3   PROBLEMS

1. *Binomial Distribution: Histograms* Consider a binomial distribution with $n = 5$ trials. Use the probabilities given in Table 3 of Appendix II to make histograms showing the probability of $r = 0, 1, 2, 3, 4, 5$ successes for each of the following. Comment on the skewness of each distribution.
   (a) The probability of success is $p = 0.50$.
   (b) The probability of success is $p = 0.25$.
   (c) The probability of success is $p = 0.75$.
   (d) What is the relationship between the distributions shown in parts (b) and (c)?
   (e) If the probability of success is $p = 0.73$, do you expect the distribution to be skewed to the right or to the left? Why?

2. *Binomial Distributions: Histograms* Figure 5-6 on the next page shows histograms of several binomial distributions with $n = 6$ trials. Match the given probability of success with the best graph.
   (a) $p = 0.30$ goes with graph _____.
   (b) $p = 0.50$ goes with graph _____.
   (c) $p = 0.65$ goes with graph _____.
   (d) $p = 0.90$ goes with graph _____.
   (e) In general, when the probability of success p is close to 0.5, would you say that the graph is more symmetrical or more skewed? In general, when the probability of success p is close to 1, would you say that the graph is skewed to the right or to the left? What about when p is close to 0?

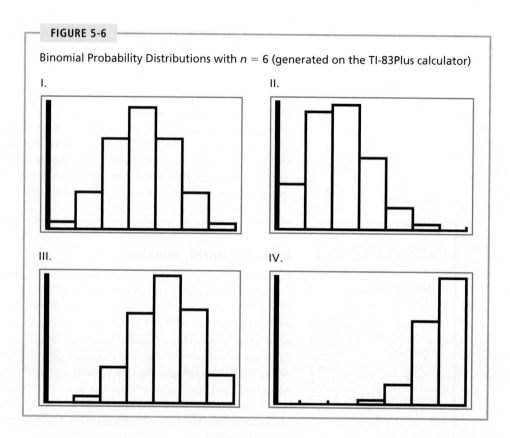

FIGURE 5-6

Binomial Probability Distributions with $n = 6$ (generated on the TI-83Plus calculator)

3. *Marketing: Photography* Does the *kid factor* make a difference? If you are talking photography, the answer may be yes! The following table is based on information from *American Demographics* (Vol. 19, No. 7).

Age of children in household, years	Under 2	None under 21
Percent of U.S. households that buy film	80%	50%

Let us say you are a market research person who interviews a random sample of 10 households.

(a) Suppose that the 10 households you interview are chosen to have children under the age of 2 years. Let r represent the number of such households that buy film. Make a histogram showing the probability distribution of r for $r = 0$ through $r = 10$. Find the mean and standard deviation of this probability distribution.

(b) Suppose that the 10 households are chosen to have no children under 21 years old. Let r represent the number of such households that buy film. Make a histogram showing the probability distribution of r for $r = 0$ through $r = 10$. Find the mean and standard deviation of this probability distribution.

(c) Compare the distributions in parts (a) and (b). You are designing TV ads to sell film. Could you justify featuring ads of parents taking pictures of toddlers? Explain your answer.

4. *Quality Control: Syringes* The quality-control inspector of a production plant will reject a batch of syringes if two or more defectives are found in a random sample of eight syringes taken from the batch. Suppose the batch contains 1% defective syringes.

(a) Make a histogram showing the probability of $r = 0, 1, 2, 3, 4, 5, 6, 7, 8$ defective syringes in a random sample of eight syringes.
(b) Find μ. What is the expected number of defective syringes the inspector will find?
(c) What is the probability that the batch will be accepted?
(d) Find σ.

5. *Private Investigation: Locating People* Old Friends Information Service is a California company that is in the business of finding addresses of long-lost friends. Old Friends claims to have a 70% success rate (Source: *Wall Street Journal*). Suppose that you have the names of six friends for whom you have no addresses and decide to use Old Friends to track them.
(a) Make a histogram showing the probability of $r = 0$ to 6 friends for whom an address will be found.
(b) Find the mean and standard deviation of this probability distribution. What is the expected number of friends for whom addresses will be found?
(c) *Quota Problem* How many names would you have to submit to be 97% sure that at least two addresses will be found?

6. *Insurance: Auto* The Mountain States Office of State Farm Insurance Company reports that approximately 85% of all automobile damage liability claims were made by people under 25 years of age. A random sample of five automobile insurance liability claims is under study.
(a) Make a histogram showing the probability that $r = 0$ to 5 claims are made by people under 25 years of age.
(b) Find the mean and standard deviation of this probability distribution. For samples of size 5, what is the expected number of claims made by people under 25 years of age?

7. *Education: Illiteracy* USA Today reported that about 20% of all people in the United States are illiterate. Suppose that you take seven people at random off a city street.
(a) Make a histogram showing the probability distribution of the number of illiterate people out of the seven people in the sample.
(b) Find the mean and standard deviation of this probability distribution. Find the expected number of people in this sample who are illiterate.
(c) *Quota Problem* How many people would you need to interview to be 98% sure that at least seven of these people can read and write (are not illiterate)?

8. *Rude Drivers: Tailgating* Do you tailgate the car in front of you? About 35% of all drivers will tailgate before passing, thinking they can make the car in front of them go faster (Source: Bernice Kanner, *Are You Normal?* St. Martin's Press). Suppose that you are driving a considerable distance on a two-lane highway and are passed by 12 vehicles.
(a) Let r be the number of vehicles that tailgate before passing. Make a histogram showing the probability distribution of r for $r = 0$ through $r = 12$.
(b) Compute the expected number of vehicles out of 12 that will tailgate.
(c) Compute the standard deviation of this distribution.

9. *Hype: Improved Products* The *Wall Street Journal* reported that approximately 25% of the people who are told a product is *improved* will believe that it is in fact improved. The remaining 75% believe that this is just hype (the same old thing with no real improvement). Suppose a marketing study consists of a random sample of eight people who are given a sales talk about a new, *improved* product.
(a) Make a histogram showing the probability that $r = 0$ to 8 people believe the product is in fact improved.

(b) Compute the mean and standard deviation of this probability distribution.
(c) *Quota Problem* How many people are needed in the marketing study to be 99% sure that at least one person believes the product to be improved? (*Hint:* Note that $P(r \geq 1) = 0.99$ is equivalent to $1 - P(0) = 0.99$, or $P(0) = 0.01$.)

10. *Forest Fires: Satellite Detection* The National Forest Service uses satellites with infrared sensors to detect forest fires in remote wilderness areas. The satellites are very sensitive and do find all the hot spots. However, the satellites register geo-thermal hot spots, cloud cover, manmade bonfires, etc., as well as hot spots caused by forest fires. Over a period of years, the Forest Service has decided that only 85% of the hot spots reported by the satellite are forest fires. The usual procedure is to send out a reconnaissance plane to check on what the satellite has detected. Let us say that the satellite is successful if it reports a hot spot that is a forest fire.

Recently, the satellite reported nine hot spots in the remote Seward Peninsula of Alaska.
(a) Find the probability $P(r)$ of r successes for r ranging from 0 to 9.
(b) Make a histogram for the probability distribution of part (a).
(c) Based on the satellite information, what is the expected number μ of real forest fires on the Seward Peninsula?
(d) What is the standard deviation σ?
(e) *Quota Problem* How many hot spots must the satellite report to be 99.9% sure of at least one real forest fire? (*Hint:* Note that $P(r \geq 1) = 0.999$ is equivalent to $1 - P(0) = 0.999$, or $P(0) = 0.001$.)

11. *Quota Problem: Sales* Vince is a computer software salesman who has a history of making a successful sales call 40% of the time. If Vince has a sales quota of at least five sales this week, how many sales calls must he make to be 95% sure of meeting the quota? (*Hint:* Note that $P(r \geq 5) = 0.95$ is equivalent to $1 - P(0) - P(1) - P(2) - P(3) - P(4) = 0.95$, or $P(0) + P(1) + P(2) + P(3) + P(4) = 0.05$. Try $n > 15$.)

12. *Quota Problem: Sales* June solicits contributions for charity by phone. She has a history of being successful at getting a donor on 55% of her calls. If June has a quota to get at least four donors each day, how many calls must she make to be 96.4% sure of meeting the quota? (*Hint:* Note that $P(r \geq 4) = 0.964$ is equivalent to $1 - P(0) - P(1) - P(2) - P(3) = 0.964$, or $P(0) + P(1) + P(2) + P(3) = 0.036$. Try $n > 9$.)

13. *Quota Problem: Archaeology* An archaeological excavation at Burnt Mesa Pueblo showed that about 10% of the flaked stone objects were finished arrow points (Source: *Bandelier Archaeological Excavation Project: Summer 1990 Excavations at Burnt Mesa Pueblo*, edited by Kohler, Washington State University). How many flaked stone objects need to be found to be 90% sure that at least one is a finished arrow point? (*Hint:* Use a calculator and note that $P(r \geq 1) \geq 0.90$ is equivalent to $1 - P(0) \geq 0.90$, or $P(0) \leq 0.10$.)

14. *Law Enforcement: Speed Traps* Do you warn oncoming traffic of a police speed trap? About 40% of all drivers will flash their lights to warn oncoming traffic of a speed trap ahead. (See reference in Problem 8.) Suppose seven cars have just driven past a police speed trap.
(a) What is the probability that at least one of the drivers will warn oncoming traffic?
(b) What is the expected number of these seven drivers who will warn oncoming traffic of a police speed trap ahead? What is the standard deviation?

(c) *Quota Problem* How many cars n would need to go by the speed trap to be 99.8% sure that at least one driver will warn oncoming traffic of the speed trap? (*Hint:* Note that $P(r \geq 1) = 0.998$ is equivalent to $1 - P(0) = 0.998$, or $P(0) = 0.002$.)

15. *Criminal Justice: Parole* USA Today reports that about 25% of all prison parolees become repeat offenders. Alice is a social worker whose job is to counsel people on parole. Let us say success means a person does not become a repeat offender. Alice has been given a group of four parolees.
    (a) Find the probability $P(r)$ for r successes ranging from 0 to 4.
    (b) Make a histogram for the probability distribution of part (a).
    (c) What is the expected number of parolees in Alice's group who will not be repeat offenders? What is the standard deviation?
    (d) *Quota Problem* How large a group should Alice counsel to be about 98% sure that three or more will not become repeat offenders?

16. *Defense: Radar Stations* The probability that a single radar station will detect an enemy plane is 0.65.
    (a) *Quota Problem* How many such stations are required to be 98% certain that an enemy plane flying over will be detected by at least one station?
    (b) If four stations are in use, what is the expected number of stations that will detect an enemy plane?

17. *Criminal Justice: Jury Duty* Have you ever tried to get out of jury duty? About 25% of those called will find an excuse (work, poor health, travel out of town, etc.) to avoid jury duty (Source: Bernice Kanner, *Are You Normal?*, St. Martin's Press, New York). If 12 people are called for jury duty,
    (a) what is the probability that all 12 will be available to serve on the jury?
    (b) what is the probability that 6 or more will *not* be available to serve on the jury?
    (c) Find the expected number of those available to serve on the jury. What is the standard deviation?
    (d) *Quota Problem* How many people n must the jury commissioner contact to be 95.9% sure of finding at least 12 people who are available to serve?

18. *Public Safety: 911 Calls* The Denver Post reported that a recent audit of the Los Angeles 911 calls showed that 85% were not emergencies. Suppose that the 911 operators in Los Angeles have just received four calls.
    (a) What is the probability that all four calls are in fact emergencies?
    (b) What is the probability that three or more calls are not emergencies?
    (c) *Quota Problem* How many calls n would the 911 operators need to answer to be 96% (or more) sure that at least one call is in fact an emergency?

19. *Law Enforcement: Property Crime* Does crime pay? The *FBI Standard Survey of Crimes* showed that for about 80% of all property crimes (burglary, larceny, car theft, etc.), the criminals are never found and the case is never solved (Source: *True Odds*, by James Walsh, Merrit Publishing). Suppose that a neighborhood district in a large city has repeated property crimes, not always by the same criminals. The police are investigating six property crime cases in this district.
    (a) What is the probability that none of the crimes will ever be solved?
    (b) What is the probability that at least one crime will be solved?
    (c) What is the expected number of crimes that will be solved? What is the standard deviation?
    (d) *Quota Problem* How many property crimes n must the police investigate before they can be at least 90% sure of solving one or more cases?

20. *Security: Burglar Alarms* A large bank vault has several automatic burglar alarms. The probability is 0.55 that a single alarm will detect a burglar.
    (a) *Quota Problem* How many such alarms should be used to be 99% certain that a burglar trying to enter is detected by at least one alarm?
    (b) Suppose the bank installs nine alarms. What is the expected number of alarms that will detect a burglar?

21. *Criminal Justice: Convictions* Innocent until proven guilty? In Japanese criminal trials, about 95% of the defendants are found guilty. In the United States, about 60% of the defendants are found guilty in criminal trials (Source: *The Book of Risks*, by Larry Laudan, John Wiley and Sons). Suppose you are a news reporter following seven criminal trials.
    (a) If the trials were in Japan, what is the probability that all the defendants would be found guilty? What is this probability if the trials were in the United States?
    (b) Of the seven trials, what is the expected number of guilty verdicts in Japan? What is the expected number in the United States? What is the standard deviation in each case?
    (c) *Quota Problem* As a U.S. news reporter, how many trails n would you need to cover to be at least 99% sure of two or more convictions? How many trials n would you need if you covered trials in Japan?

22. *Focus Problem: Personality Types* We now have the tools to solve the Chapter Focus Problem. In the book *A Guide to the Development and Use of the Myers-Briggs Type Indicators* by Myers and McCaully, it was reported that approximately 45% of all university professors are extroverted. Suppose you have classes with six different professors.
    (a) What is the probability that all six are extroverts?
    (b) What is the probability that none of your professors is an extrovert?
    (c) What is the probability that at least two of your professors are extroverts?
    (d) In a group of six professors selected at random, what is the *expected number* of extroverts? What is the *standard deviation* of the distribution?
    (e) *Quota Problem* Suppose you were assigned to write an article for the student newspaper and you were given a quota (by the editor) of interviewing at least three extroverted professors. How many professors selected at random would you need to interview to be at least 90% sure of filling the quota?

23. *Quota Problem: Motel Rooms* The owners of a motel in Florida have noticed that in the long run about 40% of the people who stop and inquire about a room for the night actually rent a room.
    (a) *Quota Problem* How many inquiries must the owner answer to be 99% sure of renting at least one room?
    (b) If 25 separate inquiries are made about rooms, what is the expected number that will result in room rentals?

24. *General: Probability Formula* Let r be a binomial random variable representing the number of successes out of n trials.
    (a) Explain why the sample space for r consists of the set $\{0, 1, 2, ..., n\}$ and why the sum of the probabilities of all the entries in the entire sample space must be 1.
    (b) Explain why $P(r \geq 1) = 1 - P(0)$.
    (c) Explain why $P(r \geq 2) = 1 - P(0) - P(1)$.
    (d) Explain why $P(r \geq m) = 1 - P(0) - P(1) - ... - P(m - 1)$ for $1 \leq m \leq n$.

5.4
The Geometric and Poisson Probability Distributions

FOCUS POINTS

✓ In many activities, the *first* to succeed wins everything! Use the geometric distribution to compute the probability that the *n*th trial is the first success.

✓ Use the Poisson distribution to compute the probability of the occurrence of events spread out over time or space.

✓ Use the Poisson distribution to approximate the binomial distribution when the number of trials is large and the probability of success is small.

In this chapter, we have studied binomial probabilities for the discrete random variable *r*, the number of successes in *n* binomial trials. Before we continue in Chapter 6 with continuous random variables, let us examine two other discrete probability distributions, the *geometric* and the *Poisson* probability distributions. These are both related to the binomial distribution. (The *hypergeometric distribution* is another discrete probability distribution related to the binomial distribution. A discussion of the hypergeometric distribution can be found in Appendix I.)

Geometric Distribution

Suppose that we have an experiment where we repeat binomial trials until we get our *first success*, and then we stop. Let *n* be the number of the trial on which we get our *first success*. In this context, *n* is not a fixed number. In fact, *n* could be any of the numbers 1, 2, 3, and so on. What is the probability that our first success comes on the *n*th trial? The answer is given by the *geometric probability distribution*.

> **Geometric probability distribution**
>
> $$P(n) = p(1 - p)^{n-1}$$
>
> where *n* is the number of the trial on which the *first success* occurs (*n* = 1, 2, 3, . . .) and *p* is the probability of success on each trial. *Note:* *p* must be the same for each trial.
>
> Using some mathematics (involving infinite series), it can be shown that the **population mean** and **standard deviation** of the geometric distribution are
>
> $$\mu = \frac{1}{p} \quad \text{and} \quad \sigma = \frac{\sqrt{1-p}}{p}$$

In many real-life situations, we keep on trying until we achieve success. This is true in areas as diverse as diplomacy, military science, real estate sales, general marketing strategies, medical science, engineering, and technology.

To Engineer Is Human: The Role of Failure in Successful Design is a fascinating book by Henry Petroski (a professor of engineering at Duke University). Reviewers for the *Los Angeles Times* describe this book as serious, amusing, probing, and sometimes frightening. The book examines topics such as the collapse of the Tacoma Narrows suspension bridge, the collapse of the Kansas City Hyatt Regency walkway, and the explosion of the space shuttle *Challenger*. Professor Petroski discusses such topics as "success in foreseeing failure" and the "limits of design." What is meant by expressions such as "foreseeing failure" and the "limits of design"? In the next example, we will see how the geometric probability distribution might help us "forecast" failure.

EXAMPLE 10

First success

An automobile assembly plant produces sheet metal door panels. Each panel moves on an assembly line. As the panel passes a robot, a mechanical arm will perform spot welding at different locations. Each location has a magnetic dot painted where the weld is to be made. The robot is programmed to locate the magnetic dot and perform the weld. However, experience shows that on each trial the robot is only 85% successful at locating the dot. If it cannot locate the magnetic dot, it is programmed to *try again*. The robot will keep trying until it finds the dot (and does the weld) or the door panel passes out of the robot's reach.

(a) What is the probability that the robot's first success will be on attempts $n = 1$, 2, or 3?

SOLUTION: Since the robot will keep trying until it is successful, the geometric distribution is appropriate. In this case, success S means that the robot finds the correct location. The probability of success is $p = P(S) = 0.85$. The probabilities are

n	$P(n) = p(1 - p)^{n-1} = 0.85(0.15)^{n-1}$
1	$0.85(0.15)^0 = 0.85$
2	$0.85(0.15)^1 = 0.1275$
3	$0.85(0.15)^2 \approx 0.0191$

(b) The assembly line moves so fast that the robot has a maximum of only three chances before the door panel is out of reach. What is the probability that the robot will be successful before the door panel is out of reach?

SOLUTION: Since $n = 1$ or 2 or 3 are mutually exclusive, then

$$P(n = 1 \text{ or } 2 \text{ or } 3) = P(1) + P(2) + P(3)$$
$$\approx 0.85 + 0.1275 + 0.0191$$
$$= 0.9966$$

This means that the weld should be correctly located about 99.7% of the time.

(c) What is the probability that the robot will not be able to locate the correct spot within three tries? If 10,000 panels are made, what is the expected number of defectives? Comment on the meaning of this answer in the context of "forecasting failure" and the "limits of design."

SOLUTION: The probability that the robot will correctly locate the weld is 0.9966, from part (b). Therefore, the probability that it cannot do so (after three unsuccessful tries) is $1 - 0.9966 = 0.0034$. If we made 10,000 panels, we would expect (forecast) $(10,000)(0.0034) = 34$ defectives. We could reduce this by inspecting every door, but such a solution is most likely too costly. If a defective weld of this type is not considered too dangerous, we can accept an expected 34 failures out of 10,000 panels due to the limits of our production design— that is, the speed of the assembly line and the accuracy of the robot. If this is not acceptable, a new (perhaps more costly) design is needed. ◇

◇ **COMMENT:** The geometric distribution deals with binomial trials that are repeated until we have our *first success* on the *n*th trial. Suppose we repeat a binomial trial *n* times until we have *k* *successes* (not just one). The probability distribution for the random variable *n* is called the *negative binomial distribution*. For more information on this topic, see Problems 24, 25, 26, and 27 at the end of this section. ◇

Poisson Probability Distribution

If we examine the binomial distribution as the number of trials n gets larger and larger while the probability of success p gets smaller and smaller, we obtain the *Poisson distribution*. Siméon Denis Poisson (1781–1840) was a French mathematician who studied probabilities of rare events that occur infrequently in space, time, volume, and so forth. The Poisson distribution applies to accident rates, arrival times, defect rates, the occurrence of bacteria in the air, and many other areas of everyday life.

As with the binomial distribution, we assume only two outcomes: A particular event occurs (success) or does not occur (failure) during the specified time period or space. The events need to be independent so that one success does not change the probability of another success during the specified interval. We are interested in computing the probability of r occurrences in the given time period, space, volume, or specified interval.

Poisson distribution

Let λ (Greek letter lambda) be the mean number of successes over time, volume, area, and so forth. Let r be the number of successes ($r = 0, 1, 2, 3, \ldots$) in a corresponding interval of time, volume, area, and so forth. Then the probability of r successes in the interval is

$$P(r) = \frac{e^{-\lambda}\lambda^r}{r!}$$

where e is approximately equal to 2.7183.

Using some mathematics (involving infinite series), it can be shown that the **population mean** and **standard deviation** of the Poisson distribution are

$$\mu = \lambda \quad \text{and} \quad \sigma = \sqrt{\lambda}$$

Note: e^x is a key found on most calculators. Simply use 1 as the exponent, and the calculator will display a decimal approximation for e.

There are many applications of the Poisson distribution. For example, if we take the point of view that waiting time can be subdivided into many small intervals, then the actual arrival (of whatever we are waiting for) during any one of the very short intervals could be thought of as an infrequent (or rare) event. This means that the Poisson distribution can be used as a mathematical model to describe the probability of arrivals such as cars to a gas station, planes to an airport, calls to a fire station, births of babies, and even fish arriving on a fisherman's line.

EXAMPLE 11

Poisson distribution

Pyramid Lake is located in Nevada on the Paiute Indian Reservation. The lake is described as a lovely jewel in a beautiful desert setting. In addition to its natural beauty, the lake contains some of the world's largest cutthroat trout. Eight- to ten-pound trout are not uncommon, and 12- to 15-pound trophies are taken each season. The Paiute Nation uses highly trained fish biologists to study and maintain this famous fishery. In one of its publications, *Creel Chronicle* (Vol. 3, No. 2), the following information was given about the November catch for boat fishermen.

Total fish per hour = 0.667

Pyramid Lake, Nevada

Suppose that you decide to fish Pyramid Lake for 7 hours during the month of November.

(a) Use the information provided by the fishery biologist in *Creel Chronicle* to find a probability distribution for *r*, the number of fish (of all sizes) you catch in a period of 7 hours.

SOLUTION: For fish of all sizes, the mean success rate per hour is 0.667.

$$\lambda = 0.667/1 \text{ hour}$$

Since we want to study a *7-hour interval*, we use a little arithmetic to adjust λ to 7 hours. That is, we adjust λ so that it represents the average number of fish expected in a 7-hour period.

$$\lambda = \frac{0.667}{1 \text{ hour}} \cdot \left(\frac{7}{7}\right) = \frac{4.669}{7 \text{ hour}}$$

For convenience, let us use the rounded value λ = 4.7 for a 7-hour period. Since *r* is the number of successes (fish caught) in the corresponding 7-hour period and λ = 4.7 for this period, we use the Poisson distribution to get

$$P(r) = \frac{e^{-\lambda}\lambda^r}{r!} = \frac{e^{-4.7}(4.7)^r}{r!}$$

Recall that *e* = 2.7183 . . . . Most calculators have **e^x**, **y^x**, and **n!** keys (see your calculator manual), so the Poisson distribution is not hard to compute.

(b) What is the probability that in 7 hours you will get 0, 1, 2, or 3 fish of any size?

SOLUTION: Using the result of part (a), we get

$$P(0) = \frac{e^{-4.7}(4.7)^0}{0!} \approx 0.0091 \approx 0.01$$

$$P(1) = \frac{e^{-4.7}(4.7)^1}{1!} \approx 0.0427 \approx 0.04$$

$$P(2) = \frac{e^{-4.7}(4.7)^2}{2!} \approx 0.1005 \approx 0.10$$

$$P(3) = \frac{e^{-4.7}(4.7)^3}{3!} \approx 0.1574 \approx 0.16$$

The probabilities of getting 0, 1, 2, or 3 fish are about 1%, 4%, 10%, and 16%, respectively.

(c) What is the probability that you will get 4 or more fish in the 7-hour fishing period?

SOLUTION: The sample space of all *r* values is *r* = 0, 1, 2, 3, 4, 5, ... The probability in the entire sample space is 1, and these events are mutually exclusive. Therefore,

$$1 = P(0) + P(1) + P(2) + P(3) + P(4) + P(5) + \ldots$$

So

$$P(r \geq 4) = P(4) + P(5) + \ldots = 1 - P(0) - P(1) - P(2) - P(3)$$
$$\approx 1 - 0.01 - 0.04 - 0.10 - 0.16$$
$$= 0.69$$

There is about a 69% chance that you will catch 4 or more fish in a 7-hour period. ◊

Use of tables

Table 4 of Appendix II is a table of the Poisson probability distribution for selected values of λ and the number of successes *r*. Table 5-15 is an excerpt from that table.

To find the value of $P(r = 2)$ when λ = 0.3, look in the column headed by 0.3 and the row headed by 2. From the table we see that $P(2) = 0.333$.

 TECH NOTE The TI-84Plus and TI-83Plus calculators have commands for the geometric and Poisson distributions. Excel and Minitab support the Poisson distribution. All the technologies have both the probability distribution and the cumulative distribution.

TI-84Plus/TI-83Plus Use the **DISTR** key and scroll to **geometpdf**(*p,n*) for the probability of first success on trial number *n*; scroll to **geomecdf**(*p,n*) for the probability of first success on trial number ≤ *n*. Use **poissonpdf**(λ,*r*) for the probability of *r* successes. Use **poissoncdf**(λ,*r*) for the probability of at least *r* successes. For example, when λ = 0.25 and *r* = 2, we get the results

```
poissonpdf(.25,2)
```
$P(r = 2)$ .0243375245
```
poissoncdf(.25,2)
```
$P(r \leq 2)$ .9978385033
∎

Excel Menu choice: **Paste Function** ⎡ f_x ⎤ ➤ **Statistical** ➤ **Poisson.** Enter the trial number *r*, and use λ for the mean. False gives the probability $P(r)$ and True gives the cumulative probability P(at least *r*).

TABLE 5-15   Excerpt from Appendix II, Table 4, "Poisson Probability Distribution"

	λ				
r	0.1	0.2	0.3	0.4	0.5 ....
0	.9048	.8187	.7408	.6703	.6065
1	.0905	.1637	.2222	.2681	.3033
2	.0045	.0164	.0333	.0536	.0758
3	.0002	.0011	.0033	.0072	.0126
4	.0000	.0001	.0003	.0007	.0016

Minitab Put the r values in a column. Then use the menu choice **Calc ➤ Probability Distribution ➤ Poisson.** In the dialogue box, select probability or cumulative, enter the column number containing the r values, and use λ for the mean.

Poisson Approximation to the Binomial Probability Distribution

In the preceding examples, we have seen how the Poisson distribution can be used over intervals of time, space, area, and so on. However, the Poisson distribution also can be used as a probability distribution for "rare" events. In the binomial distribution, if the number of trials n is large while the probability p of success is quite small, we call the event (success) a "rare" event. Put another way, it can be shown that for most practical purposes, the Poisson distribution will be a very good *approximation to the binomial* distribution provided the number of trials n is larger than or equal to 100 and $\lambda = np$ is less than 10. As n gets larger and p gets smaller, the approximation becomes better and better.

PROCEDURE

How to approximate binomial probabilities using Poisson probabilities

Suppose you have a binomial distribution with

n = number of trials
r = number of successes
p = probability of success on each trial

If $n \geq 100$ and $np < 10$, then r has a binomial distribution that is approximated by a Poisson distribution with $\lambda = np$.

$$P(r) \approx \frac{e^{-\lambda}\lambda^r}{r!}$$

Note: $\lambda = np$ is the expected value of the binomial distribution.

EXAMPLE 12

Poisson approximation to the binomial

Isabel Briggs Myers was a pioneer in the study of personality types. Today the Myers-Briggs Type Indicator is used in many career counseling programs as well as in many industrial settings where people must work closely together as a team. The 16 personality types are discussed in detail in the book *A Guide to the Development and Use of the Myers-Briggs Type Indicators,* by Myers and McCaulley. Each personality type has its own special contribution in any group activity. One of the more "rare" types is INFJ (introverted, intuitive, feeling, judgmental), which occurs in only about 2.1% of the population. Suppose that a high-school graduating class has 167 students, and suppose that we call success the event that a student is of personality type INFJ.

(a) Let r be the number of successes (INFJ students) in the $n = 167$ trials (graduating class). If $p = P(S) = 0.021$, will the Poisson distribution be a good approximation to the binomial?

   SOLUTION: Since $n = 167$ is greater than 100 and $\lambda = np = 167(0.021) \approx 3.5$ is less than 10, the Poisson distribution should be a good approximation to the binomial.

(b) Estimate the probability that this graduating class has 0, 1, 2, 3, or 4 people who have the INFJ personality type.

SOLUTION: Since Table 4 (Appendix II) for the Poisson distribution includes the values $\lambda = 3.5$ and $r = 0, 1, 2, 3,$ or 4, we may simply look up the values for $P(r)$, $r = 0, 1, 2, 3, 4$:

$P(r = 0) = 0.0302 \qquad P(r = 1) = 0.1057$

$P(r = 2) = 0.1850 \qquad P(r = 3) = 0.2158$

$P(r = 4) = 0.1888$

Since the outcomes $r = 0, 1, 2, 3,$ or 4 successes are mutually exclusive, we can compute the probability of 4 or fewer INFJ types by using the addition rule for mutually exclusive events:

$$P(r \leq 4) = P(0) + P(1) + P(2) + P(3) + P(4)$$
$$= 0.0302 + 0.1057 + 0.1850 + 0.2158 + 0.1888$$
$$= 0.7255$$

The probability that the graduating class will have 4 or fewer INFJ personality types is about 0.73.

(c) Estimate the probability that this class has 5 or more INFJ personality types.

SOLUTION: Because the outcomes of a binomial experiment are all mutually exclusive, we have

$$P(r \leq 4) + P(r \geq 5) = 1$$

or $P(r \geq 5) = 1 - P(r \leq 4) = 1 - 0.7255 = 0.2745$

The probability is approximately 0.27 that there will be 5 or more INFJ personality types in the graduating class. ◊

Summary

In this section, we have studied two discrete probability distributions. The Poisson distribution gives us the probability of r successes in an interval of time or space. The Poisson distribution also can be used to approximate the binomial distribution when $n \geq 100$ and $np < 10$. The geometric distribution gives us the probability that our first success will occur on the nth trial. In the next guided exercise, we will see situations in which each of these distributions applies.

PROCEDURE		
How to identify discrete probability distributions		
Distribution	*Conditions and Setting*	*Formulas*
Binomial distribution	1. There are n independent trials, each repeated under identical conditions. 2. Each trial has two outcomes, S = success and F = failure.	The probability of exactly r successes out of n trials is $P(r) = \dfrac{n!}{r!(n-r)!}p^r q^{n-r}$ $= C_{n,r}p^r q^{n-r}$ *Continued*

How to identify discrete probability distributions *continued*

Distribution	*Conditions and Setting*	*Formulas*
	3. $P(S) = p$ is the same for each trial, as is $P(F)$ $= q = 1 - p$. 4. The random variable r represents the number of successes out of n trials. $0 \leq r \leq n$.	For r, $$\mu = np \text{ and } \sigma = \sqrt{npq}$$ Table 3 of Appendix II has $P(r)$ values for selected n and p.
Geometric distribution	1. There are n independent trials, each repeated under identical conditions. 2. Each trial has two outcomes, S = success and F = failure. 3. $P(S) = p$ is the same for each trial, as is $P(F)$ $= q = 1 - p$. 4. The random variable n represents the number of the trial on which the *first* success occurs. $n = 1, 2, 3, \ldots$	The probability that the first success occurs on the nth trial is $$P(n) = pq^{n-1}$$ For n, $$\mu = \frac{1}{p} \text{ and } \sigma = \frac{\sqrt{q}}{p}$$
Poisson distribution	1. Consider a random process that occurs over time, volume, area, or any other quantity that can (in theory) be subdivided into smaller and smaller intervals. 2. Identify success in the context of the interval (time, volume, area, ...) you are studying. 3. Based on long-term experience, compute the mean or average number of successes that occur over the interval (time, volume, area, ...) you are studying. λ = mean number of successes over designated interval 4. The random variable r represents the number of successes that occur over the interval on which you perform the random process. $r = 0, 1, 2, 3, \ldots$	The probability of r successes in the interval is $$P(r) = \frac{e^{-\lambda}\lambda^r}{r!}$$ For r, $$\mu = \lambda \text{ and } \sigma = \sqrt{\lambda}$$ Table 4 of Appendix II gives $P(r)$ for selected values of λ and r.
Poisson approximation to the binomial distribution	1. There are n independent trials, each repeated under identical conditions. 2. Each trial has two outcomes, S = success and F = failure. 3. $P(S) = p$ is the same for each trial. 4. In addition, $n \geq 100$ and $np < 10$. 5. The random variable r represents the number of successes out of n trials in a binomial distribution.	$\lambda = np$, the expected value of r. The probability of r successes on n trials is $$P(r) \approx \frac{e^{-\lambda}\lambda^r}{r!}$$ Table 4 of Appendix II gives values of $P(r)$ for selected λ and r.

GUIDED EXERCISE 9

Select appropriate distribution

For each problem, first identify the type of probability distribution needed to solve the problem: binomial, geometric, Poisson, or Poisson approximation to the binomial. Then solve the problem.

(I) Denver, Colorado, is prone to severe hailstorms. Insurance agents claim that a homeowner in Denver can expect to replace his or her roof (due to hail damage) once every 10 years. What is the probability that in 12 years a homeowner in Denver will need to replace the roof twice because of hail?

(a) Consider the problem stated in part (I). What is success in this case? We are interested in the probability of two successes over a specified time interval of 12 years. Which distribution should we use?

⟹ Here we can say success is needing to replace a roof because of hail. Because we are interested in the probability of two successes over a time interval, we use the Poisson distribution.

(b) In part (I), we are told that the average roof replacement is once every 10 years. What is the average number of times the roof needs to be replaced in 12 years? What is λ for the 12-year period?

⟹ We are given a value of $\lambda = 1$ for 10 years. To compute λ for 12 years, we convert the denominator to 12 years.

$$\lambda = \frac{0.1}{1 \text{ year}} \cdot \frac{12}{12} = \frac{1.2}{12 \text{ years}}$$

For 12 years, we have $\lambda = 1.2$.

(c) To finish part (I), use the Poisson distribution to find the probability of two successes in the 12-year period.

⟹ We may use Table 4 of Appendix II because $\lambda = 1.2$ and $r = 2$ are values in the table. The table gives $P(r = 2) = 0.2169$. Using the formula and a calculator gives the same result.

$$P(r) = \frac{e^{-\lambda}\lambda^r}{r!}$$

$$P(r = 2) = \frac{e^{-1.2}(1.2)^2}{2!} \approx 0.2169$$

There is about a 21.7% chance the roof will be damaged twice by hail during a 12-year period.

(II) A telephone network substation will keep trying to connect a long-distance call to a trunk line until the fourth attempt has been made. After the fourth unsuccessful attempt, the call number goes into a buffer memory bank, and the caller gets a recorded message to be patient. During peak calling periods, the probability of a call connecting into a trunk line is 65% on each try. What percentage of all calls during peak time will wind up in the buffer memory bank?

Continued

GUIDED EXERCISE 9 continued

(d) Consider part (II). What is success? We are interested in the probability that a call will wind up in the buffer memory. This will occur if success does not occur before which trial? Since we are looking at the probability of a first success by a specified trial number, which probability distribution do we use?

Success is connecting a long-distance call to a trunk line. The call will go into the buffer memory if success is not achieved during the first four attempts. In symbols, the call will go into the buffer if the trial number n of the first success is such that $n \geq 5$. We use the geometric distribution.

(e) What is the probability of success on a single trial? Use this information and the formula for the geometric distribution to compute the probability that the first success occurs on trial 1, 2, 3, or 4. Then use this information to compute $P(n \geq 5)$, where n is the trial number of the first success. What percentage of the calls go to the buffer?

Success means the call connects to the trunk line. According to the description in the problem,

$$P(S) = 0.65 = p$$

By the formula for the geometric probability distribution, when n represents the trial number of the first success,

$$P(n) = p(1 - p)^{n-1}$$

Therefore,

$$P(1) = (0.65)(0.35)^0 = 0.65$$
$$P(2) = (0.65)(0.35)^1 = 0.2275$$
$$P(3) = (0.65)(0.35)^2 \approx 0.0796$$
$$P(4) = (0.65)(0.35)^3 \approx 0.0279$$
$$P(n \geq 5) = 1 - P(1) - P(2) - P(3) - P(4)$$
$$\approx 1 - 0.65 - 0.2275 - 0.0796$$
$$- 0.0279$$
$$= 0.015$$

About 1.5% of the calls go to the buffer.

(III) In Colorado, the murder rate is 3.6 murders per 100,000 inhabitants (Reference: U.S. Department of Justice, Federal Bureau of Investigation). In a large high school graduating class of 1254 graduates, what is the probability that at least one graduate will be murdered?

(f) Consider part (III). What is success in this case? What is the value of n? Find p, the probability of success on a single trial, to six places after the decimal.

Success is a graduate being murdered.

$$n = 1254$$

$$p = \frac{3.6}{100,000}$$
$$= 0.000036$$

(g) Compute np to three decimal places. Is it appropriate to use the Poisson approximation to the binomial? What is the value of λ to three decimal places?

$np \approx 0.045$

Yes.

$\lambda = np \approx 0.045$

Continued

GUIDED EXERCISE 9 continued

(h) Estimate $P(r = 0)$ to three decimal places.

⟹ $P(r) \approx \dfrac{e^{-\lambda}\lambda^r}{r!} \approx \dfrac{e^{-0.045}(0.045)^0}{0!} \approx 0.956$

Recall that $0! = 1$.

(i) Use the relation $P(r \geq 1) = 1 - P(0)$ to estimate the probability that at least one graduate will be murdered.

⟹ $P(r \geq 1) \approx 1 - 0.956$
≈ 0.044

VIEWPOINT

When Do Cracks Become Breakthroughs?

No one *wants* to learn by mistakes! However, learning by our successes will not take us beyond the state of the art! Each new idea, technology, social plan, or engineering structure can be considered a new trial. In the meantime, we the laypeople, whose spokesperson is often a poet or writer, will be threatened by both *failures* and *successes*. This is the nature not only of science, technology, and engineering but also of all human endeavors. [For more discussion on this topic, see Problem 12, as well as *To Engineer Is Human: The Role of Failure in Successful Design* by Professor Petroski (Duke University Press).]

SECTION 5.4   PROBLEMS

1. *College: Core Requirement* Susan is taking Western Civilization this semester on a pass/fail basis. The department teaching the course has a history of passing 77% of the students in Western Civilization each term. Let $n = 1, 2, 3, \ldots$ represent the number of times a student takes Western Civilization until the *first* passing grade is received. (Assume the trials are independent.)
   (a) Write out a formula for the probability distribution of the random variable n.
   (b) What is the probability that Susan passes on the first try ($n = 1$)?
   (c) What is the probability that Susan first passes on the second try ($n = 2$)?
   (d) What is the probability that Susan needs three or more tries to pass Western Civilization?
   (e) What is the expected number of attempts at Western Civilization Susan must make to have her (first) pass? *Hint:* Use μ for the geometric distribution and round.

2. *Law: Bar Exam* Bob is a recent law school graduate who intends to take the state bar exam. According to the National Conference on Bar Examiners, about 57% of all people who take the state bar exam pass (Source: *The Book of Odds,* by Shook and Shook, Signet). Let $n = 1, 2, 3, \ldots$ represent the number of times a person takes the bar exam until the *first* pass.
   (a) Write out a formula for the probability distribution of the random variable n.
   (b) What is the probability that Bob first passes the bar exam on the second try ($n = 2$)?

(c) What is the probability that Bob needs three attempts to pass the bar exam?

(d) What is the probability that Bob needs more than three attempts to pass the bar exam?

(e) What is the expected number of attempts at the state bar exam Bob must make for his (first) pass? *Hint:* Use μ for the geometric distribution and round.

3. *Anthropology: Pot Shards* Anthropological studies at Casa del Rito indicate that approximately 5% of all pot shards at the excavation site are from the traditional type of pot known as *Socorro black on white* (Source: *Bandelier Archaeological Excavation Project: Summer 1990 Excavations at Burnt Mesa Pueblo and Casa del Rito*, edited by Kohler, Washington State University Department of Anthropology). Let $n = 1, 2, 3, \ldots$ represent the number of pot shards that must be discovered (and examined) until the *first* Socorro black on white is found.

   (a) Write out a formula for the probability distribution of the random variable n.

   (b) What is the probability that the first Socorro black on white pot shard is found on trial $n = 5$?

   (c) What is the probability that the first Socorro black on white pot shard is found on trial $n = 10$?

   (d) What is the probability that more than three pot shards have to be examined before finding the first Socorro black on white?

   (e) What is the expected number of pot shards that must be examined to find the first Socorro black on white? *Hint:* Use μ for the geometric distribution and round.

4. *Sociology: Hawaiians* On the leeward side of the island of Oahu, in the small village of Nanakuli, about 80% of the residents are of Hawaiian ancestry (Source: *The Honolulu Advertiser*). Let $n = 1, 2, 3, \ldots$ represent the number of people you must meet until you encounter the *first* person of Hawaiian ancestry in the village of Nanakuli.

   (a) Write out a formula for the probability distribution of the random variable n.

   (b) Compute the probability that $n = 1$, $n = 2$, $n = 3$.

   (c) Compute the probability that $n \geq 4$.

   (d) In Waikiki it is estimated that about 4% of the residents are of Hawaiian ancestry. Repeat parts (a), (b), and (c) for Waikiki.

5. *Sociology: Values* Approximately 71% of all modern college students claim that the main reason they are attending college is to make more money after graduation. In 1967, approximately 83% of all college students claimed that they were attending college primarily to develop a meaningful philosophy of life (Source: *Chances: Risk and Odds in Everyday Life*, by James Burke). Let $n = 1, 2, 3, \ldots$ represent the *first* person who is a college student selected at random who says he or she is in college primarily to make more money after graduation.

   (a) Write out a formula for the probability distribution of the random variable n.

   (b) Find the probability that $n = 1$, $n = 2$, $n \geq 3$.

   (c) Repeat parts (a) and (b), where n represents the *first* person who was a college student in 1967 selected at random who claimed the primary reason for attending college was to develop a meaningful philosophy of life.

6. *Agriculture: Apples* Approximately 3.6% of all (untreated) Jonathan apples had bitter pit in a study conducted by the botanists Ratkowsky and Martin (Source: *Australian Journal of Agricultural Research*, Vol. 25, pp. 783–790). (Bitter pit is a disease of apples resulting in a soggy core, which can be caused either by overwatering the apple tree or by a calcium deficiency in the soil.) Let n be a random variable that represents the first Jonathan apple chosen at random that has bitter pit.

   (a) Write out a formula for the probability distribution of the random variable n.

   (b) Find the probability that $n = 3$, $n = 5$, $n = 12$.

(c) Find the probability that $n \geq 5$.

(d) What is the expected number of apples that must be examined to find the first one with bitter pit? *Hint:* Use μ for the geometric distribution and round.

7. *Fishing: Lake Trout* At Fontaine Lake Camp on Lake Athabasca in northern Canada, history shows that about 30% of the guests catch lake trout over 20 pounds on a 4-day fishing trip (Source: Athabasca Fishing Lodges, Saskatoon, Canada). Let n be a random variable that represents the *first* trip to Fontaine Lake Camp on which a guest catches a lake trout over 20 pounds.

(a) Write out a formula for the probability distribution of the random variable n.

(b) Find the probability that a guest catches a lake trout weighing at least 20 pounds for the *first* time on trip number 3.

(c) Find the probability that it takes more than three trips for a guest to catch a lake trout weighing at least 20 pounds.

(d) What is the expected number of fishing trips that must be taken to catch the first lake trout over 20 pounds? *Hint:* Use μ for the geometric distribution and round.

8. *Archaeology: Artifacts* At Burnt Mesa Pueblo, in one of the archaeological excavation sites, the artifact density (number of prehistoric artifacts per 10 liters of sediment) was 1.5 (see source in Problem 3). Suppose you are going to dig up and examine 50 liters of sediment at this site. Let $r = 0, 1, 2, 3, \ldots$ be a random variable that represents the number of prehistoric artifacts found in your 50 liters of sediment.

(a) Explain why the Poisson distribution would be a good choice for the probability distribution of r. What is λ? Write out the formula for the probability distribution of the random variable r.

(b) Compute the probability that in your 50 liters of sediment you will find two prehistoric artifacts; that you will find three artifacts; that you will find four artifacts.

(c) Find the probability that you will find three or more artifacts in the 50 liters of sediment.

(d) Find the probability that you will find fewer than three prehistoric artifacts in the 50 liters of sediment.

9. *Ecology: River Otters* In his doctoral thesis, L. A. Beckel (University of Minnesota, 1982) studied the social behavior of river otters during the mating season. An important role in the bonding process of river otters is very short periods of social grooming. After extensive observations, Dr. Beckel found that one group of river otters under study had a frequency of initiating grooming of approximately 1.7 for each 10 minutes. Suppose that you are observing river otters for 30 minutes. Let $r = 0, 1, 2, \ldots$ be a random variable that represents the number of times (in a 30-minute interval) that one otter initiates social grooming of another.

(a) Explain why the Poisson distribution would be a good choice for the probability distribution of r. What is λ? Write out the formula for the probability distribution of the random variable r.

(b) Find the probability that in your 30 minutes of observation, one otter will initiate social grooming four times, five times, or six times.

(c) Find the probability that one otter will initiate social grooming four or more times during the 30-minute observation period.

(d) Find the probability that one otter will initiate social grooming less than four times during the 30-minute observation period.

10. *Law Enforcement: Shoplifting* The *Denver Post* reported that a large shopping center had an incident of shoplifting (that was caught by security) on the average of once every three hours. The shopping center is open from 10 A.M. to 9 P.M.

(11 hours). Let *r* be the number of shoplifting incidents caught by security in an 11-hour period during which the center is open.
(a) Explain why the Poisson probability distribution would be a good choice for the random variable *r*. What is λ?
(b) What is the probability that from 10 A.M. to 9 P.M. there will be at least one shoplifting incident caught by security?
(c) What is the probability that from 10 A.M. to 9 P.M. there will be at least three shoplifting incidents caught by security?
(d) What is the probability that from 10 A.M. to 9 P.M. there will be no shoplifting incidents caught by security?

11. *Vital Statistics: Birth Rate* USA Today reported that the U.S. (annual) birth rate is about 16 per 1000 people and the death rate is about 8 per 1000 people.
(a) Explain why the Poisson probability distribution would be a good choice for the random variable *r* = number of births (or deaths) for a community of a given population size.
(b) In a community of 1000 people, what is the probability of 10 births? What is the probability of 10 deaths? What is the probability of 16 births? 16 deaths?
(c) Repeat part (b) for a community of 1500 people. You will need to use a calculator to compute *P*(10 births) and *P*(16 births).
(d) Repeat part (b) for a community of 750 people.

12. *Engineering: Cracks* Henry Petroski is a professor of civil engineering at Duke University. In his book *To Engineer Is Human: The Role of Failure in Successful Design*, Professor Petroski says that up to 95% of all structural failures, including those of bridges, airplanes, and other commonplace products of technology, are believed to be the result of crack growth. In most cases, the cracks grow slowly. It is only when the cracks reach intolerable proportions and still go undetected that catastrophe can occur. In a cement retaining wall, occasional hairline cracks are normal and nothing to worry about. If these cracks are spread out and not too close together, the wall is considered safe. However, if a number of cracks group together in a small region, there may be real trouble. Suppose that a given cement retaining wall is considered safe if hairline cracks are evenly spread out and occur on the average of 4.2 cracks per 30-foot section of wall.
(a) Explain why a Poisson probability distribution would be a good choice for the random variable *r* = number of hairline cracks for a given length of retaining wall.
(b) In a 50-foot section of safe wall, what is the probability of three (evenly spread out) hairline cracks? What is the probability of three *or more* (evenly spread out) hairline cracks?
(c) Answer part (b) for a 20-foot section of wall.
(d) Answer part (b) for a 2-foot section of wall. Round λ to the nearest tenth.
(e) Consider your answers for parts (b), (c), and (d). If you had three hairline cracks evenly spread out over a 50-foot section of wall, should this be cause for concern? The probability is low. Could this mean that you are lucky to have so few cracks? On a 20-foot section of wall [part (c)] the probability of three cracks is higher. Does this mean that this distribution of cracks is closer to what we should expect? For part (d), the probability is very small. Could this mean you are not so lucky and have something to worry about? Explain your answers.

13. *Meteorology: Winter Conditions* Much of Trail Ridge Road in Rocky Mountain National Park is over 12,000 feet high. Although it is a beautiful drive in summer months, in winter the road is closed because of severe weather conditions. *Winter Wind Studies in Rocky Mountain National Park*, by Glidden (published by Rocky Mountain Nature Association), states that sustained gale-force winds (over 32 miles per hour and often over 90 miles per hour) occur on the average of once every 60 hours at a Trail Ridge Road weather station.

(a) Let r = frequency with which gale-force winds occur in a given time interval. Explain why the Poisson probability distribution would be a good choice for the random variable r.

(b) For an interval of 108 hours, what is the probability that $r = 2, 3,$ or 4? What is the probability that $r < 2$?

(c) For an interval of 180 hours, what is the probability that $r = 3, 4,$ or 5? What is the probability that $r < 3$?

14. *Earthquakes: San Andreas Fault* USA Today reported that Parkfield, California, is dubbed the world's earthquake capital because it sits on top of the notorious San Andreas fault. Since 1857, Parkfield has had a major earthquake on the average of once every 22 years.

(a) Explain why a Poisson probability distribution would be a good choice for r = number of earthquakes in a given time interval.

(b) Compute the probability of at least one major earthquake in the next 22 years. Round λ to the nearest hundredth, and use a calculator.

(c) Compute the probability that there will be no major earthquake in the next 22 years. Round λ to the nearest hundredth, and use a calculator.

(d) Compute the probability of at least one major earthquake in the next 50 years. Round λ to the nearest hundredth, and use a calculator.

(e) Compute the probability of no major earthquakes in the next 50 years. Round λ to the nearest hundredth, and use a calculator.

15. *Real Estate: Sales* Jim is a real estate agent who sells large commercial buildings. Because his commission is so large on a single sale, he does not need to sell many buildings to make a good living. History shows that Jim has a record of selling an average of eight large commercial buildings in 275 days.

(a) Explain why a Poisson probability distribution would be a good choice for r = number of buildings sold in a given time interval.

(b) In a 60-day period, what is the probability that Jim will make no sales? one sale? two or more sales?

(c) In a 90-day period, what is the probability that Jim will make no sales? two sales? three or more sales?

16. *Law Enforcement: Burglaries* The Honolulu Advertiser stated that in Honolulu there was an average of 661 burglaries per 100,000 households in a given year. In the Kohola Drive neighborhood there are 316 homes. Let r = number of these homes that will be burglarized in a year.

(a) Explain why the Poisson approximation to the binomial would be a good choice for the random variable r. What is n? What is p? What is λ to the nearest tenth?

(b) What is the probability that there will be no burglaries this year in the Kohola Drive neighborhood?

(c) What is the probability that there will be no more than one burglary in the Kohola Drive neighborhood?

(d) What is the probability that there will be two or more burglaries in the Kohola Drive neighborhood?

17. *Criminal Justice: Drunk Drivers* Harper's Index reported that the number of (Orange County, California) convicted drunk drivers whose sentence included a tour of the morgue was 569, out of which only 1 became a repeat offender.

(a) Suppose that out of 1000 newly convicted drunk drivers, all were required to take a tour of the morgue. Let us assume that the probability of a repeat offender is still $p = 1/569$. Explain why the Poisson approximation to the binomial would be a good choice for r = number of repeat offenders out of 1000 convicted drunk drivers who toured the morgue. What is λ to the nearest tenth?

(b) What is the probability that $r = 0$?
(c) What is the probability that $r > 1$?
(d) What is the probability that $r > 2$?
(e) What is the probability that $r > 3$?

18. *Airlines: Lost Bags USA Today* reported that for all airlines, the number of lost bags was

    May: 6.02 per 1000 passengers   December: 12.78 per 1000 passengers

    Note: A passenger could lose more than one bag.
    (a) Let r = number of bags lost per 1000 passengers in May. Explain why the Poisson distribution would be a good choice for the random variable r. What is λ to the nearest tenth?
    (b) In the month of May, what is the probability that out of 1000 passengers, no bags are lost? 3 or more bags are lost? 6 or more bags are lost?
    (c) In the month of December, what is the probability that out of 1000 passengers, no bags are lost? 6 or more bags are lost? 12 or more bags are lost? (Round λ to the nearest whole number.)

19. *Law Enforcement: Officers Killed Chances: Risk and Odds in Everyday Life,* by James Burke, reports that the probability that a police officer will be killed in the line of duty is 0.5% (or less).
    (a) In a police precinct with 175 officers, let r = number of police officers killed in the line of duty. Explain why the Poisson approximation to the binomial would be a good choice for the random variable r. What is n? What is p? What is λ to the nearest tenth?
    (b) What is the probability that no officer in this precinct will be killed in the line of duty?
    (c) What is the probability that one or more officers in this precinct will be killed in the line of duty?
    (d) What is the probability that two or more officers in this precinct will be killed in the line of duty?

20. *Business Franchise: Shopping Center Chances: Risk and Odds in Everyday Life,* by James Burke, reports that only 2% of all local franchises are business failures. A Colorado Springs shopping complex has 137 franchises (restaurants, print shops, convenience stores, hair salons, etc.).
    (a) Let r be the number of these franchises that are business failures. Explain why a Poisson approximation to the binomial would be appropriate for the random variable r. What is n? What is p? What is λ (round to the nearest tenth)?
    (b) What is the probability that none of the franchises will be a business failure?
    (c) What is the probability that two or more franchises will be business failures?
    (d) What is the probability that four or more franchises will be business failures?

21. *Poisson Approximation to Binomial: Comparisons*
    (a) For $n = 100$, $p = 0.02$, and $r = 2$, compute $P(r)$ using the formula for the binomial distribution and your calculator:

    $$P(r) = C_{n,r}p^r(1 - p)^{n - r}$$

    (b) For $n = 100$, $p = 0.02$, and $r = 2$, estimate $P(r)$ using the Poisson approximation to the binomial.
    (c) Compare the results of parts (a) and (b). Does it appear that the Poisson distribution with $\lambda = np$ provides a good approximation for $P(r = 2)$?
    (d) Repeat parts (a) to (c) for $r = 3$.

22. *Expand Your Knowledge: Conditional Probability* Pyramid Lake is located in Nevada on the Paiute Indian Reservation. This lake is famous for large cutthroat trout. The mean number of trout (large and small) caught from a boat is 0.667 fish per hour (Reference: *Creel Chronicle*, Vol. 3, No. 2). Suppose you rent a boat and go fishing for 8 hours. Let r be a random variable that represents the number of fish you catch in the 8-hour period.

   (a) Explain why a Poisson probability distribution is appropriate for r. What is λ for the 8-hour fishing trip? Round λ to one place after the decimal so that you can use Table 4 of Appendix II for Poisson probabilities.

   (b) If you have already caught three trout, what is the probability you will catch a total of seven or more trout? Compute $P(r \geq 7,\ given\ r \geq 3)$. See Hint below.

   (c) If you have already caught four trout, what is the probability you will catch a total of less than nine trout? Compute $P(r < 9,\ given\ r \geq 4)$. See Hint below.

   (d) List at least three other areas besides fishing where you think conditional Poisson probabilities can be applied.

   Hint for solution: Review item 6, conditional probability, in the summary of basic probability rules at the end of Section 4.2. Note that

   $$P(A,\ given\ B) = \frac{P(A\ and\ B)}{P(B)}$$

   and show that in part (b)

   $$P(r \geq 7,\ given\ r \geq 3) = \frac{P((r \geq 7)\ and\ (r \geq 3))}{P(r \geq 3)} = \frac{P(r \geq 7)}{P(r \geq 3)}$$

23. *Conditional Probability: Hail Damage* In western Kansas the summer density of hailstorms is estimated at about 2.1 storms per 5 square miles. In most cases a hailstorm only damages a relatively small area in a square mile (Reference: *Agricultural Statistics*, United States Department of Agriculture). A crop insurance company has insured a tract of 8 square miles of Kansas wheat land against hail damage. Let r be a random variable that represents the number of hailstorms this summer in the 8-square-mile tract.

   (a) Explain why a Poisson probability distribution is appropriate for r. What is λ for the 8-square-mile tract of land? Round λ to one place after the decimal so that you can use Table 4 of Appendix II for Poisson probabilities.

   (b) If there have already been two hailstorms this summer, what is the probability that there will be a total of four or more hailstorms in this tract of land? Compute $P(r \geq 4,\ given\ r \geq 2)$.

   (c) If there have already been three hailstorms this summer, what is the probability that there will be a total of fewer than six hailstorms? Compute $P(r < 6,\ given\ r \geq 3)$.

   Hint: See Problem 22.

24. *Expand Your Knowledge: Negative Binomial Distribution* Suppose you have binomial trials for which the probability of success on each trial is p and the probability of failure is $q = 1 - p$. Let k be a fixed whole number greater than or equal to 1. Let n be the number of the trial on which the kth success occurs. This means that the first $k - 1$ successes occur within the first $n - 1$ trials, while the kth success actually occurs on the nth trial. Now, if we are going to have k successes, we must have at least k trials. So $n = k,\ k + 1,\ k + 2,\ \ldots$ and n is a random variable. The probability distribution for n is called the *negative binomial distribution*. The formula for the probability distribution of n is shown in the next display (see Problem 27 for a derivation).

Negative binomial distribution

Let $k \geq 1$ be a fixed whole number. The probability that the kth success occurs on trial number n is

$$P(n) = C_{n-1, \, k-1} \, p^k q^{n-k}$$

where

$$C_{n-1, \, k-1} = \frac{(n-1)!}{(k-1)!(n-k)!}$$

$$n = k, k+1, k+2, \ldots$$

The expected value and standard deviation of this probability distribution are

$$\mu = \frac{k}{p} \text{ and } \sigma = \frac{\sqrt{kq}}{p}$$

Note: If $k = 1$, the negative binomial distribution is called the *geometric distribution*.

In eastern Colorado there are many dry land wheat farms. The success of a spring wheat crop is dependent on sufficient moisture in March and April. Assume that the probability of a successful wheat crop in this region is about 65%. So the probability of success in a single year is $p = 0.65$ and the probability of failure is $q = 0.35$. The Wagner farm has taken out a loan and needs $k = 4$ successful crops to repay it. Let n be a random variable representing the year in which the fourth successful crop occurs (after the loan was made).

(a) Write out the formula for $P(n)$ in the context of this application.

(b) Compute $P(n = 4)$, $P(n = 5)$, $P(n = 6)$, and $P(n = 7)$.

(c) What is the probability that the Wagners can repay the loan within 4 to 7 years? *Hint:* Compute $P(4 \leq n \leq 7)$.

(d) What is the probability that the Wagners will need to farm for 8 or more years before they can repay the loan? *Hint:* Compute $P(n \geq 8)$.

(e) What are the expected value μ and standard deviation σ of the random variable n? Interpret these values in the context of this application.

25. *Negative Binomial Distribution: Marketing* Susan is a sales representative who has a history of making a successful sale from about 80% of her sales contacts. If she makes 12 successful sales this week, Susan will get a bonus. Let n be a random variable representing the number of contacts needed for Susan to get the 12th sale.

(a) Explain why a negative binomial distribution is appropriate for the random variable n. Write out the formula for $P(n)$ in the context of this application. *Hint:* See Problem 24.

(b) Compute $P(n = 12)$, $P(n = 13)$, and $P(n = 14)$.

(c) What is the probability that Susan will need from 12 to 14 contacts to get the bonus?

(d) What is the probability that Susan will need more than 14 contacts to get the bonus?

(e) What are the expected value μ and standard deviation σ of the random variable n? Interpret these values in the context of this application.

26. *Negative Binomial Distribution: Type A Blood Donors* Blood type A occurs in about 41% of the population (Reference: *Laboratory and Diagnostic Tests*, F. Fischbach). A clinic needs 3 pints of type A blood. A donor usually gives a pint

of blood. Let n be a random variable representing the number of donors needed to provide 3 pints of type A blood.

(a) Explain why a negative binomial distribution is appropriate for the random variable n. Write out the formula for $P(n)$ in the context of this application. *Hint:* See Problem 24.

(b) Compute $P(n = 3)$, $P(n = 4)$, $P(n = 5)$, and $P(n = 6)$.

(c) What is the probability that the clinic will need from 3 to 6 donors to obtain the needed 3 pints of type A blood?

(d) What is the probability that the clinic will need more than 6 donors to obtain 3 pints of type A blood?

(e) What are the expected value μ and standard deviation σ of the random variable n? Interpret these values in the context of this application.

27. *Expand Your Knowledge: Brain Teaser* If you enjoy a little abstract thinking, you may want to derive the formula for the negative binomial probability distribution. Use the notation of Problem 24. Consider two events, A and B.

A = {event the first $n - 1$ trials contain $k - 1$ successes}

B = {event the nth trial is a success}

(a) Use the binomial probability distribution to show that the probability of A is $P(A) = C_{n-1,\,k-1}\, p^{k-1} q^{(n-1)-(k-1)}$.

(b) Show that the probability of B is that of a single trial in a binomial experiment, $P(B) = p$.

(c) Why is $P(A \text{ and } B) = P(A) \cdot P(B)$? *Hint:* Binomial trials are independent.

(d) Use parts (a), (b), and (c) to compute and simplify $P(A \text{ and } B)$.

(e) Compare $P(A \text{ and } B)$ with the negative binomial formula and comment on the meaning of your results.

SUMMARY

The concepts of discrete and continuous random variables were introduced in this chapter. We looked at the general probability distribution for a discrete random variable and saw how to compute the expected value μ and the standard deviation σ of a discrete probability distribution.

Then we turned our attention to a special discrete probability distribution, the binomial probability distribution. This distribution is used to determine the probability of outcomes from a binomial experiment.

A binomial experiment must meet the following criteria:

1. There are a fixed number of trials, denoted by n.

2. The trials are independent and repeated under identical conditions.

3. Each trial has only two outcomes: success S and failure F.

4. For each trial the probability p of success remains the same. The probability of failure is $q = 1 - p$.

5. The central problem is to find the probability of r successes out of n trials.

The formula for the binomial probability distribution is

$$P(r) = C_{n,r}\, p^r q^{n-r}$$

where $C_{n,r}$ is the binomial coefficient as found in Table 2 of Appendix II. For certain values of p and n, $P(r)$ can be found directly in Table 3 of Appendix II.

The mean or expected value and standard deviation of the binomial distribution are given by the formulas

$$\mu = np$$
$$\sigma = \sqrt{npq} \qquad \text{where } q = 1 - p$$

The binomial probability distribution is a distribution of a discrete random variable. Other distributions that relate to the binomial distribution are the geometric distribution and the Poisson distribution. These are also probability distributions of discrete random variables. The geometric distribution is used to find the probability that the first success of a binomial experiment occurs on trial number n. The Poisson distribution is used to compute the probability of r successes in an interval of time, volume, area, and so forth. We also use the Poisson distribution as an approximation to the binomial when n is large and the probability of success p on a single trial is small. Appendix I contains a discussion of another discrete probability distribution, the hypergeometric distribution.

IMPORTANT WORDS & SYMBOLS

Section 5.1
Random variable
  Discrete
  Continuous
Mean μ of a probability distribution
Standard deviation σ of a probability distribution
Expected value μ
Linear function of a random variable
Linear combination of two independent random
  variables

Section 5.2
Binomial experiment
Independent trials
Successes and failures in a binomial experiment
Probability of success $P(S) = p$
Probability of failure $P(F) = q = 1 - p$
Binomial coefficient $C_{n,r}$
Binomial probability distribution $P(r) = C_{n,r} p^r q^{n-r}$

Section 5.3
Mean for the binomial distribution $\mu = np$
Standard deviation for the binomial distribution
  $\sigma = \sqrt{npq}$
Quota problem

Section 5.4
Geometric probability distribution
Poisson probability distribution
Poisson approximation to the binomial
Negative binomial distribution

VIEWPOINT   *What's Your Type?*

Are students and professors *really* compatible? One way of answering this question is to look at Myers-Briggs Type Indicators for personality preferences. What is the probability that your professor is introverted and judgmental? What is the probability that you are extroverted and perceptive? Are most of the leaders in student government extroverted and judgmental? Is it true that members of Phi Beta Kappa have personality types more like the professors'? We will consider questions such as these in more detail in Chapter 8 (estimation) and Chapter 9 (hypothesis testing), where we will continue our work with binomial probabilities. In the meantime, you can find many answers regarding careers, probability, and personality types in *Applications of the Myers-Briggs Type Indicator in Higher Education,* edited by J. Provost and S. Anchors.

CHAPTER REVIEW PROBLEMS

1. *Probability Distribution: Auto Leases* Consumer Banker Association released a report showing the lengths of automobile leases for new automobiles. The results are

Lease Length in Months	Percent of Leases
13–24	12.7%
25–36	37.1%
37–48	28.5%
49–60	21.5%
More than 60	0.2%

(a) Use the midpoint of each class, and call the midpoint of the last class 66.5 months, for purposes of computing the expected lease term. Also find the standard deviation of the distribution.

(b) Sketch a graph of the probability distribution for the duration of new auto leases.

2. *Ecology: Predator and Prey* Isle Royale, an island in Lake Superior, has provided an important study site of wolves and prey. In the National Park Service Scientific Monograph Series 11, *Wolf Ecology and Prey Relationships on Isle Royale,* Peterson gives results of many wolf–moose studies. Of special interest is the study of the number of moose killed by wolves. In the period from 1958 to 1974, there were 296 moose deaths identified as wolf kills. The age distribution of the kills is

Age of Moose in Years	Number Killed by Wolves
Calf (0.5 yr)	112
1–5	53
6–10	73
11–15	56
16–20	2

(a) For each age group, compute the probability that a moose in that age group is killed by a wolf.

(b) Consider all ages in a class equal to the class midpoint. Find the expected age of a moose killed by a wolf and the standard deviation of the ages.

3. *Insurance: Auto* State Farm Insurance studies show that in Colorado, 55% of the auto insurance claims submitted for property damage were submitted by males under 25 years of age. Suppose 10 property damage claims involving automobiles are selected at random.

(a) Let r be the number of claims that are made by males under age 25. Make a histogram for the r-distribution probabilities.

(b) What is the probability that six or more claims are made by males under age 25?

(c) What is the expected number of claims made by males under age 25? What is the standard deviation of the r-probability distribution?

4. *Quality Control: Pens* A stationery store has decided to accept a large shipment of ball-point pens if an inspection of 20 randomly selected pens yields no more than two defective pens.

(a) Find the probability that this shipment is accepted if 5% of the total shipment is defective.

(b) Find the probability that this shipment is not accepted if 15% of the total shipment is defective.

5. *Criminal Justice: Inmates* According to *Harper's Index,* 50% of all federal inmates are serving time for drug dealing. A random sample of 16 federal inmates is selected.

(a) What is the probability that 12 or more are serving time for drug dealing?

(b) What is the probability that 7 or fewer are serving time for drug dealing?

(c) What is the expected number of inmates serving time for drug dealing?

6. *Airlines: On-Time Arrivals* *Consumer Reports* rated airlines and found that 80% of the flights involved in the study arrived on time (that is, within 15 minutes of scheduled arrival time). Assuming that the on-time arrival rate is representative of the entire commercial airline industry, consider a random sample of 200 flights. What is the expected number that will arrive on time? What is the standard deviation of this distribution?

7. *Agriculture: Grapefruit* It is estimated that 75% of a grapefruit crop is good; the other 25% have rotten centers that cannot be detected unless the grapefruit are cut open. The grapefruit are sold in sacks of 10. Let r be the number of good grapefruit in a sack.

(a) Make a histogram of the probability distribution of r.

(b) What is the probability of getting no more than one bad grapefruit in a sack? What is the probability of getting at least one good grapefruit in a sack?

(c) What is the expected number of good grapefruit in a sack?

(d) What is the standard deviation of the r probability distribution?

8. *Restaurants: Reservations* The Orchard Café has found that about 5% of the diners who make reservations don't show up. If 82 reservations have been made, how many diners can be expected to show up? Find the standard deviation of this distribution.

9. *College Life: Student Government* The student government claims that 85% of all students favor an increase in student fees to buy indoor potted plants for the classrooms. A random sample of 12 students produced 2 in favor of the project. What is the probability that 2 or fewer in the sample will favor the project, assuming that

the student government is correct? Do the data support the student government claim, or does it seem that the percentage favoring the increase in fees is less than 85%?

10. *Quota Problem: Financial* Suppose you are a (junk) bond broker who buys only bonds that have a 50% chance of default. You want a portfolio with at least five bonds that do not default. You can dispose of the other bonds in the portfolio with no great loss. How many such bonds should you buy if you want to be 94.1% sure that five or more will not default?

11. *Theater: Coughs* A person with a cough is a *persona non grata* on airplanes, elevators, or at the theater. In theaters especially, the irritation level rises with each muffled explosion. According to Dr. Brian Carlin, a Pittsburgh pulmonologist, in any large audience you'll hear about 11 coughs per minute (Source: *USA Today*).
    (a) Let r = number of coughs in a given time interval. Explain why the Poisson distribution would be a good choice for the probability distribution of r.
    (b) Find the probability of 3 or fewer coughs (in a large auditorium) in a 1-minute period.
    (c) Find the probability of at least 3 coughs (in a large auditorium) in a 30-second period.

12. *Accident Rate: Small Planes* Flying over the western states with mountainous terrain in a small aircraft is 40% riskier than flying over similar distances in flatter portions of the nation, according to a General Accounting Office study completed in response to a congressional request. The accident rate for small aircraft in the 11 mountainous western states is 2.4 per 100,000 flight operations (Source: *Denver Post*).
    (a) Let r = number of accidents for a given number of operations. Explain why the Poisson distribution would be a good choice for the probability distribution of r.
    (b) Find the probability of no accidents in 100,000 flight operations.
    (c) Find the probability of at least 4 accidents in 200,000 flight operations.

13. *Banking: Loan Defaults* Records over the past year show that 1 out of 350 loans made by Mammon Bank have defaulted. Find the probability that 2 or more out of 300 loans will default. *Hint:* Is it appropriate to use the Poisson approximation to the binomial distribution?

14. *Car Theft: Hawaii* In Hawaii, the rate of motor vehicle theft is 551 thefts per 100,000 vehicles (Reference: U.S. Department of Justice, Federal Bureau of Investigation). A large parking structure in Honolulu has issued 482 parking permits.
    (a) What is the probability that none of the vehicles with a permit will eventually be stolen?
    (b) What is the probability that at least one of the vehicles with a permit will eventually be stolen?
    (c) What is the probability that two or more of the vehicles with a permit will eventually be stolen?
    Note: The vehicles may or may not be stolen from the parking structure. *Hint:* Is it appropriate to use the Poisson approximation to the binomial? Explain.

15. *General: Coin Flip* An experiment consists of tossing a coin a specified number of times and recording the outcomes.
    (a) What is the probability that the *first* head will occur on the second trial? Does this probability change if we toss the coin three times? What if we toss the coin four times? What probability distribution model do we use to compute these probabilities?
    (b) What is the probability that the *first* head will occur on the fourth trial? after the fourth trial?

16. *Testing: CPA Exam* Cathy is planning to take the Certified Public Accountant Examination (CPA exam). Records kept by the college of business from which she graduated indicate that 83% of the students who graduated pass the CPA exam. Assume that the exam is changed each time it is given. Let $n = 1, 2, 3, \ldots$ represent the number of times a person takes the CPA exam until the *first* pass. (Assume the trials are independent.)
    (a) What is the probability that Cathy passes the CPA exam on the first try?
    (b) What is the probability that Cathy passes the CPA exam on the second or third try?

DATA HIGHLIGHTS: GROUP PROJECTS

Break into small groups and discuss the following topics. Organize a brief outline in which you summarize the main points of your group discussion.

1. Powerball! Imagine, you could win a jackpot worth at least $10 million. Some jackpots have been more than $250 million! Powerball is a multistate lottery. To play Powerball, you purchase a $1 ticket. On the ticket you select five distinct white balls (numbered 1 through 53) and then one red Powerball (numbered 1 through 42). The red Powerball number may be any of the numbers 1 through 42, including any of the numbers you selected for the white balls. Every Wednesday and Saturday there is a drawing. If your chosen numbers match those drawn, you win! Figure 5-7 shows all the prizes and the probability of winning each prize and specifies how many numbers on your ticket must match those drawn to win the prize. The Multi-State Lottery Association maintains a web site that displays the results of each drawing, as well as a history of the results of previous drawings. To find out more about Powerball, visit the Brase/Brase statistics site at **http://math.college.hmco.com/students** and find the link to the Multi-State Lottery Association.
    (a) Assume that the jackpot is $10 million and that there will be only one jackpot winner. Figure 5-7 lists the prizes and the probability of winning each prize. What is the probability of *not winning* any prize? Consider all the prizes and their respective probabilities and the prize of $0 (no win) and its probability. Use all these values to estimate your expected winnings μ if you play one ticket. How much do you effectively contribute to the state where you purchased the ticket (ignoring the overhead cost of operating Powerball)?
    (b) Suppose that the jackpot increased to $25 million (and that there was to be only one winner). Compute your expected winnings if you buy one ticket. Does the probability of winning the jackpot change because the jackpot is higher?
    (c) Pretend that you are going to buy 10 Powerball tickets when the jackpot is $10 million. Use the random-number table to select your numbers. Check the Multi-State Lottery Association web site (or any other Powerball site) for the most recent drawing results to see if you would have won a prize.
    (d) The probability of winning any prize is about 0.0277. Suppose that you decide to buy five tickets. Use the binomial distribution to compute the probability of winning (any prize) at least once. *Note:* You will need to use the binomial formula. Carry at least three digits after the decimal.
    (e) The probability of winning *any* prize is about 0.0277. Suppose that you play Powerball 100 times. Explain why it is appropriate to use the Poisson approximation to the binomial to compute the probability of winning at least one prize.

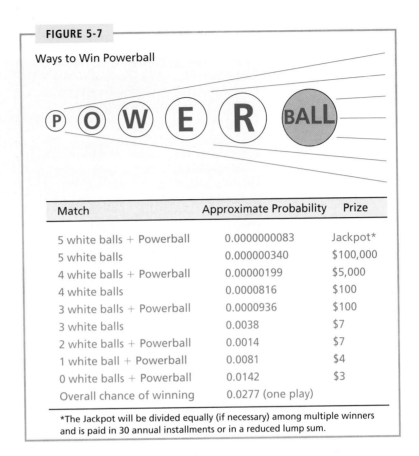

FIGURE 5-7

Ways to Win Powerball

Match	Approximate Probability	Prize
5 white balls + Powerball	0.0000000083	Jackpot*
5 white balls	0.000000340	$100,000
4 white balls + Powerball	0.00000199	$5,000
4 white balls	0.0000816	$100
3 white balls + Powerball	0.0000936	$100
3 white balls	0.0038	$7
2 white balls + Powerball	0.0014	$7
1 white ball + Powerball	0.0081	$4
0 white balls + Powerball	0.0142	$3
Overall chance of winning	0.0277 (one play)	

*The Jackpot will be divided equally (if necessary) among multiple winners and is paid in 30 annual installments or in a reduced lump sum.

Compute $\lambda = np$. Use the Poisson table to estimate the probability of winning at least one prize.

2. Would you like to travel in space, if given a chance? According to Opinion Research for Space Day Partners, if your answer is yes, you are not alone. Forty-four percent of adults surveyed agreed that they would travel in space if given a chance. Look at Figure 5-8 on the next page, and use the information presented to answer the following questions.

   (a) According to Figure 5-8, the probability that an adult selected at random agrees with the statement that humanity should explore planets is 64%. Round this probability to 65%, and use this estimate with the binomial distribution table to determine the probability that of 10 adults selected at random, at least half agree that humanity should explore planets.

   (b) Does space exploration have an impact on daily life? Find the probability that of 10 adults selected at random, at least 9 agree that space exploration does have an impact on daily life. *Hint:* Use the formula for the binomial distribution.

   (c) In a room of 35 adults, what is the expected number who would travel in space, given a chance? What is the standard deviation?

   (d) What is the probability that the first adult (selected at random) you asked would agree with the statement that space will be colonized in the person's lifetime? *Hint:* Use the geometric distribution.

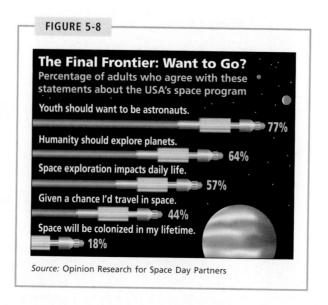

FIGURE 5-8

The Final Frontier: Want to Go?
Percentage of adults who agree with these statements about the USA's space program

Youth should want to be astronauts. **77%**

Humanity should explore planets. **64%**

Space exploration impacts daily life. **57%**

Given a chance I'd travel in space. **44%**

Space will be colonized in my lifetime. **18%**

Source: Opinion Research for Space Day Partners

LINKING CONCEPTS: WRITING PROJECTS

Discuss each of the following topics in class or review the topics on your own. Then write a brief but complete essay in which you summarize the main points. Please include formulas and graphs as appropriate.

1. Discuss what we mean by a binomial experiment. As you can see, a binomial process or binomial experiment involves a lot of assumptions! For example, all the trials are supposed to be independent and repeated under identical conditions. Is this always true? Can we always be completely certain that the probability of success does not change from one trial to the next? In the real world there is almost nothing we can be absolutely sure about, so the *theoretical* assumptions of the binomial probability distribution often will not be completely satisfied. Does that mean we cannot use the binomial distribution to solve practical problems? Looking at this chapter, the answer seems to be that we can indeed use the binomial distribution even if not all the assumptions are *exactly* met. We find in practice that the conclusions are sufficiently accurate for our intended application. List three applications of the binomial distribution for which you think, although some of the assumptions are not exactly met, there is adequate reason to apply the binomial distribution anyhow.

2. Why do we need to learn the formula for the binomial probability distribution? Using the formula repeatedly can be very tedious. To cut down on tedious calculations, most people will use a binomial table such as the one found in Appendix II of this book.
   (a) However, there are many applications for which a table in the back of *any* book is not adequate. For instance, compute

   $$P(r = 3) \quad \text{where } n = 5 \text{ and } p = 0.735$$

   Can you find the result in the table? Do the calculation by using the formula. List some other situations in which a table might not be adequate to solve a particular binomial distribution problem.

(b) The formula itself also has limitations. For instance, consider the difficulty of computing

$$P(r \geq 285) \quad \text{where } n = 500 \text{ and } p = 0.6$$

What are some of the difficulties you run into? Consider the calculation of $P(r = 285)$. You will be raising 0.6 and 0.4 to very high powers; this will give you very, very small numbers. Then you need to compute $C_{500,285}$, which is a very, very large number. When combining extremely large and extremely small numbers in the same calculation, most accuracy is lost unless you carry a huge number of significant digits. If this isn't tedious enough, consider the steps you need to compute

$$P(r \geq 285) = P(r = 285) + P(r = 286) + \cdots + P(r = 500)$$

Does it seem clear that we need a better way to estimate $P(r \geq 285)$? In Chapter 6, you will find a much better way to estimate binomial probabilities when the number of trials is large.

3. In Chapter 3, we learned about means and standard deviations. In Section 5.1, we learned that probability distributions also can have a mean and standard deviation. Discuss what is meant by the expected value and standard deviation of a binomial distribution. How does this relate back to the material we learned in Chapter 3 and Section 5.1?

4. In Chapter 2, we looked at the shapes of distributions. Review the concepts of skewness and symmetry; then categorize the following distributions as to skewness or symmetry:
   (a) A binomial distribution with $n = 11$ trials and $p = 0.50$
   (b) A binomial distribution with $n = 11$ trials and $p = 0.10$
   (c) A binomial distribution with $n = 11$ trials and $p = 0.90$

In general, does it seem true that binomial probability distributions in which the probability of success is close to 0 are skewed right, whereas those with probability of success close to 1 are skewed left?

Using Technology

Binomial Distributions

Although tables of binomial probabilities can be found in most libraries, such tables are often inadequate. Either the value of p (the probability of success on a trial) you are looking for is not in the table, or the value of n (the number of trials) you are looking for is too large for the table. In Chapter 6, we will study the normal approximation to the binomial. This approximation is a great help in many practical applications. Even so, we sometimes use the formula for the binomial probability distribution on a computer or graphing calculator to compute the probability we want.

APPLICATIONS

The following percentages were obtained over many years of observation by the U.S. Weather Bureau. All data listed are for the month of December.

Location	Long-Term Mean % of Clear Days in Dec.
Juneau, Alaska	18%
Seattle, Washington	24%
Hilo, Hawaii	36%
Honolulu, Hawaii	60%
Las Vegas, Nevada	75%
Phoenix, Arizona	77%

Adapted from *Local Climatological Data*, U.S. Weather Bureau publication, "Normals, Means, and Extremes" Table.

In the locations listed, the month of December is a relatively stable month with respect to weather. Since weather patterns from one day to the next are more or less the same, it is reasonable to use a binomial probability model.

1. Let r be the number of clear days in December. Since December has 31 days, $0 \le r \le 31$. Using appropriate computer software or calculators available to you, find the probability $P(r)$ for each of the listed locations when $r = 0, 1, 2, \ldots, 31$.

2. For each location, what is the expected value of the probability distribution? What is the standard deviation?

You may find that using cumulative probabilities and appropriate subtraction of probabilities will make finding the solutions of Applications 3 to 7 easier than adding probabilities.

3. Estimate the probability that Juneau will have at most 7 clear days in December.

4. Estimate the probability that Seattle will have from 5 to 10 (including 5 and 10) clear days in December.

5. Estimate the probability that Hilo will have at least 12 clear days in December.

6. Estimate the probability that Phoenix will have 20 or more clear days in December.

7. Estimate the probability that Las Vegas will have from 20 to 25 (including 20 and 25) clear days in December.

Technology Hints

TI-84Plus/TI-83Plus, Excel, Minitab

The Tech Note in Section 5.2 gives specific instructions for binomial distribution functions on the TI-84Plus and TI-83Plus calculators, Excel, and Minitab.

SPSS

In SPSS, the function **PDF.BINOM(q,n,p)** gives the probability of q successes out of n trials, where p is the probability of success on a single trial. In the data editor, name a variable r and enter values 0 through n. Name another variable Prob_r. Then use the menu choices **Transform ➤ Compute.** In the dialogue box use Prob_r for the target variable. In the function box select **PDF.BINOM(q,n,p).** Use the variable r for q and appropriate values for n and p. Note that the function **CDF.BINOM(q,n,p)** gives the cumulative probability of 0 through q successes.

6

Normal Distributions

One cannot escape the feeling that these mathematical formulas have an independent existence and an intelligence of their own, that they are wiser than we are, wiser even than their discoverers, that we get more out of them than was originally put into them.

—Heinrich Hertz

How can it be that mathematics, a product of human thought independent of experience, is so admirably adapted to the objects of reality?

—Albert Einstein

Heinrich Hertz was a pioneer in the study of radio waves. His work and the later work of Maxwell and Marconi led the way to modern radio, television, and radar. Albert Einstein is world renowned for his great discoveries in relativity and quantum mechanics. Everyone who has worked in both mathematics and real-world applications cannot help but marvel at how the "pure thought" of the mathematical sciences can predict and explain events in other realms. In this chapter, we will study the most important type of probability distribution in all of mathematical statistics: the normal distribution. Why is the normal distribution so important? Two of the reasons are that it applies to a wide variety of situations and that other distributions tend to become normal under certain conditions.

Heinrich Rudolf Hertz (1857–1894)

This German physicist was largely responsible for doing pioneering work in electromagnetic theory.

For on-line student resources, visit **math.college.hmco.com/students** and follow the Statistics links to the Brase/Brase, *Understandable Statistics,* 8th edition web site.

PREVIEW QUESTIONS

◊ What are some characteristics of a normal distribution? What does the empirical rule tell you about data spread around the mean? How can this information be used in quality control?   (SECTION 6.1)

◊ Can you compare apples and oranges, or maybe elephants and butterflies? In most cases, the answer is no . . . unless you first *standardize* your measurements. What are a *standard normal distribution* and a *standard z score*?   (SECTION 6.2)

◊ How do you convert *any* normal distribution to a *standard normal* distribution? How do you find probabilities of "standardized events"?   (SECTION 6.3)

◇ The binomial and normal distributions are two of the most important probability distributions in statistics. Under certain limiting conditions, the binomial can be thought to evolve (or envelope) into the normal distribution. How can you apply this in the real world?   (SECTION 6.4)

FOCUS PROBLEMS

Large Auditorium Shows: How Many Will Attend?

1. For many years, Denver, as well as most other cities, has hosted large exhibition shows in big auditoriums. These shows include house and gardening shows, fishing and hunting shows, car shows, boat shows, Native American powwows, and so on. Information provided by Denver exposition sponsors indicates that most shows have an average

attendance of about 8000 people per day with an estimated standard deviation of about 500 people. Suppose that the daily attendance figures follow a normal distribution.

(a) What is the probability that the daily attendance will be fewer than 7200 people?

(b) What is the probability that the daily attendance will be more than 8900 people?

(c) What is the probability that the daily attendance will be between 7200 and 8900 people?

2. Most exhibition shows open in the morning and close in the late evening. A study of Saturday arrival times showed that the average arrival time was 3 hours and 48 minutes after the doors open, and the standard deviation was estimated at about 52 minutes. Suppose that the arrival times follow a normal distribution.

(a) At what time after the doors open will 90% of the people who are coming to the Saturday show have arrived?

(b) At what time after the doors open will only 15% of the people who are coming to the Saturday show have arrived?

(c) Do you think the probability distribution of arrival times for Friday might be different from the distribution of arrival times for Saturday? Explain. (See Problems 36 and 37 of Section 6.3.)

6.1
Graphs of Normal Probability Distributions

FOCUS POINTS

✓ Graph a normal curve and summarize its important properties.

✓ Apply the empirical rule to solve real-world problems.

✓ Use control limits to construct control charts. Examine the chart for three possible out-of-control signals.

One of the most important examples of a continuous probability distribution is the *normal distribution*. This distribution was studied by the French mathematician Abraham de Moivre (1667–1754) and later by the German mathematician Carl Friedrich Gauss (1777–1855), whose work is so important that the normal distribution is sometimes called *Gaussian*. The work of these mathematicians provided a foundation on which much of the theory of statistical inference is based.

Applications of a normal probability distribution are so numerous that some mathematicians refer to it as "a veritable Boy Scout knife of statistics." However, before we can apply it, we must examine some of the properties of a normal distribution.

A rather complicated formula, presented later in this section, defines a normal distribution in terms of μ and σ, the mean and standard deviation of the population distribution. It is only through this formula that we can verify if a distribution is normal. However, we can look at the graph of a normal distribution and get a good pictorial idea of some of the essential features of any normal distribution.

Normal curve

The graph of a normal distribution is called a *normal curve*. It possesses a shape very much like the cross section of a pile of dry sand. Because of its shape, blacksmiths would sometimes use a pile of dry sand in the construction of a mold for a bell. Thus the normal curve is also called a *bell-shaped curve* (see Figure 6-1).

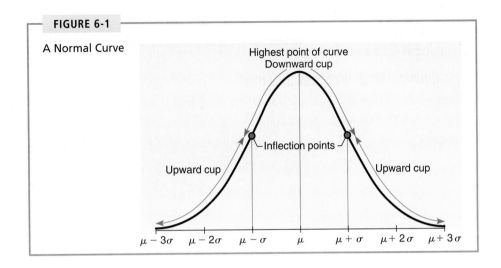

FIGURE 6-1

A Normal Curve

We see that a general normal curve is smooth and symmetrical about the vertical line extending upward from the mean μ. Notice that the highest point of the curve occurs over μ. If the distribution were graphed on a piece of sheet metal, cut out, and placed on a knife edge, the balance point would be at μ. We also see that the curve tends to level out and approach the horizontal (x axis) like a glider making a landing. However, in mathematical theory, such a glider would never quite finish its landing because a normal curve never touches the horizontal axis.

The parameter σ controls the spread of the curve. The curve is quite close to the horizontal axis at $\mu + 3\sigma$ and $\mu - 3\sigma$. Thus, if the standard deviation σ is large, the curve will be more spread out; if it is small, the curve will be more peaked. Figure 6-1 shows the normal curve cupped downward for an interval on either side of the mean μ. Then it begins to cup upward as we go to the lower part of the bell. The exact places where the *transition* between the upward and downward cupping occur are above the points $\mu + \sigma$ and $\mu - \sigma$. In the terminology of calculus, transition points such as these are called *inflection points*.

Important properties of a normal curve

1. The curve is bell-shaped with the highest point over the mean μ.

2. It is symmetrical about a vertical line through μ.

3. The curve approaches the horizontal axis but never touches or crosses it.

4. The inflection (transition) points between cupping upward and downward occur above $\mu + \sigma$ and $\mu - \sigma$.

GUIDED EXERCISE 1

Curves that are not normal

Each of the curves in Figure 6-2 fails to be a normal curve. Give reasons why these curves are not normal curves.

FIGURE 6-2

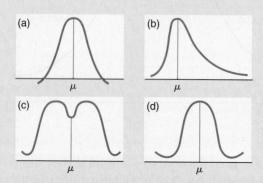

(a) A normal curve gets closer and closer to the horizontal axis, but it never touches or crosses it.

(b) A normal curve must be symmetrical. This curve is not.

(c) A normal curve is bell-shaped with one peak. Because this curve has two peaks, it is not normal.

(d) The tails of a normal curve must get closer and closer to the *x* axis. In this curve the tails are going away from the *x* axis.

GUIDED EXERCISE 2

Identify μ and σ on a normal curve

The points *A*, *B*, and *C* are indicated on the normal curve in Figure 6-3. One of these points is μ, one is $\mu + \sigma$, and one is $\mu - 2\sigma$.

FIGURE 6-3 A Normal Curve

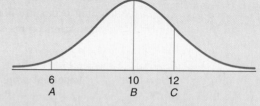

(a) Which point corresponds to the mean? What is the value of μ?

The mean μ is under the peak of the normal curve. The point *B* corresponds to the mean, so $\mu = 10$.

(b) Which point corresponds to $\mu + \sigma$? Use the values of $\mu + \sigma$ and μ to compute σ.

The point *C* where the curve changes from cupped down to cupped up is one standard deviation σ from the mean. The point *C* is $\mu + \sigma$. Since $\mu + \sigma = 12$ and $\mu = 10$, $\sigma = 2$.

(c) Which point corresponds to $\mu - 2\sigma$?

Since $\mu = 10$ and $\sigma = 2$, we see that

$$\mu - 2\sigma = 10 - 2(2) = 6$$

Point *A* corresponds to $\mu - 2\sigma$.

The parameters that control the shape of a normal curve are the mean μ and the standard deviation σ. When both μ and σ are specified, a specific normal curve is determined. In brief, μ locates the balance point, and σ determines the extent of the spread.

GUIDED EXERCISE 3

Identify μ and σ on a normal curve

Look at the normal curves in Figure 6-4.

FIGURE 6-4

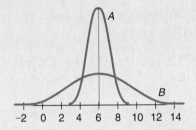

(a) Do these distributions have the same mean? If so, what is it?

⟹ The means are the same, since both graphs have the high point over 6. $\mu = 6$.

(b) One of the curves corresponds to a normal distribution with $\sigma = 3$ and the other to one with $\sigma = 1$. Which curve has which σ?

⟹ Curve A has $\sigma = 1$, and curve B has $\sigma = 3$. (Since curve B is more spread out, it has the larger σ value.)

◊ **COMMENT** The normal distribution curve is always above the horizontal axis. The area beneath the curve and above the axis is exactly one. As such, the normal distribution curve is an example of a *density curve*. The formula used to generate the shape of the normal distribution curve is called the *normal density function*. If x is a normal random variable with mean μ and standard deviation σ, the formula for the normal density function is

$$f(x) = \frac{e^{(-1/2)((x-\mu)/\sigma)^2}}{\sigma\sqrt{2\pi}}$$

In this text, we will not use this formula explicitly. However, we will use tables of areas based on the normal density function. ◊

The total area under any normal curve studied in this book will *always* be 1. The graph of the normal distribution is important because the portion of the *area* under the curve above a given interval represents the *probability* that a measurement will lie in that interval.

In Section 3.2, we studied Chebyshev's theorem. This theorem gives us information about the *smallest* proportion of data that lies within 2, 3, or k standard deviations of the mean. This result applies to *any* distribution. However, for normal distributions, we can get a much more precise result, which is given by the *empirical rule*.

Empirical rule

Empirical rule

For a distribution that is symmetrical and bell-shaped (in particular, for a normal distribution):

Approximately 68% of the data values will lie within one standard deviation on each side of the mean.

Approximately 95% of the data values will lie within two standard deviations on each side of the mean.

Approximately 99.7% (or almost all) of the data values will lie within three standard deviations on each side of the mean.

The preceding statement is called the *empirical rule* because, for symmetrical, bell-shaped distributions, the given percentages are observed in practice. Furthermore, for the normal distribution, the empirical rule is a direct consequence of the very nature of the distribution (see Figure 6-5). Notice that the empirical rule is a stronger statement than Chebyshev's theorem in that it gives *definite percentages*, not just lower limits. Of course, the empirical rule applies only to normal or symmetrical, bell-shaped distributions, whereas Chebyshev's theorem applies to all distributions.

EXAMPLE 1

Empirical rule

The playing life of a Sunshine radio is normally distributed with mean $\mu = 600$ hours and standard deviation $\sigma = 100$ hours. What is the probability that a radio selected at random will last from 600 to 700 hours?

SOLUTION: The probability that the playing time will be between 600 and 700 hours is equal to the percentage of the total area under the curve that is shaded in Figure 6-6. Since $\mu = 600$ and $\mu + \sigma = 600 + 100 = 700$, we see that the shaded area is simply the area between μ and $\mu + \sigma$. The area from μ to $\mu + \sigma$ is 34% of the

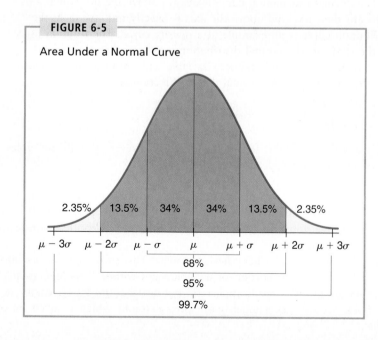

FIGURE 6-5

Area Under a Normal Curve

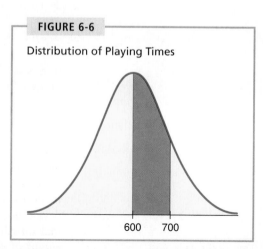

FIGURE 6-6

Distribution of Playing Times

total area. This tells us that the probability a Sunshine radio will last between 600 and 700 playing hours is about 0.34.   ◇

GUIDED EXERCISE 4

Empirical rule

The yearly wheat yield per acre on a particular farm is normally distributed with mean $\mu = 35$ bushels and standard deviation $\sigma = 8$ bushels.

(a) Shade the area under the curve in Figure 6-7 that represents the probability that an acre will yield between 19 and 35 bushels.

⇒ See Figure 6-8.

(b) Is the area the same as the area between $\mu - 2\sigma$ and μ?

⇒ Yes, since $\mu = 35$ and $\mu - 2\sigma = 35 - 2(8) = 19$.

FIGURE 6-7

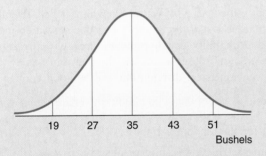

Bushels

FIGURE 6-8 Completion of Figure 6-7

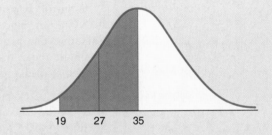

(c) Use Figure 6-5 to find the percentage of area over the interval between 19 and 35.

⇒ The area between the values $\mu - 2\sigma$ and μ is 47.5% of the total area.

(d) What is the probability that the yield will be between 19 and 35 bushels per acre?

⇒ It is 47.5% of the total area, which is 1. Therefore, the probability is 0.475 that the yield will be between 19 and 35 bushels.

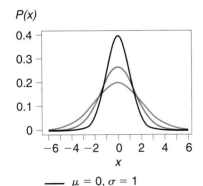

$P(x)$

— $\mu = 0, \sigma = 1$

— $\mu = 0, \sigma = 1.5$

— $\mu = 0, \sigma = 2$

TECH NOTE We can graph normal distributions using the TI-84Plus and TI-83Plus calculators, Excel, and Minitab. In each technology, set the range of x values between -3.5σ and 3.5σ. Then use the built-in normal density functions to generate the corresponding y values.

TI-84Plus/TI-83Plus Press the **Y =** key. Then, under **DISTR**, select **1:normalpdf** (x,μ,σ) and fill in desired μ and σ values. Press the **WINDOW** key. Set **Xmin** to $\mu - 3\sigma$ and **Xmax** to $\mu + 3\sigma$. Finally, press the **ZOOM** key and select option **0:ZoomFit.**

Excel In one column, enter x values from -3.5σ to 3.5σ in increments of 0.2σ. In the next column, enter y values by using the menu choices **Paste function** $\boxed{f_x}$ ➤ **Statistical** ➤ **NORMDIST**$(x, \mu, \sigma, \text{false})$. Next, use the chart wizard, and select **XY(scatter).** Choose the first picture with the dots connected and fill in the dialogue boxes.

Minitab In one column, enter x values from -3.5σ to 3.5σ in increments of 0.2σ. In the next column, enter y values by using the menu choices **Calc ➤ Probability Distribution ➤ Normal**. Fill in the dialogue box. Next, use menu choices **Graph ➤ Plot**. Fill in the dialogue box. Under Display, select connect.

Control Charts

If we are examining data over a period of equally spaced time intervals or in some sequential order, then *control charts* are especially useful. Business managers and people in charge of production processes are aware that there exists an inherent amount of variability in any sequential set of data. For example, the sugar content of bottled drinks taken sequentially off a production line, the extent of clerical errors in a bank from day to day, advertising expenses from month to month, or even the number of new customers from year to year are examples of sequential data. There is a certain amount of variability in each.

A random variable x is said to be in *statistical control* if it can be described by the *same* probability distribution when it is observed at successive points in time. Control charts combine graphic and numerical descriptions of data with probability distributions.

Control charts were invented in the 1920s by Walter Shewhart at Bell Telephone Laboratories. Since a control chart is a *warning device,* it is not absolutely necessary that our assumptions and probability calculations be precisely correct. For example, the x distributions need not follow a normal distribution exactly. Any mound-shaped and more or less symmetrical distribution will be good enough.

PROCEDURE

How to make a control chart for the random variable x

A control chart for a random variable x is a plot of observed x values in time sequence order.

1. Find the mean μ and standard deviation σ of the x distribution by
   (a) using past data from a period during which the process was "in control" or
   (b) using specified "target" values for μ and σ.
2. Create a graph where the vertical axis represents x values and the horizontal axis represents time.
3. Draw a horizontal line at height μ and horizontal, dashed control-limit lines at $\mu \pm 2\sigma$ and $\mu \pm 3\sigma$.
4. Plot the variable x on the graph in time sequence order. Use line segments to connect the points in time sequence order.

How do we pick values for μ and σ? In most practical cases, values for μ (population mean) and σ (population standard deviation) are computed from past data for which the process we are studying was known to be *in control*. Methods for choosing the sample size to fit given error tolerances can be found in Chapter 8.

Sometimes values for μ and σ are chosen as *target values*. That is, μ and σ values are chosen as set goals or targets that reflect the production level or service level at which a company hopes to perform. To be realistic, such target assignments for μ and σ should be reasonably close to actual data taken when the process was operating at a satisfactory production level. In Example 2, we will make a control chart; then we will discuss ways to analyze it to see if a process or service is "in control."

EXAMPLE 2
Control chart

Susan Tamara is director of personnel at the Antlers Lodge in Denali National Park, Alaska. Every summer Ms. Tamara hires many part-time employees from all over the United States. Most are college students seeking summer employment. One of the biggest activities for the lodge staff is that of "making up" the rooms each day. Although the rooms are supposed to be ready by 3:30 P.M., there are always some rooms not made up by this time because of high personnel turnover.

Every 15 days Ms. Tamara has a general staff meeting where she shows a control chart of the number of rooms not made up by 3:30 P.M. each day. From extensive experience Ms. Tamara is aware that the distribution of rooms not made up by 3:30 P.M. is approximately normal, with mean $\mu = 19.3$ rooms and standard deviation $\sigma = 4.7$ rooms. This distribution of x values is acceptable to the top administration of Antlers Lodge. For the past 15 days, the housekeeping unit has reported the number of rooms not ready by 3:30 P.M. (Table 6-1). Make a control chart for these data.

TABLE 6-1   Number of Rooms x Not Made Up by 3:30 P.M.

Day	1	2	3	4	5	6	7	8	9	10	11	12	13	14	15
x	11	20	25	23	16	19	8	25	17	20	23	29	18	14	10

SOLUTION: A control chart for a variable x is a plot of the observed x values (vertical scale) in time sequence order (the horizontal scale represents time). Place horizontal lines at

The mean $\mu = 19.3$

The control limits $\mu \pm 2\sigma = 19.3 \pm 2(4.7)$ or 9.90 and 28.70

The control limits $\mu \pm 3\sigma = 19.3 \pm 3(4.7)$ or 5.20 and 33.40

Then plot the data from Table 6-1. (See Figure 6-9.)

Mt. McKinley, Denali National Park

FIGURE 6-9

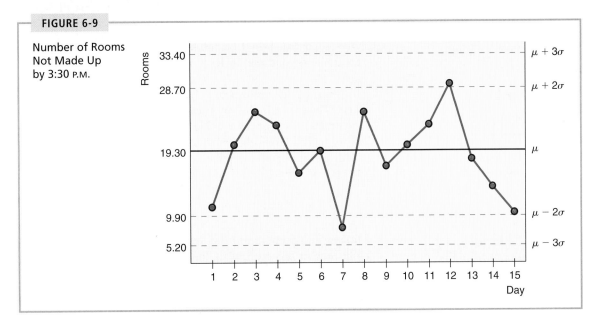

Number of Rooms Not Made Up by 3:30 P.M.

Once we have made a control chart, the main question is the following: As time goes on, is the x variable continuing in this same distribution, or is the distribution of x values changing? If the x distribution is continuing in more or less the same manner, we say it is in *statistical control*. If it is not, we say it is *out of control*.

Out-of-control warning signals

Many popular methods can set off a warning signal that a process is out of control. Remember, a random variable x is said to be *out of control* if successive time measurements of x indicate that it is no longer following the target probability distribution. We will assume that the target distribution is (approximately) normal and has (user-set) target values for μ and σ.

Three of the most popular warning signals are described next.

Out-of-Control Signal I

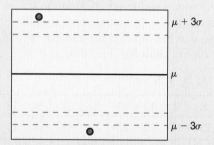

Out-of-Control Signal II

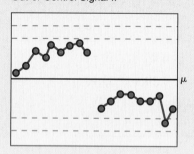

Out-of-Control Signal III

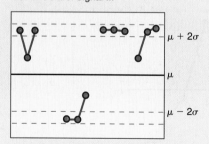

Out-of-control signals

1. **Out-of-Control Signal I: One point falls beyond the 3σ level**
   What is the probability that signal I will be a false alarm? By the empirical rule, the probability that a point lies within 3σ of the mean is 0.997. The probability that signal I will be a false alarm is $1 - 0.997 = 0.003$. Remember, a false alarm means that the x distribution is really on the target distribution, and we simply have a very rare (probability of 0.0003) event.

2. **Out-of-Control Signal II: A run of nine consecutive points on one side of the center line (the line at target value μ)**
   To find the probability that signal II is a false alarm, we observe that if the x distribution and the target distribution are the same, then there is a 50% chance that the x values will lie above or below the center line at μ. Because the samples are (time) independent, the probability of a run of nine points on one side of the center line is $(0.5)^9 = 0.002$. If we consider both sides, this probability becomes 0.004. Therefore, the probability that signal II is a false alarm is approximately 0.004.

3. **Out-of-Control Signal III: At least two of three consecutive points lie beyond the 2σ level on the same side of the center line**
   To determine the probability that signal III will produce a false alarm we use the empirical rule. By this rule, the probability that an x value will be above the 2σ level is about 0.023. Using the binomial probability distribution (with success being the point is above 2σ), the probability of two or more successes out of three trials is

$$\frac{3!}{2!1!}(0.023)^2(0.997) + \frac{3!}{3!0!}(0.023)^3 \approx 0.002$$

Taking into account *both* above or below the center line, it follows that the probability that signal III is a false alarm is about 0.004.

Remember, a control chart is only a warning device, and it is possible to get a false alarm. A false alarm happens when one (or more) of the out-of-control signals occurs, but the x distribution is really on the target or assigned distribution. In this case, we simply have a rare event (probability of 0.003 or 0.004). In practice, whenever a control chart indicates that a process is out of control, it is usually a good precaution to examine what is going on. If the process is out of control, corrective steps can be taken before things get a lot worse. The rare false alarm is a small price to pay if we can avert what might become real trouble.

Type of Warning Signal	Probability of a False Alarm
Type I: Point beyond 3σ	0.003
Type II: Run of nine consecutive points all below center line μ or all above center line μ	0.004
Type III: At least two out of three consecutive points beyond 2σ	0.004

From an intuitive point of view, signal I could be thought of as a blowup, something dramatically out of control. Signal II could be thought of as a slow drift out of control. Signal III is between a blowup and a slow drift.

EXAMPLE 3

Control chart

Ms. Tamara of the Antlers Lodge examines the control chart for housekeeping. During the staff meeting, she makes recommendations about improving service, or if all is going well, she gives her staff a well-deserved "pat on the back." Look at the control chart created in Example 2 (Figure 6-9 on page 299) to determine if the housekeeping process is out of control.

SOLUTION: The x values are more or less evenly distributed about the mean $\mu = 19.3$. None of the points are outside the $\mu \pm 3\sigma$ limit (i.e., above 33.40 or below 5.20 rooms). There is no run of nine consecutive points above or below μ. No two of three consecutive points are beyond the $\mu \pm 2\sigma$ limit (i.e., above 28.7 or below 9.90 rooms).

It appears that the x distribution is "in control." At the staff meeting, Ms. Tamara should tell her employees that they are doing a reasonably good job and they should keep up the fine work!   ◊

GUIDED EXERCISE 5

Control chart

Over the next 15-day period, let's suppose that housekeeping again reported the numbers of rooms not made up by 3:30 P.M. to Ms. Tamara of the Antlers Lodge. The data in Table 6-2 show the results.

Continued

GUIDED EXERCISE 5 continued

TABLE 6-2   Next 15-Day Report of Rooms Not Made Up by 3:30 P.M.

Day	1	2	3	4	5	6	7	8
x = number of rooms	25	8	23	15	26	24	31	21
Day	9	10	11	12	13	14	15	
x = number of rooms	27	20	25	21	27	11	16	

(a) We assume that we are still working with the symmetrical, bell-shaped distribution of x values, with mean $\mu = 19.3$ and $\sigma = 4.7$. Compute the "control limits" of $\mu \pm 2\sigma$ and $\mu \pm 3\sigma$. Draw a control chart showing the solid line at the mean and the dashed lines at the control limits. Plot the data for the 15-day period.

FIGURE 6-10 Next 15-Day Report of Rooms Not Made Up by 3:30 P.M.

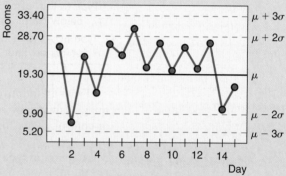

(b) Interpret the control chart of part (a).

Days 5 to 13 are above $\mu = 19.3$. We have nine consecutive days on one side of the mean. This is a warning signal! It would appear that the mean μ is slowly drifting up beyond the target value of 19.3. The chart indicates that housekeeping is "out of control." Ms. Tamara should take corrective measures at her staff meeting.

(c) Over another 15-day period Ms. Tamara obtained the data shown in Table 6-3 for housekeeping. Make a control chart using target values $\mu = 19.3$ and $\sigma = 4.7$.

FIGURE 6-11 Third Housekeeping Data Report

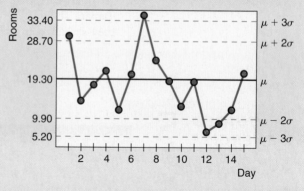

Continued

GUIDED EXERCISE 5 continued

TABLE 6-3 Third Housekeeping Data Report

Day	1	2	3	4	5	6	7	8
Number of rooms	29	14	18	21	11	20	35	24

Day	9	10	11	12	13	14	15
Number of rooms	19	12	19	6	8	11	20

(d) Interpret the control chart of part (c).

 On day 7 we have a data value beyond $\mu + 3\sigma$ (i.e., above 33.40). On days 11, 12, and 13 we have two of three data values beyond $\mu - 2\sigma$ (i.e., below 9.90). The occurrences during both these periods are out-of-control warning signals. Ms. Tamara might ask her staff about both these periods. There may be a lesson to be learned about day 7, when housekeeping apparently had a lot of trouble. Also, days 11, 12, and 13 were very good days. Perhaps a lesson could be learned about why things went so well.

VIEWPOINT   *In Control? Out of Control?*

If you care about quality, you also must care about control! Dr. Walter Shewhart invented control charts when he was working for Bell Laboratories. The great contribution of control charts is to separate variation into two sources: (1) random or chance causes (in control) and (2) special or assignable causes (out of control). A process is said to be in *statistical control* when it is no longer afflicted with special or assignable causes. The performance of a process that is in statistical control is predictable. Predictability and quality control tend to be closely associated.

(Source: Adapted from the classic text *Statistical Methods from the Viewpoint of Quality Control*, by W. A. Shewhart, with foreword by W. E. Deming, Dover Publications.)

SECTION 6.1   PROBLEMS

1. *General: Curves* Which, if any, of the curves in Figure 6-12 on the next page look(s) like a normal curve? If a curve is not a normal curve, tell why.

2. *General: Normal Curves* Look at the normal curve in Figure 6-13 on the next page, and find μ, $\mu + \sigma$, and σ.

FIGURE 6-12

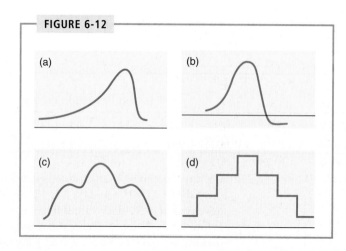

(a)

(b)

(c)

(d)

FIGURE 6-13

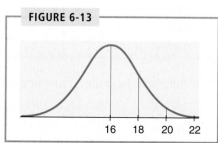

16 18 20 22

3. *General: Normal Curves* Look at the two normal curves in Figures 6-14 and 6-15. Which has the larger standard deviation? What is the mean of the curve in Figure 6-14? What is the mean of the curve in Figure 6-15?

FIGURE 6-15

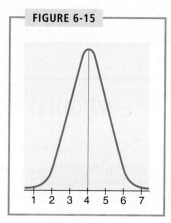

1 2 3 4 5 6 7

FIGURE 6-14

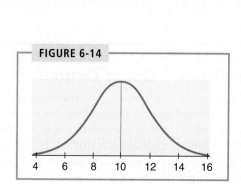

4   6   8   10   12   14   16

4. *General: Normal Curves* Sketch a normal curve
   (a) with mean 15 and standard deviation 2.
   (b) with mean 15 and standard deviation 3.
   (c) with mean 12 and standard deviation 2.
   (d) with mean 12 and standard deviation 3.
   (e) Consider two normal curves. If the first one has a larger mean than the second one, must it have a larger standard deviation as well? Explain your answer.

5. *General: Normal Curves* What percentage of the area under the normal curve lies
   (a) to the left of μ?
   (b) between $\mu - \sigma$ and $\mu + \sigma$?
   (c) between $\mu - 3\sigma$ and $\mu + 3\sigma$?

6. *General: Normal Curves* What percentage of the area under the normal curve lies
   (a) to the right of μ?
   (b) between $\mu - 2\sigma$ and $\mu + 2\sigma$?
   (c) to the right of $\mu + 3\sigma$?

7. *Distribution: Heights of Coeds* Assuming that the heights of college women are normally distributed, with mean 65 in. and standard deviation 2.5 in. (based on information from *Statistical Abstract of the United States,* 112th Edition), answer the following questions. (*Hint:* Use Problems 5 and 6 and Figure 6-5.)
   (a) What percentage of women are taller than 65 in.?
   (b) What percentage of women are shorter than 65 in.?
   (c) What percentage of women are between 62.5 in. and 67.5 in.?
   (d) What percentage of women are between 60 in. and 70 in.?

8. *Distribution: Rhode Island Red Chickens* The incubation time for Rhode Island Red chicks is normally distributed with a mean of 21 days and standard deviation of approximately 1 day (based on information from *World Book Encyclopedia*). Look at Figure 6-5 and answer the following questions. If 1000 eggs are being incubated, how many chicks do we expect will hatch
   (a) in 19 to 23 days?
   (b) in 20 to 22 days?
   (c) in 21 days or fewer?
   (d) in 18 to 24 days? (Assume all eggs eventually hatch.)
   (*Note:* In this problem, let us agree to think of a single day or a succession of days as a continuous interval of time.)

9. *Archaeology: Tree Rings* At Burnt Mesa Pueblo, archaeological studies have used the method of tree-ring dating in an effort to determine when prehistoric people lived in the pueblo. Wood from several excavations gave a mean of (year) 1243 with a standard deviation of 36 years (*Bandelier Archaeological Excavation Project: Summer 1989 Excavations at Burnt Mesa Pueblo,* edited by Kohler, Washington State University Department of Anthropology). The distribution of dates was more or less mound-shaped and symmetrical about the mean. Use the empirical rule to
   (a) estimate a range of years centered about the mean in which about 68% of the data (tree-ring dates) will be found.
   (b) estimate a range of years centered about the mean in which about 95% of the data (tree-ring dates) will be found.
   (c) estimate a range of years centered about the mean in which almost all the data (tree-ring dates) will be found.

10. *Vending Machine: Soft Drinks* A vending machine automatically pours soft drinks into cups. The amount of soft drink dispensed into a cup is normally distributed with a mean of 7.6 oz and standard deviation of 0.4 oz. Examine Figure 6-5 and answer the following questions.
    (a) Estimate the probability that the machine will overflow an 8-oz cup.
    (b) Estimate the probability that the machine will not overflow an 8-oz cup.
    (c) The machine has just been loaded with 850 cups. How many of these do you expect will overflow when served?

11. *Pain Management: Laser Therapy* "Effect of Helium-Neon Laser Auriculotherapy on Experimental Pain Threshold" is the title of an article in the journal *Physical Therapy* (Vol. 70, No. 1, pp. 24–30). In this article, laser therapy was discussed as a useful alternative to drugs in pain management of chronically ill patients. To measure pain threshold, a machine was used that delivered low-voltage direct current to different parts of the body (wrist, neck, and back). The machine measured current in milliamperes (mA). The pretreatment experimental group in the study had an average threshold of pain (pain was first detectable) at $\mu = 3.15$ mA with standard deviation $\sigma = 1.45$ mA. Assume that the distribution of threshold pain so

measured in milliamperes is symmetrical and more or less mound-shaped. Use the empirical rule to

(a) estimate a range of milliamperes centered about the mean in which about 68% of the experimental group will have a threshold of pain.

(b) estimate a range of milliamperes centered about the mean in which about 95% of the experimental group will have a threshold of pain.

12. *Control Charts: Yellowstone National Park* Yellowstone Park Medical Services (YPMS) provides emergency health care for park visitors. Such health care includes treatment for everything from indigestion and sunburn to more serious injuries. A recent issue of *Yellowstone Today* (National Park Service Publication) indicated that the average number of visitors treated each day by YPMS was 21.7. The estimated standard deviation was 4.2 (summer data). The distribution of numbers treated is approximately mound-shaped and symmetrical.

(a) For a 10-day summer period, the following data show the number of visitors treated each day by YPMS:

Day	1	2	3	4	5	6	7	8	9	10
Number treated	25	19	17	15	20	24	30	19	16	23

Make a control chart for the daily number of visitors treated by YPMS, and plot the data on the control chart. Do the data indicate that the number of visitors treated by YPMS is "in control"? Explain your answer.

(b) For another 10-day summer period, the following data were obtained:

Day	1	2	3	4	5	6	7	8	9	10
Number treated	20	15	12	21	24	28	32	36	35	37

Make a control chart, and plot the data on the chart. Do the data indicate that the number of visitors treated by YPMS is "in control" or "out of control"? Explain your answer. Identify all out-of-control signals by type (I, II, or III). If you were the park superintendent, do you think YPMS might need some (temporary) extra help? Explain.

13. *Control Charts: Bank Loans* Tri-County Bank is a small independent bank in central Wyoming. This is a rural bank that makes loans on items as small as horses and pickup trucks to items as large as ranch land. Total monthly loan requests are used by bank officials as an indicator of economic business conditions in this rural community. The mean monthly loan request for the past several years has been 615.1 (in thousands of dollars) with a standard deviation of 11.2 (in thousands of dollars). The distribution of loan requests is approximately mound-shaped and symmetrical.

(a) For 12 months, the following monthly loan requests (in thousands of dollars) were made to Tri-County Bank:

Month	1	2	3	4	5	6
Loan request	619.3	625.1	610.2	614.2	630.4	615.9

Month	7	8	9	10	11	12
Loan request	617.2	610.1	592.7	596.4	585.1	588.2

Make a control chart for the total monthly loan requests, and plot the preceding data on the control chart. From the control chart, would you say the local business economy is heating up or cooling down? Explain your answer by referring to any trend you may see on the control chart. Identify all out-of-control signals by type (I, II, or III).

(b) For another 12-month period, the following monthly loan requests (in thousands of dollars) were made to Tri-County Bank:

Month	1	2	3	4	5	6
Loan request	608.3	610.4	615.1	617.2	619.3	622.1

Month	7	8	9	10	11	12
Loan request	625.7	633.1	635.4	625.0	628.2	619.8

Make a control chart for the total monthly loan requests, and plot the preceding data on the control chart. From the control chart, would you say the local business economy is heating up, cooling down, or about normal? Explain your answer by referring to the control chart. Identify all out-of-control signals by type (I, II, or III).

14. *Control Charts: Motel Rooms* The manager of Motel 11 has 316 rooms in Palo Alto, California. From observation over a long time, she knows that on an average night 268 rooms will be rented. The long-term standard deviation is 12 rooms. This distribution is approximately mound-shaped and symmetrical.

(a) For 10 consecutive nights, the following numbers of rooms were rented each night:

Night	1	2	3	4	5	6
Number of rooms	234	258	265	271	283	267

Night	7	8	9	10
Number of rooms	290	286	263	240

Make a control chart for the number of rooms rented each night, and plot the preceding data on the control chart. Looking at the control chart, would you say the number of rooms rented during this 10-night period has been unusually low? unusually high? about what was expected? Explain your answer. Identify all out-of-control signals by type (I, II, or III).

(b) For another 10 consecutive nights, the following numbers of rooms were rented each night:

Night	1	2	3	4	5	6
Number of rooms	238	245	261	269	273	250

Night	7	8	9	10
Number of rooms	241	230	215	217

Make a control chart for the number of rooms rented each night, and plot the preceding data on the control chart. Would you say the room occupancy has been high? low? about what was expected? Explain your answer. Identify all out-of-control signals by type (I, II, or III).

15. *Control Chart: Air Pollution* The visibility standard index (VSI) is a measure of Denver air pollution that is reported each day in the *Rocky Mountain News*. The index ranges from 0 (excellent air) to 200 (very bad air). During winter months, when air pollution is higher, the index has a mean of about 90 (rated as fair) with a standard deviation of approximately 30. Suppose that for 15 days the following VSI measures were reported each day:

Day	1	2	3	4	5	6	7	8	9
VSI	80	115	100	90	15	10	53	75	80

Day	10	11	12	13	14	15
VSI	110	165	160	120	140	195

Make a control chart for the VSI, and plot the preceding data on the control chart. Identify all out-of-control signals (high or low) that you find in the control chart by type (I, II, or III).

6.2 Standard Units and Areas Under the Standard Normal Distribution

FOCUS POINTS
✓ Given μ and σ, convert raw data to z scores.
✓ Given μ and σ, convert z scores to raw data.
✓ Graph the standard normal distribution, and find areas under the standard normal curve.

z Scores and Raw Scores

Normal distributions vary from one another in two ways: The mean μ may be located anywhere on the x axis, and the bell shape may be more or less spread according to the size of the standard deviation σ. The differences among the normal distributions cause difficulties when we try to compute the area under the curve in a specified interval of x values and, hence, the probability that a measurement will fall into that interval.

It would be a futile task to try to set up a table of areas under the normal curve for each different μ and σ combination. We need a way to standardize the distributions so that we can use *one* table of areas for *all* normal distributions. We achieve this standardization by considering how many standard deviations a measurement lies from the mean. In this way, we can compare a value in one normal distribution with a value in another, different normal distribution. The next situation shows how this is done.

Suppose Tina and Jack are in two different sections of the same course. Each section is quite large, and the scores on the midterm exams of each section follow a normal distribution. In Tina's section, the average (mean) was 64 and her score was 74. In Jack's section, the mean was 72 and his score was 82. Both Tina and Jack were pleased that their scores were each 10 points above the average of each respective section. However, the fact that each was 10 points above average does not really tell us how each did *with respect to the other students in the section*. In Figure 6-16, we see the normal distribution of grades for each section.

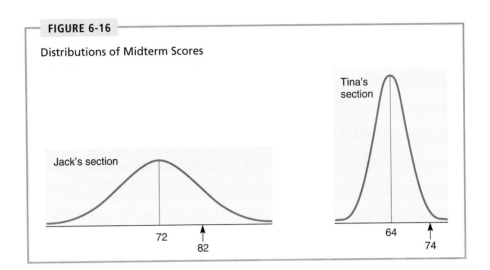

FIGURE 6-16

Distributions of Midterm Scores

Tina's 74 was higher than most of the other scores in her section, while Jack's 82 is only an upper-middle score in his section. Tina's score is far better with respect to her class than Jack's score with respect to his class.

Standard score

The preceding situation demonstrates that it is not sufficient to know the difference between a measurement (x value) and the mean of a distribution. We need also to consider the spread of the curve, or the standard deviation. What we really want to know is the number of standard deviations between a measurement and the mean. This "distance" takes both μ and σ into account.

We can use a simple formula to compute the number z of standard deviations between a measurement x and the mean μ of a normal distribution with standard deviation σ:

$$\begin{pmatrix} \text{Number of standard deviations} \\ \text{between the measurement and} \\ \text{the mean} \end{pmatrix} = \begin{pmatrix} \dfrac{\text{Difference between the}}{\text{measurement and the mean}} \\ \overline{\text{Standard deviation}} \end{pmatrix}$$

z score

The z **value** or z **score** gives the number of standard deviations between the original measurement x and the mean μ of the x distribution.

$$z = \frac{x - \mu}{\sigma}$$

The mean is a special value of a distribution. Let's see what happens when we convert $x = \mu$ to a z value:

$$z = \frac{x - \mu}{\sigma} = \frac{\mu - \mu}{\sigma} = 0$$

The mean of the original distribution is always zero, in standard units. This makes sense because the mean is zero standard variations from itself.

An x value in the original distribution that is *above* the mean μ has a corresponding z value that is *positive*. Again, this makes sense because a measurement above the mean would be a positive number of standard deviations from the mean. Likewise, an x value *below* the mean has a *negative* z value. (See Table 6-4.)

TABLE 6-4

x **Values and Corresponding** *z* **Values**

x Value in Original Distribution	Corresponding z Value or Standard Unit
$x = \mu$	$z = 0$
$x > \mu$	$z > 0$
$x < \mu$	$z < 0$

Note

Unless otherwise stated, in the remainder of the book we will take the word *average* to be either the sample arithmetic mean $\bar{x}$ or the population mean μ.

EXAMPLE 4
Standard score

A pizza parlor franchise specifies that the average (mean) amount of cheese on a large pizza should be 8 oz and the standard deviation only 0.5 oz. An inspector picks out a large pizza at random in one of the pizza parlors and finds that it is made with 6.9 oz of cheese. Assume that the amount of cheese on a pizza follows a normal distribution. If the amount of cheese is below the mean by more than *three* standard deviations, the parlor will be in danger of losing its franchise.

(Remember, in a normal distribution we are unlikely to find measurements more than three standard deviations from the mean, since 99.7% of all measurements fall within three standard deviations of the mean.)

How many standard deviations from the mean is 6.9? Is the pizza parlor in danger of losing its franchise?

SOLUTION: Since we want to know the number of standard deviations from the mean, we want to convert 6.9 to standard z units.

$$z = \frac{x - \mu}{\sigma} = \frac{6.9 - 8}{0.5} = -2.20$$

Therefore, the amount of cheese on the selected pizza is only 2.20 standard deviations below the mean. Note that the fact that z is negative indicates that the amount of cheese was 2.20 standard deviations *below* the mean. The parlor will not lose its franchise based on this sample. ◇

GUIDED EXERCISE 6

Standard score

A student has computed that it takes an average (mean) of 17 minutes with a standard deviation of 3 minutes to drive from home, park the car, and walk to an early morning class.

(a) One day it took the student 21 minutes to get to class. How many standard deviations from the average is that? Is the z value positive or negative? Explain why it should be either positive or negative.

The number of standard deviations from the mean is given by the z value:

$$z = \frac{x - \mu}{\sigma} = \frac{21 - 17}{3} \approx 1.33$$

The z value is positive. We should expect a positive z value, since 21 minutes is *more* than the mean of 17.

Continued

GUIDED EXERCISE 6 continued

(b) Another day it took only 12 minutes for the student to get to class. What is this measurement in standard units? Is the z value positive or negative? Why should it be positive or negative?

 The measurement in standard units is

$$z = \frac{x - \mu}{\sigma} = \frac{12 - 17}{3} \approx -1.67$$

Here the z value is negative, as we should expect, because 12 minutes is less than the mean of 17 minutes.

(c) Another day it took 17 minutes for the student to go from home to class. What is the z value? Why should you expect this answer?

In this case, the z value is

$$z = \frac{x - \mu}{\sigma} = \frac{17 - 17}{3} = 0.00$$

We expect this result because 17 minutes is the mean, and the z value of the mean is always zero.

Raw score

We have seen how to convert from x measurements to standard units z. We can easily reverse the process to find the original *raw score* x if we know the mean and standard deviation of the original x distribution. Simply solve the z score formula for x.

> Given an x distribution with mean μ and standard deviation σ, the **raw score** x corresponding to a z score is
>
> $$x = z\sigma + \mu$$

EXAMPLE 5

Raw score

In Example 4, we talked about the amount of cheese required by a franchise for a large pizza. Again, the mean amount of cheese required is 8 oz with a standard deviation of 0.5 oz. The franchise specifies that the minimum amount of cheese for a large pizza is three standard deviations below the mean. A pizza parlor can lose its franchise if the amount of cheese on a large pizza is less than the specified minimum. What is the minimum amount of cheese that can be placed on a large pizza according to the franchise?

SOLUTION: Here we need to convert $z = -3$ to information about x oz of cheese. We use the formula

$$x = z\sigma + \mu = -3(0.5) + 8 = 6.5 \text{ oz}$$

The franchise will not approve a large pizza with less than 6.5 oz of cheese.   ◇

In many testing situations, we hear the terms *raw score* and *z score*. The raw score is just the score in the original measuring units, and the z score is the score in standard units. Guided Exercise 7 illustrates these different units.

GUIDED EXERCISE 7

Raw score

Marulla's z score on a college entrance exam is 1.3. If the raw scores have a mean of 480 and a standard deviation of 70 points, what is her raw score?

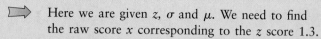 Here we are given z, σ and μ. We need to find the raw score x corresponding to the z score 1.3.

$$x = z\sigma + \mu$$
$$= 1.3(70) + 480$$
$$= 571$$

Standard Normal Distribution

If the original distribution of x values is *normal*, then the corresponding z values *have a normal distribution as well*. The z distribution has a mean of 0 and a standard deviation of 1. The normal curve with these properties has a special name.

> The **standard normal distribution** is a normal distribution with mean $\mu = 0$ and standard deviation $\sigma = 1$ (Figure 6-17).

Any normal distribution of x values can be converted to the standard normal distribution by converting all x values to their corresponding z values. Let's look at the graphic interpretation of this transformation in Figure 6-18.

The resulting standard distribution will always have mean $\mu = 0$ and standard deviation $\sigma = 1$.

Areas Under the Standard Normal Curve

We have seen how to convert *any* normal distribution to the *standard* normal distribution. We can change any x value to a z value and back again. But what is the

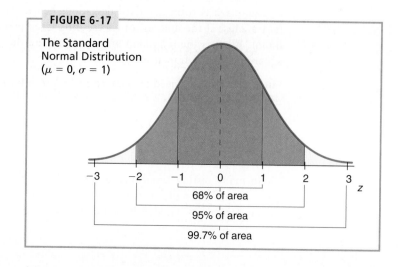

FIGURE 6-17

The Standard Normal Distribution ($\mu = 0$, $\sigma = 1$)

68% of area

95% of area

99.7% of area

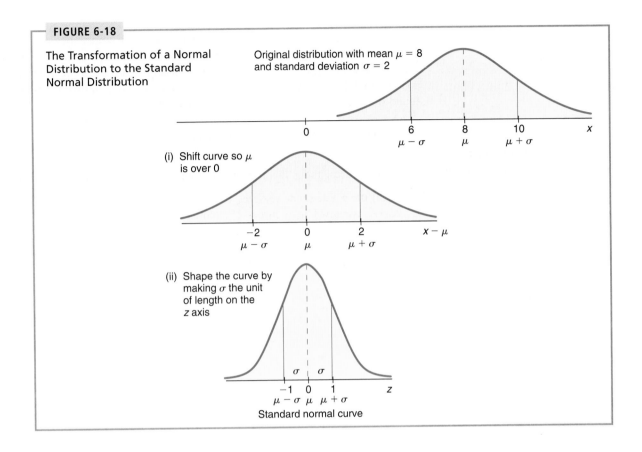

FIGURE 6-18

The Transformation of a Normal Distribution to the Standard Normal Distribution

Original distribution with mean $\mu = 8$ and standard deviation $\sigma = 2$

(i) Shift curve so μ is over 0

(ii) Shape the curve by making σ the unit of length on the z axis

Standard normal curve

advantage of all this work? The advantage is that there are extensive tables that show the *area under the standard normal curve* for almost any interval along the z axis. The areas are important because each area is equal to the *probability* that the measurement of an item selected at random falls in this interval. Thus, the *standard* normal distribution can be a tremendously helpful tool.

For instance, Sunshine Stereo guarantees their cassette decks for a period of 2 years. The company statistician has computed that the cassette deck life is normally distributed with a mean of 2.3 years and a standard deviation 0.4 year. What is the probability that a cassette deck will stop working during the guarantee period?

To answer questions of this type, we convert the given normal distribution to the standard normal distribution. Then we use a table to find the area over the interval in question and, hence, the probability an item selected at random will fall into that interval. Before we can carry out this plan, though, we must practice using Table 5 of Appendix II to find areas under the standard normal curve.

Using a Standard Normal Distribution Table

Using a table to find areas and probabilities associated with the standard normal distribution is a fairly straightforward activity. However, it is important to first observe the range of z values for which areas are given. This range is usually depicted in a picture that accompanies the table.

Left-tail style table

In this text, *we will use the left-tail style table.* This style table gives cumulative areas to the left of a specified z. Determining other areas under the curve utilizes the fact that the area under the entire curve is 1. Taking advantage of the symmetry of the normal distribution is also useful. The procedures you learn for using the left-tail style normal distribution table apply directly to cumulative normal distribution areas found on calculators and in computer software packages such as Excel and Minitab.

EXAMPLE 6

Standard normal distribution table

Use Table 5 of Appendix II to find the described areas under the standard normal curve.

(a) Find the area under the standard normal curve to the left of $z = -1.00$.

SOLUTION: First, shade the area to be found on the standard normal distribution curve, as shown in Figure 6-19. Notice that the z value we are using is negative. This means that we will look at the portion of Table 5 of Appendix II for which the z values are negative. In the upper-left corner of the table we see the letter z. The column under z gives us the units value and tenths for z. The other column headings indicate the hundredths value of z. Table entries give areas under the standard normal curve to the left of the listed z values. To find the area to the left of $z = -1.00$, we use the row headed by -1.0 and then move to the column headed by the hundredths position .00. This entry is shaded in Table 6-5. We see that the area is 0.1587.

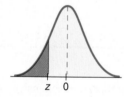

TABLE 6-5   **Excerpt from Table 5 of Appendix II Showing Negative z Values**

z	.00	.01	...	.07	.08	.09
−3.4	.0003	.0003	...	.0003	.0003	.0002
⋮						
−1.1	.1357	.1335	...	.1210	.1190	.1170
−1.0	.1587	.1562	...	.1423	.1401	.1379
−0.9	.1841	.1814	...	.1660	.1635	.1611
⋮						
−0.0	.5000	.4960	...	.4721	.4681	.4641

(b) Find the area to the left of $z = 1.18$, illustrated in Figure 6-20.

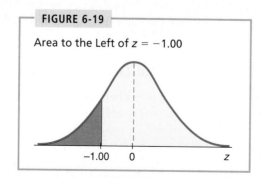

FIGURE 6-19

Area to the Left of $z = -1.00$

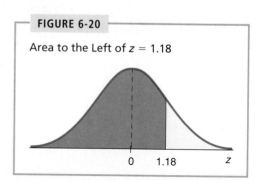

FIGURE 6-20

Area to the Left of $z = 1.18$

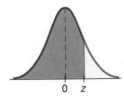

TABLE 6-6   Excerpt from Table 5 of Appendix II Showing Positive z Values

z	.00	.01	.02	...	.08	.09
0.0	.5000	.5040	.5080	...	.5319	.5359
:						
0.9	.8159	.8186	.8212	...	.8365	.8359
1.0	.8413	.8438	.8461	...	.8599	.8621
1.1	.8643	.8665	.8686	...	.8810	.8830
:						
3.4	.9997	.9997	.9997	...	.9997	.9998

SOLUTION: In this case, we are looking for an area to the left of a positive z value, so we look in the portion of Table 5 that shows positive z values. Again we first sketch the area to be found on a standard normal curve, as shown in Figure 6-20. Look in the row headed by 1.1 and move to the column headed by .08. The desired area is shaded (see Table 6-6). We see that the area to the left of 1.18 is 0.8810. ◊

GUIDED
EXERCISE **8**

Using the standard normal distribution table

Table 5, Areas of a Standard Normal Distribution, is located in Appendix II as well as in the endpapers of the text. Spend a little time studying the table, and then answer these questions.

(a) As z values increase, do the areas to the left of z increase?

⟹ Yes, as z values increase, we move to the right on the normal curve, and the areas increase.

(b) If a z value is negative, is the area to the left of z less than 0.5000?

⟹ Yes. Remember that a negative z value is on the left side of the standard normal distribution. The entire left half of the normal distribution has area 0.5, so any area to the left of $z = 0$ will be less than 0.5.

(c) If a z value is positive, is the area to the left of z greater than 0.5000?

⟹ Yes. Positive z values are on the right side of the standard normal distribution, and any area to the left of a positive z value includes the entire left half of the normal distribution.

Using Table 5 to find other areas   Table 5 gives areas under the standard normal distribution that are to the *left of a z value*. How do we find other areas under the standard normal curve?

PROCEDURE

How to use a left-tail style standard normal distribution table

1. For areas to the left of a specified z value, use the table entry directly.

2. For areas to the right of a specified z value, look up the table entry for z and subtract the area from 1.
   Note: Another way to find the same area is to use the symmetry of the normal curve and look up the table entry for $-z$.

3. For areas between two z values, z_1 and z_2 (where $z_2 > z_1$), *subtract* the table area for z_1 from the table area for z_2.

Figure 6-21 illustrates the procedure for using Table 5, Areas of a Standard Normal Distribution, to find any specified area under the standard normal distribution. Again, it is useful to sketch the area in question before you use Table 5.

◇ **COMMENT:** Notice that the z values shown in Table 5 of Appendix II are formatted to the hundredths position. It is convenient to *round or format z values to the hundredths position* before using the table. The areas are all given to four places after the decimal, so give your answers to four places after the decimal. ◇

FIGURE 6-21

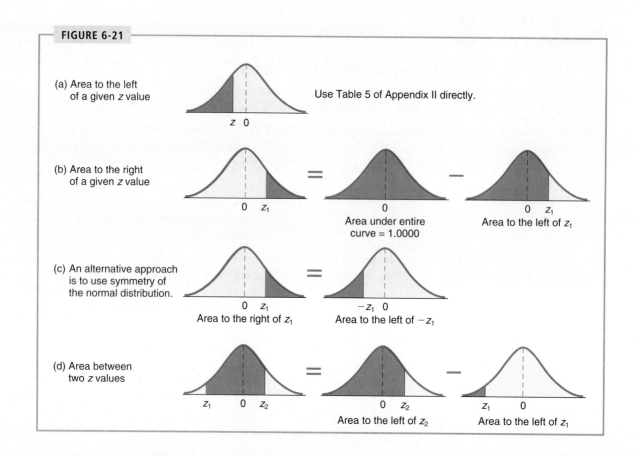

(a) Area to the left of a given z value

Use Table 5 of Appendix II directly.

(b) Area to the right of a given z value

Area under entire curve = 1.0000   Area to the left of z_1

(c) An alternative approach is to use symmetry of the normal distribution.

Area to the right of z_1 Area to the left of $-z_1$

(d) Area between two z values

Area to the left of z_2 Area to the left of z_1

◇ **COMMENT:** The smallest z value shown in Table 5 is -3.49, while the largest value is 3.49. These values are, respectively, far to the left and far to the right on the standard normal distribution, with very little area beyond either value. We will follow the common convention of treating any area to the left of a z value smaller than -3.49 as 0.000. Similarly, we will consider any area to the right of a z value greater than 3.49 as 0.000. We understand that there is some area in these extreme tails. However, these areas are each less than 0.0002. Now let's get real about this! Some very specialized applications, beyond the scope of this book, do need to measure areas and corresponding probabilities in these extreme tails. But in most practical applications, *we follow the convention of treating the areas in the extreme tails as zero.* ◇

Convention for using Table 5 of Appendix II

1. Treat any area to the left of a z value smaller than -3.49 as 0.000.

2. Treat any area to the left of a z value greater than 3.49 as 1.000.

EXAMPLE 7

Using table to find areas

Use Table 5 of Appendix II to find the specified areas.

(a) Find the area between $z = 1.00$ and $z = 2.70$.

SOLUTION: First, sketch a diagram showing the area (see Figure 6-22). Because we are finding the area between two z values, we subtract corresponding table entries.

$$(\text{Area between } 1.00 \text{ and } 2.70) = (\text{Area left of } 2.70) - (\text{Area left of } 1.00)$$
$$= 0.9965 - 0.8413$$
$$= 0.1552$$

(b) Find the area to the right of $z = 0.94$.

SOLUTION: First, sketch the area to be found (see Figure 6-23).

$$(\text{Area to right of } 0.94) = (\text{Area under entire curve}) - (\text{Area to left of } 0.94)$$
$$= 1.000 - 0.8264$$
$$= 0.1736$$

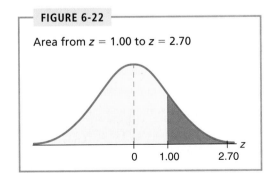

FIGURE 6-22

Area from $z = 1.00$ to $z = 2.70$

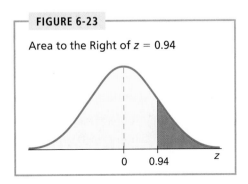

FIGURE 6-23

Area to the Right of $z = 0.94$

Alternatively,

(Area to right of 0.94) = (Area to left of −0.94)

= 0.1736   ◇

Probabilities associated with the
standard normal distribution

We have practiced the skill of finding areas under the standard normal curve for various intervals along the z axis. This skill is important since *the probability that z lies in an interval* is given by the area under the standard normal curve above that interval.

Because the normal distribution is continuous, there is no area under the curve exactly over a specific z. Therefore, probabilities such as $P(z \geq z_1)$ are the same as $P(z > z_1)$. When dealing with probabilities or areas under a normal curve that are specified with inequalities, *strict inequality* symbols can be used *interchangeably* with *inequality-or-equal* symbols.

GUIDED EXERCISE 9

Probabilities associated with the standard normal distribution

Let z be a random variable with a standard normal distribution.

(a) $P(z \geq 1.15)$ refers to the probability that z values lie to the right of 1.15. Shade the corresponding area under the standard normal curve and find $P(z \geq 1.15)$.

⟹ **FIGURE 6-24** Area to Be Found

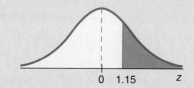

$P(z \geq 1.15) = 1.000 - P(z \leq 1.15) = 1.000 - 0.8749 = 0.1251$

Alternatively,

$P(z \geq 1.15) = P(z \leq -1.15) = 0.1251$

(b) Find $P(-1.78 \leq z \leq 0.35)$. First, sketch the area under the standard normal curve corresponding to the area.

⟹ **FIGURE 6-25** Area to Be Found

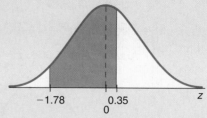

$P(-1.78 \leq z \leq 0.35) = P(z \leq 0.35) - P(z \leq -1.78)$

$= 0.6368 - 0.0375 = 0.5993$

TECH NOTE The TI-84Plus and TI-83Plus calculators, Excel, and Minitab all provide cumulative areas under any normal distribution, including the standard normal. The Tech Note of Section 6.3 shows examples.

VIEWPOINT

Mighty Oaks from Little Acorns Grow!

Just how big is that acorn? What if we compare it with other acorns? Is that oak tree taller than an average oak tree? How does it compare with other oak trees? What do you mean, this oak tree has a larger geographic range? Compared with what? Answers to questions such as these can be given only if we resort to *standardized statistical units*. Can you compare a single oak tree with an entire forest of oak trees? The answer is yes, if you use *standardized z scores*. For more information about sizes of acorns, oak trees, and geographic locations, visit the Brase/Brase statistics site at **http://math.college.hmco.com/students** and find the link to DASL, the Carnegie Mellon University Data and Story Library. From the DASL site, find Biology under Data Subjects, and select Acorns. Follow the links to Data Subjects, Biology, and Acorns.

SECTION 6.2   PROBLEMS

In these problems, assume that all the distributions are *normal*. In all problems in Chapter 6, *average* is always taken to be the arithmetic mean $\bar{x}$ or μ.

1. *z Scores: First Aid Course* The college Physical Education Department offered an Advanced First Aid course last semester. The scores on the comprehensive final exam were normally distributed, and the *z* scores for some of the students are shown below:

Robert, 1.10	Juan, 1.70	Susan, −2.00
Joel, 0.00	Jan, −0.80	Linda, 1.60

   (a) Which of these students scored above the mean?
   (b) Which of these students scored on the mean?
   (c) Which of these students scored below the mean?
   (d) If the mean score was $\mu = 150$ with standard deviation $\sigma = 20$, what was the final exam score for each student?

2. *z Scores: Teaching Duties* What do professors do with their time? They do research, teach classes, serve on academic committees, serve the student body (advise students, sponsor student clubs, attend student events), serve the community (consult, address civic groups), and a lot more! The specific answer depends on the individual professor and his or her special interests. Well, how much time does a professor spend on teaching activities? *The NEA Almanac of Higher Education*, published by the National Education Association, reports that the mean percentage of time professors spend on teaching activities is about $\mu = 51\%$ with standard deviation

$\sigma = 25\%$. Find the standardized z values corresponding to the following professors' percentages of time allocated to teaching duties.
(a) Dr. Taylor, 45%   (b) Mr. Patterson, 72%   (c) Dr. Lee, 75%
(d) Ms Simms, 65%   (e) Dr. Adams, 33%   (f) Dr. Riley, 55%

3. *z Scores: Honolulu Temperatures* Data collected over a period of years show that the average daily temperature in Honolulu is $\mu = 73°F$ with standard deviation $\sigma = 5°F$ (U.S. Department of Commerce, Environmental Data Service). Convert each of the following intervals in °F to an interval of z values.
(a) $53°F < x < 93°F$ (b) $x < 65°F$ (c) $78°F < x$

Convert each of the following intervals of z values to intervals in °F.
(d) $1.75 < z$ (e) $z < -1.90$ (f) $-1.80 < z < 1.65$

4. *z Scores: Fawns* Fawns between 1 and 5 months old in Mesa Verde National Park have a body weight that is approximately normally distributed with mean $\mu = 27.2$ kilograms and standard deviation $\sigma = 4.3$ kilograms (based on information from *The Mule Deer of Mesa Verde National Park,* by G. W. Mierau and J. L. Schmidt, Mesa Verde Museum Association). Let x be the weight of a fawn in kilograms. Convert each of the following x intervals to z intervals.
(a) $x < 30$ (b) $19 < x$ (c) $32 < x < 35$

Convert each of the following z intervals to x intervals.
(d) $-2.17 < z$ (e) $z < 1.28$ (f) $-1.99 < z < 1.44$
(g) If a fawn weighs 14 kilograms, would you say it is an unusually small animal? Explain using z values and Figure 6-17.
(h) If a fawn is unusually large, would you say that the z value for the weight of the fawn will be close to 0, -2, or 3? Explain.

5. *z Scores: Deer Population* The fall deer population in Mesa Verde National Park is approximately normally distributed with mean 4400 deer and standard deviation 620 deer (see reference in Problem 4). Let x be the random variable that represents the size of the deer population in Mesa Verde National Park in the fall of a given year. Convert each of the following x intervals to z intervals.
(a) $3300 < x$ (b) $x < 5400$ (c) $3500 < x < 5300$

Convert each of the following z intervals to x intervals.
(d) $-1.12 < z < 2.43$ (e) $z < 1.96$ (f) $2.58 < z$
(g) If the fall deer population were 2800 deer, would that be considered an unusually low number? If the fall population were 6300, would that be considered an unusually high population? Explain using z values and Figure 6-17.

6. *z Scores: White Blood Cell Count* Let x = white blood cell (WBC) count per cubic millimeter of whole blood. Then x has a distribution that is approximately normal with mean $\mu = 7500$ and standard deviation $\sigma = 1750$ (based on information from *Diagnostic Tests with Nursing Implications,* edited by S. Loeb, Springhouse Press). Convert each of the following x intervals to z intervals.
(a) $9000 < x$ (b) $x < 6000$ (c) $3500 < x < 4500$

Convert each of the following z intervals to x intervals.
(d) $z < 1.15$ (e) $2.19 < z$ (f) $0.25 < z < 1.25$
(g) If someone had a WBC count of 2500, would that be considered unusually high or low? Explain using z values and Figure 6-17.

7. *z Scores: Red Blood Cell Count* Let x = red blood cell (RBC) count in millions per cubic millimeter of whole blood. For healthy females x has an approximately normal distribution with mean $\mu = 4.8$ and standard deviation $\sigma = 0.3$. (See reference

in Problem 6.) Convert each of the following x intervals from laboratory tests to z intervals.
(a) $4.5 < x$ (b) $x < 4.2$ (c) $4.0 < x < 5.5$

Convert each of the following z intervals to x intervals.
(d) $z < -1.44$ (e) $1.28 < z$ (f) $-2.25 < z < -1.00$
(g) If a female had an RBC count of 5.9 or higher, would that be considered unusually high? Explain using z values and Figure 6-17.

8. *Normal Curve: Tree Rings* Tree-ring dates were used extensively in archaeological studies at Burnt Mesa Pueblo (*Bandelier Archaeological Excavation Project: Summer 1989 Excavations at Burnt Mesa Pueblo*, edited by Kohler, Washington State University Department of Anthropology). At one site on the mesa, tree-ring dates (for many samples) gave a mean date of $\mu_1 =$ year 1272 with standard deviation $\sigma_1 = 35$ years. At a second, removed site, the tree-ring dates gave a mean of $\mu_2 =$ year 1122 with standard deviation $\sigma_2 = 40$ years. Assume that both sites had dates that were approximately normally distributed. In the first area, an object was found and dated as $x_1 =$ year 1250. In the second area, another object was found and dated as $x_2 =$ year 1234.
   (a) Convert both x_1 and x_2 to z values, and locate both these values under the standard normal curve of Figure 6-17.
   (b) Which of these two items is the more unusual as an archaeological find in its location?

In Problems 9–28, sketch the areas under the standard normal curve over the indicated intervals, and find the specified areas.

9. To the right of $z = 0$.

10. To the left of $z = 0$.

11. To the left of $z = -1.32$.

12. To the left of $z = -0.47$.

13. To the left of $z = 0.45$.

14. To the left of $z = 0.72$.

15. To the right of $z = 1.52$.

16. To the right of $z = 0.15$.

17. To the right of $z = -1.22$.

18. To the right of $z = -2.17$.

19. Between $z = 0$ and $z = 3.18$.

20. Between $z = 0$ and $z = 2.92$.

21. Between $z = 0$ and $z = -2.01$.

22. Between $z = 0$ and $z = -1.93$.

23. Between $z = -2.18$ and $z = 1.34$.

24. Between $z = -1.40$ and $z = 2.03$.

25. Between $z = 0.32$ and $z = 1.92$.

26. Between $z = 1.42$ and $z = 2.17$.

27. Between $z = -2.42$ and $z = -1.77$.

28. Between $z = -1.98$ and $z = -0.03$.

In Problems 29–48, let z be a random variable with a standard normal distribution. Find the indicated probability, and shade the corresponding area under the standard normal curve.

29. $P(z \leq 0)$.

30. $P(z \geq 0)$.

31. $P(z \leq -0.13)$.

32. $P(z \leq -2.15)$.

33. $P(z \leq 1.20)$.

34. $P(z \leq 3.20)$.

35. $P(z \geq 1.35)$.

36. $P(z \geq 2.17)$.

37. $P(z \geq -1.20)$.   38. $P(z \geq -1.50)$.

39. $P(-1.20 \leq z \leq 2.64)$.   40. $P(-2.20 \leq z \leq 1.04)$.

41. $P(-2.18 \leq z \leq -0.42)$.   42. $P(-1.78 \leq z \leq -1.23)$.

43. $P(0 \leq z \leq 1.62)$.   44. $P(0 \leq z \leq 0.54)$.

45. $P(-0.82 \leq z \leq 0)$.   46. $P(-2.37 \leq z \leq 0)$.

47. $P(-0.45 \leq z \leq 2.73)$.   48. $P(-0.73 \leq z \leq 3.12)$.

6.3
Areas Under Any Normal Curve

FOCUS POINTS

✓ Compute the probability of "standardized events."

✓ Find a z score from a given normal probability (inverse normal).

✓ Use the inverse normal to solve guarantee problems.

Normal Distribution Areas

In many applied situations, the original normal curve is not the standard normal curve. Generally, there will not be a table of areas available for the original normal curve. This does not mean that we cannot find the probability that a measurement x will fall into an interval from a to b. What we must do is *convert* the original measurements x, a, and b to z values.

PROCEDURE

How to work with normal distributions

To find areas and probabilities for a random variable x that follows a normal distribution with mean μ and standard deviation σ, convert x values to z values using the formula

$$z = \frac{x - \mu}{\sigma}$$

Then use Table 5 of Appendix II to find corresponding areas and probabilities.

EXAMPLE 8

Normal distribution probability

Let x have a normal distribution with $\mu = 10$ and $\sigma = 2$. Find the probability that an x value selected at random from this distribution is between 11 and 14. In symbols, find $P(11 \leq x \leq 14)$.

SOLUTION: Since probabilities correspond to areas under the distribution curve, we want to find the area under the x curve above the interval from $x = 11$ to $x = 14$. To do so, we will convert the x values to standard z values (see Figure 6-26) and then use Table 5 of Appendix II to find the corresponding area under the standard curve.

We use the formula

$$z = \frac{x - \mu}{\sigma}$$

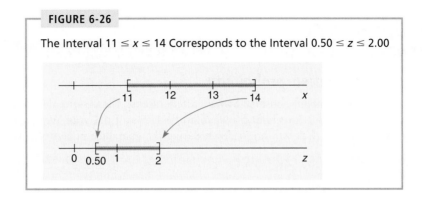

FIGURE 6-26

The Interval $11 \leq x \leq 14$ Corresponds to the Interval $0.50 \leq z \leq 2.00$

to convert the given x interval to a z interval.

$$z_1 = \frac{11 - 10}{2} = 0.50 \qquad \text{(Use } x = 11, \; \mu = 10, \; \sigma = 2.)$$

$$z_2 = \frac{14 - 10}{2} = 2.00 \qquad \text{(Use } x = 14, \; \mu = 10, \; \sigma = 2.)$$

The corresponding areas under the x and z curves are shown in Figure 6-27. From Figure 6-27 we see that

$$
\begin{aligned}
P(11 \leq x \leq 14) &= P(0.50 \leq z \leq 2.00) \\
&= P(z \leq 2.00) - P(z \leq 0.50) \\
&= 0.9772 - 0.6915 \qquad \text{(From Table 5, Appendix II)} \\
&= 0.2857
\end{aligned}
$$

The probability is 0.2857 that an x value selected at random from a normal distribution with mean 10 and standard deviation 2 lies between 11 and 14.   ◊

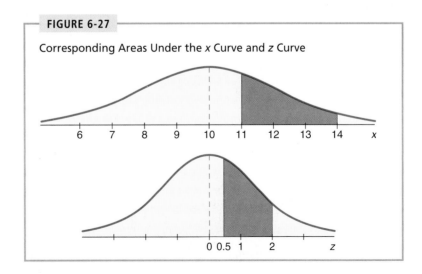

FIGURE 6-27

Corresponding Areas Under the x Curve and z Curve

GUIDED EXERCISE 10

Normal distribution probability

In Section 6.2, we talked about Sunshine Stereo cassette decks. The cassette deck life was normally distributed with a mean of 2.3 years and a standard deviation of 0.4 year. We wanted to know the probability that a cassette deck will break down during the guarantee period of 2 years.

(a) Let x represent the life of a cassette deck. The statement that the cassette deck breaks during the 2-year guarantee period means the life is less than 2 years, or $x \leq 2$. Convert this to a statement about z.

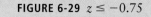 $z = \dfrac{x - \mu}{\sigma} = \dfrac{2 - 2.3}{0.4} = -0.75$

So $x \leq 2$ means $z \leq -0.75$.

(b) Indicate the area to be found in Figure 6-28. Does this area correspond to the probability that $z \leq -0.75$?

See Figure 6-29.
Yes, the shaded area does correspond to the probability that $z \leq -0.75$.

FIGURE 6-28

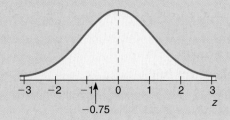

FIGURE 6-29 $z \leq -0.75$

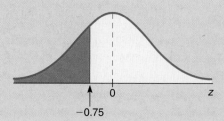

(c) Use Table 5 of Appendix II to find $P(z \leq -0.75)$.

0.2266

(d) What is the probability that the cassette deck will break before the end of the guarantee period? [*Hint:* $P(x \leq 2) = P(z \leq -0.75)$.]

The probability is

$P(x \leq 2) = P(z \leq -0.75)$
$\qquad\qquad = 0.2266$

This means that the company will repair or replace about 23% of the cassette decks.

TECH NOTE   The TI-84Plus and TI-83Plus calculators, Excel, and Minitab all provide areas under any normal distribution. Excel and Minitab give the left-tail area to the left of a specified x value. The TI-84Plus/TI-83Plus has you specify an interval from a lower bound to an upper bound and provides the area under the normal curve for that interval. For example, to solve Guided Exercise 10 regarding the probability a cassette deck will break during the guarantee period, we find $P(x \leq 2)$ for a normal distribution with $\mu = 2.3$ and $\sigma = 0.4$.

TI-84Plus/TI-83Plus Press the **DISTR** key, select **2:normalcdf (lower bound, upper bound, μ, σ)** and press Enter. Type in the specified values. For a left-tail area, use a lower bound setting at about 4 standard deviations below the mean. Likewise, for a right-tail area, use an upper bound setting about 4 standard deviations above the mean. For our example, use a lower bound of $\mu - 4\sigma = 2.3 - 4(0.4) = 0.7$.

```
normalcdf(.7,2,2.3,
.4)
            .2265955934
```

Excel Select **Paste Function** $\boxed{f_x}$ ➤ **Statistical** ➤ **NORMDIST.** Fill in the dialogue box, using True for cumulative.

=	=NORMDIST(2,2.3,0.4, TRUE)		
C	D	E	
0.226627			

Minitab Use the menu selection **Calc** ➤ **Probability Distribution** ➤ **Normal.** Fill in the dialogue box, marking cumulative.

```
Cumulative Distribution Function
Normal with mean = 2.3 and
standard deviation = 0.4
      x       P(X <= x)
    2.0        0.2266
```

Inverse Normal Distribution

Finding *z* or *x*, given a probability

Sometimes we need to find z or x values that correspond to a given area under the normal curve. This situation arises when we want to specify a guarantee period such that a given percentage of the total products produced by a company last at least as long as the duration of the guarantee period. In such cases, we use the standard normal distribution table "in reverse." When we look up an area and find the corresponding z value, we are using the *inverse normal probability distribution.*

EXAMPLE 9
Find x, given probability

Magic Video Games, Inc., sells an expensive video computer games package. Because the package is so expensive, the company wants to advertise an impressive guarantee for the life expectancy of its computer control system. The guarantee policy will refund the full purchase price if the computer fails during the guarantee period. The research department has done tests which show that the mean life for the computer is 30 months, with standard deviation of 4 months. The computer life is normally distributed. How long can the guarantee period be if management does not want to refund the purchase price on more than 7% of the Magic Video packages?

SOLUTION: Let us look at the distribution of lifetimes for the computer control system, and shade the portion of the distribution in which the computer lasts fewer months than the guarantee period. (See Figure 6-30 on the next page.)

If a computer system lasts fewer months than the guarantee period, a full-price refund will have to be made. The lifetimes requiring a refund are in the shaded region in Figure 6-30. This region represents 7% of the total area under the curve.

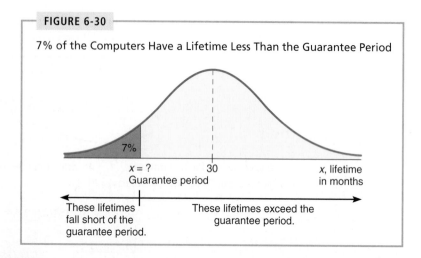

FIGURE 6-30

7% of the Computers Have a Lifetime Less Than the Guarantee Period

We can use Table 5 of Appendix II to find the z value such that 7% of the total area under the *standard* normal curve lies to the left of the z value. Then we convert the z value to its corresponding x value to find the guarantee period.

We want to find the z value with 7% of the area under the standard normal curve to the left of z. Since we are given the area in a left tail, we can use Table 5 of Appendix II directly to find z. The area value is 0.0700. However, this area is not in our table, so we use the closest area, which is 0.0694, and the corresponding z value of $z = -1.48$ (see Table 6-7).

To translate this value back to an x value (in months), we use the formula

$$x = z\sigma + \mu$$
$$= -1.48(4) + 30 \qquad \text{(Use } \sigma = 4 \text{ months and } \mu = 30 \text{ months.)}$$
$$= 24.08 \text{ months}$$

The company can guarantee the Magic Video Games package for $x = 24$ months. For this guarantee period, they expect to refund the purchase price of no more than 7% of the video games packages. ◊

Example 9 had us find a z value corresponding to a given area to the left of z. What if the specified area is to the right of z or between $-z$ and z? Figure 6-31 shows us how to proceed.

◊ **COMMENT** When we use Table 5 of Appendix II to find a z value corresponding to a given area, we usually use the nearest area value rather than interpolating between values. However, when the area value given is exactly halfway

TABLE 6-7   Excerpt from Table 5 of Appendix II

z	.00	...	.07		.08	.09
:						
−1.4	.0808		.0708		.0694	.0681
				↑		
				0.0700		

FIGURE 6-31

Inverse Normal: Use Table 5 of Appendix II to Find *z* Corresponding to a Given Area *A* (0 < *A* < 1)

(a) **Left-tail case:**
The given area *A*
is to the left of *z*.

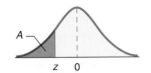 or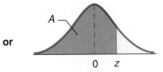

For the left-tail case, look up the number *A* in the body of the table and use the corresponding *z* value.

(b) **Right-tail case:**
The given area *A*
is to the right of *z*.

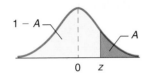 or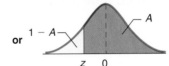

For the right-tail case, look up the number 1 − *A* in the body of the table and use the corresponding *z* value.

(c) **Center case:**
The given area *A* is
symmetric and centered
above *z* = 0. Half
of *A* lies to the left
and half lies to the
right of *z* = 0.

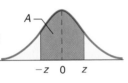

For the center case, look up the number $\dfrac{1-A}{2}$ in the body of the table and use the corresponding ± *z* value.

---

between two area values of the table, we use the *z* value halfway between the *z* values of the corresponding table areas. Example 10 demonstrates this procedure. However, this interpolation convention is not always used, especially if the area is changing slowly, as it does in the tail ends of the distribution. *When the z value corresponding to an area is smaller than −2, the standard convention is to use the z value corresponding to the smaller area. Likewise, when the z value is larger than 2, the standard convention is to use the z value corresponding to the larger area.* We will see an example of this special case in Guided Exercise 1 of the next chapter. ◇

EXAMPLE 10

Find z

Find the *z* value such that 90% of the area under the standard normal curve lies between −*z* and *z*.

SOLUTION: Sketch a picture showing the described area (see Figure 6-32).

FIGURE 6-32

Area Between −*z* and *z* Is 90%

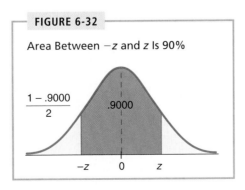

TABLE 6-8 Excerpt from Table 5 of Appendix II

z	...	.04		.05
:				
−1.6		.0505		.0495
			↑	
			0.0500	

We find the corresponding area in the left tail.

$$(\text{Area left of } -z) = \frac{1 - 0.9000}{2}$$

$$= 0.0500$$

Looking in Table 6-8, we see that 0.0500 lies exactly between areas 0.0495 and 0.0505. The halfway value between $z = -1.65$ and $z = -1.64$ is $z = -1.645$. Therefore, we conclude that 90% of the area under the standard normal curve lies between the z values -1.645 and 1.645. ◊

GUIDED EXERCISE 11

Find z

Find the z value such that 3% of the area under the standard normal curve lies to the right of z.

(a) Draw a sketch of the standard normal distribution showing the described area.

⟹ **FIGURE 6-33** 3% of Total Area Lies to the Right of z

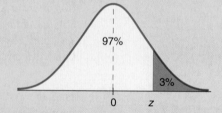

(b) Find the area to the left of z.

⟹ Area to the left of $z = 1 - 0.0300 = 0.9700$.

(c) Look up the area in Table 6-9 and find the corresponding z.

⟹ The closest area is 0.9699. This area is to the left of $z = 1.88$.

TABLE 6-9 Excerpt from Table 5 of Appendix II

z	.00	.01	.02	.03	.04	.05	.06	.07	.08	.09
1.8	.9641	.9649	.9656	.9664	.9671	.9678	.9686	.9693	.9699	.9706
1.9	.9713	.9719	.9726	.9732	.9738	.9744	.9750	.9756	.9761	.9767

Continued

GUIDED EXERCISE 11 *continued*

(d) Suppose the time to complete a test is normally distributed with $\mu = 40$ minutes and $\sigma = 5$ minutes. After how many minutes can we expect all but about 3% of the tests to be completed?

 We are looking for an x value such that 3% of the normal distribution lies to the right of x. In part (c), we found that 3% of the standard normal curve lies to the right of $z = 1.88$. We convert $z = 1.88$ to an x value.

$$x = z\sigma + \mu$$
$$= 1.88(5) + 40 = 49.4 \text{ minutes}$$

All but about 3% of the tests will be complete after 50 minutes.

(e) Use Table 6-10 to find a z value such that 3% of the area under the standard normal curve lies to the left of z.

The closest area is 0.0301. This is the area to the left of $z = -1.88$.

TABLE 6-10   Excerpt from Table 5 of Appendix II

z	.00	.01	.02	.03	.04	.05	.06	.07	.08	.09
−1.9	.0287	.0281	.0274	.0268	.0262	.0256	.0250	.0244	.0239	.0233
−1.8	.0359	.0351	.0344	.0336	.0329	.0322	.0314	.0307	.0301	.0294

(f) Compare the z value of part (c) with the z value of part (e). Is there any relationship between the z values?

One z value is the negative of the other. This result is expected because of the symmetry of the normal distribution.

 TECH NOTE   When we are given a z value and we find an area to the left of z, we are using a normal distribution function. When we are given an area to the left of z and we find the corresponding z, we are using an inverse normal distribution function. The TI-84Plus and TI-83Plus calculators, Excel, and Minitab all have inverse normal distribution functions for any normal distribution. For instance, to find an x value from a normal distribution with mean 40 and standard deviation 5 such that 97% of the area lies to the left of x, use the described instructions.

TI-84Plus/TI-83Plus   Press the **DISTR** key and select **3:invNorm(area,μ,σ)**.

```
invNorm(.97,40,5)
          49.40396805
```

Excel   Select **Paste Function** [f_x] ➤ **Statistical** ➤ **NORMINV**. Fill in the dialogue box.

=	=NORMINV(0.97,40,5)	
C	D	
49.40395		

Minitab Use the menu selection **Calc ➤ Probability Distribution ➤ Normal.** Fill in the dialogue box, marking Inverse Cumulative.

```
Inverse Cumulative Distribution Function
Normal with mean = 40.000 and
  standard deviation = 5.00000
P(X <= x)          x
  0.9700      49.4040
```

VIEWPOINT   *Want to Be an Archaeologist?*

Each year about 4500 students work with professional archaeologists in scientific research at the Crow Canyon Archaeological Center, Cortez, Colorado. In fact, Crow Canyon was included in *The Princeton Review Guide to America's Top 100 Internships.* The nonprofit, multidisciplinary program at Crow Canyon enables students and laypeople with little or no background to get started in archaeological research. The only requirement is that you be interested in Native American culture and history. By the way, a knowledge of introductory statistics could come in handy in this internship. For more information about the program, visit the Brase/Brase statistics site at **http://math.college.hmco.com/students** and find the link to Crow Canyon.

SECTION 6.3   PROBLEMS

In Problems 1–10, assume that x has a normal distribution, with the specified mean and standard deviation. Find the indicated probabilities.

1. $P(3 \leq x \leq 6)$; $\mu = 4$; $\sigma = 2$
2. $P(10 \leq x \leq 26)$; $\mu = 15$; $\sigma = 4$
3. $P(50 \leq x \leq 70)$; $\mu = 40$; $\sigma = 15$
4. $P(7 \leq x \leq 9)$; $\mu = 5$; $\sigma = 1.2$
5. $P(8 \leq x \leq 12)$; $\mu = 15$; $\sigma = 3.2$
6. $P(40 \leq x \leq 47)$; $\mu = 50$; $\sigma = 15$
7. $P(x \geq 30)$; $\mu = 20$; $\sigma = 3.4$
8. $P(x \geq 120)$; $\mu = 100$; $\sigma = 15$
9. $P(x \geq 90)$; $\mu = 100$; $\sigma = 15$
10. $P(x \geq 2)$; $\mu = 3$; $\sigma = 0.25$

In Problems 11–20, find the z value described and sketch the area described.

11. Find z such that 6% of the standard normal curve lies to the left of z.

12. Find z such that 5.2% of the standard normal curve lies to the left of z.

13. Find z such that 55% of the standard normal curve lies to the left of z.

14. Find z such that 97.5% of the standard normal curve lies to the left of z.

15. Find z such that 8% of the standard normal curve lies to the right of z.

16. Find z such that 5% of the standard normal curve lies to the right of z.

17. Find z such that 82% of the standard normal curve lies to the right of z.

18. Find z such that 95% of the standard normal curve lies to the right of z.

19. Find the z value such that 98% of the standard normal curve lies between $-z$ and z.

20. Find the z value such that 95% of the standard normal curve lies between $-z$ and z.

21. *Medical: Blood Glucose* A person's level of blood glucose and diabetes are closely related. Let x be a random variable measured in milligrams of glucose per deciliter (1/10 of a liter) of blood. After a 12-hour fast, the random variable x will have a distribution that is approximately normal with mean $\mu = 85$ and standard deviation $\sigma = 25$ (*Diagnostic Tests with Nursing Implications*, edited by S. Loeb, Springhouse Press). *Note:* After 50 years of age, both the mean and standard deviation tend to increase. What is the probability that, for an adult (under 50 years old) after a 12-hour fast,
    (a) x is more than 60?
    (b) x is less than 110?
    (c) x is between 60 and 110?
    (d) x is greater than 140 (borderline diabetes starts at 140)?

22. *Medical: Blood Protoplasm* Porphyrin is a pigment in blood protoplasm and other body fluids that is significant in body energy and storage. Let x be a random variable that represents the number of milligrams of porphyrin per deciliter of blood. In healthy adults, x is approximately normally distributed with mean $\mu = 38$ and standard deviation $\sigma = 12$ (see reference in Problem 21). What is the probability that
    (a) x is less than 60?
    (b) x is greater than 16?
    (c) x is between 16 and 60?
    (d) x is more than 60? (This may indicate an infection, anemia, or another type of illness.)

23. *Education: SAT and ACT Scores* For a given population of high school seniors, the Scholastic Aptitude Test (SAT) in mathematics has a mean score of 500 with a standard deviation of 100. Another widely used test is the American College Testing (ACT) exam. The mathematics portion of the ACT has a mean of 18 and a standard deviation of 6. (Visit the Brase/Brase statistics site at **http://math.college.hmco.com/ students** and find the link to the College Board.) Both SAT and ACT scores are normally distributed. What is the probability that a randomly selected high school senior's score on the mathematics part of the SAT will be
    (a) more than 675?   (b) less than 450?   (c) between 450 and 675?

    What is the probability that a randomly selected high school senior's score on the mathematics part of the ACT will be
    (d) more than 28?   (e) more than 12?   (f) between 12 and 28?

24. *Inverse Normal Distribution: SAT and ACT Scores* Please refer to the SAT and ACT information from Problem 23.
    (a) Suppose that an engineering school honors program will accept only high school seniors with a mathematics SAT or ACT score in the top 10%. What is the minimum SAT score in mathematics for this program? What is the minimum ACT score in mathematics for this program?
    (b) Suppose that an engineering school will accept only high school seniors with a mathematics SAT or ACT score in the top 20%. What is the minimum SAT score in mathematics for this program? What is the minimum ACT score in mathematics for this program?
    (c) Suppose that an engineering school will accept only high school seniors with a mathematics SAT or ACT score in the top 60%. What is the minimum SAT score in mathematics for this program? What is the minimum ACT score in mathematics for this program?

25. *Archaeology: Hopi Village* Thickness measurements of ancient prehistoric Native American pot shards discovered in a Hopi village are approximately normally distributed with a mean of 5.1 mm and a standard deviation of 0.9 mm. (Source: *Homol'ovi II: Archaeology of an Ancestral Hopi Village, Arizona*, edited by E. C. Adams and K. A. Hays, University of Arizona Press.) For a randomly found shard, what is the probability that the thickness is
    (a) less than 3.0 mm?
    (b) more than 7.0 mm?
    (c) between 3.0 mm and 7.0 mm?

26. *Law Enforcement: Police Response Time* Police response time to an emergency call is the difference between the time the call is first received by the dispatcher and the time a patrol car radios that it has arrived at the scene (based on information from the *Denver Post*). Over a long period of time, it has been determined that the police response time has a normal distribution with a mean of 8.4 minutes and a standard deviation of 1.7 minutes. For a randomly received emergency call, what is the probability that the response time will be
    (a) between 5 and 10 minutes?
    (b) less than 5 minutes?
    (c) more than 10 minutes?

27. *Fuel Consumption: Boeing 747* Average fuel consumption for a Boeing 747 commercial jet in cruising position is 3213 gallons of jet fuel per hour (based on information from Canadian Pacific Air). Assume that the fuel consumption distribution is mound-shaped and approximately normal with a standard deviation of 180 gallons of jet fuel per hour. When a 747 is in cruising position, what is the probability the fuel consumption is
    (a) between 3000 and 3500 gallons per hour?
    (b) less than 3000 gallons per hour?
    (c) more than 3500 gallons per hour?

28. *Vermont Skiing: Temperatures* At a ski area in Vermont, the daytime high temperature is normally distributed during January, with a mean of 22°F and a standard deviation of 10°F (U.S. Department of Commerce, Environmental Data Services). You are planning to ski there this January. What is the probability that you will encounter daytime highs of
    (a) 42°F or higher?   (b) 15°F or lower?   (c) between 29°F and 40°F?

29. *Guarantee: Batteries* Quick Start Company makes 12-volt car batteries. After many years of product testing, the company knows that the average life of a Quick Start battery is normally distributed, with a mean of 45 months and a standard deviation of 8 months.
    (a) If Quick Start guarantees a full refund on any battery that fails within the 36-month period after purchase, what percentage of its batteries will the company expect to replace?
    (b) *Inverse Normal Distribution* If Quick Start does not want to make refunds for more than 10% of its batteries under the full-refund guarantee policy, for how long should the company guarantee the batteries (to the nearest month)?

30. *Guarantee: Watches* Accrotime is a manufacturer of quartz crystal watches. Accrotime researchers have shown that the watches have an average life of 28 months before certain electronic components deteriorate, causing the watch to become unreliable. The standard deviation of watch lifetimes is 5 months, and the distribution of lifetimes is normal.
    (a) If Accrotime guarantees a full refund on any defective watch for 2 years after purchase, what percentage of total production will the company expect to replace?

(b) *Inverse Normal Distribution* If Accrotime does not want to make refunds on more than 12% of the watches it makes, how long should the guarantee period be (to the nearest month)?

31. *Expand Your Knowledge: Estimating the Standard Deviation* Consumer Reports gave information about the ages at which various household products are replaced. For example, color TVs are replaced at an average age of $\mu = 8$ years after purchase, and the (95% of data) range was from 5 to 11 years. Thus, the range was $11 - 5 = 6$ years. Let x be the age (in years) at which a color TV is replaced. Assume that x has a distribution that is approximately normal.

(a) The empirical rule (Section 6.1) indicates that for a symmetrical and bell-shaped distribution, approximately 95% of the data lies within two standard deviations of the mean. Therefore, a 95% range of data values extending from $\mu - 2\sigma$ to $\mu + 2\sigma$ is often used for "commonly occurring" data values. Note that the interval from $\mu - 2\sigma$ to $\mu + 2\sigma$ is 4σ in length. This leads to a "rule of thumb" for estimating the standard deviation from a 95% range of data values.

From the Empirical Rule

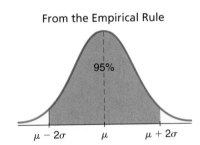

Estimating the standard deviation

For a symmetric, bell-shaped distribution,

$$\text{standard deviation} \approx \frac{\text{range}}{4} \approx \frac{\text{high value} - \text{low value}}{4}$$

where it is estimated that about 95% of the commonly occurring data values fall into this range.

Use this "rule of thumb" to approximate the standard deviation of x values, where x is the age (in years) at which a color TV is replaced.

(b) What is the probability that someone will keep a color TV more than 5 years before replacement?

(c) What is the probability that someone will keep a color TV fewer than 10 years before replacement?

(d) *Inverse Normal Distribution* Assume that the average life of a color TV is 8 years with a standard deviation of 1.5 years before it breaks. Suppose that a company guarantees color TVs and will replace a TV that breaks while under guarantee with a new one. However, the company does not want to replace more than 10% of the TVs under guarantee. For how long should the guarantee be made (rounded to the nearest tenth of a year)?

32. *Estimating the Standard Deviation: Refrigerator Replacement* Consumer Reports indicated that the average life of a refrigerator before replacement is $\mu = 14$ years with a (95% of data) range from 9 to 19 years. Let $x =$ age at which a refrigerator is replaced. Assume that x has a distribution that is approximately normal.

(a) Find a good approximation for the standard deviation of x values. *Hint:* See Problem 31.

(b) What is the probability that someone will keep a refrigerator fewer than 11 years before replacement?

(c) What is the probability that someone will keep a refrigerator more than 18 years before replacement?

(d) *Inverse Normal Distribution* Assume that the average life of a refrigerator is 14 years, with the standard deviation given in part (a) before it breaks. Suppose that a company guarantees refrigerators and will replace a refrigerator that breaks while under guarantee with a new one. However, the company does not want to replace more than 5% of the refrigerators under guarantee. For how long should the guarantee be made (rounded to the nearest tenth of a year)?

33. *Estimating the Standard Deviation: Veterinary Science* The resting heart rate for an adult horse should average about $\mu = 46$ beats per minute with a (95% of data) range from 22 to 70 beats per minute, based on information from *The Merck Veterinary Manual* (a classic reference used in most veterinary colleges). Let x be a random variable that represents the resting heart rate for an adult horse. Assume that x has a distribution that is approximately normal.
   (a) Estimate the standard deviation of the x distribution. *Hint:* See Problem 31.
   (b) What is the probability that the heart rate is less than 25 beats per minute?
   (c) What is the probability that the heart rate is greater than 60 beats per minute?
   (d) What is the probability that the heart rate is between 25 and 60 beats per minute?
   (e) *Inverse Normal Distribution* A horse whose resting heart rate is in the upper 10% of the probability distribution of heart rates may have a secondary infection or illness that needs to be treated. What is the heart rate corresponding to the upper 10% cutoff point of the probability distribution?

34. *Estimating the Standard Deviation: Veterinary Science* How much should a healthy kitten weigh? A healthy 10-week-old (domestic) kitten should weigh an average of $\mu = 24.5$ oz with a (95% of data) range from 14 to 35 oz. (See reference in Problem 33.) Let x be a random variable that represents the weight (in ounces) of a healthy 10-week-old kitten. Assume that x has a distribution that is approximately normal.
   (a) Estimate the standard deviation of the x distribution. *Hint:* See Problem 31.
   (b) What is the probability that a healthy 10-week-old kitten will weigh less than 14 oz?
   (c) What is the probability that a healthy 10-week-old kitten will weigh more than 33 oz?
   (d) What is the probability that a healthy 10-week-old kitten will weigh between 14 and 33 oz?
   (e) *Inverse Normal Distribution* A kitten whose weight is in the bottom 10% of the probability distribution of weights is called *undernourished*. What is the cutoff point for the weight of an undernourished kitten?

35. *Insurance: Satellites* A relay microchip in a telecommunications satellite has a life expectancy that follows a normal distribution with a mean of 90 months and a standard deviation of 3.7 months. When this computer-relay microchip malfunctions, the entire satellite is useless. A large London insurance company is going to insure the satellite for 50 million dollars. Assume that the only part of the satellite in question is the microchip. All other components will work indefinitely.
   (a) *Inverse Normal Distribution* For how many months should the satellite be insured to be 99% confident that it will last beyond the insurance date?
   (b) If the satellite is insured for 84 months, what is the probability that it will malfunction before the insurance coverage ends?
   (c) If the satellite is insured for 84 months, what is the expected loss to the insurance company?
   (d) If the insurance company charges $3 million for 84 months of insurance, how much profit does the company expect to make?

36. *Focus Problem: Exhibition Show Attendance* The Focus Problem at the beginning of the chapter indicates that attendance at large exhibition shows in Denver averages about 8000 people per day, with standard deviation of about 500. Assume that the daily attendance figures follow a normal distribution.

(a) What is the probability that the daily attendance will be fewer than 7200 people?
(b) What is the probability that the daily attendance will be more than 8900 people?
(c) What is the probability that the daily attendance will be between 7200 and 8900 people?

37. *Focus Problem: Inverse Normal Distribution* Most exhibition shows open in the morning and close in the late evening. A study of Saturday arrival times showed that the average arrival time was 3 hours and 48 minutes after the doors opened, and the standard deviation was estimated at about 52 minutes. Assume that the arrival times follow a normal distribution.
  (a) At what time after the doors open will 90% of the people who are coming to the Saturday show have arrived?
  (b) At what time after the doors open will only 15% of the people who are coming to the Saturday show have arrived?
  (c) Do you think the probability distribution of arrival times for Friday might be different from the distribution of arrival times for Saturday? Explain.

38. *Budget: Maintenance* The amount of money spent weekly on cleaning, maintenance, and repairs at a large restaurant was observed over a long period of time to be approximately normally distributed with mean $\mu = \$615$ and standard deviation $\sigma = \$42$.
  (a) If $646 is budgeted for next week, what is the probability that the actual costs will exceed the budgeted amount?
  (b) *Inverse Normal Distribution* How much should be budgeted for weekly repairs, cleaning, and maintenance so that the probability that the budgeted amount will be exceeded in a given week is only 0.10?

39. *Expand Your Knowledge: Conditional Probability* Suppose you want to eat lunch at a popular restaurant. The restaurant does not take reservations, so there is usually a waiting time before you can be seated. Let x represent the length of time waiting to be seated. From past experience, you know that the mean waiting time is $\mu = 18$ minutes with $\sigma = 4$ minutes. You assume that the x distribution is approximately normal.
  (a) What is the probability that the waiting time will *exceed* 20 minutes, given that it has exceeded 15 minutes? *Hint:* Compute $P(x > 20, \text{given } x > 15)$.
  (b) What is the probability that the waiting time will exceed 25 minutes, given that it has exceeded 18 minutes? *Hint:* Compute $P(x > 25, \text{given } x > 18)$.
  (c) *Hint for solution:* Review item 6, conditional probability, in the summary of basic probability rules at the end of Section 4.2. Note that

$$P(A, \text{given } B) = \frac{P(A \text{ and } B)}{P(B)}$$

and show that in part (a),

$$P(x > 20, \text{given } x > 15) = \frac{P((x > 20) \text{ and } (x > 15))}{P(x > 15)} = \frac{P(x > 20)}{P(x > 15)}$$

40. *Conditional Probability: Cycle Time* A cement truck delivers mixed cement to a large construction site. Let x represent the cycle time in minutes for the truck to leave the construction site, go back to the cement plant, fill up, and return to the construction site with another load of cement. From past experience, it is known that the mean cycle time is $\mu = 45$ minutes with $\sigma = 12$ minutes. The x distribution is approximately normal.

(a) What is the probability that the cycle time will *exceed* 60 minutes, given that it has exceeded 50 minutes? *Hint:* See Problem 39, part (c).

(b) What is the probability that the cycle time will exceed 55 minutes, given that it has exceeded 40 minutes?

6.4
Normal Approximation to the Binomial Distribution

FOCUS POINTS

✓ State the assumptions needed for the normal approximation to the binomial distribution.

✓ Compute μ and σ for the normal approximation.

✓ Use the continuity correction to convert a range of r values to a corresponding range of normal x values.

✓ Convert the x values to a range of standardized z scores and find desired probabilities.

Criteria $np > 5$ and $nq > 5$

The probability that a new vaccine will protect adults from cholera is known to be 0.85. It is administered to 300 adults who must enter an area where the disease is prevalent. What is the probability that more than 280 of these adults will be protected from cholera by the vaccine?

This question falls into the category of a binomial experiment with the number of trials n equal to 300, the probability of success p equal to 0.85, and the number of successes r greater than 280. It is possible to use the formula for the binomial distribution to compute the probability that r is greater than 280. However, this approach would involve a number of tedious and long calculations. There is an easier way to do this problem, for under the conditions stated below, the normal distribution can be used to approximate the binomial distribution.

Normal approximation to the binomial distribution

Consider a binomial distribution where

  n = number of trials

  r = number of successes

  p = probability of success on a single trial

  $q = 1 - p$ = probability of failure on a single trial

If $np > 5$ and $nq > 5$, then r has a binomial distribution that is approximated by a normal distribution with

  $$\mu = np \quad \text{and} \quad \sigma = \sqrt{npq}$$

Note: As n increases, the approximation becomes better.

Example 11 demonstrates that as n increases, the normal approximation to the binomial distribution improves.

EXAMPLE 11

Binomial distribution graphs

Graph the binomial distributions where $p = 0.25$, $q = 0.75$, and the number of trials is first $n = 3$, then $n = 10$, then $n = 25$, and finally $n = 50$.

SOLUTION: The authors used a computer program to obtain the binomial distributions for the given values of p, q, and n. The results have been organized and graphed in Figures 6-34, 6-35, 6-36, and 6-37.

When $n = 3$, the outline of the histogram does not even begin to take the shape of a normal curve. But when $n = 10$, 25, or 50, it does begin to take a normal shape, indicated by the red curve. From a theoretical point of view, the histograms in Figures 6-35, 6-36, and 6-37 would have bars for all values of r from $r = 0$ to $r = n$. However, in the construction of these histograms, the bars of height less than 0.001 unit have been omitted—that is, in this example, probabilities less than 0.001 have been rounded to 0. ◆

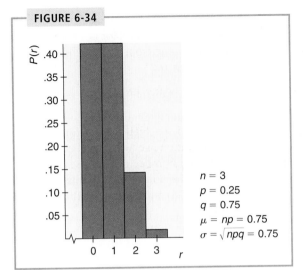

FIGURE 6-34

$n = 3$
$p = 0.25$
$q = 0.75$
$\mu = np = 0.75$
$\sigma = \sqrt{npq} = 0.75$

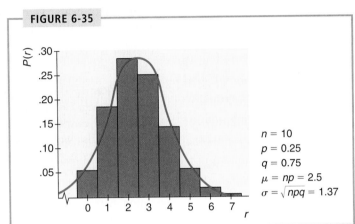

FIGURE 6-35

$n = 10$
$p = 0.25$
$q = 0.75$
$\mu = np = 2.5$
$\sigma = \sqrt{npq} = 1.37$

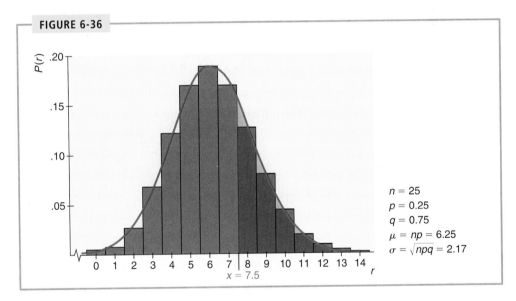

FIGURE 6-36

$x = 7.5$

$n = 25$
$p = 0.25$
$q = 0.75$
$\mu = np = 6.25$
$\sigma = \sqrt{npq} = 2.17$

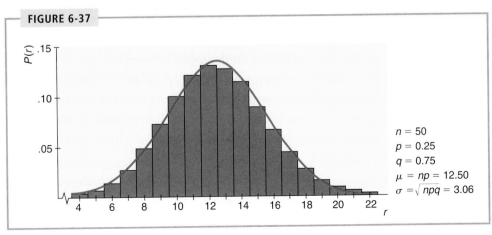

FIGURE 6-37

$n = 50$
$p = 0.25$
$q = 0.75$
$\mu = np = 12.50$
$\sigma = \sqrt{npq} = 3.06$

EXAMPLE 12

Normal approximation

The owner of a new apartment building must install 25 water heaters. From past experience in other apartment buildings, she knows that Quick Hot is a good brand. A Quick Hot heater is guaranteed for 5 years only, but from her past experience, she knows that the probability it will last 10 years is 0.25.

(a) What is the probability that 8 or more of the 25 water heaters will last at least 10 years?

SOLUTION: In this example, $n = 25$ and $p = 0.25$, so Figure 6-36 (on the preceding page) represents the probability distribution we will use. Let r be the binomial random variable corresponding to the number of successes out of $n = 25$ trials. We want to find $P(r \geq 8)$ by using the normal approximation. This probability is represented graphically (Figure 6-36) by the area of the bar over 8 and all bars to the right of the bar over 8.

Let x be a normal random variable corresponding to a normal distribution with $\mu = np = 25(0.25) = 6.25$ and $\sigma = \sqrt{npq} = \sqrt{25(0.25)0.75} \approx 2.17$. This normal curve is represented by the red line in Figure 6-36. The area under the normal curve from $x = 7.5$ to the right is approximately the same as the area of the bars from the bar over $r = 8$ to the right. It is important to notice that we start with $x = 7.5$ because the bar over $r = 8$ really starts at $x = 7.5$.

The area of the bars and the area under the corresponding red (normal) curve are approximately equal, so we conclude that $P(r \geq 8)$ is approximately equal to $P(x \geq 7.5)$.

When we convert $x = 7.5$ to standard units, we get

$$z = \frac{x - \mu}{\sigma} = \frac{7.5 - 6.25}{2.17} \qquad \text{(use } \mu = 6.25 \text{ and } \sigma = 2.17\text{)}$$

$$\approx 0.58$$

The probability we want is

$$P(x \geq 7.5) = P(z \geq 0.58) = 1 - P(z \leq 0.58) = 1 - 0.7190 = 0.2810$$

(b) How does this result compare with the result we can obtain by using the formula for the binomial probability distribution with $n = 25$ and $p = 0.25$?

SOLUTION: Using the binomial distribution function on the TI-84Plus/TI-83Plus model calculators, the authors computed that $P(r \geq 8) \approx 0.2735$. This means that the probability is approximately 0.27 that 8 or more water heaters will last at least 10 years.

(c) How do the results of parts (a) and (b) compare?

SOLUTION: The error of approximation is the difference between the approximate normal value (0.2810) and the binomial value (0.2735). The error is only $0.2810 - 0.2735 = 0.0075$, which is negligible for most practical purposes.

We knew in advance that the normal approximation to the binomial probability would be good, since $np = 25(0.25) = 6.25$ and $nq = 25(0.75) = 18.75$ are both greater than 5. These are the conditions that assure us that the normal approximation will be sufficiently close to the binomial probability for most practical purposes. ◊

Remember that when using the normal distribution to approximate the binomial, we are computing the areas under bars. The bar over the discrete variable r extends from $r - 0.5$ to $r + 0.5$. This means that the corresponding continuous normal variable x extends from $r - 0.5$ to $r + 0.5$. Adjusting the values of discrete random variables to obtain a corresponding range for a continuous random variable is called making a *continuity correction*.

Continuity correction: converting r values to x values

PROCEDURE

How to make the continuity correction

Convert the discrete random variable r (number of successes) to the continuous normal random variable x by doing the following:

1. If r is a **left-point** of an interval, subtract 0.5 to obtain the corresponding normal variable x; that is, $x = r - 0.5$.

2. If r is a **right-point** of an interval, add 0.5 to obtain the corresponding normal variable x: that is, $x = r + 0.5$.

For instance, $P(6 \leq r \leq 10)$, where r is a binomial random variable, is approximated by $P(5.5 \leq x \leq 10.5)$, where x is the corresponding normal random variable (see Figure 6-38).

◇ **COMMENT** Both the binomial and Poisson distributions are for *discrete* random variables. Therefore, adding or subtracting 0.5 to r was not necessary when we approximated the binomial distribution by the Poisson distribution (Section 5.4). However, the normal distribution is for a *continuous* random variable. In this case, adding or subtracting 0.5 to or from (as appropriate) r will improve the approximation of the normal to the binomial distribution.   ◇

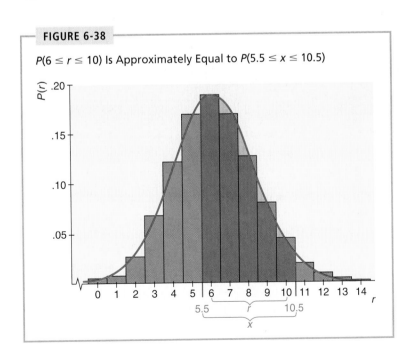

FIGURE 6-38

$P(6 \leq r \leq 10)$ Is Approximately Equal to $P(5.5 \leq x \leq 10.5)$

GUIDED EXERCISE 12

Continuity correction

From many years of observation, a biologist knows that the probability is only 0.65 that any given Arctic tern will survive the migration from its summer nesting area to its winter feeding grounds. A random sample of 500 Arctic terns were banded at their summer nesting area. Use the normal approximation to the binomial and the following steps to find the probability that between 310 and 340 of the banded Arctic terns will survive the migration. Let r be the number of surviving terns.

Arctic tern

(a) To approximate $P(310 \leq r \leq 340)$, we use the normal curve with $\mu = \underline{\hspace{1cm}}$ and $\sigma = \underline{\hspace{1cm}}$.

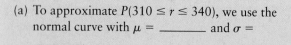 We use the normal curve with

$\mu = np = 500(0.65) = 325$ and
$\sigma = \sqrt{npq} = \sqrt{500(0.65)(0.35)} \approx 10.67$

(b) $P(310 \leq r \leq 340)$ is approximately equal to $P(\underline{\hspace{1cm}} \leq x \leq \underline{\hspace{1cm}})$, where x is a variable from the normal distribution described in part (a).

Since 310 is the left endpoint, we subtract 0.5, and since 340 is the right endpoint, we add 0.5. Consequently,

$P(310 \leq r \leq 340) \approx P(309.5 \leq x \leq 340.5)$

(c) Convert the condition $309.5 \leq x \leq 340.5$ to a condition in standard units.

Since $\mu = 325$ and $\sigma \approx 10.67$, the condition $309.5 \leq x \leq 340.5$ becomes

$$\frac{309.5 - 325}{10.67} \leq z \leq \frac{340.5 - 325}{10.67}$$

or

$-1.45 \leq z \leq 1.45$

(d) $P(310 \leq r \leq 340) = P(309.5 \leq x \leq 340.5)$
$\qquad\qquad\qquad\quad = P(-1.45 \leq z \leq 1.45)$
$\qquad\qquad\qquad\quad = \underline{\hspace{1cm}}$

$P(-1.45 \leq z \leq 1.45) = P(z \leq 1.45) - P(z \leq -1.45)$
$\qquad\qquad\qquad\qquad\quad = 0.9265 - 0.0735$
$\qquad\qquad\qquad\qquad\quad = 0.8530$

(e) Will the normal distribution make a good approximation to the binomial for this problem? Explain your answer.

Since

$np = 500(0.65) = 325$

and

$nq = 500(0.35) = 175$

are both greater than 5, the normal distribution will be a good approximation to the binomial.

VIEWPOINT   *Sunspots, Tree Rings, and Statistics*

Ancient Chinese astronomers recorded extreme sunspot activity with a peak around 1200 A.D. Mesa Verde tree rings in the period between 1276 and 1299 were unusually narrow, indicating a drought and/or a severe cold spell in the region at that time. A cooling trend could have narrowed the window of frost-free days below the approximately 80 days needed for cultivation of aboriginal corn and beans. Is this the reason the ancient Anasazi dwellings in Mesa Verde were abandoned? Is there a connection with the extreme sunspot activity? Much research and statistical work continues to be done on this topic.

Reference: *Prehistoric Astronomy in the Southwest,* by J. McKim Malville and C. Putnam, Department of Astronomy, University of Colorado.

SECTION 6.4   PROBLEMS

Note: When we say *between a* and *b,* we mean every value from *a* to *b, including a* and *b.* Due to rounding, your answers might vary slightly from answers given in the text.

1. *Health: Lead Contamination* More than a decade ago high levels of lead in the blood put 88% of children at risk. A concerted effort was made to remove lead from the environment. Now, according to the *Third National Health and Nutrition Examination Survey (NHANES III)* conducted by the Centers for Disease Control, only 9% of children in the United States are at risk of high blood-lead levels.
    (a) In a random sample of 200 children taken more than a decade ago, what is the probability that 50 or more had high blood-lead levels?
    (b) In a random sample of 200 children taken now, what is the probability that 50 or more have high blood-lead levels?

2. *Insurance: Claims* Do you try to *pad* an insurance claim to cover your deductible? About 40% of all U.S. adults will try to pad their insurance claims! (Source: *Are You Normal?,* by Bernice Kanner, St. Martin's Press.) Suppose that you are the director of an insurance adjustment office. Your office has just received 128 insurance claims to be processed in the next few days. What is the probability that
    (a) half or more of the claims have been padded?
    (b) fewer than 45 of the claims have been padded?
    (c) from 40 to 64 of the claims have been padded?
    (d) more than 80 of the claims are *not* padded?

3. *Law Enforcement: Arrests* In Colorado Springs, a local newspaper ran a full page of nearly 100 mug shots of people the police wanted to arrest for serious crimes. Within 1 week, the police received enough information to locate and arrest about 17% of these "wanted" people (reported in *Rocky Mountain News*). If next month the newspaper runs a full page of 125 mug shots of fugitives, what is the probability that the police will receive enough information to locate and arrest (within 1 week)
    (a) at least 15 fugitives?
    (b) 28 or more fugitives?

(c) between 15 and 28 fugitives?

(d) In the solution to this problem, what is n? p? q? Does it appear that both np and nq are larger than 5? Why is this an important consideration?

4. *Novels: Romance* USA Today reported that 11% of all books sold are of the romance genre. If a local bookstore sells 316 books on a given day, what is the probability that

(a) fewer than 40 are romances?

(b) at least 25 are romances?

(c) between 25 and 40 are romances?

(d) In the solution to this problem, what is n? p? q? Does it appear that both np and nq are larger than 5? Why is this an important consideration?

5. *Longevity: 90th Birthday* It is estimated that 3.5% of the general population will live past their 90th birthday (*Statistical Abstract of the United States*, 112th Edition). In a graduating class of 753 high school seniors, what is the probability that

(a) 15 or more will live beyond their 90th birthday?

(b) 30 or more will live beyond their 90th birthday?

(c) between 25 and 35 will live beyond their 90th birthday?

(d) more than 40 will live beyond their 90th birthday?

6. *Fishing: Billfish* Ocean fishing for billfish is very popular in the Cozumel region of Mexico. In *World Record Game Fishes* (published by the International Game Fish Association), it was stated that in the Cozumel region about 44% of strikes (while trolling) resulted in a catch. Suppose that on a given day a fleet of fishing boats got a total of 24 strikes. What is the probability that the number of fish caught was

(a) 12 or fewer?

(b) 5 or more?

(c) between 5 and 12?

(d) In the solution to this problem, what is n? p? q? Does it appear that both np and nq are larger than 5? Why is this an important consideration?

7. *Grocery Stores: New Products* The *Denver Post* stated that 80% of all new products introduced in grocery stores fail (are taken off the market) within 2 years. If a grocery store chain introduces 66 new products, what is the probability that within 2 years

(a) 47 or more fail?

(b) 58 or fewer fail?

(c) 15 or more succeed?

(d) fewer than 10 succeed?

8. *Crime: Murder* What are the chances that a person who is murdered actually knew the murderer? The answer to this question explains why a lot of police detective work begins with relatives and friends of the victim! About 64% of the people who are murdered actually knew the person who committed the murder (*Chances: Risk and Odds in Everyday Life*, by James Burke). Suppose that a detective file in New Orleans has 63 current unsolved murders. What is the probability that

(a) at least 35 of the victims knew their murderer?

(b) at most 48 of the victims knew their murderer?

(c) fewer than 30 victims did *not* know their murderer?

(d) more than 20 victims did *not* know their murderer?

9. *Private Investigation: Finding People* Old Friends Information Service is a California company that finds addresses for people who have lost track of each other. Old Friends claims to be 70% successful in reuniting people (*Wall Street Journal*). In December, Old Friends had 430 requests for addresses of lost acquaintances. What is the probability that the number of addresses found was

(a) more than 280?

(b) at least 320?

(c) between 280 and 320?

(d) In the solution to this problem, what is n? p? q? Does it appear that both np and nq are larger than 5? Why is this an important consideration?

10. *Archaeology: Pottery* Santa Fe black-on-white is a style of pottery that occurs in about 61% of the pot shards found in the Bandelier National Monument area (*Bandelier Archaeological Excavation Project: Summer 1990 Excavations at Burnt Mesa Pueblo*, edited by Kohler, Washington State University). At one excavation site 8641 pot shards have been found that have not yet been cleaned and identified. What is the probability that

(a) fewer than 5200 are Santa Fe black-on-white?

(b) more than 5400 are Santa Fe black-on-white?

(c) between 5200 and 5400 are Santa Fe black-on-white?

(d) In the solution to this problem, what is n? p? q? Does it appear that both np and nq are larger than 5? Why is this an important consideration?

11. *Lawyers: Bar Exam* Over the years, it has been observed that of all the lawyers who take the state bar exam, only 57% pass (information from the National Conference on Bar Examiners, referenced in *The Book of Odds*, by Shook and Shook, Signet). Suppose that this year 850 lawyers are going to take the Ohio bar exam. What is the probability that

(a) 540 or more pass?

(b) 500 or fewer pass?

(c) between 485 and 525 pass?

12. *Coupons: Redemption* More than 200 billion grocery coupons are distributed each year for discounts exceeding $84 billion. However, according to a report in *USA Today*, only 3.2% of the coupons are redeemed. If a company distributes 5000 coupons, what is the probability that

(a) more than 100 are redeemed?

(b) fewer than 200 are redeemed?

(c) between 100 and 200 are redeemed?

13. *Supermarkets: Free Samples* Do you take the free samples offered in supermarkets? About 60% of all customers will take free samples. Furthermore, of those who take the free samples, about 37% will buy what they have sampled. (See reference in Problem 2.) Suppose that you set up a counter in a supermarket offering free samples of a new product. The day you were offering free samples, 317 customers passed by your counter.

(a) What is the probability that more than 180 will take your free sample?

(b) What is the probability that fewer than 200 will take your free sample?

(c) What is the probability that a customer will take a free sample *and* buy the product? *Hint:* Use the multiplication rule for *dependent* events. Notice that we are given the conditional probability P(buy, *given* sample) = 0.37, while P(sample) = 0.60.

(d) What is the probability that between 60 and 80 customers will take the free sample *and* buy the product? *Hint:* Use the probability of success calculated in part (c).

14. *Ice Cream: Flavors* What's your favorite ice cream? For people who buy ice cream, the all-time favorite is still vanilla. About 25% of ice cream sales are vanilla. Chocolate accounts for only 9% of ice cream sales. (See reference in Problem 2.) Suppose

that 175 customers go to a grocery store in Cheyenne, Wyoming, today to buy ice cream.
(a) What is the probability that 50 or more will buy vanilla?
(b) What is the probability that 12 or more will buy chocolate?
(c) A customer who buys ice cream is not limited to one container or one flavor. What is the probability that someone who is buying ice cream will buy chocolate or vanilla? *Hint:* Chocolate flavor and vanilla flavor are not mutually exclusive events. Assume that the choice to buy one flavor is independent of the choice to buy another flavor. Then use the multiplication rule for independent events together with the addition rule for events that are not mutually exclusive to compute the requested probability. (See Section 4.2.)
(d) What is the probability that between 50 and 60 customers buy chocolate or vanilla ice cream? *Hint:* Use the probability of success computed in part (c).

15. *Airline Flights: No-Shows* Based on long experience, an airline found that about 6% of the people making reservations on a flight from Miami to Denver do not show up for the flight. Suppose the airline overbooks this flight by selling 267 ticket reservations for an airplane with only 255 seats.
(a) What is the probability that a person holding a reservation will show up for the flight?
(b) Let $n = 267$ represent the number of ticket reservations. Let r represent the number of people with reservations who show up for the flight. Which expression represents the probability that a seat will be available for everyone who shows up holding a reservation:

$$P(255 \leq r); \qquad P(r \leq 255); \qquad P(r \leq 267); \qquad P(r = 255)$$

(c) Use the normal approximation to the binomial distribution and part (b) to answer the question: What is the probability that a seat will be available for every person who shows up holding a reservation?

16. *General: Approximations* We have studied *two* approximations to the binomial, the normal approximation and the Poisson approximation (Section 5.4). Write a brief but complete essay in which you discuss and summarize the *conditions* under which each approximation would be used, the *formulas* involved, and the *assumptions* made for each approximation. Give details and examples in your essay. How could you apply these statistical methods in your own everyday life?

SUMMARY

In this chapter, we have examined graphs of normal distributions, control charts, standard units, z scores, and areas under the standard normal curve.

It is important to remember that a normal distribution with mean μ and standard deviation σ can be transformed into the standard normal distribution with mean 0 and standard deviation 1 by the formula

$$z = \frac{x - \mu}{\sigma}$$

Values of z and Table 5 of Appendix II can be used to obtain the area under the standard normal curve to the left of z. Areas under the normal curve represent probabilities that a z value will fall into the interval over which the area lies.

Given a probability associated with an interval on the standard normal curve, we can use Table 5 of Appendix II to obtain the associated z values. When x follows a normal distribution, we can find the x values associated with a given probability by (1) finding the corresponding z values, and (2) converting to x values by using the formula

$$x = z\sigma + \mu$$

In the last section, we saw that we can use the normal distribution to approximate the binomial distribution if $np > 5$ and $nq > 5$, where n is the number of trials, p is the probability of success on a single trial, and $q = 1 - p$.

IMPORTANT WORDS & SYMBOLS

Section 6.1
Normal distributions
Normal curves
Upward cup and downward cup on normal curves
Symmetry of normal curves
Empirical rule
Control chart
Out-of-control signals

Section 6.2
z value or z score
Standard units

Standard normal distribution ($\mu = 0$ and $\sigma = 1$)
Raw score, x
Area under the standard normal curve

Section 6.3
Areas under any normal curve

Section 6.4
Normal approximation to the binomial distribution
Continuity correction

VIEWPOINT

Nenana Ice Classic

The Nenana Ice Classic is a betting pool offering a large cash prize to the lucky winner who can guess the time, to the nearest minute, of the ice breakup on the Tanana River in the town of Nenana, Alaska. Official breakup time is defined as the time when the surging river dislodges a tripod on the ice. This breaks an attached line and stops a clock set to Yukon Standard Time. The event is so popular that the first state legislature of Alaska (1959) made the Nenana Ice Classic an official statewide lottery. Since 1918, the earliest breakup was April 20, 1940, at 3:27 P.M., and the latest recorded breakup was May 20, 1964, at 11:41 A.M. Want to make a statistical guess predicting when the ice will break up? Breakup times from 1918 to 1996 are recorded in *The Alaska Almanac,* published by Alaska Northwest Books, Anchorage.

CHAPTER REVIEW PROBLEMS

1. Given that z is the standard normal variable (with mean 0 and standard deviation 1), find
   (a) $P(0 \le z \le 1.75)$ (b) $P(-1.29 \le z \le 0)$
   (c) $P(1.03 \le z \le 1.21)$ (d) $P(z \ge 2.31)$
   (e) $P(z \le -1.96)$ (f) $P(z \le 1.00)$

2. Given that z is the standard normal variable (with mean 0 and standard deviation 1), find
   (a) $P(0 \le z \le 0.75)$ (b) $P(-1.50 \le z \le 0)$
   (c) $P(-2.67 \le z \le -1.74)$ (d) $P(z \ge 1.56)$
   (e) $P(z \le -0.97)$ (f) $P(z \le 2.01)$

3. Given that x is a normal variable with mean $\mu = 47$ and standard deviation $\sigma = 6.2$, find
   (a) $P(x \le 60)$ (b) $P(x \ge 50)$ (c) $P(50 \le x \le 60)$

4. Given that x is a normal variable with mean $\mu = 110$ and standard deviation $\sigma = 12$, find
   (a) $P(x \le 120)$ (b) $P(x \ge 80)$ (c) $P(108 \le x \le 117)$

5. Find z such that 5% of the area under the standard normal curve lies to the right of z.

6. Find z such that 1% of the area under the standard normal curve lies to the left of z.

7. Find z such that 95% of the area under the standard normal curve lies between $-z$ and z.

8. Find z such that 99% of the area under the standard normal curve lies between $-z$ and z.

9. *Nursing: Exams* On a practical nursing licensing exam, the mean score is 79 and the standard deviation is 9 points.
   (a) What is the standardized score of a student with a raw score of 87?
   (b) What is the standardized score of a student with a raw score of 79?
   (c) Assuming the scores follow a normal distribution, what is the probability that a score selected at random is above 85?

10. *Aptitude Tests: Mechanical* On an auto mechanic aptitude test, the mean score is 270 points and the standard deviation is 35 points.
   (a) If a student has a standardized score of 1.9, how many points is that?
   (b) If a student has a standardized score of -0.25, how many points is that?
   (c) Assuming the scores follow a normal distribution, what is the probability that a student will get between 200 and 340 points?

11. *Recycling: Aluminum Cans* One environmental group did a study of recycling habits in a California community. It found that 70% of the aluminum cans sold in the area were recycled.
   (a) If 400 cans are sold today, what is the probability that 300 or more will be recycled?
   (b) Of the 400 cans sold, what is the probability that between 260 and 300 will be recycled?

12. *Guarantee: Disc Players* Future Electronics makes compact disc players. Its research department found that the life of the laser beam device is normally distributed, with mean 5000 hours and standard deviation 450 hours.
   (a) Find the probability that the laser beam device will wear out in 5000 hours or less.

(b) *Inverse Normal Distribution* Future Electronics wants to place a guarantee on the players so that no more than 5% fail during the guarantee period. Because the laser pickup is the part most likely to wear out first, the guarantee period will be based on the life of the laser beam device. How many playing hours should the guarantee cover? (Round to the next playing hour.)

13. *Guarantee: Package Delivery* Express Courier Service has found that the delivery time for packages is normally distributed, with mean 14 hours and standard deviation 2 hours.
    (a) For a package selected at random, what is the probability that it will be delivered in 18 hours or less?
    (b) *Inverse Normal Distribution* What should be the guaranteed delivery time on all packages in order to be 95% sure that the package will be delivered before this time? (*Hint:* Note that 5% of the packages will be delivered at a time beyond the guaranteed time period.)

14. *Control Chart: Landing Gear* Hydraulic pressure in the main cylinder of the landing gear of a commercial jet is very important for a safe landing. If the pressure is not high enough, the landing gear may not lower properly. If it is too high, the connectors in the hydraulic line may spring a leak.

    In-flight landing tests show that the actual pressure in the main cylinders is a variable with mean 819 pounds per square inch and standard deviation 23 pounds per square inch. Assume that these values for the mean and standard deviation are considered safe values by engineers.
    (a) For nine consecutive test landings, the pressure in the main cylinder is recorded as follows:

Landing number	1	2	3	4	5	6	7	8	9
Pressure	870	855	830	815	847	836	825	810	792

    Make a control chart for the pressure in the main cylinder of the hydraulic landing gear, and plot the data on the control chart. Looking at the control chart, would you say the pressure is "in control" or "out of control"? Explain your answer. Identify any out-of-control signals by type (I, II, or III).
    (b) For 10 consecutive test landings, the pressure was recorded on another plane as follows:

Landing number	1	2	3	4	5	6	7	8	9	10
Pressure	865	850	841	820	815	789	801	765	730	725

    Make a control chart and plot the data on the chart. Would you say the pressure is "in control" or not? Explain your answer. Identify any out-of-control signals by type (I, II, or III).

15. *Electronic Scanners: Errors* Instead of hearing the jingle of prices being rung up manually on cash registers, we now hear the beep of prices being scanned by electronic scanners. How accurate is price scanning? There are errors, and according to a *Denver Post* article, when the error occurs in the store's favor, it is larger than when it occurs in the customer's favor. An investigation of large discount stores by the Colorado state inspectors showed that the average error in the store's favor was $2.66. Assume that the distribution of scanner errors is more or less mound-shaped. If the standard deviation of scanner errors (in the store's favor) is $0.85, use the empirical rule to
    (a) estimate a range of scanner errors centered about the mean in which 68% of the errors will lie.

(b) estimate a range of scanner errors centered about the mean in which 95% of the errors will lie.

(c) estimate a range of scanner errors centered about the mean in which almost all the errors will lie.

16. *Customer Complaints: Time* The Customer Service Center in a large New York department store has determined that the amount of time spent with a customer about a complaint is normally distributed, with a mean of 9.3 minutes and a standard deviation of 2.5 minutes. What is the probability that for a randomly chosen customer with a complaint the amount of time spent resolving the complaint will be

(a) less than 10 minutes?

(b) longer than 5 minutes?

(c) between 8 and 15 minutes?

17. *Medical: Flight for Life* The Flight for Life emergency helicopter service is available for medical emergencies occurring from 15 to 90 miles from the hospital. Emergencies that occur closer to the hospital can be handled effectively by ambulance service. A long-term study of the service shows that the response time from receipt of the dispatch call to arrival at the scene of the emergency is normally distributed, with a mean of 42 minutes and a standard deviation of 8 minutes. For a randomly received call, what is the probability that the response time will be

(a) between 30 and 45 minutes?

(b) less than 30 minutes?

(c) longer than 60 minutes?

18. *Unlisted Phones: Sacramento* How easy is it to get into contact with a person in Sacramento, California? If you don't know the telephone number, it could be difficult. The data from Survey Sampling of Fairfield, Connecticut, reported in *American Demographics,* show that 68% of the telephone-owning households in Sacramento have unlisted numbers. For a random sample of 150 Sacramento households with telephones, what is the probability that

(a) 100 or more have unlisted numbers?

(b) fewer than 100 have unlisted numbers?

(c) between 50 and 65 (including 50 and 65) households have *listed* numbers?

19. *Medical: Blood Type* Blood type AB is found in only 3% of the population (*Textbook of Medical Physiology,* by A. Guyton, M.D.). If 250 people are chosen at random, what is the probability that

(a) 5 or more will have this blood type?

(b) between 5 and 10 will have this blood type?

DATA HIGHLIGHTS: GROUP PROJECTS

Break into small groups and discuss the following topics. Organize a brief outline in which you summarize the main points of your group discussion.

1. Examine Figure 6-39. Government documents and the Census Bureau show that the age at first marriage for U.S. citizens is approximately normally distributed for both men and women. For men, the average age is about 27 years, and for women, the average is about 24 years. For both sexes, the standard deviation is about 2.5 years.

(a) If the distribution is symmetrical and mound-shaped (such as the normal distribution), why would you expect the median, mean, and mode to be equal?

(b) Consider the age at first marriage in 1995. What is the probability that a man selected at random was over age 30 at the time of his first marriage? What is the probability that he was under age 20? What is the probability that he was between 20 and 30?

(c) Consider the age at first marriage in 1995. What is the probability that a woman selected at random was over age 28 at the time of her first marriage? What is the probability that she was under age 18? What is the probability that she was between 18 and 28?

(d) At what age were only 10% of eligible men (who had never been married before) left? At what age were only 5% left?

(e) At what age were only 10% of eligible women (who had never been married before) left? At what age were only 5% left?

(f) The Census Bureau tracks data about marriages and age at first marriage. The *Statistical Abstract of the United States* is published each year and contains tables giving this information. For more information, visit the Brase/Brase statistics site at **http://math.college.hmco.com/students** and find the link to the Census Bureau. Look for marriage under the subject index, and follow the links to the table. Using either the Abstract or the Census Bureau web site, find the most recent information about median age at first marriage. Although the median age changes from year to year, the standard deviation usually does not change much. Under the assumption that the age at first marriage follows a distribution that is approximately normal, the mean age at first marriage equals the median age. Using a standard deviation of about 2.5 years, repeat parts (b) through (e) for the most recent year for which median age at first marriage is available.

2. Examine Figure 6-40, "Time Shopping."

(a) Notice that 52% of the people who go to a shopping center spend less than 1 hour. However, the figure also states that people spend an average of 69 minutes on each visit to a shopping center. How could *both* these claims be correct? Write a brief, complete essay in which you discuss mean, median, and

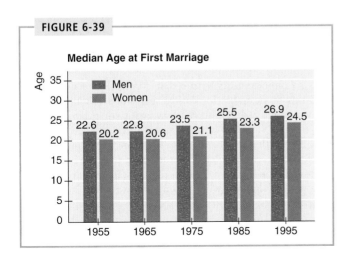

FIGURE 6-39
Median Age at First Marriage

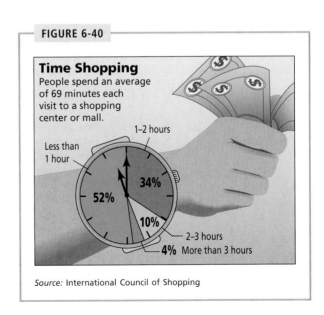

FIGURE 6-40

Time Shopping
People spend an average of 69 minutes each visit to a shopping center or mall.

Source: International Council of Shopping

mode in the context of symmetrical distribution. Also discuss mean, median, and mode for distributions that are skewed left, skewed right, or general distributions. Then answer the question: How could 52% of the people spend less than 1 hour in the shopping center while the average (we don't know which average was used) time spent was 69 minutes?

(b) Ala Moana Shopping Center in Honolulu is sometimes advertised as the largest shopping center for 2500 miles and the best shopping center in the middle of the Pacific Ocean. There are many interesting Hawaiian, Asian, and other ethnic shops in Ala Moana, so this center is a favorite of tourists. Suppose that a tour group of 75 people has just arrived at the shopping center. The International Council of Shopping Centers indicates that 86% (52% plus 34%) of the people will spend less than 2 hours in a shopping center. Let us assume this statement applies to our tour group.

(i) For the tour group of 75 people, what is the expected number who finish shopping on or before 2 hours? What is the standard deviation?

(ii) For the tour group of 75 people, what is the probability that 55 or more will finish shopping in 2 hours or less?

(iii) For the tour group, what is the probability that 70 or more will finish shopping in 2 hours or less?

(iv) What is the probability that between 50 and 70 (including 50 and 70) people in the tour group will finish shopping in 2 hours or less?

(v) If you are a tour director, how could you use this information to plan an appropriate length of time for the stop at Ala Moana shopping center? You do not want to frustrate your group by allowing too little time for shopping, but you also do not want to spend too much time at the center.

LINKING CONCEPTS: WRITING PROJECTS

Discuss each of the following topics in class or review the topics on your own. Then write a brief but complete essay in which you summarize the main points. Please include formulas and graphs as appropriate.

1. If you look up the word *normal* in a dictionary, you will find that it is synonymous with the words *standard* or *usual*. Consider the very wide and general applications of the normal probability distribution. Comment on why good synonyms for *normal probability distribution* might be *standard probability distribution* or *usual probability distribution*. List at least three random variables from everyday life for which you think the normal probability distribution could be applicable.

2. Why are standard z values so important? Is it true that z values have no units of measurement? Why would this be desirable for comparing data sets with *different* units of measurement? How can we assess differences in quality or performance by simply comparing z values under a standard normal curve? Examine the formula to compute standard z values. Notice that it involves *both* the mean and standard deviation. Recall that in Chapter 2 we commented that the mean of a data collection is not entirely adequate to describe the data; you need the standard deviation as well. Discuss this topic again in the light of what you now know about normal distributions and standard z values.

3. If you look up the word *empirical* in a dictionary, you will find that it means relying on experiment and observation rather than on theory. Discuss the empirical rule in this context. The empirical rule certainly applies to the normal distribution, but does it also apply to a wide variety of other distributions that are not *exactly* (theoretically) normal? Discuss the terms *mound-shaped* and *symmetrical*. Draw several sketches of distributions that are mound-shaped *and* symmetrical. Draw sketches of distributions that are not mound-shaped or not symmetrical. To which distributions will the empirical rule apply?

4. Most companies that manufacture a product have a division of quality control or quality assurance. The purpose of the quality-control division is to make reasonably certain that the products manufactured are up to company standards. Write a brief essay in which you describe how the statistics you have learned so far could be applied to an industrial application (such as control charts and the Antlers Lodge example).

Using Technology

APPLICATION 1

How much money do people earn in a month? One way to answer this question is to look at government employees. The average earnings of a city government employee for the month of March are given for a sample of 40 large cities in the United States (*Statistical Abstract of the United States*, 120th Edition).

(a) To compare the earnings from one city to another, we will look at z values for each city. Use the sample mean and sample standard deviation to compute the z values. You may do this "by hand" using a calculator, or you may use a computer software package.

(b) Look at the z values for each salary. Which are above average? Which are below average?

(c) Which salaries are within one standard deviation of the mean?

City	Average Earnings ($) for March	City	Average Earnings ($) for March
Albuquerque	2494	Memphis	2973
Anchorage	3571	Miami	3654
Arlington	3069	Milwaukee	3636
Atlanta	2494	Mobile	3756
Baltimore	3229	New York	3694
Birmingham	3961	Newark	2507
Boston	3526	Norfolk	2577
Cincinnati	3399	Oakland	5084
Cleveland	2899	Philadelphia	3511
Dallas	3326	Phoenix	3909
Denver	3324	Portland	2899
Detroit	3301	Raleigh	3026
Honolulu	3479	San Antonio	2427
Houston	2813	San Diego	4072
Indianapolis	2756	San Francisco	4487
Kansas City	3023	San Jose	5227
Lincoln	2882	Seattle	4462
Las Vegas	4512	St. Louis	3033
Los Angeles	4534	Washington, D.C.	3725
Louisville	2674	Wichita	2928

Technology Hints: Standardizing Raw Scores

TI-84Plus/TI-83Plus

On the TI-84Plus and TI-83Plus calculators, enter the salary data in list L_1. Then use ➤ STAT ➤ CALC ➤ 1-Var Stats to compute the sample mean $\bar{x}$ and the standard deviation s. Then go back to ➤ STAT ➤ EDIT. Arrow up to the header label L_2. At the L_2 = prompt, type in $(x - \bar{x})/s$ and press Enter. You will find the $\bar{x}$ and s symbols under the ➤ VARS ➤ Statistics ... keys. The z values will then appear in list L_2.

Excel

In Excel, you need to compute the sample mean $\bar{x}$ and standard deviation s ahead of time. To do so, enter the salary data in column A. To compute $\bar{x}$, use the menu choices ➤ Paste function $\boxed{f_x}$ ➤ Statistical ➤ AVERAGE. To compute s, use the menu choices ➤ Paste function $\boxed{f_x}$ ➤ Statistical ➤ STDEV. Finally, to generate the z values, use the menu choices ➤ Paste function $\boxed{f_x}$ ➤ Statistical ➤ STANDARDIZED. Remember to highlight the cell in which you want each value to appear before you use the commands.

Minitab

In Minitab, enter the salaries in column C1. To generate z values and store the results in column C2, use the following menu choices: ➤ Calc ➤ Standardize. In the dialogue box, select C1 for the input column and C2 for the output column. Then choose the option "subtract mean and divide by standard deviation." Minitab will compute the sample mean $\bar{x}$ and standard deviation s for the salaries and then compute z using the formula $z = (x - \bar{x})/s$.

SPSS

Enter your data in one column. Use the menu choices Analyze ➤ Descriptive Statistics ➤ Descriptives. In the dialogue box, move the variable containing data into the variables box. Check the option "Save standardized values as variables." Standardized values will appear in a column of the data editor.

APPLICATION 2

How can we determine if data originated from a normal distribution? We can look at a stem-and-leaf plot or histogram of the data to check for general symmetry, skewness, clusters of data, or outliers. However, a more sensitive way to check that a distribution is normal is to look at a special graph called a *normal quantile plot* (or a variation of this plot called a *normal probability plot* in some software packages). It really is not feasible to make a normal quantile plot by hand, but statistical software packages provide such plots. A simple version of the basic idea behind normal quantile plots involves the following process:

(a) Arrange the observed data values in order from smallest to largest, and determine the percentile occupied by each value. For instance, if there are 20 data values, the smallest datum is at the 5% point, the next smallest is at the 10% point, and so on.

(b) Find the z values that correspond to the percentile points. For instance, the z value that corresponds to the percentile 5% (i.e., % in the left tail of the distribution) is $z = -1.645$.

(c) Plot each data value x against the corresponding percentile z score. If the data are close to a normal distribution, the plotted points will lie close to a straight line. (If the data are close to a standard normal distribution, the points will lie close to the line $x = z$.)

The actual process that statistical software packages use to produce the z scores for the data is more complicated.

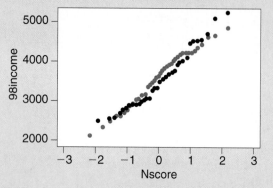

Interpreting normal quantile plots

If the points of a normal quantile plot lie close to a straight line, the plot indicates that the data follow a normal distribution. Systematic deviations from a straight line or bulges in the plot indicate that the data distribution is not normal. Individual points off the line may be outliers.

Consider Figure 6-41. This figure shows Minitab-generated quantile plots for two data sets. The black dots show the normal quantile plot for the salary data of the first application. The red dots show the normal quantile plot for a random sample of 42 data values drawn from a theoretical normal distribution with the same mean and standard deviation as the salary data ($\mu \approx 3421$, $\sigma \approx 709$).

(a) Do the black dots lie close to a straight line? Do the salaries appear to follow a normal distribution?

FIGURE 6-41 Normal Quantile Plots

- Salary data for (city) government employees
- A random sample of 42 values from a theoretical normal distribution with the same mean and standard deviation as the salary data.

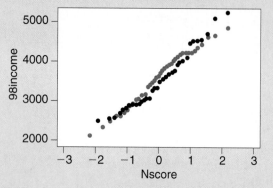

Are there any outliers on the low or high side? Would you say that any of the salaries are "out of line" for a normal distribution?

(b) Do the red dots lie close to a straight line? We know the red dots represent a sample drawn from a normal distribution. Is the normal quantile plot for the red dots consistent with this fact? Are there any outliers shown?

Technology Hints

TI-84Plus/TI-83Plus

Enter the data. Press **STATPLOT** and select one of the plots. Highlight **ON**. Then highlight the sixth plot option. To get a plot similar to that of Figure 6-41, choose Y as the data axis.

Minitab

Minitab has several types of normal quantile plots that use different types of scales. To create a normal quantile plot similar to that of Figure 6-41, enter the data in column C1. Then use the menu choices **Calc ➤ Calculator**. In the dialogue box listing the functions, scroll to **Normal Scores**. Use **NSCOR(C1)** and store the results in column C2. Finally, use the menu choices **Graph ➤ Plot**. In the dialogue box, use C1 for variable "y" and C2 for variable "x."

SPSS

Enter the data. Use the menu choices **Analyze ➤ Descriptive Statistics ➤ Explore**. In the dialogue box, move your data variable to the dependent list. Check **Plots...** . Check "Normality plots with tests." The graph appears in the output window.

Cumulative Review Problems

CHAPTERS 4–6

The Hill of Tara is located in south central Meath, not far from Dublin, Ireland. Tara is of great cultural and archaeological importance, since it is by legend the seat of the ancient high kings of Ireland. For more information, see *Tara: An Archaeological Survey*, by Conor Newman, Royal Irish Academy, Dublin.

Magnetic surveying is one technique used by archaeologists to determine anomalies arising from variations in magnetic susceptibility. Unusual changes in magnetic susceptibility might (or might not) indicate an important archaeological discovery. Let x be a random variable that represents a magnetic susceptibility (MS) reading for a randomly chosen site on the Hill of Tara. A random sample of 120 sites gave the readings shown in Table A below.

Table A   Magnetic Susceptibility Readings, centimeter-gram-second $\times$ 10^{-6} (cmg $\times$ 10^{-6})

Comment	Magnetic Susceptibility	Number of Readings	Estimated Probability
"cool"	$0 \leq x < 10$	30	$30/120 = 0.25$
"neutral"	$10 \leq x < 20$	54	$54/120 = 0.45$
"warm"	$20 \leq x < 30$	18	$18/120 = 0.15$
"very interesting"	$30 \leq x < 40$	12	$12/120 = 0.10$
"hot spot"	$40 \leq x$	6	$6/120 = 0.05$

1. *Sample Space* What is a statistical experiment? How could the magnetic susceptibility intervals $0 \leq x < 10$, $10 \leq x < 20$, and so on be considered events in the sample space of all possible readings?

2. *Estimated Probability* What is probability? What do we mean by relative frequency as a probability estimate for events? What is the law of large numbers? How would the law of large numbers apply in this context?

3. *Probability Distribution* Do the probabilities shown in Table A add up to 1? Why should they total to 1?

4. *Probability Rules* For a site chosen at random, estimate the following probabilities.
   (a) $P(0 \leq x < 30)$ (b) $P(10 \leq x < 40)$ (c) $P(x < 20)$
   (d) $P(x \geq 20)$ (e) $P(30 \leq x)$ (f) $P(x$ *not* less than 10$)$
   (g) $P(0 \leq x < 10$ or $40 \leq x)$ (h) $P(40 \leq x$ and $20 \leq x)$

5. *Conditional Probability* Suppose you are working in a "warm" region where all MS readings are 20 or higher. In this same region, what is the probability that you will find a "hot spot" where the readings are 40 or higher? Use conditional probability to estimate $P(40 \leq x$, *given* $20 \leq x)$. *Hint:* See Problem 39 of Section 6.3.

355

6. *Discrete Probability Distribution* Consider the midpoint of each interval. Assign the value 45 as the midpoint for the interval $40 \leq x$. The midpoints constitute the sample space for a discrete random variable. Using Table A, compute the expected value μ and the standard deviation σ.

Midpoint x	5	15	25	35	45
$P(x)$					

7. *Binomial Distribution* Suppose a reading between 30 and 40 is called "very interesting" from an archaeological point of view. Let us say you take readings at $n = 12$ sites chosen at random. Let r be a binomial random variable that represents the number of "very interesting" readings from these 12 sites.
   (a) Let us call "very interesting" a binomial success. Use Table A to find p, the probability of success on a single trial, where $p = P(\text{success}) = P(30 \leq x < 40)$.
   (b) What is the expected value μ and standard deviation σ for the random variable r?
   (c) What is the probability that you will find *at least* one "very interesting" reading in the 12 sites?
   (d) What is the probability that you will find *fewer than* three "very interesting" readings in the 12 sites?

8. *Geometric Distribution* Suppose a "hot spot" is a site with a reading of 40 or higher.
   (a) In a binomial setting, let us call success a "hot spot." Use Table A to find $p = P(\text{success}) = P(40 \leq x)$ for a single trial.
   (b) Suppose you decide to take readings at random until you get your *first* "hot spot." Let n be a random variable representing the trial on which you get your first "hot spot." Use the geometric probability distribution to write out a formula for $P(n)$.
   (c) What is the probability that you will need more than four readings to find the first "hot spot"? Compute $P(n > 4)$.

9. *Poisson Approximation to the Binomial* Suppose an archaeologist is looking for geomagnetic "hot spots" in an unexplored region of Tara. As in Problem 8, we have a binomial setting where success is a "hot spot." In this case, the probability of success is $p = P(40 \leq x)$. The archaeologist takes $n = 100$ magnetic susceptibility readings in the new, unexplored area. Let r be a binomial random variable representing the number of "hot spots" in the 100 readings.
   (a) We want to approximate the binomial random variable r by a Poisson distribution. Is this appropriate? What requirements must be satisfied before we can do this? Do you think these requirements are satisfied in this case? Explain. What is the value of λ?
   (b) What is the probability that the archaeologists will find six or fewer "hot spots"? *Hint:* Use Table 4 of Appendix II.
   (c) What is the probability that the archaeologists will find more than eight "hot spots"?

10. *Normal Approximation to the Binomial* Consider a binomial setting in which "neutral" is defined to be a success. So $p = P(\text{success}) = P(10 \leq x < 20)$. Suppose $n = 65$ geomagnetic readings are taken. Let r be a binomial random variable that represents the number of "neutral" geomagnetic readings.
   (a) We want to approximate the binomial random variable r by a normal variable x. Is this appropriate? What requirements must be satisfied before we can do this? Do you think these requirements are satisfied in this case? Explain.
   (b) What is the probability that there will be at least 20 "neutral" readings out of these 65 trials?
   (c) Why would the Poisson approximation to the binomial *not* be appropriate in this case? Explain.

11. *Normal Distribution Oxygen demand* is a term biologists use to describe the oxygen needed by fish and other aquatic organisms for survival. The Environmental Protection Agency conducted a study of a wetland area in Marin County, California. In this wetland environment, the mean oxygen demand was $\mu = 9.9$ mg/L with 95% of the data ranging from 6.5 mg/L to 13.3 mg/L (Reference: EPA Report 832-R-93-005). Let x be a random variable that represents oxygen demand in this wetland environment. Assume x has a probability distribution that is approximately normal.
   (a) Use the 95% data range to estimate the standard deviation for oxygen demand. *Hint:* See Problem 31 of Section 6.3.
   (b) An oxygen demand below 8 indicates that some organisms in the wetland environment may be dying. What is the probability that the oxygen demand will fall below 8 mg/L?
   (c) A high oxygen demand can also indicate trouble. An oxygen demand above 12 may indicate an overabundance of organisms that endanger some types of plant life. What is the probability that the oxygen demand will exceed 12 mg/L?

12. *Summary* Write a brief but complete essay in which you describe the probability distributions you have studied so far. Which apply to discrete random variables? Which apply to continuous random variables? Under what conditions can the binomial distribution be approximated by the normal? by the Poisson?

7

Introduction to Sampling Distributions

No one wants to learn by mistakes, but we cannot learn enough from success to go beyond the state of the art. . . . Such is the nature not only of science and engineering, but of all human endeavors.

—Henry Petroski

Experience isn't what happens to you. It's what you make out of what happens to you.

—Aldous Huxley

**Aldous Huxley
(1894–1963)**
This British novelist and critic wrote about the theme of the human being confronted by the modern world.

Henry Petroski is a professor of engineering at Duke University, and Aldous Huxley was a well-known modern writer. Both quotes imply that experience, mistakes, information, and life itself are closely related. Life and uncertainty appear to be inseparable. Only those who are no longer living can escape chance happenings. Mistakes are bound to occur. However, not all mistakes are bad. The discovery of penicillin was a "mistake" when mold (penicillin) was accidentally introduced into a bacterial culture by Alexander Fleming in 1928.

Most of the really important decisions in life will involve incomplete information. In one lifetime, we simply cannot experience *everything*. Nor should we even want to! This is one reason why *experience by way of sampling* is so important. Statistics can help you have the experiences and yet maintain some control over mistakes. Remember, it is what you make out of experience (sample data) that is of real value.

In this chapter, we will study how information from samples relates to information about populations. We cannot be certain that the information from a sample reflects corresponding information about the entire population, but we can describe likely differences. Study this chapter and the following material carefully. We believe that your effort will be rewarded by helping you appreciate the joy and wonder of living in an uncertain universe.

 For on-line student resources, visit **math.college.hmco.com/students** and follow the Statistics links to the Brase/Brase, *Understandable Statistics*, 8th edition web site.

PREVIEW QUESTIONS

◇ As humans, our experiences are finite and limited. Consequently, most of the important decisions in our lives are based on sample (incomplete) information. What is a probability sampling distribution? How will sampling distributions help us make good decisions based on incomplete information? (SECTION 7.1)

◇ There is an old saying: All roads lead to Rome. In statistics, we could recast this saying: All probability distributions average out to be normal distributions (as the sample size increases). How can we take advantage of this in our study of sampling distributions? (SECTION 7.2)

◇ Many issues in life come down to success or failure. In most cases, we will not be successful all the time, so proportions of successes are very important. What is the probability sampling distribution for proportions? (SECTION 7.3)

FOCUS PROBLEM

Impulse Buying

The Food Marketing Institute, Progressive Grocer, New Products News, and Point of Purchaser Advertising Institute are organizations that analyze supermarket sales. One of the interesting discoveries was that the average amount of impulse buying in a grocery store was very time-dependent. As reported in the *Denver Post*, "when you dilly dally in a store for 10 unplanned minutes, you can kiss nearly $20 goodbye." For this reason, it is in the best interest of the supermarket to keep you in the store longer. In the *Post* article, it was pointed out that long check-out lines (near end-aisle displays), "samplefest" events of tasting free samples, video kiosks, magazine and book sections, and so on help keep customers in the store longer. On average, a single customer who strays from his or her grocery list can plan on impulse spending of $20 for every 10 minutes spent wandering about in the supermarket.

Let x represent the dollar amount spent on supermarket impulse buying in a 10-minute (unplanned) shopping interval. Based on the *Post* article, the mean of the x distribution is about $20 and the (estimated) standard deviation is about $7.

(a) Consider a random sample of $n = 100$ customers, each of whom has 10 minutes of unplanned shopping time in a supermarket. From the central limit theorem, what can you say about the probability distribution of $\bar{x}$, the *average* amount spent by these customers due to impulse buying? Is the $\bar{x}$ distribution approximately normal? What are the mean and standard deviation of the $\bar{x}$ distribution? Is it necessary to make any assumption about the x distribution? Explain.

(b) What is the probability that $\bar{x}$ is between $18 and $22?

(c) Let us assume that x has a distribution that is approximately normal. What is the probability that x is between $18 and $22?

(d) In part (b), we used $\bar{x}$, the *average* amount spent, computed for 100 customers. In part (c), we used x, the amount spent by only *one* individual customer. The answers for parts (b) and (c) are very different. Why would this happen? In this example, $\bar{x}$ is a much more predictable or reliable statistic than x. Consider that almost all marketing strategies and sales pitches are designed for the *average* customer and *not* the *individual* customer. How does the central limit theorem tell us that the average customer is much more predictable than the individual customer? (See Problem 16 of Section 7.2.)

7.1
Sampling Distributions

FOCUS POINTS

✓ Review such commonly used terms as random sample, relative frequency, parameter, statistic, and sampling distribution.

✓ From raw data, construct a relative frequency distribution for $\bar{x}$ values and compare the result to a theoretical sampling distribution.

Let us begin with some common statistical terms. Most of these have been discussed before, but this is a good time to review them.

From a statistical point of view, a *population* can be thought of as a set of measurements (or counts), either existing or conceptual. We discussed populations at some length in Chapter 1. A *sample* is a subset of measurements from the population. For our purposes, the most important samples are *random samples*, which were discussed in Section 1.2.

When we compute a descriptive measure such as an average, it makes a difference whether it was computed from a population or from a sample.

Statistic
Parameter

> A **statistic** is a numerical descriptive measure of a *sample*.
> A **parameter** is a numerical descriptive measure of a *population*.

It is important to notice that for a given population, a specified parameter is a fixed quantity. On the other hand, the value of a statistic might vary depending on which sample has been selected.

Some commonly used statistics and corresponding parameters		
Measure	*Statistic*	*Parameter*
Mean	$\bar{x}$ (x bar)	μ (mu)
Variance	s^2	σ^2 (sigma squared)
Standard deviation	s	σ (sigma)
Proportion	$\hat{p}$ (p hat)	p

Often we do not have access to all the measurements of an entire population because of time, money, effort constraints, etc. So we must use measurements from a sample instead. In such cases, we will use a statistic (such as $\bar{x}$, s, or $\hat{p}$) to make *inferences* about corresponding population parameters (e.g., μ, σ, or p). The principal types of inferences we will make are the following.

> **Types of inferences**
>
> 1. **Estimation:** In this type of inference, we estimate the *value* of a population parameter.
>
> 2. **Testing:** In this type of inference, we formulate a *decision* about the value of a population parameter.
>
> 3. **Regression:** In this type of inference, we make *predictions* or *forecasts* about the value of a statistical variable.

Sampling distribution

To evaluate the reliability of our inferences, we will need to know the probability distribution for the statistic we are using. Such a probability distribution is called a *sampling distribution*. Perhaps Example 3 below will help clarify this discussion.

> A **sampling distribution** is a probability distribution of a sample statistic based on all possible simple random samples of the *same* size from the same population.

EXAMPLE 1

Sampling distribution for $\bar{x}$

Pinedale, Wisconsin, is a rural community with a children's fishing pond. Posted rules state that all fish under 6 inches must be returned to the pond, only children under 12 years old may fish, and a limit of five fish may be kept per day. Susan is a college student who was hired by the community last summer to make sure the rules were obeyed and to see that the children were safe from accidents. The pond contains only rainbow trout and has been well stocked for many years. Each child has no difficulty catching his or her limit of five trout.

As a project for her biometrics class, Susan kept a record of the lengths (to the nearest inch) of all trout caught last summer. Hundreds of children visited the pond and caught their limit of five trout, so Susan has a lot of data. To make Table 7-1, Susan selected 100 children at random and listed the lengths of each of the five trout caught by a child in the sample. Then, for each child, she listed the mean length of the five trout that child caught.

Now let us turn our attention to the following question: What is the average (mean) length of a trout taken from the Pinedale children's pond last summer?

SOLUTION: We can get an idea of the average length by looking at the far-right column of Table 7-1. But just looking at 100 of the $\bar{x}$ values doesn't tell us much. Let's organize our $\bar{x}$ values into a frequency table. We used a class width of 0.38 to make Table 7-2.

Note: Techniques of Section 2.2 dictate a class width of 0.4. However, this choice results in the tenth class being beyond the data. Consequently, we shortened the

TABLE 7-1 Length Measurements of Trout Caught by a Random Sample of 100 Children at the Pinedale Children's Pond

Sample	Length (to nearest inch)					$\bar{x}$ = Sample Mean	Sample	Length (to nearest inch)					$\bar{x}$ = Sample Mean
1	11	10	10	12	11	10.8	51	9	10	12	10	9	10.0
2	11	11	9	9	9	9.8	52	7	11	10	11	10	9.8
3	12	9	10	11	10	10.4	53	9	11	9	11	12	10.4
4	11	10	13	11	8	10.6	54	12	9	8	10	11	10.0
5	10	10	13	11	12	11.2	55	8	11	10	9	10	9.6
6	12	7	10	9	11	9.8	56	10	10	9	9	13	10.2
7	7	10	13	10	10	10.0	57	9	8	10	10	12	9.8
8	10	9	9	9	10	9.4	58	10	11	9	8	9	9.4
9	10	10	11	12	8	10.2	59	10	8	9	10	12	9.8
10	10	11	10	7	9	9.4	60	11	9	9	11	11	10.2
11	12	11	11	11	13	11.6	61	11	10	11	10	11	10.6
12	10	11	10	12	13	11.2	62	12	10	10	9	11	10.4
13	11	10	10	9	11	10.2	63	10	10	9	11	7	9.4
14	10	10	13	8	11	10.4	64	11	11	12	10	11	11.0
15	9	11	9	10	10	9.8	65	10	10	11	10	9	10.0
16	13	9	11	12	10	11.0	66	8	9	10	11	11	9.8
17	8	9	7	10	11	9.0	67	9	11	11	9	8	9.6
18	12	12	8	12	12	11.2	68	10	9	10	9	11	9.8
19	10	8	9	10	10	9.4	69	9	9	11	11	11	10.2
20	10	11	10	10	10	10.2	70	13	11	11	9	11	11.0
21	11	10	11	9	12	10.6	71	12	10	8	8	9	9.4
22	9	12	9	10	9	9.8	72	13	7	12	9	10	10.2
23	8	11	10	11	10	10.0	73	9	10	9	8	9	9.0
24	9	12	10	9	11	10.2	74	11	11	10	9	10	10.2
25	9	9	8	9	10	9.0	75	9	11	14	9	11	10.8
26	11	11	12	11	11	11.2	76	14	10	11	12	12	11.8
27	10	10	10	11	13	10.8	77	8	12	10	10	9	9.8
28	8	7	9	10	8	8.4	78	8	10	13	9	8	9.6
29	11	11	8	10	11	10.2	79	11	11	11	13	10	11.2
30	8	11	11	9	12	10.2	80	12	10	11	12	9	10.8
31	11	9	12	10	10	10.4	81	10	9	10	10	13	10.4
32	10	11	10	11	12	10.8	82	11	10	9	9	12	10.2
33	12	11	8	8	11	10.0	83	11	11	10	10	10	10.4
34	8	10	10	9	10	9.4	84	11	10	11	9	9	10.0
35	10	10	10	10	11	10.2	85	10	11	10	9	7	9.4
36	10	8	10	11	13	10.4	86	7	11	10	9	11	9.6
37	11	10	11	11	10	10.6	87	10	11	10	10	10	10.2
38	7	13	9	12	11	10.4	88	9	8	11	10	12	10.0
39	11	11	8	11	11	10.4	89	14	9	12	10	9	10.8
40	11	10	11	12	9	10.6	90	9	12	9	10	10	10.0
41	11	10	9	11	12	10.6	91	10	10	8	6	11	9.0
42	11	13	10	12	9	11.0	92	8	9	11	9	10	9.4
43	10	9	11	10	11	10.2	93	8	10	9	9	11	9.4
44	10	9	11	10	9	9.8	94	12	11	12	13	10	11.6
45	12	11	9	11	12	11.0	95	11	11	9	9	9	9.8
46	13	9	11	8	8	9.8	96	8	12	8	11	10	9.8
47	10	11	11	11	10	10.6	97	13	11	11	12	8	11.0
48	9	9	10	11	11	10.0	98	10	11	8	10	11	10.0
49	10	9	9	10	10	9.6	99	13	10	7	11	9	10.0
50	10	10	6	9	10	9.0	100	9	9	10	12	12	10.4

TABLE 7-2   **Frequency Table for 100 Values of $\bar{x}$**

Class	Class Limits		f = Frequency	$f/100$ = Relative Frequency
	Lower	Upper		
1	8.39	8.76	1	0.01
2	8.77	9.14	5	0.05
3	9.15	9.52	10	0.10
4	9.53	9.90	19	0.19
5	9.91	10.28	27	0.27
6	10.29	10.66	18	0.18
7	10.67	11.04	12	0.12
8	11.05	11.42	5	0.05
9	11.43	11.80	3	0.03

class width slightly and also started the first class with a value slightly smaller than the smallest data value.

The far-right column of Table 7-2 contains relative frequencies $f/100$. Recall that the relative frequencies may be thought of as probabilities, so we effectively have a probability distribution. Because $\bar{x}$ represents the mean length of a trout (based on samples of five trout caught by each child), we estimate the probability of $\bar{x}$ falling into each class by using the relative frequencies. Figure 7-1 is a relative-frequency or probability distribution of the $\bar{x}$ values.

The bars of Figure 7-1 represent our estimated probabilities of $\bar{x}$ values based on the data of Table 7-1. The bell-shaped curve represents the theoretical probability distribution that would be obtained if the number of children (i.e., number of $\bar{x}$ values) were much larger.

Figure 7-1 represents a *probability sampling distribution* for the sample mean $\bar{x}$ of trout lengths based on random samples of size 5. We see that the distribution is

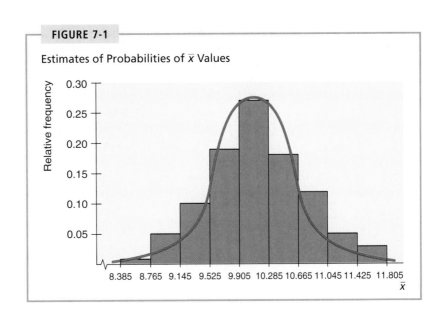

FIGURE 7-1

Estimates of Probabilities of $\bar{x}$ Values

mound-shaped and even somewhat bell-shaped. Irregularities are due to the small number of samples used (only 100 sample means) and the rather small sample size (five trout per child). These irregularities would become less obvious and even disappear if the sample of children became much larger, if we used a larger number of classes in Figure 7-1, and if the number of trout used in each sample became larger. In fact, the curve would eventually become a perfect bell-shaped curve. We will discuss this property at some length in the next section, which introduces the *central limit theorem.*   ◇

There are other sampling distributions besides the $\bar{x}$ distribution. Section 7.3 shows the sampling distribution for $\hat{p}$. In the chapters ahead, we will see that other statistics have different sampling distributions. However, the $\bar{x}$ sampling distribution is very important. It will serve us well in our inferential work in Chapters 8 and 9 on estimation and testing.

Let us summarize the information about sampling distributions in the following exercise.

GUIDED EXERCISE 1

Terminology

(a) What is a population parameter? Give an example.

⟹ A population parameter is a numerical descriptive measure of a population. Examples are μ, σ, and p. (There are many others.)

(b) What is a sample statistic? Give an example.

⟹ A sample statistic or a statistic is a numerical descriptive measure of a sample. Examples are $\bar{x}$, s, and $\hat{p}$.

(c) What is a sampling distribution?

⟹ A sampling distribution is a probability distribution for the sample statistic we are using.

(d) In Table 7-1, what makes up the members of the sample? What is the sample statistic corresponding to each sample? What is the sampling distribution? To which population parameter does this sampling distribution correspond?

⟹ There are 100 samples, each of which has five trout lengths. The first sample of five trout has lengths 11, 10, 10, 12, and 11. The sample statistic is the sample mean $\bar{x} = 10.8$. The sampling distribution is shown in Figure 7-1. This sampling distribution relates to the population mean μ of all lengths of trout taken from the Pinedale children's pond (i.e., trout over 6 inches long).

(e) Where will sampling distributions be used in our study of statistics?

⟹ Sampling distributions will be used for statistical inference. (Chapter 8 will concentrate on a method of inference called *estimation.* Chapter 9 will concentrate on a method of inference called *testing.*)

VIEWPOINT   *"Chance Favors the Prepared Mind"*
                                      —*Louis Pasteur*

It also has been said that a discovery is nothing more than an accident that meets a prepared mind. Sampling can be one of the best forms of preparation. In fact, sampling may be the primary way we humans venture into the unknown. Probability sampling distributions can provide new information for the sociologist, scientist, or economist. In addition, ordinary human sampling of life can help writers and artists develop preferences, style, and insight. Ansel Adams became famous for photographing lyrical, unforgettable landscapes such as "Moonrise, Hernandez, New Mexico." Adams claimed that he was a strong believer in the quote by Pasteur. In fact, he claims that the Hernandez photograph was just such a favored chance happening that his prepared mind readily grasped. During his lifetime, Adams made over $25 million from sales and royalties on the Hernandez photograph.

SECTION 7.1   PROBLEMS

This is a good time to review several important concepts, some of which we have studied earlier. Please write out a careful but brief answer to each of the following questions.

1. What is a population? Give three examples.

2. What is a random sample from a population? (*Hint:* See Section 1.2.)

3. What is a population parameter? Give three examples.

4. What is a sample statistic? Give three examples.

5. What is the meaning of the term *statistical inference*? What types of inferences will we make about population parameters?

6. What is a sampling distribution?

7. How do frequency tables, relative frequencies, and histograms using relative frequencies help us understand sampling distributions?

8. How can relative frequencies be used to help us estimate probabilities occurring in sampling distributions?

9. Give an example of a specific sampling distribution we studied in this section. Outline other possible examples of sampling distributions from areas such as business administration, economics, finance, psychology, political science, sociology, biology, medical science, sports, engineering, chemistry, linguistics, and so on.

7.2
The Central Limit Theorem

FOCUS POINTS

✔ For a normal distribution, use μ and σ to construct the theoretical sampling distribution for the statistic $\bar{x}$.

✔ For large samples, use sample estimates to construct a good approximate sampling distribution for the statistic $\bar{x}$.

✔ Learn the statement and underlying meaning of the central limit theorem well enough to explain it to a friend who is intelligent, but (unfortunately) doesn't know much about statistics.

The $\bar{x}$ Distribution, Given x Is Normal

In Section 7.1, we began a study of the distribution of $\bar{x}$ values, where $\bar{x}$ was the (sample) mean length of five trout caught by children at the Pinedale children's fishing pond. Let's consider this example again in the light of a very important theorem of mathematical statistics.

◊ **THEOREM 7.1 For a Normal Probability Distribution** Let x be a random variable with a *normal distribution* whose mean is μ and whose standard deviation is σ. Let $\bar{x}$ be the sample mean corresponding to random samples of size n taken from the x distribution. Then the following are true:

(a) The $\bar{x}$ distribution is a *normal distribution*.

(b) The mean of the $\bar{x}$ distribution is μ.

(c) The standard deviation of the $\bar{x}$ distribution is $\sigma/\sqrt{n}$.   ◊

We conclude from Theorem 7.1 that when x has a normal distribution, the $\bar{x}$ distribution will be normal *for any sample size n*. Furthermore, we can convert the $\bar{x}$ distribution to the standard normal z distribution using the following formulas.

$$\mu_{\bar{x}} = \mu$$

$$\sigma_{\bar{x}} = \frac{\sigma}{\sqrt{n}}$$

$$z = \frac{\bar{x} - \mu_{\bar{x}}}{\sigma_{\bar{x}}} = \frac{\bar{x} - \mu}{\sigma/\sqrt{n}}$$

where n is the sample size,
μ is the mean of the x distribution, and
σ is the standard deviation of the x distribution.

Theorem 7.1 is a wonderful theorem! It states that the $\bar{x}$ distribution will be normal provided the x distribution is normal. The sample size n could be 2, 3, 4, or any (fixed) sample size we wish. Furthermore, the mean of the $\bar{x}$ distribution is μ (same as for the x distribution), but the standard deviation is $\sigma/\sqrt{n}$ (which is, of course, smaller than σ). The next example illustrates Theorem 7.1.

EXAMPLE 2

Probability regarding x; regarding $\bar{x}$

Suppose that a team of biologists has been studying the Pinedale children's fishing pond. Let x represent the length of a single trout taken at random from the pond. This group of biologists has determined that x has a normal distribution with mean $\mu = 10.2$ inches and standard deviation $\sigma = 1.4$ inches.

(a) What is the probability that a *single trout* taken at random from the pond is between 8 and 12 inches long?

SOLUTION: We use the methods of Chapter 6 with $\mu = 10.2$ and $\sigma = 1.4$ to get

$$z = \frac{x - \mu}{\sigma} = \frac{x - 10.2}{1.4}$$

Therefore,

$$P(8 < x < 12) = P\left(\frac{8 - 10.2}{1.4} < z < \frac{12 - 10.2}{1.4}\right)$$
$$= P(-1.57 < z < 1.29)$$
$$= 0.9015 - 0.0582 = 0.8433$$

Therefore, the probability is about 0.8433 that a *single* trout taken at random is between 8 and 12 inches long.

(b) What is the probability that the *mean length* $\bar{x}$ of five trout taken at random is between 8 and 12 inches?

SOLUTION: If we let $\mu_{\bar{x}}$ represent the mean of the distribution, then Theorem 7.1, part (b), tells us that

$$\mu_{\bar{x}} = \mu = 10.2$$

If $\sigma_{\bar{x}}$ represents the standard deviation of the $\bar{x}$ distribution, then Theorem 7.1, part (c), tells us that

$$\sigma_{\bar{x}} = \sigma/\sqrt{n} = 1.4/\sqrt{5} \approx 0.63$$

To create a standard z variable from $\bar{x}$, we subtract $\mu_{\bar{x}}$ and divide by $\sigma_{\bar{x}}$:

$$z = \frac{\bar{x} - \mu_{\bar{x}}}{\sigma_{\bar{x}}} = \frac{\bar{x} - \mu}{\sigma/\sqrt{n}} \approx \frac{\bar{x} - 10.2}{0.63}$$

To standardize the interval $8 < \bar{x} < 12$, we use 8 and then 12 in place of $\bar{x}$ in the preceding formula for z.

$$8 < \bar{x} < 12$$
$$\frac{8 - 10.2}{0.63} < z < \frac{12 - 10.2}{0.63}$$
$$-3.49 < z < 2.86$$

Theorem 7.1, part (a), tells us that $\bar{x}$ has a normal distribution. Therefore,

$$P(8 < \bar{x} < 12) = P(-3.49 < z < 2.86) = 0.9979 - 0.0002 = 0.9977$$

The probability is about 0.9977 that the mean length based on a sample size of 5 is between 8 and 12 inches.

(c) Looking at the results of parts (a) and (b), we see that the probabilities (0.8433 and 0.9977) are quite different. Why is this the case?

SOLUTION: According to Theorem 7.1, both x and $\bar{x}$ have a normal distribution, and both have the same mean of 10.2 inches. The difference is in the standard deviation for x and $\bar{x}$. The standard deviation of the x distribution is $\sigma = 1.4$. The standard deviation of the $\bar{x}$ distribution is

$$\sigma_{\bar{x}} = \sigma/\sqrt{n} = 1.4/\sqrt{5} \approx 0.63$$

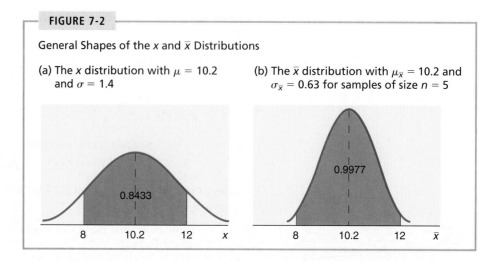

FIGURE 7-2

General Shapes of the x and $\bar{x}$ Distributions

(a) The x distribution with $\mu = 10.2$ and $\sigma = 1.4$

(b) The $\bar{x}$ distribution with $\mu_{\bar{x}} = 10.2$ and $\sigma_{\bar{x}} = 0.63$ for samples of size $n = 5$

0.8433

0.9977

The standard deviation of $\bar{x}$ is less than half the standard deviation of x. Figure 7-2 shows the distribution of x and $\bar{x}$.

Looking at Figure 7-2(a) and (b), we see that both curves use the same scale on the horizontal axis. The means are the same, and the shaded area is above the interval from 8 to 12 on each graph. It becomes clear that the smaller standard deviation of the $\bar{x}$ distribution has the effect of gathering together much more of the total probability into the region over its mean. Therefore, the region from 8 to 12 has a much higher probability for the $\bar{x}$ distribution. ◊

Theorem 7.1 describes the distribution of a particular statistic: namely, the distribution of sample means $\bar{x}$. The standard deviation of a statistic is referred to as the *standard error* of that statistic.

Standard error of the mean

> The **standard error** is the standard deviation of a sampling distribution. For the $\bar{x}$ sampling distribution,
>
> standard error $= \sigma_{\bar{x}} = \sigma/\sqrt{n}$

Statistical software

The expression *standard error* appears commonly on printouts and refers to the standard deviation of the sampling distribution being used. (In Minitab, the expression SE MEAN refers to the standard error of the mean.)

The $\bar{x}$ Distribution, Given x Follows Any Distribution

Theorem 7.1 gives complete information about the $\bar{x}$ distribution, provided the original x distribution is known to be normal. What happens if we don't have information about the shape of the original x distribution? The *central limit theorem* tells us what to expect.

Central limit theorem

◊ **THEOREM 7.2 The Central Limit Theorem for Any Probability Distribution** If x possesses *any* distribution with mean μ and standard deviation σ, then the sample mean $\bar{x}$ based on a random sample of size n will have a distribution that approaches the distribution of a normal random variable with mean μ and standard deviation $\sigma/\sqrt{n}$ as n increases without limit. $\Diamond$

The central limit theorem is indeed surprising! It says that x can have *any* distribution whatsoever, but as the sample size gets larger and larger, the distribution of $\bar{x}$ will approach a *normal* distribution. From this relation, we begin to appreciate the scope and significance of the normal distribution.

In the central limit theorem, the degree to which the distribution of $\bar{x}$ values fits a normal distribution depends on both the selected value of n and the original distribution of x values. A natural question is: How large should the sample size be if we want to apply the central limit theorem? After a great deal of theoretical as well as empirical study, statisticians agree that if n is 30 or larger, the $\bar{x}$ distribution will appear to be normal and the central limit theorem will apply. However, this rule should not be applied blindly. If the x distribution is definitely not symmetrical about its mean, then the $\bar{x}$ distribution also will display a lack of symmetry. In such a case, a sample size larger than 30 may be required to get a reasonable approximation to the normal.

In practice, it is a good idea, when possible, to make a histogram of sample x values. If the histogram is approximately mound-shaped, and if it is more or less symmetrical, then we may be assured that, for all practical purposes, the $\bar{x}$ distribution will be well approximated by a normal distribution and the central limit theorem will apply when the sample size is 30 or larger. The main thing to remember is that in almost all practical applications, a sample size of 30 or more is adequate for the central limit theorem to hold. However, in a few rare applications, you may need a sample size larger than 30 to get reliable results.

Let's summarize this information for convenient reference: For almost all x distributions, if we use a random sample of size 30 or larger, the $\bar{x}$ distribution will be approximately normal, and the larger the sample size becomes, the closer the $\bar{x}$ distribution gets to the normal. Furthermore, we may convert the $\bar{x}$ distribution to a standard normal distribution using the following formulas.

Large sample

Using the central limit theorem to convert the $\bar{x}$ distribution to the standard normal distribution

$$\mu_{\bar{x}} = \mu$$
$$\sigma_{\bar{x}} = \frac{\sigma}{\sqrt{n}}$$
$$z = \frac{\bar{x} - \mu_{\bar{x}}}{\sigma_{\bar{x}}} = \frac{\bar{x} - \mu}{\sigma/\sqrt{n}}$$

where n is the sample size ($n \geq 30$),
μ is the mean of the x distribution, and
σ is the standard deviation of the x distribution.

Guided Exercise 2 shows how to standardize $\bar{x}$ when appropriate. Then Example 3 demonstrates the use of the central limit theorem in a decision-making process.

GUIDED EXERCISE 2

Central limit theorem

(a) Suppose x has a *normal* distribution with mean $\mu = 18$ and standard deviation $\sigma = 3$. If you draw random samples of size 5 from the x distribution and $\bar{x}$ represents the sample mean, what can you say about the $\bar{x}$ distribution? How could you standardize the $\bar{x}$ distribution?

Since the x distribution is given to be *normal*, the $\bar{x}$ distribution also will be normal even though the sample size is much less than 30. The mean is $\mu_{\bar{x}} = \mu = 18$. The standard deviation is

$$\sigma_{\bar{x}} = \sigma/\sqrt{n} = 3/\sqrt{5} \approx 1.3$$

We could standardize $\bar{x}$ as follows:

$$z = \frac{\bar{x} - \mu}{\sigma/\sqrt{n}} \approx \frac{\bar{x} - 18}{1.3}$$

(b) Suppose you know that the x distribution has mean $\mu = 75$ and standard deviation $\sigma = 12$, but you have no information as to whether or not the x distribution is normal. If you draw samples of size 30 from the x distribution and $\bar{x}$ represents the sample mean, what can you say about the $\bar{x}$ distribution? How could you standardize the $\bar{x}$ distribution?

Since the sample size is large enough, the $\bar{x}$ distribution will be approximately a normal distribution. The mean of the $\bar{x}$ distribution is

$$\mu_{\bar{x}} = \mu = 75$$

The standard deviation of the distribution is

$$\sigma_{\bar{x}} = \sigma/\sqrt{n} = 12/\sqrt{30} \approx 2.2$$

We could standardize $\bar{x}$ as follows:

$$z = \frac{\bar{x} - \mu}{\sigma/\sqrt{n}} \approx \frac{\bar{x} - 75}{2.2}$$

(c) Suppose you did not know that x had a normal distribution. Would you be justified in saying that the $\bar{x}$ distribution is approximately normal if the sample size were $n = 8$?

No, the sample size should be 30 or larger if we don't know that x has a normal distribution.

EXAMPLE 3

Central limit theorem

A certain strain of bacteria occurs in all raw milk. Let x be the bacteria count per milliliter of milk. The health department has found that if the milk is not contaminated, then x has a distribution that is more or less mound-shaped and symmetrical. The mean of the x distribution is $\mu = 2500$, and the standard deviation is $\sigma = 300$. In a large commercial dairy, the health inspector takes 42 random samples of the milk produced each day. At the end of the day, the bacteria count in each of the 42 samples is averaged to obtain the sample mean bacteria count $\bar{x}$.

(a) Assuming that the milk is not contaminated, what is the distribution of $\bar{x}$?

SOLUTION: The sample size is $n = 42$. Since this value exceeds 30, the central limit theorem applies, and we know that $\bar{x}$ will be approximately normal with mean and standard deviation

$$\mu_{\bar{x}} = \mu = 2500$$
$$\sigma_{\bar{x}} = \sigma/\sqrt{n} = 300/\sqrt{42} \approx 46.3$$

(b) Assuming that the milk is not contaminated, what is the probability that the average bacteria count $\bar{x}$ for one day is between 2350 and 2650 bacteria per milliliter?

SOLUTION: We convert the interval

$$2350 \leq \bar{x} \leq 2650$$

to a corresponding interval on the standard z axis.

$$z = \frac{\bar{x} - \mu}{\sigma/\sqrt{n}} \approx \frac{\bar{x} - 2500}{46.3}$$

$\bar{x} = 2350$ converts to $z = \dfrac{2350 - 2500}{46.3} \approx -3.24$

$\bar{x} = 2650$ converts to $z = \dfrac{2650 - 2500}{46.3} \approx 3.24$

Therefore,

$$P(2350 \leq \bar{x} \leq 2650) = P(-3.24 \leq z \leq 3.24)$$
$$= 0.9994 - 0.0006$$
$$= 0.9988$$

The probability is 0.9988 that $\bar{x}$ is between 2350 and 2650.

(c) At the end of each day, the inspector must decide to accept or reject the accumulated milk that has been held in cold storage awaiting shipment. Suppose that the 42 samples taken by the inspector have a mean bacteria count $\bar{x}$ that is *not* between 2350 and 2650. If you were the inspector, what would be your comment on this situation?

SOLUTION: The probability that $\bar{x}$ is between 2350 and 2650 is very high. If the inspector finds that the average bacteria count for the 42 samples is not between 2350 and 2650, then it is reasonable to conclude that there is something wrong with the milk. If $\bar{x}$ is less than 2350, you might suspect someone added chemicals to the milk to artificially reduce the bacteria count. If $\bar{x}$ is above 2650, you might suspect some other kind of biologic contamination.   ◇

PROCEDURE

How to find probabilities regarding $\bar{x}$
Given a probability distribution of x values where

n = sample size
μ = mean of the x distribution
σ = standard deviation of the x distribution

1. If the x distribution is *normal*, then the $\bar{x}$ distribution is *normal*.

2. Even if the x distribution is *not* normal, if the *sample size $n \geq 30$*, then, by the central limit theorem, the $\bar{x}$ distribution is *approximately normal*.

3. Convert $\bar{x}$ to z using the formula

$$z = \frac{\bar{x} - \mu_{\bar{x}}}{\sigma_{\bar{x}}} = \frac{\bar{x} - \mu}{\sigma/\sqrt{n}}$$

4. Use the standard normal distribution to find the corresponding probability of events regarding $\bar{x}$.

GUIDED EXERCISE 3

Probability regarding x̄

In mountain country, major highways sometimes use tunnels instead of long, winding roads over high passes. However, too many vehicles in a tunnel at the same time can cause a hazardous situation. Traffic engineers are studying a long tunnel in Colorado. If x represents the time for a vehicle to go through the tunnel, it is known that the x distribution has mean $\mu = 12.1$ minutes and standard deviation $\sigma = 3.8$ minutes under ordinary traffic conditions. From a histogram of x values, it was found that the x distribution is mound-shaped with some symmetry about the mean.

Engineers have calculated that, *on average,* vehicles should spend from 11 to 13 minutes in the tunnel. If the time is less than 11 minutes, traffic is moving too fast for safe travel in the tunnel. If the time is more than 13 minutes, there is a problem of bad air (too much carbon monoxide and other pollutants).

Under ordinary conditions, there are about 50 vehicles in the tunnel at one time. What is the probability that the mean time for 50 vehicles in the tunnel will be from 11 to 13 minutes?

We will answer this question in steps.

(a) Let $\bar{x}$ represent the sample mean based on samples of size 50. Describe the $\bar{x}$ distribution. $\Rightarrow$ From the central limit theorem we expect the $\bar{x}$ distribution to be approximately normal with mean and standard deviation

$$\mu_{\bar{x}} = \mu = 12.1 \qquad \sigma_{\bar{x}} = \frac{\sigma}{\sqrt{n}} = \frac{3.8}{\sqrt{50}} \approx 0.54$$

(b) Find $P(11 < \bar{x} < 13)$. $\Rightarrow$ We convert the interval

$$11 < \bar{x} < 13$$

to a standard z interval and use the standard normal probability table to find our answer. Since

$$z = \frac{\bar{x} - \mu}{\sigma/\sqrt{n}} \approx \frac{\bar{x} - 12.1}{0.54}$$

$\bar{x} = 11$ converts to $z \approx \dfrac{11 - 12.1}{0.54} = -2.04$

and $\bar{x} = 13$ converts to $z \approx \dfrac{13 - 12.1}{0.54} = 1.67$

Therefore,

$$P(11 < \bar{x} < 13) = P(-2.04 < z < 1.67)$$
$$= 0.9525 - 0.0207$$
$$= 0.9318$$

(c) Comment on your answer for part (b). $\Rightarrow$ It seems that about 93% of the time there should be no safety hazard for average traffic flow.

VIEWPOINT   *Chaos!*

Is there a different side to random sampling? Can sampling be used as a weapon? According to the *Wall Street Journal*, the answer could be yes! The acronym for **C**reate **H**avoc **A**round **O**ur **S**ystem is **CHAOS**. The Association of Flight Attendants (AFA) is a union that successfully used **CHAOS** against Alaska Airlines in 1994 as a negotiation tool. **CHAOS** involves a small sample of random strikes—a few flights at a time—instead of a mass walkout. The president of the AFA claims that by striking randomly, "we take control of the schedule." The entire schedule becomes unreliable, and that is something management cannot tolerate. In 1986, TWA flight attendants struck in a mass walkout, and all were permanently replaced! Using **CHAOS**, only a few jobs are put at risk, and these are usually not lost. It appears that random sampling can be used as a weapon.

SECTION 7.2   PROBLEMS

In these problems, the word *average* refers to the arithmetic mean $\bar{x}$ or μ, as appropriate.

1. *General* Suppose that x has a distribution with $\mu = 15$ and $\sigma = 14$.
   (a) If a random sample of size $n = 49$ is drawn, find $\mu_{\bar{x}}$, $\sigma_{\bar{x}}$, and $P(15 \leq \bar{x} \leq 17)$.
   (b) If a random sample of size $n = 64$ is drawn, find $\mu_{\bar{x}}$, $\sigma_{\bar{x}}$, and $P(15 \leq \bar{x} \leq 17)$.
   (c) Why should you expect the probability of part (b) to be higher than that of part (a)? (*Hint:* Consider the standard deviations in parts (a) and (b).)

2. *General* Suppose that x has a distribution with $\mu = 100$ and $\sigma = 48$.
   (a) If a random sample of size $n = 81$ is drawn, find $\mu_{\bar{x}}$, $\sigma_{\bar{x}}$, and $P(92 \leq \bar{x} \leq 100)$.
   (b) If a random sample of size $n = 121$ is drawn, find $\mu_{\bar{x}}$, $\sigma_{\bar{x}}$, and $P(92 \leq \bar{x} \leq 100)$.
   (c) Again, comment on the differences in the probabilities in parts (a) and (b). Why do you expect the differences?

3. *General* Suppose that x has a distribution with $\mu = 25$ and $\sigma = 3.5$.
   (a) If random samples of size $n = 9$ are selected, can we say anything about the $\bar{x}$ distribution of sample means?
   (b) If the original x distribution is normal, can we say anything about the $\bar{x}$ distribution from samples of size $n = 9$? Find $P(23 \leq \bar{x} \leq 26)$.

4. *General* Suppose that x has a distribution with $\mu = 72$ and $\sigma = 8$.
   (a) If random samples of size $n = 16$ are selected, can we say anything about the $\bar{x}$ distribution of sample means?
   (b) If the original x distribution is *normal*, can we say anything about the $\bar{x}$ distribution of random samples of size 16? Find $P(68 \leq \bar{x} \leq 73)$.

5. *Coal: Automatic Loader* Coal is carried from a mine in West Virginia to a power plant in New York in hopper cars on a long train. The automatic hopper car loader is set to put 75 tons of coal into each car. The actual weights of coal loaded into each car are *normally distributed* with mean $\mu = 75$ tons and standard deviation $\sigma = 0.8$ ton.
   (a) What is the probability that one car chosen at random will have less than 74.5 tons of coal?

(b) What is the probability that 20 cars chosen at random will have a mean load weight $\bar{x}$ of less than 74.5 tons of coal?

(c) Suppose that the weight of coal in one car was less than 74.5 tons. Would that fact make you suspect that the loader had slipped out of adjustment? Suppose the weight of coal in 20 cars selected at random had an average $\bar{x}$ less than 74.5 tons. Would that fact make you suspect that the loader had slipped out of adjustment? Why?

6. *Vital Statistics: Heights of Men* The heights of 18-year-old men are approximately *normally distributed*, with mean 68 inches and standard deviation 3 inches (based on information from *Statistical Abstract of the United States*, 112th Edition).

(a) What is the probability that an 18-year-old man selected at random is between 67 and 69 inches tall?

(b) If a random sample of nine 18-year-old men is selected, what is the probability that the mean height $\bar{x}$ is between 67 and 69 inches?

(c) Compare your answers for parts (a) and (b). Is the probability in part (b) much higher? Why would you expect this?

7. *Medical: Blood Glucose* Let x be a random variable that represents the level of glucose in the blood (milligrams per deciliter of blood) after a 12-hour fast. Assume for people under 50 years old that x has a distribution that is approximately normal with mean $\mu = 85$ and estimated standard deviation $\sigma = 25$ (based on information from *Diagnostic Tests with Nursing Applications*, edited by S. Loeb, Springhouse). A test result $x < 40$ is an indication of severe excess insulin, and medication is usually prescribed.

(a) What is the probability that on a single test $x < 40$?

(b) Suppose a doctor uses the average $\bar{x}$ for two tests taken about a week apart. What can we say about the probability distribution of $\bar{x}$? *Hint:* See Theorem 7.1. What is the probability that $\bar{x} < 40$?

(c) Repeat part (b) for $n = 3$ tests taken a week apart.

(d) Repeat part (b) for $n = 5$ tests taken a week apart.

(e) Compare your answers for parts (a), (b), (c), and (d). Did the probabilities decrease as n increased? Explain what this might say if you were a doctor or a nurse. If a patient had a test result of $\bar{x} < 40$ based on five tests, explain why either you are looking at an extremely rare event or (more likely) the person has a case of excess insulin.

8. *Medical: White Blood Cells* Let x be a random variable that represents white blood cell count per cubic milliliter of whole blood. Assume that x has a distribution that is approximately normal with mean $\mu = 7500$ and estimated standard deviation $\sigma = 1750$ (see reference in Problem 7). A test result of $x < 3500$ is an indication of leukopenia. This indicates bone marrow depression that may be the result of a viral infection.

(a) What is the probability that on a single test x is less than 3500?

(b) Suppose a doctor uses the average $\bar{x}$ for two tests taken about a week apart. What can we say about the probability distribution of $\bar{x}$? What is the probability of $\bar{x} < 3500$?

(c) Repeat part (b) for $n = 3$ tests taken a week apart.

(d) Compare your answers for parts (a), (b), and (c). How did the probabilities change as n increased? If a person had $\bar{x} < 3500$ based on three tests, what conclusion would you draw as a doctor or a nurse?

9. *Wildlife: Deer* Let x be a random variable that represents the weights in kilograms (kg) of healthy adult female deer (does) in December in Mesa Verde National Park. Then x has a distribution that is approximately normal with mean $\mu = 63.0$ kg and standard deviation $\sigma = 7.1$ kg (Source: *The Mule Deer of Mesa Verde National Park*,

by G. W. Mierau and J. L. Schmidt, Mesa Verde Museum Association). Suppose a doe that weighs less than 54 kg is considered undernourished.

(a) What is the probability that a single doe captured (weighed and released) at random in December is undernourished?

(b) If the park has about 2200 does, what number do you expect to be undernourished in December?

(c) To estimate the health of the December doe population, park rangers use the rule that the average weight of $n = 50$ does should be more than 60 kg. If the average weight is less than 60 kg, it is thought that the entire population of does might be undernourished. What is the probability that the average weight $\bar{x}$ for a random sample of 50 does is less than 60 kg (assume a healthy population)?

(d) Compute the probability that $\bar{x} < 64.2$ kg for 50 does (assume a healthy population). Suppose park rangers captured, weighed, and released 50 does in December, and the average weight was $\bar{x} = 64.2$ kg. Do you think the doe population is undernourished or not? Explain.

10. *Wildlife: Hummingbirds* Selasphorus sasin is the scientific name for what is commonly called "Allen's hummingbird." This beautiful hummingbird lives on the West Coast of the United States and is named for C. A. Allen (1841–1930), who studied these birds extensively. Let x be a random variable that represents the incubation time for Allen hummingbird eggs. Based on information from *The Hummingbird Book,* by Donald and Lillian Stokes (Little, Brown and Company), the x distribution has a mean of $\mu = 16$ days. Let us assume that the standard deviation is approximately $\sigma = 2$ days. The distribution of x values is more or less mound-shaped and symmetrical but not necessarily normal. Suppose that we have $n = 30$ eggs in an incubator. Let $\bar{x}$ be the average incubation time for these eggs.

(a) What can we say about the probability distribution of $\bar{x}$? Is it approximately normal? What are the mean and standard deviation?

(b) What is the probability that $\bar{x}$ is between 16 and 17 days?

(c) What is the probability that $\bar{x}$ is less than 15 days?

11. *Finance: Templeton Funds* Templeton World is a mutual fund that invests in both U.S. and foreign markets. Let x be a random variable that represents the monthly percentage return for the Templeton World fund. Based on information from the *Morningstar Guide to Mutual Funds* (available in most libraries), x has mean $\mu = 1.6\%$ and standard deviation $\sigma = 0.9\%$.

(a) Templeton World fund has over 250 stocks that combine together to give the overall monthly percentage return x. We can consider the monthly return of the stocks in the fund to be a sample from the population of monthly returns of all world stocks. Then we see that the overall monthly return x for Templeton World fund is itself an average return computed using all 250 stocks in the fund. Why would this indicate that x has an approximately normal distribution? Explain. *Hint:* See the discussion after Theorem 7.2.

(b) After 6 months, what is the probability that the *average* monthly percentage return $\bar{x}$ will be between 1% and 2%? *Hint:* See Theorem 7.1, and assume that x has a normal distribution as based on part (a).

(c) After 2 years, what is the probability that $\bar{x}$ will be between 1% and 2%?

(d) Compare your answers for parts (b) and (c). Did the probability increase as n (number of months) increased? Why would this happen?

(e) If after 2 years the average monthly percentage return $\bar{x}$ was less than 1%, would that tend to shake your confidence in the statement that $\mu = 1.6\%$? Might you suspect that μ has slipped below 1.6%? Explain.

12. *Finance: Dean Witter Funds* Dean Witter European Growth is a mutual fund that specializes in stocks from the British Isles, continental Europe, and Scandinavia. The

fund has over 100 stocks. Let x be a random variable that represents the monthly percentage return for this fund. Based on information from *Morningstar* (see Problem 11), x has mean $\mu = 1.4\%$ and standard deviation $\sigma = 0.8\%$.

(a) Let's consider the monthly return of the stocks in the Dean Witter fund to be a sample from the population of monthly returns of all European stocks. Is it reasonable to assume that $\bar{x}$ (the average monthly return on the 100 stocks in the Dean Witter European Growth fund) has a distribution that is approximately normal? Explain. *Hint:* See Problem 11, part (a).

(b) After 9 months, what is the probability that the *average* monthly percentage return $\bar{x}$ will be between 1% and 2%? *Hint:* See Theorem 7.1 and the results of part (a).

(c) After 18 months, what is the probability that the *average* monthly percentage return $\bar{x}$ will be between 1% and 2%?

(d) Compare your answers for parts (b) and (c). Did the probability increase as n (number of months) increased? Why would this happen?

(e) If after 18 months the average monthly percentage return $\bar{x}$ is more than 2%, would that tend to shake your confidence in the statement that $\mu = 1.4\%$? If this happened, do you think the European stock market might be heating up? Explain.

13. *Finance: Invesco Funds High-yield bonds* is a polite term for "junk bonds." Good companies with good products can fall on bad times (poor management, too rapid expansion, wrong marketing approach, etc.). Many of these companies will bounce back to profitability and handsomely reward investors who picked up their "bad debt" when the company was in trouble. Invesco High Yield is a mutual fund that specializes in high-yield bonds. It has approximately 80 or more bonds at the B or below rating (S&P rating for junk bonds). Let x be a random variable that represents the annual percentage return for the Invesco High Yield fund. Based on information from *Morningstar* (see Problem 11), x has mean $\mu = 10.8\%$ and standard deviation $\sigma = 4.9\%$.

(a) Let's consider the annual yield of the bonds in the Invesco fund to be a sample from the population of annual yields of all high-yield bonds. Explain why it would be reasonable to assume that $\bar{x}$ (the average annual return of all bonds in the Invesco fund) has a distribution that is approximately normal. *Hint:* See Problem 11, part (a).

(b) Compute the probability that after 5 years $\bar{x}$ is less than 6%. After 5 years, if the average annual percentage return $\bar{x}$ is less than 6%, would that seem to indicate that μ is less than 10.8% and that the junk bond market is not as strong? *Hint:* See Theorem 7.1 and the results of part (a).

(c) Compute the probability that after 5 years $\bar{x}$ is greater than 16%. After 5 years, if the average annual percentage return $\bar{x}$ is greater than 16%, would that seem to indicate that μ is more than 10.8% and that the junk bond market is heating up?

14. *Security: Night Watchman* Arthur is a night watchman in a large warehouse. During one complete round of the warehouse, he must check in at 40 different checkpoints, all of which are about the same distance apart. At each checkpoint he inserts a key that tells a central computer the time he checked in. Let x be a random variable representing the length of time from one check-in to the next. While monitoring Arthur's check-in times for the past year, the computer found the mean of the x distribution to be $\mu = 6.4$ minutes with standard deviation $\sigma = 1.5$ minutes.

(a) In one complete round of the warehouse, there are 40 check-in time intervals. What is the probability that the average check-in time interval will be from 6 to 7 minutes?

(b) Answer part (a) for two complete rounds of the warehouse (i.e., use a sample of 80 check-in time intervals).

(c) If in two complete rounds of the warehouse the average check-in time interval is not between 6 and 7 minutes, do you think a second security guard should drop in for a look? Would this seem to indicate that Arthur is going too slowly or too fast for some unexplained reason? Assume that Arthur begins a round at a time randomly selected by the computer to foil burglars looking for a time schedule.

15. *General: Distribution of Sample Means*
    (a) If we have a distribution of x values that is more or less mound-shaped and somewhat symmetrical, what is the sample size needed to claim that the distribution of sample means $\bar{x}$ from random samples of that size is approximately normal?
    (b) If the original distribution of x values is known to be normal, do we need to make any restriction about sample size in order to claim that the distribution of sample means $\bar{x}$ taken from random samples of a given size is normal?

16. *Focus Problem: Impulse Buying* Let x represent the dollar amount spent on supermarket impulse buying in a 10-minute (unplanned) shopping interval. Based on a *Denver Post* article, the mean of the x distribution is about \$20 and the estimated standard deviation is about \$7.
    (a) Consider a random sample of $n = 100$ customers, each of whom has 10 minutes of unplanned shopping time in a supermarket. From the central limit theorem, what can you say about the probability distribution of $\bar{x}$, the average amount spent by these customers due to impulse buying? What are the mean and standard deviation of the $\bar{x}$ distribution? Is it necessary to make any assumption about the x distribution? Explain.
    (b) What is the probability that $\bar{x}$ is between \$18 and \$22?
    (c) Let us assume that x has a distribution that is approximately normal. What is the probability that x is between \$18 and \$22?
    (d) In part (b) we used $\bar{x}$, the *average* amount spent, computed for 100 customers. In part (c) we used x, the amount spent by only *one* customer. The answers for parts (b) and (c) are very different. Why would this happen? In this example $\bar{x}$ is a much more predictable or reliable statistic than x. Consider that almost all marketing strategies and sales pitches are designed for the *average* customer and *not the individual* customer. How does the central limit theorem tell us that the average customer is much more predictable than the individual customer?

17. *Expand Your Knowledge: Totals Instead of Averages* Let x be a random variable that represents checkout time (time spent in the actual checkout process) in minutes in the express lane of a large grocery. Based on a consumer survey, the mean of the x distribution is about $\mu = 2.7$ minutes with standard deviation $\sigma = 0.6$ minute. Assume that the express lane always has customers waiting to be checked out and that the distribution of x values is more or less symmetrical and mound-shaped. What is the probability that the *total* checkout time for the next 30 customers is less than 90 minutes? Let us solve this problem in steps.
    (a) Let x_i (for $i = 1, 2, 3, \ldots, 30$) represent the checkout time for each customer. For example, x_1 is the checkout time for the first customer, x_2 is the checkout time for the second customer, and so forth. Each x_i has a mean $\mu = 2.7$ minutes and standard deviation $\sigma = 0.6$ minute. Let $w = x_1 + x_2 + \cdots + x_{30}$. Explain why the problem is asking us to compute the probability that w is less than 90.
    (b) Use a little algebra and explain why $w < 90$ is mathematically equivalent to $w/30 < 3$. Since w is the total of the 30 x values, then $w/30 = \bar{x}$. Therefore, the statement $\bar{x} < 3$ is equivalent to the statement $w < 90$. From this we conclude that the probabilities $P(\bar{x} < 3)$ and $P(w < 90)$ are equal.

(c) What does the central limit theorem say about the probability distribution of $\overline{x}$? Is it approximately normal? What are the mean and standard deviation of the $\overline{x}$ distribution?

(d) Use the result of part (c) to compute $P(\overline{x} < 3)$. What does this result tell you about $P(w < 90)$?

 18. *Totals Instead of Averages: Airplane Takeoff Time* The taxi and takeoff time for commercial jets is a random variable x with a mean of 8.5 minutes and a standard deviation of 2.5 minutes. Assume that the distribution of taxi and takeoff times is approximately normal. You may assume that the jets are lined up on a runway so that one taxies and takes off immediately after the other, and that they take off one at a time on a given runway. What is the probability that for 36 jets on a given runway total taxi and takeoff time will be

(a) less than 320 minutes?

(b) more than 275 minutes?

(c) between 275 and 320 minutes?

Hint: See Problem 17.

 19. *Totals Instead of Averages: Archaeological Stone Tools* Stone Age Native American dwellings were discovered at the Turquoise Ridge site near Fort Bliss, Texas. Let x be a random variable that represents grams (g) of chipped stone tools per cubic meter of excavated soil from prehistoric house dwellings at Turquoise Ridge. The x distribution has approximate mean $\mu = 240$ and standard deviation $\sigma = 84$ (based on information from *Turquoise Ridge and Late Prehistoric Residential Mobility in the Desert Mogollon Region*, by M. E. Whalen, University of Utah Press). Suppose that 45 cubic meters of excavated soil from Turquoise Ridge house dwellings is scheduled to be dug up and examined. What is the probability that the total weight of chipped stone tools in this soil is

(a) less than 9500 g?

(b) more than 12,000 g?

(c) between 9500 and 12,000 g?

Hint: See Problem 17.

 20. *Totals Instead of Averages: Manufacturing* It is important that each operation on an assembly line be completed in a predictable amount of time. In the assembly-line production of the Road Runner four-wheel-drive sport vehicle, the headlight installation process is designed to take an average of $\mu = 6.3$ minutes with standard deviation $\sigma = 1.2$ minutes for each vehicle.

(a) Assume that the assembly times follow a *normal* distribution and that the vehicles are lined up so that headlight units are installed on one vehicle right after another. What is the probability that the assembly time to install headlight units on nine vehicles is less than 60 minutes? more than 65 minutes? (*Hint:* See Problem 17 and Theorem 7.1.)

(b) What is the probability that the assembly time to install headlight units on 50 vehicles is less than 342 minutes? Is the normal assumption of part (a) necessary for a sample size this large? Why?

 21. *Totals Instead of Averages: Escape Dunes* It's true—sand dunes in Colorado rival sand dunes of the Great Sahara Desert! The highest dunes at Great Sand Dunes National Monument can exceed the highest dunes in the Great Sahara, extending over 700 feet in height. However, like all sand dunes, they tend to move around in the wind. This can cause a bit of trouble for temporary structures located near the "escaping" dunes. Roads, parking lots, campgrounds, small buildings, trees, and

other vegetation are destroyed when a sand dune moves in and takes over. Such dunes are called "escape dunes" in the sense that they move out of the main body of sand dunes and by the force of nature (prevailing winds) take over whatever space they choose to occupy. In most cases, dune movement does not occur quickly. An escape dune can take years to relocate itself. Just how fast does an escape dune move? Let x be a random variable representing movement (in feet per year) of such sand dunes (measured from the crest of the dune). Let us assume that x has a normal distribution with $\mu = 17$ ft/yr and $\sigma = 3.3$ ft/yr. (For more information, see *Hydrologic, Geologic, and Biologic Research at Great Sand Dunes National Monument and Vicinity, Colorado*, proceedings of the National Park Service Research Symposium.)

Under the influence of prevailing wind patterns, what is the probability that
(a) an escape dune will move a total distance of more than 90 feet in 5 years?
(b) an escape dune will move a total distance of less than 80 feet in 5 years?
(c) an escape dune will move a total distance of between 80 and 90 feet in 5 years?
Hint: See Problem 17 and Theorem 7.1.

7.3
Sampling Distributions for Proportions

FOCUS POINTS

✓ Compute the mean and standard deviation for the proportion $\hat{p} = r/n$.

✓ Use the normal approximation to compute probabilities for proportions $\hat{p} = r/n$.

✓ Construct *P*-Charts and interpret what they tell you.

In Section 6.4, we discussed the normal approximation to the binomial. There are many important situations where we prefer to work with the *proportion* of successes r/n rather than the actual *number* of successes r in binomial experiments. With this in mind, we make the following summary about the *sampling distribution* of the proportion $\hat{p} = r/n$.

Sampling distribution for the proportion $\hat{p} = \dfrac{r}{n}$

Given n = number of binomial trials (fixed constant)

r = number of successes

p = probability of success on each trial

$q = 1 - p$ = probability of failure on each trial

If $np > 5$ and $nq > 5$, then the random variable $\hat{p} = r/n$ can be approximated by a normal random variable (x) with mean and standard deviation

$$\mu_{\hat{p}} = p \quad \text{and} \quad \sigma_{\hat{p}} = \sqrt{\frac{pq}{n}}$$

◇ **TERMINOLOGY** The *standard error* for $\hat{p}$ is the standard deviation $\sigma_{\hat{p}}$ of the $\hat{p}$ sampling distribution. ◇

◇ **COMMENT** To obtain the information regarding the sampling distribution for the proportion $\hat{p} = r/n$, we consider the sampling distribution for r, the number of successes out of n binomial trials. In Section 6.4, we saw that when $np > 5$ and $nq > 5$, the r distribution is approximately normal with mean $\mu_r = np$

and standard deviation $\sigma_r = \sqrt{npq}$. Notice that $\hat{p} = r/n$ is a linear function of r. This means that the $\hat{p}$ distribution is also approximately normal when np and nq are both greater than 5. In addition, from our work in Section 5.1 with linear functions of random variables, we know that $\mu_{\hat{p}} = \mu_r/n = np/n = p$ and $\sigma_{\hat{p}} = \sigma_r/n = \sqrt{npq}/n = \sqrt{pq/n}$. ◇

If $np > 5$ and $nq > 5$, then $\hat{p} = r/n$ can be approximated by a normal random variable, which we will call x. However, $\hat{p}$ is *discrete* while x is *continuous*. To adjust for this discrepancy, we apply an appropriate *continuity correction*. In Section 6.4, we noted that in the probability histogram for the binomial random variable r, the bar centered over r actually starts at $r - 0.5$ and ends at $r + 0.5$. See Figure 7-3(a).

When we shift our focus from r to $\hat{p} = r/n$, the bar centered at r/n actually starts at $(r - 0.5)/n$ and ends at $(r + 0.5)/n$ as shown in Figure 7-3(b).

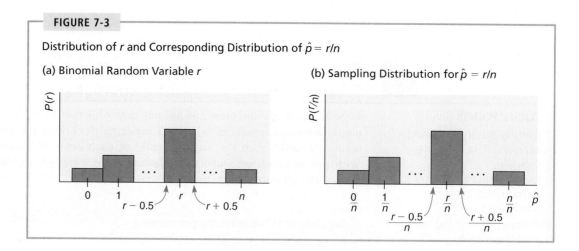

FIGURE 7-3

Distribution of r and Corresponding Distribution of $\hat{p} = r/n$

(a) Binomial Random Variable r

(b) Sampling Distribution for $\hat{p} = r/n$

This leads us to the conclusion that the appropriate continuity correction for $\hat{p}$ is to add or subtract $0.5/n$ to the endpoints of a $\hat{p}$ (discrete) interval to convert it to an x (continuous normal) interval.

PROCEDURE

How to make continuity corrections to $\hat{p}$ intervals

1. If r/n is the *right* endpoint of a $\hat{p}$ interval, we *add* $0.5/n$ to get the corresponding right endpoint of the x interval.
2. If r/n is the *left* endpoint of a $\hat{p}$ interval, we *subtract* $0.5/n$ to get the corresponding left endpoint of the x interval.

The next example illustrates the process of using the continuity correction to convert a $\hat{p}$ interval to an x (normal) interval.

EXAMPLE 4

Continuity correction

Suppose $n = 25$ and we have a $\hat{p}$ interval from $10/25 = 0.40$ to $15/25 = 0.60$. Use the continuity correction to convert this interval to an x interval.

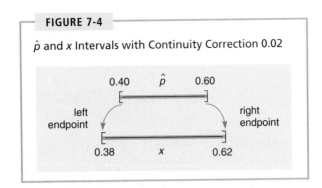

FIGURE 7-4

$\hat{p}$ and x Intervals with Continuity Correction 0.02

SOLUTION: Since $n = 25$, then $0.5/n = 0.5/25 = 0.02$. This means that we subtract 0.02 from the left endpoint and add 0.02 to the right endpoint of the $\hat{p}$ interval (see Figure 7-4).

$\hat{p}$ interval: 0.40 to 0.60

x interval: $0.40 - 0.02$ to $0.60 + 0.02$ or 0.38 to 0.62

◇ **COMMENT** If n is large, the continuity correction for $\hat{p}$ won't change the x interval much. However, for smaller n values, it can make a difference.   ◇

EXAMPLE 5

Sampling distribution of $\hat{p}$

The annual crime rate in the Capital Hill neighborhood of Denver is 111 victims per 1000 residents. This means that 111 out of 1000 residents have been the victim of at least one crime (Source: *Neighborhood Facts*, Piton Foundation). For more information, visit the Brase/Brase statistics site at **http://math.college.hmco.com/students** and find the link to the Piton Foundation. These crimes range from relatively minor crimes (stolen hubcaps or purse snatching) to major crimes (murder). The Arms is an apartment building in this neighborhood that has 50 year-round residents. Suppose we view each of the $n = 50$ residents as a binomial trial. The random variable r (which takes on values 0, 1, 2, ... , 50) represents the number of victims of at least one crime in the next year.

(a) What is the population probability p that a resident in the Capital Hill neighborhood will be the victim of a crime next year? What is the probability q that a resident will not be a victim?

SOLUTION: Using the Piton Foundation report, we take

$$p = 111/1000 = 0.111 \quad \text{and} \quad q = 1 - p = 0.889$$

(b) Consider the random variable

$$\hat{p} = \frac{r}{n} = \frac{r}{50}$$

Do you think we can approximate $\hat{p}$ with a normal distribution? Explain.

SOLUTION: $np = 50(0.111) = 5.55$

$nq = 50(0.889) = 44.45$

Since both np and nq are greater than 5, we can approximate $\hat{p}$ with a normal distribution.

(c) What are the mean and standard deviation for $\hat{p}$?

SOLUTION: $\mu_{\hat{p}} = p = 0.111$

$$\sigma_{\hat{p}} = \sqrt{\frac{pq}{n}}$$

$$= \sqrt{\frac{(0.111)(0.889)}{50}} \approx 0.044$$

(d) What is the probability that between 10% and 20% of the Arms residents will be victims of a crime next year?

SOLUTION: First we find the continuity correction so we can convert the $\hat{p}$ interval to an x interval. Since $n = 50$,

Continuity correction $= 0.5/n = 0.5/50 = 0.01$

We subtract 0.01 from the left $\hat{p}$ endpoint and add 0.01 to the right $\hat{p}$ endpoint (see Figure 7-5). The x interval is from 0.09 to 0.21. Therefore,

$$P(0.10 \le \hat{p} \le 0.20) \approx P(0.09 \le x \le 0.21)$$

$$\approx P\left(\frac{0.09 - 0.111}{0.044} \le z \le \frac{0.21 - 0.111}{0.044}\right)$$

$$\approx P(-0.48 \le z \le 2.25)$$

$$\approx 0.6722$$

FIGURE 7-5

$\hat{p}$ and x Intervals with Continuity Correction 0.01

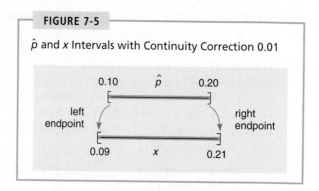

There is about a 67% chance that between 10% and 20% of the Arms residents will be crime victims next year. ◇

GUIDED EXERCISE 4

Sampling distribution of $\hat{p}$

The general ethnic profile of Denver is about 42% minority and 58% Caucasian (Source: *Neighborhood Facts*, Piton Foundation). Suppose the city of Denver recently hired 56 new grounds and maintenance workers. It was claimed that the hiring practice was completely impartial with regard to ethnic background. However, only 27% of the new employees are

Continued

GUIDED EXERCISE 4 continued

minorities, and now there is a complaint. What is the probability that at most 27% of the new hires are minorities if the selection is impartial and the applicant pool reflects the ethnic profile of Denver?

(a) We take the point of view that each new hire is a binomial experiment with success being a minority hire. What are the values of n, p, q?

$\implies$ $n = 56$; $p = 0.42$; $q = 0.58$

(b) For the new hires, what is the sample proportion $\hat{p}$ of minority hires?

$\implies$ $\hat{p} = 0.27$

(c) Is the normal approximation for the distribution of $\hat{p}$ appropriate? Explain.

$\implies$ $np = 56(0.42) \approx 23.5$;
$nq = 56(0.58) \approx 32.5$

Both products are larger than 5, so the approximation is appropriate.

(d) Compute $\mu_{\hat{p}}$ and $\sigma_{\hat{p}}$.

$\implies$ $\mu_{\hat{p}} = p = 0.42$

$$\sigma_{\hat{p}} = \sqrt{\frac{pq}{n}} = \sqrt{\frac{(0.42)(0.58)}{56}} \approx 0.066$$

(e) Compute $P(\hat{p} \le 0.27)$.

$\implies$ First find the continuity correction and convert $\hat{p} \le 0.27$ to an x interval (see Figure 7-6).

FIGURE 7-6 $\hat{p}$ and x Intervals with Continuity Correction 0.009

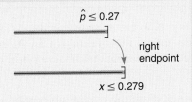

$\hat{p} \le 0.27$

right endpoint

$x \le 0.279$

Continuity correction: $\dfrac{0.5}{56} \approx 0.009$

x interval: $x \le 0.279$

$P(\hat{p} \le 0.27) \approx P(x \le 0.279)$

$$\approx P\left(z \le \frac{0.279 - 0.42}{0.066}\right)$$

$$\approx P(z \le -2.14)$$

$$\approx 0.0162$$

(f) What is your conclusion?

$\implies$ Assuming all the conditions for binomial trials have been met, the probability is smaller than 2% that the proportion of minority hires would be 27% or less. It seems the hiring process might not be completely impartial or the applicant pool does not reflect the ethnic profile of Denver.

Control Charts for Proportions (*P*-Charts)

We conclude this section with an example of a control chart for proportions r/n. Such a chart is often called a *P-Chart*.

The control charts discussed in Section 6.1 were for *quantitative* data, where the *size* of something is being measured. There are occasions where we prefer to examine a *quality* or *attribute* rather than just size. One way to do this is to use a binomial distribution in which success is defined as the quality or attribute we wish to study.

The basic idea for using P-Charts is to select samples of a fixed size n at regular time intervals and count the number of successes r from the n trials. We use the normal approximation for r/n and methods of Section 6.1 to plot control limits and r/n values, and to interpret results.

As in Section 6.1, we remind ourselves that control charts are used as warning devices tailored by a user for a particular need. Our assumptions and probability calculations need not be absolutely precise to achieve our purpose. For example, $\hat{p} = r/n$ need not follow a normal distribution exactly. A mound-shaped and more or less symmetric distribution to which the empirical rule applies will be sufficient.

EXAMPLE 6

P-Chart

Anatomy and Physiology is taught each semester. The course is required for several popular health-science majors, so it always fills up to its maximum of 60 students. The dean of the college asked the Biology Department to make a control chart for the proportion of A's given in the course each semester for the past 14 semesters. Using information from the registrar's office, the following data were obtained. Make a control chart and interpret the result.

Semester	1	2	3	4	5	6	7
r = no. of A's	9	12	8	15	6	7	13
$\hat{p} = r/60$	0.15	0.20	0.13	0.25	0.10	0.12	0.22

Semester	8	9	10	11	12	13	14
r = no. of A's	7	11	9	8	21	11	10
$\hat{p} = r/60$	0.12	0.18	0.15	0.13	0.35	0.18	0.17

SOLUTION: Let us view each student as a binomial trial where success is the quality or attribute we wish to study. Success means the student got an A, and failure is not getting an A. Since the class size is 60 students each semester, the number of trials is $n = 60$.

(a) The first step is to use the data to estimate the overall proportion of successes. To do this, we pool the data for all 14 semesters, and use the symbol $\bar{p}$ (not to be confused with $\hat{p}$) to designate the *pooled proportion* of success.

$$\bar{p} = \frac{\text{Total number of A's from all 14 semesters}}{\text{Total number of students from all 14 semesters}}$$

$$\bar{p} = \frac{9 + 12 + 8 + \cdots + 10}{14(60)} = \frac{147}{840} = 0.175$$

Since the pooled estimate for the proportion of successes is $\bar{p} = 0.175$, the estimate for the proportion of failures is $\bar{q} = 1 - \bar{p} = 0.825$.

(b) For the random variable $\hat{p} = r/n$, we know the mean is $\mu_{\hat{p}} = p$, and the standard deviation is $\sigma_{\hat{p}} = \sqrt{pq/n}$. In our case, we don't have given values for p and q, so we use the pooled estimates $\bar{p} = 0.175$ and $\bar{q} = 0.825$. The number of trials is the class size $n = 60$. Therefore,

$$\mu_{\hat{p}} = p \approx \bar{p} = 0.175$$

$$\sigma_{\hat{p}} = \sqrt{\frac{pq}{n}} \approx \sqrt{\frac{\bar{p}\,\bar{q}}{n}} = \sqrt{\frac{(0.175)(0.825)}{60}} \approx 0.049$$

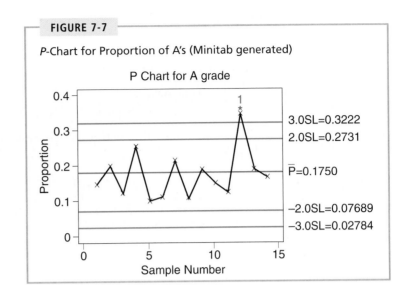

FIGURE 7-7

P-Chart for Proportion of A's (Minitab generated)

(c) Since a control chart is a *warning device*, it is not necessary that our probability calculations be absolutely precise. For instance, the empirical rule would substitute quite well for the normal distribution. However, it is a good idea to check that both $n\bar{p} = 60(0.175) = 10.5$ and $n\bar{q} = 60(0.825) = 49.5$ are larger than 5. This means the normal approximation should be reasonably good.

(d) Now we use the same basic methods of Section 6.1 to construct the control limits and control chart shown in Figure 7-7. The center line is at $\bar{p} = 0.175$.

$$\text{Control limits at } \bar{p} \pm 2\sqrt{\frac{\bar{p}\,\bar{q}}{n}} = 0.175 \pm 2(0.049) \text{ or } 0.077 \text{ and } 0.273$$

$$\text{Control limits at } \bar{p} \pm 3\sqrt{\frac{\bar{p}\,\bar{q}}{n}} = 0.175 \pm 3(0.049) \text{ or } 0.028 \text{ and } 0.322$$

(e) Interpretation: We use the three out-of-control signals discussed in Section 6.1.

Signal I—beyond the 3σ level.
    We see semester number 12 was above the 3σ level. That semester the class must have been very good indeed!

Signal II—run of nine *consecutive* points on one side of center line.
    Since this did not happen, there is no slow drift either up or down.

Signal III—at least two out of three *consecutive* points beyond the 2σ level (on the same side of center).
    This out-of-control signal did not occur.

(f) Conclusion: The Biology Department can tell the dean that the proportion of A's given in Anatomy and Physiology is in statistical control with the exception of one unusually good class two semesters ago.   ◇

PROCEDURE

How to make a *P*-Chart

1. Estimate $\bar{p}$, the overall proportion of successes.

$$\bar{p} = \frac{\text{Total number of observed successes in all samples}}{\text{Total number of trials in all samples}}$$

2. The center line of the control chart is assigned to be $\mu_{\hat{p}} = \bar{p}$.

3. Control limits are located at

$$\bar{p} \pm 2\sqrt{\frac{\bar{p}\,\bar{q}}{n}} \quad \text{and} \quad \bar{p} \pm 3\sqrt{\frac{\bar{p}\,\bar{q}}{n}}$$

4. Interpretation: Out-of-control signals

(a) Signal I: any point beyond a $\bar{p} \pm 3\sqrt{\dfrac{\bar{p}\,\bar{q}}{n}}$ control limit.

(b) Signal II: run of nine *consecutive* points on *one side* of the center line $\mu_{\hat{p}} = \bar{p}$.

(c) Signal III: at least two out of three *consecutive* points beyond a $\bar{p} \pm 2\sqrt{\dfrac{\bar{p}\,\bar{q}}{n}}$ control limit (on the same side).

If no out-of-control signals occur, we say that the process is "in control," while keeping a watchful eye on what occurs next.

◇ **COMMENT** In some *P*-Charts the value of $\bar{p}$ may be near 0 or near 1. In this case, the control limits may drop below 0 or rise above 1. If this happens, we follow the usual convention of rounding negative control limits to 0 and rounding control limits above 1 to 1.   ◇

VIEW⊙INT

Happy Memories! False Memories!!!

"Memory isn't a record; it's an interpretation," says psychologist Mark Reinitz of the University of Puget Sound, Washington. Research indicates that about 68% of all people occasionally "fill in the blanks" in their memories. They claim to remember things that did not actually occur. In another study, it was found that 35% of visitors to Disneyland claimed they shook hands with Bugs Bunny, who welcomed them at the entrance. However, Bugs Bunny is *not* a Disney character and was *not* at the Disneyland entrance.

Psychologists say memory is malleable for a reason. It helps us view ourselves in a more positive light. Statistical interpretation of proportions $\hat{p}$ are useful in this memory study, as well as all areas of natural science, business, linguistics, and social science. For more information about the memory study, see the July 2001 issue of the *Journal of Experimental Psychology*.

SECTION 7.3   PROBLEMS

1. *General Discussion* Suppose we have a binomial experiment in which success is defined to be a particular quality or attribute that interests us.
   (a) Examples of some attributes are an opinion about gun control (Problem 4), or identifying a special cell in bone marrow tissue (Problem 8). List at least three other attributes that could be used to define success in a binomial trial.
   (b) Our binomial experiment has n trials. The probability of success is p, and the number of successes is the random variable r. In this section, we study the proportion $\hat{p} = r/n$. Under what conditions can the random variable $\hat{p}$ be approximated by a normal random variable? What are the formulas for $\mu_{\hat{p}}$ and $\sigma_{\hat{p}}$?
   (c) Suppose $n = 33$ and $p = 0.21$. Can we approximate $\hat{p}$ by a normal distribution? Why? What are the values of $\mu_{\hat{p}}$ and $\sigma_{\hat{p}}$? What is the value of the continuity correction? Compute $P(0.15 \leq \hat{p} \leq 0.25)$.
   (d) Suppose $n = 25$ and $p = 0.15$. Can we safely approximate $\hat{p}$ by a normal distribution? Why or why not?
   (e) Suppose $n = 48$ and $p = 0.15$. Can we approximate $\hat{p}$ by a normal distribution? Why? What are the values of $\mu_{\hat{p}}$ and $\sigma_{\hat{p}}$? If a survey, experiment, or laboratory work gives us a $\hat{p}$ value of 0.22, what is the probability of getting a $\hat{p}$ value this high or higher?

2. *General Discussion* Suppose we have a binomial distribution with n trials and probability of success p. The random variable r is the number of successes in the n trials, and the random variable representing the proportion of successes is $\hat{p} = r/n$.
   (a) $n = 50$; $p = 0.36$; Compute $P(0.30 \leq \hat{p} \leq 0.45)$.
   (b) $n = 38$; $p = 0.25$; Compute the probability that $\hat{p}$ will exceed 0.35.
   (c) $n = 41$; $p = 0.09$; Can we approximate $\hat{p}$ by a normal distribution? Explain.

3. *Sociology: Criminal Justice* Courts sometimes make mistakes, but which do you believe is the worse mistake: convicting an innocent person or letting a guilty person go free? It turns out that about 60% of all Americans believe that convicting an innocent person is the worse mistake. (Source: *American Attitudes* by S. Mitchell, Sociology Department, Ithaca College.) Suppose you are taking a sociology class with 30 students enrolled. The question discussed today is: Do you agree with the statement that convicting an innocent person is worse than letting the guilty go free? What is the probability that the proportion of the class who agree is
   (a) at least one half?
   (b) at least two thirds?
   (c) no more than one third?
   (d) Is the normal approximation to the proportion $\hat{p} = r/n$ valid? Explain.

4. *Sociology: Gun Permits* Do you favor a law requiring a police permit to buy a gun? About 73% of American men and 86% of American women would favor such a law. (Source: See Problem 3.)
   (a) A candidate for city council is speaking to a breakfast group of 38 men. The topic of gun permits comes up. What is the probability that the majority of the audience (at least two thirds) will support gun permits? Assume the group is representative of all U.S. men.
   (b) Answer part (a) if our candidate is speaking to a women's seminar with 45 women in the audience. Assume the group is representative of all U.S. women.
   (c) Is the normal approximation to the proportion $\hat{p} = r/n$ valid in both applications? Explain.

5. *Who's Who: Misinformation* About 11% of Americans believe that Joan of Arc was Noah's wife. (Source: *Harper's Index*, Volume 3.) At a large freshman symposium, a college professor (jokingly) says that Joan of Arc was Noah's wife. Assume that college freshmen are representative of the general American population regarding biblical knowledge.
   (a) If the symposium was attended by 55 freshmen, what is the probability that up to 15% of the freshmen believe the professor's claim?
   (b) What is the probability that between 10% and 15% (including 10% and 15%) of the freshmen believe the professor's claim?
   (c) Is the normal approximation to the proportion $\hat{p} = r/n$ valid in this application? Explain.

6. *Grand Canyon: Boating Accidents* Thomas Myers is a staff physician at the clinic in Grand Canyon Village. Based on reports in recent years, Dr. Myers estimates that about 31% of the boating accidents on the Colorado River in Grand Canyon National Park occur at Crystal Rapids (mile 98). These range from small accidents (a few bruises) to major accidents (death). (Source: *Fateful Journey*, Myers, Becker, and Stevens.) In the next 28 boating accidents to be reported:
   (a) What is the probability that at least 25% of these accidents occurred at Crystal Rapids?
   (b) What is the probability that between 25% and 50% (including 25% and 50%) of these accidents occurred at Crystal Rapids?
   (c) Is the normal approximation to the proportion $\hat{p} = r/n$ valid in this application? Explain.

7. *Manufacturing: Defective Toys* A mechanical press is used to mold shapes for plastic toys. When the machine is adjusted and working well, it still produces about 6% defective toys. The toys are manufactured in lots of $n = 100$. Let r be a random variable representing the number of defective toys in a lot. Then $\hat{p} = r/n$ is the proportion of defective toys in a lot.
   (a) Explain why $\hat{p}$ can be approximated by a normal random variable. What are $\mu_{\hat{p}}$ and $\sigma_{\hat{p}}$?
   (b) Suppose a lot of 100 toys had a 7% proportion of defective toys. What is the probability that a situation this bad or worse could occur? Compute $P(0.07 \le \hat{p})$.
   (c) Suppose a lot of 100 toys had an 11% proportion of defective toys. What is the probability that a situation this bad or worse could occur? Compute $P(0.11 \le \hat{p})$. Do you think the machine might need an adjustment? Explain.

8. *Medical Tests: Leukemia* Healthy adult bone marrow contains about 56.5% neutrophils (a particular type of white blood cell). However, if this level is significantly reduced, it may be an early indicator of leukemia (Reference: *Diagnostic Tests with Nursing Implications*, edited by S. Loeb, Springhouse).
   (a) In a laboratory biopsy, a field of $n = 50$ bone marrow cells are observed under a microscope. A special dye is inserted, which only the neutrophils absorb. Then the number r of neutrophils in the field is counted. Although the field size $n = 50$ is fixed, the number of neutrophils r is a random variable. So the proportion $\hat{p} = r/n$ is also a random variable. Explain why $\hat{p}$ can be approximated by a normal random variable. What are $\mu_{\hat{p}}$ and $\sigma_{\hat{p}}$?
   (b) Suppose Jan had a bone marrow biopsy and $\hat{p}$ was observed to be 0.53. Assuming nothing is wrong (no leukemia), what is the probability of getting a biopsy result this low or lower? Compute $P(\hat{p} \le 0.53)$.
   (c) Suppose Meredith had a bone marrow biopsy and $\hat{p}$ was observed to be 0.41. Assuming nothing is wrong (no leukemia), what is the probability of getting a biopsy result this low or lower? Compute $P(\hat{p} \le 0.41)$.
   (d) Based on the probability estimates in parts (b) and (c), which do you think is the more serious case, Jan or Meredith? Explain.

9. *P-Chart: Property Crime* Lee is a cadet at the Honolulu Police Academy. He was asked to make a *P*-Chart for reported (minor) property crimes. Lee chose a small neighborhood with 92 families. Each family is viewed as a binomial trial. Success means that the family was a victim of at least one minor property crime in the past 3 months. Police reports gave the following data for the past 12 quarters (4 years). Assume the 92 families lived in the neighborhood all 4 years.

Quarter	1	2	3	4	5	6
r = no. of successes	11	14	18	23	19	15
$\hat{p} = r/92$	0.12	0.15	0.20	0.25	0.21	0.16

Quarter	7	8	9	10	11	12
r = no. of successes	12	16	13	22	24	19
$\hat{p} = r/92$	0.13	0.17	0.14	0.24	0.26	0.21

Make a *P*-Chart, and list any out-of-control signals by type (I, II, or III).

10. *P-Chart: Aluminum Cans* A high-speed metal stamp machine produces 12-oz. aluminum beverage cans. The cans are mass produced in lots of 110 cans for each square sheet of aluminum fed into the machine. However, some of the cans come out of the die stamp with folds and wrinkles. These are defective cans that must be recycled. Let us view each can as a binomial trial, where success is defined to mean the can is defective. So we have $n = 110$ trials (cans), and the random variable r is the number of defective cans. A test run of 15 consecutive aluminum sheets gave the following numbers r of defective cans.

Test sheet	1	2	3	4	5	6	7	8
r	8	11	6	9	12	8	7	11
$\hat{p} = r/110$	0.07	0.10	0.05	0.08	0.11	0.07	0.06	0.10

Test sheet	9	10	11	12	13	14	15
r	10	7	9	6	12	7	10
$\hat{p} = r/110$	0.09	0.06	0.08	0.05	0.11	0.06	0.09

Make a *P*-Chart and list any out-of-control signals by type (I, II, or III). Does it appear from the sequential test runs that the production process is in reasonable control? Explain.

11. *P-Chart: Temporary Work* Jobs for the homeless! A philanthropic foundation bought a used school bus that stops at homeless shelters early every weekday morning. The bus picks up people looking for temporary, unskilled day jobs. The bus delivers these people to a work center. Later it picks them up after work. The bus can hold 75 people, and it fills up every morning. Not everyone finds work, so at 11 A.M. the bus goes to a soup kitchen where those not finding work that day volunteer their time. Let us view each person on the bus looking for work as a binomial trial. Success means he or she got a day job. The random variable r represents the number who got jobs. The foundation requested a *P*-Chart for the success ratios. For the past three weeks, we have the following data.

Day	1	2	3	4	5	6	7	8
r	60	53	61	66	67	55	53	58
$\hat{p} = r/75$	0.80	0.71	0.81	0.88	0.89	0.73	0.71	0.77

Day	9	10	11	12	13	14	15
r	60	52	46	52	61	70	58
$\hat{p} = r/75$	0.80	0.69	0.61	0.69	0.81	0.93	0.77

Make a *P*-Chart, list any out-of-control signals, and interpret the results.

VIEWPOINT   Why Wait? Apply Now for a College Loan!

The cost of education is high. The cost of not having an education is higher! What kinds of costs can you expect? What about tuition and student fees? What about room and board? What is the total cost for 1 year at college? Perhaps some averages based on random samples of colleges would be useful. For more information, visit the Brase/Brase statistics site at **http://math.college. hmco.com/students** and find the link to the U.S. News site. Then select education. Search for the geographic regions of the colleges of interest.

SUMMARY

Sampling distributions give us the basis for inferential statistics. By studying the distribution of sample statistics, we can learn about a population parameter.

The central limit theorem describes the sampling distribution of sample means taken from samples of size *n*. It tells us that for increasing sample size *n*, the distribution of sample means $\bar{x}$ approaches a normal distribution with mean $\mu_{\bar{x}} = \mu$ and standard deviation $\sigma_{\bar{x}} = \sigma/\sqrt{n}$. The values of μ and σ are the population mean and standard deviation, respectively, of the original *x* distribution.

In the last section, we studied the proportion of successes $\hat{p} = r/n$ in binomial trials. When both *np* and *nq* are greater than 5, the sampling distribution for proportions is approximately normal with mean $\mu_{\hat{p}} = p$ and standard deviation $\sigma_{\hat{p}} = \sqrt{pq/n}$. We use the normal distribution to compute the probability that $\hat{p}$ lies in a specified interval. However, we first make continuity corrections on the interval by adding $0.5/n$ to the right endpoint and subtracting $0.5/n$ from the left endpoint.

Finally, we looked at *P*-Charts, which are control charts for proportions.

IMPORTANT WORDS & SYMBOLS

Section 7.1
Population parameter
Statistic
Sampling distribution

Section 7.2
$\mu_{\bar{x}}$
$\sigma_{\bar{x}}$
Standard error of the mean
Central limit theorem

Section 7.3
Sampling distribution for $\hat{p}$
$\mu_{\hat{p}}$
$\sigma_{\hat{p}}$
Continuity correction, $0.5/n$
P-Chart

CHAPTER REVIEW PROBLEMS

1. *General Discussion* Let x be a random variable representing the amount of sleep each adult in New York City got last night. Consider a sampling distribution of sample means $\bar{x}$.
   (a) As the sample size becomes increasingly large, what distribution does the $\bar{x}$ distribution approach?
   (b) As the sample size becomes increasingly large, what value will the mean $\mu_{\bar{x}}$ of the $\bar{x}$ distribution approach?
   (c) What value will the standard deviation $\sigma_{\bar{x}}$ of the sampling distribution approach?
   (d) How do the two $\bar{x}$ distributions for sample size $n = 50$ and $n = 100$ compare?

2. *Normal Distributions: General Discussion* If x has a normal distribution with mean $\mu = 15$ and standard deviation $\sigma = 3$, describe the distribution of $\bar{x}$ values for sample size n, where $n = 4$, $n = 16$, and $n = 100$. How do the $\bar{x}$ distributions compare for the various sample sizes?

3. *Job Interview: Length* The personnel office at a large electronics firm regularly schedules job interviews and maintains records of the interviews. From the past records, they have found that the length of a first interview is normally distributed with mean $\mu = 35$ minutes and standard deviation $\sigma = 7$ minutes.
   (a) What is the probability that a first interview will last 40 minutes or longer?
   (b) Nine first interviews are usually scheduled per day. What is the probability that the average length of time for the nine interviews will be 40 minutes or longer?

4. *Drugs: Effects* A new muscle relaxant is available. Researchers from the firm developing the relaxant have done studies that indicate that the time lapse between administration of the drug and beginning effects of the drug is normally distributed, with mean $\mu = 38$ minutes and standard deviation $\sigma = 5$ minutes.
   (a) The drug is administered to one patient selected at random. What is the probability that the time it takes to go into effect is 35 minutes or less?
   (b) The drug is administered to a random sample of 10 patients. What is the probability that the average time before it is effective for all 10 patients is 35 minutes or less?
   (c) Comment on the differences of the results in parts (a) and (b).

5. *Psychology: IQ Scores* Assume that IQ scores are normally distributed with standard deviation of 15 points and mean of 100 points. If 100 people are chosen at random, what is the probability that the sample mean of IQ scores will not differ from the population mean by more than 2 points?

6. *Hatchery Fish: Length* A large tank of fish from a hatchery is being delivered to a lake. The hatchery claims that the mean length of fish in the tank is 15 inches, and the standard deviation is 2 inches. A random sample of 36 fish is taken from the tank. Let $\bar{x}$ be the mean sample length of these fish. What is the probability that $\bar{x}$ is within 0.5 inch of the claimed population mean?

7. *Light Bulbs: Hours of Life* A company that makes light bulbs claims that its bulbs have an average life of 750 hours with standard deviation of 20 hours. A random sample of 64 light bulbs is taken. Let $\bar{x}$ be the mean life of this sample.
   (a) What is the probability that $\bar{x} \geq 750$?
   (b) What is the probability that $745 \leq \bar{x} \leq 755$?

8. *Meteorology: Miami and Fairbanks* Let x be a random variable that represents daily high temperatures (in degrees Fahrenheit) in January. The following information is based on a report from the U.S. Department of Commerce Environmental Data Services. For Miami, Florida, the mean of the x distribution is $\mu = 76$, and the standard deviation is approximately $\sigma = 1.9$. For Fairbanks, Alaska, the mean of the x distribution is $\mu = 0$ with approximate standard deviation $\sigma = 5.3$. Assume that x has a normal distribution.
   (a) For one day chosen at random in January, what is the probability that the high temperature in Miami will be less than 77°F? What is the probability that the high temperature in Fairbanks will be less than 3°F?
   (b) If we choose $n = 7$ days in January, what can we say about the probability distribution of $\bar{x}$, the average high temperature? What is the probability that $\bar{x}$ is less than 77°F for Miami? less than 3°F for Fairbanks?
   (c) Suppose that we cannot assume that x has a normal distribution, but we can say that the distribution is approximately symmetrical and mound-shaped. In this case, what can we say about the $\bar{x}$ probability distribution? If we use all 31 days in January, what is the probability that $\bar{x} < 77$°F in Miami? less than 3°F in Fairbanks?

9. *General Discussion* Suppose we have a binomial distribution with n trials and probability of success p. The random variable r is the number of successes in the n trials, and the random variable representing the proportion of successes is $\hat{p} = r/n$.
   (a) $n = 50$; $p = 0.22$; Compute $P(0.20 \leq \hat{p} \leq 0.25)$.
   (b) $n = 38$; $p = 0.27$; Compute the probability that $\hat{p}$ will equal or exceed 0.35.
   (c) $n = 51$; $p = 0.05$; Can we approximate $\hat{p}$ by a normal distribution? Explain.

DATA HIGHLIGHTS: GROUP PROJECTS

Break into small groups and discuss the following topics. Organize a brief outline in which you summarize the main points of your group discussion.

Iris setosa is a beautiful wildflower that is found in such diverse places as Alaska, the Gulf of St. Lawrence, much of North America, and even in English meadows and parks. R. A. Fisher, with his colleague Dr. Edgar Anderson, studied these flowers extensively. Dr. Anderson described how he collected information on irises:

I have studied such irises as I could get to see, in as great detail as possible, measuring iris standard after iris standard and iris fall after iris fall, sitting

Wild iris

squat-legged with record book and ruler in mountain meadows, in cypress swamps, on lake beaches, and in English parks. [Anderson, E., "The Irises of the Gaspé Peninsula," *Bulletin, American Iris Society*, 59:2–5, 1935.]

The data in Table 7-3 were collected by Dr. Anderson and were published by his friend and colleague R. A. Fisher in a paper entitled "The Use of Multiple Measurements in Taxonomic Problems" (*Annals of Eugenics*, part II, 179–188, 1936). To find these data, visit the Brase/Brase statistics site at **http://math.college.hmco.com/students** and find the link to DASL, the Carnegie Mellon University Data and Story Library. From the DASL site, look under famous data sets.

Let x be a random variable representing petal length. Using a TI-84Plus/TI-83Plus calculator, it was found that the sample mean is $\bar{x} = 1.46$ cm and the sample standard deviation is $s = 0.17$ cm. Figure 7-8 shows a histogram for the given data generated on a TI-84Plus/TI-83Plus calculator.

(a) Examine the histogram for petal lengths. Would you say that the distribution is approximately mound-shaped and symmetrical? Our sample has only 50 irises; if many thousands of irises had been used, do you think that the distribution would look even more like a normal curve? Let x be the petal length of *Iris setosa*. Research has shown that x has an approximately normal distribution with mean $\mu = 1.5$ cm and standard deviation $\sigma = 0.2$ cm.

(b) Use the empirical rule with $\mu = 1.5$ and $\sigma = 0.2$ to get an interval in which approximately 68% of the petal lengths will fall. Repeat this for 95% and 99.7%. Examine the raw data and compute the percentage of the raw data that actually falls into each of these intervals (the 68% interval, the 95% interval, and the 99.7% interval). Compare your computed percentages with those given by the empirical rule.

(c) Compute the probability that a petal length is between 1.3 and 1.6 cm. Compute the probability that a petal length is greater than 1.6 cm.

(d) Suppose that a random sample of 30 irises is obtained. Compute the probability that the average petal length for this sample is between 1.3 and 1.6 cm. Compute the probability that the average petal length is greater than 1.6 cm.

(e) Compare your answers for parts (c) and (d). Do you notice any differences? Why would these differences occur?

TABLE 7-3   Petal Length in Centimeters for
Iris setosa

1.4	1.4	1.3	1.5	1.4
1.7	1.4	1.5	1.4	1.5
1.5	1.6	1.4	1.1	1.2
1.5	1.3	1.4	1.7	1.5
1.7	1.5	1	1.7	1.9
1.6	1.6	1.5	1.4	1.6
1.6	1.5	1.5	1.4	1.5
1.2	1.3	1.4	1.3	1.5
1.3	1.3	1.3	1.6	1.9
1.4	1.6	1.4	1.5	1.4

FIGURE 7-8

Petal Length (cm) for *Iris setosa*
(TI-84Plus/TI-83Plus)

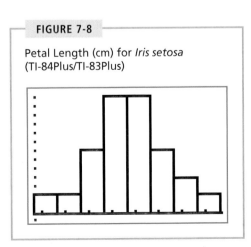

LINKING CONCEPTS: WRITING PROJECTS

Discuss each of the following topics in class, or review the topics on your own. Then write a brief but complete essay in which you summarize the main points. Please include formulas and graphs as appropriate.

1. Most people would agree that increased information should give better predictions. Discuss how sampling distributions actually enable better predictions by providing more information. Examine Theorem 7.1 again. Suppose that x is a random variable with a *normal* distribution. Then $\bar{x}$, the sample mean based on random samples of size n, also will have a normal distribution for *any* value of $n = 1, 2, 3, \ldots$.

   What happens to the standard deviation of the $\bar{x}$ distribution as n (the sample size) increases? Consider the following table for different values of n.

n	1	2	3	4	10	50	100
$\sigma/\sqrt{n}$	1σ	0.71σ	0.58σ	0.50σ	0.32σ	0.14σ	0.10σ

   In this case, "increased information" means a larger sample size n. Give a brief explanation as to why a *large* standard deviation will usually result in poor statistical predictions, whereas a *small* standard deviation usually results in much better predictions. Since the standard deviation of the sampling distribution $\bar{x}$ is $\sigma/\sqrt{n}$, we can decrease the standard deviation by increasing n. In fact, if we look at the preceding table, we see that if we use a sample size of only $n = 4$, we cut the standard deviation of $\bar{x}$ by 50% of the standard deviation σ of x. If we were to use a sample of size $n = 100$, we would cut the standard deviation of $\bar{x}$ to 10% of the standard deviation σ of x.

   Give the preceding discussion some thought and explain why you should get much better predictions for μ by using $\bar{x}$ from a sample of size n rather than by just using x. Write a brief essay in which you explain why sampling distributions are an important tool in statistics.

2. In a way, the central limit theorem can be thought of as a kind of "grand central station." It is a connecting hub or center for a great deal of statistical work. We will use it extensively in Chapters 8, 9, and 10. Put in a very elementary way, the central limit theorem states that as the sample size n increases, the mean $\bar{x}$ will always approach a normal distribution, no matter where the original x variable came from. For most people, it is the complete generality of the central limit theorem that is so awe inspiring: It applies to practically everything. List and discuss at least three variables from everyday life for which you expect the variable x itself does *not* follow a normal or bell-shaped distribution. Then discuss what would happen to the sampling distribution $\bar{x}$ if the sample size were increased. Sketch diagrams of the $\bar{x}$ distributions as the sample size n increases.

As we have seen in this chapter, the value of a sample statistic such as $\bar{x}$ varies from one sample to another. The central limit theorem describes the distribution of the sample statistic $\bar{x}$ when samples are sufficiently large.

We can use technology tools to generate samples of the same size from the same population. Then we can look at the statistic $\bar{x}$ for each sample, and the resulting $\bar{x}$ distribution.

Project Illustrating the Central Limit Theorem

Step 1: Generate random samples of specified size n from a population.

    The random-number table enables us to sample from the uniform distribution of digits 0 through 9. Use either the random-number table or a random-number generator to generate 30 samples of size 10.

Step 2: Compute the sample mean $\bar{x}$ of the digits in each sample.

Step 3: Compute the sample mean of the means (i.e., $\bar{x}_{\bar{x}}$) as well as the standard deviation $s_{\bar{x}}$ of the sample means.

The population mean of the uniform distribution of digits from 0 through 9 is 4.5. How does $\bar{x}_{\bar{x}}$ compare to this value?

Step 4: Compare the sample distribution of $\bar{x}$ values to a normal distribution having the mean and standard deviation computed in Step 3.

    (a) Use the values of $\bar{x}_{\bar{x}}$ and $s_{\bar{x}}$ computed in Step 3 to create the intervals shown in column 1 of Table 7-4.

    (b) Tally the sample means computed in Step 2 to determine how many fall into each interval of column 2. Then compute the percent of data in each interval and record the results in column 3.

    (c) The percentages listed in column 4 are those from a normal distribution (see Figure 6-5 showing the empirical rule). Compare the percentages in column 3 to those in column 4. How do the sample percentages compare with the hypothetical normal distribution?

Step 5: Create a histogram showing the sample means computed in Step 2.

TABLE 7-4 Frequency Table of Sample Means

1. Interval	2. Frequency	3. Percent	4. Hypothetical Normal Distribution
$\bar{x} - 3s$ to $\bar{x} - 2s$	Tally the sample means computed in step 2 and place here.	Compute percents from column 2 and place here.	2 or 3%
$\bar{x} - 2s$ to $\bar{x} - s$			13 or 14%
$\bar{x} - s$ to $\bar{x}$			About 34%
$\bar{x}$ to $\bar{x} + s$			About 34%
$\bar{x} + s$ to $\bar{x} + 2s$			13 or 14%
$\bar{x} + 2s$ to $\bar{x} + 3s$			2 or 3%

Look at the histogram, and compare it to a normal distribution with the mean and standard deviation of the $\bar{x}$s (as computed in Step 3).

Step 6: Compare the results of this project to the central limit theorem.

Increase the sample size of Step 1 to 20, 30, and 40 and repeat Steps 1 to 5.

Technology Hints

The TI-84Plus and TI-83Plus calculators, Excel, Minitab, and SPSS all support the process of drawing random samples from a variety of distributions. Macros can be written in Excel, Minitab, and the professional version of SPSS to repeat the six steps of the project.

Figure 7-9 shows histograms generated by SPSS for random samples of size 30 and size 100. The samples are taken from a uniform probability distribution.

TI-84Plus/TI-83Plus

You can generate random samples from uniform, normal, and binomial distributions. Press **MATH**, and select **PRB**. Selection **5:randInt(lower, upper, sample size m)** generates m random integers from the specified interval. Selection **6:randNorm(μ, σ, sample size m)** generates m random numbers from a normal distribution with mean μ and standard deviation σ. Selection **7:randBin(number of trials n, p, sample size m)** generates m random values (number of successes out of n trials) for a binomial distribution with probability of

FIGURE 7-9 SPSS-Generated Histograms for Samples of Size 30 and Size 100

(a) $n = 30$

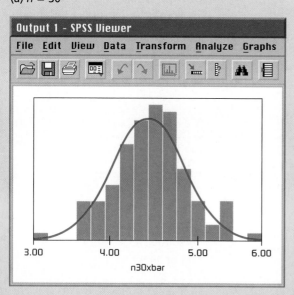

(b) $n = 100$

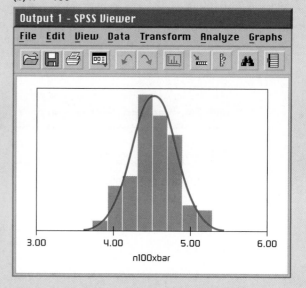

success p on each trial. You can put these values in lists by using **Edit** under **Stat.** Highlight the list header, press Enter, and then select one of the options discussed.

Excel

Use the menu selection **Tools ➤ Data Analysis ➤ Random Number Generator.** The dialogue box provides choices for the population distribution, including uniform, binomial, and normal distributions. Fill in the required parameters and designate the location for the output.

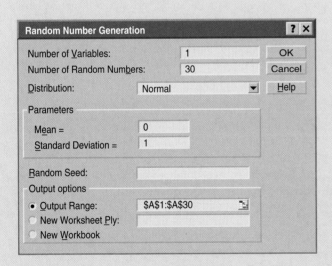

Minitab

Use the menu selections **Calc ➤ Random Data.** Then select the population distribution. The choices include uniform, binomial, and normal distributions. Fill in the dialogue box, where the number of rows indicates the number of data in the sample.

SPSS

SPSS supports random samples from a variety of distributions, including binomial, normal, and uniform. In data view, generate a column of consecutive integers from 1 to n, where n is the sample size. In variable view, name the variables sample1, sample2, and so on through sample30. These variables head the columns containing each of the 30 samples of size n. Then use the menu choices **Transform ➤ Compute.** In the dialogue box, use sample 1 as the target variable for the first sample, and so forth. In the function box, select **RV.UNIFORM(min,max)** for samples from a uniform distribution. Functions **RV.NORMAL(mean,stddev)** and **RV.BINOM(n,p)** provide random samples from normal and binomial distributions, respectively.

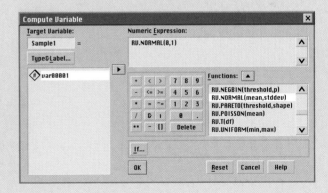

8

Estimation

We dance round in a ring and suppose,
But the Secret sits in the middle and knows.

—Robert Frost,
"The Secret Sits"*

In Chapter 1 we said that statistics is the study of how to collect, organize, analyze, and interpret numerical data. That part of statistics concerned with analysis, interpretation, and forming conclusions about the source of the data is called *statistical inference*. Problems of statistical inference require us to draw a *sample* of observations from a larger *population*. A sample usually contains incomplete information, so in a sense we must "dance round in a ring and suppose." Nevertheless, conclusions about the population can be obtained from sample data by use of statistical estimates. This chapter introduces you to several widely used methods of estimation.

*Source: From *The Poetry of Robert Frost*, edited by Edward Connery Lathem. Copyright 1942 by Robert Frost, © 1970 by Lesley Frost Ballantine, © 1969 by Henry Holt and Company, Inc. Reprinted by permission of Henry Holt and Company, Inc.

**Robert Lee Frost
(1874–1963)**

This celebrated American poet drew poetic symbols largely from common experiences observed in his rural New England.

PREVIEW QUESTIONS

◇ How do you estimate the expected value of a random variable? What assumptions are needed? How much confidence should be placed in such estimates?   (SECTION 8.1)

◇ What famous statistician worked for Guinness brewing company in Ireland? What has this to do with constructing estimates from sample data?   (SECTION 8.2)

◇ How about estimating the proportion *p* for success in a binomial experiment? How does the normal approximation fit into this process?   (SECTION 8.3)

◇ If you start out in the beginning design stage of a statistical project, how large a sample size should you plan to get? (SECTION 8.4)

◇ So what is the big difference? Sometimes differences in life can be important. How do you estimate differences?   (SECTION 8.5)

For on-line student resources, visit
math.college.hmco.com/students
and follow the Statistics links to the Brase/Brase, *Understandable Statistics,* 8th edition web site.

FOCUS PROBLEM

The Trouble with Wood Ducks

The National Wildlife Federation published an article entitled "The Trouble with Wood Ducks" (*National Wildlife*, Vol. 31, No. 5). In this article, wood ducks are described as beautiful birds living in forested areas such as the Pacific Northwest and Southeast United States. Because of overhunting and habitat destruction, these birds were in danger of extinction. A federal ban on hunting wood ducks in 1918 helped save the species from extinction. Wood ducks like to nest in tree cavities. However, many such trees were disappearing due to heavy timber cutting. For a period of time it seemed that nesting boxes were the solution to disappearing trees. At first, the wood duck population grew, but after a few seasons, the population declined sharply. Good biology research combined with good statistics provided an answer to this disturbing phenomenon.

Cornell University professors of ecology Paul Sherman and Brad Semel found that the nesting boxes were placed too close to each other.

Female wood ducks prefer a secluded nest that is a considerable distance from the next wood duck nest. In fact, female wood duck behavior changed when the nests were too close to each other. Some females would lay their eggs in another female's nest. The result was too many eggs in one nest. The biologists found that if there were too many eggs in a nest, the proportion of eggs that hatched was considerably reduced. In the long run, this meant a decline in the population of wood ducks.

In their study, Sherman and Semel used two placements of nesting boxes. Group I boxes were well separated from each other and well hidden by available brush. Group II boxes were highly visible and grouped closely together.

In group I boxes, there were a total of 474 eggs, of which a field count showed that about 270 hatched. In group II boxes, there were a total of 805 eggs, of which a field count showed that, again, about 270 hatched.

The material in Chapter 8 will enable us to answer many questions about the hatch ratios of eggs from nests in the two groups.

(a) Find a point estimate $\hat{p}_1$ for p_1, the proportion of eggs that hatch in group I nest box placements. Find a 95% confidence interval for p_1.

(b) Find a point estimate $\hat{p}_2$ for p_2, the proportion of eggs that hatch in group II nest box placements. Find a 95% confidence interval for p_2.

(c) Find a 95% confidence interval for $p_1 - p_2$. Does the interval indicate that the proportion of eggs hatched from group I nest box placements is higher than, lower than, or not different from the proportion of eggs hatched from group II nest boxes?

(d) What conclusions about placement of nest boxes can be drawn? In the article, additional concerns are raised about the higher cost of placing and maintaining group I nest boxes. At issue is also the cost efficiency per successful wood duck hatch. Data in the article do not include information that would help us answer questions of *cost* efficiency. However, the data presented do help us answer questions about proportion of successful hatches in the two nest box configurations. (See Problem 16 of Section 8.5.)

8.1
Estimating μ When σ Is Known

FOCUS POINTS

✓ Explain the meaning of confidence level, error of estimate, and critical value.

✓ Find the critical value corresponding to a given confidence level.

✓ Compute confidence intervals for μ when σ is known. Interpret the results.

Because of time and money constraints, difficulty in finding population members, and so forth, we usually do not have access to *all* measurements of an *entire* population. Instead we rely on information from a sample.

In this section, we develop techniques for estimating the population mean μ using sample data. We assume the population standard deviation σ is known.

Let's begin by listing some basic assumptions used in the development of our formulas for estimating μ when σ is known.

> **Assumptions about the random variable *x***
>
> 1. We have a *simple random sample* of size *n* drawn from a population of *x* values.
>
> 2. The value of σ, the population standard deviation of *x*, *is known.*
>
> 3. If the *x distribution is normal,* then our methods work for *any sample size n.*
>
> 4. If *x* has an unknown distribution, then we require a *sample size n ≥ 30.* However, if the *x* distribution is distinctly skewed and definitely not mound-shaped, a sample of size 50 or even 100 or higher may be necessary.

Point estimate

An estimate of a population parameter given by a single number is called a *point estimate* for that parameter. It will come as no great surprise that we use $\bar{x}$ (the sample mean) as the point estimate for μ (the population mean).

> A **point estimate** of a population parameter is an estimate of the parameter using a single number.
>
> $\bar{x}$ is the **point estimate** for μ.

Margin of error

Even with a large random sample, the value of $\bar{x}$ usually is not *exactly* equal to the population mean μ. The *margin of error* is the magnitude of the difference between the sample point estimate and the true population parameter value.

> When using $\bar{x}$ as a point estimate for μ, the **margin of error** is the magnitude of $\bar{x} - \mu$ or $|\bar{x} - \mu|$.

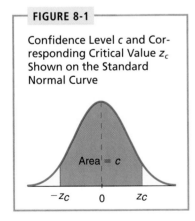

FIGURE 8-1

Confidence Level c and Corresponding Critical Value z_c Shown on the Standard Normal Curve

We cannot say exactly how close $\bar{x}$ is to μ when μ is unknown. Therefore, the exact margin of error is unknown when the population parameter is unknown. Of course, μ is usually not known or there would be no need to estimate it. In this section, we will use the language of probability to give us an idea of the size of the margin of error when we use $\bar{x}$ as a point estimate for μ.

First, we need to learn about *confidence levels.* The reliability of an estimate will be measured by the confidence level.

Suppose we want a confidence level of *c* (see Figure 8-1). Theoretically, you can choose *c* to be any value between 0 and 1, but usually *c* is equal to a number such as 0.90, 0.95, or 0.99. In each case, the value z_c is the number such that the area under the standard normal curve falling between $-z_c$ and z_c is equal to *c*. The value z_c is called the *critical value* for a confidence level of *c*.

Finding the critical value

> For a confidence level *c*, the **critical value** z_c is the number such that the area under the standard normal curve between $-z_c$ and z_c equals *c*.

The area under the normal curve from $-z_c$ to z_c is the probability that the standardized normal variable z lies in that interval. This means that

$$P(-z_c < z < z_c) = c$$

EXAMPLE 1

Find a critical value

Let us use Table 5 of Appendix II to find a number $z_{0.99}$ such that 99% of the area under the standard normal curve lies between $-z_{0.99}$ and $z_{0.99}$. That is, we will find $z_{0.99}$ such that

$$P(-z_{0.99} < z < z_{0.99}) = 0.99$$

SOLUTION: In Section 6.3, we saw how to find the z value when we were given an area between $-z$ and z. The first thing we did was to find the corresponding area to the left of $-z$. If A is the area between $-z$ and z, then $(1 - A)/2$ is the area to the left of z. In our case, the area between $-z$ and z is 0.99. The corresponding area in the left tail is $(1 - 0.99)/2 = 0.005$ (see Figure 8-2).

Next, we use Table 5 of Appendix II to find the z value corresponding to a left-tail area of 0.0050. Table 8-1 shows an excerpt from Table 5 of Appendix II.

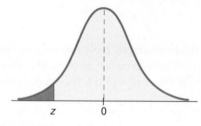

TABLE 8-1   Excerpt from Table 5 of Appendix II

z	.00	...	.07	.08	.09
−3.4	.0003		.0003	.0003	.0002
⋮					
−2.5	.0062		.0051	.0049	.0048
				↑	
				.0050	

FIGURE 8-2

Area Between $-z$ and z Is 0.99

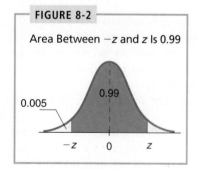

From Table 8-1, we see that the desired area, 0.0050, is exactly halfway between the areas corresponding to $z = -2.58$ and $z = -2.57$. Because the two area values are so close together, we use the more conservative z value -2.58 rather than interpolate. In fact, $z_{0.99} \approx 2.576$. However, to two decimal places, we use $z_{0.99} = 2.58$ as the critical value for a confidence level of $c = 0.99$. We have

$$P(-2.58 < z < 2.58) = 0.99$$

The results of Example 1 will be used a great deal in our later work. For convenience, Table 8-2 gives some levels of confidence and corresponding critical values z_c. The same information is provided in Table 5(b) of Appendix II.

An estimate is not very valuable unless we have some kind of measure of how "good" it is. The language of probability can give us an idea of the size of the margin of error caused by using the sample mean $\bar{x}$ as an estimate for the population mean.

Remember that $\bar{x}$ is a random variable. Each time we draw a sample of size n from a population, we can get a different value for $\bar{x}$. According to the central limit

TABLE 8-2   Some Levels of Confidence and Their Corresponding Critical Values

Level of Confidence c	Critical Value z_c
0.70, or 70%	1.04
0.75, or 75%	1.15
0.80, or 80%	1.28
0.85, or 85%	1.44
0.90, or 90%	1.645
0.95, or 95%	1.96
0.98, or 98%	2.33
0.99, or 99%	2.58

theorem, if the sample size is large, then $\bar{x}$ has a distribution that is approximately normal with mean $\mu_{\bar{x}} = \mu$, the population mean we are trying to estimate. The standard deviation is $\sigma_{\bar{x}} = \sigma/\sqrt{n}$. If x has a normal distribution, these results are true *for any sample size.* (See Theorem 7.1.)

This information, together with our work on confidence levels, leads us (as shown in the optional derivation that follows) to the probability statement

$$P\left(-z_c \frac{\sigma}{\sqrt{n}} < \bar{x} - \mu < z_c \frac{\sigma}{\sqrt{n}}\right) = c \tag{1}$$

Equation (1) uses the language of probability to give us an idea of the size of the margin of error for the corresponding confidence level c. In words, Equation (1) states that the probability is c that our point estimate $\bar{x}$ is within a distance $\pm z_c(\sigma/\sqrt{n})$ of the population mean μ. This relationship is shown in Figure 8-3.

In the following optional discussion, we derive Equation (1). If you prefer, you may jump ahead to the discussion about the margin of error.

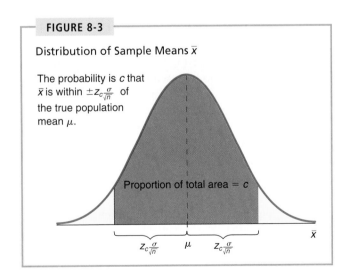

FIGURE 8-3

Distribution of Sample Means $\bar{x}$

The probability is c that $\bar{x}$ is within $\pm z_c \frac{\sigma}{\sqrt{n}}$ of the true population mean μ.

Proportion of total area $= c$

$z_c \frac{\sigma}{\sqrt{n}}$ μ $z_c \frac{\sigma}{\sqrt{n}}$ $\bar{x}$

Optional derivation of Equation (1)

For a c confidence level, we know that

$$P(-z_c < z < z_c) = c \tag{2}$$

This statement gives us information about the size of z, but we want information about the size of $\bar{x} - \mu$. Is there a relationship between z and $\bar{x} - \mu$? The answer is yes since, by the central limit theorem, $\bar{x}$ has a distribution that is approximately normal with mean μ and standard deviation $\sigma/\sqrt{n}$. We can convert $\bar{x}$ to a standard z score by using the formula

$$z = \frac{\bar{x} - \mu}{\sigma/\sqrt{n}} \tag{3}$$

Substituting this expression for z in Equation (2) gives

$$P\left(-z_c < \frac{\bar{x} - \mu}{\sigma/\sqrt{n}} < z_c\right) = c \tag{4}$$

Multiplying all parts of the inequality in (4) by $\sigma/\sqrt{n}$ gives us

$$P\left(-z_c \frac{\sigma}{\sqrt{n}} < \bar{x} - \mu < z_c \frac{\sigma}{\sqrt{n}}\right) = c \tag{1}$$

Equation (1) is precisely the equation we set out to derive.

Maximal margin of error, E

The *margin of error* (or absolute error) using $\bar{x}$ as a point estimate for μ is $|\bar{x} - \mu|$. In most practical problems, μ is unknown, so the margin of error is also unknown. However, Equation (1) allows us to compute an *error tolerance E*, which serves as a bound on the margin of error. Using a $c\%$ level of confidence, we can say that the point estimate $\bar{x}$ differs from the population mean μ by a *maximal margin of error*

$$E = z_c \frac{\sigma}{\sqrt{n}} \tag{5}$$

Note: Formula (5) for E is based on the fact that the sampling distribution for $\bar{x}$ is exactly normal, with mean μ and standard deviation $\sigma/\sqrt{n}$. This occurs whenever the x distribution is normal with mean μ and standard deviation σ. If the x distribution is not normal, then according to the central limit theorem, large samples ($n \geq 30$) produce an $\bar{x}$ distribution that is approximately normal with mean μ and standard deviation $\sigma/\sqrt{n}$.

Using Equations (1) and (5), we conclude that

$$P(-E < \bar{x} - \mu < E) = c \tag{6}$$

Equation (6) states that the probability is c that the difference between $\bar{x}$ and μ is no more than the maximal error tolerance E. If we use a little algebra on the inequality

$$-E < \bar{x} - \mu < E \tag{7}$$

for μ, we can rewrite it in the following mathematically equivalent way:

$$\bar{x} - E < \mu < \bar{x} + E \tag{8}$$

Confidence interval for μ with σ known

Since formulas (7) and (8) are mathematically equivalent, their probabilities are the same. Therefore, from (6), (7), and (8) we obtain

$$P(\overline{x} - E < \mu < \overline{x} + E) = c \qquad (9)$$

Equation (9) states that there is a chance of c that the interval from $\overline{x} - E$ to $\overline{x} + E$ contains the population mean μ. We call this interval a c *confidence interval for* μ.

> A c **confidence interval for** μ is an interval computed from sample data in such a way that c is the probability of generating an interval containing the actual value of μ.

We may get a different confidence interval for each different sample that is taken. Some intervals will contain the population mean μ and others will not. However, in the long run, the proportion of confidence intervals that contain μ is c.

> **PROCEDURE**
>
> ### How to find a confidence interval for μ when σ is known
>
> Let x be a random variable appropriate to your application. Obtain a simple random sample (of size n) of x values from which you compute the sample mean $\overline{x}$. The value of σ is already known (perhaps from a previous study).
>
> If you can assume that x has a normal distribution, then any sample size n will work. If you cannot assume this, then use a sample size of $n \geq 30$.
>
> *Confidence interval for* μ *when* σ *is known*
>
> $$\overline{x} - E < \mu < \overline{x} + E \qquad (10)$$
>
> where $\overline{x}$ = sample mean of a simple random sample
>
> $$E = z_c \frac{\sigma}{\sqrt{n}}$$
>
> c = confidence level $(0 < c < 1)$
>
> z_c = critical value for confidence level c based on the standard normal distribution (See Table 5(b) of Appendix II for frequently used values.)

EXAMPLE 2

Confidence interval for μ with σ known

Julia enjoys jogging. She has been jogging over a period of several years, during which time her physical condition has remained constantly good. Usually, she jogs 2 miles per day. The standard deviation of her times is $\sigma = 1.80$ min. During the past year Julia has recorded her times required to run 2 miles. She has a random sample of 90 of these times. For these 90 times the mean was $\overline{x} = 15.60$ minutes. Let μ be the mean jogging time for the entire distribution of Julia's 2-mile running times (taken over the past year). Find a 0.95 confidence interval for μ.

SOLUTION: The interval from $\overline{x} - E$ to $\overline{x} + E$ will be a 95% confidence interval for μ. In this case, $c = 0.95$, so $z_c = 1.96$ (see Table 8-2). The sample size $n = 90$ is

large enough for the $\bar{x}$ distribution to be approximately normal with mean μ and standard deviation $\sigma/\sqrt{n}$. Therefore,

$$E = z_c \frac{\sigma}{\sqrt{n}}$$

$$E = 1.96\left(\frac{1.80}{\sqrt{90}}\right)$$

$$E \approx 0.37$$

Using Equation (10), the given value of $\bar{x}$, and our computed value for E, we get the 95% confidence interval for μ.

$$\bar{x} - E < \mu < \bar{x} + E$$

$$15.60 - 0.37 < \mu < 15.60 + 0.37$$

$$15.23 < \mu < 15.97$$

We conclude with 95% confidence that the interval from 15.23 min. to 15.97 min. is one that contains the population mean μ of jogging times for Julia.   ◊

A few comments are in order about the general meaning of the term *confidence interval*. It is important to realize that the endpoints $\bar{x} \pm E$ are really statistical *variables*. Equation (9) states that we have a chance c of obtaining a sample such that the interval, once it is computed, will contain the parameter μ. Of course, after the confidence interval is numerically fixed, it either does or does not contain μ. So the probability is 1 or 0 that the interval, when it is fixed, will contain μ. A nontrivial probability statement can be made only about variables, not constants. Therefore, Equation (9) really states that if we repeat the experiment many times and get lots of confidence intervals (for the same sample size), then the proportion of all intervals that will turn out to contain the mean μ is c.

In Figure 8-4, the horizontal lines represent 0.90 confidence intervals for various samples of the same size from a distribution. Some of these intervals contain μ, and others do not. Since the intervals are 0.90 confidence intervals, about 90% of all such intervals should contain μ. For each sample, the interval goes from $\bar{x} - E$ to $\bar{x} + E$.

◊ **COMMENT** Please see Using Technology at the end of this chapter for a computer demonstration of this discussion about confidence intervals.   ◊

FIGURE 8-4

0.90 Confidence Intervals for Samples of the Same Size

For each sample the interval goes from $\bar{x} - E$ to $\bar{x} + E$

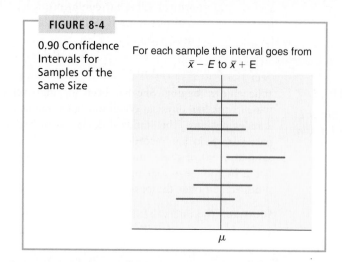

GUIDED EXERCISE 1

Confidence interval for μ with σ known

Walter usually meets Julia at the track. He prefers to jog 3 miles. From long experience, he knows that $\sigma = 2.40$ minutes for his jogging times. For a random sample of 90 jogging sessions, the mean time was $\bar{x} = 22.50$ minutes. Let μ be the mean jogging time for the entire distribution of Walter's 3-mile running times over the past several years. Find a 0.99 confidence interval for μ.

(a) What is the value of $z_{0.99}$? (See Table 8-2.)

⟹ $z_{0.99} = 2.58$

(b) Is the $\bar{x}$ distribution approximately normal?

⟹   Yes; we know this from the central limit theorem.

(c) What is the value of E?

⟹ $E = z_c \dfrac{\sigma}{\sqrt{n}} = 2.58 \left(\dfrac{2.40}{\sqrt{90}} \right) \approx 0.65$

(d) What are the endpoints for a 0.99 confidence interval for μ?

⟹   The endpoints are given by

$$\bar{x} - E \approx 22.50 - 0.65 = 21.85$$
$$\bar{x} + E \approx 22.50 + 0.65 = 23.15$$

(e) How can we interpret the confidence interval?

⟹   We are 99% certain that the interval from 21.85 to 23.15 is an interval that contains the population mean time μ.

When we use samples to estimate the mean of a population, we generate a small error. However, samples are useful even when it is possible to survey the entire population because the use of a sample may yield savings of time or effort in collecting data.

TECH NOTE The TI-84Plus and TI-83Plus calculators, Excel, and Minitab all support confidence intervals for μ from large samples. The level of support varies according to the technology. When a confidence interval is given, the standard mathematical notation (lower value, upper value) is used. For instance, the notation (15.23, 15.97) means the interval from 15.23 to 15.97.

TI-84Plus/TI-83Plus This calculator gives the most extensive support. The user can opt to enter raw data or just summary statistics. In each case, the value of σ must be specified. Press the **STAT** key and select **TESTS**, use **7:ZInterval**. The TI-84Plus/ TI-83Plus output shows the results for Example 2.

```
ZInterval
 Inpt:Data Stats
 σ:1.8
 x̄:15.6
 n:90
 C-Level:95
 Calculate
```

```
ZInterval
 (15.228, 15.972)
 x̄=15.6
 n=90
```

Excel Excel gives only the value of the maximal error of estimate *E*. Use the menu choice **Paste Function** (*f*ₓ) ➤ **Statistics** ➤ **Confidence(alpha, σ, n)**. In the dialogue box, the value of alpha is 1 − confidence level. The Excel output shows the value of *E* for Example 2.

=	=CONFIDENCE(0.05,1.8,90)	
C	D	E
0.371876		

An alternate approach incorporating raw data (using the Student's *t* distribution presented in the next section) uses the menu choices **Tools** ➤ **Data Analysis** ➤ **Describe Statistics**. Again, the value of *E* for the interval is given.

Minitab Raw data are required. Use the menu choices **Stat** ➤ **Basic Statistics** ➤ **1-SampleZ**.

VIEWPOINT   *Music and Techno Theft*

Performing rights organizations ASCAP (American Society of Composers, Authors, and Publishers) and BMI (Broadcast Music, Inc.) collect royalties for song writers and music publishers. Radio, television, cable, nightclubs, restaurants, elevators, and even beauty parlors play music that is copyrighted by a composer or publisher. The royalty payment for this music turns out to be more than a billion dollars a year (Source: *The Wall Street Journal*). How do ASCAP and BMI know who is playing what music? The answer is, they don't know! Instead of tracking *exactly* what gets played, they use random sampling and *confidence intervals*. For example, each radio station (there are more than 10,000 in the U.S.) has randomly chosen days of programming analyzed every year. The results are used to assess royalty fees. In fact, Deloitte & Touche (a financial services company) administers the sampling process.

Although the system is not perfect, it helps bring order into an otherwise chaotic accounting system. Such methods of "copyright policing" help prevent techno theft, ensuring that many song writers and recording artists get a reasonable return for their creative work.

SECTION 8.1   PROBLEMS

Answers may vary slightly due to rounding.

1. *Zoology: Hummingbirds* Allen's hummingbird (*Selasphorus sasin*) has been studied by zoologist Bill Alther (Reference: *Hummingbirds*, K. Long and W. Alther). A small group of 15 Allen's hummingbirds has been under study in Arizona. The average weight for these birds is $\bar{x} = 3.15$ gm. Based on previous studies, we can assume that the weights of Allen's hummingbirds have a normal distribution with $\sigma = 0.33$ gm.
   (a) Find an 80% confidence interval for the average weights of Allen's hummingbirds in the study region. What is the margin of error?
   (b) What conditions are necessary for your calculations?
   (c) Give a brief interpretation of your results in the context of this problem.

2. *Diagnostic Tests: Uric Acid* Overproduction of uric acid in the body can be an indication of cell breakdown. This may be an advance indication of illness such as gout, leukemia, or lymphoma (Reference: *Manual of Laboratory and Diagnostic Tests*, F. Fischbach). Over a period of months, an adult male patient has taken eight blood tests for uric acid. The mean concentration was $\bar{x} = 5.35$ mg/dl. The distribution of uric acid in healthy adult males can be assumed to be normal with $\sigma = 1.85$ mg/dl.
   (a) Find a 95% confidence interval for the population mean concentration of uric acid in this patient's blood. What is the margin of error?
   (b) What conditions are necessary for your calculations?
   (c) Give a brief interpretation of your results in the context of this problem.

3. *Diagnostic Tests: Plasma Volume* Total plasma volume is important in determining the required plasma component in blood replacement therapy for a person undergoing surgery. Plasma volume is influenced by the overall health and physical activity of an individual. (Reference: See Problem 2.) Suppose that a random sample of 45 male firefighters are tested and that they have a plasma volume sample mean of $\bar{x} = 37.5$ ml/kg (milliliters plasma per kilogram body weight). Assume that $\sigma = 7.50$ ml/kg for the distribution of blood plasma.
   (a) Find a 99% confidence interval for the population mean blood plasma volume in male firefighters. What is the margin of error?
   (b) What conditions are necessary for your calculations?
   (c) Give a brief interpretation of your results in the context of this problem.

4. *Agriculture: Watermelon* What price do farmers get for their watermelon crops? In the third week of July, a random sample of 40 farming regions gave a sample mean of $\bar{x} = \$6.88$ per 100 pounds of watermelon. Assume that σ is known to be $1.92 per 100 pounds (Reference: *Agricultural Statistics*, U.S. Department of Agriculture).
   (a) Find a 90% confidence interval for the population mean price (per 100 pounds) that farmers in this region get for their watermelon crop. What is the margin of error?
   (b) A farm brings 15 tons of watermelon to market. Find a 90% confidence interval for the population mean cash value of this crop. What is the margin of error? *Hint:* 1 ton is 2000 pounds.

5. *FBI Report: Larceny* Thirty small communities in Connecticut (population near 10,000 each) gave an average of $\bar{x} = 138.5$ reported cases of larceny per year. Assume that σ is known to be 42.6 cases per year (Reference: *Crime in the United States*, Federal Bureau of Investigation).
   (a) Find a 90% confidence interval for the population mean annual number of reported larceny cases in such communities. What is the margin of error?
   (b) Find a 95% confidence interval for the population mean annual number of reported larceny cases in such communities. What is the margin of error?
   (c) Find a 99% confidence interval for the population mean annual number of reported larceny cases in such communities. What is the margin of error?
   (d) Compare the margins of error for parts (a) through (c). As the confidence levels increase, do the margins of error increase?
   (e) Compare the lengths of the confidence intervals for parts (a) through (c). As the confidence levels increase, do the confidence intervals increase in length?

6. *Salaries: Student Services* Consider college officials in admissions, registration, counseling, financial aid, campus ministry, food services, and so on. How much money do these people make each year? Suppose you read in your local newspaper that 45 officials in student services earned an average of $\bar{x} = \$50,340$ each year (Reference: *Chronicle of Higher Education*).

(a) Assume that $\sigma = \$16,920$ for salaries of college officials in student services. Find a 90% confidence interval for the population mean salaries of such personnel. What is the margin of error?

(b) Assume that $\sigma = \$10,780$ for salaries of college officials in student services. Find a 90% confidence interval for the population mean salaries of such personnel. What is the margin of error?

(c) Assume that $\sigma = \$4830$ for salaries of college officials in student services. Find a 90% confidence interval for the population mean salaries of such personnel. What is the margin of error?

(d) Compare the margins of error for parts (a) through (c). As the standard deviation decreases, does the margin of error decrease?

(e) Compare the lengths of the confidence intervals for parts (a) through (c). As the standard deviation decreases, does the length of a 90% confidence interval decrease?

7. *Salaries: College Administrators* How much do college administrators (not teachers or service personnel) make each year? Suppose you read the local newspaper and find that the average annual salary of administrators in the local college is $\bar{x} = \$58,940$. Assume that σ is known to be $18,490 for college administrator salaries (Reference: *The Chronicle of Higher Education*).

(a) Suppose that $\bar{x} = \$58,940$ is based on a random sample of $n = 36$ administrators. Find a 90% confidence interval for the population mean annual salary of local college administrators. What is the margin of error?

(b) Suppose that $\bar{x} = \$58,940$ is based on a random sample of $n = 64$ administrators. Find a 90% confidence interval for the population mean annual salary of local college administrators. What is the margin of error?

(c) Suppose that $\bar{x} = \$58,940$ is based on a random sample of $n = 121$ administrators. Find a 90% confidence interval for the population mean annual salary of local college administrators. What is the margin of error?

(d) Compare the margins of error for parts (a) through (c). As the sample size increases, does the margin of error decrease?

(e) Compare the lengths of the confidence intervals for parts (a) through (c). As the sample size increases, does the length of a 90% confidence interval decrease?

8. *Ecology: Sand Dunes* At wind speeds above 1000 cm/sec, significant sand-moving events begin to occur. Wind speeds below 1000 cm/sec deposit sand and wind speeds above 1000 cm/sec move sand to new locations. The cyclic nature of wind and moving sand determines the shape and location of large dunes (Reference: *Hydraulic, Geologic, and Biologic Research at Great Sand Dunes National Monument and Vicinity, Colorado,* Proceedings of the National Park Service Research Symposium). At a test site, the prevailing direction of the wind did not change noticeably. However, the velocity did change. Sixty wind speed readings gave an average velocity of $\bar{x} = 1075$ cm/sec. Based on long-term experience, σ can be assumed to be 265 cm/sec.

(a) Find a 95% confidence interval for the population mean wind speed at this site.

(b) Does the confidence interval indicate that the population mean wind speed is such that the sand is always moving at this site? Explain.

9. *Profits: Banks* Jobs and productivity! How do banks rate? One way to answer this question is to examine annual profits per employee. *Forbes Top Companies,* edited by J. T. Davis (John Wiley & Sons), gave the following data about annual profits per employee (in units of one thousand dollars per employee) for representative companies in financial services. Companies such as Wells Fargo, First Bank System, and Key Banks were included. Assume $\sigma \approx 10.2$ thousand dollars.

42.9	43.8	48.2	60.6	54.9	55.1	52.9	54.9	42.5	33.0	33.6
36.9	27.0	47.1	33.8	28.1	28.5	29.1	36.5	36.1	26.9	27.8
28.8	29.3	31.5	31.7	31.1	38.0	32.0	31.7	32.9	23.1	54.9
43.8	36.9	31.9	25.5	23.2	29.8	22.3	26.5	26.7		

(a) Use a calculator or appropriate computer software to verify that, for the preceding data, $\bar{x} \approx 36.0$.

(b) Let us say that the preceding data are representative of the entire sector of (successful) financial services corporations. Find a 75% confidence interval for μ, the average annual profit per employee for all successful banks.

(c) Let us say that you are the manager for a local bank with a large number of employees. Suppose the annual profits per employee are less than 30 thousand dollars per employee. Do you think that this might be somewhat low compared with other successful financial institutions? Explain by referring to the confidence interval you computed in part (b).

(d) Suppose the annual profits are more than 40 thousand dollars per employee. As manager of the bank, would you feel somewhat better? Explain by referring to the confidence interval you computed in part (b).

(e) Repeat parts (b), (c), and (d) for a 90% confidence level.

10. *Profits: Retail* Jobs and productivity! How do retail stores rate? One way to answer this question is to examine annual profits per employee. The following data give annual profits per employee (in units of one thousand dollars per employee) for companies in retail sales. See reference in Problem 9. Companies such as Gap, Nordstrom, Circuit City, Dillards, JCPenney, Sears, Wal-Mart, Office Depot, and Toys 'Я' Us are included. Assume $\sigma \approx 3.8$ thousand dollars.

4.4	6.5	4.2	8.9	8.7	8.1	6.1	6.0	2.6	2.9	8.1	-1.9
11.9	8.2	6.4	4.7	5.5	4.8	3.0	4.3	-6.0	1.5	2.9	4.8
-1.7	9.4	5.5	5.8	4.7	6.2	15.0	4.1	3.7	5.1	4.2	

(a) Use a calculator or appropriate computer software to verify that, for the preceding data, $\bar{x} \approx 5.1$.

(b) Let us say that the preceding data are representative of the entire sector of retail sales companies. Find an 80% confidence interval for μ, the average annual profit per employee for retail sales.

(c) Let us say that you are the manager of a retail store with a large number of employees. Suppose the annual profits per employee are less than 3 thousand dollars per employee. Do you think that this might be low compared with other retail stores? Explain by referring to the confidence interval you computed in part (b).

(d) Suppose the annual profits are more than 6.5 thousand dollars per employee. As store manager, would you feel somewhat better? Explain by referring to the confidence interval you computed in part (b).

(e) Repeat parts (b), (c), and (d) for a 95% confidence interval.

11. *January Temperatures: Phoenix* The U.S. Department of Commerce Environmental Data Service gave the following information about average temperature (°F) in January in Phoenix, Arizona, for the past 40 years. Assume $\sigma \approx 3.04$°F.

52.8	52.2	52.7	53.8	54.5	48.5	53.3	52.4
51.7	43.2	51.4	42.8	48.5	52.3	51.6	43.7
49.7	49.9	52.6	51.2	50.7	54.2	48.7	56.0
54.0	51.9	50.4	50.7	54.0	52.4	51.5	48.4
46.7	53.0	51.4	49.6	54.6	52.3	54.9	52.1

(a) Use a calculator or appropriate computer software to verify that the sample mean is $\bar{x} = 51.16°F$.

(b) Find a 90% confidence interval for the January mean temperature in Phoenix.

(c) Find a 99% confidence interval for the January mean temperature in Phoenix.

(d) If someone told you that the earth was heating up and the average January temperature in Phoenix was now 53°F, what might you think about such a claim? Is it possible that a few more years of observation might be needed before such a claim could be made? Explain.

12. *Ballooning: Air Temperature* How hot is the air in the top (crown) of a hot air balloon? Information from *Ballooning: The Complete Guide to Riding the Winds*, by Wirth and Young (Random House), claims that the air in the crown should be an average of 100°C for a balloon to be in a state of equilibrium. However, the temperature does not need to be exactly 100°C. What is a reasonable and safe range of temperatures? This may vary with the size and (decorative) shape of the balloon. All balloons have a temperature gauge in the crown. Suppose that 56 readings (for a balloon in equilibrium) gave a mean temperature of $\bar{x} = 97°C$. For this balloon, $\sigma \approx 17°C$.

(a) Compute a 95% confidence interval for the average temperature at which this balloon will be in a steady-state equilibrium.

(b) If the average temperature in the crown of the balloon goes above the high end of your confidence interval, do you expect that the balloon will go up or down? Explain.

8.2
Estimating μ When σ Is Unknown

FOCUS POINTS

✓ Learn about degrees of freedom and Student's *t* distributions.

✓ Find critical values using degrees of freedom and confidence level.

✓ Compute confidence intervals for μ when σ is unknown. What does this information tell you?

In order to use the normal distribution to find confidence intervals for a population mean μ, we need to know the value of σ, the population standard deviation. However, much of the time, when μ is unknown, σ is unknown as well. In such cases, we use the sample standard deviation *s* to approximate σ. When we use *s* to approximate σ, the sampling distribution for $\bar{x}$ follows a new distribution called a *Student's t distribution*.

Student's *t* Distributions

Student's *t* distributions were discovered in 1908 by W. S. Gosset. He was employed as a statistician by Guinness brewing company, a company that discouraged publication of research by its employees. As a result, Gosset published his research under the pseudonym *Student*. Gosset was the first to recognize the importance of developing statistical methods for obtaining reliable information from samples of populations with unknown σ. Gosset used the variable *t* when he introduced the distribution in 1908. To this day and in his honor it is still called a Student's *t* distribution. It might be more fitting to call this distribution *Gosset's t distribution*; however, in the literature of mathematical statistics, it is known as a *Student's t distribution*.

The variable *t* is defined as follows. A Student's *t* distribution depends on sample size *n*.

Assume that x has a normal distribution with mean μ. For samples of size n with sample mean $\overline{x}$ and sample standard deviation s, the **t variable**

$$t = \frac{\overline{x} - \mu}{\dfrac{s}{\sqrt{n}}} \tag{11}$$

has a **Student's t distribution** with **degrees of freedom** $d.f. = n - 1$.

If many random samples of size n are drawn, then we get many t values from Equation (11). These t values can be organized into a frequency table, and a histogram can be drawn, thereby giving us an idea of the shape of the t distribution (for a given n).

Fortunately, all this work is not necessary because mathematical theorems can be used to obtain a formula for the t distribution. However, it is important to observe that these theorems say that the shape of the t distribution depends only on n, provided the basic variable x has a normal distribution. So *when we use a t distribution, we will assume that the x distribution is normal.*

Table 6 of Appendix II gives values of the variable t corresponding to what we call the number of *degrees of freedom*, abbreviated *d.f.* For the methods used in this section, the number of degrees of freedom is given by the formula

Degrees of freedom

$$d.f. = n - 1 \tag{12}$$

where *d.f.* stands for the degrees of freedom and n is the sample size being used. Each choice for *d.f.* gives a different t distribution.

The graph of a t distribution is always symmetrical about its mean, which (as for the z distribution) is 0. The main observable difference between a t distribution and the standard normal z distribution is that a t distribution has somewhat thicker tails.

Figure 8-5 shows a standard normal z distribution and Student's t distribution with $d.f. = 3$ and $d.f. = 5$.

FIGURE 8-5

A Standard Normal Distribution and Student's t Distribution with $d.f. = 3$ and $d.f. = 5$

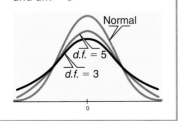

Properties of a Student's t distribution

1. The distribution is *symmetric* about the mean 0.

2. The distribution depends on the *degrees of freedom, d.f.* ($d.f. = n - 1$ for μ confidence intervals).

3. The distribution is *bell-shaped,* but has thicker tails than the standard normal distribution.

4. As the degrees of freedom increase, the t distribution *approaches* the standard normal distribution.

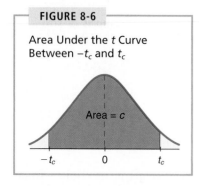

FIGURE 8-6

Area Under the t Curve Between $-t_c$ and t_c

Area = c

$-t_c$ 0 t_c

Using Table 6 to Find Critical Values for Confidence Intervals

Table 6 of Appendix II gives various t values for different degrees of freedom $d.f.$ We will use this table to find *critical values* t_c for a c confidence level. In other words, we want to find t_c such that an area equal to c under the t distribution for a given number of degrees of freedom falls between $-t_c$ and t_c. In the language of probability, we want to find t_c such that

$$P(-t_c < t < t_c) = c$$

This probability corresponds to the area shaded in Figure 8-6.

Table 6 of Appendix II has been arranged so that c is one of the column headings, and the degrees of freedom $d.f.$ are the row headings. To find t_c for any specific c, we find the column headed by that c value and read down until we reach the row headed by the appropriate number of degrees of freedom $d.f.$ (You will notice two other column headings: one-tail area and two-tail area. We will use these later, but for the time being, ignore them.)

> **Convention for using a Student's t distribution table**
>
> If the degrees of freedom $d.f.$ you need are not in the table, use the closest $d.f.$ in the table that is *smaller*. This procedure results in a critical value t_c that is more conservative in the sense that it is larger. The resulting confidence interval will be longer and have a probability that is slightly higher than c.

EXAMPLE 3

Student's t distribution

Use Table 8-3 (an excerpt from Table 6 of Appendix II) to find the critical value t_c for a 0.99 confidence level for a t distribution with sample size $n = 5$.

SOLUTION:

(a) First, we find the column with c heading 0.990.

(b) Next, we compute the number of degrees of freedom:
$d.f. = n - 1 = 5 - 1 = 4$.

(c) We read down the column under the heading $c = 0.99$ until we reach the row headed by 4 (under $d.f.$). The entry is 4.604. Therefore, $t_{0.99} = 4.604$. ◇

TABLE 8-3   Student's t Distribution Critical Values (Excerpt from Table 6, Appendix II)

one-tail area		—	—	—	—
two-tail area		—	—	—	—
$d.f.$ \ c		... 0.900	0.950	0.980	0.990 ...
⋮					
3		... 2.353	3.182	4.541	5.841 ...
4		... 2.132	2.776	3.747	4.604 ...
⋮					
7		... 1.895	2.365	2.998	3.449 ...
8		... 1.860	2.306	2.896	3.355 ...

> ## GUIDED EXERCISE 2
>
> ### Student's t distribution table
>
> Use Table 6 of Appendix II (or Table 8-3 showing an excerpt from the table) to find t_c for a 0.90 confidence level for a t distribution with sample size $n = 9$.
>
> (a) We find the column headed by $c =$ _____. $\Longrightarrow$ $c = 0.900$.
>
> (b) The degrees of freedom are given by $d.f. = n - 1 =$ _____. $\Longrightarrow$ $d.f. = n - 1 = 9 - 1 = 8$.
>
> (c) Read down the column found in part (a) until you reach the entry in the row headed by $d.f. = 8$. The value of $t_{0.90}$ is _____ for a sample of size 9. $\Longrightarrow$ $t_{0.90} = 1.860$ for a sample of size $n = 9$.
>
> (d) Find t_c for a 0.95 confidence level for a t distribution with sample size $n = 9$. $\Longrightarrow$ $t_{0.95} = 2.306$ for a sample of size $n = 9$.

Maximal margin of error, E

In Section 8.1, we found bounds $\pm E$ on the margin of error for a c confidence level. Using the same basic approach, we arrive at the conclusion that

$$E = t_c \frac{s}{\sqrt{n}}$$

is the maximal margin of error for a c confidence level when σ is unknown (i.e., $|\bar{x} - \mu| < E$ with probability c). The analogue of Equation (1) in Section 8.1 is

$$P\left(-t_c \frac{s}{\sqrt{n}} < \bar{x} - \mu < t_c \frac{s}{\sqrt{n}}\right) = c \tag{13}$$

◇ **COMMENT** Comparing Equation (13) with Equation (1) in Section 8.1, it becomes evident that we are using the same basic method on the t distribution that we did on the z distribution. ◇

Likewise, for samples from normal populations with unknown σ, Equation (9) of Section 8.1 becomes

$$P(\bar{x} - E < \mu < \bar{x} + E) = c \tag{14}$$

where $E = t_c(s/\sqrt{n})$. Let us organize what we have been doing in a convenient summary.

Confidence interval for μ with
σ unknown

PROCEDURE

How to find a confidence interval for μ when σ is unknown

Let x be a random variable appropriate to your application. Obtain a simple random sample (of size n) of x values from which you compute the sample mean $\bar{x}$ and the sample standard deviation s.

If you can assume that x has a normal distribution or simply a mound-shaped symmetric distribution, then any sample size n will work. If you cannot assume this, then use a sample size of $n \geq 30$.

Confidence interval for μ when σ is unknown

$$\bar{x} - E < \mu < \bar{x} + E \qquad (15)$$

where $\bar{x}$ = sample mean of a simple random sample

$$E = t_c \frac{s}{\sqrt{n}}$$

c = confidence level $(0 < c < 1)$

t_c = critical value for confidence level c and degrees of freedom
$d.f. = n - 1$
(See Table 6 of Appendix II.)

◊ **COMMENT** In our applications of Student's t distributions, we have made the basic assumption that x has a normal distribution. However, the same methods apply even if x is only approximately normal. In fact, the main requirement for using a Student's t distribution is that the distribution of x values be reasonably symmetrical and mound-shaped. If this is the case, then the methods we employ with the t distribution can be considered valid for most practical applications. ◊

EXAMPLE 4

Confidence interval for μ,
σ unknown

Suppose an archaeologist discovers only seven fossil skeletons from a previously unknown species of miniature horse. Reconstructions of the skeletons of these seven miniature horses show the shoulder heights (in centimeters) to be

45.3   47.1   44.2   46.8   46.5   45.5   47.6

For this sample data, the mean is $\bar{x} \approx 46.14$ and the sample standard deviation is $s \approx 1.19$. Let μ be the mean shoulder height (in centimeters) for this entire species of miniature horse, and assume that the population of shoulder heights is approximately normal.

Find a 99% confidence interval for μ, the mean shoulder height of the entire population of such horses.

SOLUTION: In this case, $n = 7$, so $d.f. = n - 1 = 7 - 1 = 6$. For $c = 0.990$, Table 6 of Appendix II gives $t_{0.99} = 3.707$ (for $d.f. = 6$). The sample standard deviation is $s = 1.19$.

$$E = t_c \frac{s}{\sqrt{n}} = (3.707)\frac{1.19}{\sqrt{7}} \approx 1.67$$

The 99% confidence interval is

$$\bar{x} - E < \mu < \bar{x} + E$$
$$46.14 - 1.67 < \mu < 46.14 + 1.67$$
$$44.5 < \mu < 47.8$$

The archaeologist can be 99% confident that the interval from 44.5 cm to 47.8 cm is an interval that contains the population mean μ for shoulder height of this species of miniature horse.   ◊

GUIDED EXERCISE 3

Confidence interval for μ, σ unknown

A company has a new process for manufacturing large artificial sapphires. In a trial run, 37 sapphires are produced. The mean weight for these 37 gems is $\bar{x} = 6.75$ carats, and the sample standard deviation is $s = 0.33$ carat. Let μ be the mean weight for the distribution of all sapphires produced by the new process.

(a) What is *d.f.* for this setting?

⟹ *d.f.* = $n - 1$ where n is the sample size. Since $n = 37$, *d.f.* = $37 - 1 = 36$.

(b) Use Table 6 of Appendix II to find $t_{0.95}$. Note that *d.f.* = 36 is not in the table. Use the *d.f.* closest to 36 that is smaller than 36.

⟹ *d.f.* = 35 is the closest *d.f.* in the table that is smaller than 36. Using *d.f.* = 35 and $c = 0.95$, we find $t_{0.95} = 2.030$.

(c) Find E.

⟹ $E = t_{0.95} \dfrac{s}{\sqrt{n}}$

$$\approx 2.030 \frac{0.33}{\sqrt{37}} \approx 0.11 \text{ carat}$$

(d) Find a 95% confidence interval for μ.

⟹ $$\bar{x} - E < \mu < \bar{x} + E$$
$$6.75 - 0.11 < \mu < 6.75 + 0.11$$
$$6.64 \text{ carats} < \mu < 6.86 \text{ carats}$$

(e) Interpret the confidence interval in the context of the problem.

⟹ The company can be 95% confident that the interval from 6.64 to 6.86 is an interval that contains the population mean weight of sapphires produced by the new process.

We have several formulas for confidence intervals for the population mean μ. How do we choose an appropriate one? We need to look at the sample size, the distribution of the original population, and whether or not the population standard deviation σ is known.

Summary: confidence intervals for the mean

Assume that you have a random sample of size n from an x distribution and that you have computed $\bar{x}$ and s. A confidence interval for μ is

$$\bar{x} - E < \mu < \bar{x} + E$$

where E is the margin of error. How do you find E? It depends on how much you know about the x distribution.

Situation I (most common)

You don't know the population standard deviation σ. In this situation you use the t distribution with margin of error

$$E = t_c \frac{s}{\sqrt{n}}$$

where degrees of freedom

$$d.f. = n - 1$$

Although a t distribution can be used in many situations, you need to observe some guidelines. If n is less than 30, x should have a distribution that is mound-shaped and approximately symmetric. It's even better if the x distribution is normal. If n is 30 or more, the central limit theorem (Chapter 7) implies these restrictions can be relaxed.

Situation II (almost never happens!)

You actually know the population value of σ. In addition, you know that x has a normal distribution. If you don't know that the x distribution is normal, then your sample size n must be 30 or larger. In this situation, you use the standard normal z distribution with margin of error

$$E = z_c \frac{\sigma}{\sqrt{n}}$$

Which distribution should you use for $\bar{x}$?

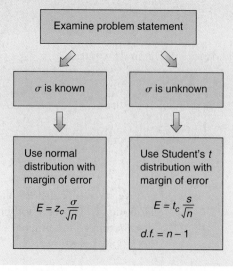

Bootstrap

◇ **COMMENT** To find confidence intervals for μ based on small samples, we need to know that the population distribution is approximately normal. What if this is not the case? A procedure called *bootstrap* utilizes computer power to generate an approximation for the $\bar{x}$ sampling distribution. Essentially, the bootstrap method treats the sample as if it were the population. Then, using repetition, it takes many samples (often thousands) from the original sample. This process is called *resampling*. The sample mean $\bar{x}$ is computed for each resample and a distribution of sample means is created. For example, a 95% confidence interval reflects the range for the middle 95% of the bootstrap $\bar{x}$ distribution. If you read Using Technology at the end of this chapter, you will find one (of many) bootstrap methods (Reference: *An Introduction to the Bootstrap*, B. Efron and R. Tibshirani). ◇

 TECH NOTE The TI-84Plus and TI-83Plus calculators, Excel, and Minitab support confidence intervals using the Student's t distribution.

TI-84Plus/TI-83Plus Press the **STAT** key, select **TESTS**, and choose the option **8:TInterval**. You may use either raw data in a list or summary statistics.

Excel Excel gives only the value of the maximal margin of error E. You can easily construct the confidence interval by computing $\bar{x} - E$ and $\bar{x} + E$. Use the menu choices **Tools ➤ Data Analysis ➤ Describe Statistics**. In the dialogue box, check summary statistics and check confidence level for mean. Then set the desired confidence level. Under these menu choices, Excel uses the Student's t distribution.

Minitab Use the menu choices **Stat ➤ Basic Statistics ➤ 1-Sample t**. In the dialogue box, indicate the column that contains the raw data. The Minitab output shows the confidence interval for Example 4.

```
T Confidence Intervals
Variable    N     Mean     StDev    SE Mean       99.0 % CI
C1          7    46.143    1.190     0.450    (44.475, 47.810)
```

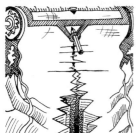

VIEWPOINT   *Earthquakes!*

California, Washington, Nevada, and even Yellowstone National Park all have earthquakes. Some earthquakes are severe! All earthquakes bring fear and anxiety to people living near the quake. Is San Francisco due for a really big quake like the 1906 major earthquake? How big are the sizes of recent earthquakes compared with really big earthquakes? What is the duration of an earthquake? How long is the time span between major earthquakes? One way to answer questions such as these is to use existing data to estimate confidence intervals on the average size, duration, and time interval between quakes. Recent data sets for computing such confidence intervals can be found at the National Earthquake Information Service of the U.S. Geological Survey web site. To access the site, visit the Brase/Brase statistics site at **http://math.college.hmco.com/students** and find the link to National Earthquake Information Service.

SECTION 8.2   PROBLEMS

1. Use Table 6 of Appendix II to find t_c for a 0.95 confidence level when the sample size is 18.

2. Use Table 6 of Appendix II to find t_c for a 0.99 confidence level when the sample size is 4.

3. Use Table 6 of Appendix II to find t_c for a 0.90 confidence level when the sample size is 22.

4. Use Table 6 of Appendix II to find the value of t_c for a 0.95 confidence level when the sample size is 12.

In Problems 5–15, assume that the population of x values has an approximately normal distribution. Answers may vary slightly due to rounding.

5. *Archaeology: Tree Rings* At Burnt Mesa Pueblo, the method of tree ring dating gave the following dates A.D. for an archaeological excavation site (*Bandelier Archaeological Excavation Project: Summer 1990 Excavations at Burnt Mesa Pueblo*, edited by Kohler, Washington State University):

| 1189 | 1271 | 1267 | 1272 | 1268 | 1316 | 1275 | 1317 | 1275 |

(a) Use a calculator with mean and standard deviation keys to verify that the sample mean date is $\bar{x} \approx 1272$ with sample standard deviation $s \approx 37$ years.
(b) Find a 90% confidence interval for the mean of all tree ring dates from this archaeological site.

6. *Camping: Cost of a Sleeping Bag* How much does a sleeping bag cost? Let's say you want a sleeping bag that should keep you warm in temperatures from 20 to 45°F. A random sample of prices ($) for sleeping bags in this temperature range was taken from *Backpacker Magazine: Gear Guide* (Vol. 25, Issue 157, No. 2). Brand names include American Camper, Cabela's, Camp 7, Caribou, Cascade, and Coleman.

| 80 | 90 | 100 | 120 | 75 | 37 | 30 | 23 | 100 | 110 |
| 105 | 95 | 105 | 60 | 110 | 120 | 95 | 90 | 60 | 70 |

(a) Use a calculator with mean and sample standard deviation keys to verify that $\bar{x} \approx \$83.75$ and $s \approx \$28.97$.
(b) Using the given data as representative of the population of all prices of summer sleeping bags, find a 90% confidence interval for the mean price μ of all summer sleeping bags.

7. *Wildlife: Mountain Lions* How much do wild mountain lions weigh? *The 77th Annual Report of the New Mexico Department of Game and Fish*, edited by Bill Montoya, gave the following information. Adult wild mountain lions (18 months or older) captured and released for the first time in the San Andres Mountains gave the following weights (lb):

| 68 | 104 | 128 | 122 | 60 | 64 |

(a) Use a calculator with mean and sample standard deviation keys to verify that $\bar{x} = 91.0$ lb and $s \approx 30.7$ lb.
(b) Find a 75% confidence interval for the population average weight μ of all adult mountain lions in the specified region.

8. *Wildlife: Wolf Pups* The number of pups in wolf dens of the southwestern United States is recorded below for 16 wolf dens (*The Wolf in the Southwest: The Making of an Endangered Species*, edited by D. E. Brown, University of Arizona Press).

5	8	7	5	3	4	3	9
5	8	5	6	5	6	4	7

(a) Use a calculator with mean and standard deviation keys to verify that the sample mean is $\bar{x} \approx 5.63$ pups with sample standard deviation $s \approx 1.78$ pups.
(b) Compute an 85% confidence interval for the population mean number of wolf pups per den in the southwestern United States.

9. *Wildlife: Fawns* The shoulder height for a random sample of six fawns (less than 5 months old) in Mesa Verde National Park was $\bar{x} = 79.25$ cm with sample standard deviation $s = 5.33$ cm (*The Mule Deer of Mesa Verde National Park*, edited by G. W. Mierau and J. L. Schmidt, Mesa Verde Museum Association). Compute an 80% confidence interval for the mean shoulder height of the population of all fawns (less than 5 months old) in Mesa Verde National Park.

10. *French Fries: Calories* How many calories are there in 3 ounces of french fries? It depends on where you get them. *Good Cholesterol Bad Cholesterol*, by Roth and Streicher, gives the data from eight popular fast-food restaurants. The data are (in calories)

222	255	254	230	249	222	237	287

Use these data to create a 99% confidence interval for the mean calorie count in 3 ounces of french fries obtained from fast-food restaurants.

11. *Diagnostic Tests: Total Calcium* Over the past several months, an adult patient has been treated for tetany (severe muscle spasms). This condition is associated with an average total calcium level below 6 mg/dl (Reference: *Manual of Laboratory and Diagnostic Tests*, F. Fischbach). Recently, the patient's total calcium tests gave the following readings (in mg/dl).

9.3	8.8	10.1	8.9	9.4	9.8	10.0
9.9	11.2	12.1				

(a) Use a calculator to verify that $\bar{x} = 9.95$ and $s \approx 1.02$.
(b) Find a 99.9% confidence interval for the population mean of total calcium in this patient's blood.
(c) Based on your results in part (b), do you think this patient still has a calcium deficiency? Explain.

12. *Franchise: Candy Store* Do you want to own your own candy store? Wow! With some interest in running your own business and a decent credit rating, you can probably get a bank loan on startup costs for franchises such as Candy Express, The Fudge Company, Karmel Corn, and Rocky Mountain Chocolate Factory. Startup costs (units in $1000) for a random sample of candy stores are given below (Source: *Entrepreneur Magazine*, Vol. 23, No. 10).

95	173	129	95	75	94	116	100	85

Use a calculator with mean and sample standard deviation keys to verify that $\bar{x} \approx 106.9$ thousand dollars and $s \approx 29.4$ thousand dollars. Find a 90% confidence interval for the population average startup costs μ for candy store franchises.

13. *Lincoln County Jail: Billy the Kid* Suppose that you are an anthropologist/historian doing research at an excavation site. How deep do you need to dig to locate artifacts of historical significance? The answer may depend on how long ago the events you hope to study occurred. If the events are relatively recent, you may not need to dig too deep. In 1881, the Lincoln County Cattle Baron Wars were in progress in the New Mexico Territory, and one special outlaw, Billy the Kid, killed two deputies in his escape from the Lincoln County Jail. In 1985, the anthropologist/historian Yvonne Oakes was commissioned by the Museum of New Mexico to study the now famous Lincoln Country Courthouse and Jail area (Source: *Archaeological Testing at Three Historic Sites at Lincoln State Monument*, by Y. R. Oakes, Museum of New Mexico).

(a) The depths (in inches) below grade at which significant artifacts were found in a random sample of trenches are

10	10.5	14	14	4	4.5	5	12	12	16
9	6	8	9	10	9	11	11	12	

Use a calculator with mean and sample standard deviation keys to verify that $\bar{x} \approx 9.8$ inches and $s \approx 3.3$ inches. Compute a 90% confidence interval for the population mean depth μ at which significant artifacts will be found.

(b) The depth (in inches) to sterile ground (no more artifacts found) for seven excavation trenches are

17	19	21.5	16	14	16	16

Use a calculator with mean and sample standard deviation keys to verify that $\bar{x} \approx 17.1$ inches and $s \approx 2.5$ inches. Compute an 80% confidence interval for the population mean depth μ to sterile ground.

14. *Hospitals: Charity Care* What percentage of hospitals provide at least some charity care? The following problem is based on information taken from *State Health Care Data: Utilization, Spending, and Characteristics* (American Medical Association). Based on a random sample of hospital reports from eastern states, the following information was obtained (units in percentage of hospitals providing at least some charity care):

57.1	56.2	53.0	66.1	59.0	64.7	70.1	64.7	53.5	78.2

Use a calculator with mean and sample standard deviation keys to verify that $\bar{x} \approx 62.3\%$ and $s \approx 8.0\%$. Find a 90% confidence interval for the population average μ of the percentage of hospitals providing at least some charity care.

15. *Box Plots and Confidence Intervals: Heights* The distribution of heights of 18-year-old men in the United States is approximately normal with mean 68 inches and standard deviation 3 inches (U.S. Census Bureau). In Minitab we can simulate the drawing of random samples of size 20 from this population (➤ **Calc** ➤ **Random Data** ➤ **Normal** with 20 rows from a distribution with mean 68 and standard deviation 3). Then we can have Minitab compute a 95% confidence interval and draw a boxplot of the data (➤ **Stat** ➤ **Basic Statistics** ➤ **1—Sample t**, with boxplot selected in the graphs). The boxplots and confidence intervals for four different samples are shown in the accompanying figures. The four confidence intervals are

VARIABLE	N	MEAN	STDEV	SEMEAN	95.0 % CI
Sample 1	20	68.050	2.901	0.649	(66.692 , 69.407)
Sample 2	20	67.958	3.137	0.702	(66.490 , 69.426)
Sample 3	20	67.976	2.639	0.590	(66.741 , 69.211)
Sample 4	20	66.908	2.440	0.546	(65.766 , 68.050)

(a) Examine the figure [parts (a) to (d)]. How do the boxplots for the four samples differ? Why should you expect the boxplots to differ?

95% Confidence Intervals for Mean Height of 18-Year-Old Men (Sample size 20)

(a) Boxplot of Sample 1
(with 95% *t*-confidence interval for the mean)

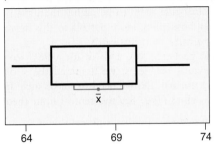

(b) Boxplot of Sample 2
(with 95% *t*-confidence interval for the mean)

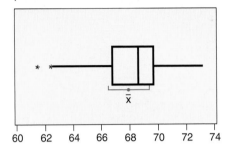

(c) Boxplot of Sample 3
(with 95% *t*-confidence interval for the mean)

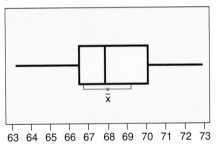

(d) Boxplot of Sample 4
(with 95% *t*-confidence interval for the mean)

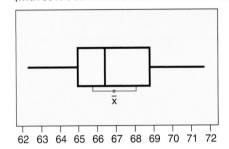

(b) Examine the 95% confidence intervals for the four samples shown in the print-out. Do the intervals differ in length? Do the intervals all contain the expected population mean of 68 inches? If we draw more samples, do you expect all of the resulting 95% confidence intervals to contain $\mu = 68$? Why or why not?

16. *Crime Rate: Denver* The following data represent crime rate per 1000 population for a random sample of 46 Denver neighborhoods (Reference: *The Piton Foundation*, Denver, Colorado).

63.2	36.3	26.2	53.2	65.3	32.0	65.0
66.3	68.9	35.2	25.1	32.5	54.0	42.4
77.5	123.2	66.3	92.7	56.9	77.1	27.5
69.2	73.8	71.5	58.5	67.2	78.6	33.2
74.9	45.1	132.1	104.7	63.2	59.6	75.7
39.2	69.9	87.5	56.0	154.2	85.5	77.5
84.7	24.2	37.5	41.1			

(a) Use a calculator with mean and sample standard deviation keys to verify that $\bar{x} \approx 64.2$ and $s \approx 27.9$ crimes per 1000 population.
(b) Let us say the preceding data are representative of the population crime rate in Denver neighborhoods. Compute an 80% confidence interval for μ, the population mean crime rate for all Denver neighborhoods.

(c) Suppose you are advising the police department about police patrol assignments. One neighborhood has a crime rate of 57 crimes per 1000 population. Do you think that this rate is below the average population crime rate and that fewer patrols could safely be assigned to this neighborhood? Use the confidence interval to justify your answer.

(d) Another neighborhood has a crime rate of 75 crimes per 1000 population. Does this crime rate seem to be higher than the population average? Would you recommend assigning more patrols to this neighborhood? Use the confidence interval to justify your answer.

(e) Repeat parts (b), (c), and (d) for a 95% confidence interval.

(f) In previous problems, we assumed the x distribution was normal or approximately normal. Do we need to make such an assumption in this problem? Why or why not? *Hint:* See the central limit theorem in Section 7.2.

17. *Finance: P/E Ratio* The price of a share of stock divided by the company's estimated future earnings per share is called the P/E ratio. High P/E ratios usually indicate "growth" stocks or maybe stocks that are simply overpriced. Low P/E ratios indicate "value" stocks or bargain stocks. A random sample of 51 of the largest companies in the United States gave the following P/E ratios (Reference: *Forbes*).

11	35	19	13	15	21	40	18	60	72	9	20
29	53	16	26	21	14	21	27	10	12	47	14
33	14	18	17	20	19	13	25	23	27	5	16
8	49	44	20	27	8	19	12	31	67	51	26
19	18	32									

(a) Use a calculator with mean and sample standard deviation keys to verify that $\bar{x} \approx 25.2$ and $s \approx 15.5$.

(b) Find a 90% confidence interval for the P/E population mean μ of all large U.S. companies.

(c) Find a 99% confidence interval for the P/E population mean μ of all large U.S. companies.

(d) Bank One (now merged with J. P. Morgan) had a P/E of 12, AT&T Wireless had a P/E of 72, and Disney had a P/E of 24. Examine the confidence intervals in parts (b) and (c). How would you describe these stocks at this time?

(e) In previous problems, we assumed the x distribution was normal or approximately normal. Do we need to make such an assumption in this problem? Why or why not? *Hint:* See the central limit theorem in Section 7.2.

18. *Baseball: Home Run Percentage* The home run percentage is the number of home runs per 100 times at bat. A random sample of 43 professional baseball players gave the following data for home run percentages (Reference: *The Baseball Encyclopedia*, Macmillan).

1.6	2.4	1.2	6.6	2.3	0.0	1.8	2.5	6.5	1.8
2.7	2.0	1.9	1.3	2.7	1.7	1.3	2.1	2.8	1.4
3.8	2.1	3.4	1.3	1.5	2.9	2.6	0.0	4.1	2.9
1.9	2.4	0.0	1.8	3.1	3.8	3.2	1.6	4.2	0.0
1.2	1.8	2.4							

(a) Use a calculator with mean and standard deviation keys to verify that $\bar{x} \approx 2.29$ and $s \approx 1.40$.

(b) Compute a 90% confidence interval for the population mean μ of home run percentages for all professional baseball players. *Hint:* If you use Table 6 of Appendix II, be sure to use the closest *d.f.* that is *smaller.*

(c) Compute a 99% confidence interval for the population mean μ of home run percentages for all professional baseball players.

(d) The home run percentages for three professional players are

Tim Huelett, 2.5   Herb Hunter, 2.0   Jackie Jensen, 3.8

Examine your confidence intervals and describe how home run percentages for these players compare to the population average.

(e) In previous problems, we assumed the *x* distribution was normal or approximately normal. Do we need to make such an assumption in this problem? Why or why not? *Hint:* See the central limit theorem in Section 7.2.

 19. *Expand Your Knowledge: Alternate Method for Confidence Intervals* When σ is unknown and the sample size $n \geq 30$, there are two methods for computing confidence intervals for μ.

Method 1: Use the Student's *t* distribution with *d.f.* = *n* − 1.

This is the method used in the text. It is widely employed in statistical studies. Also, most statistical software packages use this method.

Method 2: When $n \geq 30$, use the sample standard deviation *s* as an estimate for σ, and then use the standard normal distribution.

This method is based on the fact that for large samples, *s* is a fairly good approximation for σ. Also, for large *n*, the critical values for the Student's *t* distribution approach those of the standard normal distribution.

Consider a random sample of size $n = 31$, with sample mean $\bar{x} = 45.2$ and sample standard deviation $s = 5.3$.

(a) Compute 90%, 95%, and 99% confidence intervals for μ using Method 1 with a Student's *t* distribution. Round endpoints to two digits after the decimal.

(b) Compute 90%, 95%, and 99% confidence intervals for μ using Method 2 with the standard normal distribution. Use *s* as an estimate for σ. Round endpoints to two digits after the decimal.

(c) Compare intervals for the two methods. Would you say that confidence intervals using a Student's *t* distribution are more conservative in the sense that they tend to be longer than intervals based on the standard normal distribution?

(d) Repeat parts (a) through (c) for a sample of size $n = 81$. With increased sample size, do the two methods give respective confidence intervals that are more similar?

8.3
Estimating *p* in the Binomial Distribution

FOCUS POINTS

✓ Compute the maximal margin of error for proportions using a given level of confidence.

✓ Compute confidence intervals for *p* and interpret the results.

✓ Interpret poll results.

The binomial distribution is completely determined by the number of trials *n* and the probability *p* of success in a single trial. For most experiments, the number of trials is chosen in advance. Then the distribution is completely determined by *p*. In this section, we will consider the problem of estimating *p* under the assumption that *n* has already been selected.

We are employing what are called *large-sample methods*. We will assume that the normal curve is a good approximation to the binomial distribution, and when necessary, we will use sample estimates for the standard deviation. Empirical studies have shown that these methods are quite good provided that *both*

$$np > 5 \quad \text{and} \quad nq > 5 \qquad \text{where } q = 1 - p$$

Let r be the number of successes out of n trials in a binomial experiment. We will take the sample proportion of successes $\hat{p}$ (read "p hat") $= r/n$ as our *point estimate for p*, the population proportion of successes.

> The **point estimates for p and q** are
>
> $$\hat{p} = \frac{r}{n}$$
>
> $$\hat{q} = 1 - \hat{p}$$
>
> where n = number of trials and r = number of successes.

For example, suppose that 800 students are selected at random from a student body of 20,000 and that they are each given shots to prevent a certain type of flu. These 800 students are then exposed to the flu, and 600 of them do not get the flu. What is the probability p that the shot will be successful for any single student selected at random from the entire population of 20,000 students? We estimate p for the entire student body by computing r/n from the sample of 800 students. The value $\hat{p} = r/n$ is 600/800, or 0.75. The value $\hat{p} = 0.75$ is then the *point estimate* for p.

The difference between the actual value of p and the estimate $\hat{p}$ is the size of our error caused by using $\hat{p}$ as a point estimate for p. The magnitude of $\hat{p} - p$ is called the *margin of error* for using $\hat{p} = r/n$ as a point estimate for p. In absolute value notation, the margin of error is $|\hat{p} - p|$.

To compute the bounds for the margin of error, we need some information about the distribution of $\hat{p} = r/n$ values for different samples of the same size n. It turns out that, for large samples, the distribution of $\hat{p}$ values is well approximated by a *normal curve* with

$$\text{mean } \mu = p \qquad \text{and} \qquad \text{standard error } \sigma = \sqrt{pq/n}$$

Since the distribution of $\hat{p} = r/n$ is approximately normal, we use features of the standard normal distribution to find the bounds for the difference $\hat{p} - p$. Recall that z_c is the number such that an area equal to c under the standard normal curve falls between $-z_c$ and z_c. Then, in terms of the language of probability,

$$P\left(-z_c\sqrt{\frac{pq}{n}} < \hat{p} - p < z_c\sqrt{\frac{pq}{n}}\right) = c \tag{16}$$

Equation (16) says that the chance is c that the numerical difference between $\hat{p}$ and p is between $-z_c\sqrt{pq/n}$ and $z_c\sqrt{pq/n}$. With the c confidence level, our estimate $\hat{p}$ differs from p by no more than

$$E = z_c\sqrt{pq/n}$$

As in Section 8.1, we call *E* the *maximal margin of error.*

Optional derivation of Equation (16)

First, we need to show that $\hat{p} = r/n$ has a distribution that is approximately normal with $\mu = p$ and $\sigma = \sqrt{pq/n}$. From Section 6.4, we know that, for sufficiently large *n*, the binomial distribution can be approximated by a normal distribution with mean $\mu = np$ and standard deviation $\sigma = \sqrt{npq}$. If *r* is the number of successes out of *n* trials of a binomial experiment, then *r* is a binomial random variable with a binomial distribution. When we convert *r* to standard *z* units, we obtain

$$z = \frac{r - \mu}{\sigma} = \frac{r - np}{\sqrt{npq}}$$

For sufficiently large *n*, *r* will be approximately normally distributed, so *z* will be too.

If we divide both numerator and denominator of the last expression by *n*, the value of *z* will not change.

$$z = \frac{\dfrac{r - np}{n}}{\dfrac{\sqrt{npq}}{n}} \quad \text{Simplified, we find} \quad z = \frac{\dfrac{r}{n} - p}{\sqrt{\dfrac{pq}{n}}}. \tag{17}$$

Equation (17) tells us that the $\hat{p} = r/n$ distribution is approximated by a normal curve with $\mu = p$ and $\sigma = \sqrt{pq/n}$.

The probability is *c* that *z* lies in the interval between $-z_c$ and z_c because an area equal to *c* under the standard normal curve lies between $-z_c$ and z_c. Using the language of probability, we write

$$P(-z_c < z < z_c) = c$$

From Equation (17), we know that

$$z = \frac{\hat{p} - p}{\sqrt{\dfrac{pq}{n}}}$$

If we put this expression for *z* into the preceding equation, we obtain

$$P\left(-z_c < \frac{\hat{p} - p}{\sqrt{\dfrac{pq}{n}}} < z_c\right) = c$$

If we multiply all parts of the inequality by $\sqrt{pq/n}$, we obtain the equivalent statement

$$P\left(-z_c\sqrt{\frac{pq}{n}} < \hat{p} - p < z_c\sqrt{\frac{pq}{n}}\right) = c \tag{16}$$

Confidence interval for p

To find a c confidence interval for p, we will use E in place of the expression $z_c\sqrt{pq/n}$ in Equation (16). Then we get

$$P(-E < \hat{p} - p < E) = c \tag{18}$$

Some algebraic manipulation produces the mathematically equivalent statement

$$P(\hat{p} - E < p < \hat{p} + E) = c \tag{19}$$

Equation (19) states that the probability is c that p lies in the interval from $\hat{p} - E$ to $\hat{p} + E$. Therefore, the interval from $\hat{p} - E$ to $\hat{p} + E$ is the c confidence interval for p that we wanted to find.

There is one technical difficulty in computing the c confidence interval for p. The expression $E = z_c\sqrt{pq/n}$ requires that we know the values of p and q. In most situations, we will not know the actual values of p or q, so we will use our point estimates

$$p \approx \hat{p} \qquad \text{and} \qquad q = 1 - p \approx 1 - \hat{p}$$

to estimate E. These estimates are safe for most practical purposes, since we are dealing with large-sample theory ($np > 5$ and $nq > 5$).

For convenient reference, we'll summarize the information about c confidence intervals for p, the probability of success in a binomial distribution.

PROCEDURE

How to find a confidence interval for a proportion p

Consider a binomial experiment with n trials where p represents the population probability of success and $q = 1 - p$ represents the population probability of failure. Let r be a random variable that represents the number of successes out of the n binomial trials.

The point estimates for p and q are

$$\hat{p} = \frac{r}{n} \qquad \text{and} \qquad \hat{q} = 1 - \hat{p}$$

The number of trials n should be sufficiently large so that both $n\hat{p} > 5$ and $n\hat{q} > 5$.

Confidence interval for p

$$\hat{p} - E < p < \hat{p} + E$$

where $E \approx z_c\sqrt{\dfrac{\hat{p}\hat{q}}{n}} = z_c\sqrt{\dfrac{\hat{p}(1-\hat{p})}{n}}$

c = confidence level ($0 < c < 1$)

z_c = critical value for confidence level c based on the standard normal distribution (See Table 5(b) of Appendix II for frequently used values.)

EXAMPLE 5

Confidence interval for p

Let's return to our flu shot experiment described at the beginning of this section. Suppose that 800 students were selected at random from a student body of 20,000 and given shots to prevent a certain type of flu. All 800 students were exposed

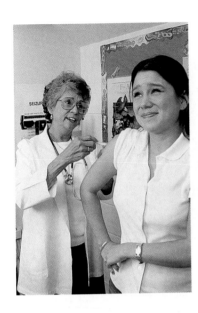

to the flu, and 600 of them did not get the flu. Let *p* represent the probability that the shot will be successful for any single student selected at random from the entire population of 20,000. Let *q* be the probability that the shot is not successful.

(a) What is the number of trials *n*? What is the value of *r*?

SOLUTION: Since each of the 800 students receiving the shot may be thought of as a trial, then $n = 800$, and $r = 600$ is the number of successful trials.

(b) What are the point estimates for *p* and *q*?

SOLUTION: We estimate *p* by the sample point estimate

$$\hat{p} = \frac{r}{n} = \frac{600}{800} = 0.75$$

We estimate *q* by

$$\hat{q} = 1 - \hat{p} = 1 - 0.75 = 0.25$$

(c) Would it seem that the number of trials is large enough to justify a normal approximation to the binomial?

SOLUTION: Since $n = 800$, $p \approx 0.75$, and $q \approx 0.25$, then

$$np \approx (800)(0.75) = 600 > 5 \qquad \text{and} \qquad nq \approx (800)(0.25) = 200 > 5$$

A normal approximation is certainly justified.

(d) Find a 99% confidence interval for *p*.

SOLUTION:

$$z_{0.99} = 2.58 \text{ (see Table 8-2 or Table 5(b) of Appendix II)}$$

$$E \approx z_{0.99}\sqrt{\frac{\hat{p}(1-\hat{p})}{n}} \approx 2.58\sqrt{\frac{(0.75)(0.25)}{800}} \approx 0.0395$$

The 99% confidence interval is then

$$\hat{p} - E < p < \hat{p} + E$$
$$0.75 - 0.0395 < p < 0.75 + 0.0395$$
$$0.71 < p < 0.79$$

◇

GUIDED EXERCISE 4

Confidence interval for p

A random sample of 188 books purchased at a local bookstore showed that 66 of the books were murder mysteries. Let *p* represent the proportion of books sold by this store that are murder mysteries.

Continued

GUIDED EXERCISE 4 continued

(a) What is a point estimate for p?

⟹ $\hat{p} = \dfrac{r}{n} = \dfrac{66}{188} = 0.35$

(b) Find a 90% confidence interval for p.

⟹ $E = z_c \sqrt{\dfrac{\hat{p}(1 - \hat{p})}{n}}$

$= 1.645 \sqrt{\dfrac{(0.35)(1 - 0.35)}{188}} \approx 0.0572$

The confidence interval is

$$\hat{p} - E < p < \hat{p} + E$$
$$0.35 - 0.0572 < p < 0.35 + 0.0572$$
$$0.29 < p < 0.41$$

(c) What is the meaning of the confidence interval you just computed?

⟹ If we had computed the interval for many different sets of 188 books, we would have found that about 90% of the intervals actually contained p, the population proportion of mysteries. Consequently, we can be 90% confident that our interval is one of the intervals that contains the unknown value p.

(d) To compute the confidence interval, we used a normal approximation. Does this seem justified?

⟹ $n = 188$; $p \approx 0.35$; $q \approx 0.65$

Since $np \approx 65.8 > 5$ and $nq \approx 122.2 > 5$, the approximation is justified.

It is interesting to note that our sample point estimate $\hat{p} = r/n$ and the confidence interval for the population proportion p do not depend on the size of the population. In our bookstore example, it made no difference how many books the store sold. On the other hand, the size of the sample does affect the accuracy of a statistical estimate. In the next section, we will study the effect of sample size on the reliability of our estimate.

 TECH NOTE   The TI-84Plus and TI-83Plus calculators and Minitab provide confidence intervals for proportions.

TI-84Plus/TI-83Plus Press the **STAT** key, select **TESTS**, and choose option **A:1-PropZInt.** The letter x represents the number of successes r. The TI-84Plus/TI-83Plus output shows the results for Guided Exercise 4.

```
1-PropZInt
 (.29381,.40832)
 p̂=.3510638298
 n=188
```

Minitab Use the menu selections **Stat ➤ Basic Statistics ➤ 1 Proportion.** In the dialogue box, select summarized data and fill in the number of trials and the number of successes. Under Options, select a confidence interval. Minitab uses the binomial distribution directly unless normal is checked. The Minitab output shows the results for Guided Exercise 4. Information from Chapter 9 material is also shown.

```
Test and Confidence Interval for One Proportion (Using Binomial)
Test of p = 0.5 vs p not = 0.5
                                                              Exact
Sample    X     N    Sample p         90.0 % CI            P-Value
  1      66   188    0.351064   (0.293222, 0.412466)         0.000
```

```
Test and Confidence Interval for One Proportion (Using Normal)
Test of p = 0.5 vs p not = 0.5
Sample    X    N    Sample p        90.0 % CI        Z-Value   P-Value
  1      66  188    0.351064   (0.293805, 0.408323)    -4.08     0.000
```

Interpreting Results from a Poll

Newspapers frequently report the results of an opinion poll. In articles that give more information, a statement about the margin of error accompanies the poll results. In most polls, the margin of error is given for a *95% confidence interval.*

General interpretation of poll results

1. When a poll states the results of a survey, the proportion reported to respond in the designated manner is $\hat{p}$, the sample estimate of the population proportion.

2. The *margin of error* is the maximal error E of a 95% confidence interval for *p*.

3. A 95% confidence interval for the population proportion *p* is

   poll report $\hat{p}$ − margin of error $E < p <$ poll report $\hat{p}$ + margin of error E.

◊ **COMMENT:** Leslie Kish, a statistician at the University of Michigan, was the first to apply the term *margin of error.* He was a pioneer in the study of population sampling techniques. His book *Survey Sampling* is still widely used all around the world. ◊

Some articles clarify the meaning of the margin of error further by saying that it is an error due to sampling. For instance, the following comments accompany results of a political poll reported in an issue of *The Wall Street Journal.*

How Poll Was Conducted

The Wall Street Journal/NBC News poll was based on nationwide telephone interviews of 1508 adults conducted last Friday through Tuesday by the polling organizations of Peter Hart and Robert Teeter.

The sample was drawn from 315 randomly selected geographic points in the continental U.S. Each region was represented in proportion to its population. Households were selected by a method that gave all telephone numbers . . . an equal chance of being included.

One adult, 18 years or older, was selected from each household by a procedure to provide the correct number of male and female respondents.

Chances are 19 of 20 that if all adults with telephones in the U.S. had been surveyed, the findings would differ from these poll results by no more than 2.6 percentage points in either direction.

GUIDED EXERCISE 5

Reading a poll

Read the last paragraph of the article, "How Poll Was Conducted."

(a) What confidence level corresponds to the phrase "chances are 19 of 20 that if . . ."

⟹ $\dfrac{19}{20} = 0.95$

A 95% confidence interval is being discussed.

(b) The article indicates that everyone in the sample was asked the question, "Which party, the Democratic Party or the Republican Party, do you think would do a better job handling . . . education?" Possible responses were Democrats, neither, both, or Republicans. The poll reported that 32% of the respondents said "Democrats." Does 32% represent the sample statistic $\hat{p}$ or the population parameter p for the proportion of adults responding "Democrat"?

⟹ 32% represents a sample statistic $\hat{p}$ because 32% represents the percentage of the adults in the *sample* who responded "Democrats."

(c) Continue reading the last paragraph of the article. It goes on to state, ". . . if all adults with telephones in the U.S. had been surveyed, the findings would differ from these poll results by no more than 2.6 percentage points in either direction." Use this information together with parts (a) and (b) to find a 95% confidence interval for the proportion p of the specified population who would respond "Democrat" to the question.

⟹ The value 2.6 percentage points represents the margin of error. Since the margin of error is for a 95% confidence interval, the confidence interval is

$$32\% - 2.6\% < p < 32\% + 2.6\%$$
$$29.4\% < p < 34.6\%$$

The poll indicates that at the time of the poll, between 29.4% and 34.6% of the specified population thought Democrats would do a better job handling education.

VIEWPOINT   *"Band-Aid Surgery"*

Faster recovery time and less pain! Sounds great. An alternate surgical technique called *laparoscopic* ("Band-Aid") *surgery* involves small incisions in which tiny video cameras and long surgical instruments are maneuvered. Instead of a 10-inch incision, surgeons might use four little stabs of about $\frac{1}{2}$-inch in length. However, not every such surgery is successful. An article in the Health Section of *The Wall Street Journal* recommends using a surgeon who has done at least 50 such surgeries. Then the prospective patient should ask about the *rate of conversion*, that is, the proportion *p* of times the surgeon has been forced by complications to switch in midoperation to conventional surgery. A confidence interval for the proportion *p* would be useful patient information!

SECTION 8.3   PROBLEMS

For all these problems, carry at least four digits after the decimal in your calculations. Answers may vary slightly due to rounding.

1. *Myers-Briggs: Actors* Isabel Myers was a pioneer in the study of personality types. The following information is taken from *A Guide to the Development and Use of the Myers-Briggs Type Indicator*, by Myers and McCaulley (Consulting Psychologists Press). In a random sample of 62 professional actors, it was found that 39 were extroverts.
   (a) Let *p* represent the proportion of all actors who are extroverts. Find a point estimate for *p*.
   (b) Find a 95% confidence interval for *p*. Give a brief interpretation of the meaning of the confidence interval you have found.
   (c) Do you think the conditions $np > 5$ and $nq > 5$ are satisfied in this problem? Explain why this would be an important consideration.

2. *Myers-Briggs: Judges* In a random sample of 519 judges, it was found that 285 were introverts (see reference of Problem 1).
   (a) Let *p* represent the proportion of all judges who are introverts. Find a point estimate for *p*.
   (b) Find a 99% confidence interval for *p*. Give a brief interpretation of the meaning of the confidence interval you have found.
   (c) Do you think the conditions $np > 5$ and $nq > 5$ are satisfied in this problem? Explain why this would be an important consideration.

3. *Navajo Lifestyle: Traditional Hogans* A random sample of 5222 permanent dwellings on the entire Navajo Indian Reservation showed that 1619 were traditional Navajo hogans (*Navajo Architecture: Forms, History, Distributions*, by Jett and Spencer, University of Arizona Press).
   (a) Let *p* be the proportion of all permanent dwellings on the entire Navajo Reservation that are traditional hogans. Find a point estimate for *p*.
   (b) Find a 99% confidence interval for *p*. Give a brief interpretation of the confidence interval.
   (c) Do you think that $np > 5$ and $nq > 5$ are satisfied for this problem? Explain why this would be an important consideration.

4. *Archaeology: Pottery* Santa Fe black-on-white is a type of pottery commonly found at archaeological excavations in Bandelier National Monument. At one excavation site a sample of 592 potsherds was found, of which 360 were identified as Santa Fe black-on-white (*Bandelier Archaeological Excavation Project: Summer 1990 Excavations at Burnt Mesa Pueblo and Casa del Rito,* edited by Kohler and Root, Washington State University).

   (a) Let p represent the population proportion of Santa Fe black-on-white potsherds at the excavation site. Find a point estimate for p.

   (b) Find a 95% confidence interval for p. Give a brief statement of the meaning of the confidence interval.

   (c) Do you think that the conditions $np > 5$ and $nq > 5$ are satisfied in this problem? Why would this be important?

5. *Health Care: Colorado Physicians* A random sample of 5792 physicians in Colorado showed that 3139 provided at least some charity care (i.e., treated poor people at no cost). These data are based on information from *State Health Care Data: Utilization, Spending, and Characteristics* (American Medical Association).

   (a) Let p represent the proportion of all Colorado physicians who provide some charity care. Find a point estimate for p.

   (b) Find a 99% confidence interval for p. Give a brief explanation of the meaning of your answer in the context of this problem.

   (c) Is the normal approximation to the binomial justified in this problem? Explain.

6. *Supermarkets: Broken Eggs* The manager of the dairy section of a large supermarket took a random sample of 250 egg cartons and found that 40 cartons had at least one broken egg.

   (a) Let p be the proportion of egg cartons with at least one broken egg out of the population of all egg cartons stocked by this store. Find a point estimate for p.

   (b) Find a 90% confidence interval for p. Give a brief interpretation of the meaning of your confidence interval.

   (c) Do you think that the conditions $np > 5$ and $nq > 5$ are satisfied? Why is this important?

7. *Law Enforcement: Arrests* "Fugitive Task Force Runs 99 Photos in (Colorado) Springs Newspaper: Police Make 17 Arrests." This was a headline in the *Rocky Mountain News.*

   (a) Let p represent the population proportion of fugitives who will be arrested after their photos are displayed in the newspaper. Find a point estimate for p.

   (b) Find an 85% confidence interval for p. Give a brief statement of the meaning of the confidence interval.

   (c) Do you think that the conditions $np > 5$ and $nq > 5$ are satisfied in this problem? Why would this be important?

8. *Law Enforcement: Escaped Convicts* Case studies showed that out of 10,351 convicts who escaped from U.S. prisons, only 7867 were recaptured (*The Book of Odds,* by Shook and Shook, Signet).

   (a) Let p represent the proportion of all escaped convicts who will eventually be recaptured. Find a point estimate for p.

   (b) Find a 99% confidence interval for p. Give a brief statement of the meaning of the confidence interval.

   (c) Is use of the normal approximation to the binomial justified in this problem? Explain.

9. *Fishing: Barbless Hooks* In a combined study of northern pike, cutthroat trout, rainbow trout, and lake trout, it was found that 26 out of 855 fish died when caught and released using barbless hooks on flies or lures. All hooks were removed from

the fish. (Source: *A National Symposium on Catch and Release Fishing,* Humboldt State University Press.)

(a) Let *p* represent the proportion of all pike and trout that die (i.e., *p* is the mortality rate) when caught and released using barbless hooks. Find a point estimate for *p*.

(b) Find a 99% confidence interval for *p*, and give a brief explanation of the meaning of the interval.

(c) Is the normal approximation to the binomial justified in this problem? Explain.

10. *Fishing: Barbed Hooks* A study of 200 rainbow trout caught on baited size 8 barbed hooks and released with the line cut at the hook (but the hook not removed from the fish) showed that 58 fish died. See reference in Problem 9.

(a) Let *p* represent the proportion of all rainbow trout that die when caught and released using the described method. Find a point estimate for *p*.

(b) Find a 95% confidence interval for *p*, and give a brief explanation of the meaning of the interval.

(c) Is the normal approximation to the binomial justified in this problem? Explain.

11. *Montana Open Range: Cattle* The U.S. Department of the Interior is checking cattle on the Windgate open range in Montana. A random sample of 900 cattle shows that 54 are undernourished.

(a) Let *p* represent the proportion of undernourished cattle on the Windgate range. Find a point estimate for *p*.

(b) Find a 0.99 confidence interval for *p*.

12. *Sports Events: Attendance* Attending sporting events is a popular source of entertainment. When 1000 people were surveyed, 590 said that getting together with friends was an important reason for attending a sporting event (*USA Today*).

(a) Let *p* be the proportion of all people attending a sporting event to be with friends. Find a point estimate for *p*.

(b) Find a 99% confidence interval for *p*.

13. *AM Radio: Audience* The Roper Organization conducted a poll of 2000 adults and found that 382 regularly listen to an AM radio station at home (*USA Today*).

(a) Let *p* represent the proportion of the adult population that regularly listens to an AM radio station at home. Find a point estimate for *p*.

(b) Find an 80% confidence interval for *p*.

14. *Physicians: Solo Practice* A random sample of 328 medical doctors showed that 171 had a solo practice. (Source: *Practice Patterns of General Internal Medicine,* American Medical Association.)

(a) Let *p* represent the proportion of all medical doctors who have a solo practice. Find a point estimate for *p*.

(b) Find a 95% confidence interval for *p*. Give a brief explanation of the meaning of the interval.

(c) As a news writer, how would you report the survey results regarding the percentage of medical doctors in solo practice? What is the margin of error based on a 95% confidence interval?

15. *Marketing: Customer Loyalty* In a marketing survey, a random sample of 730 women shoppers revealed that 628 remained loyal to their favorite supermarket during the past year (i.e., did not switch stores). (Source: *Trends in the United States: Consumer Attitudes and the Supermarket,* The Research Department, Food Marketing Institute.)

(a) Let *p* represent the proportion of all women shoppers who remain loyal to their favorite supermarket. Find a point estimate for *p*.

(b) Find a 95% confidence interval for p. Give a brief explanation of the meaning of the interval.

(c) As a news writer, how would you report the survey results regarding the percentage of supermarket shoppers who remained loyal to their favorite supermarket during the past year? What is the margin of error based on a 95% confidence interval?

16. *Marketing: Bargain Hunters* In a marketing survey, a random sample of 1001 supermarket shoppers revealed that 273 always stock up on an item when they find that item at a real bargain price. See reference in Problem 15.

(a) Let p represent the proportion of all supermarket shoppers who always stock up on an item when they find a real bargain. Find a point estimate for p.

(b) Find a 95% confidence interval for p. Give a brief explanation of the meaning of the interval.

(c) As a news writer, how would you report the survey results on the percentage of supermarket shoppers who stock up on items when they find the item is a real bargain? What is the margin of error based on a 95% confidence interval?

17. *Lifestyle: Smoking* In a survey of 1000 large corporations, 250 said that, given a choice between a job candidate who smokes and an equally qualified nonsmoker, the nonsmoker would get the job (*USA Today*).

(a) Let p represent the proportion of all corporations preferring a nonsmoking candidate. Find a point estimate for p.

(b) Find a 0.95 confidence interval for p.

(c) As a news writer, how would you report the survey results regarding the proportion of corporations that would hire the equally qualified nonsmoker? What is the margin of error based on a 95% confidence interval?

18. *Opinion Poll: Crime and Violence* A *New York Times*/CBS poll asked the question, "What do you think is the most important problem facing this country today?" Nineteen percent of the respondents answered "crime and violence." The margin of sampling error was plus or minus 3 percentage points. Following the convention that the margin of error is based on a 95% confidence interval, find a 95% confidence interval for the percentage of the population that would respond "crime and violence" to the question asked by the pollsters.

8.4
Choosing the Sample Size

FOCUS POINTS

✓ Compute the sample size to be used for estimating a mean μ.

✓ Compute the sample size to be used for estimating a proportion p when we have an estimate for p.

✓ Compute the sample size to be used for estimating a proportion p when we have no estimate for p.

In the design stages of statistical research projects, it is a good idea to decide in advance on the confidence level you wish to use and to select the *maximum* margin of error E you want for your project. How you choose to make these decisions depends on the requirements of the project and the practical nature of the problem. Whatever specifications you make, the next step is to determine the sample size. In this section, we will assume that the distribution of sample means $\bar{x}$ is approximately normal.

Sample Size for Estimating μ

Let's say that at a confidence level of c, we want our point estimate $\bar{x}$ for μ to be in error either way by less than some quantity E. In other words, E is the maximum margin of error we can tolerate. Using the language of probability, we want the following to be true:

$$P(-E < \bar{x} - \mu < E) = c \qquad (20)$$

This is essentially the same as Equation (1) of Section 8.1. Let's compare them.

$$P(-E < \bar{x} - \mu < E) = c \tag{20}$$

$$P\left(-z_c \frac{\sigma}{\sqrt{n}} < \bar{x} - \mu < z_c \frac{\sigma}{\sqrt{n}}\right) = c \tag{1}$$

From this comparison, we see that we want E to be

$$E = z_c \frac{\sigma}{\sqrt{n}}$$

Solving this equation for n, we get

$$n = \left(\frac{z_c \sigma}{E}\right)^2 \tag{21}$$

◇ **COMMENT:** To compute n from Equation (21), you must know the value of σ. If the value of σ is not known, you may be able to estimate σ from an earlier study. Otherwise, conduct a pilot study using a sample size of $n \geq 30$ and using s as an estimate for σ. As you obtain more sample data, you can improve the estimate for σ. ◇

EXAMPLE 6

Sample size for estimating μ

A wildlife study is designed to find the mean weight of salmon caught by an Alaskan fishing company. As a preliminary study, a random sample of 50 freshly caught salmon is weighed. The sample standard deviation of the weights of these 50 fish is $s = 2.15$ lb. How large a sample should be taken to be 99% confident that the sample mean $\bar{x}$ is within 0.20 lb of the true mean weight μ?

SOLUTION: In this problem, $z_{0.99} = 2.58$ (see Table 8-2) and $E = 0.20$. The preliminary study of 50 fish is large enough to permit a good approximation of σ by $s = 2.15$. Therefore, Equation (21) becomes

$$n = \left(\frac{z_c \sigma}{E}\right)^2 \approx \left(\frac{(2.58)(2.15)}{0.20}\right)^2 = 769.2$$

Note: In determining sample size, any fractional value of n is always rounded to the *next higher whole number*. We conclude that a sample size of 770 will be large enough to satisfy the specifications. Of course, a sample size larger than 770 also works. ◇

Salmon moving upstream

EXAMPLE 7

Sample size for estimating μ

A certain company makes light fixtures on an assembly line. An efficiency expert wants to determine the mean time it takes an employee to assemble the switch on one of these fixtures. A preliminary study used a random sample of 45 observations and found that the sample standard deviation was $s = 78$ seconds. How many more observations are necessary for the efficiency expert to be 95% sure that the point estimate $\bar{x}$ will be "off" from the true mean μ by at most 15 seconds?

SOLUTION: In this example, we approximate σ by $s = 78$. We use $z_{0.95} = 1.96$ (see Table 8-2). The maximum margin of error is specified to be $E = 15$ seconds. Equation (21) gives us

$$n = \left(\frac{z_c \sigma}{E}\right)^2 = \left(\frac{(1.96)(78)}{15}\right)^2 = 103.9$$

The efficiency expert should use a sample of minimum size 104. Since the preliminary study has 45 observations, an additional $104 - 45 = 59$ observations are necessary. ◇

GUIDED EXERCISE 6

Sample size for estimating μ

A large state university has over 1800 faculty members. The dean of faculty wants to estimate the average teaching experience (in years) of the faculty members. A preliminary random sample of 60 faculty members yields a sample standard deviation of $s = 3.4$ years. The dean wants to be 99% confident that the sample mean $\bar{x}$ does not differ from the population mean by more than half a year. How large a sample should be used? Let's answer this question in parts.

(a) What value can we use to approximate σ? Why can we do this?

⟹ $s = 3.4$ years is a good approximation because a preliminary sample of 60 is fairly large.

(b) What is $z_{0.99}$? (*Hint:* See Table 8-2.)

⟹ $z_{0.99} = 2.58$

(c) What is E for this problem?

⟹ $E = 0.5$ year

(d) Which is the correct formula for n:

$$\left(\frac{z_c \sigma}{n}\right)^2, \quad \left(\frac{z_c \sigma}{E}\right)^2, \quad \text{or} \quad \left(\frac{z_c E}{\sigma}\right)^2$$

⟹ $n = \left(\dfrac{z_c \sigma}{E}\right)^2$

(e) Use the formula for n to find the minimum sample size. Should your answer be rounded up or down to a whole number?

⟹ $n = \left(\dfrac{(2.58)(3.4)}{0.5}\right)^2 = (17.54)^2 = 307.8$

Always round n up to the next whole number. Our final answer $n = 308$ is the minimum size.

Sample Size for Estimating $\hat{p} = r/n$

(If you omitted the binomial distribution, omit the rest of this section.)

Next, we will determine the minimum sample size when we use the sample proportion $\hat{p} = r/n$ as a point estimate for p in a binomial distribution. We will use the methods of normal approximation (large samples) discussed in Section 8.3. Suppose for a confidence level c we want the estimate $\hat{p} = r/n$ for p to be in error either way by less than some quantity E. Using the language of probability, we want the following to be true.

$$P(-E < \hat{p} - p < E) = c \tag{22}$$

Let's compare this with Equation (16) of Section 8.3. For convenience, they both are written together:

$$P(-E < \hat{p} - p < E) = c \tag{22}$$

$$P\left(-z_c \sqrt{\frac{pq}{n}} < \hat{p} - p < z_c \sqrt{\frac{pq}{n}}\right) = c \tag{16}$$

The comparison of the two equations gives a formula for E:

$$E = z_c \sqrt{\frac{pq}{n}}$$

Solving the last equation for n, we get

$$n = pq \left(\frac{z_c}{E} \right)^2$$

Since $q = 1 - p$, our equation for n can be written

$$n = p(1 - p) \left(\frac{z_c}{E} \right)^2 \tag{23}$$

Equation (23) cannot be used unless we already have a preliminary estimate for p. To get around this difficulty, we will use the equation $p(1 - p) = \frac{1}{4} - (p - \frac{1}{2})^2$. This is an algebraic identity that you are asked to verify in an optional exercise at the end of this section. In this exercise, you are also asked to use a little logical deduction to show that the maximum possible value of $p(1 - p)$ is $\frac{1}{4}$. Therefore, *when we have no preliminary estimate for p, we use the formula*

$$n = \frac{1}{4} \left(\frac{z_c}{E} \right)^2 \tag{24}$$

Since Equation (24) may make the sample size unnecessarily large, we can say the probability is *at least* (and possibly more than) c that the point estimate $\hat{p} = r/n$ for p will be in error either way by less than the quantity E.

EXAMPLE 8

Sample size for estimating p

A company is in the business of selling wholesale popcorn to grocery stores. The company buys directly from farmers. A buyer for the company is examining a large amount of corn from a certain farmer. Before the purchase is made, the buyer wants to estimate p, the probability that a kernel will pop.

Suppose that a random sample of n kernels is taken and r of these kernels pop. The buyer wants to be 95% sure that the point estimate $\hat{p} = r/n$ for p will be in error either way by less than 0.01.

(a) If no preliminary study is made to estimate p, how large a sample should the buyer use?

SOLUTION: In this case, we use Equation (24) with $z_{0.95} = 1.96$ (see Table 8-2) and $E = 0.01$.

$$n = \frac{1}{4} \left(\frac{z_c}{E} \right)^2 = \frac{1}{4} \left(\frac{1.96}{0.01} \right)^2 = 0.25(38{,}416) = 9604$$

The buyer would need a sample of $n = 9604$ kernels.

(b) A preliminary study showed that p was approximately 0.86. If the buyer uses the results of the preliminary study, how large a sample should be used?

SOLUTION: In this case, we use Equation (23) with $p \approx 0.86$. Again, from Table 8-2, $z_{0.95} = 1.96$, and from the problem, $E = 0.01$.

$$n = p(1-p)\left(\frac{z_c}{E}\right)^2 = (0.86)(0.14)\left(\frac{1.96}{0.01}\right)^2 = 4625.29$$

The sample size should be at least $n = 4626$ kernels. This sample is less than half the sample size necessary without the preliminary study.   ◊

GUIDED EXERCISE 7

Sample size for estimating p

In Indianapolis, the department of public health wants to estimate the proportion of children (grades 1–8) who require corrective lenses for their vision. A random sample of n children is taken, and r of these children are found to require corrective lenses. Let p be the true proportion of children requiring corrective lenses. The health department wants to be 99% sure that the point estimate $\hat{p} = r/n$ for p will be in error either way by less than 0.03.

(a) If no preliminary study is made to estimate p, how large a sample should the health department use? Let's answer this question in parts.

(i) Which formula shall we use: (23) or (24)?

⟹ (i) We use formula (24) because we do not have an estimate for p.

(ii) What is the value of E, and what is the value of z_c in this problem?

⟹ (ii) $E = 0.03$ and $z_{0.99} = 2.58$ (see Table 8-2).

(iii) What is the value of n?

⟹ (iii) $n = \frac{1}{4}\left(\frac{z_c}{E}\right)^2 = \frac{1}{4}\left(\frac{2.58}{0.03}\right)^2 = 1849$

So without a preliminary study to find p, we will need a sample size of at least $n = 1849$ children.

(b) A preliminary random sample of 100 children indicates that 23 require corrective lenses. Using the results of this preliminary study, how large a sample should the health department use? Again, let's answer this question in parts.

(i) Which formula should we use: (23) or (24)?

⟹ We use formula (23) because we have an estimate of p from a preliminary study.

(ii) What are the values of E and z_c for this problem?

⟹ $E = 0.03$ and $z_{0.99} = 2.58$

(iii) What approximate value shall we use for p?

⟹ $p \approx 0.23$

(iv) What is the value of n?

⟹ $n = p(1-p)\left(\frac{z_c}{E}\right)^2 = (0.23)(0.77)\left(\frac{2.58}{0.03}\right)^2 = 1309.83$

Therefore, the sample size should be at least 1310 children.

> ### PROCEDURE
>
> **How to find the sample size n**
>
> E = specified margin of error
>
> c = specified confidence level ($0 < c < 1$)
>
> z_c = critical value from the standard normal distribution (See Table 8-2 for frequently used values.)
>
> **For μ:** $n = \left(\dfrac{z_c \sigma}{E}\right)^2$ If σ is unknown, take a preliminary sample of size $n \geq 30$ and use s as an estimate for σ.
>
> **For p:** $\begin{cases} n = p(1-p)\left(\dfrac{z_c}{E}\right)^2 & \text{if you have a preliminary estimate for } p. \\[2ex] n = \dfrac{1}{4}\left(\dfrac{z_c}{E}\right)^2 & \text{if you do } not \text{ have a preliminary estimate for } p. \end{cases}$
>
> In all cases, if n is not a whole number, round n up to the next highest whole number. For proportions, increase the sample size n to ensure that both $np \geq 5$ and $nq \geq 5$ if necessary.

VIEWPOINT

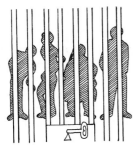

Profiles in Crime!

What proportion of the U.S. population will eventually spend time in prison? (*Answer:* About 5.1%.) What proportion of federal prison inmates have at least some college education? (*Answer:* About 28%.) If a person is released from prison, what is the probability that he or she will commit a felony and be returned to prison within 3 years? (*Answer:* About 41%.) What are the gender and age distributions of prison inmates? How accurate are these statistics? Sample size plays an important role in statistical accuracy. Methods of this section and data from the Bureau of Justice statistics can help you determine the implied level of accuracy. For more information, visit the Brase/Brase statistics site at **http://math.college.hmco.com/students** and find the link to the U.S. Justice Department.

SECTION 8.4   PROBLEMS

For each of the following problems,

(i) identify whether we are going to estimate a population mean μ or a population proportion p.

(ii) write down the appropriate sample size formula(s) for the problem, and then solve the problem.

1. *Botany: Yellowstone National Park* Test plots in Yellowstone National Park were used to study tree reproduction of lodgepole pine (*Yellowstone Vegetation,* by D. G. Despain, Roberts Rinehart). In plots of 50 square meters, the number x of new lodgepole saplings was counted. In a given region, based on long observation, the standard deviation of x values is estimated at $\sigma = 44$. How many 50-square-meter plots should be studied in such a region to be 95% sure that the sample mean $\bar{x}$ of lodgepole saplings is within 10 saplings of the population mean μ of lodgepole saplings in all 50-square-meter plots in this area?

2. *Botany: Yellowstone National Park* Root depth of grasses and shrubs in a type of soil known as glacial outwash was studied in Yellowstone National Park by D. G. Despain (see reference in Problem 1). Let x be a random variable representing root depth in this type of soil. It was found that the standard deviation of x values is approximately $\sigma = 8.94$ in. In a proposed study region of glacial outwash, how many plants should be carefully dug up and studied to be 90% sure that the sample mean root depth $\bar{x}$ is within 0.5 in. of the population mean root depth?

*3. *Medical: Blood Type* A random sample of medical files is used to estimate the proportion p of all people who have blood type B.
   (a) If you have no preliminary estimate for p, how many medical files should you include in a random sample in order to be 85% sure that the point estimate $\hat{p}$ will be within a distance of 0.05 from p?
   (b) Answer part (a) if you use the preliminary estimate that about 8 out of 90 people have blood type B. (Reference: *Manual of Laboratory and Diagnostic Tests,* F. Fischbach.)

4. *Pro Basketball: Heights of Players* A random sample of 41 basketball players from the "All-Time Player Directory" of *The Official NBA Basketball Encyclopedia* (Villard Books) gave a sample standard deviation for height of players of $s = 3.32$ inches. How many more basketball players from the "All-Time Player Directory" should be included in the sample to be 95% sure that the sample mean $\bar{x}$ is within 0.75 inch of the population mean μ of all players listed in the NBA encyclopedia?

5. *Pro Basketball: Weights of Players* The NBA "All-Time Player Directory" also gives the weight of each basketball player. A random sample of 56 basketball players from the directory (see reference in Problem 4) gave a sample standard deviation of $s = 26.58$ pounds for the weights of players. How many more basketball players from the "All-Time Player Directory" should be included in the sample to be 90% sure that the sample mean player weight $\bar{x}$ is within 4 pounds of the population mean μ?

*6. *Business: Phone Contact* How hard is it to reach a businessperson by phone? Let p be the proportion of calls to businesspeople for which the caller reaches the person being called on the *first* try.
   (a) If you have no preliminary estimate for p, how many business phone calls should you include in a random sample to be 80% sure that the point estimate $\hat{p}$ will be within a distance of 0.03 from p?
   (b) The *Book of Odds,* by Shook and Shook (Signet), reports that businesspeople can be reached by a single phone call approximately 17% of the time. Using this (national) estimate for p, answer part (a).

*7. *Campus Life: Coeds* What percentage of the campus student body is female? Let p be the proportion of women students on your campus.
   (a) If no preliminary study is made to estimate p, how large a sample is needed to be 99% sure that a point estimate $\hat{p}$ will be within a distance of 0.05 from p?

*Omit problems marked with an asterisk if you omitted the binomial distribution.

(b) The *Statistical Abstract of the United States,* 112th Edition, indicates that approximately 54% of college students are females. Answer part (a) using this estimate for *p*.

*8. *Gasoline Stations: Self-Service* At many gasoline stations, customers have the option of using self-service pumps and receiving a discount instead of using full-service pumps. The question is: What proportion of customers in your neighborhood take advantage of this option and use the self-service pumps?
   (a) If no preliminary study is made to estimate *p*, how large a sample of customers is necessary to be 90% sure that the point estimate $\hat{p}$ will be within a distance of 0.08 of *p*?
   (b) Nationally, about 81% of gasoline customers use self-service pumps (Source: Amoco Oil Corporation). Answer part (a) for your neighborhood using this estimate for *p*.

9. *Anthropology: Pottery* A random sample of 83 reconstructed clay vessels from the Turquoise Ridge archaeological site indicated the standard deviation of diameters to be approximately 5.5 cm (based on information from *Anthropological Paper Number 118,* University of Utah Press). How many more such clay vessels must be found and reconstructed to be 95% sure that the sample mean $\bar{x}$ of diameters is within 1 cm of the population mean μ of all such reconstructed clay vessels at this archaeological site?

10. *Wildlife: Bighorn Sheep* A random sample of 37 adult male desert bighorn sheep indicated the standard deviation of the sheep weights to be 15.8 lb (Source: *The Bighorn of Death Valley,* Fauna of the National Parks of the United States Monograph Number 6, U.S. Government Printing Office). How many more such adult male desert bighorn sheep should be included in the sample to be 90% sure that the sample mean weight $\bar{x}$ is within 2.5 lb of the population mean weight μ of all such bighorn sheep in this region?

*11. *Forestry: Pine Beetle* A ponderosa pine forest in Colorado has a pine beetle infestation. The beetles bore into a tree and carry a fungus that ultimately kills the tree. Let *p* be the proportion of trees in the forest that are infested.
   (a) If no preliminary sample is taken to estimate *p*, how large a sample is necessary to be 85% sure that a point estimate $\hat{p}$ will be within a distance of 0.06 from *p*?
   (b) A preliminary study of 58 trees showed that 19 were infested. How many *more* trees should be included in the sample to be 85% sure that a point estimate $\hat{p}$ will be within a distance of 0.06 from *p*?

12. *Hardware Store: Cash Flow* Gordon is thinking of buying a combination hardware/sporting goods store in Dove Creek, Montana. However, daily cash flow is an important consideration. A random sample of 40 business days from the past year was taken from the store records. For each day, the net income was determined. The sample standard deviation was found to be $57.19. How many *more* business days should be included in the sample to be 85% confident that the sample mean $\bar{x}$ of daily net incomes is within $10 of the population mean μ of daily net incomes?

*13. *Political Science: Capital Punishment* David is doing a research project in political science to determine the proportion *p* of voters in his district who favor capital punishment.
   (a) If no preliminary sample of voters is taken to estimate *p*, how large a sample is necessary to be 99% sure that a point estimate $\hat{p}$ will be within a distance of 0.01 from *p*?

*Omit problems marked with an asterisk if you omitted the binomial distribution.

(b) The National Opinion Research Center at the University of Chicago found that approximately 67% of people in the United States favor capital punishment. Use this estimate to answer part (a).

14. *Sociology: Marriage Customs* A sociologist is studying marriage customs in a rural community in Denmark. A random sample of 35 women who have been married was used to determine the age of the woman at the time of her first marriage. The sample standard deviation of these ages was 2.3 years. The sociologist wants to estimate the population mean age of a woman at the time of her first marriage. How many *more* women should be included in the sample to be 95% confident that the sample mean $\bar{x}$ of ages is within 0.25 year of the population mean μ?

15. *Airline Reservations: Waiting Time* When customers phone an airline to make reservations, they usually find it irritating if they are kept on hold for a long time. In an effort to determine how long phone customers are kept on hold, one airline took a random sample of 167 phone calls and determined the length of time (in minutes) each caller was kept on hold. The sample standard deviation was 3.8 minutes. How many more phone customers should be included in the sample to be 99% sure that the sample mean $\bar{x}$ of hold times is within 30 seconds of the population mean μ of hold times?

*16. *Small Business: Bankruptcy* The National Council of Small Businesses is interested in the proportion of small businesses that declared Chapter 11 bankruptcy last year. Since there are so many small businesses, the National Council intends to estimate the proportion from a random sample. Let p be the proportion of small businesses that declared Chapter 11 bankruptcy last year.
(a) If no preliminary sample is taken to estimate p, how large a sample is necessary to be 95% sure that a point estimate $\hat{p}$ will be within a distance of 0.10 from p?
(b) In a preliminary random sample of 38 small businesses, it was found that six had declared Chapter 11 bankruptcy. How many *more* small businesses should be included in the sample to be 95% sure that a point estimate $\hat{p}$ will be within a distance of 0.10 from p?

*17. *Women: Pickup Trucks* Let p be the proportion of all pickup truck owners in Cheyenne, Wyoming, who are women.
(a) If no preliminary study is made to estimate p, how large a sample is necessary to be 90% sure that a point estimate $\hat{p}$ will be within a distance of 0.1 from p?
(b) *USA Today* reported that nationally, approximately 24% of all pickup trucks are owned by women. Answer part (a) using this estimate for p.

*18. *Political Science: Voter Opinion* Linda Silbers is a social scientist studying voter opinion about a city bond proposal for a light-rail mass transit system in Denver.
(a) If Linda wants to be 90% sure that her sample estimate of the proportion of voters who favor the bond is within 5% of the population percent p who favor the bond, how large a sample should she use?
(b) If a preliminary study showed that p is approximately 73%, how large a sample is required?

*19. *Brain Teaser: Algebra* Why do we use 1/4 in place of $p(1 - p)$ in formula (24) for sample size when the probability of success p is unknown?
(a) Show that $p(1 - p) = 1/4 - (p - 1/2)^2$.
(b) Why is $p(1 - p)$ never greater than 1/4?

*Omit problems marked with an asterisk if you omitted the binomial distribution.

*20. *Polling: Votes* You are working for a local polling firm. Your project involves interviewing a random sample of registered voters to determine the percentage favoring the use of state lottery proceeds for park improvements. The firm wants to ensure that the margin of error is no more than 3 percentage points either way. Assuming that there is no preliminary estimate for the percentage of registered voters favoring this use of lottery funds, what is the *minimum* number of respondents required? (*Hint:* Convert the margin of error to decimal and use the *New York Times*/CBS convention that the margin of error is based on a 95% confidence level.)

*21. *Election Results: Florida* A heavily populated county in Florida is told by the election commission to estimate the proportion p of popular vote count for the Democratic candidate for president.

   (a) The maximal margin of error is to be 0.001 with a 99% confidence level. If no preliminary estimate for p can be agreed upon, how many ballots must be checked?

   (b) If $p = 0.5$ were used as a preliminary estimate for p, would the answer to part (a) change? Explain.

8.5
Estimating $\mu_1 - \mu_2$ and $p_1 - p_2$

Independent Samples and Dependent Samples

FOCUS POINTS

✓ Distinguish between independent and dependent samples.

✓ Compute confidence intervals for $\mu_1 - \mu_2$ when σ_1 and σ_2 are known.

✓ Compute confidence intervals for $\mu_1 - \mu_2$ when σ_1 and σ_2 are unknown.

✓ Compute confidence intervals for $p_1 - p_2$ using the normal approximation.

✓ Interpret the meaning and implications of an all-positive, all-negative, or mixed confidence interval.

How can we tell if two populations are different? One way is to compare the difference in population means or the difference in population proportions. In this section, we will use samples from two populations to create confidence intervals for the difference between population parameters.

To make a statistical estimate about the difference between two population parameters, we need to have a sample from each population. Samples may be *independent* or *dependent* according to how they are selected.

> Two samples are **independent** if sample data drawn from one population is completely unrelated to the selection of sample data from the other population.

> Two samples are **dependent** if each data value in one sample can be paired with a corresponding data value in the other sample.

Dependent samples and data pairs occur very naturally in "before and after" situations where the *same object* or item is *measured twice*. We will devote an entire section (9.4) to the study of dependent samples and paired data. However, in this section, we will confine our interest to independent samples.

Independent samples occur very naturally when we draw *two random samples*, one from the first population and one from the second population. Because *both* samples are random samples, there is no pairing of measurements between the two populations. All the examples of this section will involve independent random samples.

*Omit problems marked with an asterisk if you omitted the binomial distribution.

GUIDED EXERCISE 8

Distinguish between independent and dependent samples

For each experiment, categorize the sampling as independent or dependent, and explain your choice.

(a) In many medical experiments, a sample of subjects is randomly divided into two groups. One group is given a specific treatment, and the other group is given a placebo. After a certain period of time, both groups are measured for the same condition. Do the measurements from these two groups constitute independent or dependent samples?

➡ Since the subjects are *randomly assigned* to the two treatment groups (one receives a treatment, the other a placebo), the resulting measurements would form independent samples.

(b) In an accountability study, a group of students in an English composition course is given a pretest. After the course, the same students are given a posttest covering similar material. Are the two groups of scores independent or dependent?

➡ Since the pretest scores and the posttest scores are from the same students, the samples are dependent. Each student has both a pretest score and a posttest score, so there is a natural pairing of data values.

Confidence Intervals for $\mu_1 - \mu_2$ (σ_1 and σ_2 known)

The $\bar{x}_1 - \bar{x}_2$ sampling distribution

In this section, we will use probability distributions that arise from a difference of means (or proportions). How do we obtain such distributions? Suppose that we have two statistical variables x_1 and x_2, each with its own distribution. We take *independent* random samples of size n_1 from the x_1 distribution and of size n_2 from the x_2 distribution. Then we compute the respective means $\bar{x}_1$ and $\bar{x}_2$. Now consider the difference $\bar{x}_1 - \bar{x}_2$. This expression represents a difference of means. If we repeat this sampling process over and over, we will create lots of $\bar{x}_1 - \bar{x}_2$ values. Figure 8-7 illustrates the sampling distribution of $\bar{x}_1 - \bar{x}_2$.

FIGURE 8-7

Sampling Distribution of $\bar{x}_1 - \bar{x}_2$

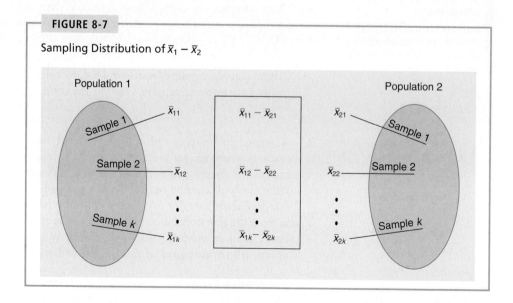

The values of $\bar{x}_1 - \bar{x}_2$ that come from repeated (independent) sampling of populations 1 and 2 can be arranged in a relative-frequency table and a relative-frequency histogram (see Section 2.2). This would give us an experimental idea of the theoretical probability distribution of $\bar{x}_1 - \bar{x}_2$.

Fortunately, it is not necessary to carry out this lengthy process for each example. The results have been worked out mathematically. The next theorem presents the main results.

◇ **THEOREM 8.1** Let x_1 and x_2 have normal distributions with means μ_1 and μ_2 and standard deviations σ_1 and σ_2, respectively. If we take independent random samples of size n_1 from the x_1 distribution and of size n_2 from the x_2 distribution, then the variable $\bar{x}_1 - \bar{x}_2$ has

1. a normal distribution

2. mean $\mu_1 - \mu_2$

3. standard deviation $\sqrt{\dfrac{\sigma_1^2}{n_1} + \dfrac{\sigma_2^2}{n_2}}$ ◇

◇ **COMMENT** The theorem requires that x_1 and x_2 have *normal* distributions. However, if *both* n_1 and n_2 are 30 or larger, then the central limit theorem (Section 7.2) assures us that $\bar{x}_1$ and $\bar{x}_2$ are approximately normally distributed. In this case, the conclusions of the theorem are again valid even if the original x_1 and x_2 distributions are not exactly normal.   ◇

Confidence intervals for $\mu_1 - \mu_2$ (σ_1 and σ_2 known)

If we use Theorem 8.1, then a discussion similar to that of Section 8.1 gives the following information.

PROCEDURE

How to find a confidence interval for $\mu_1 - \mu_2$ when both σ_1 and σ_2 are known

Let σ_1 and σ_2 be the population standard deviations of populations 1 and 2. Obtain two *independent* random samples from populations 1 and 2, where

$\bar{x}_1$ and $\bar{x}_2$ are sample means from populations 1 and 2
n_1 and n_2 are sample sizes from populations 1 and 2

If you can assume that both population distributions 1 and 2 are normal, any sample sizes n_1 and n_2 will work. If you cannot assume this, then use sample sizes $n_1 \geq 30$ and $n_2 \geq 30$.

Confidence interval for $\mu_1 - \mu_2$

$$(\bar{x}_1 - \bar{x}_2) - E < \mu_1 - \mu_2 < (\bar{x}_1 - \bar{x}_2) + E$$

where $E = z_c \sqrt{\dfrac{\sigma_1^2}{n_1} + \dfrac{\sigma_2^2}{n_2}}$

c = confidence level $(0 < c < 1)$

z_c = critical value for confidence level c based on the standard normal distribution (See Table 5(b) of Appendix II for commonly used values.)

EXAMPLE 9

Confidence interval for
$\mu_1 - \mu_2$, σ_1 and σ_2 known

Yellowstone National Park

In the summer of 1988, Yellowstone National Park had some major fires that destroyed large tracts of old timber near many famous trout streams. Fishermen were concerned about the long-term effect of the fire on these streams. However, biologists claimed that the new meadows that would spring up under dead trees would produce a lot more insects, which would in turn mean better fishing in the years ahead. Guide services registered with the park provided data about the daily catch for fishermen over many years. Ranger checks on the streams also provided data about the daily number of fish caught by fishermen. *Yellowstone Today* (a national park publication) indicated that the biologists' claim is basically correct and that Yellowstone anglers are delighted by their average increased catch.

Suppose you are a biologist studying fishing data from Yellowstone streams before and after the fire. Fishing reports include the number of trout caught per day per fisherman. A random sample of $n_1 = 167$ reports from the period before the fire showed that $\bar{x}_1 = 5.2$ trout per day. Assume that the standard deviation of daily catch per fisherman during this period was $\sigma_1 = 1.9$. Another random sample of $n_2 = 125$ fishing reports 5 years after the fire showed that the average catch per day was $\bar{x}_2 = 6.8$ trout. Assume that the standard deviation during this period was $\sigma_2 = 2.3$.

(a) For each sample, what is the population? Are the samples dependent or independent? Explain.

SOLUTION: The population for the first sample is the number of trout caught per day by fishermen before the fire. The population of the second sample is the number of trout caught per day after the fire. Both samples were random samples taken in their respective time periods. There was no effort to pair individual data values. Therefore, the samples can be thought of as independent samples.

(b) Compute a 95% confidence interval for $\mu_1 - \mu_2$, the difference of population means.

SOLUTION: Since $n_1 = 167$, $\bar{x}_1 = 5.2$, $\sigma_1 = 1.9$, $n_2 = 125$, $\bar{x}_2 = 6.8$, $\sigma_2 = 2.3$, and $z_{0.95} = 1.96$ (see Table 8-2), then

$$E = z_c\sqrt{\frac{\sigma_1^2}{n_1} + \frac{\sigma_2^2}{n_2}}$$

$$= 1.96\sqrt{\frac{(1.9)^2}{167} + \frac{(2.3)^2}{125}} \approx 1.96\sqrt{0.0639} \approx 0.4955 \approx 0.50$$

The 95% confidence interval is

$$(\bar{x}_1 - \bar{x}_2) - E < \mu_1 - \mu_2 < (\bar{x}_1 - \bar{x}_2) + E$$
$$(5.2 - 6.8) - 0.50 < \mu_1 - \mu_2 < (5.2 - 6.8) + 0.50$$
$$-2.10 < \mu_1 - \mu_2 < -1.10$$

(c) Explain the meaning of the confidence interval you computed in part (b).

SOLUTION: We are 95% confident that the interval -2.10 to -1.10 fish per day is one of the intervals containing the population difference $\mu_1 - \mu_2$, where μ_1

represents the population average daily catch before the fire and μ_2 represents the population average daily catch after the fire. Put another way, since the confidence interval contains only *negative values*, we can be 95% sure that $\mu_1 - \mu_2 < 0$. This means that we are 95% sure that $\mu_1 < \mu_2$. In words, we are 95% sure that the average catch before the fire is less than the average catch after the fire. ◇

◇ **COMMENT:** In the case of large samples ($n_1 \geq 30$ and $n_2 \geq 30$), it is not unusual to see σ_1 and σ_2 approximated by s_1 and s_2. Then Theorem 8.1 is used as a basis for approximating confidence intervals for $\mu_1 - \mu_2$. In other words, when samples are large, sample estimates for σ_1 and σ_2 can be used together with the standard normal distribution to find confidence intervals for $\mu_1 - \mu_2$. However, in this text, we follow the more common convention of using a Student's t distribution whenever σ_1 and σ_2 are unknown. ◇

Confidence Intervals for $\mu_1 - \mu_2$ When σ_1 and σ_2 Are Unknown

When σ_1 and σ_2 are unknown, we turn to a Student's t distribution. As before, when we use a Student's t distribution, we require that our populations be normal or approximately normal (mound-shaped and symmetric) when the sample sizes n_1 and n_2 are less than 30. We also replace σ_1 by s_1 and σ_2 by s_2. Then we consider the approximate t value attributed to Welch (*Biometrika*, Vol. 29, pp. 350–362).

$$t \approx \frac{(\bar{x}_1 - \bar{x}_2) - (\mu_1 - \mu_2)}{\sqrt{\dfrac{s_1^2}{n_1} + \dfrac{s_2^2}{n_2}}}$$

Unfortunately, this approximation is *not* exactly a Student's t distribution. However, it will be a good approximation provided we adjust the degrees of freedom by one of the following methods.

1. The adjustment for the degrees of freedom is calculated from sample data. The formula is called *Satterthwaite's approximation*. It is rather complicated. Satterthwaite's approximation is used in statistical software packages such as Minitab and in the TI-84Plus/TI-83Plus calculators. See Problem 20 for the formula.

2. An alternative method, which is much simpler, is to approximate the degrees of freedom using the *smaller* of $n_1 - 1$ and $n_2 - 1$.

For confidence intervals, we take the degrees of freedom *d.f.* to be the smaller of $n_1 - 1$ and $n_2 - 1$. This commonly used choice for the degrees of freedom is more conservative than Satterthwaite's approximation in the sense that it produces a slightly larger margin of error. The resulting confidence interval will be *at least* at the c level, or a little higher.

Applying methods similar to those used to find confidence intervals for μ when σ is unknown, and using the Welch approximation for t, we obtain the following results.

> ## PROCEDURE
>
> ### How to find a confidence interval for $\mu_1 - \mu_2$ when σ_1 and σ_2 are unknown
>
> Obtain two independent random samples from populations 1 and 2, where
>
> > $\bar{x}_1$ and $\bar{x}_2$ are sample means from populations 1 and 2
> >
> > s_1 and s_2 are sample standard deviations from populations 1 and 2
> >
> > n_1 and n_2 are sample sizes from populations 1 and 2
>
> If you can assume that both population distributions 1 and 2 are normal or at least mound-shaped and symmetric, then any sample sizes n_1 and n_2 will work. If you cannot assume this, then use sample sizes $n_1 \geq 30$ and $n_2 \geq 30$.
>
> *Confidence interval for $\mu_1 - \mu_2$*
>
> $$(\bar{x}_1 - \bar{x}_2) - E < \mu_1 - \mu_2 < (\bar{x}_1 - \bar{x}_2) + E$$
>
> where $E \approx t_c \sqrt{\dfrac{s_1^2}{n_1} + \dfrac{s_2^2}{n_2}}$
>
> > c = confidence level $(0 < c < 1)$
> >
> > t_c = critical value for confidence level c
> >
> > *d.f.* = *smaller* of $n_1 - 1$ and $n_2 - 1$. Note that statistical software gives a more accurate and larger *d.f.* based on Satterthwaite's approximation.

EXAMPLE 10

Confidence interval for $\mu_1 - \mu_2$, σ_1 and σ_2 unknown

Alexander Borbely is a professor at the Medical School of the University of Zurich, where he is director of the Sleep Laboratory. Dr. Borbely and his colleagues are experts on sleep, dreams, and sleep disorders. In his book *Secrets of Sleep*, Dr. Borbely discusses brain waves, which are measured in hertz, the number of oscillations per second. Rapid brain waves (wakefulness) are in the range of 16 to 25 hertz. Slow brain waves (sleep) are in the range of 4 to 8 hertz. During normal sleep, a person goes through several cycles (each cycle is about 90 minutes) of brain waves, from rapid to slow and back to rapid. During deep sleep, brain waves are at their slowest.

In his book, Professor Borbely comments that alcohol is a *poor* sleep aid. In one study, a number of subjects were given 1/2 liter of red wine before they went to sleep. The subjects fell asleep quickly but did not remain asleep the entire night. Toward morning, between 4 and 6 A.M., they tended to wake up and have trouble going back to sleep.

Suppose that a random sample of 29 college students was randomly divided into two groups. The first group of $n_1 = 15$ people was given 1/2 liter of red wine before going to sleep. The second group of $n_2 = 14$ people was given no alcohol before going to sleep. Everyone in both groups went to sleep at 11 P.M. The average brain wave activity (4 to 6 A.M.) was determined for each individual in the groups. The results follow:

Group 1 (x_1 values): $n_1 = 15$ (with alcohol)
Average brain wave activity in the hours 4 to 6 A.M.

16.0	19.6	19.9	20.9	20.3	20.1	16.4	20.6
20.1	22.3	18.8	19.1	17.4	21.1	22.1	

For group 1, we have the sample mean and standard deviation of

$$\bar{x}_1 \approx 19.65 \qquad \text{and} \qquad s_1 \approx 1.86$$

Group 2 (x_2 values): $n_2 = 14$ (no alcohol)
Average brain wave activity in the hours 4 to 6 A.M.

8.2	5.4	6.8	6.5	4.7	5.9	2.9
7.6	10.2	6.4	8.8	5.4	8.3	5.1

For group 2, we have the sample mean and standard deviation of

$$\bar{x}_2 \approx 6.59 \qquad \text{and} \qquad s_2 \approx 1.91$$

(a) Do you think that the samples are independent or dependent? Explain.

SOLUTION: Since the original random sample of 29 students was randomly divided into two groups, it is reasonable to say that the samples are independent.

(b) What assumptions are we making about the data?

SOLUTION: We are assuming that the populations of x_1 and x_2 values are each approximately normally distributed.

(c) Compute a 90% confidence interval for $\mu_1 - \mu_2$, the difference of population means.

SOLUTION: First we find $t_{0.90}$. We approximate the degrees of freedom *d.f.* by using the smaller of $n_1 - 1$ and $n_2 - 1$. Since n_2 is smaller, *d.f.* $= n_2 - 1 = 14 - 1 = 13$. This gives us $t_{0.90} \approx 1.771$. The margin of error is then

$$E \approx t_c\sqrt{\frac{s_1^2}{n_1} + \frac{s_2^2}{n_2}} = 1.771\sqrt{\frac{1.86^2}{15} + \frac{1.91^2}{14}} \approx 1.24$$

The c confidence interval is

$$(\bar{x}_1 - \bar{x}_2) - E < \mu_1 - \mu_2 < (\bar{x}_1 - \bar{x}_2) + E$$
$$(19.65 - 6.59) - 1.24 < \mu_1 - \mu_2 < (19.65 - 6.59) + 1.24$$
$$11.82 < \mu_1 - \mu_2 < 14.30$$

After further rounding we have

$$11.8 \text{ hertz} < \mu_1 - \mu_2 < 14.3 \text{ hertz}$$

(d) Explain the meaning of the confidence interval you computed in part (c).

SOLUTION: μ_1 represents the population average brain wave activity for people who drink 1/2 liter of wine before sleeping. μ_2 represents the population average brain wave activity for people who take no alcohol before sleeping. Both periods of measurement are from 4 to 6 A.M. We are 90% confident that the interval between 11.8 and 14.3 hertz is one that contains the difference $\mu_1 - \mu_2$. It would seem reasonable to conclude that people who drink before sleeping might wake up in the early morning and have trouble going back to sleep. Since the confidence interval from 11.8 to 14.3 contains only *positive values*, we could express this by saying that we are 90% confident that $\mu_1 - \mu_2$ is *positive*. This means that $\mu_1 - \mu_2 > 0$. Thus we are 90% confident that $\mu_1 > \mu_2$ (that is, average brain wave activity from 4 to 6 A.M. for the group drinking wine is more than average brain wave activity for the group not drinking). ◊

There is another method of constructing confidence intervals for $\mu_1 - \mu_2$ when σ_1 and σ_2 are unknown. Suppose the sample values s_1 and s_2 are sufficiently close, and there is reason to believe that $\sigma_1 = \sigma_2$. Methods shown in Section 11.4 use sample standard deviations s_1 and s_2 to determine if $\sigma_1 = \sigma_2$. When you can assume that $\sigma_1 = \sigma_2$, it is best to use a *pooled standard deviation* to compute the margin of error. The $\bar{x}_1 - \bar{x}_2$ distribution has an *exact* Student's t distribution with $d.f. = n_1 + n_2 - 2$. Problem 21 of this section gives the details.

Summary

What should a person do? You have independent random samples from two populations. You can compute $\bar{x}_1, \bar{x}_2, s_1,$ and s_2 and you have the sample sizes n_1 and n_2. In any case, a confidence interval for the difference $\mu_1 - \mu_2$ of population means is

$$(\bar{x}_1 - \bar{x}_2) - E < \mu_1 - \mu_2 < (\bar{x}_1 - \bar{x}_2) + E$$

where E is the margin of error. How do you compute E? The answer depends on how much you know about the x_1 and x_2 distributions.

Situation I (the usual case)

You simply don't know the population values of σ_1 and σ_2. In this situation you use a t distribution with margin of error

$$E = t_c \sqrt{\frac{s_1^2}{n_1} + \frac{s_2^2}{n_2}}$$

where a conservative estimate for the degrees of freedom is

$$d.f. = \text{minimum of } n_1 - 1 \text{ and } n_2 - 1$$

Like a good friend, the t distribution has a reputation for being robust and forgiving. Nevertheless, some guidelines should be observed. If n_1 and n_2 are both less than 30, then x_1 and x_2 should have distributions that are mound-shaped and approximately symmetric (or, even better, normal). If both n_1 and n_2 are 30 or more, the central limit theorem (Chapter 7) implies these restrictions can be relaxed.

Situation II (almost never happens)

You actually know the population values of σ_1 and σ_2. In addition, you know that x_1 and x_2 have normal distributions. If you know σ_1 and σ_2, but are not sure about the x_1 and x_2 distributions, then you must have $n_1 \geq 30$ and $n_2 \geq 30$. In this situation you use a z distribution with margin of error

$$E = z_c \sqrt{\frac{\sigma_1^2}{n_1} + \frac{\sigma_2^2}{n_2}}$$

Situation III (yes, this does sometimes occur)

You don't know σ_1 and σ_2, but the sample values s_1 and s_2 are close to each other and there is reason to believe that $\sigma_1 = \sigma_2$. This can happen when you make a slight change or alteration to a known process or method of production. The standard deviation may not change much, but the outputs or means could be very different. In this situation you are advised to use a t distribution with a pooled standard deviation. See Problem 21 at the end of this section.

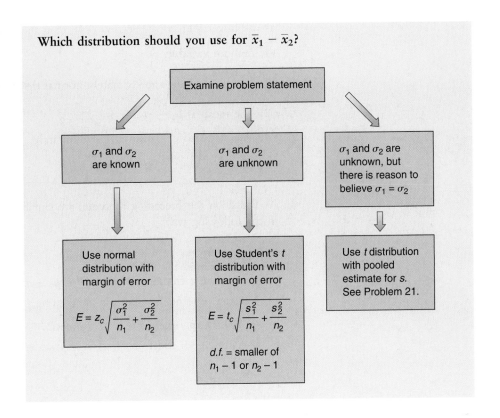

Estimating the Difference of Proportions $p_1 - p_2$

We conclude this section with a discussion of confidence intervals for $p_1 - p_2$, the difference of two proportions from binomial probability distributions. The main result on this topic is the following theorem.

◇ **THEOREM 8.2** Consider two binomial probability distributions

Distribution 1	*Distribution 2*
n_1 = number of trials	n_2 = number of trials
r_1 = number of successes out of n_1 trials	r_2 = number of successes out of n_2 trials
p_1 = probability of success on each trial	p_2 = probability of success on each trial
$q_1 = 1 - p_1$ = probability of failure on each trial	$q_2 = 1 - p_2$ = probability of failure on each trial
$\hat{p}_1 = \dfrac{r_1}{n_1}$ = point estimate for p_1	$\hat{p}_2 = \dfrac{r_2}{n_2}$ = point estimate for p_2
$\hat{q}_1 = 1 - \dfrac{r_1}{n_1}$ = point estimate for q_1	$\hat{q}_2 = 1 - \dfrac{r_2}{n_2}$ = point estimate for q_2

For most practical applications, if the four quantities

$$n_1\hat{p}_1 \qquad n_1\hat{q}_1 \qquad n_2\hat{p}_2 \qquad n_2\hat{q}_2$$

are all larger than 5 (see Section 6.4), then the following statements are true about the random variable $\frac{r_1}{n_1} - \frac{r_2}{n_2}$:

1. $\frac{r_1}{n_1} - \frac{r_2}{n_2}$ has an approximately normal distribution.

2. The mean is $p_1 - p_2$.

3. The standard deviation is approximately

$$\hat{\sigma} = \sqrt{\frac{\hat{p}_1 \hat{q}_1}{n_1} + \frac{\hat{p}_2 \hat{q}_2}{n_2}} \quad \Diamond$$

Based on the preceding theorem, we can find confidence intervals for $p_1 - p_2$ in the following way:

PROCEDURE

How to find a confidence interval for $p_1 - p_2$

Consider two independent binomial experiments.

Binomial Experiment 1

n_1 = number of trials

r_1 = number of successes out of n_1 trials

$\hat{p}_1 = \dfrac{r_1}{n_1}$

p_1 = population probability of success

Binomial Experiment 2

n_2 = number of trials

r_2 = number of successes out of n_2 trials

$\hat{p}_2 = \dfrac{r_2}{n_2}$

p_2 = population probability of success

The number of trials should be sufficiently large so that all four of the following inequalities are true:

$$n_1 \hat{p}_1 > 5; \quad n_1 \hat{q}_1 > 5; \quad n_2 \hat{p}_2 > 5; \quad n_2 \hat{q}_2 > 5$$

Confidence interval for $p_1 - p_2$

$$(\hat{p}_1 - \hat{p}_2) - E \leq p_1 - p_2 \leq (\hat{p}_1 - \hat{p}_2) + E$$

where

$$E = z_c \sigma = z_c \sqrt{\frac{\hat{p}_1 \hat{q}_1}{n_1} + \frac{\hat{p}_2 \hat{q}_2}{n_2}}$$

c = confidence level, $0 < c < 1$

z_c = critical value for confidence level c based on the standard normal distribution (See Table 5(b) of Appendix II for commonly used values.)

EXAMPLE 11

Confidence interval for $p_1 - p_2$

In his book *Secrets of Sleep*, Professor Borbely describes research on dreams in the sleep laboratory at the University of Zurich Medical School. During normal sleep, there is a phase known as *REM* (rapid eye movement). For most people, REM sleep occurs about every 90 minutes or so, and it is thought that dreams occur just before or during the REM phase. Using electronic equipment in the sleep laboratory, it is possible to detect the REM phase in a sleeping person. If a person is wakened immediately after the REM phase, he or she usually can describe a dream that has just taken place. Based on a study of over 650 people in the Zurich sleep laboratory, it was found that about one-third of all dream reports contain feelings of fear, anxiety, or aggression. There is a conjecture that if a person is in a good mood when going to sleep, the proportion of "bad" dreams (fear, anxiety, aggression) might be reduced.

Suppose that two groups of subjects were randomly chosen for a sleep study. In group I, before going to sleep, the subjects spent 1 hour watching a comedy movie. In this group, there were a total of $n_1 = 175$ dreams recorded, of which $r_1 = 49$ were dreams with feelings of anxiety, fear, or aggression. In group II, the subjects did not watch a movie but simply went to sleep. In this group, there were a total of $n_2 = 180$ dreams recorded, of which $r_2 = 63$ were dreams with feelings of anxiety, fear, or aggression.

(a) Why could groups I and II be considered independent binomial distributions? Why do we have a "large-sample" situation?

SOLUTION: Since the two groups were chosen randomly, it is reasonable to assume that neither group's response would be related to the other. In both groups, each recorded dream could be thought of as a trial, with success being a dream with feelings of fear, anxiety, or aggression.

$$\hat{p}_1 = \frac{r_1}{n_1} = \frac{49}{175} = 0.28 \qquad \text{and} \qquad \hat{q}_1 = 1 - \hat{p}_1 = 0.72$$

$$\hat{p}_2 = \frac{r_2}{n_2} = \frac{63}{180} = 0.35 \qquad \text{and} \qquad \hat{q}_2 = 1 - \hat{p}_2 = 0.65$$

Since

$$n_1\hat{p}_1 = 49 > 5 \qquad n_1\hat{q}_1 = 126 > 5$$
$$n_2\hat{p}_2 = 63 > 5 \qquad n_2\hat{q}_2 = 117 > 5$$

then large-sample theory is appropriate.

(b) What is $p_1 - p_2$? Compute a 95% confidence interval for $p_1 - p_2$.

SOLUTION: p_1 is the population proportion of successes (bad dreams) for all people who watch comedy movies before bed. Thus, p_1 can be thought of as the percentage of bad dreams for all people who are in a "good mood" when they go to bed. Likewise, p_2 is the percentage of bad dreams for the population of all people who just go to bed (no movie). The difference $p_1 - p_2$ is the population difference.

To find a confidence interval for $p_1 - p_2$, we need the values of z_c, $\hat{\sigma}$, and then E. From Table 8-2, we see that $z_{0.95} = 1.96$, so

$$\hat{\sigma} = \sqrt{\frac{\hat{p}_1\hat{q}_1}{n_1} + \frac{\hat{p}_2\hat{q}_2}{n_2}} = \sqrt{\frac{(0.28)(0.72)}{175} + \frac{(0.35)(0.65)}{180}}$$

$$\approx \sqrt{0.0024} \approx 0.0492$$

$$E = z_c\hat{\sigma} = 1.96(0.0492) \approx 0.096$$

$$(\hat{p}_1 - \hat{p}_2) - E < p_1 - p_2 < (\hat{p}_1 - \hat{p}_2) + E$$

$$(0.28 - 0.35) - 0.096 < p_1 - p_2 < (0.28 - 0.35) + 0.096$$

$$-0.166 < p_1 - p_2 < 0.026$$

(c) Explain the meaning of the confidence interval that you constructed in part (b).

> **SOLUTION:** We are 95% sure that the interval between -16.6% and 2.6% is one that contains the percentage difference of "bad" dreams for group I and group II. Since the interval -0.166 to 0.026 is not all negative (or all positive), we cannot say that $p_1 - p_2 < 0$ (or $p_1 - p_2 > 0$). Thus, at the 95% confidence level, we *cannot* conclude that $p_1 < p_2$ or $p_1 > p_2$. The comedy movies before bed help some people reduce the percentage of "bad" dreams, but at the 95% confidence level, we cannot say the *population difference* is reduced.   ◇

PROCEDURE

How to interpret confidence intervals for differences

Suppose that we construct a $c\%$ confidence interval for $\mu_1 - \mu_2$ (or $p_1 - p_2$). Then three cases arise:

1. The $c\%$ confidence interval contains only *negative values* (see Example 9). In this case, we conclude that $\mu_1 - \mu_2 < 0$ (or $p_1 - p_2 < 0$), and we are therefore $c\%$ confident that $\mu_1 < \mu_2$ (or $p_1 < p_2$).

2. The $c\%$ confidence interval contains only *positive values* (see Example 10). In this case, we conclude that $\mu_1 - \mu_2 > 0$ (or $p_1 - p_2 > 0$), and we can be $c\%$ confident that $\mu_1 > \mu_2$ (or $p_1 > p_2$).

3. The $c\%$ confidence interval contains *both positive and negative values*. In this case, we cannot at the $c\%$ confidence level conclude that either μ_1 or μ_2 (or p_1 or p_2) is larger. However, if we *reduce* the confidence level c to a *smaller value*, then the confidence interval will, in general, be shorter (explain why). A shorter confidence interval *might* put us back into case 1 or case 2 above (again, explain why).

GUIDED EXERCISE 9

Interpret a confidence interval

(a) A study reported a 90% confidence interval for the difference of means to be

$$10 < \mu_1 - \mu_2 < 20$$

For this interval, what can you conclude about the respective values of μ_1 and μ_2?

⟹ At a 90% level of confidence, we can say that the difference $\mu_1 - \mu_2$ is positive, so $\mu_1 - \mu_2 > 0$ and $\mu_1 > \mu_2$.

(b) A study reported a 95% confidence interval for the difference of proportions to be

$$-0.32 < p_1 - p_2 < 0.16$$

From this interval, what can you conclude about the respective values of p_1 and p_2?

⟹ At the 95% confidence level, we see that the difference of proportions ranges from negative to positive values. We cannot tell from this interval if p_1 is greater than p_2 or p_1 is less than p_2.

TECH NOTE   The TI-84Plus and TI-83Plus calculators and Minitab supply confidence intervals for the difference of means and for the difference of proportions.

TI-84Plus/TI-83Plus Use the **STAT** key and highlight **TESTS**. The choice **9:2-SampZInt** finds confidence intervals for differences of means when σ_1 and σ_2 are known. Choice **0:2-SampTInt** finds confidence intervals for differences of means when σ_1 and σ_2 are unknown. In general, use No for Pooled. However, if $\sigma_1 \approx \sigma_2$, use Yes for Pooled. Choice **B:2-PropZInt** provides confidence intervals for proportions.

Minitab Use the menu choice **STAT ➤ Basic Statistics ➤ 2 sample t** or **2 proportions.** Minitab always uses the Student's t distribution for $\mu_1 - \mu_2$ confidence intervals. If the variances are equal, check "assume equal variances."

VIEWPOINT

What's the Difference?

Will two 15-minute piano lessons a week significantly improve a child's analytical reasoning skills? Why piano? Why not computer keyboard instruction or maybe voice lessons? Professor Frances Rauscher, University of Wisconsin, and Professor Gordon Shaw, University of California at Irvine, claim that there is a difference! How could this be measured? A large number of piano students were given complicated tests of mental ability. Independent control groups of other students were given the same tests. Techniques involving the study of differences of means were used to draw the conclusion that students taking piano lessons did better on tests measuring analytical reasoning skills. (Reported in *The Denver Post.*)

SECTION 8.5   PROBLEMS

Answers may vary slightly due to rounding.

1. *Archaeology: Ireland* Inorganic phosphorous is a naturally occurring element in all plants and animals, with concentrations increasing progressively up the food chain (fruit < vegetables < cereals < nuts < corpse). Geochemical surveys take soil samples to determine phosphorous content (in ppm, parts per million). A high phosphorous content may or may not indicate an ancient burial site, food storage site, or even a garbage dump. The Hill of Tara is a very important archaeological site in Ireland. It is by legend the seat of Ireland's ancient high kings (Reference: *Tara, An Archaeological Survey* by Conor Newman, Royal Irish Academy, Dublin). Independent random samples from two regions in Tara gave the following phosphorous measurements (ppm). Assume the population distributions of phosphorous are mound-shaped and symmetric for these two regions.

Region I: x_1; $n_1 = 12$

540	810	790	790	340	800	890	860
820	640	970	720				

Region II: x_2; $n_2 = 16$

750	870	700	810	965	350	895	850
635	955	710	890	520	650	280	993

(a) Use a calculator with mean and standard deviation keys to verify that $\bar{x}_1 \approx$ 747.5, $s_1 \approx 170.4$, $\bar{x}_2 \approx 738.9$, and $s_2 \approx 212.1$.

(b) Let μ_1 be the population mean for x_1 and let μ_2 be the population mean for x_2. Find a 90% confidence interval for $\mu_1 - \mu_2$.

(c) Examine the confidence interval and explain what it means in the context of this problem. Does the interval consist of numbers that are all positive? all negative? of different signs? At the 90% level of confidence, is one region more interesting than the other from a geochemical perspective?

(d) Which distribution (standard normal or Student's t) did you use? Why?

2. *Archaeology: Ireland* Please see the setting and reference in Problem 1. Independent random samples from two regions (not those cited in Problem 1) gave the following phosphorous measurements (in ppm). Assume the distribution of phosphorous is mound-shaped and symmetric for these two regions.

Region I: x_1; $n_1 = 15$

855	1550	1230	875	1080	2330	1850	1860
2340	1080	910	1130	1450	1260	1010	

Region II: x_2; $n_2 = 14$

540	810	790	1230	1770	960	1650	860
890	640	1180	1160	1050	1020		

(a) Use a calculator with mean and standard deviation keys to verify that $\bar{x}_1 \approx$ 1387.3, $s_1 \approx 498.3$, $\bar{x}_2 \approx 1039.3$, and $s_2 \approx 346.7$.

(b) Let μ_1 be the population mean for x_1 and let μ_2 be the population mean for x_2. Find an 80% confidence interval for $\mu_1 - \mu_2$.

(c) Examine the confidence interval and explain what it means in the context of this problem. Does the interval consist of numbers that are all positive? all negative? of different signs? At the 80% level of confidence, is one region more interesting than the other from a geochemical perspective?

(d) Which distribution (standard normal or Student's t) did you use? Why?

3. *Large U.S. Companies: Foreign Revenue* For large U.S. companies, what percentage of their total income comes from foreign sales? A random sample of technology companies (IBM, Hewlett-Packard, Intel, and others) gave the following information.

Technology companies, % foreign revenue: x_1; $n_1 = 16$

62.8	55.7	47.0	59.6	55.3	41.0	65.1	51.1
53.4	50.8	48.5	44.6	49.4	61.2	39.3	41.8

Another independent random sample of basic consumer product companies (Goodyear, Sarah Lee, H.J. Heinz, Toys 'Я' Us) gave the following information.

Basic consumer product companies, % foreign revenue: x_2; $n_2 = 17$

28.0	30.5	34.2	50.3	11.1	28.8	40.0	44.9
40.7	60.1	23.1	21.3	42.8	18.0	36.9	28.0
32.5							

(Reference: *Forbes Top Companies.*) Assume that the distributions of percentage foreign revenue are mound-shaped and symmetric for these two company types.

(a) Use a calculator with mean and standard deviation keys to verify that $\bar{x}_1 \approx$ 51.66, $s_1 \approx 7.93$, $\bar{x}_2 = 33.60$, and $s_2 \approx 12.26$.

(b) Let μ_1 be the population mean for x_1 and let μ_2 be the population mean for x_2. Find an 85% confidence interval for $\mu_1 - \mu_2$.

(c) Examine the confidence interval and explain what it means in the context of this problem. Does the interval consist of numbers that are all positive? all negative? of different signs? At the 85% level of confidence, do technology companies have a greater percentage foreign revenue than basic consumer product companies?

(d) Which distribution (standard normal or Student's t) did you use? Why?

4. *Pro Football and Basketball: Weights of Players* Independent random samples of professional football and basketball players gave the following information (References: *Sports Encyclopedia of Pro Football* and *Official NBA Basketball Encyclopedia*). Note: These data are also available with other software on the statSpace CD-ROM. Assume that the weight distributions are mound-shaped and symmetric.

Weights (in lb.) of pro football players: $x_1; n_1 = 21$

245	262	255	251	244	276	240	265	257	252	282
256	250	264	270	275	245	275	253	265	270	

Weights (in lb.) of pro basketball players: $x_2; n_2 = 19$

205	200	220	210	191	215	221	216	228	207
225	208	195	191	207	196	181	193	201	

(a) Use a calculator with mean and standard deviation keys to verify that $\bar{x}_1 \approx 259.6$, $s_1 \approx 12.1$, $\bar{x}_2 \approx 205.8$, and $s_2 \approx 12.9$.

(b) Let μ_1 be the population mean for x_1 and let μ_2 be the population mean for x_2. Find a 99% confidence interval for $\mu_1 - \mu_2$.

(c) Examine the confidence interval and explain what it means in the context of this problem. Does the interval consist of numbers that are all positive? all negative? of different signs? At the 99% level of confidence, do professional football players tend to have a higher population mean weight than professional basketball players?

(d) Which distribution (standard normal or Student's t) did you use? Why?

5. *Pro Football and Basketball: Heights of Players* Independent random samples of professional football and basketball players gave the following information (References: *Sports Encyclopedia of Pro Football* and *Official NBA Basketball Encyclopedia*). Note: These data are also available with other software on the statSpace CD-ROM.

Heights (in ft.) of pro football players: $x_1; n_1 = 45$

6.33	6.50	6.50	6.25	6.50	6.33	6.25	6.17	6.42	6.33
6.42	6.58	6.08	6.58	6.50	6.42	6.25	6.67	5.91	6.00
5.83	6.00	5.83	5.08	6.75	5.83	6.17	5.75	6.00	5.75
6.50	5.83	5.91	5.67	6.00	6.08	6.17	6.58	6.50	6.25
6.33	5.25	6.67	6.50	5.83					

Heights (in ft.) of pro basketball players: $x_2; n_2 = 40$

6.08	6.58	6.25	6.58	6.25	5.92	7.00	6.41	6.75	6.25
6.00	6.92	6.83	6.58	6.41	6.67	6.67	5.75	6.25	6.25
6.50	6.00	6.92	6.25	6.42	6.58	6.58	6.08	6.75	6.50
6.83	6.08	6.92	6.00	6.33	6.50	6.58	6.83	6.50	6.58

(a) Use a calculator with mean and standard deviation keys to verify that $\bar{x}_1 \approx 6.179$, $s_1 \approx 0.366$, $\bar{x}_2 \approx 6.453$, and $s_2 \approx 0.314$.

(b) Let μ_1 be the population mean for x_1 and let μ_2 be the population mean for x_2. Find a 90% confidence interval for $\mu_1 - \mu_2$.

(c) Examine the confidence interval and explain what it means in the context of this problem. Does the interval consist of numbers that are all positive? all negative? of different signs? At the 90% level of confidence, do professional football players tend to have a higher population mean height than professional basketball players?

(d) Which distribution (standard normal or Student's t) did you use? Why? Do we need information about the height distributions? Explain.

 6. *Botany: Iris* The following data represent petal lengths (in cm) for independent random samples of two species of iris (Reference: E. Anderson, *Bulletin American Iris Society*). *Note:* These data are also available with other software on the statSpace CD-ROM.

Petal length (in cm) of *iris virginica*: x_1; $n_1 = 35$

5.1 5.8 6.3 6.1 5.1 5.5 5.3 5.5 6.9 5.0 4.9 6.0 4.8 6.1 5.6 5.1

5.6 4.8 5.4 5.1 5.1 5.9 5.2 5.7 5.4 4.5 6.1 5.3 5.5 6.7 5.7 4.9

4.8 5.8 5.1

Petal length (in cm) of *iris setosa*: x_2; $n_2 = 38$

1.5 1.7 1.4 1.5 1.5 1.6 1.4 1.1 1.2 1.4 1.7 1.0 1.7 1.9 1.6 1.4

1.5 1.4 1.2 1.3 1.5 1.3 1.6 1.9 1.4 1.6 1.5 1.4 1.6 1.2 1.9 1.5

1.6 1.4 1.3 1.7 1.5 1.7

(a) Use a calculator with mean and standard deviation keys to verify that $\bar{x}_1 \approx 5.48$, $s_1 \approx 0.55$, $\bar{x}_2 \approx 1.49$, and $s_2 \approx 0.21$.

(b) Let μ_1 be the population mean for x_1 and let μ_2 be the population mean for x_2. Find a 99% confidence interval for $\mu_1 - \mu_2$.

(c) Examine the confidence interval and explain what it means in the context of this problem. Does the interval consist of numbers that are all positive? all negative? of different signs? At the 99% level of confidence, is the population mean petal length of *iris virginica* longer than that of *iris setosa*?

(d) Which distribution (standard normal or Student's t) did you use? Why? Do we need information about the petal length distributions? Explain.

7. *Myers-Briggs: Marriage Counseling* Isabel Myers was a pioneer in the study of personality types. She identified four basic personality preferences that are described at length in the book *A Guide to the Development and Use of the Myers-Briggs Type Indicator*, by Myers and McCaulley (Consulting Psychologists Press). Marriage counselors know that couples who have none of the four preferences in common may have a stormy marriage. Myers took a random sample of 375 married couples and found that 289 had two or more personality preferences in common. In another random sample of 571 married couples, it was found that only 23 had no preferences in common. Let p_1 be the population proportion of all married couples who have two or more personality preferences in common. Let p_2 be the population proportion of all married couples who have no personality perferences in common.

(a) Find a 99% confidence interval for $p_1 - p_2$.

(b) Explain the meaning of the confidence interval in part (a) in the context of this problem. Does the confidence interval contain all positive, all negative, or both positive and negative numbers? What does this tell you (at the 99% confidence level) about the proportion of married couples with two or more personality preferences in common compared with the proportion of married couples sharing no personality preferences in common?

8. *Myers-Briggs: Marriage Counseling* Most married couples have two or three personality preferences in common (see reference in Problem 7). Myers used a random sample of 375 married couples and found that 132 had three preferences in common. Another random sample of 571 couples showed that 217 had two personality preferences in common. Let p_1 be the population proportion of all married couples who have three personality preferences in common. Let p_2 be the population proportion of all married couples who have two personality preferences in common.
   (a) Find a 90% confidence interval for $p_1 - p_2$.
   (b) Examine the confidence interval in part (a) and explain what it means in the context of this problem. Does the confidence interval contain all positive, all negative, or both positive and negative numbers? What does this tell you about the proportion of married couples with three personality preferences in common compared with the proportion of couples with two preferences in common (at the 90% confidence level)?

9. *Yellowstone National Park: Old Faithful Geyser* The U.S. Geological Survey compiled historical data about Old Faithful Geyser (Yellowstone National Park) from 1870 to 1987. Some of these data are published in the book *The Story of Old Faithful*, by G. D. Marler (Yellowstone Association Press). Let x_1 be a random variable that represents the time interval (in minutes) between Old Faithful eruptions for the years 1948 to 1952. Based on 9340 observations, the sample mean interval was $\bar{x}_1 = 63.3$ minutes. Let x_2 be a random variable that represents the time interval in minutes between Old Faithful eruptions for the years 1983 to 1987. Based on 25,111 observations, the sample mean time interval was $\bar{x}_2 = 72.1$ minutes. Historical data suggests that $\sigma_1 = 9.17$ minutes and $\sigma_2 = 12.67$ minutes. Let μ_1 be the population mean of x_1 and let μ_2 be the population mean of x_2.
   (a) Compute a 99% confidence interval for $\mu_1 - \mu_2$.
   (b) Comment on the meaning of the confidence interval in the context of this problem. Does the interval consist of positive numbers only? negative numbers only? a mix of positive and negative numbers? Does it appear (at the 99% confidence level) that a change in the interval length between eruptions has occurred? Many geologic experts believe that the distribution of eruption times of Old Faithful changed after the major earthquake that occurred in 1959.

10. *Psychology: Parental Sensitivity* "Parental Sensitivity to Infant Cues: Similarities and Differences Between Mothers and Fathers," by M. V. Graham (*Journal of Pediatric Nursing*, Vol. 8, No. 6), reports a study of parental empathy for sensitivity cues and baby temperament (higher scores mean more empathy). Let x_1 be a random variable that represents the score of a mother on an empathy test (as regards her baby). Let x_2 be the empathy score of a father. A random sample of 32 mothers gave a sample mean of $\bar{x}_1 = 69.44$. Another random sample of 32 fathers gave $\bar{x}_2 = 59$. Assume that $\sigma_1 = 11.69$ and $\sigma_2 = 11.60$.
   (a) Let μ_1 be the population mean of x_1 and let μ_2 be the population mean of x_2. Find a 99% confidence interval for $\mu_1 - \mu_2$.
   (b) Examine the confidence interval and explain what it means in the context of this problem. Does the confidence interval contain all positive, all negative, or both positive and negative numbers? What does this tell you about the relationship between average empathy scores for mothers compared with those for fathers at the 99% confidence level?

11. *Navajo Culture: Traditional Hogans* S. C. Jett is a professor of geography at the University of California, Davis. He and a colleague, V. E. Spencer, are experts on

modern Navajo culture and geography. The following information is taken from their book *Navajo Architecture: Forms, History, Distributions* (University of Arizona Press). On the Navajo Reservation, a random sample of 210 permanent dwellings in the Fort Defiance region showed that 65 were traditional Navajo hogans. In the Indian Wells region, a random sample of 152 permanent dwellings showed that 18 were traditional hogans. Let p_1 be the population proportion of all traditional hogans in the Fort Defiance region, and let p_2 be the population proportion of all traditional hogans in the Indian Wells region.

(a) Find a 99% confidence interval for $p_1 - p_2$.

(b) Examine the confidence interval and comment on its meaning. Does it include numbers that are all positive? all negative? mixed? What if it is hypothesized that Navajo who follow the traditional culture of their people tend to occupy hogans? Comment on the confidence interval for $p_1 - p_2$ in this context.

12. *Archaeology: Culture Affiliation* "Unknown cultural affiliations and loss of identity at high elevations." These are words used to propose the hypothesis that archaeological sites tend to lose their identity as altitude extremes are reached. This idea is based on the notion that prehistoric people tended *not* to take trade wares to temporary settings and/or isolated areas (Source: *Prehistoric New Mexico: Background for Survey*, by D. E. Stuart and R. P. Gauthier, University of New Mexico Press). As elevation zones of prehistoric people (in what is now the state of New Mexico) increased, there seemed to be a loss of artifact identification. Consider the following information.

Elevation Zone	Number of Artifacts	Number Unidentified
7000–7500 ft	112	69
5000–5500 ft	140	26

Let p_1 be the population proportion of unidentified archaeological artifacts at the elevation zone 7000–7500 ft in the given archaeological area. Let p_2 be the population proportion of unidentified archaeological artifacts at the elevation zone 5000–5500 ft in the given archaeological area.

(a) Find a 99% confidence interval for $p_1 - p_2$.

(b) Explain the meaning of the confidence interval in part (a) in the context of this problem. Does the confidence interval contain all positive numbers? all negative numbers? both positive and negative numbers? What does this tell you (at the 99% confidence level) about the comparison of the population proportion of unidentified artifacts at high elevations (7000–7500 ft) with the population proportion of unidentified artifacts at lower elevations (5000–5500 ft)? How does this relate to the stated hypothesis?

13. *Wildlife: Wolves* David E. Brown is an expert in wildlife conservation. In his book *The Wolf in the Southwest: The Making of an Endangered Species* (University of Arizona Press), he records the following weights of adult grey wolves from two regions in Old Mexico.

Chihuahua region: x_1 variable in pounds

86	75	91	70	79
80	68	71	74	64

Durango region: x_2 variable in pounds

68	72	79	68	77	89	62	55	68
68	59	63	66	58	54	71	59	67

(a) Use a calculator with mean and standard deviation keys to verify that $\bar{x}_1 = 75.80$ pounds, $s_1 = 8.32$ pounds, $\bar{x}_2 = 66.83$ pounds, and $s_2 = 8.87$ pounds.

(b) Let μ_1 be the mean weight of the population of all grey wolves in the Chihuahua region. Let μ_2 be the mean weight of the population of all grey wolves in the Durango region. Find an 85% confidence interval for $\mu_1 - \mu_2$.

(c) Examine the confidence interval and explain what it means in the context of this problem. Does the interval consist of numbers that are all positive? all negative? of different signs? At the 85% level of confidence, what can you say about the comparison of the average weight of grey wolves in the Chihuahua region with the average weight of grey wolves in the Durango region?

14. *Medical: Plasma Compress* At Community Hospital, the burn center is experimenting with a new plasma compress treatment. A random sample of $n_1 = 316$ patients with minor burns received the plasma compress treatment. Of these patients, it was found that 259 had no visible scars after treatment. Another random sample of $n_2 = 419$ patients with minor burns received no plasma compress treatment. For this group, it was found that 94 had no visible scars after treatment. Let p_1 be the population proportion of all patients with minor burns receiving the plasma compress treatment who have no visible scars. Let p_2 be the population proportion of all patients with minor burns not receiving the plasma compress treatment who have no visible scars.

(a) Find a 95% confidence interval for $p_1 - p_2$.

(b) Explain the meaning of the confidence interval found in part (a) in the context of the problem. Does the interval contain numbers that are all positive? all negative? both positive and negative? At the 95% level of confidence, does treatment with plasma compresses seem to make a difference in the proportion of patients with visible scars from minor burns?

15. *Psychology: Self-Esteem* Female undergraduates in randomized groups of 15 took part in a self-esteem study ("There's More to Self-Esteem than Whether It Is High or Low: The Importance of Stability of Self-Esteem," by M. H. Kernis et al., *Journal of Personality and Social Psychology*, Vol. 65, No. 6). The study measured an index of self-esteem from the point of view of competence, social acceptance, and physical attractiveness. Let x_1, x_2, and x_3 be random variables representing the measure of self-esteem through x_1 (competence), x_2 (social acceptance), and x_3 (attractiveness). Higher index values mean a more positive influence on self-esteem.

Variable	Sample Size	Mean $\bar{x}$	Standard Deviation s	Population Mean
x_1	15	19.84	3.07	μ_1
x_2	15	19.32	3.62	μ_2
x_3	15	17.88	3.74	μ_3

(a) Find an 85% confidence interval for $\mu_1 - \mu_2$.

(b) Find an 85% confidence interval for $\mu_1 - \mu_3$.

(c) Find an 85% confidence interval for $\mu_2 - \mu_3$.

(d) Comment on the meaning of each of the confidence intervals found in parts (a), (b), and (c). At the 85% confidence level, what can you say about the average differences in influence on self-esteem between competence and social acceptance? between competence and attractiveness? between social acceptance and attractiveness?

16. *Focus Problem: Wood Duck Nests* In the Focus Problem at the beginning of this chapter, a study was described comparing the hatch ratios of wood duck nesting boxes. Group I nesting boxes were well separated from each other and well hidden by available brush. There were a total of 474 eggs in group I boxes, of which a field count

showed about 270 hatched. Group II nesting boxes were placed in highly visible locations and grouped closely together. There were a total of 805 eggs in group II boxes, of which a field count showed about 270 hatched.

(a) Find a point estimate $\hat{p}_1$ for p_1, the proportion of eggs that hatch in group I nest box placements. Find a 95% confidence interval for p_1.

(b) Find a point estimate $\hat{p}_2$ for p_2, the proportion of eggs that hatch in group II nest box placements. Find a 95% confidence interval for p_2.

(c) Find a 95% confidence interval for $p_1 - p_2$. Does the interval indicate that the proportion of eggs hatched from group I nest boxes is higher than, lower than, or equal to the proportion of eggs hatched from group II nest boxes?

(d) What conclusions about placement of nest boxes can be drawn? In the article discussed in the Focus Problem, additional concerns are raised about the higher cost of placing and maintaining group I nest box placements. At issue also is the cost efficiency per successful wood duck hatch.

17. *General: Different Confidence Levels*

(a) Suppose that a 95% confidence interval for the difference of means contains both positive and negative numbers. Will a 99% confidence interval based on the same data necessarily contain both positive and negative numbers? Explain. What about a 90% confidence interval? Explain.

(b) Suppose that a 95% confidence interval for the difference of proportions contains all positive numbers. Will a 99% confidence interval based on the same data necessarily contain all positive numbers as well? Explain. What about a 90% confidence interval? Explain.

18. *Expand Your Knowledge: Sample Size, Difference of Means* What about sample size? If we want a confidence interval with maximal margin of error E and level of confidence c, then Section 8.4 shows us which formulas to apply for a *single* mean μ or a *single* proportion p.

(a) How about a *difference of means*? When σ_1 and σ_2 are known, the margin of error E for a $c\%$ confidence interval is

$$E = z_c \sqrt{\frac{\sigma_1^2}{n_1} + \frac{\sigma_2^2}{n_2}}$$

Let us make the simplifying assumption that we have *equal sample size n* so that $n = n_1 = n_2$. Also assume that $n \geq 30$. In this context, we get

$$E = z_c \sqrt{\frac{\sigma_1^2}{n} + \frac{\sigma_2^2}{n}} = \frac{z_c}{\sqrt{n}} \sqrt{\sigma_1^2 + \sigma_2^2}$$

Solve this equation for n and show that

$$n = \left(\frac{z_c}{E}\right)^2 (\sigma_1^2 + \sigma_2^2)$$

(b) In Problem 5 (football and basketball player heights), suppose we want to be 95% sure that our estimate $\bar{x}_1 - \bar{x}_2$ for the difference $\mu_1 - \mu_2$ has a margin of error $E = 0.05$ feet. How large should the sample size be (assuming equal sample size, i.e., $n = n_1 = n_2$)? Since we do not know σ_1 or σ_2 and $n \geq 30$, use s_1 and s_2, respectively, from the preliminary sample of Problem 5.

(c) In Problem 6 (petal lengths of two iris species), suppose we want to be 90% sure that our estimate $\bar{x}_1 - \bar{x}_2$ for the difference $\mu_1 - \mu_2$ has a margin of error $E = 0.1$ cm. How large should the sample size be (assuming equal sample size, i.e., $n = n_1 = n_2$)? Since we do not know σ_1 or σ_2 and $n \geq 30$, use s_1 and s_2, respectively, from the preliminary sample of Problem 6.

19. *Expand Your Knowledge: Sample Size, Difference of Proportions* What about the sample size n for confidence intervals for the difference of proportions $p_1 - p_2$? Let us make the following assumptions: *equal sample size $n = n_1 = n_2$ and all four quantities $n_1\hat{p}_1$, $n_1\hat{q}_1$, $n_2\hat{p}_2$, and $n_2\hat{q}_2$ are greater than 5*. Those readers familiar with algebra can use the procedure outlined in Problem 18 to show that if we have preliminary estimates $\hat{p}_1$ and $\hat{p}_2$ and a given maximal margin of error E for a specified confidence level c, then the sample size n should be at least

$$n = \left(\frac{z_c}{E}\right)^2 (\hat{p}_1\hat{q}_1 + \hat{p}_2\hat{q}_2)$$

However, if we have no preliminary estimates for $\hat{p}_1$ and $\hat{p}_2$, theory similar to that used in Section 8.4 tells us that the sample size n should be at least

$$n = \frac{1}{2}\left(\frac{z_c}{E}\right)^2$$

(a) In Problem 7 (Myers-Briggs personality type indicators in common for married couples), suppose we want to be 99% confident that our estimate $\hat{p}_1 - \hat{p}_2$ for the difference $p_1 - p_2$ has a maximum margin of error $E = 0.04$. Use the preliminary estimates $\hat{p}_1 = 289/375$ for the proportion of couples sharing two personality traits and $\hat{p}_2 = 23/571$ for the proportion having no traits in common. How large should the sample size be (assuming equal sample size, i.e., $n = n_1 = n_2$)?

(b) Suppose that in Problem 7 we have no preliminary estimates for $\hat{p}_1$ and $\hat{p}_2$ and we want to be 95% confident that our estimate $\hat{p}_1 - \hat{p}_2$ for the difference $p_1 - p_2$ has a maximum margin of error $E = 0.05$. How large should the sample size be (assuming equal sample size, i.e., $n = n_1 = n_2$)?

20. *Expand Your Knowledge: Software Approximation for Degrees of Freedom* Given x_1 and x_2 distributions that are normal or approximately normal with unknown σ_1 and σ_2, the value of t corresponding to $\bar{x}_1 - \bar{x}_2$ has a distribution that is approximated by a Student's t distribution. We use the convention that the degrees of freedom is approximately the smaller of $n_1 - 1$ and $n_2 - 1$. However, a more accurate estimate for the appropriate degrees of freedom is given by *Satterthwaite's formula*

$$d.f. \approx \frac{\left(\dfrac{s_1^2}{n_1} + \dfrac{s_2^2}{n_2}\right)^2}{\dfrac{1}{n_1 - 1}\left(\dfrac{s_1^2}{n_1}\right)^2 + \dfrac{1}{n_2 - 1}\left(\dfrac{s_2^2}{n_2}\right)^2}$$

where s_1, s_2, n_1, and n_2 are the respective sample standard deviations and sample sizes of independent random samples from the x_1 and x_2 distributions. This is the approximation used by most statistical software. When both n_1 and n_2 are 5 or larger, it is quite accurate. The degrees of freedom computed from this formula are either truncated or not rounded.

(a) Use the data of Problem 4 (weights of pro football and pro basketball players) to compute $d.f.$ using the formula. Compare the result to 36, the value generated by Minitab. Did Minitab truncate?

(b) Compute a 99% confidence interval using $d.f. \approx 36$. (Using Table 6 requires using $d.f. = 35$.) Compare this confidence interval to the one you computed in Problem 4. Which $d.f.$ gives the longer interval?

21. *Expand Your Knowledge: Pooled Two-Sample Procedures* Under the condition that both populations have equal standard deviations ($\sigma_1 = \sigma_2$), we can pool the standard deviations and use a Student's t distribution with degrees of freedom $d.f. = n_1 + n_2 - 2$ to find the margin of error of a c confidence interval for $\mu_1 - \mu_2$. This technique demonstrates another commonly used method of computing confidence intervals for $\mu_1 - \mu_2$.

> **PROCEDURE**
>
> **How to find a confidence interval for $\mu_1 - \mu_2$ when $\sigma_1 = \sigma_2$**
>
> Consider two *independent* random samples where
>
> $\bar{x}_1$ and $\bar{x}_2$ are sample means from populations 1 and 2
>
> s_1 and s_2 are sample standard deviations from populations 1 and 2
>
> n_1 and n_2 are sample sizes from populations 1 and 2
>
> If you can assume that both population distributions 1 and 2 are normal or at least mound-shaped and symmetric, then any sample sizes n_1 and n_2 will work. If you cannot assume this, then use sample sizes $n_1 \geq 30$ and $n_2 \geq 30$.
>
> *Confidence interval for $\mu_1 - \mu_2$ when $\sigma_1 = \sigma_2$*
>
> $$(\bar{x}_1 - \bar{x}_2) - E < \mu_1 - \mu_2 < (\bar{x}_1 - \bar{x}_2) + E$$
>
> where
>
> $$E = t_c s \sqrt{\frac{1}{n_1} + \frac{1}{n_2}}$$
>
> $$s = \sqrt{\frac{(n_1 - 1)s_1^2 + (n_2 - 1)s_2^2}{n_1 + n_2 - 2}} \quad \textbf{(pooled standard deviation)}$$
>
> c = confidence level ($0 < c < 1$)
>
> t_c = critical value for confidence level c and degrees of freedom $d.f. = n_1 + n_2 - 2$ (See Table 6 of Appendix II.)
>
> *Note:* With statistical software, select pooled variance or equal variance options.

(a) There are many situations in which we want to compare means from populations having standard deviations that are equal. The pooled standard deviation method applies even if the standard deviations are known to be only approximately equal. (See Section 11.4 for methods to test that $\sigma_1 = \sigma_2$.) Consider Problem 13 regarding weights of grey wolves in two regions. Notice that $s_1 = 8.32$ pounds and $s_2 = 8.87$ pounds are fairly close. Use the method of pooled standard deviation to find an 85% confidence interval for the difference in population mean weights of grey wolves in the Chihuahua region compared with those in the Durango region.

(b) Compare the confidence interval computed in part (a) with that computed in Problem 13. Which method has the larger degrees of freedom? Which method has the longer confidence interval?

SUMMARY

How do you get information about a population by looking at a sample? One way is to use point estimates and confidence intervals. In this chapter you studied point estimates and confidence intervals for population parameters μ, p, $\mu_1 - \mu_2$, and $p_1 - p_2$. The respective point estimates are $\bar{x}$, $\hat{p}$, $\bar{x}_1 - \bar{x}_2$, and $\hat{p}_1 - \hat{p}_2$. Confidence intervals are created by subtracting and adding the margin of error E for a specified confidence level.

The general structure for a c confidence interval is

$$\text{point estimate} - E < \text{parameter} < \text{point estimate} + E$$

Specific formulas for E depend on the parameter being estimated, the level of confidence, whether population standard deviations are known, sample sizes, and the shapes of the original population distributions. When estimating μ or $\mu_1 - \mu_2$, follow the convention of using the standard normal distribution for critical values only if population standard deviations are known. Otherwise, use a Student's t distribution.

Confidence intervals for p and $p_1 - p_2$ require large-sample techniques so that the standard normal distribution can be used for critical values.

Confidence intervals have an associated probability c called the confidence level. The probability is c that the c confidence interval you compute is one of the many possible intervals containing the population parameter.

How do you choose the sample size for a specific maximal margin of error E and confidence level c? Section 8.4 addresses this question for the parameters μ and p. Problems 18 and 19 of Section 8.5 address the question for parameters $\mu_1 - \mu_2$ and $p_1 - p_2$.

IMPORTANT WORDS & SYMBOLS

Section 8.1
Large samples, $n \geq 30$
Maximal margin of error E
Confidence level c
Critical values z_c
Point estimate for μ
Confidence interval for μ
c confidence interval

Section 8.2
Student's t variable
Degrees of freedom ($d.f.$)
Critical values t_c

Section 8.3
Point estimate for p, $\hat{p}$
Confidence interval for p
Margin of error for polls

Section 8.4
Sample size n

Section 8.5
Independent samples
Dependent samples
Confidence interval for $\mu_1 - \mu_2$ (σ_1 and σ_2 known)
Confidence interval for $\mu_1 - \mu_2$ (σ_1 and σ_2 unknown)
Confidence interval for $p_1 - p_2$

VIEWPOINT   *All Systems Go?*

On January 28, 1986, the Space Shuttle *Challenger* caught fire and blew up only seconds after launch. A great deal of good engineering went into the design of the *Challenger*. However, when a system has several confidence levels operating at once, it can happen, in rare cases, that risks will increase rather than cancel out. (See Chapter Review Problem 17.) Diane Vaughn is a professor of sociology at Boston College and author of the book *The Challenger Launch Decision* (University of Chicago Press). Her book contains an excellent discussion of risks, the normalization of deviants, and cost/safety tradeoffs. Vaughn's book is described as "a remarkable and important analysis of how social structures can induce consequential errors in a decision process" (Robert K. Merton, Columbia University).

CHAPTER REVIEW PROBLEMS

1. In your own words, carefully explain the meaning of the following terms: point estimate, critical value, maximal margin of error, confidence level, and confidence interval.

For Problems 2–17, categorize each problem according to parameter being estimated, proportion p, mean μ, difference of means $\mu_1 - \mu_2$, or difference of proportions $p_1 - p_2$. Then solve the problem.

2. *Auto Insurance: Claims* Anystate Auto Insurance Company took a random sample of 370 insurance claims paid out during a 1-year period. The average claim paid was \$1570. Assume $\sigma = \$250$. Find 0.90 and 0.99 confidence intervals for the mean claim payment.

3. *Psychology: Closure* Three experiments investigating the relation between need for cognitive closure and persuasion were reported in "Motivated Resistance and Openness to Persuasion in the Presence or Absence of Prior Information," by A. W. Kruglanski (*Journal of Personality and Social Psychology*, Vol. 65, No. 5, pp. 861–874). Part of the study involved administering a "need for closure scale" to a group of students enrolled in an introductory psychology course. The "need for closure scale" has scores ranging from 101 to 201. For the 73 students in the highest quartile of the distribution, the mean score was $\bar{x} = 178.70$. Assume the population standard deviation $\sigma = 7.81$. These students were all classified as high on their need for closure. Assume that the 73 students represent a random sample of all students who are classified as high on their need for closure. Find a 95% confidence interval for the population mean score μ on the "need for closure scale" for all students with a high need for closure.

4. *Psychology: Closure* How large a sample is needed in Problem 3 if we wish to be 99% confident that the sample mean score is within 2 points of the population mean score for students who are high on the need for closure?

5. *Archaeology: Excavations* The Wind Mountain archaeological site is located in southwestern New Mexico. Wind Mountain was home to an ancient culture of prehistoric Native Americans called Anasazi. A random sample of excavations at Wind Mountain gave the following depths (in centimeters) from present-day sur-

face grade to the location of significant archaeological artifacts (Source: *Mimbres Mogollon Archaeology,* by A. Woosley and A. McIntyre, University of New Mexico Press).

85	45	120	80	75	55	65	60
65	95	90	70	75	65	68	

(a) Use a calculator with mean and sample standard deviation keys to verify that $\bar{x} \approx 74.2$ cm and $s \approx 18.3$ cm.

(b) Compute a 95% confidence interval for the mean depth μ at which archaeological artifacts from the Wind Mountain excavation site can be found.

6. *Archaeology: Pottery* Sherds of clay vessels were put together to reconstruct rim diameters of the original ceramic vessels at the Wind Mountain archaeological site (see source in Problem 5). A random sample of ceramic vessels gave the following rim diameters (in centimeters):

15.9	13.4	22.1	12.7	13.1	19.6	11.7	13.5	17.7	18.1

(a) Use a calculator with mean and sample standard deviation keys to verify that $\bar{x} \approx 15.8$ cm and $s \approx 3.5$ cm.

(b) Compute an 80% confidence interval for the population mean μ of rim diameters for such ceramic vessels found at the Wind Mountain archaeological site.

7. *Telephone Interviews: Survey* The National Study of the Changing Work Force conducted an extensive survey of 2958 wage and salaried workers on issues ranging from relationship with their bosses to household chores. The data were gathered through hour-long telephone interviews with a nationally representative sample (*The Wall Street Journal*). In response to the question, "What does success mean to you?" 1538 responded, "Personal satisfaction from doing a good job." Let p be the population proportion of all wage and salaried workers who would respond the same way to the stated question. Find a 90% confidence interval for p.

8. *Telephone Interviews: Survey* How large a sample is needed in Problem 7 if we wish to be 95% confident that the sample percentage of those equating success with personal satisfaction is within 1% of the population percentage? (*Hint:* Use $p \approx 0.52$ as a preliminary estimate.)

9. *Archaeology: Pottery* Three-circle, red-on-white is one distinctive pattern painted on ceramic vessels of the Anasazi period found at the Wind Mountain archaeological site (see source for Problem 5). At one excavation a sample of 167 potsherds indicated that 68 were of the three-circle, red-on-white pattern.

(a) Find a point estimate $\hat{p}$ for the proportion of all ceramic potsherds at this site that are of the three-circle, red-on-white pattern.

(b) Compute a 95% confidence interval for the population proportion p of all ceramic potsherds with this distinctive pattern found at the site.

10. *Archaeology: Pottery* Consider the three-circle, red-on-white pattern discussed in Problem 9. How many ceramic potsherds must be found and identified if we are to be 95% confident that the sample proportion $\hat{p}$ of such potsherds is within 6% of the population proportion of three-circle, red-on-white patterns found at this excavation site? (*Hint:* Use the results of Problem 9 as a preliminary estimate.)

 11. *Agriculture: Bell Peppers* The following data represent soil water content (percent water by volume) for independent random samples of soil taken from two experimental fields growing bell peppers (Reference: *Journal of Agricultural, Biological,*

and Environmental Statistics). *Note:* These data are also available with other software on the statSpace CD-ROM.

Soil water content from field I: x_1; $n_1 = 72$

15.1	11.2	10.3	10.8	16.6	8.3	9.1	12.3	9.1	14.3
10.7	16.1	10.2	15.2	8.9	9.5	9.6	11.3	14.0	11.3
15.6	11.2	13.8	9.0	8.4	8.2	12.0	13.9	11.6	16.0
9.6	11.4	8.4	8.0	14.1	10.9	13.2	13.8	14.6	10.2
11.5	13.1	14.7	12.5	10.2	11.8	11.0	12.7	10.3	10.8
11.0	12.6	10.8	9.6	11.5	10.6	11.7	10.1	9.7	9.7
11.2	9.8	10.3	11.9	9.7	11.3	10.4	12.0	11.0	10.7
8.8	11.1								

Soil water content from field II: x_2; $n_2 = 80$

12.1	10.2	13.6	8.1	13.5	7.8	11.8	7.7	8.1	9.2
14.1	8.9	13.9	7.5	12.6	7.3	14.9	12.2	7.6	8.9
13.9	8.4	13.4	7.1	12.4	7.6	9.9	26.0	7.3	7.4
14.3	8.4	13.2	7.3	11.3	7.5	9.7	12.3	6.9	7.6
13.8	7.5	13.3	8.0	11.3	6.8	7.4	11.7	11.8	7.7
12.6	7.7	13.2	13.9	10.4	12.8	7.6	10.7	10.7	10.9
12.5	11.3	10.7	13.2	8.9	12.9	7.7	9.7	9.7	11.4
11.9	13.4	9.2	13.4	8.8	11.9	7.1	8.5	14.0	14.2

(a) Use a calculator with mean and standard deviation keys to verify that $\bar{x}_1 \approx 11.42$, $s_1 \approx 2.08$, $\bar{x}_2 \approx 10.65$, and $s_2 \approx 3.03$.

(b) Let μ_1 be the population mean for x_1 and let μ_2 be the population mean for x_2. Find a 95% confidence interval for $\mu_1 - \mu_2$.

(c) Examine the confidence interval and explain what it means in the context of this problem. Does the interval consist of numbers that are all positive? all negative? of different signs? At the 95% level of confidence, is the population mean soil water content of the first field higher than that of the second field?

(d) Which distribution (standard normal or Student's t) did you use? Why? Do you need information about the soil water content distributions?

12. *Stocks: Retail and Utility* How profitable are different sectors of the stock market? One way to answer such a question is to examine profit as a percentage of stockholder equity. A random sample of 32 retail stocks such as Toys 'Я' Us, Best Buy, and Gap was studied for x_1, profit as a percentage of stockholder equity. The result was $\bar{x}_1 = 13.7$. A random sample of 34 utility (gas and electric) stocks such as Boston Edison, Wisconsin Energy, and Texas Utilities was studied for x_2, profit as a percentage of stockholder equity. The result was $\bar{x}_2 = 10.1$. (Source: *Fortune 500*, Vol. 135, No. 8.) Assume $\sigma_1 = 4.1$ and $\sigma_2 = 2.7$.

(a) Let μ_1 represent the population mean profit as a percentage of stockholder equity for retail stocks, and let μ_2 represent the population mean profit as a percentage of stockholder equity for utility stocks. Find a 95% confidence interval for $\mu_1 - \mu_2$.

(b) Examine the confidence interval and explain what it means in the context of this problem. Does the interval consist of numbers that are all positive? all negative? of different signs? At the 95% level of confidence, does it appear that the profit as a percentage of stockholder equity for retail stocks is higher than that for utility stocks?

13. *Wildlife: Wolves* A random sample of 18 adult male wolves from the Canadian Northwest Territories gave an average weight $\bar{x}_1 = 98$ lb with estimated sample standard deviation $s_1 = 6.5$ lb. Another sample of 24 adult male wolves from Alaska gave an average weight $\bar{x}_2 = 90$ lb with estimated sample standard deviation $s_2 = 7.3$ lb (Source: *The Wolf*, by L. D. Mech, University of Minnesota Press).
    (a) Let μ_1 represent the population mean weight of adult male wolves from the Northwest Territories, and let μ_2 represent the population mean weight of adult male wolves from Alaska. Find a 75% confidence interval for $\mu_1 - \mu_2$.
    (b) Examine the confidence interval and explain what it means in the context of this problem. Does the interval consist of numbers that are all positive? all negative? of different signs? At the 75% level of confidence, does it appear that the average weight of adult male wolves from the Northwest Territories is greater than that of the Alaska wolves?

14. *Wildlife: Wolves* A random sample of 17 wolf litters in Ontario, Canada, gave an average of $\bar{x}_1 = 4.9$ wolf pups per litter with estimated sample standard deviation $s_1 = 1.0$. Another random sample of 6 wolf litters in Finland gave an average of $\bar{x}_2 = 2.8$ wolf pups per litter with sample standard deviation $s_2 = 1.2$ (see source for Problem 13).
    (a) Find an 85% confidence interval for $\mu_1 - \mu_2$, the difference in population mean litter size between Ontario and Finland.
    (b) Examine the confidence interval and explain what it means in the context of this problem. Does the interval consist of numbers that are all positive? all negative? of different signs? At the 85% level of confidence, does it appear that the average litter size of wolf pups in Ontario is greater than the average litter size in Finland?

15. *Survey Response: Validity* The book *Survey Responses: An Evaluation of Their Validity*, by E. J. Wentland and K. Smith (Academic Press), includes studies reporting accuracy of answers to questions from surveys. A study by Locander et al. considered the question, "Are you a registered voter?" Accuracy of response was confirmed by a check of city voting records. Two methods of survey were used: a face-to-face interview and a telephone interview. A random sample of 93 people was asked the voter registration question face to face. Seventy-nine respondents gave accurate answers (as verified by city records). Another random sample of 83 people was asked the same question during a telephone interview. Seventy-four respondents gave accurate answers. Assume that the samples are representative of the general population.
    (a) Let p_1 be the population proportion of all people who answer the voter registration question accurately during a face-to-face interview. Let p_2 be the population proportion of all people who answer the question accurately during a telephone interview. Find a 95% confidence interval for $p_1 - p_2$.
    (b) Does the interval contain numbers that are all positive? all negative? mixed? Comment on the meaning of the confidence interval in the context of this problem. At the 95% level, do you detect any difference in the proportion of accurate responses from face-to-face interviews compared with the proportion of accurate responses from telephone interviews?

16. *Survey Response: Validity* Locander et al. (see reference in Problem 15) also studied the accuracy of responses on questions involving more sensitive material than voter registration. From public records, individuals were identified as having been charged with drunken driving not less than 6 months or more than 12 months from the starting date of the study. Two random samples from this group were studied. In the first sample of 30 individuals, the respondents were asked in a face-to-face interview if they had been charged with drunken driving in the last 12 months. Of

these 30 people interviewed face to face, 16 answered the question accurately. The second random sample consisted of 46 people who had been charged with drunken driving. During a telephone interview, 25 of these responded accurately to the question asking if they had been charged with drunken driving during the past 12 months. Assume that the samples are representative of all people recently charged with drunken driving.

(a) Let p_1 represent the population proportion of all people with recent charges of drunken driving who respond accurately to a face-to-face interview asking if they have been charged with drunken driving during the past 12 months. Let p_2 represent the population proportion of people who respond accurately to the question when it is asked in a telephone interview. Find a 90% confidence interval for $p_1 - p_2$.

(b) Does the interval found in part (a) contain numbers that are all positive? all negative? mixed? Comment on the meaning of the confidence interval in the context of this problem. At the 90% level, do you detect any differences in the proportion of accurate responses to the question from face-to-face interviews as compared with the proportion of accurate responses from telephone interviews?

 17. *Expand Your Knowledge: Two Confidence Intervals* What happens if we want several confidence intervals to hold at the same time (concurrently)? Do we still have the same level of confidence we had for *each* individual interval?

(a) Suppose we have two independent random variables x_1 and x_2 with respective population means μ_1 and μ_2. Let us say that we use sample data to construct two 80% confidence intervals.

Confidence Interval	Confidence Level
$A_1 < \mu_1 < B_1$	0.80
$A_2 < \mu_2 < B_2$	0.80

Now, what is the probability that *both* intervals hold together? Use methods of Section 4.2 to show that

$$P(A_1 < \mu_1 < B_1 \quad and \quad A_2 < \mu_2 < B_2) = 0.64$$

Hint: We are combining independent events. If the confidence is 64% that both intervals hold together, explain why the risk that at least one interval does not hold (i.e., fails) must be 36%.

(b) Suppose that we want *both* intervals to hold with 90% confidence (i.e., only 10% risk level). How much confidence c should each interval have to achieve this combined level of confidence? (Assume that each interval has the same confidence level c.)

Hint: $P(A_1 < \mu_1 < B_1 \quad and \quad A_2 < \mu_2 < B_2) = 0.90$

$$P(A_1 < \mu_1 < B_1) \times P(A_2 < \mu_2 < B_2) = 0.90$$

$$c \times c = 0.90$$

Now solve for c.

(c) If we want *both* intervals to hold at the 90% level of confidence, then the individual intervals must hold at a *higher* level of confidence. Write a brief but detailed explanation of how this could be of importance in a large, complex engineering design such as a rocket booster or a spacecraft.

DATA HIGHLIGHTS: GROUP PROJECTS

Break into small groups and discuss the following topics. Organize a brief outline in which you summarize the main points of your group discussion.

Digging clams

1. Garrison Bay is a small bay in Washington state. A popular recreational activity in the bay is clam digging. For several years, this harvest has been monitored and the size distribution of clams recorded. Data for lengths and widths of little neck clams (*Protothaca staminea*) were recorded by a method of systematic sampling in a study done by S. Scherba and V. F. Gallucci ("The Application of Systematic Sampling to a Study of Infaunal Variation in a Soft Substrate Intertidal Environment," *Fishery Bulletin* 74:937–948). The data in Tables 8-4 and 8-5 give lengths and widths for 35 little neck clams.
   (a) Use a calculator to compute the sample mean and sample standard deviation for the lengths and widths. Compute the coefficient of variation for each.
   (b) Compute a 95% confidence interval for the population mean length of all Garrison Bay little neck clams.
   (c) How many more little neck clams would be needed in a sample if you wanted to be 95% sure that the sample mean length is within a maximal margin of error of 10 mm of the population mean length?
   (d) Compute a 95% confidence interval for the population mean width of all Garrison Bay little neck clams.
   (e) How many more little neck clams would be needed in a sample if you wanted to be 95% sure that the sample mean width is within a maximal margin of error of 10 mm of the population mean width?
   (f) The *same* 35 clams were used for measures of length and width. Are the sample measurements length and width independent or dependent? Why?

2. Examine Figure 8-8, "Fall Back."
   (a) Of the 1024 adults surveyed, 66% were reported to favor daylight saving time. How many people in the sample preferred daylight saving time? Using the statistic $\hat{p} = 0.66$ and sample size $n = 1024$, find a 95% confidence interval for the proportion of people p who favor daylight saving time. How could you report this information in terms of a margin of error?
   (b) Look at Figure 8-8 to find the sample statistic $\hat{p}$ for the proportion of people preferring standard time. Find a 95% confidence interval for the population proportion p of people who favor standard time. Report the same information in terms of a margin of error.

TABLE 8-4 Lengths of Little Neck Clams (mm)

530	517	505	512	487	481	485	479	452	468
459	449	472	471	455	394	475	335	508	486
474	465	420	402	410	393	389	330	305	169
91	537	519	509	511					

TABLE 8-5 Widths of Little Neck Clams (mm)

494	477	471	413	407	427	408	430	395	417
394	397	402	401	385	338	422	288	464	436
414	402	383	340	349	333	356	268	264	141
77	498	456	433	447					

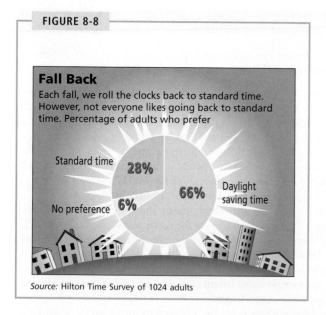

FIGURE 8-8

Fall Back

Each fall, we roll the clocks back to standard time. However, not everyone likes going back to standard time. Percentage of adults who prefer

Standard time **28%**

No preference **6%** **66%** Daylight saving time

Source: Hilton Time Survey of 1024 adults

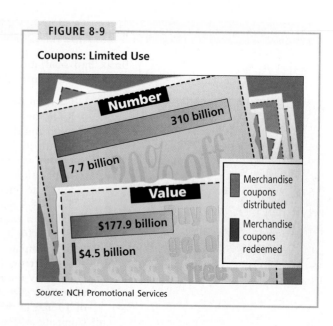

FIGURE 8-9

Coupons: Limited Use

Number

310 billion

7.7 billion

Value

$177.9 billion

$4.5 billion

Merchandise coupons distributed

Merchandise coupons redeemed

Source: NCH Promotional Services

3. Examine Figure 8-9, "Coupons: Limited Use."

(a) Use Figure 8-9 to estimate the percentage of merchandise coupons that were redeemed. Also estimate the percentage dollar value of the coupons that were redeemed. Are these numbers approximately equal?

(b) Suppose that you are a marketing executive working for a national chain of toy stores. You wish to estimate the percentage of coupons that will be redeemed for the toy stores. How many coupons should you check to be 95% sure that the percentage of coupons redeemed is within 1% of the population proportion of all coupons redeemed for the toy store?

(c) Use the results of part (a) as a preliminary estimate for p, the percentage of coupons that are redeemed, and redo part (b).

(d) Suppose that you sent out 937 coupons and found that 27 were redeemed. Explain why you could be 95% confident that the proportion of such coupons redeemed in the future would be between 1.9% and 3.9%.

(e) Suppose that the dollar value of a collection of coupons was $10,000. Use the data in Figure 8-9 to find the expected value and standard deviation of the dollar value of the redeemed coupons. What is the probability that between $225 and $275 (out of the $10,000) is redeemed?

LINKING CONCEPTS: WRITING PROJECTS

Discuss each of the following topics in class or review the topics on your own. Then write a brief but complete essay in which you summarize the main points. Please include formulas and graphs as appropriate.

1. In this chapter, we have studied confidence intervals. Carefully read the following statements about confidence intervals:

(a) Once the endpoints of the confidence interval are numerically fixed, then the parameter in question (either μ or p) does or does not fall inside the "fixed" interval.

(b) A given fixed interval either does or does not contain the parameter μ or p; therefore, the probability is 1 or 0 that the parameter is in the interval.

Next, read the following statements. Then discuss all four statements in the context of what we actually mean by a confidence interval.
(c) Nontrivial probability statements can be made only about variables, not constants.
(d) The confidence level c represents the proportion of all (fixed) intervals that would contain the parameter if we repeated the process many, many times.

2. Throughout Chapter 8, we have used the normal distribution, the central limit theorem, or the Student's t distribution.
   (a) Give a brief outline describing how confidence intervals for means use the central limit theorem or Student's t distribution in their basic construction.
   (b) Give a brief outline describing how the normal approximation to the binomial distribution is used in the construction of confidence intervals for a proportion p.
   (c) Give a brief outline describing how the sample size for a predetermined error tolerance and level of confidence is determined from the normal distribution or the central limit theorem.

3. When the results of a survey or a poll are published, the sample size is usually given, as well as the margin of error. For example, suppose the *Honolulu Star Bulletin* reported that it surveyed 385 Honolulu residents and 78% said they favor mandatory jail sentences for people convicted of driving under the influence of drugs or alcohol (with margin of error of 3 percentage points in either direction). Usually the confidence level of the interval is not given, but it is standard practice to use the margin of error for a 95% confidence interval when no other confidence level is given.
   (a) The paper reported a point estimate of 78% with margin of error of $\pm 3\%$. Write this information in the form of a confidence interval for p, the population proportion of residents favoring mandatory jail sentences for people convicted of driving under the influence. What is the assumed confidence level?
   (b) The margin of error is simply the error due to using a sample instead of the entire population. It does not take into account the bias that might be introduced by the wording of the question, by the truthfulness of the respondents, or by other factors. Suppose the question was asked in this fashion: "Considering the devastating injuries suffered by innocent victims in auto accidents caused by drunken or drugged drivers, do you favor a mandatory jail sentence for those convicted of driving under the influence of drugs or alcohol?" Do you think the wording of the question would influence the respondents? Do you think the population proportion of those favoring mandatory jail sentences is accurately represented by a confidence interval based on responses to such a question? Explain your answer.

   Suppose the question had been: "Considering the existing overcrowding of our prisons, do you favor a mandatory jail sentence for people convicted of driving under the influence of drugs or alcohol?" Do you think the population proportion of those favoring mandatory jail sentences is accurately represented by a confidence interval based on responses to such a question? Explain your answer.

Using Technology

APPLICATION 1

Finding a Confidence Interval for a Population Mean μ

Cryptanalysis, the science of breaking codes, makes extensive use of language patterns. The frequency of various letter combinations is an important part of the study. A letter combination consisting of a single letter is a monograph, while combinations consisting of two letters are called digraphs, and those with three letters are called trigraphs. In the English language the most frequent digraph is the letter combination TH.

The *characteristic rate* of a letter combination is a measurement of its rate of occurrence. To compute the characteristic rate, count the number of occurrences of a given letter combination and divide by the number of letters in the text. For instance, to estimate the characteristic rate of the digraph TH, you could select a newspaper text and pick a random starting place. From that place mark off 2000 letters and count the number of times that TH occurs. Then divide the number of occurrences by 2000.

The characteristic rate of a digraph can vary slightly depending on the style of the author, so to estimate an overall characteristic frequency, you want to consider several samples of newspaper text by different authors. Suppose you did this with a random sample of 15 articles and found the characteristic rate of the digraph TH in the articles. The results follow.

0.0275	0.0230	0.0300	0.0255
0.0280	0.0295	0.0265	0.0265
0.0240	0.0315	0.0250	0.0265
0.0290	0.0295	0.0275	

(a) Find a 95% confidence interval for the mean characteristic rate of the digraph TH.

(b) Repeat part (a) for a 90% confidence interval.

(c) Repeat part (a) for an 80% confidence interval.

(d) Repeat part (a) for a 70% confidence interval.

(e) Repeat part (a) for a 60% confidence interval.

(f) For each confidence interval in parts (a)–(e), compute the length of the given interval. Do you notice a relation between the confidence level and the length of the interval?

A good reference for cryptanalysis is a book by Sinkov:

Sinkov, Abraham. *Elementary Cryptanalysis.* New York: Random House.

In the book, other common digraphs and trigraphs are given.

APPLICATION 2

Confidence Interval Demonstration

When we generate different random samples of the same size from a population, we discover that $\bar{x}$ varies from sample to sample. Likewise, different samples produce different confidence intervals for μ. The endpoints $\bar{x} \pm E$ of a confidence interval are statistical variables. A 90% confidence interval tells us that if we obtain lots of confidence intervals (for the same sample size), then the proportion of all intervals that will turn out to contain μ is 90%.

(a) Use the technology of your choice to generate 10 large random samples from a population with a known mean μ.

(b) Construct a 90% confidence interval for the mean for each sample.

(c) Examine the confidence intervals and note the percentage of the intervals that contain the population mean μ. We have 10 confidence intervals. Will exactly 90% of 10 intervals always contain μ? Explain. What if we have 1000 intervals?

Technology Hints for Confidence Interval Demonstration

TI-84Plus/TI-83Plus

The TI-84Plus/TI-83Plus generates random samples from uniform, normal, and binomial distributions. Press the **MATH** key and select **PRB**. Choice **5:randInt(lower, upper, sample size n)** generates random samples of size n from the integers between the specified lower and upper values. Choice **6:randNorm(μ, σ, sample size n)** generates random samples of size n from a normal distribution with specified mean and standard deviation. Choice **7:randBin(number of trials, p, sample size)** generates samples of the specified size from the designated binomial distribution. Under **STAT**, select **EDIT** and highlight the list name such as L1. At the = sign, use the **MATH** key to access the desired population distribution. Finally, use the **Zinterval** under the **TESTS** option of the **STAT** key to generate 90% confidence intervals.

Excel

Use the menu choices **Tools ➤ Data Analysis ➤ Random Number Generator**. In the dialogue box, the number of variables refers to the number of samples. The number of random numbers refers to the number of data in each sample. Select the population distribution (uniform, normal, binomial). The command **Paste function** $\boxed{f_x}$ **➤ Statistical ➤ Confidence(1 − confidence level, σ, sample size)** gives the maximal margin of error E. To find a 90% confidence interval for each sample, use **Confidence(0.10, σ, sample size)** to find the maximal margin of error E. Note that if you use the population standard deviation σ in the function, the value of E will be the same for all samples of the same size. Next, find the sample mean $\overline{x}$ for each sample (use **Paste function** $\boxed{f_x}$ **➤ Statistical ➤ Average**). Finally, construct the endpoints $\overline{x} \pm E$ of the confidence interval for each sample.

Minitab

Minitab provides options for sampling from a variety of distributions. To generate random samples from a specific distribution, use the menu selection **Calc ➤ Random Data ➤** and then select the population distribution. In the dialogue box, the *number of rows of data* represents the *sample size*. The *number of samples* corresponds to the number of columns selected for data storage. For example, c1 − c10 in data storage produces 10 different random samples of the specified size. Use the menu selection **Stat ➤ Basic Statistics ➤ 1 sample z** to generate confidence intervals for the mean μ from each sample. In the variables box, list all the columns containing your samples. For instance, using c1 − c10 in the variables list will produce confidence intervals for each of the 10 samples stored in columns c1 through c10.

The Minitab display shows 90% confidence intervals for 10 different random samples of size 50 taken from a normal distribution with $\mu = 30$ and $\sigma = 4$. Notice that, as expected, 9 out of 10 of the intervals contain $\mu = 30$.

Minitab Display

Z Confidence Intervals (Samples from a Normal
Population with μ = 30 and σ = 4)
The assumed sigma = 4.00

Variable	N	Mean	StDev	SE Mean	90.0 % CI
C1	50	30.265	4.300	0.566	(29.334, 31.195)
C2	50	31.040	3.957	0.566	(30.109, 31.971)
C3	50	29.940	4.195	0.566	(29.010, 30.871)
C4	50	30.753	3.842	0.566	(29.823, 31.684)
C5	50	30.047	4.174	0.566	(29.116, 30.977)
C6	50	29.254	4.423	0.566	(28.324, 30.185)
C7	50	29.062	4.532	0.566	(28.131, 29.992)
C8	50	29.344	4.487	0.566	(28.414, 30.275)
C9	50	30.062	4.199	0.566	(29.131, 30.992)
C10	50	29.989	3.451	0.566	(29.058, 30.919)

SPSS

SPSS uses a Student's *t* distribution to generate confidence intervals for the mean and difference of means. Use the menu choices **Analyze ➤ Compare Means** and then **One-Sample T Test** or **Independent-Sample T Tests** for confidence intervals for a single mean or difference of means, respectively. In the dialogue box, use 0 for the test value. Click **Options...** to provide the confidence level.

To generate 10 random samples of size $n = 30$ from a normal distribution with $\mu = 30$ and $\sigma = 4$, first enter consecutive integers from 1 to 30 in a column of the data editor. Then, under variable view, enter the variable names Sample1 through Sample10. Use the menu choices **Transform ➤ Compute**. In the dialogue box, use Sample1 for the target variable, then select the function **RV.Normal(mean, stddev)**. Use 30 for the mean and 4 for the standard deviation. Continue until you have 10 samples. To sample from other distributions, use appropriate functions in the Compute dialogue box.

The SPSS display shows 90% confidence intervals for 10 different random samples of size 30 taken from a normal

distribution with $\mu = 30$ and $\sigma = 4$. Notice that, as expected, 9 of the 10 intervals contain the population mean $\mu = 30$.

SPSS Display

90% t-confidence intervals for random samples of size
n = 30 from a normal distribution with μ = 30
and σ = 4.

	t	df	Sig(2-tail)	Mean	Lower	Upper
SAMPLE1	42.304	29	.000	29.7149	28.5214	30.9084
SAMPLE2	43.374	29	.000	30.1552	28.9739	31.3365
SAMPLE3	53.606	29	.000	31.2743	30.2830	32.2656
SAMPLE4	35.648	29	.000	30.1490	28.7120	31.5860
SAMPLE5	47.964	29	.000	31.0161	29.9173	32.1148
SAMPLE6	34.718	29	.000	30.3519	28.8665	31.8374
SAMPLE7	34.698	29	.000	30.7665	29.2599	32.2731
SAMPLE8	39.731	29	.000	30.2388	28.9456	31.5320
SAMPLE9	44.206	29	.000	29.7256	28.5831	30.8681
SAMPLE10	49.981	29	.000	29.7273	28.7167	30.7379

APPLICATION 3

Bootstrap Demonstration

Bootstrap can be used to construct confidence intervals for μ when traditional methods cannot be used. For example, if the sample size is small and the sample shows extreme outliers or extreme lack of symmetry, use of the Student's *t* distribution is inappropriate. Bootstrap makes no assumptions about the population.

Consider the following random sample of size 20:

12	15	21	2	6	3	15	51	22	18
37	12	25	19	33	15	14	17	12	27

A stem-and-leaf display shows that the data are skewed with one outlier.

```
0 | 2   represents 2
0 | 236
1 | 2224555789
2 | 1257
3 | 37
4 |
5 | 1
```

We can use Minitab to model the bootstrap method for constructing confidence intervals for μ. (The Professional edition of Minitab is required because of spreadsheet size and other limitations of the Student edition.) This demonstration uses only 1000 samples. Bootstrap uses many thousands.

STEP 1: Create 1000 new samples, each of size 20, by sampling *with replacement* from the original data. To do this in Minitab, we enter the original 20 data values in column C1. Then, in column C2, place equal probabilities of 0.05 beside each of the original data values. Use the menu choices **Calc ➤ Random Data ➤ Discrete**. In the dialogue box, fill in 1000 as the number of rows, store the data in columns C11–C30, and use column C1 for values and column C2 for probabilities.

STEP 2: Find the sample mean of each of the 1000 samples. To do this in Minitab, use the menu choices **Calc ➤ Row Statistics**. In the dialogue box, select **mean**. Use columns C11–C30 as the input variables and store the results in column C31.

STEP 3: Order the 1000 means from smallest to largest. In Minitab, use the menu choices **Manip ➤ Sort**. In the dialogue box, indicate C31 as the column to be sorted. Store the results in column C32. Sort by values in column C31.

STEP 4: Create a 95% confidence interval by finding the boundaries for the middle 95% of the data. In other words, you need to find the values of the 2.5 percentile ($P_{2.5}$) and the 97.5 percentile ($P_{97.5}$). Since there are 1000 data values, the 2.5 percentile is the data value in position 25, while the 97.5 percentile is the data value in position 975. The confidence interval is $P_{2.5} < \mu < P_{97.5}$.

Demonstration Results

Figure 8-10 shows a histogram of the 1000 $\bar{x}$ values from one bootstrap simulation. Three bootstrap simulations produced the following 95% confidence intervals.

13.90 to 23.90

14.00 to 24.15

14.05 to 23.8

Using the t distribution on the sample data, Minitab produced the interval 13.33 to 24.27. The results of the bootstrap simulations and the t distribution method are quite close.

FIGURE 8-10 Bootstrap Simulation, $\bar{x}$ Distribution

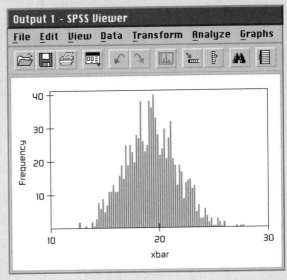

9

Hypothesis Testing

Charles Lutwidge Dodgson (1832–1898)

Using the pseudonym Lewis Carroll, this English mathematician and author wrote *Alice's Adventures in Wonderland*.

For on-line student resources, visit **math.college.hmco.com/students** and follow the Statistics links to the Brase/Brase, *Understandable Statistics,* 8th edition web site.

480

"Would you tell me, please, which way I ought to go from here?"
"That depends a good deal on where you want to get to," said the Cat.
"I don't much care where—" said Alice.
"Then it doesn't matter which way you go," said the Cat.

—Lewis Carroll
Alice's Adventures in Wonderland

Charles Dodgson was an English mathematician who loved to write children's stories in his free time. The dialogue above between Alice and the Cheshire Cat occurs in the masterpiece *Alice's Adventures in Wonderland*, written by Dodgson under the pen name Lewis Carroll. These lines relate to our study of hypothesis testing. Statistical tests cannot answer all of life's questions. They cannot always tell us "where to go," but after this decision is made on other grounds, they can help us find the best way to get there.

PREVIEW QUESTIONS

◊ Many of life's questions require a yes or no answer. When you must act on incomplete (sample) information, how do you decide whether to accept or reject a proposal?   (SECTION 9.1)

◊ What is the *P*-value of a statistical test? What does this measurement have to do with performance reliability?   (SECTION 9.1)

◊ How do you construct statistical tests for μ? Does it make a difference whether σ is known or unknown?   (SECTION 9.2)

◊ How do you construct statistical tests for the proportion *p* of successes in a binomial experiment?   (SECTION 9.3)

◊ What are the advantages of pairing data values? How do you construct statistical tests for paired differences?   (SECTION 9.4)

◊ How do you construct statistical tests for differences of independent random variables?   (SECTION 9.5)

FOCUS PROBLEM

Benford's Law: The Importance of Being Number 1

Benford's Law states that in a wide variety of circumstances, numbers have "1" as their first nonzero digit disproportionately often. Benford's Law applies to such diverse topics as the drainage areas of rivers; properties of chemicals; populations of towns; figures in newspapers, magazines, and government reports; and the half-lives of radioactive atoms!

Specifically, such diverse measurements begin with "1" about 30% of the time, with "2" about 18% of time, and with "3" about 12.5% of the time. Larger digits occur less often. For example, less than 5% of the numbers in circumstances such as these begin with the digit 9. This is in dramatic contrast to a random sampling situation, where each of the digits 1 through 9 has an equal chance of appearing.

The first nonzero digits of numbers taken from large bodies of numerical records such as tax returns, population studies, government records, and so forth show the following probabilities of occurrence.

481

First nonzero digit	1	2	3	4	5	6	7	8	9
Probability	0.301	0.176	0.125	0.097	0.079	0.067	0.058	0.051	0.046

More than 100 years ago, the astronomer Simon Newcomb noticed that books of logarithm tables were much dirtier near the fronts of the tables. It seemed that people were more frequently looking up numbers with a low first digit. This was regarded as an odd phenomenon and a strange curiosity. The phenomenon was rediscovered in 1938 by physicist Frank Benford (hence the name *Benford's Law*).

More recently, Ted Hill, a mathematician at the Georgia Institute of Technology, studied situations that might demonstrate Benford's Law. Professor Hill showed that such probability distributions are likely to occur when we have a "distribution of distributions." Put another way, large random collections of random samples tend to follow Benford's Law. This seems to be especially true for samples taken from large government data banks, accounting reports for large corporations, large collections of astronomical observations, and so forth. For more information, see *American Scientist*, Vol. 86, pp. 358–363, and *Chance*, American Statistical Association, Vol. 12, No. 3, pp. 27–31.

Can Benford's Law be applied to help solve a real-world problem? Well, one application might be accounting fraud! Suppose the first nonzero digits of the entries in the accounting records of a large corporation (such as Enron or WorldCom) did not follow Benford's Law. Should this set off an accounting alarm for the FBI or the stockholders? How "significant" would this be? Such questions are the subject of statistics.

In Section 9.3 you will see how to use sample data to test whether the proportion of first nonzero digits of the entries in a large accounting report follow Benford's Law. Problems 1 and 2 of Section 9.3 relate to Benford's Law and accounting discrepancies. In one problem you are asked to use sample data to determine if accounting books have been "cooked" by "pumping numbers up" to make the company look more attractive or perhaps to provide a cover for money laundering. In the other problem you are asked to determine if accounting books have been "cooked" by artificially lowered numbers, perhaps to hide profits from the Internal Revenue Service or to divert company profits to unscrupulous employees. (See Problems 1 and 2 of Section 9.3.)

9.1
Introduction to Statistical Tests

FOCUS POINTS

✓ Understand the rationale for statistical tests.

✓ Identify the null and alternate hypotheses in a statistical test.

✓ Identify right-tailed, left-tailed, and two-tailed tests.

✓ Use a test statistic to compute a *P*-value.

✓ Recognize types of errors, level of significance, and power of a test.

✓ Understand the meaning and risks of rejecting or not rejecting the null hypothesis.

In Chapter 1, we emphasized the fact that one of a statistician's most important jobs is to draw inferences about populations based on samples taken from the populations. Most statistical inference centers around the parameters of a population (often the mean or probability of success in a binomial trial). Methods for drawing inferences about parameters are of two types: Either we make decisions concerning the value of the parameter, or we actually estimate the value of the parameter. When we estimate the value (or location) of a parameter, we are using methods of estimation such as those studied in Chapter 8. Decisions concerning the value of a parameter are obtained by *hypothesis testing*, the topic we shall study in this chapter.

Students often ask which method should be used on a particular problem—that is, should the parameter be estimated, or should we test a *hypothesis* involving the parameter? The answer lies in the practical nature of the problem and the questions posed about it. Some people prefer to test theories concerning the parameters.

Others prefer to express their inferences as estimates. Both estimation and hypothesis testing are found extensively in the literature of statistical applications.

Stating Hypotheses

Null hypothesis

Our first step is to establish a working hypothesis about the population parameter in question. This hypothesis is called the *null hypothesis,* denoted by the symbol H_0. The value specified in the null hypothesis is often a historical value, a claim, or a production specification. For instance, if the average height of a professional male basketball player was 6.5 feet 10 years ago, we might use a null hypothesis H_0: $\mu = 6.5$ feet for a study involving the average height of this year's professional male basketball players. If television networks claim that the average length of time devoted to commercials in a 60-minute program is 12 minutes, we would use H_0: $\mu = 12$ minutes as our null hypothesis in a study regarding the length of time devoted to commercials. Finally, if a repair shop claims that it should take an average of 25 minutes to install a new muffler on a passenger automobile, we would use H_0: $\mu = 25$ minutes as the null hypothesis for a study of how well the repair shop is conforming to specified times for a muffler installation.

Alternate hypothesis

Any hypothesis that differs from the null hypothesis is called an *alternate hypothesis.* An alternate hypothesis is constructed in such a way that it is the one to be accepted when the null hypothesis must be rejected. The alternate hypothesis is denoted by the symbol H_1. For instance, if we believe the average height of professional male basketball players is taller than it was 10 years ago, we would use an alternate hypothesis H_1: $\mu > 6.5$ feet with the null hypothesis H_0: $\mu = 6.5$ feet.

> **Null hypothesis H_0:** This is the statement that is under investigation or being tested. Usually the null hypothesis represents a statement of "no effect," "no difference," or, put another way, "things haven't changed."
>
> **Alternate hypothesis H_1:** This is the statement you will adopt in the situation where the evidence (data) is so strong that you reject H_0. A statistical test is designed to assess the strength of the evidence (data) against the null hypothesis.

EXAMPLE 1

Null and alternate hypotheses

A car manufacturer advertises that its new subcompact models get 47 miles per gallon (mpg). Let μ be the mean of the mileage distribution for these cars. You assume that the manufacturer will not underrate the car, but you suspect that the mileage might be overrated.

(a) What shall we use for H_0?

   SOLUTION: We want to see if the manufacturer's claim that $\mu = 47$ can be rejected. Therefore, our null hypothesis is simply that $\mu = 47$. We denote the null hypothesis as

   H_0: $\mu = 47$

(b) What shall we use for H_1?

   SOLUTION: From experience with this manufacturer, we have every reason to believe that the advertised mileage is too high. If μ is not 47, we are sure it is less than 47. Therefore, the alternate hypothesis is

   H_1: $\mu < 47$ ◇

GUIDED EXERCISE 1

Null and alternate hypotheses

A company manufactures ball bearings for precision machines. The average diameter of a certain type of ball bearing should be 6.0 mm. To check that the average diameter is correct, the company formulates a statistical test.

(a) What should be used for H_0? (*Hint:* What is the company trying to test?)

⟹ If μ is the mean diameter of the ball bearings, the company wants to test whether $\mu = 6.0$ mm. Therefore, H_0: $\mu = 6.0$.

(b) What should be used for H_1? (*Hint:* An error either way, too small or too large, would be serious.)

⟹ An error either way could occur, and it would be serious. Therefore, H_1: $\mu \neq 6.0$ (μ is either smaller than or larger than 6.0).

◇ **COMMENT: NOTATION REGARDING THE NULL HYPOTHESIS** In statistical testing, the null hypothesis H_0 always contains the equals symbol. However, in the null hypothesis, some statistical software packages and texts also include the inequality symbol that is opposite that shown in the alternate hypothesis. For instance, if the alternate hypothesis is "μ is less than 3" ($\mu < 3$), then the corresponding null hypothesis is sometimes written as "μ is greater than or equal to 3" ($\mu \geq 3$). The mathematical construction of a statistical test uses the null hypothesis to assign a specific number (rather than a range of numbers) to the parameter μ in question. The null hypothesis establishes a single fixed value for μ, so we are working with a single distribution having a specific mean. In this case, H_0 assigns $\mu = 3$. So when H_1: $\mu < 3$ is the alternate hypothesis, we follow the commonly used convention of writing the null hypothesis simply as H_0: $\mu = 3$. ◇

Types of Tests

The null hypothesis H_0 always states that the parameter of interest *equals* a specified value. The alternate hypothesis H_1 states that the parameter is *less than, greater than,* or simply *not equal to* the same value. We categorize a statistical test as *left-tailed, right-tailed,* or *two-tailed* according to the alternate hypothesis.

> **Types of statistical tests**
>
> A statistical test is:
>
> **left-tailed** if H_1 states that the parameter is less than the value claimed in H_0
>
> **right-tailed** if H_1 states that the parameter is greater than the value claimed in H_0
>
> **two-tailed** if H_1 states that the parameter is different from (or not equal to) the value claimed in H_0

TABLE 9-1   The Null and Alternate Hypotheses for Tests of the Mean μ

Null Hypothesis	Alternate Hypotheses and Type of Test		
Claim about μ or historical value of μ H_0: $\mu = k$	You believe that μ is less than value stated in H_0. H_1: $\mu < k$ Left-tailed test	You believe that μ is more than value stated in H_0. H_1: $\mu > k$ Right-tailed test	You believe that μ is different from value stated in H_0. H_1: $\mu \neq k$ Two-tailed test

In this introduction to statistical tests, we discuss tests involving a population mean μ. However, you should keep an open mind and be aware that the methods outlined apply to testing other parameters as well (e.g., p, σ, $\mu_1 - \mu_2$, $p_1 - p_2$, and so on). Table 9-1 shows how tests of the mean μ are categorized.

Hypothesis Tests of μ, Given x Is Normal and σ Is Known

Once you have selected the null and alternate hypotheses, how do you decide which hypothesis is likely to be valid? Data from a simple random sample and the sample test statistic, together with the corresponding sampling distribution of the test statistic, will help you decide. Example 2 leads you through the decision process.

First, a quick review of Section 7.1 is in order. Recall that a population *parameter* is a numerical descriptive measurement of the entire population. Examples of population parameters are μ, p, and σ. It is important to remember that for a given population, the parameters are *fixed* values. They do not vary! The null hypothesis H_0 makes a statement about a population parameter.

A *statistic* is a numerical descriptive measurement of a sample. Examples of statistics are $\bar{x}, \hat{p}$, and s. Statistics usually *vary* from one sample to the next. The probability distribution of the statistic we are using is called a *sampling distribution*.

For hypothesis testing, we take a simple random sample and compute a *test statistic* corresponding to the parameter in H_0. Based on the sampling distribution of the statistic, we can assess how compatible the test statistic is with H_0.

In this section, we use hypothesis tests about the mean to introduce the concepts and vocabulary of hypothesis testing. In particular, let's suppose that x has a *normal distribution* with mean μ and standard deviation σ. Then, Theorem 7.1 tells us that $\bar{x}$ has a *normal distribution* with mean μ and standard deviation $\sigma/\sqrt{n}$.

Test statistic for μ, given x normal and σ known

Given that x has a *normal distribution* with known standard deviation σ, then

$$\text{test statistic} = z = \frac{\bar{x} - \mu}{\sigma/\sqrt{n}}$$

where $\bar{x}$ = mean of a simple random sample
μ = value stated in H_0
n = sample size

EXAMPLE 2

Statistical testing preview

Rosie is an aging sheep dog in Montana who gets regular check-ups from her owner, the local veterinarian. Let x be a random variable that represents Rosie's resting heart rate (in beats per minute). From past experience, the vet knows that x has a normal distribution with $\sigma = 12$. The vet checked the *Merck Veterinary Manual* and found that for dogs of this breed, $\mu = 115$ beats per minute.

Over the past six weeks, Rosie's heart rate (beats/min) measured

| 93 | 109 | 110 | 89 | 112 | 117 |

The sample mean is $\bar{x} = 105.0$. The vet is concerned that Rosie's heart rate may be slowing. Do the data indicate that this is the case?

SOLUTION:

(a) Establish the null and alternate hypotheses.

If "nothing has changed" from Rosie's earlier life, then her heart rate should be nearly average. This point of view is represented by the null hypothesis

$H_0: \mu = 115$

However, the vet is concerned about Rosie's heart rate slowing. This point of view is represented by the alternate hypothesis

$H_1: \mu < 115$

(b) Are the observed sample data compatible with the null hypothesis?

Are the six observations of Rosie's heart rate compatible with the null hypothesis $H_0: \mu = 115$? To answer this question, you need to know the *probability* of obtaining a sample mean of 105.0 or less from a population with true mean $\mu = 115$. If this probability is small, we conclude that $H_0: \mu = 115$ is not the case. Rather, $H_1: \mu < 115$ and Rosie's heart rate is slowing.

(c) How do you compute the probability in part (b)?

Well, you probably guessed it! We use the sampling distribution for $\bar{x}$ and compute $P(\bar{x} < 105.0)$. Figure 9-1 shows the $\bar{x}$ distribution and the corresponding standard normal distribution with the desired probability shaded.

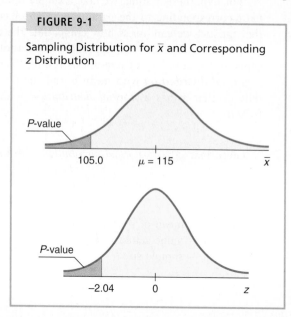

FIGURE 9-1

Sampling Distribution for $\bar{x}$ and Corresponding z Distribution

Since x has a normal distribution, $\bar{x}$ will also have a normal distribution for any sample size n and given σ (see Theorem 7.1). Note that using $\mu = 115$ from H_0, $\sigma = 12$, and $n = 6$, the sample $\bar{x} = 105.0$ converts to

$$\text{test statistic} = z = \frac{\bar{x} - \mu}{\sigma/\sqrt{n}} = \frac{105.0 - 115}{12/\sqrt{6}} \approx -2.04$$

Using the standard normal distribution table, we find that

$$P(\bar{x} < 105.0) = P(z < -2.04) = 0.0207$$

P-value

The area in the left tail that is more extreme than $\bar{x} = 105.0$ is called the *P-value* of the test. In this example, *P*-value $= 0.0207$. We will learn more about *P*-values later.

(d) What conclusion can be drawn about Rosie's average heart rate?

If $H_0\colon \mu = 115$ is in fact true, the probability of getting a sample mean of $\bar{x} \leq 105.0$ is only about 2%. Because this probability is small, we reject $H_0\colon \mu = 115$ and conclude that $H_1\colon \mu < 115$. Rosie's average heart rate seems to be slowing.

(e) Have we proved $H_0\colon \mu = 115$ to be false and $H_1\colon \mu < 115$ to be true?

No! The sample data does not prove H_0 to be false and H_1 to be true! We do say that H_0 has been "discredited" by a small *P*-value of 0.0207. Therefore, we abandon the claim $H_0\colon \mu = 115$ and adopt the claim $H_1\colon \mu < 115$. ◊

The *P*-value of a Statistical Test

Rosie the sheep dog has helped us to "sniff out" an important statistical concept.

P-value

Assuming H_0 is true, the *probability* that the test statistic will take on values as extreme as or more extreme than the observed test statistic (computed from sample data) is called the **P-value** of the test. The smaller the *P*-value computed from sample data, the stronger the evidence against H_0.

The *P*-value is sometimes called the *probability of chance*. The *P*-value can be thought of as the probability that the results of a statistical experiment are due only to chance. The lower the *P*-value, the greater the likelihood of obtaining the same results (or very similar results) in a repetition of the statistical experiment. Thus a low *P*-value is a good indication that your results are not due to random chance alone.

The *P*-value associated with the observed test statistic takes on different values depending on the alternate hypothesis and the type of test. Let's look at *P*-values and types of tests when the test involves the mean and standard normal distribution. Notice that in Example 2, part (c), we computed a *P*-value for a left-tailed test. Guided Exercise 3 asks you to compute a *P*-value for a two-tailed test.

P-values and types of tests

Let $z_{\bar{x}}$ represent the standardized sample test statistic for testing a mean μ using the standard normal distribution. That is, $z_{\bar{x}} = (\bar{x} - \mu)/(\sigma/\sqrt{n})$.

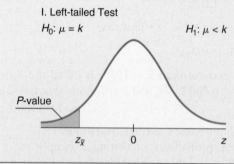

I. Left-tailed Test
$H_0: \mu = k$ $H_1: \mu < k$

P-value $= P(z < z_{\bar{x}})$
This is the probability of getting a test statistic as low as or lower than $z_{\bar{x}}$.

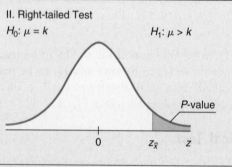

II. Right-tailed Test
$H_0: \mu = k$ $H_1: \mu > k$

P-value $= P(z > z_{\bar{x}})$
This is the probability of getting a test statistic as high as or higher than $z_{\bar{x}}$.

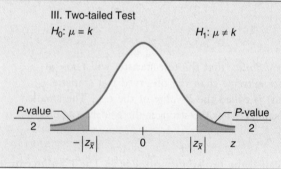

III. Two-tailed Test
$H_0: \mu = k$ $H_1: \mu \neq k$

$$\frac{\text{P-value}}{2} = P(z > |z_{\bar{x}}|); \text{ therefore,}$$

$$\textbf{P-value} = 2P(z > |z_{\bar{x}}|)$$

This is the probability of getting a test statistic either lower than $-|z_{\bar{x}}|$ or higher than $|z_{\bar{x}}|$.

Types of Errors

If we *reject the null hypothesis when it is,* in fact, *true,* we have made an error that is called a *type I error.* On the other hand, if we *accept the null hypothesis when it is,* in fact, *false,* we have made an error that is called a *type II error.* Table 9-2 indicates how these errors occur.

For tests of hypotheses to be well constructed, they must be designed to minimize possible errors of decision. (Usually, we do not know if an error has been made, and therefore, we can talk only about the probability of making an error.) Usually, for a given sample size, an attempt to reduce the probability of one type

TABLE 9-2   Type I and Type II Errors

	Our Decision	
Truth of H_0	And if we do not reject H_0	And if we reject H_0
If H_0 is true	Correct decision; no error	Type I error
If H_0 is false	Type II error	Correct decision; no error

of error results in an increase in the probability of the other type of error. In practical applications, one type of error may be more serious than another. In such a case, careful attention is given to the more serious error. If we increase the sample size, it is possible to reduce both types of errors, but increasing the sample size may not be possible.

Good statistical practice requires that we announce in advance how much evidence against H_0 will be required to reject H_0. The probability with which we are willing to risk a type I error is called the *level of significance* of a test. The level of significance is denoted by the Greek letter α (pronounced "alpha").

Level of significance

> The **level of significance** $\boldsymbol{\alpha}$ is the probability of rejecting H_0 when it is true. This is the probability of a type I error.

The *probability of making a type II error* is denoted by the Greek letter β (pronounced "beta"). Methods of hypothesis testing require us to choose α and β values to be as small as possible. In elementary statistical applications, we usually choose α first.

Power of a test

The quantity $1 - \beta$ is called the *power of the test* and represents the probability of rejecting H_0 when it is in fact false. For a given level of significance, how much power can we expect from a test? The actual value of the power is usually difficult (and sometimes impossible) to obtain, since it requires us to know the H_1 distribution. However, we can make the following general comments:

1. The power of a statistical test increases as the level of significance α increases. A test performed at the $\alpha = 0.05$ level has more power than one performed at $\alpha = 0.01$. This means that the less stringent we make our significance level α, the more likely we will reject the null hypothesis when it is false.

2. Using a larger value of α will increase the power, but it also will increase the probability of a type I error. Despite this fact, most business executives, administrators, social scientists, and scientists use *small* α values. This choice reflects the conservative nature of administrators and scientists, who are usually more willing to make an error by failing to reject a claim (i.e., H_0) than to make an error by accepting another claim (i.e., H_1) that is false. Table 9-3 on the next page summarizes the probabilities of errors associated with a statistical test.

◊ **COMMENT** Since the calculation of the probability of a type II error is treated in advanced statistics courses, we will restrict our attention to the probability of a type I error. ◊

TABLE 9-3 Probabilities Associated with a Statistical Test

Truth of H_0	Our Decision	
	And if we accept H_0 as true	And if we reject H_0 as false
H_0 is true	Correct decision, with corresponding probability $1 - \alpha$	Type I error, with corresponding probability α, called the *level of significance of the test*
H_0 is false	Type II error, with corresponding probability β	Correct decision, with corresponding probability $1 - \beta$, called the *power of the test*

GUIDED EXERCISE 2

Types of errors

Let's reconsider Guided Exercise 1, in which we were considering the manufacturing specifications for the diameter of ball bearings. The hypotheses were

H_0: $\mu = 6.0$ mm (manufacturer's specification) H_1: $\mu \neq 6.0$ mm (cause for adjusting process)

(a) Suppose the manufacturer requires a 1% level of significance. Describe a type I error, its consequence, and its probability.

A type I error is caused when sample evidence indicates that we should reject H_0 when, in fact, the average diameter of the ball bearings being produced is 6.0 mm. A type I error will cause a needless adjustment and delay of the manufacturing process. The probability of such an error is 1% because $\alpha = 0.01$.

(b) Discuss a type II error and its consequences.

A type II error occurs if the sample evidence tells us not to reject the null hypothesis H_0: $\mu = 6.0$ mm when, in fact, the average diameter of the ball bearing is either too large or too small to meet specifications. Such an error would mean that the production process would not be adjusted when it really needed to be adjusted. This could possibly result in a large production of ball bearings that do not meet specifications.

Concluding a Statistical Test

Usually, α is specified in advance before any samples are drawn so that results will not influence the choice for the level of significance. To conclude a statistical test, we compare our α value with the P-value computed using sample data and the sampling distribution.

> **PROCEDURE**
>
> **How to conclude a test using the *P*-value and level of significance α**
>
> If *P*-value $\leq \alpha$, we **reject** the null hypothesis and say the data are **statistically significant** at the level α.
>
> If *P*-value $> \alpha$, we **do not reject** the null hypothesis.

Statistical significance

In what sense are we using the word "significant"? *Webster's Dictionary* gives two interpretations of *significance*: (1) having or signifying *meaning*; or (2) important or momentous.

In statistical work, significance does not necessarily imply momentous importance. For us, "significant" at the α level has a special *meaning*. It says that at the α level of risk, the evidence (sample data) against the null hypothesis H_0 is sufficient to discredit H_0, so we adopt the alternate hypothesis H_1.

In any case, we do not claim that we have "proved" or "disproved" the null hypothesis H_0. We can say that the probability of a type I error (rejecting H_0 when it is in fact true) is α.

> **Basic components of a statistical test**
>
> A statistical test can be thought of as a package of five basic ingredients.
>
> 1. **Null hypothesis H_0, alternate hypothesis H_1, and preset level of significance α**
>   If the evidence (sample data) against H_0 is strong enough, we reject H_0 and adopt H_1. The level of significance α is the probability of rejecting H_0 when it is in fact true.
>
> 2. **Test statistic and sampling distribution**
>   These are mathematical tools used to measure compatibility of sample data and the null hypothesis.
>
> 3. ***P*-value**
>   This is the probability of obtaining a test statistic from the sampling distribution that is as extreme as or more extreme (as specified by H_1) than the sample test statistic computed from the data under the assumption that H_0 is true.
>
> 4. **Test conclusion**
>   If *P*-value $\leq \alpha$, we reject H_0 and say that the data are significant at level α. If *P*-value $> \alpha$, we do not reject H_0.
>
> 5. **Interpretation of the test results**
>   Give a simple explanation of your conclusions in the context of the application.

GUIDED EXERCISE 3

Constructing a statistical test for μ (normal distribution)

The Environmental Protection Agency has been studying Miller Creek regarding ammonia nitrogen concentration. For many years, the concentration has been 2.3 mg/l. However, a new golf course and housing developments are raising concern that the concentration may have changed because of lawn fertilizer. Any change (either an increase or a decrease) in the ammonia nitrogen concentration can affect plant and animal life in and around the creek (Reference: *EPA Report* 832-R-93-005). Let x be a random variable representing ammonia nitrogen concentration (in mg/l). Based on recent studies of Miller Creek, we may assume that x has a normal distribution with $\sigma = 0.30$. Recently, a random sample of 8 water tests from the creek gave the following x values.

 2.1   2.5   2.2   2.8   3.0   2.2   2.4   2.9

The sample mean is $\bar{x} \approx 2.51$.

Let us construct a statistical test to examine the claim that the concentration of ammonia nitrogen has changed from 2.3 mg/l. Use level of significance $\alpha = 0.01$.

(a) What is the null hypothesis? What is the alternate hypothesis? What is the level of significance α?

$\implies$ H_0: $\mu = 2.3$

H_1: $\mu \neq 2.3$

$\alpha = 0.01$

(b) Is this a right-tailed, left-tailed, or two-tailed test?

$\implies$ Since H_1: $\mu \neq 2.3$, this is a two-tailed test.

(c) What sampling distribution shall we use? Note that the value of μ is given in the null hypothesis, H_0.

$\implies$ Since the x distribution is normal and σ is known, use the standard normal distribution with

$$z = \frac{\bar{x} - \mu}{\dfrac{\sigma}{\sqrt{n}}} = \frac{\bar{x} - 2.3}{\dfrac{0.3}{\sqrt{8}}}$$

(d) What is the sample test statistic? Convert the sample mean $\bar{x}$ to a standard z value.

$\implies$ The sample of 8 measurements has mean $\bar{x} = 2.51$. Converting this measurement to z, we have

$$\text{test statistic} = z = \frac{2.51 - 2.3}{\dfrac{0.3}{\sqrt{8}}} \approx 1.98$$

(e) Draw a sketch showing the P-value area on the standard normal distribution. Find the P-value.

$\implies$ $P\text{-value} = 2P(z > 1.98) = 2(0.0239) = 0.0478$

FIGURE 9-2 P-value

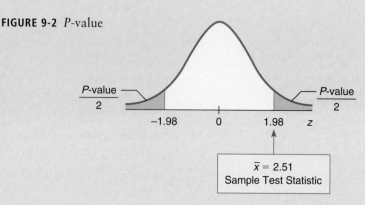

Continued

GUIDED EXERCISE 3 continued

(f) Compare the level of significance
     α and the *P*-value. What is your
     conclusion?

⟹ Since *P*-value $0.0478 \geq 0.01$, we see that

P-value $> \alpha$

We fail to reject H_0.

(g) Summarize your results in the
     context of this problem.

⟹ The sample data are not significant at the $\alpha = 1\%$ level. At this
    point in time there is not enough evidence to conclude that the
    ammonia nitrogen concentration has changed in Miller Creek.

Meaning of accepting H_0

In most statistical applications, the level of significance is specified to be
$\alpha = 0.05$ or $\alpha = 0.01$, although other values can be used. If $\alpha = 0.05$, then we say
we are using a 5% level of significance. This means that in 100 similar situations,
H_0 will be rejected 5 times, on average, when it should not have been rejected.
Using Technology at the end of this chapter shows a simulation of this phenomenon.

When we accept (or fail to reject) the null hypothesis, we should understand
that we are *not proving the null hypothesis*. We are saying only that the sample
evidence (data) is not strong enough to justify rejection of the null hypothesis. The
word *accept* sometimes has a stronger meaning in common English usage than we
are willing to give it in our application of statistics. Therefore, we often use the
expression *fail to reject H_0* instead of *accept H_0*. *Fail to reject* the null hypothesis
simply means the evidence in favor of rejection was not strong enough (see Table
9-4). Often, in the case that H_0 cannot be rejected, a confidence interval is used to
estimate the parameter in question. The confidence interval gives the statistician a
range of possible values for the parameter.

Some comments about *P*-values and level of significance α should be made. The
level of significance α should be a fixed, pre-specified value. Usually α is chosen
before any samples are drawn. The level of significance α is the probability of a
type I error. So, α is the probability of rejecting H_0 when in fact H_0 is true.

The *P*-value should *not* be interpreted as the probability of a type I error. The
level of significance (in theory) is set in advance before any samples are drawn. The
P-value cannot be set in advance, since it is determined from the random sample.
The *P*-value, together with α, should be regarded as tools used to conclude the test.
If *P*-value $\leq \alpha$, then reject H_0, and if *P*-value $> \alpha$, then do not reject H_0.

TABLE 9-4   Meaning of the Terms *Fail to Reject H_0* and *Reject H_0*

Term	Meaning
Fail to reject H_0	There is not enough evidence in the data (and the test being used) to justify a rejection of H_0. This means that we retain H_0 with the understanding that we have not proved it to be true beyond all doubt.
Reject H_0	There is enough evidence in the data (and the test employed) to justify rejection of H_0. This means that we choose the alternate hypothesis H_1 with the understanding that we have not proved H_1 to be true beyond all doubt.

In most computer applications and journal articles, only the *P*-value is given. It is understood that the person using this information will supply an appropriate level of significance α. From an historical point of view, the English statistician F. Y. Edgeworth (1845–1926) was one of the first to use the term *significant* to imply that the sample data indicated a "meaningful" difference from a previously held view.

In this book, we are using the most popular method of testing, which is called the *P-value method*. At the end of the next section, you will learn about another (equivalent) method of testing called the *critical region method*. An extensive discussion regarding the *P*-value method of testing versus the critical region method can be found in *The American Statistician,* Vol. 57, No. 3, pp. 171–178, American Statistical Association.

VIEWPOINT   *Lovers Take Heed!!!*

If you are going to whisper sweet nothings to your sweetheart, be sure to whisper in the *left* ear. Professor Sim of Sam Houston State University (Huntsville, Texas) found that emotionally loaded words had a higher recall rate when spoken into a person's left ear, not the right. Professor Sim presented his findings at the British Psychology Society European Congress. He told the Congress that his findings are consistent with the hypothesis that the brain's right hemisphere has more influence in the processing of emotional stimuli. The left ear is controlled by the right side of the brain. Sim's research involved statistical tests like the ones you will study in this chapter.

SECTION 9.1   PROBLEMS

1. Discuss each of the following topics in class or review the topics on your own. Then write a brief but complete essay in which you answer the following questions.
   (a) What is a null hypothesis H_0?
   (b) What is an alternate hypothesis H_1?
   (c) What is a type I error? a type II error?
   (d) What is the level of significance of a test? What is the probability of a type II error?

2. In a statistical test, we have a choice of a left-tailed test, right-tailed test, or two-tailed test. Is it the null hypothesis or the alternate hypothesis that determines which type of test is used? Explain your answer.

3. If we fail to reject (i.e., "accept") the null hypothesis, does this mean that we have *proved* it to be true beyond *all* doubt? Explain your answer.

4. If we reject the null hypothesis, does this mean that we have *proved* it to be false beyond *all* doubt? Explain your answer.

5. *Veterinary Science: Colts* The body weight of a healthy 3-month-old colt should be about $\mu = 60$ kg. (Source: *The Merck Veterinary Manual,* a standard reference manual used in most veterinary colleges.)
   (a) If you want to set up a statistical test to challenge the claim that $\mu = 60$ kg, what would you use for the null hypothesis H_0?

(b) In Nevada, there are many herds of wild horses. Suppose that you want to test the claim that the average weight of a wild Nevada colt (3 months old) is less than 60 kg. What would you use for the alternate hypothesis H_1?

(c) Suppose that you want to test the claim that the average weight of such a wild colt is greater than 60 kg. What would you use for the alternate hypothesis?

(d) Suppose that you want to test the claim that the average weight of such a wild colt is *different* from 60 kg. What would you use for the alternate hypothesis?

(e) For each of the tests in parts (b), (c), and (d), would the area corresponding to the *P*-value be on the left, right, or both sides of the mean? Explain your answer in each case.

6. *Marketing: Shopping Time* How much customers buy is a direct result of how much time they spend in the store. A study of average shopping time in a large national houseware store gave the following information (Source: *Why We Buy: The Science of Shopping* by P. Underhill):

   Women with female companion: 8.3 min.
   Women with male companion: 4.5 min.

   Suppose you want to set up a statistical test to challenge the claim that a woman with a female friend spends an average of 8.3 minutes shopping in such a store.
   (a) What would you use for the null and alternate hypotheses if you believe the average shopping time is less than 8.3 minutes? Is this a right-tailed, left-tailed, or two-tailed test?
   (b) What would you use for the null and alternate hypotheses if you believe the average shopping time is different from 8.3 minutes? Is this a right-tailed, left-tailed, or two-tailed test?

   Stores that sell mainly to women should figure out a way to engage the interest of men! Perhaps comfortable seats and a big TV with sports programs. Suppose such an entertainment center was installed and you now wish to challenge the claim that a woman with a male friend spends only 4.5 minutes shopping in a houseware store.
   (c) What would you use for the null and alternate hypotheses if you believe the average shopping time is more than 4.5 minutes? Is this a right-tailed, left-tailed, or two-tailed test?
   (d) What would you use for the null and alternate hypotheses if you believe the average shopping time is different from 4.5 minutes? Is this a right-tailed, left-tailed, or two-tailed test?

7. *Meteorology: Storms Weatherwise* magazine is published in association with the American Meteorological Society. Volume 46, Number 6 has a rating system to classify Nor'easter storms that frequently hit New England states and can cause much damage near the ocean coast. A *severe* storm has an average peak wave height of 16.4 feet for waves hitting the shore. Suppose that a Nor'easter is in progress at the severe storm class rating.
   (a) Let us say that we want to set up a statistical test to see if the wave action (i.e., height) is dying down or getting worse. What would be the null hypothesis regarding average wave height?
   (b) If you wanted to test the hypothesis that the storm is getting worse, what would you use for the alternate hypothesis?
   (c) If you wanted to test the hypothesis that the waves are dying down, what would you use for the alternate hypothesis?
   (d) Suppose that you do not know if the storm is getting worse or dying out. You just want to test the hypothesis that the average wave height is *different* (either up or down) from the severe storm class rating. What would you use for the alternate hypothesis?

(e) For each of the tests in parts (b), (c), and (d) would the area corresponding to the *P*-value be on the left, right, or both sides of the mean? Explain your answer in each case.

8. *Chrysler Concorde: Acceleration Consumer Reports* stated that the mean time for a Chrysler Concorde to go from 0 to 60 miles per hour was 8.7 seconds.
   (a) If you want to set up a statistical test to challenge the claim of 8.7 seconds, what would you use for the null hypothesis?
   (b) The town of Leadville, Colorado, has an elevation over 10,000 feet. Suppose that you wanted to test the claim that the average time to accelerate from 0 to 60 miles per hour is longer in Leadville (because of less oxygen). What would you use for the alternate hypothesis?
   (c) Suppose that you made an engine modification and you think the average time to accelerate from 0 to 60 miles per hour is reduced. What would you use for the alternate hypothesis?
   (d) For each of the tests in parts (b) and (c), would the *P*-value area be on the left, right, or both sides of the mean? Explain your answer in each case.

For Problems 9–14, please provide the following information.
(a) What is the level of significance? State the null and alternate hypotheses. Will you use a left-tailed, right-tailed, or two-tailed test?
(b) What sampling distribution will you use? Explain the rationale for your choice of sampling distribution. What is the value of the sample test statistic?
(c) Find (or estimate) the *P*-value. Sketch the sampling distribution and show the area corresponding to the *P*-value.
(d) Based on your answers in parts (a) to (c), will you reject or fail to reject the null hypothesis? Are the data statistically significant at level α?
(e) State your conclusion in the context of the application.

9. *Dividend Yield: Australian Bank Stocks* Let *x* be a random variable representing dividend yield of Australian bank stocks. We may assume that *x* has a normal distribution with $\sigma = 2.4\%$. A random sample of 10 Australian bank stocks gave the following yields.

5.7	4.8	6.0	4.9	4.0	3.4	6.5	7.1	5.3	6.1

   The sample mean is $\bar{x} = 5.38\%$. For the entire Australian stock market, the mean dividend yield is $\mu = 4.7\%$ (Reference: *Forbes*). Do these data indicate that the dividend yield of all Australian bank stocks is higher than 4.7%? Use $\alpha = 0.01$.

10. *Glucose Level: Horses* Gentle Ben is a Morgan horse at a Colorado dude ranch. Over the past 8 weeks, a veterinarian took the following glucose readings from this horse (in mg/100 ml).

93	88	82	105	99	110	84	89

    The sample mean is $\bar{x} \approx 93.8$. Let *x* be a random variable representing glucose readings taken from Gentle Ben. We may assume that *x* has a normal distribution, and we know from past experience that $\sigma = 12.5$. The mean glucose level for horses should be $\mu = 85$ mg/100 ml (Reference: *Merck Veterinary Manual*). Do these data indicate that Gentle Ben has an overall average glucose level higher than 85? Use $\alpha = 0.05$.

11. *Ecology: Hummingbirds* Bill Alther is a zoologist who studies Anna's hummingbird (*Calypte anna*). (Reference: *Hummingbirds*, K. Long, W. Alther.) Suppose that in a

remote part of the Grand Canyon a random sample of six of these birds was caught, weighed, and released. The weights (in gm) were

| 3.7 | 2.9 | 3.8 | 4.2 | 4.8 | 3.1 |

The sample mean is $\bar{x} = 3.75$ gm. Let x be a random variable representing weights of Anna's hummingbirds in this part of the Grand Canyon. We assume that x has a normal distribution and $\sigma = 0.70$ gm. It is known that for the population of all Anna's hummingbirds, the mean weight is $\mu = 4.55$ gm. Do the data indicate that the mean weight of these birds in this part of the Grand Canyon is less than 4.55 gm? Use $\alpha = 0.01$.

12. *Finance: P/E of Stocks* The price to earnings ratio (P/E) is an important tool in financial work. A random sample of 14 large U.S. banks (J. P. Morgan, Bank of America, and others) gave the following P/E ratios (Reference: *Forbes*).

| 24 | 16 | 22 | 14 | 12 | 13 | 17 |
| 22 | 15 | 19 | 23 | 13 | 11 | 18 |

The sample mean is $\bar{x} \approx 17.1$. Generally speaking, a low P/E ratio indicates a "value" or bargain stock. A recent copy of *The Wall Street Journal* indicated that the P/E ratio of the entire S&P 500 stock index is $\mu = 19$. Let x be a random variable representing the P/E ratio of all large U.S. bank stocks. We assume that x has a normal distribution and $\sigma = 4.5$. Do these data indicate that the P/E ratio of all U.S. bank stocks is less than 19? Use $\alpha = 0.05$.

13. *Insurance: Hail Damage* Nationally, about 11% of the total U.S. wheat crop is destroyed each year by hail (Reference: *Agricultural Statistics*, U.S. Department of Agriculture). An insurance company is studying wheat hail damage claims in Weld County, Colorado. A random sample of 16 claims in Weld County gave the following data (% wheat crop lost to hail).

| 15 | 8 | 9 | 11 | 12 | 20 | 14 | 11 |
| 7 | 10 | 24 | 20 | 13 | 9 | 12 | 5 |

The sample mean is $\bar{x} = 12.5\%$. Let x be a random variable that represents the percentage of wheat crop in Weld County lost to hail. Assume that x has a normal distribution and $\sigma = 5.0\%$. Do these data indicate that the percentage of wheat crops lost to hail in Weld County is different (either way) from the national mean of 11%? Use $\alpha = 0.01$.

14. *Medical: Red Blood Cell Volume* Total blood volume (in ml) per body weight (in kg) is important in medical research. For healthy adults, the red blood cell volume mean is about $\mu = 28$ ml/kg (Reference: *Laboratory and Diagnostic Tests*, F. Fischbach). Red blood cell volume that is too low or too high can indicate a medical problem (see reference). Suppose that Roger has had seven blood tests, and the red blood cell volumes were

| 32 | 25 | 41 | 35 | 30 | 37 | 29 |

The sample mean is $\bar{x} \approx 32.7$ ml/kg. Let x be a random variable that represents Roger's red blood cell volume. Assume that x has a normal distribution and $\sigma = 4.75$. Do the data indicate that Roger's red blood cell volume is different (either way) from $\mu = 28$ ml/kg? Use a 0.01 level of significance.

9.2
Testing the Mean μ

FOCUS POINTS

✓ Review the general procedure for testing using *P*-values.

✓ Test μ when σ is known using the normal distribution.

✓ Test μ when σ is unknown using a Student's *t* distribution.

✓ Understand the "traditional" method of testing that uses critical regions and critical values instead of *P*-values.

In this section we continue our study of testing the mean μ. The method we are using is called the *P*-value method. It was used extensively by the famous statistician R. A. Fisher and is the most popular method of testing in use today. At the end of this section, we present another method of testing called the *critical region method* (or *traditional method*). The critical region method was used extensively by the statisticians J. Neyman and E. Pearson. In recent years, the use of this method has been declining. It is important to realize that for a fixed, preset level of significance α, both methods are logically equivalent.

In Section 9.1 we discussed the vocabulary and method of hypothesis testing using *P*-values. Let's quickly review the basic process.

1. We first state a proposed value for a population parameter in the null hypothesis H_0. The alternate hypothesis H_1 states alternative values of the parameter, either $<$, $>$, or $\neq$ the value proposed in H_0. We also set the level of significance α. This is the risk we are willing to take of committing a type I error. That is, α is the probability of rejecting H_0 when it is in fact true.

2. We use a corresponding sample statistic from a simple random sample to challenge the statement made in H_0. We convert the sample statistic to a test statistic, which is the corresponding value of the appropriate sampling distribution.

3. We use the sampling distribution of the test statistic and the type of test to compute the *P*-value of this statistic. Under the assumption that the null hypothesis is true, the *P*-value is the probability of getting a sample statistic as extreme as or more extreme than the observed statistic from our random sample.

4. Finally, we conclude the test. If the *P*-value is very small, we have evidence to reject H_0 and adopt H_1. What do we mean by "very small"? We compare the *P*-value to the preset level of significance α. If the *P*-value $\leq \alpha$, then we say we have evidence to reject H_0 and adopt H_1. Otherwise, we say that the sample evidence is insufficient to reject H_0.

Knowing the sampling distribution of the sample test statistic is an essential part of the hypothesis testing process. For tests of μ, we use one of two sampling distributions for $\bar{x}$: the standard normal distribution or a Student's *t* distribution. As discussed in Chapters 7 and 8, the appropriate distribution depends upon our knowledge of the population standard deviation σ, the nature of the x distribution, and the sample size.

Part I: Testing μ When σ Is Known

In most real world situations σ is simply not known. However, in some cases a preliminary study or other information can be used to get a realistic and accurate value for σ.

> ## PROCEDURE
>
> ### How to test μ when σ is known
>
> Let x be a random variable appropriate to your application. Obtain a simple random sample (of size n) of x values from which you compute the sample mean $\bar{x}$. The value of σ is already known (perhaps from a previous study).
>
> 1. In the context of the application, state the *null and alternate hypotheses* and set the *level of significance* α.
>
> 2. If you can assume that x has a normal distribution, then any sample size n will work. If you cannot assume this, then use a sample size $n \geq 30$. Use the known σ, the sample size n, the value of $\bar{x}$ from the sample, and μ from the null hypothesis to compute the standardized sample *test statistic*.
>
> $$z = \frac{\bar{x} - \mu}{\dfrac{\sigma}{\sqrt{n}}}$$
>
> 3. Use the standard normal distribution and the type of test, one-tailed or two-tailed, to find the *P-value* corresponding to the test statistic.
>
> 4. *Conclude* the test. If P-value $\leq \alpha$, then reject H_0. If P-value $> \alpha$, then do not reject H_0.
>
> 5. *State your conclusion* in the context of the application.

In Section 9.1, we examined P-value tests for normal distributions with relatively small sample size ($n < 30$). The next example does not assume a normal distribution, but has a large sample size ($n \geq 30$).

EXAMPLE 3

Testing μ, σ known

Sunspots have been observed for many centuries. Records of sunspots from ancient Persian and Chinese astronomers go back thousands of years. Some archaeologists think sunspot activity may somehow be related to prolonged periods of drought in the southwestern United States. Let x be a random variable representing the number of sunspots observed in a four-week period. A random sample of 40 such periods from Spanish colonial times gave the following data (Reference: M. Waldmeir, *Sun Spot Activity*, International Astronomical Union Bulletin).

12.5	14.1	37.6	48.3	67.3	70.0	43.8	56.5	59.7	24.0
12.0	27.4	53.5	73.9	104.0	54.6	4.4	177.3	70.1	54.0
28.0	13.0	6.5	134.7	114.0	72.7	81.2	24.1	20.4	13.3
9.4	25.7	47.8	50.0	45.3	61.0	39.0	12.0	7.2	11.3

The sample mean is $\bar{x} \approx 47.0$. Previous studies of sunspot activity during this period indicate that $\sigma = 35$. It is thought that for thousands of years, the mean number of sunspots per four-week period was about $\mu = 41$. Sunspot activity above this level may (or may not) be linked to gradual climate change. Do the data indicate that the mean sunspot activity during the Spanish colonial period was higher than 41? Use $\alpha = 0.05$.

SOLUTION:

(a) Establish the null and alternate hypotheses.
Since we want to know whether the average sunspot activity during the Spanish colonial period was higher than the long-term average of $\mu = 41$,

$$H_0: \mu = 41 \quad \text{and} \quad H_1: \mu > 41$$

(b) Compute the test statistic from the sample data.
Since $n \geq 30$ and we know σ, we use the standard normal distribution. Using $\bar{x} = 47$ from the sample, $\sigma = 35$, $\mu = 41$ from H_0, and $n = 40$,

$$z = \frac{\bar{x} - \mu}{\sigma/\sqrt{n}} \approx \frac{47 - 41}{35/\sqrt{40}} \approx 1.08$$

(c) Find the P-value of the test statistic.
Figure 9-3 shows the P-value. Since we have a right-tailed test, the P-value is the area to the right of $z = 1.08$ shown in Figure 9-3. Using Table 5 of Appendix II, we find that

$$P\text{-value} = P(z > 1.08) \approx 0.1401.$$

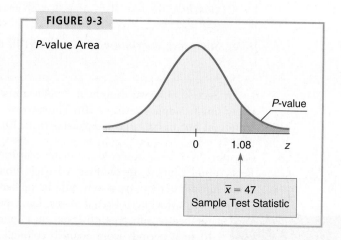

FIGURE 9-3

P-value Area

P-value

0   1.08   *z*

$\bar{x} = 47$
Sample Test Statistic

(d) Conclude the test.
Since the P-value of $0.1401 > 0.05$ for α, we do not reject H_0.

(e) Interpret the results.
At the 5% level of significance, the evidence is not sufficient to reject H_0. Based on the sample data, we do not think the average sunspot activity during the Spanish colonial period was higher than the long-term mean. ◊

Part II: Testing μ When σ Is Unknown

In many real-world situations, you have only a random sample of data values. In addition, you may have some limited information about the probability distribution of your data values. Can you still test μ under these circumstances? In most cases the answer is yes!

PROCEDURE

How to test μ when σ is unknown

Let x be a random variable appropriate to your application. Obtain a simple random sample (of size n) of x values from which you compute the sample mean $\bar{x}$ and the sample standard deviation s.

1. In the context of the application, state the *null and alternate hypotheses* and set the *level of significance α*.

2. If you can assume that x has a normal distribution or simply has a mound-shaped symmetric distribution, then any sample size n will work. If you cannot assume this, then use a sample size $n \geq 30$. Use $\bar{x}$, s, and n from the sample with μ from H_0 to compute the sample *test statistic*.

$$t = \frac{\bar{x} - \mu}{\dfrac{s}{\sqrt{n}}} \qquad \text{with degrees of freedom } d.f. = n - 1$$

3. Use the Student's t distribution and the type of test, one-tailed or two-tailed, to find (or estimate) the *P-value* corresponding to the test statistic.

4. *Conclude* the test. If P-value $\leq \alpha$, then reject H_0. If P-value $> \alpha$, then do not reject H_0.

5. *State your conclusion* in the context of the application.

Using the Student's t table to estimate P-values

In Sections 8.2 and 8.5, we used Table 6 of Appendix II, Student's t Distribution, to find critical values t_c for confidence intervals. The critical values are in the body of the table. We find P-values in the *rows* headed by "one-tail area" and "two-tail area," depending on whether we have a one-tailed or two-tailed test. If the test statistic t for the sample statistic $\bar{x}$ is negative, look up the P-value for the corresponding *positive* value of t (i.e., look up the P-value for $|t|$).

Note: In Table 6, areas are given in *one tail* beyond positive t on the right or negative t on the left, and in *two tails* beyond $\pm t$. Notice that in each column, two-tail area = 2(one-tail area). Consequently, we use *one-tail areas* as endpoints of the interval containing the P-value for *one-tailed tests*. We use *two-tail areas* as endpoints of the interval containing the P-value for *two-tailed tests*. (See Figure 9-4.)

Example 4 and Guided Exercise 4 show how to use Table 6 of Appendix II to find an interval containing the P-value corresponding to a test statistic t.

FIGURE 9-4

P-value for One-Tailed Tests and for Two-Tailed Tests

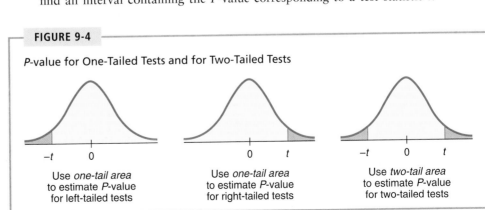

Use *one-tail area* to estimate *P*-value for left-tailed tests

Use *one-tail area* to estimate *P*-value for right-tailed tests

Use *two-tail area* to estimate *P*-value for two-tailed tests

EXAMPLE 4

Testing μ, σ unknown

The drug 6-mP (6-mercaptopurine) is used to treat leukemia. The following data represent the remission times (in weeks) for a random sample of 21 patients using 6-mP (Reference: E. A. Gehan, University of Texas Cancer Center).

10	7	32	23	22	6	16	34	32	25	11
20	19	6	17	35	6	13	9	6	10	

The sample mean is $\bar{x} \approx 17.1$ weeks with sample standard deviation $s \approx 10.0$. Let x be a random variable representing the remission time (in weeks) for all patients using 6-mP. Assume the x distribution is mound-shaped and symmetric. A previously used drug treatment had a mean remission time of $\mu = 12.5$ weeks. Do the data indicate that the mean remission time using the drug 6-mP is different (either way) from 12.5 weeks? Use $\alpha = 0.01$.

SOLUTION:

(a) Establish the null and alternate hypotheses.

Since we want to determine if the drug 6-mP provides a mean remission time that is different from that provided by a previously used drug having $\mu = 12.5$ weeks,

$$H_0: \mu = 12.5 \text{ weeks} \quad \text{and} \quad H_1: \mu \neq 12.5 \text{ weeks}$$

(b) Compute the test statistic from the sample data.

Since the x distribution is assumed to be mound-shaped and symmetric, we use the Student's t distribution. Using $\bar{x} \approx 17.1$ and $s \approx 10.0$ from the sample data, $\mu = 12.5$ from H_0, and $n = 21$,

$$t \approx \frac{\bar{x} - \mu}{s/\sqrt{n}} \approx \frac{17.1 - 12.5}{10.0/\sqrt{21}} \approx 2.108$$

(c) Find the P-value or the interval containing the P-value.

Figure 9-5 shows the P-value. Using Table 6 of Appendix II, we find an interval containing the P-value. Since this is a two-tailed test, we use entries from the row headed by *two-tail area*. Look up the t value in the row headed by $d.f. = n - 1 = 21 - 1 = 20$. The sample statistic $t = 2.108$ falls between 2.086 and 2.528. The P-value for the sample t falls between the corresponding two-tail areas 0.050 and 0.020. (See Table 9-5, Excerpt from Table 6.)

$$0.020 < P\text{-value} < 0.050$$

FIGURE 9-5

P-value

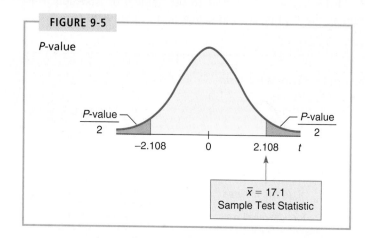

TABLE 9-5   Excerpt from Student's t Distribution (Table 6, Appendix II)

one-tail area	...	...
✓two-tail area	0.050	0.020
$d.f. = 20$	2.086	2.528
		Sample $t = 2.108$

(d) Conclude the test.

The following diagram shows the interval that contains the single P-value corresponding to the test statistic. Note that there is just one P-value corresponding to the test statistic. Table 6 of Appendix II does not give that specific value, but it does give a range that contains the specific P-value. As the diagram shows, the entire range is greater than α. This means the specific P-value is greater than α, so we cannot reject H_0.

$$
\begin{array}{ccc}
\alpha & & \\
+ & (\!\!===\!\!\!\! &)\!\!- \\
0.01 & 0.020 & 0.050
\end{array}
$$

Note: Using the raw data, computer software gives P-value ≈ 0.048. This value is in the interval we estimated. It is larger than the α value of 0.01, so we do not reject H_0.

(e) Interpret the results.

At the 1% level of significance, the evidence is not sufficient to reject H_0. Based on the sample data, we cannot say that the drug 6-mP provides a different average remission time than the previous drug. ◇

GUIDED EXERCISE 4

Testing μ, σ unknown

Archaeologists become excited when they find an anomaly in discovered artifacts. The anomaly may (or may not) indicate a new trading region or a new method of craftsmanship. Suppose the lengths of projectile points (arrowheads) at a certain archaeological site have mean length $\mu = 2.6$ cm. A random sample of 61 recently discovered projectile points in an adjacent cliff dwelling gave the following lengths (in cm) (Reference: A. Woosley and A. McIntyre, *Mimbres Mogollon Archaeology*, University of New Mexico Press).

3.1	4.1	1.8	2.1	2.2	1.3	1.7	3.0	3.7	2.3	2.6	2.2	2.8	3.0
3.2	3.3	2.4	2.8	2.8	2.9	2.9	2.2	2.4	2.1	3.4	3.1	1.6	3.1
3.5	2.3	3.1	2.7	2.1	2.0	4.8	1.9	3.9	2.0	5.2	2.2	2.6	1.9
4.0	3.0	3.4	4.2	2.4	3.5	3.1	3.7	3.7	2.9	2.6	3.6	3.9	3.5
1.9	4.0	4.0	4.6	1.9									

The sample mean is $\bar{x} \approx 2.92$ cm and the sample standard deviation is $s \approx 0.85$, where x is a random variable that represents the lengths (in cm) of all projectile points found at the adjacent cliff dwelling site. Do these data indicate that the mean length of projectile points in the adjacent cliff dwelling is longer than 2.6 cm? Use a 1% level of significance.

(a) State H_0, H_1, and α.

⟹ H_0: $\mu = 2.6$ cm; H_1: $\mu > 2.6$ cm; $\alpha = 0.01$

(b) What sampling distribution should you use? What is the t value of the sample test statistic?

⟹ Because $n \geq 30$ and σ is unknown, use the Student's t distribution with $d.f. = n - 1 = 61 - 1 = 60$. Using $\bar{x} \approx 2.92$, $s \approx 0.85$, $\mu = 2.6$ from H_0, and $n = 61$,

$$
t = \frac{\bar{x} - \mu}{\sigma/\sqrt{n}} \approx \frac{2.92 - 2.6}{0.85/\sqrt{61}} \approx 2.940
$$

Continued

GUIDED EXERCISE 4 continued

(c) When you use Table 6, Appendix II, to find an interval containing the *P*-value, do you use one-tail or two-tail areas? Why? Sketch a figure showing the *P*-value. Find an interval for the *P*-value.

⇒ This is a right-tailed test, so use a one-tail area.

FIGURE 9-6 *P*-value

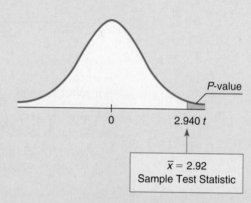

TABLE 9-6   Excerpt from Student's *t* Table

✓ one-tail area	...0.005	0.0005
two-tail area	...0.010	0.0010
d.f. = 60	...2.660	3.460

↑
Sample *t* = 2.940

Using *d.f.* = 60, we find the sample $t = 2.940$ is between the critical values 2.660 and 3.460. The sample *P*-value is then between the one-tail areas 0.005 and 0.0005.

$$0.0005 < P\text{-value} < 0.005$$

(d) Do we reject or fail to reject H_0?

⇒ Since the interval containing the *P*-value lies to the left of $\alpha = 0.01$, we reject H_0.

Note: Using the raw data, computer software gives $P\text{-value} \approx 0.0022$. This value is in our estimated range and is less than $\alpha = 0.01$, so we reject H_0.

(e) Interpret your results in the context of the application.

⇒ At the 1% level of significance, sample evidence is sufficiently strong to reject H_0 and conclude that the average projectile point length at the adjacent cliff dwelling site is longer than 2.6 cm.

TECH NOTE The TI-84Plus and TI-83Plus calculators, Excel, and Minitab all support testing of μ using the standard normal distribution. The TI-84Plus/TI-83Plus and Minitab support testing of μ using a Student's *t* distribution. All the technologies return a *P*-value for the test.

TI-84Plus/TI-83Plus You can select to enter raw data (**Data**) or summary statistics (**Stats**). Enter the value of μ_0 used in the null hypothesis H_0: $\mu = \mu_0$. Select the symbol used in the alternate hypothesis ($\neq\mu_0$, $<\mu_0$, $>\mu_0$). To test μ using the standard normal distribution, press **Stat**, select **Tests**, and use option **1:Z-Test**. The value for σ is required. To test μ using a Student's *t* distribution, use option **2:T-Test**. Using data from Example 4 regarding remission times, we have the following displays.

```
T-Test
 Inpt:Data Stats
 μ₀:12.5
 List:L1
 Freq:1
 μ:≠μ₀ <μ₀ >μ₀
 Calculate Draw
```

```
T-Test
 μ≠12.5
 t=2.105902924
 p=.0480466063
 x̄=17.0952381
 Sx=9.999523798
 n=21
```

Excel In Excel, the **ZTEST** function finds the *P*-values for a right-tailed test. (*Note:* Ignore the Excel documentation that mistakenly says ZTEST gives the *P*-value for a two-tailed test.) Use the menu choice **Paste Function** (f_x) ➤ **ZTEST**. In the dialogue box, give the cell range containing your data for the array. Use the value of μ stated in H_0 for *x*. Provide σ. Otherwise, Excel uses the sample standard deviation computed from the data.

Minitab Enter the raw data from a sample. Use the menu selections **Stat ➤ Basic Stat ➤ 1-Sample z** for tests using the standard normal distribution. For tests of μ using a Student's *t* distribution, select **1-Sample t.**

Part III: Testing μ Using Critical Regions (Traditional Method)

The most popular method of statistical testing is the *P*-value method. For that reason, the *P*-value method is emphasized in this book. Another method of testing is called the *critical region method* or *traditional method*.

Critical region method

For a fixed preset value of the level of significance α, both methods are logically equivalent. Because of this, we treat the traditional method as an "optional" topic and consider only the case of testing μ when σ is known.

Consider the null hypothesis $H_0: \mu = k$. We use information from a random sample, together with the sampling distribution for $\bar{x}$ and the level of significance α, to determine whether or not we should reject the null hypothesis. The essential question is, "How much can $\bar{x}$ vary from $\mu = k$ before we suspect that $H_0: \mu = k$ is false and reject it?"

The answer to the question regarding the relative sizes of $\bar{x}$ and μ, as stated in the null hypothesis, depends on the sampling distribution of $\bar{x}$, the alternate hypothesis H_1, and the level of significance α. If the sample test statistic $\bar{x}$ is sufficiently different from the claim about μ made in the null hypothesis, we reject the null hypothesis.

The values of $\bar{x}$ for which we reject H_0 are called the *critical region* of the $\bar{x}$ distribution. Depending on the alternate hypothesis, the critical region is located on the left side, the right side, or both sides of the $\bar{x}$ distribution. Figure 9-7 on the next page shows the relationship of the critical region to the alternate hypothesis and the level of significance α.

Notice that the total area in the critical region is preset to be the level of significance α. This is *not* the *P*-value discussed earlier! In fact, you cannot set the *P*-value in advance because it is determined from a random sample. Recall that the level of significance α should (in theory) be a fixed, preset number assigned before drawing any samples.

The most commonly used levels of significance are $\alpha = 0.05$ and $\alpha = 0.01$. Critical regions of a standard normal distribution are shown for these levels of significance in Figure 9-8 on the following page. *Critical values* are the boundaries of the critical region. Critical values designated as z_0 for the standard normal

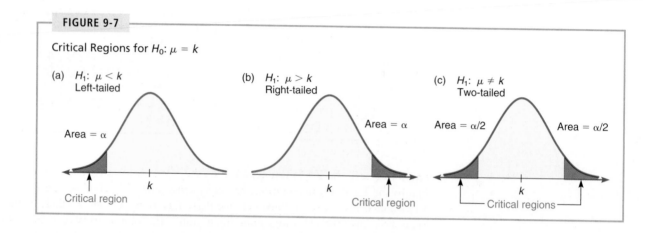

FIGURE 9-7

Critical Regions for H_0: $\mu = k$

(a) H_1: $\mu < k$
Left-tailed

(b) H_1: $\mu > k$
Right-tailed

(c) H_1: $\mu \neq k$
Two-tailed

Area = α

Critical region

Area = α

Critical region

Area = $\alpha/2$

Area = $\alpha/2$

Critical regions

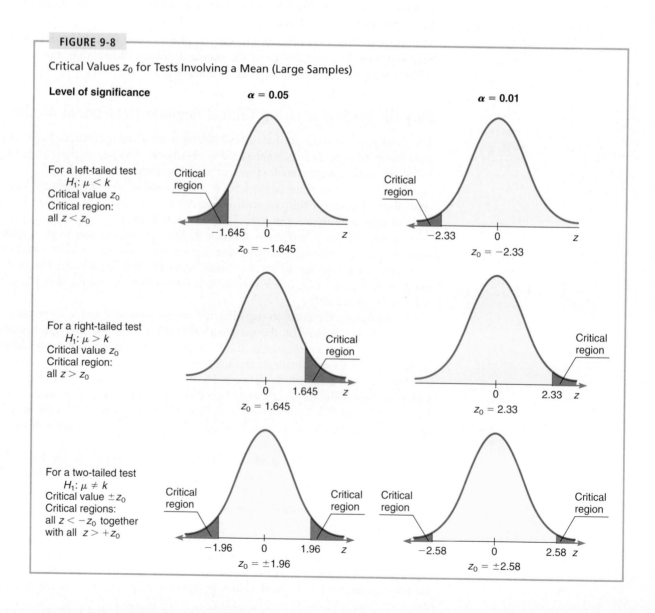

FIGURE 9-8

Critical Values z_0 for Tests Involving a Mean (Large Samples)

Level of significance

$\alpha = 0.05$

$\alpha = 0.01$

For a left-tailed test
H_1: $\mu < k$
Critical value z_0
Critical region:
all $z < z_0$

Critical region

-1.645 0 z

$z_0 = -1.645$

Critical region

-2.33 0 z

$z_0 = -2.33$

For a right-tailed test
H_1: $\mu > k$
Critical value z_0
Critical region:
all $z > z_0$

Critical region

0   1.645 z

$z_0 = 1.645$

Critical region

0   2.33 z

$z_0 = 2.33$

For a two-tailed test
H_1: $\mu \neq k$
Critical value $\pm z_0$
Critical regions:
all $z < -z_0$ together
with all $z > +z_0$

Critical region

Critical region

-1.96 0   1.96 z

$z_0 = \pm 1.96$

Critical region

Critical region

-2.58 0   2.58 z

$z_0 = \pm 2.58$

distribution are shown in Figure 9-8. For easy reference, they are also included in Table 5 of Appendix II, Areas of a Standard Normal Distribution.

The procedure for hypothesis testing using critical regions follows the same first two steps as the procedure using P-values. However, instead of finding a P-value for the sample test statistic, we check if the sample test statistic falls in the critical region. If it does, we reject H_0. Otherwise, we do not reject H_0.

PROCEDURE

How to test μ when σ is known (critical region method)

Let x be a random variable appropriate to your application. Obtain a simple random sample (of size n) of x values from which you compute the sample mean $\bar{x}$. The value of σ is already known (perhaps from a previous study).

1. In the context of the application, state the *null and alternate hypotheses* and set the *level of significance* α. We use the most popular choices, $\alpha = 0.05$ or $\alpha = 0.01$.

2. If you can assume that x has a normal distribution, then any sample size n will work. If you cannot assume this, then use a sample size $n \geq 30$. Use the known σ, the sample size n, the value of $\bar{x}$ from the sample, and μ from the null hypothesis to compute the standardized sample *test statistic*.

$$z = \frac{\bar{x} - \mu}{\frac{\sigma}{\sqrt{n}}}$$

3. Show the *critical region and critical value(s)* on a graph of the sampling distribution. The level of significance α and the alternate hypothesis determine the locations of critical regions and critical values.

4. *Conclude* the test. If the test statistic z computed in Step 2 is in the critical region, then reject H_0. If the test statistic z is not in the critical region, then do not reject H_0.

5. *State your conclusion* in the context of the application.

EXAMPLE 5

Critical region method of testing μ

Consider Example 3 regarding sunspots. Let x be a random variable representing the number of sunspots observed in a four-week period. A random sample of 40 such periods from Spanish colonial times gave the number of sunspots per period. The raw data are given in Example 3. The sample mean is $\bar{x} \approx 47.0$. Previous studies indicate that for this period, $\sigma = 35$. It is thought that for thousands of years, the mean number of sunspots per four-week period was about $\mu = 41$. Do the data indicate that the mean sunspot activity during the Spanish colonial period was higher than 41? Use $\alpha = 0.05$.

SOLUTION:

(a) Set the null and alternate hypotheses.

As in Example 3, we use H_0: $\mu = 41$ and H_1: $\mu > 41$.

(b) Compute the sample test statistic.

As in Example 3, we use the standard normal distribution with $\bar{x} = 47$, $\sigma = 35$, $\mu = 41$ from H_0, and $n = 40$.

$$z = \frac{\bar{x} - \mu}{\sigma/\sqrt{n}} \approx \frac{47 - 41}{35/\sqrt{40}} \approx 1.08$$

(c) Determine the critical region and critical value based on H_1 and $\alpha = 0.05$.

Since we have a right-tailed test, the critical region is the rightmost 5% of the standard normal distribution. According to Figure 9-8, the critical value is $z_0 = 1.645$.

(d) Conclude the test.

We conclude the test by showing the critical region, critical value, and sample test statistic $z = 1.08$ on the standard normal curve. For a right-tailed test with $\alpha = 0.05$, the critical value is $z_0 = 1.645$. Figure 9-9 shows the critical region. As we can see, the sample test statistic does not fall in the critical region. Therefore, we fail to reject H_0.

(e) Interpret the results.

At the 5% level of significance, the sample evidence is insufficient to justify rejecting H_0. It seems that the average sunspot activity during the Spanish colonial period was the same as the historical average.

(f) How do results of the critical region method compare to the results of the P-value method?

The results, as expected, are the same. In both cases we fail to reject H_0.

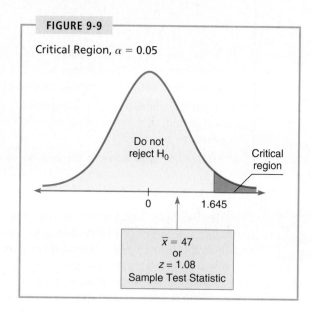

FIGURE 9-9

Critical Region, $\alpha = 0.05$

The critical region method of testing as outlined applies to tests of other parameters. As with the P-value method, you need to know the sampling distribution of the sample test statistic. Critical values for distributions are usually found in tables rather than in computer software output. For example, Table 6 of Appendix II provides critical values for Student t distributions.

PROCEDURE

How to conclude tests using the critical region method

Compare the sample test statistic to the critical value determined by α and the nature of the test: right-tailed, left-tailed, or two-tailed.

1. For a right-tailed test,
   - if sample test statistic ≥ critical value, reject H_0
   - if sample test statistic < critical value, fail to reject H_0

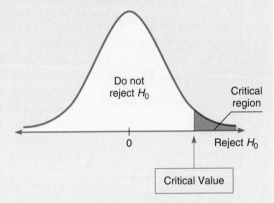

2. For a left-tailed test,
   - if sample test statistic ≤ critical value, reject H_0
   - if sample test statistic > critical value, fail to reject H_0

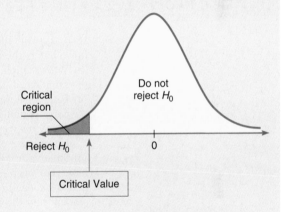

3. For a two-tailed test,
   - if sample test statistic lies beyond critical values, reject H_0
   - if sample test statistic lies between critical values, fail to reject H_0

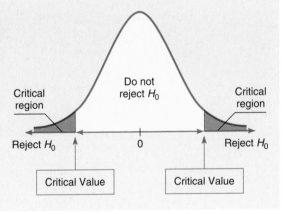

VIEWPOINT   *Predator or Prey?*

Consider animals such as the arctic fox, gray wolf, desert lion, and South American jaguar. Each animal is a predator. What are the total sleep time (hours per day), maximum life span (years), and overall danger index from other animals? Now consider prey such as rabbits, deer, wild horses, and the Brazilian tapir (a wild pig). Is there a statistically significant difference in average sleep time, life span, and danger index? What about other variables such as the ratio of brain weight to body weight or the sleep exposure index (sleeping in a well-protected den or out in the open)? How did prehistoric humans fit into this picture? Scientists have collected a lot of data, and a great deal of statistical work has been done regarding such questions. For more information, see the web site <http://lib.stat.cmu.edu/> and follow the links to Datasets and then Sleep.

SECTION 9.2   PROBLEMS

Please provide the following information for Problems 1–16.
(a) What is the level of significance? State the null and alternate hypotheses.
(b) What sampling distribution will you use? Explain the rationale for your choice of sampling distribution. What is the value of the sample test statistic?
(c) Find (or estimate) the P-value. Sketch the sampling distribution and show the area corresponding to the P-value.
(d) Based on your answers in parts (a) to (c), will you reject or fail to reject the null hypothesis? Are the data statistically significant at level α?
(e) State your conclusion in the context of the application.

Note: For degrees of freedom d.f. not given in the Student's t table, use the closest d.f. that is *smaller*. In some situations, this choice of d.f. may increase the P-value by a small amount and therefore produce a slightly more "conservative" answer.

1. *Meteorology: Storms Weatherwise* is a magazine published by the American Meteorological Society. One issue gives a rating system used to classify Nor'easter storms that frequently hit New England and can cause much damage near the ocean. A severe storm has an average peak wave height of $\mu = 16.4$ feet for waves hitting the shore. Suppose that a Nor'easter is in progress at the severe storm class rating. Peak wave heights are usually measured from land (using binoculars) off fixed cement piers. Suppose that a reading of 36 waves showed an average wave height of $\bar{x} = 17.3$ feet. Previous studies of severe storms indicate that $\sigma = 3.5$ feet. Does this information suggest that the storm is (perhaps temporarily) increasing above the severe rating? Use $\alpha = 0.01$.

2. *Ford Taurus: Assembly Time* Let x be a random variable that represents assembly time for the Ford Taurus. *The Wall Street Journal* reported that the average assembly time is $\mu = 38$ hours. A modification to the assembly procedure has been made. Experience with this new method indicates that $\sigma = 1.2$ hours. It is thought that the average assembly time may be reduced by this modification. A random sample of 47 new Ford Taurus automobiles coming off the assembly line showed the average assembly time of the new method to be $\bar{x} = 37.5$ hours. Does this indicate that the average assembly time has been reduced? Use $\alpha = 0.01$.

3. *E-mails: Priority Lists* Message mania! A professional employee in a large corporation receives an average of $\mu = 41.7$ e-mails per day. Most of these e-mails are from other employees in the company. Because of the large number of e-mails, employees find themselves distracted and are unable to concentrate when they return to their tasks (Reference: *The Wall Street Journal*). In an effort to reduce distraction caused by such interruptions, one company established a priority list that all employees were to use before sending an e-mail. One month after the new priority list was put into place, a random sample of 45 employees showed that they were receiving an average of $\bar{x} = 36.2$ e-mails per day. The computer server through which the e-mails are routed showed that $\sigma = 18.5$. Has the new policy had any effect? Use a 5% level of significance to test the claim that there has been a change (either way) in the average number of e-mails received per day per employee.

4. *Medical: Blood Plasma* Let x be a random variable that represents the pH of arterial plasma (i.e., acidity of the blood). For healthy adults the mean of the x distribution is $\mu = 7.4$ (Reference: *Merck Manual*, a commonly used reference in medical schools and nursing programs). A new drug for arthritis has been developed. However, it is thought that this drug may change blood pH. A random sample of 31 patients with arthritis took the drug for 3 months. Blood tests showed that $\bar{x} = 8.1$ with sample standard deviation $s = 1.9$. Use a 5% level of significance to test the claim that the drug has changed (either way) the mean pH level of the blood.

5. *Wildlife: Coyotes* A random sample of 46 adult coyotes in a region of northern Minnesota showed the average age to be $\bar{x} = 2.05$ years with sample standard deviation $s = 0.82$ years (based on information from the book *Coyotes: Biology, Behavior and Management* by M. Bekoff, Academic Press). However, it is thought that the overall population mean age of coyotes is $\mu = 1.75$. Does the sample data indicate that coyotes in this region of northern Minnesota tend to live longer than the average of 1.75 years? Use $\alpha = 0.01$.

6. *Fishing: Trout* Pyramid Lake is on the Paiute Indian Reservation in Nevada. The lake is famous for cutthroat trout. Suppose a friend tells you that the average length of trout caught in Pyramid Lake is $\mu = 19$ inches. However, the Creel Survey (published by the Pyramid Lake Paiute Tribe Fisheries Association) reported that of a random sample of 51 fish caught, the mean length was $\bar{x} = 18.5$ inches with estimated standard deviation $s = 3.2$ inches. Do these data indicate that the average length of a trout caught in Pyramid Lake is less than $\mu = 19$ inches? Use $\alpha = 0.05$.

7. *Investing: Stocks* Socially conscious investors screen out stocks of alcohol and tobacco makers, firms with poor environmental records, and companies with poor labor practices. Some examples of "good," socially conscious companies are Johnson and Johnson, Dell Computers, Bank of America, and Home Depot. The question is, are such stocks overpriced? One measure of value is the P/E, or price to earnings ratio. High P/E ratios may indicate a stock is overpriced. For the S&P Stock Index of all major stocks, the mean P/E ratio is $\mu = 19.4$. A random sample of 36 "socially conscious" stocks gave a P/E ratio sample mean of $\bar{x} = 17.9$ with sample standard deviation $s = 5.2$ (Reference: *Morningstar*, a financial analysis company in Chicago). Does this indicate that the mean P/E ratio of all socially conscious stocks is different (either way) from the mean P/E ratio of the S&P Stock Index? Use $\alpha = 0.05$.

8. *Agriculture: Ground Water* Unfortunately, arsenic occurs naturally in some ground water (Reference: *Union Carbide Technical Report K/UR-1*). A mean arsenic level of $\mu = 8.0$ parts per billion (ppb) is considered safe for agricultural use. A well in Texas is used to water cotton crops. This well is tested on a regular basis for arsenic. A random sample of 37 tests gave a sample mean of $\bar{x} = 7.2$ ppb arsenic with

$s = 1.9$ ppb. Does this information indicate that the mean level of arsenic in this well is less than 8 ppb? Use $\alpha = 0.01$.

9. *Medical: Red Blood Cell Count* Let x be a random variable that represents red blood cell count (RBC) in millions of cells per cubic millimeter of whole blood. Then x has a distribution that is approximately normal. For the population of healthy female adults, the mean of the x distribution is about 4.8 (based on information from *Diagnostic Tests with Nursing Implications,* Springhouse Corporation). Suppose that a female patient has taken six laboratory blood tests over the past several months and that the RBC count data sent to the patient's doctor are

4.9	4.2	4.5	4.1	4.4	4.3

   i. Use a calculator with sample mean and sample standard deviation keys to verify that $\bar{x} = 4.40$ and $s \approx 0.28$.
   ii. Do the given data indicate that the population mean RBC count for this patient is lower than 4.8? Use $\alpha = 0.05$.

10. *Medical: Hemoglobin Count* Let x be a random variable that represents hemoglobin count (HC) in grams per 100 milliliters of whole blood. Then x has a distribution that is approximately normal, with population mean of about 14 for healthy adult women (see reference in Problem 9). Suppose that a female patient has taken 10 laboratory blood tests during the past year. The HC data sent to the patient's doctor are

15	18	16	19	14	12	14	17	15	11

   i. Use a calculator with sample mean and sample standard deviation keys to verify that $\bar{x} = 15.1$ and $s \approx 2.51$.
   ii. Does this information indicate that the population average HC for this patient is higher than 14? Use $\alpha = 0.01$.

11. *Ski Patrol: Avalanches* Snow avalanches can be a real problem for travelers in the western United States and Canada. A very common type of avalanche is called the slab avalanche. These have been studied extensively by David McClung, a professor of civil engineering at the University of British Columbia. Slab avalanches studied in Canada had an average thickness of $\mu = 67$ cm (Source: *Avalanche Handbook,* by D. McClung and P. Schaerer). The ski patrol at Vail, Colorado, is studying slab avalanches in their region. A random sample of avalanches in spring gave the following thicknesses (in cm):

59	51	76	38	65	54	49	62
68	55	64	67	63	74	65	79

   i. Use a calculator with mean and standard deviation keys to verify that $\bar{x} \approx 61.8$ cm and $s \approx 10.6$ cm.
   ii. Assume the slab thickness has an approximately normal distribution. Use a 1% level of significance to test the claim that the mean slab thickness in the Vail region is different from that in Canada.

12. *Longevity: Honolulu* USA Today reported that the state with the longest mean life span is Hawaii, where the population mean life span is 77 years. A random sample of 20 obituary notices in the *Honolulu Advertizer* gave the following information about life span (in years) of Honolulu residents:

72	68	81	93	56	19	78	94	83	84
77	69	85	97	75	71	86	47	66	27

i. Use a calculator with mean and standard deviation keys to verify that $\bar{x} = 71.4$ years and $s \approx 20.65$ years.

ii. Assuming that life span in Honolulu is approximately normally distributed, does this information indicate that the population mean life span for Honolulu residents is less than 77 years? Use a 5% level of significance.

13. *Veterinary Science: Lions* The heart rate of a healthy lion is approximately normally distributed with mean $\mu = 40$ beats per minute. (Source: *The Merck Veterinary Manual*, a reference used in most veterinary colleges.) A heart rate that is too slow or too fast can indicate a health problem. A veterinarian has removed an abscessed tooth from a young, healthy zoo lion. As the animal slowly starts to come out of the anesthetic, its heart rate (in beats per minute) is taken and recorded for half an hour:

$$30 \qquad 37 \qquad 43 \qquad 38 \qquad 35 \qquad 36$$

i. Use a calculator with mean and standard deviation keys to verify that $\bar{x} = 36.5$ and $s \approx 4.2$.

ii. Use a 5% level of significance to test the claim that the population average heart rate of the lion is different (either way) from 40 beats per minute.

14. *Shopping Time: Housewares* How much customers buy is a direct result of how much time they spend in the store. The mean shopping time for a woman accompanied by children in national houseware stores is 7.3 minutes. (Source: *Why We Buy: The Science of Shopping* by P. Underhill.) A retail research team is studying shopping habits in the Cherry Creek Mall (Denver). A random sample of women shoppers with children in a large houseware store gave the following shopping times (in minutes):

$$7.7 \qquad 8.1 \qquad 8.2 \qquad 9.0 \qquad 5.8 \qquad 9.3 \qquad 8.4 \qquad 6.9 \qquad 12.1 \qquad 9.4$$
$$8.1 \qquad 6.2 \qquad 7.3 \qquad 7.9 \qquad 8.2 \qquad 8.5 \qquad 7.2 \qquad 6.3 \qquad 9.1 \qquad 8.8$$

i. Use a calculator with mean and standard deviation keys to verify that $\bar{x} \approx 8.1$ min and $s \approx 1.4$ min.

ii. Assume shopping time follows an approximately normal distribution. Use a 5% level of significance to test the claim that the average shopping time for women with children in the Cherry Creek Mall is higher than the national average for this type of store.

15. *Fishing: Atlantic Salmon* Homser Lake, Oregon, has an Atlantic salmon catch and release program that has been very successful. The average fisherman's catch has been $\mu = 8.8$ Atlantic salmon per day. (Source: *National Symposium on Catch and Release Fishing*, Humboldt State University.) Suppose that a new quota system restricting the number of fishermen has been put into effect this season. A random sample of fishermen gave the following catches per day:

$$12 \qquad 6 \qquad 11 \qquad 12 \qquad 5 \qquad 0 \qquad 2$$
$$7 \qquad 8 \qquad 7 \qquad 6 \qquad 3 \qquad 12 \qquad 12$$

i. Use a calculator with mean and sample standard deviation keys to verify that $\bar{x} \approx 7.36$ and sample standard deviation $s \approx 4.03$.

ii. Assuming that the catch per day has an approximately normal distribution, use a 5% level of significance to test the claim that the population average catch per day is now different from 8.8.

16. *Archaeology: Tree Rings* Tree-ring dating from archaeological excavation sites is used in conjunction with other chronologic evidence to estimate occupation dates

of prehistoric Indian ruins in the southwestern United States. It is thought that Burnt Mesa Pueblo was occupied around 1300 A.D. (based on evidence from potsherds and stone tools). The following data give tree-ring dates (A.D.) from adjacent archaeological sites (*Bandelier Archaeological Excavation Project: Summer 1990 Excavations at Burnt Mesa Pueblo*, edited by T. Kohler, Washington State University Department of Anthropology, 1992):

| 1189 | 1267 | 1268 | 1275 | 1275 |
| 1271 | 1272 | 1316 | 1317 | 1230 |

i. Use a calculator with mean and standard deviation keys to verify that $\bar{x} = 1268$ and $s \approx 37.29$ years.

ii. Assuming that the tree-ring dates in this excavation area follow a distribution that is approximately normal, does this information indicate that the population mean of tree-ring dates in the area is different from (either higher or lower than) that in 1300 A.D.? Use a 1% level of significance.

17. *General: One-Tailed versus Two-Tailed Tests*

(a) For the same data and null hypothesis, is the *P*-value of a one-tailed test (right or left) larger or smaller than that of a two-tailed test? Explain.

(b) For the same data, null hypothesis, and level of significance, is it possible that a one-tailed test results in the conclusion to reject H_0 while a two-tailed test results in the conclusion to fail to reject H_0? Explain.

(c) For the same data, null hypothesis, and level of significance, if the conclusion is to reject H_0 based on a two-tailed test, do you also reject H_0 based on a one-tailed test? Explain.

(d) If a report states that certain data were used to reject a given hypothesis, would it be a good idea to know what type of test (one-tailed or two-tailed) was used? Explain.

18. *General: Comparing Hypothesis Tests to U.S. Courtroom System* Compare similarities of statistical testing with legal methods used in a U.S. court setting. Then discuss the following topics in class or consider the topics on your own. Please write a brief but complete essay in which you answer the following questions.

(a) In a court setting, the person charged with a crime is initially considered to be innocent. The claim of innocence is maintained until the jury returns with a decision. Explain how the claim of innocence could be taken to be the null hypothesis. Do we assume that the null hypothesis is true throughout the testing procedure? What would the alternate hypothesis be in a court setting?

(b) The court claims that a person is innocent if the evidence against the person is not adequate to find him or her guilty. This does not mean, however, that the court has necessarily *proved* the person to be innocent. It simply means that the evidence against the person was not adequate for the jury to find him or her guilty. How does this situation compare with a statistical test for which the conclusion is "do not reject" (i.e., accept) the null hypothesis? What would be a type II error in this context?

(c) If the evidence against a person is adequate for the jury to find him or her guilty, then the court claims that the person is guilty. Remember, this does not mean that the court has necessarily *proved* the person to be guilty. It simply means that the evidence against the person was strong enough to find him or her guilty. How does this situation compare with a statistical test for which the conclusion is to "reject" the null hypothesis? What would be a type I error in this context?

(d) In a court setting, the final decision as to whether the person charged is innocent or guilty is made at the end of the trial, usually by a jury of impartial people. In hypothesis testing, the final decision to reject or not reject the null hypothesis is made at the end of the test by using information or data from an (impartial) random sample. Discuss these similarities between statistical hypothesis testing and a court setting.

(e) We hope that you are able to use this discussion to increase your understanding of statistical testing by comparing it with something that is a well-known part of our American way of life. However, all analogies have weak points. It is important not to take the analogy between statistical hypothesis testing and legal court methods too far. For instance, the judge does not set a level of significance and tell the jury to determine a verdict that is wrong only 5% or 1% of the time. Discuss some of these weak points in the analogy between the court setting and hypothesis testing.

 19. *Expand Your Knowledge: Confidence Intervals and Two-Tailed Hypothesis Tests* Is there a relationship between confidence intervals and two-tailed hypothesis tests? Let c be the level of confidence used to construct a confidence interval from sample data. Let α be the level of significance for a two-tailed hypothesis test. The following statement applies to hypothesis tests of the mean.

> For a two-tailed hypothesis test with level of significance α and null hypothesis H_0: $\mu = k$, we *reject* H_0 whenever k falls *outside* the $c = 1 - \alpha$ confidence interval for μ based on the sample data. When k falls within the $c = 1 - \alpha$ confidence interval, we do not reject H_0.

(A corresponding relationship between confidence intervals and two-tailed hypothesis tests also is valid for other parameters such as p, $\mu_1 - \mu_2$, or $p_1 - p_2$, which we will study in Sections 9.3 and 9.5.) Whenever the value of k given in the null hypothesis falls *outside* the $c = 1 - \alpha$ confidence interval for the parameter, we *reject* H_0. For example, consider a two-tailed hypothesis test with $\alpha = 0.01$ and

$$H_0: \mu = 20 \qquad H_1: \mu \neq 20$$

A random sample of size 36 has a sample mean $\bar{x} = 22$ from a population with standard deviation $\sigma = 4$.

(a) What is the value of $c = 1 - \alpha$? Using the methods of Chapter 8, construct a $1 - \alpha$ confidence interval for μ from the sample data. What is the value of μ given in the null hypothesis (i.e., what is k)? Is this value in the confidence interval? Do we reject or fail to reject H_0 based on this information?

(b) Using methods of Chapter 9, find the P-value for the hypothesis test. Do we reject or fail to reject H_0? Compare your result to that of part (a).

 20. *Confidence Intervals and Two-Tailed Hypothesis Tests* Change the null hypothesis of Problem 19 to H_0: $\mu = 21$. Repeat parts (a) and (b).

21. *Critical Region Method: Standard Normal* Solve Problem 1 using the critical region method of testing (i.e., traditional method). Compare your conclusion with the conclusion obtained by using the P-value method. Are they the same?

22. *Critical Region Method: Standard Normal* Solve Problem 2 using the critical region method of testing. Compare your conclusion with the conclusion obtained by using the P-value method. Are they the same?

23. *Critical Region Method: Standard Normal* Solve Problem 3 using the critical region method of testing. Compare your conclusion with the conclusion obtained by using the P-value method. Are they the same?

24. *Critical Region Method: Student's t* Table 6 of Appendix II gives critical values for the Student's t distribution. Use an appropriate *d.f.* as the row header. For a *right-tailed* test, the column header is the value of α found in the *one-tail area* row. For a *left-tailed* test, the column header is the value of α found in the *one-tail area* row, but you must change the sign of the critical value t to $-t$. For a *two-tailed* test, the column header is the value of α from the *two-tail area* row. The critical values are the $\pm t$ values shown. Solve Problem 4 using the critical region method of testing. Compare your conclusion with the conclusion obtained by using the *P*-value method. Are they the same?

25. *Critical Region Method: Student's t* Solve Problem 5 using the critical region method of testing. *Hint:* See Problem 24. Compare your conclusion with the conclusion obtained by using the *P*-value method. Are they the same?

26. *Critical Region Method: Student's t* Solve Problem 6 using the critical region method of testing. *Hint:* See Problem 24. Compare your conclusion with the conclusion obtained by using the *P*-value method. Are they the same?

9.3
Testing a Proportion *p*

FOCUS POINTS

✓ Identify the components needed for testing a proportion.

✓ Compute the sample test statistic.

✓ Find the *P*-value and conclude the test.

Tests for a single proportion

Many situations arise that call for tests of proportions or percentages rather than means. For instance, a college registrar may want to determine if the proportion of students wanting 3-week intensive courses has increased.

How can we make such a test? In this section, we will study tests involving proportions (i.e., percentages or proportions). Such tests are similar to those in Sections 9.1 and 9.2. The main difference is that we are working with a distribution of proportions.

Throughout this section, we will assume that the situations we are dealing with satisfy the conditions underlying the binomial distribution. In particular, we will let r be a binomial random variable. This means that r is the number of successes out of n independent binomial trials (for the definition of binomial trial, see Section 5.2). We will use $\hat{p} = r/n$ as our estimate for p, the population probability of success on each trial. The letter q again represents the population probability of failure on each trial, and so $q = 1 - p$. We also assume that the samples are large (i.e., $np > 5$ and $nq > 5$).

For large samples, the distribution of $\hat{p} = r/n$ values is well approximated by a *normal curve* with mean μ and standard deviation σ as follows:

$$\mu = p$$

$$\sigma = \sqrt{\frac{pq}{n}}$$

The null and alternate hypotheses for tests of proportions are

Left-Tailed Test	Right-Tailed Test	Two-Tailed Test
$H_0: p = k$	$H_0: p = k$	$H_0: p = k$
$H_1: p < k$	$H_1: p > k$	$H_1: p \neq k$

depending on what is asked for in the problem. Notice that since p is a probability, the value k must be between 0 and 1.

Sample test statistic

For tests of proportions, we need to convert the sample test statistic $\hat{p}$ to a z value. Then we can find a P-value appropriate for the test. The $\hat{p}$ distribution is approximately normal with mean p and standard deviation $\sqrt{pq/n}$. Therefore, the conversion of $\hat{p}$ to z follows the formula

$$z = \frac{\hat{p} - p}{\sqrt{\dfrac{pq}{n}}}$$

where $\hat{p} = r/n$ is the sample test statistic

   n = number of trials

   p = proportion specified in H_0

   $q = 1 - p$

Using this mathematical information about the sampling distribution for $\hat{p}$, the basic procedure is similar to tests you have conducted before.

> **PROCEDURE**
>
> **How to test a proportion p**
>
> Consider a binomial experiment with n trials, where p represents the population probability of success and $q = 1 - p$ represents the population probability of failure. Let r be a random variable that represents the number of successes out of the n binomial trials.
>
> 1. In the context of the application, state the *null and alternate hypotheses* and set the *level of significance* α.
> 2. The number of trials n should be sufficiently large so that both $np > 5$ and $nq > 5$ (use p from the null hypothesis). In this case, $\hat{p} = r/n$ can be approximated by the normal distribution using the standardized sample *test statistic*
>
> $$z = \frac{\hat{p} - p}{\sqrt{\dfrac{pq}{n}}}$$
>
>   where p is the value specified in H_0 and $q = 1 - p$.
> 3. Use the standard normal distribution and the type of test, one-tailed or two-tailed, to find the *P-value* corresponding to the test statistic.
> 4. *Conclude* the test. If P-value $\leq \alpha$, then reject H_0. If P-value $> \alpha$, then do not reject H_0.
> 5. *State your conclusion* in the context of the application.

EXAMPLE 6

Testing p

A team of eye surgeons has developed a new technique for a risky eye operation to restore the sight of people blinded from a certain disease. Under the old method, it is known that only 30% of the patients who undergo this operation recover their eyesight.

Suppose that surgeons in various hospitals have performed a total of 225 operations using the new method and that 88 have been successful (the patients fully recovered their sight). Can we justify the claim that the new method is better than the old one? (Use a 1% level of significance.)

SOLUTION:

(a) Establish H_0 and H_1 and note the level of significance.

The level of significance is $\alpha = 0.01$. Let p be the probability that a patient fully recovers his or her eyesight. The null hypothesis is that p is still 0.30, even for the new method. The alternate hypothesis is that the new method has improved the chances of a patient recovering his or her eyesight. Therefore,

$$H_0: p = 0.30 \quad \text{and} \quad H_1: p > 0.30$$

(b) Find the sample test statistic $\hat{p}$ and convert it to a z value, if appropriate.

Using p from H_0, we note that $np = 225(0.3) = 67.5$ is greater than 5 and $nq = 225(0.7) = 157.5$ is also greater than 5, so we can use the normal distribution for the sample statistic $\hat{p}$.

$$\hat{p} = \frac{r}{n} = \frac{88}{225} \approx 0.39$$

The z value corresponding to $\hat{p}$ is

$$z = \frac{\hat{p} - p}{\sqrt{\dfrac{pq}{n}}} \approx \frac{0.39 - 0.30}{\sqrt{\dfrac{0.30(0.70)}{225}}} \approx 2.95$$

In the formula, the value for p is from the null hypothesis. H_0 specifies that $p = 0.30$, so $q = 1 - 0.30 = 0.70$.

(c) Find the P-value of the test statistic.

Figure 9-10 shows the P-value. Since we have a right-tailed test, the P-value is the area to the right of $z = 2.95$ shown in Figure 9-10. Using the normal distribution (Table 5 of Appendix II), we find that P-value $= P(z > 2.95) \approx 0.0016$.

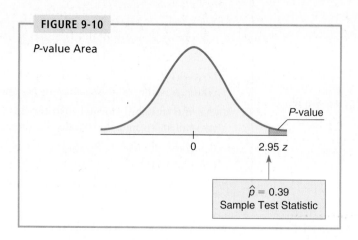

FIGURE 9-10

P-value Area

P-value

0   2.95 *z*

$\hat{p} = 0.39$
Sample Test Statistic

(d) Conclude the test.

Since the P-value of $0.0016 \leq 0.01$ for α, we reject H_0.

(e) Interpret the results.

At the 1% level of significance, the evidence shows that the population probability of success for the new surgery technique is higher than that of the old technique.   ◇

GUIDED EXERCISE 5

Testing p

A botanist has produced a new variety of hybrid wheat that is better able to withstand drought than other varieties. The botanist knows that for the parent plants, the proportion of seeds germinating is 80%. The proportion of seeds germinating for the hybrid variety is unknown, but the botanist claims that it is 80%. To test this claim, 400 seeds from the hybrid plant are tested, and it is found that 312 germinated. Use a 5% level of significance to test the claim that the proportion germinating for the hybrid is 80%.

(a) Let p be the proportion of hybrid seeds that will germinate. Notice that we have no prior knowledge about the germination proportion for the hybrid plant. State H_0 and H_1. What is the required level of significance?

⟹ H_0: $p = 0.80$; H_1: $p \neq 0.80$; $\alpha = 0.05$

(b) Calculate the sample test statistic $\hat{p}$. Using the value of p in H_0, are both $np > 5$ and $nq > 5$? Can we use the normal distribution for $\hat{p}$?

⟹   The number of trials is $n = 400$, and the number of successes is $r = 312$. Thus,

$$\hat{p} = \frac{r}{n} = \frac{312}{400} = 0.78$$

From H_0, $p = 0.80$ and $q = 1 - p = 0.20$.

$np = 400(0.8) = 320 > 5$

$nq = 400(0.2) = 80 > 5$

So, we can use the normal distribution for $\hat{p}$.

(c) Next, we convert the sample test statistic $\hat{p} = 0.78$ to a z value. Based on our choice for H_0, what value should we use for p in our formula? Since $q = 1 - p$, what value should we use for q? Using these values for p and q, convert $\hat{p}$ to a z value.

⟹   According to H_0, $p = 0.80$. Then $q = 1 - p = 0.20$. Using these values in the following formula gives

$$z = \frac{\hat{p} - p}{\sqrt{\dfrac{pq}{n}}} = \frac{0.78 - 0.80}{\sqrt{\dfrac{0.80(0.20)}{400}}} = -1.00$$

● **CALCULATOR NOTE**   If you evaluate the denominator separately, be sure to carry at least 4 digits after the decimal.

(d) Is the test right-tailed, left-tailed, or two-tailed? Find the P-value of the sample test statistic and sketch a standard normal curve showing the P-value.

⟹   For a two-tailed test, using the normal distribution (Table 5 of Appendix II), we find that

P-value $= 2P(z < -1.00) = 2(0.1587) = 0.3174$

Continued

GUIDED EXERCISE 5 continued

FIGURE 9-11 *P-value*

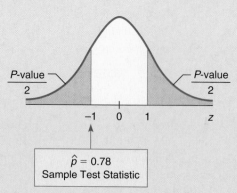

$\dfrac{P\text{-value}}{2}$ $\dfrac{P\text{-value}}{2}$

$\hat{p} = 0.78$
Sample Test Statistic

(e) Do we reject or fail to reject H_0? State your conclusion in the context of the application.   ⇨   Since

P-value of $0.3174 > 0.05$ for α

we fail to reject H_0. At the 5% level of significance, there is insufficient evidence to say that the botanist is wrong.

Critical region method

Since the $\hat{p}$ sampling distribution is approximately normal, we use Table 5, "Areas of a Standard Normal Distribution," in Appendix II to find critical values.

EXAMPLE 7

Critical region method for testing p

Let's solve Guided Exercise 5 using the critical region approach. In that problem, 312 of 400 seeds from a hybrid wheat variety germinated. For the parent plants, the proportion of germinating seeds was 80%. Use a 5% level of significance to test the claim that the population proportion of germinating seeds from the hybrid wheat is different from that of the parent plants.

SOLUTION:

(a) As in Guided Exercise 5, we have $\alpha = 0.05$, H_0: $p = 0.80$, and H_1: $p \neq 0.80$. The next step is to find the sample statistic $\hat{p}$ and the corresponding test statistic z. This was done in Guided Exercise 5, where we found that $\hat{p} = 0.78$ with corresponding $z = -1.00$.

(b) Now we find the critical value z_0 for a two-tailed test using $\alpha = 0.05$. This means that we want the total area 0.05 divided between two tails, one to the right of z_0 and one to the left of $-z_0$. As shown in Figure 9-8 of Section 9.2, the critical value(s) are ± 1.96. (See also Table 5, part (c), of Appendix II for critical values of the z distribution.)

(c) Figure 9-12 shows the critical regions and the location of the sample test statistic.

(d) Finally, we conclude the test and compare the results to Guided Exercise 5. Since the sample test statistic does not fall in the critical region, we fail to reject H_0 and conclude that at the 5% level of significance, the evidence is not strong

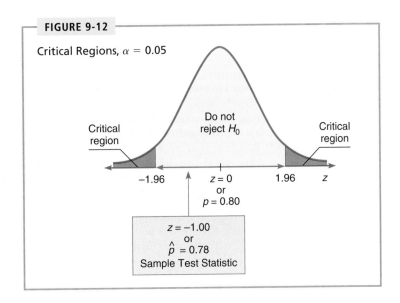

FIGURE 9-12

Critical Regions, $\alpha = 0.05$

enough to reject the botanist's claim. This result, as expected, is consistent with the conclusion obtained by using the *P*-value method.   ◇

TECH NOTE   The TI-84Plus/TI-83Plus calculators and Minitab support tests of proportions. The output for both technologies includes the sample proportion $\hat{p}$ and the *P*-value of $\hat{p}$. Minitab also includes the z value corresponding to $\hat{p}$.

TI-84Plus/TI-83Plus Press **STAT**, select **TESTS**, and use option **5:1-PropZTest**. The value of p_0 is from the null hypothesis H_0: $p = p_0$. The number of successes is the value for x.

Minitab Menu selections: **Stat ➤ Basic Statistics ➤ 1 Proportion.** Under options, set the test proportion as the value in H_0. Choose to use the normal distribution.

VIEWP◉INT

Who Did What?

Art, music, literature, and science share a common need to classify things: Who painted that picture? Who composed that music? Who wrote that document? Who should get that patent? In statistics, such questions are called *classification problems.* For example, the *Federalist Papers* were published anonymously in 1787–1788 by Alexander Hamilton, John Jay, and James Madison. But who wrote what? That question is addressed by F. Mosteller (Harvard University) and D. Wallace (University of Chicago) in the book *Statistics: A Guide to the Unknown,* edited by J. M. Tanur. Other scholars have studied authorship regarding Plato's *Republic* and Plato's *Dialogues,* including the *Symposium.* For more information on this topic, see the source in Problems 9 and 10 of this exercise set.

SECTION 9.3   PROBLEMS

Please provide the following information for Problems 1–17.

(a) What is the level of significance? State the null and alternate hypotheses.

(b) What sampling distribution will you use? Do you think that the sample size is sufficiently large? Explain. What is the value of the sample test statistic?

(c) Find the P-value of the test statistic. Sketch the sampling distribution and show the area corresponding to the P-value.

(d) Based on your answers in parts (a) to (c), will you reject or fail to reject the null hypothesis? Are the data statistically significant at level α?

(e) State your conclusion in the context of the application.

1. *Focus Problem: Benford's Law* Please read the focus problem at the beginning of this chapter. Recall that Benford's Law claims that numbers chosen from very large data files tend to have "1" as the first nonzero digit disproportionately often. In fact, research has shown that if you randomly draw a number from a very large data file, the probability of getting a number with "1" as the leading digit is about 0.301 (see the reference in this chapter's Focus Problem).

   Now suppose you are an auditor for a very large corporation. The revenue report involves millions of numbers in a large computer file. Let us say you took a random sample of $n = 215$ numerical entries from the file and $r = 46$ of the entries had a first nonzero digit of 1. Let p represent the population proportion of all numbers in the corporate file that have a first nonzero digit of 1.

   i. Test the claim that p is less than 0.301. Use $\alpha = 0.01$.

   ii. If p is in fact less than 0.301, would it make you suspect that there are not enough numbers in the data file with leading 1's? Could this indicate that the books have been "cooked" by "pumping up" or inflating the numbers? Comment from the viewpoint of a stockholder. Comment from the perspective of the Federal Bureau of Investigation as it looks for money laundering in the form of false profits.

   iii. Comment on the following statement: If we reject the null hypothesis at level of significance α, we have not *proved* H_0 to be false. We can say that the probability is α that we made a mistake in rejecting H_0. Based on the outcome of the test, would you recommend further investigation before accusing the company of fraud?

2. *Focus Problem: Benford's Law* Again suppose you are the auditor for a very large corporation. The revenue file contains millions of numbers in a large computer data bank (see Problem 1). You draw a random sample of $n = 228$ numbers from this file and $r = 92$ have a first nonzero digit of 1. Let p represent the population proportion of all numbers in the computer file that have a leading digit of 1.

   i. Test the claim that p is more than 0.301. Use $\alpha = 0.01$.

   ii. If p is in fact larger than 0.301, it would seem there are too many numbers in the file with leading 1's. Could this indicate that the books have been "cooked" by artificially lowering numbers in the file? Comment from the point of view of the Internal Revenue Service. Comment from the perspective of the Federal Bureau of Investigation as it looks for "profit skimming" by unscrupulous employees.

   iii. Comment on the following statement: If we reject the null hypothesis at level of significance α, we have not *proved* H_0 to be false. We can say that the probability is α that we made a mistake in rejecting H_0. Based on the outcome of the test, would you recommend further investigation before accusing the company of fraud?

3. *Sociology: Crime Rate* Is the national crime rate really going down? Some sociologists say yes! They say that the reason for the decline in crime rates in the 1980s and 1990s is demographics. It seems that the population is aging, and older people commit fewer crimes. According to the FBI and the Justice Department, 70% of all arrests are of males aged 15 to 34 years. (Source: *True Odds*, by J. Walsh, Merritt Publishing.) Suppose that you are a sociologist in Rock Springs, Wyoming, and a random sample of police files showed that of 32 arrests last month, 24 were of males aged 15 to 34 years. Use a 1% level of significance to test the claim that the population proportion of such arrests in Rock Springs is different from 70%.

4. *College Athletics: Graduation Rate* Women athletes at the University of Colorado, Boulder, have a long-term graduation rate of 67% (Source: *The Chronicle of Higher Education*). Over the past several years, a random sample of 38 women athletes at the school showed that 21 eventually graduated. Does this indicate that the population proportion of women athletes who graduate from the University of Colorado, Boulder, is now less than 67%? Use a 5% level of significance.

5. *Highway Accidents: DUI* The U.S. Department of Transportation, National Highway Traffic Safety Administration, reported that 77% of all fatally injured automobile drivers were intoxicated. A random sample of 27 records of automobile driver fatalities in Kit Carson County, Colorado, showed that 15 involved an intoxicated driver. Do these data indicate that the population proportion of driver fatalities related to alcohol is less than 77% in Kit Carson County? Use $\alpha = 0.01$.

6. *Preference: Color* What is your favorite color? A large survey of countries including the United States, China, Russia, France, Turkey, Kenya, and others indicated that most people prefer the color blue. In fact, about 24% of the population claim blue as their favorite color. (Reference: Study by J. Bunge and A. Freeman-Gallant, Statistics Center, Cornell University.) Suppose a random sample of $n = 56$ college students were surveyed and $r = 12$ of them said that blue is their favorite color. Does this information imply that the color preference of all college students is different (either way) from that of the general population? Use $\alpha = 0.05$.

7. *Wildlife: Wolves* The following is based on information from *The Wolf in the Southwest: The Making of an Endangered Species*, by David E. Brown (University of Arizona Press). Before 1918, the proportion of female wolves in the general population of all southwestern wolves was about 50%. However, after 1918, southwestern cattle ranchers began a widespread effort to destroy wolves. In a recent sample of 34 wolves, there were only 10 females. One theory is that male wolves tend to return sooner than females to their old territory, where their predecessors were exterminated. Do these data indicate that the population proportion of female wolves is now less than 50% in the region? Use $\alpha = 0.01$.

8. *Fishing: Northern Pike* Athabasca Fishing Lodge is located on Lake Athabasca in northern Canada. In one of its recent brochures, the lodge advertises that 75% of its guests catch northern pike over 20 pounds. Suppose that last summer 64 out of a random sample of 83 guests did, in fact, catch northern pike weighing over 20 pounds. Does this indicate that the population proportion of guests who catch pike over 20 pounds is different from 75% (either higher or lower)? Use $\alpha = 0.05$.

9. *Plato's* Republic: *Syllable Patterns* Prose rhythm is characterized as the occurrence of five-syllable sequences in long passages of text. This characterization may be used to assess the similarity among passages of text and sometimes the identity of authors. The following information is based on an article by D. Wishart and S. V. Leach appearing in *Computer Studies of the Humanities and Verbal Behavior* (Vol. 3, pp. 90–99). Syllables were categorized as long or short. On analyzing Plato's *Republic,* Wishart and Leach found that about 26.1% of the five-syllable sequences are of the type in which two are short and three are long. Suppose that Greek archaeologists have found an ancient manuscript dating back to Plato's time (about 427–347 B.C.). A random sample of 317 five-syllable sequences from the newly discovered manuscript showed that 61 are of the type two short and three long. Do the data indicate that the population proportion of this type of five-syllable sequence is different (either way) from the text of Plato's *Republic?* Use $\alpha = 0.01$.

10. *Plato's* Dialogues: *Prose Rhythm* Symposium is part of a larger work referred to as Plato's *Dialogues.* Wishart and Leach (see source in Problem 9) found that about 21.4% of five-syllable sequences in *Symposium* are of the type in which four are short and one is long. Suppose that an antiquities store in Athens has a very old manuscript that the owner claims is part of Plato's *Dialogues.* A random sample of 493 five-syllable sequences from this manuscript showed that 136 were of the type four short and one long. Do the data indicate that the population proportion of this type of five-syllable sequence is higher than that found in Plato's *Symposium?* Use $\alpha = 0.01$.

11. *Consumers: Product Loyalty* USA Today reported that about 47% of the general consumer population in the United States is loyal to the automobile manufacturer of their choice. Suppose that Chevrolet did a study of a random sample of 1006 Chevrolet owners and found that 490 said that they would buy another Chevrolet. Does this indicate that the population proportion of consumers loyal to Chevrolet is more than 47%? Use $\alpha = 0.01$.

12. *Supermarket: Prices* Harper's Index reported that 80% of all supermarket prices end in the digit 9 or 5. Suppose that you check a random sample of 115 items in a supermarket and find that 88 have prices that end in 9 or 5. Does this indicate that less than 80% of the prices in the store end in the digits 9 or 5? Use $\alpha = 0.05$.

13. *Medical: Hypertension* This problem is based on information taken from *The Merck Manual* (a reference manual used in most medical and nursing schools). Hypertension is defined as a blood pressure over 140 mm Hg systolic and/or over 90 mm Hg diastolic. Hypertension, if not corrected, can cause long-term health problems. In the college-age population (18–24 years), about 9.2% have hypertension. Suppose that a blood donor program is occurring in a college dormitory this week (final exams week). Before each student gives blood, the nurse takes a blood pressure reading. Of 196 donors, it was found that 29 have hypertension. Do these data indicate that the population proportion of students with hypertension during final exams week is higher than 9.2%? Use a 5% level of significance.

14. *Medical: Hypertension* Diltiazem is a commonly prescribed drug for hypertension (see source in Problem 13). However, diltiazem causes headaches in about 12% of patients using the drug. It is hypothesized that regular exercise might help reduce the headaches. If a random sample of 209 patients using diltiazem exercised regularly and only 16 had headaches, would this indicate a reduction in the population proportion of patients having headaches? Use a 1% level of significance.

15. *Myers-Briggs: Extroverts* Are most student government leaders extroverts? According to Myers-Briggs estimates, about 82% of college student government leaders are extroverts. (Source: *Myers-Briggs Type Indicator Atlas of Type Tables.*) Suppose that a Myers-Briggs personality preference test was given to a random sample of 73 student government leaders attending a large national leadership conference and that 56 were found to be extroverts. Does this indicate that the population proportion of extroverts among college student government leaders is different (either way) from 82%? Use $\alpha = 0.01$.

16. *American Attitudes: NAFTA* Generally speaking, would you say that America benefits from being a member of NAFTA (North American Free Trade Agreement)? Nationally, about 28% of the U.S. population believes NAFTA benefits America (Source: *American Attitudes* by S. Mitchell, Sociology Department, Ithaca College). A random sample of 48 interstate truck drivers showed that 19 believe NAFTA benefits America. Does this indicate that the population proportion of interstate truckers who believe NAFTA benefits America is higher than 28%? Use a 5% level of significance.

17. *Careers: College Professors* If you could start your career all over again, would you still choose to be a college professor? About 76% of all U.S. college professors responded yes to this question (Source: *The Chronicle of Higher Education*). A random sample of 59 college professors in Colorado showed that 47 claim they would choose college teaching again. Does this indicate that the proportion of professors in Colorado who would choose the career again is different from the national rate of 76%? Use a 1% level of significance.

18. *Critical Region Method: Testing Proportions* Solve Problem 3 using the critical region method of testing. Since the sampling distribution of $\hat{p}$ is the normal distribution, you can use critical values from the standard normal distribution as shown in Figure 9-8 or part (c) of Table 5, Appendix II. Compare your conclusions with the conclusions obtained by using the *P*-value method. Are they the same?

19. *Critical Region Method: Testing Proportions* Solve Problem 5 using the critical region method of testing. *Hint:* See Problem 18. Compare your conclusions with the conclusions obtained by using the *P*-value method. Are they the same?

20. *Critical Region Method: Testing Proportions* Solve Problem 11 using the critical region method of testing. *Hint:* See Problem 18. Compare your conclusions with the conclusions obtained by using the *P*-value method. Are they the same?

9.4
Tests Involving Paired Differences (Dependent Samples)

FOCUS POINTS

✓ Identify paired data and dependent samples.

✓ Explain the advantages of paired data tests.

✓ Compute differences and the sample test statistic.

✓ Estimate the *P*-value and conclude the test.

Creating data pairs

Many statistical applications use *paired data* samples to draw conclusions about the difference between two population means. Data *pairs* occur very naturally in "before and after" situations, where the *same* object or item is measured both before and after a treatment. Applied problems in social science, natural science, and business administration frequently involve a study of matching pairs. Psychological studies of identical twins; biological studies of plant growth on plots of land matched for soil type, moisture, and sun; and business studies on sales of matched inventories are examples of paired data studies.

When working with paired data, it is very important to have a definite and uniform method of creating data pairs that clearly utilizes a natural matching of characteristics. The next example and exercise demonstrate this feature.

EXAMPLE 8

Paired data

A shoe manufacturer claims that among the general population of adults in the United States, the average length of the left foot is longer than that of the right. To compare the average length of the left foot with that of the right, we can take a random sample of 15 U.S. adults and measure the length of the left foot and then the length of the right foot for each person in the sample. Is there a natural way of pairing the measurements? How many pairs will we have?

SOLUTION: In this case, we can pair each left foot measurement with the same person's right foot measurement. The person serves as the "matching link" between the two distributions. We will have 15 pairs of measurements.   ◊

GUIDED EXERCISE 6

Paired data

A psychologist has developed a series of exercises called the Instrumental Enrichment (IE) Program, which he claims is useful in overcoming cognitive deficiencies in mentally retarded children. To test the program, extensive statistical tests are being conducted. In one experiment, a random sample of 10-year-old students with IQ scores below 80 was selected. An IQ test was given to these students before they spent 2 years in an IE Program, and an IQ test was given to the same students after the program.

(a) On what basis can you pair the IQ scores?

⟹ Take the "before and after" IQ scores of each individual student.

(b) If there were 20 students in the sample, how many data pairs would you have?

⟹ Twenty data pairs. Note that there would be 40 IQ scores, but only 20 pairs.

◊ **COMMENT** To compare two populations, we cannot always employ paired data tests, but when we can, what are the advantages? Using matched or paired data often can reduce the danger of introducing extraneous or uncontrollable factors into our sample measurements because the matched or paired data have essentially the *same* characteristics except for the *one* characteristic that is being measured. Furthermore, it can be shown that pairing data has the theoretical effect of reducing measurement variability (i.e., variance), which increases the accuracy of statistical conclusions. ◇

When we wish to compare the means of two samples, the first item to be determined is whether or not there is a natural pairing between the data in the two samples. Again, data pairs are created from "before and after" situations, or from matching data by using studies of the same object, or by a process of taking measurements of closely matched items.

Testing the differences d

When testing *paired* data, we take the difference *d* of the data pairs *first* and look at the mean difference $\overline{d}$. Then we use a test on $\overline{d}$. Theorem 9.1 provides the basis for our work with paired data.

◇ **THEOREM 9.1** Consider a random sample of *n* data pairs. Suppose the differences *d* between the first and second members of each data pair are (approximately) normally distributed with population mean μ_d. Then the *t* values

$$t = \frac{\overline{d} - \mu_d}{s_d/\sqrt{n}}$$

where $\overline{d}$ is the sample mean of the *d* values, *n* is the number of data pairs, and

$$s_d = \sqrt{\frac{\Sigma(d - \overline{d})^2}{n - 1}}$$

is the sample standard deviation of the *d* values, follow a Student's *t* distribution with degrees of freedom *d.f.* = *n* − 1. ◇

Hypotheses for testing the mean of paired differences

When testing the mean of the differences of paired data values, the null hypothesis is that there is no difference among the pairs. That is, the mean of the differences μ_d is zero.

H_0: $\mu_d = 0$

The alternate hypothesis depends on the problem and can be

H_1: $\mu_d < 0$	H_1: $\mu_d > 0$	H_1: $\mu_d \neq 0$
(left-tailed)	(right-tailed)	(two-tailed)

Sample test statistic

For paired difference tests, we make our decision regarding H_0 according to the evidence of the sample mean $\overline{d}$ of the differences of measurements. By Theorem 9.1, we convert the sample test statistic $\overline{d}$ to a *t* value using the formula

$$t = \frac{\overline{d} - \mu_d}{(s_d/\sqrt{n})} \text{ with } d.f. = n - 1$$

where s_d = sample standard deviation of the differences *d*

n = number of data pairs

μ_d = 0 as specified in H_0

To find the *P*-value (or an interval containing the *P*-value) corresponding to the test statistic *t* computed from $\overline{d}$, we use the Student's *t* distribution table (Table 6, Appendix II). Recall from Section 9.2 that we find the test statistic *t* (or, if *t* is negative, $|t|$) in the row headed by *d.f.* = *n* − 1, where *n* is the number of data pairs. The *P*-value for the test statistic is the column entry in the *one-tail area* row for one-tailed tests (right or left). For two-tailed tests, the *P*-value is the column entry in the *two-tail area* row. Usually the exact test statistic *t* is not in the table, so we obtain an interval that contains the *P*-value by using adjacent entries in the table. Table 9-7 gives the basic structure for using the Student's *t* distribution table to find the *P*-value or an interval containing the *P*-value.

TABLE 9-7   Using Student's *t* Distribution Table for *P*-values

For one-tailed tests:	one-tail area	*P*-value	*P*-value
For two-tailed tests:	two-tail area	*P*-value	*P*-value
Use row header	*d.f.* = *n* − 1	↑ Find *t* value	

With the preceding information, you are now ready to test paired differences. First let's summarize the procedure.

PROCEDURE

How to test paired differences using the Student's *t* distribution

Obtain a simple random sample of *n* matched data pairs *A*, *B*. Let *d* be a random variable representing the difference between the values in a matched data pair. Compute the sample mean $\overline{d}$ and sample standard deviation s_d.

1. Use the *null hypothesis* of *no difference*, H_0: $\mu_d = 0$. In the context of the application, choose the *alternate hypothesis* to be H_1: $\mu_d > 0$, or $\mu_d < 0$, or $\mu_d \neq 0$. Set the *level of significance* α.

2. If you can assume that *d* has a normal distribution or simply has a mound-shaped symmetric distribution, then any sample size *n* will work. If you cannot assume this, then use a sample size $n \geq 30$. Use $\overline{d}$, s_d, the sample size *n*, and $\mu_d = 0$ from the null hypothesis to compute the sample *test statistic*

$$t = \frac{\overline{d} - 0}{\dfrac{s_d}{\sqrt{n}}} = \frac{\overline{d}\sqrt{n}}{s_d}$$

with degrees of freedom *d.f.* = *n* − 1.

3. Use the Student's *t* distribution and the type of test, one-tailed or two-tailed, to find (or estimate) the *P-value* corresponding to the test statistic.

4. *Conclude* the test. If *P*-value $\leq \alpha$, then reject H_0. If *P*-value $> \alpha$, then do not reject H_0.

5. *State your conclusion* in the context of the application.

EXAMPLE 9

Paired difference test

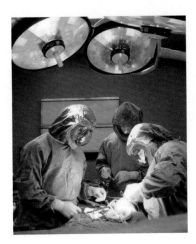

A team of heart surgeons at Saint Ann's Hospital knows that many patients who undergo corrective heart surgery have a dangerous buildup of anxiety before their scheduled operations. The staff psychiatrist at the hospital has started a new counseling program intended to reduce this anxiety. A test of anxiety is given to patients who know they must undergo heart surgery. Then each patient participates in a series of counseling sessions with the staff psychiatrist. At the end of the counseling sessions, each patient is retested to determine anxiety level. Table 9-8 indicates the results for a random sample of nine patients. Higher scores mean higher levels of anxiety.

From the given data, can we conclude that the counseling sessions reduce anxiety? Use a 0.01 level of significance.

SOLUTION: Before we answer this question, let us notice two important points: (1) we have a *random sample* of nine patients, and (2) we have a *pair* of measurements taken on the same patient before and after counseling sessions. In our problem, the sample size is $n = 9$ pairs (i.e., patients), and the d values are found in the fourth column of Table 9-8.

(a) Note the level of significance and set the hypotheses.

In the problem statement, $\alpha = 0.01$. We want to test the claim that the counseling sessions reduce anxiety. This means that the anxiety level before counseling is expected to be higher than the anxiety level after counseling. In symbols, $d = B - A$ should tend to be positive, and the population mean of differences μ_d also should be positive. Therefore, we have

$$H_0: \mu_d = 0 \quad \text{and} \quad H_1: \mu_d > 0$$

(b) Find the sample test statistic $\bar{d}$ and convert it to a corresponding test statistic t. First we need to compute $\bar{d}$ and s_d. Using formulas or a calculator and the d values shown in Table 9-8, we find that

$$\bar{d} \approx 33.33 \quad \text{and} \quad s_d \approx 22.92$$

Using these values together with $n = 9$ and $\mu_d = 0$, we have

$$t = \frac{\bar{d} - 0}{(s_d/\sqrt{n})} \approx \frac{33.33}{22.92/\sqrt{9}} \approx 4.363$$

TABLE 9-8

Patient	B Score before Counseling	A Score after Counseling	$d = B - A$ Difference
Jan	121	76	45
Tom	93	93	0
Diane	105	64	41
Barbara	115	117	−2
Mike	130	82	48
Bill	98	80	18
Frank	142	79	63
Carol	118	67	51
Alice	125	89	36

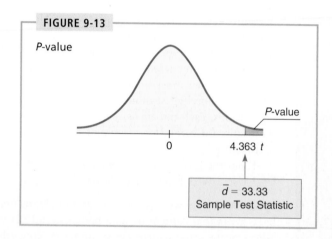

FIGURE 9-13

(c) Find the *P*-value for the test statistic and sketch the *P*-value on the *t* distribution. Since we have a right-tailed test, the *P*-value is the area to the right of $t = 4.363$, as shown in Figure 9-13. In Table 6 of Appendix II, we find an interval containing the *P*-value. Use entries from the row headed by $d.f. = n - 1 = 9 - 1 = 8$. The test statistic $t = 4.636$ falls between 3.355 and 5.041. The *P*-value for the sample *t* falls between the corresponding one-tail areas 0.005 and 0.0005. (See Table 9-9, Excerpt from Table 6, Appendix II.)

$$0.0005 < P\text{-value} < 0.005$$

TABLE 9-9   Excerpt from Student's *t* Distribution Table (Table 6, Appendix II)

✓ one-tail area	0.005	0.0005
two-tail area	0.010	0.0010
d.f. = 8	3.355	5.041

↑
Sample *t* = 4.363

(d) Conclude the test.

——(▬▬▬▬)——_α—|—
0.0005   0.005   0.01

Since the interval containing the *P*-value lies to the left of $\alpha = 0.01$, we reject H_0. *Note:* Using the raw data and software, the *P*-value ≈ 0.0012.

(e) Interpret the results.
    At the 1% level of significance, we conclude that the counseling sessions reduce the average anxiety level of patients about to undergo corrective heart surgery.   ◊

The problem we have just solved is a paired difference problem of the "before and after" type. The next guided exercise demonstrates a paired difference problem of the "matched pair" type.

GUIDED EXERCISE 7

Paired difference test

Do educational toys make a difference in the age at which a child learns to read? To study this question, researchers designed an experiment in which one group of preschool children spent 2 hours each day (for 6 months) in a room well supplied with "educational" toys such as alphabet blocks, puzzles, ABC readers, coloring books featuring letters, and so forth. A control group of children spent 2 hours a day for 6 months in a "noneducational" toy room. It was anticipated that IQ differences and home environment might be uncontrollable factors unless identical twins could be used. Therefore, six pairs of identical twins of preschool age were randomly selected. From each pair, one member was randomly selected to participate in the experimental (i.e., educational toy room) group and the other in the control (i.e., noneducational toy room) group. For each twin the data item recorded is the age in months when the child began reading at the primary level (Table 9-10).

TABLE 9-10   Reading Ages for Identical Twins in Months

Twin Pair	Experimental Group B = Reading Age	Control Group A = Reading Age	Difference $d = B - A$
1	58	60	
2	61	64	
3	53	52	
4	60	65	
5	71	75	
6	62	63	

(a) Compute the entries in the $d = B - A$ column of Table 9-10. Using formulas for the mean and sample standard deviation or a calculator with mean and sample standard deviation keys, compute $\bar{d}$ and s_d.

Pair	$d = B - A$
1	−2
2	−3
3	1
4	−5
5	−4
6	−1

$\bar{d} \approx -2.33$
$s_d \approx 2.16$

(b) What is the null hypothesis?

$H_0: \mu_d = 0$

(c) To test the claim that the experimental group learned to read at a *different age* (either younger or older), what should the alternate hypothesis be?

$H_1: \mu_d \neq 0$

(d) Convert the sample test statistic $\bar{d}$ to a t value. Find the degrees of freedom.

Using $\mu_d = 0$ from H_0, $\bar{d} = -2.33$, $n = 6$, and $s_d = 2.16$, we get

$$t = \frac{\bar{d} - \mu_d}{(s_d/\sqrt{n})} \approx \frac{-2.33 - 0}{(2.16/\sqrt{6})} \approx -2.642$$

$$d.f. = n - 1 = 6 - 1 = 5$$

Continued

GUIDED EXERCISE 7 continued

(e) When we use Table 6 of Appendix II to find an interval containing the *P*-value, do we use one-tail or two-tail areas? Why? Sketch a figure showing the *P*-value. Find an interval containing the *P*-value.

 This is a two-tailed test, so we use two-tail areas.

FIGURE 9-14 *P*-value

TABLE 9-11 **Excerpt from Student's *t* Table**

one-tail area	0.025	0.010
✓ two-tail area	0.050	0.020
d.f. = 5	2.571	3.365

                 ↑
             Sample *t* = 2.642

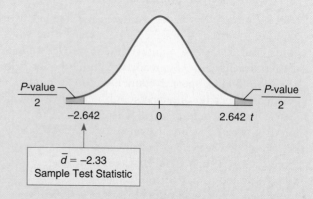

The sample *t* is between 2.571 and 3.365.

$0.020 < P\text{-value} < 0.050$

(f) Using $\alpha = 0.05$, do we reject or fail to reject H_0? Interpret your results in the context of this application.

Since the interval containing the *P*-value has values that are all smaller than 0.05, we reject H_0.

$$\underline{\quad\underset{0.020}{(}\underline{\qquad\qquad}\overset{\alpha}{\underset{0.050}{)}}\quad}$$

At the 5% level of significance, the experiment indicates that educational toys make a difference in the age at which a child learns to read.

Note: Using the raw data and software, *P*-value ≈ 0.0457.

◇ **COMMENT:** The test for paired differences used in this section is called a *parametric test.* Such tests usually require certain assumptions, such as a normal distribution or a large sample size. In Section 12.1 you will find the sign test for matched pairs. This is a *non-parametric test.* Such tests are useful when you cannot make assumptions about the population distribution. The disadvantage of non-parametric tests is that they are less sensitive in that they tend to accept the null hypothesis more often than they should. Which type of test should you use? If it is reasonable to assume the underlying population is normal (or at least mound-shaped and symmetric), or if you have a large sample size, then use the more powerful parametric test described in this section. ◇

TECH NOTE Both Excel and Minitab support paired difference tests directly. On the TI-84Plus and TI-83Plus calculators, construct a column of differences and then do a t test on the data in that column. For each technology, be sure to relate the alternate hypothesis to the "before and after" assignments. All the displays show the results for the data of Guided Exercise 7.

TI-84Plus/TI-83Plus Enter the "before" data in column L1 and the "after" data in column L2. Highlight L3, type L1 − L2 and press enter. The column L3 now contains the $B - A$ differences. To conduct the test, press **STAT**, select **TESTS**, and use option **2:T-Test.** Note that the letter x is used in place of d.

```
L1      L2      L3      3
58      60      -2
61      64      -3
53      52      1
60      65      -5
71      75      -4
62      63      -1

L3(7)  =
```

```
T-Test
 μ≠0
 t=-2.645751311
 p=.0456591238
 x̄=-2.333333333
 Sx=2.160246899
 n=6
```

Excel Enter the data in two columns. Use the menu choices **Tools ➤ Data Analysis ➤ t-Test: Paired Two-Sample for Means.** Fill in the dialogue box with the hypothesized mean difference of 0. Set alpha.

B	C	D
t-Test: Paired Two Sample for Means		
	Variable 1	Variable 2
Mean	60.83333	63.16666667
Variance	34.96667	55.76666667
Observations	6	6
Pearson Correlation	0.974519	
Hypothesized Mean Difference	0	
df	5	
t Stat	−2.64575	
P(T<=t) one-tail	0.02283	
t Critical one-tail	2.015049	
P(T<=t) two-tail	0.045659	
t Critical two-tail	2.570578	

P-value points to the P(T<=t) two-tail row.

Minitab Enter the data in two columns. Use the menu selection **Stat ➤ Basic Statistics ➤ Paired *t*.** Under Options, set the null and alternate hypotheses.

```
Paired T-Test and Confidence Interval
Paired T for B − A
                N       Mean      St Dev SE    Mean
 B              6       60.83     5.91         2.41
 A              6       63.17     7.47         3.05
 Difference     6       −2.333    2.160        0.882
 95% CI for mean difference: (−4.601, −0.066)
 T-Test of mean difference = 0 (vs not = 0):
        T-Value = −2.65 P-Value = 0.046
```

EXAMPLE 10

Critical region method

Let's revisit Guided Exercise 7 regarding educational toys and reading age and conclude the test using the critical region method. Recall that there were six pairs of twins. One twin of each set was given educational toys and the other was not. The difference d in reading ages for each pair of twins was measured, and $\alpha = 0.05$.

SOLUTION: From Guided Exercise 7, we have

$$H_0: \mu_d = 0 \qquad \text{and} \qquad H_1: \mu_d \neq 0$$

We computed the sample test statistic $\bar{d} \approx -2.33$ with corresponding $t \approx -2.642$.

(a) Find the critical values for $\alpha = 0.05$.
Since the number of pairs is $n = 6$, $d.f. = n - 1 = 5$. In the Student's t distribution table (Table 6, Appendix II), look in the row headed by 5. To find the column, locate $\alpha = 0.05$ in the *two-tail area* row, since we have a two-tailed test. The critical values are $\pm t_0 = \pm 2.571$.

(b) Sketch the critical regions and place the t value of the sample test statistic $\bar{d}$ on the sketch. Conclude the test. Compare the result to the result given by the *P*-value method of Guided Exercise 7.
Since the sample test statistic falls in the critical region (see Figure 9-15), we reject H_0 at the 5% level of significance. At this level, educational toys seem to make a difference in reading age. Notice that this conclusion is consistent with the conclusion obtained using the *P*-value.   ◊

FIGURE 9-15

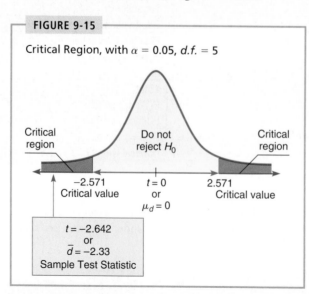

Critical Region, with $\alpha = 0.05$, *d.f.* = 5

VIEWPOINT   *DUI*

DUI usually means "driving under the influence" of *alcohol,* but driving under the influence of *sleep loss* can be just as dangerous. Researchers in Australia have found that after staying awake for 24 hours straight, a person will be about as impaired as if he or she had had enough alcohol to be legally drunk in most U.S. states (Source: *Rocky Mountain News*). Using driver simulation exams and statistical tests (paired difference tests) found in this section, it is possible to show that the null hypothesis $H_0: \mu_d = 0$ cannot be rejected. Or put another way, the average level of impairment for a given individual from alcohol (at the DUI level) is about the same as the average level of impairment for sleep loss (24 hours without sleep).

SECTION 9.4   PROBLEMS

Please provide the following information for Problems 1–16.
(a) What is the level of significance? State the null and alternate hypotheses. Will you use a left-tailed, right-tailed, or two-tailed test?
(b) What sampling distribution will you use? What assumptions are you making? What is the value of the sample test statistic?
(c) Find (or estimate) the *P*-value. Sketch the sampling distribution and show the area corresponding to the *P*-value.
(d) Based on your answers in parts (a) to (c), will you reject or fail to reject the null hypothesis? Are the data statistically significant at level α?
(e) State your conclusion in the context of the application.
In these problems, assume that the distribution of differences is approximately normal.

Note: For degrees of freedom *d.f.* not in the Student's *t* table, use the closest *d.f.* that is *smaller*. In some situations, this choice of *d.f.* may increase the *P*-value a small amount, and therefore produce a slightly more "conservative" answer.

1. *Business: CEO Raises* Are America's top chief executive officers (CEOs) really worth all that money? One way to answer this question is to look at row *B*, the annual company percentage increase in revenue, versus row *A*, the CEO's annual percentage salary increase in that same company. (Source: *Forbes*, Vol. 159, No. 10.) A random sample of companies such as John Deere & Co., General Electric, Union Carbide, and Dow Chemical yielded the following data:

B: Percent for company	24	23	25	18	6	4	21	37
A: Percent for CEO	21	25	20	14	−4	19	15	30

Do these data indicate that the population mean percentage increase in corporate revenue (row *B*) is different from the population mean percentage increase in CEO salary? Use a 5% level of significance.

2. *Fishing: Shore or Boat?* Is fishing better from a boat or from the shore? Pyramid Lake is on the Paiute Indian Reservation in Nevada. Presidents, movie stars, and people who just want to catch fish go to Pyramid Lake for really large cutthroat trout. Let row *B* represent hours per fish fishing from the shore, and let row *A*

represent hours per fish using a boat. The following data are paired by month from October through April. (Source: *Pyramid Lake Fisheries*, Paiute Reservation, Nevada.)

	Oct.	Nov.	Dec.	Jan.	Feb.	March	April
B: Shore	1.6	1.8	2.0	3.2	3.9	3.6	3.3
A: Boat	1.5	1.4	1.6	2.2	3.3	3.0	3.8

Use a 1% level of significance to test if there is a difference in the population mean hours per fish using a boat compared with fishing from the shore.

3. *Ecology: Rocky Mountain National Park* The following is based on information taken from *Winter Wind Studies in Rocky Mountain National Park,* by D. E. Glidden (Rocky Mountain Nature Association). At five weather stations on Trail Ridge Road in Rocky Mountain National Park, the peak wind gusts (in miles per hour) in January and April are recorded below.

Weather Station	1	2	3	4	5
January	139	122	126	64	78
April	104	113	100	88	61

Does this information indicate that the peak wind gusts are higher in January than in April? Use $\alpha = 0.01$.

4. *Wildlife: Highways* The western United States has a number of four-lane interstate highways that cut through long tracts of wilderness. To prevent car accidents with wild animals, the highways are bordered on both sides with 12-foot-high woven wire fences. Although the fences prevent accidents, they also disturb the winter migration pattern of many animals. To compensate for this disturbance, the highways have frequent wilderness underpasses designed for exclusive use by deer, elk, and other animals.

In Colorado, there is a large group of deer that spend their summer months in a region on one side of a highway and survive the winter months in a lower region on the other side. To determine if the highway has disturbed deer migration to the winter feeding area, the following data were gathered on a random sample of 10 wilderness districts in the winter feeding area. Row *B* represents the average January deer count for a 5-year period before the highway was built, and row *A* represents the average January deer count for a 5-year period after the highway was built. The highway department claims that the January population has not changed. Test this against the claim that the January population has dropped. Use a 5% level of significance. Units used in the table are hundreds of deer.

Wilderness District	1	2	3	4	5	6	7	8	9	10
B: Before highway	10.3	7.2	12.9	5.8	17.4	9.9	20.5	16.2	18.9	11.6
A: After highway	9.1	8.4	10.0	4.1	4.0	7.1	15.2	8.3	12.2	7.3

5. *Wildlife: Wolves* In environmental studies, sex ratios are of great importance. Wolf society, packs, and ecology have been studied extensively at different locations in the U.S. and foreign countries. Sex ratios for eight study sites in northern Europe are shown below (based on *The Wolf* by L. D. Mech, University of Minnesota Press).

Gender Study of Large Wolf Packs

Location of Wolf Pack	% Males (Winter)	% Males (Summer)
Finland	72	53
Finland	47	51
Finland	89	72
Lapland	55	48
Lapland	64	55
Russia	50	50
Russia	41	50
Russia	55	45

It is hypothesized that in winter, "loner" males (not present in summer packs) join the pack to increase survival rate. Use a 5% level of significance to test the claim that the average percentage of males in a wolf pack is higher in winter.

6. *Demographics: Birth Rate and Death Rate* In the following data pairs, *A* represents birth rate and *B* represents death rate per 1000 resident population. The data are paired by counties in the Midwest. A random sample of 16 counties gave the following information.

A:	12.7	13.4	12.8	12.1	11.6	11.1	14.2	15.1
B:	9.8	14.5	10.7	14.2	13.0	12.9	10.9	10.0

A:	12.5	12.3	13.1	15.8	10.3	12.7	11.1	15.7
B:	14.1	13.6	9.1	10.2	17.9	11.8	7.0	9.2

(Reference: *County and City Data Book*, U.S. Department of Commerce.)
Do the data indicate a difference (either way) between population average birth rate and death rate in this region? Use $\alpha = 0.01$.

7. *Navajo Reservation: Hogans* The following data are based on information taken from the book *Navajo Architecture: Forms, History, Distributions*, by S. C. Jett and V. E. Spencer (University of Arizona Press). A survey of houses and traditional hogans was made in a number of different regions of the modern Navajo Indian Reservation. The following table is the result of a random sample of eight regions on the Navajo Reservation.

Area on Navajo Reservation	Number of Inhabited Houses	Number of Inhabited Hogans
Bitter Springs	18	13
Rainbow Lodge	16	14
Kayenta	68	46
Red Mesa	9	32
Black Mesa	11	15
Canyon de Chelly	28	47
Cedar Point	50	17
Burnt Water	50	18

Does this information indicate that the population mean number of inhabited houses is greater than that of hogans on the Navajo Reservation? Use a 5% level of significance.

8. *Archaeology: Stone Tools* The following is based on information taken from *Bandelier Archaeological Excavation Project: Summer 1990 Excavations at Burnt Mesa Pueblo and Casa del Rito*, edited by T. A. Kohler (Washington State University, Department of Anthropology). The artifact frequency for an excavation of a kiva in Bandelier National Monument gave the following information.

Stratum	Flaked Stone Tools	Nonflaked Stone Tools
1	7	3
2	3	2
3	10	1
4	1	3
5	4	7
6	38	32
7	51	30
8	25	12

Does this information indicate that there tend to be more flaked stone tools than nonflaked stone tools at this excavation site? Use a 5% level of significance.

9. *Archaeology: Pot Sherds* From the same stratum of an excavated block of rooms at Bandelier National Monument, the following information was obtained about sherds of service ware in two different subareas (see reference in Problem 8):

Service Ware	Subarea 1	Subarea 2
Socorro black-on-white	10	4
Santa Fe black-on-white	42	39
Galisteo black-on-white	15	21
Puerco black-on-red	6	9
Wingate black-on-red	11	6

Does this information indicate that there is a difference (either higher or lower) in the population mean number of service ware sherds in subarea 1 as compared with subarea 2? Use a 5% level of significance.

10. *Psychology: Babies* Many mothers say that they can recognize the cries of their own babies and that they can distinguish between a cry of pain and a hunger cry. A psychologist studied this phenomenon using the following experiment. A random sample of mothers listened to a tape-recorded set of five cries from different babies, one of which was their own. They had to decide which was their baby. Each mother heard 20 such sets, in which 10 were cries of hungry babies and 10 were cries produced by a slight pin prick on a foot. The results are shown in the following table, where row B is the correct number of identifications (out of 10) for a hunger cry, and row A is the correct number of identifications (out of 10) for a pain cry. The psychologist claims that the mothers are more successful in picking out their own babies when a hunger cry is involved, since the mothers have more experience with that situation. Test this claim at the 5% level of significance.

Mother	1	2	3	4	5	6	7	8
B: Hunger cry	6	6	6	5	3	7	9	2
A: Pain cry	5	4	7	3	2	6	4	3

11. *Economics: Cost of Living Index* In the following data pairs, A represents the cost of living index for housing and B represents the cost of living index for groceries. The data are paired by metropolitan areas in the United States. A random sample of 36 metropolitan areas gave the following information. (Reference: *Statistical Abstract of the United States*, 121st edition.)

A:	132	109	128	122	100	96	100	131	97
B:	125	118	139	104	103	107	109	117	105

A:	120	115	98	111	93	97	111	110	92
B:	110	109	105	109	104	102	100	106	103

A:	85	109	123	115	107	96	108	104	128
B:	98	102	100	95	93	98	93	90	108

A:	121	85	91	115	114	86	115	90	113
B:	102	96	92	108	117	109	107	100	95

 i. Let d be the random variable $d = A - B$. Use a calculator to verify that $\bar{d} \approx 2.472$ and $s_d \approx 12.124$.

 ii. Do the data indicate that the U.S. population mean cost of living index for housing is higher than that for groceries in these areas? Use $\alpha = 0.05$.

12. *Economics: Cost of Living Index* In the following data pairs, A represents the cost of living index for utilities and B represents the cost of living index for transportation. The data are paired by metropolitan areas in the United States. A random sample of 46 metropolitan areas gave the following information. (Reference: *Statistical Abstract of the United States*, 121st edition.)

A:	90	84	85	106	83	101	89	125	105
B:	100	91	103	103	109	109	94	114	113

A:	118	133	104	84	80	77	90	92	90
B:	120	130	117	109	107	104	104	113	101

A:	106	95	110	112	105	93	119	99	109
B:	96	109	103	107	103	102	101	86	94

A:	109	113	90	121	120	85	91	91	97
B:	88	100	104	119	116	104	121	108	86

A:	95	115	99	86	88	106	80	108	90	87
B:	100	83	88	103	94	125	115	100	96	127

i. Let d be the random variable $d = A - B$. Use a calculator to verify that $\bar{d} \approx -5.739$ and $s_d \approx 15.910$.

ii. Do the data indicate that the U.S. population mean cost of living index for utilities is less than that for transportation in these areas? Use $\alpha = 0.05$.

13. *Golf: Tournaments* Do professional golfers play better in their first round? Let row B represent the score in the fourth (and final) round, and let row A represent the score in the first round of a professional golf tournament. A random sample of finalists in the British Open gave the following data for their first and last rounds in the tournament. (Source: *Golf Almanac*.)

B: Last	73	68	73	71	71	72	68	68	74
A: First	66	70	64	71	65	71	71	71	71

Do the data indicate that the population mean score on the last round is higher than that on the first? Use a 5% level of significance.

14. *Psychology: Training Rats* The following data are based on information from the Regis University Psychology Department. In an effort to determine if rats perform certain tasks more quickly if offered larger rewards, the following experiment was performed. On day 1, a group of 3 rats was given a reward of one food pellet each time they ran a maze. A second group of 3 rats was given a reward of five food pellets each time they ran the maze. On day 2, the groups were reversed, so the first group now got five food pellets for running the maze and the second group got only one pellet for running the same maze. The average times in seconds for each rat to run the maze 30 times are shown in the following table.

Rat	A	B	C	D	E	F
Time with one food pellet	3.6	4.2	2.9	3.1	3.5	3.9
Time with five food pellets	3.0	3.7	3.0	3.3	2.8	3.0

Do these data indicate that rats receiving larger rewards tend to run the maze in less time? Use a 5% level of significance.

15. *Psychology: Training Rats* The same experimental design discussed in Problem 14 also was used to test rats trained to climb a sequence of short ladders. Times in seconds for eight rats to perform this task are shown in the following table.

Rat	A	B	C	D	E	F	G	H
Time 1 pellet	12.5	13.7	11.4	12.1	11.0	10.4	14.6	12.3
Time 5 pellets	11.1	12.0	12.2	10.6	11.5	10.5	12.9	11.0

Do these data indicate that rats receiving larger rewards tend to perform the ladder climb in less time? Use a 5% level of significance.

16. *Political Science: Democrat versus Republican* In the following data pairs, *A* represents the percentage of voters who voted Democrat and *B* represents the percentage of voters who voted Republican. Because of other political parties, *A* + *B* need not equal 100%. The data are paired by urban counties in the southern United States. A random sample of 17 counties gave the following information. (Reference: *County and City Data Book*, U.S. Department of Commerce.)

A:	42.2	44.0	34.1	41.8	40.7	43.3	39.5	49.7	37.4
B:	35.4	39.4	40.0	39.2	40.2	37.3	40.8	32.8	38.5

A:	44.1	41.0	42.1	46.9	42.8	40.8	36.4	40.6
B:	36.8	35.5	36.0	41.1	33.2	38.3	47.7	41.1

Do the data indicate that the population mean percentage of Democrat votes is higher than that of Republican votes in this region? Use $\alpha = 0.05$.

17. *Critical Region Method: Student's t* Solve Problem 1 using the critical region method of testing. Compare your conclusions with the conclusion obtained by using the *P*-value method. Are they the same?

18. *Critical Region Method: Student's t* Solve Problem 3 using the critical region method of testing. Compare your conclusions with the conclusion obtained by using the *P*-value method. Are they the same?

9.5   Testing $\mu_1 - \mu_2$ and $p_1 - p_2$ (Independent Samples)

Independent Samples

FOCUS POINTS

✓ Identify independent samples and sampling distributions.

✓ Compute the sample test statistic and *P*-value for $\mu_1 - \mu_2$ and conclude the test.

✓ Compute the sample test statistic and *P*-value for $p_1 - p_2$ and conclude the test.

Many practical applications of statistics involve a comparison of two population means or two population proportions. In Section 9.4, we considered tests of differences of means for *dependent samples*. With dependent samples, we could pair the data and then consider the difference of data measurements *d*. In this section, we will turn our attention to tests of differences of means from *independent samples*. We will see new techniques for testing the difference of means from *independent samples*.

First, let's consider independent samples. We say that two sampling distributions are **independent** if there is no relation whatsoever between specific values of the two distributions.

EXAMPLE 11

Independent sample

A teacher wishes to compare the effectiveness of two teaching methods. Students are randomly divided into two groups: The first group is taught by method 1; the second group, by method 2. At the end of the course, a comprehensive exam is given to all students, and the mean score $\bar{x}_1$ for group 1 is compared with the mean score $\bar{x}_2$ for group 2. Are the samples independent or dependent?

SOLUTION: Because the students were *randomly* divided into two groups, it is reasonable to say that the $\bar{x}_1$ distribution is independent of the $\bar{x}_2$ distribution.   ◊

EXAMPLE 12

Dependent sample

In Section 9.4, we considered a situation in which a shoe manufacturer claims that for the general population of adult U.S. citizens, the average length of the left foot is longer than the average length of the right foot. To study this claim, the manufacturer gathers data in this fashion: Sixty adult U.S. citizens are drawn at random, and for these 60 people, both their left and right feet are measured. Let $\bar{x}_1$ be the mean length of the left feet and $\bar{x}_2$ be the mean length of the right feet.

Are the $\bar{x}_1$ and $\bar{x}_2$ distributions independent for this method of collecting data?

SOLUTION: In this method, there is only *one* random sample of people drawn, and both the left and right feet are measured from this sample. The length of a person's left foot is usually related to the length of the right foot, so in this case the $\bar{x}_1$ and $\bar{x}_2$ distributions are *not* independent. In fact, we could pair the data and consider the distribution of the differences, left foot length minus right foot length. Then we would use the techniques of paired difference tests as found in Section 9.4.   ◊

GUIDED EXERCISE 8

Independent sample

Suppose the shoe manufacturer of Example 12 gathers data in the following way: Sixty adult U.S. citizens are drawn at random and their left feet are measured; then another 60 adult U.S. citizens are drawn at random and their right feet are measured. Again, $\bar{x}_1$ is the mean of the left foot measurements and $\bar{x}_2$ is the mean of the right foot measurements.

Are the $\bar{x}_1$ and $\bar{x}_2$ distributions independent for this method of collecting data?

    For this method of gathering data, two random samples are drawn: one for the left foot measurements and one for the right foot measurements. The first sample is not related to the second sample. The $\bar{x}_1$ and $\bar{x}_2$ distributions are independent.

Part I: Testing $\mu_1 - \mu_2$ When σ_1 and σ_2 Are Known

Properties of $\bar{x}_1 - \bar{x}_2$ distribution, σ_1 and σ_2 known

In this part, we will use distributions that arise from a difference of means from independent samples. How do we obtain such distributions? If we have two statistical variables x_1 and x_2, each with its own distribution, we take independent random samples of size n_1 from the x_1 distribution and of size n_2 from the x_2 distribution. Then we can compute the respective means $\bar{x}_1$ and $\bar{x}_2$. Consider the difference $\bar{x}_1 - \bar{x}_2$. This represents a difference of means. If we repeat the sampling process over and over, we will come up with lots of $\bar{x}_1 - \bar{x}_2$ values. These values can be arranged in a frequency table, and we can make a histogram for the distribution of $\bar{x}_1 - \bar{x}_2$ values. This will give us an experimental idea of the theoretical distribution of $\bar{x}_1 - \bar{x}_2$.

Fortunately, it is not necessary to carry out this lengthy process for each example. The results have already been worked out mathematically. The next theorem presents the main results.

◇ **THEOREM 9.2** Let x_1 have a normal distribution with mean μ_1 and standard deviation σ_1. Let x_2 have a normal distribution with mean μ_2 and standard deviation σ_2. If we take independent random samples of size n_1 from the x_1 distribution and of size n_2 from the x_2 distribution, then the variable $\bar{x}_1 - \bar{x}_2$ has

1. A normal distribution

2. Mean $\mu_1 - \mu_2$

3. Standard deviation

$$\sqrt{\frac{\sigma_1^2}{n_1} + \frac{\sigma_2^2}{n_2}} \quad ◇$$

◇ **COMMENT** Theorem 9.2 requires that x_1 and x_2 have normal distributions. However, if both n_1 and n_2 are 30 or larger, then for most practical applications, the central limit theorem assures us that $\bar{x}_1$ and $\bar{x}_2$ are approximately normally distributed. In this case, the conclusions of the theorem are again valid even if the original x_1 and x_2 distributions were not normal.   ◇

Hypotheses for testing difference of means

When testing the difference of means, it is customary to use the null hypothesis

$$H_0\text{: } \mu_1 - \mu_2 = 0 \text{ or, equivalently, } H_0\text{: } \mu_1 = \mu_2$$

As mentioned in Section 9.1, the null hypothesis is set up to see if it can be rejected. When testing the difference of means, we first set up the hypothesis H_0 that there is no difference. The alternate hypothesis could then be any of the ones listed in Table 9-12. The alternate hypothesis and consequent type of test used depend on the particular problem. Note that μ_1 is always listed first.

Using Theorem 9.2 and the central limit theorem (Section 7.2), we can summarize the procedure for testing $\mu_1 - \mu_2$ when both σ_1 and σ_2 are known.

TABLE 9-12   Alternate Hypotheses and Type of Test: Difference of Two Means

H_1			Type of Test
H_1: $\mu_1 - \mu_2 < 0$	or equivalently	H_1: $\mu_1 < \mu_2$	Left-tailed test
H_1: $\mu_1 - \mu_2 > 0$	or equivalently	H_1: $\mu_1 > \mu_2$	Right-tailed test
H_1: $\mu_1 - \mu_2 \neq 0$	or equivalently	H_1: $\mu_1 \neq \mu_2$	Two-tailed test

PROCEDURE

How to test $\mu_1 - \mu_2$ when both σ_1 and σ_2 are known

Let σ_1 and σ_2 be the population standard deviations of populations 1 and 2. Obtain two independent random samples from populations 1 and 2, where

$\bar{x}_1$ and $\bar{x}_2$ are sample means from populations 1 and 2

n_1 and n_2 are sample sizes from populations 1 and 2

1. In the context of the application, state the *null and alternate hypotheses* and set the *level of significance* α. It is customary to use $H_0: \mu_1 - \mu_2 = 0$.

2. If you can assume that both population distributions 1 and 2 are normal, any sample sizes n_1 and n_2 will work. If you cannot assume this, then use sample sizes $n_1 \geq 30$ and $n_2 \geq 30$. Use $\mu_1 - \mu_2 = 0$ from the null hypothesis together with $\bar{x}_1, \bar{x}_2, \sigma_1, \sigma_2, n_1$, and n_2 to compute the sample *test statistic*.

$$z = \frac{(\bar{x}_1 - \bar{x}_2) - (\mu_1 - \mu_2)}{\sqrt{\dfrac{\sigma_1^2}{n_1} + \dfrac{\sigma_2^2}{n_2}}} = \frac{\bar{x}_1 - \bar{x}_2}{\sqrt{\dfrac{\sigma_1^2}{n_1} + \dfrac{\sigma_2^2}{n_2}}}$$

3. Use the standard normal distribution and the type of test, one-tailed or two-tailed, to find the *P-value* corresponding to the sample test statistic.

4. *Conclude the test.* If P-value $\leq \alpha$, then reject H_0. If P-value $> \alpha$, then do not reject H_0.

5. *State your conclusion* in the context of the application.

EXAMPLE 13

Testing the difference of means (σ_1 and σ_2 known)

A consumer group is testing camp stoves. To test the heating capacity of a stove, it measures the time required to bring 2 quarts of water from 50°F to boiling (at sea level). Two competing models are under consideration. Ten stoves of the first model and 12 stoves of the second model are tested. The following results are obtained.

Model 1: Mean time $\bar{x}_1 = 11.4$ min; $\sigma_1 = 2.5$ min; $n_1 = 10$

Model 2: Mean time $\bar{x}_2 = 9.9$ min; $\sigma_2 = 3.0$ min; $n_2 = 12$

Assume that the time required to bring water to a boil is normally distributed for each stove. Is there any difference (either way) between the performances of these two models? Use a 5% level of significance.

SOLUTION:

(a) State the null and alternate hypotheses and note the value of α.

Let μ_1 and μ_2 be the mean of the distribution of times for models 1 and 2, respectively. We set up the null hypothesis to state that there is no difference:

$H_0: \mu_1 = \mu_2$ or $H_0: \mu_1 - \mu_2 = 0$

The alternate hypothesis states that there is a difference:

$H_1: \mu_1 \neq \mu_2$ or $H_1: \mu_1 - \mu_2 \neq 0$

The level of significance is $\alpha = 0.05$.

(b) Compute the sample test statistic $\bar{x}_1 - \bar{x}_2$ and then convert it to a z value. Note that we use the standard normal distribution because the original distributions are normal and the standard deviations are known.

We are given the values $\bar{x}_1 = 11.4$ and $\bar{x}_2 = 9.9$. Therefore, the sample test statistic is $\bar{x}_1 - \bar{x}_2 = 11.4 - 9.9 = 1.5$. To convert this to a z value, we use the values $\sigma_1 = 2.5$, $\sigma_2 = 3.0$, $n_1 = 10$, and $n_2 = 12$. From the null hypothesis, $\mu_1 - \mu_2 = 0$.

$$z = \frac{(\bar{x}_1 - \bar{x}_2) - (\mu_1 - \mu_2)}{\sqrt{\dfrac{\sigma_1^2}{n_1} + \dfrac{\sigma_2^2}{n_2}}} = \frac{1.5}{\sqrt{\dfrac{2.5^2}{10} + \dfrac{3.0^2}{12}}} \approx 1.28$$

(c) Find the P-value and sketch the area on the standard normal curve.
   Figure 9-16 shows the P-value. Use the standard normal distribution (Table 5 of Appendix II) and the fact that we have a two-tailed test. P-value $\approx 2(0.1003) = 0.2006$.

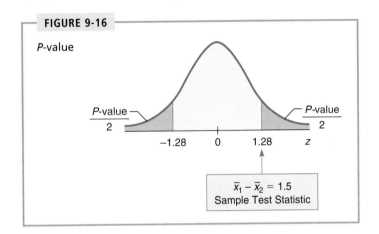

FIGURE 9-16

(d) Conclude the test.
   The P-value is 0.2006 and $\alpha = 0.05$. Since P-value $> \alpha$, do not reject H_0.

(e) Interpret the results.
   At the 5% level of significance, the sample data do not indicate any difference in the population mean times for boiling water for the two stove models. ◇

GUIDED EXERCISE 9

Testing the difference of means (σ_1 and σ_2 known)

Let us return to Example 11 at the beginning of this section. A teacher wishes to compare the effectiveness of two teaching methods for her students. Students are randomly divided into two groups. The first group is taught by method 1; the second group, by method 2. At the end of the course, a comprehensive exam is given to all students.

The first group consists of $n_1 = 49$ students with a mean score of $\bar{x}_1 = 74.8$ points. The second group has $n_2 = 50$ students with a mean score of $\bar{x}_2 = 81.3$ points. The teacher claims that the second method will increase the mean score on the comprehensive exam. Is this claim justified at the 5% level of significance? Earlier research for the two methods indicates that $\sigma_1 = 14$ points and $\sigma_2 = 15$ points.

Continued

GUIDED EXERCISE 9 continued

Let μ_1 and μ_2 be the mean score of the distribution of all scores using method 1 and method 2, respectively.

(a) What is the null hypothesis?

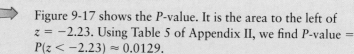 $H_0: \mu_1 = \mu_2$ or $H_0: \mu_1 - \mu_2 = 0$

(b) To examine the validity of the teacher's claim, what should the alternate hypothesis be? What is α?

$H_1: \mu_1 < \mu_2$ (the second method gives a higher average score) or $H_1: \mu_1 - \mu_2 < 0$.

$\alpha = 0.05$

(c) Compute the sample test statistic $\bar{x}_1 - \bar{x}_2$.

$\bar{x}_1 - \bar{x}_2 = 74.8 - 81.3 = -6.5$

(d) Convert $\bar{x}_1 - \bar{x}_2 = -6.5$ to a z value.

Since σ_1 and σ_2 are both known and the samples are large, we use the standard normal distribution. Using $\sigma_1 = 14$, $\sigma_2 = 15$, $n_1 = 49$, $n_2 = 50$, and $\mu_1 - \mu_2 = 0$ from H_0, we have

$$z = \frac{(\bar{x}_1 - \bar{x}_2) - (\mu_1 - \mu_2)}{\sqrt{\dfrac{\sigma_1^2}{n_1} + \dfrac{\sigma_2^2}{n_2}}} = \frac{-6.5 - 0}{\sqrt{\dfrac{14^2}{49} + \dfrac{15^2}{50}}} \approx -2.23$$

(e) Find the P-value and sketch the area on the standard normal curve.

Figure 9-17 shows the P-value. It is the area to the left of $z = -2.23$. Using Table 5 of Appendix II, we find P-value $= P(z < -2.23) \approx 0.0129$.

FIGURE 9-17 P-value

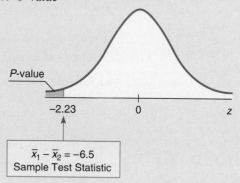

(f) Conclude the test and interpret the results in the context of the application.

Since P-value of $0.0129 \leq 0.05$ for α, reject H_0. At the 5% level of significance, there is sufficient evidence to show that the second teaching method increased the population mean score on the exam.

Part II: Testing $\mu_1 - \mu_2$ When σ_1 and σ_2 Are Unknown

To test $\mu_1 - \mu_2$ when σ_1 and σ_2 are unknown, we use distribution methods similar to those in Chapter 8 for estimating $\mu_1 - \mu_2$. In particular, if the two distributions are normal or approximately mound-shaped, or if both sample sizes are large (≥ 30), we use a Student's t distribution. Let's summarize the method of testing $\mu_1 - \mu_2$.

> **PROCEDURE**
>
> **How to test $\mu_1 - \mu_2$ when σ_1 and σ_2 are unknown**
>
> Obtain two independent random samples from populations 1 and 2, where
>
> $\bar{x}_1$ and $\bar{x}_2$ are sample means from populations 1 and 2
>
> s_1 and s_2 are sample standard deviations from populations 1 and 2
>
> n_1 and n_2 are sample sizes from populations 1 and 2
>
> 1. In the context of the application, state the *null and alternate hypotheses* and set the *level of significance* α. It is customary to use H_0: $\mu_1 - \mu_2 = 0$.
>
> 2. If you can assume that both population distributions 1 and 2 are normal or at least mound-shaped and symmetric, then any sample sizes n_1 and n_2 will work. If you cannot assume this, then use sample sizes $n_1 \geq 30$ and $n_2 \geq 30$. Use $\mu_1 - \mu_2 = 0$ from the null hypothesis together with $\bar{x}_1, \bar{x}_2, s_1, s_2, n_1$, and n_2 to compute the sample *test statistic*.
>
> $$t = \frac{(\bar{x}_1 - \bar{x}_2) - (\mu_1 - \mu_2)}{\sqrt{\dfrac{s_1^2}{n_1} + \dfrac{s_2^2}{n_2}}} = \frac{\bar{x}_1 - \bar{x}_2}{\sqrt{\dfrac{s_1^2}{n_1} + \dfrac{s_2^2}{n_2}}}$$
>
> The sample test statistic distribution is approximately that of a Student's t with *degrees of freedom d.f. = smaller of* $n_1 - 1$ and $n_2 - 1$.
> Note that statistical software gives a more accurate and larger *d.f.* based on Satterthwaite's approximation (see Problem 15).
>
> 3. Use a Student's t distribution and the type of test, one-tailed or two-tailed, to find the *P-value* corresponding to the sample test statistic.
>
> 4. *Conclude the test.* If P-value $\leq \alpha$, then reject H_0. If P-value $> \alpha$, then do not reject H_0.
>
> 5. *State your conclusion* in the context of the application.

EXAMPLE 14

Testing the difference of means (σ_1 and σ_2 unknown)

Two competing headache remedies claim to give fast-acting relief. An experiment was performed to compare the mean lengths of time required for bodily absorption of brand A and brand B headache remedies.

Twelve people were randomly selected and given an oral dosage of brand A. Another 12 were randomly selected and given an equal dosage of brand B. The lengths of time in minutes for the drugs to reach a specified level in the blood were recorded. The means, standard deviations, and sizes of the two samples follow.

Brand A: $\bar{x}_1 = 21.8$ min; $s_1 = 8.7$ min; $n_1 = 12$
Brand B: $\bar{x}_2 = 18.9$ min; $s_2 = 7.5$ min; $n_2 = 12$

Past experience with the drug composition of the two remedies permits researchers to assume that both distributions are approximately normal. Let us use a 5% level of significance to test the claim that there is no difference in the mean time required for bodily absorption. Also, find or estimate the *P-value* of the sample test statistic.

SOLUTION:

(a) $\alpha = 0.05$. The null hypothesis is

$$H_0: \mu_1 = \mu_2 \qquad \text{or} \qquad H_0: \mu_1 - \mu_2 = 0$$

Since we have no prior knowledge about which brand is faster, the alternate hypothesis is

$$H_1: \mu_1 \neq \mu_2 \quad \text{or} \quad H_0: \mu_1 - \mu_2 \neq 0$$

(b) Compute the sample test statistic.

We're given $\bar{x}_1 = 21.8$ and $\bar{x}_2 = 18.9$, so the sample difference is $\bar{x}_1 - \bar{x}_2 = 21.8 - 18.9 = 2.9$. Using $s_1 = 8.7$, $s_2 = 7.5$, $n_1 = 12$, $n_2 = 12$, and $\mu_1 - \mu_2 = 0$ from H_0, we compute the sample test statistic.

$$t = \frac{(\bar{x}_1 - \bar{x}_2) - (\mu_1 - \mu_2)}{\sqrt{\dfrac{s_1^2}{n_1} + \dfrac{s_2^2}{n_2}}} = \frac{2.9}{\sqrt{\dfrac{8.7^2}{12} + \dfrac{7.5^2}{12}}} \approx 0.875$$

(c) Estimate the P-value and sketch the area on a t graph.

Figure 9-18 shows the P-value. The degrees of freedom is $d.f. = 11$ (since both samples are of size 12). Because the test is a two-tailed test, the P-value is the area to the right of 0.875 together with the area to the left of -0.875. In the Student's t distribution table (Table 6 of Appendix II), we find an interval containing the P-value. Find 0.875 in the row headed by $d.f. = 11$. The test statistic 0.875 falls between the entries 0.697 and 1.214. Because this is a two-tailed test, we use the corresponding P-values 0.500 and 0.250 from the *two-tail area* row (see Table 9-13, Excerpt from Table 6). The P-value for the sample t is in the interval

$$0.250 < P\text{-value} < 0.500$$

(d) Conclude the test.

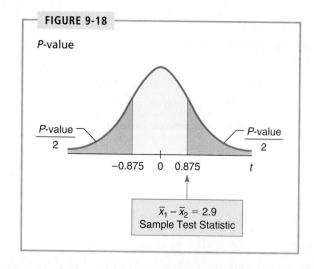

Since the interval containing the P-value lies to the right of $\alpha = 0.05$, we fail to reject H_0.

Note: Using the raw data and a calculator with Satterthwaite's approximation for the degrees of freedom, $d.f. \approx 21.53$, the P-value ≈ 0.3915. This value is in the interval we computed.

(e) Interpret the results.

FIGURE 9-18

P-value

$\dfrac{P\text{-value}}{2}$

$\dfrac{P\text{-value}}{2}$

$-0.875 \quad 0 \quad 0.875 \qquad t$

$\bar{x}_1 - \bar{x}_2 = 2.9$
Sample Test Statistic

TABLE 9-13   Excerpt from Table 6, Appendix II

	0.250	0.125
one-tail area	0.250	0.125
✓ two-tail area	0.500	0.250
$d.f. = 11$	0.697	1.214

Sample $t = 0.875$

At the 5% level of significance, there is insufficient evidence to conclude that there is a difference in mean times for the remedies to reach the specified level in the bloodstream.   ◇

GUIDED EXERCISE 10

Testing the difference of means (σ_1 and σ_2 unknown)

Suppose the experiment to measure the time in minutes for the headache remedies to enter the bloodstream (Example 14) yielded sample means, sample standard deviations, and sample sizes as follows:

Brand A: $\bar{x}_1 = 20.1$ min; $s_1 = 8.7$ min; $n_1 = 12$
Brand B: $\bar{x}_2 = 11.2$ min; $s_2 = 7.5$ min; $n_2 = 8$

Brand B claims to be faster. Is this claim justified at the 1% level of significance? (Use the following steps to obtain the answer.)

(a) What is α? State H_0 and H_1.

⇨ $\alpha = 0.01$.

$H_0\colon \mu_1 = \mu_2$ or $H_0\colon \mu_1 - \mu_2 = 0$

$H_1\colon \mu_1 > \mu_2$ (or $H_1\colon \mu_1 - \mu_2 > 0$). This says that the mean time for brand B is less than the mean time for brand A.

(b) Compute the sample test statistic $\bar{x}_1 - \bar{x}_2$ and convert it to a t value.

⇨ $\bar{x}_1 - \bar{x}_2 = 20.1 - 11.2 = 8.9$. Using $s_1 = 8.7$, $s_2 = 7.5$, $n_1 = 12$, $n_2 = 8$, and $\mu_1 - \mu_2 = 0$ from H_0, we have

$$t = \frac{\bar{x}_1 - \bar{x}_2}{\sqrt{\dfrac{s_1^2}{n_1} + \dfrac{s_2^2}{n_2}}} = \frac{8.9}{\sqrt{\dfrac{8.7^2}{12} + \dfrac{7.5^2}{8}}} \approx 2.437$$

(c) What degrees of freedom do you use? To find an interval containing the P-value, do you use one-tail or two-tail areas of Table 6, Appendix II? Sketch a figure showing the P-value. Find an interval for the P-value.

⇨   Since $n_2 < n_1$, d.f. $= n_2 - 1 = 8 - 1 = 7$. Use *one-tail area* of Table 6.

FIGURE 9-19 P-value

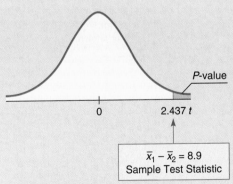

TABLE 9-14   Excerpt from Student's t Table

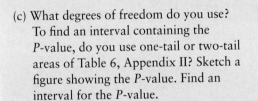

✓ one-tail area	0.025	0.010
two-tail area	0.050	0.020
d.f. = 7	2.365	2.998

Sample $t = 2.437$

The sample t is between 2.365 and 2.998.

$0.010 < P\text{-value} < 0.025$

Continued

GUIDED EXERCISE 10 continued

(d) Do we reject or fail to reject H_0?

➡ Since the interval containing the *P*-value has values that are all less than 0.05, we reject H_0.

$$\overline{\quad(\!\blacksquare\!)\quad}\overset{\alpha}{\underset{\big|}{\quad}}$$
0.010   0.025   0.05

Note: On the calculator with Satterthwaite's approximation for *d.f.*, we have *d.f.* = 16.66 and *P*-value ≈ 0.013.

(e) Interpret the results in the context of the application.

➡ At the 5% level of significance, there is evidence that the mean time for brand B to enter the bloodstream is less than that of brand A.

Alternate method using pooled standard deviation

There is another method of testing $\mu_1 - \mu_2$ when σ_1 and σ_2 are unknown. Suppose that the sample values s_1 and s_2 are sufficiently close and that there is reason to believe $\sigma_1 = \sigma_2$ (or the standard deviations are approximately equal). This situation can happen when you make a slight change or alteration to a known process or method of production. The standard deviation may not change much, but the outputs or means could be very different. When there is reason to believe that $\sigma_1 = \sigma_2$, it is best to use a *pooled standard deviation*. The sample test statistic $\overline{x}_1 - \overline{x}_2$ has a corresponding *t* variable with an *exact* Student's *t* distribution and degrees of freedom *d.f.* = $n_1 + n_2 - 2$. Problem 16 at the end of the section provides the details.

Under the null hypothesis H_0: $\mu_1 = \mu_2$, which distribution should you use for the sample test statistic $\overline{x}_1 - \overline{x}_2$?

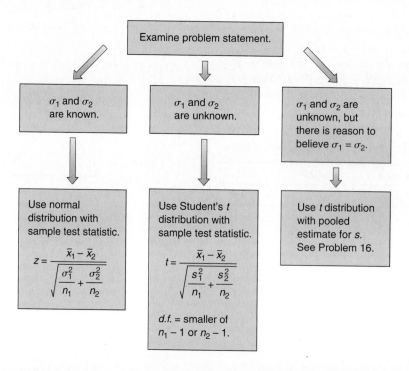

Part III: Testing a Difference of Proportions $p_1 - p_2$

Suppose we have two independent binomial experiments. That is, outcomes from one binomial experiment are in no way paired with outcomes from the other. We use the notation

Binomial Experiment 1

n_1 = number of trials

r_1 = number of successes

p_1 = population probability of success on a single trial

Binomial Experiment 2

n_2 = number of trials

r_2 = number of successes

p_2 = population probability of success on a single trial

For *large* values of n_1 and n_2, the distribution of sample differences

$$\hat{p}_1 - \hat{p}_2 = \frac{r_1}{n_1} - \frac{r_2}{n_2}$$

is closely approximated by a *normal distribution* with mean μ and standard deviation σ as shown:

$$\mu = p_1 - p_2 \qquad \sigma = \sqrt{\frac{p_1 q_1}{n_1} + \frac{p_2 q_2}{n_2}}$$

where $q_1 = 1 - p_1$ and $q_2 = 1 - p_2$.

Pooled estimate $\bar{p}$

For most practical problems involving a comparison of two binomial populations, the experimenters will want to test the null hypothesis $p_1 = p_2$. Consequently, this is the type of test we shall consider. Since the values of p_1 and p_2 are unknown, and since specific values are not assumed under the null hypothesis $p_1 = p_2$, the best estimate for the common value is the total number of successes $(r_1 + r_2)$ divided by the total number of trials $(n_1 + n_2)$. If we denote this *pooled estimate of proportion* by $\bar{p}$ (read "p bar"), then

$$\bar{p} = \frac{r_1 + r_2}{n_1 + n_2}$$

This formula gives the best sample estimate $\bar{p}$ for p_1 and p_2 *under the assumption that $p_1 = p_2$*. Also, $\bar{q} = 1 - \bar{p}$.

Criteria for using the normal approximation to the binomial

◇ **COMMENT** For most practical applications, the sample sizes n_1 and n_2 are considered large samples if each of the four quantities

$$n_1 \bar{p} \qquad n_1 \bar{q} \qquad n_2 \bar{p} \qquad n_2 \bar{q}$$

is larger than 5 (see Section 6.4). ◇

Sample test statistic

As stated earlier, the sample statistic $\hat{p}_1 - \hat{p}_2$ has a normal distribution with mean $\mu = p_1 - p_2$ and standard deviation $\sigma = \sqrt{p_1 q_1 / n_1 + p_2 q_2 / n_2}$. Under the null hypothesis, we assume that $p_1 = p_2$ and then use the pooled estimate $\bar{p}$ in place of each p. Using all this information, we find that the sample test statistic is

$$z = \frac{\hat{p}_1 - \hat{p}_2}{\sqrt{\dfrac{\overline{p}\,\overline{q}}{n_1} + \dfrac{\overline{p}\,\overline{q}}{n_2}}}$$

where $\overline{p} = \dfrac{r_1 + r_2}{n_1 + n_2}$ and $\overline{q} = 1 - \overline{p}$

$$\hat{p}_1 = \frac{r_1}{n_1} \quad \text{and} \quad \hat{p}_2 = \frac{r_2}{n_2}$$

Using this information, we summarize the procedure for testing $p_1 - p_2$.

PROCEDURE

How to test a difference of proportions $p_1 - p_2$

Consider two independent binomial experiments.

Binomial Experiment 1

n_1 = number of trials

r_1 = number of successes out of n_1 trials

$\hat{p}_1 = \dfrac{r_1}{n_1}$

p_1 = population probability of success on a single trial

Binomial Experiment 2

n_2 = number of trials

r_2 = number of successes out of n_2 trials

$\hat{p}_2 = \dfrac{r_2}{n_2}$

p_2 = population probability of success on a single trial

1. Use the *null hypothesis* of no difference, H_0: $p_1 - p_2 = 0$. In the context of the application, choose the *alternate hypothesis*. Set the *level of significance* α.

2. The null hypothesis claims that $p_1 = p_2$; therefore, *pooled best estimates* for the population probabilities of success and failure are

$$\overline{p} = \frac{r_1 + r_2}{n_1 + n_2} \quad \text{and} \quad \overline{q} = 1 - \overline{p}$$

The number of trials should be sufficiently large so that all four quantities $n_1\overline{p}$, $n_1\overline{q}$, $n_2\overline{p}$, and $n_2\overline{q}$ are each larger than 5. In this case you compute the sample *test statistic*

$$z = \frac{\hat{p}_1 - \hat{p}_2}{\sqrt{\dfrac{\overline{p}\,\overline{q}}{n_1} + \dfrac{\overline{p}\,\overline{q}}{n_2}}}$$

3. Use the standard normal distribution and a type of test, one-tailed or two-tailed, to find the *P-value* corresponding to the sample test statistic.

4. *Conclude the test.* If P-value $\leq \alpha$, then reject H_0. If P-value $> \alpha$, then do not reject H_0.

5. *State your conclusion* in the context of the application.

EXAMPLE 15

Testing the difference of proportions

The Macek County Clerk wishes to improve voter registration. One method under consideration is to send reminders in the mail to all citizens in the county who are eligible to register. As part of a pilot study to determine if this method will actually improve voter registration, a random sample of 1250 potential voters was taken. Then this sample was randomly divided into two groups.

Group 1: There were 625 people in this group. No reminders to register were sent to them. The number of potential voters from this group who registered was 295.

Group 2: This group also contained 625 people. Reminders were sent in the mail to each member in the group, and the number who registered to vote was 350.

The county clerk claims that the proportion of people who registered was significantly greater in group 2. On the basis of this claim, the clerk recommends that the project be funded for the entire population of Macek County. Use a 5% level of significance to test the claim that the proportion of potential voters who registered was greater in group 2, the group that received reminders.

SOLUTION:

(a) Note that $\alpha = 0.05$. Let p_1 be the proportion of voters who registered from group 1, and let p_2 be the proportion who registered from group 2. The null hypothesis is that there is no difference in proportions, so

$$H_0: p_1 = p_2 \qquad \text{or} \qquad H_0: p_1 - p_2 = 0$$

The alternate hypothesis is that the proportion of voters who registered was greater in the group that received reminders.

$$H_1: p_1 < p_2 \qquad \text{or} \qquad H_1: p_1 - p_2 < 0$$

(b) Compute the sample statistic $\hat{p}_1 - \hat{p}_2$ and convert it to a z value.

● **CALCULATOR NOTE** Carry the values for $\hat{p}_1, \hat{p}_2, \hat{q}_1, \hat{q}_2,$ and the pooled estimates $\overline{p}$ and $\overline{q}$ out to at least three places after the decimal. Then round the z value of the corresponding test statistic to two places after the decimal.

For the first group, the number of successes is $r_1 = 295$ out of $n_1 = 625$ trials. For the second group, there are $r_2 = 350$ successes out of $n_2 = 625$ trials. Since

$$\hat{p}_1 = \frac{r_1}{n_1} = \frac{295}{625} = 0.472 \qquad \text{and} \qquad \hat{p}_2 = \frac{r_2}{n_2} = \frac{350}{625} = 0.560$$

then

$$\hat{p}_1 - \hat{p}_2 = 0.472 - 0.560 = -0.088$$

To convert this $\hat{p}_1 - \hat{p}_2$ to a z value, we need to find the *pooled estimate* $\overline{p}$ for the common values of p_1 and p_2 and the corresponding value for $\overline{q}$.

$$\overline{p} = \frac{r_1 + r_2}{n_1 + n_2} = \frac{295 + 350}{625 + 625} = 0.516 \quad \text{and} \quad \overline{q} = 1 - \overline{p} = 0.484$$

Using these values, we find that

$$z = \frac{\hat{p}_1 - \hat{p}_2}{\sqrt{\dfrac{\overline{p}\,\overline{q}}{n_1} + \dfrac{\overline{p}\,\overline{q}}{n_2}}} = \frac{-0.088}{\sqrt{\dfrac{(0.516)(0.484)}{625} + \dfrac{(0.516)(0.484)}{625}}} \approx -3.11$$

(c) Find the P-value and sketch the area on the standard normal curve.

Figure 9-20 shows the P-value. This is a left-tailed test, so the P-value is the area to the left of -3.11. Using the standard normal distribution (Table 5 of Appendix II), we find P-value $= P(z < -3.11) \approx 0.0009$.

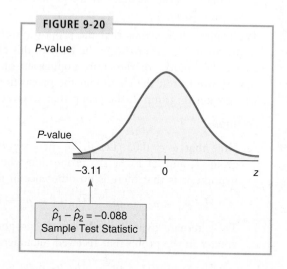

FIGURE 9-20

P-value

P-value

−3.11   0   *z*

$\hat{p}_1 - \hat{p}_2 = -0.088$
Sample Test Statistic

(d) Conclude the test.

Since P-value of $0.0009 \leq 0.05$ for α, we reject H_0.

(e) Interpret the results.

At the 5% level of significance, the data indicate that the population proportion of potential voters who registered was greater in group 2, the group that received reminders.   ◇

GUIDED EXERCISE 11

Testing the difference of proportions

In Example 15 about voter registration, suppose that a random sample of 1100 potential voters was randomly divided into two groups.

Group 1: 500 potential voters; no registration reminders sent; 248 registered to vote

Group 2: 600 potential voters; registration reminders sent; 332 registered to vote

Do these data support the claim that the proportion of voters who registered was greater in the group that received reminders than in the group that did not? Use a 1% level of significance.

Continued

GUIDED EXERCISE 11 continued

(a) What is α? State H_0 and H_1.

⟹ $\alpha = 0.01$. As before, H_0: $p_1 = p_2$ and H_1: $p_1 < p_2$.

(b) Under the null hypothesis $p_1 = p_2$, calculate the *pooled estimates* $\overline{p}$ and $\overline{q}$.

⟹ $n_1 = 500$, $r_1 = 248$; $n_2 = 600$, $r_2 = 332$.

$$\overline{p} = \frac{r_1 + r_2}{n_1 + n_2} = \frac{248 + 332}{500 + 600} \approx 0.527$$

$$\overline{q} = 1 - \overline{p} \approx 1 - 0.527 \approx 0.473$$

(c) What is the value of the sample test statistic $\hat{p}_1 - \hat{p}_2$?

⟹ $\hat{p}_1 = \dfrac{r_1}{n_1} = \dfrac{248}{500} = 0.496$ $\hat{p}_2 = \dfrac{r_2}{n_2} = \dfrac{332}{600} \approx 0.553$

$\hat{p}_1 - \hat{p}_2 = -0.057$

(d) Convert the sample test statistic $\hat{p}_1 - \hat{p}_2 = -0.057$ to a z value.

⟹ $$z = \frac{\hat{p}_1 - \hat{p}_2}{\sqrt{\dfrac{\overline{p}\,\overline{q}}{n_1} + \dfrac{\overline{p}\,\overline{q}}{n_2}}} = \frac{-0.057}{\sqrt{\dfrac{(0.527)(0.473)}{500} + \dfrac{(0.527)(0.473)}{600}}} \approx -1.89$$

(e) Find the *P*-value and sketch the area on the standard normal curve.

⟹ Figure 9-21 shows the *P*-value. It is the area to the left of $z = -1.89$. Using Table 5 of Appendix II, we find *P*-value = $P(z < -1.89) = 0.0294$.

FIGURE 9-21 *P*-value

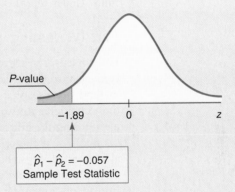

P-value

−1.89   0   z

$\hat{p}_1 - \hat{p}_2 = -0.057$
Sample Test Statistic

(f) Conclude the test and interpret the results in the context of the application.

⟹ Since *P*-value of 0.0294 > 0.01 for α, we cannot reject H_0. At the 1% level of significance, the data do not support the claim that the reminders increase the proportion of registered voters.

TECH NOTE The TI-84Plus and TI-83Plus calculators, Excel, and Minitab all support testing the difference of means for independent samples. The TI-84Plus/TI-83Plus calculators and Minitab also support testing the difference of proportions. When testing the difference of means using the normal distribution, the technologies require the population standard deviations for the distributions of the two samples. When testing the difference of means using a Student's *t* distribution, the technologies give the option of using the pooled standard deviation. As discussed in Problem 16 of this section, the pooled standard deviation is appropriate when the standard deviations of the two populations are approximately equal. If the pooled standard deviation option is not selected, the technologies compute the sample test statistic for $\overline{x}_1 - \overline{x}_2$ using the procedures described in this section. However, Satterthwaite's approximation for the degrees of freedom is used.

TI-84Plus/TI-83Plus Enter the data. Press **STAT** and select **TESTS**. Options **3: 2-SampZTest, 4: 2-SampTTest, 6: 2-PropZTest** perform tests for the difference of means using the normal distribution, difference of means using a Student's *t* distribution, and difference of proportions, respectively. The calculator uses the symbol $\hat{p}$ to designate the pooled estimate for *p*.

Excel Enter the data in columns. Use the menu choices **Tools ➤ Data Analysis.** The choice **z-Test Two Sample Means** conducts a test for the difference of means using the normal distribution. The choice **t-Test: Two-Sample Assuming Unequal Variances** conducts a test using a Student's *t* distribution with Satterthwaite's approximation for the degrees of freedom. The choice **t-Test: Two-Sample Assuming Equal Variances** conducts a test using the pooled standard deviation.

Minitab Enter the data in two columns. Use the menu choices **Stat ➤ Basic Statistics.** The choice **2 sample t** tests the difference of means using a Student's *t* distribution. In the dialogue box, leaving the box **Assume equal variances** unchecked produces a test using Satterthwaite's approximation for the degrees of freedom. Checking the box **Assume equal variances** produces a test using the pooled standard deviation. Minitab does not support testing the difference of means using the normal distribution. The menu item **2 Proportions** tests the difference of proportions. Under Options, elect the null and alternate hypotheses.

Part IV: Testing $\mu_1 - \mu_2$ and $p_1 - p_2$ Using Critical Regions

For a fixed preset level of significance α, the *P*-value method of testing is logically equivalent to the critical region method of testing. This book emphasizes the *P*-value method because of its great popularity and because it is readily compatible with most computer software. However, for completeness, we provide an optional example utilizing the critical region method.

Recall that the critical region method and the *P*-value method of testing share a number of steps. Both methods use the same *null and alternate hypotheses*, the same *sample test statistic*, and the same *sampling distribution* for the test statistic. Instead of computing the *P*-value and comparing it to the level of significance α, the critical region method compares the sample test statistic to a *critical value* from the sampling distribution that is based on α and the alternate hypothesis (left-tailed, right-tailed, or two-tailed).

Test conclusions based on critical values

For a *right-tailed test,* if the sample *test statistic* $\geq$ *critical value,* reject H_0.

For a *left-tailed test,* if the sample *test statistic* $\leq$ *critical value,* reject H_0.

For a *two-tailed test,* if the sample *test statistic lies beyond the critical values* (that is, $\leq$ negative critical value or $\geq$ positive critical value), reject H_0.

Otherwise, in each case, do not reject H_0.

Critical values z_0 for tests using the standard normal distribution can be found in Table 5(c) of Appendix II. Critical values t_0 for tests using a Student's *t* distribution are found in Table 6 of Appendix II. Use the row headed by the appropriate degrees of freedom and the column that includes the value of α (level of significance) in the *one-tail area* row for one-tailed tests or the *two-tail area* row for two-tailed tests.

EXAMPLE 16

Critical region method

Use the critical region method to solve the application in Example 14 (test $\mu_1 - \mu_2$ when σ_1 and σ_2 are unknown).

SOLUTION: Example 14 involves testing the difference in average time for two headache remedies to reach the bloodstream. For brand A, $\bar{x}_1 = 21.8$ min, $s_1 = 8.7$ min, and $n_1 = 12$; for brand B, $\bar{x}_2 = 18.9$ min, $s_2 = 7.5$ min, and $n_2 = 12$. The level of significance α is 0.05. The Student's t distribution is appropriate because both populations are approximately normal.

(a) To use the critical region method to test for a difference in average time, we use the same hypotheses and the same sample test statistic as in Example 14.

$$H_0: \mu_1 = \mu_2; H_1: \mu_1 \neq \mu_2;$$
sample test statistic: $\bar{x}_1 - \bar{x}_2 = 2.9$ min; sample $t = 0.875$

(b) Instead of finding the P-value of the sample test statistic, we use α and H_1 to find the critical values in Table 6 of Appendix II. We have $d.f. = 11$ (since both samples are of size 12). We find $\alpha = 0.05$ in the *two-tail area* row since we have a two-tailed test. The critical values are $\pm t_0 = \pm 2.201$.

Next compare the sample test statistic $t = 0.875$ to the critical values. Figure 9-22 shows the critical regions and the sample test statistic. We see that the sample test statistic falls in the "do not reject H_0" region. At the 5% level of significance, sample evidence does not show a difference in time for drugs to reach the bloodstream. The result is consistent with the result obtained by the P-value method of Example 14.   ◊

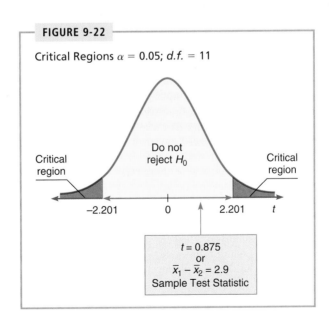

FIGURE 9-22

Critical Regions $\alpha = 0.05$; $d.f. = 11$

Critical region

Do not reject H_0

Critical region

−2.201   0   2.201 t

$t = 0.875$
or
$\bar{x}_1 - \bar{x}_2 = 2.9$
Sample Test Statistic

VIEWPOINT   *Temper! Temper!*

In her book *Red Ink Behaviors,* Jean Hollands discusses inappropriate, problem behaviors of professional employees in the corporate business world. Temper tantrums, flaming e-mails, omitting essential information, sabotaging fellow workers, and the arrogant opinion that others are "dumb and dispensable" create personnel problems that cost companies a lot in the form of wasted time, reduced productivity, and lost revenues. A study of major industries in the Silicon Valley area gave Hollands data for estimating just how much time and money are wasted by such "red ink behaviors." For more information, see Problems 11 and 12 in this section.

SECTION 9.5   PROBLEMS

Please provide the following information for Problems 1–14 and 17–25.
(a) What is the level of significance? State the null and alternate hypotheses.
(b) What sampling distribution will you use? What assumptions are you making? What is the value of the sample test statistic?
(c) Find (or estimate) the *P*-value. Sketch the sampling distribution and show the area corresponding to the *P*-value.
(d) Based on your answers in parts (a) to (c), will you reject or fail to reject the null hypothesis? Are the data statistically significant at level α?
(e) State your conclusion in the context of the application.
   Note: For degrees of freedom *d.f.* not in the Student's *t* table, use the closest *d.f.* that is *smaller.* In some situations, this choice of *d.f.* may increase the *P*-value a small amount, and therefore produce a slightly more "conservative" answer.
Answers may vary due to rounding.

1. *Medical: REM Sleep* REM (rapid eye movement) sleep is sleep during which most dreams occur. Each night a person has both REM and non-REM sleep. However, it is thought that children have more REM sleep than adults (Reference: *Secrets of Sleep* by Dr. A. Borbely). Assume that REM sleep time is normally distributed for both children and adults. A random sample of $n_1 = 10$ children (9 years old) showed that they had an average REM sleep time of $\bar{x}_1 = 2.8$ hours per night. From previous studies it is known that $\sigma_1 = 0.5$ hour. Another random sample of $n_2 = 10$ adults showed that they had an average REM sleep time of $\bar{x}_2 = 2.1$ hours per night. Previous studies show that $\sigma_2 = 0.7$ hour. Do these data indicate that on average, children tend to have more REM sleep than adults? Use a 1% level of significance.

2. *Environment: Pollution Index* Based on information from the *Rocky Mountain News,* a random sample of $n_1 = 12$ winter days in Denver gave a sample mean pollution index of $\bar{x}_1 = 43$. Previous studies show that $\sigma_1 = 21$. For Englewood (a suburb of Denver), a random sample of $n_2 = 14$ winter days gave a sample mean pollution index of $\bar{x}_2 = 36$. Previous studies show that $\sigma_2 = 15$. Assume the pollution index is normally distributed in both Englewood and Denver. Do these data indicate that the mean population pollution index of Englewood is different (either way) from that of Denver in the winter? Use a 1% level of significance.

3. *Survey: Outdoor Activities* A Michigan study concerning preference for outdoor activities used a questionnaire with a six-point Likert-type response in which 1

designated "not important" and 6 designated "extremely important." A random sample of $n_1 = 46$ adults were asked about fishing as an outdoor activity. The mean response was $\bar{x}_1 = 4.9$. Another random sample of $n_2 = 51$ adults were asked about camping as an outdoor activity. For this group, the mean response was $\bar{x}_2 = 4.3$. From previous studies it is known that $\sigma_1 = 1.5$ and $\sigma_2 = 1.2$. Does this indicate a difference (either way) regarding preference for camping versus preference for fishing as an outdoor activity? Use a 5% level of significance. Note: A *Likert scale* usually has to do with approval of or agreement with a statement in a questionnaire. For example, respondents are asked to indicate whether they "strongly agree," "agree," "disagree," or "strongly disagree" with the statement.

4. *Generation Gap: Education* Education influences attitude and lifestyle. Differences in education are a big factor in the "generation gap." Is the younger generation really better educated? Large surveys of people age 65 and older were taken in $n_1 = 32$ U.S. cities. The sample mean for these cities showed that $\bar{x}_1 = 15.2\%$ of the older adults had attended college. Large surveys of young adults (age 25–34) were taken in $n_2 = 35$ U.S. cities. The sample mean for these cities showed that $\bar{x}_2 = 19.7\%$ of the young adults had attended college. From previous studies it is known that $\sigma_1 = 7.2\%$ and $\sigma_2 = 5.2\%$ (Reference: *American Generations*, S. Mitchell). Does this information indicate that the population mean percentage of young adults who attended college is higher? Use $\alpha = 0.05$.

5. *Crime Rate: FBI* A random sample of $n_1 = 10$ regions in New England gave the following violent crime rate (per million population).

x_1: **New England Crime Rate**

3.5	3.7	4.0	3.9	3.3	4.1	1.8	4.8	2.9	3.1

Another random sample of $n_2 = 12$ regions in the Rocky Mountain states gave the following violent crime rate (per million population).

x_2: **Rocky Mountain States**

3.7	4.3	4.5	5.3	3.3	4.8	3.5	2.4	3.1	3.5	5.2	2.8

(Reference: *Crime in the United States*, Federal Bureau of Investigation.) Assume that the crime rate distribution is approximately normal in both regions.
i. Use a calculator to verify that $\bar{x}_1 \approx 3.51$, $s_1 \approx 0.81$, $\bar{x}_2 \approx 3.87$, and $s_2 \approx 0.94$.
ii. Do the data indicate that the violent crime rate in the Rocky Mountain region is higher than in New England? Use $\alpha = 0.01$.

6. *Medical: Hay Fever* A random sample of $n_1 = 16$ communities in western Kansas gave the following information for people under 25 years of age.

x_1: **Rate of hay fever per 1000 population for people under 25**

98	90	120	128	92	123	112	93
125	95	125	117	97	122	127	88

A random sample of $n_2 = 14$ regions in western Kansas gave the following information for people over 50 years old.

x_2: **Rate of hay fever per 1000 population for people over 50**

95	110	101	97	112	88	110
79	115	100	89	114	85	96

(Reference: National Center for Health Statistics.)

i. Use a calculator to verify that $\bar{x}_1 \approx 109.50$, $s_1 \approx 15.41$, $\bar{x}_2 \approx 99.36$, and $s_2 \approx 11.57$.

ii. Assume that the hay fever rate in each age group has an approximately normal distribution. Do the data indicate that the age group over 50 has a lower rate of hay fever? Use $\alpha = 0.05$.

7. *Education: Tutoring* In the journal *Mental Retardation*, an article reported the results of a peer tutoring program to help mildly mentally retarded children learn to read. In the experiment, the mildly retarded children were randomly divided into two groups: the experimental group received peer tutoring along with regular instruction, and the control group received regular instruction with no peer tutoring. There were $n_1 = n_2 = 30$ children in each group. The Gates-MacGintie Reading Test was given to both groups before instruction began. For the experimental group, the mean score on the vocabulary portion of the test was $\bar{x}_1 = 344.5$ with sample standard deviation $s_1 = 49.1$. For the control group, the mean score on the same test was $\bar{x}_2 = 354.2$ with sample standard deviation $s_2 = 50.9$. Use a 5% level of significance to test the hypothesis that there was no difference in the vocabulary scores of the two groups before the instruction began.

8. *Education: Tutoring* In the article cited in Problem 7, the results of the following experiment were reported. Form 2 of the Gates-MacGintie Reading Test was administered to both an experimental group and a control group after 6 weeks of instruction during which the experimental group received peer tutoring and the control group did not. For the experimental group $n_1 = 30$ children, the mean score on the vocabulary portion of the test was $\bar{x}_1 = 368.4$ with sample standard deviation $s_1 = 39.5$. The average score on the vocabulary portion of the test for the $n_2 = 30$ subjects in the control group was $\bar{x}_2 = 349.2$, with sample standard deviation $s_2 = 56.6$. Use a 1% level of significance to test the claim that the experimental group performed better than the control group.

9. *Wildlife: Fox Rabies* A study of fox rabies in southern Germany gave the following information about different regions and the occurrence of rabies in each region (Reference: B. Sayers, et al., "A Pattern Analysis Study of a Wildlife Rabies Epizootic," *Medical Informatics* 2:11–34). Based on information from this article, a random sample of $n_1 = 16$ locations in region I gave the following information about the number of cases of fox rabies near that location.

x_1: Region I data	1	8	8	8	7	8	8	1
	3	3	3	2	5	1	4	6

A second random sample of $n_2 = 15$ locations in region II gave the following information about the number of cases of fox rabies near that location.

x_2: Region II data	1	1	3	1	4	8	5	4
	4	4	2	2	5	6	9	

i. Use a calculator with sample mean and sample standard deviation keys to verify that $\bar{x}_1 = 4.75$ with $s_1 \approx 2.82$ in region I and $\bar{x}_2 \approx 3.93$ with $s_2 \approx 2.43$ in region II.

ii. Does this information indicate that there is a difference (either way) in the mean number of cases of fox rabies between the two regions? Use a 5% level of significance. (Assume the distribution of rabies cases in both regions is mound-shaped and approximately normal.)

10. *Agriculture: Bell Peppers* The pathogen *Phytophthora capsici* causes bell peppers to wilt and die. Because bell peppers are an important commercial crop, this disease

has undergone a great deal of agricultural research. It is thought that too much water aids the spread of the pathogen. Two fields are under study. The first step in the research project is to compare the mean soil water content for the two fields (Source: *Journal of Agricultural, Biological, and Environmental Statistics*, Vol. 2, No. 2). Units are percent water by volume of soil.

Field A samples, x_1:

10.2	10.7	15.5	10.4	9.9	10.0	16.6
15.1	15.2	13.8	14.1	11.4	11.5	11.0

Field B samples, x_2:

8.1	8.5	8.4	7.3	8.0	7.1	13.9	12.2
13.4	11.3	12.6	12.6	12.7	12.4	11.3	12.5

i. Use a calculator with mean and standard deviation keys to verify that $\bar{x}_1 \approx$ 12.53, $s_1 \approx 2.39$, $\bar{x}_2 \approx 10.77$, and $s_2 \approx 2.40$.

ii. Assuming the distribution of soil water content in each field is mound-shaped and symmetric, use a 5% level of significance to test the claim that field A has, on average, a higher soil water content than field B.

11. *Management: Lost Time* In her book *Red Ink Behaviors,* Jean Hollands reports on the assessment of leading Silicon Valley companies regarding a manager's lost time due to inappropriate behavior of employees. Consider the following independent random variables. The first variable x_1 measures manager's hours per week lost due to hot tempers, flaming e-mails, and general unproductive tensions:

x_1:	1	5	8	4	2	4	10

The variable x_2 measures manager's hours per week lost due to disputes regarding technical workers' superior attitudes that their colleagues are "dumb and dispensable":

x_2:	10	5	4	7	9	4	10	3

i. Use a calculator with sample mean and standard deviation keys to verify that $\bar{x}_1 \approx 4.86$, $s_1 \approx 3.18$, $\bar{x}_2 = 6.5$, and $s_2 \approx 2.88$.

ii. Does the information indicate that the population mean time lost due to hot tempers is different (either way) from population mean time lost due to disputes arising from technical workers' superior attitudes? Use $\alpha = 0.05$. Assume that the two lost-time population distributions are mound-shaped and symmetric.

12. *Management: Intimidators and Stressors* This problem is based on information regarding productivity in leading Silicon Valley companies (see reference in Problem 11). In large corporations, an "intimidator" is an employee who tries to stop communication, sometimes sabotages others, and, above all, likes to listen to him- or herself talk. Let x_1 be a random variable representing productive hours per week lost by peer employees of an intimidator.

x_1:	8	3	6	2	2	5	2

A "stressor" is an employee with a hot temper that leads to unproductive tantrums in corporate society. Let x_2 be a random variable representing productive hours per week lost by peer employees of a stressor.

x_2:	3	3	10	7	6	2	5	8

i. Use a calculator with mean and standard deviation keys to verify that $\bar{x}_1 = 4.00$, $s_1 \approx 2.38$, $\bar{x}_2 = 5.5$, and $s_2 \approx 2.78$.

ii. Assuming that the variables x_1 and x_2 are independent, do the data indicate that the population mean time lost due to stressors is greater than the population mean time lost due to intimidators? Use a 5% level of significance. (Assume that the population distributions of time lost due to intimidators and time lost due to stressors are each mound-shaped and symmetric.)

13. *Environment: Power Plants* A large electric power plant uses ocean water for its cooling system (and returns the water to the ocean). A random sample of $n_1 = 11$ temperature readings showed the following increases in surface water temperature (in °F):

x_1:   6   8   4   5   10   3   9   11   7   9   7

A new generator was added to the plant, and environmentalists fear that the average change in water temperature has increased. A random sample of $n_2 = 12$ temperature readings taken after addition of the new generator showed the following increases in surface temperature (in °F):

x_2:   9   11   15   12   7   12   10   13   8   11   14   8

i. Use a calculator with mean and standard deviation keys to verify that $\bar{x}_1 \approx 7.2°F$, $s_1 \approx 2.5°F$, $\bar{x}_2 \approx 10.8°F$, and $s_2 \approx 2.5°F$.
ii. Use a 1% level of significance to test the claim that the mean increase in water temperature at the surface has increased since the addition of the new generator. Assume that the population distribution of increase in surface temperature for each generator is mound-shaped and symmetric.

14. *Paramedics: Night Shift* Paramedics in a large city say they need more staff at night because they get more emergency calls then. A random sample of $n_1 = 7$ days showed that the paramedics received the following numbers of emergency calls during the day.

x_1:   65   54   81   67   75   83   79

An independent sample of $n_2 = 7$ nights showed that the paramedics received the following numbers of emergency calls during the night.

x_2:   72   81   85   80   88   82   56

i. Use a calculator with mean and standard deviation keys to verify that $\bar{x}_1 = 72$ calls, $s_1 \approx 10.47$ calls, $\bar{x}_2 \approx 77.7$ calls, and $s_2 \approx 10.78$ calls.
ii. Use a 1% level of significance to test the claim that there is a difference (either way) between the mean number of calls during the day and the mean number of calls during the night. (Assume that the population distributions of daytime calls and nighttime calls are mound-shaped and symmetric.)

15. *Expand Your Knowledge: Software Approximation for Degrees of Freedom* Given x_1 and x_2 distributions that are normal or approximately normal with unknown σ_1 and σ_2, the value of t corresponding to $\bar{x}_1 - \bar{x}_2$ has a distribution that is approximated by a Student's t distribution. We use the convention that the degrees of freedom is approximately the smaller of $n_1 - 1$ and $n_2 - 1$. However, a more accurate estimate for the appropriate degrees of freedom is given by Satterthwaite's formula:

$$d.f. \approx \frac{\left(\dfrac{s_1^2}{n_1} + \dfrac{s_2^2}{n_2}\right)^2}{\dfrac{1}{n_1 - 1}\left(\dfrac{s_1^2}{n_1}\right)^2 + \dfrac{1}{n_2 - 1}\left(\dfrac{s_2^2}{n_2}\right)^2}$$

where s_1, s_2, n_1, and n_2 are the respective sample standard deviations and sample sizes of independent random samples from the x_1 and x_2 distributions. This is the approximation used by most statistical software. When both n_1 and n_2 are 5 or larger, it is quite accurate. The degrees of freedom computed from this formula are either truncated or not rounded.

(a) In Problem 5 we tested whether the population average crime rate μ_2 in the Rocky Mountain region is higher than that in New England, μ_1. The data were $n_1 = 10$, $\bar{x}_1 \approx 3.51$, $s_1 \approx 0.81$, $n_2 = 12$, $\bar{x}_2 \approx 3.87$, and $s_2 \approx 0.94$. Use Satterthwaite's formula to compute the degrees of freedom for the Student's t distribution.

(b) When you did Problem 5, you followed the convention that degrees of freedom $d.f. = smaller$ of $n_1 - 1$ and $n_2 - 1$. Compare this $d.f.$ with that found by Satterthwaite's formula.

16. *Expand Your Knowledge: Pooled Two-Sample Procedure* Consider independent random samples from two populations that are normal or approximately normal, or the case in which both sample sizes are at least 30. Then, if σ_1 and σ_2 are unknown but we have reason to believe that $\sigma_1 = \sigma_2$, we can pool the standard deviations. Using sample sizes n_1 and n_2, the sample test statistic $\bar{x}_1 - \bar{x}_2$ has a Student's t distribution, where

$$t = \frac{\bar{x}_1 - \bar{x}_2}{s\sqrt{\dfrac{1}{n_1} + \dfrac{1}{n_2}}} \text{ with degrees of freedom } d.f. = n_1 + n_2 - 2$$

where the **pooled standard deviation** s is

$$s = \sqrt{\frac{(n_1 - 1)s_1^2 + (n_2 - 1)s_2^2}{n_1 + n_2 - 2}}$$

Note: With statistical software, select the pooled variance or equal variance options.

(a) There are many situations in which we want to compare means from populations having standard deviations that are equal. This method applies even if the standard deviations are known to be only approximately equal (see Section 11.4 for methods to test that $\sigma_1 = \sigma_2$). Consider Problem 9 regarding average incidence of fox rabies in two regions. For region I, $n_1 = 16$, $\bar{x}_1 = 4.75$, and $s_1 \approx 2.82$ and for region II, $n_2 = 15$, $\bar{x}_2 \approx 3.93$, and $s_2 \approx 2.43$. The two sample standard deviations are sufficiently close that we can assume $\sigma_1 = \sigma_2$. Use the method of pooled standard deviation to redo Problem 9, where we tested if there was a difference in population mean average incidence of rabies at the 5% level of significance.

(b) Compare the t value calculated in part (a) using the pooled standard deviation with the t value calculated in Problem 9 using the unpooled standard deviation. Compare the degrees of freedom for the sample test statistic. Compare the conclusions.

17. *Federal Tax Money: Art Funding* Would you favor spending more federal tax money on the arts? This question was asked by a research group on behalf of *The National Institute* (Reference: *Painting by Numbers*, J. Wypijewski, University of California Press). Of a random sample of $n_1 = 220$ women, $r_1 = 59$ responded yes. Another random sample of $n_2 = 175$ men showed that $r_2 = 56$ responded yes. Does this information indicate a difference (either way) between the population proportion

of women and the population proportion of men who favor spending more federal tax dollars on the arts? Use $\alpha = 0.05$.

18. *Art Funding: Politics* Would you favor spending more federal tax money on the arts? This question was asked by a research group on behalf of *The National Institute* (Reference: *Painting by Numbers*, J. Wypijewski, University of California Press). Of a random sample of $n_1 = 93$ politically conservative voters, $r_1 = 21$ responded yes. Another random sample of $n_2 = 83$ politically moderate voters showed that $r_2 = 22$ responded yes. Does this information indicate that the population proportion of conservative voters inclined to spend more federal tax money on funding the arts is less than the proportion of moderate voters so inclined? Use $\alpha = 0.05$.

19. *Sociology: High School Dropouts* This problem is based on information taken from *Life in America's Fifty States*, by G. S. Thomas. A random sample of $n_1 = 153$ people ages 16 to 19 were taken from the island of Oahu, Hawaii, and 12 were found to be high school dropouts. Another random sample of $n_2 = 128$ people ages 16 to 19 were taken from Sweetwater County, Wyoming, and 7 were found to be high school dropouts. Do these data indicate that the population proportion of high school dropouts on Oahu is different (either way) from that of Sweetwater County? Use a 1% level of significance.

20. *Political Science: Voters* A random sample of $n_1 = 288$ voters registered in the state of California showed that 141 voted in the last general election. A random sample of $n_2 = 216$ registered voters in the state of Colorado showed that 125 voted in the most recent general election. (See reference in Problem 19.) Do these data indicate that the population proportion of voter turnout in Colorado is higher than that in California? Use a 5% level of significance.

21. *Extraterrestrials: Believe It?* Based on information from *Harper's Index*, $r_1 = 37$ out of a random sample of $n_1 = 100$ adult Americans who did not attend college believe in extraterrestrials. However, out of a random sample of $n_2 = 100$ adult Americans who did attend college, $r_2 = 47$ claim that they believe in extraterrestrials. Does this indicate that the proportion of people who attended college and who believe in extraterrestrials is higher than the proportion who did not attend college? Use $\alpha = 0.01$.

22. *Art: Politics* Do you prefer paintings in which the people are fully clothed? This question was asked by a professional survey group on behalf of the National Arts Society (see reference in Problem 18). A random sample of $n_1 = 59$ people who are conservative voters showed that $r_1 = 45$ said yes. Another random sample of $n_2 = 62$ people who are liberal voters showed that $r_2 = 36$ said yes. Does this indicate that the population proportion of conservative voters who prefer art with fully clothed people is higher? Use $\alpha = 0.05$.

23. *Hotels: Nonsmoking* A random sample of $n_1 = 378$ hotel guests was taken 1 year ago, and it was found that $r_1 = 194$ requested nonsmoking rooms. Recently, a random sample of $n_2 = 516$ hotel guests showed that $r_2 = 320$ requested nonsmoking rooms. Do these data indicate that the proportion of hotel guests requesting nonsmoking rooms has increased? Use a 1% level of significance.

24. *Sociology: College Degrees* A random sample of $n_1 = 78$ women ages 21–29 in Denver showed that $r_1 = 23$ have a college degree. Another random sample of $n_2 = 73$ men in Denver in the same age group showed that $r_2 = 20$ have a college degree

(based on information from *Educational Attainment in the United States*, Bureau of the Census). Does this indicate that the population proportion of Denver women ages 21–29 with college degrees is different (either way) from that of men in this age group? Use $\alpha = 0.05$.

25. *Sociology: Trusting People* Generally speaking, would you say that most people can be trusted? A random sample of $n_1 = 250$ people in Chicago ages 18–25 showed that $r_1 = 45$ said yes. Another random sample of $n_2 = 280$ people in Chicago ages 35–45 showed that $r_2 = 71$ said yes (based on information from the *National Opinion Research Center*, University of Chicago). Does this indicate that the population proportion of trusting people in Chicago is higher for the older group? Use $\alpha = 0.05$.

26. *Critical Region Method: Testing $\mu_1 - \mu_2$; σ_1, σ_2 Known* Redo Problem 1 using the critical region method and compare your results to those obtained using the *P*-value method.

27. *Critical Region Method: Testing $\mu_1 - \mu_2$; σ_1, σ_2 Unknown* Redo Problem 5 using the critical region method and compare your results to those obtained using the *P*-value method.

28. *Critical Region Method: Testing $p_1 - p_2$* Redo Problem 17 using the critical region method and compare your results to those obtained using the *P*-value method.

SUMMARY

In this chapter, we studied statistical inference methods called *hypothesis testing*. We establish an initial claim about the value of a parameter. This claim is the null hypothesis H_0, which claims the parameter in question equals a certain value. Then we propose an alternate hypothesis H_1, which indicates the parameter is less than, greater than, or different from the value in the null hypothesis. To determine whether or not to reject the null hypothesis, we use the evidence of the sample data and the predetermined level of significance α.

The basic steps we follow in the procedure of hypothesis testing are

1. Choose the level of significance α. State the null and alternate hypotheses H_0 and H_1.

2. Determine the sampling distribution of the sample test statistic. Convert the sample test statistic to a z value or a t value as appropriate.

3. Find (or estimate) the *P*-value of the sample test statistic.

4. If *P*-value $\leq \alpha$, reject H_0. If *P*-value $> \alpha$, do not reject H_0.

5. Interpret the results in the context of the application.

An alternate way to conclude a test of hypotheses is to use critical regions based on the alternate hypothesis and α. Critical values z_0 are found in Table 5(c) of Appendix II. Critical values t_0 are found in Table 6 of Appendix II. If the sample test statistic falls in the critical region, reject H_0.

In this chapter, we used hypothesis testing to conduct tests involving a single mean μ (σ known or unknown), a single proportion p, a paired difference of means, differences of means from independent samples (σ_1 and σ_2 known or unknown), and differences of proportions. The methods of hypothesis testing are very general, and we will see them used again in later chapters with other parameters and other probability distributions.

IMPORTANT WORDS & SYMBOLS

Section 9.1
Hypothesis testing
Hypotheses
Null hypothesis H_0
Alternate hypothesis H_1
right-tailed test
left-tailed test
two-tailed test
sample test statistic
P-value
statistical significance
Type I error
Type II error
α, the level of significance of a test and the probability of a type I error
β, the probability of a type II error
Power of a test $(1 - \beta)$

Section 9.2
$d.f.$ for testing μ when σ is unknown
Critical region
Critical value

Section 9.3
Criteria for using normal approximation to binomial, $np > 5$ and $nq > 5$

Section 9.4
Paired data
Dependent samples

Section 9.5
Independent samples
$d.f.$ for testing $\mu_1 - \mu_2$ when σ_1 and σ_2 are unknown
Pooled estimate of proportion $\bar{p}$
Pooled standard deviation

VIEWPOINT   *Will It Rain?*

Do cloud seed experiments ever work? If you seed the clouds, will it rain? If it does rain, who will benefit? Who will be displeased by the rain? If you seed the clouds and nothing happens, will taxpayers (who support the effort) complain or rejoice? Maybe this should be studied over a remote island—such as Tasmania (near Australia). Using what you already know about statistical testing, you can conduct your own tests, given the appropriate data. Remember, there are sociological questions (pleased/displeased with result) as well as technical questions (number of inches of rain produced). For data regarding cloud-seeding experiments over Tasmania, visit the Brase/Brase statistics site at **http://math.college.hmco.com/students** and find the link to DASL, the Carnegie Mellon University Data and Story Library. From the DASL site, look under Datasets for Cloud.

CHAPTER REVIEW PROBLEMS

Before you solve each problem, first categorize it by answering the following question: Are we testing a single mean, a difference of means, a single proportion, or a difference of proportions?

Then provide the following information for Problems 1–17.

(a) What is the level of significance? State the null and alternate hypotheses.

(b) What sampling distribution will you use? What assumptions are you making? What is the value of the sample test statistic?

(c) Find (or estimate) the *P*-value. Sketch the sampling distribution and show the area corresponding to the *P*-value.

(d) Based on your answers in parts (a) to (c), will you reject or fail to reject the null hypothesis? Are the data statistically significant at level *α*?

(e) State your conclusion in the context of the application.

Note: For degrees of freedom *d.f.* not in the Student's *t* table, use the closest *d.f.* that is *smaller*. In some situations, this choice of *d.f.* may increase the *P*-value by a small amount, and therefore produce a slightly more "conservative" answer. Answers may vary due to rounding.

1. *Vehicles: Mileage* Based on information in *Statistical Abstract of the United States* (116th Edition), the average annual miles driven per vehicle in the United States is 11.1 thousand miles with $\sigma \approx 600$ miles. Suppose that a random sample of 36 vehicles owned by residents of Chicago showed that the average mileage driven last year was 10.8 thousand miles. Does this indicate that the average miles driven per vehicle in Chicago is different from (higher or lower than) the national average? Use a 0.05 level of significance.

2. *Student Life: Employment* Professor Jennings claims that only 35% of the students at Flora College work while attending school. Dean Renata thinks that the professor has underestimated the number of students with part-time or full-time jobs. A random sample of 81 students shows that 39 have jobs. Do the data indicate that more than 35% of the students have jobs? (Use a 5% level of significance.)

3. *Toys: Electric Trains* The Toylot Company makes an electric train with a motor that it claims will draw an average of only 0.8 ampere (A) under a normal load. A sample of nine motors was tested, and it was found that the mean current was $\bar{x} = 1.4$ A with a sample standard deviation of $s = 0.41$ A. Do the data indicate that the Toylot claim of 0.8 A is too low? (Use a 1% level of significance.)

4. *Highways: Reflective Paint* The highway department is testing two types of reflecting paint for concrete bridge end pillars. The two kinds of paint are alike in every respect except that one is orange and the other is yellow. The orange paint is applied to 12 bridges, and the yellow paint is applied to 12 bridges. After a period of 1 year, reflectometer readings were made on all these bridge end pillars. (A higher reading means better visibility.) For the orange paint the mean reflectometer reading was $\bar{x}_1 = 9.4$ with standard deviation $s_1 = 2.1$. For the yellow paint the mean was $\bar{x}_2 = 6.9$ with standard deviation $s_2 = 2.0$. Based on these data, can we conclude that the yellow paint has less visibility after 1 year? (Use a 1% level of significance.)

5. *Medical: Plasma Compress* A hospital reported that the normal death rate for patients with extensive burns (more than 40% of skin area) has been significantly reduced by the use of new fluid plasma compresses. Before the new treatment, the mortality rate for extensive burn patients was about 60%. Using the new

compresses, the hospital found that only 40 of 90 patients with extensive burns died. Use a 1% level of significance to test the claim that the mortality rate has dropped.

6. *Unions: Salaries* The Fleetfoot Shoe Company claims that the average yearly salary of its workers is $29,800. The union believes that the average salary is much less. A random sample of 61 employees shows their average salary to be $29,500 with a sample standard deviation of $800. Use a 5% level of significance to test the company's claim.

7. *Student Government: Opinions* The student council is thinking about discontinuing the student poetry magazine because only 20% of the students read it. A vote was taken, and it was decided to continue the magazine if more than 20% of the students are known to read it. A random sample of 200 students showed that 58 of them had read the last issue. Use a 1% level of significance to determine whether the magazine should be continued.

8. *Bus Lines: Schedules* A comparison is made between two bus lines to determine if arrival times of their regular buses from Denver to Durango are off schedule by the same amount of time. For 51 randomly selected runs, bus line A was observed to be off schedule an average time of 53 min with standard deviation of 19 min. For 60 randomly selected runs, bus line B was observed to be off schedule an average of 62 min with standard deviation 15 min. Do the data indicate a significant difference in average off-schedule times? Use a 5% level of significance.

9. *Matches: Number per Box* The Nero Match Company sells matchboxes that are supposed to have an average of 40 matches per box with $\sigma = 9$. A random sample of 94 Nero matchboxes shows the average number of matches per box to be 43.1. Using a 1% level of significance, can you say that the average number of matches per box is more than 40?

10. *Magazines: Subscriptions* A study is made of residents in Phoenix and its suburbs concerning the proportion of residents that subscribe to *Sporting News*. A random sample of 88 urban residents showed that 12 subscribed, and a random sample of 97 suburban residents showed that 18 subscribed. Does this indicate that a higher proportion of suburban residents subscribe to *Sporting News*? (Use a 5% level of significance.)

11. *Fast Food: Service* An independent rating service is trying to determine which of two hamburger stands has quicker service. Over a period of 16 randomly selected times, the average waiting period at Burger Queen is 4.8 min with standard deviation 2.0 min. The average waiting period at McGregor over a period of 14 randomly selected times is 5.8 min with standard deviation 1.8 min. Using a 5% level of significance, can we say there is a difference in the average waiting time between Burger Queen and McGregor?

12. *Civil Service: College Degrees* The Congressional Budget Office reports that 36% of federal civilian employees have a bachelor's degree or higher (*The Wall Street Journal*). A random sample of 120 employees in the private sector showed that 33 have a bachelor's degree or higher. Does this indicate that the percentage of employees holding bachelor's degrees or higher in the private sector is less than in the federal civilian sector? Use $\alpha = 0.05$.

13. *Vending Machines: Coffee* A machine in the student lounge dispenses coffee. The average cup of coffee is supposed to contain 7.0 oz. Eight cups of coffee from this machine show the average content to be 7.3 oz with a standard deviation of 0.5 oz. Do you think that the machine has slipped out of adjustment and that the average amount of coffee per cup is different from 7 oz? Use a 5% level of significance.

14. *Psychology: Creative Thinking* Six sets of identical twins were randomly selected from a population of identical twins. One child was taken at random from each pair to form an experimental group. These children participated in a program designed to promote creative thinking. The other child from each pair was part of the control group that did not participate in the program to promote creative thinking. At the end of the program, a creative problem-solving test was given with the results shown in the following table:

Twin pair	A	B	C	D	E	F
Experimental group	53	35	12	25	33	47
Control group	39	21	5	18	21	42

Higher scores indicate better performance in creative problem solving. Do the data support the claim that the program of the experimental group did promote creative problem solving? (Use $\alpha = 0.01$.)

15. *Marketing: Sporting Goods* A marketing consultant was hired to visit a random sample of five sporting goods stores across the state of California. Each store was part of a large franchise of sporting goods stores. The consultant taught the managers of each store better ways to advertise and display their goods. The net sales for 1 month before and 1 month after the consultant's visit were recorded as follows for each store (in thousands of dollars):

Store	1	2	3	4	5
Before visit	57.1	94.6	49.2	77.4	43.2
After visit	63.5	101.8	57.8	81.2	41.9

Do the data indicate that the average net sales improved? (Use $\alpha = 0.05$.)

16. *Sports Car: Fuel Injection* The manufacturer of a sports car claims that the fuel injection system lasts 48 months before it needs to be replaced. A consumer group tests this claim by surveying a random sample of 10 owners who had the fuel

injection system replaced. The ages of the cars at the time of replacement were (in months):

29   42   49   48   53   46   30   51   42   52

   i. Use your calculator to verify that the mean age of a car when the fuel injection system fails is $\bar{x} = 44.2$ months with standard deviation $s \approx 8.61$ months.

  ii. Test the claim that the fuel injection system lasts less than an average of 48 months before needing replacement. Use a 5% level of significance.

17. *Archaeology: Arrowheads* The Wind Mountain archaeological site is in southwest New Mexico. Prehistoric Native Americans called Anasazi once lived and hunted small game in this region. A stemmed projectile point is an arrowhead that has a notch on each side of the base. Both stemmed and stemless projectile points were found at the Wind Mountain site. A random sample of $n_1 = 55$ stemmed projectile points showed the mean length to be $\bar{x}_1 = 3.0$ cm with sample standard deviation $s_1 = 0.8$ cm. Another random sample of $n_2 = 51$ stemless projectile points showed the mean length to be $\bar{x}_2 = 2.7$ cm with $s_2 = 0.9$ cm. (Source: *Mimbres Mogollon Archaeology*, by A. I. Woosley and A. J. McIntyre, University of New Mexico Press.) Do these data indicate a difference (either way) in the population mean length of the two types of projectile points? Use a 5% level of significance.

DATA HIGHLIGHTS: GROUP PROJECTS

Break into small groups and discuss the following topics. Organize a brief outline in which you summarize the main points of your group discussion.

1. "With Sampling, There Is Too a Free Lunch"—This is a headline that appeared in *The Wall Street Journal*. The article is about food product samples available at grocery stores. Giving out food samples is expensive and labor-intensive. It clogs supermarket aisles. It is risky. What if a customer tries an item and spits it out on the floor or says the product is awful? It creates litter. Some customers drop toothpicks or small paper cups on the floor or spill the product. However, the budget that companies are willing to spend to have their products sampled is growing. The director of communications for Bigg's "hypermarket" (a combination grocery and general-merchandise store) says that more than 60% of customers sample products and about 37% of those who sample buy the product.

  (a) Let's test the hypothesis that 60% of customers sample a particular product. What is the null hypothesis? Do you believe that the percentage of customers who sample products is less than, more than, or just different from 60%? What will you use for the alternate hypothesis?

  (b) Choose a level of significance α.

  (c) Go to a grocery store when special products are being sampled (not just the usual in-house store samples often available at the deli or bakery). Count the number of customers going by the display when a sample is available and the number of customers who try the sample. Be sure the number of customers n is large enough to use the normal distribution to approximate the binomial.

  (d) Using your sample data, conclude the hypothesis test. What is your conclusion?

  (e) Do you think different food products might have a higher or lower percentage of customers trying them? For instance, does a higher percentage of customers try samples of pizza than samples of yogurt? How could you use statistics to justify your answer?

(f) Do you want to include young children in your sample? Do they pick up items to include in the customer's basket, or do they just munch the samples?

2. "Sweets May Not Be Culprit in Hyper Kids"—This is a *USA Today* headline reporting results of a study that appeared in the *New England Journal of Medicine*. In this study, the subjects were 25 normal preschoolers, aged 3 to 5, and 23 kids, aged 6 to 10, who had been described as "sensitive to sugar." The kids and their families were put on three different diets for 3 weeks each. One diet was high in sugar, one was low in sugar and contained aspartame, and one was low in sugar and contained saccharin. The diets were all free of additives, artificial food coloring, preservatives, and chocolate. All food in the household was removed, and the meals were delivered to the families. Researchers gathered information about the kids' behavior from parents, babysitters, and teachers. In addition, researchers tested the kids for memory, concentration, reading, and math skills. The result: "We couldn't find any difference in terms of their behavior or their learning on any of the three diets," says Mark Wolraich, professor of pediatrics at Vanderbilt University Medical Center, who oversaw the project. In another interview, Dr. Wolraich is quoted as saying, "Our study would say there is no evidence sugar has an adverse effect on children's behavior."

(a) This research involved comparing several means, not just two. (An introduction to such methods, called *analysis of variance*, is found in Chapter 11.) However, let us take a simplified view of the problem and consider the difference of behavior when children consumed the diet with sugar compared with their behavior when they consumed the diet with aspartame and low sugar. List some variables that might be measured to reflect the behavior of the children.

(b) Let's assume that the general null hypothesis was that there is no difference in children's behavior when they have a diet high in sugar. Was the evidence sufficient to allow the researchers to reject the null hypothesis and conclude that there are differences in children's behavior when they have a diet high in sugar? When we cannot reject H_0, have we *proved* that H_0 is true? In your own words, paraphrase the comments made by Dr. Wolraich.

LINKING CONCEPTS: WRITING PROJECTS

Discuss each of the following topics in class or review the topics on your own. Then write a brief but complete essay in which you summarize the main points. Please include formulas and graphs as appropriate.

The most important questions in life usually cannot be answered with absolute certainty. Many important questions are answered by giving an estimate and a measure of confidence in the estimate. This was the focus of Chapter 8. However, sometimes important questions must be answered in a more straightforward manner by a simple *yes* or *no*. Hypothesis testing is the statistical process of answering questions with a straightforward yes or no *and* providing an estimate of the risk in accepting the answer.

(a) Review and discuss type I and type II errors associated with hypothesis testing.

(b) Review and discuss the level of significance and power of a statistical test.

(c) The following statements are very important. Give them some careful thought and discuss them.

(i) When we fail to reject the null hypothesis, we do not claim it is absolutely true. We simply claim that at the given level of significance, the data were not sufficient to reject the null hypothesis.

(ii) When we accept the alternate hypothesis, we do not claim the null hypothesis is absolutely false. We do claim that at the given level of significance, the data presented enough evidence to reject the null hypothesis.

(d) In the text, it is said that a statistical test is a package of five basic ingredients. List these ingredients, discuss them in class, and write a short description of how these ingredients relate to the above discussion questions.

(e) As access to computers becomes more and more prevalent, we see the P-value reported in hypothesis testing more frequently. Review the use of the P-value in hypothesis testing. What is the difference between the level of significance of a test and the P-value? Considering both the P-value and level of significance, under what conditions do we reject or fail to reject the null hypothesis?

Using Technology

SIMULATION

Recall that the level of significance α is the probability of mistakenly rejecting a true null hypothesis. If $\alpha = 0.05$, then we expect to mistakenly reject a true null hypothesis about 5% of the time. The following simulation conducted with Minitab demonstrates this phenomenon.

We draw 40 random samples of size 50 from a population that is normally distributed with mean $\mu = 30$ and standard deviation $\sigma = 2.5$. The display shows the results of a hypothesis test with

$$H_0: \mu = 30 \qquad H_1: \mu > 30$$

for each of the 40 samples labeled C1 through C40. Because each of the 40 samples is drawn from a population with mean $\mu = 30$, the null hypothesis $H_0: \mu = 30$ is true for the test based on each sample. However, as the display shows, for some samples we reject the true null hypothesis.

(a) How many of the 40 samples have a sample mean $\bar{x}$ above $\mu = 30$? below $\mu = 30$?

(b) Look at the P-value of the sample statistic $\bar{x}$ in each of the 40 samples. How many P-values are less than or equal to $\alpha = 0.05$? What percent of the P-values are less than or equal to α? What percent of the samples have us reject H_0 when, in fact, each of the samples was drawn from a normal distribution with $\mu = 30$, as hypothesized in the null hypothesis?

(c) If you have access to computer or calculator technology that creates random samples from a normal distribution with a specified mean and standard deviation, repeat this simulation. Do you expect to get the same results? Why or why not?

Minitab Display: Random samples of size 50 from a normal population with $\mu = 30$ and $\sigma = 2.5$

```
Z-Test
Test of mu = 30.000 vs. mu > 30.000
The assumed sigma = 2.50
Variable   N    Mean    StDev   SE Mean      Z      P
C1        50   30.002   2.776    0.354    0.01   0.50
C2        50   30.120   2.511    0.354    0.34   0.37
C3        50   30.032   2.721    0.354    0.09   0.46
C4        50   30.504   2.138    0.354    1.43   0.077
C5        50   29.901   2.496    0.354   -0.28   0.61
C6        50   30.059   2.836    0.354    0.17   0.43
C7        50   30.443   2.519    0.354    1.25   0.11
C8        50   29.775   2.530    0.354   -0.64   0.74
C9        50   30.188   2.204    0.354    0.53   0.30
C10       50   29.907   2.302    0.354   -0.26   0.60
C11       50   30.036   2.762    0.354    0.10   0.46
C12       50   30.656   2.399    0.354    1.86   0.032
C13       50   30.158   2.884    0.354    0.45   0.33
C14       50   29.830   3.129    0.354   -0.48   0.68
C15       50   30.308   2.241    0.354    0.87   0.19
C16       50   29.751   2.165    0.354   -0.70   0.76
C17       50   29.833   2.358    0.354   -0.47   0.68
C18       50   29.741   2.836    0.354   -0.73   0.77
C19       50   30.441   2.194    0.354    1.25   0.11
C20       50   29.820   2.156    0.354   -0.51   0.69
C21       50   29.611   2.360    0.354   -1.10   0.86
C22       50   30.569   2.659    0.354    1.61   0.054
C23       50   30.294   2.302    0.354    0.83   0.20
C24       50   29.978   2.298    0.354   -0.06   0.53
C25       50   29.836   2.438    0.354   -0.46   0.68
C26       50   30.102   2.322    0.354    0.29   0.39
C27       50   30.066   2.266    0.354    0.19   0.43
C28       50   29.071   2.219    0.354   -2.63   1.00
C29       50   30.597   2.426    0.354    1.69   0.046
C30       50   30.092   2.296    0.354    0.26   0.40
C31       50   29.803   2.495    0.354   -0.56   0.71
C32       50   29.546   2.335    0.354   -1.28   0.90
C33       50   29.702   1.902    0.354   -0.84   0.80
C34       50   29.233   2.657    0.354   -2.17   0.98
C35       50   30.097   2.472    0.354    0.28   0.39
C36       50   29.733   2.588    0.354   -0.76   0.78
C37       50   30.379   2.976    0.354    1.07   0.14
C38       50   29.424   2.827    0.354   -1.63   0.95
C39       50   30.288   2.396    0.354    0.81   0.21
C40       50   30.195   3.051    0.354    0.55   0.29
```

573

Technology Hints

TI-84Plus/TI-83Plus

Press **STAT** and select **EDIT.** Highlight the list name such as L1. Then press **MATH,** select **PRB,** and highlight **6:randNorm(μ, σ, sample size).** Press enter. Fill in the values of $\mu = 30$, $\sigma = 2.5$, and sample size = 50. Press enter. Now list L1 contains a random sample from the normal distribution specified.

To test the hypothesis H_0: $\mu = 30$ against H_1: $\mu > 30$, press **STAT,** select **TESTS,** and use option **1:Z-Test.** Fill in the value 30 for μ_0, 2.5 for σ, and $> \mu_0$. The output provides the value of the sample statistic $\bar{x}$, its corresponding z value, and the P-value of the sample statistic.

Excel

To draw random samples from a normal distribution with $\mu = 30$ and $\sigma = 2.5$, use the menu choices **Tools ➤ Data Analysis ➤ Random Number Generator.** In the dialogue box below, the number of variables is the number of samples. Fill in the rest of the dialogue box as shown.

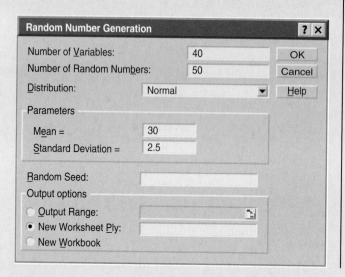

To conduct a hypothesis test of H_0: $\mu = 30$ against H_1: $\mu > 30$, use the command **ZTEST(data range, 30, 2.5).** This command is described as returning the two-tailed P-value of the z test. However, it appears to give the P-value of a right-tailed test. Use the **ZTEST** command with caution and check your results against the table results.

Minitab

To generate random samples from a normal distribution, use the menu choices **Calc ➤ Random Data ➤ Normal.** In the dialogue box, the number of rows refers to the sample size. Use 50 rows. Then designate the columns for the samples. Using C1–C40 will generate 40 random samples and put the samples in columns C1 through C40.

To test the hypothesis H_0: $\mu = 30$ against H_1: $\mu > 30$, use the menu choices **Stat ➤ Basic Statistics ➤ 1-SampleZ.** Use columns C1–C40 as the variables. Fill in 30 for the test mean, use greater than for the alternate hypothesis, and use 2.5 for sigma.

SPSS

SPSS uses a Student's t distribution to test the mean and difference of means. SPSS uses the sample standard deviation s even if the population σ is known. Use the menu choices **Analyze ➤ Compare Means** and then **One-Sample T Test** or **Independent-Sample T Tests** for tests of a single mean or a difference of means, respectively. In the dialogue box, fill in the test value of the null hypothesis.

To generate 40 random samples of size $n = 50$ from a normal distribution with $\mu = 30$ and $\sigma = 2.5$, first enter consecutive integers from 1 to 50 in a column of the data editor. Then, under variable view, enter the variable names Sample1 through Sample40. Use the menu choices **Transform ➤ Compute.** In the dialogue box, use

Sample1 for the target variable, and then select the function I Normal(mean, stddev). Use 30 for the mean and 2.5 for the standard deviation. Continue until you have 40 samples. To sample from other distributions, use appropriate functions in the Compute dialogue box.

The SPSS display shows the test results (H_0: $\mu = 30$; H_1: $\mu \neq 30$) for a sample of size $n = 50$ drawn from a normal distribution with $\mu = 30$ and $\sigma = 2.5$. The P-value is given as the significance for a two-tailed test. For a one-tailed test, divide the significance by 2. In the display, the significance is 0.360 for a two-tailed test. So, for a one-tailed test, the P-value is 0.360/2 or 0.180.

SPSS Display

T-Test

One-Sample Statistics

	N	Mean	Std. Deviation	Std. Error Mean
SAMPLE1	50	30.3228	2.46936	.34922

One-Sample Test

	Test Value = 30				90% Confidence Interval of the Difference	
	t	df	Sig. (2-tailed)	Mean Difference	Lower	Upper
SAMPLE1	.924	49	.360	.3228	−.2627	.9083

575

Cumulative Review Problems

CHAPTERS 7–9

Answers may vary due to rounding.

1. *Terminology* Please give a careful but brief answer to each of the following questions.
   (a) What is a population? How do you get a simple random sample? Give examples.
   (b) What is a sample statistic? What is a sampling distribution? Give examples.
   (c) Give a careful and complete statement of the central limit theorem.
   (d) List at least three areas of everyday life to which the above concepts can be applied. Be specific.

2. *Sampling Distribution $\bar{x}$* Workers at a large toxic cleanup project are concerned that their white blood cell counts may have been reduced. Let x be a random variable that represents white blood cell count per cubic millimeter of whole blood in a healthy adult. Then $\mu = 7500$ and $\sigma \approx 1750$ (Reference: *Diagnostic Tests with Nursing Applications*, S. Loeb). A random sample of $n = 50$ workers from the toxic cleanup site were given a blood test that showed $\bar{x} = 6820$. What is the probability that for healthy adults $\bar{x}$ will be this low or lower?
   (a) How does the central limit theorem apply? Explain.
   (b) Compute $P(\bar{x} \leq 6820)$.
   (c) Based on your answer to part (b), would you recommend that additional facts be obtained, or would you recommend that the workers' claims be dismissed? Explain.

3. *Sampling Distribution $\hat{p}$* Do you have a great deal of confidence in the advice given to you by your medical doctor? About 45% of all adult Americans claim they do have a great deal of confidence in their M.D.s (Reference: *National Opinion Research Center*, University of Chicago). Suppose that a random sample of $n = 32$ adults in a health insurance program are asked about their confidence in the medical advice their doctors give.
   (a) What is the probability that at least 18 out of 32 will say they have a great deal of confidence in the medical advice they receive?
   (b) What is the probability that 10 or fewer out of 32 will say they have a great deal of confidence in the medical advice they receive?
   (c) Is the normal approximation to the proportion $\hat{p} = r/n$ valid in both parts (a) and (b)? Explain. What is the expected value and standard deviation of $\hat{p}$?

In Problems 4–9, please use the following steps (i) through (v) for all hypothesis tests.
 (i) What is the level of significance? State the null and alternate hypotheses.
(ii) What sampling distribution will you use? What assumptions are you making? What is the value of the sample test statistic?
(iii) Find (or estimate) the P-value. Sketch the sampling distribution and show the area corresponding to the P-value.
(iv) Based on your answers in parts (i) to (iii), will you reject or fail to reject the null hypothesis? Are the data statistically significant at level α?
 (v) State your conclusion in the context of the application.

Note: For degrees of freedom *d.f.* not in the Student's *t* table, use the closest *d.f.* that is *smaller*. In some situations, this choice of *d.f.* may increase the *P*-value a small amount, and thereby produce a slightly more "conservative" answer.

4. *Testing and Estimating μ, σ Known* Let *x* be a random variable that represents micrograms of lead per liter of water (ug/l). An industrial plant discharges water into a creek. The Environmental Protection Agency has studied the discharged water and found *x* to have a normal distribution with $\sigma = 0.7$ ug/l (Reference: *EPA Wetlands Case Studies*).
   (a) The industrial plant says that the population mean value of *x* is $\mu = 2.0$ ug/l. However, a random sample of $n = 10$ water samples showed that $\bar{x} = 2.56$ ug/l. Does this indicate that the lead concentration population mean is higher than the industrial plant claims? Use $\alpha = 1\%$.
   (b) Find a 95% confidence interval for μ using the sample data and the EPA value for σ.
   (c) How large a sample should be taken to be 95% confident that the sample mean $\bar{x}$ is within a margin of error $E = 0.2$ ug/l of the population mean?

5. *Testing and Estimating μ, σ Unknown* Carboxyhemoglobin is formed when hemoglobin is exposed to carbon monoxide. Heavy smokers tend to have a high percentage of carboxyhemoglobin in their blood (Reference: *Laboratory and Diagnostic Tests*, F. Fishbach). Let *x* be a random variable representing percentage of carboxyhemoglobin in the blood. For a person who is a regular heavy smoker, *x* has a distribution that is approximately normal. A random sample of $n = 12$ blood tests given to a heavy smoker gave the following results (percent carboxyhemoglobin in the blood).

   9.1   9.5   10.2   9.8   11.3   12.2   11.6   10.3   8.9   9.7   13.4   9.9

   (a) Use a calculator to verify that $\bar{x} \approx 10.49$ and $s \approx 1.36$.
   (b) A long-term population mean $\mu = 10\%$ is considered a health risk. However, a long-term population mean above 10% is considered a clinical alert that the person may be asymptomatic. Do the data indicate that the population mean percentage is higher than 10% for this patient? Use $\alpha = 0.05$.
   (c) Use the given data to find a 99% confidence interval for μ for this patient.

6. *Testing and Estimating a Proportion p* Although older Americans are most afraid of crime, it is young people who are more likely to be the actual victims of crime. It seems that older people are more cautious about the people with whom they associate. A national survey showed that 10% of all people ages 16–19 have been victims of crime (Reference: *Bureau of Justice Statistics*). At Jefferson High School, a random sample of $n = 68$ students (ages 16–19) showed that $r = 10$ had been victims of a crime.
   (a) Do these data indicate that the population proportion of students in this school (ages 16–19) who have been victims of a crime is different (either way) from

the national rate for this age group? Use $\alpha = 0.05$. Do you think the conditions $np > 5$ and $nq > 5$ are satisfied in this setting? Why is this important?

(b) Find a 90% confidence interval for the proportion of students in this school (ages 16–19) who have been victims of a crime.

(c) How large a sample size should be used to be 95% sure that the sample proportion $\hat{p}$ is within a margin of error $E = 0.05$ of the population proportion of all students in this school (ages 16–19) who have been victims of a crime? *Hint:* Use sample data $\hat{p}$ as a preliminary estimate for p.

7. *Testing Paired Differences* Phosphorous is a chemical that is found in many household cleaning products. Unfortunately, phosphorous also finds its way into surface water where it can harm fish, plants, and other wildlife. Two methods of phosphorous reduction are being studied. At a random sample of 7 locations, both methods were used and the total phosphorous reduction (mg/l) was recorded. (Reference: *Environmental Protection Agency Case Study 832-R-93-005.*)

Site	1	2	3	4	5	6	7
Method I:	0.013	0.030	0.015	0.055	0.007	0.002	0.010
Method II:	0.014	0.058	0.017	0.039	0.017	0.001	0.013

Do these data indicate a difference (either way) in the average reduction of phosphorous between the two methods? Use $\alpha = 0.05$.

8. *Testing and Estimating $\mu_1 - \mu_2$, σ_1 and σ_2 Unknown* In the airline business, "on-time" flight arrival is important for connecting flights and general customer satisfaction. Is there a difference between summer and winter average on-time flight arrivals? Let x_1 be a random variable that represents percentage of on-time arrivals at major airports in the summer. Let x_2 be a random variable that represents percentage of on-time arrivals at major airports in the winter. A random sample of $n_1 = 16$ major airports showed that $\bar{x}_1 = 74.8\%$ with $s_1 = 5.2\%$. A random sample of $n_2 = 18$ major airports showed that $\bar{x}_2 = 70.1\%$ with $s_2 = 8.6\%$. (Reference: *Statistical Abstract of the United States.*)

(a) Does this information indicate a difference (either way) in the population mean percentage of on-time arrivals for summer compared to winter? Use $\alpha = 0.05$.

(b) Find an 95% confidence interval for $\mu_1 - \mu_2$.

(c) What assumptions about the original populations have you made for the methods used?

9. *Testing and Estimating a Difference of Proportions $p_1 - p_2$* How often do you go out dancing? This question was asked by a professional survey group on behalf of the National Arts Survey. A random sample of $n_1 = 95$ single men showed that $r_1 = 23$ went out dancing occasionally. Another random sample of $n_2 = 92$ single women showed that $r_2 = 19$ went out dancing occasionally.

(a) Do these data indicate that the proportion of single men who go out dancing occasionally is higher than the proportion of single women? Use a 5% level of significance. List the assumptions you made in solving this problem. Do you think these assumptions are realistic?

(b) Compute a 90% confidence interval for the population difference of proportions $p_1 - p_2$ of single men and single women who occasionally go out dancing.

10. *Essay and Project* In Chapters 7, 8, and 9 you have studied sampling distributions, estimation, and hypothesis testing.

(a) Write a brief essay in which you discuss using information from samples to infer information about populations. Be sure to include methods of estimation and hypothesis testing in your discussion. What two sampling distributions are used in estimation and hypothesis testing of population means, proportions, paired differences, differences of means, and differences of proportions? What are the criteria for determining the appropriate sampling distribution? What is the level of significance of a test? What is the P-value? How is the P-value related to the alternate hypothesis? How is the null hypothesis related to the sample test statistic? Explain.

(b) Suppose you want to study the length of time devoted to commercial breaks for two different types of television programs. Identify the types of programs you want to study (e.g., sitcoms, sports events, movies, news, children's programs, etc.). Write a brief outline for your study. Consider whether you will used paired data (such as same time slot on two different channels) or independent samples. Discuss how to obtain random samples. How large should the sample be for a specified margin of error? Describe the protocol you will follow to measure the times of the commercial breaks. Determine whether you are going to compare the average time devoted to commercials or the proportion of time devoted to commercials. What assumptions will you make regarding population distributions? What graphics might be appropriate? What methods of estimation will you use? What methods of testing will you use?

10

Correlation and Regression

When it is not in our power to determine what is true, we ought to follow what is most probable.

—René Descartes

It is important to realize that statistics and probability do not deal in the realm of certainty. If there is any realm of human knowledge where genuine certainty exists, you may be sure that our statistical methods are not needed there. In most human endeavors, and in almost all of the natural world around us, the element of chance happenings cannot be avoided. When we cannot expect something with true certainty, we must rely on probability to be our guide. In this chapter we will study regression, correlation, and forecasting. One of the tools we use is a scatter plot. René Decartes was the first mathematician to systematically use rectangular coordinate plots. For this reason, such a coordinate axis is called a Cartesian axis.

**René Descartes
(1596–1650)**

French mathematician and philosopher.

PREVIEW QUESTIONS

◇ How can you use a scatter diagram to visually estimate the degree of linear correlation of two random variables?   (SECTION 10.1)

◇ How do you compute the correlation coefficient and what does it tell you about the strength of the linear relationship between two random variables?   (SECTION 10.1)

◇ What is the least-squares criterion? How do you find the equation of the least-squares line?   (SECTION 10.2)

◇ What is the coefficient of determination and what does it tell you about explained variation of *y* in a random sample of data pairs (*x, y*)?   (SECTION 10.2)

◇ How do you determine if the sample correlation coefficient is statistically significant?   (SECTION 10.3)

◇ How do you find a confidence interval for predictions based on the least-squares model?   (SECTION 10.3)

 For on-line student resources, visit **math.college.hmco.com/students** and follow the Statistics links to the Brase/Brase, *Understandable Statistics*, 8th edition web site.

580

◇ How do you test the slope β of the population least-squares line? How do you construct a confidence interval for β? (SECTION 10.4)

◇ What if you have more than just two random variables? How do you construct a linear regression model for three, four, or more random variables? (SECTION 10.4)

Changing Populations and Crime Rate

Is the crime rate higher in neighborhoods where people might not know each other very well? Is there a relationship between crime rate and population change? If so, can we make predictions based on such a relationship? Is the relationship statistically significant? Is it possible to predict crime rate from population changes?

Denver is a city that has had a lot of growth and consequently a lot of population change in recent years. Sociologists studying population changes and crime rate could find a wealth of information in Denver statistics. Let x be a random variable representing percentage change in neighborhood population in the past few years, and let y be a random variable representing crime rate (crimes per 1,000 population). A random sample of six Denver neighborhoods gave the following information (Source: *Neighborhood Facts*, The Piton Foundation). To find out more about the Piton Foundation, visit the Brase/Brase statistics site at **http://math.college. hmco.com/students** and find the link to the Piton Foundation.

x	29	2	11	17	7	6
y	173	35	132	127	69	53

Using information presented in this chapter, you will be able to analyze the relationship between the variables x and y using the following tools.

• Scatter diagram

• Sample correlation coefficient and coefficient of determination

• Least-squares line equation

• Predictions for y using the least-squares line

• Tests of population correlation coefficient and of slope of least-squares line

• Confidence intervals for slope and for predictions

(See Problem 6 in the Chapter Review Problems.)

10.1
Scatter Diagrams and Linear Correlation

FOCUS POINTS

✓ Make a scatter diagram.
✓ Visually estimate the location of the "best-fitting" line for a scatter diagram.
✓ Use sample data to compute the sample correlation coefficient r.
✓ Investigate the meaning of the correlation coefficient r.

Scatter diagram

Studies of correlation and regression of two variables usually begin with a graph of *paired data values* (x, y). We call such a graph a *scatter diagram*.

> A **scatter diagram** is a graph in which data pairs (x, y) are plotted as individual points on a grid with horizontal axis x and vertical axis y. We call x the **explanatory** variable and y the **response** variable.

By looking at a scatter diagram of data pairs, you can observe if there seems to be a linear relationship between the x and y values.

EXAMPLE 1

Scatter diagram

Phosphorous is a chemical used in many household and industrial cleaning compounds. Unfortunately, phosphorous tends to find its way into surface water, where it can kill fish, plants, and other wetland creatures. Phosphorous reduction programs are required by law and are monitored by the Environmental Protection Agency (EPA). (Reference: *EPA Case Study 832-R-93-005*.)

A random sample of eight sites in a California wetlands study gave the following information about phosphorous reduction in drainage water. In this study, x is

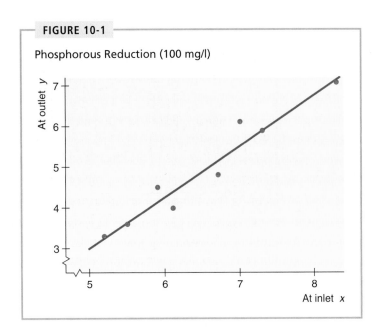

FIGURE 10-1

Phosphorous Reduction (100 mg/l)

a random variable that represents phosphorous concentration (in 100 mg/l) at the inlet of a passive biotreatment facility, and y is a random variable that represents total phosphorous concentration (in 100 mg/l) at the outlet of the passive biotreatment facility.

x	5.2	7.3	6.7	5.9	6.1	8.3	5.5	7.0
y	3.3	5.9	4.8	4.5	4.0	7.1	3.6	6.1

(a) Make a scatter diagram for these data.

> **SOLUTION:** Figure 10-1 shows points corresponding to the given data pairs. These plotted points constitute the scatter diagram. To make the diagram, first scan the data and decide on an appropriate scale for each axis. Figure 10-1 shows the scatter diagram (points) along with a line segment showing the basic trend. Notice a "jump scale" on both axes.

(b) Comment on the relationship between x and y shown in Figure 10-1.

> **SOLUTION:** By inspecting the figure, we see that smaller values of x are associated with smaller values of y and larger values of x tend to be associated with larger values of y. Roughly speaking, the general trend seems to be reasonably well represented by an upward-sloping line segment, as shown in the diagram.   ◊

Of course, it is possible to draw many curves close to the points in Figure 10-1, but a straight line is the simplest and most widely used for elementary studies of paired data. We can draw many lines in Figure 10-1, but in some sense, the "best" line should be the one that comes closest to each of the points of the scatter diagram. To single out one line as the "best-fitting line," we must find a mathematical criterion for this line and a formula representing the line. This will be done in Section 10.2 using the *method of least squares*.

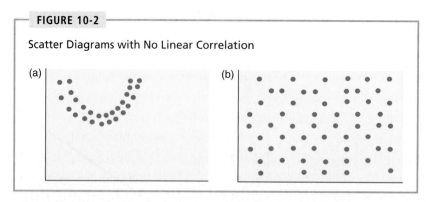

FIGURE 10-2

Scatter Diagrams with No Linear Correlation

(a)   (b)

Introduction to linear correlation

Another problem precedes that of finding the "best-fitting line." That is the problem of determining how well the points of the scatter diagram are suited for fitting *any* line. Certainly, if the points are a very poor fit to *any* line, there is little use in trying to find the "best" line.

If the points of a scatter diagram are located so that *no* line is realistically a "good" fit, we then say that the points possess *no linear correlation*. We see some examples of scatter diagrams for which there is no linear correlation in Figure 10-2.

GUIDED EXERCISE 1

Scatter diagram

A large industrial plant has seven divisions that do the same type of work. A safety inspector visits each division of 20 workers quarterly. The number *x* of work-hours devoted to safety training and the number *y* of work-hours lost due to industry-related accidents are recorded for each separate division in Table 10-1.

TABLE 10-1   Safety Report

Division	*x*	*y*
1	10.0	80
2	19.5	65
3	30.0	68
4	45.0	55
5	50.0	35
6	65.0	10
7	80.0	12

(a) Make a scatter diagram for these pairs. Use the *x* values on the horizontal axis and the *y* values on the vertical axis.

FIGURE 10-3   Scatter Diagram for Safety Report

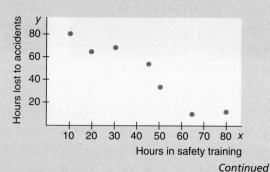

Continued

GUIDED EXERCISE 1 continued

(b) As the number of hours spent on safety training increases, what happens to the number of hours lost due to industry-related accidents?

⟹ In general, as the number of hours in safety training goes up, the number of hours lost due to accidents goes down.

(c) Does a line fit the data reasonably well?

⟹ A line fits reasonably well.

(d) Draw a line that you think "fits best."

⟹ Use a downward-sloping line that lies close to the points. Later, you will find the equation of the line that is a "best fit."

If the points seem close to a straight line, we say the linear correlation is low to moderate, depending on how close the points lie to a line. If all the points do, in fact, lie on a line, then we have *perfect linear correlation*. In Figure 10-4, we see some diagrams with perfect linear correlation. In statistical applications, perfect linear correlation almost never occurs.

Positive correlation

The variables x and y are said to have *positive correlation* if low values of x are associated with low values of y and high values of x are associated with high values of y. Figure 10-4 parts (a) and (c) show scatter diagrams in which the variables are positively correlated. On the other hand, if low values of x are associated with high values of y and high values of x are associated with low values of y, the variables are said to be *negatively correlated*. Figure 10-4 parts (b) and (d) show variables that are negatively correlated.

Negative correlation

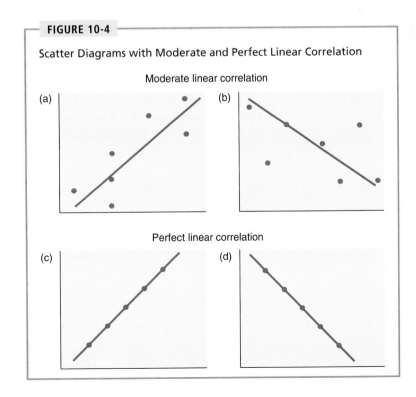

FIGURE 10-4

Scatter Diagrams with Moderate and Perfect Linear Correlation

Moderate linear correlation

(a)   (b)

Perfect linear correlation

(c)   (d)

GUIDED EXERCISE 2

Scatter diagram and linear correlation

Examine the scatter diagrams in Figure 10-5 and then answer the following questions.

FIGURE 10-5 Scatter Diagrams

(a)
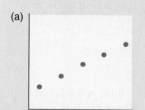

(b)
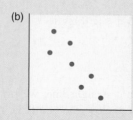

(c)
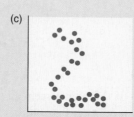

(a) Which diagram has no linear correlation?

⇨ Figure 10-5(c) has no linear correlation. No straight-line fit should be attempted.

(b) Which has perfect linear correlation?

⇨ Figure 10-5(a) has perfect linear correlation and can be fitted exactly by a straight line.

(c) Which can be reasonably fitted by a straight line?

⇨ Figure 10-5(b) can be reasonably fitted by a straight line.

TECH NOTE   The TI-84Plus and TI-83Plus calculators, Excel, and Minitab all produce scatter plots. For each technology, enter the x values in one column and the corresponding y values in another column. The displays show the data from Guided Exercise 1 regarding safety training and hours lost because of accidents. Notice that the scatter plots do not necessarily show the origin.

TI-84Plus/TI-83Plus Enter the data into two columns. Use **Stat Plot** and choose the first type. Use option **9: ZoomStat** under **Zoom**. To check the scale, look at the settings displayed under **Window**.

Excel Enter the data into two columns. Use the menu choices **Chart wizard ➤ Scatter Diagram**. Dialogue box choices permit you to label the axes and title the chart. Changing the size of the diagram box changes the scale on the axes.

Minitab Enter the data into two columns. Use the menu selections **Stat ➤ Regression ➤ Fitted Line Plot**. The best-fit line is automatically plotted on the scatter diagram.

TI-84Plus/TI-83Plus Display

Excel Display

Minitab Display

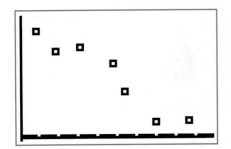

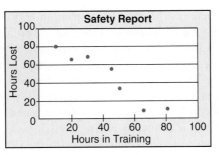

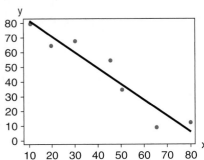

Sample Correlation Coefficient *r*

Looking at a scatter diagram to see whether a line best describes the relationship between the values of data pairs is useful. In fact, whenever you are looking for a relationship between two variables, making a scatter diagram is a good first step.

There is a mathematical measurement that describes the strength of the linear association between two variables. This measure is the *sample correlation coefficient r*. The full name for *r* is the *Pearson product-moment correlation coefficient*, named in honor of the English statistician Karl Pearson (1857–1936), who is credited with formulating *r*.

The **correlation coefficient *r*** is a numerical measurement that assesses the strength of a *linear* relationship between two variables *x* and *y*.

1. *r* is a unitless measurement between -1 and 1. In symbols, $-1 \leq r \leq 1$. If $r = 1$, there is perfect positive linear correlation. If $r = -1$, there is perfect negative linear correlation. If $r = 0$, there is no linear correlation. The closer *r* is to 1 or -1, the better a line describes the relationship between the two variables *x* and *y*.

2. Positive values of *r* imply that as *x* increases, *y* tends to increase. Negative values of *r* imply that as *x* increases, *y* tends to decrease.

3. The value of *r* is the same regardless of which variable is the explanatory variable and which is the response variable. In other words, the value of *r* is the same for the pairs (x, y) and the corresponding pairs (y, x).

4. The value of *r* does not change when either variable is converted to different units.

We'll develop the defining formula for *r* and then give a more convenient computation formula.

Development of Formula for *r*

If there is a *positive* linear relation between variables *x* and *y*, then high values of *x* are paired with high values of *y*, and low values of *x* are paired with low values of *y*. [See Figure 10-6(a).] In the case of *negative* linear correlation, high values of *x* are paired with low values of *y*, and low values of *x* are paired with high values of *y*. This relation is pictured in Figure 10-6(b). If there is *little or no linear correlation* between *x* and *y*, however, then we will find both high and low *x* values sometimes paired with high *y* values and sometimes paired with low *y* values. This relation is shown in Figure 10-6(c).

These observations lead us to the development of the formula for the correlation coefficient *r*. Taking *high* to mean "above the mean," we can express the relationships pictured in Figure 10-6 by considering the products

$$(x - \bar{x})(y - \bar{y})$$

If both *x* and *y* are high, both factors will be positive, and the product will be positive as well. The sign of this product will depend on the relative values of *x* and *y* compared with their respective means.

$$(x - \bar{x})(y - \bar{y}) \begin{cases} \text{is positive if } x \text{ and } y \text{ are both "high"} \\ \text{is positive if } x \text{ and } y \text{ are both "low"} \\ \\ \text{is negative if } x \text{ is "low," but } y \text{ is "high"} \\ \text{is negative if } x \text{ is "high," but } y \text{ is "low"} \end{cases}$$

In the case of positive linear correlation, most of the products $(x - \bar{x})(y - \bar{y})$ will be positive and so will the sum over all the data pairs

$$\Sigma(x - \bar{x})(y - \bar{y})$$

FIGURE 10-6

Patterns for Linear Correlation

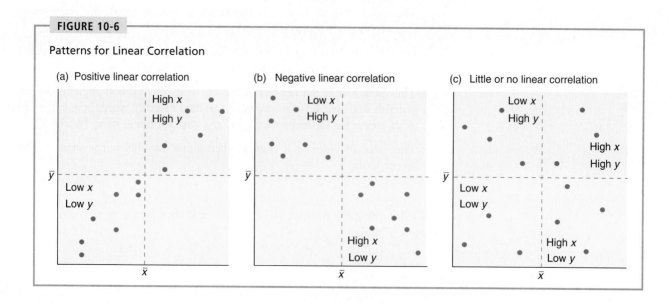

For negative linear correlation, the products will tend to be negative, so the sum also will be negative. On the other hand, in the case of little, if any, linear correlation, the sum will tend to be zero.

One trouble with the preceding sum is that it will be larger or smaller, depending on the units of x and y. Because we want r to be unitless, we standardize both x and y of a data pair by dividing each factor $(x - \bar{x})$ by the sample standard deviation s_x and each factor $(y - \bar{y})$ by s_y. Finally, we take an average of all the products. For technical reasons, we take the average by dividing by $n - 1$ instead of by n. This process leads us to the desired measurement, r.

$$r = \frac{1}{n - 1} \Sigma \frac{(y - \bar{y})}{s_y} \cdot \frac{(x - \bar{x})}{s_x} \tag{1}$$

Computation Formula for r

The defining formula for r shows how the mean and standard deviation of each variable in the data pair enter into the formulation of r. However, the defining formula is technically difficult to work with because of all the subtractions and products. A computation formula for r uses the raw data values of x and y directly.

PROCEDURE

How to compute the sample correlation coefficient r

Obtain a random sample of n data pairs (x, y). The data pairs should have a *bivariate normal distribution*. This means that for a fixed value of x, the y values should have a normal distribution (or at least a mound-shaped and symmetric distribution), and for a fixed y, the x values should have their own (approximately) normal distribution.

1. Using the data pairs, compute Σx, Σy, Σx^2, Σy^2, and Σxy.

2. With n = sample size, Σx, Σy, Σx^2, Σy^2, and Σxy, you are ready to compute the sample correlation coefficient r using the computation formula

$$r = \frac{n\Sigma xy - (\Sigma x)(\Sigma y)}{\sqrt{n\Sigma x^2 - (\Sigma x)^2} \ \sqrt{n\Sigma y^2 - (\Sigma y)^2}} \tag{2}$$

Be careful! The notation Σx^2 means first square x and then calculate the sum, whereas $(\Sigma x)^2$ means first sum the x values, then square the result.

It can be shown mathematically that r is always a number between $+1$ and -1 ($-1 \leq r \leq +1$). Table 10-2 on the next page gives a quick summary of some basic facts about r.

For most applications you will use a calculator or computer software to compute r directly. However, to build some familiarity with the structure of the correlation coefficient, it is useful to do some calculations for yourself. Example 2 and Guided Exercise 3 show how to use the computation formula to compute r.

TABLE 10-2   Some Facts About the Correlation Coefficient

If r Is	Then	The Scatter Diagram Might Look Something Like
0	There is no linear relation for the points of the scatter diagram.	
1 or -1	There is a perfect linear relation between x and y values; all points lie on the least-squares line.	$r = -1$ $r = 1$
Between 0 and 1 $(0 < r < 1)$	The x and y values have a *positive correlation.* By this, we mean that *large x* values are associated with *large y* values, and *small x* values are associated with *small y* values.	As we go from left to right, the least-squares line goes *up.*
Between -1 and 0 $(-1 < r < 0)$	The x and y values have a *negative correlation.* By this, we mean *large x* values are associated with *small y* values, and *small x* values are associated with *large y* values.	As we go from left to right, the least-squares line goes *down.*

EXAMPLE 2

Computing r

Sand driven by wind creates large beautiful dunes at the Great Sand Dunes National Monument, Colorado. Of course, the same natural forces also create large dunes in the Great Sahara and Arabia. Is there a linear correlation between wind velocity and sand drift rate? Let x be a random variable representing wind velocity (in 10 cm/sec) and let y be a random variable representing drift rate of sand (in 100 g/cm/sec). A test site at the Great Sand Dunes National Monument gave the following information about x and y. (Reference: *Hydrologic, Geologic, and Biologic Research at Great Sand Dunes National Monument,* Proceedings of the National Park Service Research Symposium.)

x	70	115	105	82	93	125	88
y	3	45	21	7	16	62	12

(a) Construct a scatter diagram. Do you expect r to be positive?

SOLUTION: Figure 10-7 displays the scatter diagram. From the scatter diagram it appears that as x values increase, y values also tend to increase. Therefore, r should be positive.

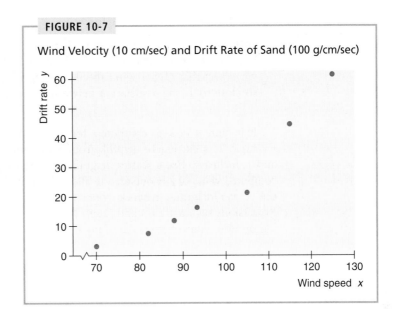

FIGURE 10-7

Wind Velocity (10 cm/sec) and Drift Rate of Sand (100 g/cm/sec)

(b) Compute r using the computation formula (formula 2).

SOLUTION: To find r, we need to compute Σx, Σx^2, Σy, Σy^2, and Σxy. It is convenient to organize the data in a table of five columns (Table 10-3) and then sum the entries in each column. Of course, many calculators give these sums directly. Using the computation formula for r, the sums from Table 10-3, and $n = 7$, we have

$$r = \frac{n\Sigma xy - (\Sigma x)(\Sigma y)}{\sqrt{n\Sigma x^2 - (\Sigma x)^2}\ \sqrt{n\Sigma y^2 - (\Sigma y)^2}} \tag{2}$$

$$= \frac{7(18,458) - (678)(166)}{\sqrt{7(67,892) - (678)^2}\ \sqrt{7(6768) - (166)^2}} \approx \frac{16,658}{(124.74)(140.78)} \approx 0.949$$

Note: Using a calculator to compute r directly gives 0.949, to three places after the decimal.

TABLE 10-3   Computation Table

x	y	x^2	y^2	xy
70	3	4900	9	210
115	45	13,225	2025	5175
105	21	11,025	441	2205
82	7	6724	49	574
93	16	8649	256	1488
125	62	15,625	3844	7750
88	12	7744	144	1056
$\Sigma x = 678$	$\Sigma y = 166$	$\Sigma x^2 = 67,892$	$\Sigma y^2 = 6768$	$\Sigma xy = 18,458$

(c) What does the value of *r* tell you?

SOLUTION: Since *r* is very close to 1, we have an indication of a strong positive linear correlation between wind velocity and drift rate of sand. In other words, we expect that higher wind speeds tend to mean greater drift rates. Because *r* is so close to 1, the association between the variables appears to be linear. ◊

It is quite a task to compute *r* for even 7 data pairs. The use of columns as in Example 2 is extremely helpful. Your value for *r* should always be between −1 and 1, inclusive. Use a scatter diagram to get a rough idea of the value of *r*. If your computed value of *r* is outside the allowable range, or if it disagrees quite a bit with the scatter diagram, recheck your calculations. Be sure you distinguish between expressions such as (Σx^2) and $(\Sigma x)^2$. Negligible rounding errors may occur, depending on how you (or your calculator) round.

GUIDED EXERCISE 3

Computing *r*

In one of the Boston city parks, there has been a problem with muggings in the summer months. A police cadet took a random sample of 10 days (out of the 90-day summer) and compiled the following data. For each day, *x* represents the number of police officers on duty in the park and *y* represents the number of reported muggings on that day.

x	10	15	16	1	4	6	18	12	14	7
y	5	2	1	9	7	8	1	5	3	6

(a) Construct a scatter diagram of *x* and *y* values.   Figure 10-8 shows the scatter diagram.

FIGURE 10-8 Scatter Diagram for Number of Police Officers versus Number of Muggings

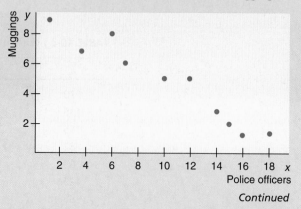

Continued

GUIDED EXERCISE 3 continued

(b) From the scatter diagram, do you think the computed value of r will be positive, negative, or zero? Explain.

 r will be negative. The general trend is that large x values are associated with small y values and vice versa. From left to right, the least-squares line goes down.

(c) Complete **TABLE 10-4**.

x	y	x^2	y^2	xy
10	5	100	25	50
15	2	225	4	30
16	1	256	1	16
1	9	1	81	9
4	7	16	49	28
6	8	___	___	___
18	1	___	___	___
12	5	___	___	___
14	3	___	___	___
7	6	49	36	42

$\Sigma x = 103$ $\Sigma y = 47$ $\Sigma x^2 =$ ___ $\Sigma y^2 =$ ___ $\Sigma xy =$ ___
$(\Sigma x)^2 =$ ___ $(\Sigma y)^2 =$ ___

TABLE 10-5   Completion of Table 10-4

x	y	x^2	y^2	xy
6	8	36	64	48
18	1	324	1	18
12	5	144	25	60
14	3	196	9	42

$\Sigma x^2 = 1347$ $\Sigma y^2 = 295$ $\Sigma xy = 343$
$(\Sigma x)^2 = 10{,}609$ $(\Sigma y)^2 = 2209$

(d) Compute r. Alternatively, find the value of r directly by using a calculator or computer software.

$$r = \frac{n\Sigma xy - (\Sigma x)(\Sigma y)}{\sqrt{n\Sigma x^2 - (\Sigma x)^2}\ \sqrt{n\Sigma y^2 - (\Sigma y)^2}}$$

$$= \frac{10(343) - (103)(47)}{\sqrt{10(1347) - (103)^2}\ \sqrt{10(295) - (47)^2}}$$

$$\approx \frac{-1411}{(53.49)(27.22)} \approx -0.969$$

TECH NOTE Most calculators that support two-variable statistics provide the value of the correlation coefficient r directly. Statistical software provides r, r^2, or both.

TI-84Plus/TI-83Plus First use **CATALOG**, find, **DiagnosticOn**, and press **Enter** twice. Then, when you use **STAT**, **CALC**, option **8:LinReg(a+bx)**, the value of r will be given (data from Example 2). In the next section we will discuss the line $y = a + bx$ and the meaning of r^2.

Excel Use the menu selection **Paste function** 〔 f_x 〕 ➤ **Statistical** ➤ **Correl.**

Minitab Use the menu selection **Stat** ➤ **Basic Statistics** ➤ **Correlation.**

```
LinReg
 y=a+bx
 a=-79.97763496
 b=1.070565553
 r²=.8997719968
 r=.9485631222
■
```

Cautions about Correlation

The correlation coefficient can be thought of as a measure of how well a linear model fits the data points on a scatter diagram. The closer r is to $+1$ or -1, the better a line "fits" the data. Values of r close to 0 indicate a poor fit to any line.

Usually a scatter diagram does not contain *all* possible data points that could be gathered. Most scatter diagrams represent only a *random sample* of data pairs taken from a very large population of all possible pairs. Because r is computed on the basis of a random sample of (x, y) pairs, we expect the values of r to vary from one sample to the next (much as the sample mean $\bar{x}$ varies from sample to sample). This brings up the question of the *significance* of r. Or, put another way, what are the chances that our random sample of data pairs indicates a high correlation when, in fact, the population x and y values are not so strongly correlated. Right now let's just say that the significance of r is a separate issue that will be treated in Section 10.3, where we test the *population correlation coefficient* ρ (Greek letter *rho*, pronounced "row").

> r = **sample** correlation coefficient computed from a random sample of (x, y) data pairs.
>
> ρ = **population** correlation coefficient computed from all population data pairs (x, y).

There is a less formal way to address the significance of r using a table of "critical values" or "cut-off values" based on the r distribution and the number of data pairs. Problem 17 at the end of this section discusses this method.

The correlation coefficient is a mathematical tool for measuring the strength of a linear relationship between two variables. As such, it makes no implication about cause or effect. The fact that two variables tend to increase or decrease together does not mean a change in one is *causing* a change in the other. A strong correlation between x and y is sometimes due to other (either known or unknown) variables. Such variables are called *lurking variables*.

> In ordered pairs (x, y), x is called the **explanatory** variable and y is called the **response** variable. When r indicates a linear correlation between x and y, changes in values of y tend to respond to changes in values of x according to a linear model. A **lurking variable** is a variable that is neither an explanatory nor a response variable. Yet, a lurking variable may be responsible for changes in both x and y.

EXAMPLE 3

Causation and lurking variables

Over a period of years, the population of a certain town increased. It was observed that during this period the correlation between x, the number of people attending church, and y, the number of people in the city jail, was $r = 0.90$. Does going to church *cause* people to go to jail? Is there a *lurking variable* that might cause both variables x and y to increase?

SOLUTION: We hope church attendance does not cause people to go to jail! During this period, there was an increase in population. Therefore, it is not too surprising that both the number of people attending church and the number of people in jail increased. The high correlation between x and y is likely due to the lurking variable of population increase.   ◇

Correlation between averages

The correlation between two variables consisting of averages is usually higher than the correlation between two variables representing corresponding raw data. One reason is that the use of averages reduces the variation existing between individual measurements (see Section 7.2 and the central limit theorem). A high correlation based on two variables consisting of averages does not necessarily imply a high correlation between two variables consisting of individual measurements. See Problem 19 at the end of this section.

VIEWPOINT

Low on Credit, High on Cost!!!

How do you measure automobile insurance risk? One way is to use a little statistics and customer credit rating. Insurers say statistics show that drivers who have a history of bad credit are more likely to be in serious car accidents. According to a high-level executive at Allstate Insurance Company, financial instability is an extremely powerful predictor of future insurance losses. In short, there seems to be a strong correlation between bad credit ratings and auto insurance claims. Consequently, insurance companies want to charge higher premiums to customers with bad credit ratings. Consumer advocates object strongly because they say bad credit *does not cause* automobile accidents. More than 20 states prohibit or restrict the use credit ratings to determine auto insurance premiums. Insurance companies respond by saying that your best defense is to pay your bills on time!

SECTION 10.1   PROBLEMS

Note: Answers may vary due to rounding.

1. *Scatter Diagrams: Linear Correlation* Look at the following diagrams. Does each diagram show high linear correlation, moderate or low linear correlation, or no linear correlation?

(a)

(b)

(c)

2. *Scatter Diagrams: Linear Correlation* Look at the following diagrams. Does each diagram show high linear correlation, moderate or low linear correlation, or no linear correlation?

(a) 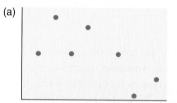   (b)    (c)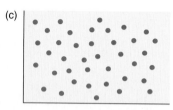

3. *Causation: Lurking Variables* Over the past few years, there has been a strong positive correlation between the annual consumption of diet soda drinks and the number of traffic accidents.
   (a) Do you think increasing consumption of diet soda drinks causes traffic accidents? Explain.
   (b) What lurking variables might be causing the increase in one or both of the variables? Explain.

4. *Causation: Lurking Variables* Over the past decade, there has been a strong positive correlation between teacher salaries and prescription drug costs.
   (a) Do you think paying teachers more causes prescription drugs to cost more? Explain.
   (b) What lurking variables might be causing the increase in one or both of the variables? Explain.

5. *Causation: Lurking Variables* Over the past 50 years, there has been a strong negative correlation between average annual income and the record time to run 1 mile. In other words, average annual incomes have been rising while the record time to run 1 mile has been decreasing.
   (a) Do you think increasing incomes cause decreasing times to run the mile? Explain.
   (b) What lurking variables might be causing the increase in one or both of the variables? Explain.

6. *Causation: Lurking Variables* Over the past 30 years in the United States, there has been a strong negative correlation between the number of infant deaths at birth and the number of people over age 65.
   (a) Is the fact that people are living longer causing a decrease in infant mortalities at birth?
   (b) What lurking variables might be causing the increase in one or both of the variables? Explain.

7. *Veterinary Science: Shetland Ponies* How much should a healthy Shetland pony weigh? Let x be the age of the pony (in months), and let y be the average weight of the pony (in kilograms). The following information is based on data taken from *The Merck Veterinary Manual* (a reference used in most veterinary colleges).

x	3	6	12	18	24
y	60	95	140	170	185

(a) Make a scatter diagram and draw the line you think best fits the data.
(b) Would you say the correlation is low, moderate, or strong? positive or negative?

(c) Use a calculator to verify that $\Sigma x = 63$, $\Sigma x^2 = 1089$, $\Sigma y = 650$, $\Sigma y^2 = 95,350$, and $\Sigma xy = 9930$. Compute r. As x increases, does the value of r imply that y should tend to increase or decrease? Explain.

8. *Health Insurance: Administrative Cost* The following data are based on information from *Domestic Affairs*. Let x be the average number of employees in a group health insurance plan, and let y be the average administrative cost as a percentage of claims.

x	3	7	15	35	75
y	40	35	30	25	18

(a) Make a scatter diagram and draw the line you think best fits the data.
(b) Would you say the correlation is low, moderate, or strong? positive or negative?
(c) Use a calculator to verify that $\Sigma x = 135$, $\Sigma x^2 = 7133$, $\Sigma y = 148$, $\Sigma y^2 = 4674$, and $\Sigma xy = 3040$. Compute r. As x increases, does the value of r imply that y should tend to increase or decrease? Explain.

9. *Meteorology: Cyclones* Can a low barometer reading be used to predict maximum wind speed of an approaching tropical cyclone? Data for this problem are based on information taken from *Weatherwise* (vol. 46, no. 1), a publication of the American Meteorological Society. For a random sample of tropical cyclones, let x be the lowest pressure (in millibars) as a cyclone approaches, and let y be the maximum wind speed (in miles per hour) of the cyclone.

x	1004	975	992	935	985	932
y	40	100	65	145	80	150

(a) Make a scatter diagram and draw the line you think best fits the data.
(b) Would you say the correlation is low, moderate, or strong? positive or negative?
(c) Use a calculator to verify that $\Sigma x = 5823$, $\Sigma x^2 = 5,655,779$, $\Sigma y = 580$, $\Sigma y^2 = 65,750$, and $\Sigma xy = 556,315$. Compute r. As x increases, does the value of r imply that y should tend to increase or decrease? Explain.

10. *Geology: Earthquakes* Is the magnitude of an earthquake related to the depth below the surface at which the quake occurs? Let x be the magnitude of an earthquake (on the Richter scale), and let y be the depth (in kilometers) of the quake below the surface at the epicenter. The following is based on information taken from the National Earthquake Information Service of the U.S. Geological Survey. Additional data may be found by visiting the Brase/Brase statistics site at **http://math.college.hmco.com/students** and finding the link to earthquakes.

x	2.9	4.2	3.3	4.5	2.6	3.2	3.4
y	5.0	10.0	11.2	10.0	7.9	3.9	5.5

(a) Make a scatter diagram and draw the line you think best fits the data.
(b) Would you say the correlation is low, moderate, or strong? positive or negative?
(c) Use a calculator to verify that $\Sigma x = 24.1$, $\Sigma x^2 = 85.75$, $\Sigma y = 53.5$, $\Sigma y^2 = 458.31$, and $\Sigma xy = 190.18$. Compute r. As x increases, does the value of r imply that y should tend to increase or decrease? Explain.

11. *Baseball: Batting Averages and Home Runs* In baseball, is there a linear correlation between batting average and home run percentage? Let x represent the batting

average of a professional baseball player. Let y represent the home run percentage (number of home runs per 100 times at bat). A random sample of $n = 7$ professional baseball players gave the following information. (Reference: *The Baseball Encyclopedia*, Macmillan Publishing Company.)

x	0.243	0.259	0.286	0.263	0.268	0.339	0.299
y	1.4	3.6	5.5	3.8	3.5	7.3	5.0

(a) Make a scatter diagram and draw the line you think best fits the data.
(b) Would you say the correlation is low, moderate, or high? positive or negative?
(c) Use a calculator to verify that $\Sigma x = 1.957$, $\Sigma x^2 \approx 0.553$, $\Sigma y = 30.1$, $\Sigma y^2 = 150.15$, and $\Sigma xy \approx 8.753$. Compute r. As x increases, does the value of r imply that y should tend to increase or decrease? Explain.

12. *University Crime: FBI Report* Do larger universities tend to have more property crime? University crime statistics are affected by a variety of factors. The surrounding community, accessibility given to outside visitors, and many other factors influence crime rate. Let x be a variable that represents student enrollment (in thousands) on a university campus. Let y be a variable that represents the number of burglaries in a year on a university campus. A random sample of $n = 8$ universities in California gave the following information about enrollments and annual burglary incidents. (Reference: *Crime in the United States*, Federal Bureau of Investigation.)

x	12.5	30.0	24.5	14.3	7.5	27.7	16.2	20.1
y	26	73	39	23	15	30	15	25

(a) Make a scatter diagram and draw the line you think best fits the data.
(b) Would you say the correlation is low, moderate, or high? positive or negative?
(c) Using a calculator, verify that $\Sigma x = 152.8$, $\Sigma x^2 = 3350.98$, $\Sigma y = 246$, $\Sigma y^2 = 10,030$, and $\Sigma xy = 5488.4$. Compute r. As x increases, does the value of r imply that y should tend to increase or decrease? Explain.

13. *Archaeology: Pottery* Wind Mountain archaeological site is located in southwest New Mexico. Ancient, prehistoric pottery vessels are usually found as sherds (broken pieces) and carefully reconstructed if enough sherds can be found. For reconstructed (or even rare unbroken) pottery vessels, let x be the body diameter (in centimeters), and let y be the height (in centimeters) of the vessel. The following data are based on information taken from *Mimbres Mogollon Archaeology*, by A. I. Woosley and A. J. McIntyre (University of New Mexico Press).

x	7.3	31.0	18.4	6.5	4.9	2.6	19.5	9.2	23.7
y	5.5	28.5	19.7	5.0	5.7	2.1	11.5	5.0	11.6

(a) Make a scatter diagram and draw the line you think best fits the data.
(b) Would you say the correlation is low, moderate, or high? positive or negative?
(c) Using a calculator, verify that $\Sigma x = 123.1$, $\Sigma x^2 = 2452.45$, $\Sigma y = 94.6$, $\Sigma y^2 = 1584.3$, and $\Sigma xy = 1897.19$. Compute r. As x increases, does the value of r imply that y should tend to increase or decrease? Explain.

14. *Physiology: Children* The following problem is based on information taken from the pediatrics section of *The Merck Manual* (a commonly used reference in medical schools and nursing programs). Let x be the body weight of a child (in kilograms), and let y be the metabolic rate of the child (in 100 kcal/24 h).

x	3.0	5.0	9.0	11.0	15.0	17.0	19.0	21.0
y	1.4	2.7	5.0	6.0	7.1	7.8	8.3	8.8

(a) Make a scatter diagram and draw the line you think best fits the data.

(b) Would you say the correlation is low, moderate, or high? positive or negative?

(c) Using a calculator, verify that $\Sigma x = 100$, $\Sigma x^2 = 1552$, $\Sigma y = 47.1$, $\Sigma y^2 = 327.83$, and $\Sigma xy = 710.3$. Compute r. As x increases, does the value of r imply that y should tend to increase or decrease? Explain.

15. *Expand Your Knowledge: Effect of Scale on Scatter Diagram* The initial visual impact of a scatter diagram depends on the scales used on the x and y axes. Consider the following data:

x	1	2	3	4	5	6
y	1	4	6	3	6	7

(a) Make a scatter diagram using the same scale on both the x and y axes (i.e., make sure the unit lengths on the two axes are equal).

(b) Make a scatter diagram using a scale on the y axis that is twice as long as that on the x axis.

(c) Make a scatter diagram using a scale on the y axis that is half as long as that on the x axis.

(d) On each of the three graphs, draw the straight line that you think best fits the data points. How do the slopes (or directions) of the three lines appear to change? (*Note:* The actual slopes will be the same; they just appear different because of the choice of scale factors.)

16. *Expand Your Knowledge: Effect on r of Exchanging x and y Values* Examine the computation formula for r, the sample correlation coefficient [formulas (1) and (2) of this section].

(a) In the formula for r, if we exchange the symbols x and y, do we get a different result or do we get the same (equivalent) result? Explain.

(b) If we have a set of x and y data values, and we exchange each corresponding x and y value to get a new data set, should the sample correlation coefficient be the same for both sets of data? Explain.

(c) Compute the sample correlation coefficient r for each of the following data sets and show that r is the same for both.

x	1	3	4
y	2	1	6

x	2	1	6
y	1	3	4

17. *Expand Your Knowledge: Using a Table to Test ρ* The correlation coefficient r is a *sample* statistic. What does it tell us about the value of the population correlation coefficient ρ (Greek letter rho)? We will build the formal structure of hypothesis tests of ρ in Section 10.3. However, there is a quick way to determine if the sample evidence based on r is strong enough to conclude that there is some population correlation between the variables. In other words, we can use the value of r to determine if $\rho \neq 0$. We do this by comparing the value $|r|$ to an entry in Table 10-6. The value of α in the table gives us the probability of concluding that $\rho \neq 0$ when in fact $\rho = 0$ and there is no population correlation. We have two choices for α: $\alpha = 0.05$ or $\alpha = 0.01$.

TABLE 10-6 Critical Values for Correlation Coefficient r

n	α = 0.05	α = 0.01	n	α = 0.05	α = 0.01	n	α = 0.05	α = 0.01
3	1.00	1.00	13	0.53	0.68	23	0.41	0.53
4	0.95	0.99	14	0.53	0.66	24	0.40	0.52
5	0.88	0.96	15	0.51	0.64	25	0.40	0.51
6	0.81	0.92	16	0.50	0.61	26	0.39	0.50
7	0.75	0.87	17	0.48	0.61	27	0.38	0.49
8	0.71	0.83	18	0.47	0.59	28	0.37	0.48
9	0.67	0.80	19	0.46	0.58	29	0.37	0.47
10	0.63	0.76	20	0.44	0.56	30	0.36	0.46
11	0.60	0.73	21	0.43	0.55			
12	0.58	0.71	22	0.42	0.54			

PROCEDURE

How to use Table 10-6 to test ρ

1. First compute r from a random sample of n data pairs (x, y).

2. Find the table entry in the row headed by n and the column headed by your choice of α. Your choice of α is the risk you are willing to take of mistakenly concluding that $\rho \neq 0$ when in fact $\rho = 0$.

3. Compare $|r|$ to the table entry.
   (a) If $|r| \geq$ table entry, then there is sufficient evidence to conclude that $\rho \neq 0$, and we say that r is **significant.** In other words, we conclude that there is some population correlation between the two variables x and y.

   (b) If $|r| <$ table entry, then the evidence is insufficient to conclude that $\rho \neq 0$, and we say that r is **not significant.** We do not have enough evidence to conclude that there is any correlation between the two variables x and y.

(a) Look at Problem 7 regarding the variables x = age of a Shetland pony and y = weight of that pony. Is the value of $|r|$ large enough to conclude that weight and age of Shetland ponies are correlated? Use $\alpha = 0.05$.

(b) Look at Problem 9 regarding the variables x = lowest barometric pressure as a cyclone approaches and y = maximum wind speed of the cyclone. Is the value of $|r|$ large enough to conclude that lowest barometric pressure and wind speed of a cyclone are correlated? Use $\alpha = 0.01$.

18. *Expand Your Knowledge: Sample Size and Significance of Correlation* In this problem we use Table 10-6 to explore the significance of r based on different sample sizes. See Problem 17.

(a) Is a sample correlation coefficient $r = 0.820$ significant at the $\alpha = 0.01$ level based on a sample size of $n = 7$ data pairs? What about $n = 9$ data pairs?

(b) Is a sample correlation coefficient $r = 0.40$ significant at the $\alpha = 0.05$ level based on a sample size of $n = 20$ data pairs? What about $n = 27$ data pairs?

(c) Is it true that in order to be significant, an r value must be larger than 0.90? larger than 0.70? larger than 0.50? What does sample size have to do with the significance of r? Explain.

19. *Expand Your Knowledge: Correlation of Averages* Fuming because you are stuck in traffic? Roadway congestion is a costly item, both in time wasted and fuel wasted. Let x represent the *average* annual hours per person spent in traffic delays and let y represent the *average* annual gallons of fuel wasted per person in traffic delays. A random sample of eight cities showed the following data. (Reference: *Statistical Abstract of the United States*, 122nd edition.)

x (hr)	28	5	20	35	20	23	18	5
y (gal)	48	3	34	55	34	38	28	9

(a) Draw a scatter diagram for the data. Verify that $\Sigma x = 154$, $\Sigma x^2 = 3712$, $\Sigma y = 249$, $\Sigma y^2 = 9959$, and $\Sigma xy = 6067$. Compute r.

The data in part (a) represent *average* annual hours lost per person and *average* annual gallons of fuel wasted per person in traffic delays. Suppose that instead of using average data for different cities, you selected one person at random from each city and measured the annual number of hours lost x for that person, and the annual gallons of fuel wasted y for the same person.

x (hr)	20	4	18	42	15	25	2	35
y (gal)	60	8	12	50	21	30	4	70

(b) Compute $\bar{x}$ and $\bar{y}$ for both sets of data pairs and compare the averages. Compute the sample standard deviations s_x and s_y for both sets of data pairs and compare the standard deviations. In which set are the standard deviations for x and y larger? Look at the defining formula for r, Equation 1. Why do smaller standard deviations s_x and s_y tend to increase the value of r?

(c) Make a scatter diagram for the second set of data pairs. Verify that $\Sigma x = 161$, $\Sigma x^2 = 4583$, $\Sigma y = 255$, $\Sigma y^2 = 12{,}565$, and $\Sigma xy = 7071$. Compute r.

(d) Compare r from part (a) with r from part (b). Do the data for averages have a higher correlation coefficient than the data for individual measurements? List some reasons why you think hours lost per individual and fuel wasted per individual might vary more than the same quantities averaged over all the people in a city.

20. *Expand Your Knowledge: Dependent Variables* In Section 5.1, we studied linear combinations of *independent* random variables. What happens if the variables are not independent? A lot of mathematics can be used to prove the following:

Let x and y be random variables with means μ_x and μ_y, variances σ_x^2 and σ_y^2, and population correlation coefficient ρ (the Greek letter rho). Let a and b be any constants and let $w = ax + by$. Then

$$\mu_w = a\mu_x + b\mu_y$$
$$\sigma_w^2 = a^2\sigma_x^2 + b^2\sigma_y^2 + 2ab\sigma_x\sigma_y\rho$$

In this formula, ρ is the population correlation coefficient theoretically computed using the population of all (x, y) data pairs. The expression $\sigma_x\sigma_y\rho$ is called the *covariance* of x and y. If x and y are independent, then $\rho = 0$ and the formula for σ_w^2 reduces to the appropriate formula for independent variables (see Section 5.1). In most real-world applications the population parameters are not known, so we use sample estimates with the understanding that our conclusions are also estimates.

Do you have to be rich to invest in bonds and real estate? No, mutual fund shares are available to you even if you aren't rich. Let x represent annual percentage return (after expenses) on the Vanguard Total Bond Index Fund, and let y represent annual percentage return on the Fidelity Real Estate Investment Fund. Over a long period of time, we have the following population estimates (based on *Morningstar Mutual Fund Report*).

$$\mu_x \approx 7.32 \qquad \sigma_x \approx 6.59 \qquad \mu_y \approx 13.19 \qquad \sigma_y \approx 18.56 \qquad \rho \approx 0.424$$

(a) Do you think the variables x and y are independent? Explain.
(b) Suppose you decide to put 60% of your investment in bonds and 40% in real estate. This means we will use a weighted average $w = 0.6x + 0.4y$. Estimate your expected percentage return μ_w and risk σ_w.
(c) Repeat part (b) if $w = 0.4x + 0.6y$.
(d) Compare your results in parts (b) and (c). Which investment has the higher expected return? Which has the greater risk as measured by σ_w?

10.2   Linear Regression and the Coefficient of Determination

FOCUS POINTS

✓ State the least-squares criterion.
✓ Use sample data to find the equation of the least-squares line. Graph the least-squares line.
✓ Use the least-squares line to predict a value of the response variable y for a specified value of the explanatory variable x.
✓ Explain the difference between interpolation and extrapolation.
✓ Explain why extrapolation beyond the sample data range might give results that are misleading or meaningless.
✓ Use r^2 to determine *explained* and *unexplained* variation of the response variable y.

In Denali National Park, Alaska, the wolf population is dependent on a large, strong caribou population. In this wild setting caribou are found in very large herds. The well-being of an entire caribou herd is not threatened by wolves. In fact, it is thought that wolves keep caribou herds strong by helping prevent overpopulation. Can the caribou population be used to predict the size of the wolf population?

Let x be a random variable that represents the fall caribou population (in hundreds) in Denali National Park. Let y be a random variable that represents the late-winter wolf population in the park. A random sample of recent years gave the following information. (Reference: U.S. Department of the Interior, National Biological Service.)

x	30	34	27	25	17	23	20
y	66	79	70	60	48	55	60

Looking at the scatter diagram in Figure 10-9 on the next page, we can ask some questions.

1. Do the data indicate a linear relationship between x and y?
2. Can you find an equation for the best-fitting line relating x and y? Can you use this relationship to predict the size of the wolf population when you know the size of the caribou population?
3. What fractional part of the variability in y can be associated with the variability in x? What fractional part of the variability in y is not associated with a corresponding variability in x?

The first step in answering these questions is to try to express the relationship as a mathematical equation. There are many possible equations, but the simplest and most widely used is the linear equation, or the equation of a straight line. Because

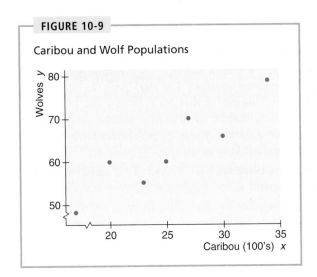

FIGURE 10-9

Caribou and Wolf Populations

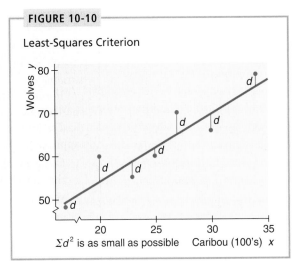

FIGURE 10-10

Least-Squares Criterion

we will be using this line to predict the y values from the x values, we call x the *explanatory variable* and y the *response variable*.

Explanatory variable

Response variable

Least-squares criterion

Our job is to find the "best" linear equation representing the points of the scatter diagram. For our criterion of best-fitting line, we use the *least-squares criterion*, which states that the line we fit to the data points must be such that *the sum of the squares of the vertical distances from the points to the line be made as small as possible*. The least-squares criterion is illustrated in Figure 10-10.

Least-squares criterion

The sum of the squares of the vertical distances from the data points (x, y) to the line is made as small as possible.

In Figure 10-10, d represents the difference between the y coordinate of the data point and the corresponding y coordinate on the line. Thus, if the data point lies above the line, d is positive, but if the data point is below the line, d is negative. As a result, the sum of the d values can be small even if the points are widely spread in the scatter diagram. However, the squares d^2 cannot be negative. By minimizing the sum of the squares, we are, in effect, not allowing positive and negative d values to "cancel out" one another in the sum. It is in this way that we can meet the least-squares criterion of minimizing the sum of the squares of the vertical distances between the points and the line over *all* points in the scatter diagram.

Least-squares Line

We use the notation $\hat{y} = a + bx$ for the least-squares line. A little algebra tells us that b is the slope and a is the intercept of the line. In this context $\hat{y}$ (read "y hat") represents the value of the response variable y estimated using the least squares line and a given value of the explanatory variable x.

Techniques of calculus can be applied to show that a and b may be computed using the following procedure.

PROCEDURE

How to find the equation for the least-squares line $\hat{y} = a + bx$

Obtain a random sample of n data pairs (x, y), where x is the *explanatory variable* and y is the *response variable*. The data pairs should have a *bivariate normal distribution*. This means that for a fixed value of x, the y values should have a normal distribution (or at least a mound-shaped and symmetric distribution), and for a fixed y, the x values should have their own (approximately) normal distribution.

1. Using the data pairs, compute Σx, Σy, Σx^2, Σy^2, and Σxy. Then compute the sample means $\bar{x}$ and $\bar{y}$.

2. With n = sample size, Σx, Σy, Σx^2, Σy^2, Σxy, $\bar{x}$, and $\bar{y}$, you are ready to compute the slope b and intercept a using the computation formulas

$$\text{Slope:} \qquad b = \frac{n\Sigma xy - (\Sigma x)(\Sigma y)}{n\Sigma x^2 - (\Sigma x)^2} \qquad\qquad (3)$$

$$\text{Intercept:} \quad a = \bar{y} - b\bar{x} \qquad\qquad\qquad\qquad (4)$$

Be careful! The notation Σx^2 means first square x and then calculate the sum, whereas $(\Sigma x)^2$ means first sum the x values, then square the result.

3. The equation of the least-squares line computed from your sample data is

$$\hat{y} = a + bx \qquad\qquad\qquad\qquad\qquad (5)$$

◇ **COMMENT:** The computation formulas for the slope of the least-squares line, the correlation coefficient r, and the standard deviations s_x and s_y use many of the same sums. There is, in fact, a relationship between the correlation coefficient r and the slope of the least-squares line b. In instances where we know r, s_x, and s_y, we can use the following formula to compute b.

$$b = r\left(\frac{s_y}{s_x}\right) \qquad\qquad\qquad\qquad\qquad (6) ◇$$

◇ **COMMENT:** In other mathematics courses, the slope-intercept form of the equation of a line is usually given as $y = mx + b$, where m refers to the slope of the line and b to the y-coordinate of the y-intercept. In statistics, when there is only one explanatory variable, it is common practice to use the letter b to designate the slope of the least-squares line and the letter a to designate the y-coordinate of the intercept. For example, these are the symbols used on the TI-84Plus and TI-83Plus calculators as well as many other calculators. ◇

Using the formulas to find the values of a and b

For most applications, you can use a calculator or computer software to compute a and b directly. However, to build some familiarity with the structure of the computation formulas, it is useful to do some calculations for yourself. Example 4 shows how to use the computation formulas to find the values of a and b and the equation of the least-squares line $\hat{y} = a + bx$.

Note: If you are using your calculator to find the values of a and b directly, then you may omit the discussion regarding use of the formulas. Go to the margin header "Using the values of a and b to construct the equation of the least-squares line."

EXAMPLE 4

Least-squares line

Let's find the least-squares equation relating the variables x = size of caribou population (in hundreds) and y = size of wolf population in Denali National Park. Use x as the explanatory variable and y as the response variable.

(a) Use the computation formulas to find the slope of the least-squares line b and the y-intercept a.

SOLUTION: Table 10-7 gives the data values x and y, along with the values x^2, y^2, and xy. First compute the sample means.

$$\bar{x} = \frac{\Sigma x}{n} = \frac{176}{7} \approx 25.14 \quad \text{and} \quad \bar{y} = \frac{\Sigma y}{n} = \frac{438}{7} \approx 62.57$$

Next compute the slope b.

$$b = \frac{n\Sigma xy - (\Sigma x)(\Sigma y)}{n\Sigma x^2 - (\Sigma x)^2} = \frac{7(11{,}337) - (176)(438)}{7(4628) - (176)^2} = \frac{2271}{1420} \approx 1.60$$

Use the values of b, $\bar{x}$, and $\bar{y}$ to compute the y-intercept a.

$$a = \bar{y} - b\bar{x} \approx 62.57 - 1.60(25.14) \approx 22.35$$

Note that calculators give the values $b \approx 1.599$ and $a \approx 22.36$. These values differ slightly from those you computed using the formulas because of rounding.

Using the values of a and b to construct the equation of the least-squares line

(b) Use the values of a and b (either computed or obtained from a calculator) to find the equation of the least-squares line.

SOLUTION:

$$\hat{y} = a + bx$$
$$\hat{y} \approx 22.35 + 1.60x \quad \text{since} \quad a \approx 22.35 \quad \text{and} \quad b \approx 1.60$$

TABLE 10-7   Sums for Computing b, $\bar{x}$, and $\bar{y}$

x	y	x^2	y^2	xy
30	66	900	4356	1980
34	79	1156	6241	2686
27	70	729	4900	1890
25	60	625	3600	1500
17	48	289	2304	816
23	55	529	3025	1265
20	60	400	3600	1200
$\Sigma x = 176$	$\Sigma y = 438$	$\Sigma x^2 = 4628$	$\Sigma y^2 = 28{,}026$	$\Sigma xy = 11{,}337$

Graphing the least squares line

(c) Graph the equation of the least-squares line on a scatter diagram.

> **SOLUTION:** To graph the least-squares line, we have several options available. The slope-intercept method of algebra is probably the quickest, but may not always be convenient if the intercept is not within the range of the sample data values. It is just as easy to select two x values in the range of the x data values and then use the least-squares line to compute two corresponding $\hat{y}$ values.
>
> In fact, we already have the coordinates of one point on the least squares line. By the formula for the intercept [Equation (4)], the point $(\bar{x}, \bar{y})$ is always on the least-squares line. For our example, $(\bar{x}, \bar{y}) = (25.14, 62.57)$.

> The point $(\bar{x}, \bar{y})$ is always on the least-squares line.

> Another x value within the data range is $x = 34$. Using the least-squares line to compute the corresponding $\hat{y}$ value gives
>
> $$\hat{y} \approx 22.35 + 1.60(34) \approx 76.75$$
>
> We place the two points (25.14, 62.57) and (34, 76.75) on the scatter diagram (using a different symbol than that used for the sample data points) and connect the points with a line segment (Figure 10-11).   ◊

Meaning of slope

In the equation $\hat{y} = a + bx$, the slope b tells us how many units $\hat{y}$ changes for each unit change in x. In Example 4 regarding size of wolf and caribou populations,

$$\hat{y} \approx 22.35 + 1.60x$$

The slope 1.60 tells us that if the number of caribou (in hundreds) changes by 1 (hundred), then we expect the sustainable wolf population to change by 1.60. In other words, our model says that an increase of 100 caribou will increase the predicted wolf population by 1.60. If the caribou population decreases by 400, we predict the sustainable wolf population to decrease by 6.4.

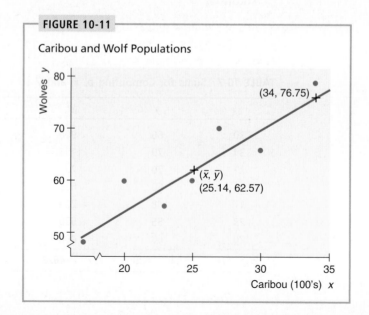

FIGURE 10-11

Caribou and Wolf Populations

> The slope of the least squares line tells how many units the response variable is expected to change for each unit change in the explanatory variable. The number of units change in the response variable for each unit change in the explanatory variable is called the **marginal change** of the response variable.

Predicting *y* for a specified *x*

Making predictions is one of the main applications of linear regression. In other words, you use the equation of the least-squares line to predict the $\hat{y}$ value for a specified *x* value. Of course, the accuracy of the prediction depends on how well the least-squares line fits the original raw data points. It is a good idea to check that the correlation coefficient indicates a strong linear correlation.

Interpolation, extrapolation

Another issue that affects the validity of predictions is whether you are *interpolating* or *extrapolating*.

> Predicting $\hat{y}$ values for *x* values that are **between** observed *x* values in the data set is called **interpolation.**

> Predicting $\hat{y}$ values of *x* values that are **beyond** observed *x* values in the data set is called **extrapolation.**

The least-squares line is developed from sample data pairs (*x*, *y*). The least-squares line may not reflect the relationship between *x* and *y* for values of *x* outside the data range. For example, there is a fairly high correlation between height and age for boys ages 1 year to 10 years. In general, the older the boy, the taller the boy. A least-squares line based on such data would give good predictions of height for ages between 1 and 10. However, it would be fairly meaningless to use the same linear regression line to predict the height of a 20-year-old or 50-year-old man.

Another consideration when working with predictions is the fact that the least-squares line is based on sample data. Each different sample will produce a slightly different equation for the least-squares line. Just as there are confidence intervals for parameters such as population means, there are confidence intervals for the prediction of *y* for a given *x*. We will examine confidence intervals for predictions in Section 10.3.

One more important fact about predictions. The least-squares line is developed with *x* as the explanatory variable and *y* as the response variable. This model can be used only to predict *y* values from specified *x* values. If you wish to begin with *y* values and predict corresponding *x* values, you must start all over and compute a new equation. Such an equation would be developed using a model with *x* as the response variable and *y* as the explanatory variable. See Problem 19 at the end of this section. Note that the equation for predicting *x* values *cannot* be derived from the least-squares line predicting *y* simply by solving the equation for *x*.

> The least-squares line developed with *x* as the explanatory variable and *y* as the response variable can be used only to predict *y* values from specified *x* values.

The next example shows how to use the least-squares line for predictions.

EXAMPLE 5

Predictions

We continue with Example 4 regarding size of the wolf population as it relates to size of the caribou population. Suppose you want to predict the size of the wolf population when the size of the caribou population is 21 (hundred).

(a) In the least-squares model developed in Example 4, which is the explanatory variable and which is the response variable? Can you use the equation to predict the size of the wolf population for a specified size of caribou population?

SOLUTION: The least-squares line $\hat{y} \approx 22.35 + 1.60x$ was developed using x = size of caribou population in hundreds as the explanatory variable and y = size of wolf population as the response variable. We can use the equation to predict the y value for a specified x value.

(b) The sample data pairs have x values ranging from 17 (hundred) to 34 (hundred) for the size of the caribou population. To predict the size of the wolf population when the size of the caribou population is 21 (hundred), will you be interpolating or extrapolating?

SOLUTION: Interpolating, since 21 (hundred) falls within the range of sample x values.

(c) Predict the size of the wolf population when the caribou population is 21 (hundred).

SOLUTION: Using the least-squares line from Example 4 and the value 21 in place of x gives

$$\hat{y} \approx 22.35 + 1.60x \approx 22.35 + 1.60(21) \approx 55.95$$

Rounding up to a whole number gives a prediction of 56 for the size of the wolf population.   ◇

GUIDED EXERCISE 4

Least-squares line

The Quick Sell car dealership has been using 1-minute spot ads on a local TV station. The ads always occur during the evening hours and advertise the different models and price ranges of cars on the lot that week. During a 10-week period, the Quick Sell dealer kept a weekly record of the number x of TV ads versus the number y of cars sold. The results are given in Table 10-8.

The manager decided that Quick Sell can afford only 12 ads per week. At that level of advertisement, how many cars can Quick Sell expect to sell each week? We'll answer this question in several steps.

TABLE 10-8

x	y
6	15
20	31
0	10
14	16
25	28
16	20
28	40
18	25
10	12
8	15

Continued

GUIDED EXERCISE 4 continued

(a) Draw a scatter diagram for the data.

⇨ The scatter diagram is shown in Figure 10-12. The plain red dots in Figure 10-12 are the points of the scatter diagram. Notice that the least-squares line is also shown with two extra points used to position the line.

FIGURE 10-12 Scatter Diagram and Least-Squares Line for Table 10-8

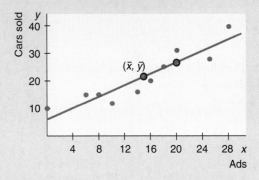

(b) Look at Equations (3) to (5) pertaining to the least-squares line (page 604). Two of the quantities that we need to find b are (Σx) and (Σxy). List the others.

⇨ We also need n, (Σy), (Σx^2), and $(\Sigma x)^2$.

(c) Complete Table 10-9(a).

⇨ The missing table entries are shown in Table 10-9(b).

TABLE 10-9(a)

x	y	x^2	xy
6	15	36	90
20	31	400	620
0	10	0	0
14	16	196	224
25	28	625	700
16	20	256	320
28	40	——	——
18	25	——	——
10	12	——	——
8	15	64	120
$\Sigma x = 145$	$\Sigma y = 212$	$\Sigma x^2 = $ ___	$\Sigma xy = $ ___

TABLE 10-9(b)

x^2	xy
$(28)^2 = 784$	$28(40) = 1120$
$(18)^2 = 324$	$18(25) = \ \ 450$
$(10)^2 = 100$	$10(12) = \ \ 120$
$\Sigma x^2 \ = 2785$	$\Sigma xy \ = 3764$

(d) Compute the sample means $\bar{x}$ and $\bar{y}$.

⇨ $\bar{x} = \dfrac{\Sigma x}{n} = \dfrac{145}{10} = 14.5$

$\bar{y} = \dfrac{\Sigma y}{n} = \dfrac{212}{10} = 21.2$

Continued

GUIDED EXERCISE 4 continued

(e) Compute a and b for the equation $\hat{y} = a + bx$ of the least-squares line.

$\Longrightarrow$

$$b = \frac{n\Sigma xy - (\Sigma x)(\Sigma y)}{n\Sigma x^2 - (\Sigma x)^2}$$

$$= \frac{10(3764) - (145)(212)}{10(2785) - (145)^2} = \frac{6900}{6825} \approx 1.01$$

$$a = \bar{y} - b\bar{x}$$

$$\approx 21.2 - 1.01(14.5) \approx 6.56$$

(f) What is the equation of the least-squares line $\hat{y} = a + bx$?

$\Longrightarrow$

Using the values of a and b computed in part (e) or values of a and b obtained directly from a calculator,

$$\hat{y} \approx 6.56 + 1.01x$$

(g) Plot the least-squares line on your scatter diagram.

$\Longrightarrow$

The least-squares line goes through the point $(\bar{x}, \bar{y}) = (14.5, 21.2)$. To get another point on the line, select a value for x and compute the corresponding y value using the equation $y = 6.56 + 1.01x$. For $x = 20$, we get $y = 6.56 + 1.01(20) = 26.8$, so the point $(20, 26.8)$ is also on the line. The least-squares line is shown in Figure 10-12.

(h) Read the y value for $x = 12$ from your graph. Then use the equation of the least-squares line to calculate y when $x = 12$. How many cars can the manager expect to sell if 12 ads per week are aired on TV?

$\Longrightarrow$

The graph gives $y \approx 19$. From the equation we get

$$y = 6.56 + 1.01x$$

$$= 6.56 + 1.01(12) \quad \text{using 12 in place of } x$$

$$= 18.68$$

To the nearest whole number, the manager can expect to sell 19 cars when 12 ads are aired on TV each week.

TECH NOTE   When we have more data pairs, it is convenient to use a technology tool such as the TI-84Plus and TI-83Plus calculators, Excel, or Minitab to find the equation of the least-squares line. The displays show results for the data of Guided Exercise 4 regarding car sales and ads.

TI-84Plus/TI-83Plus Press **STAT**, choose **Calculate**, and use option **8:LinReg(a+bx)**. For a graph showing the scatter plot and the least-squares line, press the **STAT PLOT** key, turn on a plot, and highlight the first type. Then press the **Y=** key. To enter the equation of the least-squares line, press **VARS**, select **5:Statistics**, highlight **EQ**, and then **1:RegEQ**. Press **ENTER**. Finally, press **ZOOM** and choose **9:ZoomStat**.

Excel There are several ways to find the equation of the least-squares line in Excel. One way is to make a scatter plot using the menu choices **Chart wizard ➤ Scatter Diagram**. When the diagram is complete, **right click** on one of the points on the diagram, select **trendline**, and under options check to display equation of line.

TI-84Plus/TI-83Plus Display   Excel Display

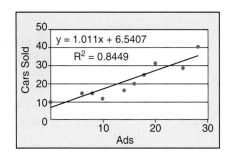

Minitab There are a number of ways to generate the least-squares line. One way is to use the menu selection **Stat ➤ Regression ➤ Fitted Line Plot.** The least-squares equation is shown with the diagram.

Coefficient of Determination

There is another way to answer the question, How good is the least-squares line as an instrument of regression? The *coefficient of determination* r^2 is the square of the sample correlation coefficient r.

Suppose we have a scatter diagram and corresponding least-squares line, as shown in Figure 10-13.

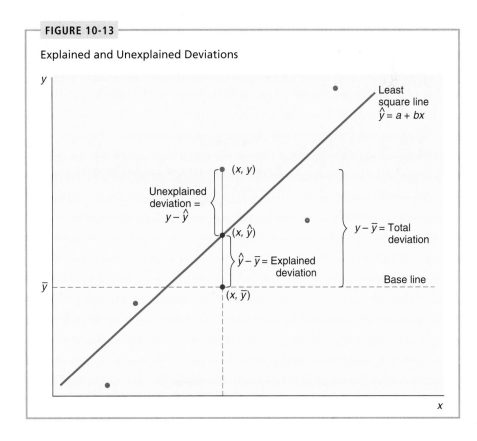

FIGURE 10-13

Explained and Unexplained Deviations

Let us take the point of view that $\bar{y}$ is a kind of baseline for the y values. If you were given an x value, and if you were completely ignorant of regression and correlation but you wanted to predict a value of y corresponding to the given x, a reasonable guess for y would be the mean $\bar{y}$. However, since we do know how to construct the least-squares regression line, we can calculate $\hat{y} = a + bx$, the predicted value corresponding to x. Now in most cases the predicted value $\hat{y}$ on the least-squares line will not be the same as the actual data value y. We will measure deviations (or differences) from the baseline $\bar{y}$. (See Figure 10-13 on the preceding page.)

$$\text{Total deviation} = y - \bar{y}$$
$$\text{Explained deviation} = \hat{y} - \bar{y}$$
$$\text{Unexplained deviation} = y - \hat{y} \qquad \text{(also known as the } \textit{residual}\text{)}$$

The total deviation $y - \bar{y}$ is a measure of how far y is from the baseline $\bar{y}$. This can be broken into two parts: the explained deviation $\hat{y} - \bar{y}$ tells us how far the estimated y value "should" be from the baseline $\bar{y}$. (The "explanation" of this part of the deviation is the least-squares line, so to speak.) The unexplained deviation $y - \hat{y}$ tells us how far our data value y is "off." This amount is called *unexplained* because it is due to random chance and other factors that the least-squares line cannot account for.

$$(y - \bar{y}) = (\hat{y} - \bar{y}) + (y - \hat{y})$$

$$\begin{pmatrix}\text{Total} \\ \text{deviation}\end{pmatrix} = \begin{pmatrix}\text{Explained} \\ \text{deviation}\end{pmatrix} + \begin{pmatrix}\text{Unexplained} \\ \text{deviation}\end{pmatrix}$$

At this point, we wish to include all the data pairs and we wish to deal only with nonnegative values (so positive and negative deviations won't cancel out). Therefore, we construct the following equation for the sum of squares. This equation can be derived using some lengthy algebraic manipulations, which we omit.

$$\Sigma(y - \bar{y})^2 = \Sigma(\hat{y} - \bar{y})^2 + \Sigma(y - \hat{y})^2$$

$$\begin{pmatrix}\text{Total} \\ \text{variation}\end{pmatrix} = \begin{pmatrix}\text{Explained} \\ \text{variation}\end{pmatrix} + \begin{pmatrix}\text{Unexplained} \\ \text{variation}\end{pmatrix}$$

Note that the sum of *squares* is taken over all data points and is then referred to as *variation* (not deviation).

The preceding concepts are connected together in the following important statement (whose proof we omit):

If r is the correlation coefficient [see Equation (2)], then it can be shown that

$$r^2 = \frac{\Sigma(\hat{y} - \bar{y})^2}{\Sigma(y - \bar{y})^2} = \frac{\text{Explained variation}}{\text{Total variation}}$$

r^2 is called the *coefficient of determination*.

Let us summarize our discussion.

> **Coefficient of determination r^2**
>
> 1. Compute the sample correlation coefficient r using the procedure of Section 10.1. Then simply compute r^2, the sample coefficient of determination.
>
> 2. The value r^2 is the ratio of explained variation over total variation. That is, r^2 is the fractional amount of total variation in y that can be explained by using the linear model $\hat{y} = a + bx$.
>
> 3. Furthermore, $1 - r^2$ is the fractional amount of total variation in y that is due to random chance or to the possibility of lurking variables that influence y.

In other words, the coefficient of determination r^2 is a measure of the proportion of variation in y that is explained by the regression line, using x as the explanatory variable. If $r = 0.90$, then $r^2 = 0.81$ is the coefficient of determination. We can say that about 81% of the (variation) behavior of the y variable can be explained by the corresponding (variation) behavior of the x variable if we use the equation of the least-squares line. The remaining 19% of the (variation) behavior of the y variable is due to random chance or to the possibility of lurking variables that influence y.

GUIDED EXERCISE 5

Coefficient of determination r^2

In Guided Exercise 4 we looked at the relationship between x = number of 1-minute spot ads on TV advertising different models of cars and y = number of cars sold each week by the sponsoring car dealership.

(a) Using the sums found in Guided Exercise 4, compute the correlation coefficient r. $n = 10$, $\Sigma x = 145$, $\Sigma y = 212$, $\Sigma x^2 = 2785$, and $\Sigma xy = 3764$. You also need $\Sigma y^2 = 5320$.

$$r = \frac{n\Sigma xy - (\Sigma x)(\Sigma y)}{\sqrt{n\Sigma x^2 - (\Sigma x)^2}\sqrt{n\Sigma y^2 - (\Sigma y)^2}}$$

$\Rightarrow$ $$r = \frac{10(3764) - (145)(212)}{\sqrt{10(2785) - (145)^2}\sqrt{10(5320) - (212)^2}}$$

$$\approx \frac{6900}{(82.61)(90.86)}$$

$$\approx 0.919$$

(b) Compute the coefficient of determination r^2.

$\Rightarrow$ $r^2 \approx 0.845$

(c) What percentage of the variation in the number of car sales can be explained by the ads and the least-squares line?

$\Rightarrow$ 84.5%

(d) What percentage of the variation in the number of car sales is not explained by the ads and the least-squares line?

$\Rightarrow$ 100% − 84.5%, or 15.5%

VIEWPOINT   *It's Freezing!*

Can we use average temperatures in January to predict how bad the rest of the winter will be? Can you predict the number of days with freezing temperatures for the entire calendar year using conditions in January? How good would such a forecast be for predicting growing season or number of frost-free days? Methods of this section can help you answer such questions. For more information, visit the Brase/Brase statistics site at **http://math.college.hmco.com/students** and find the link to temperatures.

SECTION 10.2   PROBLEMS

For Problems 1–16, please do the following.
(a) Draw a scatter diagram displaying the data.
(b) Verify the given sums Σx, Σy, Σx^2, Σy^2, and Σxy and the value of the sample correlation coefficient r.
(c) Find $\bar{x}$, $\bar{y}$, a, and b. Then find the equation of the least squares line $\hat{y} = a + bx$.
(d) Graph the least-squares line on your scatter diagram. Be sure to use the point $(\bar{x}, \bar{y})$ as one of the points on the line.
(e) Find the value of the coefficient of determination r^2. What percentage of the variation in y can be *explained* by the corresponding variation in x and the least-squares line? What percentage is *unexplained*?

Answers may vary slightly due to rounding.

1. *Economics: Entry-Level Jobs* An economist is studying the job market in Denver area neighborhoods. Let x represent the total number of jobs in a given neighborhood, and let y represent the number of entry-level jobs in the same neighborhood. A sample of six Denver neighborhoods gave the following information (units in 100s of jobs).

x	16	33	50	28	50	25
y	2	3	6	5	9	3

Source: Neighborhood Facts, The Piton Foundation. To find out more, visit the Brase/Brase statistics site at http://math.college.hmco.com/students and find the link to the Piton Foundation.

Complete parts (a) through (e), given $\Sigma x = 202$, $\Sigma y = 28$, $\Sigma x^2 = 7754$, $\Sigma y^2 = 164$, $\Sigma xy = 1096$, and $r \approx 0.860$.
(f) For a neighborhood with $x = 40$ jobs, how many are predicted to be entry-level jobs?

2. *Ranching: Cattle* You are the foreman of the Bar-S cattle ranch in Colorado. A neighboring ranch has calves for sale, and you are going to buy some calves to add to the Bar-S herd. How much should a healthy calf weigh? Let x be the age of the calf (in weeks), and let y be the weight of the calf (in kilograms). The following

information is based on data taken from *The Merck Veterinary Manual* (a reference used by many ranchers).

x	1	3	10	16	26	36
y	42	50	75	100	150	200

Complete parts (a) through (e), given $\Sigma x = 92$, $\Sigma y = 617$, $\Sigma x^2 = 2338$, $\Sigma y^2 = 82{,}389$, $\Sigma xy = 13{,}642$, and $r \approx 0.998$.

(f) The calves you want to buy are 12 weeks old. What does the least-squares line predict for a healthy weight?

3. *Weight of Car: Miles per Gallon* Do heavier cars really use more gasoline? Suppose that a car is chosen at random. Let x be the weight of the car (in hundreds of pounds), and let y be the miles per gallon (mpg). The following information is based on data taken from *Consumer Reports* (vol. 62, no. 4).

x	27	44	32	47	23	40	34	52
y	30	19	24	13	29	17	21	14

Complete parts (a) through (e), given $\Sigma x = 299$, $\Sigma y = 167$, $\Sigma x^2 = 11{,}887$, $\Sigma y^2 = 3773$, $\Sigma xy = 5814$, and $r \approx -0.946$.

(f) Suppose that a car weighs $x = 38$ (hundred pounds). What does the least-squares line forecast for $y =$ miles per gallon?

4. *Basketball: Fouls* Data for this problem are based on information from *STATS Basketball Scoreboard*. It is thought that basketball teams that make too many fouls in a game tend to lose the game even if they otherwise play well. Let x be the number of fouls more than (i.e., over and above) the opposing team. Let y be the percentage of times the team with the larger number of fouls wins the game.

x	0	2	5	6
y	50	45	33	26

Complete parts (a) through (e), given $\Sigma x = 13$, $\Sigma y = 154$, $\Sigma x^2 = 65$, $\Sigma y^2 = 6290$, $\Sigma xy = 411$, and $r \approx -0.988$.

(f) If a team had $x = 4$ fouls over and above the opposing team, what does the least-squares equation forecast for y?

5. *Auto Accidents: Age* Data for this problem are based on information taken from *The Wall Street Journal*. Let x be the age in years of a licensed automobile driver. Let y be the percentage of all fatal accidents (for a given age) due to speeding. For example, the first data pair indicates that 36% of all fatal accidents of 17-year-olds are due to speeding.

x	17	27	37	47	57	67	77
y	36	25	20	12	10	7	5

Complete parts (a) through (e), given $\Sigma x = 329$, $\Sigma y = 115$, $\Sigma x^2 = 18{,}263$, $\Sigma y^2 = 2639$, $\Sigma xy = 4015$, and $r \approx -0.959$.

(f) Predict the percentage of all fatal accidents due to speeding for 25-year-olds.

6. *Auto Accidents: Age* Let x be the age of a licensed driver in years. Let y be the percentage of all fatal accidents (for a given age) due to failure to yield the right of way. For example, the first data pair says that 5% of all fatal accidents of 37-year-olds are due to failure to yield the right of way. *The Wall Street Journal* article referenced in Problem 5 reported the following data:

x	37	47	57	67	77	87
y	5	8	10	16	30	43

Complete parts (a) through (e), given $\Sigma x = 372$, $\Sigma y = 112$, $\Sigma x^2 = 24{,}814$, $\Sigma y^2 = 3194$, $\Sigma xy = 8254$, and $r \approx 0.943$.
(f) Predict the percentage of all fatal accidents due to failing to yield the right of way for 70-year-olds.

7. *Income: Medical Care* Let x be per capita income in thousands of dollars. Let y be the number of medical doctors per 10,000 residents. Six small cities in Oregon gave the following information about x and y (based on information from *Life in America's Small Cities*, by G. S. Thomas, Prometheus Books).

x	8.6	9.3	10.1	8.0	8.3	8.7
y	9.6	18.5	20.9	10.2	11.4	13.1

Complete parts (a) through (e), given $\Sigma x = 53$, $\Sigma y = 83.7$, $\Sigma x^2 = 471.04$, $\Sigma y^2 = 1276.83$, $\Sigma xy = 755.89$, and $r \approx 0.934$.
(f) Suppose a small city in Oregon has a per capita income of 10 thousand dollars. What is the predicted number of M.D.s per 10,000 residents?

8. *Violent Crimes: Prisons* Does prison really deter violent crime? Let x represent percent change in the rate of violent crime and y represent percent change in the rate of imprisonment in the general U.S. population. For 7 recent years the following data have been obtained (Source: *The Crime Drop in America*, edited by Blumstein and Wallman, Cambridge University Press).

x	6.1	5.7	3.9	5.2	6.2	6.5	11.1
y	−1.4	−4.1	−7.0	−4.0	3.6	−0.1	−4.4

Complete parts (a) through (e), given $\Sigma x = 44.7$, $\Sigma y = -17.4$, $\Sigma x^2 = 315.85$, $\Sigma y^2 = 116.1$, $\Sigma xy = -107.18$, and $r \approx 0.084$.
(f) Considering the values of r and r^2, does it make sense to use the least-squares line for prediction? Explain.

9. *Education: Violent Crime* The following data are based on information from the book *Life in America's Small Cities* (by G. S. Thomas, Prometheus Books). Let x be the percentage of 16- to 19-year-olds not in school and not high school graduates. Let y be the reported violent crimes per 1000 residents. Six small cities in Arkansas (Blytheville, El Dorado, Hot Springs, Jonesboro, Rogers, and Russellville) reported the following information about x and y:

x	24.2	19.0	18.2	14.9	19.0	17.5
y	13.0	4.4	9.3	1.3	0.8	3.6

Complete parts (a) through (e), given $\Sigma x = 112.8$, $\Sigma y = 32.4$, $\Sigma x^2 = 2167.14$, $\Sigma y^2 = 290.14$, $\Sigma xy = 665.03$, and $r \approx 0.764$.

(f) If the percentage of 16- to 19-year-olds not in school and not graduates reaches 24% in a similar city, what is the predicted rate of violent crimes per 1000 residents?

10. *Research: Patents* The following data are based on information from the *Harvard Business Review* (vol. 72, no. 1). Let x be the number of different research programs, and let y be the mean number of patents per program. As in any business, a company can spread itself too thin. For example, too many research programs might lead to a decline in overall research productivity. The following data are for a collection of pharmaceutical companies and their research programs:

x	10	12	14	16	18	20
y	1.8	1.7	1.5	1.4	1.0	0.7

Complete parts (a) through (e), given $\Sigma x = 90$, $\Sigma y = 8.1$, $\Sigma x^2 = 1420$, $\Sigma y^2 = 11.83$, $\Sigma xy = 113.8$, and $r \approx -0.973$.

(f) Suppose that a pharmaceutical company had 15 different research programs. What does the least-squares equation forecast for y = mean number of patents per program?

11. *Archaeology: Artifacts* Data for this problem are based on information taken from *Prehistoric New Mexico: Background for Survey* (by D. E. Stuart and R. P. Gauthier, University of New Mexico Press). It is thought that prehistoric Indians did not take their best tools, pottery, and household items when they visited higher elevations for their summer camps. It is hypothesized that archaeological sites tend to lose their cultural identity and specific cultural affiliation as the elevation of the site increases. Let x be the elevation (in thousands of feet) for an archaeological site in the southwestern United States. Let y be the percentage of unidentified artifacts (no specific cultural affiliation) at a given elevation. The following data were obtained for a collection of archaeological sites in New Mexico:

x	5.25	5.75	6.25	6.75	7.25
y	19	13	33	37	62

Complete parts (a) through (e), given $\Sigma x = 31.25$, $\Sigma y = 164$, $\Sigma x^2 \approx 197.813$, $\Sigma y^2 = 6832$, $\Sigma xy = 1080$, and $r \approx 0.913$.

(f) At an archaeological site with elevation 6.5 (thousand feet), what does the least-squares equation forecast for y = percentage of culturally unidentified artifacts?

12. *Psychiatry: Irrelevant Responses* A child psychiatrist is studying the mental development of children. A random sample of nine children were given a standard set of questions appropriate to the age of each child. The number of irrelevant responses to the questions was recorded for each child. In the following data, x = age of child in years and y = number of irrelevant responses:

x	2	3	4	5	7	9	10	11	12
y	15	15	12	13	11	10	8	6	5

Complete parts (a) through (e), given $\Sigma x = 63$, $\Sigma y = 95$, $\Sigma x^2 = 549$, $\Sigma y^2 = 1109$, $\Sigma xy = 561$, and $r \approx -0.971$.

(f) If a child is 9.5 years old, what does the least-squares line predict for the number of irrelevant responses?

13. *Climatology: Frost* Data for this problem are from *Climatology Report No. 77-3* (by J. F. Benci and T. B. McKee, Department of Atmospheric Science, Colorado State University). Let x be the elevation (in thousands of feet), and let y be the average number of frost-free days in a year. For Denver, Gunnison, Aspen, Crested Butte, and Dillon, Colorado, the following data were obtained:

x	5.3	7.7	7.9	8.9	9.8
y	162	63	73	49	21

Complete parts (a) through (e), given $\Sigma x = 39.6$, $\Sigma y = 368$, $\Sigma x^2 = 325.04$, $\Sigma y^2 = 38{,}384$, $\Sigma xy = 2562.3$, and $r \approx -0.981$.

(f) Colorado Springs is at an elevation of 6 thousand feet. What does the least-squares equation forecast for the average number of frost-free days per year in Colorado Springs?

14. *Medical: Metabolic Rate* This problem is based on information taken from the pediatrics section of *The Merck Manual* (a commonly used reference in medical schools and nursing programs). Let x be the body weight of a child (in kilograms), and let y be the metabolic rate of the child (in 100 kcal/24 h).

x	3	5	9	11	15	17	19	21
y	1.4	2.7	5.0	6.0	7.1	7.8	8.3	8.8

Complete parts (a) through (e), given $\Sigma x = 100$, $\Sigma y = 47.1$, $\Sigma x^2 = 1552$, $\Sigma y^2 = 327.83$, $\Sigma xy = 710.3$, and $r \approx 0.984$.

(f) Suppose that a child weighs 16 kg. What does the least-squares line forecast for $y =$ metabolic rate of the child?

15. *Physics: CO_2* The following data are taken from the *Handbook of Physics and Chemistry* (CRC Publishing Company). Here $x =$ water temperature in degrees Celsius and $y =$ weight of carbon dioxide in grams that will dissolve in 100 g of water at 1 atmosphere of pressure for the corresponding temperature.

x	3	6	9	12	15
y	0.298	0.268	0.240	0.224	0.210

Complete parts (a) through (e), given $\Sigma x = 45$, $\Sigma y = 1.24$, $\Sigma x^2 = 495$, $\Sigma y^2 = 0.312504$, $\Sigma xy = 10.5$, and $r \approx -0.985$.

(f) If the temperature is 10°C, what does the least-squares line predict for the weight of carbon dioxide that will dissolve in 100 g of water?

 16. *Cricket Chirps: Temperature* Anyone who has been outdoors on a summer evening has probably heard crickets. Did you know that it is possible to use the cricket as a thermometer? Crickets tend to chirp more frequently as temperatures increase.

This phenomenon was studied in detail by George W. Pierce, a physics professor at Harvard. In the following data, x is a random variable representing chirps per second and y is a random variable representing temperature (°F). These data are on the statSpace CD-ROM.

x	20.0	16.0	19.8	18.4	17.1	15.5	14.7	17.1
y	88.6	71.6	93.3	84.3	80.6	75.2	69.7	82.0

x	15.4	16.2	15.0	17.2	16.0	17.0	14.4
y	69.4	83.3	79.6	82.6	80.6	83.5	76.3

Source: Reprinted by permission of the publisher from *The Songs of Insects* by George W. Pierce, Cambridge, Mass.: Harvard University Press, Copyright © 1948 by the President and Fellows of Harvard College.

Complete parts (a) through (e), given $\Sigma x = 249.8$, $\Sigma y = 1200.6$, $\Sigma x^2 = 4200.56$, $\Sigma y^2 = 96{,}725.86$, $\Sigma xy = 20{,}127.47$, and $r \approx 0.835$.

(f) What is the predicted temperature when $x = 19$ chirps per second?

17. *Expand Your Knowledge: Residual Plot* The least-squares line usually does not go through all the sample data points (x, y). In fact, for a specified x value from a data pair (x, y), there is usually a difference between the predicted value $\hat{y}$ and the y value paired with x. This difference is called the *residual*.

> The **residual** is the difference between the y value in a specified data pair (x, y) and the value $\hat{y} = a + bx$ predicted by the least-squares line for the same x.
>
> $y - \hat{y}$ is the **residual.**

One way to assess how well a least-squares line serves as a model for the data is a **residual plot.** To make a residual plot, we put the x values in order on the horizontal axis and plot the corresponding residuals $y - \hat{y}$ in the vertical direction. Because for a least-squares model the mean of the residuals is always zero, we dash in a horizontal line at zero. The accompanying figure shows a residual plot for the data of Guided Exercise 4, in which the relationship between the number of ads run per week and the number of cars sold that week was explored. To make the residual plot, first compute all the residuals. Remember that x and y are the given data values, and $\hat{y}$ is computed from the least-squares line $\hat{y} \approx 6.56 + 1.01x$.

Residual

x	y	$\hat{y}$	$y - \hat{y}$
6	15	12.6	2.4
20	31	26.8	4.2
0	10	6.6	3.4
14	16	20.7	−4.7
25	28	31.8	−3.8

Residual

x	y	$\hat{y}$	$y - \hat{y}$
16	20	22.7	−2.7
28	40	34.8	5.2
18	25	24.7	0.3
10	12	16.7	−4.7
8	15	14.6	0.4

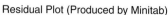

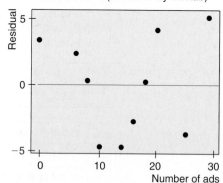

(a) If the least-squares line provides a reasonable model for the data, the pattern of points in the plot will seem random and unstructured around the horizontal line at 0. Is this the case for the residual plot?

(b) If a point on the residual plot seems far outside the pattern of other points, it might reflect an unusual data point (x, y), called an *outlier*. Such points may have quite an influence on the least-squares model. Do there appear to be any outliers in the data for the residual plot?

18. *Residual Plot: Miles per Gallon* Consider the data of Problem 3.
   (a) Make a residual plot for the least-squares model.
   (b) Use the residual plot to comment about the appropriateness of the least-squares model for these data. See Problem 17.

19. *Least-Squares Equation: Exchange x and y*
   (a) Suppose that you are given the following x, y data pairs:

x	1	3	4
y	2	1	6

   Show that the least-squares equation for these data is $y = 1.071x + 0.143$ (rounded to three digits after the decimal).

   (b) Now suppose that you are given these x, y data pairs:

x	2	1	6
y	1	3	4

   Show that the least-squares equation for these data is $y = 0.357x + 1.595$ (rounded to three digits after the decimal).

   (c) In the data for parts (a) and (b), did we simply exchange the x and y values of each data pair?

   (d) Solve $y = 0.143 + 1.071x$ for x. Do you get the least-squares equation of part (b) with the symbols x and y exchanged?

   (e) In general, suppose that we have the least-squares equation $y = a + bx$ for a set of data pairs x and y. If we solve this equation for x, will we *necessarily* get the least-squares equation for the set of data pairs y, x (with x and y exchanged)? Explain using parts (a) through (d).

10.3
Inferences for Correlation and Regression

FOCUS POINTS

✓ Test the correlation coefficient ρ.

✓ Use sample data to compute the standard error of estimate S_e.

✓ Find a confidence interval for the value of y predicted for a specified value of x.

✓ Test the slope β of the least-squares line.

✓ Find a confidence interval for the slope β of the least-squares line and interpret its meaning.

Learn more, earn more! We have probably all heard this platitude. The question is whether or not there is some truth in the statement. Do college graduates have an improved chance at a better income? Is there a trend in the general population to support the "learn more, earn more" statement?

Consider the following variables: x = percentage of the population 25 or older with at least four years of college and y = percentage *growth* in per capita income over the past seven years. A random sample of six communities in Ohio gave the information (based on *Life in America's Small Cities*, by G. S. Thomas) shown in Table 10-10.

If we use what we learned in Sections 10.1 and 10.2, we can compute the correlation coefficient r and the least-squares line $\hat{y} = a + bx$ using the data of Table 10-10. However, r is only a *sample* correlation coefficient and $\hat{y} = a + bx$ is only a "sample-based" least-squares line. What if we used *all* possible data pairs (x, y) from *all* U.S. cities, not just the six towns in Ohio? If we accomplished this seemingly impossible task, we would have the *population* of all (x, y) pairs.

From this population of (x, y) pairs we could (in theory) compute the *population correlation coefficient*, which we call ρ (Greek letter rho, pronounced like "row"). We could also compute the least-squares line for the entire population, which we denote as $y = \alpha + \beta x$ using more Greek letters, α (alpha) and β (beta).

Sample Statistic		Population Parameter
r	$\rightarrow$	ρ
a	$\rightarrow$	α
b	$\rightarrow$	β
$\hat{y} = a + bx$	$\rightarrow$	$y = \alpha + \beta x$

Assumptions for inferences concerning linear regression

To make inferences regarding the population correlation coefficient ρ and the slope β of the population least-squares line, we need to be sure that

(a) The set (x, y) of ordered pairs is a *random sample* from the population of all possible such (x, y) pairs.

(b) For each fixed value of x, the y values have a normal distribution. All of the y distributions have the same variance, and, for a given x value, the distribution of y values has a mean that lies on the least-squares line. We also assume that for a fixed y, each x has its own normal distribution. In most cases the results are still accurate if the distributions are simply mound-shaped and symmetric, and the y variances are approximately equal.

We assume these conditions are met for all inferences presented in this section.

TABLE 10-10   Education and Income Growth Percentages

x	9.9	11.4	8.1	14.7	8.5	12.6
y	37.1	43.0	33.4	47.1	26.5	40.2

Testing the Correlation Coefficient

The first topic we want to study is the statistical significance of the sample correlation coefficient r. To do this, we construct a statistical test of ρ, the population correlation coefficient. The test will be based on the following theorem.

◇ **THEOREM 10.1** Let r be the sample correlation coefficient computed using data pairs (x, y). We use the null hypothesis

H_0: x and y have no linear correlation, so $\rho = 0$

The alternate hypothesis may be

H_1: $\rho > 0$ or H_1: $\rho < 0$ or H_1: $\rho \neq 0$

The conversion of r to a Student's t distribution is

$$t = \frac{r\sqrt{n-2}}{\sqrt{1-r^2}} \quad \text{with } d.f. = n-2$$

where n is the number of sample data pairs (x, y) ($n \geq 3$). ◇

PROCEDURE

How to test the population correlation coefficient ρ

1. Use the *null hypothesis* H_0: $\rho = 0$. In the context of the application, state the *alternate hypothesis* ($\rho > 0$ or $\rho < 0$ or $\rho \neq 0$) and set the *level of significance* α.

2. Obtain a random sample of $n \geq 3$ data pairs (x, y) and compute the sample *test statistic*

$$t = \frac{r\sqrt{n-2}}{\sqrt{1-r^2}} \quad \text{with degrees of freedom } d.f. = n-2$$

3. Use a Student's t distribution and the type of test, one-tailed or two-tailed, to find (or estimate) the *P-value* corresponding to the test statistic.

4. *Conclude* the test. If P-value $\leq \alpha$, then reject H_0. If P-value $> \alpha$, then do not reject H_0.

5. *State your conclusion* in the context of the application.

EXAMPLE 6

Testing ρ

Let's return to our data from Ohio regarding the percentage of the population with at least four years of college and the percentage of growth in per capita income (Table 10-10). We'll develop a test for the population correlation coefficient ρ.

SOLUTION: First, we compute the sample correlation coefficient r. Using a calculator, statistical software, or "by-hand" calculation from Section 10.1, we find

$r \approx 0.887$

Now we test the correlation coefficient ρ. Remember that x represents percentage college graduates and y represents percentage salary increases in the general

TABLE 10-11   Excerpt from Student's *t* Distribution

✓one-tail area	0.010	0.005
two-tail area	0.020	0.010
d.f. = 4	3.747	4.604

Sample *t* = 3.84 (↑)

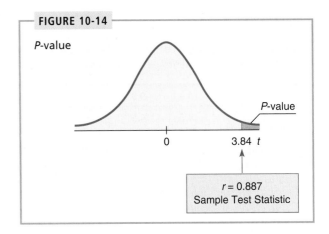

FIGURE 10-14

P-value

P-value

0   3.84 *t*

r = 0.887
Sample Test Statistic

population. We suspect the population correlation is positive, $\rho > 0$. Let's use a 1% level of significance:

H_0: $\rho = 0$ (no linear correlation)

H_1: $\rho > 0$ (positive linear correlation)

Convert the sample test statistic $r = 0.887$ to t using $n = 6$.

$$t = \frac{r\sqrt{n-2}}{\sqrt{1-r^2}} = \frac{0.887\sqrt{6-2}}{\sqrt{1-0.887^2}} \approx 3.84 \quad \text{with } d.f. = n - 2 = 6 - 2 = 4$$

The *P*-value for the sample test statistic $t = 3.84$ is shown in Figure 10-14. Since we have a right-tailed test, we use the one-tail area in the Student's *t* distribution (Table 6 of Appendix II).

From Table 10-11 we see that

$$0.005 < P\text{-value} < 0.010$$

Since the interval containing the *P*-value is less than the level of significance $\alpha = 0.01$, we reject H_0 and conclude that the population correlation coefficient between x and y is positive.

α
(———)
0.005   0.010

Note: Although we have shown that x and y are positively correlated, we have not shown that an increase in education *causes* an increase in earnings.   ◊

GUIDED EXERCISE 6

Testing ρ

A medical research team is studying the effect of a new drug on red blood cells. Let x be a random variable representing milligrams of the drug given to a patient. Let y be a random

Continued

GUIDED EXERCISE 6 continued

variable representing red blood cells per cubic milliliter of whole blood. A random sample of $n = 7$ volunteer patients gave the following results.

x	9.2	10.1	9.0	12.5	8.8	9.1	9.5
y	5.0	4.8	4.5	5.7	5.1	4.6	4.2

Use a calculator to verify that $r \approx 0.689$. Then use a 1% level of significance to test the claim that $\rho \neq 0$.

(a) State the null and alternate hypotheses. What is the level of significance α?

➡ $H_0: \rho = 0$; $H_1: \rho \neq 0$; $\alpha = 0.01$

(b) Compute the sample test statistic.

➡ $t = \dfrac{r\sqrt{n-2}}{\sqrt{1-r^2}} \approx \dfrac{0.689\sqrt{7-2}}{\sqrt{1-0.689^2}} \approx \dfrac{1.5406}{0.7248} \approx 2.126$

(c) Use the Student's t distribution, Table 6 of Appendix II, to estimate the P-value.

➡ $d.f. = n - 2 = 7 - 2 = 5$; two-tailed test

✓ two-tail area	0.100	0.050
$d.f. = 5$	2.015	2.571

Sample $t = 2.126$

$0.050 < P\text{-value} < 0.100$

(d) Do we reject or fail to reject H_0?

➡ Since the interval containing the P-value lies to the right of $\alpha = 0.01$, we do not reject H_0.

α

0.01   0.050   0.100

(e) State the conclusion in the context of the application.

➡ At the 1% level of significance, the evidence is not strong enough to indicate any correlation between the amount of drug administered and the red blood cell count.

Standard Error of Estimate

Sometimes a scatter diagram clearly indicates the existence of a linear relationship between x and y, but it can happen that the points are widely scattered around the least-squares line. We need a method (besides just looking) for measuring the spread of a set of points about the least-squares line. There are three common methods of measuring the spread. One method uses the *standard error of estimate*. The others are the *coefficient of correlation* and the *coefficient of determination*.

For the standard error of estimate, we use a measure of spread that is in some ways like the standard deviation of measurements of a single variable. Let

$\hat{y} = a + bx$

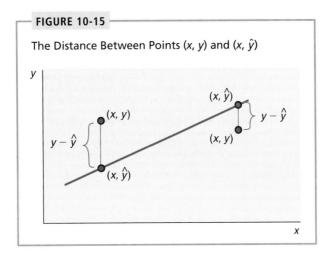

FIGURE 10-15

The Distance Between Points (x, y) and $(x, \hat{y})$

be the predicted value of y from the least-squares line. Then $y - \hat{y}$ is the difference between the y value of the *data point* (x, y) shown on the scatter diagram (Figure 10-15) and the $\hat{y}$ value of the point on the *least-squares line* with the same x value. The quantity $y - \hat{y}$ is known as the *residual*. To avoid the difficulty of having some positive and some negative values, we square the quantity $(y - \hat{y})$. Then we sum the squares and, for technical reasons, divide this sum by $n - 2$. Finally, we take the square root to obtain the *standard error of estimate*, denoted by S_e.

Residual

$$\text{Standard error of estimate} = S_e = \sqrt{\frac{\Sigma(y - \hat{y})^2}{n - 2}} \qquad (7)$$

where $\hat{y} = a + bx$ and $n \geq 3$.

Note: To compute the standard error of estimate, we require that there be at least three points on the scatter diagram. If we had only two points, the line would be a perfect fit, since two points determine a line. In such a case, there would be no need to compute S_e.

The nearer the scatter points lie to the least-squares line, the smaller S_e will be. In fact, if $S_e = 0$, it follows that each $y - \hat{y}$ is also zero. This means that all the scatter points lie *on* the least-squares line if $S_e = 0$. The larger S_e becomes, the more scattered the points are.

The formula for the standard error of estimate is reminiscent of the formula for the standard deviation. It, too, is a measure of dispersion. However, the standard deviation involves differences of data values from a mean, whereas the standard error of estimate involves the differences between experimental and predicted y values for a given x (i.e., $y - \hat{y}$).

The actual computation of S_e using Equation (7) is quite long because the formula requires us to use the least-squares line equation to compute a predicted value $\hat{y}$ for *each* x value in the data pairs. There is a computational formula that we strongly recommend you use. However, as with all the computation formulas, be careful about rounding. This formula is sensitive to rounding, and you should carry as many digits as seems reasonable for your problem. Answers will vary, depending on rounding used. We give the formula here and follow it with an example of its use.

> **PROCEDURE**
>
> **How to find the standard error of estimate S_e**
>
> 1. Obtain a random sample of $n \geq 3$ data pairs (x, y).
> 2. Use the procedures of Section 10.2 to find a and b from the sample least-squares line $\hat{y} = a + bx$.
> 3. The standard error of estimate is
>
> $$S_e = \sqrt{\frac{\Sigma y^2 - a\Sigma y - b\Sigma xy}{n - 2}} \qquad (8)$$

With a considerable amount of algebra, Equations (7) and (8) can be shown to be mathematically equivalent. Equation (7) shows the strong similarity between the standard error of estimate and standard deviation. Equation (8) is a shortcut calculation formula because it involves few subtractions. The sums Σx, Σy, Σx^2, Σy^2, and Σxy are provided directly on most calculators that support two-variable statistics.

In the next example, we show you how to compute the standard error of estimate using the computation formula.

EXAMPLE 7

Least-squares line and S_e

June and Jim are partners in the chemistry lab. Their assignment is to determine how much copper sulfate ($CuSO_4$) will dissolve in water at 10, 20, 30, 40, 50, 60, and 70°C. Their lab results are shown in Table 10-12, where y is the weight in grams of copper sulfate that will dissolve in 100 g of water at x°C.

Sketch a scatter diagram, find the equation of the least-squares line, and compute S_e.

SOLUTION: Figure 10-16 includes a scatter diagram for the data of Table 10-12. To find the equation of the least-squares line and the value of S_e, we set up a computational table (Table 10-13).

$$\bar{x} = \frac{\Sigma x}{n} = \frac{280}{7} = 40 \qquad \text{and} \qquad \bar{y} = \frac{\Sigma y}{n} = \frac{213}{7} \approx 30.429$$

$$b = \frac{n\Sigma xy - (\Sigma x)(\Sigma y)}{n\Sigma x^2 - (\Sigma x)^2} = \frac{7(9940) - (280)(213)}{7(14,000) - (280)^2} = \frac{9940}{19,600} \approx 0.50714$$

$$a = \bar{y} - b\bar{x} \approx 30.429 - 0.507(40) \approx 10.149$$

The equation of the least-squares line is

$$\hat{y} = a + bx$$
$$\hat{y} \approx 10.14 + 0.51x$$

The graph of the least-squares line is shown in Figure 10-16. Notice that it passes through the point $(\bar{x}, \bar{y}) = (40, 30.4)$. Another point on the line can be found by using $x = 15$ in the equation of the line $\hat{y} = 10.14 + 0.51x$. When we use 15 in place of x, we obtain $\hat{y} = 10.14 + 0.51(15) = 17.8$. The point $(15, 17.8)$ is the other point we used to graph the least-squares line in Figure 10-16.

The standard error of estimate is computed using the computational formula

$$S_e = \sqrt{\frac{\Sigma y^2 - a\Sigma y - b\Sigma xy}{n - 2}}$$

$$\approx \sqrt{\frac{7229 - 10.149(213) - 0.507(9940)}{7 - 2}} \approx \sqrt{\frac{27.683}{5}} \approx 2.35$$

Note: This formula is very sensitive to rounded values of a and b.

TABLE 10-12 Lab Results (x = °C, y = amount of CuSO₄)

x	y
10	17
20	21
30	25
40	28
50	33
60	40
70	49

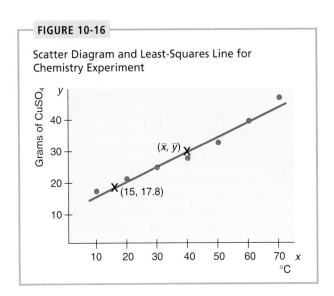

FIGURE 10-16

Scatter Diagram and Least-Squares Line for Chemistry Experiment

TABLE 10-13 Computational Table

x	y	x^2	y^2	xy
10	17	100	289	170
20	21	400	441	420
30	25	900	625	750
40	28	1,600	784	1,120
50	33	2,500	1,089	1,650
60	40	3,600	1,600	2,400
70	49	4,900	2,401	3,430
$\Sigma x = 280$	$\Sigma y = 213$	$\Sigma x^2 = 14{,}000$	$\Sigma y^2 = 7229$	$\Sigma xy = 9940$

TECH NOTE Although many calculators that support two-variable statistics and linear regression do not provide the value of the standard error of estimate S_e directly, they do provide the sums required for the calculation of S_e. The TI-84Plus/TI-83Plus, Excel, and Minitab all provide the value of S_e.

TI-84Plus/TI-83Plus The value for S_e is given as s under **STAT, TEST,** option **E: LinRegTTest.**

Excel Use the paste function (f_x), select **Statistical,** and choose the function **STEYX.**

Minitab Use the menu choices **Stat ➤ Regression ➤ Regression.** The value for S_e is given as s in the display.

Confidence Intervals for y

The least-squares line gives us a predicted value $\hat{y}$ for a specified x value. However, we used sample data to get the equation of the line. The line derived from the population of all data pairs is likely to have a slightly different slope, which we designate by the symbol β for population slope, and a slightly different y intercept, which we designate by the symbol α for population intercept. In addition, there is some random error ϵ, so the true y value would be

$$y = \alpha + \beta x + \epsilon$$

Because of the random variable ϵ, for each x value there is a corresponding distribution of y values. The methods of linear regression were developed so that the distribution of y values for a given x is centered on the population regression line. Furthermore, the distributions of y values corresponding to each x value all have the same standard deviation, estimated by the standard error of estimate S_e.

Using all this background, the theory tells us that for a specific x, a *c confidence interval for y* is given by the next procedure.

PROCEDURE

How to find a confidence interval for a predicted y from the least-squares line

1. Obtain a random sample of $n \geq 3$ data pairs (x, y).

2. Use the procedure of Section 10.2 to find $\hat{y} = a + bx$. You also need to find $\bar{x}$ from the sample data and the standard error of estimate S_e using equation (8) of this section.

3. The c confidence interval for y for a **specified value of x** is

$$\hat{y} - E < y < \hat{y} + E$$

where

$$E = t_c S_e \sqrt{1 + \frac{1}{n} + \frac{n(x - \bar{x})^2}{n\Sigma x^2 - (\Sigma x)^2}}$$

$\hat{y} = a + bx$ is the predicted value of y from the least-squares line for a *specified x* value

c = confidence level $(0 < c < 1)$

n = number of data pairs $(n \geq 3)$

t_c = critical value from Student's t distribution for c confidence level using $d.f. = n - 2$

S_e = standard error of estimate

The formulas involved in the computation of a c confidence interval look complicated. However, they involve quantities we have already computed or values we can easily look up in tables. The next example illustrates this point.

EXAMPLE 8
Confidence interval for prediction

Using the data of Table 10-12 on the preceding page, find a 95% confidence interval for the amount of copper sulfate that will dissolve in 100 g of water at 45°C.

SOLUTION: First, we need to find $\hat{y}$ for $x = 45$°C. We use the equation of the least-squares line that we found in Example 7.

$\hat{y} \approx 10.14 + 0.51x$ from Example 7

$\hat{y} \approx 10.14 + 0.51(45)$ using 45 in place of x

$\hat{y} \approx 33$

A 95% confidence interval is then

$$\hat{y} - E < y < \hat{y} + E$$

$$33 - E < y < 33 + E$$

where $E = t_c S_e \sqrt{1 + \dfrac{1}{n} + \dfrac{n(x - \bar{x})^2}{n\Sigma x^2 - (\Sigma x)^2}}$.

From Example 7, we have $n = 7$, $\Sigma x = 280$, $\Sigma x^2 = 14,000$, $\bar{x} = 40$, and $S_e \approx 2.35$. Using $n - 2 = 7 - 2 = 5$ degrees of freedom, we find from Table 6 of Appendix II that $t_{0.95} = 2.571$.

$$E \approx (2.571)(2.35)\sqrt{1 + \dfrac{1}{7} + \dfrac{7(45 - 40)^2}{7(14,000) - (280)^2}}$$

$$\approx (2.571)(2.35)\sqrt{1.15179} \approx 6.5$$

A 95% confidence interval for y is

$$33 - 6.5 \le y \le 33 + 6.5$$

$$26.5 \le y \le 39.5$$

This means that we are 95% sure that the interval between 26.5 g and 39.5 g is one that contains the predicted amount of copper sulfate that will dissolve in 100 g of water at 45°C. The interval is fairly wide but would decrease with more sample data.   ◇

GUIDED EXERCISE 7

Confidence interval for prediction

Let's use the data of Example 7 to compute a 95% confidence interval for y = amount of copper sulfate that will dissolve at $x = 15$°C.

(a) From Example 7, we have

$$\hat{y} \approx 10.14 + 0.51x$$

Evaluate $\hat{y}$ for $x = 15$.

⟹ $\hat{y} \approx 10.14 + 0.51x$

$\approx 10.14 + 0.51(15)$

≈ 17.8

(b) The bound E on the error of estimate is

$$E = t_c S_e \sqrt{1 + \dfrac{1}{n} + \dfrac{n(x - \bar{x})^2}{n\Sigma x^2 - (\Sigma x)^2}}$$

From Example 7, we know that $S_e \approx 2.35$, $\Sigma x = 280$, $\Sigma x^2 = 14,000$, $\bar{x} = 40$, and $n = 7$. Find $t_{0.95}$ and compute E.

⟹ $t_{0.95} = 2.571$ for $d.f. = n - 2 = 5$

$$E \approx (2.571)(2.35)\sqrt{1 + \dfrac{1}{7} + \dfrac{7(15 - 40)^2}{7(14,000) - (280)^2}}$$

$$\approx (2.571)(2.35)\sqrt{1.366071} \approx 7.1$$

(c) Find a 95% confidence interval for y.

$$\hat{y} - E \le y \le \hat{y} + E$$

⟹ The confidence interval is

$$17.8 - 7.1 \le y \le 17.8 + 7.1$$

$$10.7 \le y \le 24.9$$

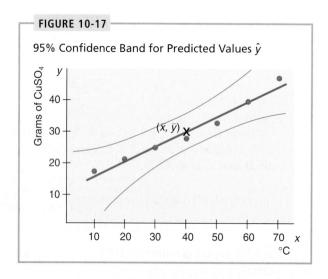

FIGURE 10-17

95% Confidence Band for Predicted Values $\hat{y}$

As we compare the results of Guided Exercise 7 and Example 8, we notice that the 95% confidence interval of y values for $x = 15°C$ is 7.1 units above and below the least-squares line, while the 95% confidence interval of y values for $x = 45°C$ is only 6.5 units above and below the least-squares line. This comparison reflects the general property that confidence intervals for y are narrower the nearer we are to the mean $\bar{x}$ of the x values. As we move near the extremes of the x distribution, the confidence intervals for y become wider. This is another reason that we should not try to use the least-squares line to predict y values for x values beyond the data extremes of the sample x distribution.

If we were to compute a 95% confidence interval for all x values in the range of the sample x values, the confidence interval band would curve away from the least-squares line, as shown in Figure 10-17.

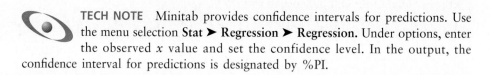 **TECH NOTE** Minitab provides confidence intervals for predictions. Use the menu selection **Stat ➤ Regression ➤ Regression.** Under options, enter the observed x value and set the confidence level. In the output, the confidence interval for predictions is designated by %PI.

Inferences about the Slope β

Recall that $\hat{y} = a + bx$ is the sample-based least-squares line and $y = \alpha + \beta x$ is the population least-squares line computed (in theory) from the population of all (x, y) data pairs. In many real world applications, the slope β is very important because β measures the rate at which y changes per unit change in x. Our next topic is to develop statistical tests and confidence intervals for β. Our work is based on the following theorem.

◇ **THEOREM 10.2** Let b be the slope of the sample least-squares line $\hat{y} = a + bx$ computed from a random sample of $n \geq 3$ data pairs (x, y). Let β be the slope of the population least-squares line $y = \alpha + \beta x$, which is in theory computed from the population of all (x, y) data pairs. Let S_e be the standard error of estimate computed from the sample. Then

$$t = \frac{b - \beta}{S_e \Big/ \sqrt{\Sigma x^2 - \frac{1}{n}(\Sigma x)^2}}$$

has a Student's t distribution with degrees of freedom $d.f. = n - 2$. ◇

◇ **COMMENT:** The expression $S_e \Big/ \sqrt{\Sigma x^2 - \frac{1}{n}(\Sigma x)^2}$ is called the *standard error* for b. ◇

Using this theorem, we can construct a procedure for statistical tests and confidence intervals for β.

PROCEDURE

How to test β and find a confidence interval for β

Obtain a random sample of $n \geq 3$ data pairs (x, y). Use the procedure of Section 10.2 to find b, the slope of the sample least-squares line. Use Equation (8) of this section to find S_e, the standard error of estimate.

For a statistical test of β

1. Use the *null hypothesis* $H_0: \beta = 0$. Use an *alternate hypothesis* H_1 appropriate to your application ($\beta > 0$ or $\beta < 0$ or $\beta \neq 0$). Set the level of significance α.

2. Use the null hypothesis $H_0: \beta = 0$ and the values of S_e, n, Σx, Σx^2, and b to compute the *sample test statistic*

$$t = \frac{b}{S_e}\sqrt{\Sigma x^2 - \frac{1}{n}(\Sigma x)^2} \qquad \text{with } d.f. = n - 2$$

3. Use a Student's t distribution and the type of test, one-tailed or two-tailed, to find (or estimate) the *P-value* corresponding to the test statistic.

4. *Conclude* the test. If P-value $\leq \alpha$, then reject H_0. If P-value $> \alpha$, then do not reject H_0.

5. *State your conclusion* in the context of the application.

To find a confidence interval for β

$$b - E < \beta < b + E$$

where $E = \dfrac{t_c S_e}{\sqrt{\Sigma x^2 - \frac{1}{n}(\Sigma x)^2}}$

   c = confidence level ($0 < c < 1$)

   n = number of data pairs (x, y), $n \geq 3$

   t_c = Student's t distribution critical value for confidence level c and $d.f. = n - 2$

   S_e = standard error of estimate

EXAMPLE 9

Testing β and finding a confidence interval for β

Plate tectonics and the spread of the ocean floor are very important in modern studies of earthquakes and earth science in general. A random sample of islands in the Indian Ocean gave the following information.

x = age of volcanic island in the Indian Ocean (units in 10^6 years)

y = distance of the island from the center of the midoceanic ridge (units in 100 km)

x	120	83	60	50	35	30	20	17
y	30	16	15.5	14.5	22	18	12	0

Source: From King, Cuchaine A. M. *Physical Geography.* Oxford: Basil Blackwell, 1980, pp. 77–86 and 196–206. Reprinted by permission of the publisher.

(a) Starting from raw data values (x, y), the first step is simple but tedious. In short, you may verify (if you wish) that

$\Sigma x = 415$, $\Sigma y = 128$, $\Sigma x^2 = 30{,}203$, $\Sigma y^2 = 2558.5$, $\Sigma xy = 8133$, $\bar{x} = 51.875$, and $\bar{y} = 16$

(b) The next step is to compute b, a, and S_e. Using a calculator, statistical software, or the formulas we get

$b \approx 0.1721$ and $a \approx 7.072$

Since $n = 8$, we get

$$S_e = \sqrt{\frac{\Sigma y^2 - a\Sigma y - b\Sigma xy}{n-2}}$$

$$\approx \sqrt{\frac{2558.5 - 7.072(128) - 0.1721(8133)}{8-2}} \approx 6.50$$

(c) Use an $\alpha = 5\%$ level of significance to test the claim that β is positive.

SOLUTION: $\alpha = 0.05$; $H_0: \beta = 0$; $H_1: \beta > 0$. The sample test statistic is

$$t = \frac{b}{S_e}\sqrt{\Sigma x^2 - \frac{1}{n}(\Sigma x)^2} \approx \frac{0.1721}{6.50}\sqrt{30{,}203 - \frac{(415)^2}{8}} \approx 2.466$$

with $d.f. = n - 2 = 8 - 2 = 6$.

We use the Student's t distribution (Table 6 of Appendix II) to find an interval containing the P-value. The test is a one-tailed test.

$0.010 < P\text{-value} < 0.025$

TABLE 10-14   Excerpt from Table 6, Appendix II

✓ one-tail area	0.025	0.010
$d.f. = 6$	2.447	3.143

Sample $t = 2.466$

Since the interval containing the P-value is less than $\alpha = 0.05$, we reject H_0 and conclude that at the 5% level of significance, the slope is positive.

(d) Find a 75% confidence interval for β.

SOLUTION: For $c = 0.75$ and $d.f. = n - 2 = 8 - 2 = 6$, the critical value $t_c = 1.273$. The margin of error E for the confidence interval is

$$E = \frac{t_c S_e}{\sqrt{\Sigma x^2 - \frac{1}{n}(\Sigma x)^2}} \approx \frac{1.273(6.50)}{\sqrt{30{,}203 - \frac{(415)^2}{8}}} \approx 0.0888$$

Using $b \approx 0.17$, a 75% confidence interval for β is

$$b - E < \beta < b + E$$
$$0.17 - 0.09 < \beta < 0.17 + 0.09$$
$$0.08 < \beta < 0.26$$

(e) What does the confidence interval mean?

Recall the units involved (x in 10^6 yr and y in 100 km). It appears that, in this part of the world, we can be 75% confident that we have an interval that shows the ocean floor is moving at a rate of between 8 mm and 26 mm per year. ◊

GUIDED EXERCISE 8

Inference for β

How fast do puppies grow? That depends on the puppy. How about male wolf pups in the Helsinki Zoo (Finland)? Let x = age in weeks and y = weight in kilograms for a random sample of male wolf pups. The following data are based on the article *Studies of the Wolf in Finland Canis lupus L* (*Ann. Zool. Fenn. 2:* 215–259) by E. Pulliainen, University of Helsinki.

x	8	10	14	20	28	40	45
y	7	13	17	23	30	34	35

$\Sigma x = 165$, $\Sigma y = 159$, $\Sigma x^2 = 5169$, $\Sigma y^2 = 4317$, $\Sigma xy = 4659$

(a) Verify the following values.

$\bar{x} \approx 23.571$ $\bar{y} \approx 22.714$,
$b \approx 0.7120$, $a \approx 5.932$,
$S_e \approx 3.368$

 Use the formulas for $\bar{x}$, $\bar{y}$, b, a, and S_e or find the results directly using your calculator or computer software.

Continued

(b) Use a 1% level of significance to test the claim that $\beta \neq 0$, and interpret the results in the context of this application.

 $\alpha = 0.01$; $H_0: \beta = 0$; $H_1: \beta \neq 0$

Convert $b \approx 0.7120$ to a t value.

$$t = \frac{b}{S_e}\sqrt{\Sigma x^2 - \frac{1}{n}(\Sigma x)^2}$$

$$\approx \frac{0.7120}{3.368}\sqrt{5169 - \frac{(165)^2}{7}} \approx 7.563$$

From Table 6, Appendix II, for a two-tailed test with $d.f. = n - 2 = 7 - 2 = 5$,

✓ two-tail area	0.001
$d.f. = 5$	6.869

Sample $t = 7.563$

Noting that areas decrease at t values increase, we have

$0.001 > P\text{-value}$

$$\begin{array}{cc} & \alpha \\ \text{)}\rule{1cm}{0.5pt} & \rule{1cm}{0.5pt} \\ 0.001 & 0.01 \end{array}$$

Since the P-value is less than $\alpha = 0.01$, we reject H_0 and conclude that the population slope β is not zero.

(c) Compute an 80% confidence interval for β and interpret the results in the context of this application.

 $d.f. = 5$. For an 80% confidence interval, the critical value $t_c = 1.476$. The confidence interval is

$$b - E < \beta < b + E$$

where $b = 0.712$ and

$$E = \frac{t_c S_e}{\sqrt{\Sigma x^2 - \frac{(\Sigma x)^2}{n}}} \approx \frac{1.476(3.368)}{\sqrt{5169 - \frac{(165)^2}{7}}}$$

$$\approx 0.139$$

The interval is from 0.57 kg to 0.85 kg. We can be 80% confident that the interval computed is one that contains β. For each week's change in age, the weight change is between 0.57 kg and 0.85 kg.

 TECH NOTE   It turns out that the t value corresponding to the correlation coefficient r is the same as the t value corresponding to b, the slope of the least-squares line (see Problem 8 at the end of this section). Consequently, the two tests H_0: $\rho = 0$ and H_0: $\beta = 0$ (with similar corresponding alternate hypotheses) have the same conclusions. The TI-84Plus/TI-83Plus uses this fact explicitly. Minitab and Excel show the two-tailed P value for the slope b of the least-squares line. Excel also shows confidence intervals for β. The displays show data from Guided Exercise 8 regarding the age and weight of wolf pups.

TI-84Plus/TI-83Plus Under **STAT**, select **TEST** and use option **E:LinRegTTest.**

```
LinRegTTest
 y=a+bx
 β≠0 and ρ≠0
 t=7.5632
 p=6.4075ᴇ⁻4
 df=5.0000
↓a=5.9317
```

```
LinRegTTest
 y=a+bx
 β≠0 and ρ≠0
↑b=.7120
 s=3.3676
 r²=.9196
 r=.9590
```

Note that the value of S_e is given as s.

Excel Use the menu selection **Tools ➤ Data Analysis ➤ Regression.**

Regression Statistics	
Multiple R	0.958966516
R Square	0.919616778
Adjusted R Square	0.903540133
Standard Error	3.367628886
Observations	7

← Value of S_e

	Coefficients	Standard Error	t Stat	P-value	Lower 95%	Upper 95%
Intercept	5.931681179	2.558126184	2.318760198	0.068158803	-0.644180779	12.50754314
X Variable 1	0.711989283	0.094138596	7.563202697	0.000640746	0.469998714	0.953979853

                  b for two-tailed test

Minitab Use the menu selection **Stat ➤ Regression ➤ Regression.** The value of S_e is S; P is the P-value of a two-tailed test. For a one-tailed test, divide the P-value by 2.

```
Regression Analysis
The regression equation is
y = 5.93 + 0.712 x
Predictor        Coef        StDev        T         P
Constant        5.932        2.558       2.32     0.068
x              0.71199      0.09414      7.56     0.001
S  = 3.368      R-Sq = 92.0%      R-Sq(adj) = 90.4%
```

VIEWPOINT   *Hawaii Island Hopping!*

Suppose you want to go camping in Hawaii. Yes! Hawaii has both state and federal parks where you can enjoy camping on the beach or in the mountains. However, you will probably need to rent a car to get to the different campgrounds. How much will the car rental cost? That depends on the islands you visit. For car rental data and regression statistics you can compute regarding costs on different Hawaiian Islands, visit the Brase/Brase statistics site at **http://math.college.hmco.com/students** and find the link to Hawaiian Islands.

SECTION 10.3   PROBLEMS

In Problems 1–6, parts (a) and (b) relate to testing ρ. Part (c) requests the value of S_e. Parts (d) and (e) relate to confidence intervals for prediction. Parts (f) and (g) relate to testing β and finding confidence intervals for β.

Answers may vary due to rounding.

1. *Basketball: Free Throws and Field Goals* Let x be a random variable that represents the percentage of successful free throws a professional basketball player makes in a season. Let y be a random variable that represents the percentage of successful field goals a professional basketball player makes in a season. A random sample of $n = 6$ professional basketball players gave the following information. (Reference: *The Official NBA Basketball Encyclopedia*, Villard Books.)

x	67	65	75	86	73	73
y	44	42	48	51	44	51

   (a) Verify that $\Sigma x = 439$, $\Sigma y = 280$, $\Sigma x^2 = 32{,}393$, $\Sigma y^2 = 13{,}142$, $\Sigma xy = 20{,}599$, and $r \approx 0.784$.
   (b) Use a 5% level of significance to test the claim that $\rho > 0$.
   (c) Verify that $S_e \approx 2.6964$, $a \approx 16.542$, $b \approx 0.4117$, and $\bar{x} \approx 73.167$.
   (d) Find the predicted percentage $\hat{y}$ of successful field goals for a player with $x = 70\%$ successful free throws.
   (e) Find a 90% confidence interval for y when $x = 70$.
   (f) Use a 5% level of significance to test the claim that $\beta > 0$.
   (g) Find a 90% confidence interval for β and interpret its meaning.

2. *Baseball: Batting Average and Strikeouts* Let x be a random variable that represents the batting average of a professional baseball player. Let y be a random variable that represents the percentage of strikeouts of a professional baseball player. A random sample of $n = 6$ professional baseball players gave the following information. (Reference: *The Baseball Encyclopedia*, Macmillan.)

x	0.328	0.290	0.340	0.248	0.367	0.269
y	3.2	7.6	4.0	8.6	3.1	11.1

   (a) Verify that $\Sigma x = 1.842$, $\Sigma y = 37.6$, $\Sigma x^2 = 0.575838$, $\Sigma y^2 = 290.78$, $\Sigma xy = 10.87$, and $r \approx -0.891$.

(b) Use a 5% level of significance to test the claim that $\rho \neq 0$.
(c) Verify that $S_e \approx 1.6838$, $a \approx 26.247$, and $b \approx -65.081$.
(d) Find the predicted percentage of strikeouts for a player with an $x = 0.300$ batting average.
(e) Find an 80% confidence interval for y when $x = 0.300$.
(f) Use a 5% level of significance to test the claim that $\beta \neq 0$.
(g) Find a 90% confidence interval for β and interpret its meaning.

3. *Scuba Diving: Depth* What is the optimal time for a scuba diver to be on the bottom of the ocean? That depends on the depth of the dive. The U.S. Navy has done a lot of research on this topic. The Navy defines the "optimal time" to be the time at each depth for the best balance between length of work period and decompression time after surfacing. Let x = depth of dive in meters, and let y = optimal time in hours. A random sample of divers gave the following data (based on information taken from *Medical Physiology* by A. C. Guyton, M.D.).

x	14.1	24.3	30.2	38.3	51.3	20.5	22.7
y	2.58	2.08	1.58	1.03	0.75	2.38	2.20

(a) Verify that $\Sigma x = 201.4$, $\Sigma y = 12.6$, $\Sigma x^2 = 6735.46$, $\Sigma y^2 = 25.607$, $\Sigma xy = 311.292$, and $r \approx -0.976$.
(b) Use a 1% level of significance to test the claim that $\rho < 0$.
(c) Verify that $S_e \approx 0.1660$, $a \approx 3.366$, and $b \approx -0.0544$.
(d) Find the predicted optimal time in hours for a dive depth of $x = 18$ meters.
(e) Find an 80% confidence interval for y when $x = 18$ meters.
(f) Use a 1% level of significance to test the claim that $\beta < 0$.
(g) Find a 90% confidence interval for β and interpret its meaning.

4. *Physiology: Oxygen* Aviation and high-altitude physiology is a specialty in the study of medicine. Let x = partial pressure of oxygen in the alveoli (air cells in the lungs) when breathing naturally available air. Let y = partial pressure when breathing pure oxygen. The (x, y) data pairs correspond to elevations from 10,000 feet up to 30,000 feet in 5000-foot intervals for a random sample of volunteers. Although the medical data were collected using airplanes, they will apply equally well to Mt. Everest climbers (summit 29,028 feet).

x	6.7	5.1	4.2	3.3	2.1 (units: mm Hg/10)
y	43.6	32.9	26.2	16.2	13.9 (units: mm Hg/10)

(Based on information taken from *Medical Physiology* by A. C. Guyton, M.D.)
(a) Verify that $\Sigma x = 21.4$, $\Sigma y = 132.8$, $\Sigma x^2 = 103.84$, $\Sigma y^2 = 4125.46$, $\Sigma xy = 652.6$, and $r \approx 0.984$.
(b) Use a 1% level of significance to test the claim that $\rho > 0$.
(c) Verify that $S_e \approx 2.5319$, $a \approx -2.869$, and $b \approx 6.876$.
(d) Find the predicted pressure when breathing pure oxygen when the pressure from breathing available air is $x = 4.0$.
(e) Find a 90% confidence interval for y when $x = 4.0$.
(f) Use a 1% level of significance to test the claim that $\beta > 0$.
(g) Find a 95% confidence interval for β and interpret its meaning.

5. *New Car: Negotiating Price* Suppose you are interested in buying a new Toyota Corolla. You are standing on the sales lot looking at a model with different options. The list price is on the vehicle. As a salesperson approaches, you wonder what the

dealer invoice price is for this model with its options. The following data are based on information taken from *Consumer Guide* (vol. 677). Let x be the list price (in thousands of dollars) for a random selection of Toyota Corollas of different models and options. Let y be the dealer invoice (in thousands of dollars) for the given vehicle.

x	12.6	13.0	12.8	13.6	13.4	14.2
y	11.6	12.0	11.5	12.2	12.0	12.8

(a) Verify that $\Sigma x = 79.6$, $\Sigma y = 72.1$, $\Sigma x^2 = 1057.76$, $\Sigma y^2 = 867.49$, $\Sigma xy = 957.84$, and $r \approx 0.956$.
(b) Use a 1% level of significance to test the claim that $\rho > 0$.
(c) Verify that $S_e \approx 0.1527$, $a \approx 1.965$, and $b \approx 0.758$.
(d) Find the predicted dealer invoice when the list price is $x = 14$ (thousand dollars).
(e) Find an 85% confidence interval for y when $x = 14$ (thousand dollars).
(f) Use a 1% level of significance to test the claim that $\beta > 0$.
(g) Find a 95% confidence interval for β and interpret its meaning.

6. *New Car: Negotiating Price* Suppose you are interested in buying a new Lincoln Navigator or Town Car. You are standing on the sales lot looking at a model with different options. The list price is on the vehicle. As a salesperson approaches, you wonder what the dealer invoice price is for this model with its options. The following data are based on information taken from *Consumer Guide* (vol. 677). Let x be the list price (in thousands of dollars) for a random selection of these cars of different models and options. Let y be the dealer invoice (in thousands of dollars) for the given vehicle.

x	32.1	33.5	36.1	44.0	47.8
y	29.8	31.1	32.0	42.1	42.2

(a) Verify that $\Sigma x = 193.5$, $\Sigma y = 177.2$, $\Sigma x^2 = 7676.71$, $\Sigma y^2 = 6432.5$, $\Sigma xy = 7023.19$, and $r \approx 0.977$.
(b) Use a 1% level of significance to test the claim that $\rho > 0$.
(c) Verify that $S_e \approx 1.5223$, $a \approx 1.4084$, and $b \approx 0.8794$.
(d) Find the predicted dealer invoice when the list price is $x = 40$ (thousand dollars).
(e) Find a 95% confidence interval for y when $x = 40$ (thousand dollars).
(f) Use a 1% level of significance to test the claim that $\beta > 0$.
(g) Find a 90% confidence interval for β and interpret its meaning.

7. *Expand Your Knowledge: Sample Size and Significance of r*
(a) Suppose $n = 6$ and the sample correlation coefficient is $r = 0.90$. Is r significant at the 1% level of significance (based on a two-tailed test)?
(b) Suppose $n = 10$ and the sample correlation coefficient is $r = 0.90$. Is r significant at the 1% level of significance (based on a two-tailed test)?
(c) Explain why the test results of parts (a) and (b) are different even though the sample correlation coefficient $r = 0.90$ in both parts. Does it appear that sample size plays an important role in determining the significance of a correlation coefficient? Explain.

8. *Expand Your Knowledge: Student's t Value for Sample r and Sample b* It is not obvious from the formulas, but the values of the sample test statistic t for the correlation coefficient and for the slope of the least-squares line are the same. This fact is based on the relation

$$b = r\frac{s_y}{s_x}$$

where s_y and s_x are the sample standard deviations of the x and y values, respectively.

(a) Many computer software packages give the t value and corresponding P-value for b. If β is significant, is ρ significant?

(b) When doing statistical tests "by hand," it is easier to compute the sample test statistic t for the sample correlation coefficient r than it is to compute the sample test statistic t for the slope b of the sample least-squares line. Compare the results of parts (b) and (f) for the first six problems of this problem set. Is the sample test statistic t for r the same as the corresponding test statistic for b? If you conclude that ρ is positive, can you conclude that β is positive at the same level of significance? If you conclude that ρ is not significant, is β also not significant at the same level of significance?

10.4
Multiple Regression

Advantages of Multiple Regression

FOCUS POINTS
✓ Learn about the advantages of multiple regression.
✓ Learn the basic ingredients that go into a multiple regression model.
✓ Discuss standard error for computed coefficients and the coefficient of multiple determination.
✓ Test coefficients in the model for statistical significance.
✓ Compute confidence intervals for predictions.

There are many examples in statistics where one variable can be predicted very accurately in terms of another *single* variable. However, predictions usually improve if we consider additional relevant information. For example, the sugar content y of golden delicious apples taken from an apple orchard in Colorado could be predicted from x_1 = number of days in growing season. If we also included information regarding x_2 = soil quality rating and x_3 = amount of available water, then we would expect our prediction of y = sugar content to be more accurate.

Likewise, the annual net income y of a new franchise auto parts store could be predicted using only x_1 = population size of sales district. However, we would probably get a better prediction of y values if we included the explanatory variables x_2 = size of store inventory, x_3 = dollar amount spent on advertising in local newspapers, and x_4 = number of competing stores in the sales district.

For most statistical applications, we gain a definite advantage in the reliability of our predictions if we include more *relevant* data and corresponding (relevant) random variables in the computation of our predictions. In this section, we will give you an idea of how this can be done by methods of *multiple regression*. You should be aware that an in-depth study of multiple regression requires the use of advanced mathematics. However, if you are willing to let the computer be a "friend who gives you useful information," then you will learn a great deal about multiple regression in this section. We will let the computer do most of the calculating work while we interpret the results.

Basic Terminology and Notation

In statistics, the most commonly used mathematical formulas for expressing linear relationships among more than two variables are *equations* of the form

$$y = b_0 + b_1 x_1 + b_2 x_2 + \cdots + b_k x_k \tag{9}$$

Here y is the variable that we want to predict or forecast. We will employ the usual terminology and call y the *response variable*. The k variables x_1, x_2, ... , x_k are specified variables on which the predictions are going to be based. Once again, we will employ the popular terminology and call x_1, x_2, ... , x_k the *explanatory variables*. This terminology is easy to remember if you just think of the explanatory variables x_1, x_2, ... , x_k as "explaining" the response y.

In Equation (9), b_0, b_1, b_2, ... , b_k are numerical constants (called *coefficients*) that must be mathematically determined from given data. The numerical values of these coefficients are obtained from the *least-squares criterion*, which we will discuss after the following exercise.

GUIDED EXERCISE 9

Components of multiple regression equation

An industrial psychologist working for a hospital supply company is studying the following variables for a random sample of company employees:

x_1 = number of years the employee has been with the company

x_2 = job training level (0 = lowest level and 5 = highest level)

x_3 = interpersonal skills (0 = lowest level and 10 = highest level)

y = job performance rating from supervisor (1 = lowest rating, 20 = highest rating)

The psychologist wants to predict y using x_1, x_2, and x_3 together in a least-squares equation.

(a) Identify the response variable and the explanatory variables.

⟹ The response variable is what we want to predict. This is y, job performance. The explanatory variables are years of experience x_1, training level x_2, and interpersonal skills x_3. In a sense, these variables "explain" the response variable.

(b) After collecting data, the psychologist used a computer with appropriate software to obtain the least-squares linear equation

$$y = 1 + 0.2x_1 + 2.3x_2 + 0.7x_3$$

Identify the constant term and each of the coefficients with its corresponding variable.

⟹ The constant term is 1.

Explanatory Variable	Coefficient
x_1	0.2
x_2	2.3
x_3	0.7

Continued

GUIDED EXERCISE 9 continued

(c) Use the equation to predict the job performance rating of an employee with 3 years of experience, a training level of 4, and an interpersonal skill rating of 2.

 Substituting $x_1 = 3$, $x_2 = 4$, and $x_3 = 2$ in the least-squares equation and multiplying by the respective coefficients, we obtain the predicted job performance rating of

$$y = 1 + 0.2(3) + 2.3(4) + 0.7(2) = 12.2$$

Of course, the *predicted* value for job performance might differ from the actual rating given by the supervisor.

Theory for the least-squares criterion (optional)

This material is a little sophisticated, so you may wish to skip ahead to the discussion of regression models and computers and omit the following explanation of basic theory.

In multiple regression, the least-squares criterion states that the following sum (over all data points),

$$\Sigma[y_i - (b_0 + b_1x_{1i} + b_2x_{2i} + \cdots + b_kx_{ki})]^2 \qquad (10)$$

must be made as small as possible. In this formula,

$y_i = i$th data value for y

$x_{1i} = i$th data value for x_1

$x_{2i} = i$th data value for x_2

$\vdots$

$x_{ki} = i$th data value for x_k

Recall that Equation (9) gives the predicted y value; therefore,

$$y_i - (b_0 + b_1x_{1i} + b_2x_{2i} + \cdots + b_kx_{ki}) \qquad (11)$$

represents the *difference* between the *observed* y value (that is, y_i) and the *predicted* y value based on the data values $x_{1i}, x_{2i}, \ldots, x_{ki}$. When we square this difference and total the result over all data points and choose the values of $b_0, b_1, b_2, \ldots, b_k$ to minimize the sum [i.e., minimize Equation (10)], then we are satisfying the least-squares criterion.

◇ **COMMENT** The algebraic expression in Equation (11) is very important. In fact, it has a special name in the theory of regression. It is called a *residual*. The residual is simply the difference between the actual data value and the predicted value of the response variable based on given data values for the explanatory variables. Advanced topics in the theory of regression will study residuals in great detail. Such a detailed treatment is beyond the scope of this text. However, from the discussion presented so far, we see that the method of least squares chooses the values of the coefficients b_i to make the sum of the squares of the residuals as small as possible. ◇

After a good deal of mathematics has been done (involving a considerable amount of calculus), the least-squares criterion can be reduced to solving a system of linear equations. These are usually called *normal equations* (not to be confused with the normal distribution).

In the simplest case, where there are only *two* explanatory variables x_1 and x_2 and we want to fit the equation

$$y = b_0 + b_1 x_1 + b_2 x_2$$

to given data, there are three normal equations that must be solved for b_0, b_1, and b_2. These normal equations are

$$\Sigma y_i = n b_0 + b_1(\Sigma x_{1i}) + b_2(\Sigma x_{2i})$$
$$\Sigma x_{1i} y_i = b_0(\Sigma x_{1i}) + b_1(\Sigma x_{1i}^2) + b_2(\Sigma x_{1i} x_{2i}) \qquad (12)$$
$$\Sigma x_{2i} y_i = b_0(\Sigma x_{2i}) + b_1(\Sigma x_{1i} x_{2i}) + b_2(\Sigma x_{2i}^2)$$

In the system of Equations (12), n represents the number of data points and x_{1i}, x_{2i}, and y_i all represent given data values.

Therefore, the only unknowns are the coefficients b_0, b_1, and b_2; we can use the system of Equations (12) to solve for these unknowns. This is the procedure that lets us obtain the least-squares regression equation in Equation (9) when we have only *two* explanatory variables.

As you can see, this is all rather complicated, and the more explanatory variables x_1, x_2, ..., x_k we have, the more involved the calculations become. In the general case, if you have k explanatory variables, there will be $k + 1$ normal equations that must be solved for the coefficients b_0, b_1, b_2, ..., b_k.

Regression Models and Computers

As you can see from the preceding optional discussion, the work required to find an equation satisfying the least-squares criterion is tremendous and can be very complex. Today, such work is conveniently left to computers. In this text, we use two computer software packages that specialize in statistical applications.

Minitab is a widely used statistical software package. It fully supports multiple regression. Excel has a multiple regression component that performs much of the multiple regression analysis. We will use Minitab in our example. Many other software packages, including SPSS, support multiple regression and have outputs similar to Minitab.

Ingredients of the regression model

In this section, we will often refer to a *regression model*. What do we mean by this? We mean a mathematical package that consists of the following ingredients:

1. A collection of random variables, *one* of which has been identified as the response variable, with *any or all* of the remaining variables being identified as explanatory variables.

2. Associated with a given application will be a collection of numerical data values for each of the variables of part 1.

3. Using the numerical data values, the least-squares criterion, and the declared response and explanatory variables, a *least-squares equation* (also called a

regression equation) will be constructed. In Section 10.2, we were able to construct the least-squares equation using only a hand calculator. However, in multiple regression, we will use a computer to construct the least-squares equation.

4. The model usually includes additional information about the variables used, the coefficients and regression equation, and a measure of "goodness of fit" of the regression equation to the data values. In modern practice, this information usually comes to you in the form of computer displays.

5. Finally, the regression model allows you to supply given values of the explanatory variables for the purpose of predicting or forecasting the corresponding value of the response variable. You also should be able to construct a $c\%$ confidence interval for your least-squares prediction. In multiple regression, this will be done by the computer at your request.

The next example demonstrates computer applications of a typical multiple regression problem. In the context of the example, we will introduce some of the basic techniques of multiple regression.

Example Utilizing Minitab

EXAMPLE 10

Multiple regression

Antelope are beautiful and graceful animals that live on the high plains of the western United States. Thunder Basin National Grasslands in Wyoming is home to hundreds of antelope. The Bureau of Land Management (BLM) has been studying the Thunder Basin antelope population for the past 8 years. The variables used are

x_1 = spring fawn count (in hundreds of fawns)

x_2 = size of adult antelope population (in hundreds)

x_3 = annual precipitation (in inches)

x_4 = winter severity index (1 = mild and 5 = extremely severe) (This is an index based on temperature and wind chill factors.)

The data obtained in the study over the 8-year period are shown in Table 10-15.

TABLE 10-15   Data for Thunder Basin Antelope Study

Year	x_1	x_2	x_3	x_4
1	2.9	9.2	13.2	2
2	2.4	8.7	11.5	3
3	2.0	7.2	10.8	4
4	2.3	8.5	12.3	2
5	3.2	9.6	12.6	3
6	1.9	6.8	10.6	5
7	3.4	9.7	14.1	1
8	2.1	7.9	11.2	3

Summary Statistics for Each Variable

It is a good idea to first look at the summary statistics for each variable. Figure 10-18 shows the Minitab display of the summary statistics.

Menu selection: **Stat ➤ Basic Statistic ➤ Display Descriptive Statistics**

FIGURE 10-18

Minitab Display of Summary Statistics for Each Variable

```
Descriptive Statistics
Variable     N        Mean      Median      TrMean      StDev     SE Mean
x1           8       2.525       2.350       2.525      0.570       0.202
x2           8       8.450       8.600       8.450      1.076       0.380
x3           8      12.037      11.900      12.037      1.229       0.435
x4           8       2.875       3.000       2.875      1.246       0.441
Variable   Minimum    Maximum          Q1          Q3
x1           1.900      3.400       2.025       3.125
x2           6.800      9.700       7.375       9.500
x3          10.600     14.100      10.900      13.050
x4           1.000      5.000       2.000       3.750
```

This type of information can be very useful because it tells you basic information about the variables you are studying. Sample means and sample standard deviations with a Student's t distribution are essential ingredients for estimating or testing population means (Chapters 8 and 9).

For example, if μ_2 represents the *population mean* of x_2 (adult antelope population), then by using the methods of Section 8.2 we can quickly estimate a 90% confidence interval for μ_2:

$$7.729 < \mu_2 < 9.171$$

Since our units are in hundreds, this means that we can be 90% sure the *population mean* μ_2 of adult antelope in the Thunder Basin Grasslands is between 773 and 917.

Correlation Between Variables

It is also useful to examine how the variables relate to each other. Figure 10-19 shows the correlation coefficients r between each of the two variables. A natural question arises: Which of the variables are closely related to each other, and which are not as closely related? Recall (from Section 10.3) that if the correlation coefficient is near 1 or -1, then the corresponding variables have a lot in common. If the correlation coefficient is near zero, the variables have much less influence on each other.

Menu selection: **Stat ➤ Basic Statistics ➤ Correlation**

FIGURE 10-19

Minitab Display of Correlation Coefficients Between Variables

```
Correlations (Pearson)
             x1           x2           x3
x2        0.939
x3        0.924        0.903
x4       -0.739       -0.836       -0.901
```

Look at Figure 10-19. Which of the variables has the greatest influence on x_1? The correlation coefficient between x_1 and x_2 is $r = 0.939$, with a corresponding coefficient of determination of $r^2 \approx 0.88$. This means that if we consider only x_1 and x_2 (and none of the other variables), then about 88% of the variation in x_1 can be explained by the corresponding variation in x_2 (by itself). Similarly, if we consider only x_1 and x_3, we see the correlation coefficient $r = 0.924$, with a corresponding coefficient of determination of $r^2 \approx 0.85$. About 85% of the variation in x_1 can be explained by the corresponding variation in x_3. The variable x_4 has much less influence on x_1 because the correlation coefficient between these two variables is $r = -0.739$, with corresponding coefficient of determination $r^2 \approx 0.55$, or only 55%.

These relationships are very reasonable in the context of our problem. It is common sense that the number of spring fawns x_1 is strongly related to x_2, the size of the adult antelope population. Furthermore, the spring fawn count x_1 is very much influenced by available food for the fawn (and its mother). Thunder Basin National Grasslands is a semiarid region, and available food (grass) is almost completely determined by annual precipitation x_3. Antelope are naturally strong and hardy animals. Therefore, the temperature and wind chill index x_4 will have much less effect on the adult does and corresponding number of spring fawns provided there is plenty of available food.

Least-Squares Equation

Figure 10-20 shows a display that gives an expression for the actual least-squares equation and a lot of information about the equation. To get this display or a similar display, the user needs to declare which variable is the response variable and which are the explanatory variables. For Figure 10-20, we designated x_1 as the response variable. This means that x_1 is the variable we choose to predict. We also designated variables x_2, x_3, and x_4 as explanatory variables. This means that x_2, x_3, and x_4 will be used *together* to predict x_1. There is a lot of flexibility here. We could have designated any *one* of the variables x_1, x_2, x_3, x_4 as the response variable and *any or all* of the remaining variables as explanatory variables. So there are a lot of possible regression models the computer can construct for you, depending on the type of information you want. In this example, we want to predict x_1 (spring fawn count) by using x_2 (adult population), x_3 (annual precipitation), and x_4 (winter index) *together*.

Menu selection: **Stat ➤ Regression ➤ Regression**. In the dialogue box, select x_1 as the response and x_2, x_3, x_4 as the predictors.

FIGURE 10-20

Minitab Display of Regression Analysis

```
Regression Analysis
The regression equation is
x1 = -5.92 + 0.338 x2 + 0.402 x3 + 0.263 x4
Predictor        Coef        StDev         T          P
Constant       -5.922        1.256      -4.72      0.009
x2            0.33822      0.09947       3.40      0.027
x3             0.4015       0.1099       3.65      0.022
x4            0.26295      0.08514       3.09      0.037
S = 0.1209    R-Sq = 97.4%     R-Sq(adj) = 95.5%
```

The least-squares regression equation is given near the top of the display. Then more information is given about the constant and coefficients. The parts of the equation are

$$x_1 = -5.92 + 0.338x_2 + 0.402x_3 + 0.263x_4 \tag{13}$$

response variable   constant   coefficient of associated explanatory variable

◇ **COMMENT** In the case of a simple regression model, where we have only one explanatory variable, the coefficient of that variable is the *slope* of the least-squares line. This slope (or coefficient) represents the change in the response variable per unit change in the explanatory variable. In a multiple regression model such as Equation (13), the coefficients also can be thought of as a slope—*provided* we hold the other variables as arbitrary and fixed constants. For example, the coefficient of x_2 in Equation (13) is $b_2 = 0.338$. This means that if x_3 (precipitation) and x_4 (winter index) are taken into account but held constant, then $b_2 = 0.338$ represents the change in x_1 (spring fawn count) per unit change in x_2 (adult antelope count). Since our units are in hundreds, this indicates that if x_3 and x_4 are taken into account as arbitrary but fixed values, then an increase of 100 adult antelope would give an expected increase of 33.8 or 34 spring fawns. ◇

A natural question arises: How good a fit is the least-squares regression Equation (13) for our given data?

One way to answer this question is to examine the *coefficient of multiple determination.* The coefficient of multiple determination is a direct generalization of the concept of coefficient of determination (between *two* variables) as discussed in Section 10.2, and it has essentially the same meaning. The coefficient of multiple determination is given in the display of Figure 10-20 as a percent. We see R-Sq = 97.4%. This means that about 97.4% of the variation in the response variable x_1 can be explained from the least-squares Equation (13) and the corresponding *joint* variation of the variables x_2, x_3, and x_4 taken together. The remaining $100\% - 97.4\% = 2.6\%$ of the variation in x_1 is due to random chance or possibly the presence of other variables not included in this regression equation. (We will discuss the *standard error* associated with each coefficient later in this section.)

Coefficient of multiple determination

Predictions

Let's use the current regression model to predict the response variable x_1. Recall that in Section 10.2 we first made predictions from the least-squares line and then constructed a confidence interval for our prediction. Although the exact details are beyond the scope of this text, this process can be generalized to multiple regression. The calculations are very tedious, but that's why we use a computer!

Suppose we ask the following question: In a year when $x_2 = 8.2$ (hundreds of adult antelope), $x_3 = 11.7$ (inches of precipitation), and $x_4 = 3$ (winter index), what do we predict for x_1 (spring fawn count)? Furthermore, let's suppose we want an 85% confidence interval for our prediction.

To answer this question, we look at Figure 10-21, which shows the Minitab prediction result for x_1 from the specified values of x_2, x_3, x_4.

Menu selection: **Stat ➤ Regression ➤ Regression.** In the dialogue box, select Options. List the new observations for x_2, x_3, and x_4 in order, separated by spaces. Specify the confidence level. Be sure that Fit Intercept is checked.

FIGURE 10-21

Minitab Display Showing the Predicted Value of x_1

```
Predicted Values
 Fit        StDev Fit        85.0% CI            85.0% PI
2.3378        0.0472      (2.2539, 2.4217)    (2.1069, 2.5687)
```

The value for Fit is 2.3378. This is the predicted value for x_1. The 85% confidence interval for the prediction is designated as 85% PI. We see that the interval for x_1 (rounded to two digits after the decimal) is $2.11 \leq x_1 \leq 2.57$. This means we are 85% confident that the number of spring fawns will be in the range from 211 to 257.

Please note that this is *not* a confidence interval for the population mean of x_1. Rather, we have constructed a confidence interval for the *actual value* of x_1 under the conditions $x_2 = 8.2$, $x_3 = 11.7$, and $x_4 = 3$.   ◊

◊ **COMMENT** Extrapolation much beyond the data range in a multiple regression model in any of the variables can produce results that might be meaningless and unrealistic. Many computer software packages warn about computing a confidence interval for a prediction when some of the values of the explanatory variables are beyond the data range in either direction.   ◊

Testing a Coefficient for Significance

In applications of multiple regression, it is possible to have many different variables. Occasionally, you might suspect that one of the explanatory variables x_i is not very useful as a tool for predicting the response variable. It simply may not influence the response variable much at all. To decide whether or not this is the case, we construct a test for the significance of the coefficient of x_i in the least-squares equation.

Recall that the general least-squares equation is

$$y = b_0 + b_1 x_1 + b_2 x_2 + \cdots + b_k x_k \tag{14}$$

where y = response variable

x_i = explanatory variable for $i = 1, 2, \ldots, k$

b_i = numerical coefficient for $i = 0, 1, 2, \ldots, k$

Equation (14) was constructed from given data. Usually, the data are only a small subset of all possible data that could have been collected.

Let us suppose (in theory) that we used *all possible data* that could ever be obtained for our regression problem and that we constructed the regression equation using the entire population of all possible data. Then we would get the *theoretical* regression equation

$$y = \beta_0 + \beta_1 x_1 + \beta_2 x_2 + \cdots + \beta_k x_k \tag{15}$$

where y and x_i are as in Equation (14), but β_i is the *theoretical* coefficient of x_i.

Now look back at the regression analysis in Figure 10-20. Beside the constant and each coefficient there is a number in the StDev column. This is the *standard error* corresponding to that coefficient. The standard error can be thought of as similar to a standard deviation that corresponds to the coefficient. The calculation of the number is beyond the scope of this text, but it is available on computer printouts, and we will use it to construct our test.

Let us call S_i the standard error for coefficient x_i (S_0 is the standard error for the constant). Under very basic and general assumptions, it can be proved that

$$t = \frac{b_i - \beta_i}{S_i} \tag{16}$$

has a Student's t distribution with degrees of freedom $d.f. = n - k - 1$, where n = number of data points and k = number of explanatory variables in the least-squares equation.

Now let us return to the question: Is x_i useful as an explanatory variable in the least-squares equation?

The answer is that it is *not* useful if $\beta_i = 0$. In this case, the (theoretical) coefficient of x_i would be zero and x_i would contribute nothing to the least-squares equation. However, if $\beta_i \neq 0$, then the explanatory variable x_i does contribute information in the least-squares equation.

Consider the following hypotheses,

$$H_0: \beta_i = 0 \quad \text{and} \quad H_1: \beta_i \neq 0$$

If we accept H_0, we conclude that $\beta_i = 0$ and x_i probably should be dropped as an explanatory variable in the least-squares equation. If we accept H_1, we conclude that $\beta_i \neq 0$ and x_i should be included as an explanatory variable in the least-squares equation.

EXAMPLE 11

Test a coefficient

We'll use the data and printouts of Example 10 and test the significance of x_3 as an explanatory variable using $\alpha = 0.05$ as level of significance.

$$H_0: \beta_3 = 0 \quad \text{and} \quad H_1: \beta_3 \neq 0$$

To find the t value corresponding to b_3, we use Equation (16) and the null hypothesis $H_0: \beta_3 = 0$. This gives us the equation

$$t = \frac{b_3}{S_3} \tag{17}$$

In the regression analysis shown in Figure 10-20, we see a t value for the constant and each coefficient. This t value is exactly the value of $t = b_i/S_i$. This is the t value corresponding to the sample test statistic. For the coefficient of x_3, we see

t value ≈ 3.65

Notice that in Figure 10-20 we are also given the P-value of the sample test statistic for each coefficient. This is the value in the column headed "p." For the sample test statistic $t \approx 3.65$, the corresponding P-value is 0.022. Since the P-value is less than the level of significance $\alpha = 0.05$, we reject H_0. In other words, at the 5% level of significance, we can say that the population correlation coefficient β_3 of x_3 is not 0.

We conclude at the 5% level of significance that x_3 (annual precipitation) should be included as an explanatory variable in the least-squares equation. Notice that Figure 10-20 also gives the P-value for each ratio, so we can conclude the test using P-values directly. Using the P-values, we see that x_2 and x_3 are also significant at the 5% level. ◇

Confidence Intervals for Coefficients

Equation (16) also gives us the basis for finding *confidence intervals* for β_i. A $c\%$ confidence interval for β_i will be

$$b_i - tS_i < \beta_i < b_i + tS_i$$

where $d.f. = n - k - 1$, t is selected according to the specified confidence level, b_i is the numerical value of the coefficient from Figure 10-20, S_i is the numerical value of the standard error from Figure 10-20, n is the number of data points, and k is the number of explanatory variables in the least-squares equation.

EXAMPLE 12

Confidence interval for a coefficient

Suppose we want to compute a 90% confidence interval for β_2, the coefficient of x_2. From Figure 10-20 we have (rounding to three digits after the decimal)

$$b_2 = 0.338, \quad S_2 = 0.099, \quad \text{and} \quad d.f. = 4$$

From the t table (Table 6, Appendix II), we find $t = 2.132$, so

$$b_2 - tS_2 < \beta_2 < b_2 + tS_2$$
$$0.338 - 2.132(0.099) < \beta_2 < 0.338 + 2.132(0.099)$$
$$0.127 < \beta_2 < 0.549$$

◊

Excel Displays

Excel gives information very similar to that supplied by Minitab. The least-squares equation is not explicitly displayed. However, the intercept (constant) and coefficients of the variables are shown with the corresponding standard errors and t values with P-values. Excel shows the confidence interval for each coefficient. However, there is no built-in function to provide predicted values or confidence intervals for predicted values. Note that as in the Minitab regression analysis, we will not make use of the ANOVA information in the Excel display.

Menu selection: **Tools ➤ Data Analysis ➤ Regression.** Note that when you enter data into the worksheet, all the explanatory variables must be together in a block. Figure 10-22 shows the Excel display for Examples 10 and 11.

FIGURE 10-22

Excel Display of Regression Analysis

Regression Statistics	
Multiple R	0.987060478
R Square	0.974288388
Adjusted R Square	0.955004679
Standard Error	0.120927579
Observations	8

ANOVA

	df	SS	MS	F	Significance F
Regression	3	2.216506083	0.738835361	50.5239104	0.001228863
Residual	4	0.058493917	0.014623479		
Total	7	2.275			

	Coefficients	Standard Error	t Stat	P-value	Lower 95%	Upper 95%
Intercept	-5.922011616	1.255623292	-4.716391972	0.009196085	-9.40818798	-2.435835251
x2	0.338217487	0.099470083	3.400193085	0.027272474	0.062043691	0.614391283
x3	0.401503945	0.109900277	3.653347874	0.021707246	0.096371226	0.706636664
x4	0.262946128	0.085136028	3.088541172	0.036626194	0.02657013	0.499322125

VIEWP●INT *Synoptic Climatology*

Synoptic means "giving a summary from the same basic point of view." In this case, the point of view is Niwot Ridge, high above the timberline in the Rocky Mountains. Vegetation, water, temperature, and wind all affect the delicate balance of this alpine environment. How do these elements of nature interact to sustain life in such a harsh land? One answer can be found by collecting data at the location and using multiple regression to study the interaction of variables. For more information, visit the Brase/Brase statistics site at **http://math.college.hmco.com/students** and find the link to Niwot ridge climate study.

SECTION 10.4   PROBLEMS

1. Given the linear regression equation

$$x_1 = 1.6 + 3.5x_2 - 7.9x_3 + 2.0x_4$$

   (a) Which variable is the response variable? Which variables are the explanatory variables?
   (b) Which number is the constant term? List the coefficients with their corresponding explanatory variables.
   (c) If $x_2 = 2$, $x_3 = 1$, and $x_4 = 5$, what is the predicted value for x_1?
   (d) Explain how each coefficient can be thought of as a "slope" under certain conditions. Suppose x_3 and x_4 were held at fixed but arbitrary values and x_2 increased by one unit. What would be the corresponding change in x_1? Suppose x_2 increased by two units. What would be the expected change in x_1? Suppose x_2 decreased by four units. What would be the expected change in x_1?
   (e) Suppose that $n = 12$ data points were used to construct the given regression equation and that the standard error for the coefficient of x_2 is 0.419. Construct a 90% confidence interval for the coefficient of x_2.
   (f) Using the information of part (e) and level of significance 5%, test the claim that the coefficient of x_2 is different from zero. Explain how the conclusion of this test would affect the regression equation.

2. Given the linear regression equation

$$x_3 = -16.5 + 4.0x_1 + 9.2x_4 - 1.1x_7$$

   (a) Which variable is the response variable? Which variables are the explanatory variables?
   (b) Which number is the constant term? List the coefficients with their corresponding explanatory variables.
   (c) If $x_1 = 10$, $x_4 = -1$, and $x_7 = 2$, what is the predicted value for x_3?
   (d) Explain how each coefficient can be thought of as a "slope." Suppose x_1 and x_7 were held as fixed but arbitrary values. If x_4 increased by one unit, what would we expect the corresponding change in x_3 to be? If x_4 increased by three units, what would be the corresponding expected change in x_3? If x_4 decreased by two units, what do we expect for the corresponding change in x_3?
   (e) Suppose that $n = 15$ data points were used to construct the given regression equation and that the standard error for the coefficient of x_4 is 0.921. Construct a 90% confidence interval for the coefficient of x_4.

(f) Using the information of part (e) and level of significance 1%, test the claim that the coefficient of x_4 is different from zero. Explain how the conclusion has a bearing on the regression equation.

 For Problems 3–6, use appropriate multiple regression software of your choice and enter the data. Note that the statSpace CD-ROM that comes with this text has the data in formats for Excel, Minitab portable files, SPSS files, and ASCII files.

3. *Medical: Blood Pressure* The systolic blood pressure of individuals is thought to be related to both age and weight. For a random sample of 11 men, the following data were obtained:

Systolic Blood Pressure x_1	Age (years) x_2	Weight (pounds) x_3	Systolic Blood Pressure x_1	Age (years) x_2	Weight (pounds) x_3
132	52	173	137	54	188
143	59	184	149	61	188
153	67	194	159	65	207
162	73	211	128	46	167
154	64	196	166	72	217
168	74	220			

(a) Generate summary statistics, including the mean and standard deviation of each variable. Compute the coefficient of variation (see Section 3.2) for each variable. Relative to its mean, which variable has the greatest spread of data values? Which variable has the smallest spread of data values relative to its mean?

(b) For each pair of variables, generate the correlation coefficient r. Compute the corresponding coefficient of determination r^2. Which variable (other than x_1) has the greatest influence (by itself) on x_1? Would you say that both variables x_2 and x_3 show a strong influence on x_1? Explain your answer. What percent of the variation in x_1 can be explained by the corresponding variation in x_2? Answer the same question for x_3.

(c) Perform a regression analysis with x_1 as the response variable. Use x_2 and x_3 as explanatory variables. Look at the coefficient of multiple determination. What percentage of the variation in x_1 can be explained by the corresponding variations in x_2 and x_3 *taken together*?

(d) Look at the coefficients of the regression equation. Write out the regression equation. Explain how each coefficient can be thought of as a slope. If age were held fixed, but a person put on 10 pounds, what would you expect for the corresponding change in systolic blood pressure? If a person kept the same weight but got 10 years older, what would you expect for the corresponding change in systolic blood pressure?

(e) Test each coefficient to determine if it is zero or not zero. Use level of significance 5%. Why would the outcome of each test help us determine whether or not a given variable should be used in the regression model?

(f) Find a 90% confidence interval for each coefficient.

(g) Suppose that Michael is 68 years old and weighs 192 pounds. Predict his systolic blood pressure, and find a 90% confidence range for your prediction (if your software produces prediction intervals).

4. *Education: Exam Scores* Professor Gill has taught General Psychology for many years. During the semester, she gives three multiple-choice exams, each

worth 100 points. At the end of the course, Dr. Gill gives a comprehensive final worth 200 points. Let x_1, x_2, and x_3 represent a student's scores on exams 1, 2, and 3, respectively. Let x_4 represent the student's score on the final exam. Last semester Dr. Gill had 25 students in her class. The student exam scores are shown below.

x_1	x_2	x_3	x_4	x_1	x_2	x_3	x_4	x_1	x_2	x_3	x_4
73	80	75	152	79	70	88	164	81	90	93	183
93	88	93	185	69	70	73	141	88	92	86	177
89	91	90	180	70	65	74	141	78	83	77	159
96	98	100	196	93	95	91	184	82	86	90	177
73	66	70	142	79	80	73	152	86	82	89	175
53	46	55	101	70	73	78	148	78	83	85	175
69	74	77	149	93	89	96	192	76	83	71	149
47	56	60	115	78	75	68	147	96	93	95	192
87	79	90	175								

Since Professor Gill has not changed the course much from last semester to the present semester, the preceding data should be useful for constructing a regression model that describes this semester as well.

(a) Generate summary statistics, including the mean and standard deviation of each variable. Compute the coefficient of variation (see Section 3.2) for each variable. Relative to its mean, would you say that each exam had about the same spread of scores? Most professors do not wish to give an exam that is extremely easy or extremely hard. Would you say that all of the exams were about the same level of difficulty? (Consider both means and spread of test scores.)

(b) For each pair of variables, generate the correlation coefficient r. Compute the corresponding coefficient of determination r^2. Of the three exams 1, 2, and 3, which do you think had the most influence on the final exam 4? Although one exam had more influence on the final exam, did the other two exams still have a lot of influence on the final? Explain each answer.

(c) Perform a regression analysis with x_4 as the response variable. Use x_1, x_2, and x_3 as explanatory variables. Look at the coefficient of multiple determination. What percentage of the variation in x_4 can be explained by the corresponding variations in x_1, x_2, and x_3 taken together?

(d) Write out the regression equation. Explain how each coefficient can be thought of as a slope. If a student were to study "extra hard" for exam 3 and increase his or her score on that exam by 10 points, what corresponding change would you expect on the final exam? (Assume that exams 1 and 2 remain "fixed" in their scores.)

(e) Test each coefficient in the regression equation to determine if it is zero or not zero. Use level of significance 5%. Why would the outcome of each hypothesis test help us decide whether or not a given variable should be used in the regression equation?

(f) Find a 90% confidence interval for each coefficient.

(g) This semester Susan has scores of 68, 72, and 75 on exams 1, 2, and 3, respectively. Make a prediction for Susan's score on the final exam and find a 90% confidence interval for your prediction (if your software supports prediction intervals).

5. *Entertainment: Movies* A motion picture industry analyst is studying movies based on epic novels. The following data were obtained for 10 Hollywood movies made in the past five years. Each movie was based on an epic novel. For these data, x_1 = first year box office receipts of the movie, x_2 = total production costs of the movie, x_3 = total promotional costs of the movie, and x_4 = total book sales prior to movie release. All units are in millions of dollars.

x_1	x_2	x_3	x_4	x_1	x_2	x_3	x_4
85.1	8.5	5.1	4.7	30.3	3.5	1.2	3.5
106.3	12.9	5.8	8.8	79.4	9.2	3.7	9.7
50.2	5.2	2.1	15.1	91.0	9.0	7.6	5.9
130.6	10.7	8.4	12.2	135.4	15.1	7.7	20.8
54.8	3.1	2.9	10.6	89.3	10.2	4.5	7.9

(a) Generate summary statistics, including the mean and standard deviation of each variable. Compute the coefficient of variation (see Section 3.2) for each variable. Relative to its mean, which variable has the largest spread of data values? Why would a variable with a large coefficient of variation be expected to change a lot relative to its average value? Although x_1 has the largest standard deviation, it has the smallest coefficient of variation. How does the mean of x_1 help explain this?

(b) For each pair of variables, generate the correlation coefficient r. Compute the corresponding coefficient of determination r^2. Which of the three variables x_2, x_3, and x_4 has the *least* influence on box office receipts? What percent of the variation in box office receipts can be attributed to the corresponding variation in production costs?

(c) Perform a regression analysis with x_1 as the response variable. Use x_2, x_3, and x_4 as explanatory variables. Look at the coefficient of multiple determination. What percentage of the variation in x_1 can be explained by the corresponding variations in x_2, x_3, and x_4 taken together?

(d) Write out the regression equation. Explain how each coefficient can be thought of as a slope. If x_2 (production costs) and x_4 (book sales) were held fixed but x_3 (promotional costs) were increased by one million dollars, what would you expect for the corresponding change in x_1 (box office receipts)?

(e) Test each coefficient in the regression equation to determine if it is zero or not zero. Use level of significance 5%. Explain why book sales x_4 are probably not contributing much information in the regression model to forecast box office receipts x_1.

(f) Find a 90% confidence interval for each coefficient.

(g) Suppose that a new movie (based on an epic novel) has just been released. Production costs were x_2 = 11.4 million; promotion costs were x_3 = 4.7 million; book sales were x_4 = 8.1 million. Make a prediction for x_1 = first year box office receipts and find an 85% confidence interval for your prediction (if your software supports prediction intervals).

(h) Construct a new regression model with x_3 as the response variable and x_1, x_2, and x_4 as explanatory variables. Suppose that Hollywood is planning a new epic movie with projected box office sales x_1 = 100 million and production costs x_2 = 12 million. The book on which the movie is based sold x_4 = 9.2 million. Forecast the dollar amount (in millions) that should be budgeted for promotion costs x_3 and find an 80% confidence interval for your prediction.

6. *Franchise Business: Market Analysis* All Greens is a franchise store that sells house plants and lawn and garden supplies. Although All Greens is a franchise, each store is owned and managed by private individuals. Some friends have asked you to go into business with them to open a new All Greens store in the suburbs of San Diego. The national franchise headquarters sent you the following information at your request. These data are about 27 All Greens stores in California. Each of the 27 stores has been doing very well, and you would like to use the information to help set up your own new store. The variables for which we have data are

x_1 = annual net sales in thousands of dollars
x_2 = number of square feet of floor display in store in thousands of square feet
x_3 = value of store inventory in thousands of dollars
x_4 = amount spent on local advertising in thousands of dollars
x_5 = size of sales district in thousands of families
x_6 = number of competing or similar stores in sales district

A sales district was defined to be the region within a 5-mile radius of an All Greens store.

x_1	x_2	x_3	x_4	x_5	x_6	x_1	x_2	x_3	x_4	x_5	x_6
231	3	294	8.2	8.2	11	65	1.2	168	4.7	3.3	11
156	2.2	232	6.9	4.1	12	98	1.6	151	4.6	2.7	10
10	0.5	149	3	4.3	15	398	4.3	342	5.5	16.0	4
519	5.5	600	12	16.1	1	161	2.6	196	7.2	6.3	13
437	4.4	567	10.6	14.1	5	397	3.8	453	10.4	13.9	7
487	4.8	571	11.8	12.7	4	497	5.3	518	11.5	16.3	1
299	3.1	512	8.1	10.1	10	528	5.6	615	12.3	16.0	0
195	2.5	347	7.7	8.4	12	99	0.8	278	2.8	6.5	14
20	1.2	212	3.3	2.1	15	0.5	1.1	142	3.1	1.6	12
68	0.6	102	4.9	4.7	8	347	3.6	461	9.6	11.3	6
570	5.4	788	17.4	12.3	1	341	3.5	382	9.8	11.5	5
428	4.2	577	10.5	14.0	7	507	5.1	590	12.0	15.7	0
464	4.7	535	11.3	15.0	3	400	8.6	517	7.0	12.0	8
15	0.6	163	2.5	2.5	14						

(a) Generate summary statistics, including the mean and standard deviation of each variable. Compute the coefficient of variation (see Section 3.2) for each variable. Relative to its mean, which variable has the largest spread of data values? Which variable has the least spread of data values relative to its mean?

(b) For each pair of variables, generate the correlation coefficient r. For all pairs involving x_1, compute the corresponding coefficient of determination r^2. Which variable has the greatest influence on annual net sales? Which variable has the least influence on annual net sales?

(c) Perform a regression analysis with x_1 as the response variable. Use x_2, x_3, x_4, x_5, and x_6 as explanatory variables. Look at the coefficient of multiple determination. What percentage of the variation in x_1 can be explained by the corresponding variations in x_2, x_3, x_4, x_5, and x_6 taken together?

(d) Write out the regression equation. If two new competing stores moved into the sales district, but the other explanatory variables did not change, what would you expect for the corresponding change in annual net sales? Explain your answer. If you increased the local advertising by a thousand dollars, but the other explanatory variables did not change, what would you expect for the corresponding change in annual net sales? Explain.

(e) Test each coefficient to determine if it is or is not zero. Use level of significance 5%.

(f) Suppose you and your business associates rent a store, get a bank loan to start up your business, and do a little research on the size of your sales district and the number of competing stores in the district. If $x_2 = 2.8$, $x_3 = 250$, $x_4 = 3.1$, $x_5 = 7.3$, and $x_6 = 2$, use the computer to forecast x_1 = annual net sales and find an 80% confidence interval for your forecast (if your software produces prediction intervals).

(g) Construct a new regression model with x_4 as the response variable and x_1, x_2, x_3, x_5, and x_6 as explanatory variables. Suppose an All Greens store in Sonoma, California, wants to estimate a range of advertising costs appropriate to its store. If it spends too little on advertising, it will not reach enough customers. However, it does not want to overspend on advertising for this type and size of store. At this store, $x_1 = 163$, $x_2 = 2.4$, $x_3 = 188$, $x_5 = 6.6$, and $x_6 = 10$. Use these data to predict x_4 (advertising costs) and find an 80% confidence interval for your prediction. At the 80% confidence level, what range of advertising costs do you think is appropriate for this store?

● **NOTE** In the Using Technology section at the end of this chapter, you will find a "mini case study" of seven important variables from the economy of the United States for the years 1976 to 1987. Readers interested in applications of multiple regression and the United States economy are referred to this material.

SUMMARY

Scatter diagrams of data pairs (x, y) are useful in helping us determine visually if there is any relation between x and y values and, if so, how strong the relation might be. We call x the explanatory variable and y the response variable.

The Pearson product-moment correlation coefficient r gives a numerical measurement assessing the strength of a *linear* relationship between x and y based on a random sample of data pairs (x, y). The value of r ranges from -1 to 1, with 1 indicating perfect positive linear correlation, -1 indicating perfect negative linear correlation, and 0 indicating no linear correlation. The closer the sample statistic r is to 1 or -1, the stronger the linear correlation. Methods of testing the population correlation coefficient ρ show whether or not the sample statistic r is significant. We test the null hypothesis H_0: $\rho = 0$ against a suitable alternate hypothesis ($\rho > 0$, $\rho < 0$, or $\rho \neq 0$).

If the scatter diagram and correlation coefficient r indicate a linear relationship, then we use the least-squares criterion to develop the equation of the least-squares line between the explanatory variable x and the response variable y

$$\hat{y} = a + bx$$

where $\hat{y}$ is the value of y predicted by the least-squares line, a is the y-intercept, and b is the slope. Methods of testing use the sample statistic b to determine whether the population slope β is significant at a given level of significance α. We use the null hypothesis $H_0: \beta = 0$ with appropriate alternate hypothesis ($\beta > 0$, $\beta < 0$, or $\beta \neq 0$). Confidence intervals for β give us a range of values for β based on the sample statistic b and a specified confidence level. Likewise, confidence intervals for predicted y give us a range of values for y for a specific x value. We base the confidence interval on the sample prediction $\hat{y}$ and a confidence level.

The coefficient of determination r^2 is a value that measures the proportion of variation in y explained by the least-squares line. The standard error of estimate S_e is a measure of data spread around the least-squares line. It is based on the differences $y - \hat{y}$ between the y value in the data pair (x, y) and the corresponding predicted value $\hat{y}$ for the same x. The difference $y - \hat{y}$ is called a residual.

Techniques of multiple regression (with computer assistance) help us analyze the linear relation among several variables.

IMPORTANT WORDS & SYMBOLS

Section 10.1
Paired data values
Explanatory variable
Response variable
Scatter diagram
Sample correlation coefficient r
Perfect linear correlation
No linear correlation
Lurking variable

Section 10.2
Least-squares criterion
Least-squares line $\hat{y} = a + bx$
Meaning of slope
Interpolation

Extrapolation
Explained variation
Unexplained variation
Coefficient of determination r^2
Residual
Residual plot

Section 10.3
Population correlation coefficient ρ
Standard error of estimate S_e
Population slope β

Section 10.4
Multiple regression
Coefficient of multiple determination

 VIEWPOINT   *Living Arrangements*

Male, female, married, single, living alone, living with friends or relatives— all these categories are of interest to the U.S. Census Bureau. In addition to these categories, there are others, such as age, income, and health needs. How strongly correlated are these variables? Can we use one or more of these variables to predict the others? How good is such a prediction? Methods of this chapter can help you answer such questions. For more information regarding such data, visit the Brase/Brase statistics site at **http://math.college.hmco.com/students** and find the link to Census Bureau.

CHAPTER REVIEW PROBLEMS

In Problems 1–6, parts (a)–(e) involve scatter diagrams, least-squares lines, correlation coefficients with coefficients of determination, tests of ρ, and predictions. Parts (f)–(i) involve standard error of estimate, confidence intervals for predictions, tests of β, and confidence intervals for β.

When solving chapter problems involving the standard error of estimate, testing the correlation coefficient, or testing β or confidence intervals for β, make the assumption that x and y are normally distributed random variables. Answers may vary slightly due to rounding.

1. *Desert Ecology: Wildlife* Bighorn sheep are beautiful wild animals found throughout the western United States. Data for this problem are based on information taken from *The Desert Bighorn*, edited by Monson and Sumner (University of Arizona Press). Let x be the age of a bighorn sheep (in years), and let y be the mortality rate (percent that die) for this age group. For example, $x = 1$, $y = 14$ means that 14% of the bighorn sheep between 1 and 2 years old died. A random sample of Arizona bighorn sheep gave the following information:

x	1	2	3	4	5
y	14	18.9	14.4	19.6	20.0

   $\Sigma x = 15$; $\Sigma y = 86.9$; $\Sigma x^2 = 55$; $\Sigma y^2 = 1544.73$; $\Sigma xy = 273.4$
   (a) Draw a scatter diagram.
   (b) Find the equation of the least-squares line.
   (c) Find r. Find the coefficient of determination r^2. Explain what these measures mean in the context of the problem.
   (d) Test the claim that the population correlation coefficient is positive at the 1% level of significance.
   (e) Given the lack of significance of r, is it practical to find estimates of y for a given x value based on the least-squares line model? Explain.

2. *Sociology: Job Changes* A sociologist is interested in the relation between $x = $ number of job changes and $y = $ annual salary (in thousands of dollars) for people living in the Nashville area. A random sample of 10 people employed in Nashville provided the following information:

x (Number of job changes)	4	7	5	6	1	5	9	10	10	3
y (Salary in $1000)	33	37	34	32	32	38	43	37	40	33

   $\Sigma x = 60$; $\Sigma y = 359$; $\Sigma x^2 = 442$; $\Sigma y^2 = 13{,}013$; $\Sigma xy = 2231$
   (a) Draw a scatter diagram for the data.
   (b) Find $\bar{x}$, $\bar{y}$, b, and the equation of the least-squares line. Plot the line on the scatter diagram of part (a).
   (c) Find the sample correlation coefficient r and the coefficient of determination. What percentage of variation in y is explained by the least-squares model?
   (d) Test the claim that the population correlation coefficient ρ is positive at the 5% level of significance.
   (e) If someone had $x = 2$ job changes, what does the least-squares line predict for y, the annual salary?
   (f) Verify that $S_e \approx 2.56$.

(g) Find a 90% confidence interval for the annual salary of an individual with $x = 2$ job changes.

(h) Test the claim that the slope β of the population least-squares line is positive at the 5% level of significance.

(i) Find a 90% confidence interval for β and interpret its meaning.

3. *Medical: Fat Babies* Modern medical practice tells us not to encourage babies to become too fat. Is there a positive correlation between the weight x of a 1-year-old baby and the weight y of the mature adult (30 years old)? A random sample of medical files produced the following information for 14 females:

x (lb)	21	25	23	24	20	15	25	21	17	24	26	22	18	19
y (lb)	125	125	120	125	130	120	145	130	130	130	130	140	110	115

$\Sigma x = 300; \Sigma y = 1775; \Sigma x^2 = 6572; \Sigma y^2 = 226{,}125; \Sigma xy = 38{,}220$

(a) Draw a scatter diagram for the data.

(b) Find $\bar{x}, \bar{y}, b$, and the equation of the least-squares line. Plot the line on the scatter diagram of part (a).

(c) Find the sample correlation coefficient r and the coefficient of determination. What percentage of the variation in y is explained by the least-squares model?

(d) Test the claim that the population correlation coefficient ρ is positive at the 1% level of significance.

(e) If a female baby weighs 20 lb at 1 year, what do you predict she will weigh at 30 years of age?

(f) Verify that $S_e \approx 8.38$.

(g) Find a 95% confidence interval for weight at age 30 of a female who weighed 20 lb at 1 year of age.

(h) Test the claim that the slope β of the population least-squares line is positive at the 1% level of significance.

(i) Find an 80% confidence interval for β and interpret its meaning.

4. *Sales: Insurance* Dorothy Kelly sells life insurance for the Prudence Insurance Company. She sells insurance by making visits to her clients' homes. Dorothy believes that the number of sales should depend, to some degree, on the number of visits made. For the past several years, she kept careful records of the number of visits (x) she made each week and the number of people (y) who bought insurance that week. For a random sample of 15 such weeks, the x and y values follow:

x	11	19	16	13	28	5	20	14	22	7	15	29	8	25	16
y	3	11	8	5	8	2	5	6	8	3	5	10	6	10	7

$\Sigma x = 248; \Sigma y = 97; \Sigma x^2 = 4856; \Sigma y^2 = 731; \Sigma xy = 1825$

(a) Draw a scatter diagram for the data.

(b) Find $\bar{x}, \bar{y}, b$, and the equation of the least-squares line. Plot the line on the scatter diagram of part (a).

(c) Find the sample correlation coefficient r and the coefficient of determination. What percentage of the variation in y is explained by the least-squares model?

(d) Test the claim that the population correlation coefficient ρ is positive at the 1% level of significance.

(e) On a week in which Dorothy makes 18 visits, how many people do you predict will buy insurance from her?

(f) Verify that $S_e \approx 1.731$.

(g) Find a 95% confidence interval for the number of sales Dorothy would make in a week in which she made 18 visits.

(h) Test the claim that the slope β of the population least-squares line is positive at the 1% level of significance.

(i) Find an 80% confidence interval for β and interpret its meaning.

5. *Marketing: Coupons* Each box of Healthy Crunch breakfast cereal contains a coupon entitling you to a free package of garden seeds. At the Healthy Crunch home office, they use the weight of incoming mail to determine how many of their employees are to be assigned to collecting coupons and mailing out seed packages on a given day. (Healthy Crunch has a policy of answering all its mail on the day it is received.)

Let x = weight of incoming mail and y = number of employees required to process the mail in one working day. A random sample of 8 days gave the following data:

x (lb)	11	20	16	6	12	18	23	25
y (Number of employees)	6	10	9	5	8	14	13	16

$\Sigma x = 131; \Sigma y = 81; \Sigma x^2 = 2435; \Sigma y^2 = 927; \Sigma xy = 1487$

(a) Draw a scatter diagram for the data.

(b) Find $\bar{x}, \bar{y}, b$, and the equation of the least-squares line. Plot the line on the scatter diagram of part (a).

(c) Find the sample correlation coefficient r and the coefficient of determination. What percentage of the variation in y is explained by the least-squares model?

(d) Test the claim that the population correlation coefficient ρ is positive at the 1% level of significance.

(e) If Healthy Crunch receives 15 lb of mail, how many employees should be assigned mail duty?

(f) Verify that $S_e \approx 1.726$.

(g) Find a 95% confidence interval for the number of employees required to process mail for 15 lb of mail.

(h) Test the claim that the slope β of the population least-squares line is positive at the 1% level of significance.

(i) Find an 80% confidence interval for β and interpret its meaning.

6. *Focus Problem: Changing Population and Crime Rate* Let x be a random variable representing percentage change in neighborhood population in the past few years, and let y be a random variable representing crime rate (crimes per 1000 population). A random sample of six Denver neighborhoods gave the following information (Source: *Neighborhood Facts*, The Piton Foundation).

x	29	2	11	17	7	6
y	173	35	132	127	69	53

$\Sigma x = 72; \Sigma y = 589; \Sigma x^2 = 1340; \Sigma y^2 = 72{,}277; \Sigma xy = 9499$

(a) Draw a scatter diagram for the data.

(b) Find $\bar{x}$, $\bar{y}$, b, and the equation of the least-squares line. Plot the line on the scatter diagram of part (a).

(c) Find the sample correlation coefficient r and the coefficient of determination. What percentage of the variation in y is explained by the least-squares model?

(d) Test the claim that the population correlation coefficient ρ is not zero at the 1% level of significance.

(e) For a neighborhood with $x = 12\%$ change in population in the past few years, predict the change in the crime rate (per 1000 residents).

(f) Verify that $S_e \approx 22.5908$.

(g) Find an 80% confidence interval for the change in crime rate when the percentage change in population is $x = 12\%$.

(h) Test the claim that the slope β of the population least-squares line is not zero at the 1% level of significance.

(i) Find an 80% confidence interval for β and interpret its meaning.

DATA HIGHLIGHTS: GROUP PROJECTS

Break into small groups and discuss the following topics. Organize a brief outline in which you summarize the main points of your group discussion.

Scatter diagrams! Are they really useful? Scatter diagrams give a first impression of a data relationship and help us assess whether a linear relation provides a reasonable model for the data. In addition, we can spot *influential points*. A data point with an extreme x value can heavily influence the position of the least-squares line. In this project, we look at data sets with an influential point.

x	1	4	5	9	10	15
y	3	7	6	10	12	4

(a) Compute r and b, the slope of the least-squares line. Find the equation of the least-squares line, and sketch the line on the scatter diagram.

(b) Notice the point boxed in blue in Figure 10-23. Does it seem to lie away from the linear pattern determined by the other points? The coordinates of that point are

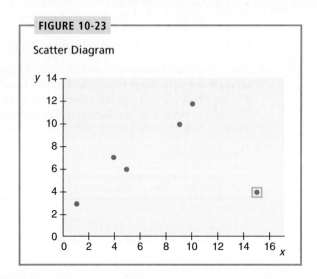

FIGURE 10-23

Scatter Diagram

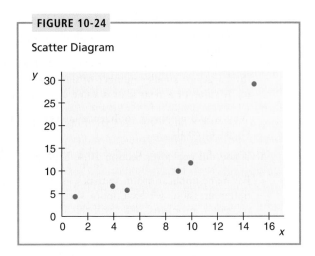

FIGURE 10-24

Scatter Diagram

(15, 4). Is it an influential point? Remove that point from the model and recompute *r, b,* and the equation of the least-squares line. Sketch this least-squares line on the diagram. How does the removal of the influential point affect the values of *r* and *b* and the position of the least-squares line?

(c) Consider the scatter diagram of Figure 10-24. Is there an influential point? If you remove the influential point, will the slope of the new least-squares line be larger or smaller than the slope of the line from the original data? Will the correlation coefficient be larger or smaller?

LINKING CONCEPTS: WRITING PROJECTS

Discuss each of the following topics in class or review the topics on your own. Then write a brief but complete essay in which you summarize the main points. Please include formulas and graphs as appropriate.

1. What do we mean when we say that two variables have a strong positive (or negative) linear correlation? What would a scatter diagram for these variables look like? Is it possible that two variables could be strongly related somehow, but have a low *linear* correlation? Explain and draw a scatter diagram to demonstrate your point.

2. What do we mean by the least-squares criterion? Give a very general description of how the least-squares criterion is involved in the construction of the least-squares line. Why do we say the least-squares line is the "best-fitting" line for the data set?

3. In this chapter, we discussed three measures for "goodness of fit" of the least-squares line to given data. These measures were standard error of estimate, correlation coefficient, and coefficient of determination. Discuss the ways these measurements are different and the ways they are similar to each other. Be sure to include a discussion of explained variation, unexplained variation, and total variation in your answer. Draw a sketch and include appropriate formulas.

4. Look at the formula for confidence bounds for least-squares predictions. Which of the following conditions do you think will result in a *shorter* confidence interval for a prediction?
   (a) Larger or smaller values for the standard error of estimate
   (b) Larger or smaller number of data pairs
   (c) A value of x near $\bar{x}$ or a value of x far away from $\bar{x}$

   Why would a shorter confidence interval for a prediction be more desirable than a longer interval?

5. If you did not cover Section 10.4, Multiple Regression, then omit this problem.

   For many applications in statistics, more data lead to more accurate results. In multiple regression, we have more variables (and data) than we have in most simple regression problems. Why will this usually lead to more accurate predictions? Will additional variables *always* lead to more accurate predictions? Explain your answer. Discuss the coefficient of multiple determination and its meaning in the context of multiple regression. How do we know if an explanatory variable has a statistically significant influence on the response variable? What do we mean by a regression model?

6. Use the Internet or go to the library and find a magazine or journal article in your field of major interest where the content of this chapter could be applied. List the variables used, method of data collection, and general type of information and conclusions drawn.

Using Technology

Simple Linear Regression (one explanatory variable)

APPLICATION 1

The data in this section are taken from this reference:

King, Cuchlaine A. M. *Physical Geography.* Oxford: Basil Blackwell, 1980, 77–86, 196–206. Reprinted with permission of Basil Blackwell Limited, Oxford, England.

Throughout the world, natural ocean beaches are beautiful sights to see. If you have visited natural beaches, you may have noticed that when the gradient or dropoff is steep, the grains of sand tend to be larger. In fact, a manmade beach with the "wrong" size granules of sand tends to be washed away and eventually replaced when the proper size grain is selected by the action of the ocean and the gradient of the bottom. Since manmade beaches are expensive, grain size is an important consideration.

In the data that follow, x = median diameter (in millimeters) of granules of sand, and y = gradient of beach slope in degrees on natural ocean beaches.

x	y
0.17	0.63
0.19	0.70
0.22	0.82
0.235	0.88
0.235	1.15
0.30	1.50
0.35	4.40
0.42	7.30
0.85	11.30

1. Find the sample mean and standard deviation for x and y.

2. Make a scatter plot. Would you expect a moderately high correlation and a good fit for the least-squares line?

3. Find the equation of the least-squares line, and graph the line on the scatter plot.

4. Find the correlation coefficient r and the coefficient of determination r^2. Is r significant at the 1% level of significance (two-tailed test)?

5. Test that $\beta > 0$ at the 1% level of significance. Find the standard error of estimate S_e and form an 80% confidence interval for β. As the diameter of granules of sand changes by 0.10 mm, how much does the gradient of beach slope change?

6. Suppose that you have a truckload of sifted sand in which the median size of granules is 0.38 mm. If you want to put this sand on a beach and you don't want the sand to wash away, then what does the least-squares line predict for the angle of the beach? *Note:* Heavy storms that produce abnormal waves may also wash out the sand. However, in the long run, the size of sand granules that remain on the beach or that are brought back to the beach by long-term wave action are determined to a large extent by the angle at which the beach drops off. What range of angles should the beach have if we want to be 90% confident that we are matching the size of our sand granules (0.38 mm) to the proper angle of the beach?

7. Suppose we now have a truckload of sifted sand in which the median size of the granules is 0.45 mm. Repeat Problem 6.

Technology Hints (Simple Regression)

TI-84Plus/TI-83Plus

Be sure to set **DiagnosticOn** (under **Catalog**).
- (a) Scatter diagram: Use **STAT PLOT,** select the first type, use **ZOOM** option **9:ZoomStat.**
- (b) Least-squares line and r: Use **STAT, CALC,** option **8:LinReg(a + bx).**
- (c) Graph least-squares line and predict: Press **Y=.** Then under **VARS,** select **5:Statistics,** then select **EQ,** and finally select item **1:RegEQ.** Press enter. This sequence of steps will automatically set $Y_1 =$ your regression equation. Press **GRAPH.** To find a predicted value, when the graph is showing, press the **CALC** key and select item **1:Value.** Enter the x value and the corresponding y value will appear.
- (d) Testing ρ and β, value for S_e: Use **STAT, TEST,** option **E:LinRegTTest.** The value of S_e is in the display as s.
- (e) Confidence intervals for β or predictions: Use formulas from Section 10.3.

Excel

- (a) Scatter plot, least-squares line, r^2: Use **Chart wizard.** Select **scatter plot.** Once plot is displayed, *right* click on any data point. Select **trend line.** Under options, check display line and display r^2.
- (b) Prediction: Use paste function $\boxed{f_x}$ ➤ **Statistical** ➤ **Forecast.**
- (c) Coefficient r: Use $\boxed{f_x}$ ➤ **Statistical** ➤ **Correl.**

- (d) Testing β and confidence intervals for β: Use menu selection **Tools** ➤ **Data Analysis** ➤ **Regression.**
- (e) Confidence interval for prediction: Use formulas from Section 10.3.

Minitab

- (a) Scatter plot, least-squares line, r^2, S_e: Use menu selection **Stat** ➤ **Regression** ➤ **Fitted line plot.** The value of S_e is displayed as the value of s.
- (b) Coefficient r: Use menu selection **Stat** ➤ **Basic Statistics** ➤ **Correlation.**
- (c) Testing β, predictions, confidence interval for predictions: Use menu selection **Stat** ➤ **Regression** ➤ **Regression.**
- (d) Confidence interval for β: Use formulas from Section 10.3.

SPSS

SPSS offers several options for finding the correlation coefficient r and the equation of the least-squares line. First enter the data in the data editor and label the variables appropriately in the variable view window. Use the menu choices **Analyze** ➤ **Regression** ➤ **Linear** and select dependent and independent variables. The output includes the correlation coefficient, the standard error of estimate, the constant, and the coefficient of the dependent variable with corresponding t values and P-values for two-tailed tests. The display shows the results for the data in this chapter's Focus Problem regarding crime rate and percentage change in population.

Model Summary

Model	R	R Square	Adjusted R Square	Std. Error of the Estimate
1	.927[a]	.859	.823	22.59076

a. Predictors: (Constant), % change in population

Coefficients[a]

Model		Unstandardized Coefficients B	Unstandardized Coefficients Std. Error	Standardized Coefficients Beta	t	Sig.
1	(Constant)	36.881	15.474		2.383	.076
	% change in population	5.107	1.035	.927	4.932	.008

a. Dependent Variable: Crime rate per 1,000

With the menu choices **Graph ➤ Interactive ➤ Scatterplot**, SPSS produces a scatter diagram with the least-squares line, least-squares equation, coefficient of determination r^2, and optional prediction bands. In the dialogue box, move the dependent variable to the box along the vertical axis and the independent variable to the box along the horizontal axis. Click the "fit" tab, highlight Regression, and check the box to include the constant in the equation. For optional prediction band, check individual, enter the confidence level, and check total. The following display shows a scatter diagram for the data in this chapter's Focus Problem regarding crime rate and percentage change in population.

SPSS Display for Focus Problem

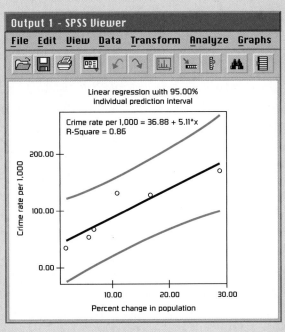

665

Multiple Regression

Data values in the following study are taken from *Statistical Abstract of the United States*, U.S. Department of Commerce, 103rd and 109th Editions (see Table 10-16).

All data values represent annual averages as determined by the U.S. Department of Commerce.

1. Construct a regression model with

   Response variable: x_3 (foreign investments)

   Explanatory variables: x_5 (GNP), x_6 (U.S. dollar), and x_7 (consumer credit)

What is the coefficient of multiple determination?

(a) Use a 1% level of significance and test each coefficient for significance (two-tailed test).
(b) Examine the coefficients of the regression equation. Then explain why you think the following statement is true or false: If the purchasing power of the U.S. dollar did not change and the GNP did not change, then an increase in consumer credit would likely be accompanied by a reduction in foreign investments.
(c) Suppose $x_5 = 3500$, $x_6 = 0.975$, and $x_7 = 450$. Predict the level of foreign investment. Find a 90% confidence interval for your prediction.

TABLE 10-16 Economic Data 1976–1987 (on the data disk)

Year	x_1	x_2	x_3	x_4	x_5	x_6	x_7
1976	10.9	7.61	31	974.9	1718	1.757	234.4
1977	12.0	7.42	35	894.6	1918	1.649	263.8
1978	12.5	8.41	42	820.2	2164	1.532	308.3
1979	17.7	9.44	54	844.4	2418	1.380	347.5
1980	28.1	11.46	83	891.4	2732	1.215	349.4
1981	35.6	13.91	109	932.9	3053	1.098	366.6
1982	31.8	13.00	125	884.4	3166	1.035	381.1
1983	29.0	11.11	137	1190.3	3406	1.000	430.4
1984	28.6	12.44	165	1178.5	3772	0.961	511.8
1985	26.8	10.62	185	1328.2	4015	0.928	592.4
1986	14.6	7.68	209	1792.8	4240	0.913	646.1
1987	17.9	8.38	244	2276.0	4527	0.880	685.5

We will use the following notation:

$x_1 =$ price of a barrel of crude oil in dollars per barrel

$x_2 =$ percent interest on 10-year U.S. Treasury notes

$x_3 =$ total foreign investments in U.S. in billions of dollars

$x_4 =$ Dow Jones Industrial Average (DJIA)

$x_5 =$ Gross National Product, GNP, in billions of dollars

$x_6 =$ purchasing power of U.S. dollar with base 1983 corresponding to $1.000

$x_7 =$ consumer credit (i.e., consumer debt) in billions of dollars

2. Construct a new regression model with

> Response variable: x_4 (DJIA)
>
> Explanatory variables: x_3 (foreign investments), x_5 (GNP), and x_7 (consumer credit)

What is the coefficient of multiple determination?

(a) Use a 5% level of significance and test each coefficient for significance (two-tailed test).

(b) Examine the coefficients of the regression equation; then explain why you think the following statement is true or false: If the GNP and consumer credit didn't change but foreign investments increased, the DJIA would likely show a strong increase.

(c) Suppose $x_3 = 210$, $x_5 = 4260$, and $x_7 = 650$. Predict the DJIA and find an 85% confidence interval for your prediction.

3. Construct a new regression model with

> Response variable: x_7 (consumer credit)
>
> Explanatory variables: x_3 (foreign investments), x_5 (GNP), and x_6 (U.S. dollar)

What is the coefficient of multiple determination?

(a) Use a 1% level of significance and test each coefficient for significance (two-tailed test).

(b) Examine the coefficients of the regression equation; then explain why you think each of the following statements is true or false: If both GNP and purchasing power of the U.S. dollar didn't change, then an increase in foreign investments would likely be accompanied by a reduction in consumer credit. If both foreign investments and purchasing power of the U.S. dollar remained fixed, then an increase in GNP would likely be accompanied by an increase in consumer credit.

(c) Suppose $x_3 = 88$, $x_5 = 2750$, and $x_6 = 1.250$. Predict consumer credit, and find an 80% confidence interval for your prediction.

Technology Hints (Multiple Regression)

TI-84Plus/TI-83Plus

Does not support multiple regression.

Excel

Use the menu selection **Tools ➤ Data Analysis ➤ Regression**. On the spreadsheet, the columns containing the explanatory variables need to be adjacent.

Minitab

Use the menu selection **Stat ➤ Regression ➤ Regression**.

SPSS

Use the menu selection **Analyze ➤ Regression ➤ Linear** and select dependent and independent variables.

11

Chi-Square and F Distributions

"So what!"

—Anonymous

We have all heard the exclamation, "So what!" Philologists (people who study cultural linguistics) tell us that this expression is a shortened version of "So what is the difference!" They also tell us that there are similar popular or slang expressions about differences in all languages and cultures. It is human nature to challenge the claim that something is better, worse, or just simply different. In this chapter, we will focus on this very human theme by studying a variety of topics regarding questions of whether or not differences exist between two population variances or among several population means.

"Girl with Black Eye" by Norman Rockwell (1894–1978)

Norman Rockwell painted everyday people and situations. In this cover for the *Saturday Evening Post* (May 23, 1953), a young lady is about to have a conference with her school principal. So what!

PREVIEW QUESTIONS

◊ How do you decide if random variables are dependent or independent?   (SECTION 11.1)

◊ How do you decide if two distributions are not only dependent, but actually the same distribution?   (SECTION 11.2)

◊ How do you compute confidence intervals and tests for σ? (SECTION 11.3)

◊ How do you test two variances σ_1^2 and σ_2^2?   (SECTION 11.4)

◊ What is one-way ANOVA? Where is it used?   (SECTION 11.5)

◊ What about two-way ANOVA? Where is it used?   (SECTION 11.6)

For on-line student resources, visit **math.college.hmco.com/students** and follow the Statistics links to the Brase/Brase, *Understandable Statistics*, 8th edition web site.

FOCUS PROBLEM

Stone Age Tools and Archaeology

Archaeologists at Washington State University did an extensive summer excavation at Burnt Mesa Pueblo in Bandelier National Monument. Their work is published in the book *Bandelier Archaeological Excavation Project: Summer 1990 Excavations at Burnt Mesa Pueblo and Casa del Rito*, edited by T. A. Kohler.

One question the archaeologists asked was: Is raw material used by prehistoric Indians for stone tool manufacture independent of the archaeological excavation site? Two different excavation sites at Burnt Mesa Pueblo gave the information in the table below.

Use a chi-square test with 5% level of significance to test the claim that raw material used for construction of stone tools and excavation site are independent. (See Problem 11 of Section 11.1.)

Stone Tool Construction Material, Burnt Mesa Pueblo

Material	Site A	Site B	Row Total
Basalt	731	584	1315
Obsidian	102	93	195
Pedernal chert	510	525	1035
Other	85	94	179
Column total	1428	1296	2724

Mesa Verde National Park

Archaeological excavation site

Overview of the Chi-Square Distribution

So far, we have used several probability distributions for hypothesis testing and confidence intervals, with the most frequently used being the normal distribution and the Student's *t* distribution. In this chapter, we will use two other probability distributions, namely, the chi-square distribution (where *chi* is pronounced like the first two letters in the word *kite*) and the *F* distribution. In Part I, we will see applications of the chi-square distribution, whereas in Part II, we will see some important applications of the *F* distribution.

Chi is a Greek letter denoted by the symbol χ, so chi-square is denoted by the symbol χ^2. Because the distribution is of chi-*square* values, the χ^2 values begin at 0 and then are all positive. The graph of the χ^2 distribution is not symmetrical, and like the Student's *t* distribution, it depends on the number of degrees of freedom. Figure 11-1 shows the χ^2 distribution for several degrees of freedom (*d.f.*).

As the degrees of freedom increase, the graph of the chi-square distribution becomes more bell-like and begins to look more and more symmetric.

> The **mode (high point)** of a chi-square distribution with *n* degrees of freedom occurs over $n - 2$ (for $n \geq 3$).

Table 7 of Appendix II shows critical values of chi-square distributions for which a designated area falls to the *right* of the critical value. Table 11-1 gives an excerpt from Table 7. Notice that the row headers are degrees of freedom, and the column headers are areas in the *right* tail of the distribution. For instance, according to the table, for a χ^2 distribution with 3 degrees of freedom, the area occurring to the *right* of $\chi^2 = 0.072$ is 0.995. For a χ^2 distribution with 4 degrees of freedom, the area falling to the *right* of $\chi^2 = 13.28$ is 0.010.

In the next three sections, we will see how to apply the chi-square distribution to different applications.

FIGURE 11-1

The χ^2 Distribution

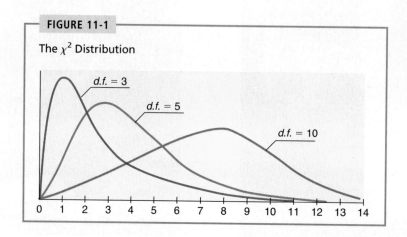

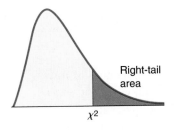

Right-tail area

χ^2

TABLE 11-1 Excerpt from Table 7 (Appendix II): The χ^2 Distribution

d.f.	Area of the Right Tail					
	0.995	0.990	0.975	...	0.010	0.005
⋮	⋮	⋮	⋮	⋮	⋮	⋮
3	0.072	0.115	0.216		11.34	12.84
4	0.207	0.297	0.484		13.28	14.86

11.1
Chi-Square: Tests of Independence

FOCUS POINTS

✓ Set up a test to investigate independence of random variables.

✓ Use contingency tables to compute the sample χ^2 statistic.

✓ Estimate the P-value and complete the test.

Innovative Machines Incorporated has developed two new letter arrangements for computer keyboards. The company wishes to see if there is any relationship between the arrangement of letters on the keyboard and the number of hours it takes a new typing student to learn to type at 20 words per minute. Or, from another point of view, is the time it takes a student to learn to type *independent* of the arrangement of the letters on a keyboard?

To answer questions of this type, we test the hypotheses

> H_0: Keyboard arrangement and learning times *are independent*.
>
> H_1: Keyboard arrangement and learning times *are not independent*.

Chi-square distribution

In problems of this sort, we are testing the *independence* of two factors. The probability distribution we use to make the decision is the *chi-square distribution*. Recall from the overview of the chi-square distribution that *chi* is pronounced like the first two letters of the word *kite* and is a Greek letter denoted by the symbol χ, so chi-square is denoted by χ^2.

The first task for Innovative Machines is to gather data. Suppose that the company took a random sample of 300 beginning typing students and randomly assigned them to learn to type on one of three keyboards. The learning times for this sample are shown in Table 11-2.

Contingency table

Table 11-2 is called a *contingency table*. The *shaded boxes* that contain observed frequencies are called *cells*. The row and column totals are not considered to be cells. This contingency table is of size 3×3 (read, "three-by-three") because there

TABLE 11-2 Keyboard versus Time to Learn to Type at 20 wpm

Keyboard	21–40 h	41–60 h	61–80 h	Row Total
A	#1 25	#2 30	#3 25	80
B	#4 30	#5 71	#6 19	120
Standard	#7 35	#8 49	#9 16	100
Column total	90	150	60	300 Sample size

are three rows of cells and three columns. When giving the size of a contingency table, we always list the number of *rows first*.

> To determine the **size** of a contingency table, count the number of rows containing data and the number of columns containing data. The size is
>
> Number of rows × Number of columns
>
> where the symbol "×" is read "by." The number of rows is always given first.

GUIDED EXERCISE 1

Size of contingency table

Give the sizes of the contingency tables in Figures 11-2 and 11-3. Also, count the number of cells in each table. (Remember, each cell is a pink shaded box.)

(a) **FIGURE 11-2** Contingency Table

⟹ There are two rows and four columns, so this is a 2 × 4 table. There are eight cells.

(b) **FIGURE 11-3** Contingency Table

⟹ Here we have three rows and two columns, so this is a 3 × 2 table with six cells.

We are testing the null hypothesis that the keyboard arrangement and the time it takes a student to learn to type are *independent*. We use this hypothesis to determine the *expected frequency* of each cell.

Expected frequency

For instance, to compute the expected frequency of cell 1 in Table 11-2, we observe that cell 1 consists of all the students in the sample who learned to type on keyboard A and who mastered the skill at the 20-words-per-minute level in 21 to 40 hours. By the assumption (null hypothesis) that the two events are independent, we use the multiplication law to obtain the probability that a student is in cell 1.

$$P(\text{cell 1}) = P(\text{keyboard A } and \text{ skill in 21–40 h})$$
$$= P(\text{keyboard A}) \cdot P(\text{skill in 21–40 h})$$

Because there are 300 students in the sample and 80 used keyboard A,

$$P(\text{keyboard A}) = \frac{80}{300}$$

Also, 90 of the 300 students learned to type in 21–40 hours, so

$$P(\text{skill in 21–40 h}) = \frac{90}{300}$$

Using these two probabilities and the assumption of independence,

$$P(\text{keyboard A } and \text{ skill in 21–40 h}) = \frac{80}{300} \cdot \frac{90}{300}$$

Finally, because there are 300 students in the sample, we have the *expected frequency E* for cell 1.

$$E = P(\text{student in cell 1}) \cdot (\text{no. of students in sample})$$
$$= \frac{80}{300} \cdot \frac{90}{300} \cdot 300 = \frac{80 \cdot 90}{300} = 24$$

We can repeat this process for each cell. However, the last step yields an easier formula for the expected frequency E.

Formula for expected frequency *E*

$$E = \frac{(\text{Row total})(\text{Column total})}{\text{Sample size}}$$

Note: If the expected value is not a whole number, do *not* round it to the nearest whole number.

Let's use this formula in Example 1 to find the expected frequency for cell 2.

EXAMPLE 1

Expected frequency

Find the expected frequency for cell 2 of contingency Table 11-2.

SOLUTION: Cell 2 is in row 1 and column 2. The *row total* is 80, and the *column total* is 150. The size of the sample is still 300.

$$E = \frac{(\text{Row total})(\text{Column total})}{\text{Sample size}}$$
$$= \frac{(80)(150)}{300} = 40$$

◇

GUIDED EXERCISE 2

Expected frequency

Table 11-3 contains the *observed frequencies* O and *expected frequencies* E for the contingency table giving keyboard arrangement and number of hours it takes a student to learn to type at 20 words per minute. Fill in the missing expected frequencies.

TABLE 11-3 Complete Contingency Table of Keyboard Arrangement and Time to Learn to Type

Keyboard	21–40 h	41–60 h	61–80 h	Row Total
A	#1 O = 25 E = 24	#2 O = 30 E = 40	#3 O = 25 E = ____	80
B	#4 O = 30 E = 36	#5 O = 71 E = ____	#6 O = 19 E = ____	120
Standard	#7 O = 35 E = ____	#8 O = 49 E = 50	#9 O = 16 E = 20	100
Column Total	90	150	60	300 Sample Size

For cell 3, we have
$$E = \frac{(80)(60)}{300} = 16$$

For cell 5, we have
$$E = \frac{(120)(150)}{300} = 60$$

For cell 6, we have
$$E = \frac{(120)(60)}{300} = 24$$

For cell 7, we have
$$E = \frac{(100)(90)}{300} = 30$$

Computing the sample test statistic χ^2

Now we are ready to compute the sample statistic χ^2 for the typing students. The χ^2 value is a measure of the sum of the differences between observed frequency O and expected frequency E in each cell. These differences are listed in Table 11-4.

As you see, if we sum the differences between the observed frequencies and the expected frequencies of the cells, we get the value zero. This total certainly does not reflect the fact that there were differences between the observed and expected

TABLE 11-4 Difference Between the Observed and Expected Frequencies

Cell	Observed O	Expected E	Difference (O − E)
1	25	24	1
2	30	40	−10
3	25	16	9
4	30	36	−6
5	71	60	11
6	19	24	−5
7	35	30	5
8	49	50	−1
9	16	20	−4
			$\Sigma(O - E) = 0$

frequencies. To obtain a measure whose sum does reflect the magnitude of the differences, we square the differences and work with the quantities $(O - E)^2$. But instead of using the terms $(O - E)^2$, we use the values $(O - E)^2/E$. We use this expression because a small difference between the observed and expected frequency is not nearly as important when the expected frequency is large as it is when the expected frequency is small. For instance, for both cells 1 and 8, the squared difference $(O - E)^2$ is 1. However, this difference is more meaningful in cell 1, where the expected frequency is 24, than it is in cell 8, where the expected frequency is 50. When we divide the quantity $(O - E)^2$ by E, we take the size of the difference with respect to the size of the expected value. We use the sum of these values to form the sample statistic χ^2:

$$\chi^2 = \Sigma \frac{(O - E)^2}{E}$$

where the sum is over all cells in the contingency table.

◇ **COMMENT** If you look up the word *irony* in a dictionary, you will find one of its meanings is described as "the difference between actual (or observed) results and expected results." Because irony is so prevalent in much of our human experience, it is not surprising that statisticians have incorporated a related chi-square distribution into their work. ◇

GUIDED EXERCISE 3

Sample χ^2

(a) Complete Table 11-5.

⇨ The last two rows of Table 11-5 are

TABLE 11-5   Data of Table 11-4

Cell	O	E	$O - E$	$(O - E)^2$	$(O - E)^2/E$
1	25	24	1	1	0.04
2	30	40	−10	100	2.50
3	25	16	9	81	5.06
4	30	36	−6	36	1.00
5	71	60	11	121	2.02
6	19	24	−5	25	1.04
7	35	30	5	25	0.83
8	49	50	___	___	___
9	16	20	___	___	___

$$\Sigma \frac{(O - E)^2}{E} = \underline{\hspace{1cm}}$$

Cell	O	E	$O - E$	$(O - E)^2$	$(O - E)^2/E$
8	49	50	−1	1	0.02
9	16	20	−4	16	0.80

$$\Sigma \frac{(O - E)^2}{E} = \text{total of last column} = 13.31$$

(b) Compute the statistic χ^2 for this sample.

⇨ Since $\chi^2 = \Sigma \dfrac{(O - E)^2}{E}$, then $\chi^2 = 13.31$.

Notice that when the observed frequency and the expected frequency are very close, the quantity $(O - E)^2$ is close to zero, and so the statistic χ^2 is near zero. As the difference increases, the statistic χ^2 also increases. To determine how large the sample statistic can be before we must reject the null hypothesis of independence, we find the P-value of the statistic in the chi-square distribution, Table 7 of Appendix II, and compare it to the specified level of significance α. The P-value depends on the number of degrees of freedom. To test independence, the degrees of freedom $d.f.$ are determined by the following formula.

> **Degrees of freedom for test of independence**
>
> Degrees of freedom = (Number of rows $- 1$) $\cdot$ (Number of columns $- 1$)
>
> or $d.f. = (R - 1)(C - 1)$
>
> where R = number of cell rows
>
> C = number of cell columns

GUIDED EXERCISE 4

Degrees of freedom

Determine the number of degrees of freedom in the example of keyboard arrangements (see Table 11-2). Recall that the contingency table had three rows and three columns.

$\Longrightarrow$ $d.f. = (R - 1)(C - 1)$
$= (3 - 1)(3 - 1) = (2)(2) = 4$

Finding the P-value for tests of independence

To test the hypothesis that the letter arrangement on a keyboard and the time it takes to learn to type at 20 words per minute are independent at the $\alpha = 0.05$ level of significance, we estimate the P-value shown in Figure 11-4 for the sample test statistic $\chi^2 = 13.31$ (calculated in Guided Exercise 3). We then compare the P-value to the specified level of significance α.

> For tests of independence, we always use a *right-tailed* test on the chi-square distribution. This is because we are testing to see if the χ^2 measure of the difference between the observed and expected frequencies is too large to be due to chance alone.

In Guided Exercise 4 we found that the degrees of freedom for the example of keyboard arrangements is 4. From Table 7 of Appendix II, in the row headed by $d.f. = 4$, we see that the sample $\chi^2 = 13.31$ falls between the entries 13.28 and 14.86. The corresponding P-value falls between 0.005 and 0.010.

α

———(———————)———+————
0.005   0.010   0.05

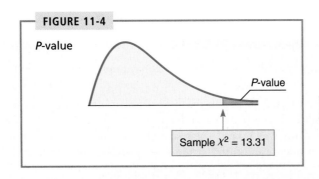

FIGURE 11-4

P-value

Right-tail Area	0.010	0.005
d.f. = 4	13.28	14.86

Sample χ^2 = 13.31

Since the *P*-value is less than the level of significance $\alpha = 0.05$, we reject the null hypothesis of independence and conclude that the keyboard arrangement and learning time are *not* independent.

Tests of independence for two statistical variables involve a number of steps. A summary of the procedure follows.

PROCEDURE

How to test for independence of two statistical variables

Construct a contingency table in which the rows represent one statistical variable and the columns represent the other. Obtain a random sample of observations, which are assigned to the cells described by the rows and columns. These assignments are called the **observed values O** from the sample.

1. Set the level of significance α and use the hypotheses

    H_0: The variables are independent.

    H_1: The variables are not independent.

2. For each cell, compute the **expected frequency E** (do not round, but give as a decimal number).

    $$E = \frac{(\text{Row total})(\text{Column total})}{\text{Sample size}}$$

    You need a sample size large enough so that, for each cell, $E \geq 5$. Now each cell has two numbers, the observed frequency O from the sample and the expected frequency E.

    Next compute the sample *chi-square test statistic*

    $$\chi^2 = \Sigma \frac{(O - E)^2}{E} \text{ with degrees of freedom } d.f. = (R - 1)(C - 1)$$

    where the sum is over all cells in the contingency table and

    R = number of rows in contingency table

    C = number of columns in contingency table

3. Use the chi-square distribution (Table 7 of Appendix II) and a *right-tailed test* to find (or estimate) the *P-value* corresponding to the test statistic.

4. *Conclude* the test. If *P*-value $\leq \alpha$, then reject H_0. If *P*-value $> \alpha$, then do not reject H_0.

5. *State your conclusion* in the context of the application.

GUIDED EXERCISE 5

Testing independence

Super Vending Machines Company is to install soda pop machines in elementary schools and high schools. The market analysts wish to know if flavor preference and school level are independent. A random sample of 200 students was taken. Their school level and soda pop preferences are given in Table 11-6. Is independence indicated at the $\alpha = 0.01$ level of significance?

Step 1: State the null and alternate hypotheses.

➥ H_0: School level and soda pop preference are independent.

H_1: School level and soda pop preference are not independent.

Step 2:

(a) Complete the contingency Table 11-6 by filling in the required expected frequencies.

➥ The expected frequency

for cell 5 is $\dfrac{(40)(80)}{200} = 16$

for cell 6 is $\dfrac{(40)(120)}{200} = 24$

for cell 7 is $\dfrac{(20)(80)}{200} = 8$

for cell 8 is $\dfrac{(20)(120)}{200} = 12$

TABLE 11-6 School Level and Soda Pop Preference

Soda Pop	High School	Elementary School	Row Total
Kula Kola	$O = 33$ #1 $E = 36$	$O = 57$ #2 $E = 54$	90
Mountain Mist	$O = 30$ #3 $E = 20$	$O = 20$ #4 $E = 30$	50
Jungle Grape	$O = 5$ #5 $E = \underline{\hspace{1cm}}$	$O = 35$ #6 $E = \underline{\hspace{1cm}}$	40
Diet Pop	$O = 12$ #7 $E = \underline{\hspace{1cm}}$	$O = 8$ #8 $E = \underline{\hspace{1cm}}$	20
Column Total	80	120	200 Sample Size

Note: In this example, the expected frequencies are all whole numbers. If the expected frequency has a decimal part such as 8.45, do *not* round the value to the nearest whole number; rather, give the expected frequency as the decimal number.

(b) Fill in Table 11-7 and use the table to find the sample statistic χ^2.

➥ The last three rows of Table 11-7 should read as follows:

TABLE 11-7 Computational Table for χ^2

Cell	O	E	$O - E$	$(O - E)^2$	$(O - E)^2/E$
1	33	36	−3	9	0.25
2	57	54	3	9	0.17
3	30	20	10	100	5.00
4	20	30	−10	100	3.33
5	5	16	−11	121	7.56
6	35	24	11	___	___
7	12	8	___	___	___
8	8	12	___	___	___

Cell	O	E	$O - E$	$(O - E)^2$	$(O - E)^2/E$
6	35	24	11	121	5.04
7	12	8	4	16	2.00
8	8	12	−4	16	1.33

χ^2 = total of last column

$$= \Sigma \frac{(O - E)^2}{E} = 24.68$$

Continued

GUIDED EXERCISE 5 continued

(c) What is the size of the contingency table? Use the number of rows and the number of columns to determine the degrees of freedom.

⇨ The contingency table is of size 4 × 2. Since there are four rows and two columns,

$$d.f. = (4 - 1)(2 - 1) = 3$$

Step 3: Use Table 7 of Appendix II to estimate the *P*-value of the sample statistic $\chi^2 = 24.68$ with $d.f. = 3$.

⇨

Right-tail Area	0.005
d.f. = 3	12.84

↑
Sample χ^2 = 24.68

As the χ^2 values increase, the area to the right decreases, so

P-value < 0.005

Step 4: Conclude the test by comparing the *P*-value of the sample statistic χ^2 to the level of significance $\alpha = 0.01$.

⇨

Since the *P*-value is less than α, we reject the null hypothesis of independence.

Step 5: Interpret the test result in the context of the application.

⇨ At the 1% level of significance, we conclude that school level and soda pop preference are dependent.

TECH NOTE The TI-84Plus and TI-83Plus calculators, Excel, and Minitab all support chi-square tests of independence. In each case, the observed data are entered in the format of the contingency table.

TI-84Plus/TI-83Plus Enter the observed data into a matrix. Set the dimension of matrix [**B**] to match that of the matrix of observed values. Expected values will be placed in matrix [**B**]. Press **STAT, TESTS,** and select option **C:χ^2-Test.** The output gives the sample χ^2 with the *P*-value.

Excel Enter the table of observed values. Use the formulas of this section to compute the expected values. Enter the corresponding table of expected values. Finally, use **paste function** ⬚ f_x ➤ **Statistical ➤ Chitest.** Excel returns the *P*-value of the sample χ^2.

Minitab Enter the contingency table of observed values. Use the menu selection **Stat ➤ Tables ➤ Chi-Square Test.** The output shows the contingency table with expected values and the sample χ^2 with *P*-value.

Multinomial Experiments (Optional Reading)

Here are some observations that may be considered "brain teasers." In Chapters 6, 7, 8, and 9, you studied normal approximations to binomial experiments. This concept resulted in some important statistical applications. Is it possible to extend this idea and obtain even more applications? Well, read on!

Consider a *binomial experiment* with n trials. The probability of success on each trial is p, and the probability of failure is $q = 1 - p$. If r is the number of successes out of n trials, then, from Chapter 5, you know that

$$P(r) = \frac{n!}{r!(n-r)!} p^r q^{n-r}$$

The binomial setting has just two outcomes: success or failure. What if you want to consider more than just two outcomes on each trial (for instance, outcomes shown in a contingency table)? Well, you need a new statistical tool.

Consider a *multinomial experiment*. This means that

1. The trials are independent and repeated under identical conditions.

2. The outcome on each trial falls into exactly one of $k \geq 2$ categories or cells.

3. The probability that the outcome of a single trial will fall into the ith category or cell is p_i (where $i = 1, 2, \ldots, k$) and remains the same for each trial. Furthermore, $p_1 + p_2 + \cdots + p_k = 1$.

4. Let r_i be a random variable that represents the number of trials in which the outcome falls into category or cell i. If you have n trials, then $r_1 + r_2 + \cdots + r_k = n$. The multinomial probability distribution is then

$$P(r_1, r_2, \ldots r_k) = \frac{n!}{r_1! r_2! \cdots r_k!} p_1^{r_1} p_2^{r_2} \cdots p_k^{r_k}$$

How are the multinomial distribution and the binomial distribution related? In the special case where $k = 2$, we use the notation $r_1 = r$, $r_2 = n - r$, $p_1 = p$, and $p_2 = q$. In this special case the multinomial distribution becomes the binomial distribution.

There are two important tests regarding the cell probabilities p_i of a multinomial distribution.

I. **Test of Independence** (Section 11.1)
   In this test, the null hypothesis of independence claims that each cell probability p_i will equal the product of its respective row and column probabilities. The alternate hypothesis claims that this is not so.

II. **Goodness-of-Fit Test** (Section 11.2)
   In this test, the null hypothesis claims that each category or cell probability p_i will equal a pre-specified value. The alternate hypothesis claims that this is not so.

So why don't we use the multinomial probability distribution in Sections 11.1 and 11.2? The reason is that the exact calculation of probabilities associated with type I errors using the multinomial distribution is very tedious and cumbersome. Fortunately, the British statistician Karl Pearson discovered that the chi-square distribution can be used for this purpose, provided the expected value of each cell or category is at least 5.

It is Pearson's chi-square methods that are presented in Sections 11.1 and 11.2. In a sense you have seen a similar application to statistical tests in Section 9.3, where you used the normal approximation to the binomial when np, the expected number of successes, and nq, the expected number of failures, were both at least 5.

VIEWPOINT

Loyalty! Going, Going, Gone!

Was there a time in the past when people worked for the same company all their lives, regularly purchased the same brand names, always voted for candidates from the same political party, and loyally cheered for the same sports team? One way to look at this question is to consider tests of *statistical independence*. Is customer loyalty independent of company profits? Can a company maintain its productivity independent of loyal workers? Can politicians do whatever they please independent of the voters back home? Americans may be ready to act on a pent-up desire to restore a sense of loyalty in their lives. For more information, see *American Demographics*, vol. 19, no. 9.

SECTION 11.1 PROBLEMS

For each problem, please provide the following information.
(a) What is the level of significance? State the null and alternate hypotheses.
(b) Find the value of the chi-square statistic for the sample. Are all the expected frequencies greater than 5? What sampling distribution will you use? What are the degrees of freedom?
(c) Find or estimate the *P*-value of the sample test statistic.
(d) Based on your answers in parts (a) to (c), will you reject or fail to reject the null hypothesis of independence?
(e) State your conclusion in the context of the application.

Use the expected values *E* to the hundredths place.

1. *Psychology: Myers-Briggs* The following table shows the Myers-Briggs personality preferences for a random sample of 406 people in the listed professions (*Atlas of Type Tables*, by Macdaid, McCaulley, and Kainz). E refers to extroverted, and I refers to introverted.

	Personality Preference Type		
Occupation	E	I	Row Total
Clergy (all denominations)	62	45	107
M.D.	68	94	162
Lawyer	56	81	137
Column total	186	220	406

Use the chi-square test to determine if the listed occupations and personality preferences are independent at the 0.05 level of significance.

2. *Psychology: Myers-Briggs* The following table shows the Myers-Briggs personality preferences for a random sample of 519 people in the listed professions (*Atlas of Type Tables*, by Macdaid, McCaulley, and Kainz). T refers to thinking, and F refers to feeling.

Occupation	Personality Preference Type		Row Total
	T	F	
Clergy (all denominations)	57	91	148
M.D.	77	82	159
Lawyer	118	94	212
Column total	252	267	519

Use the chi-square test to determine if the listed occupations and personality preferences are independent at the 0.01 level of significance.

3. *Archaeology: Pottery* The following table shows site type and type of pottery for a random sample of 628 sherds at a location in Sand Canyon Archaeological Project, Colorado (*The Sand Canyon Archaeological Project,* edited by Lipe).

Site Type	Pottery Type			Row Total
	Mesa Verde Black-on-White	McElmo Black-on-White	Mancos Black-on-White	
Mesa Top	75	61	53	189
Cliff-Talus	81	70	62	213
Canyon Bench	92	68	66	226
Column total	248	199	181	628

Use a chi-square test to determine if site type and pottery type are independent at the 0.01 level of significance.

4. *Archaeology: Pottery* The following table shows ceremonial ranking and type of pottery sherd for a random sample of 434 sherds at a location in the Sand Canyon Archaeological Project, Colorado (*The Architecture of Social Integration in Prehistoric Pueblos,* edited by Lipe and Hegmon).

Ceremonial Ranking	Cooking Jar Sherds	Decorated Jar Sherds (Noncooking)	Row Total
A	86	49	135
B	92	53	145
C	79	75	154
Column total	257	177	434

Use a chi-square test to determine if ceremonial ranking and pottery type are independent at the 0.05 level of significance.

5. *Ecology: Buffalo* The following table shows age distribution and location of a random sample of 166 buffalo in Yellowstone National Park (based on information from *The Bison of Yellowstone National Park,* National Park Service Scientific Monograph Series).

Age	Lamar District	Nez Perce District	Firehole District	Row Total
Calf	13	13	15	41
Yearling	10	11	12	33
Adult	34	28	30	92
Column total	57	52	57	166

Use a chi-square test to determine if age distribution and location are independent at the 0.05 level of significance.

6. *Psychology: Myers-Briggs* The following table shows the Myers-Briggs personality preference and area of study for a random sample of 519 college students (*Applications of the Myers-Briggs Type Indicator in Higher Education*, edited by Provost and Anchors). In the table IN refers to introvert, intuitive; EN refers to extrovert, intuitive; IS refers to introvert, sensing; and ES refers to extrovert, sensing.

Myers-Briggs Preference	Arts & Science	Business	Allied Health	Row Total
IN	64	15	17	96
EN	82	42	30	154
IS	68	35	12	115
ES	75	42	37	154
Column total	289	134	96	519

Use a chi-square test to determine if Myers-Briggs preference type is independent of area of study at the 0.05 level of significance.

7. *Sociology: Movie Preference* Mr. Acosta, a sociologist, is doing a study to see if there is a relationship between the age of a young adult (18 to 35 years old) and the type of movie preferred. A random sample of 93 adults revealed the following data. Test if age and type of movie preferred are independent at the 0.05 level.

Movie	18–23 yr	24–29 yr	30–35 yr	Row Total
Drama	8	15	11	34
Science fiction	12	10	8	30
Comedy	9	8	12	29
Column total	29	33	31	93

8. *Sociology: Ethnic Groups* After a large fund drive to help the Boston City Library, the following information was obtained from a random sample of contributors to the library fund. Using a 1% level of significance, test the claim that the amount contributed to the library fund is independent of ethnic group.

Ethnic Group	Number of People Making Contribution					Row Total
	$1–50	$51–100	$101–150	$151–200	Over $200	
A	83	62	53	35	18	251
B	94	77	48	25	20	264
C	78	65	51	40	32	266
D	105	89	63	54	29	340
Column total	360	293	215	154	99	1121

9. *Marketing: Movies* Blue Bird Consolidated Theaters has more than 600 theaters located across the country. Each theater has four separate screens, and a customer can choose from one of four different movies. The president of Blue Bird Consolidated wants to know if a variety of shows (spy, comedy, horror, children's) or a coordinated bill (all spy, all comedy, all horror, all children's) has any effect on the total ticket sales at a theater. The president randomly assigned 47 theaters to use a variety of shows and 53 other theaters to use a coordinated bill of shows. For all theaters, total ticket sales for one week were recorded. Using the following data and a 5% level of significance, test the claim that total ticket sales are independent of the four shows being varied or coordinated.

Type of Billing	Ticket Sales for One Week				Row Total
	Less than 1000	1001 to 2000	2001 to 3000	More than 3000	
Variety	10	12	18	7	47
Coordinated	6	16	22	9	53
Column total	16	28	40	16	100

10. *Political Affiliation: Funding* A random sample of senators and representatives in Washington, D.C., gave the following information about party affiliation and number of dollars spent on federal projects in their home districts. Using a 1% level of significance, test the claim that federal spending level in home districts is independent of party affiliation.

Party	Dollars Spent on Federal Projects in Home Districts			Row Total
	Less than 5 Billion	5 to 10 Billion	More than 10 Billion	
Democratic	8	15	22	45
Republican	12	19	16	47
Column total	20	34	38	92

11. *Focus Problem: Archaeology* The Focus Problem at the beginning of the chapter refers to excavations at Burnt Mesa Pueblo in Bandelier National Monument. One question the archaeologists asked was: Is raw material used by prehistoric Indians for stone tool manufacture independent of the archaeological excavation site? Two different excavation sites at Burnt Mesa Pueblo gave the information in the following table. Use a chi-square test with 5% level of significance to test the claim that raw material used for construction of stone tools and excavation site are independent.

| Material | Stone Tool Construction Material, Burnt Mesa Pueblo | | Row Total |
	Site A	Site B	
Basalt	731	584	1315
Obsidian	102	93	195
Pedernal chert	510	525	1035
Other	85	94	179
Column total	1428	1296	2724

11.2
Chi-Square: Goodness of Fit

FOCUS POINTS

✓ Set up a test to investigate how well a sample distribution fits a given distribution.

✓ Use observed and expected frequencies to compute the sample χ^2 statistic.

✓ Estimate the *P*-value and complete the test.

Hypotheses

Last year the labor union bargaining agents listed five categories and asked each employee to mark the *one* most important to her or him. The categories and corresponding percentages of favorable responses are shown in Table 11-8. The bargaining agents need to determine if the distribution of responses *now* "fits" last year's distribution or if it is different.

In questions of this type, we are asking if a population follows a specified distribution. In other words, we are testing the hypotheses

H_0: The population fits the given distribution.

H_1: The population has a different distribution.

We use the chi-square distribution to test "goodness-of-fit" hypotheses.

TABLE 11-8   Bargaining Categories (last year)

Category	Percentage of Favorable Responses
Vacation time	4%
Salary	65%
Safety regulations	13%
Health and retirement benefits	12%
Overtime policy and pay	6%

Computing sample χ^2

Just as with tests of independence, we compute the sample statistic:

$$\chi^2 = \Sigma \frac{(O - E)^2}{E} \text{ with degrees of freedom} = k - 1$$

where E = expected frequency

O = observed frequency

$\dfrac{(O - E)^2}{E}$ is summed for each category in the distribution

k = number of categories in the distribution

Next we use the chi-square distribution table (Table 7, Appendix II) to estimate the P-value of the sample χ^2 statistic. Finally, we compare the P-value to the level of significance α and conclude the test.

In the case of a *goodness-of-fit test,* we use the null hypothesis to compute the expected values for the categories. Let's look at the bargaining category problem to see how this is done.

In the bargaining category problem, the two hypotheses are

H_0: The present distribution of responses is the same as last year's.

H_1: The present distribution of responses is different.

The null hypothesis tells us that the expected frequencies of the present response distribution should follow the percentages indicated in last year's survey. To test this hypothesis, a random sample of 500 employees was taken. If the null hypothesis is true, then there should be 4%, or 20 responses, out of the 500 rating vacation time as the most important bargaining issue. Table 11-9 gives the other expected values and all the information necessary to compute the sample statistic χ^2. We see that the sample statistic is

$$\chi^2 = \Sigma \frac{(O - E)^2}{E} = 14.15$$

Larger values of the sample statistic χ^2 indicate greater differences between the proposed distribution and the distribution followed by the sample. The larger the

Type of test

TABLE 11-9   Observed and Expected Frequencies for Bargaining Categories

Category	O	E	$(O - E)^2$	$(O - E)^2/E$
Vacation time	30	4% of 500 = 20	100	5.00
Salary	290	65% of 500 = 325	1225	3.77
Safety	70	13% of 500 = 65	25	0.38
Health and retirement	70	12% of 500 = 60	100	1.67
Overtime	40	6% of 500 = 30	100	3.33
	$\Sigma O = 500$	$\Sigma E = 500$		$\Sigma \dfrac{(O - E)^2}{E} = 14.15$

χ^2 statistic, the stronger the evidence is to reject the null hypothesis that the population distribution fits the given distribution. Consequently, goodness-of-fit tests are always *right-tailed* tests.

> For *goodness-of-fit tests*, we use a *right-tailed* test on the chi-square distribution. This is because we are testing to see if the χ^2 measure of the difference between the observed and expected frequencies is too large to be due to chance alone.

Degrees of freedom

To test the hypothesis that the present distribution of responses to bargaining categories is the same as last year's, we use the chi-square distribution (Table 7 of Appendix II) to estimate the *P*-value of the sample statistic $\chi^2 = 14.15$. To estimate the *P*-value, we need to know the number of degrees of freedom. In the case of a goodness-of-fit test, the degrees of freedom are found by the following formula.

> **Degrees of freedom for goodness-of-fit test**
>
> $$d.f. = k - 1$$
>
> where k = number of categories

Notice that when we compute the expected values E, we must use the null hypothesis to compute all but the last one. To compute the last one, we can subtract the previous expected values from the sample size. For instance, for the bargaining issues, we could have found the number of responses for overtime policy by adding up the other expected values and subtracting that sum from the sample size 500. We would again get an expected value of 30 responses. The degrees of freedom, then, is the number of E values that *must* be computed by using the null hypothesis.

For the bargaining issues, we have

$$d.f. = 5 - 1 = 4$$

where $k = 5$ is the number of categories.

P-value

We now have the tools necessary to use Table 7 of Appendix II to estimate the *P*-value of $\chi^2 = 14.15$. Figure 11-5 shows the *P*-value. In Table 7, we use the row

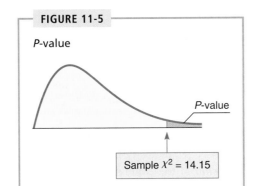

FIGURE 11-5

P-value

P-value

Sample $\chi^2 = 14.15$

Right-tail area	0.010	0.005
d.f. = 4	13.28	14.86

Sample $\chi^2 = 14.15$

headed by *d.f.* = 4. We see that $\chi^2 = 14.15$ falls between the entries 13.28 and 14.86. Therefore, the *P*-value falls between the corresponding right-tail areas 0.005 and 0.010.

To test the hypothesis that the distribution of responses to bargaining issues is the same as last year's at the 1% level of significance, we compare the *P*-value of the statistic to $\alpha = 0.01$.

$$\underset{0.005\qquad 0.010}{\overline{\quad(\underline{\qquad\qquad})\overset{\alpha}{\quad}\quad}}$$

We see that the *P*-value is less than α, so we reject the null hypothesis that the distribution of responses to bargaining issues is the same as last year's. At the 1% level of significance, we can say that the evidence supports the conclusion that this year's responses to the issues are different from last year's.

Goodness-of-fit tests involve several steps that can be summarized as follows.

PROCEDURE

How to test for goodness of fit

The members of a population need to be classified into exactly one of several different categories. Next you need a specific (theoretical) distribution that assigns a fixed probability (or percentage) that a member of the population will fall into one of the categories. You then need a random sample size *n* from the population. Let *O* represent the *observed number* of data from the sample that fall into each category. Let *E* represent the *expected number* of data from the sample that in theory would fall into each category.

O = observed frequency count of a category using sample data

E = expected frequency of a category

= (sample size *n*)(probability assigned to category)

The sample size *n* should be large enough so that $E \geq 5$ in each category.

1. Set the *level of significance* α and use the *hypotheses*

   H_0: The population fits the specified distribution of categories.

   H_1: The population has a different distribution.

2. For each category compute $(O - E)^2/E$, then compute the sample *test statistic*

   $$\chi^2 = \Sigma\frac{(O - E)^2}{E} \quad\text{with } d.f. = k - 1$$

   where the sum is taken over all categories and *k* = number of categories.

3. Use the chi-square distribution (Table 7 of Appendix II) and a *right-tailed test* to find (or estimate) the *P-value* corresponding to the sample test statistic.

4. *Conclude* the test. If *P*-value < α, then reject H_0. If *P*-value > α, then do not reject H_0.

5. *State your conclusion* in the context of the application.

One important application of goodness-of-fit tests is to genetic theories. Such an application is shown in Guided Exercise 6.

GUIDED EXERCISE 6

Goodness-of-fit test

According to genetics theory, red-green colorblindness in humans is a recessive sex-linked characteristic. In this case, the gene is carried on the X chromosome only. We will denote an X chromosome with the gene by X_c and one without the gene by X_n. Women have two X chromosomes, and they will be red-green colorblind only if both chromosomes have the gene, designated $X_c X_c$. A woman can have normal vision but still carry the colorblind gene if only one of the chromosomes has the gene, designated $X_c X_n$. A man carries an X and a Y chromosome; if the X chromosome carries the colorblind gene ($X_c Y$), the man is colorblind.

TABLE 11-10
Red-Green Colorblindness

Mother	Father	
	X_n	Y
X_c	$X_c X_n$	$X_c Y$
X_n	$X_n X_n$	$X_n Y$

According to genetics theory, if a man with normal vision ($X_n Y$) and a woman carrier ($X_c X_n$) have a child, the probabilities that the child will have red-green colorblindness, will have normal vision and not carry the gene, or will have normal vision and carry the gene are given by the *equally likely* events in Table 11-10.

$P(\text{child has normal vision and is not a carrier}) = P(X_n Y) + P(X_n X_n) = \dfrac{1}{2}$

$P(\text{child has normal vision and is a carrier}) = P(X_c X_n) = \dfrac{1}{4}$

$P(\text{child is red-green colorblind}) = P(X_c Y) = \dfrac{1}{4}$

To test this genetics theory, Genetics Labs took a random sample of 200 children whose mothers were carriers of the colorblind gene and whose fathers had normal vision. The results are shown in Table 11-11. We wish to test the hypothesis that the population follows the distribution predicted by the genetics theory (see Table 11-10). Use a 1% level of significance.

(a) State the null and alternate hypotheses. What is α?

⟹ H_0: The population fits the distribution predicted by genetics theory.

H_1: The population does not fit the distribution predicted by genetics theory.

$\alpha = 0.01$

Continued

GUIDED EXERCISE 6 continued

(b) Fill in the rest of Table 11-11 and use the table to compute the sample statistic χ^2.

TABLE 11-11   Colorblindness Sample

Event	O	E	$(O - E)^2$	$(O - E)^2/E$
Red-green colorblind	35	50	225	4.50
Normal vision, noncarrier	105	___	___	___
Normal vision, carrier	60	___	___	___

TABLE 11-12   Completion of Table 11-11

Event	O	E	$(O - E)^2$	$(O - E)^2/E$
Red-green colorblind	35	50	225	4.50
Normal vision, noncarrier	105	100	25	0.25
Normal vision, carrier	60	50	100	2.00

The sample statistic is $\chi^2 = \Sigma \dfrac{(O - E)^2}{E} = 6.75$.

(c) There are $k = 3$ categories listed in Table 11-11. Use this information to compute the degrees of freedom.

$d.f. = k - 1$
$= 3 - 1 = 2$

(d) Find the *P*-value for $\chi^2 = 6.75$.

Using Table 7 of Appendix II and the fact that goodness-of-fit tests are right-tailed tests, we see that

Right-tail area	0.050	0.025
$d.f. = 2$	5.99	7.38

↑ Sample $\chi^2 = 6.75$

$0.025 < P\text{-value} < 0.050$

(e) Conclude the test for $\alpha = 0.01$.

For $\alpha = 0.01$, we have

```
         α
 ────┼───────(═══════)────
   0.01   0.025      0.050
```

Since *P*-value > α, do not reject H_0.

(f) State the conclusion in the context of the application.

At the 1% level of significance, there is insufficient evidence to conclude that the population follows a distribution different from that predicted by genetics theory.

VIEWPOINT   *Run! Run! Run!*

What description would you use for marathon runners? How about age distribution? Body weight? Length of stride? Heart rate? Blood pressure? What countries do these runners come from? What are their best running times? Make your own estimated distribution for these variables, and then consider a goodness-of-fit test for your distribution compared with available data. For more information on marathon runners, visit the Brase/Brase statistics site at **http://math.college.hmco.com/students** and find links to the Honolulu marathon site and to the *Runners World* site.

SECTION 11.2   PROBLEMS

For Problems 1–12, please provide the following information.
(a) What is the level of significance? State the null and alternate hypotheses.
(b) Find the value of the chi-square statistic for the sample. Are all the expected frequencies greater than 5? What sampling distribution will you use? What are the degrees of freedom?
(c) Find or estimate the *P*-value of the sample test statistic.
(d) Based on your answers in parts (a) to (c), will you reject or fail to reject the null hypothesis that the population fits the specified distribution of categories?
(e) State your conclusion in the context of the application.

1. *Census: Age* The age distribution of the Canadian population and the age distribution of a random sample of 455 residents in the Indian community of Red Lake (Northwest Territories) are shown below (based on *U.S. Bureau of the Census, International Data Base*).

Age (years)	Percent of Canadian Population	Observed Number in Red Lake Village
Under 5	7.2%	47
5 to 14	13.6%	75
15 to 64	67.1%	288
65 and older	12.1%	45

Use a 5% level of significance to test the claim that the age distribution of the general Canadian population fits the age distribution of the residents of Red Lake Village.

2. *Census: Type of Household* The type of household for the U.S. population and for a random sample of 411 households of the community of Dove Creek, Montana, are shown (based on *Statistical Abstract of the United States*).

Type of Household	Percent of U.S. Households	Observed Number of Households in Dove Creek
Married, with children	26%	102
Married, no children	29%	112
Single parent	9%	33
One person	25%	96
Other (e.g., roommates, siblings)	11%	68

Use a 5% level of significance to test the claim that the distribution of U.S. households fits the Dove Creek distribution.

3. *Archaeology: Stone Tools* The types of raw material used to construct stone tools found at the archaeological site Casa del Rito are shown below (*Bandelier Archaeological Excavation Project*, edited by Kohler and Root). A random sample of 1486 stone tools were obtained from a current excavation site.

Raw Material	Regional Percent of Stone Tools	Observed Number of Tools at Current Excavation Site
Basalt	61.3%	906
Obsidian	10.6%	162
Welded tuff	11.4%	168
Pedernal chert	13.1%	197
Other	3.6%	53

Use a 1% level of significance to test the claim that the regional distribution of raw materials fits the distribution at the current excavation site.

4. *Ecology: Deer* The type of browse favored by deer is shown in the following table (*The Mule Deer of Mesa Verde National Park*, edited by Mierau and Schmidt). Using binoculars, volunteers observed feeding habits of a random sample of 320 deer.

Type of Browse	Plant Composition in Study Area	Observed Number of Deer Feeding on This Plant
Sage brush	32%	102
Rabbit brush	38.7%	125
Salt brush	12%	43
Service berry	9.3%	27
Other	8%	23

Use a 5% level of significance to test the claim that the natural distribution of browse fits the deer feeding pattern.

5. *Meteorology: Normal Distribution* The following problem is based on information from the *National Oceanic and Atmospheric Administration (NOAA) Environmental Data Service*. Let *x* be a random variable that represents the average daily temperature (in degrees Fahrenheit) in July in the town of Kit Carson, Colorado. The *x* distribution has a mean μ of approximately 75°F and standard deviation σ of approximately 8°F. A 20-year study (620 July days) gave the entries in the rightmost column of the following table.

I	II	III	IV
Region under Normal Curve	$x°F$	Expected % from Normal Curve	Observed Number of Days in 20 Years
$\mu - 3\sigma \leq x < \mu - 2\sigma$	$51 \leq x < 59$	2.35%	16
$\mu - 2\sigma \leq x < \mu - \sigma$	$59 \leq x < 67$	13.5%	78
$\mu - \sigma \leq x < \mu$	$67 \leq x < 75$	34%	212
$\mu \leq x < \mu + \sigma$	$75 \leq x < 83$	34%	221
$\mu + \sigma \leq x < \mu + 2\sigma$	$83 \leq x < 91$	13.5%	81
$\mu + 2\sigma \leq x < \mu + 3\sigma$	$91 \leq x < 99$	2.35%	12

(i) Remember that $\mu = 75$ and $\sigma = 8$. Examine Figure 6-5 in Chapter 6. Write a brief explanation for columns I, II, and III in the context of this problem.

(ii) Use a 1% level of significance to test the claim that the average daily July temperature follows a normal distribution with $\mu = 75$ and $\sigma = 8$.

6. *Meteorology: Normal Distribution* Let x be a random variable that represents the average daily temperature (in degrees Fahrenheit) in January at the town of Hana, Maui. The x variable has a mean μ of approximately 68°F and standard deviation σ of approximately 4°F (see reference in Problem 5). A 20-year study (620 January days) gave the entries in the rightmost column of the following table.

I	II	III	IV
Region under Normal Curve	$x°F$	Expected % from Normal Curve	Observed Number of Days in 20 Years
$\mu - 3\sigma \leq x < \mu - 2\sigma$	$56 \leq x < 60$	2.35%	14
$\mu - 2\sigma \leq x < \mu - \sigma$	$60 \leq x < 64$	13.5%	86
$\mu - \sigma \leq x < \mu$	$64 \leq x < 68$	34%	207
$\mu \leq x < \mu + \sigma$	$68 \leq x < 72$	34%	215
$\mu + \sigma \leq x < \mu + 2\sigma$	$72 \leq x < 76$	13.5%	83
$\mu + 2\sigma \leq x < \mu + 3\sigma$	$76 \leq x < 80$	2.35%	15

(i) Remember that $\mu = 68$ and $\sigma = 4$. Examine Figure 6-5 in Chapter 6. Write a brief explanation for columns I, II, and III in the context of this problem.

(ii) Use a 1% level of significance to test the claim that the average daily January temperature follows a normal distribution with $\mu = 68$ and $\sigma = 4$.

7. *Ecology: Fish* The Fish and Game Department stocked Lake Lulu with fish in the following proportions: 30% catfish, 15% bass, 40% bluegill, and 15% pike. Five years later it sampled the lake to see if the distribution of fish had changed. It found that the 500 fish in the sample were distributed as follows.

Catfish	Bass	Bluegill	Pike
120	85	220	75

In the 5-year interval, did the distribution of fish change at the 0.05 level?

8. *Library: Book Circulation* The director of library services at Fairmont College did a survey of types of books (by subject) in the circulation library. Then she used

694 Chapter 11   Chi-Square and *F* Distributions

library records to take a random sample of 888 books checked out last term and classified the books in the sample by subject. The results are shown below.

Subject Area	Percent of Books in Circulation Library on This Subject	Number of Books in Sample on This Subject
Business	32%	268
Humanities	25%	214
Natural science	20%	215
Social science	15%	115
All other subjects	8%	76

Using a 5% level of significance, test the claim that the subject distribution of books in the library fits the distribution of books checked out by students.

9. *Census: California* The accuracy of a census report on a city in southern California was questioned by some government officials. A random sample of 1215 people living in the city was used to check the report, and the results are shown here:

Ethnic Origin	Census Percent	Sample Result
Black	10%	127
Asian	3%	40
Anglo	38%	480
Latino/Latina	41%	502
Native American	6%	56
All others	2%	10

Using a 1% level of significance, test the claim that the census distribution and the sample distribution agree.

10. *Marketing: Compact Discs* Snoop Incorporated is a firm that does market surveys. The Rollum Sound Company hired Snoop to study the age distribution of people who buy compact discs. To check the Snoop report, Rollum used a random sample of 519 customers and obtained the following data:

Customer Age (years)	Percent of Customers from Snoop Report	Number of Customers from Sample
Less than 14	12%	88
14–18	29%	135
19–23	11%	52
24–28	10%	40
29–33	14%	76
More than 33	24%	128

Using a 1% level of significance, test the claim that the distribution of customer ages in the Snoop report agrees with that of the sample report.

11. *Accounting Records: Benford's Law* Benford's Law states that the first nonzero digits of numbers drawn at random from a large complex data file have the following

probability distribution. (Reference: American Statistical Association, *Chance*, vol. 12, no. 3, pp. 27–31; see also the Focus Problem of Chapter 9.)

First nonzero digit	1	2	3	4	5	6	7	8	9
Probability	0.301	0.176	0.125	0.097	0.079	0.067	0.058	0.051	0.046

Suppose that $n = 275$ numerical entries were drawn at random from a large accounting file of a major corporation. The first nonzero digits were recorded for the sample.

First nonzero digit	1	2	3	4	5	6	7	8	9
Sample frequency	83	49	32	22	25	18	13	17	16

Use a 1% level of significance to test the claim that the distribution of first nonzero digits in this accounting file follows Benford's Law.

12. *Fair Dice: Uniform Distribution* A gambler complained about the dice. They seemed to be loaded! The dice were taken off the table and tested one at a time. One die was rolled 300 times and the following frequencies were recorded.

Outcome	1	2	3	4	5	6
Observed frequency O	62	45	63	32	47	51

Do these data indicate that the die is unbalanced? Use a 1% level of significance. *Hint:* If the die is balanced, all outcomes should have the same expected frequency.

13. *Highway Accidents: Poisson Distribution* A civil engineer has been studying the frequency of vehicle accidents on a certain stretch of interstate highway. Long-term history indicates that there has been an average of 1.72 accidents per day on this section of the interstate. Let r be a random variable that represents number of accidents per day. Let O represent the number of observed accidents per day based on local highway patrol reports. A random sample of 90 days gave the following information.

r	0	1	2	3	4 or more
O	22	21	15	17	15

(a) The civil engineer wants to use a Poisson distribution to represent the probability of r, the number of accidents per day. The Poisson distribution is

$$P(r) = \frac{e^{-\lambda}\lambda^r}{r!}$$

where $\lambda = 1.72$ is the average number of accidents per day. Compute $P(r)$ for $r = 0, 1, 2, 3$, and 4 or more.

(b) Compute the expected number of accidents $E = 90P(r)$ for $r = 0, 1, 2, 3$, and 4 or more.

(c) Compute the sample statistic $\chi^2 = \Sigma \frac{(O - E)^2}{E}$ and the degrees of freedom.

(d) Test the statement that the Poisson distribution fits the sample data. Use a 1% level of significance.

14. *Bacteria Colonies: Poisson Distribution* A pathologist has been studying the frequency of bacterial colonies within the field of a microscope using samples of throat

cultures from healthy adults. Long-term history indicates that there is an average of 2.80 bacteria colonies per field. Let *r* be a random variable that represents the number of bacteria colonies per field. Let *O* represent the number of observed bacteria colonies per field for throat cultures from healthy adults. A random sample of 100 healthy adults gave the following information.

r	0	1	2	3	4	5 or more
O	12	15	29	18	19	7

(a) The pathologist wants to use a Poisson distribution to represent the probability of *r*, the number of bacteria colonies per field. The Poisson distribution is

$$P(r) = \frac{e^{-\lambda}\lambda^r}{r!}$$

where $\lambda = 2.80$ is the average number of bacteria colonies per field. Compute $P(r)$ for $r = 0, 1, 2, 3, 4,$ and 5 or more.

(b) Compute the expected number of colonies $E = 100P(r)$ for $r = 0, 1, 2, 3, 4,$ and 5 or more.

(c) Compute the sample statistic $\chi^2 = \Sigma\frac{(O-E)^2}{E}$ and the degrees of freedom.

(d) Test the statement that the Poisson distribution fits the sample data. Use a 5% level of significance.

11.3 Testing and Estimating a Single Variance or Standard Deviation

Testing σ^2

FOCUS POINTS

✓ Set up a test for a single variance σ^2.

✓ Compute the sample χ^2 statistic.

✓ Use the χ^2 distribution to estimate a *P*-value and conclude the test.

✓ Compute confidence intervals for σ^2 or σ.

Many problems arise that require us to make decisions about variability. In this section, we will study two kinds of problems: (1) we will test hypotheses about the variance (or standard deviation) of a population, and (2) we will find confidence intervals for the variance (or standard deviation) of a population. It is customary to talk about variance instead of standard deviation because our techniques employ the sample variance rather than the standard deviation. Of course, the standard deviation is just the square root of the variance, so any discussion about variance is easily converted to a similar discussion about standard deviation.

Let us consider a specific example in which we might wish to test a hypothesis about the variance. Almost everyone has had to wait in line. In a grocery store, bank, post office, or registration center, there are usually several checkout or service areas. Frequently, each service area has its own independent line. However, many businesses and government offices are adopting a "single-line" procedure.

In a single-line procedure there is only one waiting line for everyone. As any service area becomes available, the next person in line gets served. The old independent-lines procedure has a line at each service center. An incoming customer simply picks the shortest line and hopes it will move quickly. In either procedure, the number of clerks and the rate at which they work is the same, so the average waiting time is the *same*. What is the advantage of the single-line procedure? The difference is in the *attitudes* of people who wait in the lines. A lengthy waiting line will be more acceptable if the variability of waiting times is smaller, even though the average waiting time is the same. When the variability is small, the inconvenience of waiting (although it might not be reduced) does become more predictable. This means impatience is reduced and people are happier.

To test the hypothesis that variability is less in a single-line process, we use the chi-square distribution. The next theorem tells us how to use the sample and population variance to compute values of χ^2.

◇ **THEOREM 11.1** If we have a *normal* population with variance σ^2 and a random sample of n measurements is taken from this population with sample variance s^2, then

$$\chi^2 = \frac{(n-1)s^2}{\sigma^2}$$

has a chi-square distribution with degrees of freedom $d.f. = n - 1$.   ◇

Recall that the chi-square distribution is *not* symmetrical and that there are different chi-square distributions for different degrees of freedom. Table 7 of Appendix II gives chi-square values for which the area α is to the *right* of the given chi-square value.

EXAMPLE 2

χ^2 *distribution*

(a) Find the χ^2 value such that the area to the right of χ^2 is 0.05 when $d.f. = 10$.

SOLUTION: Since the area to the *right* of χ^2 is to be 0.05, we look in the right-tail area = 0.050 column and the row with $d.f. = 10$. $\chi^2 = 18.31$ (see Figure 11-6a).

(b) Find the χ^2 value such that the area to the *left* of χ^2 is 0.05 when $d.f. = 10$.

SOLUTION: When the area to the left of χ^2 is 0.05, the corresponding area to the *right* is $1 - 0.05 = 0.95$, so we look in the right-tail area = 0.950 column and the row with $d.f. = 10$. We find $\chi^2 = 3.94$ (see Figure 11-6b).   ◇

FIGURE 11-6

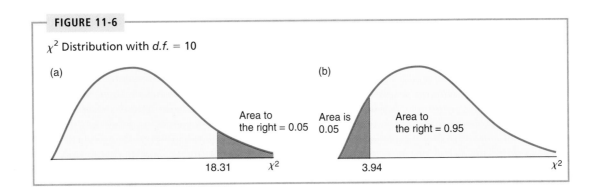

χ^2 Distribution with $d.f. = 10$

(a) Area to the right = 0.05 — 18.31 — χ^2

(b) Area is 0.05 — Area to the right = 0.95 — 3.94 — χ^2

GUIDED EXERCISE 7

χ^2 *distribution*

(a) Find the area to the *right* of $\chi^2 = 37.57$ when $d.f. = 20$.

⟹ Use Table 7 of Appendix II. In the row headed by $d.f. = 20$, find the column with $\chi^2 = 37.57$. The column header 0.010 is the area to the right (see Figure 11-7).

(b) Find the area to the *left* of $\chi^2 = 8.26$ when $d.f. = 20$.

   (i) First use Table 7 of Appendix II to find the area to the right of $\chi^2 = 8.26$.

   (ii) To get the area to the *left* of $\chi^2 = 8.26$, subtract the area to the right from 1.

⟹ Find the column with $\chi^2 = 8.26$ in the row headed by $d.f. = 20$. The column header 0.990 gives the area to the *right* of $\chi^2 = 8.26$.

Next, subtract the area to the right from 1.

Area to *left* = 1 − Area to *right* = 1 − 0.990 = 0.010 (see Figure 11-8).

FIGURE 11-7 χ^2 Distribution with $d.f. = 20$

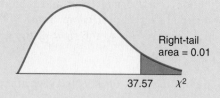

Right-tail area = 0.01

37.57 χ^2

FIGURE 11-8 χ^2 Distribution with $d.f. = 20$

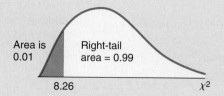

Area is 0.01   Right-tail area = 0.99

8.26 χ^2

Table 11-13 summarizes the techniques for using the chi-square distribution (Table 7 of Appendix II) to find *P*-values for a right-tailed test, a left-tailed test, and a two-tailed test. Example 3 demonstrates the technique of finding *P*-values for a left-tailed test. Example 4 demonstrates the technique for a two-tailed test, and Guided Exercise 8 uses a right-tailed test.

Now let's use Theorem 11.1 and our knowledge of the chi-square distribution to determine if a single-line procedure has less variance of waiting times than independent lines.

EXAMPLE 3

Testing the variance (left-tailed test)

A large discount hardware store in San Antonio has been using the independent-lines procedure to check out customers. After long observation, the manager knows that the standard deviation of waiting times is 7 minutes. The manager decides to introduce the single-line procedure on a trial basis to see if a reduction in waiting time variability occurs. A random sample of 25 customers are monitored, and their waiting times for checkout are determined. The sample standard deviation is $s = 5$ minutes. We will use a 5% level of significance to test the claim that the variance of waiting times has been reduced.

Establish H_0 and H_1

SOLUTION: As a null hypothesis, we assume that the variance of waiting times is the same as that of the former independent-lines procedure. The alternate hypothesis is

TABLE 11-13   *P*-values for Chi-Square Distribution Table (Table 7, Appendix II)

(a) Right-tailed test Since the chi-square table gives right-tail probabilities, you can use the table directly to find or estimate the *P*-value.	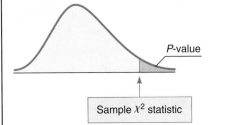
(b) Left-tailed test Since the chi-square table gives right-tail probabilities, you first find or estimate the quantity *1 − (P*-value) from the right tail. Then subtract from 1 to get the *P*-value of the left-tail.	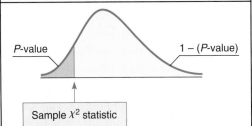
(c) Two-tailed test Remember that the *P*-value is the probability of getting a test statistic as extreme as or more extreme than the test statistic computed from the sample. For a two-tailed test, we need to account for corresponding equal areas in *both* the upper and lower tails. This means that in each tail we have an area of *P*-value/2. The total *P*-value is then $P\text{-value} = 2\left(\dfrac{P\text{-value}}{2}\right)$	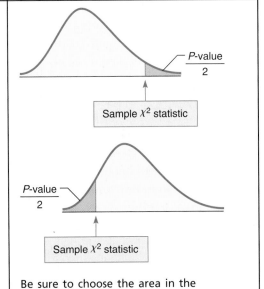 Be sure to choose the area in the appropriate tail (left or right) so that $\dfrac{P\text{-value}}{2} \leq 0.5$.

Checkout lines

that the variance for the single-line procedure is less than that for the independent-lines procedure. If we let σ be the standard deviation of waiting times for the single-line procedure, then σ^2 is the variance, and we have

$H_0: \sigma^2 = 49 \qquad$ (use $7^2 = 49$)

$H_1: \sigma^2 < 49$

We use the chi-square distribution to test the hypotheses. Assuming that the waiting times are normally distributed, we compute our observed value of χ^2 by using Theorem 11.1.

Sample χ^2 value and degrees of freedom

$$n = 25$$

$$s = 5 \quad \text{so} \quad s^2 = 25 \qquad \text{(observed from sample)}$$

$$\sigma = 7 \quad \text{so} \quad \sigma^2 = 49 \qquad \text{(from } H_0\text{: } \sigma^2 = 49\text{)}$$

$$\chi^2 = \frac{(n-1)s^2}{\sigma^2} = \frac{(25-1)25}{49} \approx 12.24$$

$$d.f. = n - 1 = 25 - 1 = 24$$

P-value

Next we estimate the *P*-value for $\chi^2 = 12.24$. Since we have a left-tailed test, the *P*-value is the area of the chi-square distribution that lies to the *left* of $\chi^2 = 12.24$, as shown in Figure 11-9.

To estimate the *P*-value on the left, we consider the fact that the area of the right tail is between 0.975 and 0.990. To find an estimate for the area of the left tail, we *subtract* each right-tail endpoint from 1. The *P*-value (area of the left tail) is in the interval

$$1 - 0.990 < P\text{-value of left tail} < 1 - 0.975$$

$$0.010 < P\text{-value} < 0.025$$

Test conclusion

To conclude the test, we compare the *P*-value to the level of significance $\alpha = 0.05$.

```
                                     α
 ──(━━━━━━━━━━)────────┼───────
 0.010      0.025      0.05
```

Since the *P*-value is less than α, we reject H_0. At the 5% level of significance, we conclude that the variance of waiting times for a single line is less than the variance of waiting times for multiple lines.   ◊

The steps used in Example 3 for testing the variance σ^2 are summarized as follows.

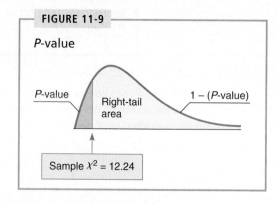

FIGURE 11-9

P-value

Right-tail Area	0.990	0.975
d.f. = 24	10.86	12.40

Sample $\chi^2 = 12.24$

PROCEDURE

How to test σ^2

You first need to know that a random variable x has a normal distribution. In testing σ^2, the normal assumption must be strictly observed (whereas in testing means, we can say normal or approximately normal). Next you need a random sample (size $n \geq 2$) of values from the x distribution for which you compute the sample variance s^2.

1. In the context of the problem, state the *null hypothesis H_0* and the *alternate hypothesis H_1*, and set the *level of significance α*.

2. Use the value of σ^2 given in the null hypothesis H_0, the sample variance s^2, and the sample size n to compute the sample *test statistic*

$$\chi^2 = \frac{(n-1)s^2}{\sigma^2} \quad \text{with degrees of freedom } d.f. = n - 1$$

3. Use a chi-square distribution and the type of test to find or estimate the *P-value*. Use the procedures shown in Table 11-13 and Table 7 of Appendix II.

4. *Conclude* the test. If P-value $\leq \alpha$, then reject H_0. If P-value $> \alpha$, then do not reject H_0.

5. *State your conclusion* in the context of the application.

EXAMPLE 4

Testing the variance (two-tailed test)

Let x be a random variable that represents weight loss (in pounds) after following a certain diet for 6 months. After extensive study, it is found that x has a normal distribution with $\sigma = 5.7$ lb. A new modification of the diet has been implemented. A random sample of $n = 21$ people use the modified diet for 6 months. For these people, the sample standard deviation of weight loss is $s = 4.1$ lb. Does this result indicate that the variance of weight loss for the modified diet is different (either way) from the variance of weight loss for the original diet? Use $\alpha = 0.01$.

(a) What is the level of significance? State the null and alternate hypotheses.

SOLUTION: We are using $\alpha = 0.01$. The standard deviation of weight loss for the original diet is $\sigma = 5.7$ lb, so the variance is $\sigma^2 = 32.49$. The null hypothesis is that the weight loss variance for the modified diet is the same as that for the original diet. The alternate hypothesis is that the variance is different.

$$H_0: \sigma^2 = 32.49 \qquad H_1: \sigma^2 \neq 32.49$$

(b) Compute the sample χ^2 statistic and the degrees of freedom.

SOLUTION: Using sample size $n = 21$, sample standard deviation $s = 4.1$ lb, and $\sigma^2 = 32.49$ from the null hypothesis, we have

$$\chi^2 = \frac{(n-1)s^2}{\sigma^2} = \frac{(21-1)4.1^2}{32.49} \approx 10.35$$

with degrees of freedom $d.f. = n - 1 = 21 - 1 = 20$.

(c) Use the chi-square distribution (Table 7 of Appendix II) to estimate the P-value.

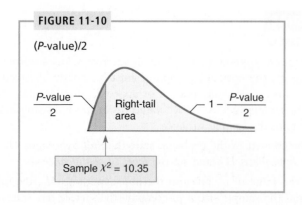

FIGURE 11-10

(*P*-value)/2

Right-tail Area	0.975	0.950
d.f. = 20	8.59	10.85

Sample $\chi^2 \approx 10.35$

SOLUTION: For a *two-tailed* test, the area beyond the sample χ^2 represents *half* the total *P*-value or (*P*-value)/2. Figure 11-10 shows this region, which is to the left of $\chi^2 \approx 10.35$. However, Table 7 of Appendix II gives the areas in the *right tail*. We use Table 7 to find the area in the right tail and then subtract from 1 to find the corresponding area in the left tail.

From the table, we see that the right-tail area falls in the interval between 0.950 and 0.975. Subtracting each endpoint of the interval from 1 gives us an interval containing (*P*-value)/2. Multiplying by 2 gives an interval for the *P*-value.

$$1 - 0.975 < \frac{P\text{-value}}{2} < 1 - 0.950 \quad \text{Subtract right-tail-area endpoints from 1.}$$

$$0.025 < \frac{P\text{-value}}{2} < 0.050$$

$$0.05 < P\text{-value} < 0.10 \quad \text{Multiply each part by 2.}$$

(d) Conclude the test.

SOLUTION: The *P*-value is greater than $\alpha = 0.01$, so we do not reject H_0.

(e) State the conclusion in the context of the application.

SOLUTION: At the 1% level of significance, there is insufficient evidence to conclude that the variance of weight loss using the modified diet is different from the variance of weight loss using the original diet.   ◇

GUIDED EXERCISE 8

Testing the variance (right-tailed test)

Certain industrial machines require overhaul when wear on their parts introduces too much variability to pass inspection. A government official is visiting a dentist's office to inspect the operation of an x-ray machine. If the machine emits too little radiation, clear photographs

Continued

GUIDED EXERCISE 8 continued

cannot be obtained. However, too much radiation can be harmful to the patient. Government regulations specify an average emission of 60 millirads with standard deviation σ of 12 millirads, and the machine has been set for these readings. After examining the machine, the inspector is satisfied that the average emission is still 60 millirads. However, there is wear on certain mechanical parts. To test variability, the inspector takes a random sample of 30 x-ray emissions and finds the sample standard deviation to be $s = 15$ millirads. Does this support the claim that the variance is too high (i.e., the machine should be overhauled)? Use a 1% level of significance.

Let σ be the (population) standard deviation of emissions (in millirads) of the machine in its present condition.

(a) What is α? State H_0 and H_1.

⟹ $\alpha = 0.01$. Government regulations specify that $\sigma = 12$. This means that the variance $\sigma^2 = 144$. We are to test the claim that the variance is higher than government specifications allow.

$H_0: \sigma^2 = 144$ and $H_1: \sigma^2 > 144$

(b) Compute the sample statistic χ^2 and corresponding degrees of freedom.

⟹ Using $n = 30$, $s = 15$, and $\sigma^2 = 144$ from H_0,

$$\chi^2 = \frac{(n-1)s^2}{\sigma^2} = \frac{(30-1)15^2}{144} \approx 45.3$$

Degrees of freedom $d.f. = n - 1 = 30 - 1 = 29$

(c) Estimate the *P*-value for the sample $\chi^2 = 45.3$ with *d.f.* = 29.

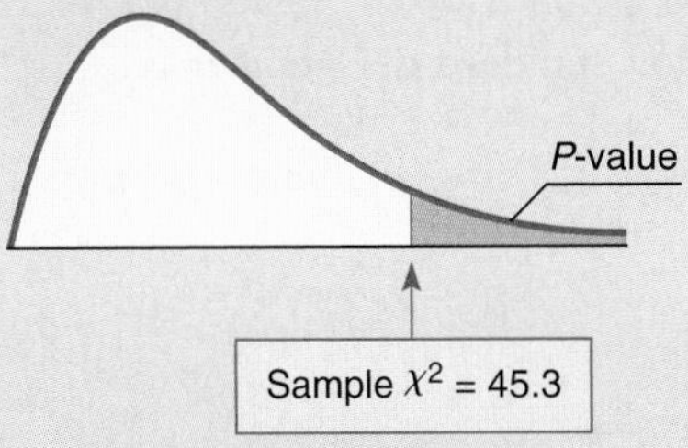

⟹ Since this is a *right-tailed* test, we look up *P*-values directly in the chi-square table (Table 7 of Appendix II).

FIGURE 11-11 *P*-value

Sample $\chi^2 = 45.3$

Right-tail area	0.050	0.025
d.f. = 29	42.56	45.72

↑
Sample $\chi^2 = 45.3$

$0.025 < P\text{-value} < 0.050$

(d) Conclude the test.

⟹ The *P*-value for $\chi^2 = 45.3$ is greater than $\alpha = 0.01$.

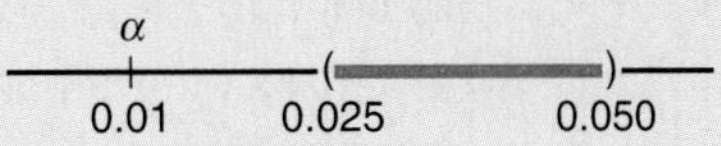

α
0.01   0.025   0.050

Fail to reject H_0.

(e) Interpret the conclusion in the context of the application.

⟹ At the 1% level of significance, there is insufficient evidence to conclude that the variance of the radiation emitted by the machine is greater than that specified by government regulations. The evidence does not indicate that an adjustment is necessary at this time.

Confidence Interval for σ^2

Sometimes it is important to have a confidence interval for the variance or standard deviation. Let us look at another example.

Mr. Wilson is a truck farmer in California who makes his living on a large single-vegetable crop of green beans. Because of modern machinery being used, the entire crop must be harvested at once. Therefore, it is important to plant a variety of green beans that mature all at once. This means that Mr. Wilson wants a small standard deviation between maturing times of individual plants. A seed company is trying to develop a new variety of green bean with a small standard deviation of maturing times. To test the new variety, Mr. Wilson planted 30 of the new seeds and carefully observed the number of days required for each plant to arrive at its peak of maturity. The maturing times for these plants had a sample standard deviation of $s = 3.4$ days. How can we find a 95% confidence interval for the population standard deviation of maturing times for this variety of green bean? The answer to this question is based on the following procedure.

PROCEDURE

How to find a confidence interval for σ^2 and σ

Let x be a random variable with a normal distribution and unknown population standard deviation σ. Take a random sample of size n from the x distribution and compute the sample standard deviation s.

Then a **confidence interval for the population variance σ^2** is

$$\frac{(n-1)s^2}{\chi_U^2} < \sigma^2 < \frac{(n-1)s^2}{\chi_L^2} \tag{1}$$

and a **confidence interval for the population standard deviation σ** is

$$\sqrt{\frac{(n-1)s^2}{\chi_U^2}} < \sigma < \sqrt{\frac{(n-1)s^2}{\chi_L^2}}$$

where
  c = confidence level $(0 < c < 1)$
  n = sample size $(n \geq 2)$
  χ_U^2 = chi-square value from Table 7 of Appendix II using $d.f. = n - 1$ and right-tail area = $(1 - c)/2$
  χ_L^2 = chi-square value from Table 7 of Appendix II using $d.f. = n - 1$ and right-tail area = $(1 + c)/2$

From Figure 11-12 we see that a c confidence level on a chi-square distribution with equal probability in each tail does not center the middle of the corresponding interval under the peak of the curve. This is to be expected because a chi-square curve is skewed to the right.

◇ **COMMENT:** Note that the method of computing intervals for variances is different from the method of computing confidence intervals for means or proportions

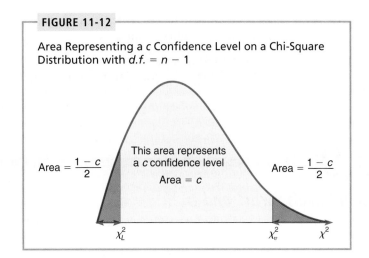

FIGURE 11-12

Area Representing a *c* Confidence Level on a Chi-Square Distribution with *d.f.* = *n* − 1

Area = $\dfrac{1-c}{2}$

This area represents a *c* confidence level
Area = *c*

Area = $\dfrac{1-c}{2}$

χ_L^2 χ_U^2 χ^2

as studied in Chapter 8. Confidence intervals for σ^2 do not involve a maximal error of estimate *E*. Rather, the endpoints of the confidence interval are computed directly using the sample statistic s^2, the sample size, and the critical values. ◊

Now let us finish our example regarding the variance of maturing times for green beans.

EXAMPLE 5

Confidence interval for σ^2 and σ

A random sample of *n* = 30 plants has a sample standard deviation of *s* = 3.4 days for maturity. Find a 95% confidence interval for the population variance σ^2.

SOLUTION: To find the confidence interval, we use the following values:

$c = 0.95$ confidence level

$n = 30$ sample size

$d.f. = n - 1 = 30 - 1 = 29$ degrees of freedom

$s = 3.4$ sample standard deviation

To find the value of χ_U^2, we use Table 7 of Appendix II with *d.f.* = 29 and right-tail area = $(1 - c)/2 = (1 - 0.95)/2 = 0.025$. From Table 7, we get

$$\chi_U^2 = 45.72$$

To find the value of χ_L^2, we use Table 7 of Appendix II with *d.f.* = 29 and right-tail area = $(1 + c)/2 = (1 + 0.95)/2 = 0.975$. From Table 7, we get

$$\chi_L^2 = 16.05$$

Formula (1) tells us that our desired 95% confidence interval for σ^2 is

$$\frac{(n - 1)s^2}{\chi_U^2} < \sigma^2 < \frac{(n - 1)s^2}{\chi_L^2}$$

$$\frac{(30 - 1)(3.4)^2}{45.72} < \sigma^2 < \frac{(30 - 1)(3.4)^2}{16.05}$$

$$7.33 < \sigma^2 < 20.89$$

To find a 95% confidence interval for σ, we simply take square roots; therefore, a 95% confidence interval for σ is

$$\sqrt{7.33} < \sigma < \sqrt{20.89}$$
$$2.71 < \sigma < 4.57$$ ◇

GUIDED EXERCISE 9

Confidence intervals for σ^2 and σ

A few miles off the Kona coast of the island of Hawaii, a research vessel lies anchored. This ship makes electrical energy from the solar temperature differential of (warm) surface water versus (cool) deep water. The basic idea is that the warm water is flushed over coils to vaporize a special fluid. The vapor is under pressure and drives electrical turbines. Then some electricity is used to pump up cold water to cool the vapor back to a liquid, and the process is repeated. Even though some electricity is used to pump up the cold water, there is plenty left to supply a moderate-sized Hawaiian town. The subtropic sun always warms up surface water to a reliable temperature, but ocean currents can change the temperature of the deep, cooler water. If the deep-water temperature is too variable, the power plant cannot operate efficiently or possibly cannot operate at all. To estimate the variability of deep ocean water temperatures, a random sample of 25 near-bottom readings gave a sample standard deviation of 7.3°C.

Find a 99% confidence interval for the variance σ^2 and standard deviation σ of the deep-water temperatures.

(a) Determine the following values: $c = $ _____; $n = $ _____; $d.f. = $ _____; $s = $ _____.

➡ $c = 0.99$; $n = 25$; $d.f. = 24$; $s = 7.3$

(b) What is the value of χ_U^2? _____ of χ_L^2? _____

➡ We use Table 7 of Appendix II with $d.f. = 24$.

For χ_U^2, right-tail area $= (1 - 0.99)/2 = 0.005$
$$\chi_U^2 = 45.56$$

For χ_L^2, right-tail area $= (1 + 0.99)/2 = 0.995$
$$\chi_L^2 = 9.89$$

(c) Find a 99% confidence interval for σ^2.

➡ $$\frac{(n-1)s^2}{\chi_U^2} < \sigma^2 < \frac{(n-1)s^2}{\chi_L^2}$$
$$\frac{(24)(7.3)^2}{45.56} < \sigma^2 < \frac{24(7.3)^2}{9.89}$$
$$28.07 < \sigma^2 < 129.32$$

(d) Find a 99% confidence interval for σ.

➡ $$\sqrt{28.07} < \sqrt{\sigma^2} < \sqrt{129.32}$$
$$5.30 < \sigma < 11.37$$

 *Adopton—A Good Choice!*

Cuckoos are birds that are known to lay their eggs in the nests of other (host) birds. The host birds then hatch the eggs and adopt the cuckoo chicks as their own. Birds such as the meadow pipit, tree pipit, hedge sparrow, robin, and wren have all played host to cuckoo eggs and adopted their chicks. L. H. C. Tippett (1902–1985) was a pioneer in the field of statistical quality control who collected data on cuckoo eggs found in the nests of other birds. For more information and data from Tippett's study, visit the Brase/Brase statistics site at **http://math.college.hmco.com/students** and find a link to DASL, the Carnegie Mellon University Data and Story Library. Find Biology under Data Subjects, and then select the Cuckoo Egg Length Data file.

SECTION 11.3   PROBLEMS

For each problem, please provide the following information.
(a) What is the level of significance? State the null and alternate hypotheses.
(b) Find the value of the chi-square statistic for the sample. What are the degrees of freedom? What assumptions are you making about the original distribution?
(c) Find or estimate the P-value of the sample test statistic.
(d) Based on your answers in parts (a) to (c), will you reject or fail to reject the null hypothesis of independence?
(e) State your conclusion in the context of the application.
(f) Find the requested confidence interval for the population variance or population standard deviation. Interpret the results in the context of the application.

In each of the following problems, assume a normal population distribution.

1. *Archaeology: Chaco Canyon* The following problem is based on information from *Archaeological Surveys of Chaco Canyon, New Mexico,* by A. Hayes, D. Brugge, and W. Judge, University of New Mexico Press. A *transect* is an archaeological study area that is 1/5 mile wide and 1 mile long. A *site* in a transect is the location of a significant archaeological find. Let x represent the number of sites per transect. In a section of Chaco Canyon, a large number of transects showed that x has a population variance $\sigma^2 = 42.3$. In a different section of Chaco Canyon, a random sample of 23 transects gave a sample variance $s^2 = 46.1$ for the number of sites per transect. Use a 5% level of significance to test the claim that the variance in the new section is greater than 42.3. Find a 95% confidence interval for the population variance.

2. *Sociology: Marriage* The following problem is based on information from an article by N. Keyfitz in *The American Journal of Sociology* (vol. 53, pp. 470–480). Let x = age in years of a rural Quebec woman at the time of her first marriage. In the year 1941, the population variance of x was approximately $\sigma^2 = 5.1$. Suppose that a recent study of age at first marriage for a random sample of 41 women in rural Quebec gave a sample variance $s^2 = 3.3$. Use a 5% level of significance to test the claim that the current variance is less than 5.1. Find a 90% confidence interval for the population variance.

3. *Mountain Climbing: Accidents* The following problem is based on information taken from *Accidents in North American Mountaineering* (jointly published by The American Alpine Club and The Alpine Club of Canada). Let x represent the number of mountain climbers killed each year. The long-term variance of x is approximately $\sigma^2 = 136.2$. Suppose that for the past 8 years the variance has been $s^2 = 115.1$. Use a 1% level of significance to test the claim that the recent variance for number of mountain-climber deaths is less than 136.2. Find a 90% confidence interval for the population variance.

4. *Professors: Salaries* The following problem is based on information taken from *Academe, Bulletin of the American Association of University Professors*. Let x represent the average annual salary of college and university professors (in thousands of dollars) in the United States. For all colleges and universities in the United States, the population variance of x is approximately $\sigma^2 = 47.1$. However, a random sample of 15 colleges and universities in Kansas showed that x has a sample variance $s^2 = 83.2$. Use a 5% level of significance to test the claim that the variance for colleges and universities in Kansas is greater than 47.1. Find a 95% confidence interval for the population variance.

5. *Medical: Clinical Test* A new kind of typhoid shot is being developed by a medical research team. The old typhoid shot was known to protect the population for a mean of 36 months with a standard deviation of 3 months. To test the variability of the new shot, a random sample of 23 people were given the new shot. Regular blood tests showed that the sample standard deviation of protection times was 1.9 months. Using a 0.05 level of significance, test the claim that the new typhoid shot has a smaller variance of protection times. Find a 90% confidence interval for the population standard deviation.

6. *Veterinary Science: Tranquilizer* Jim Mead is a veterinarian who visits a Vermont farm to examine prize bulls. In order to examine a bull, Jim first gives the animal a tranquilizer shot. The effect of the shot is supposed to last an average of 65 minutes, and it usually does. However, Jim sometimes gets chased out of the pasture by a bull that recovers too soon, and other times he becomes worried about prize bulls that take too long to recover. By reading journals, Jim found that the tranquilizer should have a mean duration of 65 minutes with standard deviation of 15 minutes. A random sample of 10 of Jim's bulls had a mean tranquilized duration time of close to 65 minutes but a standard deviation of 24 minutes. At the 1% level of significance, is Jim justified in the claim that the variance is larger than that stated in his journal? Find a 95% confidence interval for the population standard deviation.

7. *Engineering: Jet Engines* The fan blades on commercial jet engines must be replaced when wear on these parts indicates too much variability to pass inspection. If a single fan blade broke during operation, it could severely endanger a flight. A large engine contains thousands of fan blades, and safety regulations require that variability measurements on the population of all blades not exceed $\sigma^2 = 0.18$ mm^2. An engine inspector took a random sample of 61 fan blades from an engine. She measured each blade and found a sample variance of 0.27 mm^2. Using a 0.01 level of significance, is the inspector justified in claiming that all the engine fan blades must be replaced? Find a 90% confidence interval for the population standard deviation.

8. *Law: Bar Exam* A factor in determining the usefulness of an examination as a measure of demonstrated ability is the amount of spread that occurs in the grades. If the spread or variation of examination scores is very small, it usually means that the

examination was either too hard or too easy. However, if the variance of scores is moderately large, then there is a definite difference in scores between "better," "average," and "poorer" students. A group of attorneys in a Midwest state has been given the task of making up this year's bar examination for the state. The examination has 500 total possible points, and from the history of past examinations, it is known that a standard deviation of around 60 points is desirable. Of course, too large or too small a standard deviation is not good. The attorneys want to test their examination to see how good it is. A preliminary version of the examination (with slight modification to protect the integrity of the real examination) is given to a random sample of 24 newly graduated law students. Their scores give a sample standard deviation of 72 points.

(i) Using a 0.01 level of significance, test the claim that the population standard deviation for the new examination is 60 against the claim that the population standard deviation is different from 60.

(ii) Find a 99% confidence interval for the population variance.

(iii) Find a 99% confidence interval for the population standard deviation.

9. *Engineering: Solar Batteries* A set of solar batteries is used in a research satellite. The satellite can run on only one battery, but it runs best if more than one battery is used. The variance σ^2 of lifetimes of these batteries affects the useful lifetime of the satellite before it goes dead. If the variance is too small, all the batteries will tend to die at once. Why? If the variance is too large, the batteries are simply not dependable. Why? Engineers have determined a variance of $\sigma^2 = 23$ months (squared) is most desirable for these batteries. A random sample of 22 batteries gave a sample variance of 14.3 months (squared).

(i) Using a 0.05 level of significance, test the claim that $\sigma^2 = 23$ against the claim that σ^2 is different from 23.

(ii) Find a 90% confidence interval for the population variance σ^2.

(iii) Find a 90% confidence interval for the population standard deviation σ.

PART II: INFERENCES USING THE *F* DISTRIBUTION*

11.4
Testing Two Variances

FOCUS POINTS

✓ Set up a test for two variances σ_1^2 and σ_2^2.

✓ Use sample variances to compute the sample *F* statistic.

✓ Use the *F* distribution to estimate a *P*-value and conclude the test.

In this section, we present a method for testing two variances (or equivalently, two standard deviations). We use independent random samples from two populations to test the claim that the population variances are equal. The concept of variation among data is very important, so there will be many possible applications in science, industry, business administration, social science, and so on.

In Section 11.3, we tested a *single* variance. The main mathematical tool we used was the chi-square probability distribution. In this section, the main tool will be the *F* probability distribution. This distribution was discovered by the English statistician Sir Ronald Fisher (1890–1962).

Let us begin by stating what we need to assume for a test of two population variances (see box at top of next page).

---

*Section 11.4, "Testing Two Variances," and Section 11.5, "One-Way ANOVA: Comparing Several Sample Means," are self-contained and can be presented independently. Section 11.5 should be presented before Section 11.6, "Introduction to Two-Way ANOVA."

Basic assumptions

> - The two populations are independent of each other. Recall from Section 9.5 that two sampling distributions are *independent* if there is no relation whatsoever between specific values of the two distributions.
> - The two populations each have a *normal* probability distribution. This is important because the test we will use is sensitive to changes away from normality.

Setup for test

Now that we know the basic assumptions, let's consider the setup.

How to Set Up the Test

STEP 1: Get Two Independent Random Samples, One from Each Population

We use the following notation:

Population I (larger s^2)	Population II (smaller s^2)
n_1 = sample size	n_2 = sample size
s_1^2 = sample variance	s_2^2 = sample variance
σ_1^2 = population variance	σ_2^2 = population variance

To simplify later discussion, we make the notational choice that

$$s_1^2 \geq s_2^2$$

This means that we *define* Population I as the population with the *larger* (or equal, as the case may be) sample variance. This is only a notational convention and does not affect the general nature of the test.

STEP 2: Set Up the Hypotheses

The null hypothesis will be that we have equal population variances.

$$H_0: \sigma_1^2 = \sigma_2^2$$

Reflecting on our notation setup, it makes sense to use an alternate hypothesis, either

$$H_1: \sigma_1^2 \neq \sigma_2^2 \quad \text{or} \quad H_1: \sigma_1^2 > \sigma_2^2$$

Notice that the test makes claims about variances. However, we can also use it for corresponding claims about standard deviations.

Hypotheses about Variances	Equivalent Hypotheses about Standard Deviations
$H_0: \sigma_1^2 = \sigma_2^2$	$H_0: \sigma_1 = \sigma_2$
$H_1: \sigma_1^2 \neq \sigma_2^2$	$H_1: \sigma_1 \neq \sigma_2$
$H_1: \sigma_1^2 > \sigma_2^2$	$H_1: \sigma_1 > \sigma_2$

STEP 3: Compute the Sample Test Statistic

$$F = \frac{s_1^2}{s_2^2}$$

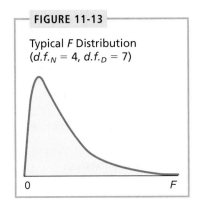

FIGURE 11-13

Typical *F* Distribution
($d.f._N = 4$, $d.f._D = 7$)

For two normally distributed populations with equal variances (H_0: $\sigma_1^2 = \sigma_2^2$), the sampling distribution we will use is the *F distribution* (see Table 8 of Appendix II).

The *F* distribution depends on *two* degrees of freedom, but a typical *F* distribution graph is shown in Figure 11-13.

Properties of the F distribution

- The *F* distribution is not symmetrical. It is skewed to the right.

- Values of the *F* distribution are always greater than or equal to zero.

- A specific *F* distribution (see Table 8 of Appendix II) is determined from *two* degrees of freedom. These are called *degrees of freedom for the numerator* $d.f._N$ and *degrees of freedom for the denominator* $d.f._D$.

For **tests of two variances,** it can be shown that

$$d.f._N = n_1 - 1 \quad \text{and} \quad d.f._D = n_2 - 1$$

STEP 4: Find (or estimate) the *P*-value of the sample test statistic

Use the *F* distribution (Table 8 of Appendix II) to find the *P*-value of the sample test statistic. You need to know the degrees of freedom for the numerator, $d.f._N = n_1 - 1$, and the degrees of freedom for the denominator, $d.f._D = n_2 - 1$. Find the block of entries with your $d.f._D$ as row header and your $d.f._N$ as column header. Within that block of values, find the position of the sample test statistic *F*. Then find the corresponding right-tail area. For instance, using Table 11-14 (Excerpt from Table 8), we see that for $d.f._D = 2$ and $d.f._N = 3$, sample $F = 55.2$ lies between 39.17 and 99.17, with corresponding right-tail areas of 0.025 and 0.010. The interval containing the *P*-value for $F = 55.2$ is $0.010 < P\text{-value} < 0.025$.

Table 11-15 gives a summary of computing the *P*-value for both right-tailed and two-tailed tests for two variances.

Now that we have steps 1 to 4 as an outline, let's look at a specific example.

TABLE 11-14   Excerpt from Table 8 (Appendix II): The *F* Distribution

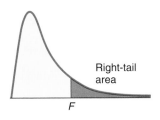

Right-tail
area

		Degrees of Freedom for Numerator $d.f._N$			
$d.f._D$	Right-tail Area	1	2	3	4 ...
⋮	⋮	⋮	⋮	⋮	⋮
	0.100	8.53	9.00	9.16	9.24
	0.050	18.51	19.00	19.16	19.25
✓2	0.025	38.51	39.00	39.17	39.25
	0.010	98.50	99.00	99.17	99.25
	0.001	998.50	999.00	999.17	9999.25

TABLE 11-15   *P*-values for Testing Two Variances (Table 8, Appendix II)

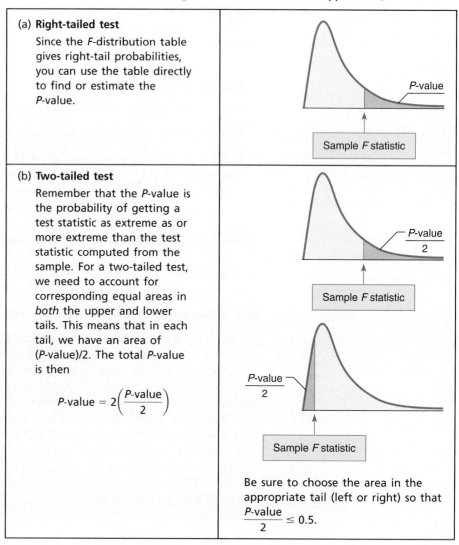

(a) **Right-tailed test**

Since the *F*-distribution table gives right-tail probabilities, you can use the table directly to find or estimate the *P*-value.

(b) **Two-tailed test**

Remember that the *P*-value is the probability of getting a test statistic as extreme as or more extreme than the test statistic computed from the sample. For a two-tailed test, we need to account for corresponding equal areas in *both* the upper and lower tails. This means that in each tail, we have an area of (*P*-value)/2. The total *P*-value is then

$$P\text{-value} = 2\left(\frac{P\text{-value}}{2}\right)$$

Be sure to choose the area in the appropriate tail (left or right) so that $\frac{P\text{-value}}{2} \le 0.5$.

EXAMPLE 6

Testing two variances

Prehistoric Native Americans smoked pipes for ceremonial purposes. Most pipes were either carved-stone pipes or ceramic pipes made from clay. Clay pipes were easier to make, whereas stone pipes required careful drilling using hollow-core-bone drills and special stone reamers. An anthropologist claims that because clay pipes were easier to make, they show a greater variance in their construction. We want to test this claim using a 5% level of significance. Data for this example are taken from the Wind Mountain Archaeological Region. (Source: *Mimbres Mogollon Archaeology,* by A. I. Woosley and A. J. McIntyre, University of New Mexico Press.)

Ceramic Pipe Bowl Diameters (cm)

1.7	5.1	1.4	0.7	2.5	4.0
3.8	2.0	3.1	5.0	1.5	

Stone Pipe Bowl Diameters (cm)

1.6	2.1	3.1	1.4	2.2	2.1
2.6	3.2	3.4			

SOLUTION:

(a) Assume that the pipe bowl diameters follow normal distributions and that the given data make up independent random samples of pipe measurements taken from archaeological excavations at Wind Mountain. Use a calculator to verify the following:

Population I: Ceramic Pipes	Population II: Stone Pipes
$n_1 = 11$	$n_2 = 9$
$s_1^2 \approx 2.266$	$s_2^2 \approx 0.504$
σ_1^2 = population variance	σ_2^2 = population variance

Note: Because the sample variance for ceramic pipes (2.266) is larger than the sample variance for stone pipes (0.504), we designate Population I as ceramic pipes.

(b) Set up the null and alternate hypotheses.

$$H_0: \sigma_1^2 = \sigma_2^2 \quad \text{(or the equivalent, } \sigma_1 = \sigma_2\text{)}$$
$$H_1: \sigma_1^2 > \sigma_2^2 \quad \text{(or the equivalent, } \sigma_1 > \sigma_2\text{)}$$

The null hypothesis states that there is no difference. The alternate hypothesis supports the anthropologist's claim that clay pipes have a larger variance.

(c) The sample test statistic is

$$F = \frac{s_1^2}{s_2^2} \approx \frac{2.266}{0.504} \approx 4.496$$

Now, if $\sigma_1^2 = \sigma_2^2$, then s_1^2 and s_2^2 also should be close in value. If this were the case, $F = s_1^2/s_2^2 \approx 1$. However, if $\sigma_1^2 > \sigma_2^2$, then we see that the sample statistic $F = s_1^2/s_2^2$ should be larger than 1.

FIGURE 11-14

P-value

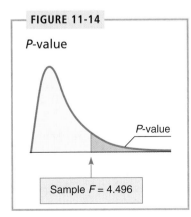

Sample $F = 4.496$

Right-tail Area		d.f._N 10
	0.100	2.54
*d.f.*_D	0.050	3.35
✓ 8	0.025	4.30
	0.010	5.81
	0.001	11.54

(d) Find an interval containing the *P*-value for $F = 4.496$.

This is a right-tailed test (see Figure 11-14 on the previous page) with degrees of freedom

$$d.f._N = n_1 - 1 = 11 - 1 = 10 \quad \text{and} \quad d.f._D = n_2 - 1 = 9 - 1 = 8$$

The interval containing the *P*-value is

$$0.010 < P\text{-value} < 0.025$$

(e) Conclude the test.

Since the *P*-value is less than $\alpha = 0.05$, we reject H_0.

At the 5% level of significance, the evidence is sufficient to conclude that the variance for the ceramic pipes is larger.   ◊

We summarize the steps involved in testing two variances with the following procedure.

PROCEDURE

How to test two variances σ_1^2 and σ_2^2

Assume that x_1 and x_2 are random variables that have *independent normal distributions* with unknown variances σ_1^2 and σ_2^2. Next you need independent random samples of x_1 values and x_2 values, from which you compute sample variances s_1^2 and s_2^2. Use samples of sizes n_1 and n_2, respectively, with both samples of size at least 2. Without loss of generality, we may assume the notational setup is such that $s_1^2 \geq s_2^2$.

1. Set the *level of significance* α. Use the *null hypothesis* H_0: $\sigma_1^2 = \sigma_2^2$. In the context of the problem, choose the *alternate hypothesis* to be H_1: $\sigma_1^2 > \sigma_2^2$ or H_1: $\sigma_1^2 \neq \sigma_2^2$.

2. Compute the sample *test statistic*

$$F = \frac{s_1^2}{s_2^2}$$

where $d.f._N = n_1 - 1$ (degrees of freedom numerator)

$\quad\quad\;\; d.f._D = n_2 - 1$ (degrees of freedom denominator)

3. Use the *F*-distribution and the type of test to find or estimate the *P-value*. Use Table 8 of Appendix II and the procedure shown in Table 11-15.

4. *Conclude* the test. If *P*-value $\leq \alpha$, then reject H_0. If *P*-value $> \alpha$, then do not reject H_0.

5. *State your conclusion* in the context of the application.

GUIDED EXERCISE 10

Testing two variances

A large variance in blood chemistry components can result in health problems as the body attempts to return to equilibrium. J. B. O'Sullivan and C. M. Mahan conducted a study reported in the *American Journal of Clinical Nutrition* (vol. 19, pp. 345–351) that concerned the glucose (blood sugar) levels of pregnant and nonpregnant women at Boston City Hospital. For both groups, a fasting (12-hour fast) blood glucose test was done. The following data are in units of milligrams of glucose per 100 milliliters of blood.

Glucose Test: Nonpregnant Women

| 73 | 61 | 104 | 75 | 85 | 65 | 62 | 98 | 92 | 106 |

Glucose Test: Pregnant Women

| 72 | 84 | 90 | 95 | 66 | 70 | 79 | 85 |

Medical researchers question if the variance of the glucose test results for nonpregnant women is *different* (either way) compared with the variance for pregnant women. Let's conduct a test using a 5% level of significance.

(a) What assumptions must be made about the two populations and the samples?

⟹ The population measurements follow independent normal distributions. The samples are random samples from each population.

(b) Use a calculator to compute the sample variance for each data group. Then complete the following:

Population I	Population II
$n_1 = $ _____	$n_2 = $ _____
$s_1^2 = $ _____	$s_2^2 = $ _____

⟹ Recall that we choose our notation so that Population I has the *larger* sample variance.

Population I	Population II
$n_1 = 10$	$n_2 = 8$
$s_1^2 \approx 298.25$	$s_2^2 \approx 103.84$

(c) What is α? State the null and alternate hypotheses.

⟹ $\alpha = 0.05$; $H_0: \sigma_1^2 = \sigma_2^2$; $H_1: \sigma_1^2 \neq \sigma_2^2$

(d) Compute the sample F statistic, $d.f._N$, and $d.f._D$.

⟹ $F = \dfrac{s_1^2}{s_2^2} \approx \dfrac{298.25}{103.84} \approx 2.87$

$d.f._N = n_1 - 1 = 10 - 1 = 9$

$d.f._D = n_2 - 1 = 8 - 1 = 7$

(e) Estimate the P-value.

FIGURE 11-15 *P-value*

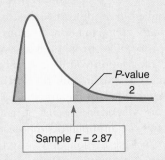

P-value / 2

Sample $F = 2.87$

⟹ Because this is a two-tailed test, we look up the area to the right of $F = 2.87$ and double it.

	Right-tail Area	$d.f._N$ 9
	0.100	2.72
$d.f._D$	0.050	3.68
✓ 7	0.025	4.82
	0.010	6.72
	0.001	14.33

Continued

GUIDED EXERCISE 10 continued

$$0.050 < \frac{P\text{-value}}{2} < 0.100$$

$$0.100 < P\text{-value} < 0.200$$

(f) Conclude the test.

⟹ Since the P-value is greater than $\alpha = 0.05$, we do not reject H_0.

At the 5% level of significance, the evidence is insufficient to reject the claim of equal variances.

TECH NOTE The TI-84Plus and TI-83Plus calculators support tests of two variances. Use **STAT, TESTS**, and option **D:2-SampFTest.** For results consistent with the notational convention that the larger variance goes in the numerator of the sample F statistic, put the data with the larger variance in **List1.**

Minitab Release 14 of Minitab supports tests of two variances. Use menu choices **Stat ➤ Basic Statistics ➤ 2 Variances.**

Variety is said to be the spice of life. However, in statistics, when we want to compare two populations, we will often need the assumption that the population variances are the same. As long as the two populations follow normal distributions, we can use the methods of this section and random samples from the populations to determine if the assumption of equal variances is reasonable at a given level of significance.

VIEWPOINT

Mercury in Bass?

Largemouth bass were studied in 53 different lakes to examine factors that influence the level of mercury contamination. In many cases, the contamination was fairly low, except for older (trophy) fish, in which the mercury levels were much higher. Using information you have learned in this section, you can test variances of mercury contamination for different lakes and/or different regions. For more information, see the article by Lange, Royals, and Connor, *Transactions of the American Fisheries Society*. To find this article, visit the Brase/Brase statistics site at **http://math.college.hmco.com/students** and find a link to DASL, the Carnegie Mellon University Data and Story Library. From the DASL site, link to Nature under Data Subjects, and select Mercury in the Bass Data file.

SECTION 11.4   PROBLEMS

For each problem, please provide the following information.
(a) What is the level of significance? State the null and alternate hypotheses.
(b) Find the value of the sample F statistic. What are the degrees of freedom? What assumptions are you making about the original distribution?
(c) Find or estimate the P-value of the sample test statistic.
(d) Based on your answers in parts (a) to (c), will you reject or fail to reject the null hypothesis of independence?
(e) State your conclusion in the context of the application.

Assume that the data values in each problem come from independent populations and that each population follows a normal distribution.

1. *Agriculture: Wheat* Rothamsted Experimental Station (England) has studied wheat production since 1852. Each year many small plots of equal size but different soil/fertilizer conditions are planted with wheat. At the end of the growing season, the yield (in pounds) of the wheat on the plot is measured. The following data are based on information taken from an article by G. A. Wiebe in the *Journal of Agricultural Research* (vol. 50, pp. 331–357). For a random sample of years, one plot gave the following annual wheat production (in pounds):

4.15	4.21	4.27	3.55	3.50	3.79	4.09	4.42
3.89	3.87	4.12	3.09	4.86	2.90	5.01	3.39

   Use a calculator to verify that, for this plot, the sample variance is $s^2 \approx 0.332$.
   Another random sample of years for a second plot gave the following annual wheat production (in pounds):

4.03	3.77	3.49	3.76	3.61	3.72	4.13	4.01
3.59	4.29	3.78	3.19	3.84	3.91	3.66	4.35

   Use a calculator to verify that the sample variance for this plot is $s^2 \approx 0.089$.
   Test the claim that the population variance of annual wheat production for the first plot is larger than that for the second plot. Use a 1% level of significance.

2. *Agriculture: Wheat* Two plots at Rothamsted Experimental Station (see reference in Problem 1) were studied for production of wheat straw. For a random sample of years, the annual wheat straw production (in pounds) from one plot was as follows:

6.17	6.05	5.89	5.94	7.31	7.18
7.06	5.79	6.24	5.91	6.14

   Use a calculator to verify that, for the preceding data, $s^2 \approx 0.318$.
   Another random sample of years for a second plot gave the following annual wheat straw production (in pounds):

6.85	7.71	8.23	6.01	7.22	5.58	5.47	5.86

   Use a calculator to verify that, for these data, $s^2 \approx 1.078$.
   Test the claim that there is a difference (either way) in the population variance of wheat straw production for these two plots. Use a 5% level of significance.

3. *Economics: Productivity* An economist wonders if corporate productivity in some countries is more *volatile* than in other countries. One measure of a company's productivity is annual percentage yield based on total company assets. Data for this problem are based on information taken from *Forbes Top Companies*, edited by J. T. Davis. A random sample of leading companies in France gave the following percentage yields based on assets:

4.4	5.2	3.7	3.1	2.5	3.5	2.8	4.4	5.7	3.4	4.1
6.8	2.9	3.2	7.2	6.5	5.0	3.3	2.8	2.5	4.5	

Use a calculator to verify that $s^2 \approx 2.044$ for this sample of French companies.

   Another random sample of leading companies in Germany gave the following percentage yields based on assets:

3.0	3.6	3.7	4.5	5.1	5.5	5.0	5.4	3.2
3.5	3.7	2.6	2.8	3.0	3.0	2.2	4.7	3.2

Use a calculator to verify that $s^2 \approx 1.038$ for this sample of German companies.

   Test the claim that there is a difference (either way) in the population variance for leading companies in France and Germany. Use a 5% level of significance. How could your test conclusion relate to the economist's question regarding *volatility* (data spread) of corporate productivity of large companies in France compared with companies in Germany?

4. *Economics: Productivity* A random sample of leading companies in South Korea gave the following percentage yields based on assets (see reference in Problem 3):

2.5	2.0	4.5	1.8	0.5	3.6	2.4
0.2	1.7	1.8	1.4	5.4	1.1	

Use a calculator to verify that $s^2 = 2.247$ for these South Korean companies.

   Another random sample of leading companies in Sweden gave the following percentage yields based on assets:

2.3	3.2	3.6	1.2	3.6	2.8	2.3	3.5	2.8

Use a calculator to verify that $s^2 = 0.624$ for these Swedish companies.

   Test the claim that the population variance of percentage yields on assets for South Korean companies is higher than for companies in Sweden. Use a 5% level of significance. How could your test conclusion relate to an economist's question regarding *volatility* of corporate productivity of large companies in South Korea compared with those in Sweden?

5. *Investing: Mutual Funds* You don't need to be rich to buy a few shares in a mutual fund. The question is, how *reliable* are mutual funds as investments? This depends on the type of fund you buy. The following data are based on information taken from *Morningstar*, a mutual fund guide available in most libraries. A random sample of percentage annual returns for mutual funds holding stocks in aggressive-growth small companies is shown below.

−1.8	14.3	41.5	17.2	−16.8	4.4	32.6	−7.3	16.2	2.8	34.3
−10.6	8.4	−7.0	−2.3	−18.5	25.0	−9.8	−7.8	−24.6	22.8	

Use a calculator to verify that $s^2 \approx 348.43$ for the sample of aggressive-growth small company funds.

Another random sample of percentage annual returns for mutual funds holding value (i.e., market underpriced) stocks in large companies is shown below.

| 16.2 | 0.3 | 7.8 | −1.6 | −3.8 | 19.4 | −2.5 | 15.9 | 32.6 | 22.1 | 3.4 |
| −0.5 | −8.3 | 25.8 | −4.1 | 14.6 | 6.5 | 18.0 | 21.0 | 0.2 | −1.6 | |

Use a calculator to verify that $s^2 \approx 137.31$ for value stocks in large companies.

Test the claim that the population variance for mutual funds holding aggressive-growth small stocks is larger than the population variance for mutual funds holding value stocks in large companies. Use a 5% level of significance. How could your test conclusion relate to the question of *reliability* of returns for each type of mutual fund?

6. *Investing: Mutual Funds* How *reliable* are mutual funds that invest in bonds? Again, this depends on the bond fund you buy (see reference in Problem 5). A random sample of annual percentage returns for mutual funds holding short-term U.S. government bonds is shown below.

| 4.6 | 4.7 | 1.9 | 9.3 | −0.8 | 4.1 | 10.5 |
| 4.2 | 3.5 | 3.9 | 9.8 | −1.2 | 7.3 | |

Use a calculator to verify that $s^2 \approx 13.59$ for the preceding data.

A random sample of annual percentage returns for mutual funds holding intermediate-term corporate bonds is shown below.

| −0.8 | 3.6 | 20.2 | 7.8 | −0.4 | 18.8 | −3.4 | 10.5 |
| 8.0 | −0.9 | 2.6 | −6.5 | 14.9 | 8.2 | 18.8 | 14.2 |

Use a calculator to verify that $s^2 \approx 72.06$ for returns from mutual funds holding intermediate-term corporate bonds.

Use $\alpha = 0.05$ to test the claim that the population variance for annual percentage returns of mutual funds holding short-term government bonds is different from the population variance for mutual funds holding intermediate-term corporate bonds. How could your test conclusion relate to the question of *reliability* of returns for each type of mutual fund?

7. *Engineering: Fuel Injection* A new fuel injection system has been engineered for pickup trucks. The new system and the old system both produce about the same average miles per gallon. However, engineers question which system (old or new) will give better *consistency* in fuel consumption (miles per gallon) under a variety of driving conditions. A random sample of 31 trucks were fitted with the new fuel injection system and driven under different conditions. For these trucks, the sample variance of gasoline consumption was 58.4. Another random sample of 25 trucks were fitted with the old fuel injection system and driven under a variety of different conditions. For these trucks, the sample variance of gasoline consumption was 31.6. Test the claim that there is a difference in population variance of gasoline consumption for the two injection systems. Use a 5% level of significance. How could your test conclusion relate to the question regarding the *consistency* of fuel consumption for the two fuel injection systems?

8. *Engineering: Thermostats* A new thermostat has been engineered for the frozen food cases in large supermarkets. Both the old and new thermostats hold temperatures at an average of 25°F. However, it is hoped that the new thermostat

might be more *dependable* in the sense that it will hold temperatures closer to 25°F. One frozen food case was equipped with the new thermostat, and a random sample of 21 temperature readings gave a sample variance of 5.1. Another similar frozen food case was equipped with the old thermostat, and a random sample of 16 temperature readings gave a sample variance of 12.8. Test the claim that the population variance of the old thermostat temperature readings is larger than that for the new thermostat. Use a 5% level of significance. How could your test conclusion relate to the question regarding the *dependability* of the temperature readings?

11.5
One-Way ANOVA: Comparing Several Sample Means

FOCUS POINTS

✓ Learn about the risk α of a type I error when we test several means at once.

✓ Learn about the notation and set up for a one-way ANOVA test.

✓ Compute mean squares between groups and within groups.

✓ Compute the sample *F* statistic.

✓ Use the *F* distribution to estimate a *P*-value and conclude the test.

In our past work, to determine the existence (or nonexistence) of a significant difference between population means, we restricted our attention to only two data groups representing the means in question. Many statistical applications in psychology, social science, business administration, and natural science involve many means and many data groups. Questions commonly asked are: Which of *several* alternative methods yields the best results in a particular setting? Which of *several* treatments leads to highest incidence of patient recovery? Which of *several* teaching methods leads to greatest student retention? Which of *several* investment schemes leads to greatest economic gain?

Using our previous methods (Sections 9.4 and 9.5) of comparing only *two* means would require many tests of significance to answer the preceding questions. For example, if we had only 5 variables, we would be required to perform 10 tests of significance in order to compare each variable to each of the other variables. If we had the time and patience, we could perform all 10 tests, but what about the risk of accepting a difference where there really is no difference (a type I error)? If the risk of a type I error on each test is $\alpha = 0.05$, then on 10 tests we expect the number of tests with a type I error to be 10(0.05) or 0.5 (see expected value, Section 5.3). This situation may not seem too serious to you, but remember that in a "real-world" problem and with the aid of a high-speed computer, a researcher may want to study the effect of 50 variables on the outcome of an experiment. Using a little mathematics, we can show that the study would require 1225 separate tests to check *each pair* of variables for a significant difference of means. At the $\alpha = 0.05$ level of significance for each test, we could expect (1225)(0.05) or 61.25 of the tests to have a type I error. In other words, these 61.25 tests would say that there are differences between means when there really are no differences.

To avoid such problems, statisticians have developed a method called *analysis of variance* (abbreviated *ANOVA*). We will study single-factor analysis of variance (also called *one-way ANOVA*) in this section and two-way ANOVA in section 11.6. With appropriate modification, methods of single-factor ANOVA generalize to *n*-dimensional ANOVA, but we leave that topic to more advanced studies.

Introduction

EXAMPLE 7

One-way ANOVA test

A psychologist is studying the effect of dream deprivation on a person's anxiety level during waking hours. Brain waves, heart rate, and eye movements can be used to determine if a sleeping person is about to enter into a dream period. Three groups of subjects were randomly chosen from a large group of college students who

TABLE 11-16   Dream Deprivation Study

Group I $n_1 = 6$ Subjects		Group II $n_2 = 7$ Subjects		Group III $n_3 = 5$ Subjects	
x_1	x_1^2	x_2	x_2^2	x_3	x_3^2
9	81	10	100	15	225
7	49	9	81	11	121
3	9	11	121	12	144
6	36	10	100	9	81
5	25	7	49	10	100
8	64	6	36		
		8	64		
$\Sigma x_1 = 38$	$\Sigma x_1^2 = 264$	$\Sigma x_2 = 61$	$\Sigma x_2^2 = 551$	$\Sigma x_3 = 57$	$\Sigma x_3^2 = 671$

$N = n_1 + n_2 + n_3 = 18$
$\Sigma x_{TOT} = \Sigma x_1 + \Sigma x_2 + \Sigma x_3 = 156$
$\Sigma x_{TOT}^2 = \Sigma x_1^2 + \Sigma x_2^2 + \Sigma x_3^2 = 1486$

Explanation of notation and formulas

volunteered to participate in the study. Group I subjects had their sleep interrupted four times each night but never during or immediately before a dream. Group II subjects had their sleep interrupted four times also, but on two occasions they were wakened at the onset of a dream. Group III subjects were wakened four times, each time at the onset of a dream. This procedure was repeated for 10 nights, and each day all subjects were given a test to determine level of anxiety. The data in Table 11-16 record the total of the test scores for each person over the entire project. Higher totals mean higher anxiety levels.

From Table 11-16, we see that group I had $n_1 = 6$ subjects, group II had $n_2 = 7$ subjects, and group III had $n_3 = 5$ subjects. For each subject, the anxiety score (x value) and the square of the test score (x^2 value) are also shown. In addition, special sums are shown.

We will outline the procedure for single-factor ANOVA in six steps. Each step will contain general methods and rationale appropriate to all single-factor ANOVA tests. As we proceed, we will use the data of Table 11-16 for a specific reference example.

Basic assumptions of ANOVA

Our application of ANOVA requires three basic assumptions. In a general problem with k groups:

1. We assume that each of our k groups of measurements is obtained from a population with a *normal* distribution.

2. Each group is randomly selected and is *independent* of all other groups. In particular, this means that we will not use the same subjects in more than one group and that the scores of one subject will not have an effect on the scores of another subject.

3. We assume that the variables from each group come from distributions with approximately the *same standard deviation*.

STEP 1: Determine the Null and Alternate Hypotheses

The purpose of an ANOVA test is to determine the existence (or nonexistence) of a statistically significant difference *among* the group means. In a general problem with k groups, we call the (population) mean of the first group μ_1, the population mean of the second group μ_2, and so forth. The null hypothesis is simply that *all* the group population means are the same. Since our basic assumptions say that each of the k groups of measurements comes from normal, independent distributions with common standard deviation, the null hypothesis says that all the sample groups come from *one and the same* population. The alternate hypothesis is that *not all* the group population means are equal. Therefore, in a problem with k groups we have

Hypotheses *(margin note)*

> **Hypotheses for one-way ANOVA**
>
> H_0: $\mu_1 = \mu_2 = \cdots = \mu_k$
>
> H_1: At least two of the means $\mu_1, \mu_2, \ldots, \mu_k$ are not equal.

Notice that the alternate hypothesis claims that *at least* two of the means are not equal. If more than two of the means are unequal, the alternate hypothesis is, of course, satisfied.

In our dream problem, we have $k = 3$; μ_1 is the population mean of group I, μ_2 is the population mean of group II, and μ_3 is the population mean of group III. Therefore,

H_0: $\mu_1 = \mu_2 = \mu_3$

H_1: At least two of the means μ_1, μ_2, μ_3 are not equal.

We will test the null hypothesis using an $\alpha = 0.05$ level of significance. Notice that only one test is being performed, even though we have $k = 3$ groups and three corresponding means. Using ANOVA avoids the problem mentioned earlier of using multiple tests.

STEP 2: Find SS_{TOT}

Sum of squares total *(margin note)*

The concept of *sum of squares* is very important in statistics. We used a sum of squares in Chapter 3 to compute the sample standard deviation and sample variance.

$$s = \sqrt{\frac{\Sigma(x - \bar{x})^2}{n - 1}} \qquad \text{sample standard deviation}$$

$$s^2 = \frac{\Sigma(x - \bar{x})^2}{n - 1} \qquad \text{sample variance}$$

The numerator of the sample variance is a special sum of squares that plays a central role in ANOVA. Since this numerator is so important, we give it the special name SS (for sum of squares).

$$SS = \Sigma(x - \bar{x})^2 \tag{2}$$

Using some college algebra, it can be shown that the following simpler formula is equivalent to Equation (2) and involves fewer calculations:

$$SS = \Sigma x^2 - \frac{(\Sigma x)^2}{n} \tag{3}$$

where n is the sample size.

In future references to SS, we will use Equation (3) because it is easier to use than Equation (2).

The **total sum of squares** SS_{TOT} can be found by using the entire collection of all data values in all groups:

$$SS_{TOT} = \Sigma x_{TOT}^2 - \frac{(\Sigma x_{TOT})^2}{N} \tag{4}$$

where $N = n_1 + n_2 + \cdots + n_k$ is the total sample size from all groups.

$\Sigma x_{TOT} = $ sum of all data $= \Sigma x_1 + \Sigma x_2 + \cdots + \Sigma x_k$

$\Sigma x_{TOT}^2 = $ sum of all data squares $= \Sigma x_1^2 + \cdots + \Sigma x_k^2$

Using the specific data given in Table 11-16 for the dream example, we have

$k = 3$ total number of groups

$N = n_1 + n_2 + n_3 = 6 + 7 + 5 = 18$ total number of subjects

$\Sigma x_{TOT} = $ total sum of x values $= \Sigma x_1 + \Sigma x_2 + \Sigma x_3 = 38 + 61 + 57 = 156$

$\Sigma x_{TOT}^2 = $ total sum of x^2 values $= \Sigma x_1^2 + \Sigma x_2^2 + \Sigma x_3^2 = 264 + 551 + 671 = 1486$

Therefore, using Equation (4), we have

$$SS_{TOT} = \Sigma x_{TOT}^2 - \frac{(\Sigma x_{TOT})^2}{N} = 1486 - \frac{(156)^2}{18} = 134$$

The numerator for the total variation for all groups in our dream example is $SS_{TOT} = 134$. What interpretation can we give to SS_{TOT}? If we let $\bar{x}_{TOT}$ be the mean of all x values for all groups, then

$$\text{Mean of all } x \text{ values} = \bar{x}_{TOT} = \frac{\Sigma x_{TOT}}{N}$$

Under the null hypothesis (all groups come from the same normal distribution), $SS_{TOT} = \Sigma(x_{TOT} - \bar{x}_{TOT})^2$ represents the numerator of the sample variance for all groups. Therefore, SS_{TOT} represents total variability of the data. Total variability can occur in two ways:

1. Scores may differ from one another because they belong to *different groups* with different means (recall that the alternate hypothesis says that the means are not all equal). This difference is called **between-group variability** and is denoted SS_{BET}.

2. Inherent differences unique to each subject and differences due to chance may cause a particular score to be different from the mean of its *own group*. This difference is called **within-group variability** and is denoted SS_W.

> Because total variability SS_{TOT} is the sum of between-group variability SS_{BET} and within-group variability SS_W, we may write
>
> $$SS_{TOT} = SS_{BET} + SS_W$$

As we will see, SS_{BET} and SS_W are going to help us decide whether or not to reject the null hypothesis. Therefore, our next two steps are to compute these two quantities.

STEP 3: Find SS_{BET}

Sum of squares between groups

Recall that $\bar{x}_{TOT}$ is the mean of all x values from all groups. Between-group variability (SS_{BET}) measures the variability of group means. Because different groups may have different numbers of subjects, we must "weight" the variability contribution from each group by the group size n_i.

$$SS_{BET} = \sum_{\text{all groups}} n_i(\bar{x}_i - \bar{x}_{TOT})^2$$

where n_i = sample size of group i

$\qquad \bar{x}_i$ = sample mean of group i

$\qquad \bar{x}_{TOT}$ = mean for values from all groups

If we use algebraic manipulations, we can write the formula for SS_{BET} in the following computationally easier form:

Sum of squares between groups

$$SS_{BET} = \sum_{\text{all groups}} \left(\frac{(\Sigma x_i)^2}{n_i} \right) - \frac{(\Sigma x_{TOT})^2}{N} \tag{5}$$

---

where, as before, $N = n_1 + n_2 + \cdots + n_k$

$\qquad \Sigma x_i$ = sum of data in group i

$\qquad \Sigma x_{TOT}$ = sum of data from all groups

Using data from Table 11-16 for the dream example, we have

$$SS_{BET} = \sum_{\text{all groups}} \left(\frac{(\Sigma x_i)^2}{n_i} \right) - \frac{(\Sigma x_{TOT})^2}{N}$$

$$= \frac{(\Sigma x_1)^2}{n_1} + \frac{(\Sigma x_2)^2}{n_2} + \frac{(\Sigma x_3)^2}{n_3} - \frac{(\Sigma x_{TOT})^2}{N}$$

$$= \frac{(38)^2}{6} + \frac{(61)^2}{7} + \frac{(57)^2}{5} - \frac{(156)^2}{18}$$

$$= 70.038$$

Therefore, the numerator of the between-group variation is

$$SS_{BET} = 70.038$$

STEP 4: Find SS_W

Sum of squares within groups

We could find the value of SS_W by using the formula relating SS_{TOT} to SS_{BET} and SS_W and solving for SS_W:

$$SS_W = SS_{TOT} - SS_{BET}$$

However, we prefer to compute SS_W in a different way and to use the preceding formula as a check on our calculations.

SS_W is the numerator of the variation within groups. Inherent differences unique to each subject and differences due to chance create the variability assigned to SS_W. In a general problem with k groups, the variability within the ith group can be represented by

$$SS_i = \Sigma(x_i - \bar{x}_i)^2$$

or by the mathematically equivalent formula

$$SS_i = \Sigma x_i^2 - \frac{(\Sigma x_i)^2}{n_i} \tag{6}$$

Because SS_i represents the variation within the ith group and we are seeking SS_W, the variability within *all* groups, we simply add SS_i for all groups:

Sum of squares within groups

$$SS_W = SS_1 + SS_2 + \cdots + SS_k \tag{7}$$

Using Equations (6) and (7) and the data of Table 11-16 with $k = 3$, we have

$$SS_1 = \Sigma x_1^2 - \frac{(\Sigma x_1)^2}{n_1} = 264 - \frac{(38)^2}{6} = 23.333$$

$$SS_2 = \Sigma x_2^2 - \frac{(\Sigma x_2)^2}{n_2} = 551 - \frac{(61)^2}{7} = 19.429$$

$$SS_3 = \Sigma x_3^2 - \frac{(\Sigma x_3)^2}{n_3} = 671 - \frac{(57)^2}{5} = 21.200$$

$$SS_W = SS_1 + SS_2 + SS_3 = 23.333 + 19.429 + 21.200 = 63.962$$

Let us check our calculation by using SS_{TOT} and $SS_{BET.}$

$$SS_{TOT} = SS_{BET} + SS_W$$
$$134 = 70.038 + 63.962 \qquad \text{(from Steps 2 and 3)}$$

We see that our calculation checks.

Mean squares

STEP 5: Find Variance Estimates (Mean Squares)

In Steps 3 and 4, we found SS_{BET} and SS_W. Although these quantities represent variability between groups and within groups, they are not yet the variance estimates we need for our ANOVA test. You may recall our study of the Student's *t* distribution, in which we introduced the concept of degrees of freedom. Degrees of freedom represent the number of values that are free to vary once we have placed certain restrictions on our data. In ANOVA, there are two types of degrees of freedom: $d.f._{BET}$, representing the degrees of freedom between groups, and $d.f._W$, representing degrees of freedom within groups. A theoretical discussion beyond the scope of this text would show

---

Degrees of freedom between and within groups

$$d.f._{BET} = k - 1 \quad \text{where } k \text{ is the number of groups}$$
$$d.f._W = N - k \quad \text{where } N \text{ is the total sample size}$$

(*Note:* $d.f._{BET} + d.f._W = N - 1$.)

The variance estimates we are looking for are designated as follows:

MS_{BET}, the variance between groups (read *mean square between*)
MS_W, the variance within groups (read *mean square within*)

In the literature of ANOVA, the variances between and within groups are usually referred to as *mean squares* between and within groups, respectively. We will use the mean-square notations because it is used so commonly. However, remember that the notations MS_{BET} and MS_W both refer to *variances,* and you might occasionally see the variance notations S^2_{BET} and S^2_W used for these quantities. The formulas for the variances between and within samples follow the pattern of the basic formula for sample variance.

$$\text{Sample variance} = s^2 = \frac{\Sigma(x - \bar{x})^2}{n - 1} = \frac{SS}{n - 1}$$

Instead of using $n - 1$ in the denominator for MS_{BET} and MS_W variances, we use their respective degrees of freedom.

$$\text{Mean square between} = MS_{BET} = \frac{SS_{BET}}{d.f._{BET}} = \frac{SS_{BET}}{k - 1}$$

$$\text{Mean square within} = MS_W = \frac{SS_W}{d.f._W} = \frac{SS_W}{N - k}$$

Using these two formulas and the data of Table 11-16, we find the mean squares within and between variances for the dream deprivation example:

$$MS_{BET} = \frac{SS_{BET}}{k-1} = \frac{70.038}{3-1} = 35.019$$

$$MS_W = \frac{SS_W}{N-k} = \frac{63.962}{18-3} = 4.264$$

STEP 6: Find the *F* Ratio and Complete the ANOVA Test

The logic of our ANOVA test rests on the fact that one of the variances, MS_{BET}, *can* be influenced by population differences among means of the several groups, whereas the other variance, MS_W, *cannot* be so influenced. For instance, in the dream deprivation and anxiety study, the variance between groups MS_{BET} will be affected if any of the treatment groups has a population mean anxiety score that is *different* from any other group. On the other hand, the variance within groups MS_W compares anxiety scores of each treatment group to its own group anxiety mean, and the fact that group means might differ *does not* affect the MS_W value.

Recall that the null hypothesis claims that all the groups are samples from populations having the *same* (normal) distributions. The alternate hypothesis says that at least two of the sample groups come from populations with *different* (normal) distributions.

If the *null* hypothesis is *true*, MS_{BET} and MS_W should both estimate the *same* quantity. Therefore, if H_0 is true, the *F ratio*

Sample *F* statistic

> **Sample *F* statistic**
>
> $$F = \frac{MS_{BET}}{MS_W}$$

should be approximately 1, and variations away from 1 should occur only because of sampling errors. The variance within groups MS_W is a good estimate of the overall population variance, but the variance between groups MS_{BET} consists of the population variance *plus* an additional variance stemming from the differences between samples. Therefore, if the *null* hypothesis is *false*, MS_{BET} will be larger than MS_W, and the *F* ratio will tend to be *larger* than 1.

The decision of whether or not to reject the null hypothesis is determined by the relative size of the *F* ratio. The *F* ratio and its corresponding probability distribution were discovered by the English statistician Sir Ronald Fisher (1890–1962). Table 8 of Appendix II gives *F* values.

For our example about dreams, the computed *F* ratio is

$$F = \frac{MS_{BET}}{MS_W} = \frac{35.019}{4.264} = 8.213$$

Because large *F* values tend to discredit the null hypothesis, we use a *right-tailed test* with the *F distribution*. To find (or estimate) the *P*-value for the sample *F* statistic, we use the *F*-distribution table, Table 8 of Appendix II. The table requires us to know *degrees of freedom for the numerator* and *degrees of freedom for the denominator.*

Degrees of freedom for sample *F*

> **Degrees of freedom for sample *F* in one-way ANOVA**
>
> Degrees of freedom numerator = $d.f._N = d.f._{BET} = k - 1$
> Degrees of freedom denominator = $d.f._D = d.f._W = N - k$
>
> where k = number of groups
> N = total sample size across all groups

For our example about dreams,

$$d.f._N = k - 1 = 3 - 1 = 2 \qquad d.f._D = N - k = 18 - 3 = 15$$

Finding the *P*-value

Let's use the *F*-distribution table (Table 8, Appendix II) to find the *P*-value of the sample statistic $F = 8.213$. The *P*-value is a *right-tail area*, as shown in Figure 11-16. In Table 8, look in the block headed by column $d.f._N = 2$ and row $d.f._D = 15$. For convenience, the entries are shown in Table 11-17 (Excerpt from Table 8). We see that the sample $F = 8.213$ falls between the entries 6.36 and 11.34 with corresponding right-tail areas 0.010 and 0.001.

Test conclusion

The *P*-value is in the interval $0.001 < P\text{-value} < 0.010$. Since $\alpha = 0.05$, we see that the *P*-value is less than α and we reject H_0.

$$\begin{array}{ccc} & & \overset{\alpha}{|} \\ \text{—(———■———)——} & & \text{——} \\ 0.001 \quad\quad 0.010 & & 0.05 \end{array}$$

At the 5% level of significance, we reject H_0 and conclude that not all the means are equal. The amount of dream deprivation *does* make a difference in mean anxiety level.   ◇

This completes our single-factor ANOVA test. Before we consider another example, let's summarize the main points.

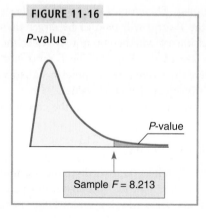

FIGURE 11-16

P-value

P-value

Sample $F = 8.213$

TABLE 11-17   Excerpt from Table 8, Appendix II

	Right-tail Area	$d.f._N$ 2
	0.100	2.70
$d.f._D$	0.050	3.68
✓ 15	0.025	4.77
	0.010	6.36
	0.001	11.34

PROCEDURE

How to construct a one-way ANOVA test

You need k independent data groups, with each group belonging to a normal distribution and all groups having (approximately) the same standard deviation. N is the total number of data values across all groups.

1. Set the *level of significance* α and the *hypotheses*

   H_0: $\mu_1 = \mu_2 = \ldots = \mu_k$

   H_1: not all of μ_1, μ_2, $\ldots$, μ_k are equal

   where μ_i is the population mean of group i.

2. Compute the sample *test statistic F* using the following steps or appropriate technology.

   (a) $SS_{TOT} = \Sigma x_{TOT}^2 - \dfrac{(\Sigma x_{TOT})^2}{N}$

   where Σx_{TOT} is the sum of all data elements from all groups

   Σx_{TOT}^2 is the sum of all data elements squared from all groups

   N is the total sample size

   (b) $SS_{TOT} = SS_{BET} + SS_W$

   where $SS_{BET} = \displaystyle\sum_{\text{all groups}} \left(\dfrac{(\Sigma x_i)^2}{n_i} \right) - \dfrac{(\Sigma x_{TOT})^2}{N}$

   n_i is the number of data elements in group i

   Σx_i is the sum of the data elements in group i

   $SS_W = \displaystyle\sum_{\text{all groups}} \left(\Sigma x_i^2 - \dfrac{(\Sigma x_i)^2}{n_i} \right)$

   (c) $MS_{BET} = \dfrac{SS_{BET}}{d.f._{BET}}$ where $d.f._{BET} = k - 1$

   $MS_W = \dfrac{SS_W}{d.f._W}$ where $d.f._W = N - k$

   (d) $F = \dfrac{MS_{BET}}{MS_W}$ with $d.f._N = k - 1$ and $d.f._D = N - k$

   Because an ANOVA test requires a number of calculations, we recommend that you summarize your results in a table such as Table 11-18. This is the type of table that is often generated by computer software.

3. Find (or estimate) the *P-value* using the F distribution (Table 8, Appendix II). The test is a *right-tailed* test.

4. *Conclude* the test. If *P*-value $< \alpha$, then reject H_0. If *P*-value $> \alpha$, then do not reject H_0.

5. *State your conclusion* in the context of the application.

TABLE 11-18   Summary of ANOVA Results

Source of Variation	Sum of Squares	Degrees of Freedom	Mean Square (Variance)	*F* Ratio	*P*-value	Test Decision
			Basic Model			
Between groups	SS_{BET}	$d.f._{BET}$	MS_{BET}	$\dfrac{MS_{BET}}{MS_W}$	From table	Reject H_0 or fail to reject H_0
Within groups	SS_W	$d.f._W$	MS_W			
Total	SS_{TOT}	$N-1$				
			Summary of ANOVA Results from Dream Experiment (Example 7)			
Between groups	70.038	2	35.019	8.213	< 0.010	Reject H_0
Within groups	63.962	15	4.264			
Total	134	17				

GUIDED EXERCISE 11

One-way ANOVA test

A psychologist is studying pattern-recognition skills under four laboratory settings. In each setting, a fourth-grade child is given a pattern-recognition test with 10 patterns to identify. In setting I, the child is given *praise* for each correct answer and no comment about wrong answers. In setting II, the child is given *criticism* for each wrong answer and no comment about correct answers. In setting III, the child is given no praise or criticism, but the observer expresses *interest* in what the child is doing. In setting IV, the observer remains *silent* in an adjacent room watching the child through a one-way mirror. A random sample of fourth-grade children was used, and each child participated in the test only once. The test scores (number correct) for each group follow. (See Table 11-19.)

(a) Fill in the missing entries of Table 11-19.

$$\Sigma x_{TOT} = \underline{\quad}$$
$$\Sigma x^2_{TOT} = \underline{\quad}$$
$$N = \underline{\quad}$$
$$k = \underline{\quad}$$

$\Rightarrow$
$$\Sigma x_{TOT} = \Sigma x_1 + \Sigma x_2 + \Sigma x_3 + \Sigma x_4$$
$$= 41 + 14 + 38 + 28 = 121$$
$$\Sigma x^2_{TOT} = \Sigma x_1^2 + \Sigma x_2^2 + \Sigma x_3^2 + \Sigma x_4^2$$
$$= 339 + 54 + 264 + 168 = 825$$
$$N = n_1 + n_2 + n_3 + n_4 = 5 + 4 + 6 + 5 = 20$$
$$k = 4 \text{ groups}$$

(b) What assumptions are we making about the data to apply a single-factor ANOVA test?

$\Rightarrow$ Because each of the groups comes from independent random samples (no child was tested twice), we need assume only that each group of data came from a normal distribution, and that all the groups came from distributions with about the same standard deviation.

Continued

GUIDED EXERCISE 11 continued

TABLE 11-19 Pattern-Recognition Experiment

Group I (Praise) $n_1 = 5$		Group II (Criticism) $n_2 = 4$		Group III (Interest) $n_3 = 6$		Group IV (Silence) $n_4 = 5$	
x_1	x_1^2	x_2	x_2^2	x_3	x_3^2	x_4	x_4^2
9	81	2	4	9	81	5	25
8	64	5	25	3	9	7	49
8	64	4	16	7	49	3	9
9	81	3	9	8	64	6	36
7	49			5	25	7	49
				6	36		
$\Sigma x_1 = 41$		$\Sigma x_2 = 14$		$\Sigma x_3 = 38$		$\Sigma x_4 = 28$	
$\Sigma x_1^2 = 339$		$\Sigma x_2^2 = 54$		$\Sigma x_3^2 = 264$		$\Sigma x_4^2 = 168$	
$\Sigma x_{TOT} = $ ___		$\Sigma x^2{}_{TOT} = $ ___		$N = $ ___		$k = $ ___	

(c) What are the null and alternate hypotheses?

$H_0: \mu_1 = \mu_2 = \mu_3 = \mu_4$

In words, all the groups have the same population mean, and this hypothesis, together with the basic assumptions of part (b), states that all the groups come from the same population.

H_1: not all the means μ_1, μ_2, μ_3, μ_4 are equal.

In words, not all the groups have the same population mean, so at least one group did not come from the same population as the others.

(d) Find the value of SS_{TOT}.

$$SS_{TOT} = \Sigma x_{TOT}^2 - \frac{(\Sigma x_{TOT})^2}{N} = 825 - \frac{(121)^2}{20}$$

$$= 92.950$$

(e) Find SS_{BET}.

$$SS_{BET} = \sum_{\text{all groups}} \left(\frac{(\Sigma x_i)^2}{n_i} \right) - \frac{(\Sigma x_{TOT})^2}{N}$$

$$= \frac{(41)^2}{5} + \frac{(14)^2}{4} + \frac{(38)^2}{6}$$

$$+ \frac{(28)^2}{5} - \frac{(121)^2}{20} = 50.617$$

Continued

GUIDED EXERCISE 11 continued

(f) Find SS_W and check your calculations using the formula

$$SS_{TOT} = SS_{BET} + SS_W$$

$\Longrightarrow$ $SS_W = \sum_{\text{all groups}} \left(\Sigma x_i^2 - \dfrac{(\Sigma x_i)^2}{n_i} \right)$

$SS_W = SS_1 + SS_2 + SS_3 + SS_4$

$SS_1 = \Sigma x_1^2 - \dfrac{(\Sigma x_1)^2}{n_1} = 339 - \dfrac{(41)^2}{5} = 2.800$

$SS_2 = \Sigma x_2^2 - \dfrac{(\Sigma x_2)^2}{n_2} = 54 - \dfrac{(14)^2}{4} = 5.000$

$SS_3 = \Sigma x_3^2 - \dfrac{(\Sigma x_3)^2}{n_3} = 264 - \dfrac{(38)^2}{6} \approx 23.333$

$SS_4 = \Sigma x_4^2 - \dfrac{(\Sigma x_4)^2}{n_4} = 168 - \dfrac{(28)^2}{5} = 11.200$

$SS_W = 42.333$

Check: $SS_{TOT} = SS_{BET} + SS_W$

$92.950 = 50.617 + 42.333$ checks

(g) Find $d.f._{BET}$ and $d.f._W$.

$\Longrightarrow$ $d.f._{BET} = k - 1 = 4 - 1 = 3$

$d.f._W = N - k = 20 - 4 = 16$

Check: $N - 1 = d.f._{BET} + d.f._W$

$20 - 1 = 3 + 16$ checks

(h) Find the mean squares MS_{BET} and MS_W.

$\Longrightarrow$ $MS_{BET} = \dfrac{SS_{BET}}{d.f._{BET}} = \dfrac{50.617}{3} \approx 16.872$

$MS_W = \dfrac{SS_W}{d.f._W} = \dfrac{42.333}{16} \approx 2.646$

(i) Find the F ratio.

$\Longrightarrow$ $F = \dfrac{MS_{BET}}{MS_W} = \dfrac{16.872}{2.646} \approx 6.376$

(j) Estimate the P-value for the sample $F = 6.376$. (Use Table 8 of Appendix II.)

$\Longrightarrow$ $d.f._N = d.f._{BET} = k - 1 = 3$

$d.f._D = d.f._W = N - k = 16$

FIGURE 11-17 *P*-value

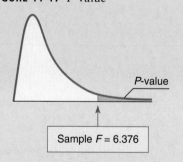

Sample $F = 6.376$

	Right-tail Area	$d.f._N$ 3
	0.100	2.46
$d.f._D$	0.050	3.24
✓ 16	0.025	4.08
	0.010	5.29
	0.001	9.01

$0.001 < P\text{-value} < 0.010$

Continued

GUIDED EXERCISE 11 continued

(k) Conclude the test using a 1% level of significance. Does the test indicate that we should reject or fail to reject the null hypothesis? Explain.

$\alpha = 0.01$.

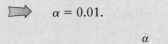

Since the *P*-value is less than 0.01, we reject H_0 and conclude that there is a significant difference in population means among the four groups. The laboratory setting *does* affect the mean scores.

(l) Make a summary table of this ANOVA test.   See Table 11-20.

TABLE 11-20   Summary of ANOVA Results for Pattern Recognition Experiment

Source of Variation	Sum of Squares	Degrees of Freedom	Mean Square (Variance)	F Ratio	P-value	Test Decision
Between groups	50.617	3	16.872	6.376	<0.01	Reject H_0
Within groups	42.333	16	2.646			
Total	92.950	19				

TECH NOTE   After you understand the process of ANOVA, technology tools offer valuable assistance in performing one-way ANOVA. The TI-84Plus and TI-83Plus calculators, Excel, and Minitab all support one-way ANOVA. Both the TI-84Plus and TI-83Plus calculators and Minitab use the terminology

Factor for Between Groups

Error for Within Groups

In all the technologies, enter data for each group in separate columns. The displays show results for Guided Exercise 11.

TI-84Plus/TI-83Plus Use **STAT, TESTS,** and option **F:ANOVA** and enter the lists containing the data.

```
One-way ANOVA
 F=6.376902887
 p=.0047646422
 Factor
  df=3
  SS=50.6166667
↓ MS=16.8722222
```

```
One-way ANOVA
↑ MS=16.8722222
 Error
  df=16
  SS=42.3333333
  MS=2.64583333
 Sxp=1.62660177
```

Excel Use Tools ➤ Data Analysis ➤ Anova: Single Factor.

Anova: Single Factor						
SUMMARY						
Groups	*Count*	*Sum*	*Average*	*Variance*		
x1	5	41	8.2	0.7		
x2	4	14	3.5	1.666666667		
x3	6	38	6.333333333	4.666666667		
x4	5	28	5.6	2.8		
ANOVA						
Source of Variation	*SS*	*df*	*MS*	*F*	*P-value*	*F crit*
Between Groups	50.61666667	3	16.87222222	6.376902887	0.004764642	5.292235983
Within Groups	42.33333333	16	2.645833333			
Total	92.95	19				

Minitab Use Stat ➤ ANOVA ➤ Oneway(unstacked).

```
One-way Analysis of Variance

Analysis of Variance
Source    DF      SS      MS      F      P
Factor     3    50.62   16.87   6.38   0.005
Error     16    42.33    2.65
Total     19    92.95
                              Individual 95% CIs For Mean
                            Based on Pooled StDev
Level    N    Mean   StDev  ---+---------+---------+---------+---
x1       5   8.200   0.837                         (-----*-----)
x2       4   3.500   1.291  (------*------)
x3       6   6.333   2.160             (-----*-----)
x4       5   5.600   1.673          (------*------)
                            ---+---------+---------+---------+---
Pooled StDev = 1.627            2.5       5.0       7.5      10.0
```

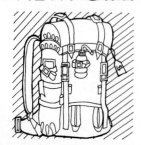

VIEWPOINT   *Gear Guide!*

How much does that backpack cost? Do brand names really make any difference in cost? One way to answer such a question is to construct a one-way ANOVA test to study list prices for various backpacks with similar features but different brand names. For more information, see *Backpacker Magazine*, vol. 25, issue 157.

In each problem, assume that the distributions are normal and have approximately the same population standard deviation. In each problem, please provide the following information.

(a) What is the level of significance? State the null and alternate hypotheses.

(b) Find SS_{TOT}, SS_{BET}, and SS_W and check that $SS_{TOT} = SS_{BET} + SS_W$. Find $d.f._{BET}$, $d.f._W$, MS_{BET}, and MS_W. Find the value of the sample F statistic. What are the degrees of freedom?

(c) Find (or estimate) the P-value of the sample test statistic.

(d) Based on your answers in parts (a) to (c), will you reject or fail to reject the null hypothesis?

(e) State your conclusion in the context of the application.

(f) Make a summary table for your ANOVA test.

1. *Archaeology: Ceramics* Wind Mountain is an archaeological study area located in southwestern New Mexico. Potsherds are broken pieces of prehistoric Native American clay vessels. One type of painted ceramic vessel is called *Mimbres classic black-on-white*. At three different sites the number of such sherds was counted in local dwelling excavations. (Source: Based on information from *Mimbres Mogollon Archaeology*, by A. I. Woosley and A. J. McIntyre, University of New Mexico Press.)

Site I	Site II	Site III
61	25	12
34	18	36
25	54	69
12	67	27
79		18
55		14
20		

Shall we reject or not reject the claim that there is no difference in population mean Mimbres classic black-on-white sherd counts for the three sites? Use a 1% level of significance.

2. *Archaeology: Ceramics* Another type of painted ceramic vessel is called *three circle red-on-white* (see reference in Problem 1). At four different sites in the Wind Mountain archaeological region, the number of such sherds was counted in local dwelling excavations.

Site I	Site II	Site III	Site IV
17	18	32	13
23	4	19	19
6	33	18	14
19	8	43	34
11	25		12
	16		15

Shall we reject or not reject the claim that there is no difference in the population mean three circle red-on-white sherd counts for the four sites? Use a 5% level of significance.

3. *Economics: Profits per Employee* How productive are U.S. workers? One way to answer this question is to study annual profits per employee. A random sample of

companies in computers (I), aerospace (II), heavy equipment (III), and broadcasting (IV) gave the following data regarding annual profits per employee (units in thousands of dollars). (Source: *Forbes Top Companies,* edited by J. T. Davis, John Wiley and Sons.)

I	II	III	IV
27.8	13.3	22.3	17.1
23.8	9.9	20.9	16.9
14.1	11.7	7.2	14.3
8.8	8.6	12.8	15.2
11.9	6.6	7.0	10.1
	19.3		9.0

Shall we reject or not reject the claim that there is no difference in population mean annual profits per employee in each of the four types of companies? Use a 5% level of significance.

4. *Economics: Profits per Employee* A random sample of companies in electric utilities (I), financial services (II), and food processing (III) gave the following information regarding annual profits per employee (units in thousands of dollars). (See reference in Problem 3.)

I	II	III
49.1	55.6	39.0
43.4	25.0	37.3
32.9	41.3	10.8
27.8	29.9	32.5
38.3	39.5	15.8
36.1		42.6
20.2		

Shall we reject or not reject the claim that there is no difference in population mean annual profits per employee in each of the three types of companies? Use a 1% level of significance.

5. *Ecology: Deer* Where are the deer? Random samples of square-kilometer plots were taken in different ecological locations of Mesa Verde National Park. The deer count per square kilometer was recorded and is shown in the following table. (Source: *The Mule Deer of Mesa Verde National Park,* edited by G. W. Mierau and J. L. Schmidt, Mesa Verde Museum Association.)

Mountain Brush	Sagebrush Grassland	Pinon Juniper
30	20	5
29	58	7
20	18	4
29	22	9

Shall we reject or accept the claim that there is no difference among the mean number of deer per square kilometer in these different ecological locations? Use a 5% level of significance.

6. *Ecology: Vegetation* Wild irises are beautiful flowers found throughout the United States, Canada, and northern Europe. This problem concerns the length of the

sepal (leaf-like part covering the flower) of different species of wild iris. Data are based on information taken from an article by R. A. Fisher in *Annals of Eugenics* (vol. 7, part 2, pp. 179–188). Measurements of sepal length in centimeters from random samples of *Iris setosa* (I), *Iris versicolor* (II), and *Iris virginica* (III) are as follows:

I	II	III
5.4	5.5	6.3
4.9	6.5	5.8
5.0	6.3	4.9
5.4	4.9	7.2
4.4	5.2	5.7
5.8	6.7	6.4
5.7	5.5	
	6.1	

Shall we reject or not reject the claim that there are no differences among the population means of sepal length for the different species of iris? Use a 5% level of significance.

7. *Insurance: Sales* An executive at the home office of Big Rock Life Insurance is considering three branch managers as candidates for promotion to vice president. The branch reports include records showing sales volume for each salesperson in the branch (in hundreds of thousands of dollars). A random sample of these records was selected for salespersons in each branch. All three branches are located in cities where per capita income is the same. The executive wishes to compare these samples to see if there is a significant difference in performance of salespersons in the three different branches. If so, the information will be used to determine which of the managers to promote.

Branch Managed by Adams	Branch Managed by McDale	Branch Managed by Vasquez
7.2	8.8	6.9
6.4	10.7	8.7
10.1	11.1	10.5
11.0	9.8	11.4
9.9		
10.6		

Use an $\alpha = 0.01$ level of significance. Shall we reject or not reject the claim that there is no difference among the salespersons in the different branches?

8. *Ecology: Pollution* The quantity of dissolved oxygen is a measure of water pollution in lakes, rivers, and streams. Water samples were taken at four different locations in a river in an effort to determine if water pollution varied from location to location. Location I was 500 m above an industrial plant water discharge point and near the shore. Location II was 200 m above the discharge point and in midstream. Location III was 50 m downstream from the discharge point and near the shore. Location IV was 200 m downstream from the discharge point and in midstream. The following table shows the results. Lower dissolved oxygen readings mean more pollution. Because of the difficulty in getting midstream samples, ecology students collecting the data had fewer of these samples. Use an $\alpha = 0.05$ level of significance.

Do we reject or not reject the claim that the quantity of dissolved oxygen does not vary from one location to another?

Location I	Location II	Location III	Location IV
7.3	6.6	4.2	4.4
6.9	7.1	5.9	5.1
7.5	7.7	4.9	6.2
6.8	8.0	5.1	
6.2		4.5	

9. *Sociology: Ethnic Groups* A sociologist studying New York City ethnic groups wants to determine if there is a difference in income for immigrants from four different countries during their first year in the city. She obtained the data in the following table from a random sample of immigrants from these countries (incomes in thousands of dollars). Use a 0.05 level of significance to test the claim that there is no difference in the earnings of immigrants from the four different countries.

Country I	Country II	Country III	Country IV
12.7	8.3	20.3	17.2
9.2	17.2	16.6	8.8
10.9	19.1	22.7	14.7
8.9	10.3	25.2	21.3
16.4		19.9	19.8

11.6
Introduction to Two-Way ANOVA

FOCUS POINTS

✓ Learn the notation and setup for two-way ANOVA tests.

✓ Learn about the three main types of deviations and how they break into additional effects.

✓ Use mean-square values to compute different sample *F* statistics.

✓ Use the *F* distribution to estimate *P*-values and conclude the test.

✓ Summarize experimental design features using a completely randomized design flowchart.

Suppose that Friendly Bank is interested in average customer satisfaction regarding the issue of obtaining bank balances and a summary of recent account transactions. Friendly Bank uses two systems, the first being a completely automated voice mail information system requiring customers to enter account numbers and passwords using the telephone keypad, and the second being the use of bank tellers or bank representatives to give the account information personally to customers. In addition, Friendly Bank wants to learn if average customer satisfaction is the same regardless of the time of day of contact. Three times of day are under study: morning, afternoon, and evening.

Friendly Bank could do two studies: one regarding average customer satisfaction with regard to type of contact (automated or bank representative) and one regarding average customer satisfaction with regard to time of day. The first study could be done using a difference-of-means test because there are only two types of contact being studied. The second study could be accomplished using one-way ANOVA.

However, Friendly Bank could use just *one* study and the technique of *two-way analysis of variance* (known as *two-way ANOVA*) to simultaneously study average customer satisfaction not only with regard to the variable type of contact and to the variable time of day but also with regard to the *interaction* between the two variables. An interaction is present if, for instance, the difference in average customer satisfaction regarding type of contact is much more pronounced during the evening hours than, say, during the afternoon hours or the morning hours.

Let's begin our study of two-way ANOVA by considering the organization of data appropriate to two-way ANOVA. Two-way ANOVA involves *two* variables. These variables are called *factors*. The *levels* of a factor are the different values the factor can assume. Example 8 demonstrates the use of this terminology for the information Friendly Bank is seeking.

EXAMPLE 8

Factors and levels

For the Friendly Bank study discussed earlier, identify the factors and their levels, and create a table displaying the information.

SOLUTION: There are two factors. Call factor 1 *time of day*. This factor has three levels: morning, afternoon, and evening. Factor 2 is *type of contact*. This factor has two levels: automated contact and personal contact through a bank representative. Table 11-21 shows how the information regarding customer satisfaction can be organized with respect to the two factors.

TABLE 11-21   Table for Recording Average Customer Response

Factor 1: Time of Day	Factor 2: Type of Contact	
	Automated	Bank Representative
Morning	Morning Automated	Morning Bank Representative
Afternoon	Afternoon Automated	Afternoon Bank Representative
Evening	Evening Automated	Evening Bank Representative

When we look at Table 11-21, we see six contact–time-of-day combinations. Each such combination is called a *cell* in the table. The number of cells in any two-way ANOVA data table equals the product of the number of levels of the row factor times the number of levels of the column factor. In the case illustrated by Table 11-21, we see that the number of cells is 3×2, or 6.   ◇

Basic assumptions of two-way ANOVA

Just as for one-way ANOVA, our application of two-way ANOVA requires some basic assumptions:

1. The measurements in each cell of a two-way ANOVA model are assumed to be drawn from a population with a normal distribution.

2. The measurements in each cell of a two-way ANOVA model are assumed to come from distributions with approximately the same variance.

3. The measurements in each cell come from independent random samples.

4. There are the *same number of measurements* in each cell.

Procedure to Conduct a Two-Way ANOVA Test (More Than One Measurement per Cell)

We will outline the procedure for two-way ANOVA in five steps. Each step will contain general methods and rationale appropriate to all two-way ANOVA tests with more than one data value in each cell. As we proceed, we will see how the method is applied to the Friendly Bank study.

Let's assume that Friendly Bank has taken random samples of customers fitting the criteria of each of the six cells described in Table 11-21. This means that a random sample of four customers fitting the morning-automated cell were surveyed. Another random sample of four customers fitting the afternoon-automated cell were surveyed, and so on. The bank measured customer satisfaction on a scale of 0 to 10 (10 representing highest customer satisfaction). The data appear in Table 11-22. Table 11-22 also shows cell means, row means, column means, and the total mean $\bar{\bar{x}}$ computed for all 24 data values. We will use these means as we conduct the two-way ANOVA test.

Overview

As in any statistical test, the first task is to establish the hypotheses for the test. Then, as in one-way ANOVA, the *F* distribution is used to determine the test conclusion. To compute the sample *F* value for a given null hypothesis, many of the same kinds of computations are done as were done in one-way ANOVA. In particular, we will use degrees of freedom $d.f. = N - 1$ (where N is the total sample size) allocated among the row factor, the column factor, the interaction, and the error (corresponding to "within groups" of one-way ANOVA). We look at sum of squares *SS* (which measures variation) for the row factor, the column factor, the interaction, and the error. Then we compute the mean square *MS* for each category by taking the *SS* value and dividing by the corresponding degrees of freedom. Finally, we compute the sample *F* statistic for each factor and for the interaction by dividing the appropriate *MS* value by the *MS* value of the error.

STEP 1: Establish the Hypotheses

Because we have two factors, we have hypotheses regarding each of the factors separately (called *main effects*) and then hypotheses regarding the interaction between the factors.

TABLE 11-22   Customer Satisfaction at Friendly Bank

Factor 1: Time of Day	Factor 2: Type of Contact		
	Automated	Bank Representative	Row Means
Morning	6, 5, 8, 4 $\bar{x} = 5.75$	8, 7, 9, 9 $\bar{x} = 8.25$	Row 1 $\bar{x} = 7.00$
Afternoon	3, 5, 6, 5 $\bar{x} = 4.75$	9, 10, 6, 8 $\bar{x} = 8.25$	Row 2 $\bar{x} = 6.50$
Evening	5, 5, 7, 5 $\bar{x} = 5.50$	9, 10, 10, 9 $\bar{x} = 9.50$	Row 3 $\bar{x} = 7.50$
Column means	Column 1 $\bar{x} = 5.33$	Column 2 $\bar{x} = 8.67$	Total $\bar{\bar{x}} = 7.00$

These three sets of hypotheses are

Hypotheses

1. H_0: There is no difference in population means among the levels of the row factor.
   H_1: At least two population means are different among the levels of the row factor.

2. H_0: There is no difference in population means among the levels of the column factor.
   H_1: At least two population means are different among the levels of the column factor.

3. H_0: There is no interaction between the factors.
   H_1: There is an interaction between the factors.

In the case of Friendly Bank, the hypotheses regarding the main effects are

H_0: There is no difference in population mean satisfaction depending on time of contact.

H_1: At least two population mean satisfaction measures are different depending on time of contact.

H_0: There is no difference in population mean satisfaction between the two types of customer contact.

H_1: There is a difference in population mean satisfaction between the two types of customer contact.

The hypotheses regarding interaction between factors are

H_0: There is no interaction between type of contact and time of contact.

H_1: There is an interaction between type of contact and time of contact.

STEP 2: Compute Sum of Squares (*SS*) Values

The calculations for the SS values are usually done on a computer. The main questions are whether population means differ according to the factors or the interaction of the factors. As we look at the Friendly Bank data in Table 11-22, we see that sample averages for customer satisfaction differ not only in each cell but also across the rows and across the columns. In addition, the total sample mean (designated $\bar{\bar{x}}$) differs from almost all the means. We know that different samples of the same size from the same population certainly can have different sample means. We need to decide if the differences are simply due to chance (sampling error) or are occurring because the samples have been taken from different populations with means that are not the same.

The tools we use to analyze the differences among the data values, the cell means, the row means, the column means, and the total mean are similar to those we used in Section 11.5 for one-way ANOVA. In particular, we first examine deviations of various measurements from the total mean $\bar{\bar{x}}$, and then we compute the sum of the squares *SS*.

There are basically three types of deviations:

Total deviation	= **Treatment deviation**	+ **Error deviation**
Compare each data value with the total mean $\bar{\bar{x}}$, $(x - \bar{\bar{x}})$.	For each data value, compare the mean of each cell with the total mean $\bar{\bar{x}}$, (cell $\bar{x} - \bar{\bar{x}}$).	Compare each data value with the mean of its cell, $(x - \text{cell } \bar{x})$.

The treatment deviation breaks down further as

Treatment deviation	= **Deviation for main effect of factor 1**	+ **Deviation for main effect of factor 2**	+ **Deviation for interaction**
For each data value, (cell $\bar{x} - \bar{\bar{x}}$).	For each data value, compare the row mean with the total mean $\bar{\bar{x}}$, (row $\bar{x} - \bar{\bar{x}}$).	For each data value, compare the column mean with the total mean $\bar{\bar{x}}$, (column $\bar{x} - \bar{\bar{x}}$).	For each data value, (cell $\bar{x}$ − corresponding row $\bar{x}$ − corresponding column $\bar{x}$ + $\bar{\bar{x}}$).

The deviations for each data value, row mean, column mean, or cell mean are then *squared and totaled over all the data*. This results in sums of squares or variations. The *treatment variations* correspond to *between-group variations* of one-way ANOVA. The *error variation* corresponds to the *within-group variation* of one-way ANOVA.

$$\text{Total variation} = \text{Treatment variation} + \text{Error variation}$$

$$\sum_{\text{all data}} (x - \bar{\bar{x}})^2 = \sum_{\text{all data}} (\text{cell } \bar{x} - \bar{\bar{x}})^2 + \sum_{\text{all data}} (x - \text{cell } \bar{x})^2$$

$$SS_{TOT} = SS_{TR} + SS_E$$

where

$$\text{Treatment variation} = \text{Factor 1 variation} + \text{Factor 2 variation} + \text{Interaction variation}$$

$$SS_{TR} = SS_{F1} + SS_{F2} + SS_{F1 \times F2}$$

$$\sum_{\text{all data}} (\text{cell } \bar{x} - \bar{\bar{x}})^2 = \sum_{\text{all data}} (\text{row } \bar{x} - \bar{\bar{x}})^2 + \sum_{\text{all data}} (\text{col } \bar{x} - \bar{\bar{x}})^2 + \sum_{\text{all data}} (\text{cell } \bar{x} - \text{row } \bar{x} - \text{col } \bar{x} + \bar{\bar{x}})^2$$

The actual calculation of all the required SS values is quite time-consuming. In most cases, computer packages are used to obtain the results. For the Friendly Bank data, the following table is a Minitab printout giving the sum of squares SS for the type-of-contact factor, the time-of-day factor, the interaction between time and type of contact, and the error.

```
Minitab Printout for Customer Satisfaction at Friendly Bank

Analysis of Variance for Response
Source            DF         SS         MS        F         P
Time               2       4.00       2.00     1.24     0.313
Type               1      66.67      66.67    41.38     0.000
Interaction        2       2.33       1.17     0.72     0.498
Error             18      29.00       1.61
Total             23     102.00
```

We see that $SS_{type} = 66.67$, $SS_{time} = 4.00$, $SS_{interaction} = 2.33$, $SS_{error} = 29.00$, and $SS_{TOT} = 102$ (the total of the other four sums of squares).

STEP 3: Compute the Mean Square (*MS*) Values

The calculations for the MS values are usually done on a computer. Although the sum of squares computed in Step 2 represents variation, we need to compute mean-square (*MS*) values for two-way ANOVA. As in one-way ANOVA, we compute *MS* values by dividing the *SS* values by respective degrees of freedom:

$$\text{Mean square } MS = \frac{\text{Corresponding sum of squares } SS}{\text{Respective degrees of freedom}}$$

For two-way ANOVA with more than one data value per cell, the degrees of freedom are

Degrees of freedom

$d.f.$ of row factor $= r - 1$ $d.f.$ of interaction $= (r - 1)(c - 1)$
$d.f.$ of column factor $= c - 1$ $d.f.$ of error $= rc(n - 1)$
$d.f.$ of total $= nrc - 1$

where r = number of rows, c = number of columns, and n = number of data in one cell.

The Minitab table shows the degrees of freedom and the *MS* values for the main effect factors, the interaction, and the error for the Friendly Bank study.

STEP 4: Compute the Sample F Statistic for Each Factor and for the Interaction

Under the assumption of the respective null hypothesis, we have

$$\text{Sample } F \text{ for row factor} = \frac{MS \text{ for row factor}}{MS \text{ for error}}$$

with degrees of freedom numerator, $d.f._N$ = $d.f.$ of row factor
degrees of freedom denominator, $d.f._D$ = $d.f.$ of error

$$\text{Sample } F \text{ for column factor} = \frac{MS \text{ for column factor}}{MS \text{ for error}}$$

with degrees of freedom numerator, $d.f._N$ = $d.f.$ of column factor
degrees of freedom denominator, $d.f._D$ = $d.f.$ of error

$$\text{Sample } F \text{ for interaction} = \frac{MS \text{ for interaction}}{MS \text{ for error}}$$

with degrees of freedom numerator, $d.f._N$ = $d.f.$ of interaction
degrees of freedom denominator, $d.f._D$ = $d.f.$ of error

For the Friendly Bank study, the sample F values are

$$\text{Sample } F \text{ for time:} \quad F = \frac{MS_{\text{time}}}{MS_{\text{error}}} = \frac{2.00}{1.61} = 1.24$$

$$d.f._N = 2 \quad \text{and} \quad d.f._D = 18$$

$$\text{Sample } F \text{ for type of contact:} \quad F = \frac{MS_{\text{type}}}{MS_{\text{error}}} = \frac{66.67}{1.61} = 41.41$$

$$d.f._N = 1 \quad \text{and} \quad d.f._D = 18$$

$$\text{Sample } F \text{ for interaction:} \quad F = \frac{MS_{\text{interaction}}}{MS_{\text{error}}} = \frac{1.17}{1.61} = 0.73$$

$$d.f._N = 2 \quad \text{and} \quad d.f._D = 18$$

Due to rounding, the sample F values we just computed differ slightly from those shown in the Minitab printout.

STEP 5: Conclude the Test

As with one-way ANOVA, larger values of the sample F statistic discredit the null hypothesis that there is no difference in population means across a given factor. The smaller the area to the right of the sample F statistic, the more likely there is an actual difference in some population means across the different factors. Smaller areas to the right of the sample F for interaction indicate greater likelihood of interaction between factors. Consequently, the P-value of a sample F statistic is the area of the F distribution to the *right* of the sample F statistic. Figure 11-18 shows the P-value associated with a sample F statistic.

Finding the P-value

Most statistical computer software packages provide P-values for the sample test statistic. You can also use the F distribution (Table 8 of Appendix II) to estimate the P-value. Once you have the P-value, compare it to the preset level of significance α. If the P-value is less than α, then reject H_0. Otherwise, do not reject H_0.

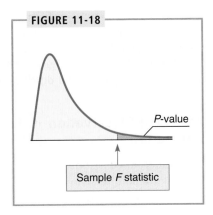

FIGURE 11-18

P-value

Sample *F* statistic

For two-way ANOVA, the *P*-value of the sample statistic is the area of the *F* distribution to the *right* of the sample *F* statistic.

Be sure to test for interaction between the factors *first*. If you *reject* the null hypothesis of no interaction, then you should *not* test for a difference of means in the levels of the row factors or a difference of means in the levels of the column factors because the interaction of the factors makes interpretation of the results of the main effects more complicated. A more extensive study of two-way ANOVA beyond the scope of this book shows how to interpret the results of the test of the main factors when there is interaction. For our purposes, we will simply stop the analysis rather than draw misleading conclusions.

In two-way ANOVA, test for *interaction* first. If you reject the null hypothesis of interaction, then do not continue with any tests of differences of means among other factors (unless you know more advanced techniques than those presented in this section).

If the test for interaction between the factors indicates that there is no evidence of interaction, then proceed to test the hypotheses regarding the levels of the row factor and the hypotheses regarding the levels of the column factor.

For the Friendly Bank study, we proceed as follows:

1. First we determine if there is any evidence of interaction between the factors. The sample test statistic for interaction is $F = 0.73$ with P-value ≈ 0.498. Since the P-value is greater than $\alpha = 0.05$, we do not reject H_0. There is no evidence of interaction. Because there is no evidence of interaction between the main effects of type of contact and time of day, we proceed to test each factor for a difference in population mean satisfaction among the respective levels of the factors.

2. Next we determine if there is a difference in mean satisfaction according to type of contact. The sample test statistic for type of contact is $F = 41.41$ with P-value ≈ 0.000 (to three places after the decimal). Since the P-value is less than $\alpha = 0.05$, we reject H_0. At the 5% level of significance, we conclude that there is a difference in average customer satisfaction between contact with an automated system and contact with a bank representative.

3. Finally, we determine if there is a difference in mean satisfaction according to time of day. The sample test statistic for time of day is $F = 1.24$ with P-value $\approx$ 0.313. Because the P-value is greater than $\alpha = 0.05$, we do not reject H_0. We conclude that at the 5% level of significance, there is no evidence that population mean customer satisfaction is different according to time of day.

Special Case: One Observation in Each Cell with No Interaction

In the case where our data consist of only one value in each cell, there are no measures for sum of squares *SS* interaction or mean square *MS* interaction, and we cannot test for interaction of factors using two-way ANOVA. If it *seems reasonable* (based on other information) to assume that there is *no* interaction between the factors, then we can use two-way ANOVA techniques to test for average response differences due to the main effects. In Guided Exercise 12, we look at two-way ANOVA applied to the special case of only one measurement per cell and no interactions.

GUIDED EXERCISE 12

Special case two-way ANOVA

Let's use two-way ANOVA to test if the average fat content (grams of fat per 3-oz serving) of potato chips is different according to the brand or according to which laboratory made the measurement. Use $\alpha = 0.05$. (See the following Minitab tables.)

Average Grams of Fat in a 3-oz Serving of Potato Chips

Brand	Lab I	Lab II	Lab III
Texas Chips	32.4	33.1	32.9
Great Chips	37.9	37.7	37.8
Chip Ooh	29.1	29.4	29.5

(header: Laboratory)

Minitab Printout for Potato Chip Data

Analysis of Variance for Fat

Source	DF	SS	MS	F	P
Brand	2	108.7022	54.3511	968.63	0.000
Lab	2	0.1422	0.0711	1.27	0.375
Error	4	0.2244	0.0561		
Total	8	109.0689			

(a) List the factors and the number of levels for each.

⟹ The factors are brand and laboratory. Each factor has three levels.

(b) Assuming that there is no interaction, list the hypotheses for each factor.

⟹ For brand,

H_0: There is no difference in population mean fat by brands.

H_1: At least two brands have different population mean fat content.

For laboratory,

H_0: There is no difference in mean fat content as measured by the labs.

H_1: At least two of the labs give different mean fat measurements.

Continued

GUIDED EXERCISE 12 continued

(c) Calculate the sample F statistic for brands and compare it to the value given in the Minitab printout. Look at the P-value in the printout. What is your conclusion regarding average fat content among brands?

 For brand,

$$\text{Sample } F = \frac{MS_{\text{brand}}}{MS_{\text{error}}} \approx \frac{54.35}{0.056} \approx 970$$

Using the Minitab printout, we see P-value ≈ 0.000 (to three places after the decimal). Using Table 8 of Appendix II, we see P-value < 0.001. Since the P-value is less than $\alpha = 0.05$, we reject H_0 and conclude that at the 5% level of significance, at least two of the brands have different mean fat content.

(d) Calculate the sample F statistic for laboratories and compare it to the value given in the Minitab printout. What is your conclusion regarding average fat content as measured by the different laboratories?

 For laboratories,

$$\text{Sample } F = \frac{MS_{\text{lab}}}{MS_{\text{error}}} \approx \frac{0.0711}{0.056} \approx 1.27$$

Using the Minitab printout, we see P-value ≈ 0.375. Using Table 8 of Appendix II, we see P-value > 0.100. Because the P-value is greater than $\alpha = 0.05$, we conclude that at the 5% level of significance, there is no evidence of differences in average measurements of fat content as determined by the different laboratories.

 TECH NOTE   The calculations involved with two-way ANOVA are usually done using statistical or spreadsheet software. Basic printouts from various software packages are similar. Specific instructions for using Excel and Minitab are given in the Using Technology section at the end of the chapter.

Experimental Design

In the preceding section and in this section, we have seen aspects of one-way and two-way ANOVA, respectively. Now let's take a brief look at some experimental design features that are appropriate for the use of these techniques.

For one-way ANOVA, we have one factor. Different levels for the factor form the treatment groups under study. In a *completely randomized design*, independent random samples of experimental subjects or objects are selected for each treatment group. For example, suppose a researcher wants to study the effects of different treatments for the condition of slightly high blood pressure. Three treatments are under study: diet, exercise, and medication. In a completely randomized design, the people participating in the experiment are *randomly* assigned to each treatment group. Table 11-23 shows the process.

TABLE 11-23   Completely Randomized Design Flowchart

Subjects with slightly high blood pressure	→	Random assignment	→	Treatment 1: Diet
			→	Treatment 2: Exercise
			→	Treatment 3: Medication

TABLE 11-24 Randomized Block Design Flowchart

	Blocks		Treatments
Subjects with slightly high blood pressure	Under 30 →	Random assignment	Treatment 1: Diet Treatment 2: Exercise Treatment 3: Medication
	Ages 31–50 →	Random assignment	Treatment 1: Diet Treatment 2: Exercise Treatment 3: Medication
	Over 50 →	Random assignment	Treatment 1: Diet Treatment 2: Exercise Treatment 3: Medication

For two-way ANOVA, there are *two* factors. When we *block* experimental subjects or objects together based on a similar characteristic that might affect responses to treatments, we have a *block design*. For example, suppose that the researcher studying treatments for slightly high blood pressure believes that the age of subjects might affect the response to the three treatments. In such a case, blocks of subjects in specified age groups are used. The factor age is used to form blocks. Suppose age has three levels: under age 30, ages 31–50, and over age 50. The same number of subjects are assigned to each block. Then the subjects in each block are randomly assigned to the different treatments of diet, exercise, or medication. Table 11-24 shows the *randomized block design*.

Experimental design is an essential component of good statistical research. The design of experiments can be quite complicated, and if the experiment is complex, the services of a professional statistician may be required. The use of blocks helps the researcher account for some of the most important sources of variability among the experimental subjects or objects. Then randomized assignments to different treatment groups help average out the effects of other remaining variability. In this way, differences among the treatment groups are more likely to be caused by the treatments themselves rather than by other sources of variability.

VIEWPOINT

Who Watches Cable TV?

Consider the following claim: Average cable TV viewers are, generally speaking, as affluent as newspaper readers and better off than radio or magazine audiences. How do we know that this claim is true? One way to answer such a question is to construct a two-way ANOVA test where the rows represent household income levels and the columns represent cable TV viewers, newspaper readers, magazine audiences, and radio listeners. The response variable is an index that represents the ratio of the specific medium compared with U.S. averages. For more information and data, see *American Demographics* (vol. 17, no. 6).

SECTION 11.6 PROBLEMS

1. *Physical Therapy: Dual Tasks* Does talking while walking slow you down? A study reported in the journal *Physical Therapy* (vol. 72, no. 4) considered mean cadence (steps per minute) for subjects using no walking device, a standard walker, and a rolling walker. In addition, the cadence was measured when the subjects had to perform dual tasks. The second task was to respond vocally to a signal while walking. Cadence was measured for subjects who were just walking (using no device, a standard walker, or a rolling walker) and for subjects required to respond to a signal while walking. List the factors and the number of levels of each factor. How many cells are there in the data table?

2. *Professors: Salary Survey Academe, Bulletin of the American Association of University Professors* (vol. 83, no. 2) presents results of salary surveys (average salary) by rank of the faculty member (professor, associate, assistant, instructor) and by type of institution (public, private). List the factors and the number of levels of each factor. How many cells are there in the data table?

3. *Physical Therapy: Dual Tasks* For the study regarding mean cadence (see Problem 1), two-way ANOVA was used. Recall that the two factors were walking device (none, standard walker, rolling walker) and dual task (being required to respond vocally to a signal or no dual task required). Results of two-way ANOVA showed that there was no evidence of interaction between the factors. However, according to the article, "the ANOVA conducted on the cadence data revealed a main effect of walking device." When the hypothesis regarding no difference in mean cadence according to which, if any, walking device is used, the sample F was 30.94, with $d.f._N = 2$ and $d.f._D = 18$. Further, the P-value for the result was reported to be less than 0.01. From this information, what is the conclusion regarding any difference in mean cadence according to the factor walking device used?

4. *Education: Media Usage* In a study of media usage versus education level (*American Demographics*, vol. 17, no. 6), an index was used to measure media usage, where a measurement of 100 represents the U.S. average. Values above 100 represent above average media usage.

Education Level	Media				
	Cable Network	Prime-Time TV	Radio	Newspaper	Magazine
Less than high school	80	112	87	76	85
High school graduate	103	105	100	99	101
Some college	107	94	106	105	107
College graduate	108	90	106	116	108

Source: From *American Demographics*, Vol. 17, No. 6. Reprinted with permission, copyright © 1995 *American Demographics*, Ithaca, NY.

(a) List the factors and the number of levels of each factor.
(b) Assume that there is no interaction between the factors. Use two-way ANOVA and the following Minitab printout to determine if there is a difference in population mean index based on education. Use $\alpha = 0.05$.
(c) Determine if there is a difference in population mean index based on media. Use $\alpha = 0.05$.

```
Minitab Printout for Media/Education Data
Analysis of Variance for Index
  Source      DF      SS      MS        F        P
  Edu          3     961     320     2.96    0.075
  Media        4       5       1     0.01    1.000
  Error       12    1299     108
  Total       19    2264
```

5. *Income: Media Usage* In the same study described in Problem 4, media usage versus household income also was considered. The media usage indices for the various media and income levels follow.

Income Level	Media				
	Cable Network	Prime-Time TV	Radio	Newspaper	Magazine
Less than $20,000	78	112	89	80	91
$20,000–$39,999	97	105	100	97	100
$40,000–$74,999	113	92	106	111	105
$75,000 or more	121	94	107	121	105

Source: From *American Demographics*, Vol. 17, No. 6. Reprinted with permission, copyright © 1995 *American Demographics*, Ithaca, NY.

(a) List the factors and the number of levels of each factor.
(b) Assume that there is no interaction between the factors. Use two-way ANOVA and the following Minitab printout to determine if there is a difference in population mean index based on income. Use $\alpha = 0.05$.
(c) Determine if there is a difference in population mean index based on media. Use $\alpha = 0.05$.

```
Minitab Printout for Media/Income Data
Analysis of Variance for Index
  Source      DF      SS      MS        F        P
  Income       3    1078     359     2.77    0.088
  Media        4      15       4     0.03    0.998
  Error       12    1558     130
  Total       19    2651
```

6. *Gender: Grade Point Average* Does college grade point average (GPA) depend on gender? Does it depend on class (freshman, sophomore, junior, senior)? In a study, the following GPA data were obtained for random samples of college students in each of the cells.

Gender	Class							
	Freshman		Sophomore		Junior		Senior	
Male	2.8	2.1	2.5	2.3	3.1	2.9	3.8	3.6
	2.7	3.0	2.9	3.5	3.2	3.8	3.5	3.1
Female	2.3	2.9	2.6	2.4	2.6	3.6	3.2	3.5
	3.5	3.9	3.3	3.6	3.3	3.7	3.8	3.6

(a) List the factors and the number of levels of each factor.
(b) Use two-way ANOVA and the following Minitab printout to determine if there is any evidence of interaction between the two factors at a level of significance of 0.05.

```
Minitab Printout of GPA Based on Gender and Class

Analysis of Variance for GPA
Source        DF      SS       MS       F       P
Gender        1     0.281    0.281    1.26    0.273
Class         3     2.226    0.742    3.32    0.037
Interaction   3     0.286    0.095    0.43    0.736
Error        24     5.365    0.224
Total        31     8.159
```

(c) If there is no evidence of interaction, use two-way ANOVA and the Minitab printout to determine if there is a difference in mean GPA based on class. Use $\alpha = 0.05$.
(d) If there is no evidence of interaction, use two-way ANOVA and the Minitab printout to determine if there is a difference in mean GPA based on gender. Use $\alpha = 0.05$.

7. *Education: Teaching Style* A researcher forms three blocks of students interested in taking a history course. The groups are based on grade point average (GPA). The first group consists of students with a GPA of less than 2.5, the second group consists of students with a GPA between 2.5 and 3.1, and the last group consists of students with a GPA greater than 3.1. History courses are taught in three ways: traditional lecture, small-group collaborative method, and independent study. The researcher randomly assigns 10 students from each block to sections of history taught each of the three ways. Sections for each teaching style then have 10 students from each block. The researcher records the scores on a common course final examination administered to each student. Draw a flowchart showing the design of this experiment. Does the design fit the model for randomized block design?

SUMMARY

In this chapter, we introduced applications of two probability distributions: the chi-square and F distributions. We used the chi-square distribution to test for independence and goodness of fit, to estimate the variance σ^2, and to test hypotheses involving the variance σ^2.

We used the F distribution to test two variances. Another application of the F distribution was for a method called analysis of variance. Analysis of variance is used to determine if there are differences among means for several groups. In the case that the groups are based on values of only one variable, we have one-way ANOVA. In the case of groups formed using two variables, we use two-way ANOVA to test for differences of means based on either variable or on an interaction between the variables.

IMPORTANT WORDS & SYMBOLS

Section 11.1
Independence test
Chi-square distribution, χ^2
Degrees of freedom, $d.f. = (R - 1)(C - 1)$ for χ^2
    distribution and tests of independence
Contingency table with cells
Row total
Column total
Expected frequency of a cell, E
Observed frequency of a cell, O

Section 11.2
Goodness-of-fit test
Degrees of freedom $d.f.$ for χ^2 distribution and
    goodness-of-fit tests

Section 11.3
Hypotheses tests about σ^2
Confidence interval for σ^2
χ_U^2, χ_L^2

Section 11.4
F distribution

F ratio
Hypothesis tests about two variances

Section 11.5
ANOVA
Sum of squares, SS
SS_{BET}, SS_W, SS_{TOT}
MS_{BET}, MS_W
F ratio
F distribution
Summary table for ANOVA
Degrees of freedom $d.f.$ for numerator for F
    distribution
Degrees of freedom $d.f.$ for denominator for F
    distribution

Section 11.6
Two-way ANOVA
Interaction
Factor
Level
Completely randomized design
Randomized block design

VIEWPOINT

Movies and Money!

Young adults are the movie industry's best customers. However, going to the movies is expensive, which may explain why attendance rates increase with household income. Using what you have learned in this chapter, you can create appropriate chi-square tests to determine how good a fit exists between national percentage rates of attendance by household income and attendance rates in your demographic area. For more information and national data, see *American Demographics* (vol. 18, no. 12).

CHAPTER REVIEW PROBLEMS

Before you solve a problem, first classify the problem as one of the following:

Chi-square test of independence
Chi-square goodness of fit

Chi-square for testing or estimating σ^2 or σ

F test for two variances

One-way ANOVA

Two-way ANOVA

Then, in each of the problems when a test is to be performed, do the following:

(i) Give the value of the level of significance. State the null and alternate hypotheses.
(ii) Find the sample test statistic.
(iii) Find or estimate the P-value of the sample test statistic.
(iv) Conclude the test.
(v) Interpret the conclusion in the context of the application.
(vi) In the case of one-way ANOVA, make a summary table.

1. *Sales: Packaging* The makers of Country Boy Corn Flakes are thinking about changing the packaging of the cereal with the hope of improving sales. In an experiment, five stores of similar size in the same region sold Country Boy Corn Flakes in different-shaped containers for 2 weeks. Total packages sold are given in the following table. Using a 0.05 level of significance, shall we reject or fail to reject the hypothesis that the mean sales are the same, no matter which shape box is used?

Cube	Cylinder	Pyramid	Rectangle
120	110	74	165
88	115	62	98
65	180	110	125
95	96	66	87
71	85	83	118

2. *Education: Exams* Professor Fair believes that extra time does not improve grades on exams. He randomly divided a group of 300 students into two groups and gave them all the same test. One group had exactly 1 hour in which to finish the test, and the other group could stay as long as desired. The results are shown in the following table. Test at the 0.01 level of significance that time to complete a test and test results are independent.

Time	A	B	C	F	Row Total
1 h	23	42	65	12	142
Unlimited	17	48	85	8	158
Column total	40	90	150	20	300

3. *Tires: Blowouts* A consumer agency is investigating the blowout pressures of Soap Stone tires. A Soap Stone tire is said to blow out when it separates from the wheel rim due to impact forces usually caused by hitting a rock or a pothole in the road. A random sample of 30 Soap Stone tires were inflated to the recommended pressure, and then forces measured in foot-pounds were applied to each tire (1 foot-pound is the force of 1 pound dropped from a height of 1 foot). The customer

complaint is that some Soap Stone tires blow out under small-impact forces, while other tires seem to be well made and don't have this fault. For the 30 test tires, the sample standard deviation of blowout forces was 1353 foot-pounds.

(a) Soap Stone claims its tires will blow out at an average pressure of 20,000 foot-pounds with a standard deviation of 1020 foot-pounds. The average blowout force is not in question, but the variability of blowout forces is in question. Using a 0.01 level of significance, test the claim that the variance of blowout pressures is more than Soap Stone claims it is.

(b) Find a 95% confidence interval for the variance of blowout pressures, using the information from the random sample.

4. *Computer Science: Data Processing* Anela is a computer scientist who is formulating a large and complicated program for a type of data processing. She has three ways of storing and retrieving data: CD, tape, and disks. As an experiment, she sets up her program in three different ways: one using CDs, one using tape, and the other using disks. Then four test runs of this type of data processing are made on each program. The time required to execute each program is shown in the following table (in minutes). Use a 0.01 level of significance to test the hypothesis that the mean processing time is the same for each method.

CD	Tape	Disks
8.7	7.2	7.0
9.3	9.1	6.4
7.9	7.5	9.8
8.0	7.7	8.2

5. *Teacher Ratings: Grades* Professor Stone complains that student teacher ratings depend on the grade the student receives. In other words, according to Professor Stone, a teacher who gives good grades gets good ratings, and a teacher who gives bad grades gets bad ratings. To test this claim, the Student Assembly took a random sample of 300 teacher ratings on which the student's grade for the course also was indicated. The results are given in the following table. Test the hypothesis that teacher ratings and student grades are independent at the 0.01 level of significance.

Rating	A	B	C	F (or withdrawal)	Row Total
Excellent	14	18	15	3	50
Average	25	35	75	15	150
Poor	21	27	40	12	100
Column total	60	80	130	30	300

6. *Packaging: Corn Flakes* A machine that puts corn flakes into boxes is adjusted to put an average of 15 oz into each box with standard deviation of 0.25 oz. If a random sample of 12 boxes gave a sample standard deviation of 0.38 oz, do these data support the claim that the variance has increased and the machine needs to be brought back into adjustment? (Use a 0.01 level of significance.)

7. *Sociology: Age Distribution* A sociologist is studying the age of the population in Blue Valley. Ten years ago the population was such that 20% were under 20 years old, 15% were in the 20- to 35-year-old bracket, 30% were between 36 and 50, 25% were between 51 and 65, and 10% were over 65. A study done this year used a random sample of 210 residents. This sample showed

Under 20	20–35	36–50	51–65	Over 65
26	27	69	68	20

At the 0.01 level of significance, has the age distribution of the population of Blue Valley changed?

8. *Engineering: Roller Bearings* Two processes for manufacturing large roller bearings are under study. In both cases, the diameters (in centimeters) are being examined. A random sample of 21 roller bearings from the old manufacturing process showed the sample variance of diameters to be $s^2 = 0.235$. Another random sample of 26 roller bearings from the new manufacturing process showed the sample variance of their diameters to be $s^2 = 0.128$. Use a 5% level of significance to test the claim that there is a difference (either way) in the population variances for the old or new manufacturing processes.

9. *Engineering: Light Bulbs* Two processes for manufacturing 60-watt light bulbs are under study. In both cases, the life (in hours) of the bulb before it burns out is being examined. A random sample of 18 light bulbs manufactured using the old process showed the sample variance of lifetimes to be $s^2 = 51.87$. Another random sample of 16 light bulbs manufactured using the new process showed the sample variance of the lifetimes to be $s^2 = 135.24$. Use a 5% level of significance to test the claim that the population variance of lifetimes for the new manufacturing process is larger than that of the old process.

10. *Advertising: Newspapers* Does the section in which a newspaper ad is placed make a difference in the average daily number of people responding to the ad? Is there a difference in average daily number of people responding to the ad if it is placed in the Sunday newspaper as compared with the Wednesday newspaper? Video Entertainment is a video club that sells videotapes featuring movies of all kinds—instructional videos, videos of TV specials, etc. To attract new customers, Video Entertainment ran ads in the Wednesday newspaper and in the Sunday newspaper offering 6 free videotapes or DVDs to new members. In addition, the ads were placed in the sports section, the entertainment section, and the business section of the local newspaper. Ads running in the different sections carried different promotion codes. Different codes also were used for Wednesday ads compared with Sunday ads. The numbers of people responding to the ads for days selected at random were recorded according to the promotion codes. The results follow:

Day	Section of Newspaper								
	Sports			Entertainment			Business		
Wed	12	15	11	22	14	17	2	4	3
	12	15	20	22	18	12	5	0	1
Sun	20	23	25	32	26	28	13	16	13
	33	15	17	31	25	41	15	14	10

(a) List the factors and the number of levels for each factor.

(b) Use the following Minitab printout and the *F* distribution table (Table 8 of Appendix II) to test for interaction between the variables. Use a 1% level of significance.

```
Minitab Printout for Mean Number of Responses per Day

Analysis of Variance for Response
Source          DF        SS        MS        F        P
Day              1     1024.0    1024.0    55.28    0.000
Section          2     1573.6     786.8    42.48    0.000
Interaction      2       38.0      19.0     1.03    0.371
Error           30      555.7      18.5
Total           35     3191.2
```

(c) If there is no evidence of interaction between the factors, test for a difference in mean number of daily responses for the levels of the day factor. Use $\alpha = 0.01$.

(d) If there is no evidence of interaction between the factors, test for a difference in mean number of daily responses for the levels of the section factor. Use $\alpha = 0.01$.

DATA HIGHLIGHTS: GROUP PROJECTS

Break into small groups and discuss the following topics. Organize a brief outline in which you summarize the main points of your group discussion.

The *Statistical Abstract of the United States* reported information about the percentage of arrests of all drunk drivers according to age group. In the following table, the entry 3.7 in the first row means that in the entire United States, about 3.7% of all people arrested for drunk driving were in the age group 16–17 years. The Freemont County Sheriff's Office obtained data about the number of drunk drivers arrested in each age group over the past several years. In the following table, the entry 8 in the first row means that eight people in the age group 16–17 years were arrested for drunk driving in Freemont County.

Distribution of Drunk Driver Arrests by Age

Age	National Percentage	Number in Freemont County
16–17	3.7	8
18–24	18.9	35
25–29	12.9	23
30–34	10.3	19
35–39	8.5	12
40–44	7.9	14
45–49	8.0	16
50–54	7.9	13
55–59	6.8	10
60–64	5.7	9
65 and over	9.4	15
	100%	174

Use a chi-square test with 5% level of significance to test the claim that the age distribution of drunk drivers arrested in Freemont County is the same as the national age distribution of drunk drivers arrested.
(a) State the null and alternate hypotheses.
(b) Find the value of the chi-square test statistic from the sample.
(c) Find the degrees of freedom and the P-value of the test statistic.
(d) Decide whether you should reject or not reject the null hypothesis.
(e) State your conclusion in the context of the problem.
(f) How could you gather data and conduct a similar test for the city or county in which you live? Explain.

LINKING CONCEPTS: WRITING PROJECTS

Discuss each of the following topics in class or review the topics on your own. Then write a brief but complete essay in which you summarize the main points. Please include formulas and graphs as appropriate.

1. In this chapter, you studied the chi-square distribution and three principal applications for the distribution.
   (a) Outline the basic ideas behind the chi-square test of independence. What is a contingency table? What are the null and alternate hypotheses? How is the test statistic constructed? What basic assumptions underlie this application of the chi-square distribution?
   (b) Outline the basic ideas behind the chi-square test of goodness of fit. What are the null and alternate hypotheses? How is the test statistic constructed? There are a number of direct similarities between tests of independence and tests for goodness of fit. Discuss and summarize these similarities.
   (c) Outline the basic ideas behind the chi-square method of testing and estimating a standard deviation. What basic assumptions underlie this process?

2. The F distribution is used to construct a one-way ANOVA test for comparing several sample means.
   (a) Outline the basic purpose of ANOVA. How does ANOVA avoid high risk due to multiple type I errors?
   (b) Outline the basic assumption for ANOVA.
   (c) What are the null and alternate hypotheses in an ANOVA test? If the test conclusion is to reject the null hypothesis, do we know which of the population means are different from each other?
   (d) What is the F distribution? How are the degrees of freedom for numerator and denominator determined?
   (e) What do we mean by a summary table of ANOVA results? What are the main components of such a table? How is the final decision made?

Using Technology

APPLICATION

Analysis of Variance (One-Way ANOVA)

The following data comprise a winter mildness/severity index for three European locations near 50° north latitude. For each decade, the number of unmistakably mild months minus the number of unmistakably severe months for December, January, and February is given.

Decade	Britain	Germany	Russia
1800	−2	−1	+1
1810	−2	−3	−1
1820	0	0	0
1830	−3	−2	−1
1840	−3	−2	+1
1850	−1	−2	+3
1860	+8	+6	+1
1870	0	0	−3
1880	−2	0	+1
1890	−3	−1	+1
1900	+2	0	+2
1910	+5	+6	+1
1920	+8	+6	+2
1930	+4	+4	+5
1940	+1	−1	−1
1950	0	+1	+2

Table is based on data from *Exchanging Climate* by H. H. Lamb; copyright © 1966. Reprinted by permission of Routledge, UK.

1. We wish to test the null hypothesis that the mean winter indices for Britain, Germany, and Russia are all equal against the alternate hypothesis that they are not all equal. Use a 5% level of significance.

2. What is the sum of squares between groups? Within groups? What is the sample F ratio? What is the P-value? Shall we reject or fail to reject the statement that the mean winter indices for these locations in Britain, Germany, and Russia are the same?

3. What is the smallest level of significance at which we could conclude that the mean winter indices for these locations are not all equal?

Technology Hints (One-Way ANOVA)

SPSS

Enter all the data in one column. In another column, use integers to designate the group to which each data value belongs. Use the menu selections **Analyze ➤ Compare Means ➤ One-Way ANOVA**. Move the column containing the data to the dependent list. Move the column containing group designation to the factor list.

Technology Hints (Two-Way ANOVA)

Excel

Excel has two commands for two-way ANOVA, depending on how many data values are in each cell. In both cases, use the menu selections **Tools ➤ Data Analysis**. Then use

ANOVA: Two-Factor with Replication if there are two or more sample measurements for each factor combination cell. Again, there must be the same number of data in each cell.

ANOVA: Two-Factor without Replication if there is only one data value in each factor combination cell.

Data entry is fairly straightforward. For example, look at the Excel spreadsheet for the data of Guided Exercise 12 regarding the fat content of different brands of potato chips as measured by different labs.

	A	B	C	D
1		**Lab 1**	**Lab 2**	**Lab 3**
2	Texas	32.4	33.1	32.9
3	Great	37.9	37.7	37.8
4	Chip Ooh	29.1	29.4	29.5

Minitab

For Minitab, all the data for the response variable (in this case, fat content) are entered into a single column. Create two more columns, one for the row number of the cell containing the data value and one for the column number of the cell containing the data value. For the potato chip example, the rows correspond to the brand and the columns to the lab doing the analysis. Use the menu choices **Stat ➤ ANOVA ➤ Two-Way.**

	C1	C2	C3
	Brand	Lab	Fat
1	1	1	32.4
2	1	2	33.1
3	1	3	32.9
4	2	1	37.9
5	2	2	37.7
6	2	3	37.8
7	3	1	29.1
8	3	2	29.4
9	3	3	29.5

SPSS

Data entry for SPSS is similar to that for Minitab. Enter all the data in one column. Use a separate column for each factor and use a label or integer to designate the group in the particular factor. Under Variable View, type appropriate labels for the columns of data. Use the menu selections **Analyze ➤ General Linear Model ➤ Univariate….** In the dialogue box, the dependent variable is the quantity represented by the data. The factors are those found in each factor column. For the special case of only one datum per cell, click the Model button. Select Custom and move the desired factors into Model.

SPSS Data Editor

File   Edit   View   Data   Transform   Analyze   Graphs

	fat	lab	brand
1	32.40	1	Texas
2	37.90	1	Great
3	29.10	1	Chip
4	33.10	2	Texas
5	37.70	2	Great
6	29.40	2	Chip
7	32.90	3	Texas
8	37.80	3	Great
9	29.50	3	Chip

12

Nonparametric Statistics

Make everything as simple as possible, but no simpler.

—Albert Einstein

Albert Einstein (1879–1955)

This brilliant German-born American physicist formulated the theory of relativity.

For on-line student resources, visit **math.college.hmco.com/students** and follow the Statistics links to the Brase/Brase, *Understandable Statistics,* 8th edition web site.

PREVIEW QUESTIONS

◇ What if you cannot make assumptions about a population distribution? Can you still use statistical methods? What are the advantages and disadvantages?   (SECTION 12.1)

◇ What are nonparametric tests? How do you handle a "before-and-after" situation?   (SECTION 12.1)

◇ If you can't make assumptions about the population, and you have independent samples, how do you set up a nonparametric test?   (SECTION 12.2)

◇ Suppose you are interested only in rank data (ordinal type data). If you have ordered pairs (x, y) of ranked data, is there a way to measure and test correlation?   (SECTION 12.3)

◇ Is a sequence random or is there a pattern associated with the sequence?   (SECTION 12.4)

How Cold? Compared to What?

Juneau is the capital of Alaska. The terrain surrounding Juneau is very rugged, and storms that sweep across the Gulf of Alaska usually hit Juneau. However, Juneau is located in southern Alaska, near the ocean, and temperatures are often comparable with those found in the lower 48 states. Madison is the capital of Wisconsin. The city is located between two large lakes. The climate of Madison is described as typical continental climate of interior North America. Consider the long-term average temperatures (in degrees Fahrenheit) paired by month for the two cities. (Source: National Weather Bureau.) Use a sign test with a 5% level of significance to test the claim that the

Month	Madison	Juneau
January	17.5	22.2
February	21.1	27.3
March	31.5	31.9
April	46.1	38.4
May	57.0	46.4
June	67.0	52.8
July	71.3	55.5
August	69.8	54.1
September	60.7	49.0
October	51.0	41.5
November	35.7	32.0
December	22.8	26.9

overall temperature distribution of Madison is different (either way) from that of Juneau. (See Problem 11 of Section 12.1.)

12.1
The Sign Test for Matched Pairs

FOCUS POINTS

✓ State the criteria for setting up a matched-pair sign test.
✓ Complete a matched-pair sign test.
✓ Interpret the results in the context of the application.

There are many situations where very little is known about the population from which samples are drawn. Therefore, we cannot make assumptions about the population distribution, such as assuming the distribution is normal or binomial. In this chapter, we will study methods that come under the heading of *nonparametric statistics*. These methods are called *nonparametric* because they require no assumptions about the population distributions from which samples are drawn. The obvious advantages of these tests are that they are quite general and (as we shall see) not difficult to apply. The disadvantages are that they tend to waste information and tend to result in acceptance of the null hypothesis more often than they should; nonparametric tests are sometimes less sensitive than other tests.

The easiest of all the nonparametric tests is probably the *sign test*. The sign test is used when we compare sample distributions from two populations that are *not independent*. This occurs when we measure the sample twice, as in "before-and-after" studies. The following example shows how the sign test is constructed and used.

Criteria for sign test

As part of their training, 15 police cadets took a special course on identification awareness. To determine how the course affects a cadet's ability to identify a suspect, the 15 cadets were first given an identification awareness exam and then, after the course, were tested again. The police school would like to use the results of the two tests to see if the identification awareness course *improves* a cadet's score. Table 12-1 gives the scores for each exam.

The sign of the difference is obtained by subtracting the precourse score from the postcourse score. If the difference is positive, we say that the sign of the difference is +, and if the difference is negative, we indicate it with −. No sign is indicated if

TABLE 12-1 Scores for 15 Police Cadets

Cadet	Postcourse Score	Precourse Score	Sign of Difference
1	93	76	+
2	70	72	−
3	81	75	+
4	65	68	−
5	79	65	+
6	54	54	No difference
7	94	88	+
8	91	81	+
9	77	65	+
10	65	57	+
11	95	86	+
12	89	87	+
13	78	78	No difference
14	80	77	+
15	76	76	No difference

the scores are identical; in essence, such scores are ignored when using the sign test. To use the sign test, we need to compute the *proportion x of plus signs* to all signs. We ignore the pairs with no difference of signs. This is done in Guided Exercise 1.

GUIDED EXERCISE 1

Proportion of plus signs

Look at Table 12-1 under the "Sign of Difference" column.

(a) How many plus signs do you see?   ⟹   10

(b) How many plus and minus signs do you see? ⟹   12

(c) The *proportion of plus signs* is   ⟹ $x = \dfrac{10}{12} = \dfrac{5}{6} \approx 0.833$

$$x = \frac{\text{Number of plus signs}}{\text{Total number of plus and minus signs}}$$

Use parts (a) and (b) to find x.

We observe that x is the sample proportion of plus signs, and we use p to represent the population proportion of plus signs (if *all* possible police cadets were used).

Null hypothesis   The null hypothesis is

$H_0: p = 0.5$ (the distributions of scores before and after the course are the same)

The null hypothesis states that the identification awareness course does *not* affect the distribution of scores. Under the null hypothesis we expect the number of plus signs and minus signs to be about equal. This means that the proportion of plus signs should be approximately 0.5.

Alternate hypothesis   The police department wants to see if the course *improves* a cadet's score. Therefore, the alternate hypothesis will be

$H_1: p > 0.5$ (the distribution of scores after the course is shifted higher than the distribution before the course)

The alternate hypothesis states that the identification awareness course tends to improve scores. This means that the proportion of plus signs should be greater than 0.5.

Sampling distribution   To test the null hypothesis $H_0: p = 0.5$ against the alternate hypothesis $H_1: p > 0.5$, we use methods of Section 9.3 for tests of proportions. As in Section 9.3, we will assume that all our samples are sufficiently large to permit a good normal approximation to the binomial distribution. For most practical work, this will be the case if the total number of plus and minus signs is 12 or more ($n \geq 12$).

When the total number of plus and minus signs is 12 or more, the sample statistic x (proportion of plus signs) has a distribution that is approximately normal with mean p and standard deviation $\sqrt{pq/n}$. (See Section 7.4.)

Under the null hypothesis H_0: $p = 0.5$, we assume that the population proportion p of plus signs is 0.5. Therefore, the z value corresponding to the sample test statistic x is

Sample test statistic

$$z = \frac{x - p}{\sqrt{\dfrac{pq}{n}}} = \frac{x - 0.5}{\sqrt{\dfrac{(0.5)(0.5)}{n}}} = \frac{x - 0.5}{\sqrt{\dfrac{0.25}{n}}}$$

where n is the total number of plus and minus signs, and x is the total number of plus signs divided by n.

For the police cadet example, we found $x \approx 0.833$ in Guided Exercise 1. The value of n is 12. (Note that of the 15 cadets in the sample, 3 had no difference in precourse and postcourse test scores, so there are no signs for these 3.) The z value corresponding to $x = 0.833$ is then

$$z \approx \frac{0.833 - 0.5}{\sqrt{\dfrac{0.25}{12}}} \approx 2.31$$

P-value

We use the standard normal distribution table (Table 5 of Appendix II) to find P-values for the sign test. This table gives areas to the left of z. Recall from Section 9.2 that Table 5 of Appendix II can be used directly to find P-values of one-tailed tests. For *two-tailed* tests, we must *double* the value given in the table. To review the process of finding areas to the right or left of z using Table 5, see Section 6.2.

The alternate hypothesis for the police cadet example is H_1: $p > 0.5$. The P-value for the sample test statistic $z = 2.31$ is shown in Figure 12-1. For a right-tailed test, the P-value is the area to the right of the sample test statistic $z = 2.31$. From Table 5 of Appendix II, $P(z > 2.31) = 0.0104$.

Conclude the test

In our example, the police department wishes to use a 5% level of significance to test the claim that the identification awareness course improves a cadets' score. Since the P-value of 0.0104 is less than $\alpha = 0.05$, we reject the null hypothesis H_0 that the course makes no difference. Instead, at the 5% level of significance, we say the results are significant. The evidence is sufficient to claim that the identification awareness course improves cadets' scores.

The steps used to construct a sign test for matched pairs are summarized in the next procedure.

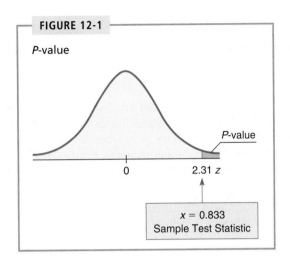

FIGURE 12-1

P-value

P-value

0   2.31 *z*

x = 0.833
Sample Test Statistic

PROCEDURE

How to construct a sign test for matched pairs

You first need a random sample of data pairs (*A*, *B*). Next, you take the differences *A* − *B* and record the sign change for each difference: plus, minus, or no change. The number of data pairs should be large enough so that the total number of plus and minus signs is at least 12. The sample proportion of plus signs is

$$x = \frac{\text{number of plus signs}}{\text{total number of plus and minus signs}}$$

Let *p* represent the population proportion of plus signs if the entire population of all possible data pairs (*A*, *B*) were to be used.

1. Set the *level of significance* α. The *null hypothesis* is $H_0\!: p = 0.5$. In the context of the application, set the *alternate hypothesis*: $p > 0.5$, $p < 0.5$, or $p \neq 0.5$.

2. The sample *test statistic* is

$$z = \frac{x - 0.5}{\sqrt{\dfrac{0.25}{n}}}$$

where $n \geq 12$ is the total number of plus and minus signs.

3. Use the standard normal distribution and the type of test, one-tailed or two-tailed, to find the *P-value* corresponding to the test statistic.

4. *Conclude* the test. If P-value ≤ α, then reject H_0. If P-value > α, then do not reject H_0.

5. *State your conclusion* in the context of the application.

GUIDED
EXERCISE 2

Sign test

Dr. Kick-a-poo's Traveling Circus made a stop at Middlebury, Vermont, where the doctor opened a booth and sold bottles of Dr. Kick-a-poo's Magic Gasoline Additive. The additive is supposed to increase gas mileage when used according to instructions. Twenty local people purchased bottles of the additive and used it according to instructions. These people carefully recorded their mileage with and without the additive. The results are shown in Table 12-2.

TABLE 12-2 Mileage Before and After Kick-a-poo's Additive

Car	With Additive	Without Additive	Sign of Difference
1	17.1	16.8	+
2	21.2	20.1	+
3	12.3	12.3	No difference (N.D.)
4	19.6	21.0	−
5	22.5	20.9	+
6	17.0	17.9	‾‾‾
7	24.2	25.4	‾‾‾
8	22.2	20.1	‾‾‾
9	18.3	19.1	‾‾‾
10	11.0	12.3	‾‾‾
11	17.6	14.2	‾‾‾
12	22.1	23.7	‾‾‾
13	29.9	30.2	‾‾‾
14	27.6	27.6	‾‾‾
15	28.4	27.7	‾‾‾
16	16.1	16.1	‾‾‾
17	19.0	19.5	‾‾‾
18	38.7	37.9	‾‾‾
19	17.6	19.7	‾‾‾
20	21.6	22.2	‾‾‾

TABLE 12-3 Completion of Table 12-2

Car	Sign of Difference
6	−
7	−
8	+
9	−
10	−
11	+
12	−
13	−
14	N.D.
15	+
16	N.D.
17	−
18	+
19	−
20	−

(a) In Table 12-2, complete the column headed "Sign of Difference." How many plus signs are there? How many total plus and minus signs are there? What is x, the proportion of plus signs?

⇒ There are 7 plus signs and 17 total plus and minus signs. The proportion of plus signs is

$$x = \frac{7}{17} \approx 0.412$$

(b) Most people claim that the additive has no effect. Let's use a 0.05 level of significance to test this claim against the alternate hypothesis that the additive did have an effect (one way or the other). State the null and alternate hypotheses.

⇒ We use

$H_0: p = 0.5$ (mileage distributions are the same)
$H_1: p \neq 0.5$ (mileage distributions are different)

Continued

GUIDED EXERCISE 2 continued

(c) Convert the sample x value, $x = 0.412$, to a z value.

To find the z value corresponding to $x = 0.412$, we use $n = 17$ (total number of signs).

$$z = \frac{x - 0.5}{\sqrt{0.25/n}} \approx \frac{0.412 - 0.5}{\sqrt{0.25/17}} \approx -0.73$$

(d) Find the corresponding P-value.

Table 5 of Appendix II gives the area to the left of $z = -0.73$.

$$P(z < -0.73) = 0.2327$$

Because this is a two-tailed test, the P-value is double this area.

$$P\text{-value} = 2(0.2327) = 0.4654$$

FIGURE 12-2 P-value

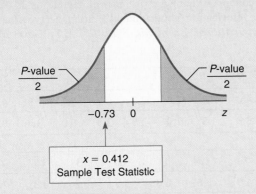

(e) Conclude the test.

For $\alpha = 0.05$, we see that the P-value $= 0.4654$ is greater than α. We fail to reject H_0. At the 5% level of significance, the data are not statistically significant, and we cannot reject the hypothesis that the mileage distribution is the same with or without the additive.

VIEWP●INT   *Yukon News*

The *Yukon News* featured an article entitled "Resurgence of the Dreaded White Plague," about the resurgence of tuberculosis (TB) in the far north. TB, also known as the white plague, has been present in Canada since it was brought in by European immigrants in the 17th century. Although antibiotics are widely used today, the disease has never been eradicated. Canadian National Health data suggest that TB is spreading faster in the Yukon than elsewhere in Canada. Because of this, the Canadian government has established many new TB clinics in remote Yukon villages. Using what you have learned in this section and Canadian National Health data, can you think of a way to use a sign test to study the claim that in these villages, the rate of TB in the population dropped after the clinics were activated?

SECTION 12.1   PROBLEMS

For each problem, please provide the following information.
(a) What is the level of significance? State the null and alternate hypotheses.
(b) Compute the sample test statistic. What is the sampling distribution?
(c) Find the *P*-value of the sample test statistic.
(d) Conclude the test.
(e) State the conclusion in the context of the application.

1. *Economic Growth: Asia* Asian economies impact some of the world's largest populations. The growth of an economy has a big influence on the everyday lives of ordinary people. Are Asian economies changing? A random sample of 15 Asian economies gave the following information about annual percentage growth rate. (Reference: *Handbook of International Economic Statistics*, U.S. Government Documents.)

Region	1	2	3	4	5	6	7	8
Modern Growth Rate %	4.0	2.3	7.8	2.8	0.7	5.1	2.9	4.2
Historic Growth Rate %	3.3	1.9	7.0	5.5	3.3	6.0	3.2	8.2

Region	9	10	11	12	13	14	15
Modern Growth Rate %	4.9	5.8	6.8	3.6	3.2	0.8	7.3
Historic Growth Rate %	6.4	7.2	6.1	1.5	1.0	2.1	5.1

Does this information indicate a change (either way) in the growth rate of Asian economies? Use a 5% level of significance.

2. *Debt: Developing Countries* Borrowing money may be necessary for business expansion. However, too much borrowed money can also mean trouble. Are developing countries tending to borrow more? A random sample of 20 developing countries gave the following information regarding foreign debt per capita (in U.S. dollars, inflation adjusted). (Reference: *Handbook of International Economic Statistics*, U.S. Government Documents.)

Country	1	2	3	4	5	6	7	8	9	10
Modern Debt per Capita	179	157	129	125	91	80	31	25	29	85
Historic Debt per Capita	144	132	88	112	53	66	31	30	40	75

Country	11	12	13	14	15	16	17	18	19	20
Modern Debt per Capita	27	20	17	21	195	189	143	126	106	76
Historic Debt per Capita	21	19	15	24	104	150	142	118	117	79

Does this information indicate that foreign debt per capita is increasing in developing countries? Use a 1% level of significance.

3. *Education: Exams* A high-school science teacher decided to give a series of lectures on current events. To determine if the lectures had any effect on student awareness of current events, an exam was given to the class before the lectures, and a similar exam was given after the lectures. The scores follow. Use a 0.05 level of significance

to test the claim that the lectures made no difference against the claim that the lectures did make some difference (one way or the other).

Student	1	2	3	4	5	6	7	8	9
After Lectures	107	115	120	78	83	56	71	89	77
Before Lectures	111	110	93	75	88	56	75	73	83

Student	10	11	12	13	14	15	16	17	18
After Lectures	44	119	130	91	99	96	83	100	118
Before Lectures	40	115	101	110	90	98	76	100	109

4. *Grain Yields: Feeding the World* With an ever-increasing world population, grain yields are extremely important. A random sample of 16 large grain-producing regions in the world gave the following information about grain production (in kg/hectare). (Reference: *Handbook of International Economic Statistics,* U.S. Government Documents.)

Region	1	2	3	4	5	6	7	8
Modern Production	1610	2230	5270	6990	2010	4560	780	6510
Historic Production	1590	2360	5161	7170	1920	4760	660	6320

Region	9	10	11	12	13	14	15	16
Modern Production	2850	3550	1710	2050	2750	2550	6750	3670
Historic Production	2920	2440	1340	2180	3110	2070	7330	2980

Does this information indicate that modern grain production is higher? Use a 5% level of significance.

5. *Identical Twins: Reading Skills* To compare two elementary schools in teaching of reading skills, 12 sets of identical twins were used. In each case, one child was selected at random and sent to school A and his or her twin was sent to school B. Near the end of fifth grade, an achievement test was given to each child. The results follow:

Twin Pair	1	2	3	4	5	6
School A	177	150	112	95	120	117
School B	86	135	115	110	116	84

Twin Pair	7	8	9	10	11	12
School A	86	111	110	142	125	89
School B	93	77	96	130	147	101

Use a 0.05 level of significance to test the hypothesis that the two schools have the same effectiveness in teaching reading skills against the alternate hypothesis that the schools are not equally effective.

6. *Incomes: Electricians and Carpenters* How do the average weekly incomes of electricians and carpenters compare? A random sample of 17 regions in the United States gave the following information about average weekly income (in dollars). (Reference: U.S. Department of Labor, Bureau of Labor Statistics.)

Region	1	2	3	4	5	6	7	8	9
Electricians	461	713	593	468	730	690	740	572	805
Carpenters	540	812	512	473	686	507	785	657	475

Region	10	11	12	13	14	15	16	17
Electricians	593	593	700	572	863	599	596	653
Carpenters	485	646	675	382	819	600	559	501

Does this information indicate a difference (either way) in the average weekly incomes of electricians compared to those of carpenters? Use a 5% level of significance.

7. *Quitting Smoking: Hypnosis* One program to help people stop smoking cigarettes uses the method of posthypnotic suggestion to remind subjects to avoid smoking. A random sample of 18 subjects agreed to test the program. All subjects counted the number of cigarettes they usually smoke a day; then they counted the number of cigarettes smoked the day after hypnosis. (*Note:* It usually takes several weeks for the subject to stop smoking completely, and the method does not work for everyone.) The results follow.

Subject	Cigarettes Smoked per Day After Hypnosis	Cigarettes Smoked per Day Before Hypnosis	Subject	Cigarettes Smoked per Day After Hypnosis	Cigarettes Smoked per Day Before Hypnosis
1	28	28	10	5	19
2	15	35	11	12	32
3	2	14	12	20	42
4	20	20	13	30	26
5	31	25	14	19	37
6	19	40	15	0	19
7	6	18	16	16	38
8	17	15	17	4	23
9	1	21	18	19	24

Using a 1% level of significance, test the claim that the number of cigarettes smoked per day was less after hypnosis.

8. *Incomes: Lawyers and Architects* How do the average weekly incomes of lawyers and architects compare? A random sample of 18 regions in the United States gave the following information about average weekly incomes (in dollars). (Reference: U.S. Department of Labor, Bureau of Labor Statistics.)

Region	1	2	3	4	5	6	7	8	9
Lawyers	709	898	848	1041	1326	1165	1127	866	1033
Architects	859	936	887	1100	1378	1295	1039	888	1012

Region	10	11	12	13	14	15	16	17	18
Lawyers	718	835	1192	992	1138	920	1397	872	1142
Architects	794	900	1150	1038	1197	939	1124	911	1171

Does this information indicate that architects tend to have a larger average weekly income? Use $\alpha = 0.05$.

9. *High School Dropouts: Male versus Female* Is the high school dropout rate higher for males or females? A random sample of population regions gave the following information about percentage of 15- to 19-year-olds who are high school dropouts. (Reference: *Statistical Abstract of the United States,* 121st edition.)

Region	1	2	3	4	5	6	7	8	9	10
Male	7.3	7.5	7.7	21.8	4.2	12.2	3.5	4.2	8.0	9.7
Female	7.5	6.4	6.0	20.0	2.6	5.2	3.1	4.9	12.1	10.8

Region	11	12	13	14	15	16	17	18	19	20
Male	14.1	3.6	3.6	4.0	5.2	6.9	15.6	6.3	8.0	6.5
Female	15.6	6.3	4.0	3.9	9.8	9.8	12.0	3.3	7.1	8.2

Does this information indicate that the dropout rates for males and females are different (either way)? Use $\alpha = 0.01$.

10. *Marketing: Ads* Enterprise Sales sent a team of 15 salespeople to Dodge City, Kansas, for door-to-door magazine sales. After one week of sales efforts, Enterprise Sales decided to buy local spot TV ads for its magazines and then continue the door-to-door sales effort for another week. The results follow.

Salesperson	Number of Sales After TV Ads	Number of Sales Before TV Ads	Salesperson	Number of Sales After TV Ads	Number of Sales Before TV Ads
1	4	3	9	3	2
2	1	0	10	0	1
3	0	1	11	1	0
4	3	4	12	4	3
5	3	2	13	4	4
6	0	0	14	5	6
7	6	5	15	3	2
8	4	3			

Using a 5% level of significance, test the claim that sales before and after the TV ads are different (either up or down).

11. *Focus Problem: Meteorology* The Focus Problem at the beginning of this chapter asks you to use a sign test with a 5% level of significance to test the claim that the overall temperature distribution of Madison, Wisconsin is different (either way) from that of Juneau, Alaska. The monthly average data (in °F) are as follows.

Month	Jan.	Feb.	March	April	May	June
Madison	17.5	21.1	31.5	46.1	57.0	67.0
Juneau	22.2	27.3	31.9	38.4	46.4	52.8

Month	July	Aug.	Sept.	Oct.	Nov.	Dec.
Madison	71.3	69.8	60.7	51.0	35.7	22.8
Juneau	55.5	54.1	49.0	41.5	32.0	26.9

What is your conclusion?

12.2
The Rank-Sum Test

FOCUS POINTS

✓ State the criteria for setting up a rank-sum test.

✓ Use the distribution of ranks to complete the test.

✓ Interpret the results in the context of the application.

Criteria for rank-sum test

The sign test is used when we have paired data values coming from dependent samples as in "before-and-after" studies. However, if the data values are *not* paired, the sign test should *not* be used.

For the situation in which we draw independent random samples from two populations, there is another nonparametric method for testing the difference between sample means; it is called the *rank-sum test* (also called the *Mann-Whitney test*). The rank-sum test can be used when assumptions about *normal* populations are not satisfied. To fix our thoughts on a definite problem, let's consider the following example.

When a scuba diver makes a deep dive, nitrogen builds up in the diver's blood. After returning to the surface, the diver must wait in a decompression chamber until the nitrogen level of the blood returns to normal. A physiologist working with the Navy has invented a pill that a diver takes 1 hour before diving. The pill is supposed to have the effect of reducing the waiting time spent in the decompression chamber. Twenty-three Navy divers volunteered to help the physiologist determine if the pill has any effect. The divers were randomly divided into two groups: group A had 11 divers who each took the pill, and group B had 12 divers who did not take the pill. All the divers worked the same length of time on a deep salvage operation and returned to the decompression chamber. A monitoring device in the decompression chamber measured the waiting time for each diver's nitrogen level to return to normal. These times are recorded in Table 12-4.

TABLE 12-4   Decompression Times for 23 Navy Divers (in min)

Group A (had pill)										
41	56	64	42	50	70	44	57	63	65	52
Mean time = 54.91 min										

Group B (no pill)											
66	43	72	62	55	80	74	75	77	78	47	60
Mean time = 65.75 min											

TABLE 12-5   Ranks for Decompression Time

Time	Group	Rank	Time	Group	Rank
41	A	1	63	A	13
42	A	2	64	A	14
43	B	3	65	A	15
44	A	4	66	B	16
47	B	5	70	A	17
50	A	6	72	B	18
52	A	7	74	B	19
55	B	8	75	B	20
56	A	9	77	B	21
57	A	10	78	B	22
60	B	11	80	B	23
62	B	12			

Rank the data

The means of our two samples are 54.91 and 65.75 minutes. We will use the rank-sum test to decide whether the difference between the means is significant. First, we arrange the two samples jointly in order of increasing time. To do this, we use the data of groups A and B as if they were one sample. The times (in minutes), groups, and ranks are shown in Table 12-5.

Group A occupies the ranks 1, 2, 4, 6, 7, 9, 10, 13, 14, 15, and 17, while group B occupies the ranks 3, 5, 8, 11, 12, 16, 18, 19, 20, 21, 22, and 23. We add up the ranks of the group with the *smaller* sample size, in this case group A.

The sum of the ranks is denoted by R:

$$R = 1 + 2 + 4 + 6 + 7 + 9 + 10 + 13 + 14 + 15 + 17 = 98$$

Let n_1 be the size of the *smaller sample* and n_2 be the size of the *larger sample*. In the case of the divers, $n_1 = 11$ and $n_2 = 12$. So R is the sum of the ranks from the smaller sample. If both samples are of the same size, then $n_1 = n_2$ and R is the sum of the ranks of either group (but not both groups).

Distribution of ranks

When both n_1 and n_2 are sufficiently large (each greater than 10), advanced mathematical statistics can be used to show that R is approximately normally distributed with mean

$$\mu_R = \frac{n_1(n_1 + n_2 + 1)}{2}$$

and standard deviation

$$\sigma_R = \sqrt{\frac{n_1 n_2(n_1 + n_2 + 1)}{12}}$$

GUIDED
EXERCISE **3**

Mean and standard deviation of ranks

For the Navy divers, compute μ_R and σ_R. (Recall that $n_1 = 11$ and $n_2 = 12$.)

$$\mu_R = \frac{n_1(n_1 + n_2 + 1)}{2} = \frac{11(11 + 12 + 1)}{2} = 132$$

$$\sigma_R = \sqrt{\frac{n_1 n_2 (n_1 + n_2 + 1)}{12}} = \sqrt{\frac{11 \cdot 12(11 + 12 + 1)}{12}} \approx 16.25$$

Sample test statistic

Since $n_1 = 11$ and $n_2 = 12$, the samples are large enough to assume that the rank R is approximately normally distributed. We convert the sample test statistic R to a z value using the following formula with $R = 98$, $\mu_R = 132$, and $\sigma_R \approx 16.25$:

$$z = \frac{R - \mu_R}{\sigma_R} \approx \frac{98 - 132}{16.25} \approx -2.09$$

Hypotheses

When using the rank-sum test, the null hypothesis is that the distributions are the same, while the alternate hypothesis is that the distributions are different. In the case of the Navy divers we have

> H_0: Decompression time distributions are the same.
>
> H_1: Decompression time distributions are different.

We'll test the decompression time distributions using level of significance 5%.

P-value

To find the *P*-value of the sample test statistic $z = -2.09$, we use the normal distribution (Table 5 of Appendix II) and the fact that we have a two-tailed test. Figure 12-3 shows the *P*-value.

The area to the left of -2.09 is 0.0183. This is a two-tailed test, so

$$P\text{-value} = 2(0.0183) = 0.0366$$

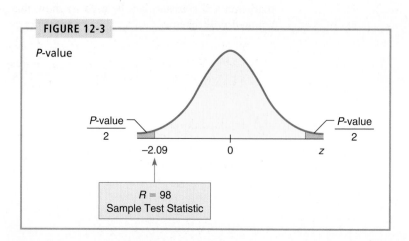

FIGURE 12-3

P-value

Since the *P*-value is less than $\alpha = 0.05$, we reject H_0. At the 5% level of significance, we have sufficient evidence to conclude that the pill changes decompression time for divers.

The steps necessary for a rank-sum test are summarized by the following procedure.

PROCEDURE

How to construct a rank-sum test

You first need independent random samples (both of size 11 or more) from two populations *A* and *B*. Let n_1 be the sample size of the smaller sample and let n_2 be the sample size of the larger sample. If the sample sizes are equal, then simply use the common value for n_1 and n_2. Next, you need to rank-order the data as if they were one big sample. Label each rank *A* or *B* according to the population from which it came. Let *R* be a random variable that represents the sum of ranks from the sample of size n_1. If $n_1 = n_2$, then *R* is the sum of ranks from either group (but not both).

1. Set the *level of significance* α. The *null* and *alternate hypotheses* are

    H_0: The two samples come from populations with the same distribution (the two populations are identical).

    H_1: The two samples come from populations with different distributions (the populations differ in some way).

2. The sample *test statistic* is

$$z = \frac{R - \mu_R}{\sigma_R}$$

    where R = sum of ranks from the sample of size n_1

$$\mu_R = \frac{n_1(n_1 + n_2 + 1)}{2}$$

$$\sigma_R = \sqrt{\frac{n_1 n_2 (n_1 + n_2 + 1)}{12}}$$

    and $n_1 > 10$, $n_2 > 10$.

3. Use the standard normal distribution with a two-tailed test to find the *P-value* corresponding to the test statistic.

4. *Conclude* the test. If *P*-value $\leq \alpha$, then reject H_0. If *P*-value $> \alpha$, then do not reject H_0.

5. *State your conclusion* in the context of the application.

◇ **NOTE** For the decompression time data, there were no ties for any rank. If a tie does occur, then each of the tied observations is given the *mean* of the ranks that they occupy. For example, if we rank the numbers

41   42   44   44   44   44

TABLE 12-6

Observation	Rank
41	1
42	2
44	4.5
44	4.5
44	4.5
44	4.5

we see that 44 occupies ranks three, four, five, and six. Therefore, we give each of the 44s a rank that is the mean of 3, 4, 5, and 6:

$$\text{Mean of ranks} = \frac{3 + 4 + 5 + 6}{4} = 4.5$$

The final ranking would then be that shown in Table 12-6. ◊

For samples wherein n_1 or n_2 is less than 11, there are statistical tables that give appropriate critical values for the rank-sum test. Most libraries contain such tables, and the interested reader can find such information by looking under the *Mann-Whitney U Test*.

GUIDED EXERCISE 4

Rank-sum test

A biologist is doing research on elk in their natural Colorado habitat. Two regions are under study, both with about the same amount of forage and natural cover. However, region A seems to have fewer predators than region B. To determine if there is a difference in elk life spans between the two regions, a sample of 11 mature elk from each region are tranquilized and have a tooth removed. A laboratory examination of the teeth reveals the ages of the elk. Results for each sample are given in Table 12-7. The biologist uses a 5% level of significance to test for a difference in life spans.

TABLE 12-7 Ages of Elk

Group A	4	10	11	2	2	3	9	4	12	6	6
Group B	7	3	8	4	8	5	6	4	2	4	3

(a) Fill in the remaining ranks of Table 12-8. Be sure to use the process of taking the mean of tied ranks.

TABLE 12-8 Ranks of Elk

Age	Group	Rank	Age	Group	Rank		Rank
2	A	2	5	B	12		12
2	A	2	6	A	—		14
2	B	2	6	A	—		14
3	A	5	6	B	—		14
3	B	5	7	B	—		16
3	B	5	8	B	—		17.5
4	A	9	8	B	—		17.5
4	A	9	9	A	—		19
4	B	9	10	A	—		20
4	B	9	11	A	—		21
4	B	9	12	A	—		22

Continued

GUIDED EXERCISE 4 continued

(b) What is α? State the null and alternate hypotheses.   ⟹ $\alpha = 0.05$

H_0: Distributions of life spans are the same.

H_1: Distributions of life spans are different.

(c) Find μ_R, σ_R, and R. Convert R to a sample z statistic.   ⟹   Since $n_1 = 11$ and $n_2 = 11$,

$$\mu_R = \frac{(11)(11 + 11 + 1)}{2} = 126.5$$

$$\sigma_R = \sqrt{\frac{11 \cdot 11(11 + 11 + 1)}{12}} \approx 15.23$$

Since $n_1 = n_2 = 11$, we can use the sum of the ranks of either the A group or the B group. Let's use the A group. The A group ranks are 2, 2, 5, 9, 9, 14, 14, 19, 20, 21, and 22. Therefore,

$R = 2 + 2 + 5 + 9 + 9 + 14 + 14 + 19 + 20 + 21 + 22 = 137$

$$z = \frac{R - \mu_R}{\sigma_R} = \frac{137 - 126.5}{15.23} \approx 0.69$$

(d) Find the *P*-value shown in Figure 12-4.   ⟹   Using Table 5 of Appendix II, the area to the right of 0.69 is 0.2451. Since this is a two-tailed test,

P-value = 2(0.2451) = 0.4902

FIGURE 12-4 *P*-value

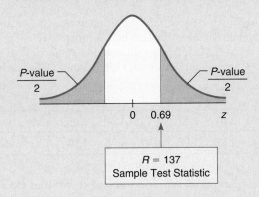

Comment: If we use the sum of ranks of group B, then $R_B = 116$ and $z = -0.69$. The *P*-value is again 0.4902, and we have the same conclusion.

(e) What is the conclusion?   ⟹   The *P*-value of 0.4902 is greater than $\alpha = 0.05$, so we do not reject H_0. The evidence does not support the claim that the age distribution of elk is different between the two regions.

VIEWPOINT   *Point Barrow, Alaska*

Point Barrow is located very near the northernmost point of land in the United States. In 1935, Will Rogers (an American humorist, social critic, and philosopher) was killed with Wiley Post (a pioneer aviator) at a landing strip near Point Barrow. Since 1920, a weather station at the (now named) Wiley Post–Will Rogers Memorial Landing Strip has recorded daily high and low temperatures. From these readings, annual mean maximum and minimum temperatures have been computed. Is Point Barrow warming up, cooling down, or neither? Can you think of a way to gather data and construct a nonparametric test to investigate long-term temperature highs and lows at Point Barrow? For weather-related data, visit the Brase/Brase statistics site at **http://math.college.hmco.com/students** and find a link to the Geophysical Institute at the University of Alaska in Fairbanks. Then follow the links to Point Barrow.

SECTION 12.2   PROBLEMS

For each problem, please provide the following information.
(a) What is the level of significance? State the null and alternate hypotheses.
(b) Compute the sample test statistic. What is the sampling distribution? What conditions are necessary to use this distribution?
(c) Find the *P*-value of the sample test statistic.
(d) Conclude the test.
(e) State the conclusion in the context of the application.

1. *Agriculture: Lima Beans* Are yields for organic farming different from conventional farming yields? Independent random samples from method A (organic farming) and method B (conventional farming) gave the following information about yield of lima beans (in tons/acre). (Reference: *Agricultural Statistics*, United States Department of Agriculture.)

Method A	1.83	2.34	1.61	1.99	1.78	2.01	2.12	1.15	1.41	1.95	1.25
Method B	2.15	2.17	2.11	1.89	1.34	1.88	1.96	1.10	1.75	1.80	1.53	2.21

Use a 5% level of significance to test that there is no difference between the yield distributions.

2. *Agriculture: Sweet Corn* Are yields for organic farming different from conventional farming yields? Independent random samples from method A (organic farming) and method B (conventional farming) gave the following information about yield of sweet corn (in tons/acre). (Reference: *Agricultural Statistics*, United States Department of Agriculture.)

Method A	6.88	6.86	7.12	5.91	6.80	6.92	6.25	6.98	7.21	7.33	5.85	6.72
Method B	5.71	6.93	7.05	7.15	6.79	6.87	6.45	7.34	5.68	6.78	6.95

Use a 5% level of significance to test the claim that there is no difference between the yield distributions.

3. *Horse Trainer: Jumps* A horse trainer teaches horses to jump by using two methods of instruction. Horses being taught by method A have a lead horse that accompanies each jump. Horses being taught by method B have no lead horse. The table shows the number of training sessions required before each horse would do the jumps properly.

Method A	28	35	19	41	37	31	38	40	25	27	36	43
Method B	42	33	26	24	44	46	34	20	48	39	45	

Use a 5% level of significance to test the claim that there is no difference between the training session distributions.

4. *Violent Crime: FBI Report* Is the crime rate in New York different from the crime rate in New Jersey? Independent random samples from region A (cities in New York) and region B (cities in New Jersey) gave the following information about violent crime rate (number of violent crimes per 100,000 population). (Reference: U.S. Department of Justice, Federal Bureau of Investigation.)

Region A	554	517	492	561	577	621	512	580	543	605	531	
Region B	475	419	505	575	395	433	521	388	375	411	586	415

Use a 5% level of significance to test the claim that there is no difference in the crime rate distributions of the two states.

5. *Psychology: Testing* A cognitive aptitude test consists of putting together a puzzle. Eleven people in group A took the test in a competitive setting (first and second to finish received a prize). Twelve people in group B took the test in a noncompetitive setting. The results follow (in minutes required to complete the puzzle).

Group A	7	12	10	15	22	17	18	13	8	16	11	
Group B	9	16	30	11	33	28	19	14	24	27	31	29

Use a 5% level of significance to test the claim that there is no difference in the distributions of time to complete the test.

6. *Psychology: Testing* A psychologist has developed a mental alertness test. She wishes to study the effects (if any) of type of food consumed on mental alertness. Twenty-one volunteers were randomly divided into two groups. Both groups were told to eat the amount they usually eat for lunch at noon. At 2:00 P.M., all subjects were given the alertness test. Group A had a low-fat lunch with no red meat, lots of vegetables, carbohydrates, and fiber. Group B had a high-fat lunch with red meat, vegetable oils, and low fiber. The only drink for both groups was water. The test scores are shown below.

Group A	76	93	52	81	68	79	88	90	67	85	60	
Group B	44	57	60	91	62	86	82	65	96	42	68	98

Use a 1% level of significance to test the claim that there is no difference in mental alertness distributions based on type of lunch.

7. *Lifestyles: Exercise* Is there a link between exercise and level of education? Independent random samples of adults from group A (college graduates) and group B (no high-school diploma) gave the following information about percentage who exercise regularly. (Reference: Centers for Disease Control and Prevention.)

A(%)	63.3	55.1	50.0	47.1	58.2	60.0	44.3	49.1	68.7	57.3	59.9	
B(%)	33.7	40.1	53.3	36.9	29.1	59.6	35.7	44.2	38.2	46.6	45.2	60.2

Use a 1% level of significance to test the claim that there is no difference in the exercise rate distributions according to education level.

8. *Doctor's Degree: Years of Study* Is the average length of time to earn a doctorate different from one field to another? Independent random samples from large graduate schools gave the following averages for length of registered time (in years) from bachelor's degree to doctorate. Sample A was taken from the humanities field, and sample B from the social sciences field. (Reference: *Education Statistics*, U.S. Department of Education.)

Field A	8.9	8.3	7.2	6.4	8.0	7.5	7.1	6.0	9.2	8.7	7.5	
Field B	7.6	7.9	6.2	5.8	7.8	8.3	8.5	7.0	6.3	5.4	5.9	7.7

Use a 1% level of significance to test the claim that there is no difference in the distributions of time to complete a doctorate for the two fields.

9. *Education: Spelling* Twenty-two fourth-grade children were randomly divided into two groups. Group A was taught spelling by a phonetic method. Group B was taught spelling by a memorization method. At the end of the fourth grade, all children were given a standard spelling exam. The scores are as follows.

Group A	77	95	83	69	85	92	61	79	87	93	65	78
Group B	62	90	70	81	63	75	80	72	82	94	65	79

Use a 1% level of significance to test the claim that there is no difference in the test score distributions based on instruction method.

10. *Industrial Chemistry: Cement* Dr. Hansen, an industrial chemist, has discovered a new catalyst that may affect the setting time of wet cement. Two groups of test slabs of cement were studied. Group A had no catalyst, and group B used the catalyst. The setting time for each slab was measured by Dr. Hansen. The results follow (in hours).

Group A	2.7	2.4	1.9	2.9	3.4	1.6	3.6	4.1	4.0	3.8	2.4	2.3
Group B	2.5	1.8	1.6	2.2	4.0	3.8	1.4	2.8	1.5	1.9	1.7	1.3

Use a 5% level of significance to test the claim that there is no difference in the setting time distributions based on the use of the catalyst.

12.3
Spearman Rank Correlation

FOCUS POINTS

✓ Learn about monotone relations and the Spearman rank correlation coefficient.

✓ Compute the Spearman correlation coefficient and conduct statistical tests for significance.

✓ Interpret the results in the context of the application.

Data given in ranked form (ordinal type) are different from data given in measurement form (interval or ratio type). For instance, if we compared the test performances of three students and, say, Elizabeth did the best, Joel did next best, and Sally did the worst, we are giving the information in ranked form. We cannot say how much better Elizabeth did than Sally or Joel, but we do know how the three scores compare. If the actual test scores for the three tests were given, we would have data in measurement form and could tell exactly how much better Elizabeth did than Joel or Sally. In Chapter 10, we studied linear correlation of data in measurement form. In this section, we will study correlation of data in ranked form.

As a specific example of a situation in which we might want to compare ranked data from two sources, consider the following. Hendricks College has a new faculty position in its political science department. A national search to fill this position has resulted in a large number of qualified candidates. The political science faculty reserves the right to make the final hiring decision. However, the faculty is interested in comparing its opinion with student opinion about the teaching ability of the candidates. A random sample of nine equally qualified candidates were asked to give a classroom presentation to a large class of students. Both faculty and students attended the lectures. At the end of each lecture, both faculty and students filled out a questionnaire about the teaching performance of the candidate. Based on these questionnaires, each candidate was given an overall rank from the faculty and an overall rank from the students. The results are shown in Table 12-9. Higher ranks mean better teaching performance.

Using data in ranked form, how can we answer the following questions:

1. Do candidates getting higher ranks from faculty tend to get higher ranks from students?

2. Is there any relation between faculty rankings and student rankings?

3. Do candidates getting higher ranks from faculty tend to get lower ranks from students?

We will use the Spearman rank correlation to answer such questions. In the early 1900s, Charles Spearman of the University of London developed the techniques that

TABLE 12-9   Faculty and Student Ranks of Candidates

Candidate	Faculty Rank	Student Rank
1	3	5
2	7	7
3	5	6
4	9	8
5	2	3
6	8	9
7	1	1
8	6	4
9	4	2

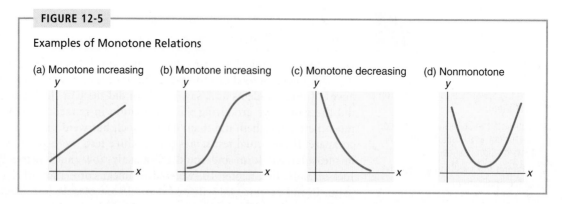

FIGURE 12-5

Examples of Monotone Relations

(a) Monotone increasing   (b) Monotone increasing   (c) Monotone decreasing   (d) Nonmonotone

now bear his name. The Spearman test of rank correlation requires us to use *ranked variables*. Because we are using only ranks, we cannot use the Spearman test to check on the existence of a linear relationship between the variables, as we did with the Pearson correlation coefficient (Section 10.1). The Spearman test checks only on the existence of a *monotone* relationship between the variables. (See Figure 12-5.) By a *monotone relationship** between variables x and y, we mean a relationship in which

1. as x increases, y also increases, or

2. as x increases, y decreases.

The relationship shown in Figure 12-5(d) is a nonmonotone relationship because as x increases, y at first decreases, but later starts to increase. Remember, for a relation to be monotone, as x increases, y must *always* increase or *always* decrease. In a nonmonotone relation, as x increases, y sometimes increases and sometimes decreases or stays unchanged.

GUIDED EXERCISE 5

Monotonic behavior

Identify each of the relations in Figure 12-6 as monotone increasing, monotone decreasing, or nonmonotone.

FIGURE 12-6

(a)   (b)   (c)   (d)

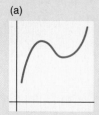   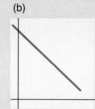   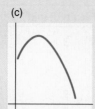   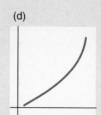

Answers: (a) nonmonotone, (b) monotone decreasing, (c) nonmonotone, (d) monotone increasing

*Some advanced texts call the monotone relationship we describe *strictly monotone*.

Before we can complete the solution of our problem about the political science department at Hendricks College, we need the following information.

Suppose we have a sample of size n of randomly obtained ordered pairs (x, y), where both the x and y values are from *ranked variables*. If there are no ties in the ranks, then the Pearson product moment correlation coefficient (Section 10.1) can be reduced to a simpler equation. The new equation produces the *Spearman rank correlation coefficient, r_s*.

Spearman rank correlation coefficient

Spearman rank correlation coefficient

$$r_s = 1 - \frac{6\Sigma d^2}{n(n^2 - 1)} \quad \text{where } d = x - y$$

The Spearman rank correlation coefficient has the following properties.

Properties of the Spearman rank correlation coefficient

1. $-1 \le r_s \le 1$. If $r_s = -1$, the relation between x and y is perfectly monotone decreasing. If $r_s = 0$, there is no monotone relation between x and y. If $r_s = 1$, the relation between x and y is perfectly monotone increasing. Values of r_s close to 1 or -1 indicate a strong tendency for x and y to have a monotone relationship (increasing or decreasing). Values of r_s close to 0 indicate a very weak (or perhaps nonexistent) monotone relationship.

2. The probability distribution of r_s depends on the sample size n. It is symmetric about $r_s = 0$. Table 9 of Appendix II gives critical values for certain specified one-tail and two-tail areas. Use of the table requires no assumptions that x and y are normally distributed variables. In addition, we make no assumption about the x and y relationship being linear.

3. The Spearman rank correlation coefficient r_s is the *sample* estimate for the *population* Spearman rank correlation coefficient ρ_s.

We construct a test of significance for the Spearman rank correlation coefficient in much the same way that we tested the Pearson correlation coefficient (Section 10.3). The null hypothesis states that there is no monotone relation between x and y (either increasing or decreasing).

Hypotheses

$$H_0: \rho_s = 0$$

The alternate hypothesis is one of the following:

$$H_1: \rho_s < 0 \qquad H_1: \rho_s > 0 \qquad H_1: \rho_s \ne 0$$
$$\text{(left-tailed)} \qquad \text{(right-tailed)} \qquad \text{(two-tailed)}$$

A left-tailed alternate hypothesis claims there is a monotone-decreasing relation between x and y. A right-tailed alternate hypothesis claims there is a monotone-increasing relation between x and y, while a two-tailed alternate hypothesis claims there is a monotone relation (either increasing or decreasing) between x and y.

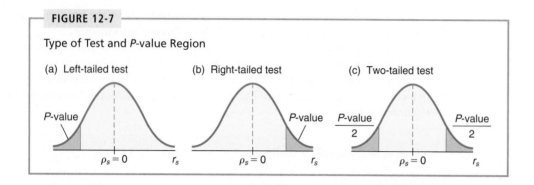

FIGURE 12-7

Type of Test and *P*-value Region

(a) Left-tailed test   (b) Right-tailed test   (c) Two-tailed test

Figure 12-7 shows the type of test and corresponding *P*-value region.

EXAMPLE 1

Testing the Spearman rank correlation coefficient

Using the information about the Spearman rank correlation coefficient, let's finish our problem about the search for a new member of the political science department at Hendricks College. Our work is organized in Table 12-10, where the rankings given by students and faculty are listed for each of the nine candidates.

(a) Using a 1% level of significance, let's test the claim that the faculty and students tend to agree about a candidate's teaching ability. This means that the x and y variables should be monotone increasing (as x increases, y increases). Since ρ_s is the population Spearman rank correlation coefficient, we have

$H_0: \rho_s = 0$ (There is no monotone relation.)

$H_1: \rho_s > 0$ (There is a monotone-increasing relation.)

(b) Compute the sample test statistic.

SOLUTION: Since the sample size is $n = 9$, and from Table 12-10 we see that $\Sigma d^2 = 16$, the Spearman rank correlation coefficient is

$$r_s = 1 - \frac{6\Sigma d^2}{n(n^2 - 1)} = 1 - \frac{6(16)}{9(81 - 1)} \approx 0.867$$

TABLE 12-10   **Student and Faculty Ranks of Candidates and Calculations for the Spearman Rank Correlation Test**

Candidate	Faculty Rank x	Student Rank y	$d = x - y$	d^2
1	3	5	−2	4
2	7	7	0	0
3	5	6	−1	1
4	9	8	1	1
5	2	3	−1	1
6	8	9	−1	1
7	1	1	0	0
8	6	4	2	4
9	4	2	2	4
				$\Sigma d^2 = 16$

P-value

(c) Find or estimate the *P*-value.

SOLUTION: To estimate the *P*-value for the sample test statistic $r_s = 0.867$, we use Table 9 of Appendix II. The sample size is $n = 9$ and the test is a one-tailed test. We find the location of the sample test statistic in row 9, and then read the corresponding one-tail area. From the Table 9, Appendix II excerpt, we see that the sample test statistic $r_s = 0.867$ falls between the entries 0.834 and 0.917 in the $n = 9$ row. These values correspond to *one-tail areas* between 0.005 and 0.001.

$$0.001 < P\text{-value} < 0.005$$

(d) Conclude the test.

SOLUTION:

✓ One-tail area	0.005	0.001
$n = 9$	0.834	0.917
		↑
	Sample $r_s = 0.867$	

Since the *P*-value is less than $\alpha = 0.01$, we reject H_0. At the 1% level of significance, we conclude that the relation between faculty and student ratings is monotone increasing. This means that faculty and students tend to rank the teaching performance of candidates in a similar way. Higher student ratings of a candidate correspond with higher faculty ratings of the same candidate.   ◇

The following procedure summarizes the steps involved in testing the Spearman rank correlation coefficient.

PROCEDURE

How to test the Spearman rank correlation coefficient ρ_s

You first need a random sample (of size *n*) of data pairs (*x*, *y*), where both the *x* and *y* values are *ranked* variables. Let ρ_s represent the population Spearman rank correlation coefficient, which is in theory computed from the population of all possible (*x*, *y*) data pairs.

1. Set the *level of significance* α. The *null hypothesis* is H_0: $\rho_s = 0$. In the context of the application, choose the *alternate hypothesis* to be H_1: $\rho_s > 0$ or H_1: $\rho_s < 0$ or H_1: $\rho_s \neq 0$.

2. If there are no ties in the ranks, or if the number of ties is small compared to the number of data pairs *n*, then compute the sample *test statistic*

$$r_s = 1 - \frac{6\Sigma d^2}{n(n^2 - 1)}$$

   where $d = x - y$ is the difference in ranks
   n = number of data pairs

   and the sum is over all sample data pairs.

3. Use Table 9 of Appendix II to find or estimate the *P-value* corresponding to r_s and n = number of data pairs.

4. *Conclude* the test. If *P*-value $\leq \alpha$, then reject H_0. If *P*-value $> \alpha$, then do not reject H_0.

5. *State your conclusion* in the context of the application.

GUIDED EXERCISE 6

Testing Spearman rank correlation coefficient

Fishermen in the Adirondack Mountains are complaining that acid rain caused by air pollution is killing fish in their region. To research this claim, a team of biologists studied a random sample of 12 lakes in the region. For each lake, they measured the level of acidity of rain in the drainage leading into the lake and the density of fish in the lake (number of fish per acre foot of water). They then did a ranking of x = acidity and y = density of fish. The results are shown in Table 12-11. Higher x ranks mean more acidity, and higher y ranks mean higher density of fish.

TABLE 12-11   Acid Rain and Density of Fish

Lake	Acidity x	Fish Density y	$d = x - y$	d^2
1	5	8	−3	9
2	8	6	2	4
3	3	9	−6	36
4	2	12	−10	100
5	6	7	−1	1
6	1	10	−9	81
7	10	2	8	64
8	12	1	——	——
9	7	5	——	——
10	4	11	——	——
11	9	4	——	——
12	11	3	——	——
			$\Sigma d^2 =$	——

(a) Complete the entries in the d and d^2 columns of Table 12-11, and find Σd^2.

Lake	x	y	d	d^2
8	12	1	11	121
9	7	5	2	4
10	4	11	−7	49
11	9	4	5	25
12	11	3	8	64
			$\Sigma d^2 =$	558

(b) Compute r_s.

$$r_s = 1 - \frac{6\Sigma d^2}{n(n^2 - 1)} = 1 - \frac{6(558)}{12(144 - 1)} \approx -0.951$$

(c) The fishermen claim that more acidity means lower density of fish. Does this claim state that x and y have a monotone-increasing relation, a monotone-decreasing relation, or no monotone relation?

The claim states that as x increases, y decreases, so the relation of x and y is monotone decreasing.

Continued

GUIDED EXERCISE 6 continued

(d) To test the fishermen's claim, what should we use for the null hypothesis and for the alternate hypothesis? Use $\alpha = 0.01$.

H_0: $\rho_s = 0$ (no monotone relation)

H_1: $\rho_s < 0$ (monotone-decreasing relation)

(e) Find the *P*-value of the sample test statistic $r_s = -0.951$.

Use Table 9 of Appendix II. There are $n = 12$ data pairs. The sample statistic r_s is negative. Because the r_s distribution is symmetric about 0, we look up the corresponding positive value 0.951 in the row headed by $n = 12$. Use one-tail areas, since this is a left-tailed test.

✓ One-tail area	0.001
$n = 12$	0.826

$\uparrow$
$-r_s = 0.951$

As positive r_s values increase, corresponding right-tail areas decrease. Therefore,

P-value < 0.001

(f) Use $\alpha = 0.01$ and conclude the test. Do the data support the claim that higher acidity means fewer fish?

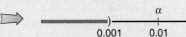

Since the *P*-value is less than $\alpha = 0.01$, we reject H_0 and conclude that there is a monotone-decreasing relationship between the acidity of the water and the number of fish. At the 1% level of significance, we conclude that higher acidity means fewer fish.

Ties of ranks

If ties occur in the assignment of ranks, we follow the usual method of averaging tied ranks. This method was discussed in Section 12.2 (The Rank-Sum Test). The next example illustrates the method.

◇ **COMMENT** Technically, the use of the given formula for r_s requires that there be no ties in rank. However, if the number of ties in rank is small relative to the number of ranks, the formula can be used with quite a bit of reliability.   ◇

EXAMPLE 2

Tied ranks

Do people who smoke more tend to drink more cups of coffee? The following data were obtained from a random sample of $n = 10$ cigarette smokers who also drink coffee.

Person	Cigarettes per Day	Cups of Coffee per Day
1	8	4
2	15	7
3	20	10
4	5	3
5	22	9
6	15	5
7	15	8
8	25	11
9	30	18
10	35	18

(a) To use the Spearman rank correlation test, we need to rank the data. It does not matter if we rank from smallest to largest or largest to smallest. The only requirement is that we be consistent in our rankings. Let us rank from smallest to largest.

First, we rank the data for each variable as though there were no ties; then we average the ties as shown in Tables 12-12 and 12-13.

TABLE 12-12   Rankings of Cigarettes Smoked per Day

Person	Cigarettes per Day	Rank	Average Rank x	
4	5	1	1	
1	8	2	2	
2	15 ⎫	3 ⎫	4 ⎫	Use the average rank for tied data.
6	15 ⎬ Ties	4 ⎬ Average rank is 4.	4 ⎬	
7	15 ⎭	5 ⎭	4 ⎭	
3	20	6	6	
5	22	7	7	
8	25	8	8	
9	30	9	9	
10	35	10	10	

TABLE 12-13   Rankings of Cups of Coffee per Day

Person	Cups of Coffee per Day	Rank	Average Rank y	
4	3	1	1	
1	4	2	2	
6	5	3	3	
2	7	4	4	
7	8	5	5	
5	9	6	6	
3	10	7	7	
8	11	8	8	
9	18 ⎫ Ties	9 ⎫ Average rank is 9.5.	9.5 ⎫	Use the average rank for tied data.
10	18 ⎭	10 ⎭	9.5 ⎭	

TABLE 12-14 Ranks to Be Used for a Spearman Rank Correlation Test

Person	Cigarette Rank x	Coffee Rank y	$d = x - y$	d^2
1	2	2	0	0
2	4	4	0	0
3	6	7	−1	1
4	1	1	0	0
5	7	6	1	1
6	4	3	1	1
7	4	5	−1	1
8	8	8	0	0
9	9	9.5	−0.5	0.25
10	10	9.5	0.5	0.25
				$\Sigma d^2 = 4.5$

(b) Using 0.01 as the level of significance, we test the claim that x and y have a monotone-increasing relationship. In other words, we test the claim that people who tend to smoke more tend to drink more cups of coffee (Table 12-14).

H_0: $\rho_s = 0$ (There is no monotone relation.)

H_1: $\rho_s > 0$ (Right-tailed test)

(c) Next, we compute the observed sample test statistic r_s using the results shown in Table 12-14.

$$r_s = 1 - \frac{6\Sigma d^2}{n(n^2 - 1)} = 1 - \frac{6(4.5)}{10(100 - 1)} \approx 0.973$$

(d) Find or estimate the P-value for the sample test statistic $r_s = 0.973$.
We use Table 9 of Appendix II to estimate the P-value. Using $n = 10$ and a one-tailed test, we see that $r_s = 0.973$ is to the right of the entry 0.879. Therefore, the P-value is smaller than 0.001.

✓ One-tail area	0.001
$n = 10$	0.879
	↑
	Sample $r_s = 0.973$

(e) Conclude the test.

Since the P-value is less than $\alpha = 0.01$, we reject H_0. At the 1% level of significance, it appears that there is a monotone-increasing relationship between the number of cigarettes smoked and the amount of coffee consumed. People who smoke more cigarettes tend to drink more coffee. ◊

VIEWP⊙INT **Rug Rats!**

When do babies start to crawl? Janette Benson, in her article "Infant Behavior and Development," claims that crawling age is related to temperature during the month in which babies first try to crawl. To find a data file for this subject, visit the Brase/Brase statistics site at **http://math.college.hmco.com/students** and find the link to DASL, the Carnegie Mellon University Data and Story Library. Then look under Psychology in the Data Subjects and select the Crawling Datafile. Can you think of a way to gather data and construct a nonparametric test to study this claim?

SECTION 12.3 PROBLEMS

For each problem, please provide the following information.
(a) What is the level of significance? State the null and alternate hypotheses.
(b) Compute the sample test statistic.
(c) Find or estimate the *P*-value of the sample test statistic.
(d) Conclude the test.
(e) State the conclusion in the context of the application.

1. *Training Program: Sales* A data processing company has a training program for new salespeople. After completing the training program, each trainee is ranked by his or her instructor. After a year of sales, the same class of trainees is again ranked by a company supervisor according to net value of the contracts they have acquired for the company. The results for a random sample of 11 salespeople trained in the last year follow, where *x* is rank in training class and *y* is rank in sales after 1 year. Lower ranks mean higher standing in class and higher net sales.

Person	1	2	3	4	5	6	7	8	9	10	11
x rank	6	8	11	2	5	7	3	9	1	10	4
y rank	4	9	10	1	6	7	8	11	3	5	2

Using a 0.05 level of significance, test the claim that the relation between *x* and *y* is monotone (either increasing or decreasing).

2. *Economics: Stocks* As an economics class project, Debbie studied a random sample of 14 stocks. For each of these stocks, she found the cost per share (in dollars) and ranked each of the stocks according to cost. After 3 months, she found the earnings per share on each stock (in dollars). Again, Debbie ranked each of the stocks according to earnings. The way Debbie ranked, higher ranks mean higher cost and higher earnings. The results follow, where *x* is the rank in cost and *y* is the rank in earnings.

Stock	1	2	3	4	5	6	7	8	9	10	11	12	13	14
x rank	5	2	4	7	11	8	12	3	13	14	10	1	9	6
y rank	5	13	1	10	7	3	14	6	4	12	8	2	11	9

Using a 0.01 level of significance, test the claim that there is a monotone relation, either way, between the ranks of cost and earnings.

3. *Psychology: Rat Colonies* A psychology professor is studying the relation between overcrowding and violent behavior in a rat colony. Eight colonies with different degrees of overcrowding are being used. By using a television monitor, lab assistants record incidents of violence. Each colony has been ranked for crowding and violence. A rank of 1 means most crowded or most violent. The results for the eight colonies are in the following table, with x being the population density rank and y the violence rank.

Colony	1	2	3	4	5	6	7	8
x rank	3	5	6	1	8	7	4	2
y rank	1	3	5	2	8	6	4	7

Using a 0.05 level of significance, test the claim that lower crowding ranks mean lower violence ranks (i.e., the variables have a monotone-increasing relationship).

4. *FBI Report: Murder and Arson* Is there a relation between murder and arson? A random sample of 15 Midwest cities (over 10,000 population) gave the following information about annual number of murder and arson cases. (Reference: Federal Bureau of Investigation, U.S. Department of Justice.)

City	1	2	3	4	5	6	7	8	9	10	11	12	13	14	15
Murder	12	7	25	4	10	15	9	8	11	18	23	19	21	17	6
Arson	62	12	153	2	36	93	31	29	47	131	175	129	162	115	4

(i) Rank-order murder using 1 as the largest data value. Also rank-order arson using 1 as the largest data value. Then construct a table of ranks to be used for a Spearman rank correlation test.

(ii) Use a 1% level of significance to test the claim that there is a monotone-increasing relationship between the ranks of murder and arson.

5. *Psychology: Testing* An army psychologist gave a random sample of seven soldiers a test to measure sense of humor and another test to measure aggressiveness. High scores mean greater sense of humor or more aggressiveness.

Soldier	1	2	3	4	5	6	7
Score on humor test	60	85	78	90	93	45	51
Score on aggressiveness test	78	42	68	53	62	50	76

(i) Ranking the data with rank 1 for highest score on a test, make a table of ranks to be used in a Spearman rank correlation test.

(ii) Using a 0.05 level of significance, test the claim that rank in humor has a monotone-decreasing relation to rank in aggressiveness.

6. *FBI Report: Child Abuse and Runaway Children* Is there a relation between incidents of child abuse and number of runaway children? A random sample of cities (over 10,000 population) gave the following information about the number of reported incidents of child abuse and the number of runaway children. (Reference: Federal Bureau of Investigation, U.S. Department of Justice.)

City	1	2	3	4	5	6	7	8	9	10	11	12	13	14	15
Abuse Cases	49	74	87	10	26	119	35	13	89	45	53	22	65	38	29
Runaways	382	510	581	163	210	791	275	153	491	351	402	209	410	312	210

(i) Rank-order abuse using 1 as the largest data value. Also rank-order runaways using 1 as the largest data value. Then construct a table of ranks to be used for a Spearman rank correlation test.

(ii) Use a 1% level of significance to test the claim that there is a monotone-increasing relationship between the ranks of incidents of abuse and number of runaway children.

7. *Demographics: Police and Fire Protection* Is there a relation between police protection and fire protection? A random sample of large population areas gave the following information about the number of local police and the number of local firefighters (units in thousands). (Reference: *Statistical Abstract of the United States*.)

Area	1	2	3	4	5	6	7	8	9	10	11	12	13
Police	11.1	6.6	8.5	4.2	3.5	2.8	5.9	7.9	2.9	18.0	9.7	7.4	1.8
Firefighters	5.5	2.4	4.5	1.6	1.7	1.0	1.7	5.1	1.3	12.6	2.1	3.1	0.6

(i) Rank-order police using 1 as the largest data value. Also rank-order firefighters using 1 as the largest data value. Then construct a table of ranks to be used for a Spearman rank correlation test.

(ii) Use a 5% level of significance to test the claim that there is a monotone relationship (either way) between the ranks of number of police and number of firefighters.

8. *Ecology: Wetlands* Turbid water is muddy or cloudy water. Sunlight is necessary for most life forms; thus turbid water is considered a threat to wetland ecosystems. Passive filtration systems are commonly used to reduce turbidity in wetlands. Suspended solids are measured in mg/l. Is there a relation between input and output turbidity for a passive filtration system and, if so, is it statistically significant? At a wetlands environment in Illinois, the inlet and outlet turbidity of a passive filtration system has been measured. A random sample of measurements are shown below. (Reference: *EPA Wetland Case Studies*.)

Reading	1	2	3	4	5	6	7	8	9	10	11	12
Inlet (mg/l)	8.0	7.1	24.2	47.7	50.1	63.9	66.0	15.1	37.2	93.1	53.7	73.3
Outlet (mg/l)	2.4	3.6	4.5	14.9	7.4	7.4	6.7	3.6	5.9	8.2	6.2	18.1

(i) Rank-order the inlet readings using 1 as the largest data value. Also rank-order the outlet readings using 1 as the largest data value. Then construct a table of ranks to be used for a Spearman rank correlation test.

(ii) Use a 1% level of significance to test the claim that there is a monotone relationship (either way) between the ranks of the inlet readings and outlet readings.

9. *Insurance: Sales* Big Rock Insurance Company did a study of per capita income and volume of insurance sales in eight Midwest cities. The volume of sales in the cities was ranked, with 1 being the largest volume. The per capita income was rounded to the nearest thousand dollars.

City	1	2	3	4	5	6	7	8
Volume of insurance sales rank	6	7	1	8	3	2	5	4
Per capita income in $1000	17	18	19	11	16	20	15	19

(i) Using a rank of 1 for the highest per capita income, make a table of ranks to be used for a Spearman rank correlation test.

(ii) Using a 0.01 level of significance, test the claim that there is a monotone relation (either way) between rank of sales volume and rank of per capita income.

10. *Economics: United States and Europe* Is there a relationship between the growth rates of Gross Domestic Product (GDP) in the United States and Europe? A random sample of recent years gave the following annual percent changes in GDP for the United States and Europe. (Reference: *Handbook of International Economic Statistics,* Government Documents.)

Year	1	2	3	4	5	6	7	8	9	10	11	12
U.S.	3.1	2.9	−1.0	2.7	2.2	3.5	2.0	2.8	3.8	2.5	2.9	3.3
Europe	3.0	2.4	2.7	0.9	−0.5	2.8	2.4	1.8	2.6	2.1	2.7	2.2

(i) Rank-order percent change in U.S. GDP, using 1 as the largest data value. Also rank-order percent change in European GDP using 1 as the largest data value. Then construct a table of ranks to be used for a Spearman rank correlation test.

(ii) Use a 5% level of significance to test the claim that there is a monotone relationship (either way) between the ranks of percent change in GDP for the U.S. and for Europe.

12.4
Runs Test for Randomness

FOCUS POINTS

✔ Test a sequence of *symbols* for randomness.

✔ Test a sequence of *numbers* for randomness around the median.

Astronomers have made an extensive study of galaxies that are ±16° above and below the celestial equator. Of special interest is the flux, or change in radio signals, that originates from large electromagnetic disturbances deep in space. The flux units (10^{-26} watts/m^2/Hz) are very small. However, modern radio astronomy can detect and analyze these signals using large antennas. (Reference: *Journal of Astrophysics,* vol. 148, pp. 321–365.)

A very important question is the following: Are changes in flux simply random, or is there some kind of non-random pattern? Let us use the symbol S to represent a strong or moderate flux, and the symbol W to represent a faint or weak flux. Astronomers have received the following signals in order of occurrence.

S S W W W S W W S S S W W W S S W W W S S

Is there a statistical test to help us decide whether or not this sequence of radio signals is random? Well, we're glad you asked, because that is the topic of this section.

We consider applications where *two* symbols are used (e.g., S or W). Applications using more than two symbols are left to specialized studies in mathematical combinatorics.

> A **sequence** is an *ordered set* of consecutive symbols.
>
> A **run** is a sequence of one or more occurrences of the *same* symbol.
>
> n_1 = number of times the first symbol occurs in a sequence
>
> n_2 = number of times the second symbol occurs in a sequence
>
> R is a random variable that represents the **number of runs in a sequence.**

EXAMPLE 3

Basic terminology

In this example we use the symbols S and W, where S is the first symbol and W is the second symbol, to demonstrate sequences and runs.

(a) S S W W W is a sequence.

SOLUTION: Table 12-15 shows the runs. There are $R = 2$ runs in the sequence. The first symbol S occurs $n_1 = 2$ times. The second symbol W occurs $n_2 = 3$ times.

TABLE 12-15   Runs

Run 1	Run 2
S S	W W W

(b) S S W W W S W W S S S S W is a sequence.

SOLUTION: The runs are shown in Table 12-16. There are $R = 6$ runs in the sequence. The first symbol S occurs $n_1 = 7$ times. The second symbol W occurs $n_2 = 6$ times.

TABLE 12-16   Runs

Run 1	Run 2	Run 3	Run 4	Run 5	Run 6
S S	W W W	S	W W	S S S S	W

Hypotheses

To test a sequence of two symbols for randomness, we use the following hypotheses.

Hypotheses for runs test of randomness

H_0: The symbols are randomly mixed in the sequence.

H_1: The symbols are not randomly mixed in the sequence.

The decision procedure will reject H_0 if either R is too small (too few runs) or R is too large (too many runs).

Sample test statistic

The number of runs R is a sample *test statistic* with its own sampling distribution. Table 10 of Appendix II gives critical values of R for a significance level $\alpha = 0.05$. There are two parameters associated with R. They are n_1 and n_2, the numbers of times the first and second symbols appear in the sequence, respectively. If either $n_1 > 20$ or $n_2 > 20$, you can apply the normal approximation to construct the test. This will be discussed in Problems 9 and 10 at the end of this section. For now we assume that $n_1 \leq 20$ and $n_2 \leq 20$.

Critical values

For each pair of n_1 and n_2 values, Table 10 of Appendix II provides two critical values: a smaller value denoted c_1 and a larger value denoted c_2. These two values are used to decide whether or not to reject the null hypothesis H_0, that the symbols are randomly mixed in the sequence.

> **Decision process: $n_1 \leq 20$ and $n_2 \leq 20$**
>
> Use Table 10 of Appendix II with n_1 and n_2 to find the critical values c_1 and c_2. At the $\alpha = 5\%$ level of significance, use the following decision process, where R is the number of runs. If either $R \leq c_1$ (too few runs) or $R \geq c_2$ (too many runs), then *reject* H_0. Otherwise, *do not reject* H_0.

Let's apply this decision process to the astronomy example regarding the sequence of strong and weak electromagnetic radio signals coming from a distant galaxy.

EXAMPLE 4

Runs test

Recall that our astronomers had received the following sequence of electromagnetic signals, where S represents a strong flux and W represents a weak flux.

S S W W W S W W S S S W W W S S W W W S S

Is this a random sequence or not? Use a 5% level of significance.

(a) What is the level of significance α? State the null and alternate hypotheses.

SOLUTION: $\alpha = 0.05$

H_0: The symbols S and W are randomly mixed in the sequence.

H_1: The symbols S and W are not randomly mixed in the sequence.

(b) Find the sample test statistic R and the parameters n_1 and n_2.

SOLUTION: We break the sequence according to runs.

Run 1	Run 2	Run 3	Run 4	Run 5	Run 6	Run 7	Run 8	Run 9
SS	WWW	S	WW	SSS	WWW	SS	WWW	SS

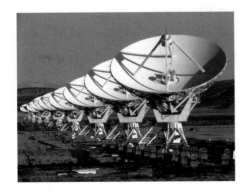

We see that there are $n_1 = 10$ S symbols and $n_2 = 11$ W symbols. The number of runs is $R = 9$.

(c) Use Table 10 of Appendix II to find the critical values c_1 and c_2.

SOLUTION: Since $n_1 = 10$ and $n_2 = 11$, then $c_1 = 6$ and $c_2 = 17$.

(d) Conclude the test.

SOLUTION:

$R \leq 6$	✓ $7 \leq R \leq 16$	$R \geq 17$
Reject H_0.	✓ Fail to reject H_0.	Reject H_0.

Since $R = 9$, we fail to reject H_0 at the 5% level of significance.

(e) Interpret the conclusion in the context of the problem.

SOLUTION: At the 5% level of significance, there is insufficient evidence to conclude that the sequence of electromagnetic signals is not random.   ◇

Randomness around the median

An important application of the runs test is to help us decide if a sequence of numbers is a random sequence around the median. This is done using the *median* of the sequence of numbers. The process is explained in the next example.

EXAMPLE 5

Runs test around the median

Silver-iodide seeding of summer clouds was done over the Santa Catalina mountains of Arizona. Of great importance is the direction of the wind during the seeding process. A sequence of consecutive days gave the following compass readings for wind direction at seeding level at 5 A.M. (0° represents true north). (Reference: *Proceedings of the National Academy of Science,* vol. 68, pp. 649–652.)

174	160	175	288	195	140	124	219	197	184
183	224	33	49	175	74	103	166	27	302
61	72	93	172						

We will test this sequence for randomness above and below the median using a 5% level of significance.

Part I: Adjust the sequence so that it has only two symbols, A and B.

SOLUTION: First rank-order the data and find the median (see Section 3.1). Doing this, we find the median to be 169. Next, give each data value in the original sequence the label A if it is *above* the median and the label B if it is *below* the median. Using the original sequence, we get

A | B | AAA | BB | AAAAA | BB | A | BBBB | A | BBB | A

We see that

$n_1 = 12$ (number of A's) $n_2 = 12$ (number of B's) $R = 11$ (number of runs)

Note: In this example, none of the data values actually equals the median. If a data value *equals the median,* we put neither A nor B in the sequence. This eliminates from the sequence any data values that equal the median.

Part II: Test the sequence of A and B symbols for randomness.

(a) What is the level of significance α? State the null and alternate hypotheses.

SOLUTION: $\alpha = 0.05$

H_0: The symbols A and B are randomly mixed in the sequence.

H_1: The symbols A and B are not randomly mixed in the sequence.

(b) Find the sample test statistic R and the parameters n_1 and n_2.

SOLUTION: As shown in Part I, for the sequence of A's and B's,

$n_1 = 12; n_2 = 12; R = 11$

(c) Use Table 10 of Appendix II to find the critical values c_1 and c_2.

SOLUTION: Since $n_1 = 12$ and $n_2 = 12$, we find $c_1 = 7$ and $c_2 = 19$.

(d) Conclude the test.

SOLUTION:

$R \leq 7$	✓ $8 \leq R \leq 18$	$R \geq 19$
Reject H_0.	✓ Fail to reject H_0.	Reject H_0.

Since $R = 11$, we fail to reject H_0 at the 5% level of significance.

(e) Interpret the conclusion in the context of the problem.

SOLUTION: At the 5% level of significance, there is insufficient evidence to conclude that the sequence of wind directions above and below the median direction is not random. ◊

PROCEDURE

How to construct a runs test for randomness

You need a sequence (ordered set) consisting of two symbols. If your sequence consists of measurements of some type, then convert it to a sequence of two symbols in the following way:

(a) Find the median of the entries in the sequence.

(b) Label an entry A if it is above the median and B if it is below the median. If an entry equals the median, then put neither A nor B in the sequence.

Now you have a sequence with two symbols.

Let n_1 = number of times the first symbol occurs in the sequence.

n_2 = number of times the second symbol occurs in the sequence.

Note: Either symbol can be called the "first" symbol.

Let R = number of runs in the sequence.

1. The *level of significance is* $\alpha = 0.05$. The *null and alternate hypotheses* are:

   H_0: The two symbols are randomly mixed in the sequence.

   H_1: The two symbols are not randomly mixed in the sequence.

2. The sample *test statistic* is the number of runs R.

3. Use Table 10, Appendix II with parameters n_1 and n_2 to find the *lower and upper critical values* c_1 and c_2.

4. Use the *critical values* c_1 and c_2 in the following *decision process.*

$R \leq c_1$	$c_1 + 1 \leq R \leq c_2 - 1$	$R \geq c_2$
Reject H_0.	Fail to reject H_0.	Reject H_0.

5. *State your conclusion* in the context of the application.

   Note: If your original sequence consisted of measurements (not just symbols), it is important to remember that you are testing for randomness about the median of these measurements. In any case, you are testing for randomness regarding a mix of two symbols in a given sequence.

◊ **COMMENT:** In many applications, $n_1 \leq 20$ and $n_2 \leq 20$. What happens if either $n_1 > 20$ or $n_2 > 20$? In this case, you can use the normal approximation, which is presented in Problems 9 and 10 at the end of this section.   ◊

GUIDED EXERCISE 7

Runs test for randomness on two symbols

The majority party of the United States Senate from 1973 to 2003 is shown below, where D and R represent Democrat and Republican, respectively. (Reference: *Statistical Abstract of the United States.*)

D   D   D   D   R   R   R   D   D   D   D   R   R   R   R   D   D   R

Test the sequence for randomness. Use a 5% level of significance.

(a) What is α? State the null and alternate hypotheses.

⇨ $\alpha = 0.05$

H_0: The two symbols are randomly mixed.

H_1: The two symbols are not randomly mixed.

(b) Block the sequence into runs. Find the values of n_1, n_2, and R.

⇨ DDDD | RRR | DDDD | RRRR | DD | R

Letting D be the first symbol, we have

$n_1 = 10$; $n_2 = 8$; $R = 6$

(c) Use Table 10 of Appendix II to find the critical values c_1 and c_2.

⇨ Lower critical value $c_1 = 5$

Upper critical value $c_2 = 15$

(d) Using critical values, do you reject or fail to reject H_0?

⇨

$R \leq 5$	✓ $6 \leq R \leq 14$	$R \geq 15$
Reject H_0.	✓ Fail to reject H_0.	Reject H_0.

Since $R = 6$, we fail to reject H_0.

(e) State the conclusion in the context of the application.

⇨ The sequence of party control of the U.S. Senate appears to be random. At the 5% level of significance, the evidence is insufficient to reject H_0, that the sequence is random.

GUIDED EXERCISE 8

Runs test for randomness about the median

The national percentage distribution of burglaries is shown by month starting in January. (Reference: *FBI Crime Report,* U.S. Department of Justice.)

7.8   6.7   7.6   7.7   8.3   8.2   9.0   9.1   8.6   9.3   8.8   8.9

Continued

GUIDED EXERCISE 8 continued

Test the sequence for randomness about the median. Use a 5% level of significance.

(a) What is α? State the null and alternate hypotheses.

⟹ $\alpha = 0.05$

H_0: The sequence of values above and below the median is random.

H_1: The sequence of values above and below the median is not random.

(b) Find the median. Assign the symbol A to values above the median and the symbol B to values below the median. Next block the sequence of A's and B's into runs. Find n_1, n_2, and R.

⟹ First order the numbers. Then find the median. Median = 8.45. The original sequence translates to

BBBBBB | AAAAAA

$n_1 = 6$; $n_2 = 6$; $R = 2$

(c) Use Table 10 of Appendix II to find the critical values c_1 and c_2.

⟹ Lower critical value $c_1 = 3$
Upper critical value $c_2 = 11$

(d) Using the critical values, do you reject or fail to reject H_0?

⟹

✓ $R \leq 3$	$4 \leq R \leq 10$	$R \geq 11$
✓ Reject H_0.	Fail to reject H_0.	Reject H_0.

Since $R = 2$, we reject H_0.

(e) Interpret the conclusion in the context of the application.

⟹ At the 5% level of significance, there is sufficient evidence to claim that the sequence of burglaries is not random about the median. It appears that from January to June, there tend to be fewer burglaries.

TECH NOTE **Minitab** Enter your sequence of numbers in a column. Use the menu choices **Stat ➤ Nonparametrics ➤ Runs.** In the dialogue box, select the column containing the sequence. The default is to test the sequence for randomness above and below the mean. Otherwise, you can test for randomness above and below any other value, such as the median.

SECTION 12.4   PROBLEMS

For Problems 1–8, please provide the following information.
(a) What is the level of significance? State the null and alternate hypotheses.
(b) Find the sample test statistic R, the number of runs.
(c) Find the upper and lower critical values in Table 10 of Appendix II.
(d) Conclude the test.
(e) State the conclusion in the context of the application.

1. *Presidents: Party Affiliation* For each successive presidential term, the party affiliation controlling the White House from Teddy Roosevelt to George W. Bush (initial term) is shown below, where R designates Republican and D designates Democrat. (Reference: *The New York Times Almanac.*)

   R R R D D R R D D D D D R D R R D R R R D D R

   Historical Note: In cases where a president died in office or resigned, the period during which the vice president finished the term is not counted as a new term. Test the sequence for randomness. Use $\alpha = 0.05$.

2. *Congress: Party Affiliation* The majority party of the United States House of Representatives from 1973 to 2003 is shown below, where D and R represent Democrat and Republican, respectively. (Reference: *Statistical Abstract of the United States.*)

   D D D D D D D D D D D R R R R R R R

   Test the sequence for randomness. Use $\alpha = 0.05$.

3. *Cloud Seeding: Arizona* Researchers experimenting with cloud seeding in Arizona want a random sequence of days for their experiments. (Reference: *Proceedings of the National Academy of Science,* vol. 68, pp. 649–652.) Suppose they have the following itinerary for consecutive days, where S indicates a day for cloud seeding and N a day for no cloud seeding.

   S S S N S N S S S S N N S N S S S N N S S S

   Test this sequence for randomness. Use $\alpha = 0.05$.

4. *Astronomy: Earth's Rotation* Changes in the earth's rotation are exceedingly small. However, a very long term trend could be important. (Reference: *Journal of Astronomy,* vol. 57, pp. 125–146.) Let I represent an increase and D a decrease in the rate of the earth's rotation. The following sequence represents historical increases and decreases measured every consecutive fifth year.

   D D D D I I I D D D D D I I I I I I I I I D I I I I I

   Test the sequence for randomness. Use $\alpha = 0.05$.

5. *Random Walk: Stocks* Many economists and financial experts claim that the *price level* of a stock or bond is not random, but the *price changes* tend to follow a random sequence over time. The following data represent annual percentage returns on Vanguard Total Stock Index for a sequence of recent years. This fund represents nearly all publicly traded U.S. stocks. (Reference: *Morningstar Mutual Fund Analysis.*)

10.4	10.6	−0.2	35.8	21.0	31.0	23.3	23.8	−10.6
−11.0	−21.0	12.8						

   (i) Convert this sequence of numbers to a sequence of symbols A and B, where A indicates a value above the median and B a value below the median.
   (ii) Test the sequence for randomness about the median. Use $\alpha = 0.05$.

6. *Random Walk: Bonds* The following data represent annual percentage returns on Vanguard Total Bond Index for a sequence of recent years. This fund represents nearly all publicly traded U.S. bonds. (Reference: *Morningstar Mutual Fund Analysis.*)

7.1	9.7	−2.7	18.2	3.6	9.4	8.6	−0.8	11.4
8.4	8.3	0.8						

(i) Convert this sequence of numbers to a sequence of symbols A and B, where A indicates a value above the median and B a value below the median.

(ii) Test the sequence for randomness about the median. Use $\alpha = 0.05$.

7. *Civil Engineering: Soil Profiles* Sand and clay studies were conducted at the West Side Field Station of the University of California. (Reference: Professor D. R. Nielsen, University of California, Davis.) Twelve consecutive depths, each about 15 cm deep, were studied and the following percentages of sand in the soil were recorded.

19.0	27.0	30.0	24.3	33.2	27.5	24.2
18.0	16.2	8.3	1.0	0.0		

(i) Convert this sequence of numbers to a sequence of symbols A and B, where A indicates a value above the median and B a value below the median.

(ii) Test the sequence for randomness about the median. Use $\alpha = 0.05$.

8. *Civil Engineering: Soil Profiles* Sand and clay studies were conducted at the West Side Field Station of the University of California. (Reference: Professor D. R. Nielsen, University of California, Davis.) Twelve consecutive depths, each about 15 cm deep, were studied and the following percentages of clay in the soil were recorded.

47.4	43.4	48.4	42.6	41.4	40.7	46.4
44.8	36.5	35.7	33.7	42.6		

(i) Convert this sequence of numbers to a sequence of symbols A and B, where A indicates a value above the median and B a value below the median.

(ii) Test the sequence for randomness about the median. Use $\alpha = 0.05$.

9. *Expand Your Knowledge: Either $n_1 > 20$ or $n_2 > 20$* For each successive presidential term, the party affiliation controlling the White House from Franklin Pierce (the 14th president, elected in 1853) to George W. Bush (43rd president) is shown below, where R designates Republican and D designates Democrat. (Reference: *The New York Times Almanac.*)

Historical Note: We start this sequence with the 14th president because earlier presidents belonged to political parties such as the Federalist or Wigg party (not Democratic or Republican). In cases where a president died in office or resigned, the period during which the vice president finished the term is not counted as a new term. The one exception is the case in which Lincoln (a Republican) was assassinated and the vice president Johnson (a Democrat) finished the term.

D D R R D R R R D R D R R R D D R R

D D D D D R R D D R R D R R R D D R

Test the sequence for randomness at the 5% level of significance. Use the following outline.

(a) State the null and alternate hypotheses.

(b) Find the number of runs R, n_1, and n_2. Let n_1 = number of Republicans and n_2 = number of Democrats.

(c) In this case, $n_1 = 21$, so we cannot use Table 10 of Appendix II to find the critical values. Whenever either n_1 or n_2 exceeds 20, the number of runs R has a distribution that is approximately normal with

$$\mu_R = \frac{2n_1 n_2}{n_1 + n_2} + 1 \quad \text{and} \quad \sigma_R = \sqrt{\frac{(2n_1 n_2)(2n_1 n_2 - n_1 - n_2)}{(n_1 + n_2)^2 (n_1 + n_2 - 1)}}$$

We convert the number of runs R to a z value, and then use the normal distribution to find the critical values. Convert the sample test statistic R to z using the formula

$$z = \frac{R - \mu_R}{\sigma_R}$$

(d) The critical values of a normal distribution for a two-tailed test with level of significance $\alpha = 0.05$ are -1.96 and 1.96 (see Table 5(c) of Appendix II). Reject H_0 if the sample test statistic $z \leq -1.96$ or if the sample test statistic $z \geq 1.96$. Otherwise, do not reject H_0.

Sample $z \leq -1.96$	$-1.96 <$ sample $z < 1.96$	Sample $z \geq 1.96$
Reject H_0.	Fail to reject H_0.	Reject H_0.

Using this decision process, do you reject or fail to reject H_0 at the 5% level of significance? What is the P-value for this two-tailed test? At the 5% level of significance, do you reach the same conclusion using the P-value that you reach using critical values? Explain.

(e) Interpret your results in the context of the application.

10. *Expand Your Knowledge: Either $n_1 > 20$ or $n_2 > 20$* Professor Cornish studied rainfall cycles and sunspot cycles. (Reference: *Australian Journal of Physics*, vol. 7, pp. 334–346.) Part of the data include amount of rain (in mm) for 6-day intervals. The following data give rain amounts for consecutive 6-day intervals at Adelaide, South Australia.

6	29	6	0	68	0	0	2	23	5	18	0	50	163
64	72	26	0	0	3	8	142	108	3	90	43	2	5
0	21	2	57	117	51	3	157	43	20	14	40	0	23
18	73	25	64	114	38	31	72	54	38	9	1	17	0
13	6	2	0	1	5	9	11						

Verify that the median is 17.5.
(a) Convert this sequence of numbers to a sequence of symbols A and B, where A indicates a value above the median and B a value below the median.
(b) Test the sequence for randomness about the median at the 5% level of significance. Use the large sample theory outlined in Problem 9.

SUMMARY

When we cannot assume that data come from a normal, binomial, or Student's t distribution, we can employ tests that make no assumptions about data distribution. Such tests are called nonparametric tests. We studied four widely used tests: the sign test, the rank-sum test, the Spearman rank correlation coefficient test, and the runs test for randomness. Nonparametric tests have the advantage of being easy to use; however, they do tend to waste information and to be less sensitive than standard tests. It is usually good advice to use standard tests when possible, keeping nonparametric tests for situations wherein assumptions about the data distribution cannot be made.

IMPORTANT WORDS & SYMBOLS

Section 12.1
Nonparametric statistics
Sign test

Section 12.2
Rank-sum test

Section 12.3
Spearman rank correlation coefficient r_s

Section 12.4
Sequence
Run
Runs test for randomness

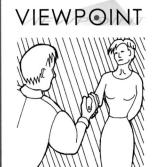

VIEWPOINT   *Lending a Hand*

Whom would you ask for help if you were sick? in need of money? upset with your spouse? depressed? Consider the following claims: People look to sisters for emotional help and brothers for physical help. After that, people look to parents, clergy, or friends. Can you think of nonparametric tests to study such claims? For more information, see *American Demographics*, vol. 18, no. 8.

CHAPTER REVIEW PROBLEMS

For each problem, please provide the following information.
(a) State the test used.
(b) Give α. State the null and alternate hypotheses.
(c) Find the sample test statistic.
(d) For the sign test, rank-sum test, and Spearman correlation coefficient test, find the *P*-value of the sample test statistic. For the runs test of randomness, find the critical values from Table 10 of Appendix II.
(e) Conclude the test and interpret the results in the context of the application.

1. *Chemistry: Lubricant* In the production of synthetic motor lubricant from coal, a new catalyst has been discovered that seems to affect the viscosity index of the lubricant. In an experiment consisting of 23 production runs, 11 used the new catalyst and 12 did not. After each production run, the viscosity index of the lubricant was determined to be as follows.

With catalyst	1.6	3.2	2.9	4.4	3.7	2.5	1.1	1.8	3.8	4.2	4.1	
Without catalyst	3.9	4.6	1.5	2.2	2.8	3.6	2.4	3.3	1.9	4.0	3.5	3.1

The two samples are independent. Use a 0.05 level of significance to test the null hypothesis that the viscosity index is unchanged by the catalyst against the alternate hypothesis that the viscosity index has changed.

2. *Self-Improvement: Memory* Professor Adams wrote a book called *Improving Your Memory*. The professor claims that if you follow the program outlined in the book, your memory will definitely improve. Fifteen people took the professor's course, in which the book and its program were used. On the first day of class, everyone took a memory exam; and on the last day, everyone took a similar exam. The paired scores for each person follow.

Last exam	225	120	115	275	85	76	114	200	99	135	170	110	216	280	78
First exam	175	110	115	200	60	85	160	190	70	110	140	10	190	200	92

Use a 0.05 level of significance to test the null hypothesis that the scores are the same whether or not people have taken the course against the alternate hypothesis that the scores of people who have taken the course are higher.

3. *Sales: Paint* A chain of hardware stores is trying to sell more paint by mailing pamphlets describing the paint. In 15 communities containing one of these hardware stores, the paint sales (in dollars) were recorded for the months before and after the ads were sent out. The paired results for each store follow.

Sales after	610	150	790	288	715	465	280	640	500	118	265	365	93	217	280
Sales before	460	216	640	250	685	430	220	470	370	118	117	360	93	291	430

Use a 0.01 level of significance to test the null hypothesis that the advertising had no effect on sales against the alternate hypothesis that it improved sales.

4. *Dogs: Obedience School* An obedience school for dogs experimented with two methods of training. One method involved rewards (food, praise); the other involved no rewards. The dogs are randomly placed into two independent groups of 11 each. The number of sessions required to train each of 22 dogs follows.

With rewards	12	17	15	10	16	20	9	23	8	14	10
No rewards	19	22	11	18	13	25	24	28	21	20	21

Use a 0.05 level of significance to test the hypothesis that the number of sessions was the same for the two groups against the alternate hypothesis that the number of sessions was not the same.

5. *Training Program: Fast Food* At McDouglas Hamburger stands, each employee must undergo a training program before he or she is hired. A group of nine people went through the training program and were hired to work in the Teton Park McDouglas Hamburger stand. Rankings in performance after the training program and after one month on the job are shown (a rank of 1 is for best performance).

Employee	1	2	3	4	5	6	7	8	9
Rank, training program	8	9	7	3	6	4	1	2	5
Rank on job	9	8	6	7	5	1	3	4	2

Using a 0.05 level of significance, test the claim that there is a monotone-increasing relation between rank in the training program and rank in performance on the job.

6. *Cooking School: Chocolate Mousse* Two expert French chefs judged chocolate mousse made by students in a Paris cooking school. Each chef ranked the best chocolate mousse as 1.

Student	1	2	3	4	5
Rank by Chef Pierre	4	2	3	1	5
Rank by Chef André	4	1	2	3	5

Use a 0.10 level of significance to test the claim that there is a monotone relation (either way) between ranks given by Chef Pierre and Chef André.

7. *Education: True–False Questions* Dr. Gill wants to arrange the answers to a true–false exam in random order. The answers in order of occurrence are shown below.

T T T F T T T F F T T T T T F F F F F F T T T T T T

Test the sequence for randomness using $\alpha = 0.05$.

8. *Agriculture: Wheat* For the past 16 years, the yields of wheat (in tons) grown on a plot at Rothamsted Experimental Station (England) are shown below. The sequence is by year.

3.8   1.9   0.6   1.7   2.0   3.5   3.0   1.4   2.7   2.3   2.6   2.1

2.4   2.7   1.8   1.9

Use level of significance 5% to test for randomness about the median.

DATA HIGHLIGHTS: GROUP PROJECTS

Break into small groups and discuss the following topics. Organize a brief outline in which you summarize the main points of your group discussion.

In the world of business and economics, to what extent do assets determine profits? Do the big companies with large assets always make more profits? Is there a rank correlation between assets and profits? The following table is based on information taken from *Fortune* (vol. 135, no. 8). A rank of 1 means highest profits or highest assets. The companies are food service companies.

Company	Asset Rank	Profit Rank
Pepsico	4	2
McDonald's	1	1
Aramark	6	4
Darden Restaurants	7	5
Flagstar	11	11
VIAD	10	8
Wendy's International	2	3
Host Marriott Services	9	10
Brinker International	5	7
Shoney's	3	6
Food Maker	8	9

(a) Compute the Spearman rank correlation coefficient for these data.

(b) Using a 5% level of significance, test the claim that there is a monotone-increasing relation between the ranks of earnings and growth.

(c) Decide whether you should reject or not reject the null hypothesis. State your conclusion in the context of the problem.

(d) As an investor, what are some other features of food companies that you might be interested in ranking? Identify any such features that you think might have a monotone relation.

LINKING CONCEPTS: WRITING PROJECTS

Discuss each of the following topics in class or review the topics on your own. Then write a brief but complete essay in which you summarize the main points. Please include formulas and graphs as appropriate.

1. (a) What do we mean by the term *nonparametric statistics*? What do we mean by the term *parametric statistics*? How do nonparametric methods differ from the methods we studied earlier?

   (b) What are the advantages of nonparametric statistical methods? How can they be used in problems to which other methods we have learned would not apply?

   (c) Are there disadvantages to nonparametric statistical methods? What do we mean when we say that nonparametric methods tend to waste information? Why do we say that nonparametric methods are not as *sensitive* as parametric methods?

   (d) List three random variables from ordinary experience to which you think nonparametric methods would definitely apply and parametric methods would be questionable.

2. Outline the basic logic and ideas behind the sign test. Describe how the binomial probability distribution was used in the construction of the sign test. What assumptions must be made about the sign test? Why is the sign test so extremely general in its possible applications? Why is it a special test for "before-and-after" studies?

3. Outline the basic logic and ideas behind the rank-sum test. Under what conditions would you use the rank-sum test and *not* the sign test? What assumptions must be made about the rank-sum test? List two advantages the rank-sum test has that the methods of Section 9.5 do not have. List some advantages the methods of Section 9.5 have that the rank-sum test does not have.

4. What do we mean by a monotone relationship between two variables x and y? What do we mean by ranked variables? Give a graphic example of two variables x and y that have a monotone relationship but do *not* have a linear relationship. Does the Spearman test check for a monotone relationship or a linear relationship? Under what conditions does the Pearson product moment correlation coefficient reduce to the Spearman rank correlation coefficient? Summarize the basic logic and ideas behind the test for Spearman rank correlation. List variables x and y from daily experience for which you think a strong Spearman rank correlation coefficient exists, although the variables are *not* linearly related.

5. What do we mean by a runs test for randomness? What is a run in a sequence? How can we test for randomness about the median? Why is this an important concept? List at least three applications from your own experience.

Cumulative Review Problems

CHAPTERS 10–12

1. *Linear Regression: Blood Glucose* Let x be a random variable that represents blood glucose level after a 12-hour fast. Let y be a random variable representing blood glucose level 1 hour after drinking sugar water (after the 12-hour fast). Units are in mg/10 ml. A random sample of eight adults gave the following information. (Reference: *American Journal of Clinical Nutrition*, vol. 19, pp. 345–351.)

x	6.2	8.4	7.0	7.5	8.1	6.9	10.0	9.7
y	9.8	10.7	10.3	11.9	14.2	7.0	14.6	12.2

$$\Sigma x = 63.8; \Sigma x^2 = 521.56; \Sigma y = 90.7; \Sigma y^2 = 1070.87; \Sigma xy = 739.65$$

(a) Draw a scatter diagram for the data.

(b) Find the equation of the least-squares line and graph it on the scatter diagram.

(c) Find the sample correlation coefficient r and the sample coefficient of determination r^2. Explain the meaning of r^2 in the context of the application.

(d) If $x = 9.0$, use the least-squares line to predict y. Find an 80% confidence interval for your prediction.

(e) Use level of significance 1% and test the claim that the population correlation coefficient ρ is not zero.

(f) Find an 85% confidence interval for the slope β of the population-based least-squares line. Explain its meaning in the context of the application.

2. *Goodness-of-Fit Test: Rare Events* This cumulative review problem uses material from Chapters 3, 5, and 11. Recall that the Poisson distribution deals with rare events. Death from the kick of a horse is a rare event, even in the Prussian army. The following data are a classic example of a Poisson application to rare events. A reproduction of the original data can be found in C. P. Winsor, *Human Biology*, vol. 19, pp. 154–161. The data represent the number of deaths from the kick of a horse per army corps per year for 10 Prussian army corps for 20 years (1875–1894). Let x represent the number of deaths and f the frequency of x deaths.

x	0	1	2	3 or more
f	109	65	22	4

(a) First we fit the data to a Poisson distribution (see Section 5.4).

Poisson distribution: $P(x) = \dfrac{e^{-\lambda}\lambda^x}{x!}$ where $\lambda \approx \bar{x}$ (sample mean of x values)

From our study of weighted averages (see Section 3.1),

$$\bar{x} = \frac{\Sigma xf}{\Sigma f}$$

Verify that $\bar{x} \approx 0.61$. *Hint:* For the category 3 or more, use 3.

(b) Now we have $P(x) = \dfrac{e^{-0.61}(0.61)^x}{x!}$ for $x = 0, 1, 2, 3, \ldots$.

Find $P(0)$, $P(1)$, $P(2)$, and $P(3 \le x)$. Round to 3 places after the decimal.

(c) The total number of observations was $\Sigma f = 200$. For a given x, the expected frequency of x deaths is $200P(x)$. The following table gives the observed frequencies O and the expected frequencies $E = 200P(x)$.

x	$O = f$	$E = 200P(x)$
0	109	$200(0.543) = 108.6$
1	65	$200(0.331) = 66.2$
2	22	$200(0.101) = 20.2$
3 or more	4	$200(0.025) = 5$

Compute $\chi^2 = \Sigma \dfrac{(O - E)^2}{E}$.

(d) State the null and alternate hypotheses for a chi-square goodness-of-fit test. Set the level of significance to be $\alpha = 0.01$. Find the P-value for a goodness-of-fit test. State your conclusion in the context of this application. Is there reason to believe that the Poisson distribution fits the raw data provided by the Prussian army? Explain.

3. *Test of Independence: Agriculture* Three types of fertilizer were used on 132 identical plots of maize. Each plot was harvested and the yield (in kg) was recorded. (Reference: Caribbean Agricultural Research and Development Institute.)

Yield (kg)	Type of Fertilizer			Row Total
	I	II	III	
0–2.9	12	10	15	37
3.0–5.9	18	21	11	50
6.0–8.9	16	19	10	45
Column total	46	50	36	132

Use a 5% level of significance to test the hypothesis that type of fertilizer and yield of maize are independent.

4. *Testing and Estimating Variances: Iris* Random samples of two species of iris gave the following petal lengths (in cm). (Reference: R. A. Fisher, *Annals of Eugenics*, vol. 7.)

x_1, Iris virginica	5.1	5.9	4.5	4.9	5.7	4.8	5.8	6.4	5.6	5.9
x_2, Iris versicolor	4.5	4.8	4.7	5.0	3.8	5.1	4.4	4.2		

(a) Use a 5% level of significance to test the claim that the population standard deviation of x_1 is larger than 0.55.
(b) Find a 90% confidence interval for the population standard deviation of x_1.
(c) Use a 1% level of significance to test the claim that the population variance of x_1 is larger than that of x_2.

5. *Sign Test: Wind Direction* The following data are paired by date. Let x and y be random variables representing wind direction at 5 A.M. and 5 P.M., respectively (units are degrees on a compass, with 0° representing true north). The readings were taken at seeding level in a cloud seeding experiment. (Reference: *Proceedings of the National Academy of Science*, vol. 68, pp. 649–652.) A random sample of days gave the following information.

x	177	140	197	224	49	175	257	72	172
y	142	142	217	125	53	245	218	35	147

x	214	265	110	193	180	190	94	8	93
y	205	218	100	170	245	117	140	99	60

Use the sign test with a 5% level of significance to test the claim that the distributions of wind directions at 5 A.M. and 5 P.M. are different.

6. *Rank-Sum Test: Apple Trees* Commercial apple trees usually consist of two parts grafted together. The upper part or graft determines the character of the fruit, while the root stock determines the size of the tree. (Reference: East Malling Research Station, England.) The following data are from two root stocks A and B. The data represent total extension growth (in meters) of the grafts after 4 years.

Stock A	2.81	2.26	1.94	2.37	3.11	2.58	2.74	2.10	3.41	2.94	2.88
Stock B	2.52	3.02	2.86	2.91	2.78	2.71	1.96	2.44	2.13	1.58	2.77

Use a 1% level of significance and the rank-sum test to test the claim that the distributions of growths are different for root stocks A and B.

7. *Spearman Rank Correlation: Calcium Tests* Random collections of 9 different solutions of a calcium compound were given to two laboratories A and B. Each laboratory measured the calcium content (in mmol. per liter) and reported the results. The data are paired by calcium compound. (Reference: *Journal of Clinical Chemistry and Clinical Biochemistry*, vol. 19, pp. 395–426.)

809

Compound	1	2	3	4	5	6	7	8	9
Lab A	13.33	15.79	14.78	11.29	12.59	9.65	8.69	10.06	11.58
Lab B	13.17	15.72	14.66	11.47	12.65	9.60	8.75	10.25	11.56

(a) Rank-order the data using 1 for the lowest calcium reading. Make a table of ranks to be used in a Spearman rank correlation test.

(b) Use a 5% level of significance to test for a monotone relation (either way) between ranks.

8. *Runs Test for Randomness: Sunspots* The January mean number of sunspots is recorded for a sequence of recent Januaries. (Reference: *International Astronomical Union Quarterly Bulletin on Solar Activity*.)

57.9   38.7   19.8   15.3   17.5   28.2   110.9   121.8   104.4   111.5   9.13

61.5   43.4   27.6   18.9   8.1   16.4   51.9

Use level of significance 5% to test for randomness about the median.

Appendix I Additional Topics

PART I: BAYES'S THEOREM

The Reverend Thomas Bayes (1702–1761) was an English mathematician who discovered an important relation for conditional probabilities. This relation is referred to as *Bayes's rule* or *Bayes's theorem*. It uses conditional probabilities to adjust calculations so that we can accommodate new relevant information. We will restrict our attention to a special case of Bayes's theorem in which an event B is partitioned into only *two* mutually exclusive events (see Figure AI-1). The general formula is a bit complicated but is a straightforward extension of the basic ideas we will present here. Most advanced texts contain such an extension.

Note: We use the following compact notation in the statement of Bayes's theorem:

Notation	Meaning
A^c	complement of A; *not A*
$P(B|A)$	probability of event B, *given* event A; P(B, *given* A)
$P(B|A^c)$	probability of event B, *given* the complement of A; P(B, *given* not A)

We will use Figure AI-1 to motivate Bayes's theorem. Let A and B be events in a sample space that have probabilities not equal to 0 or 1. Let A^c be the complement of A.

Here is Bayes's theorem: $P(A|B) = \dfrac{P(B|A)P(A)}{P(B|A)P(A) + P(B|A^c)P(A^c)}$ \hfill (1)

Overview of Bayes's Theorem

Suppose we have an event A, and we calculate $P(A)$, the unconditional probability of A standing by itself. Now suppose we have a "new" event B and we know the

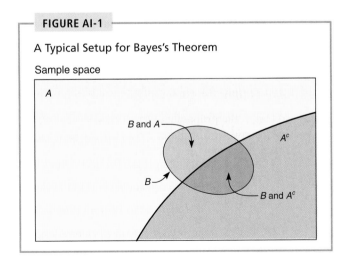

FIGURE AI-1

A Typical Setup for Bayes's Theorem

Sample space

A1

probability of B, given that A occurs P(B|A), as well as the probability of B, given that A does not occur P(B|A^c). Where does such an event B come from? The event B can be constructed in many possible ways. For example, B can be constructed as the result of a consulting service or a testing procedure or a sorting activity. In the examples and problems, you will find more ways to construct such an event B.

How can we use this "new" information concerning the event B to adjust our calculation of the probability of event A, given B? That is, how can we make our calculation of the probability of A more realistic by including information about the event B? The answer is that we will use Equation (1) of Bayes's theorem.

Let's look at some examples that use Equation (1) of Bayes's theorem. We are grateful to personal friends in the oil and natural gas business in Colorado who provided the basic information in the following example.

EXAMPLE 1

Bayes's theorem

A geologist has examined seismic data and other geologic formations in the vicinity of a proposed site for an oil well. Based on this information, the geologist reports a 65% chance of finding oil. The oil company decides to go ahead and start drilling. As the drilling progresses, sample cores are taken from the well and studied by the geologist. These sample cores have a history of predicting oil *when there is oil* about 85% of the time. However, about 6% of the time the sample cores will predict oil *when there is no oil*. (Note that these probabilities need not add up to 1.) Our geologist is delighted because the sample cores predict oil for this well.

Use the "new" information from the sample cores to revise the geologist's original probability that the well will hit oil. What is the new probability?

SOLUTION: To use Bayes's theorem, we need to identify the events A and B. Then we need to find $P(A)$, $P(A^c)$, $P(B|A)$, and $P(B|A^c)$. From the description of the problem, we have

> A is the event that the well strikes oil.
>
> A^c is the event that the well is dry (no oil).
>
> B is the event that the core samples indicate oil.

Again, from the description, we have

$$P(A) = 0.65, \quad \text{so} \quad P(A^c) = 1 - 0.65 = 0.35$$

These are our *prior* (before new information) probabilities. New information comes from the sample cores. Probabilities associated with the new information are

$$P(B|A) = 0.85$$

This is the probability that core samples indicate oil when there actually is oil.

$$P(B|A^c) = 0.06$$

This is the probability that core samples indicate oil when there is no oil (dry well).

Now we use Bayes's theorem to revise the probability that the well will hit oil based on the "new" information from core samples. The revised probability is the *posterior* probability we compute that uses the new information from the sample cores:

$$P(A|B) = \frac{P(B|A)P(A)}{P(B|A)P(A) + P(B|A^c)P(A^c)} = \frac{(0.85)(0.65)}{(0.85)(0.65) + (0.06)(0.35)} = 0.9634$$

We see that the revised (*posterior*) probability indicates about a 96% chance for the well to hit oil. This is why sample cores that are good can attract money in the form of venture capital (for independent drillers) on a big, expensive well. ◇

GUIDED EXERCISE 1

Bayes's theorem

Anasazi were prehistoric pueblo people who lived in what is now the southwestern United States. Mesa Verde, Pecos Pueblo, and Chaco Canyon are beautiful national parks and monuments, but long ago they were home to many Anasazi. In prehistoric times, there were several Anasazi migrations, until finally their pueblo homes were completely abandoned. The delightful book *Proceedings of the Anasazi Symposium, 1981,* published by Mesa Verde Museum Association, contains a very interesting discussion about methods anthropologists use to (approximately) date Anasazi objects. There are two popular ways. One is to compare environmental data to other objects of known dates. The other is radioactive carbon dating.

Carbon dating has some variability in its accuracy, depending on how far back in time the age estimate goes and also on the condition of the specimen itself. Suppose experience has shown that the carbon method is correct 75% of the time it is used on an object from a known (given) time period. However, there is a 10% chance that the carbon method will predict that an object is from a certain period when we know the object is not from that period.

Using environmental data, an anthropologist reported the probability to be 40% that a fossilized deer bone bracelet was from a certain Anasazi migration period. Then, as a follow-up study, the carbon method also indicated that the bracelet was from this migration period. How can the anthropologist adjust her estimated probability to include the "new" information from the carbon dating?

(a) To use Bayes's theorem, we must identify the events A and B. From the description of the problem, what are A and B?

A is the event that the bracelet is from the given migration period. B is the event that carbon dating indicates that the bracelet is from the given migration period.

(b) Find $P(A)$, $P(A^c)$, $P(B|A)$, and $P(B|A^c)$.

From the description,

$$P(A) = 0.40$$
$$P(A^c) = 0.60$$
$$P(B|A) = 0.75$$
$$P(B|A^c) = 0.10$$

(c) Compute $P(A|B)$, and explain the meaning of this number.

Using Bayes's theorem and the results of part (b), we have

$$P(A|B) = \frac{P(B|A)P(A)}{P(B|A)P(A) + P(B|A^c)P(A^c)}$$

$$= \frac{(0.75)(0.40)}{(0.75)(0.40) + (0.10)(0.60)} = 0.8333$$

The prior (before carbon dating) probability was only 40%. However, the carbon dating allowed us to revise this probability to 83%. Thus, we are about 83% sure that the bracelet came from the given migration period. Perhaps additional research at the site will uncover more information to which Bayes's theorem could be applied again.

PROBLEM: Bayes's theorem applied to quality control

A company that makes steel bolts knows from long experience that about 12% of its bolts are defective. If the company simply ships all bolts that it produces, then 12% of the shipment the customer receives will be defective. To decrease the percentage of defective bolts shipped to customers, an electronic scanner is installed. The scanner is positioned over the production line and is supposed to pick out the good bolts. However, the scanner itself is not perfect. To test the scanner, a large number of (pretested) "good" bolts were run under the scanner, and it accepted 90% of the bolts as good. Then a large number of (pretested) defective bolts were run under the scanner, and it accepted 3% of these as good bolts.

(a) If the company does not use the scanner, what percentage of a shipment is expected to be good? What percentage is expected to be defective?

(b) The scanner itself makes mistakes, and the company is questioning the value of using it. Suppose the company does use the scanner and ships only what the scanner passes as "good" bolts. In this case, what percentage of the shipment is expected to be good? What percentage is expected to be defective?

Partial Answer

To solve this problem, we use Bayes's theorem. The result of using the scanner is a dramatic improvement in the quality of the shipped product. If the scanner is not used, only 88% of the shipped bolts will be good. However, if the scanner is used and only the bolts it passes as good are shipped, then 99.6% of the shipment is expected to be good. Even though the scanner itself makes a considerable number of mistakes, it is definitely worth using. Not only does it increase the quality of a shipment, the bolts it rejects can be recycled into new bolts.

PART II: THE HYPERGEOMETRIC PROBABILITY DISTRIBUTION

In Chapter 5, we examined the binomial distribution. The binomial probability distribution assumes *independent trials*. If the trials are constructed by drawing samples from a population, then we have two possibilities: We sample either *with replacement* or *without replacement*. If we draw random samples with replacement, the trials can be taken to be independent. If we draw random samples without replacement and the population is very large, then it is reasonable to say that the trials are approximately independent. In this case, we go ahead and use the binomial distribution. However, if the population is relatively small and we draw samples without replacement, the assumption of independent trials is not valid, and we should not use the binomial distribution.

The *hypergeometric distribution* is a probability distribution of a random variable that has two outcomes when sampling is done *without replacement*.

Consider the following notational setup (see Figure AI-2). Suppose we have a population with only *two* distinct types of objects. Such a population might be made up of females and males, students and faculty, residents and nonresidents, defective

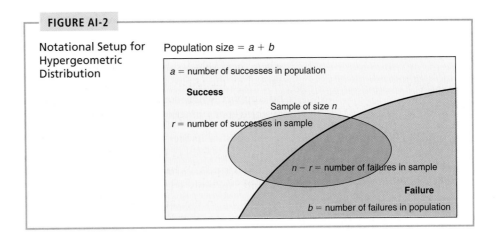

FIGURE AI-2

Notational Setup for Hypergeometric Distribution

Population size $= a + b$

a = number of successes in population

Success

Sample of size n

r = number of successes in sample

$n - r$ = number of failures in sample

Failure

b = number of failures in population

and nondefective items, and so on. For simplicity of reference, let us call one type of object (your choice) "success" and the other "failure." Let's use the letter a to designate the number of successes in the population and the letter b to designate the number of failures in the population. Thus, the total population size is $a + b$. Next, we draw a random sample (without replacement) of size n from this population. Let r be the number of successes in this sample. Then $n - r$ is the number of failures in the sample. The hypergeometric distribution gives us the probability of r successes in the sample of size n.

Recall from Section 4.3 that the number of combinations of k objects taken j at a time can be computed as

$$C_{k,j} = \frac{k!}{j!(k - j)!}$$

Using the notation of Figure AI-2 and the formula for combinations, the hypergeometric distribution can be calculated.

Hypergeometric distribution

Given that a population has two distinct types of objects, success and failure,

   a counts the number of successes in the population.

   b counts the number of failures in the population.

For a random sample of size n taken *without replacement* from this population, the probability $P(r)$ of getting r successes in the *sample* is

$$P(r) = \frac{C_{a,r}C_{b,n-r}}{C_{(a+b),n}} \tag{2}$$

The expected value and standard deviation are

$$\mu = \frac{na}{a + b} \quad \text{and} \quad \sigma = \sqrt{n\left(\frac{a}{a + b}\right)\left(\frac{b}{a + b}\right)\left(\frac{a + b - n}{a + b - 1}\right)}$$

EXAMPLE 2

Hypergeometric distribution

A section of an Interstate 95 bridge across the Mianus River in Connecticut collapsed suddenly on the morning of June 28, 1983. (See *To Engineer Is Human: The Role of Failure in Successful Designs,* by Henry Petroski.) Three people were killed when their vehicles fell off the bridge. It was determined that the collapse was caused by the failure of a metal hanger design that left a section of the bridge with no support when something went wrong with the pins. Subsequent inspection revealed many cracked pins and hangers in bridges across the United States.

(a) Suppose a hanger design uses 4 pins in the upper part and 6 pins in the lower part, as shown in Figure AI-3. The hangers come in a kit consisting of the hanger and 10 pins. When a work crew installs a hanger, they start with the top part and randomly select a pin, which is put into place. This is repeated until all 4 pins are in the top. Then they finish the lower part.

Assume that 3 pins in the kit are faulty. The other 7 are all right. What is the probability that all 3 faulty pins get put into the top part of the hanger? This means that the support is held up, in effect, by only one good pin.

SOLUTION: The population consists of 10 pins identical in appearance. However, 3 are faulty and 7 are good. The sampling of 4 pins for the top part of the hanger is done *without replacement*. Since we are interested in the faulty pins, let us label them "success" (only a convenient label). Using the notation of Figure AI-2 and the hypergeometric distribution, we have

a = number of successes in the population (bad pins) = 3

b = number of failures in the population (good pins) = 7

n = sample size (number of pins put in top) = 4

r = number of successes in sample (number of bad pins in top) = 3

The hypergeometric distribution applies because the population is relatively small (10 pins) and sampling is done without replacement. By Equation (2), we compute $P(r)$:

$$P(r) = \frac{C_{a,r} C_{b,n-r}}{C_{(a+b),n}}$$

Using the preceding information about a, b, n, and r, we get

$$P(r = 3) = \frac{C_{3,3} C_{7,1}}{C_{10,4}}$$

Using the formula for $C_{k,j}$, or Table 2 of Appendix II, or the combinations key on a calculator, we get

$$P(r = 3) = \frac{1 \cdot 7}{210} = 0.0333$$

We see that there is a better than 3.3% chance of getting 3 out of 4 bad pins in the top part of the hanger.

(b) Suppose that all the hanger kits are like the one described in part (a). On a long bridge that used 200 such hangers, how many do you expect are held up by only one good pin? How might this affect the safety of the bridge?

FIGURE AI-3

Steel Hanger Design for Bridge Support

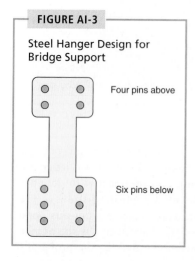

Four pins above

Six pins below

SOLUTION: We would expect

$$200(0.0333) = 6.66$$

That is, between 6 and 7 hangers are expected to be held up by only one good pin. As time goes on, this pin will corrode and show signs of wear as the bridge vibrates. With only one good pin, there is much less margin of safety.

Professor Petroski discusses the bridge on I-95 across the Mianus River in his book mentioned earlier. He points out that this dramatic accidental collapse resulted in better quality control (for hangers and pins) as well as better overall design of bridges. In addition to this, the government has greatly increased programs for maintenance and inspection of bridges. ◊

GUIDED EXERCISE 2

Hypergeometric distribution

The biology club weekend outing has two groups. One group with 7 people will camp at Diamond Lake. The other group with 10 people will camp at Arapahoe Pass. Seventeen duffels were prepacked by the outing committee, but 6 of these had the tents accidentally left out of the duffel. The group going to Diamond Lake picked up their duffels at random from the collection and started off on the trail. The group going to Arapahoe Pass used the remaining duffels. What is the probability that all 6 duffels without tents were picked up by the group going to Diamond Lake?

(a) What is success? Are the duffels selected with or without replacement? Which probability distribution applies?

⟹ Success is taking a duffel without a tent. The duffels are selected without replacement. The hypergeometric distribution applies.

(b) Use the hypergeometric distribution to compute the probability of $r = 6$ successes in the sample of 7 people going to Diamond Lake.

⟹ To use the hypergeometric distribution, we need to know the values of

a = number of successes in population = 6

b = number of failures in population = 11

n = sample size = 7, since 7 people are going to Diamond Lake

r = number of successes in sample = 6

Then, $P(r = 6) = \dfrac{C_{6,6} \, C_{11,1}}{C_{17,7}} = \dfrac{1 \cdot 11}{19448} = 0.0006$

The probability that all 6 duffels without tents are taken by the 7 hikers to Diamond Lake is 0.0006.

Appendix II Tables

TABLE 1 Random Numbers

92630	78240	19267	95457	53497	23894	37708	79862	76471	66418
79445	78735	71549	44843	26104	67318	00701	34986	66751	99723
59654	71966	27386	50004	05358	94031	29281	18544	52429	06080
31524	49587	76612	39789	13537	48086	59483	60680	84675	53014
06348	76938	90379	51392	55887	71015	09209	79157	24440	30244
28703	51709	94456	48396	73780	06436	86641	69239	57662	80181
68108	89266	94730	95761	75023	48464	65544	96583	18911	16391
99938	90704	93621	66330	33393	95261	95349	51769	91616	33238
91543	73196	34449	63513	83834	99411	58826	40456	69268	48562
42103	02781	73920	56297	72678	12249	25270	36678	21313	75767
17138	27584	25296	28387	51350	61664	37893	05363	44143	42677
28297	14280	54524	21618	95320	38174	60579	08089	94999	78460
09331	56712	51333	06289	75345	08811	82711	57392	25252	30333
31295	04204	93712	51287	05754	79396	87399	51773	33075	97061
36146	15560	27592	42089	99281	59640	15221	96079	09961	05371
29553	18432	13630	05529	02791	81017	49027	79031	50912	09399
23501	22642	63081	08191	89420	67800	55137	54707	32945	64522
57888	85846	67967	07835	11314	01545	48535	17142	08552	67457
55336	71264	88472	04334	63919	36394	11196	92470	70543	29776
10087	10072	55980	64688	68239	20461	89381	93809	00796	95945
34101	81277	66090	88872	37818	72142	67140	50785	21380	16703
53362	44940	60430	22834	14130	96593	23298	56203	92671	15925
82975	66158	84731	19436	55790	69229	28661	13675	99318	76873
54827	84673	22898	08094	14326	87038	42892	21127	30712	48489
25464	59098	27436	89421	80754	89924	19097	67737	80368	08795
67609	60214	41475	84950	40133	02546	09570	45682	50165	15609
44921	70924	61295	51137	47596	86735	35561	76649	18217	63446
33170	30972	98130	95828	49786	13301	36081	80761	33985	68621
84687	85445	06208	17654	51333	02878	35010	67578	61574	20749
71886	56450	36567	09395	96951	35507	17555	35212	69106	01679
00475	02224	74722	14721	40215	21351	08596	45625	83981	63748
25993	38881	68361	59560	41274	69742	40703	37993	03435	18873

TABLE 1 *continued*

92882	53178	99195	93803	56985	53089	15305	50522	55900	43026
25138	26810	07093	15677	60688	04410	24505	37890	67186	62829
84631	71882	12991	83028	82484	90339	91950	74579	03539	90122
34003	92326	12793	61453	48121	74271	28363	66561	75220	35908
53775	45749	05734	86169	42762	70175	97310	73894	88606	19994
59316	97885	72807	54966	60859	11932	35265	71601	55577	67715
20479	66557	50705	26999	09854	52591	14063	30214	19890	19292
86180	84931	25455	26044	02227	52015	21820	50599	51671	65411
21451	68001	72710	40261	61281	13172	63819	48970	51732	54113
98062	68375	80089	24135	72355	95428	11808	29740	81644	86610
01788	64429	14430	94575	75153	94576	61393	96192	03227	32258
62465	04841	43272	68702	01274	05437	22953	18946	99053	41690
94324	31089	84159	92933	99989	89500	91586	02802	69471	68274
05797	43984	21575	09908	70221	19791	51578	36432	33494	79888
10395	14289	52185	09721	25789	38562	54794	04897	59012	89251
35177	56986	25549	59730	64718	52630	31100	62384	49483	11409
25633	89619	75882	98256	02126	72099	57183	55887	09320	73463
16464	48280	94254	45777	45150	68865	11382	11782	22695	41988

Source: Reprinted from *A Million Random Digits with 100,000 Normal Deviates* by the Rand Corporation (New York: The Free Press, 1955). Copyright 1955 and 1983 by the Rand Corporation. Used by permission.

TABLE 2 Binomial Coefficients $C_{n,r}$

n \ r	0	1	2	3	4	5	6	7	8	9	10
1	1	1									
2	1	2	1								
3	1	3	3	1							
4	1	4	6	4	1						
5	1	5	10	10	5	1					
6	1	6	15	20	15	6	1				
7	1	7	21	35	35	21	7	1			
8	1	8	28	56	70	56	28	8	1		
9	1	9	36	84	126	126	84	36	9	1	
10	1	10	45	120	210	252	210	120	45	10	1
11	1	11	55	165	330	462	462	330	165	55	11
12	1	12	66	220	495	792	924	792	495	220	66
13	1	13	78	286	715	1,287	1,716	1,716	1,287	715	286
14	1	14	91	364	1,001	2,002	3,003	3,432	3,003	2,002	1,001
15	1	15	105	455	1,365	3,003	5,005	6,435	6,435	5,005	3,003
16	1	16	120	560	1,820	4,368	8,008	11,440	12,870	11,440	8,008
17	1	17	136	680	2,380	6,188	12,376	19,448	24,310	24,310	19,448
18	1	18	153	816	3,060	8,568	18,564	31,824	43,758	48,620	43,758
19	1	19	171	969	3,876	11,628	27,132	50,388	75,582	92,378	92,378
20	1	20	190	1,140	4,845	15,504	38,760	77,520	125,970	167,960	184,756

TABLE 3 Binomial Probability Distribution $C_{n,r}\, p^r q^{n-r}$

This table shows the probability of r successes in n independent trials, each with probability of success p.

n	r	.01	.05	.10	.15	.20	.25	.30	.35	.40	.45	.50	.55	.60	.65	.70	.75	.80	.85	.90	.95
2	0	.980	.902	.810	.723	.640	.563	.490	.423	.360	.303	.250	.203	.160	.123	.090	.063	.040	.023	.010	.002
	1	.020	.095	.180	.255	.320	.375	.420	.455	.480	.495	.500	.495	.480	.455	.420	.375	.320	.255	.180	.095
	2	.000	.002	.010	.023	.040	.063	.090	.123	.160	.203	.250	.303	.360	.423	.490	.563	.640	.723	.810	.902
3	0	.970	.857	.729	.614	.512	.422	.343	.275	.216	.166	.125	.091	.064	.043	.027	.016	.008	.003	.001	.000
	1	.029	.135	.243	.325	.384	.422	.441	.444	.432	.408	.375	.334	.288	.239	.189	.141	.096	.057	.027	.007
	2	.000	.007	.027	.057	.096	.141	.189	.239	.288	.334	.375	.408	.432	.444	.441	.422	.384	.325	.243	.135
	3	.000	.000	.001	.003	.008	.016	.027	.043	.064	.091	.125	.166	.216	.275	.343	.422	.512	.614	.729	.857
4	0	.961	.815	.656	.522	.410	.316	.240	.179	.130	.092	.062	.041	.026	.015	.008	.004	.002	.001	.000	.000
	1	.039	.171	.292	.368	.410	.422	.412	.384	.346	.300	.250	.200	.154	.112	.076	.047	.026	.011	.004	.000
	2	.001	.014	.049	.098	.154	.211	.265	.311	.346	.368	.375	.368	.346	.311	.265	.211	.154	.098	.049	.014
	3	.000	.000	.004	.011	.026	.047	.076	.112	.154	.200	.250	.300	.346	.384	.412	.422	.410	.368	.292	.171
	4	.000	.000	.000	.001	.002	.004	.008	.015	.026	.041	.062	.092	.130	.179	.240	.316	.410	.522	.656	.815
5	0	.951	.774	.590	.444	.328	.237	.168	.116	.078	.050	.031	.019	.010	.005	.002	.001	.000	.000	.000	.000
	1	.048	.204	.328	.392	.410	.396	.360	.312	.259	.206	.156	.113	.077	.049	.028	.015	.006	.002	.000	.000
	2	.001	.021	.073	.138	.205	.264	.309	.336	.346	.337	.312	.276	.230	.181	.132	.088	.051	.024	.008	.001
	3	.000	.001	.008	.024	.051	.088	.132	.181	.230	.276	.312	.337	.346	.336	.309	.264	.205	.138	.073	.021
	4	.000	.000	.000	.002	.006	.015	.028	.049	.077	.113	.156	.206	.259	.312	.360	.396	.410	.392	.328	.204
	5	.000	.000	.000	.000	.000	.001	.002	.005	.010	.019	.031	.050	.078	.116	.168	.237	.328	.444	.590	.774
6	0	.941	.735	.531	.377	.262	.178	.118	.075	.047	.028	.016	.008	.004	.002	.001	.000	.000	.000	.000	.000
	1	.057	.232	.354	.399	.393	.356	.303	.244	.187	.136	.094	.061	.037	.020	.010	.004	.002	.000	.000	.000
	2	.001	.031	.098	.176	.246	.297	.324	.328	.311	.278	.234	.186	.138	.095	.060	.033	.015	.006	.001	.000
	3	.000	.002	.015	.042	.082	.132	.185	.236	.276	.303	.312	.303	.276	.236	.185	.132	.082	.042	.015	.002
	4	.000	.000	.001	.006	.015	.033	.060	.095	.138	.186	.234	.278	.311	.328	.324	.297	.246	.176	.098	.031
	5	.000	.000	.000	.000	.002	.004	.010	.020	.037	.061	.094	.136	.187	.244	.303	.356	.393	.399	.354	.232
	6	.000	.000	.000	.000	.000	.000	.001	.002	.004	.008	.016	.028	.047	.075	.118	.178	.262	.377	.531	.735
7	0	.932	.698	.478	.321	.210	.133	.082	.049	.028	.015	.008	.004	.002	.001	.000	.000	.000	.000	.000	.000
	1	.066	.257	.372	.396	.367	.311	.247	.185	.131	.087	.055	.032	.017	.008	.004	.001	.000	.000	.000	.000
	2	.002	.041	.124	.210	.275	.311	.318	.299	.261	.214	.164	.117	.077	.047	.025	.012	.004	.001	.000	.000
	3	.000	.004	.023	.062	.115	.173	.227	.268	.290	.292	.273	.239	.194	.144	.097	.058	.029	.011	.003	.000
	4	.000	.000	.003	.011	.029	.058	.097	.144	.194	.239	.273	.292	.290	.268	.227	.173	.115	.062	.023	.004
	5	.000	.000	.000	.001	.004	.012	.025	.047	.077	.117	.164	.214	.261	.299	.318	.311	.275	.210	.124	.041
	6	.000	.000	.000	.000	.000	.001	.004	.008	.017	.032	.055	.087	.131	.185	.247	.311	.367	.396	.372	.257
	7	.000	.000	.000	.000	.000	.000	.000	.001	.002	.004	.008	.015	.028	.049	.082	.133	.210	.321	.478	.698

TABLE 3 *continued*

											p										
n	r	.01	.05	.10	.15	.20	.25	.30	.35	.40	.45	.50	.55	.60	.65	.70	.75	.80	.85	.90	.95
8	0	.923	.663	.430	.272	.168	.100	.058	.032	.017	.008	.004	.002	.001	.000	.000	.000	.000	.000	.000	.000
	1	.075	.279	.383	.385	.336	.267	.198	.137	.090	.055	.031	.016	.008	.003	.001	.000	.000	.000	.000	.000
	2	.003	.051	.149	.238	.294	.311	.296	.259	.209	.157	.109	.070	.041	.022	.010	.004	.001	.000	.000	.000
	3	.000	.005	.033	.084	.147	.208	.254	.279	.279	.257	.219	.172	.124	.081	.047	.023	.009	.003	.000	.000
	4	.000	.000	.005	.018	.046	.087	.136	.188	.232	.263	.273	.263	.232	.188	.136	.087	.046	.018	.005	.000
	5	.000	.000	.000	.003	.009	.023	.047	.081	.124	.172	.219	.257	.279	.279	.254	.208	.147	.084	.033	.005
	6	.000	.000	.000	.000	.001	.004	.010	.022	.041	.070	.109	.157	.209	.259	.296	.311	.294	.238	.149	.051
	7	.000	.000	.000	.000	.000	.000	.001	.003	.008	.016	.031	.055	.090	.137	.198	.267	.336	.385	.383	.279
	8	.000	.000	.000	.000	.000	.000	.000	.000	.001	.002	.004	.008	.017	.032	.058	.100	.168	.272	.430	.663
9	0	.914	.630	.387	.232	.134	.075	.040	.021	.010	.005	.002	.001	.000	.000	.000	.000	.000	.000	.000	.000
	1	.083	.299	.387	.368	.302	.225	.156	.100	.060	.034	.018	.008	.004	.001	.000	.000	.000	.000	.000	.000
	2	.003	.063	.172	.260	.302	.300	.267	.216	.161	.111	.070	.041	.021	.010	.004	.001	.000	.000	.000	.000
	3	.000	.008	.045	.107	.176	.234	.267	.272	.251	.212	.164	.116	.074	.042	.021	.009	.003	.001	.000	.000
	4	.000	.001	.007	.028	.066	.117	.172	.219	.251	.260	.246	.213	.167	.118	.074	.039	.017	.005	.001	.000
	5	.000	.000	.001	.005	.017	.039	.074	.118	.167	.213	.246	.260	.251	.219	.172	.117	.066	.028	.007	.001
	6	.000	.000	.000	.001	.003	.009	.021	.042	.074	.116	.164	.212	.251	.272	.267	.234	.176	.107	.045	.008
	7	.000	.000	.000	.000	.000	.001	.004	.010	.021	.041	.070	.111	.161	.216	.267	.300	.302	.260	.172	.063
	8	.000	.000	.000	.000	.000	.000	.000	.001	.004	.008	.018	.034	.060	.100	.156	.225	.302	.368	.387	.299
	9	.000	.000	.000	.000	.000	.000	.000	.000	.000	.001	.002	.005	.010	.021	.040	.075	.134	.232	.387	.630
10	0	.904	.599	.349	.197	.107	.056	.028	.014	.006	.003	.001	.000	.000	.000	.000	.000	.000	.000	.000	.000
	1	.091	.315	.387	.347	.268	.188	.121	.072	.040	.021	.010	.004	.002	.000	.000	.000	.000	.000	.000	.000
	2	.004	.075	.194	.276	.302	.282	.233	.176	.121	.076	.044	.023	.011	.004	.001	.000	.000	.000	.000	.000
	3	.000	.010	.057	.130	.201	.250	.267	.252	.215	.166	.117	.075	.042	.021	.009	.003	.001	.000	.000	.000
	4	.000	.001	.011	.040	.088	.146	.200	.238	.251	.238	.205	.160	.111	.069	.037	.016	.006	.001	.000	.000
	5	.000	.000	.001	.008	.026	.058	.103	.154	.201	.234	.246	.234	.201	.154	.103	.058	.026	.008	.001	.000
	6	.000	.000	.000	.001	.006	.016	.037	.069	.111	.160	.205	.238	.251	.238	.200	.146	.088	.040	.011	.001
	7	.000	.000	.000	.000	.001	.003	.009	.021	.042	.075	.117	.166	.215	.252	.267	.250	.201	.130	.057	.010
	8	.000	.000	.000	.000	.000	.000	.001	.004	.011	.023	.044	.076	.121	.176	.233	.282	.302	.276	.194	.075
	9	.000	.000	.000	.000	.000	.000	.000	.000	.002	.004	.010	.021	.040	.072	.121	.188	.268	.347	.387	.315
	10	.000	.000	.000	.000	.000	.000	.000	.000	.000	.001	.001	.003	.006	.014	.028	.056	.107	.197	.349	.599
11	0	.895	.569	.314	.167	.086	.042	.020	.009	.004	.001	.000	.000	.000	.000	.000	.000	.000	.000	.000	.000
	1	.099	.329	.384	.325	.236	.155	.093	.052	.027	.013	.005	.002	.001	.000	.000	.000	.000	.000	.000	.000
	2	.005	.087	.213	.287	.295	.258	.200	.140	.089	.051	.027	.013	.005	.002	.001	.000	.000	.000	.000	.000

TABLE 3 *continued*

n	r	.01	.05	.10	.15	.20	.25	.30	.35	.40	.45	.50	.55	.60	.65	.70	.75	.80	.85	.90	.95
11	3	.000	.014	.071	.152	.221	.258	.257	.225	.177	.126	.081	.046	.023	.010	.004	.001	.000	.000	.000	.000
	4	.000	.001	.016	.054	.111	.172	.220	.243	.236	.206	.161	.113	.070	.038	.017	.006	.002	.000	.000	.000
	5	.000	.000	.002	.013	.039	.080	.132	.183	.221	.236	.226	.193	.147	.099	.057	.027	.010	.002	.000	.000
	6	.000	.000	.000	.002	.010	.027	.057	.099	.147	.193	.226	.236	.221	.183	.132	.080	.039	.013	.002	.000
	7	.000	.000	.000	.000	.002	.006	.017	.038	.070	.113	.161	.206	.236	.243	.220	.172	.111	.054	.016	.001
	8	.000	.000	.000	.000	.000	.001	.004	.010	.023	.046	.081	.126	.177	.225	.257	.258	.221	.152	.071	.014
	9	.000	.000	.000	.000	.000	.000	.001	.002	.005	.013	.027	.051	.089	.140	.200	.258	.295	.287	.213	.087
	10	.000	.000	.000	.000	.000	.000	.000	.000	.001	.002	.005	.013	.027	.052	.093	.155	.236	.325	.384	.329
	11	.000	.000	.000	.000	.000	.000	.000	.000	.000	.000	.000	.001	.004	.009	.020	.042	.086	.167	.314	.569
12	0	.886	.540	.282	.142	.069	.032	.014	.006	.002	.001	.000	.000	.000	.000	.000	.000	.000	.000	.000	.000
	1	.107	.341	.377	.301	.206	.127	.071	.037	.017	.008	.003	.001	.000	.000	.000	.000	.000	.000	.000	.000
	2	.006	.099	.230	.292	.283	.232	.168	.109	.064	.034	.016	.007	.002	.001	.000	.000	.000	.000	.000	.000
	3	.000	.017	.085	.172	.236	.258	.240	.195	.142	.092	.054	.028	.012	.005	.001	.000	.000	.000	.000	.000
	4	.000	.002	.021	.068	.133	.194	.231	.237	.213	.170	.121	.076	.042	.020	.008	.002	.001	.000	.000	.000
	5	.000	.000	.004	.019	.053	.103	.158	.204	.227	.223	.193	.149	.101	.059	.029	.011	.003	.001	.000	.000
	6	.000	.000	.000	.004	.016	.040	.079	.128	.177	.212	.226	.212	.177	.128	.079	.040	.016	.004	.000	.000
	7	.000	.000	.000	.001	.003	.011	.029	.059	.101	.149	.193	.223	.227	.204	.158	.103	.053	.019	.004	.002
	8	.000	.000	.000	.000	.001	.002	.008	.020	.042	.076	.121	.170	.213	.237	.231	.194	.133	.068	.021	.002
	9	.000	.000	.000	.000	.000	.000	.001	.005	.012	.028	.054	.092	.142	.195	.240	.258	.236	.172	.085	.017
	10	.000	.000	.000	.000	.000	.000	.000	.001	.002	.007	.016	.034	.064	.109	.168	.232	.283	.292	.230	.099
	11	.000	.000	.000	.000	.000	.000	.000	.000	.000	.001	.003	.008	.017	.037	.071	.127	.206	.301	.377	.341
	12	.000	.000	.000	.000	.000	.000	.000	.000	.000	.000	.000	.001	.002	.006	.014	.032	.069	.142	.282	.540
15	0	.860	.463	.206	.087	.035	.013	.005	.002	.000	.000	.000	.000	.000	.000	.000	.000	.000	.000	.000	.000
	1	.130	.366	.343	.231	.132	.067	.031	.013	.005	.002	.000	.000	.000	.000	.000	.000	.000	.000	.000	.000
	2	.009	.135	.267	.286	.231	.156	.092	.048	.022	.009	.003	.001	.000	.000	.000	.000	.000	.000	.000	.000
	3	.000	.031	.129	.218	.250	.225	.170	.111	.063	.032	.014	.005	.002	.000	.000	.000	.000	.000	.000	.000
	4	.000	.005	.043	.116	.188	.225	.219	.179	.127	.078	.042	.019	.007	.002	.001	.000	.000	.000	.000	.000
	5	.000	.001	.010	.045	.103	.165	.206	.212	.186	.140	.092	.051	.024	.010	.003	.001	.001	.000	.000	.000
	6	.000	.000	.002	.013	.043	.092	.147	.191	.207	.191	.153	.105	.061	.030	.012	.003	.001	.000	.000	.000
	7	.000	.000	.000	.003	.014	.039	.081	.132	.177	.201	.196	.165	.118	.071	.035	.013	.003	.001	.000	.000
	8	.000	.000	.000	.001	.003	.013	.035	.071	.118	.165	.196	.201	.177	.132	.081	.039	.014	.003	.000	.000
	9	.000	.000	.000	.000	.001	.003	.012	.030	.061	.105	.153	.191	.207	.191	.147	.092	.043	.013	.002	.000
	10	.000	.000	.000	.000	.000	.001	.003	.010	.024	.051	.092	.140	.186	.212	.206	.165	.103	.045	.010	.001

TABLE 3 *continued*

n	r	.01	.05	.10	.15	.20	.25	.30	.35	.40	.45	.50	.55	.60	.65	.70	.75	.80	.85	.90	.95
15	11	.000	.000	.000	.000	.000	.000	.001	.002	.007	.019	.042	.078	.127	.179	.219	.225	.188	.116	.043	.005
	12	.000	.000	.000	.000	.000	.000	.000	.000	.002	.005	.014	.032	.063	.111	.170	.225	.250	.218	.129	.031
	13	.000	.000	.000	.000	.000	.000	.000	.000	.000	.001	.003	.009	.022	.048	.092	.156	.231	.286	.267	.135
	14	.000	.000	.000	.000	.000	.000	.000	.000	.000	.000	.000	.002	.005	.013	.031	.067	.132	.231	.343	.366
	15	.000	.000	.000	.000	.000	.000	.000	.000	.000	.000	.000	.000	.000	.002	.005	.013	.035	.087	.206	.463
16	0	.851	.440	.185	.074	.028	.010	.003	.001	.000	.000	.000	.000	.000	.000	.000	.000	.000	.000	.000	.000
	1	.138	.371	.329	.210	.113	.053	.023	.009	.003	.001	.000	.000	.000	.000	.000	.000	.000	.000	.000	.000
	2	.010	.146	.275	.277	.211	.134	.073	.035	.015	.006	.002	.001	.000	.000	.000	.000	.000	.000	.000	.000
	3	.000	.036	.142	.229	.246	.208	.146	.089	.047	.022	.009	.003	.001	.000	.000	.000	.000	.000	.000	.000
	4	.000	.006	.051	.131	.200	.225	.204	.155	.101	.057	.028	.011	.004	.001	.000	.000	.000	.000	.000	.000
	5	.000	.001	.014	.056	.120	.180	.210	.201	.162	.112	.067	.034	.014	.005	.001	.000	.000	.000	.000	.000
	6	.000	.000	.003	.018	.055	.110	.165	.198	.198	.168	.122	.075	.039	.017	.006	.001	.000	.000	.000	.000
	7	.000	.000	.000	.005	.020	.052	.101	.152	.189	.197	.175	.132	.084	.044	.019	.006	.001	.000	.000	.000
	8	.000	.000	.000	.001	.006	.020	.049	.092	.142	.181	.196	.181	.142	.092	.049	.020	.006	.001	.000	.000
	9	.000	.000	.000	.000	.001	.006	.019	.044	.084	.132	.175	.197	.189	.152	.101	.052	.020	.005	.000	.000
	10	.000	.000	.000	.000	.000	.001	.006	.017	.039	.075	.122	.168	.198	.198	.165	.110	.055	.018	.003	.000
	11	.000	.000	.000	.000	.000	.000	.001	.005	.014	.034	.067	.112	.162	.201	.210	.180	.120	.056	.014	.001
	12	.000	.000	.000	.000	.000	.000	.000	.001	.004	.011	.028	.057	.101	.155	.204	.225	.200	.131	.051	.006
	13	.000	.000	.000	.000	.000	.000	.000	.000	.001	.003	.009	.022	.047	.089	.146	.208	.246	.229	.142	.036
	14	.000	.000	.000	.000	.000	.000	.000	.000	.000	.001	.002	.006	.015	.035	.073	.134	.211	.277	.275	.146
	15	.000	.000	.000	.000	.000	.000	.000	.000	.000	.000	.000	.001	.003	.009	.023	.053	.113	.210	.329	.371
	16	.000	.000	.000	.000	.000	.000	.000	.000	.000	.000	.000	.000	.000	.001	.003	.010	.028	.074	.185	.440
20	0	.818	.358	.122	.039	.012	.003	.001	.000	.000	.000	.000	.000	.000	.000	.000	.000	.000	.000	.000	.000
	1	.165	.377	.270	.137	.058	.021	.007	.002	.000	.000	.000	.000	.000	.000	.000	.000	.000	.000	.000	.000
	2	.016	.189	.285	.229	.137	.067	.028	.010	.003	.001	.000	.000	.000	.000	.000	.000	.000	.000	.000	.000
	3	.001	.060	.190	.243	.205	.134	.072	.032	.012	.004	.001	.000	.000	.000	.000	.000	.000	.000	.000	.000
	4	.000	.013	.090	.182	.218	.190	.130	.074	.035	.014	.005	.001	.000	.000	.000	.000	.000	.000	.000	.000
	5	.000	.002	.032	.103	.175	.202	.179	.127	.075	.036	.015	.005	.001	.000	.000	.000	.000	.000	.000	.000
	6	.000	.000	.009	.045	.109	.169	.192	.171	.124	.075	.036	.015	.005	.001	.000	.000	.000	.000	.000	.000
	7	.000	.000	.002	.016	.055	.112	.164	.184	.166	.122	.074	.037	.015	.004	.001	.000	.000	.000	.000	.000
	8	.000	.000	.000	.005	.022	.061	.114	.161	.180	.162	.120	.073	.035	.014	.004	.001	.000	.000	.000	.000
	9	.000	.000	.000	.001	.007	.027	.065	.116	.160	.177	.160	.119	.071	.034	.012	.003	.000	.000	.000	.000

p

TABLE 3 *continued*

n	r	p																			
		.01	.05	.10	.15	.20	.25	.30	.35	.40	.45	.50	.55	.60	.65	.70	.75	.80	.85	.90	.95
20	10	.000	.000	.000	.000	.002	.010	.031	.069	.117	.159	.176	.159	.117	.069	.031	.010	.002	.000	.000	.000
	11	.000	.000	.000	.000	.000	.003	.012	.034	.071	.119	.160	.177	.160	.116	.065	.027	.007	.001	.000	.000
	12	.000	.000	.000	.000	.000	.001	.004	.014	.035	.073	.120	.162	.180	.161	.114	.061	.022	.005	.000	.000
	13	.000	.000	.000	.000	.000	.000	.001	.005	.015	.037	.074	.122	.166	.184	.164	.112	.055	.016	.002	.000
	14	.000	.000	.000	.000	.000	.000	.000	.001	.005	.015	.037	.075	.124	.171	.192	.169	.109	.045	.009	.000
	15	.000	.000	.000	.000	.000	.000	.000	.000	.001	.005	.015	.036	.075	.127	.179	.202	.175	.103	.032	.002
	16	.000	.000	.000	.000	.000	.000	.000	.000	.000	.001	.005	.014	.035	.074	.130	.190	.218	.182	.090	.013
	17	.000	.000	.000	.000	.000	.000	.000	.000	.000	.000	.001	.004	.012	.032	.072	.134	.205	.243	.190	.060
	18	.000	.000	.000	.000	.000	.000	.000	.000	.000	.000	.000	.001	.003	.010	.028	.067	.137	.229	.285	.189
	19	.000	.000	.000	.000	.000	.000	.000	.000	.000	.000	.000	.000	.000	.002	.007	.021	.058	.137	.270	.377
	20	.000	.000	.000	.000	.000	.000	.000	.000	.000	.000	.000	.000	.000	.000	.001	.003	.012	.039	.122	.358

TABLE 4 Poisson Probability Distribution

For a given value of λ, entry indicates the probability
of obtaining a specified value of r.

r	0.1	0.2	0.3	0.4	0.5	0.6	0.7	0.8	0.9	1.0
0	.9048	.8187	.7408	.6703	.6065	.5488	.4966	.4493	.4066	.3679
1	.0905	.1637	.2222	.2681	.3033	.3293	.3476	.3595	.3659	.3679
2	.0045	.0164	.0333	.0536	.0758	.0988	.1217	.1438	.1647	.1839
3	.0002	.0011	.0033	.0072	.0126	.0198	.0284	.0383	.0494	.0613
4	.0000	.0001	.0003	.0007	.0016	.0030	.0050	.0077	.0111	.0153
5	.0000	.0000	.0000	.0001	.0002	.0004	.0007	.0012	.0020	.0031
6	.0000	.0000	.0000	.0000	.0000	.0000	.0001	.0002	.0003	.0005
7	.0000	.0000	.0000	.0000	.0000	.0000	.0000	.0000	.0000	.0001

r	1.1	1.2	1.3	1.4	1.5	1.6	1.7	1.8	1.9	2.0
0	.3329	.3012	.2725	.2466	.2231	.2019	.1827	.1653	.1496	.1353
1	.3662	.3614	.3543	.3452	.3347	.3230	.3106	.2975	.2842	.2707
2	.2014	.2169	.2303	.2417	.2510	.2584	.2640	.2678	.2700	.2707
3	.0738	.0867	.0998	.1128	.1255	.1378	.1496	.1607	.1710	.1804
4	.0203	.0260	.0324	.0395	.0471	.0551	.0636	.0723	.0812	.0902
5	.0045	.0062	.0084	.0111	.0141	.0176	.0216	.0260	.0309	.0361
6	.0008	.0012	.0018	.0026	.0035	.0047	.0061	.0078	.0098	.0120
7	.0001	.0002	.0003	.0005	.0008	.0011	.0015	.0020	.0027	.0034
8	.0000	.0000	.0001	.0001	.0001	.0002	.0003	.0005	.0006	.0009
9	.0000	.0000	.0000	.0000	.0000	.0000	.0001	.0001	.0001	.0002

r	2.1	2.2	2.3	2.4	2.5	2.6	2.7	2.8	2.9	3.0
0	.1225	.1108	.1003	.0907	.0821	.0743	.0672	.0608	.0550	.0498
1	.2572	.2438	.2306	.2177	.2052	.1931	.1815	.1703	.1596	.1494
2	.2700	.2681	.2652	.2613	.2565	.2510	.2450	.2384	.2314	.2240
3	.1890	.1966	.2033	.2090	.2138	.2176	.2205	.2225	.2237	.2240
4	.0992	.1082	.1169	.1254	.1336	.1414	.1488	.1557	.1622	.1680
5	.0417	.0476	.0538	.0602	.0668	.0735	.0804	.0872	.0940	.1008
6	.0146	.0174	.0206	.0241	.0278	.0319	.0362	.0407	.0455	.0504
7	.0044	.0055	.0068	.0083	.0099	.0118	.0139	.0163	.0188	.0216
8	.0011	.0015	.0019	.0025	.0031	.0038	.0047	.0057	.0068	.0081
9	.0003	.0004	.0005	.0007	.0009	.0011	.0014	.0018	.0022	.0027
10	.0001	.0001	.0001	.0002	.0002	.0003	.0004	.0005	.0006	.0008
11	.0000	.0000	.0000	.0000	.0000	.0001	.0001	.0001	.0002	.0002
12	.0000	.0000	.0000	.0000	.0000	.0000	.0000	.0000	.0000	.0001

TABLE 4 *continued*

					λ					
r	3.1	3.2	3.3	3.4	3.5	3.6	3.7	3.8	3.9	4.0
0	.0450	.0408	.0369	.0334	.0302	.0273	.0247	.0224	.0202	.0183
1	.1397	.1304	.1217	.1135	.1057	.0984	.0915	.0850	.0789	.0733
2	.2165	.2087	.2008	.1929	.1850	.1771	.1692	.1615	.1539	.1465
3	.2237	.2226	.2209	.2186	.2158	.2125	.2087	.2046	.2001	.1954
4	.1734	.1781	.1823	.1858	.1888	.1912	.1931	.1944	.1951	.1954
5	.1075	.1140	.1203	.1264	.1322	.1377	.1429	.1477	.1522	.1563
6	.0555	.0608	.0662	.0716	.0771	.0826	.0881	.0936	.0989	.1042
7	.0246	.2078	.0312	.0348	.0385	.0425	.0466	.0508	.0551	.0595
8	.0095	.0111	.0129	.0148	.0169	.0191	.0215	.0241	.0269	.0298
9	.0033	.0040	.0047	.0056	.0066	.0076	.0089	.0102	.0116	.0132
10	.0010	.0013	.0016	.0019	.0023	.0028	.0033	.0039	.0045	.0053
11	.0003	.0004	.0005	.0006	.0007	.0009	.0011	.0013	.0016	.0019
12	.0001	.0001	.0001	.0002	.0002	.0003	.0003	.0004	.0005	.0006
13	.0000	.0000	.0000	.0000	.0001	.0001	.0001	.0001	.0002	.0002
14	.0000	.0000	.0000	.0000	.0000	.0000	.0000	.0000	.0000	.0001

					λ					
r	4.1	4.2	4.3	4.4	4.5	4.6	4.7	4.8	4.9	5.0
0	.0166	.0150	.0136	.0123	.0111	.0101	.0091	.0082	.0074	.0067
1	.0679	.0630	.0583	.0540	.0500	.0462	.0427	.0395	.0365	.0337
2	.1393	.1323	.1254	.1188	.1125	.1063	.1005	.0948	.0894	.0842
3	.1904	.1852	.1798	.1743	.1687	.1631	.1574	.1517	.1460	.1404
4	.1951	.1944	.1933	.1917	.1898	.1875	.1849	.1820	.1789	.1755
5	.1600	.1633	.1662	.1687	.1708	.1725	.1738	.1747	.1753	.1755
6	.1093	.1143	.1191	.1237	.1281	.1323	.1362	.1398	.1432	.1462
7	.0640	.0686	.0732	.0778	.0824	.0869	.0914	.0959	.1002	.1044
8	.0328	.0360	.0393	.0428	.0463	.0500	.0537	.0575	.0614	.0653
9	.0150	.0168	.0188	.0209	.0232	.0255	.0280	.0307	.0334	.0363
10	.0061	.0071	.0081	.0092	.0104	.0118	.0132	.0147	.0164	.0181
11	.0023	.0027	.0032	.0037	.0043	.0049	.0056	.0064	.0073	.0082
12	.0008	.0009	.0011	.0014	.0016	.0019	.0022	.0026	.0030	.0034
13	.0002	.0003	.0004	.0005	.0006	.0007	.0008	.0009	.0011	.0013
14	.0001	.0001	.0001	.0001	.0002	.0002	.0003	.0003	.0004	.0005
15	.0000	.0000	.0000	.0000	.0001	.0001	.0001	.0001	.0001	.0002

TABLE 4 *continued*

					λ					
r	5.1	5.2	5.3	5.4	5.5	5.6	5.7	5.8	5.9	6.0
0	.0061	.0055	.0050	.0045	.0041	.0037	.0033	.0030	.0027	.0025
1	.0311	.0287	.0265	.0244	.0225	.0207	.0191	.0176	.0162	.0149
2	.0793	.0746	.0701	.0659	.0618	.0580	.0544	.0509	.0477	.0446
3	.1348	.1293	.1239	.1185	.1133	.1082	.1033	.0985	.0938	.0892
4	.1719	.1681	.1641	.1600	.1558	.1515	.1472	.1428	.1383	.1339
5	.1753	.1748	.1740	.1728	.1714	.1697	.1678	.1656	.1632	.1606
6	.1490	.1515	.1537	.1555	.1571	.1584	.1594	.1601	.1605	.1606
7	.1086	.1125	.1163	.1200	.1234	.1267	.1298	.1326	.1353	.1377
8	.0692	.0731	.0771	.0810	.0849	.0887	.0925	.0962	.0998	.1033
9	.0392	.0423	.0454	.0486	.0519	.0552	.0586	.0620	.0654	.0688
10	.0200	.0220	.0241	.0262	.0285	.0309	.0334	.0359	.0386	.0413
11	.0093	.0104	.0116	.0129	.0143	.0157	.0173	.0190	.0207	.0225
12	.0039	.0045	.0051	.0058	.0065	.0073	.0082	.0092	.0102	.0113
13	.0015	.0018	.0021	.0024	.0028	.0032	.0036	.0041	.0046	.0052
14	.0006	.0007	.0008	.0009	.0011	.0013	.0015	.0017	.0019	.0022
15	.0002	.0002	.0003	.0003	.0004	.0005	.0006	.0007	.0008	.0009
16	.0001	.0001	.0001	.0001	.0001	.0002	.0002	.0002	.0003	.0003
17	.0000	.0000	.0000	.0000	.0000	.0000	.0001	.0001	.0001	.0001

					λ					
r	6.1	6.2	6.3	6.4	6.5	6.6	6.7	6.8	6.9	7.0
0	.0022	.0020	.0018	.0017	.0015	.0014	.0012	.0011	.0010	.0009
1	.0137	.0126	.0116	.0106	.0098	.0090	.0082	.0076	.0070	.0064
2	.0417	.0390	.0364	.0340	.0318	.0296	.0276	.0258	.0240	.0223
3	.0848	.0806	.0765	.0726	.0688	.0652	.0617	.0584	.0552	.0521
4	.1294	.1249	.1205	.1162	.1118	.1076	.1034	.0992	.0952	.0912
5	.1579	.1549	.1519	.1487	.1454	.1420	.1385	.1349	.1314	.1277
6	.1605	.1601	.1595	.1586	.1575	.1562	.1546	.1529	.1511	.1490
7	.1399	.1418	.1435	.1450	.1462	.1472	.1480	.1486	.1489	.1490
8	.1066	.1099	.1130	.1160	.1188	.1215	.1240	.1263	.1284	.1304
9	.0723	.0757	.0791	.0825	.0858	.0891	.0923	.0954	.0985	.1014
10	.0441	.0469	.0498	.0528	.0558	.0588	.0618	.0649	.0679	.0710
11	.0245	.0265	.0285	.0307	.0330	.0353	.0377	.0401	.0426	.0452
12	.0124	.0137	.0150	.0164	.0179	.0194	.0210	.0227	.0245	.0264
13	.0058	.0065	.0073	.0081	.0089	.0098	.0108	.0119	.0130	.0142
14	.0025	.0029	.0033	.0037	.0041	.0046	.0052	.0058	.0064	.0071
15	.0010	.0012	.0014	.0016	.0018	.0020	.0023	.0026	.0029	.0033
16	.0004	.0005	.0005	.0006	.0007	.0008	.0010	.0011	.0013	.0014
17	.0001	.0002	.0002	.0002	.0003	.0003	.0004	.0004	.0005	.0006
18	.0000	.0001	.0001	.0001	.0001	.0001	.0001	.0002	.0002	.0002
19	.0000	.0000	.0000	.0000	.0000	.0000	.0000	.0001	.0001	.0001

TABLE 4 *continued*

					λ					
r	7.1	7.2	7.3	7.4	7.5	7.6	7.7	7.8	7.9	8.0
0	.0008	.0007	.0007	.0006	.0006	.0005	.0005	.0004	.0004	.0003
1	.0059	.0054	.0049	.0045	.0041	.0038	.0035	.0032	.0029	.0027
2	.0208	.0194	.0180	.0167	.0156	.0145	.0134	.0125	.0116	.0107
3	.0492	.0464	.0438	.0413	.0389	.0366	.0345	.0324	.0305	.0286
4	.0874	.0836	.0799	.0764	.0729	.0696	.0663	.0632	.0602	.0573
5	.1241	.1204	.1167	.1130	.1094	.1057	.1021	.0986	.0951	.0916
6	.1468	.1445	.1420	.1394	.1367	.1339	.1311	.1282	.1252	.1221
7	.1489	.1486	.1481	.1474	.1465	.1454	.1442	.1428	.1413	.1396
8	.1321	.1337	.1351	.1363	.1373	.1382	.1388	.1392	.1395	.1396
9	.1042	.1070	.1096	.1121	.1144	.1167	.1187	.1207	.1224	.1241
10	.0740	.0770	.0800	.0829	.0858	.0887	.0914	.0941	.0967	.0993
11	.0478	.0504	.0531	.0558	.0585	.0613	.0640	.0667	.0695	.0722
12	.0283	.0303	.0323	.0344	.0366	.0388	.0411	.0434	.0457	.0481
13	.0154	.0168	.0181	.0196	.0211	.0227	.0243	.0260	.0278	.0296
14	.0078	.0086	.0095	.0104	.0113	.0123	.0134	.0145	.0157	.0169
15	.0037	.0041	.0046	.0051	.0057	.0062	.0069	.0075	.0083	.0090
16	.0016	.0019	.0021	.0024	.0026	.0030	.0033	.0037	.0041	.0045
17	.0007	.0008	.0009	.0010	.0012	.0013	.0015	.0017	.0019	.0021
18	.0003	.0003	.0004	.0004	.0005	.0006	.0006	.0007	.0008	.0009
19	.0001	.0001	.0001	.0002	.0002	.0002	.0003	.0003	.0003	.0004
20	.0000	.0000	.0001	.0001	.0001	.0001	.0001	.0001	.0001	.0002
21	.0000	.0000	.0000	.0000	.0000	.0000	.0000	.0000	.0001	.0001

					λ					
r	8.1	8.2	8.3	8.4	8.5	8.6	8.7	8.8	8.9	9.0
0	.0003	.0003	.0002	.0002	.0002	.0002	.0002	.0002	.0001	.0001
1	.0025	.0023	.0021	.0019	.0017	.0016	.0014	.0013	.0012	.0011
2	.0100	.0092	.0086	.0079	.0074	.0068	.0063	.0058	.0054	.0050
3	.0269	.0252	.0237	.0222	.0208	.0195	.0183	.0171	.0160	.0150
4	.0544	.0517	.0491	.0466	.0443	.0420	.0398	.0377	.0357	.0337
5	.0882	.0849	.0816	.0784	.0752	.0722	.0692	.0663	.0635	.0607
6	.1191	.1160	.1128	.1097	.1066	.1034	.1003	.0972	.0941	.0911
7	.1378	.1358	.1338	.1317	.1294	.1271	.1247	.1222	.1197	.1171
8	.1395	.1392	.1388	.1382	.1375	.1366	.1356	.1344	.1332	.1318
9	.1256	.1269	.1280	.1290	.1299	.1306	.1311	.1315	.1317	.1318
10	.1017	.1040	.1063	.1084	.1104	.1123	.1140	.1157	.1172	.1186
11	.0749	.0776	.0802	.0828	.0853	.0878	.0902	.0925	.0948	.0970
12	.0505	.0530	.0555	.0579	.0604	.0629	.0654	.0679	.0703	.0728
13	.0315	.0334	.0354	.0374	.0395	.0416	.0438	.0459	.0481	.0504
14	.0182	.0196	.0210	.0225	.0240	.0256	.0272	.0289	.0306	.0324
15	.0098	.0107	.0116	.0126	.0136	.0147	.0158	.0169	.0182	.0194

TABLE 4 *continued*

					λ					
r	8.1	8.2	8.3	8.4	8.5	8.6	8.7	8.8	8.9	9.0
16	.0050	.0055	.0060	.0066	.0072	.0079	.0086	.0093	.0101	.0109
17	.0024	.0026	.0029	.0033	.0036	.0040	.0044	.0048	.0053	.0058
18	.0011	.0012	.0014	.0015	.0017	.0019	.0021	.0024	.0026	.0029
19	.0005	.0005	.0006	.0007	.0008	.0009	.0010	.0011	.0012	.0014
20	.0002	.0002	.0002	.0003	.0003	.0004	.0004	.0005	.0005	.0006
21	.0001	.0001	.0001	.0001	.0001	.0002	.0002	.0002	.0002	.0003
22	.0000	.0000	.0000	.0000	.0001	.0001	.0001	.0001	.0001	.0001

					λ					
r	9.1	9.2	9.3	9.4	9.5	9.6	9.7	9.8	9.9	10
0	.0001	.0001	.0001	.0001	.0001	.0001	.0001	.0001	.0001	.0000
1	.0010	.0009	.0009	.0008	.0007	.0007	.0006	.0005	.0005	.0005
2	.0046	.0043	.0040	.0037	.0034	.0031	.0029	.0027	.0025	.0023
3	.0140	.0131	.0123	.0115	.0107	.0100	.0093	.0087	.0081	.0076
4	.0319	.0302	.0285	.0269	.0254	.0240	.0226	.0213	.0201	.0189
5	.0581	.0555	.0530	.0506	.0483	.0460	.0439	.0418	.0398	.0378
6	.0881	.0851	.0822	.0793	.0764	.0736	.0709	.0682	.0656	.0631
7	.1145	.1118	.1091	.1064	.1037	.1010	.0982	.0955	.0928	.0901
8	.1302	.1286	.1269	.1251	.1232	.1212	.1191	.1170	.1148	.1126
9	.1317	.1315	.1311	.1306	.1300	.1293	.1284	.1274	.1263	.1251
10	.1198	.1210	.1219	.1228	.1235	.1241	.1245	.1249	.1250	.1251
11	.0991	.1012	.1031	.1049	.1067	.1083	.1098	.1112	.1125	.1137
12	.0752	.0776	.0799	.0822	.0844	.0866	.0888	.0908	.0928	.0948
13	.0526	.0549	.0572	.0594	.0617	.0640	.0662	.0685	.0707	.0729
14	.0342	.0361	.0380	.0399	.0419	.0439	.0459	.0479	.0500	.0521
15	.0208	.0221	.0235	.0250	.0265	.0281	.0297	.0313	.0330	.0347
16	.0118	.0127	.0137	.0147	.0157	.0168	.0180	.0192	.0204	.0217
17	.0063	.0069	.0075	.0081	.0088	.0095	.0103	.0111	.0119	.0128
18	.0032	.0035	.0039	.0042	.0046	.0051	.0055	.0060	.0065	.0071
19	.0015	.0017	.0019	.0021	.0023	.0026	.0028	.0031	.0034	.0037
20	.0007	.0008	.0009	.0010	.0011	.0012	.0014	.0015	.0017	.0019
21	.0003	.0003	.0004	.0004	.0005	.0006	.0006	.0007	.0008	.0009
22	.0001	.0001	.0002	.0002	.0002	.0002	.0003	.0003	.0004	.0004
23	.0000	.0001	.0001	.0001	.0001	.0001	.0001	.0001	.0002	.0002
24	.0000	.0000	.0000	.0000	.0000	.0000	.0000	.0001	.0001	.0001

TABLE 4 *continued*

					λ					
r	11	12	13	14	15	16	17	18	19	20
0	.0000	.0000	.0000	.0000	.0000	.0000	.0000	.0000	.0000	.0000
1	.0002	.0001	.0000	.0000	.0000	.0000	.0000	.0000	.0000	.0000
2	.0010	.0004	.0002	.0001	.0000	.0000	.0000	.0000	.0000	.0000
3	.0037	.0018	.0008	.0004	.0002	.0001	.0000	.0000	.0000	.0000
4	.0102	.0053	.0027	.0013	.0006	.0003	.0001	.0001	.0000	.0000
5	.0224	.0127	.0070	.0037	.0019	.0010	.0005	.0002	.0001	.0001
6	.0411	.0255	.0152	.0087	.0048	.0026	.0014	.0007	.0004	.0002
7	.0646	.0437	.0281	.0174	.0104	.0060	.0034	.0018	.0010	.0005
8	.0888	.0655	.0457	.0304	.0194	.0120	.0072	.0042	.0024	.0013
9	.1085	.0874	.0661	.0473	.0324	.0213	.0135	.0083	.0050	.0029
10	.1194	.1048	.0859	.0663	.0486	.0341	.0230	.0150	.0095	.0058
11	.1194	.1144	.1015	.0844	.0663	.0496	.0355	.0245	.0164	.0106
12	.1094	.1144	.1099	.0984	.0829	.0661	.0504	.0368	.0259	.0176
13	.0926	.1056	.1099	.1060	.0956	.0814	.0658	.0509	.0378	.0271
14	.0728	.0905	.1021	.1060	.1024	.0930	.0800	.0655	.0514	.0387
15	.0534	.0724	.0885	.0989	.1024	.0992	.0906	.0786	.0650	.0516
16	.0367	.0543	.0719	.0866	.0960	.0992	.0963	.0884	.0772	.0646
17	.0237	.0383	.0550	.0713	.0847	.0934	.0963	.0936	.0863	.0760
18	.0145	.0256	.0397	.0554	.0706	.0830	.0909	.0936	.0911	.0844
19	.0084	.0161	.0272	.0409	.0557	.0699	.0814	.0887	.0911	.0888
20	.0046	.0097	.0177	.0286	.0418	.0559	.0692	.0798	.0866	.0888
21	.0024	.0055	.0109	.0191	.0299	.0426	.0560	.0684	.0783	.0846
22	.0012	.0030	.0065	.0121	.0204	.0310	.0433	.0560	.0676	.0769
23	.0006	.0016	.0037	.0074	.0133	.0216	.0320	.0438	.0559	.0669
24	.0003	.0008	.0020	.0043	.0083	.0144	.0226	.0328	.0442	.0557
25	.0001	.0004	.0010	.0024	.0050	.0092	.0154	.0237	.0336	.0446
26	.0000	.0002	.0005	.0013	.0029	.0057	.0101	.0164	.0246	.0343
27	.0000	.0001	.0002	.0007	.0016	.0034	.0063	.0109	.0173	.0254
28	.0000	.0000	.0001	.0003	.0009	.0019	.0038	.0070	.0117	.0181
29	.0000	.0000	.0001	.0002	.0004	.0011	.0023	.0044	.0077	.0125
30	.0000	.0000	.0000	.0001	.0002	.0006	.0013	.0026	.0049	.0083
31	.0000	.0000	.0000	.0000	.0001	.0003	.0007	.0015	.0030	.0054
32	.0000	.0000	.0000	.0000	.0001	.0001	.0004	.0009	.0018	.0034
33	.0000	.0000	.0000	.0000	.0000	.0001	.0002	.0005	.0010	.0020
34	.0000	.0000	.0000	.0000	.0000	.0000	.0001	.0002	.0006	.0012
35	.0000	.0000	.0000	.0000	.0000	.0000	.0000	.0001	.0003	.0007
36	.0000	.0000	.0000	.0000	.0000	.0000	.0000	.0001	.0002	.0004
37	.0000	.0000	.0000	.0000	.0000	.0000	.0000	.0000	.0001	.0002
38	.0000	.0000	.0000	.0000	.0000	.0000	.0000	.0000	.0000	.0001
39	.0000	.0000	.0000	.0000	.0000	.0000	.0000	.0000	.0000	.0001

Source: Extracted from William H. Beyer (ed.), *CRC Basic Statistical Tables* (Cleveland, Ohio: The Chemical Rubber Co., 1971).

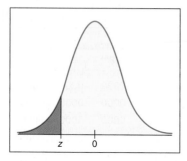

The table entry for z is the area to the left of z.

TABLE 5   Areas of a Standard Normal Distribution

(a) Table of Areas to the Left of z

z	.00	.01	.02	.03	.04	.05	.06	.07	.08	.09
−3.4	.0003	.0003	.0003	.0003	.0003	.0003	.0003	.0003	.0003	.0002
−3.3	.0005	.0005	.0005	.0004	.0004	.0004	.0004	.0004	.0004	.0003
−3.2	.0007	.0007	.0006	.0006	.0006	.0006	.0006	.0005	.0005	.0005
−3.1	.0010	.0009	.0009	.0009	.0008	.0008	.0008	.0008	.0007	.0007
−3.0	.0013	.0013	.0013	.0012	.0012	.0011	.0011	.0011	.0010	.0010
−2.9	.0019	.0018	.0018	.0017	.0016	.0016	.0015	.0015	.0014	.0014
−2.8	.0026	.0025	.0024	.0023	.0023	.0022	.0021	.0021	.0020	.0019
−2.7	.0035	.0034	.0033	.0032	.0031	.0030	.0029	.0028	.0027	.0026
−2.6	.0047	.0045	.0044	.0043	.0041	.0040	.0039	.0038	.0037	.0036
−2.5	.0062	.0060	.0059	.0057	.0055	.0054	.0052	.0051	.0049	.0048
−2.4	.0082	.0080	.0078	.0075	.0073	.0071	.0069	.0068	.0066	.0064
−2.3	.0107	.0104	.0102	.0099	.0096	.0094	.0091	.0089	.0087	.0084
−2.2	.0139	.0136	.0132	.0129	.0125	.0122	.0119	.0116	.0113	.0110
−2.1	.0179	.0174	.0170	.0166	.0162	.0158	.0154	.0150	.0146	.0143
−2.0	.0228	.0222	.0217	.0212	.0207	.0202	.0197	.0192	.0188	.0183
−1.9	.0287	.0281	.0274	.0268	.0262	.0256	.0250	.0244	.0239	.0233
−1.8	.0359	.0351	.0344	.0336	.0329	.0322	.0314	.0307	.0301	.0294
−1.7	.0446	.0436	.0427	.0418	.0409	.0401	.0392	.0384	.0375	.0367
−1.6	.0548	.0537	.0526	.0516	.0505	.0495	.0485	.0475	.0465	.0455
−1.5	.0668	.0655	.0643	.0630	.0618	.0606	.0594	.0582	.0571	.0559
−1.4	.0808	.0793	.0778	.0764	.0749	.0735	.0721	.0708	.0694	.0681
−1.3	.0968	.0951	.0934	.0918	.0901	.0885	.0869	.0853	.0838	.0823
−1.2	.1151	.1131	.1112	.1093	.1075	.1056	.1038	.1020	.1003	.0985
−1.1	.1357	.1335	.1314	.1292	.1271	.1251	.1230	.1210	.1190	.1170
−1.0	.1587	.1562	.1539	.1515	.1492	.1469	.1446	.1423	.1401	.1379
−0.9	.1841	.1814	.1788	.1762	.1736	.1711	.1685	.1660	.1635	.1611
−0.8	.2119	.2090	.2061	.2033	.2005	.1977	.1949	.1922	.1894	.1867
−0.7	.2420	.2389	.2358	.2327	.2296	.2266	.2236	.2206	.2177	.2148
−0.6	.2743	.2709	.2676	.2643	.2611	.2578	.2546	.2514	.2483	.2451
−0.5	.3085	.3050	.3015	.2981	.2946	.2912	.2877	.2843	.2810	.2776
−0.4	.3446	.3409	.3372	.3336	.3300	.3264	.3228	.3192	.3156	.3121
−0.3	.3821	.3783	.3745	.3707	.3669	.3632	.3594	.3557	.3520	.3483
−0.2	.4207	.4168	.4129	.4090	.4052	.4013	.3974	.3936	.3897	.3859
−0.1	.4602	.4562	.4522	.4483	.4443	.4404	.4364	.4325	.4286	.4247
−0.0	.5000	.4960	.4920	.4880	.4840	.4801	.4761	.4721	.4681	.4641

For values of z less than −3.49, use 0.000 to approximate the area.

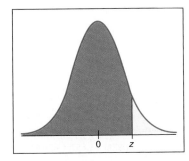

The table entry for z is the area to the left of z.

TABLE 5(a) *continued*

z	.00	.01	.02	.03	.04	.05	.06	.07	.08	.09
0.0	.5000	.5040	.5080	.5120	.5160	.5199	.5239	.5279	.5319	.5359
0.1	.5398	.5438	.5478	.5517	.5557	.5596	.5636	.5675	.5714	.5753
0.2	.5793	.5832	.5871	.5910	.5948	.5987	.6026	.6064	.6103	.6141
0.3	.6179	.6217	.6255	.6293	.6331	.6368	.6406	.6443	.6480	.6517
0.4	.6554	.6591	.6628	.6664	.6700	.6736	.6772	.6808	.6844	.6879
0.5	.6915	.6950	.6985	.7019	.7054	.7088	.7123	.7157	.7190	.7224
0.6	.7257	.7291	.7324	.7357	.7389	.7422	.7454	.7486	.7517	.7549
0.7	.7580	.7611	.7642	.7673	.7704	.7734	.7764	.7794	.7823	.7852
0.8	.7881	.7910	.7939	.7967	.7995	.8023	.8051	.8078	.8106	.8133
0.9	.8159	.8186	.8212	.8238	.8264	.8289	.8315	.8340	.8365	.8389
1.0	.8413	.8438	.8461	.8485	.8508	.8531	.8554	.8577	.8599	.8621
1.1	.8643	.8665	.8686	.8708	.8729	.8749	.8770	.8790	.8810	.8830
1.2	.8849	.8869	.8888	.8907	.8925	.8944	.8962	.8980	.8997	.9015
1.3	.9032	.9049	.9066	.9082	.9099	.9115	.9131	.9147	.9162	.9177
1.4	.9192	.9207	.9222	.9236	.9251	.9265	.9279	.9292	.9306	.9319
1.5	.9332	.9345	.9357	.9370	.9382	.9394	.9406	.9418	.9429	.9441
1.6	.9452	.9463	.9474	.9484	.9495	.9505	.9515	.9525	.9535	.9545
1.7	.9554	.9564	.9573	.9582	.9591	.9599	.9608	.9616	.9625	.9633
1.8	.9641	.9649	.9656	.9664	.9671	.9678	.9686	.9693	.9699	.9706
1.9	.9713	.9719	.9726	.9732	.9738	.9744	.9750	.9756	.9761	.9767
2.0	.9772	.9778	.9783	.9788	.9793	.9798	.9803	.9808	.9812	.9817
2.1	.9821	.9826	.9830	.9834	.9838	.9842	.9846	.9850	.9854	.9857
2.2	.9861	.9864	.9868	.9871	.9875	.9878	.9881	.9884	.9887	.9890
2.3	.9893	.9896	.9898	.9901	.9904	.9906	.9909	.9911	.9913	.9916
2.4	.9918	.9920	.9922	.9925	.9927	.9929	.9931	.9932	.9934	.9936
2.5	.9938	.9940	.9941	.9943	.9945	.9946	.9948	.9949	.9951	.9952
2.6	.9953	.9955	.9956	.9957	.9959	.9960	.9961	.9962	.9963	.9964
2.7	.9965	.9966	.9967	.9968	.9969	.9970	.9971	.9972	.9973	.9974
2.8	.9974	.9975	.9976	.9977	.9977	.9978	.9979	.9979	.9980	.9981
2.9	.9981	.9982	.9982	.9983	.9984	.9984	.9985	.9985	.9986	.9986
3.0	.9987	.9987	.9987	.9988	.9988	.9989	.9989	.9989	.9990	.9990
3.1	.9990	.9991	.9991	.9991	.9992	.9992	.9992	.9992	.9993	.9993
3.2	.9993	.9993	.9994	.9994	.9994	.9994	.9994	.9995	.9995	.9995
3.3	.9995	.9995	.9995	.9996	.9996	.9996	.9996	.9996	.9996	.9997
3.4	.9997	.9997	.9997	.9997	.9997	.9997	.9997	.9997	.9997	.9998

For z values greater than 3.49, use 1.000 to approximate the area.

TABLE 5 *continued*

(b) Confidence Interval Critical Values z_c

Level of Confidence c	Critical Value z_c
0.70, or 70%	1.04
0.75, or 75%	1.15
0.80, or 80%	1.28
0.85, or 85%	1.44
0.90, or 90%	1.645
0.95, or 95%	1.96
0.98, or 98%	2.33
0.99, or 99%	2.58

TABLE 5 *continued*

(c) Hypothesis Testing, Critical Values z_0

Level of Significance	$\alpha = 0.05$	$\alpha = 0.01$
Critical value z_0 for a left-tailed test	−1.645	−2.33
Critical value z_0 for a right-tailed test	1.645	2.33
Critical values $\pm z_0$ for a two-tailed test	±1.96	±2.58

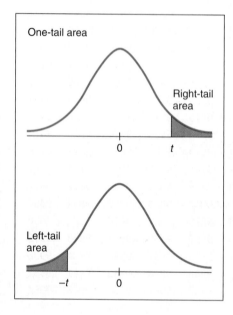

c is a confidence level

Area *c*

−*t*   0   *t*

One-tail area

Right-tail area

0   *t*

Left-tail area

−*t*   0

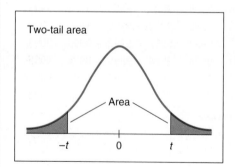

Two-tail area

Area

−*t*   0   *t*

TABLE 6 Critical Values for Student's *t* Distribution

one-tail area	0.250	0.125	0.100	0.075	0.050	0.025	0.010	0.005	0.0005
two-tail area	0.500	0.250	0.200	0.150	0.100	0.050	0.020	0.010	0.0010
d.f.　　*c*	0.500	0.750	0.800	0.850	0.900	0.950	0.980	0.990	0.999
1	1.000	2.414	3.078	4.165	6.314	12.706	31.821	63.657	636.619
2	0.816	1.604	1.886	2.282	2.920	4.303	6.965	9.925	31.599
3	0.765	1.423	1.638	1.924	2.353	3.182	4.541	5.841	12.924
4	0.741	1.344	1.533	1.778	2.132	2.776	3.747	4.604	8.610
5	0.727	1.301	1.476	1.699	2.015	2.571	3.365	4.032	6.869
6	0.718	1.273	1.440	1.650	1.943	2.447	3.143	3.707	5.959
7	0.711	1.254	1.415	1.617	1.895	2.365	2.998	3.499	5.408
8	0.706	1.240	1.397	1.592	1.860	2.306	2.896	3.355	5.041
9	0.703	1.230	1.383	1.574	1.833	2.262	2.821	3.250	4.781
10	0.700	1.221	1.372	1.559	1.812	2.228	2.764	3.169	4.587
11	0.697	1.214	1.363	1.548	1.796	2.201	2.718	3.106	4.437
12	0.695	1.209	1.356	1.538	1.782	2.179	2.681	3.055	4.318
13	0.694	1.204	1.350	1.530	1.771	2.160	2.650	3.012	4.221
14	0.692	1.200	1.345	1.523	1.761	2.145	2.624	2.977	4.140
15	0.691	1.197	1.341	1.517	1.753	2.131	2.602	2.947	4.073
16	0.690	1.194	1.337	1.512	1.746	2.120	2.583	2.921	4.015
17	0.689	1.191	1.333	1.508	1.740	2.110	2.567	2.898	3.965
18	0.688	1.189	1.330	1.504	1.734	2.101	2.552	2.878	3.922
19	0.688	1.187	1.328	1.500	1.729	2.093	2.539	2.861	3.883
20	0.687	1.185	1.325	1.497	1.725	2.086	2.528	2.845	3.850
21	0.686	1.183	1.323	1.494	1.721	2.080	2.518	2.831	3.819
22	0.686	1.182	1.321	1.492	1.717	2.074	2.508	2.819	3.792
23	0.685	1.180	1.319	1.489	1.714	2.069	2.500	2.807	3.768
24	0.685	1.179	1.318	1.487	1.711	2.064	2.492	2.797	3.745
25	0.684	1.198	1.316	1.485	1.708	2.060	2.485	2.787	3.725
26	0.684	1.177	1.315	1.483	1.706	2.056	2.479	2.779	3.707
27	0.684	1.176	1.314	1.482	1.703	2.052	2.473	2.771	3.690
28	0.683	1.175	1.313	1.480	1.701	2.048	2.467	2.763	3.674
29	0.683	1.174	1.311	1.479	1.699	2.045	2.462	2.756	3.659
30	0.683	1.173	1.310	1.477	1.697	2.042	2.457	2.750	3.646
35	0.682	1.170	1.306	1.472	1.690	2.030	2.438	2.724	3.591
40	0.681	1.167	1.303	1.468	1.684	2.021	2.423	2.704	3.551
45	0.680	1.165	1.301	1.465	1.679	2.014	2.412	2.690	3.520
50	0.679	1.164	1.299	1.462	1.676	2.009	2.403	2.678	3.496
60	0.679	1.162	1.296	1.458	1.671	2.000	2.390	2.660	3.460
70	0.678	1.160	1.294	1.456	1.667	1.994	2.381	2.648	3.435
80	0.678	1.159	1.292	1.453	1.664	1.990	2.374	2.639	3.416
100	0.677	1.157	1.290	1.451	1.660	1.984	2.364	2.626	3.390
500	0.675	1.152	1.283	1.442	1.648	1.965	2.334	2.586	3.310
1000	0.675	1.151	1.282	1.441	1.646	1.962	2.330	2.581	3.300
∞	0.674	1.150	1.282	1.440	1.645	1.960	2.326	2.576	3.291

For degrees of freedom *d.f.* not in the table, use the closest *d.f.* that is *smaller*.

TABLE 7   The χ^2 Distribution

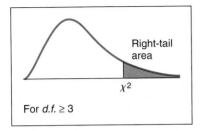

For *d.f.* ≥ 3

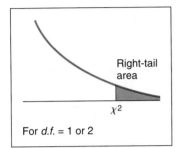

For *d.f.* = 1 or 2

d.f.	Right-tail Area									
	.995	.990	.975	.950	.900	.100	.050	.025	.010	.005
1	0.0^4393	0.0^3157	0.0^3982	0.0^2393	0.0158	2.71	3.84	5.02	6.63	7.88
2	0.0100	0.0201	0.0506	0.103	0.211	4.61	5.99	7.38	9.21	10.60
3	0.072	0.115	0.216	0.352	0.584	6.25	7.81	9.35	11.34	12.84
4	0.207	0.297	0.484	0.711	1.064	7.78	9.49	11.14	13.28	14.86
5	0.412	0.554	0.831	1.145	1.61	9.24	11.07	12.83	15.09	16.75
6	0.676	0.872	1.24	1.64	2.20	10.64	12.59	14.45	16.81	18.55
7	0.989	1.24	1.69	2.17	2.83	12.02	14.07	16.01	18.48	20.28
8	1.34	1.65	2.18	2.73	3.49	13.36	15.51	17.53	20.09	21.96
9	1.73	2.09	2.70	3.33	4.17	14.68	16.92	19.02	21.67	23.59
10	2.16	2.56	3.25	3.94	4.87	15.99	18.31	20.48	23.21	25.19
11	2.60	3.05	3.82	4.57	5.58	17.28	19.68	21.92	24.72	26.76
12	3.07	3.57	4.40	5.23	6.30	18.55	21.03	23.34	26.22	28.30
13	3.57	4.11	5.01	5.89	7.04	19.81	22.36	24.74	27.69	29.82
14	4.07	4.66	5.63	6.57	7.79	21.06	23.68	26.12	29.14	31.32
15	4.60	5.23	6.26	7.26	8.55	22.31	25.00	27.49	30.58	32.80
16	5.14	5.81	6.91	7.96	9.31	23.54	26.30	28.85	32.00	34.27
17	5.70	6.41	7.56	8.67	10.09	24.77	27.59	30.19	33.41	35.72
18	6.26	7.01	8.23	9.39	10.86	25.99	28.87	31.53	34.81	37.16
19	6.84	7.63	8.91	10.12	11.65	27.20	30.14	32.85	36.19	38.58
20	7.43	8.26	8.59	10.85	12.44	28.41	31.41	34.17	37.57	40.00
21	8.03	8.90	10.28	11.59	13.24	29.62	32.67	35.48	38.93	41.40
22	8.64	9.54	10.98	12.34	14.04	30.81	33.92	36.78	40.29	42.80
23	9.26	10.20	11.69	13.09	14.85	32.01	35.17	38.08	41.64	44.18
24	9.89	10.86	12.40	13.85	15.66	33.20	36.42	39.36	42.98	45.56
25	10.52	11.52	13.12	14.61	16.47	34.38	37.65	40.65	44.31	46.93
26	11.16	12.20	13.84	15.38	17.29	35.56	38.89	41.92	45.64	48.29
27	11.81	12.88	14.57	16.15	18.11	36.74	40.11	43.19	46.96	49.64
28	12.46	13.56	15.31	16.93	18.94	37.92	41.34	44.46	48.28	50.99
29	13.21	14.26	16.05	17.71	19.77	39.09	42.56	45.72	49.59	52.34
30	13.79	14.95	16.79	18.49	20.60	40.26	43.77	46.98	50.89	53.67
40	20.71	22.16	24.43	26.51	29.05	51.80	55.76	59.34	63.69	66.77
50	27.99	29.71	32.36	34.76	37.69	63.17	67.50	71.42	76.15	79.49
60	35.53	37.48	40.48	43.19	46.46	74.40	79.08	83.30	88.38	91.95
70	43.28	45.44	48.76	51.74	55.33	85.53	90.53	95.02	100.4	104.2
80	51.17	53.54	57.15	60.39	64.28	96.58	101.9	106.6	112.3	116.3
90	59.20	61.75	65.65	69.13	73.29	107.6	113.1	118.1	124.1	128.3
100	67.33	70.06	74.22	77.93	82.36	118.5	124.3	129.6	135.8	140.2

Source: From H. L. Herter, *Biometrika*, June 1964. Printed by permission of the Biometrika Trustees.

TABLE 8   Critical Values For *F* Distribution

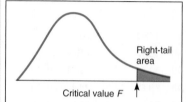

Critical value *F*

Right-tail area

	Right-tail area	Degrees of freedom numerator, $d.f._N$								
		1	2	3	4	5	6	7	8	9
1	0.100	39.86	49.50	53.59	55.83	57.24	58.20	58.91	59.44	59.86
	0.050	161.45	199.50	215.71	224.58	230.16	233.99	236.77	238.88	240.54
	0.025	647.79	799.50	864.16	899.58	921.85	937.11	948.22	956.66	963.28
	0.010	4052.2	4999.5	5403.4	5624.6	5763.6	5859.0	5928.4	5981.1	6022.5
	0.001	405284	500000	540379	562500	576405	585937	592873	598144	602284
2	0.100	8.53	9.00	9.16	9.24	9.29	9.33	9.35	9.37	9.38
	0.050	18.51	19.00	19.16	19.25	19.30	19.33	19.35	19.37	19.38
	0.025	38.51	39.00	39.17	39.25	39.30	39.33	39.36	39.37	39.39
	0.010	98.50	99.00	99.17	99.25	99.30	99.33	99.36	99.37	99.39
	0.001	998.50	999.00	999.17	999.25	999.30	999.33	999.36	999.37	999.39
3	0.100	5.54	5.46	5.39	5.34	5.31	5.28	5.27	5.25	5.24
	0.050	10.13	9.55	9.28	9.12	9.01	8.94	8.89	8.85	8.81
	0.025	17.44	16.04	15.44	15.10	14.88	14.73	14.62	14.54	14.47
	0.010	34.12	30.82	29.46	28.71	28.24	27.91	27.67	27.49	27.35
	0.001	167.03	148.50	141.11	137.10	134.58	132.85	131.58	130.62	129.86
4	0.100	4.54	4.32	4.19	4.11	4.05	4.01	3.98	3.95	3.94
	0.050	7.71	6.94	6.59	6.39	6.26	6.16	6.09	6.04	6.00
	0.025	12.22	10.65	9.98	9.60	9.36	9.20	9.07	8.98	8.90
	0.010	21.20	18.00	16.69	15.98	15.52	15.21	14.98	14.80	14.66
	0.001	74.14	61.25	56.18	53.44	51.71	50.53	49.66	49.00	48.47
5	0.100	4.06	3.78	3.62	3.52	3.45	3.40	3.37	3.34	3.32
	0.050	6.61	5.79	5.41	5.19	5.05	4.95	4.88	4.82	4.77
	0.025	10.01	8.43	7.76	7.39	7.15	6.98	6.85	6.76	6.68
	0.010	16.26	13.27	12.06	11.39	10.97	10.67	10.46	10.29	10.16
	0.001	47.18	37.12	33.20	31.09	29.75	28.83	28.16	27.65	27.24
6	0.100	3.78	3.46	3.29	3.18	3.11	3.05	3.01	2.98	2.96
	0.050	5.99	5.14	4.76	4.53	4.39	4.28	4.21	4.15	4.10
	0.025	8.81	7.26	6.60	6.23	5.99	5.82	5.70	5.60	5.52
	0.010	13.75	10.92	9.78	9.15	8.75	8.47	8.26	8.10	7.98
	0.001	35.51	27.00	23.70	21.92	20.80	20.03	19.46	19.03	18.69
7	0.100	3.59	3.26	3.07	2.96	2.88	2.83	2.78	2.75	2.72
	0.050	5.59	4.74	4.35	4.12	3.97	3.87	3.79	3.73	3.68
	0.025	8.07	6.54	5.89	5.52	5.29	5.12	4.99	4.90	4.82
	0.010	12.25	9.55	8.45	7.85	7.46	7.19	6.99	6.84	6.72
	0.001	29.25	21.69	18.77	17.20	16.21	15.52	15.02	14.63	14.33
8	0.100	3.46	3.11	2.92	2.81	2.73	2.67	2.62	2.59	2.56
	0.050	5.32	4.46	4.07	3.84	3.69	3.58	3.50	3.44	3.39
	0.025	7.57	6.06	5.42	5.05	4.82	4.65	4.53	4.43	4.36
	0.010	11.26	8.65	7.59	7.01	6.63	6.37	6.18	6.03	5.91
	0.001	25.41	18.49	15.83	14.39	13.48	12.86	12.40	12.05	11.77

Degrees of freedom denominator, $d.f._D$

TABLE 8 *continued*

	Right-tail area	Degrees of freedom numerator, $d.f._N$										
		10	12	15	20	25	30	40	50	60	120	1000
1	0.100	60.19	60.71	61.22	61.74	62.05	62.26	62.53	62.69	62.79	63.06	63.30
	0.050	241.88	243.91	245.95	248.01	249.26	250.10	251.14	251.77	252.20	253.25	254.19
	0.025	968.63	976.71	984.87	993.10	998.08	1001.4	1005.6	1008.1	1009.8	1014.0	1017.7
	0.010	6055.8	6106.3	6157.3	6208.7	6239.8	6260.6	6286.8	6302.5	6313.0	6339.4	6362.7
	0.001	605621	610668	615764	620908	624017	626099	628712	630285	631337	633972	636301
2	0.100	9.39	9.41	9.42	9.44	9.45	9.46	9.47	9.47	9.47	9.48	9.49
	0.050	19.40	19.41	19.43	19.45	19.46	19.46	19.47	19.48	19.48	19.49	19.49
	0.025	39.40	39.41	39.43	39.45	39.46	39.46	39.47	39.48	39.48	39.49	39.50
	0.010	99.40	99.42	99.43	99.45	99.46	99.47	99.47	99.48	99.48	99.49	99.50
	0.001	999.40	999.42	999.43	999.45	999.46	999.47	999.47	999.48	999.48	999.49	999.50
3	0.100	5.23	5.22	5.20	5.18	5.17	5.17	5.16	5.15	5.15	5.14	5.13
	0.050	8.79	8.74	8.70	8.66	8.63	8.62	8.59	8.58	8.57	8.55	8.53
	0.025	14.42	14.34	14.25	14.17	14.12	14.08	14.04	14.01	13.99	13.95	13.91
	0.010	27.23	27.05	26.87	26.69	26.58	26.50	26.41	26.35	26.32	26.22	26.14
	0.001	129.25	128.32	127.37	126.42	125.84	125.45	124.96	124.66	124.47	123.97	123.53
4	0.100	3.92	3.90	3.87	3.84	3.83	3.82	3.80	3.80	3.79	3.78	3.76
	0.050	5.96	5.91	5.86	5.80	5.77	5.75	5.72	5.70	5.69	5.66	5.63
	0.025	8.84	8.75	8.66	8.56	8.50	8.46	8.41	8.38	8.36	8.31	8.26
	0.010	14.55	14.37	14.20	14.02	13.91	13.84	13.75	13.69	13.65	13.56	13.47
	0.001	48.05	47.41	46.76	46.10	45.70	45.43	45.09	44.88	44.75	44.40	44.09
5	0.100	3.30	3.27	3.24	3.21	3.19	3.17	3.16	3.15	3.14	3.12	3.11
	0.050	4.74	4.68	4.62	4.56	4.52	4.50	4.46	4.44	4.43	4.40	4.37
	0.025	6.62	6.52	6.43	6.33	6.27	6.23	6.18	6.14	6.12	6.07	6.02
	0.010	10.05	9.89	9.72	9.55	9.45	9.38	9.29	9.24	9.20	9.11	9.03
	0.001	26.92	26.42	25.91	25.39	25.08	24.87	24.60	24.44	24.33	24.06	23.82
6	0.100	2.94	2.90	2.87	2.84	2.81	2.80	2.78	2.77	2.76	2.74	2.72
	0.050	4.06	4.00	3.94	3.87	3.83	3.81	3.77	3.75	3.74	3.70	3.67
	0.025	5.46	5.37	5.27	5.17	5.11	5.07	5.01	4.98	4.96	4.90	4.86
	0.010	7.87	7.72	7.56	7.40	7.30	7.23	7.14	7.09	7.06	6.97	6.89
	0.001	18.41	17.99	17.56	17.12	16.85	16.67	16.44	16.31	16.21	15.98	15.77
7	0.100	2.70	2.67	2.63	2.59	2.57	2.56	2.54	2.52	2.51	2.49	2.47
	0.050	3.64	3.57	3.51	3.44	3.40	3.38	3.34	3.32	3.30	3.27	3.23
	0.025	4.76	4.67	4.57	4.47	4.40	4.36	4.31	4.28	4.25	4.20	4.15
	0.010	6.62	6.47	6.31	6.16	6.06	5.99	5.91	5.86	5.82	5.74	5.66
	0.001	14.08	13.71	13.32	12.93	12.69	12.53	12.33	12.20	12.12	11.91	11.72
8	0.100	2.54	2.50	2.46	2.42	2.40	2.38	2.36	2.35	2.34	2.32	2.30
	0.050	3.35	3.28	3.22	3.15	3.11	3.08	3.04	3.02	3.01	2.97	2.93
	0.025	4.30	4.20	4.10	4.00	3.94	3.89	3.84	3.81	3.78	3.73	3.68
	0.010	5.81	5.67	5.52	5.36	5.26	5.20	5.12	5.07	5.03	4.95	4.87
	0.001	11.54	11.19	10.84	10.48	10.26	10.11	9.92	9.80	9.73	9.53	9.36

Degrees of freedom denominator, $d.f._D$

TABLE 8 *continued*

	Right-tail area	Degrees of freedom numerator, $d.f._N$								
		1	2	3	4	5	6	7	8	9
9	0.100	3.36	3.01	2.81	2.69	2.61	2.55	2.51	2.47	2.44
	0.050	5.12	4.26	3.86	3.63	3.48	3.37	3.29	3.23	3.18
	0.025	7.21	5.71	5.08	4.72	4.48	4.32	4.20	4.10	4.03
	0.010	10.56	8.02	6.99	6.42	6.06	5.80	5.61	5.47	5.35
	0.001	22.86	16.39	13.90	12.56	11.71	11.13	10.70	10.37	10.11
10	0.100	3.29	2.92	2.73	2.61	2.52	2.46	2.41	2.38	2.35
	0.050	4.96	4.10	3.71	3.48	3.33	3.22	3.14	3.07	3.02
	0.025	6.94	5.46	4.83	4.47	4.24	4.07	3.95	3.85	3.78
	0.010	10.04	7.56	6.55	5.99	5.64	5.39	5.20	5.06	4.94
	0.001	21.04	14.91	12.55	11.28	10.48	9.93	9.52	9.20	8.96
11	0.100	3.23	2.86	2.66	2.54	2.45	2.39	2.34	2.30	2.27
	0.050	4.84	3.98	3.59	3.36	3.20	3.09	3.01	2.95	2.90
	0.025	6.72	5.26	4.63	4.28	4.04	3.88	3.76	3.66	3.59
	0.010	9.65	7.21	6.22	5.67	5.32	5.07	4.89	4.74	4.63
	0.001	19.69	13.81	11.56	10.35	9.58	9.05	8.66	8.35	8.12
12	0.100	3.18	2.81	2.61	2.48	2.39	2.33	2.28	2.24	2.21
	0.050	4.75	3.89	3.49	3.26	3.11	3.00	2.91	2.85	2.80
	0.025	6.55	5.10	4.47	4.12	3.89	3.73	3.61	3.51	3.44
	0.010	9.33	6.93	5.95	5.41	5.06	4.82	4.64	4.50	4.39
	0.001	18.64	12.97	10.80	9.63	8.89	8.38	8.00	7.71	7.48
13	0.100	3.14	2.76	2.56	2.43	2.35	2.28	2.23	2.20	2.16
	0.050	4.67	3.81	3.41	3.18	3.03	2.92	2.83	2.77	2.71
	0.025	6.41	4.97	4.35	4.00	3.77	3.60	3.48	3.39	3.31
	0.010	9.07	6.70	5.74	5.21	4.86	4.62	4.44	4.30	4.19
	0.001	17.82	12.31	10.21	9.07	8.35	7.86	7.49	7.21	6.98
14	0.100	3.10	2.73	2.52	2.39	2.31	2.24	2.19	2.15	2.12
	0.050	4.60	3.74	3.34	3.11	2.96	2.85	2.76	2.70	2.65
	0.025	6.30	4.86	4.24	3.89	3.66	3.50	3.38	3.29	3.21
	0.010	8.86	6.51	5.56	5.04	4.69	4.46	4.28	4.14	4.03
	0.001	17.14	11.78	9.73	8.62	7.92	7.44	7.08	6.80	6.58
15	0.100	3.07	2.70	2.49	2.36	2.27	2.21	2.16	2.12	2.09
	0.050	4.54	3.68	3.29	3.06	2.90	2.79	2.71	2.64	2.59
	0.025	6.20	4.77	4.15	3.80	3.58	3.41	3.29	3.20	3.12
	0.010	8.68	6.36	5.42	4.89	4.56	4.32	4.14	4.00	3.89
	0.001	16.59	11.34	9.34	8.25	7.57	7.09	6.74	6.47	6.26
16	0.100	3.05	2.67	2.46	2.33	2.24	2.18	2.13	2.09	2.06
	0.050	4.49	3.63	3.24	3.01	2.85	2.74	2.66	2.59	2.54
	0.025	6.12	4.69	4.08	3.73	3.50	3.34	3.22	3.12	3.05
	0.010	8.53	6.23	5.29	4.77	4.44	4.20	4.03	3.89	3.78
	0.001	16.12	10.97	9.01	7.94	7.27	6.80	6.46	6.19	5.98

Degrees of freedom denominator, $d.f._D$

TABLE 8 *continued*

	Right-tail area	\multicolumn{11}{c}{Degrees of freedom numerator, $d.f._N$}
		10	12	15	20	25	30	40	50	60	120	1000
9	0.100	2.42	2.38	2.34	2.30	2.27	2.25	2.23	2.22	2.21	2.18	2.16
	0.050	3.14	3.07	3.01	2.94	2.89	2.86	2.83	2.80	2.79	2.75	2.71
	0.025	3.96	3.87	3.77	3.67	3.60	3.56	3.51	3.47	3.45	3.39	3.34
	0.010	5.26	5.11	4.96	4.81	4.71	4.65	4.57	4.52	4.48	4.40	4.32
	0.001	9.89	9.57	9.24	8.90	8.69	8.55	8.37	8.26	8.19	8.00	7.84
10	0.100	2.32	2.28	2.24	2.20	2.17	2.16	2.13	2.12	2.11	2.08	2.06
	0.050	2.98	2.91	2.85	2.77	2.73	2.70	2.66	2.64	2.62	2.58	2.54
	0.025	3.72	3.62	3.52	3.42	3.35	3.31	3.26	3.22	3.20	3.14	3.09
	0.010	4.85	4.71	4.56	4.41	4.31	4.25	4.17	4.12	4.08	4.00	3.92
	0.001	8.75	8.45	8.13	7.80	7.60	7.47	7.30	7.19	7.12	6.94	6.78
11	0.100	2.25	2.21	2.17	2.12	2.10	2.08	2.05	2.04	2.03	2.00	1.98
	0.050	2.85	2.79	2.72	2.65	2.60	2.57	2.53	2.51	2.49	2.45	2.41
	0.025	3.53	3.43	3.33	3.23	3.16	3.12	3.06	3.03	3.00	2.94	2.89
	0.010	4.54	4.40	4.25	4.10	4.01	3.94	3.86	3.81	3.78	3.69	3.61
	0.001	7.92	7.63	7.32	7.01	6.81	6.68	6.52	6.42	6.35	6.18	6.02
12	0.100	2.19	2.15	2.10	2.06	2.03	2.01	1.99	1.97	1.96	1.93	1.91
	0.050	2.75	2.69	2.62	2.54	2.50	2.47	2.43	2.40	2.38	2.34	2.30
	0.025	3.37	3.28	3.18	3.07	3.01	2.96	2.91	2.87	2.85	2.79	2.73
	0.010	4.30	4.16	4.01	3.86	3.76	3.70	3.62	3.57	3.54	3.45	3.37
	0.001	7.29	7.00	6.71	6.40	6.22	6.09	5.93	5.83	5.76	5.59	5.44
13	0.100	2.14	2.10	2.05	2.01	1.98	1.96	1.93	1.92	1.90	1.88	1.85
	0.050	2.67	2.60	2.53	2.46	2.41	2.38	2.34	2.31	2.30	2.25	2.21
	0.025	3.25	3.15	3.05	2.95	2.88	2.84	2.78	2.74	2.72	2.66	2.60
	0.010	4.10	3.96	3.82	3.66	3.57	3.51	3.43	3.38	3.34	3.25	3.18
	0.001	6.80	6.52	6.23	5.93	5.75	5.63	5.47	5.37	5.30	5.14	4.99
14	0.100	2.10	2.05	2.01	1.96	1.93	1.91	1.89	1.87	1.86	1.83	1.80
	0.050	2.60	2.53	2.46	2.39	2.34	2.31	2.27	2.24	2.22	2.18	2.14
	0.025	3.15	3.05	2.95	2.84	2.78	2.73	2.67	2.64	2.61	2.55	2.50
	0.010	3.94	3.80	3.66	3.51	3.41	3.35	3.27	3.22	3.18	3.09	3.02
	0.001	6.40	6.13	5.85	5.56	5.38	5.25	5.10	5.00	4.94	4.77	4.62
15	0.100	2.06	2.02	1.97	1.92	1.89	1.87	1.85	1.83	1.82	1.79	1.76
	0.050	2.54	2.48	2.40	2.33	2.28	2.25	2.20	2.18	2.16	2.11	2.07
	0.025	3.06	2.96	2.86	2.76	2.69	2.64	2.59	2.55	2.52	2.46	2.40
	0.010	3.80	3.67	3.52	3.37	3.28	3.21	3.13	3.08	3.05	2.96	2.88
	0.001	6.08	5.81	5.54	5.25	5.07	4.95	4.80	4.70	4.64	4.47	4.33
16	0.100	2.03	1.99	1.94	1.89	1.86	1.84	1.81	1.79	1.78	1.75	1.72
	0.050	2.49	2.42	2.35	2.28	2.23	2.19	2.15	2.12	2.11	2.06	2.02
	0.025	2.99	2.89	2.79	2.68	2.61	2.57	2.51	2.47	2.45	2.38	2.32
	0.010	3.69	3.55	3.41	3.26	3.16	3.10	3.02	2.97	2.93	2.84	2.76
	0.001	5.81	5.55	5.27	4.99	4.82	4.70	4.54	4.45	4.39	4.23	4.08

Degrees of freedom denominator, $d.f._D$

TABLE 8 *continued*

	Right-tail area	Degrees of freedom numerator, $d.f._N$								
		1	2	3	4	5	6	7	8	9
	0.100	3.03	2.64	2.44	2.31	2.22	2.15	2.10	2.06	2.03
	0.050	4.45	3.59	3.20	2.96	2.81	2.70	2.61	2.55	2.49
17	0.025	6.04	4.62	4.01	3.66	3.44	3.28	3.16	3.06	2.98
	0.010	8.40	6.11	5.19	4.67	4.34	4.10	3.93	3.79	3.68
	0.001	15.72	10.66	8.73	7.68	7.02	6.56	6.22	5.96	5.75
	0.100	3.01	2.62	2.42	2.29	2.20	2.13	2.08	2.04	2.00
	0.050	4.41	3.55	3.16	2.93	2.77	2.66	2.58	2.51	2.46
18	0.025	5.98	4.56	3.95	3.61	3.38	3.22	3.10	3.01	2.93
	0.010	8.29	6.01	5.09	4.58	4.25	4.01	3.84	3.71	3.60
	0.001	15.38	10.39	8.49	7.46	6.81	6.35	6.02	5.76	5.56
	0.100	2.99	2.61	2.40	2.27	2.18	2.11	2.06	2.02	1.98
	0.050	4.38	3.52	3.13	2.90	2.74	2.63	2.54	2.48	2.42
19	0.025	5.92	4.51	3.90	3.56	3.33	3.17	3.05	2.96	2.88
	0.010	8.18	5.93	5.01	4.50	4.17	3.94	3.77	3.63	3.52
	0.001	15.08	10.16	8.28	7.27	6.62	6.18	5.85	5.59	5.39
	0.100	2.97	2.59	2.38	2.25	2.16	2.09	2.04	2.00	1.96
	0.050	4.35	3.49	3.10	2.87	2.71	2.60	2.51	2.45	2.39
20	0.025	5.87	4.46	3.86	3.51	3.29	3.13	3.01	2.91	2.84
	0.010	8.10	5.85	4.94	4.43	4.10	3.87	3.70	3.56	3.46
	0.001	14.82	9.95	8.10	7.10	6.46	6.02	5.69	5.44	5.24
	0.100	2.96	2.57	2.36	2.23	2.14	2.08	2.02	1.98	1.95
	0.050	4.32	3.47	3.07	2.84	2.68	2.57	2.49	2.42	2.37
21	0.025	5.83	4.42	3.82	3.48	3.25	3.09	2.97	2.87	2.80
	0.010	8.02	5.78	4.87	4.37	4.04	3.81	3.64	3.51	3.40
	0.001	14.59	9.77	7.94	6.95	6.32	5.88	5.56	5.31	5.11
	0.100	2.95	2.56	2.35	2.22	2.13	2.06	2.01	1.97	1.93
	0.050	4.30	3.44	3.05	2.82	2.66	2.55	2.46	2.40	2.34
22	0.025	5.79	4.38	3.78	3.44	3.22	3.05	2.93	2.84	2.76
	0.010	7.95	5.72	4.82	4.31	3.99	3.76	3.59	3.45	3.35
	0.001	14.38	9.61	7.80	6.81	6.19	5.76	5.44	5.19	4.99
	0.100	2.94	2.55	2.34	2.21	2.11	2.05	1.99	1.95	1.92
	0.050	4.28	3.42	3.03	2.80	2.64	2.53	2.44	2.37	2.32
23	0.025	5.75	4.35	3.75	3.41	3.18	3.02	2.90	2.81	2.73
	0.010	7.88	5.66	4.76	4.26	3.94	3.71	3.54	3.41	3.30
	0.001	14.20	9.47	7.67	6.70	6.08	5.65	5.33	5.09	4.89
	0.100	2.93	2.54	2.33	2.19	2.10	2.04	1.98	1.94	1.91
	0.050	4.26	3.40	3.01	2.78	2.62	2.51	2.42	2.36	2.30
24	0.025	5.72	4.32	3.72	3.38	3.15	2.99	2.87	2.78	2.70
	0.010	7.82	5.61	4.72	4.22	3.90	3.67	3.50	3.36	3.26
	0.001	14.03	9.34	7.55	6.59	5.98	5.55	5.23	4.99	4.80

Degrees of freedom denominator, $d.f._D$

TABLE 8 *continued*

| | Right-tail area | \multicolumn{11}{c}{Degrees of freedom numerator, $d.f._N$} |
		10	12	15	20	25	30	40	50	60	120	1000
17	0.100	2.00	1.96	1.91	1.86	1.83	1.81	1.78	1.76	1.75	1.72	1.69
	0.050	2.45	2.38	2.31	2.23	2.18	2.15	2.10	2.08	2.06	2.01	1.97
	0.025	2.92	2.82	2.72	2.62	2.55	2.50	2.44	2.41	2.38	2.32	2.26
	0.010	3.59	3.46	3.31	3.16	3.07	3.00	2.92	2.87	2.83	2.75	2.66
	0.001	5.58	5.32	5.05	4.78	4.60	4.48	4.33	4.24	4.18	4.02	3.87
18	0.100	1.98	1.93	1.89	1.84	1.80	1.78	1.75	1.74	1.72	1.69	1.66
	0.050	2.41	2.34	2.27	2.19	2.14	2.11	2.06	2.04	2.02	1.97	1.92
	0.025	2.87	2.77	2.67	2.56	2.49	2.44	2.38	2.35	2.32	2.26	2.20
	0.010	3.51	3.37	3.23	3.08	2.98	2.92	2.84	2.78	2.75	2.66	2.58
	0.001	5.39	5.13	4.87	4.59	4.42	4.30	4.15	4.06	4.00	3.84	3.69
19	0.100	1.96	1.91	1.86	1.81	1.78	1.76	1.73	1.71	1.70	1.67	1.64
	0.050	2.38	2.31	2.23	2.16	2.11	2.07	2.03	2.00	1.98	1.93	1.88
	0.025	2.82	2.72	2.62	2.51	2.44	2.39	2.33	2.30	2.27	2.20	2.14
	0.010	3.43	3.30	3.15	3.00	2.91	2.84	2.76	2.71	2.67	2.58	2.50
	0.001	5.22	4.97	4.70	4.43	4.26	4.14	3.99	3.90	3.84	3.68	3.53
20	0.100	1.94	1.89	1.84	1.79	1.76	1.74	1.71	1.69	1.68	1.64	1.61
	0.050	2.35	2.28	2.20	2.12	2.07	2.04	1.99	1.97	1.95	1.90	1.85
	0.025	2.77	2.68	2.57	2.46	2.40	2.35	2.29	2.25	2.22	2.16	2.09
	0.010	3.37	3.23	3.09	2.94	2.84	2.78	2.69	2.64	2.61	2.52	2.43
	0.001	5.08	4.82	4.56	4.29	4.12	4.00	3.86	3.77	3.70	3.54	3.40
21	0.100	1.92	1.87	1.83	1.78	1.74	1.72	1.69	1.67	1.66	1.62	1.59
	0.050	2.32	2.25	2.18	2.10	2.05	2.01	1.96	1.94	1.92	1.87	1.82
	0.025	2.73	2.64	2.53	2.42	2.36	2.31	2.25	2.21	2.18	2.11	2.05
	0.010	3.31	3.17	3.03	2.88	2.79	2.72	2.64	2.58	2.55	2.46	2.37
	0.001	4.95	4.70	4.44	4.17	4.00	3.88	3.74	3.64	3.58	3.42	3.28
22	0.100	1.90	1.86	1.81	1.76	1.73	1.70	1.67	1.65	1.64	1.60	1.57
	0.050	2.30	2.23	2.15	2.07	2.02	1.98	1.94	1.91	1.89	1.84	1.79
	0.025	2.70	2.60	2.50	2.39	2.32	2.27	2.21	2.17	2.14	2.08	2.01
	0.010	3.26	3.12	2.98	2.83	2.73	2.67	2.58	2.53	2.50	2.40	2.32
	0.001	4.83	4.58	4.33	4.06	3.89	3.78	3.63	3.54	3.48	3.32	3.17
23	0.100	1.89	1.84	1.80	1.74	1.71	1.69	1.66	1.64	1.62	1.59	1.55
	0.050	2.27	2.20	2.13	2.05	2.00	1.96	1.91	1.88	1.86	1.81	1.76
	0.025	2.67	2.57	2.47	2.36	2.29	2.24	2.18	2.14	2.11	2.04	1.98
	0.010	3.21	3.07	2.93	2.78	2.69	2.62	2.54	2.48	2.45	2.35	2.27
	0.001	4.73	4.48	4.23	3.96	3.79	3.68	3.53	3.44	3.38	3.22	3.08
24	0.100	1.88	1.83	1.78	1.73	1.70	1.67	1.64	1.62	1.61	1.57	1.54
	0.050	2.25	2.18	2.11	2.03	1.97	1.94	1.89	1.86	1.84	1.79	1.74
	0.025	2.64	2.54	2.44	2.33	2.26	2.21	2.15	2.11	2.08	2.01	1.94
	0.010	3.17	3.03	2.89	2.74	2.64	2.58	2.49	2.44	2.40	2.31	2.22
	0.001	4.64	4.39	4.14	3.87	3.71	3.59	3.45	3.36	3.29	3.14	2.99

Degrees of freedom denominator, $d.f._D$

TABLE 8 *continued*

	Right-tail area	\multicolumn{9}{c}{Degrees of freedom numerator, $d.f._N$}								
		1	2	3	4	5	6	7	8	9
	0.100	2.92	2.53	2.32	2.18	2.09	2.02	1.97	1.93	1.89
	0.050	4.24	3.39	2.99	2.76	2.60	2.49	2.40	2.34	2.28
25	0.025	5.69	4.29	3.69	3.35	3.13	2.97	2.85	2.75	2.68
	0.010	7.77	5.57	4.68	4.18	3.85	3.63	3.46	3.32	3.22
	0.001	13.88	9.22	7.45	6.49	5.89	5.46	5.15	4.91	4.71
	0.100	2.91	2.52	2.31	2.17	2.08	2.01	1.96	1.92	1.88
	0.050	4.23	3.37	2.98	2.74	2.59	2.47	2.39	2.32	2.27
26	0.025	5.66	4.27	3.67	3.33	3.10	2.94	2.82	2.73	2.65
	0.010	7.72	5.53	4.64	4.14	3.82	3.59	3.42	3.29	3.18
	0.001	13.74	9.12	7.36	6.41	5.80	5.38	5.07	4.83	4.64
	0.100	2.90	2.51	2.30	2.17	2.07	2.00	1.95	1.91	1.87
	0.050	4.21	3.35	2.96	2.73	2.57	2.46	2.37	2.31	2.25
27	0.025	5.63	4.24	3.65	3.31	3.08	2.92	2.80	2.71	2.63
	0.010	7.68	5.49	4.60	4.11	3.78	3.56	3.39	3.26	3.15
	0.001	13.61	9.02	7.27	6.33	5.73	5.31	5.00	4.76	4.57
	0.100	2.89	2.50	2.29	2.16	2.06	2.00	1.94	1.90	1.87
	0.050	4.20	3.34	2.95	2.71	2.56	2.45	2.36	2.29	2.24
28	0.025	5.61	4.22	3.63	3.29	3.06	2.90	2.78	2.69	2.61
	0.010	7.64	5.45	4.57	4.07	3.75	3.53	3.36	3.23	3.12
	0.001	13.50	8.93	7.19	6.25	5.66	5.24	4.93	4.69	4.50
	0.100	2.89	2.50	2.28	2.15	2.06	1.99	1.93	1.89	1.86
	0.050	4.18	3.33	2.93	2.70	2.55	2.43	2.35	2.28	2.22
29	0.025	5.59	4.20	3.61	3.27	3.04	2.88	2.76	2.67	2.59
	0.010	7.60	5.42	4.54	4.04	3.73	3.50	3.33	3.20	3.09
	0.001	13.39	8.85	7.12	6.19	5.59	5.18	4.87	4.64	4.45
	0.100	2.88	2.49	2.28	2.14	2.05	1.98	1.93	1.88	1.85
	0.050	4.17	3.32	2.92	2.69	2.53	2.42	2.33	2.27	2.21
30	0.025	5.57	4.18	3.59	3.25	3.03	2.87	2.75	2.65	2.57
	0.010	7.56	5.39	4.51	4.02	3.70	3.47	3.30	3.17	3.07
	0.001	13.29	8.77	7.05	6.12	5.53	5.12	4.82	4.58	4.39
	0.100	2.84	2.44	2.23	2.09	2.00	1.93	1.87	1.83	1.79
	0.050	4.08	3.23	2.84	2.61	2.45	2.34	2.25	2.18	2.12
40	0.025	5.42	4.05	3.46	3.13	2.90	2.74	2.62	2.53	2.45
	0.010	7.31	5.18	4.31	3.83	3.51	3.29	3.12	2.99	2.89
	0.001	12.61	8.25	6.59	5.70	5.13	4.73	4.44	4.21	4.02
	0.100	2.81	2.41	2.20	2.06	1.97	1.90	1.84	1.80	1.76
	0.050	4.03	3.18	2.79	2.56	2.40	2.29	2.20	2.13	2.07
50	0.025	5.34	3.97	3.39	3.05	2.83	2.67	2.55	2.46	2.38
	0.010	7.17	5.06	4.20	3.72	3.41	3.19	3.02	2.89	2.78
	0.001	12.22	7.96	6.34	5.46	4.90	4.51	4.22	4.00	3.82

Degrees of freedom denominator, $d.f._D$

TABLE 8 *continued*

	Right-tail area	Degrees of freedom numerator, $d.f._N$										
		10	12	15	20	25	30	40	50	60	120	1000
	0.100	1.87	1.82	1.77	1.72	1.68	1.66	1.63	1.61	1.59	1.56	1.52
	0.050	2.24	2.16	2.09	2.01	1.96	1.92	1.87	1.84	1.82	1.77	1.72
25	0.025	2.61	2.51	2.41	2.30	2.23	2.18	2.12	2.08	2.05	1.98	1.91
	0.010	3.13	2.99	2.85	2.70	2.60	2.54	2.45	2.40	2.36	2.27	2.18
	0.001	4.56	4.31	4.06	3.79	3.63	3.52	3.37	3.28	3.22	3.06	2.91
	0.100	1.86	1.81	1.76	1.71	1.67	1.65	1.61	1.59	1.58	1.54	1.51
	0.050	2.22	2.15	2.07	1.99	1.94	1.90	1.85	1.82	1.80	1.75	1.70
26	0.025	2.59	2.49	2.39	2.28	2.21	2.16	2.09	2.05	2.03	1.95	1.89
	0.010	3.09	2.96	2.81	2.66	2.57	2.50	2.42	2.36	2.33	2.23	2.14
	0.001	4.48	4.24	3.99	3.72	3.56	3.44	3.30	3.21	3.15	2.99	2.84
	0.100	1.85	1.80	1.75	1.70	1.66	1.64	1.60	1.58	1.57	1.53	1.50
	0.050	2.20	2.13	2.06	1.97	1.92	1.88	1.84	1.81	1.79	1.73	1.68
27	0.025	2.57	2.47	2.36	2.25	2.18	2.13	2.07	2.03	2.00	1.93	1.86
	0.010	3.06	2.93	2.78	2.63	2.54	2.47	2.38	2.33	2.29	2.20	2.11
	0.001	4.41	4.17	3.92	3.66	3.49	3.38	3.23	3.14	3.08	2.92	2.78
	0.100	1.84	1.79	1.74	1.69	1.65	1.63	1.59	1.57	1.56	1.52	1.48
	0.050	2.19	2.12	2.04	1.96	1.91	1.87	1.82	1.79	1.77	1.71	1.66
28	0.025	2.55	2.45	2.34	2.23	2.16	2.11	2.05	2.01	1.98	1.91	1.84
	0.010	3.03	2.90	2.75	2.60	2.51	2.44	2.35	2.30	2.26	2.17	2.08
	0.001	4.35	4.11	3.86	3.60	3.43	3.32	3.18	3.09	3.02	2.86	2.72
	0.100	1.83	1.78	1.73	1.68	1.64	1.62	1.58	1.56	1.55	1.51	1.47
	0.050	2.18	2.10	2.03	1.94	1.89	1.85	1.81	1.77	1.75	1.70	1.65
29	0.025	2.53	2.43	2.32	2.21	2.14	2.09	2.03	1.99	1.96	1.89	1.82
	0.010	3.00	2.87	2.73	2.57	2.48	2.41	2.33	2.27	2.23	2.14	2.05
	0.001	4.29	4.05	3.80	3.54	3.38	3.27	3.12	3.03	2.97	2.81	2.66
	0.100	1.82	1.77	1.72	1.67	1.63	1.61	1.57	1.55	1.54	1.50	1.46
	0.050	2.16	2.09	2.01	1.93	1.88	1.84	1.79	1.76	1.74	1.68	1.63
30	0.025	2.51	2.41	2.31	2.20	2.12	2.07	2.01	1.97	1.94	1.87	1.80
	0.010	2.98	2.84	2.70	2.55	2.45	2.39	2.30	2.25	2.21	2.11	2.02
	0.001	4.24	4.00	3.75	3.49	3.33	3.22	3.07	2.98	2.92	2.76	2.61
	0.100	1.76	1.71	1.66	1.61	1.57	1.54	1.51	1.48	1.47	1.42	1.38
	0.050	2.08	2.00	1.92	1.84	1.78	1.74	1.69	1.66	1.64	1.58	1.52
40	0.025	2.39	2.29	2.18	2.07	1.99	1.94	1.88	1.83	1.80	1.72	1.65
	0.010	2.80	2.66	2.52	2.37	2.27	2.20	2.11	2.06	2.02	1.92	1.82
	0.001	3.87	3.64	3.40	3.14	2.98	2.87	2.73	2.64	2.57	2.41	2.25
	0.100	1.73	1.68	1.63	1.57	1.53	1.50	1.46	1.44	1.42	1.38	1.33
	0.050	2.03	1.95	1.87	1.78	1.73	1.69	1.63	1.60	1.58	1.51	1.45
50	0.025	2.32	2.22	2.11	1.99	1.92	1.87	1.80	1.75	1.72	1.64	1.56
	0.010	2.70	2.56	2.42	2.27	2.17	2.10	2.01	1.95	1.91	1.80	1.70
	0.001	3.67	3.44	3.20	2.95	2.79	2.68	2.53	2.44	2.38	2.21	2.05

Degrees of freedom denominator, $d.f._D$

TABLE 8 *continued*

	Right-tail area	Degrees of freedom numerator, $d.f._N$								
		1	2	3	4	5	6	7	8	9
60	0.100	2.79	2.39	2.18	2.04	1.95	1.87	1.82	1.77	1.74
	0.050	4.00	3.15	2.76	2.53	2.37	2.25	2.17	2.10	2.04
	0.025	5.29	3.93	3.34	3.01	2.79	2.63	2.51	2.41	2.33
	0.010	7.08	4.98	4.13	3.65	3.34	3.12	2.95	2.82	2.72
	0.001	11.97	7.77	6.17	5.31	4.76	4.37	4.09	3.86	3.69
100	0.100	2.76	2.36	2.14	2.00	1.91	1.83	1.78	1.73	1.69
	0.050	3.94	3.09	2.70	2.46	2.31	2.19	2.10	2.03	1.97
	0.025	5.18	3.83	3.25	2.92	2.70	2.54	2.42	2.32	2.24
	0.010	6.90	4.82	3.98	3.51	3.21	2.99	2.82	2.69	2.59
	0.001	11.50	7.41	5.86	5.02	4.48	4.11	3.83	3.61	3.44
200	0.100	2.73	2.33	2.11	1.97	1.88	1.80	1.75	1.70	1.66
	0.050	3.89	3.04	2.65	2.42	2.26	2.14	2.06	1.98	1.93
	0.025	5.10	3.76	3.18	2.85	2.63	2.47	2.35	2.26	2.18
	0.010	6.76	4.71	3.88	3.41	3.11	2.89	2.73	2.60	2.50
	0.001	11.15	7.15	5.63	4.81	4.29	3.92	3.65	3.43	3.26
1000	0.100	2.71	2.31	2.09	1.95	1.85	1.78	1.72	1.68	1.64
	0.050	3.85	3.00	2.61	2.38	2.22	2.11	2.02	1.95	1.89
	0.025	5.04	3.70	3.13	2.80	2.58	2.42	2.30	2.20	2.13
	0.010	6.66	4.63	3.80	3.34	3.04	2.82	2.66	2.53	2.43
	0.001	10.89	6.96	5.46	4.65	4.14	3.78	3.51	3.30	3.13

Degrees of freedom denominator, $d.f._D$

TABLE 8 *continued*

	Right-tail area	Degrees of freedom numerator, $d.f._N$										
		10	12	15	20	25	30	40	50	60	120	1000
60	0.100	1.71	1.66	1.60	1.54	1.50	1.48	1.44	1.41	1.40	1.35	1.30
	0.050	1.99	1.92	1.84	1.75	1.69	1.65	1.59	1.56	1.53	1.47	1.40
	0.025	2.27	2.17	2.06	1.94	1.87	1.82	1.74	1.70	1.67	1.58	1.49
	0.010	2.63	2.50	2.35	2.20	2.10	2.03	1.94	1.88	1.84	1.73	1.62
	0.001	3.54	3.32	3.08	2.83	2.67	2.55	2.41	2.32	2.25	2.08	1.92
100	0.100	1.66	1.61	1.56	1.49	1.45	1.42	1.38	1.35	1.34	1.28	1.22
	0.050	1.93	1.85	1.77	1.68	1.62	1.57	1.52	1.48	1.45	1.38	1.30
	0.025	2.18	2.08	1.97	1.85	1.77	1.71	1.64	1.59	1.56	1.46	1.36
	0.010	2.50	2.37	2.22	2.07	1.97	1.89	1.80	1.74	1.69	1.57	1.45
	0.001	3.30	3.07	2.84	2.59	2.43	2.32	2.17	2.08	2.01	1.83	1.64
200	0.100	1.63	1.58	1.52	1.46	1.41	1.38	1.34	1.31	1.29	1.23	1.16
	0.050	1.88	1.80	1.72	1.62	1.56	1.52	1.46	1.41	1.39	1.30	1.21
	0.025	2.11	2.01	1.90	1.78	1.70	1.64	1.56	1.51	1.47	1.37	1.25
	0.010	2.41	2.27	2.13	1.97	1.87	1.79	1.69	1.63	1.58	1.45	1.30
	0.001	3.12	2.90	2.67	2.42	2.26	2.15	2.00	1.90	1.83	1.64	1.43
1000	0.100	1.61	1.55	1.49	1.43	1.38	1.35	1.30	1.27	1.25	1.18	1.08
	0.050	1.84	1.76	1.68	1.58	1.52	1.47	1.41	1.36	1.33	1.24	1.11
	0.025	2.06	1.96	1.85	1.72	1.64	1.58	1.50	1.45	1.41	1.29	1.13
	0.010	2.34	2.20	2.06	1.90	1.79	1.72	1.61	1.54	1.50	1.35	1.16
	0.001	2.99	2.77	2.54	2.30	2.14	2.02	1.87	1.77	1.69	1.49	1.22

Degrees of freedom denominator, $d.f._D$

Source: From *Biometrika Tables for Statisticians,* Vol. I. Printed by permission of the Biometrika Trustees.

TABLE 9   Critical Values for Spearman Rank Correlation, r_s

For a right- (left-) tailed test, use the positive (negative) critical value found in the table under one-tail area. For a two-tailed test, use both the positive and negative of the critical value found in the table under two-tail area, n = number of pairs.

	One-tail area			
	0.05	0.025	0.005	0.001
	Two-tail area			
n	0.10	0.05	0.01	0.002
5	0.900	1.000		
6	0.829	0.886	1.000	
7	0.715	0.786	0.929	1.000
8	0.620	0.715	0.881	0.953
9	0.600	0.700	0.834	0.917
10	0.564	0.649	0.794	0.879
11	0.537	0.619	0.764	0.855
12	0.504	0.588	0.735	0.826
13	0.484	0.561	0.704	0.797
14	0.464	0.539	0.680	0.772
15	0.447	0.522	0.658	0.750
16	0.430	0.503	0.636	0.730
17	0.415	0.488	0.618	0.711
18	0.402	0.474	0.600	0.693
19	0.392	0.460	0.585	0.676
20	0.381	0.447	0.570	0.661
21	0.371	0.437	0.556	0.647
22	0.361	0.426	0.544	0.633
23	0.353	0.417	0.532	0.620
24	0.345	0.407	0.521	0.608
25	0.337	0.399	0.511	0.597
26	0.331	0.391	0.501	0.587
27	0.325	0.383	0.493	0.577
28	0.319	0.376	0.484	0.567
29	0.312	0.369	0.475	0.558
30	0.307	0.363	0.467	0.549

Source: From G. J. Glasser and R. F. Winter, "Critical Values of the Coefficient of Rank Correlation for Testing the Hypothesis of Independence," *Biometrika, 48,* 444 (1961). Reprinted by permission of Biometrika Trustees.

TABLE 10   Critical Values for Number of Runs R (Level of significance $\alpha = 0.05$)

Value of n_1	Value of n_2																		
	2	3	4	5	6	7	8	9	10	11	12	13	14	15	16	17	18	19	20
2	1	1	1	1	1	1	1	1	1	1	2	2	2	2	2	2	2	2	2
	6	6	6	6	6	6	6	6	6	6	6	6	6	6	6	6	6	6	6
3	1	1	1	1	2	2	2	2	2	2	2	2	2	3	3	3	3	3	3
	6	8	8	8	8	8	8	8	8	8	8	8	8	8	8	8	8	8	8
4	1	1	1	2	2	2	3	3	3	3	3	3	3	3	4	4	4	4	4
	6	8	9	9	9	10	10	10	10	10	10	10	10	10	10	10	10	10	10
5	1	1	2	2	3	3	3	3	3	4	4	4	4	4	4	4	5	5	5
	6	8	9	10	10	11	11	12	12	12	12	12	12	12	12	12	12	12	12
6	1	2	2	3	3	3	3	4	4	4	4	5	5	5	5	5	5	6	6
	6	8	9	10	11	12	12	13	13	13	13	14	14	14	14	14	14	14	14
7	1	2	2	3	3	3	4	4	5	5	5	5	5	6	6	6	6	6	6
	6	8	10	11	12	13	13	14	14	14	14	15	15	15	16	16	16	16	16
8	1	2	3	3	3	4	4	5	5	5	6	6	6	6	6	7	7	7	7
	6	8	10	11	12	13	14	14	15	15	16	16	16	16	17	17	17	17	17
9	1	2	3	3	4	4	5	5	5	6	6	6	7	7	7	7	8	8	8
	6	8	10	12	13	14	14	15	16	16	16	17	17	18	18	18	18	18	18
10	1	2	3	3	4	5	5	5	6	6	7	7	7	7	8	8	8	8	9
	6	8	10	12	13	14	15	16	16	17	17	18	18	18	19	19	19	20	20
11	1	2	3	4	4	5	5	6	6	7	7	7	8	8	8	9	9	9	9
	6	8	10	12	13	14	15	16	17	17	18	19	19	19	20	20	20	21	21
12	2	2	3	4	4	5	6	6	7	7	7	8	8	8	9	9	9	10	10
	6	8	10	12	13	14	16	16	17	18	19	19	20	20	21	21	21	22	22
13	2	2	3	4	5	5	6	6	7	7	8	8	9	9	9	10	10	10	10
	6	8	10	12	14	15	16	17	18	19	19	20	20	21	21	22	22	23	23
14	2	2	3	4	5	5	6	7	7	8	8	9	9	9	10	10	10	11	11
	6	8	10	12	14	15	16	17	18	19	20	20	21	22	22	23	23	23	24
15	2	3	3	4	5	6	6	7	7	8	8	9	9	10	10	11	11	11	12
	6	8	10	12	14	15	16	18	18	19	20	21	22	22	23	23	24	24	25
16	2	3	4	4	5	6	6	7	8	8	9	9	10	10	11	11	11	12	12
	6	8	10	12	14	16	17	18	19	20	21	21	22	23	23	24	25	25	25
17	2	3	4	4	5	6	7	7	8	9	9	10	10	11	11	11	12	12	13
	6	8	10	12	14	16	17	18	19	20	21	22	23	23	24	25	25	26	26
18	2	3	4	5	5	6	7	8	8	9	9	10	10	11	11	12	12	13	13
	6	8	10	12	14	16	17	18	19	20	21	22	23	24	25	25	26	26	27
19	2	3	4	5	6	6	7	8	8	9	10	10	11	11	12	12	13	13	13
	6	8	10	12	14	16	17	18	20	21	22	23	23	24	25	26	26	27	27
20	2	3	4	5	6	6	7	8	9	9	10	10	11	12	12	13	13	13	14
	6	8	10	12	14	16	17	18	20	21	22	23	24	25	25	26	27	27	28

From "Tables for testing randomness of groupings in a sequence of alternatives," *The Annals of Mathematical Statistics*, Vol. 14, No. 1. Reprinted with permission of the Institute of Mathematical Statistics.

Photo Credits

Chapter 1 p. 2: © Roman Soumar/Corbis; p. 3: *(left)* © Bruce Coleman, Inc./PictureQuest, *(right)* Courtesy of Corrinne and Charles Brase; p. 6: © Geoffrey Bryant/Photo Researchers, Inc.; p. 16: © Catherine Ursillo/Photo Researchers, Inc.; p. 24: © Tim Davis/Photo Researchers, Inc.; p. 27: © R. Lord/The Image Works

Chapter 2 p. 38: © Brown Brothers; p. 39: *(left)* © Judy Gelles/Stock Boston, *(right)* © Jean-Marc Loubat/Vandystadt/Photo Researchers, Inc.; p. 42: © Michael Newman/PhotoEdit; p. 46: © Myrleen Ferguson Cate/PhotoEdit; p. 53: © Russell D. Curtis/Photo Researchers, Inc.; p. 64: © Ph. Royer/Explorer/Photo Researchers, Inc.; p. 75: © Picture Press/Corbis; p. 77: © Michael J. Doolittle/The Image Works

Chapter 3 p. 96: © Wood River Gallery/PictureQuest; p. 97: *(left)* © Nancy Sheehan/PhotoEdit, *(right)* © Myrleen Ferguson Cate/PhotoEdit; p. 99: © Steve Skjold/PhotoEdit; p. 101: © Jose Carillo/PhotoEdit; p. 111: © David Young-Wolff/PhotoEdit; p. 114: © Tony Freeman/PhotoEdit; p. 118: © Ron Watts/Corbis; p. 120: © Bob Daemmrich/The Image Works; p. 128: © Rhoda Sydney/PhotoEdit; p. 137: © Gary Conner/PhotoEdit; p. 152: © Peter Southwick/Stock Boston; p. 158: © Dave G. Houser/Corbis

Chapter 4 p. 160: © North Wind Picture Archives; p. 161: *(left)* © David Young-Wolff/PhotoEdit, *(right)* © John Neubauer/PhotoEdit; p. 166: © Bonnie Kamen/PhotoEdit; p. 170: © Randy Wells/Corbis; p. 176: © Royalty-Free/Corbis; p. 185: © Mark Richards/PhotoEdit

Chapter 5 p. 216: © National Portrait Gallery, Smithsonian Institution/Art Resource, NY; p. 217: *(left)* © Peter Vandermark/Stock Boston, *(right)* © Mitch Wojnarowicz/The Image Works; p. 223: © Kelly-Mooney Photography/Corbis; p. 239: © Ted Curtin/Stock Boston; p. 248: © Mark Richards/PhotoEdit; p. 264: © Richard Rowan/Photo Researchers, Inc.

Chapter 6 p. 290: © Historical Pictures/Stock Montage; p. 291: *(2 photos)* © Jeff Greenberg/PhotoEdit; p. 299: © Scott T. Smith/Corbis; p. 310: © Lois Ellen Frank/Corbis; p. 326: © David Young-Wolff/PhotoEdit; p. 340: © William Mullins/Photo Researchers, Inc.; p. 355: © Hubert Stadler/Corbis

Chapter 7 p. 358: © Ralph Steiner; p. 359: *(left)* © Dana White/PhotoEdit, *(right)* © Syracuse Newspapers/David Lassman/The Image Works; p. 361: © Philip James Corwin/Corbis; p. 367: © Picture Press/Corbis; p. 393: © Mike Mazzaschi/Stock Boston

Chapter 8 p. 398: © Culver Pictures; p. 399: *(left)* © Paul Lally/Stock Boston, *(right)* © R. J. Erwin/Photo Researchers, Inc.; p. 406: © Myrleen Ferguson Cate/PhotoEdit; p. 429: © Bob Daemmrich/Stock Boston; p. 437: © François Gohier/Photo Researchers, Inc.; p. 448: © Jeff Foott/Discovery Images/PictureQuest; p. 473: © J. Griesdieck/Corbis

Chapter 9 p. 480: © Brown Brothers; p. 481: *(left)* © Comstock Images, *(right)* © Reuters/Corbis; p. 486: © Martin Ruegner/ImageState-Pictor/PictureQuest; p. 499: © Comstock Images; p. 520: © John Elk/Stock Boston; p. 529: © Fritz Hoffman/The Image Works; p. 544: © Bob Winsett/Corbis; p. 553: © Bob Daemmrich/The Image Works; p. 579: © Royalty-Free/Corbis

Chapter 10 p. 580: © Archivo Iconografico/S.A./Corbis; p. 581: *(left)* © David Young-Wolff/PhotoEdit, *(right)* © Peter Menzel/Stock Boston; p. 583: © Cindy Kassab/Corbis; p. 590: © David Muench/Corbis; p. 605: © Joe McDonald/Corbis; p. 608: © Joe McDonald/Corbis; p. 626: © Jeffrey Greenberg/Photo Researchers, Inc.; p. 632: © Douglas Faulkner/Photo Researchers, Inc.; p. 633: © Erwin and Peggy Bauer/Animals, Animals; p. 643: © D. Robert & Lorri Franz/Corbis

Chapter 11 p. 668: © The Norman Rockwell Family Trust; p. 669: *(left)* © Nancy Richmond/The Image Works, *(right)* © Robert Brenner/PhotoEdit; p. 673: © Toney Freeman/PhotoEdit; p. 686: © Steve Skjold/PhotoEdit; p. 699: © Mark Richards/PhotoEdit; p. 713: © Richard A. Cooke/Corbis; p. 721: © Bob Daemmrich/Stock Boston

Chapter 12 p. 760: © Keystone Press Agency; p. 761: *(left)* © James Shaffer/PhotoEdit, *(right)* © Peter Vandermark/Stock Boston; p. 762: © Richard Hutching/Photo Researchers, Inc.; p. 773: © Andrew Wood/Photo Researchers, Inc.; p. 784: © Getty Images/Kaluzny/Thatcher; p. 795: © Eastcott-Momatiuk/The Image Works; p. 796: © University Corporation for Atmospheric Research; p. 807: © Jacob Halaska/Index Stock Imagery/PictureQuest; p. 809: © Eastcott-Momatiuk/The Image Works

A38

Answers and Key Steps to Odd-Numbered Problems

CHAPTER 1

Section 1.1

1. (a) Response regarding frequency of eating at fast-food restaurants. (b) Qualitative. (c) Responses for *all* adults in the U.S.
3. (a) Student/faculty ratio at colleges. (b) Quantitative. (c) Student/faculty ratio at *all* colleges in the nation.
5. (a) Nitrogen concentration (mg nitrogen/l water). (b) Quantitative. (c) Nitrogen concentration (mg nitrogen/l water) in the entire lake.
7. (a) Ratio. (b) Interval. (c) Nominal. (d) Ordinal. (e) Ratio. (f) Ratio.
9. (a) Nominal. (b) Ratio. (c) Interval. (d) Ordinal. (e) Ratio. (f) Interval.

Section 1.2

1. See text.
3. Select a starting place in the table and group the digits in groups of four. Scan the table by rows and include the first six groups with numbers between 0001 and 8615.
5. (a) One way is to number the subjects 01 through 40. Make groups of two digits in the random-number table. The first valid number is included in Group 1 while the second valid number is included in Group 2. Continue alternating the group assignments until both groups are filled. (b) Use the process of part a, limited to numbers 01 through 22. (c) Label the two groups of healthy subjects A and B and the two groups of sick subjects C and D. Select a starting place in the random-number table. If the first digit is even, use healthy Group A in the first combined group. If the second digit is even, use Group C of the sick subjects in the first combined group. If either digit is odd, use the other group of healthy or sick subjects. The second combined group contains the two groups not selected for the first combined group.
7. (a) Yes, when a die is rolled several times, the same number may appear more than once. Outcome on the 4th roll is 2. (b) No, for a fair die, the outcomes are random.
9. Use a random-number table to select four distinct numbers corresponding to people in your class. (a) Reasons may vary. For instance, the first four students may make a special effort to get to class on time. (b) Reasons may vary. For instance, four students who come in late might all be nursing students enrolled in an anatomy and physiology class that meets the hour before in a far-away building. They may be more motivated than other students to complete a degree requirement. (c) Reasons may vary. For instance, four students sitting in the back row might be less inclined to participate in class discussions. (d) Reasons may vary. For instance, the tallest students might all be male.
11. (a) Assign each sheep a distinct number from 1 to 250. Because the largest number has three digits, read groups of three digits from a random-number table. Select a starting place, and proceed until you have 15 distinct numbers from 001 to 250. Numbers included in the sample will vary according to the starting place and pattern for reading the table. (b) Because the largest number has four digits, read groups of four digits from a random-number table. Select a starting place, and proceed until you have 10 distinct numbers from 1024 to 8342. Numbers included in the sample will vary according to the starting place and pattern for reading the table. (c) Number the pieces of luggage as they come off the conveyor belt in the next 25 minutes. Use a random-number table to choose five distinct numbers that correspond to pieces of luggage. Numbers will vary according to the starting place and pattern for reading the table. (d) Give the survey to as many people as will take the time to complete the survey between 6 and 7 P.M. Number all the surveys obtained. Use a random-number table to choose 12 distinct numbers corresponding to surveys. Note that the population you are sampling consists of survey data from people who are willing to complete surveys, not from everyone who comes to the shopping center during the designated time period.
13. Since there are five possible outcomes for each question, read single digits from a random-number table. Select a starting place, and proceed until you have 10 digits from 1 to 5. Repetition is required. The correct answer for each question will be the letter choice corresponding to the digit chosen for that question.
15. (a) Simple random sample. (b) Cluster sample. (c) Convenience sample. (d) Systematic sample. (e) Stratified sample.

Section 1.3

1. (a) Observational study. (b) Experiment.
   (c) Experiment. (d) Observational study.
3. (a) Sampling. (b) Simulation. (c) Census.
   (d) Experiment.
5. (a) Use random selection to pick 10 calves to inoculate;
   test all calves; no placebo. (b) Use random selection to
   pick 9 schools to visit; survey all schools; no placebo.
   (c) Use random selection to pick 40 volunteers for skin
   patch with drug; survey all volunteers; placebo used.

CHAPTER REVIEW PROBLEMS

1. Depends on article.
3. See text.
5. In the random-number table use groups of two digits.
   Select the first six distinct groups of two digits that fall in
   the range from 01 to 42. Choices vary according to the
   starting place in the random-number table.
7. (a) Observational study. (b) Experiment.
9. Possible directions on survey questions: Give height in
   inches, give age as of last birthday, give GPA to one
   decimal place, and so forth. Think about the types of
   responses you wish to have on each question.
11. (a) Experiment, since a treatment is imposed on one
    colony. (b) The control group receives normal daylight/
    darkness conditions. The treatment group has light 24
    hours per day. (c) The number of fireflies living at the
    end of 72 hours. (d) Ratio.

CHAPTER 2

Section 2.1

1. Highest Level of Education and Average Annual Household Income (in thousands of dollars)

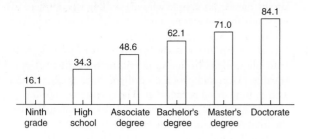

3. Annual Harvest (1000 Metric Tons)—Pareto Chart

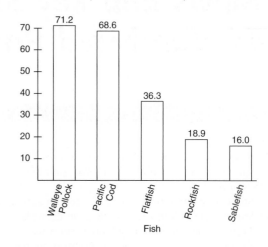

5. Where We Hide the Mess

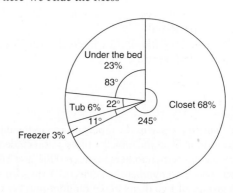

7. How College Professors Spend Time

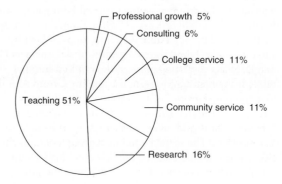

9. (a) Hawaii Crime Rate per 100,000 Population

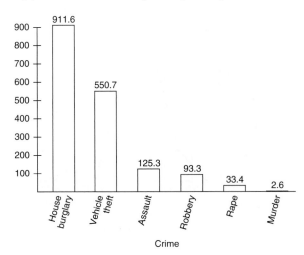

(b) A circle graph is not appropriate because the data do not reflect all types of crime. Also, the same person may have been the victim of more than one crime.

11. Elevation of Pyramid Lake Surface—Time Plot

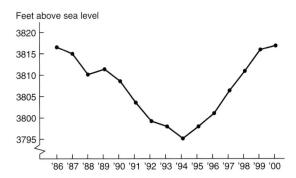

13. The Coca-Cola stock shows price volatility, first with price decreases, then increases, and finally a decrease to an ending price very close to the initial price of the time period. McDonald's stock also shows an initial price decrease, followed by a much stronger increase. After a slight decrease, the ending price of the stock is higher than the initial price was in February. McDonald's had the larger percentage price increase (about 40%).

Section 2.2

1. (a) Class width = 25.
   (b)

Class Limits	Boundaries	Midpoint	Frequency	Relative Frequency	Cumulative Frequency
236–260	235.5–260.5	248	4	0.07	4
261–285	260.5–285.5	273	9	0.16	13
286–310	285.5–310.5	298	25	0.44	38
311–335	310.5–335.5	323	16	0.28	54
336–360	335.5–360.5	348	3	0.05	57

(c–e) Hours to Complete the Iditarod—Histogram, Frequency Polygon, Relative-Frequency Histogram

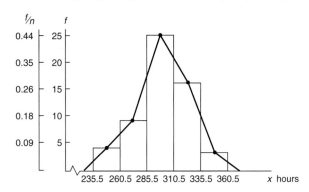

(f) Hours to Complete the Iditarod—Ogive

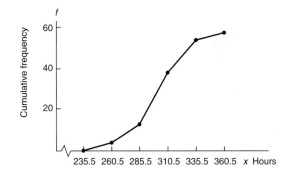

3. (a) Class width = 12.
   (b)

Class Limits	Boundaries	Midpoint	Frequency	Relative Frequency	Cumulative Frequency
1–12	0.5–12.5	6.5	6	0.14	6
13–24	12.5–24.5	18.5	10	0.24	16
25–36	24.5–36.5	30.5	5	0.12	21
37–48	36.5–48.5	42.5	13	0.31	34
49–60	48.5–60.5	54.5	8	0.19	42

(c–e) Months Before Tumor Recurrence—Histogram,
      Frequency Polygon, Relative-Frequency Histogram

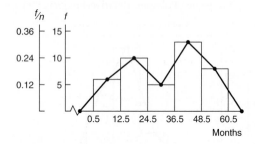

(f) Months Before Tumor Recurrence—Ogive

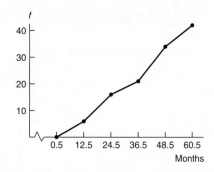

5. (a) Class width = 9.
   (b)

Class Limits	Boundaries	Midpoint	Frequency	Relative Frequency	Cumulative Frequency
10–18	9.5–18.5	14	6	0.11	6
19–27	18.5–27.5	23	26	0.47	32
28–36	27.5–36.5	32	20	0.36	52
37–45	36.5–45.5	41	1	0.02	53
46–54	45.5–54.5	50	2	0.04	55

(c–e) Fuel Consumption (mpg)—Histogram, Frequency
      Polygon, Relative-Frequency Histogram

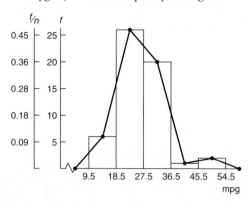

(f) Fuel Consumption (mpg)—Ogive

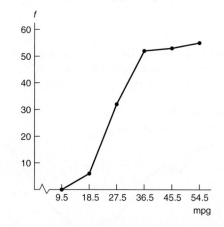

7. (a) Class midpoints: 34.5; 44.5; 54.5; 64.5; 74.5; 84.5.
   (b) Age of Senators—Frequency Polygon

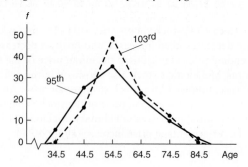

(c) In general, the ages in the 103rd Congress are older.

9. (a)

Profit as a Percent of Sales—Food Companies (class width = 3)

Class	Frequency	Midpoint
−3−−1	2	−2
0–2	16	1
3–5	10	4
6–8	9	7
9–11	2	10

Profit as a Percent of Sales—Electronic Companies (class width = 5)

Class	Frequency	Midpoint
−6−−2	3	−4
−1–3	13	1
4–8	20	6
9–13	7	11
14–18	1	16

Profit as a Percent of Sales

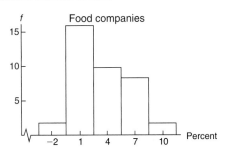

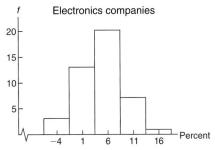

(b) Because the classes and class widths are different for the two company types, it is difficult to compare profits. We can notice that for the electronics companies the percentage of profits does extend as high as 18, while for the food companies the highest percent of profits is 11. On the other hand, some of the electronics companies also have greater losses than the food companies. Had we made the class limits the same for both company types, it would have been easier to compare the data.

11. (a) 85; 84.2%. (b) 25; 24.8%.

13. (a) Version 1 is skewed left; version 2 is uniform; version 3 is symmetrical; version 4 is bimodal; version 5 is skewed right. (b) Answers will vary.

15. (a) Class width = 0.40.
    (b, c)

Class Limits	Boundaries	Midpoint	Frequency
0.46–0.85	0.455–0.855	0.655	4
0.86–1.25	0.855–1.255	1.055	5
1.26–1.65	1.255–1.655	1.455	10
1.66–2.05	1.655–2.055	1.855	5
2.06–2.45	2.055–2.455	2.255	5
2.46–2.85	2.455–2.855	2.655	3

(c) Tonnes of Wheat—Histogram

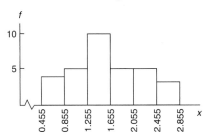

17. (a) One. (b) 5/51 or 9.8%. (c) Interval from 650 to 750.

19. Dotplot for Months Before Tumor Recurrence

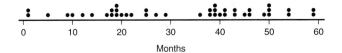

Section 2.3

1. (a) Longevity of Cowboys

4	7 = 47 years	
4		7
5		2 7 8 8
6		1 6 6 8 8
7		0 2 2 3 3 5 6 7
8		4 4 4 5 6 6 7 9
9		0 1 1 2 3 7

(b) Yes, certainly these cowboys lived long lives.

3. Average Length of Hospital Stay

5	2 = 5.2 days
5	2 3 5 5 6 7
6	0 2 4 6 6 7 7 8 8 8 8 9 9
7	0 0 0 0 0 0 1 1 1 2 2 2 3 3 3 3 4 4 5 5 6 6 8
8	4 5 7
9	4 6 9
10	0 3
11	1

The distribution is skewed right.

5. (a) Minutes Beyond 2 Hours (1961–1980)

0	9 = 9 minutes past 2 hours
0	9 9
1	0 0 2 3 3 4
1	5 5 6 6 7 8 8 9
2	0 2 3 3

(b) Minutes Beyond 2 Hours (1981–2000)

0	7 = 7 minutes past 2 hours
0	7 7 7 8 8 8 8 9 9 9 9 9 9 9 9
1	0 0 1 1 4

(c) In more recent times, the winning times have been closer to 2 hours, with all the times between 7 and 14 minutes over two hours. In the earlier period, more than half the times were more than 2 hours and 14 minutes.

7. Angular Momentum of Stars

00	14 = 0.014 arc sec/century		
00	08 14 38 42 50 57	11	69 69
01	73	12	60 60
02	16 19 51	13	
03	51 69	14	38
04	30	15	
05		16	16 60
06	23 67	17	
07	59 88	18	08
08	88		
09			
10	24 57		

No large gaps. There are a greater number with angular momentum below 0.888 than above.

9. Milligrams of Tar per Cigarette

1	0 = 1.0 mg tar		
1	0	11	4
2		12	0 4 8
3		13	7
4	1 5	14	1 5 9
5		15	0 1 2 8
6		16	0 6
7	3 8	17	0
8	0 6 8		
9	0		
10		29	8

11. Milligrams of Nicotine per Cigarette

0	1 = 0.1 milligram
0	1 4 4
0	5 6 6 6 7 7 7 8 8 9 9 9
1	0 0 0 0 0 0 1 2
1	
2	0

13. (a) $49,000 to $126,000 for California; $45,000 to $120,000 for New York.
(b) New York; California.
(c) California has slightly higher average salaries.

Chapter 2 Review

1. (a) Yes, with lines used instead of bars. However, because of the perspective nature of the drawing, the lengths of the bars do not represent the mileages. The scale for each bar changes. (b) Yes. The scale does not change, and the viewer is not distracted by the graphic of the highway. (c) The trend was steeply up at the beginning. Then there was a drop in mileage. After rising again to the 1985 level, the mileage stayed the same for 10 years. The 1985- and 1999-model cars have the same required fuel efficiency.

Fuel Economy Standards for New Cars (1978–1999)

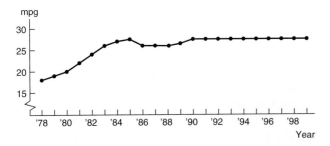

(d) The mileage requirements for light trucks are much lower than for cars, and change much more slowly.

Fuel Economy Standards for Light Trucks (1982–1999)

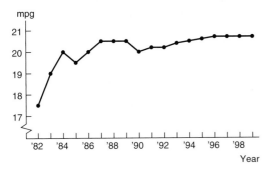

3. Problems with Tax Returns

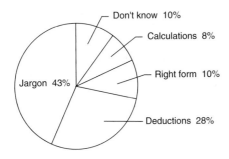

5. (a) Class width = 11.

Class Limits	Boundaries	Midpoint	Frequency	Relative Frequency	Cumulative Frequency
69–79	68.5–79.5	74	2	0.03	2
80–90	79.5–90.5	85	3	0.05	5
91–101	90.5–101.5	96	8	0.13	13
102–112	101.5–112.5	107	19	0.32	32
113–123	112.5–123.5	118	22	0.37	54
124–134	123.5–134.5	129	3	0.05	57
135–145	134.5–145.5	140	3	0.05	60

(b–d) Trunk Circumference (mm)—Histogram, Frequency Polygon, Relative-Frequency Histogram

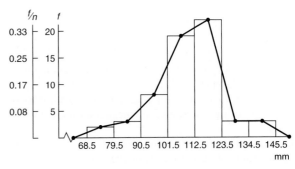

(e) Trunk Circumference (mm)—Ogive

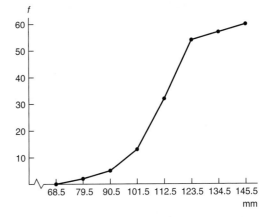

7. (a) 1240s had 40 data. (b) 75. (c) From 1203 to 1212. Little if any repairs or new construction.
9. (a) 65 to 84. (b) 56%. (c) 44%.

CHAPTER 3

Section 3.1

1. Mean ≈ 156.33; median = 157; mode = 157. A gardener in Colorado should look at seed and plant descriptions to determine if the plant can thrive and mature in the designated number of frost-free days. The mean, median, and mode are all close. About half the locations have 157 or fewer frost-free days.
3. $\bar{x} \approx 167.3$ °F; median = 171 °F; mode = 178 °F.
5. (a) $\bar{x} \approx 3.27$; median = 3; mode = 3. (b) $\bar{x} \approx 4.21$; median = 2; mode = 1. (c) Lower Canyon mean is greater; median and mode are less. (d) Trimmed mean = 3.75 and is closer to Upper Canyon mean.
7. (a) Mean ≈ 82.33. (b) Median = 37; median. (c) Mean = 30.9; median = 32.5. (d) Extreme values affect the mean more.
9. (a) For the first week, mean ≈ 14.57 meteoroids; median = 15 meteoroids; mode = 15 meteoroids.

(b) For all nine nights, mean ≈ 24.56 meteoroids; median = 15 meteoroids; mode = 15 meteoroids. (c) Extreme values affect the mean far more than they do the median or mode.

11. (a) $\bar{x}$ = \$136.15; median = \$66.50; mode = \$60. (b) 5% trimmed mean ≈ \$121.28; yes, but still higher than the median. (c) Median. The low and high prices would be useful.

13. (a) Mode if it exists. (b) Mean, median, mode if it exists. (c) Mode if it exists; median, mean if 24-hour clock is used.

15. (a) If the largest data value is *replaced* by a larger value, the mean will increase because the sum of the data values will increase, but the number of them will remain the same. The median will not change. The same value will still be in the eighth position when the data are ordered. (b) If the largest value is replaced by a value that is smaller (but still higher than the median), the mean will decrease because the sum of the data values will decrease. The median will not change. The same value will be in the eighth position in increasing order. (c) If the largest value is replaced by a value that is smaller than the median, the mean will decrease because the sum of the data values will decrease. The median also will decrease because the value formerly in the eighth position will move to the ninth position in increasing order. The median will be the new value in the eighth position.

17. Σwx = 87.65; Σw = 1; weighted average = 87.65.

19. Σwx = 85; Σw = 10; weighted average = 8.5.

21. (a) 3.7 percent. (b) 5.5 years. (c) 3.4 percent. (d) 4.8 years.

23. Answers vary.

Section 3.2

1. (a) 15. (b) Use a calculator. (c) 37; 608. (d) 37; 6.08. (e) σ^2 ≈ 29.59; σ ≈ 5.44.

3. (a) 7.87. (b) Use a calculator. (c) $\bar{x}$ ≈ 1.24; s^2 ≈ 1.78; s ≈ 1.33. (d) CV ≈ 107%. The standard deviation of the time to failure is just slightly larger than the average time.

5. (a) Use a calculator. (b) $\bar{x}$ = 49; s^2 ≈ 687.49; s ≈ 26.22. (c) $\bar{y}$ = 44.8; s^2 ≈ 508.50; s ≈ 22.55. (d) Mallard nests, CV ≈ 53.5%; Canada goose nests, CV ≈ 50.3%. The CV gives the ratio of the standard deviation to the mean; the CV for mallard nests is slightly higher.

7. (a) 75% of the cycles should fall within 2 standard deviations of the mean: 6.67 to 15.35 years. (b) 93.8% of the cycles should fall within 4 standard deviations of the mean: 2.33 to 19.69 years.

9. (a) Range = 737; $\bar{x}$ ≈ 566.9. (b) s^2 ≈ 71,202; s ≈ 266.8. (c) CV ≈ 47.1%. (d) 33 to 1100.

11. 4.1% to 14.5%.

13. Construction artifacts have highest average and lowest relative standard deviation.

15. (a) Pax, CV ≈ 146.7%; Vanguard, CV ≈ 138.6%. Vanguard fund has slightly less risk per unit of return. (b) Pax, −18.52% to 37.68%; Vanguard, −15.98% to 34.02%. Vanguard has a narrower range of returns, with less downside, but also less upside.

17. Since $CV = s/\bar{x}$, then $s = CV(\bar{x})$; s = 0.033.

19. Answers vary.

Section 3.3

1. Midpoints: 25.5, 35.5, 45.5; $\bar{x}$ ≈ 35.80; s^2 ≈ 61.1; s ≈ 7.82.

3. Midpoints: 10.55, 14.55, 18.55, 22.55, 26.55; $\bar{x}$ ≈ 15.6; s^2 ≈ 23.4; s ≈ 4.8.

5. Midpoints: 21, 29.5, 39.5, 49.5, 59.5, 72.5; $\bar{x}$ ≈ 39.12; s ≈ 17.02; CV ≈ 43.5%.

7. Midpoints and frequencies are shown on the figure. $\bar{x}$ ≈ 7.9 hours; s ≈ 1.05 hours; CV ≈ 13.29.

9. (a) $\bar{x}$ ≈ 3.97; s ≈ 2.415. (b) The results of entering the 31 individual values into a calculator are the same. The grouped-data method should give the same results, since each group consists of only one value. When you have many repeated values in a data set, you might consider using the method of grouped data. It is generally faster.

11. $\bar{x}$ ≈ 4.11; s^2 ≈ 3.02; s ≈ 1.74.

Section 3.4

1. 82% or more of the scores were at or below Angela's score; 18% or fewer of the scores were above Angela's score.

3. No, the score 82 might have a percentile rank less than 70.

5. Low = 0.52; Q_1 = 0.735; median = 0.875; Q_3 = 1.325; high = 1.92; IQR = 0.59.

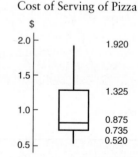

Cost of Serving of Pizza

7. Low = 2; Q_1 = 9.5; median = 23; Q_3 = 28.5; high = 42; IQR = 19.

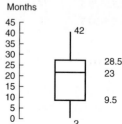

Nurses' Length of Employment (months)

9. Suburban: low = 808; Q_1 = 972; median = 1081; Q_3 = 1216; high = 1292; IQR = 244.
Urban: low = 1768; Q_1 = 1968; median = 2231.5; Q_3 = 2674; high = 2910; IQR = 706.

Auto Insurance Premiums for Suburban and Urban Customers (dollars)

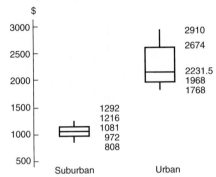

11. (a) Low = 17; Q_1 = 22; median = 24; Q_3 = 27; high = 38; IQR = 5.
(b) 3rd quartile, since it is between the median and Q_3.

Bachelor's Degree Percentage by State

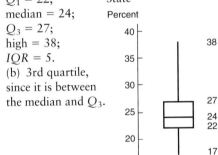

13. (a) California has the lowest premium. Pennsylvania has the highest. (b) Pennsylvania has the highest median premium. (c) California has the smallest range. Texas has the smallest interquartile range. (d) Part (a) is the five-number summary for Texas. It has the smallest IQR. Part (b) is the five-number summary for Pennsylvania. It has the largest minimum. Part (c) is the five-number summary for California. It has the lowest minimum.

15. (a) Smallest median, assistant; highest increase, associate. (b) Instructor. (c) Assistant. (d) Professor; yes. (e) Associate, 9.16; instructor, 10.23; yes, the points indicated by asterisks are above the upper limit for each rank.

Chapter 3 Review

1. (a) $\bar{x}$ = 109.5; s ≈ 31.7; CV ≈ 28.9%; range = 69.
(b) $\bar{x}$ = 110.125; s ≈ 7.2; CV ≈ 6.5%; range = 20.
(c) The first distribution is more spread than the second.

3. (a) Low = 31; Q_1 = 40; median = 45; Q_3 = 52.5; high = 68; IQR = 12.5.

Percentage of Democratic Vote by County

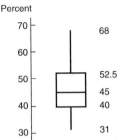

(b) Class width = 8.

Class	Midpoint	f
31–38	34.5	11
39–46	42.5	24
47–54	50.5	15
55–62	58.5	7
63–70	66.5	3

$\bar{x}$ ≈ 46.1; s ≈ 8.64; 28.82 to 63.38.
(c) $\bar{x}$ = 46.15; s ≈ 8.63.
5. Mean weight = 156.25 lb.
7. (a) $\bar{x}$ ≈ 7.83 lb; s ≈ 2.32 lb; CV ≈ 29.6%; range = 4.8 lb. (b) $\bar{x}$ ≈ 9.95 lb; s ≈ 0.29 lb; CV ≈ 2.9%; range = 0.7 lb. (c) Second line has more consistent performance as reflected by the smaller standard deviation, CV, and range.
9. (a) No. (b) $23,478 to $57,478. (c) $7,775.
11. Σw = 16, Σwx = 121, average = 7.56.
13. (a) It is possible for the range and the standard deviation to be the same. For instance, for data values that are all the same, such as 1, 1, 1, 1, 1, the range and standard deviation are both 0. (b) It is possible for the mean, median, and mode to be all the same. For instance, the data set 1, 2, 3, 3, 3, 4, 5 has mean, median, and mode all equal to 3. The averages can all be different, as in the data set 1, 2, 3, 3. In this case, the mean is 2.25, the median is 2.5, and the mode is 3.

CUMULATIVE REVIEW PROBLEMS CHAPTERS 1–3

1. Assign consecutive numbers to all the wells in the study region. Then use a random number table, computer, or calculator to select 102 values that are less than or equal to the highest number assigned to a well in the study region. The sample consists of the wells with numbers corresponding to those selected.
2. Ratio.

3.   7 | 0 represents a pH level of 7.0

7	000000001111111111
7	22222222223333333333
7	4444444455555555
7	666666666777777
7	8888899999
8	01111111
8	2222222
8	45
8	67
8	88

4. Clear the decimals. Then the highest value is 88 and the lowest is 70. The class width for the whole numbers is 4. For the actual data, the class width is 0.4.

Class Limits	Boundaries	Midpoint	Frequency	Relative Frequency	Cumulative Frequency
7.0–7.3	6.95–7.35	7.15	39	0.38	39
7.4–7.7	7.35–7.75	7.55	32	0.31	71
7.8–8.1	7.75–8.15	7.95	18	0.18	89
8.2–8.5	8.15–8.55	8.35	9	0.09	98
8.6–8.9	8.55–8.95	8.75	4	0.04	102

Levels of pH in West Texas Wells Histogram, Relative-Frequency Histogram, Frequency Polygon

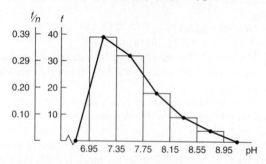

5. Levels of pH in West Texas Wells, Ogive

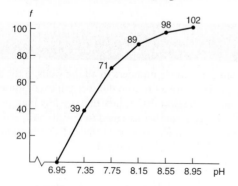

6. Range = 1.8; $\bar{x} \approx 7.58$; median = 7.5; mode = 7.3.

7. Use a calculator or computer.
8. $s^2 \approx 0.20$; $s \approx 0.45$; $CV \approx 5.9\%$.
9. 6.68 to 8.48.
10. Levels of pH in West Texas Wells

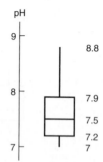

$IQR = 0.7$.
11. Skewed right. Lower values are more common.
12. 89%; 50%.
13. No, there are no gaps in the plot, but only 6 out of 102, or about 6%, have pH levels at or above 8.4. Eight wells are neutral.
14. Half the wells have pH levels between 7.2 and 7.9. The data are skewed toward the high values, with the upper half of the pH levels spread out more than the lower half. The upper half ranges between 7.5 and 8.8, while the lower half is clustered between 7 and 7.5.
15. The report should emphasize the relatively low mean, median, and mode, and the fact that half the wells have a pH level less than 7.5. The data are clustered at the low end of the range.

CHAPTER 4

Section 4.1

1. See text.
3. b, since 4.1 is greater than 1; d, since −0.5 is less than 0; h, since 150% is greater than 100% or 1.
5. Answers vary. Probability as a relative frequency. One concern is whether the students in the class are more or less adept at wiggling their ears than people in the general population.
7. (a) $P(0) = 15/375$; $P(1) = 71/375$; $P(2) = 124/375$; $P(3) = 131/375$; $P(4) = 34/375$.   (b) Yes, the listed numbers of similar preferences form the sample space.
9. (a) P(best idea 6 A.M.–12 noon) $= 290/966 \approx 0.30$; P(best idea 12 noon–6 P.M.) $= 135/966 \approx 0.14$; P(best idea 6 P.M.–12 midnight) $= 319/966 \approx 0.33$; P(best idea from 12 midnight–6 A.M.) $= 222/966 \approx 0.23$.   (b) The probabilities add up to 1. They should add up to 1 provided that the intervals do not overlap and each inventor chose only one interval. The sample space is the set of four time intervals.

11. (a) These events form a sample space. Everyone in the survey gave a response that fell into one of the three categories: P(left alone) = 770/1000 = 0.77; P(waited on) = 160/1000 = 0.16; P(different treatment) = 70/1000 = 0.07.   (b) P(not left alone) = 1 − P(left alone) = 1 − 0.77 = 0.23; P(not waited on) = 1 − P(waited on) = 1 − 0.16 = 0.84.

13. (b) P(success) = 2/17 ≈ 0.118.   (c) P(make shot) = 3/8 or 0.375.

15. (a) P(enter if walks by) = 58/127 ≈ 0.46.   (b) P(buy if entered) = 25/58 ≈ 0.43.   (c) P(walk in and buy) = 25/127 ≈ 0.20.   (d) P(not buy) = 1 − P(buy) ≈ 1 − 0.43 = 0.57.

Section 4.2

1. (a) 0.2; yes.   (b) 0.4; yes.   (c) 1.0 − 0.2 = 0.8.

3. (a) 0.332; yes.   (b) 0.332; yes.   (c) 1 (no purple).

5. (a) Yes.   (b) P(5 on green *and* 3 on red) = P(5) · P(3) = (1/6)(1/6) = 1/36 ≈ 0.028.   (c) P(3 on green *and* 5 on red) = P(3) · P(5) = (1/6)(1/6) = 1/36 ≈ 0.028.   (d) P((5 on green *and* 3 on red) *or* (3 on green *and* 5 on red)) = (1/36) + (1/36) = 1/18 ≈ 0.056.

7. (a) P(sum of 6) = P(1 *and* 5) + P(2 *and* 4) + P(3 *and* 3) + P(4 *and* 2) + P(5 *and* 1) = (1/36) + (1/36) + (1/36) + (1/36) + (1/36) = 5/36.   (b) P(sum of 4) = P(1 *and* 3) + P(2 *and* 2) + P(3 *and* 1) = (1/36) + (1/36) + (1/36) = 3/36 or 1/12.   (c) P(sum of 6 *or* sum of 4) = P(sum of 6) + P(sum of 4) = (5/36) + (3/36) = 8/36 or 2/9; yes.

9. (a) No, after the first draw the sample space becomes smaller and probabilities for events on the second draw change.   (b) P(ace on 1st *and* king on 2nd) = P(ace) · P(king, *given* ace) = (4/52)(4/51) = 4/663.   (c) P(king on 1st *and* ace on 2nd) = P(king) · P(ace, *given* king) = (4/52)(4/51) = 4/663.   (d) P(ace and king in either order) = P(ace on 1st *and* king on 2nd) + P(king on 1st *and* ace on 2nd) = (4/663) + (4/663) = 8/663.

11. (a) Yes, replacement of the card restores the sample space and all probabilities for the second draw remain unchanged regardless of the outcome of the first card.   (b) P(ace on 1st *and* king on 2nd) = P(ace) · P(king) = (4/52)(4/52) = 1/169.   (c) P(king on 1st *and* ace on 2nd) = P(king) · P(ace) = (4/52)(4/52) = 1/169.   (d) P(ace and king in either order) = P(ace on 1st *and* king on 2nd) + P(king on 1st *and* ace on 2nd) = (1/169) + (1/169) = 2/169.

13. (a) P(6 years old *or* older) = P(6–9) + P(10–12) + P(13 and over) = 0.27 + 0.14 + 0.22 = 0.63.   (b) P(12 years old *or* younger) = P(2 and under) + P(3–5) + P(6–9) + P(10–12) = 0.15 + 0.22 + 0.27 + 0.14 = 0.78.   (c) P(between 6 and 12) = P(6–9) + P(10–12) = 0.27 + 0.14 = 0.41.   (d) P(between 3 and 9) = P(3–5) + P(6–9) = 0.22 + 0.27 = 0.49. The category 13 and over contains far more ages than the group

10–12. It is not surprising that more toys are purchased for this group, since there are more children in this group.

15. The information from James Burke can be viewed as conditional probabilities. P(report lie, *given* person is lying) = 0.72 and P(report lie, *given* person is not lying) = 0.07.   (a) P(person is not lying) = 0.90; P(person is not lying *and* polygraph reports lie) = P(person is not lying) × P(reports lie, *given* person not lying) = (0.90)(0.07) = 0.063 or 6.3%.   (b) P(person is lying) = 0.10; P(person is lying *and* polygraph reports lie) = P(person is lying) × P(reports lie, *given* person is lying) = (0.10)(0.72) = 0.072 or 7.2%.   (c) P(person is not lying) = 0.5; P(person is lying) = 0.5; P(person is not lying *and* polygraph reports lie) = P(person is not lying) × P(reports lie, *given* person not lying) = (0.50)(0.07) = 0.035 or 3.5%. P(person is lying *and* polygraph reports lie) = P(person is lying) × P(reports lie, *given* person is lying) = (0.50)(0.72) = 0.36 or 36%.   (d) P(person is not lying) = 0.15; P(person is lying) = 0.85; P(person is not lying *and* polygraph reports lie) = P(person is not lying) × P(reports lie, *given* person is not lying) = (0.15)(0.07) = 0.0105 or 1.05%. P(person is lying *and* polygraph reports lie) = P(person is lying) × P(reports lie, *given* person is lying) = (0.85)(0.72) = 0.612 or 61.2%.

17. (a) P(glasses *and* woman) = P(glasses) × P(woman, *given* glasses) = (0.56)(0.554) ≈ 0.310.   (b) P(glasses *and* man) = P(glasses) × P(man, *given* glasses) = (0.56)(0.446) ≈ 0.250.   (c) P(contacts *and* woman) = P(contacts) × P(woman, *given* contacts) = (0.036)(0.631) ≈ 0.023.   (d) P(contacts *and* man) = P(contacts) × P(man, *given* contacts) = (0.036)(0.369) ≈ 0.013.   (e) Since the preceding events are all disjoint, P(any one of the above) ≈ 0.310 + 0.250 + 0.023 + 0.013 = 0.596; P(none) ≈ 1 − 0.596 = 0.404.

19. (a) 686/1160; 270/580; 416/580.   (b) No.   (c) 270/1160; 416/1160.   (d) 474/1160; 310/580.   (e) No.   (f) 686/1160 + 580/1160 − 270/1160 = 996/1160.

21. (a) 72/154.   (b) 82/154.   (c) 79/116.   (d) 37/116.   (e) 72/270.   (f) 82/270.

23. (a) 932/1894.   (b) 353/739.   (c) 142/1894.   (d) 22/224.   (e) 1007/1894.   (f) 39/66.   (g) No; Probabilities computed in parts (a) and (b) are not equal. (Note: more than once is two or more.)

25. (a) $P(A)$ = 0.65.   (b) $P(B)$ = 0.71.   (c) $P(B$, *given* $A)$ = 0.87.   (d) $P(A$ and $B)$ = $P(A)$ · $P(B$, *given* $A)$ = (0.65)(0.87) ≈ 0.57.   (e) $P(A$ or $B)$ = $P(A)$ + $P(B)$ − $P(A$ and $B)$ ≈ 0.65 + 0.71 − 0.57 = 0.79.   (f) P(not close) = P(profit 1st year *or* profit 2nd year) = $P(A$ or $B)$ ≈ 0.79; P(close) = 1 − P(not close) ≈ 1 − 0.79 = 0.21.

27. (a) P(TB *and* positive) = P(TB)P(positive, *given* TB) = (0.04)(0.82) ≈ 0.033.   (b) P(does not have TB) = 1 −

$P(\text{TB}) = 1 - 0.04 = 0.96.$　(c) $P(\text{no TB } and \text{ positive}) = P(\text{no TB})P(\text{positive, } given \text{ no TB}) = (0.96)(0.09) \approx 0.086.$

Section 4.3

1. (a) Outcomes for Tossing a Coin Three Times

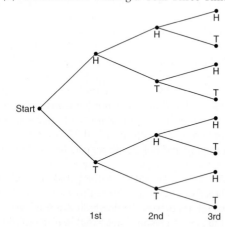

(b) 3.　(c) 3/8.

3. (a) Outcomes for Drawing Two Balls (without replacement)

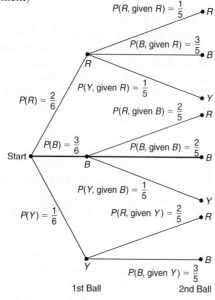

(b) $P(R \text{ and } R) = 2/6 \cdot 1/5 = 1/15.$
$P(R \text{ 1st } and \text{ B 2nd}) = 2/6 \cdot 3/5 = 1/5.$
$P(R \text{ 1st } and \text{ Y 2nd}) = 2/6 \cdot 1/5 = 1/15.$
$P(B \text{ 1st } and \text{ R 2nd}) = 3/6 \cdot 2/5 = 1/5.$
$P(B \text{ 1st } and \text{ B 2nd}) = 3/6 \cdot 2/5 = 1/5.$
$P(B \text{ 1st } and \text{ Y 2nd}) = 3/6 \cdot 1/5 = 1/10.$
$P(Y \text{ 1st } and \text{ R 2nd}) = 1/6 \cdot 2/5 = 1/15.$
$P(Y \text{ 1st } and \text{ B 2nd}) = 1/6 \cdot 3/5 = 1/10.$

5. (a) Choices for Three True/False Questions

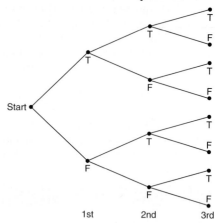

(b) 1/8.
7. $4 \cdot 3 \cdot 2 \cdot 1 = 24$ ways.
9. (a) $52 \cdot 52 = 2704.$　(b) $4 \cdot 4 = 16.$
　(c) $16/2704 \approx 0.006.$
11. $4 \cdot 3 \cdot 3 = 36.$
13. $P_{5,2} = (5!/3!) = 5 \cdot 4 = 20.$
15. $P_{7,7} = (7!/0!) = 7! = 5040.$
17. $C_{5,2} = (5!/(2!3!)) = 10.$
19. $C_{7,7} = (7!/(7!0!)) = 1.$
21. $P_{15,3} = 2730.$
23. (a) $8! = 40{,}320.$　(b) $8 \cdot 7 \cdot 6 \cdot 5 \cdot 4 = 6720.$
25. $5 \cdot 4 \cdot 3 = 60.$
27. $C_{15,5} = (15!/(5!10!)) = 3003.$
29. (a) $C_{12,6} = (12!/(6!6!)) = 924.$
　(b) $C_{7,6} = (7!/(6!1!)) = 7.$　(c) $7/924 \approx 0.008.$

Chapter 4 Review

1. $P(\text{asked}) = 24\%;$ $P(\text{received, } given \text{ asked}) = 45\%;$ $P(\text{ask } and \text{ receive}) = (0.24)(0.45) = 10.8\%.$
3. (a) If the first card is replaced, the outcomes are independent. Replacing the first card restores the original sample space. If the first card is not replaced, the outcomes are not independent, because removing the first card changes the sample space.
　(b) $P(\text{heart } and \text{ heart}) = (13/52)(13/52) \approx 0.063.$
　(c) $P(\text{heart } and \text{ heart}) = (13/52)(12/51) \approx 0.059.$
5. (a) Drop a fixed number of tacks and count how many land flat side down. Then form the ratio of the number landing flat side down to the total number dropped.
　(b) Up, down.　(c) $P(\text{up}) = 160/500 = 0.32;$ $P(\text{down}) = 340/500 = 0.68.$

7. (a)

Outcomes x	2	3	4	5	6
$P(x)$	0.028	0.056	0.083	0.111	0.139

(b)

x	7	8	9	10	11	12
$P(x)$	0.167	0.139	0.111	0.083	0.056	0.028

9. $C_{8,2} = (8!/(2!6!)) = (8 \cdot 7/2) = 28$.

11. $3 \cdot 2 \cdot 1 \approx 6$.

13. $4 \cdot 4 \cdot 4 \cdot 4 \cdot 4 = 1024$ choices; $P(\text{all correct}) = 1/1024 \approx 0.00098$.

15. $10 \cdot 10 \cdot 10 = 1000$.

CHAPTER 5

Section 5.1

1. (a) Discrete. (b) Continuous. (c) Continuous.
   (d) Discrete. (e) Continuous.

3. (a) Yes. (b) No; probabilities total to more than 1.

5. (a) Yes, events are distinct and probabilities total to 1.
   (b) Income Distribution ($1000)

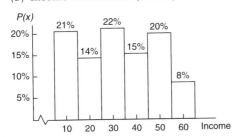

(c) 32.3 thousand dollars. (d) 16.12 thousand dollars.

7. (a)

x	36	37	38	39	40	41
$P(x)$	0.029	0.048	0.053	0.096	0.125	0.154

x	42	43	44	45
$P(x)$	0.163	0.135	0.120	0.077

(b) Number of Nighttime Calls Requiring a Nurse

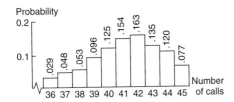

(c) 0.673. (d) 0.351. (e) 41.288. (f) 2.326.

9. (a) Number of Fish Caught in a 6-Hour Period at Pyramid Lake, Nevada

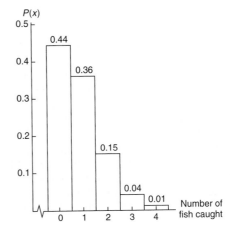

(b) 0.56. (c) 0.20. (d) 0.82. (e) 0.899.

11. (a) 15/719; 704/719. (b) $0.73; $14.27.

13. (a) 0.01191; $595.50. (b) $646; $698; $751.50; $806.50; $3497.50 total. (c) $4197.50. (d) $1502.50.

15. (a) $\mu_W = 15$; $\sigma_W^2 = 208$; $\sigma_W \approx 14.4$.
    (b) $\mu_W = 107.5$; $\sigma_W^2 = 52$; $\sigma_W \approx 7.2$.
    (c) $\mu_L = 90$; $\sigma_L^2 = 92.16$; $\sigma_L = 9.6$.
    (d) $\mu_L = 90$; $\sigma_L^2 = 57.76$; $\sigma_L = 7.6$.

17. (a) $\mu_W = 50.2$; $\sigma_W^2 = 66.125$; $\sigma_W \approx 8.13$.
    (b) The means are the same. (c) The standard deviation for two policies is smaller. (d) As we include more policies, the coefficients in W decrease, resulting in smaller σ_W^2 and σ_W. For instance, for three policies, $W = (\mu_1 + \mu_2 + \mu_3)/3 \approx 0.33\mu_1 + 0.33\mu_2 + 0.33\mu_3$ and $\sigma_W^2 \approx (0.33)^2\sigma_1^2 + (0.33)^2\sigma_2^2 + (0.33)^2\sigma_3^2$. Yes, the risk appears to decrease by a factor of $1/\sqrt{n}$.

Section 5.2

1. A trial is one flip of a fair quarter. Success = coin shows heads. Failure = coin shows tails. $n = 3$; $p = 0.5$; $q = 0.5$. (a) $P(r = 3 \text{ heads}) = C_{3,3}p^3q^0 = 1(0.5)^3(0.5)^0 = 0.125$. To find this value in Table 3 of Appendix II, use the group in which $n = 3$, the column headed by $p = 0.5$, and the row headed by $r = 3$. (b) $P(r = 2 \text{ heads}) = C_{3,2}p^2q^1 = 3(0.5)^2(0.5)^1 = 0.375$. To find this value in Table 3 of Appendix II, use the group in which $n = 3$, the column headed by $p = 0.5$, and the row headed by $r = 2$. (c) $P(r \text{ is 2 or more}) = P(r = 2 \text{ heads}) + P(r = 3 \text{ heads}) = 0.375 + 0.125 = 0.500$. (d) The probability of getting three tails when you toss a coin three times is the same as getting zero heads. Therefore, $P(3 \text{ tails}) = P(r = 0 \text{ heads}) = C_{3,0}p^0q^3 = 1(0.5)^0(0.5)^3 = 0.125$. To find this value in Table 3 of Appendix II, use the group in which $n = 3$, the column headed by $p = 0.5$, and the row headed by $r = 0$.

3. (a) A trial is a man's response to the question, "Would you marry the same woman again?" Success = a positive response. Failure = a negative response. $n = 10$; $p = 0.80$; $q = 0.20$. Using values in Table 3 of Appendix II, $P(r$ is at least 7) = $P(r = 7) + P(r = 8) + P(r = 9) + P(r = 10) = 0.201 + 0.302 + 0.268 + 0.107 = 0.878$. $P(r$ is less than half of 10) = $P(r < 5) = P(r = 0) + P(r = 1) + P(r = 2) + P(r = 3) + P(r = 4) = 0.000 + 0.000 + 0.000 + 0.001 + 0.006 = 0.007$. (b) A trial is a woman's response to the question, "Would you marry the same man again?" Success = a positive response. Failure = a negative response. $n = 10$; $p = 0.5$; $q = 0.5$. Using values in Table 3 of Appendix II, $P(r$ is at least 7) = $P(r = 7) + P(r = 8) + P(r = 9) + P(r = 10) = 0.117 + 0.044 + 0.010 + 0.001 = 0.172$. $P(r$ is less than half of 10) = $P(r < 5) = P(r = 0) + P(r = 1) + P(r = 2) + P(r = 3) + P(r = 4) = 0.001 + 0.010 + 0.044 + 0.117 + 0.205 = 0.377$.

5. A trial consists of a woman's response regarding her mother-in-law. Success = dislike. Failure = like. $n = 6$; $p = 0.90$; $q = 0.10$. (a) $P(r = 6) = 0.531$. (b) $P(r = 0) = 0.000$ (to 3 digits). (c) $P(r \geq 4) = P(r = 4) + P(r = 5) + P(r = 6) = 0.098 + 0.354 + 0.531 = 0.983$. (d) $P(r \leq 3) = 1 - P(r \geq 4) \approx 1 - 0.983 = 0.017$ or 0.016 directly from table.

7. A trial is taking a polygraph exam. Success = pass. Failure = fail. $n = 9$; $p = 0.85$; $q = 0.15$. (a) $P(r = 9) = 0.232$. (b) $P(r \geq 5) = P(r = 5) + P(r = 6) + P(r = 7) + P(r = 8) + P(r = 9) = 0.028 + 0.107 + 0.260 + 0.368 + 0.232 = 0.995$. (c) $P(r \leq 4) = 1 - P(r \geq 5) \approx 1 - 0.995 = 0.005$ or 0.006 directly from table. (d) $P(r = 0) = 0.000$ (to 3 digits).

9. A trial consists of checking the gross receipts of the Green Parrot Italian Restaurant for one business day. Success = gross is over $2200. Failure = gross is at or below $2200. $p = 0.85$; $q = 0.15$. (a) $n = 7$; $P(r = 5) = P(r = 5) + P(r = 6) + P(r = 7) = 0.210 + 0.396 + 0.321 = 0.927$. (b) $n = 10$; $P(r \geq 5) = P(r = 5) + P(r = 6) + P(r = 7) + P(r = 8) + P(r = 9) + P(r = 10) = 0.008 + 0.040 + 0.130 + 0.276 + 0.347 + 0.197 = 0.998$. (c) $n = 5$; $P(r < 3) = P(r = 0) + P(r = 1) + P(r = 2) = 0.000 + 0.002 + 0.024 = 0.026$. (d) $n = 10$; $P(r < 7) = P(r = 0) + P(r = 1) + P(r = 2) + P(r = 3) + P(r = 4) + P(r = 5) + P(r = 6) = 0.000 + 0.000 + 0.000 + 0.000 + 0.001 + 0.008 + 0.040 = 0.049$. (e) $n = 7$; $P(r < 3) = P(r = 0) + P(r = 1) + P(r = 2) = 0.000 + 0.000 + 0.001 = 0.001$. Yes. If p were really 0.85, then the event of a 7-day period with gross income exceeding $2200 fewer than 3 days would be very rare. If it happened again, we would suspect that $p = 0.85$ is too high.

11. A trial is catching and releasing a pike. Success = pike dies. Failure = pike lives. $n = 16$; $p = 0.05$; $q = 0.95$. (a) $P(r = 0) = 0.440$. (b) $P(r < 3) = 0.957$. (c) $P(r = 0) = 0.440$ (all live is equivalent to none die). (d) Change success to live; $p = 0.95$; $P(r > 14) = 0.811$.

13. (a) A trial consists of using the Myers-Briggs instrument to determine if a person in marketing is an extrovert. Success = extrovert. Failure = not extrovert. $n = 15$; $p = 0.75$; $q = 0.25$. $P(r \geq 10) = 0.851$; $P(r \geq 5) = 0.999$; $P(r = 15) = 0.013$. (b) A trial consists of using the Myers-Briggs instrument to determine if a computer programmer is an introvert. Success = introvert. Failure = not introvert. $n = 5$; $p = 0.60$; $q = 0.40$. $P(r = 0) = 0.010$; $P(r \geq 3) = 0.683$; $P(r = 5) = 0.078$.

15. (a) $n = 10$; $p = 0.40$; $P(r = 0) = 0.006$. (b) $n = 10$; $p = 0.40$; $P(r < 5) = 0.633$. (c) $n = 10$; $p = 0.30$; $P(r \leq 2) = 0.382$. (d) $n = 10$; $p = 0.70$; $P(r \geq 6) = 0.849$.

17. $n = 8$; $p = 0.53$; $q = 0.47$. (a) 0.812515; yes, truncated at 5 digits. (b) 0.187486; 0.18749; yes, rounded to 5 digits.

19. A trial consists of determining the kind of stone in a chipped stone tool. (a) $n = 11$. Success = obsidian. Failure = not obsidian. $p = 0.15$; $q = 0.85$; $P(r \geq 3) = 0.221$. (b) $n = 5$. Success = basalt. Failure = not basalt. $p = 0.55$; $q = 0.45$; $P(r \geq 2) = 0.869$. (c) $n = 10$. Success = neither obsidian nor basalt. Failure = either obsidian or basalt. The two outcomes, tool is obsidian or tool is basalt, are mutually exclusive. Therefore, $P(\text{obsidian } or \text{ basalt}) = 0.55 + 0.15 = 0.70$. $P(\text{neither obsidian nor basalt}) = 1 - 0.70 = 0.30$. Therefore, $p = 0.30$; $P(r \geq 4) = 0.350$.

21. (a) They are the same. (b) They are the same. (c) $r = 1$. (d) The one headed by $p = 0.80$.

23. (a) $n = 8$; $p = 0.65$; $P(6 \leq r, \text{ given } 4 \leq r) = P(6 \leq r)/P(4 \leq r) = 0.428/0.895 \approx 0.478$. (b) $n = 10$; $p = 0.65$; $P(8 \leq r, \text{ given } 6 \leq r) = P(8 \leq r)/P(6 \leq r) = 0.262/0.752 \approx 0.348$. (c) Essay. (d) Use event $A = 6 \leq r$ and event $B = 4 \leq r$ in the formula.

Section 5.3

1. (a) Binomial Distribution
   The distribution is symmetrical.

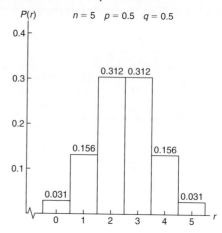

(b) Binomial Distribution
The distribution is skewed right.

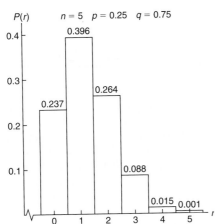

(c) Binomial Distribution
The distribution is skewed left.

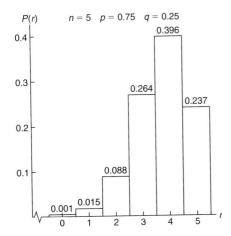

(d) The distributions are mirror images of one another.
(e) The distribution would be skewed left for $p = 0.73$ because the more likely numbers of successes are to the right of the middle.

3. (a) Households with Children Under 2 That Buy Film

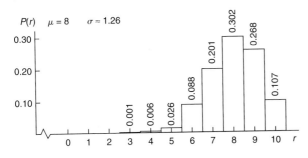

(b) Households with No Children Under 21 That Buy Film

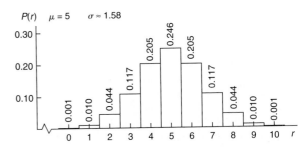

(c) Yes. Adults with children seem to buy more film.

5. (a) Binomial Distribution for Number of Addresses Found

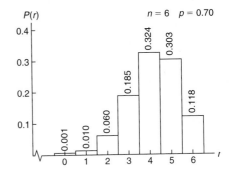

(b) $\mu = 4.2$; $\sigma \approx 1.122$.
(c) $n = 5$. Note that $n = 5$ gives $P(r \geq 2) = 0.97$.

7. (a) Binomial Distribution for Number of Illiterate People

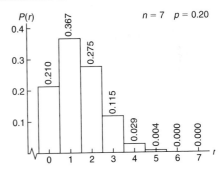

(b) $\mu = 1.4$; $\sigma \approx 1.058$.
(c) $n = 12$. Note that $n = 12$ gives $P(r \geq 7) = 0.98$, where success = literate and $p = 0.80$.

9. (a) Binomial Distribution for Number of Gullible Consumers

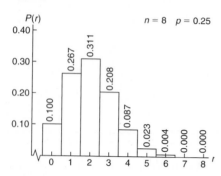

(b) $\mu = 2$; $\sigma \approx 1.225$.
(c) $n = 16$. Note that $n = 16$ gives $P(r \geq 1) = 0.99$.

11. $n = 20$ gives $P(r \geq 5) = 0.95$.

13. $P(r \geq 1) = 1 - P(r = 0)$. From the formula for the binomial distribution with $p = 0.1$ and $q = 0.9$, $P(r = 0) = C_{n,0}p^0 q^n = 1(0.1)^0(0.9)^n$. Therefore, $P(r \geq 1) = 1 - 0.9^n$. Computing this probability for various values of n shows that $n = 22$ is the smallest value for which $P(r \geq 1)$ is at least 0.90.

15. (a) $P(r = 0) = 0.004$; $P(r = 1) = 0.047$; $P(r = 2) = 0.211$; $P(r = 3) = 0.422$; $P(r = 4) = 0.316$.

(b) Binomial Distribution for Number of Parolees Who Do Not Become Repeat Offenders

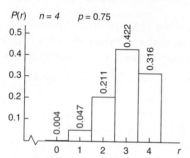

(c) $\mu = 3$; $\sigma \approx 0.866$.
(d) $n = 7$. Note that $n = 7$ gives $P(r \geq 3) = 0.987$.

17. $n = 12$; $p = 0.25$ do not serve; $p = 0.75$ serve.
(a) $P(r = 12 \text{ serve}) = 0.032$. (b) $P(r \geq 6 \text{ do not serve}) = 0.053$. (c) For serving, $\mu = 9$; $\sigma = 1.50$. (d) To be at least 95.9% sure that 12 are available to serve, call 20.

19. $n = 6$; $p = 0.80$ do not solve; $p = 0.20$ solve. (a) $P(r = 6 \text{ not solved}) = 0.262$. (b) $P(r \geq 1 \text{ solved}) = 0.738$. (c) For solving crime, $\mu = 1.2$; $\sigma \approx 0.98$. (d) To be 90% sure of solving 1 or more crimes, investigate $n = 11$ crimes.

21. (a) $P(r = 7 \text{ guilty in U.S.}) = 0.028$; $P(r = 7 \text{ guilty in Japan}) = 0.698$. (b) For guilty in Japan, $\mu = 6.65$, $\sigma \approx 0.58$; for guilty in U.S., $\mu = 4.2$; $\sigma \approx 1.30$. (c) To be 99% sure of at least 2 guilty convictions in the U.S., look

at $n = 8$ trials. To be 99% sure of at least 2 guilty convictions in Japan, look at $n = 3$ trials.

23. (a) 9. (b) 10.

Section 5.4

1. (a) $p = 0.77$; $P(n) = (0.77)(0.23)^{n-1}$. (b) $P(1) = 0.77$. (c) $P(2) = 0.1771$. (d) $P(3 \text{ or more tries}) = 1 - P(1) - P(2) = 0.0529$. (e) 1.29 or 1.

3. (a) $P(n) = (0.05)(0.95)^{n-1}$. (b) $P(5) \approx 0.0407$. (c) $P(10) \approx 0.0315$. (d) $P(n > 3) = 1 - P(1) - P(2) - P(3) \approx 1 - 0.05 - 0.0475 - 0.0451 = 0.8574$. (e) 20.

5. (a) $P(n) = (0.71)(0.29)^{n-1}$. (b) $P(1) = 0.71$; $P(2) = 0.2059$; $P(n \geq 3) = 1 - P(1) - P(2) = 0.0841$. (c) $P(n) = (0.83)(0.17)^{n-1}$; $P(1) = 0.83$; $P(2) = 0.1411$; $P(n \geq 3) = 1 - P(1) - P(2) = 0.0289$.

7. (a) $P(n) = (0.30)(0.70)^{n-1}$. (b) $P(3) = 0.147$. (c) $P(n > 3) = 1 - P(1) - P(2) - P(3) = 1 - 0.300 - 0.210 - 0.147 = 0.343$. (d) 3.33 or 3.

9. (a) $\lambda = (1.7/10) \times (3/3) = 5.1$ per 30-minute interval; $P(r) = e^{-5.1}(5.1)^r/r!$. (b) Using Table 4 of Appendix II with $\lambda = 5.1$, we find $P(4) = 0.1719$; $P(5) = 0.1753$; $P(6) = 0.1490$. (c) $P(r \geq 4) = 1 - P(0) - P(1) - P(2) - P(3) = 1 - 0.0061 - 0.0311 - 0.0793 - 0.1348 = 0.7487$. (d) $P(r < 4) = 1 - P(r \geq 4) = 1 - 0.7487 = 0.2513$.

11. (a) Births and deaths occur somewhat rarely in a group of 1000 people in a given year. For 1000 people, $\lambda = 16$ births; $\lambda = 8$ deaths. (b) By Table 4 of Appendix II, $P(10 \text{ births}) = 0.0341$; $P(10 \text{ deaths}) = 0.0993$; $P(16 \text{ births}) = 0.0992$; $P(16 \text{ deaths}) = 0.0045$. (c) $\lambda(\text{births}) = (16/1000) \times (1500/1500) = 24$ per 1500 people. $\lambda(\text{deaths}) = (8/1000) \times (1500/1500) = 12$ per 1500 people. By the table, $P(10 \text{ deaths}) = 0.1048$; $P(16 \text{ deaths}) = 0.0543$. Since $\lambda = 24$ is not in the table, use the formula for $P(r)$ to find $P(10 \text{ births}) = 0.00066$; $P(16 \text{ births}) = 0.02186$. (d) $\lambda(\text{births}) = (16/1000) \times (750/750) = 12$ per 750 people. $\lambda(\text{deaths}) = (8/1000) \times (750/750) = 6$ per 750 people. By Table 4 of Appendix II, $P(10 \text{ births}) = 0.1048$; $P(10 \text{ deaths}) = 0.0413$; $P(16 \text{ births}) = 0.0543$; $P(16 \text{ deaths}) = 0.0003$.

13. (a) The Poisson distribution is a good choice for r because gale-force winds occur rather rarely. The occurrences are usually independent. (b) For interval of 108 hours, $\lambda = (1/60) \times (108/108) = 1.8$ per 108 hours. Using Table 4 of Appendix II, we find that $P(2) = 0.2678$; $P(3) = 0.1607$; $P(4) = 0.0723$; $P(r < 2) = P(0) + P(1) = 0.1653 + 0.2975 = 0.4628$. (c) For interval of 180 hours, $\lambda = (1/60) \times (180/180) = 3$ per 180 hours. Table 4 of Appendix II gives $P(3) = 0.2240$; $P(4) = 0.1680$; $P(5) = 0.1008$; $P(r < 3) = P(0) + P(1) + P(2) = 0.0498 + 0.1494 + 0.2240 = 0.4232$.

15. (a) The sales of large buildings are rare events. It is reasonable to assume that they are independent. The

variable r = number of sales in a fixed time interval.
(b) For a 60-day period, $\lambda = (8/275) \times (60/60) = 1.7$ per 60 days. By Table 4 of Appendix II, $P(0) = 0.1827$; $P(1) = 0.3106$; $P(r \geq 2) = 1 - P(0) - P(1) = 0.5067$.
(c) For a 90-day period, $\lambda = (8/275) \times (90/90) = 2.6$ per 90 days. By Table 4 of Appendix II, $P(0) = 0.0743$; $P(2) = 0.2510$; $P(r \geq 3) = 1 - P(0) - P(1) - P(2) = 1 - 0.0743 - 0.1931 - 0.2510 = 0.4816$.

17. (a) The problem satisfies the conditions for a binomial experiment with small $p = 0.0018$ and large $n = 1000$. $np = 1.8$, which is less than 10, so the Poisson approximation to the binomial distribution would be a good choice. $\lambda = np = 1.8$. (b) By Table 4, Appendix II, $P(0) = 0.1653$. (c) $P(r > 1) = 1 - P(0) - P(1) = 1 - 0.1653 - 0.2975 = 0.5372$. (d) $P(r > 2) = 1 - P(0) - P(1) - P(2) = 1 - 0.1653 - 0.2975 - 0.2678 = 0.2694$. (e) $P(r > 3) = 1 - P(0) - P(1) - P(2) - P(3) = 1 - 0.1653 - 0.2975 - 0.2678 - 0.1607 = 0.1087$.

19. (a) The problem satisfies the conditions for a binomial experiment with n large, $n = 175$, and p small. $np = (175)(0.005) = 0.875 < 10$. The Poisson distribution would be a good approximation to the binomial. $n = 175$; $p = 0.005$; $\lambda = np = 0.9$. (b) By Table 4 of Appendix II, $P(0) = 0.4066$. (c) $P(r \geq 1) = 1 - P(0) = 0.5934$. (d) $P(r \geq 2) = 1 - P(0) - P(1) = 0.2275$.

21. (a) $n = 100$; $p = 0.02$, $r = 2$; $P(2) = C_{100,2}(0.02)^2(0.98)^{98} \approx 0.2734$. (b) $\lambda = np = 2$; $P(2) = [e^{-2}(2)^2]/2! \approx 0.2707$. (c) The approximation is correct to two decimal places. (d) $n = 100$; $p = 0.02$; $r = 3$. By the formula for the binomial distribution, $P(3) \approx 0.1823$. By the Poisson approximation, $P(3) \approx 0.1804$. The approximation is correct to two decimal places.

23. (a) $\lambda \approx 3.4$. (b) $P(r \geq 4, \text{given } r \geq 2) = P(r \geq 4)/P(r \geq 2) \approx 0.4416/0.8531 \approx 0.5176$. (c) $P(r < 6, \text{given } r \geq 3) = P(3 \leq r < 6)/P(r \geq 3) \approx 0.5308/0.6602 \approx 0.8040$.

25. (a) $P(n) = C_{n-1,11}(0.80^{12})(0.20^{n-12})$. (b) $P(12) \approx 0.0687$; $P(13) \approx 0.1649$; $P(14) \approx 0.2144$. (c) 0.4480. (d) 0.5520. (e) $\mu = 15$; $\sigma \approx 1.94$. Susan can expect to get the bonus if she makes 15 contacts, with a standard deviation of about 2 contacts.

Chapter 5 Review

1. (a) 38; 11.6.
(b) Duration of Leases in Months

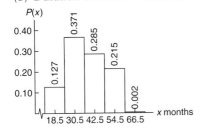

3. (a) Number of Claimants Under 25

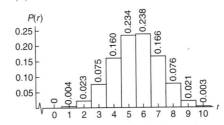

(b) $P(r \geq 6) = 0.504$. (c) $\mu = 5.5$; $\sigma \approx 1.57$.
5. (a) 0.039. (b) 0.403. (c) 8.
7. (a) Number of Good Grapefruit

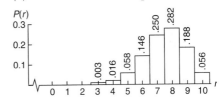

(b) 0.244, 0.999. (c) 7.5. (d) 1.37.
9. $P(r \leq 2) = 0.000$ (to 3 digits). The data seem to indicate that the percent favoring the increase in fees is less than 85%.
11. (a) Coughs are a relatively rare occurrence. It is reasonable to assume that they are independent events, and the variable is the number of coughs in a fixed time interval. (b) $\lambda = 11$ coughs per minute; $P(r \leq 3) = P(0) + P(1) + P(2) + P(3) = 0.000 + 0.002 + 0.0010 + 0.0037 = 0.0049$. (c) $\lambda = (11/1) \times (0.5/0.5) = 5.5$ coughs per 30-second period. $P(r \geq 3) = 1 - P(0) - P(1) - P(2) = 1 - 0.0041 - 0.0225 - 0.0618 = 0.9116$.
13. The loan-default problem satisfies the conditions for a binomial experiment. Moreover, p is small, n is large, and $np < 10$. Use of the Poisson approximation to the binomial distribution is appropriate. $n = 300$; $p = 1/350 \approx 0.0029$, and $\lambda = np \approx 300(0.0029) = 0.86 \approx 0.9$; $P(r \geq 2) = 1 - P(0) - P(1) = 1 - 0.4066 - 0.3659 = 0.2275$.
15. (a) Use the geometric distribution with $p = 0.5$. $P(n = 2) = (0.5)(0.5) = 0.25$. As long as you toss the coin at least twice, it does not matter how many more times you toss it. To get the first head on the second toss, you must get a tail on the first and a head on the second. (b) $P(n = 4) = (0.5)(0.5)^3 = 0.0625$; $P(n > 4) = 1 - P(1) - P(2) - P(3) - P(4) = 1 - 0.5 - 0.5^2 - 0.5^3 - 0.5^4 = 0.0625$.

CHAPTER 6

Section 6.1

1. (a) No, it's skewed. (b) No, it crosses the horizontal axis. (c) No, it has three peaks. (d) No, the curve is not smooth.

3. Figure 6-14 has the larger standard deviation. The mean of Figure 6-14 is $\mu = 10$. The mean of Figure 6-15 is $\mu = 4$.

5. (a) 50%. (b) 68%. (c) 99.7%.

7. (a) 50%. (b) 50%. (c) 68%. (d) 95%.

9. (a) From 1207 to 1279. (b) From 1171 to 1315.
   (c) From 1135 to 1351.

11. (a) From 1.70 mA to 4.60 mA. (b) From 0.25 mA to 6.05 mA.

13. (a) Tri-County Bank Monthly Loan Request—First Year (thousands of dollars)

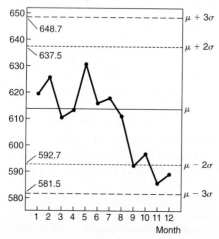

The process is out of control with a type III warning signal, since two of three consecutive points are more than 2 standard deviations below the mean. The trend is down.

(b) Tri-County Bank Monthly Loan Requests—Second Year (thousands of dollars)

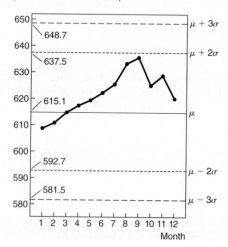

The process shows warning signal II, a run of nine consecutive points above the mean. The economy is probably heating up.

15. Visibility Standard Index

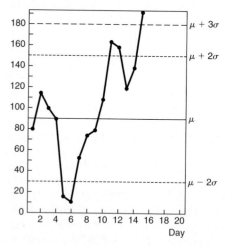

There is one point above 3σ. Thus control signal I indicates "out of control." Control signal III is present. There are two consecutive points below $\mu - 2\sigma$ and two consecutive points above $\mu + 2\sigma$. The out-of-control signals that cause the most concern are those above the mean. Special pollution regulations may be appropriate for those periods.

Section 6.2

1. (a) Robert, Juan, and Linda each scored above the mean.
   (b) Joel scored on the mean. (c) Susan and Jan scored below the mean. (d) Robert, 172; Juan, 184; Susan, 110; Joel, 150; Jan, 134; Linda, 182.

3. (a) $-4.00 < z < 4.00$. (b) $z < -1.6$. (c) $1.00 < z$.
   (d) $81.75°F < x$. (e) $x < 63.5°F$.
   (f) $64°F < x < 81.25°F$.

5. (a) $-1.77 < z$. (b) $z < 1.61$. (c) $-1.45 < z < 1.45$.
   (d) $3706 < x < 5907$. (e) $x < 5615$. (f) $6000 < x$.
   (g) A population of 2800 deer corresponds to a z value of -2.58. Data values this far below the mean occur less than 2.5% of the time. This would be an unusually low number. The population 6300 corresponds to a z value of 3.06. Fall deer populations are practically never so large. Such a population would be considered an unusually high population.

7. (a) $-1.00 < z$. (b) $z < -2.00$.
   (c) $-2.67 < z < 2.33$. (d) $x < 4.4$. (e) $5.2 < x$.
   (f) $4.1 < x < 4.5$.
   (g) A red blood cell count of 5.9 or higher corresponds to a standard z score of 3.67. Practically no data values occur this far above the mean. Such a count would be considered unusually high for a healthy female.

9. 0.5000. 11. 0.0934. 13. 0.6736. 15. 0.0643.

17. 0.8888. 19. 0.4993. 21. 0.4778. 23. 0.8953.

25. 0.3471. 27. 0.0306. 29. 0.5000. 31. 0.4483.

33. 0.8849.   35. 0.0885.   37. 0.8849.   39. 0.8808.
41. 0.3226.   43. 0.4474.   45. 0.2939.   47. 0.6704.

Section 6.3

1. $P(3 \leq x \leq 6) = P(-0.50 \leq z \leq 1.00) = 0.5328.$
3. $P(50 \leq x \leq 70) = P(0.67 \leq z \leq 2.00) = 0.2286.$
5. $P(8 \leq x \leq 12) = P(-2.19 \leq z \leq -0.94) = 0.1593.$
7. $P(x \geq 30) = P(z \geq 2.94) = 0.0016.$
9. $P(x \geq 90) = P(z \geq -0.67) = 0.7486.$
11. $-1.555.$ 13. $0.13.$ 15. $1.41.$ 17. $-0.92.$
19. $\pm 2.33.$
21. (a) $P(x > 60) = P(z > -1) = 0.8413.$ (b) $P(x < 110)$
    $= P(z < 1) = 0.8413.$ (c) $P(60 \leq x \leq 110) =$
    $P(-1.00 \leq z \leq 1.00) = 0.8413 - 0.1587 = 0.6826.$
    (d) $P(x > 140) = P(z > 2.20) = 0.0139.$
23. (a) $P(x > 675) = P(z > 1.75) = 0.0401.$
    (b) $P(x < 450) = P(z < -0.50) = 0.3085.$
    (c) $P(450 \leq x \leq 675) = P(-0.50 \leq z \leq 1.75) =$
    $0.6514.$ (d) $P(x > 28) = P(z > 1.67) = 0.0475.$
    (e) $P(x > 12) = P(z > -1.00) = 0.8413.$
    (f) $P(12 \leq x \leq 28) = P(-1.00 \leq z \leq 1.67) = 0.7938.$
25. (a) $P(x < 3.0 \text{ mm}) = P(z < -2.33) = 0.0099.$
    (b) $P(x > 7.0 \text{ mm}) = P(z > 2.11) = 0.0174.$
    (c) $P(3.0 \text{ mm} < x < 7.0 \text{ mm}) = P(-2.33 < z < 2.11) =$
    $0.9727.$
27. (a) $P(3000 < x < 3500) = P(-1.18 < z < 1.59) =$
    $0.8251.$ (b) $P(x < 3000) = P(z < -1.18) = 0.1190.$
    (c) $P(x > 3500) = P(z > 1.59) = 0.0559.$
29. (a) $P(x < 36 \text{ mo}) = P(z < -1.13) = 0.1292.$ The com-
    pany will replace 13% of its batteries.   (b) $P(z < z_0) =$
    10% for $z_0 = -1.28$; $x = -1.28(8) + 45 = 34.76.$
    Guarantee the batteries for 35 months.
31. (a) According to the empirical rule, about 95% of the
    data lies between $\mu - 2\sigma$ and $\mu + 2\sigma$. Since this interval
    is 4σ wide, we have $4\sigma \approx 6$ years, so $\sigma \approx 1.5$ years.   (b)
    $P(x > 5) = P(z > -2.00) = 0.9772.$ (c) $P(x < 10) =$
    $P(z < 1.33) = 0.9082.$ (d) $P(z < z_0) = 0.10$ for $z_0 =$
    -1.28; $x = -1.28(1.5) + 8 = 6.08$ years. Guarantee the
    TVs for about 6.1 years.
33. (a) $\sigma \approx 12$ beats/min.   (b) $P(x < 25) = P(z < -1.75) =$
    $0.0401.$ (c) $P(x > 60) = P(z > 1.17) = 0.1210.$
    (d) $P(25 \leq x \leq 60) = P(-1.75 \leq z \leq 1.17) = 0.8389.$
    (e) $P(z \leq z_0) = 0.90$ for $z_0 = 1.28$; $x = 1.28(12) + 46 =$
    61.36 beats/min. A heart rate of 61 beats/min corre-
    sponds to the 90% cutoff point of the distribution.
35. (a) $P(z \geq z_0) = 0.99$ for $z_0 = -2.33$; $x = -2.33(3.7) +$
    $90 \approx 81.38$ mo. Guarantee the microchips for 81 months.
    (b) $P(x \leq 84) = P(z \leq -1.62) = 0.0526.$ (c) Expected
    loss $= (50,000,000)(0.0526) = \$2,630,000.$ (d) Profit
    $= \$370,000.$
37. (a) $z = 1.28$; $x \approx 4.9$ hours.   (b) $z = -1.04$; $x \approx 2.9$
    hours.   (c) Yes; work and/or school schedules may be
    different on Saturday.

39. (a) In general, $P(A, \text{given } B) = P(A \text{ and } B)/P(B)$;
    $P(x > 20) = P(z > 0.50) = 0.3085$; $P(x > 15) =$
    $P(z > -0.75) = 0.7734$; $P(x > 20, \text{given } x > 15) =$
    $0.3989.$ (b) $P(x > 25) = P(z > 1.75) = 0.0401$;
    $P(x > 18) = P(z > 0.00) = 0.5000$; $P(x > 25,$
    $\text{given } x > 18) = 0.0802.$ (c) Use event $A = x > 20$
    and event $B = x > 15$ in the formula.

Section 6.4

Note: Answers may differ slightly depending on how many
digits are carried in the computation of the standard deviation and z.

1. (a) $P(r \geq 50) = P(x \geq 49.5) = P(z \geq -27.53) \approx 1$ or
    almost certain.   (b) $P(r \geq 50) = P(x \geq 49.5) =$
    $P(z \geq 7.78) \approx 0$ or almost impossible for a random
    sample.
3. (a) $P(r \geq 15) = P(x \geq 14.5) = P(z \geq -1.61) = 0.9463.$
    (b) $P(r \geq 28) = P(x \geq 27.5) = P(z \geq 1.49) = 0.0681.$
    (c) $P(15 \leq r \leq 28) = P(14.5 \leq x \leq 28.5) =$
    $P(-1.61 \leq z \leq 1.73) = 0.9045.$ (d) Since both np and
    nq are larger than 5, the normal approximation is
    appropriate.
5. (a) $P(r \geq 15) = P(x \geq 14.5) = P(z \geq -2.35) = 0.9906.$
    (b) $P(r \geq 30) = P(x \geq 29.5) = P(z \geq 0.62) = 0.2676.$
    (c) $P(25 \leq r \leq 35) + P(24.5 \leq x \leq 35.5) =$
    $P(-0.37 \leq z \leq 1.81) = 0.6092.$ (d) $P(r > 40) =$
    $P(r \geq 41) = P(x \geq 40.5) = P(z \geq 2.80) = 0.0026.$
7. (a) $P(r \geq 47) = P(x \geq 46.5) = P(z \geq -1.94) = 0.9738.$
    (b) $P(r \leq 58) = P(x \leq 58.5) = P(z \leq 1.75) = 0.9599.$ In
    parts (c) and (d), let r be the number of products that
    succeed, and use $p = 1 - 0.80 = 0.20.$ (c) $P(r \geq 15) =$
    $P(x \geq 14.5) = P(z \geq 0.40) = 0.3446.$ (d) $P(r < 10) =$
    $P(r \leq 9) = P(x \leq 9.5) = P(z \leq -1.14) = 0.1271.$
9. (a) $P(r > 280) = P(r \geq 281) = P(x > 280.5) =$
    $P(z \geq -2.16) = 0.9846.$ (b) $P(r \geq 320) =$
    $P(x \geq 319.5) = P(z \geq 1.95) = 0.0256.$
    (c) $P(280 \leq r \leq 320) = P(279.5 \leq x \leq 320.5) =$
    $P(-2.26 \leq z \leq 2.05) = 0.9679.$ (d) $n = 430$;
    $p = 0.70$; $q = 0.30$; np and nq are both greater than 5.
    These conditions mean that the normal approximation to
    the binomial is appropriate.
11. (a) $P(r \geq 540) = P(x \geq 539.5) = P(z \geq 3.81) \approx 0.000.$
    (b) $P(r \leq 500) = P(x \leq 500.5) = P(z \leq 1.11) = 0.8665.$
    (c) $P(485 \leq r \leq 525) = P(484.5 \leq x \leq 525.5) =$
    $P(0 \leq z \leq 2.84) = 0.4977.$
13. (a) $P(r > 180) = P(x \geq 180.5) = P(z > -1.11) =$
    $0.8665.$ (b) $P(r < 200) = P(x \leq 199.5) = P(z \leq 1.07)$
    $= 0.8577.$ (c) $P(\text{take sample and buy product}) =$
    $P(\text{take sample}) \cdot P(\text{buy, given take sample}) = 0.222.$
    (d) $P(60 \leq r \leq 80) = P(59.5 \leq x \leq 80.5) =$
    $P(-1.47 \leq z \leq 1.37) = 0.8439.$
15. (a) $0.94.$ (b) $P(r \leq 255).$ (c) $P(r \leq 255) =$
    $P(x \leq 255.5) = P(z \leq 1.16) = 0.8770.$

Chapter 6 Review

1. (a) 0.4599. (b) 0.4015. (c) 0.0384. (d) 0.0104. (e) 0.0250. (f) 0.8413.
3. (a) 0.9821. (b) 0.3156. (c) 0.2977.
5. 1.645.
7. $z = \pm 1.96$.
9. (a) 0.89. (b) 0. (c) 0.2514.
11. (a) 0.0166. (b) 0.975.
13. (a) 0.9772. (b) 17.3 hr.
15. (a) From \$1.81 to \$3.51 is a 68% range of errors.
    (b) From \$0.96 to \$4.36 is a 95% range of errors.
    (c) Almost all errors are from \$0.11 to \$5.21.
17. (a) 0.5812. (b) 0.0668. (c) 0.0122.
19. (a) 0.8665. (b) 0.7330.

CUMULATIVE REVIEW PROBLEMS

1. The specified ranges of readings are disjoint and cover all possible readings.
2. Essay.
3. Yes; the events constitute the entire sample space.
4. (a) 0.85. (b) 0.70. (c) 0.70.
   (d) 0.30. (e) 0.15. (f) 0.75.
   (g) 0.30. (h) 0.05.
5. 0.17
6.

x	$P(x)$
5	0.25
15	0.45
25	0.15
35	0.10
45	0.05

$\mu \approx 17.5; \sigma \approx 10.9$.

7. (a) $p = 0.10$. (b) $\mu = 1.2; \sigma \approx 1.04$. (c) 0.718.
   (d) 0.889.
8. (a) 0.05. (b) $P(n) = (0.05)(0.95)^n; n \geq 1$. (c) 0.81.
9. (a) Yes; since $n = 100$ and $np = 5$, the criteria $n \geq 100$ and $np < 10$ are satisfied. $\lambda = 5$. (b) 0.7622.
   (c) 0.0680.
10. (a) Yes; both np and np exceed 5. (b) 0.9925.
    (c) np is too large ($np > 10$) and n is too small ($n < 100$).
11. (a) $\sigma \approx 1.7$. (b) 0.1314. (c) 0.1075.
12. Essay.

CHAPTER 7

Section 7.1

1. A set of measurements or counts either existing or conceptual. For example, the population of ages of all people in Colorado; the population of weights of all students in your school; the population count of all antelope in Wyoming.

3. A numerical descriptive measure of a population, such as μ, the population mean; σ, the population standard deviation; or σ^2, the population variance.
5. A statistical inference is a conclusion about the value of a population parameter. We will do both estimation and testing.
7. They help us visualize the sampling distribution by using tables and graphs that approximately represent the sampling distribution.
9. We studied the sampling distribution of mean trout lengths based on samples of size 5. Other such sampling distributions abound.

Section 7.2

Note: Answers may differ slightly depending on the number of digits carried in the standard deviation.

1. (a) $\mu_{\bar{x}} = 15; \sigma_{\bar{x}} = 2.0; P(15 \leq \bar{x} \leq 17) = P(0 \leq z \leq 1.00) = 0.3413$. (b) $\mu_{\bar{x}} = 15; \sigma_{\bar{x}} = 1.75; P(15 \leq \bar{x} \leq 17) = P(0 \leq z \leq 1.14) = 0.3729$. (c) The standard deviation is smaller in part (b) because of the larger sample size. Therefore, the distribution about $\mu_{\bar{x}}$ is narrower in part (b).
3. (a) No; the sample size is only 9 and so is too small.
   (b) Yes; the $\bar{x}$ distribution also will be normal with $\mu_{\bar{x}} = 25; \sigma_{\bar{x}} = 3.5/3; P(23 \leq \bar{x} \leq 26) = P(-1.71 \leq z \leq 0.86) = 0.7615$.
5. (a) $P(x < 74.5) = P(z < -0.63) = 0.2643$.
   (b) $P(\bar{x} < 74.5) = P(z < -2.79) = 0.0026$. (c) No. If the weight of only one car were less than 74.5 tons, we could not conclude that the loader is out of adjustment. If the mean weight for a sample of 20 cars were less than 74.5 tons, we would suspect that the loader is malfunctioning. As we see in part (b), the probability of this happening is very low if the loader is correctly adjusted.
7. (a) $P(x < 40) = P(z < -1.80) = 0.0359$. (b) Since the x distribution is approximately normal, the $\bar{x}$ distribution is approximately normal with mean 85 and standard deviation 17.678. $P(\bar{x} < 40) = P(z < -2.55) = 0.0054$.
   (c) $P(\bar{x} < 40) = P(z < -3.12) = 0.0009$.
   (d) $P(\bar{x} < 40) = P(z < -4.02) < 0.0002$. (e) Yes; if the average value based on five tests were less than 40, the patient is almost certain to have excess insulin.
9. (a) $P(x < 54) = P(z < -1.27) = 0.1020$. (b) The expected number undernourished is 2200(0.1020), or about 224. (c) $P(\bar{x} \leq 60) = P(z \leq -2.99) = 0.0014$.
   (d) $P(\bar{x} < 64.2) = P(z < 1.20) = 0.8849$. Since the sample average is above the mean, it is quite unlikely that the doe population is undernourished.
11. (a) Since x itself represents a sample mean return based on a large (random) sample of stocks, x has a distribution that is approximately normal (central limit theorem). (b) $P(1\% \leq \bar{x} \leq 2\%) = P(-1.63 \leq z \leq 1.09) = 0.8105$. (c) $P(1\% \leq \bar{x} \leq 2\%) =$

$P(-3.27 \leq z \leq 2.18) = 0.9849.$ (d) Yes. The standard deviation decreases as the sample size increases.
(e) $P(\bar{x} < 1\%) = P(z < -3.27) = 0.0005.$ This is very unlikely if $\mu = 1.6\%$. One would suspect that μ has slipped below 1.6%.

13. (a) Since x itself represents a sample mean from a large (random) sample of bonds, x is approximately normally distributed according to the central limit theorem.
(b) $P(\bar{x} < 6\%) = P(z < -2.19) = 0.0143.$ Yes, it is very unlikely that $\bar{x}$ would be less than 6% if $\mu = 10.8\%$. The junk bond market appears to be weaker.
(c) $P(\bar{x} > 16\%) = P(z > 2.37) = 0.0089.$ Yes, it is very unlikely that $\bar{x}$ would be greater than 16% if $\mu = 10.8\%$. The junk bond market may be heating up.

15. (a) 30 or more. (b) No.

17. (a) The total checkout time for 30 customers is the sum of the checkout times for each individual customer. Thus, $w = x_1 + x_2 + \cdots + x_{30}$, and the probability that the total checkout time for the next 30 customers is less than 90 is $P(w < 90)$. (b) $w < 90$ is equivalent to $x_1 + x_2 + \cdots + x_{30} < 90$. Divide both sides by 30 to get $\bar{x} < 3$ for samples of size 30. Therefore, $P(w < 90) = P(\bar{x} < 3)$.
(c) By the central limit theorem, $\bar{x}$ is approximately normal with $\mu_{\bar{x}} = 2.7$ min and $\sigma_{\bar{x}} = 0.1095$.
(d) $P(\bar{x} < 3) = P(z < 2.74) = 0.9969.$

19. (a) $P(w < 9500\text{ g}) = P(\bar{x} < 211.11) = P(z < -2.31) = 0.0104.$ (b) $P(w > 12{,}000\text{ g}) = P(\bar{x} > 266.67) = P(z > 2.13) = 0.0166.$ (c) $P(9500 \leq w \leq 12{,}000) = P(211.11 \leq \bar{x} \leq 266.67) = P(-2.31 \leq z \leq 2.13) = 0.9730.$

21. (a) $P(w > 90) = P(\bar{x} > 18) = P(z > 0.68) = 0.2483.$
(b) $P(w < 80) = P(\bar{x} < 16) = P(z < -0.68) = 0.2483.$
(c) $P(80 < w < 90) = P(16 < \bar{x} < 18) = P(-0.68 < z < 0.68) = 0.5034.$

Section 7.3

1. (a) Answers vary. (b) When np and nq both exceed 5; $\mu_{\hat{p}} = p$; $\sigma_{\hat{p}} = \sqrt{pq/n}$. (c) Yes; both np and nq exceed 5; $\mu_{\hat{p}} = 0.21$; $\sigma_{\hat{p}} \approx 0.071$; continuity correction ≈ 0.015. $P(0.15 \leq \hat{p} \leq 0.25) \approx P(0.135 \leq x \leq 0.265) \approx P(-1.06 \leq z \leq 0.77) \approx 0.6348.$ (d) No; $np < 5$.
(e) Yes; both np and nq exceed 5; $\mu_{\hat{p}} = 0.15$; $\sigma_{\hat{p}} \approx 0.052$; continuity correction ≈ 0.010. $P(\hat{p} \geq 0.22) \approx P(x \geq 0.21) \approx P(z \geq 1.15) \approx 0.1251.$

3. $\mu_{\hat{p}} = 0.60$; $\sigma_{\hat{p}} \approx 0.089$; continuity correction ≈ 0.017.
(a) $P(\hat{p} \geq 0.5) \approx P(x \geq 0.483) \approx P(z \geq -1.31) \approx 0.9049.$ (b) $P(\hat{p} \geq 0.667) \approx P(x \geq 0.65) \approx P(z \geq 0.56) \approx 0.2877.$ (c) $P(\hat{p} \leq 0.33) \approx P(x \leq 0.35) \approx P(z \leq -2.81) = 0.0025.$ (d) Yes; both np and nq exceed 5.

5. $\mu_{\hat{p}} = 0.11$; $\sigma_{\hat{p}} \approx 0.042$; continuity correction ≈ 0.009.
(a) $P(\hat{p} \leq 0.15) \approx P(x \leq 0.159) \approx P(z \leq 1.17) \approx 0.8790.$ (b) $P(0.10 \leq \hat{p} \leq 0.15) \approx P(0.091 \leq x \leq$

$0.159) = P(-0.45 \leq z \leq 1.17) = 0.5526.$ (c) Yes, both np and nq exceed 5.

7. (a) Both np and nq exceed 5; $\mu_{\hat{p}} = 0.06$; $\sigma_{\hat{p}} = 0.024$; continuity correction $= 0.005$. (b) $P(\hat{p} \geq 0.07) \approx P(x \geq 0.065) \approx P(z \geq 0.21) = 0.4168.$ (c) $P(\hat{p} \geq 0.11) \approx P(x \geq 0.105) \approx P(z \geq 1.88) \approx 0.0301.$ Yes, the probability of producing this proportion of defective toys is only about 3%.

9.

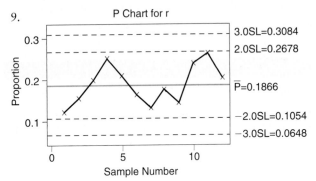

No out-of-control signals.

11.

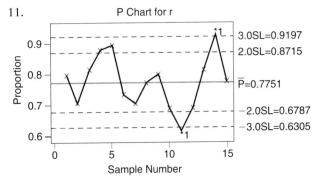

Out-of-control signal III occurs on days 4 and 5; out-of-control signal I occurs on day 11 on the low side and day 14 on the high side. Out-of-control signals on the low side are of most concern for the homeless seeking work. The foundation should look to see what happened on that day. The foundation might take a look at the out-of-control periods on the high side to see if there is a possibility of cultivating more jobs.

Chapter 7 Review

1. (a) A normal distribution. (b) The mean μ of the x distribution. (c) $\sigma/\sqrt{n}$, where σ is the standard deviation of the x distribution. (d) They will both be approximately normal with the same mean, but the standard deviations will be $\sigma/\sqrt{50}$ and $\sigma/\sqrt{100}$, respectively.

3. (a) $P(x \geq 40) = P(z \geq 0.71) = 0.2389.$ (b) $P(\bar{x} \geq 40) = P(z \geq 2.14) = 0.0162.$

5. $P(98 \leq \bar{x} \leq 102) = P(-1.33 \leq z \leq 1.33) = 0.8164$.

7. (a) $P(\bar{x} \geq 750) = P(z \geq 0) = 0.5000$.
(b) $P(745 \leq \bar{x} \leq 755) = P(-2.00 \leq z \leq 2.00) = 0.9544$.

9. (a) $\mu_{\hat{p}} = 0.22$; $\sigma_{\hat{p}} \approx 0.059$; continuity correction $= 0.01$; $P(0.20 \leq \hat{p} \leq 0.25) \approx P(0.19 \leq \hat{p} \leq 0.26) \approx P(-0.51 \leq z \leq 0.68) \approx 0.4467$. (b) $\mu_{\hat{p}} = 0.27$; $\sigma_{\hat{p}} \approx 0.072$; continuity correction ≈ 0.013; $P(\hat{p} \geq 0.35) \approx P(\hat{p} \geq 0.337) \approx P(z \geq 0.93) \approx 0.1762$. (c) No, $np < 5$.

CHAPTER 8

Section 8.1

1. (a) 3.04 gm to 3.26 gm; 0.11 gm. (b) Distribution of weights is normal with known σ. (c) There is an 80% chance that the confidence interval is one of the intervals that contains the population average weight of Allen's hummingbirds in this region.

3. (a) 34.62 ml/kg to 40.38 ml/kg; 2.88 ml/kg. (b) The sample size is large (30 or more) and σ is known. (c) There is a 99% chance that the confidence interval is one of the intervals that contains the population average blood plasma level for male firefighters.

5. (a) 125.7 to 151.3 larceny cases; 12.8 larceny cases. (b) 123.3 to 153.7 larceny cases; 15.2 larceny cases. (c) 118.4 to 158.6 larceny cases; 20.1 larceny cases. (d) Yes. (e) Yes.

7. (a) $53,871 to $64,009; $5069. (b) $55,138 to $62,742; $3802. (c) $56,175 to $61,705; $2765. (d) Yes. (e) Yes.

9. (a) The mean and standard deviation round to the values given. (b) Using the rounded values of part (a), the 75% interval is from 34.19 thousand to 37.81 thousand. (c) Yes. 30 thousand dollars is below the lower bound of the 75% confidence interval. We can say with 75% confidence that the mean lies between 34.19 thousand and 37.81 thousand. (d) Yes. 40 thousand is above the upper bound of the 75% confidence interval. (e) 33.41 thousand to 38.59 thousand. We can say with 90% confidence that the mean lies between 33.4 thousand and 38.6 thousand dollars. 30 thousand is below the lower bound and 40 thousand is above the upper bound.

11. (a) The values for the mean and standard deviation round to those given. (b) Using the rounded values for the mean and standard deviation given in part (a), the interval is from 50.37 to 51.95. (c) Using the rounded values for the mean and standard deviation given in part (a), the interval is from 49.92 to 52.40. (d) We can be 99% sure that the average January temperature is between 49.92°F and 52.4°F. It is possible that the average is 53°F, but not very likely. It is possible that a few more years of observation might be needed before such a claim could be made.

Section 8.2

1. 2.110.

3. 1.721.

5. (a) The mean and standard deviation round to the values given. (b) Using the rounded values for the mean and standard deviation given in part (a), the interval is from 1249 to 1295.

7. (a) Use a calculator. (b) 74.7 lb to 107.3 lb.

9. 76.04 to 82.46 cm.

11. (a) The mean and standard deviation round to the given values. (b) 8.41 to 11.49. (c) Since all values in the 99.9% confidence interval are above 6, we can be almost certain that this patient no longer has a calcium deficiency.

13. (a) Use a calculator; 8.5 to 11.1 in. (b) Use a calculator; 15.7 to 18.5 in.

15. (a) Boxplots differ in length of interquartile box, location of median, and length of whiskers. The boxplots come from different samples. (b) Yes; no; for 95% confidence intervals, we expect about 95% of the samples to generate intervals that contain the mean of the population.

17. (a) The mean and standard deviation round to the given values. (b) 21.6 to 28.8. (c) 19.4 to 31.0. (d) Using both confidence intervals, we can say that the P/E for Bank One is well below the population average. The P/E for AT&T Wireless is well above the population average. The P/E for Disney is within both confidence intervals. It appears that the P/E for Disney is close to the population average P/E. (e) By the central limit theorem, when n is large, the $\bar{x}$ distribution is approximately normal. In general, $n \geq 30$ is considered large.

19. (a) $d.f. = 30$; 43.59 to 46.82; 43.26 to 47.14; 42.58 to 47.81. (b) 43.63 to 46.77; 43.33 to 47.07; 42.74 to 47.66. (c) Yes; the respective intervals based on the Student's t distribution are slightly longer. (d) For Student's t, $d.f. = 80$; 44.22 to 46.18; 44.03 to 46.37; 43.65 to 46.75. For standard normal, 44.23 to 46.17; 44.05 to 46.35; 43.68 to 46.72. The intervals using the t distribution are still slightly longer than corresponding intervals using the standard normal distribution. However, with a larger sample size, the differences between the two methods is less pronounced.

Section 8.3

1. (a) $\hat{p} = 39/62 = 0.6290$. (b) 0.51 to 0.75. If this experiment were repeated many times, about 95% of the intervals would contain p. (c) Both np and nq are

greater than 5. If either is less than 5, the normal curve will not necessarily give a good approximation to the binomial.

3. (a) $\hat{p} = 1619/5222 = 0.3100$. (b) 0.29 to 0.33. If we repeat the survey with many different samples of 5222 dwellings, about 99% of the intervals will contain p. (c) Both np and nq are greater than 5. If either is less than 5, the normal curve will not necessarily give a good approximation to the binomial.

5. (a) $\hat{p} = 0.5420$. (b) 0.53 to 0.56. (c) Yes. Both np and nq are greater than 5.

7. (a) $\hat{p} = 17/99 = 0.1717$. (b) 0.12 to 0.23. (c) Yes. Both np and nq are greater than 5.

9. (a) $\hat{p} = 0.0304$. (b) 0.02 to 0.05. (c) Yes. Both np and nq are greater than 5.

11. (a) $\hat{p} = 0.0600$. (b) 0.04 to 0.08.

13. (a) $\hat{p} = 0.1910$. (b) 0.18 to 0.20.

15. (a) $\hat{p} = 0.8603$. (b) 0.84 to 0.89. (c) A recent study shows that 86% of women shoppers remained loyal to their favorite supermarket last year. The margin of error was 2.5 percentage points.

17. (a) $\hat{p} = 0.25$. (b) 0.22 to 0.28. (c) A survey of 1000 large corporations has shown that 25% will choose a nonsmoking job candidate over an equally qualified smoker. The margin of error was 2.7%.

Section 8.4

1. Estimate a mean. Use 75 plots.

3. (a) Estimate a proportion; 208. (b) 68.

5. Estimate a mean; 120 total or 64 more.

7. (a) Estimate a proportion; 666. (b) 662.

9. Estimate a mean; 117 or 34 more.

11. (a) Estimate a proportion; 144. (b) 127 total or 69 more.

13. (a) Estimate a proportion; 16,641. (b) 14,718.

15. Estimate a mean; 385 or 218 more.

17. (a) Estimate a proportion; 68. (b) 50.

19. (a) $1/4 - (p - 1/2)^2 = 1/4 - (p^2 - p + 1/4) = -p^2 + p = p(1 - p)$. (b) Since $(p - 1/2)^2 \geq 0$, then $1/4 - (p - 1/2)^2 \leq 1/4$ because we are subtracting $(p - 1/2)^2$ from 1/4.

21. (a) 1,664,100. (b) No. When $p = 0.5$, the formula for sample size without a preliminary estimate is the same as the formula with a preliminary estimate.

Section 8.5

1. (a) Use a calculator. (b) $d.f. \approx 11$; $E \approx 129.9$; interval from -121.3 to 138.5 ppm. (c) Because the interval contains both positive and negative numbers, we cannot say at the 90% confidence level that one region is more interesting than the other. (d) Student's t because σ_1 and σ_2 are unknown.

3. (a) Use a calculator. (b) $d.f. \approx 15$; $E \approx 5.42$; interval from 12.64% to 23.48% foreign revenue. (c) Because the interval contains only positive values, we can say at the 85% confidence level that technology companies have a higher population mean % foreign revenue. (d) Student's t because σ_1 and σ_2 are unknown.

5. (a) Use a calculator. (b) $d.f. \approx 39$; to use Table 6, round down to $d.f. \approx 35$; $E \approx 0.125$; interval from -0.399 to -0.149 feet. (c) Since the interval contains all negative numbers, it seems that at the 90% confidence level the population mean height of pro football players is less than that of pro basketball players. (d) Student's t distribution because σ_1 and σ_2 are unknown. Both samples are large, so no assumptions about the original distribution are needed.

7. (a) $\hat{\sigma} = 0.0232$; $E \approx 0.0599$; the interval is from 0.67 to 0.79. (b) The confidence interval contains values that are all positive, so we can be 99% sure that $p_1 > p_2$.

9. (a) $E = 0.3201$; the interval is from -9.12 to -8.48. (b) The interval consists of negative values only. At the 99% confidence level we can conclude that $\mu_1 < \mu_2$.

11. (a) $\hat{p}_1 = 0.3095$; $\hat{p}_2 = 0.1184$; $\hat{\sigma} = 0.0413$; interval from 0.085 to 0.297. (b) The interval contains numbers that are all positive. A greater proportion of hogans occur in Fort Defiance.

13. (a) Use a calculator. (b) $d.f. \approx 9$; $E \approx 5.3$; 3.7 to 14.3 pounds. (c) Interval contains all positive values. At the 85% confidence level it appears that the population mean weight of grey wolves in Chihuahua is greater than that of grey wolves in Durango.

15. (a) -1.35 to 2.39. (b) 0.06 to 3.86. (c) -0.61 to 3.49. (d) At the 85% confidence level, we can say that the mean index of self-esteem based on competence is greater than the mean index of self-esteem based on physical attractiveness. We cannot conclude that there is a difference between the mean index of self-esteem based on competence and that based on social acceptance. We cannot conclude that there is a difference in the mean indices based on social acceptance and physical attractiveness.

17. (a) Based on the same data, a 99% confidence interval is longer than a 95% confidence interval. Therefore, if the 95% confidence interval has both positive and negative values, so will the 99% confidence interval. However, for the same data, a 90% confidence interval is shorter than a 95% confidence interval. The 90% confidence interval might contain only positive or only negative values even if the 95% interval contains both. (b) Based on the same data, a 99% confidence interval is longer than a 95% confidence interval. Even if the 95% confidence interval contains values that are all positive, the longer 99% interval could contain both positive and negative

values. Since, for the same data, a 90% confidence interval is shorter than a 95% confidence interval, if the 95% confidence interval contains only positive values, so will the 90% confidence interval.

19. (a) $n = 896.1$ or 897 couples in each sample.
(b) $n = 768.3$ or 769 couples in each sample.

21. (a) Pooled standard deviation $s \approx 8.6836$; interval from 3.9 to 14.1.   (b) The pooled standard deviation method has a shorter interval and a larger $d.f.$

Chapter 8 Review

1. See text.

3. Interval for a mean; 176.91 to 180.49.

5. Interval for a mean.
(a) Use a calculator.   (b) 64.1 to 84.3.

7. Interval for a proportion; 0.50 to 0.54.

9. Interval for a proportion.
(a) $\hat{p} = 0.4072$.   (b) 0.333 to 0.482.

11. Difference of means.
(a) Use a calculator.   (b) $d.f. \approx 71$; to use Table 6, round down to $d.f. \approx 70$; $E \approx 0.83$; interval from -0.06 to 1.6.   (c) Because the interval contains both positive and negative values, we cannot conclude at the 95% confidence level that there is any difference in soil water content in the two fields.   (d) Student's t distribution because σ_1 and σ_2 are unknown. Both samples are large, so no assumptions about the original distributions are needed.

13. Difference of means.
(a) $d.f. \approx 17$; $E \approx 2.5$; interval from 5.5 to 10.5 lb.
(b) Yes. The interval contains values that are all positive. At the 75% level of confidence it appears that the average weight of adult male wolves from the Northwest Territories is greater.

15. Difference of proportions.
(a) $\hat{p}_1 = 0.8495$; $\hat{p}_2 = 0.8916$; -0.1409 to 0.0567.
(b) No. The interval contains both negative and positive numbers. We do not detect a difference in the proportions at the 95% confidence level.

17. (a) $P(A_1 < \mu_1 < B_1 \text{ and } A_2 < \mu_2 < B_2) = (0.80)(0.80) = 0.64$. The complement of the event $A_1 < \mu_1 < B_1$ and $A_2 < \mu_2 < B_2$ is that either μ_1 is not in the first interval or μ_2 is not in the second interval or both. Thus, $P(\text{at least one interval fails}) = 1 - P(A_1 < \mu_1 < B_1 \text{ and } A_2 < \mu_2 < B_2) = 1 - 0.64 = 0.36$.   (b) Suppose $P(A_1 < \mu_1 < B_1) = c$ and $P(A_2 < \mu_2 < B_2) = c$. If we want the probability that both hold to be 90%, and if x_1 and x_2 are independent, then $P(A_1 < \mu_1 < B_1 \text{ and } A_2 < \mu_2 < B_2) = 0.90$ means $P(A_1 < \mu_1 < B_1) \cdot P(A_2 < \mu_2 < B_2) = 0.90$ so $c^2 = 0.90$ or $c = 0.9487$.
(c) In order to have a high probability of success for the whole project, the probability that each component will perform as specified must be significantly higher.

CHAPTER 9

Section 9.1

1. See text.

3. No, if we fail to reject the null hypothesis, we have not proven it beyond all doubt. We have failed only to find sufficient evidence to reject it.

5. (a) H_0: $\mu = 60$ kg.   (b) H_1: $\mu < 60$ kg.   (c) H_1: $\mu > 60$ kg.   (d) H_1: $\mu \neq 60$ kg.   (e) For part b, the P-value area region is on the left. For part c, the P-value area is on the right. For part d, the P-value area is on both sides of the mean.

7. (a) H_0: $\mu = 16.4$ feet.   (b) H_1: $\mu > 16.4$ feet.   (c) H_1: $\mu < 16.4$ feet.   (d) H_1: $\mu \neq 16.4$ feet.   (e) For part b, the P-value area is on the right. For part c, the P-value area is on the left. For part d, the P-value area is on both sides of the mean.

9. (a) $\alpha = 0.01$; H_0: $\mu = 4.7\%$; H_1: $\mu > 4.7\%$; right-tailed.
(b) Normal; $\bar{x} = 5.38$; $z \approx 0.90$.   (c) P-value ≈ 0.1841; on standard normal curve, shade area to the right of 0.90.   (d) P-value of $0.1841 > 0.01$ for α; fail to reject H_0.   (e) Insufficient evidence at the 0.01 level to reject claim that average yield for bank stocks equals average yield for all stocks.

11. (a) $\alpha = 0.01$; H_0: $\mu = 4.55$ gm; H_1: $\mu < 4.55$ gm; left-tailed.   (b) Normal; $\bar{x} = 3.75$ gm; $z \approx -2.80$.
(c) P-value ≈ 0.0026; on standard normal curve, shade area to the left of -2.80.   (d) P-value of $0.0026 \leq 0.01$ for α; reject H_0.   (e) The sample evidence is sufficient at the 0.01 level to justify rejecting H_0. It seems that the hummingbirds in the Grand Canyon region have a lower average weight.

13. (a) $\alpha = 0.01$; H_0: $\mu = 11\%$; H_1: $\mu \neq 11\%$; two-tailed.
(b) Normal; $\bar{x} = 12.5\%$; $z = 1.20$.   (c) P-value $= 2(0.1151) = 0.2302$; on standard normal curve, shade areas to the right of 1.20 and to the left of -1.20.
(d) P-value of $0.2302 > 0.01$ for α; fail to reject H_0.
(e) There is insufficient evidence at the 0.01 level to reject H_0. It seems that the average hail damage to wheat crops in Weld County matches the national average.

Section 9.2

1. (a) $\alpha = 0.01$; H_0: $\mu = 16.4$ ft; H_1: $\mu > 16.4$ ft.
(b) Standard normal; $z \approx 1.54$.   (c) P-value ≈ 0.0618; on standard normal curve shade area to the right of $z \approx 1.54$.   (d) P-value of $0.0618 > 0.01$ for α; fail to reject H_0.   (e) At the 1% level, there is insufficient evidence to say that the average storm level is increasing.

3. (a) $\alpha = 0.05$; H_0: $\mu = 41.7$; H_1: $\mu \neq 41.7$.
(b) Standard normal; $z \approx -1.99$.   (c) P-value $\approx 2(0.0233) \approx 0.0466$; on standard normal curve shade areas to the right of 1.99 and to the left of -1.99.
(d) P-value of $0.0466 \leq 0.05$ for α; reject H_0.

(e) At the 5% level, there is sufficient evidence to say that the average number of e-mails is different with the new priority system.

5. (a) $\alpha = 0.01$; H_0: $\mu = 1.75$ yr; H_1: $\mu > 1.75$ yr. (b) Student's t, $d.f. = 45$; $t \approx 2.481$. (c) $0.005 <$ P-value < 0.010; on t graph shade area to the right of 2.481. (d) Entire P-interval ≤ 0.01 for α; reject H_0. (e) At the 1% level of significance, the sample data indicate that the average age of the Minnesota region coyotes is higher than 1.75 years.

7. (a) $\alpha = 0.05$; H_0: $\mu = 19.4$; H_1: $\mu \neq 19.4$ (b) Student's t, $d.f. = 35$; $t \approx -1.731$. (c) $0.050 < P$-value < 0.100; on t graph shade area to the right of 1.731 and to the left of -1.731. (d) P-value interval > 0.05 for α; fail to reject H_0. (e) At the 5% level of significance, the sample evidence does not support rejecting the claim that the average P/E of socially responsible funds is different from that of the S&P stock index.

9. i. Use a calculator. Rounded values are used in part ii.
ii. (a) $\alpha = 0.05$; H_0: $\mu = 4.8$; H_1: $\mu < 4.8$. (b) Student's t, $d.f. = 5$; $t \approx -3.499$. (c) $0.005 < P$-value $<$ 0.010; on t graph shade area to the left of -3.499 (d) P-value interval ≤ 0.05 for α; reject H_0. (e) At the 5% level of significance, sample evidence supports the claim that the average RBC count for this patient is less than 4.8.

11. i. Use a calculator. Rounded values are used in part ii.
ii. (a) $\alpha = 0.01$; H_0: $\mu = 67$; H_1: $\mu \neq 67$. (b) Student's t, $d.f. = 15$; $t \approx -1.962$. (c) $0.050 < P$-value $<$ 0.100; on t graph shade area to the right of 1.962 and to the left of -1.962. (d) P-value interval > 0.01; fail to reject H_0. (e) At the 1% level of significance, the sample evidence does not support a claim that the average thickness of slab avalanches in Vail is different from that in Canada.

13. i. Use a calculator. Rounded values are used in part ii.
ii. (a) $\alpha = 0.05$; H_0: $\mu = 40$ beats per min; H_1: $\mu \neq 40$ beats per min. (b) Student's t, $d.f. = 5$; $t \approx -2.041$. (c) $0.050 < P$-value < 0.100; on t graph shade area to the right of 2.041 and to the left of -2.041. (d) P-value interval > 0.05; fail to reject H_0. (e) At the 5% level of significance, the population average heart rate for the lion is not significantly different.

15. i. Use a calculator. Rounded values are used in part ii.
ii. (a) $\alpha = 0.05$; H_0: $\mu = 8.8$; H_1: $\mu \neq 8.8$. (b) Student's t, $d.f. = 13$; $t \approx -1.337$. (c) $0.200 <$ P-value < 0.250; on t graph shade area to the right of 1.337 and to the left of -1.337. (d) P-value interval > 0.05; fail to reject H_0. (e) At the 5% level of significance, we cannot conclude that the catch is different from 8.8 fish per day.

17. (a) The P-value of a one-tailed test is smaller. For a two-tailed test, the P-value is doubled because it includes the area in both tails. (b) Yes; the P-value of a one-tailed test is smaller, so it might be smaller than α, whereas the P-value of a two-tailed test is larger than α. (c) Yes; if the two-tailed P-value is less than α, the smaller one-tail area is also less than α. (d) Yes, the conclusions can be different. The conclusion based on the two-tailed test is more conservative in the sense that the sample data must be more extreme (differ more from H_0) in order to reject H_0.

19. (a) For $\alpha = 0.01$, confidence level $c = 0.99$; interval from 20.28 to 23.72; hypothesized $\mu = 20$ is not in the interval; reject H_0. (b) H_0: $\mu = 20$; H_1: $\mu \neq 20$; $z = 3.000$; P-value ≈ 0.0026; P-value of $0.0026 \leq 0.01$ for α; reject H_0; conclusions are the same.

21. Critical value $z_0 = 2.33$; critical region is values to the right of 2.33; since the sample statistic $z = 1.54$ is not in the critical region, fail to reject H_0. At the 1% level, there is insufficient evidence to say that the average storm level is increasing. Conclusion is same as with P-value method.

23. Critical values $z_0 = \pm 1.96$; critical regions are values to left of -1.96 together with values to the right of 1.96. Since the sample test statistic $z = -1.99$ is in the critical region, reject H_0. At the 5% level, there is sufficient evidence to say that the average number of e-mails is different with the new priority system. Conclusion is same as with P-value method.

25. Critical value is $t_0 = 2.412$ for one-tailed test with $d.f. = 45$; critical region is values to the right of 2.412. Since the sample test statistic $t = 2.481$ is in the critical region, reject H_0. At the 1% level, the sample data indicate that the average age of Minnesota region coyotes is higher than 1.75 yr. Conclusion is same as with P-value method.

Section 9.3

1. i. (a) $\alpha = 0.01$; H_0: $p = 0.301$; H_1: $p < 0.301$. (b) Standard normal; yes, $np \approx 64.7 > 5$ and $nq \approx$ $150.3 > 5$; $\hat{p} \approx 0.214$; $z \approx -2.78$. (c) P-value $\approx$ 0.0027; on standard normal curve shade area to the left of -2.78. (d) P-value of $0.0027 \leq 0.01$ for α; reject H_0. (e) At the 1% level of significance, the sample data indicate that the population proportion of numbers with a leading "1" in the revenue file is less than 0.301, predicted by Benford's Law.
ii. Yes; the revenue data file seems to include more numbers with higher first nonzero digits than Benford's Law predicts.
iii. We have not proved H_0 to be false. However, because our sample data led us to reject H_0 and to conclude that there are too few numbers with a leading digit of 1, more investigation is merited.

3. (a) $\alpha = 0.01$; H_0: $p = 0.70$; H_1: $p \neq 0.70$.   (b) Standard normal; $\hat{p} = 0.75$; $z \approx 0.62$.   (c) P-value = $2(0.2676) = 0.5352$; on standard normal curve shade areas to the right of 0.62 and to the left of -0.62.   (d) P-value of $0.5352 > 0.01$ for α; fail to reject H_0.   (e) At the 1% level of significance, we cannot say that the population proportion of arrests of males aged 15 to 34 in Rock Springs is different from 70%.

5. (a) $\alpha = 0.01$; H_0: $p = 0.77$; H_1: $p < 0.77$.   (b) Standard normal; $\hat{p} \approx 0.5556$; $z \approx -2.65$.   (c) P-value ≈ 0.004; on standard normal curve shade area to the left of -2.65.   (d) P-value of $0.004 \leq 0.01$ for α; reject H_0.   (e) At the 1% level of significance, the data show that the population proportion of driver fatalities related to alcohol is less than 77% in Kit Carson County.

7. (a) $\alpha = 0.01$; H_0: $p = 0.50$; H_1: $p < 0.50$.   (b) Standard normal; $\hat{p} \approx 0.2941$; $z \approx -2.40$.   (c) P-value = 0.0082; on standard normal curve shade region to the left of -2.40.   (d) P-value of $0.0082 \leq 0.01$ for α; reject H_0.   (e) At the 1% level of significance, the data indicate that the population proportion of female wolves is now less than 50% in the region.

9. (a) $\alpha = 0.01$; H_0: $p = 0.261$; H_1: $p \neq 0.261$.   (b) Standard normal; $\hat{p} \approx 0.1924$; $z \approx -2.78$.   (c) P-value = $2(0.0027) = 0.0054$; on standard normal curve shade area to the right of 2.78 and to the left of -2.78.   (d) P-value of $0.0054 \leq 0.01$ for α; reject H_0.   (e) At the 1% level of significance, the sample data indicate that the population proportion of the five-syllable sequence is different from that of Plato's *Republic*.

11. (a) $\alpha = 0.01$; H_0: $p = 0.47$; H_1: $p > 0.47$.   (b) Standard normal; $\hat{p} \approx 0.4871$; $z \approx 1.09$.   (c) P-value = 0.1379; on standard normal curve shade area to the right of 1.09.   (d) P-value of $0.1379 > 0.01$ for α; fail to reject H_0.   (e) At the 1% level of significance, there is insufficient evidence to support the claim that the population proportion of customers loyal to Chevrolet is more than 47%.

13. (a) $\alpha = 0.05$; H_0: $p = 0.092$; H_1: $p > 0.092$.   (b) Standard normal; $\hat{p} \approx 0.1480$; $z \approx 2.71$.   (c) P-value = 0.0034; on standard normal curve shade region to the right of 2.71.   (d) P-value of $0.0034 \leq 0.05$ for α; reject H_0.   (e) At the 5% level of significance, the data indicate that the population proportion of students with hypertension during final exams week is higher than 9.2%.

15. (a) $\alpha = 0.01$; H_0: $p = 0.82$; H_1: $p \neq 0.82$.   (b) Standard normal; $\hat{p} \approx 0.7671$; $z \approx -1.18$.   (c) P-value = $2(0.1190) = 0.2380$; on standard normal curve shade area to the right of 1.18 and to the left of -1.18.   (d) P-value of $0.2380 > 0.01$ for α; fail to reject H_0.   (e) At the 1% level of significance, the evidence is insufficient to indicate that the population proportion of extroverts among college student government leaders is different from 82%.

17. (a) $\alpha = 0.01$; H_0: $p = 0.76$; H_1: $p \neq 0.76$.   (b) Standard normal; $\hat{p} \approx 0.7966$; $z = 0.66$.   (c) P-value = $2(0.2546) = 0.5092$; on standard normal curve shade area to the right of 0.66 and to the left of -0.66.   (d) P-value of $0.5092 > 0.01$ for α; fail to reject H_0.   (e) At the 1% level of significance, the evidence is insufficient to conclude that the population proportion of professors in Colorado who would choose the career again is different from the national rate of 76%.

19. Critical value is $z_0 = -2.33$. The critical region consists of values less than -2.33. The sample test statistic $z = -2.65$ is in the critical region, so we reject H_0. This result is consistent with the P-value conclusion.

Section 9.4

1. (a) $\alpha = 0.05$; H_0: $\mu_d = 0$; H_1: $\mu_d \neq 0$.   (b) Student's t, $d.f. = 7$; $\bar{d} \approx 2.25$; $t \approx 0.818$.   (c) $0.250 <$ P-value < 0.500; on t graph shade area to the left of -0.818 and to the right of 0.818.   (d) P-value interval > 0.05 for α; fail to reject H_0.   (e) At the 5% level of significance, the evidence is insufficient to claim a difference in population mean percentage increases for corporate revenue and CEO salary.

3. (a) $\alpha = 0.01$; H_0: $\mu_d = 0$; H_1: $\mu_d > 0$.   (b) Student's t, $d.f. = 4$; $\bar{d} \approx 12.6$; $t \approx 1.243$.   (c) $0.125 <$ P-value < 0.250; on t graph shade area to the right of 1.243.   (d) P-value interval > 0.01 for α; fail to reject H_0.   (e) At the 1% level of significance, the evidence is insufficient to claim that the average peak wind gusts are higher in January.

5. (a) $\alpha = 0.05$; H_0: $\mu_d = 0$; H_1: $\mu_d > 0$.   (b) Student's t, $d.f. = 7$; $\bar{d} \approx 6.125$; $t \approx 1.762$.   (c) $0.050 <$ P-value < 0.075; on t graph shade area to the right of 1.762.   (d) P-value interval > 0.05 for α; fail to reject H_0.   (e) At the 5% level of significance, the evidence is insufficient to indicate that the population average percentage of male wolves in winter is higher.

7. (a) $\alpha = 0.05$; H_0: $\mu_d = 0$; H_1: $\mu_d > 0$.   (b) Student's t, $d.f. = 7$; $\bar{d} \approx 6.0$; $t \approx 0.789$.   (c) $0.125 <$ P-value < 0.250; on t graph shade area to the right of 0.789.   (d) P-value interval > 0.05 for α; fail to reject H_0.   (e) At the 5% level of significance, the evidence is insufficient to show that the population mean number of inhabited houses is greater than that of hogans.

9. (a) $\alpha = 0.05$; H_0: $\mu_d = 0$; H_1: $\mu_d \neq 0$.   (b) Student's t, $d.f. = 4$; $\bar{d} \approx 1.0$; $t \approx 0.427$.   (c) P-value > 0.500 (note that the t value 0.427 is smaller than any entry in the $d.f. = 4$ row, so the P-value is larger than the largest value 0.500 in the two-tail area row); on t graph shade area to the left of -0.427 and to the right of 0.427.   (d) P-value interval > 0.05 for α; fail to reject H_0.   (e) At the 5% level of significance, the evidence is insufficient to indicate a difference in the population mean number of service ware sherds in subarea 1 as compared with subarea 2.

11. i. Use a calculator. Non-rounded results are used in part ii.
    ii. (a) $\alpha = 0.05$; H_0: $\mu_d = 0$; H_1: $\mu_d > 0$. (b) Student's t, $d.f. = 35$; $\bar{d} \approx 2.472$; $t \approx 1.223$. (c) $0.100 <$ P-value < 0.125; on t graph shade area to the right of 1.223. (d) P-value interval > 0.05 for α; fail to reject H_0. (e) At the 5% level of significance, the evidence is insufficient to claim that the population mean cost of living index for housing is higher than that for groceries.

13. (a) $\alpha = 0.05$; H_0: $\mu_d = 0$; H_1: $\mu_d > 0$. (b) Student's t, $d.f. = 8$; $\bar{d} = 2.0$; $t \approx 1.333$. (c) $0.100 < P$-value < 0.125; on t graph shade area to the right of 1.333. (d) P-value interval > 0.05 for α; fail to reject H_0. (e) At the 5% level of significance, the evidence is insufficient to claim that the population score on the last round is higher than that on the first.

15. (a) $\alpha = 0.05$; H_0: $\mu_d = 0$; H_1: $\mu_d > 0$. (b) Student's t, $d.f. = 7$; $\bar{d} \approx 0.775$; $t \approx 2.080$. (c) $0.025 < P$-value < 0.050; on t graph shade area to the right of 2.080. (d) P-value interval ≤ 0.05 for α; reject H_0. (e) At the 5% level of significance, the evidence is sufficient to claim that the population mean time for rats receiving larger rewards to climb the ladder is less.

17. For a two-tailed test with $\alpha = 0.05$ and $d.f. = 7$, the critical values are $\pm t_0 = \pm 2.365$. The sample test statistic $t = 0.818$ is between -2.365 and 2.365, so we do not reject H_0. This conclusion is the same as that reached by the P-value method.

Section 9.5

1. (a) $\alpha = 0.01$; H_0: $\mu_1 = \mu_2$; H_1: $\mu_1 > \mu_2$. (b) Standard normal; $\bar{x}_1 - \bar{x}_2 = 0.7$; $z \approx 2.57$. (c) P-value $= P(z > 2.57) \approx 0.0051$; on standard normal curve shade area to the right of 2.57. (d) P-value of $0.0051 \le 0.01$ for α; reject H_0. (e) At the 1% level of significance, the evidence is sufficient to indicate that the population mean REM sleep time for children is more than that for adults.

3. (a) $\alpha = 0.05$; H_0: $\mu_1 = \mu_2$; H_1: $\mu_1 \ne \mu_2$. (b) Standard normal; $\bar{x}_1 - \bar{x}_2 = 0.6$; $z \approx 2.16$. (c) P-value $= 2P(z > 2.16) \approx 2(0.0154) = 0.0308$; on standard normal curve shade area to the right of 2.16 and to the left of -2.16. (d) P-value of $0.0308 \le 0.05$ for α; reject H_0. (e) At the 5% level of significance, the evidence is sufficient to show that there is a difference between mean response regarding preference for camping or fishing.

5. i. Use rounded results to compute t.
   ii. (a) $\alpha = 0.01$; H_0: $\mu_1 = \mu_2$; H_1: $\mu_1 < \mu_2$. (b) Student's t, $d.f. = 9$; $\bar{x}_1 - \bar{x}_2 = -0.36$; $t \approx -0.965$. (c) $0.125 < P$-value < 0.250; on t graph shade area to the left of -0.965. (d) P-value interval > 0.01 for α; do not reject H_0. (e) At the 1% level of significance, the evidence is insufficient to indicate that violent crime in the Rocky Mountain region is higher than in New England.

7. (a) $\alpha = 0.05$; H_0: $\mu_1 = \mu_2$; H_1: $\mu_1 \ne \mu_2$. (b) Student's t, $d.f. = 29$; $\bar{x}_1 - \bar{x}_2 = -9.7$; $t \approx -0.751$. (c) $0.250 < P$-value < 0.500; on t graph shade area to the right of 0.751 and to the left of -0.751. (d) P-value interval > 0.05 for α; do not reject H_0. (e) At the 5% level of significance, the evidence is insufficient to indicate that there is a difference between the control and experimental groups in the mean score on the vocabulary portion of the test.

9. i. Use rounded results to compute t.
   ii. (a) $\alpha = 0.05$; H_0: $\mu_1 = \mu_2$; H_1: $\mu_1 \ne \mu_2$. (b) Student's t, $d.f. = 14$; $\bar{x}_1 - \bar{x}_2 = 0.82$; $t \approx 0.869$. (c) $0.250 < P$-value < 0.500; on t graph shade area to the right of 0.869 and to the left of -0.869. (d) P-value interval > 0.05 for α; do not reject H_0. (e) At the 5% level of significance, the evidence is insufficient to indicate that there is a difference in the mean number of cases of fox rabies between the two regions.

11. i. Use rounded results to compute t.
    ii. (a) $\alpha = 0.05$; H_0: $\mu_1 = \mu_2$; H_1: $\mu_1 \ne \mu_2$. (b) Student's t, $d.f. = 6$; $\bar{x}_1 - \bar{x}_2 = -1.64$; $t \approx -1.041$. (c) $0.250 < P$-value < 0.500; on t graph shade area to the right of 1.041 and to the left of -1.041. (d) P-value interval > 0.05 for α; do not reject H_0. (e) At the 5% level of significance, the evidence is insufficient to indicate that the mean time lost due to hot tempers is different from that lost due to technical workers' attitudes.

13. i. Use rounded results to compute t.
    ii. (a) $\alpha = 0.01$; H_0: $\mu_1 = \mu_2$; H_1: $\mu_1 < \mu_2$. (b) Student's t, $d.f. = 10$; $\bar{x}_1 - \bar{x}_2 = -3.6$; $t \approx -3.450$. (c) $0.0005 < P$-value < 0.005; on t graph shade area to the left of -3.450. (d) P-value interval ≤ 0.01 for α; reject H_0. (e) At the 1% level of significance, the evidence is sufficient to indicate that the mean increase in water temperature at the surface has increased since the addition of the new generator.

15. (a) $d.f. = 19.96$ (Some software will truncate this to 19.) (b) $d.f. = 9$; the convention of using the smaller of $n_1 - 1$ and $n_2 - 1$ leads to a $d.f.$ that is always less than or equal to that computed by Satterthwaite's formula.

17. (a) $\alpha = 0.05$; H_0: $p_1 = p_2$; H_1: $p_1 \ne p_2$. (b) Standard normal; $\bar{p} \approx 0.2911$; $\hat{p}_1 - \hat{p}_2 \approx -0.052$; $z \approx -1.13$. (c) P-value $\approx 2P(z < -1.13) \approx 2(0.1292) = 0.2584$; on standard normal curve shade area to the right of 1.13 and to the left of -1.13. (d) P-value of $0.2584 > 0.05$ for α; fail to reject H_0. (e) At the 5% level of significance, there is insufficient evidence to conclude that the population proportion of women favoring more tax dollars for the arts is different from the proportion of men.

19. (a) $\alpha = 0.01$; H_0: $p_1 = p_2$; H_1: $p_1 \ne p_2$. (b) Standard normal; $\bar{p} \approx 0.0676$; $\hat{p}_1 - \hat{p}_2 \approx 0.0237$; $z \approx 0.79$. (c) P-value $\approx 2P(z > 0.79) \approx 2(0.2148) = 0.4296$; on standard normal curve shade area to the right of 0.79

and to the left of -0.79.   (d) *P*-value of $0.4296 > 0.01$ for α; fail to reject H_0.   (e) At the 1% level of significance, there is insufficient evidence to conclude that the population proportion of high school dropouts on Oahu is different from that of Sweetwater County.

21. (a) $\alpha = 0.01$; H_0: $p_1 = p_2$; H_1: $p_1 < p_2$.   (b) Standard normal; $\bar{p} = 0.42$; $\hat{p}_1 - \hat{p}_2 = -0.10$; $z \approx -1.43$.   (c) *P*-value $\approx P(z < -1.43) \approx 0.0764$; on standard normal curve shade area to the left of -1.43.   (d) *P*-value of $0.0764 > 0.01$ for α; fail to reject H_0.   (e) At the 1% level of significance, there is insufficient evidence to conclude that the population proportion of adults who believe in extraterrestrials and who attended college is higher than the proportion who did not attend college.

23. (a) $\alpha = 0.01$; H_0: $p_1 = p_2$; H_1: $p_1 < p_2$.   (b) Standard normal; $\bar{p} \approx 0.5749$; $\hat{p}_1 - \hat{p}_2 \approx -0.1070$; $z \approx -3.19$.   (c) *P*-value $\approx P(z < -3.19) \approx 0.0007$; on standard normal curve shade area to the left of -3.19.   (d) *P*-value of $0.0007 \leq 0.01$ for α; reject H_0.   (e) At the 1% level of significance, there is sufficient evidence to conclude that the population proportion of guests requesting non-smoking rooms has increased.

25. (a) $\alpha = 0.05$; H_0: $p_1 = p_2$; H_1: $p_1 < p_2$.   (b) Standard normal; $\bar{p} \approx 0.0204$; $\hat{p}_1 - \hat{p}_2 \approx -0.074$; $z \approx -2.04$.   (c) *P*-value $\approx P(z < -2.04) \approx 0.0207$; on standard normal curve shade area to the left of -2.04.   (d) *P*-value of $0.0207 \leq 0.05$ for α; reject H_0.   (e) At the 5% level of significance, there is sufficient evidence to conclude that the population proportion of trusting people in Chicago is higher for the older group.

27. H_0: $\mu_1 = \mu_2$; H_1: $\mu_1 < \mu_2$; for *d.f.* = 9, $\alpha = 0.01$ in the *one-tail area* row, the critical value $t_0 = -2.821$; sample test statistic $t = -0.965$ is not in the critical region; fail to reject H_0. This result is consistent with that obtained by the *P*-value method.

Chapter 9 Review

1. (a) $\alpha = 0.05$; H_0: $\mu = 11.1$; H_1: $\mu \neq 11.1$.   (b) Standard normal; $z = -3.00$.   (c) *P*-value = 0.0026; on standard normal curve shade area to the right of 3.00 and to the left of -3.00.   (d) *P*-value of 0.0026 ≤ 0.05 for α; reject H_0.   (e) At the 5% level of significance, the evidence is sufficient to say that the miles driven per vehicle in Chicago is different from the national average.

3. (a) $\alpha = 0.01$; H_0: $\mu = 0.8$; H_1: $\mu > 0.8$.   (b) Student's *t*, *d.f.* = 8; $t \approx 4.390$.   (c) $0.0005 <$ *P*-value < 0.005; on *t* graph shade area to the right of 4.390.   (d) *P*-value interval ≤ 0.01 for α; reject H_0.   (e) At the 5% level of significance, the evidence is sufficient to say that the Toylot claim of 0.8 A is too low.

5. (a) $\alpha = 0.01$; H_0: $p = 0.60$; H_1: $p < 0.60$.   (b) Standard normal; $z = -3.01$.   (c) *P*-value = 0.0013; on standard normal curve shade area to the left of -3.01.

(d) *P*-value of $0.0013 \leq 0.01$ for α; reject H_0.   (e) At the 1% level of significance, the evidence is sufficient to show that the mortality rate has dropped.

7. (a) $\alpha = 0.01$; H_0: $p = 0.20$; H_1: $p > 0.20$.   (b) Standard normal; $z = 2.83$.   (c) *P*-value = 0.0023; on standard normal curve shade area to the right of 2.83.   (d) *P*-value of $0.0023 \leq 0.01$ for α; reject H_0.   (e) At the 1% level of significance, the evidence is sufficient to show that the population proportion of students who read the magazine is larger than 0.20.

9. (a) $\alpha = 0.01$; H_0: $\mu = 40$; H_1: $\mu > 40$.   (b) Standard normal; $z = 3.34$.   (c) *P*-value = 0.0004; on standard normal curve shade area to the right of 3.34.   (d) *P*-value of $0.0004 \leq 0.01$ for α; reject H_0.   (e) At the 1% level of significance, the evidence is sufficient to say that the population average number of matches is larger than 40.

11. (a) $\alpha = 0.05$; H_0: $\mu_1 = \mu_2$; H_1: $\mu_1 \neq \mu_2$.   (b) Student's *t*, *d.f.* = 13; $t \approx -1.441$.   (c) $0.150 <$ *P*-value < 0.200; on *t* graph shade area to the right of 1.441 and to the left of -1.441.   (d) *P*-value interval > 0.05 for α; do not reject H_0.   (e) At the 5% level of significance, the evidence is insufficient to show that there is a difference in the population mean waiting times.

13. (a) $\alpha = 0.05$; H_0: $\mu = 7$ oz; H_1: $\mu \neq 7$ oz.   (b) Student's *t*, *d.f.* = 7; $t \approx 1.697$.   (c) $0.100 <$ *P*-value < 0.150; on *t* graph shade area to the right of 1.697 and to the left of -1.697.   (d) *P*-value interval > 0.05 for α; do not reject H_0.   (e) At the 5% level of significance, the evidence is insufficient to show that the population mean amount of coffee per cup is different from 7 oz.

15. (a) $\alpha = 0.05$; H_0: $\mu_d = 0$; H_1: $\mu_d < 0$.   (b) Student's *t*, *d.f.* = 4; $\bar{d} \approx -4.94$; $t = -2.832$.   (c) $0.010 <$ *P*-value < 0.025; on *t* graph shade area to the left of -2.832.   (d) *P*-value interval ≤ 0.05 for α; reject H_0.   (e) At the 5% level of significance, there is sufficient evidence to claim that the population average net sales improved.

17. (a) $\alpha = 0.05$; H_0: $\mu_1 = \mu_2$; H_1: $\mu_1 \neq \mu_2$.   (b) Student's *t*, *d.f.* = 50; $\bar{x}_1 - \bar{x}_2 = 0.3$ cm; $t \approx 1.808$.   (c) $0.050 <$ *P*-value < 0.100; on *t* graph shade area to the right of 1.808 and to the left of -1.808.   (d) *P*-value interval > 0.05 for α; do not reject H_0.   (e) At the 5% level of significance, the evidence is insufficient to indicate a difference in population mean length of the two types of projectile points.

CUMULATIVE REVIEW PROBLEMS

1. Essay based on material from Chapter 7 and Section 1.2.
2. (a) Because of the large sample size, the central limit theorem describes the $\bar{x}$ distribution (approximately).   (b) $P(\bar{x} \leq 6820) = P(z \leq -2.75) = 0.0030$.   (c) The probability that the average white blood cell count for 50 healthy adults is as low as or lower than 6820 is very

small, 0.0030. Based on this result, it would be reasonable to gather additional facts.

3. $n = 32$; $\mu_{\hat{p}} = p = 0.45$; $\sigma_{\hat{p}} \approx 0.08$; continuity correction $= 0.5/32 \approx 0.0156$. (a) $P(\hat{p} \geq 18/32) = P(\hat{p} \geq 0.5625) = P(x \geq 0.5469) = P(z \geq 1.10) = 0.1357$.
(b) $P(\hat{p} \leq 10/32) = P(\hat{p} \leq 0.3125) = P(x \leq 0.3281) = P(z \leq -1.39) = 0.0823$. (c) $np = 14.4$ and $nq = 17.6$, so both exceed 5. We can approximate the $\hat{p}$ distribution by a normal distribution with expected value $\mu_{\hat{p}} = p = 0.45$ and $\sigma_{\hat{p}} \approx 0.08$.

4. (a) i. $\alpha = 0.01$; H_0: $\mu = 2.0$ ug/L; H_1: $\mu > 2.0$ ug/L.
ii. Standard normal; $z = 2.53$.
iii. P-value ≈ 0.0057; on standard normal curve shade area to the right of 2.53.
iv. P-value of $0.0057 \leq 0.01$ for α; reject H_0.
v. At the 1% level of significance, the evidence is sufficient to say that the population mean discharge level of lead is higher.
(b) 2.13 ug/L to 2.99 ug/L. (c) $n = 48$.

5. (a) Use rounded results to compute t in part (b).
(b) i. $\alpha = 0.05$; H_0: $\mu = 10\%$; H_1: $\mu > 10\%$.
ii. Student's t, $d.f. = 11$; $t \approx 1.248$.
iii. $0.100 < P$-value < 0.125; on t graph shade area to the right of 1.248.
iv. P-value interval > 0.05 for α; fail to reject H_0.
v. At the 5% level of significance, the evidence does not indicate that the patient is asymptomatic.
(c) 9.27% to 11.71%.

6. (a) i. $\alpha = 0.05$; H_0: $p = 0.10$; H_1: $p \neq 0.10$; yes, $np > 5$ and $nq > 5$; necessary to use normal approximation to the binominal.
ii. Standard normal; $\hat{p} \approx 0.147$; $z = 1.29$.
iii. P-value $= 2P(z > 1.29) \approx 0.1970$; on standard normal curve shade area to the right of 1.29 and to the left of -1.29.
iv. P-value of $0.1970 > 0.05$ for α; fail to reject H_0.
v. At the 5% level of significance, the data do not indicate any difference from the national average for the population proportion of crime victims.
(b) 0.063 to 0.231. (c) From sample, $p \approx \hat{p} \approx 0.147$; $n = 193$.

7. (a) i. $\alpha = 0.05$; H_0: $\mu_d = 0$; H_1: $\mu_d \neq 0$.
ii. Student's t, $d.f. = 6$; $\bar{d} \approx -0.0039$, $t \approx -0.771$.
iii. $0.250 < P$-value < 0.500; on t graph shade area to the right of 0.771 and to the left of -0.771.
iv. P-value interval > 0.05 for α; fail to reject H_0.
v. At the 5% level of significance, the evidence does not show a population mean difference in phosphorous reduction between the two methods.

8. (a) i. $\alpha = 0.05$; H_0: $\mu_1 = \mu_2$; H_1: $\mu_1 \neq \mu_2$.
ii. Student's t, $d.f. = 15$; $t \approx 1.952$.
iii. $0.050 < P$-value < 0.100; on t graph shade area to the right of 1.952 and to the left of -0.1952.
iv. P-value interval > 0.05 for α; fail to reject H_0.

v. At the 5% level of significance, the evidence does not show any difference in the population mean proportion of on-time arrivals in summer versus winter.
(b) -0.43% to 9.835%. (c) x_1 and x_2 distributions are approximately normal (mound-shaped and symmetric).

9. (a) i. $\alpha = 0.05$; H_0: $p_1 = p_2$; H_1: $p_1 > p_2$.
ii. Standard normal; $\hat{p}_1 \approx 0.242$; $\hat{p}_2 \approx 0.207$; $\bar{p} \approx 0.2246$; $z \approx 0.58$.
iii. P-value ≈ 0.2810; on standard normal curve shade area to the right of 0.58.
iv. P-value interval > 0.05 for α; fail to reject H_0.
v. At the 5% level of significance, the evidence does not indicate that the population proportion of single men who go out dancing occasionally differs from the proportion of single women.
Since $n_1\bar{p}$, $n_1\bar{q}$, $n_2\bar{p}$, and $n_2\bar{q}$ are all greater than 5, the normal approximation to the binomial is justified.
(b) -0.065 to 0.139.

10. (a) Essay. (b) Outline of study.

CHAPTER 10

Section 10.1

1. (a) Moderate. (b) None. (c) High.
3. (a) No. (b) Increasing population might be a lurking variable causing both variables to increase.
5. (a) No. (b) One lurking variable responsible for average annual income increases is inflation. Better training might be a lurking variable responsible for short times to run the mile.
7. (a) Ages and Average Weights of Shetland Ponies

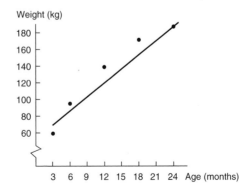

Line slopes upward.
(b) Strong; positive. (c) $r \approx 0.972$; increase.

9. (a) Lowest Barometric Pressure and Maximum Wind Speed for Tropical Cyclones

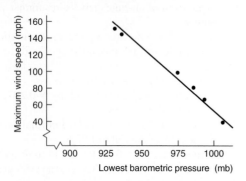

Line slopes downward.
  (b) Strong; negative. (c) $r \approx -0.990$; decrease.

11. (a) Batting Average and Home Run Percentage

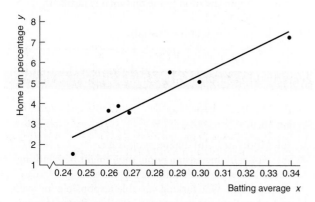

Line slopes upward.
  (b) High; positive. (c) $r \approx 0.948$; increase.

13. (a) Body Diameter and Weight of Prehistoric Pottery

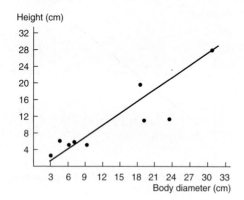

Line slopes upward.
  (b) High; positive. (c) $r \approx 0.896$; increase.

15. (a) Unit Length on y Same as That on x

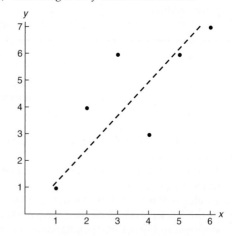

  (b) Unit Length on y Twice That on x

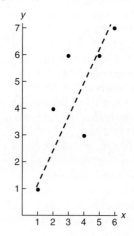

  (c) Unit Length on y Half That on x

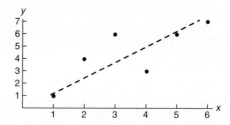

  (d) The line in part b appears steeper than the line in part a, while the line in part c appears flatter than the line in part a. The slopes actually are all the same, but the lines look different because of the change in unit lengths on the y and x axes.

17. (a) $r \approx 0.972$ with $n = 5$ is significant for $\alpha = 0.05$. For this α, we conclude that age and weight of Shetland ponies are correlated. (b) $r \approx -0.990$ with $n = 6$ is significant for $\alpha = 0.01$. For this α, we conclude that lowest barometric pressure reading and maximum wind speed for cyclones are correlated.

19. (a) Average Hours Lost per Person versus Average Fuel Wasted per Person in Traffic Delays

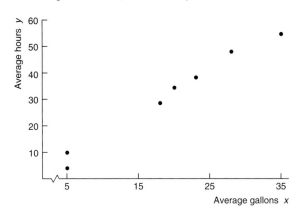

$r \approx 0.991$.

(b) For variables based on averages, $\bar{x} = 19.25$ hr; $s_x \approx 10.33$ hr; $\bar{y} = 31.13$ gal; $s_y \approx 17.76$ gal. For variables based on single individuals, $\bar{x} = 20.13$ hr; $s_x \approx 13.84$ hr; $\bar{y} = 31.87$ gal; $s_y \approx 25.18$. Dividing by larger numbers results in a smaller value.

(c) Hours Lost per Person versus Fuel Wasted per Person in Traffic Delays

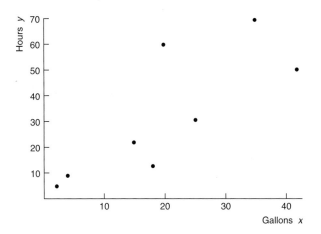

$r \approx 0.794$.

(d) Yes; by the central limit theorem, the $\bar{x}$ distribution has a smaller standard deviation than the corresponding x distribution.

Section 10.2

1. (a) Total Number of Jobs and Number of Entry-Level Jobs

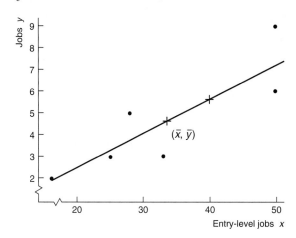

(b) Use a calculator. (c) $\bar{x} \approx 33.67$ jobs; $\bar{y} \approx 4.67$ entry-level jobs; $a \approx -0.748$; $b \approx 0.161$; $\hat{y} \approx -0.748 + 0.161x$. (d) See figure in part a. (e) $r^2 \approx 0.740$; 74.0% of variation explained and 26.0% unexplained. (f) 5.69 jobs.

3. (a) Weight of Cars and Gasoline Mileage

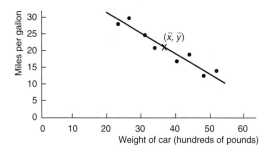

(b) Use a calculator. (c) $\bar{x} = 37.375$; $\bar{y} = 20.875$ mpg; $a \approx 43.326$; $b \approx -0.6007$; $\hat{y} \approx 43.326 - 0.6007x$. (d) See figure in part a. (e) $r^2 \approx 0.895$; 89.5% of variation explained and 10.5% unexplained. (f) 20.5 mpg.

5. (a) Age and Percentage of Fatal Accidents Due to Speeding

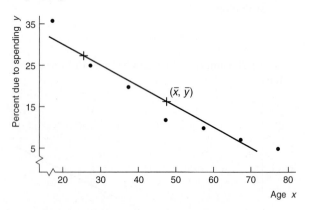

(b) Use a calculator. (c) $\bar{x} = 47$ years; $\bar{y} \approx 16.43\%$; $a \approx 39.761$; $b \approx -0.496$; $\hat{y} \approx 39.761 - 0.496x$. (d) See figure of part a. (e) $r^2 \approx 0.920$; 92.0% of variation explained and 8.0% unexplained. (f) 27.36%.

7. (a) Per Capita Income ($1000) and M.D.s per 10,000 Residents

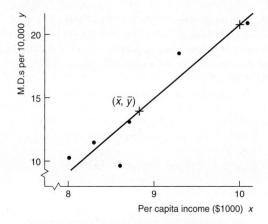

(b) Use a calculator. (c) $\bar{x} = \$8.83$; $\bar{y} \approx 13.95$ M.D.s; $a \approx -36.898$; $b \approx 5.756$; $\hat{y} \approx -36.898 + 5.756x$. (d) See figure of part a. (e) $r^2 \approx 0.872$; 87.2% of variation explained, 12.8% unexplained. (f) 20.7 M.D.s per 10,000 residents.

9. (a) Percentage of 16- to 19-Year-Olds Not in School and Violent Crime Rate per 1000 Residents

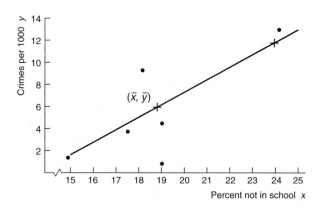

(b) Use a calculator. (c) $\bar{x} = 18.8\%$; $\bar{y} = 5.4$; $a \approx -17.204$; $b \approx 1.202$; $\hat{y} \approx -17.204 + 1.202x$. (d) See figure of part a. (e) $r^2 \approx 0.584$; 58.4% of variation explained, 41.6% unexplained. (f) 11.6 crimes per 1000 residents.

11. (a) Elevation of Archaeological Sites and Percentage of Unidentified Artifacts

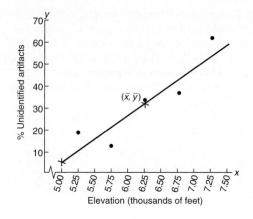

(b) Use a calculator. (c) $\bar{x} = 6.25$; $\bar{y} = 32.8$; $a = -104.7$; $b = 22$; $\hat{y} = -104.7 + 22x$. (d) See figure of part a. (e) $r^2 \approx 0.833$; 83.3% of variation explained, 16.7% unexplained. (f) 38.3.

13. (a) Elevation and the Number of Frost-Free Days

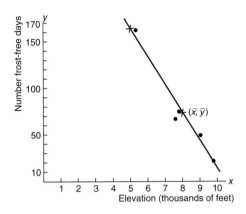

(b) Use a calculator. (c) $\bar{x} = 7.92$; $\bar{y} = 73.6$; $a \approx 318.16$; $b \approx -30.88$; $\hat{y} \approx 318.16 - 30.88x$. (d) See figure of part a. (e) $r^2 \approx 0.963$; 96.3% of variation explained, 3.7% unexplained. (f) 132.89.

15. (a) Solubility of Carbon Dioxide in Water

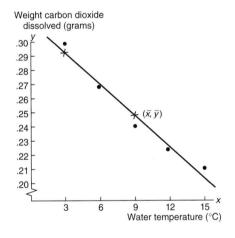

(b) Use a calculator. (c) $\bar{x} = 9$; $\bar{y} = 0.248$; $a = 0.314$; $b \approx -0.00733$; $\hat{y} \approx 0.314 - 0.00733x$. (d) See figure of part a. (e) $r^2 \approx 0.971$; 97.1% of variation explained, 2.9% unexplained. (f) 0.241 grams.

17. (a) Yes. The pattern of residuals appears randomly scattered around the horizontal line at 0. (b) No. There do not appear to be any outliers.

19. (a) Result checks. (b) Result checks. (c) Yes. (d) The equation $x = 0.9337y - 0.1335$ does not match part b. (e) No. The least-squares equation changes depending on which variable is the explanatory variable and which is the response variable.

Section 10.3

1. (a) Use a calculator. (b) $\alpha = 0.05$; H_0: $\rho = 0$; H_1: $\rho > 0$; sample $t \approx 2.522$; $d.f. = 4$; $0.025 < P\text{-value} < 0.050$; reject H_0. There seems to be a positive correlation between x and y. (c) Use a calculator. (d) 45.36%. (e) Interval from 39.05 to 51.67. (f) $\alpha = 0.05$; H_0: $\beta = 0$; H_1: $\beta > 0$; sample $t \approx 2.522$; $d.f. = 4$; $0.025 < P\text{-value} < 0.050$; reject H_0. There seems to be a positive slope between x and y. (g) Interval from 0.064 to 0.760. For every percentage increase in successful free throws, the percentage of successful field goals increases by an amount between 0.06 and 0.76.

3. (a) Use a calculator. (b) $\alpha = 0.01$; H_0: $\rho = 0$; H_1: $\rho < 0$; sample $t \approx -10.06$; $d.f. = 5$; $P\text{-value} < 0.0005$; reject H_0. The sample evidence supports a negative correlation. (c) Use a calculator. (d) 2.39 hours. (e) Interval from 2.12 to 2.66 hours. (f) $\alpha = 0.01$; H_0: $\beta = 0$; H_1: $\beta < 0$; sample $t \approx -10.06$; $d.f. = 5$; $P\text{-value} < 0.0005$; reject H_0. The sample evidence supports a negative slope. (g) Interval from -0.065 to -0.044. For every additional meter of depth, the optimal time decreases by between 0.04 and 0.07 hour.

5. (a) Use a calculator. (b) $\alpha = 0.01$; H_0: $\rho = 0$; H_1: $\rho > 0$; sample $t \approx 6.534$; $d.f. = 4$; $0.0005 < P\text{-value} < 0.005$; reject H_0. The sample evidence supports a positive correlation. (c) Use a calculator. (d) $12.577 thousand. (e) Interval from 12.247 to 12.907 (thousand dollars). (f) $\alpha = 0.01$; H_0: $\beta = 0$; H_1: $\beta > 0$; sample $t \approx 6.534$; $d.f. = 4$; $0.0005 < P\text{-value} < 0.005$; reject H_0. The sample evidence supports a positive slope. (g) Interval from 0.436 to 1.080. For every $1000 increase in list price, the dealer price increase is between $436 and $1080 higher.

7. (a) H_0: $\rho = 0$; H_1: $\rho \neq 0$; $d.f. = 4$; sample $t = 4.129$; $0.01 < P\text{-value} < 0.02$; do not reject H_0; r is not significant at the 0.01 level of significance. (b) H_0: $\rho = 0$; H_1: $\rho \neq 0$; $d.f. = 8$; sample $t = 5.840$; $P\text{-value} < 0.001$; reject H_0; r is significant at the 0.01 level of significance. (c) As n increases, the t value corresponding to r also increases, resulting in a smaller $P\text{-value}$.

Section 10.4

1. (a) Response variable is x_1. Explanatory variables are x_2, x_3, x_4. (b) 1.6 is the constant term; 3.5 is the coefficient of x_2; -7.9 is the coefficient of x_3; and 2.0 is the coefficient of x_4. (c) $x_1 = 10.7$. (d) 3.5 units; 7 units; -14 units. (e) $d.f. = 8$; $t = 1.860$; 2.72 to 4.28. (f) $\alpha = 0.05$; H_0: $\beta_2 = 0$; H_1: $\beta_2 \neq 0$; $d.f. = 8$; $t = 8.35$; $P\text{-value} < 0.001$; reject H_0.

3. (a) $CVx_1 \approx 9.08$; $CVx_2 \approx 14.59$; $CVx_3 \approx 8.88$; x_2 has greatest spread; x_3 has smallest. (b) $r^2 x_1 x_2 \approx 0.958$; $r^2 x_1 x_3 \approx 0.942$; $r^2 x_2 x_3 \approx 0.895$; x_2; yes; 95.8%; 94.2%. (c) 97.7%. (d) $x_1 = 30.99 + 0.861 x_2 + 0.335 x_3$; 3.35; 8.61. (e) $\alpha = 0.05$; H_0: coefficient = 0; H_1: coefficient $\neq 0$; $d.f. = 8$; for β_2, $t = 3.47$ with P-value = 0.008; for β_3, $t = 2.56$ with P-value = 0.034; reject H_0 for each coefficient and conclude that the coefficients of x_2 and x_3 are not zero. (f) $d.f. = 8$; $t = 1.86$; C.I. for β_2 is 0.40 to 1.32; C.I. for β_3 is 0.09 to 0.58. (g) 153.9; 148.3 to 159.4.

5. (a) $CVx_1 \approx 39.64$; $CVx_2 \approx 44.45$; $CVx_3 \approx 50.62$; $CVx_4 \approx 52.15$; x_4; x_1 has a small CV because we divide by a large mean. (b) $r^2 x_1 x_2 \approx 0.842$; $r^2 x_1 x_3 \approx 0.865$; $r^2 x_1 x_4 \approx 0.225$; $r^2 x_2 x_3 \approx 0.624$; $r^2 x_2 x_4 \approx 0.184$; $r^2 x_3 x_4 \approx 0.089$; x_4; 84.2%. (c) 96.7%. (d) $x_1 = 7.68 + 3.66 x_2 + 7.62 x_3 + 0.83 x_4$; 7.62 million dollars. (e) $\alpha = 0.05$; H_0: coefficient = 0; H_1: coefficient $\neq 0$; $d.f. = 6$; for β_2, $t = 3.28$ with P-value = 0.017; for β_3, $t = 4.60$ with P-value = 0.004; for β_4, $t = 1.54$ with P-value = 0.175; reject H_0 for β_2 and β_3 and conclude that the coefficients of x_2 and x_3 are not zero. For β_4, fail to reject H_0 and conclude that the coefficient of x_4 could be zero. (f) $d.f. = 6$; $t = 1.943$; C.I. for β_2 is 1.49 to 5.83; C.I. for β_3 is 4.40 to 10.84; C.I. for β_4 is -0.22 to 1.88. (g) 91.95; 77.6 to 106.3. (h) 5.63; 4.21 to 7.04.

Chapter 10 Review

1. (a) Age and Mortality Rate for Bighorn Sheep

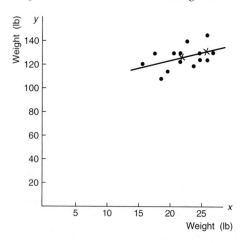

(b) $\bar{x} = 3$; $\bar{y} \approx 17.38$; $b \approx 1.27$; $\hat{y} \approx 13.57 + 1.27x$. (c) $r \approx 0.685$; $r^2 \approx 0.469$. (d) $\alpha = 0.01$; H_0: $\rho = 0$; H_1: $\rho > 0$; $d.f. = 3$; $t = 1.629$; $0.100 < P$-value < 0.125; do not reject H_0. There does not seem to be a positive correlation between age and mortality rate of bighorn sheep. (e) No. Based on these limited data, predictions from the least-squares line model might be misleading. There appear to be other lurking variables that affect the mortality rate of sheep in different age groups.

3. (a) Weight of One-Year-Old versus Weight of Adult

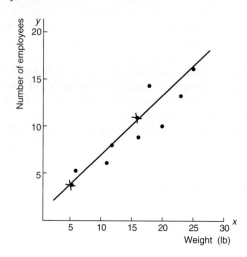

(b) $\bar{x} \approx 21.43$; $\bar{y} \approx 126.79$; $b \approx 1.285$; $\hat{y} \approx 99.25 + 1.285x$. (c) $r \approx 0.468$; $r^2 \approx 0.219$; 21.9% explained. (d) $\alpha = 0.01$; H_0: $\rho = 0$; H_1: $\rho > 0$; $d.f. = 12$; $t = 1.835$; $0.025 < P$-value < 0.050; do not reject H_0. At the 1% level of significance, there does not seem to be a positive correlation between weight of baby and weight of adult. (e) 124.95 lb. However, since r is not significant, this prediction may not be useful. Other lurking variables seem to have an effect on adult weight. (f) $S_e \approx 8.38$. (g) 105.91 to 143.99 lb. (h) $\alpha = 0.01$; H_0: $\beta = 0$; H_1: $\beta > 0$; $d.f. = 12$; $t = 1.835$; $0.025 < P$-value < 0.050; do not reject H_0. At the 1% level of significance, there does not seem to be a positive slope between weight of baby x and weight of adult y. (i) 0.347 to 2.223. At the 80% confidence level, we can say that for each additional pound a female infant weights at 1 year, the female's adult weight changes by 0.35 to 2.22 lb.

5. (a) Weight of Mail versus Number of Employees Required

(b) $\bar{x} \approx 16.38$; $\bar{y} \approx 10.13$; $b \approx 0.554$; $\hat{y} \approx 1.051 + 0.554x$.
(c) $r \approx 0.913$; $r^2 \approx 0.833$; 83.3% explained. (d) $\alpha = 0.01$; H_0: $\rho = 0$; H_1: $\rho > 0$; d.f. = 6; $t = 5.467$; 0.0005 $< P$-value < 0.005; reject H_0. At the 1% level of significance, there is sufficient evidence to show a positive correlation between pounds of mail and number of employees required to process the mail. (e) 9.36.
(f) $S_e \approx 1.73$. (g) 4.86 to 13.86. (h) $\alpha = 0.01$; H_0: $\beta = 0$; H_1: $\beta > 0$; d.f. = 6; $t = 5.467$; 0.0005 $< P$-value < 0.005; reject H_0. At the 1% level of significance, there is sufficient evidence to show a positive slope between pounds of mail x and number of employees required to process the mail y. (i) 0.408 to 0.700. At the 80% confidence level, we can say that for each additional pound of mail, between 0.4 and 0.7 additional employees are needed.

CHAPTER 11

Section 11.1

1. (a) $\alpha = 0.05$; H_0: Myers-Briggs preference and profession are independent; H_1: Myers-Briggs preference and profession are not independent. (b) $\chi^2 = 8.649$; d.f. = 2. (c) 0.010 $< P$-value < 0.025. (d) Reject H_0. (e) At the 5% level of significance, there is sufficient evidence to conclude that Myers-Briggs preference and profession are not independent.

3. (a) $\alpha = 0.01$; H_0: Site type and pottery type are independent; H_1: Site type and pottery type are not independent. (b) $\chi^2 = 0.5552$; d.f. = 4. (c) 0.950 $< P$-value < 0.975. (d) Do not reject H_0. (e) At the 1% level of significance, there is insufficient evidence to conclude that site and pottery type are not independent.

5. (a) $\alpha = 0.05$; H_0: Age distribution and location are independent; H_1: Age distribution and location are not independent. (b) $\chi^2 = 0.6704$; d.f. = 4. (c) 0.950 $< P$-value < 0.975. (d) Do not reject H_0. (e) At the 5% level of significance, there is insufficient evidence to conclude that age distribution and location are not independent.

7. (a) $\alpha = 0.05$; H_0: Age of young adult and movie preference are independent; H_1: Age of young adult and movie preference are not independent. (b) $\chi^2 = 3.6230$; d.f. = 4. (c) 0.100 $< P$-value < 0.900. (d) Do not reject H_0. (e) At the 5% level of significance, there is insufficient evidence to conclude that age of young adult and movie preference are not independent.

9. (a) $\alpha = 0.05$; H_0: Ticket sales and type of billing are independent; H_1: Ticket sales and type of billing are not independent. (b) $\chi^2 = 1.8685$; d.f. = 3.

(c) 0.100 $< P$-value < 0.900. (d) Do not reject H_0.
(e) At the 5% level of significance, there is insufficient evidence to conclude that ticket sales and type of billing are not independent.

11. (a) $\alpha = 0.05$; H_0: Stone tool construction material and site are independent; H_1: Stone tool construction material and site are not independent. (b) $\chi^2 = 11.15$; d.f. = 3. (c) 0.010 $< P$-value < 0.025. (d) Reject H_0. (e) At the 5% level of significance, there is sufficient evidence to conclude that stone tool construction material and site are not independent.

Section 11.2

1. (a) $\alpha = 0.05$; H_0: The distributions are the same; H_1: The distributions are different. (b) Sample $\chi^2 = 11.788$; d.f. = 3. (c) 0.005 $< P$-value < 0.010. (d) Reject H_0. (e) At the 5% level of significance, the evidence is sufficient to conclude that the age distribution of the Red Lake Village population does not fit the age distribution of the general Canadian population.

3. (a) $\alpha = 0.01$; H_0: The distributions are the same; H_1: The distributions are different. (b) Sample $\chi^2 = 0.1984$; d.f. = 4. (c) P-value > 0.995. (Note that as the χ^2 values decrease, the area in the right tail increases, so $\chi^2 < 0.207$ means that the corresponding P-value > 0.995.) (d) Do not reject H_0. (e) At the 1% level of significance, the evidence is insufficient to conclude that the regional distribution of raw materials does not fit the distribution at the current excavation site.

5. (i) Essay. (ii) (a) $\alpha = 0.01$; H_0: The distributions are the same; H_1: The distributions are different. (b) Sample $\chi^2 = 1.5693$; d.f. = 5. (c) 0.900 $< P$-value < 0.950. (d) Do not reject H_0. (e) At the 1% level of significance, the evidence is insufficient to conclude that the average daily July temperature does not follow a normal distribution.

7. (a) $\alpha = 0.05$; H_0: The distributions are the same; H_1: The distributions are different. (b) Sample $\chi^2 = 9.333$; d.f. = 3. (c) 0.025 $< P$-value < 0.050. (d) Reject H_0. (e) At the 5% level of significance, the evidence is sufficient to conclude that the current fish distribution is different than it was 5 years ago.

9. (a) $\alpha = 0.01$; H_0: The distributions are the same; H_1: The distributions are different. (b) Sample $\chi^2 = 13.70$; d.f. = 5. (c) 0.010 $< P$-value < 0.025. (d) Do not reject H_0. (e) At the 1% level of significance, the evidence is insufficient to conclude that the census ethnic origin distribution and the ethnic origin distribution of city residents are different.

11. (a) $\alpha = 0.01$; H_0: The distributions are the same; H_1: The distributions are different. (b) Sample $\chi^2 = 3.559$; $d.f. = 8$. (c) $0.100 < P\text{-value} < 0.900$. (d) Do not reject H_0. (e) At the 1% level of significance, the evidence is insufficient to conclude that the distribution of first nonzero digits in the accounting file does not follow Benford's Law.

13. (a) $P(0) \approx 0.179$; $P(1) \approx 0.308$; $P(2) \approx 0.265$; $P(3) \approx 0.152$; $P(r \geq 4) \approx 0.096$. (b) For $r = 0$, $E \approx 16.11$; for $r = 1$, $E \approx 27.72$; for $r = 2$, $E \approx 23.85$; for $r = 3$, $E \approx 13.68$; for $r \geq 4$, $E \approx 8.64$. (c) $\chi^2 \approx 12.55$ with $d.f. = 4$. (d) $\alpha = 0.01$; H_0: The Poisson distribution fits; H_1: The Poisson distribution does not fit; $0.01 < P\text{-value} < 0.025$; do not reject H_0. At the 1% level of significance, we cannot say that the Poisson distribution does not fit.

Section 11.3

1. (a) $\alpha = 0.05$; H_0: $\sigma^2 = 42.3$; H_1: $\sigma^2 > 42.3$. (b) $\chi^2 \approx 23.98$; $d.f. = 22$. (c) $0.100 < P\text{-value} < 0.900$. (d) Do not reject H_0. (e) At the 5% level of significance, there is insufficient evidence to conclude that the variance is greater in the new section. (f) $\chi_U^2 = 36.78$; $\chi_L^2 = 10.98$. Interval for σ^2 is from 27.57 to 92.37.

3. (a) $\alpha = 0.01$; H_0: $\sigma^2 = 136.2$; H_1: $\sigma^2 < 136.2$ (b) $\chi^2 \approx 5.92$; $d.f. = 7$. (c) Right-tailed area between 0.900 and 0.100; $0.100 < P\text{-value} < 0.900$. (d) Do not reject H_0. (e) At the 1% level of significance, there is insufficient evidence to conclude that the variance for number of mountain-climber deaths is less than 136.2. (f) $\chi_U^2 = 14.07$; $\chi_L^2 = 2.17$. Interval for σ^2 is from 57.26 to 371.29.

5. (a) $\alpha = 0.05$; H_0: $\sigma^2 = 9$; H_1: $\sigma^2 < 9$. (b) $\chi^2 \approx 8.82$; $d.f. = 22$. (c) Right-tail area is between 0.995 and 0.990; $0.005 < P\text{-value} < 0.010$. (d) Reject H_0. (e) At the 5% level of significance, there is sufficient evidence to conclude that the variance of protection times for the new typhoid shot is less than 9. (f) $\chi_U^2 = 33.92$; $\chi_L^2 = 12.34$. Interval for σ is from 1.53 to 2.54.

7. (a) $\alpha = 0.01$; H_0: $\sigma^2 = 0.18$; H_1: $\sigma^2 > 0.18$. (b) $\chi^2 = 90$; $d.f. = 60$. (c) $0.005 < P\text{-value} < 0.010$. (d) Reject H_0. (e) At the 1% level of significance, there is sufficient evidence to conclude that the variance of measurements for the fan blades is higher than the specified amount. The inspector is justified in claiming that the blades must be replaced. (f) $\chi_U^2 = 79.08$; $\chi_L^2 = 43.19$. Interval for σ is from 0.45 mm to 0.61 mm.

9. (i) (a) $\alpha = 0.05$; H_0: $\sigma^2 = 23$; H_1: $\sigma^2 \neq 23$. (b) $\chi^2 \approx 13.06$; $d.f. = 21$. (c) The area to the left of

$\chi^2 = 13.06$ is less than 50%, so we double the left-tail area to find the P-value for the two-tailed test. Right-tail area is between 0.950 and 0.900. Subtracting each value from 1, we find that the left-tail area is between 0.050 and 0.100. Doubling the left-tail area for a two-tailed test gives $0.100 < P\text{-value} < 0.200$. (d) Do not reject H_0. (e) At the 5% level of significance, there is insufficient evidence to conclude that the variance of battery life is different from 23. (ii) $\chi_U^2 = 32.67$; $\chi_L^2 = 11.59$. Interval for σ^2 is from 9.19 to 25.91. (iii) Interval for σ is from 3.03 to 5.09.

Section 11.4

1. (a) $\alpha = 0.01$; population 1 is annual production from the first plot; H_0: $\sigma_1^2 = \sigma_2^2$; H_1: $\sigma_1^2 > \sigma_2^2$. (b) $F \approx 3.73$; $d.f._N = 15$; $d.f._D = 15$. (c) $0.001 < P\text{-value} < 0.010$. (d) Reject H_0. (e) At the 1% level of significance, there is sufficient evidence to show that the variance in annual wheat production of the first plot is greater than that of the second plot.

3. (a) $\alpha = 0.05$; population 1 has data from France; H_0: $\sigma_1^2 = \sigma_2^2$; H_1: $\sigma_1^2 \neq \sigma_2^2$. (b) $F \approx 1.97$; $d.f._N = 20$; $d.f._D = 17$. (c) $0.050 < \text{right-tail area} < 0.100$; $0.100 < P\text{-value} < 0.200$. (d) Do not reject H_0. (e) At the 5% level of significance, there is insufficient evidence to show that the variance in corporate productivity of large companies in France and of those in Germany differ. Volatility of corporate productivity does not appear to differ.

5. (a) $\alpha = 0.05$; population 1 has data from aggressive growth companies; H_0: $\sigma_1^2 = \sigma_2^2$; H_1: $\sigma_1^2 > \sigma_2^2$. (b) $F \approx 2.54$; $d.f._N = 20$; $d.f._D = 20$. (c) $0.010 < P\text{-value} < 0.025$. (d) Reject H_0. (e) At the 5% level of significance, there is sufficient evidence to show that the variance in percentage annual returns for funds holding aggressive-growth small stocks is larger than that for funds holding value stocks.

7. (a) $\alpha = 0.05$; population 1 has data from the new system; H_0: $\sigma_1^2 = \sigma_2^2$; H_1: $\sigma_1^2 \neq \sigma_2^2$. (b) $F \approx 1.85$; $d.f._N = 30$; $d.f._D = 24$. (c) $0.050 < \text{right-tail area} < 0.100$; $0.100 < P\text{-value} < 0.200$. (d) Do not reject H_0. (e) At the 5% level of significance, there is insufficient evidence to show that the variance in gasoline consumption for the two injection systems is different.

Section 11.5

1. (a) $\alpha = 0.01$; H_0: $\mu_1 = \mu_2 = \mu_3$; H_1: Not all the means are equal.
   (b–f)

Source of Variation	Sum of Squares	Degrees of Freedom	MS	F Ratio	P-value	Test Decision
Between groups	520.280	2	260.14	0.48	> 0.100	Do not reject H_0
Within groups	7544.190	14	538.87			
Total	8064.470	16				

3. (a) $\alpha = 0.05$; H_0: $\mu_1 = \mu_2 = \mu_3 = \mu_4$; H_1: Not all the means are equal.
   (b–f)

Source of Variation	Sum of Squares	Degrees of Freedom	MS	F Ratio	P-value	Test Decision
Between groups	89.637	3	29.879	0.846	> 0.100	Do not reject H_0
Within groups	635.827	18	35.324			
Total	725.464	21				

5. (a) $\alpha = 0.05$; H_0: $\mu_1 = \mu_2 = \mu_3$; H_1: Not all the means are equal.
   (b–f)

Source of Variation	Sum of Squares	Degrees of Freedom	MS	F Ratio	P-value	Test Decision
Between groups	1303.167	2	651.58	5.005	between	Reject H_0
Within groups	1171.750	9	130.19		0.025 and 0.050	
Total	2474.917	11				

7. (a) $\alpha = 0.01$; H_0: $\mu_1 = \mu_2 = \mu_3$; H_1: Not all the means are equal.
   (b–f)

Source of Variation	Sum of Squares	Degrees of Freedom	MS	F Ratio	P-value	Test Decision
Between groups	2.042	2	1.021	0.336	> 0.100	Do not reject H_0
Within groups	33.428	11	3.039			
Total	35.470	13				

9. (a) $\alpha = 0.05$; H_0: $\mu_1 = \mu_2 = \mu_3 = \mu_4$; H_1: Not all the means are equal.
   (b–f)

Source of Variation	Sum of Squares	Degrees of Freedom	MS	F Ratio	P-value	Test Decision
Between groups	238.225	3	79.408	4.611	between	Reject H_0
Within groups	258.340	15	17.223		0.010 and 0.025	
Total	496.565	18				

Section 11.6

1. 2 factors; walking device with 3 levels and task with 2 levels; data table has 6 cells.
3. Since the P-value is less than 0.01, there is a significant difference in mean cadence according to the factor walking device used.
5. (a) 2 factors: income with 4 levels and media type with 5 levels. (b) $\alpha = 0.05$; For income level, H_0: There is no difference in population mean index based on income level; H_1: At least two income levels have different population mean indices; $F_{\text{income}} \approx 2.77$ with P-value ≈ 0.088. At the 5% level of significance, do not reject H_0. The data do not indicate any differences in population mean index according to income level. (c) $\alpha = 0.05$; For media, H_0: There is no difference in population mean index according to media type; H_1: At least two media types have different population mean indices; $F_{\text{media}} \approx 0.03$ with P-value ≈ 0.998. At the 5% level of significance, do not reject H_0. The data do not indicate any differences in population mean index according to media type.
7. Randomized Block Design

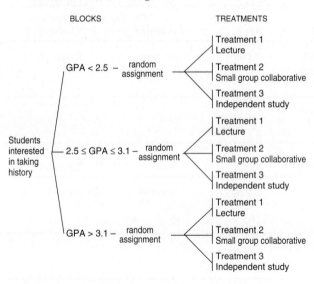

Yes, the design fits the model for randomized block design.

Chapter 11 Review

1. One-way ANOVA. $\alpha = 0.05$; H_0: $\mu_1 = \mu_2 = \mu_3 = \mu_4$; H_1: Not all the means are equal.

Chapter 11 Review Problem 1

Source of Variation	Sum of Squares	Degrees of Freedom	MS
Between groups	6149.75	3	2049.917
Within groups	12454.80	16	778.425
Total	18604.55	19	

F Ratio	P-value	Test Decision
2.633	between 0.050 and 0.100	Do not reject H_0

3. (a) Chi-square test of σ^2. (i) $\alpha = 0.01$; H_0: $\sigma^2 = 1{,}040{,}400$; H_1: $\sigma^2 > 1{,}040{,}400$. (ii) $\chi^2 \approx 51.03$; $d.f. = 29$. (iii) $0.005 < P$-value < 0.010. (iv) Reject H_0. (v) At the 1% level of significance, there is sufficient evidence to conclude that the variance is greater than claimed. (b) $\chi^2_U = 45.72$; $\chi^2_L = 16.05$; $1{,}161{,}147.4 < \sigma^2 < 3{,}307{,}642.4$.
5. Chi-square test of independence. (i) $\alpha = 0.01$; H_0: Student grade and teacher rating are independent; H_1: Student grade and teacher rating are not independent. (ii) $\chi^2 \approx 9.80$; $d.f. = 6$. (iii) $0.100 < P$-value < 0.900. (iv) Do not reject H_0. (v) At the 1% level of significance, there is insufficient evidence to claim that student grade and teacher rating are not independent.
7. Chi-square test of goodness of fit. (i) $\alpha = 0.01$; H_0: The distributions are the same; H_1: The distributions are different. (ii) $\chi^2 \approx 11.93$; $d.f. = 4$. (iii) $0.010 < P$-value < 0.025. (iv) Do not reject H_0. (v) At the 1% level of significance, there is insufficient evidence to claim that the age distribution of the population of Blue Valley has changed.
9. F test for two variances. (i) $\alpha = 0.05$; H_0: $\sigma_1^2 = \sigma_2^2$; H_1: $\sigma_1^2 > \sigma_2^2$. (ii) $F \approx 2.61$; $d.f._N = 15$; $d.f._D = 17$. (iii) $0.025 < P$-value < 0.050. (iv) Reject H_0. (v) At the 5% level of significance, there is sufficient evidence to show that the variance for the lifetimes of bulbs manufactured using the new process is larger than that for bulbs made by the old process.

CHAPTER 12

Section 12.1

1. (a) $\alpha = 0.05$; H_0: Distributions are the same; H_1: Distributions are different. (b) $x = 7/15 \approx 0.4667$; $z \approx -0.26$. (c) P-value $= 2(0.3974) = 0.7948$. (d) Do not reject H_0. (e) At the 5% level of significance, the data are not significant. The evidence is insufficient to conclude that the economic growth rates are different.

3. (a) $\alpha = 0.05$; H_0: Distributions are the same; H_1: Distributions are different. (b) $x = 10/16 = 0.625$; $z \approx 1.00$. (c) P-value $= 2(0.1587) = 0.3174$. (d) Do not reject H_0. (e) At the 5% level of significance, the data are not significant. The evidence is insufficient to conclude that the lectures have any effect on student awareness of current events.

5. (a) $\alpha = 0.05$; H_0: Distributions are the same; H_1: Distributions are different. (b) $x = 7/12 \approx 0.5833$; $z \approx 0.58$. (c) P-value $= 2(0.2810) = 0.5620$. (d) Do not reject H_0. (e) At the 5% level of significance, the data are not significant. The evidence is insufficient to conclude that the schools are not equally effective.

7. (a) $\alpha = 0.01$; H_0: Distributions are the same; H_1: Distribution after hypnosis is lower. (b) $x = 3/16 = 0.1875$; $z \approx -2.50$. (c) P-value $= 0.0062$. (d) Reject H_0. (e) At the 1% level of significance, the data are significant. The evidence is sufficient to conclude that the number of cigarettes smoked per day was less after hypnosis.

9. (a) $\alpha = 0.01$; H_0: Distributions are the same; H_1: Distributions are different. (b) $x = 10/20 = 0.5000$; $z = 0$. (c) P-value $= 2(0.5000) = 1$. (d) Do not reject H_0. (e) At the 1% level of significance, the data are not significant. The evidence is insufficient to conclude that the distribution of dropout rates is different for males and females.

11. (a) $\alpha = 0.05$; H_0: Distributions are the same; H_1: Distributions are different. (b) $x = 8/12 \approx 0.67$; $z = 1.15$. (c) P-value $= 2(0.1251) = 0.2502$. (d) Do not reject H_0. (e) At the 5% level of significance, the data are not significant. The evidence is insufficient to conclude that the temperature distributions in Juneau and Madison are different.

Section 12.2

1. (a) $\alpha = 0.05$; H_0: Distributions are the same; H_1: Distributions are different. (b) $R_A = 126$; $\mu_R = 132$; $\sigma_R \approx 16.25$; $z \approx -0.37$. (c) P-value $\approx 2(0.3557) = 0.7114$. (d) Do not reject H_0. (e) At the 5% level of significance, the evidence is insufficient to conclude that the yield distributions for organic and conventional farming methods are different.

3. (a) $\alpha = 0.05$; H_0: Distributions are the same; H_1: Distributions are different. (b) $R_B = 148$; $\mu_R = 132$; $\sigma_R \approx 16.25$; $z \approx 0.98$. (c) P-value $\approx 2(0.1635) = 0.3270$. (d) Do not reject H_0. (e) At the 5% level of significance, the evidence is insufficient to conclude that the distributions of the training sessions are different.

5. (a) $\alpha = 0.05$; H_0: Distributions are the same; H_1: Distributions are different. (b) $R_A = 92$; $\mu_R = 132$; $\sigma_R \approx 16.25$; $z \approx -2.46$. (c) P-value $\approx 2(0.0069) = 0.0138$. (d) Reject H_0. (e) At the 5% level of significance, the evidence is sufficient to conclude that the completion time distributions for the two settings are different.

7. (a) $\alpha = 0.01$; H_0: Distributions are the same; H_1: Distributions are different. (b) $R_A = 176$; $\mu_R = 132$; $\sigma_R \approx 16.25$; $z \approx 2.71$. (c) P-value $\approx 2(0.0034) = 0.0068$. (d) Reject H_0. (e) At the 1% level of significance, the evidence is sufficient to conclude that the distributions showing percentage of exercisers differ by education level.

9. (a) $\alpha = 0.01$; H_0: Distributions are the same; H_1: Distributions are different. (b) $R_A = 166$; $\mu_R = 150$; $\sigma_R \approx 17.32$; $z \approx 0.92$. (c) P-value $\approx 2(0.1788) = 0.3576$. (d) Do not reject H_0. (e) At the 1% level of significance, the evidence is insufficient to conclude that the distributions of test scores differ according to instruction method.

Section 12.3

1. (a) $\alpha = 0.05$; H_0: $\rho_s = 0$; H_1: $\rho_s \neq 0$. (b) $r_s \approx 0.682$. (c) $n = 11$; $0.01 < P$-value < 0.05. (d) Reject H_0. (e) At the 5% level of significance, we conclude that there is a monotone relationship (either increasing or decreasing) between rank in training class and rank in sales.

3. (a) $\alpha = 0.05$; H_0: $\rho_s = 0$; H_1: $\rho_s > 0$. (b) $r_s \approx 0.571$. (c) $n = 8$; P-value > 0.05. (d) Do not reject H_0. (e) At the 5% level of significance, there is insufficient evidence to indicate a monotone-increasing relationship between crowding and violence.

5. (ii) (a) $\alpha = 0.05$; H_0: $\rho_s = 0$; H_1: $\rho_s < 0$. (b) $r_s \approx -0.214$. (c) $n = 7$; P-value > 0.05. (d) Do not reject H_0. (e) At the 5% level of significance, the evidence is insufficient to conclude that there is a monotone-decreasing relationship between the ranks of humor and aggressiveness.

7. (ii) (a) $\alpha = 0.05$; H_0: $\rho_s = 0$; H_1: $\rho_s \neq 0$. (b) $r_s \approx 0.930$. (c) $n = 13$; P-value < 0.002. (d) Reject H_0. (e) At the 5% level of significance, we conclude that there is a monotone relationship between number of firefighters and number of police.

9. (ii) (a) $\alpha = 0.01$; H_0: $\rho_s = 0$; H_1: $\rho_s \neq 0$. (b) $r_s \approx 0.661$. (c) $n = 8$; $0.05 < P$-value < 0.10. (d) Do not

reject H_0.   (e) At the 1% level of significance, we conclude that there is insufficient evidence to reject the null hypothesis of no monotone relationship between rank of insurance sales and rank of per capita income.

Section 12.4

1. (a) $\alpha = 0.05$; H_0: The symbols are randomly mixed in the sequence; H_1: The symbols are not randomly mixed in the sequence.   (b) $R = 11$.   (c) $n_1 = 12$; $n_2 = 11$; $c_1 = 7$; $c_2 = 18$.   (d) Do not reject H_0.   (e) At the 5% level of significance, the evidence is insufficient to conclude that the sequence of presidential party affiliations is not random.

3. (a) $\alpha = 0.05$; H_0: The symbols are randomly mixed in the sequence; H_1: The symbols are not randomly mixed in the sequence.   (b) $R = 11$.   (c) $n_1 = 16$; $n_2 = 7$; $c_1 = 6$; $c_2 = 16$.   (d) Do not reject H_0.   (e) At the 5% level of significance, the evidence is insufficient to conclude that the sequence of days for seeding and not seeding is not random.

5. (i) Median = 11.7; BBBBAAAAABBBA.   (ii) (a) $\alpha = 0.05$; H_0: The numbers are randomly mixed about the median; H_1: The numbers are not randomly mixed about the median.   (b) $R = 4$.   (c) $n_1 = 6$; $n_2 = 6$; $c_1 = 3$; $c_2 = 11$.   (d) Do not reject H_0.   (e) At the 5% level of significance, the evidence is insufficient to conclude that the sequence of returns is not random about the median.

7. (i) Median = 21.6; BAAAAAABBBBB.   (ii) (a) $\alpha = 0.05$; H_0: The numbers are randomly mixed about the median; H_1: The numbers are not randomly mixed about the median.   (b) $R = 3$.   (c) $n_1 = 6$; $n_2 = 6$; $c_1 = 3$; $c_2 = 11$.   (d) Reject H_0.   (e) At the 5% level of significance, we can conclude that the sequence of percentages of sand in the soil at successive depths is not random about the median.

9. (a) H_0: The symbols are randomly mixed in the sequence. H_1: The symbols are not randomly mixed in the sequence.   (b) $n_1 = 21$; $n_2 = 17$; $R = 18$.   (c) $\mu_R \approx 19.80$; $\sigma_R \approx 3.01$; $z \approx -0.60$.   (d) Since $-1.96 < z < 1.96$, do not reject H_0; P-value $\approx 2(0.2743) = 0.5486$; at the 5% level of significance, the P-value also tells us not to reject H_0.   (e) At the 5% level of significance, the evidence is insufficient to reject the null hypothesis of a random sequence of Democratic and Republican presidential terms.

Chapter 12 Review

1. (a) Rank-sum test.   (b) $\alpha = 0.05$; H_0: Distributions are the same; H_1: Distributions are different.   (c) $R_A = $

134; $\mu_R = 132$; $\sigma_R \approx 16.25$; $z \approx 0.12$.   (d) P-value = $2(0.4522) = 0.9044$.   (e) Do not reject H_0. At the 5% level of significance, there is insufficient evidence to conclude that the viscosity index distribution has changed with use of the catalyst.

3. (a) Sign test.   (b) $\alpha = 0.01$; H_0: Distributions are the same; H_1: Distribution after ads is higher.   (c) $x = 0.77$; $z = 1.95$.   (d) P-value = 0.0256.   (e) Do not reject H_0. At the 1% level of significance, the evidence is insufficient to claim that the distribution is higher after the ads.

5. (a) Spearman rank correlation coefficient test.   (b) $\alpha = 0.05$; H_0: $\rho = 0$; H_1: $\rho > 0$.   (c) $r_s \approx 0.617$.   (d) $n = 9$; $0.025 < P$-value < 0.05.   (e) Reject H_0. At the 5% level of significance, we conclude that there is a monotone-increasing relation between the ranks for the training program and the ranks on the job.

7. (a) Runs test for randomness.   (b) $\alpha = 0.05$; H_0: The symbols are randomly mixed in the sequence; H_1: The symbols are not randomly mixed in the sequence.   (c) $R = 7$.   (d) $n_1 = 16$; $n_2 = 9$; $c_1 = 7$; $c_2 = 18$.   (e) Reject H_0. At the 5% level of significance, we can conclude that the sequence of answers is not random.

Cumulative Review Problems

1. (a) Blood Glucose Level

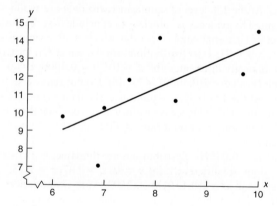

(b) $\hat{y} \approx 1.135 + 1.279x$.   (c) $r \approx 0.700$; $r^2 \approx 0.490$; 49% of the variance in y is explained by the model and the variance in x.   (d) 12.65; 9.64 to 15.66.   (e) $\alpha = 0.01$; H_0: $\rho = 0$; H_1: $\rho \neq 0$; $r \approx 0.700$ with $t \approx 2.40$; $d.f. = 6$; $0.05 < P$-value < 0.10; do not reject H_0. At the 1% level of significance, the evidence is insufficient to conclude that there is a correlation.   (f) $S_e \approx 1.901$; $t_c = 1.645$; 0.40 to 2.16.

2. (a) $\bar{x} \approx 0.61$.   (b) $P(0) \approx 0.543$; $P(1) \approx 0.331$; $P(2) \approx 0.101$; $P(3) \approx 0.025$.   (c) 0.3836; $d.f. = 3$.   (d) $\alpha = 0.01$; H_0: The distributions are the same; H_1: The distri-

butions are different; $\chi^2 \approx 0.3836$; $0.900 < P\text{-value} < 0.950$; do not reject H_0. At the 1% level of significance, the evidence is insufficient to claim that the distribution does not fit the Poisson distribution.

3. $\alpha = 0.05$; H_0: Yield and fertilizer type are independent; H_1: Yield and fertilizer type are not independent; $\chi^2 \approx 5.005$; $d.f. = 4$; $0.100 < P\text{-value} < 0.900$; do not reject H_0. At the 5% level of significance, the evidence is insufficient to conclude that fertilizer type and yield are not independent.

4. (a) $\alpha = 0.05$; H_0: $\sigma = 0.55$; H_1: $\sigma > 0.55$; $s \approx 0.602$; $d.f. = 9$; $\chi^2 \approx 10.78$; $0.100 < P\text{-value} < 0.900$; do not reject H_0. At the 5% level of significance, there is insufficient evidence to conclude that the standard deviation of petal lengths is greater than 0.55. (b) Interval from 0.44 to 0.99. (c) $\alpha = 0.01$; H_0: $\sigma_1^2 = \sigma_2^2$; H_1: $\sigma_1^2 > \sigma_2^2$; $F \approx 1.95$; $d.f._N = 9$, $d.f._D = 7$; $P\text{-value} > 0.100$; do not reject H_0. At the 1% level of significance, the evidence is insufficient to conclude that the variance of the petal lengths for *Iris virginica* is greater than that for *Iris versicolor*.

5. $\alpha = 0.05$; H_0: $p = 0.5$ (wind direction distributions are the same); H_1: $p \neq 0.5$ (wind direction distributions are

different); $x = 11/18$; $z \approx 0.94$; $P\text{-value} = 2(0.1736) = 0.3472$; do not reject H_0. At the 5% level of significance, the evidence is insufficient to conclude that the wind direction distributions are different.

6. $\alpha = 0.01$; H_0: Growth distributions are the same; H_1: Growth distributions are different; $\mu_R = 126.5$; $\sigma_R \approx 15.23$; $R_A = 135$; $z \approx 0.56$; $P\text{-value} = 2(0.2877) = 0.5754$; do not reject H_0. At the 1% level of significance, the evidence is insufficient to conclude that the growth distributions are different for the two root stocks.

7. (b) $\alpha = 0.05$; H_0: $\rho_s = 0$; H_1: $\rho_s \neq 0$; $r_s = 1$; $P\text{-value} < 0.002$; reject H_0. At the 5% level of significance, we can say that there is a monotone relationship between the calcium contents as measured by the labs.

8. Median $= 33.45$; AABBBBAAAABAABBBBA; $\alpha = 0.05$; H_0: Numbers are random about the median; H_1: Numbers are not random about the median; $R = 7$; $n_1 = n_2 = 9$; $c_1 = 5$; $c_2 = 15$; do not reject H_0. At the 5% level of significance, there is insufficient evidence to conclude that the sunspot activity about the median is not random.

Index

FREQUENTLY USED FORMULAS

n = sample size N = population size f = frequency

Chapter 2

Class Width $= \dfrac{\text{high} - \text{low}}{\text{number classes}}$ (increase to next integer)

Class Midpoint $= \dfrac{\text{upper limit} + \text{lower limit}}{2}$

Lower boundary = lower boundary of previous class
+ class width

Chapter 3

Sample mean $\bar{x} = \dfrac{\Sigma x}{n}$

Population mean $\mu = \dfrac{\Sigma x}{N}$

Weighted average $= \dfrac{\Sigma xw}{\Sigma w}$

Range = largest data value − smallest data value

Sample standard deviation $s = \sqrt{\dfrac{\Sigma(x - \bar{x})^2}{n - 1}}$

Computation formula $s = \sqrt{\dfrac{\Sigma x^2 - (\Sigma x)^2/n}{n - 1}}$

Population standard deviation $\sigma = \sqrt{\dfrac{\Sigma(x - \mu)^2}{N}}$

Sample variance s^2

Population variance σ^2

Sample Coefficient of Variation $CV = \dfrac{s}{\bar{x}} \cdot 100$

Sample mean for grouped data $\bar{x} = \dfrac{\Sigma xf}{n}$

Sample standard deviation for grouped data

$$s = \sqrt{\dfrac{\Sigma(x - \bar{x})^2 f}{n - 1}} = \sqrt{\dfrac{\Sigma x^2 f - (\Sigma xf)^2/n}{n - 1}}$$

Chapter 4

Probability of the complement of event A
$P(not\ A) = 1 - P(A)$

Multiplication rule for independent events
$P(A\ and\ B) = P(A) \cdot P(B)$

General multiplication rules
$P(A\ and\ B) = P(A) \cdot P(B,\ given\ A)$
$P(A\ and\ B) = P(B) \cdot P(A,\ given\ B)$

Addition rule for mutually exclusive events
$P(A\ or\ B) = P(A) + P(B)$

General addition rule
$P(A\ or\ B) = P(A) + P(B) - P(A\ and\ B)$

Permutation rule $P_{n,r} = \dfrac{n!}{(n - r)!}$

Combination rule $C_{n,r} = \dfrac{n!}{r!(n - r)!}$

Chapter 5

Mean of a discrete probability distribution $\mu = \Sigma x P(x)$

Standard deviation of a discrete probability distribution
$\sigma = \sqrt{\Sigma(x - \mu)^2 P(x)}$

Given $L = a + bx$

$\mu_L = a + b\mu$

$\sigma_L = |b|\sigma$

Given $W = ax_1 + bx_2$ (x_1 and x_2 independent)

$\mu_W = a\mu_1 + b\mu_2$

$\sigma_W = \sqrt{a^2\sigma_1^2 + b^2\sigma_2^2}$

For Binomial Distributions

r = number of successes; p = probability of success;
$q = 1 - p$

Binomial probability distribution $P(r) = C_{n,r} p^r q^{n-r}$

Mean $\mu = np$

Standard deviation $\sigma = \sqrt{npq}$

Geometric Probability Distribution

n = number of trial on which first success occurs
$P(n) = p(1 - p)^{n-1}$

Poisson Probability Distribution

r = number of successes

λ = mean number of successes over given interval
$$P(r) = \dfrac{e^{-\lambda}\lambda^r}{r!}$$

Chapter 6

Raw score $x = z\sigma + \mu$ Standard score $z = \dfrac{x - \mu}{\sigma}$

Chapter 7

Mean of $\bar{x}$ distribution $\mu_{\bar{x}} = \mu$

Standard deviation of $\bar{x}$ distribution $\sigma_{\bar{x}} = \dfrac{\sigma}{\sqrt{n}}$

Standard score for $\bar{x}$ $z = \dfrac{\bar{x} - \mu}{\sigma/\sqrt{n}}$

Mean of $\hat{p}$ distribution $\mu_{\hat{p}} = p$

Standard deviation of $\hat{p}$ distribution $\sigma_{\hat{p}} = \sqrt{\dfrac{pq}{n}}$; $q = 1 - p$

Chapter 8

Confidence Interval

for μ

$$\bar{x} - E < \mu < \bar{x} + E$$

where $E = z_c \dfrac{\sigma}{\sqrt{n}}$ when σ is known

$E = t_c \dfrac{s}{\sqrt{n}}$ when σ is unknown

with $d.f. = n - 1$

for p ($np > 5$ and $n(1 - p) > 5$)

$$\hat{p} - E < p < \hat{p} + E$$

where $E = z_c \sqrt{\dfrac{p(1 - p)}{n}}$

$$\hat{p} = \dfrac{r}{n}$$

for $\mu_1 - \mu_2$ (independent samples)

$$(\bar{x}_1 - \bar{x}_2) - E < \mu_1 - \mu_2 < (\bar{x}_1 - \bar{x}_2) + E$$

where $E = z_c \sqrt{\dfrac{\sigma_1^2}{n_1} + \dfrac{\sigma_2^2}{n_2}}$ when σ_1 and σ_2 are known

$E = t_c \sqrt{\dfrac{s_1^2}{n_1} + \dfrac{s_2^2}{n_2}}$ when σ_1 or σ_2 is unknown

with $d.f. =$ smaller of $n_1 - 1$ and $n_2 - 1$

(*Note:* Software uses Satterthwaite's approximation for degrees of freedom $d.f.$)

for difference of proportions $p_1 - p_2$

$$(\hat{p}_1 - \hat{p}_2) - E < p_1 - p_2 < (\hat{p}_1 - \hat{p}_2) + E$$

where $E = z_c \sqrt{\dfrac{\hat{p}_1 \hat{q}_1}{n_1} + \dfrac{\hat{p}_2 \hat{q}_2}{n_2}}$

$$\hat{p}_1 = r_1/n_1; \hat{p}_2 = r_2/n_2$$
$$\hat{q}_1 = 1 - \hat{p}_1; \hat{q}_2 = 1 - \hat{p}_2$$

Sample Size for Estimating

means $n = \left(\dfrac{z_c \sigma}{E}\right)^2$

proportions

$n = p(1 - p)\left(\dfrac{z_c}{E}\right)^2$ with preliminary estimate for p

$n = \dfrac{1}{4}\left(\dfrac{z_c}{E}\right)^2$ without preliminary estimate for p

Chapter 9

Sample Test Statistics for Tests of Hypotheses

for μ (σ known) $\quad z = \dfrac{\bar{x} - \mu}{\sigma/\sqrt{n}}$

for μ (σ unknown) $\quad t = \dfrac{\bar{x} - \mu}{s/\sqrt{n}}$; $d.f. = n - 1$

for p ($np > 5$ and $nq > 5$) $\quad z = \dfrac{\hat{p} - p}{\sqrt{pq/n}}$

where $q = 1 - p$; $\hat{p} = r/n$

for paired differences $d \quad t = \dfrac{\bar{d} - \mu_{\bar{d}}}{s_d/\sqrt{n}}$; $d.f. = n - 1$

for difference of means, σ_1 and σ_2 known

$$z = \dfrac{\bar{x}_1 - \bar{x}_2}{\sqrt{\dfrac{\sigma_1^2}{n_1} + \dfrac{\sigma_2^2}{n_2}}}$$

for difference of means, σ_1 or σ_2 unknown

$$t = \dfrac{\bar{x}_1 - \bar{x}_2}{\sqrt{\dfrac{s_1^2}{n_1} + \dfrac{s_2^2}{n_2}}}$$

$d.f. =$ smaller of $n_1 - 1$ and $n_2 - 1$

(*Note:* Software uses Satterthwaite's approximation for degrees of freedom $d.f.$)

for difference of proportions

$$z = \dfrac{\hat{p}_1 - \hat{p}_2}{\sqrt{\dfrac{\bar{p}\bar{q}}{n_1} + \dfrac{\bar{p}\bar{q}}{n_2}}}$$

where $\bar{p} = \dfrac{r_1 + r_2}{n_1 + n_2}$ and $\bar{q} = 1 - \bar{p}$

$$\hat{p}_1 = r_1/n_1; \hat{p}_2 = r_2/n_2$$

Chapter 10

Regression and Correlation

Pearson product moment correlation coefficient

$$r = \dfrac{n\Sigma xy - (\Sigma x)(\Sigma y)}{\sqrt{n\Sigma x^2 - (\Sigma x)^2}\sqrt{n\Sigma y^2 - (\Sigma y)^2}}$$

Least-squares line $\hat{y} = a + bx$

where $b = \dfrac{n\Sigma xy - (\Sigma x)(\Sigma y)}{n\Sigma x^2 - (\Sigma x)^2}$

$$a = \bar{y} - b\bar{x}$$

Coefficient of determination $= r^2$

Sample test statistic for r

$$t = \frac{r\sqrt{n-2}}{\sqrt{1-r^2}} \text{ with } d.f. = n-2$$

Standard error of estimate $S_e = \sqrt{\dfrac{\Sigma y^2 - a\Sigma y - b\Sigma xy}{n-2}}$

Confidence interval for y

$$\hat{y} - E < y < \hat{y} + E$$

$$\text{where } E = t_c S_e \sqrt{1 + \frac{1}{n} + \frac{n(x-\bar{x})^2}{n\Sigma x^2 - (\Sigma x)^2}}$$

$$\text{with } d.f. = n-2$$

Sample test statistic for slope b

$$t = \frac{b}{S_e}\sqrt{\Sigma x^2 - \frac{1}{n}(\Sigma x)^2} \text{ with } d.f. = n-2$$

Confidence interval for β

$$b - E < \beta < b + E$$

$$\text{where } E = \frac{t_c S_e}{\sqrt{\Sigma x^2 - \frac{1}{n}(\Sigma x)^2}} \text{ with } d.f. = n-2$$

Chapter 11

$$\chi^2 = \Sigma \frac{(O-E)^2}{E} \text{ where } E = \frac{(\text{row total})(\text{column total})}{\text{sample size}}$$

Tests of Independence $d.f. = (R-1)(C-1)$

Goodness of fit $d.f. = (\text{number of categories}) - 1$

Confidence Interval for σ^2; $d.f. = n-1$

$$\frac{(n-1)s^2}{\chi_U^2} < \sigma^2 < \frac{(n-1)s^2}{\chi_L^2}$$

Sample test statistic for σ^2

$$\chi^2 = \frac{(n-1)s^2}{\sigma^2} \text{ with } d.f. = n-1$$

Testing Two Variances

Sample test statistic $F = \dfrac{s_1^2}{s_2^2}$

$$\text{where } s_1^2 \geq s_2^2$$

$$d.f._N = n_1 - 1; \ d.f._D = n_2 - 1$$

ANOVA

k = number of groups; N = total sample size

$$SS_{TOT} = \Sigma x_{TOT}^2 - \frac{(\Sigma x_{TOT})^2}{N}$$

$$SS_{BET} = \sum_{all\ groups} \left(\frac{(\Sigma x_i)^2}{n_i} \right) - \frac{(\Sigma x_{TOT})^2}{N}$$

$$SS_W = \sum_{all\ groups} \left(\Sigma x_i^2 - \frac{(\Sigma x_i)^2}{n_i} \right)$$

$$SS_{TOT} = SS_{BET} + SS_W$$

$$MS_{BET} = \frac{SS_{BET}}{d.f._{BET}} \text{ where } d.f._{BET} = k-1$$

$$MS_W = \frac{SS_W}{d.f._W} \text{ where } d.f._W = N-k$$

$$F = \frac{MS_{BET}}{MS_W} \text{ where } d.f. \text{ numerator} = d.f._{BET} = k-1;$$

$$d.f. \text{ denominator} = d.f._W = N-k$$

Two-Way ANOVA

r = number of rows; c = number of columns

$$\text{Row factor } F: \frac{MS \text{ row factor}}{MS \text{ error}}$$

$$\text{Column factor } F: \frac{MS \text{ column factor}}{MS \text{ error}}$$

$$\text{Interaction } F: \frac{MS \text{ interaction}}{MS \text{ error}}$$

with degrees of freedom for

row factor $= r-1$ interaction $= (r-1)(c-1)$

column factor $= c-1$ error $= rc(n-1)$

Chapter 12

Sample test statistic for x = proportion of plus signs to all signs ($n \geq 12$)

$$z = \frac{x - 0.5}{\sqrt{0.25/n}}$$

Sample test statistic for R = sum of ranks

$$z = \frac{R - \mu_R}{\sigma_R} \text{ where } \mu_R = \frac{n_1(n_1 + n_2 + 1)}{2} \text{ and}$$

$$\sigma_R = \sqrt{\frac{n_1 n_2 (n_1 + n_2 + 1)}{12}}$$

Spearman rank correlation coefficient

$$r_s = 1 - \frac{6\Sigma d^2}{n(n^2-1)} \text{ where } d = x - y$$

Sample test statistic for runs test

R = number of runs in sequence

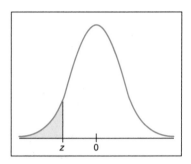

Table entry for z is the area to the left of z.

Areas of a Standard Normal Distribution

(a) Table of Areas to the Left of z

z	.00	.01	.02	.03	.04	.05	.06	.07	.08	.09
−3.4	.0003	.0003	.0003	.0003	.0003	.0003	.0003	.0003	.0003	.0002
−3.3	.0005	.0005	.0005	.0004	.0004	.0004	.0004	.0004	.0004	.0003
−3.2	.0007	.0007	.0006	.0006	.0006	.0006	.0006	.0005	.0005	.0005
−3.1	.0010	.0009	.0009	.0009	.0008	.0008	.0008	.0008	.0007	.0007
−3.0	.0013	.0013	.0013	.0012	.0012	.0011	.0011	.0011	.0010	.0010
−2.9	.0019	.0018	.0018	.0017	.0016	.0016	.0015	.0015	.0014	.0014
−2.8	.0026	.0025	.0024	.0023	.0023	.0022	.0021	.0021	.0020	.0019
−2.7	.0035	.0034	.0033	.0032	.0031	.0030	.0029	.0028	.0027	.0026
−2.6	.0047	.0045	.0044	.0043	.0041	.0040	.0039	.0038	.0037	.0036
−2.5	.0062	.0060	.0059	.0057	.0055	.0054	.0052	.0051	.0049	.0048
−2.4	.0082	.0080	.0078	.0075	.0073	.0071	.0069	.0068	.0066	.0064
−2.3	.0107	.0104	.0102	.0099	.0096	.0094	.0091	.0089	.0087	.0084
−2.2	.0139	.0136	.0132	.0129	.0125	.0122	.0119	.0116	.0113	.0110
−2.1	.0179	.0174	.0170	.0166	.0162	.0158	.0154	.0150	.0146	.0143
−2.0	.0228	.0222	.0217	.0212	.0207	.0202	.0197	.0192	.0188	.0183
−1.9	.0287	.0281	.0274	.0268	.0262	.0256	.0250	.0244	.0239	.0233
−1.8	.0359	.0351	.0344	.0336	.0329	.0322	.0314	.0307	.0301	.0294
−1.7	.0446	.0436	.0427	.0418	.0409	.0401	.0392	.0384	.0375	.0367
−1.6	.0548	.0537	.0526	.0516	.0505	.0495	.0485	.0475	.0465	.0455
−1.5	.0668	.0655	.0643	.0630	.0618	.0606	.0594	.0582	.0571	.0559
−1.4	.0808	.0793	.0778	.0764	.0749	.0735	.0721	.0708	.0694	.0681
−1.3	.0968	.0951	.0934	.0918	.0901	.0885	.0869	.0853	.0838	.0823
−1.2	.1151	.1131	.1112	.1093	.1075	.1056	.1038	.1020	.1003	.0985
−1.1	.1357	.1335	.1314	.1292	.1271	.1251	.1230	.1210	.1190	.1170
−1.0	.1587	.1562	.1539	.1515	.1492	.1469	.1446	.1423	.1401	.1379
−0.9	.1841	.1814	.1788	.1762	.1736	.1711	.1685	.1660	.1635	.1611
−0.8	.2119	.2090	.2061	.2033	.2005	.1977	.1949	.1922	.1894	.1867
−0.7	.2420	.2389	.2358	.2327	.2296	.2266	.2236	.2206	.2177	.2148
−0.6	.2743	.2709	.2676	.2643	.2611	.2578	.2546	.2514	.2483	.2451
−0.5	.3085	.3050	.3015	.2981	.2946	.2912	.2877	.2843	.2810	.2776
−0.4	.3446	.3409	.3372	.3336	.3300	.3264	.3228	.3192	.3156	.3121
−0.3	.3821	.3783	.3745	.3707	.3669	.3632	.3594	.3557	.3520	.3483
−0.2	.4207	.4168	.4129	.4090	.4052	.4013	.3974	.3936	.3897	.3859
−0.1	.4602	.4562	.4522	.4483	.4443	.4404	.4364	.4325	.4286	.4247
−0.0	.5000	.4960	.4920	.4880	.4840	.4801	.4761	.4721	.4681	.4641

For values of z less than −3.49, use 0.000 to approximate the area.